What's What

What's What

A Visual Glossary of the Physical World

REVISED EDITION

Reginald Bragonier Jr. and David Fisher

HAMMOND®
INCORPORATED
MAPLEWOOD, NEW JERSEY

Printed in the United States of America

Library of Congress Cataloging-in-Publication Data

Bragonier, Reginald.
    What's what, a visual glossary of the physical world/
Reginald Bragonier Jr., and David Fisher.—Rev. ed.
      p. cm.
    Includes index
    Summary: Pictures of common objects and their parts,
each identified individually by name, are classed under
such general categories as living things, transportation, and
personal items.
    ISBN 0-8437-3322-5
    1. Picture dictionaries, English. [1. Picture dictionaries.
2. Vocabulary. 3. English language—Terms and phrases.
4. Technology—Dictionaries.] I. Fisher, David, 1946-
II. Title. III. Title: What's what.
AG250.B7 1990   89-51862
031.02—dc20   CIP
                                                    AC

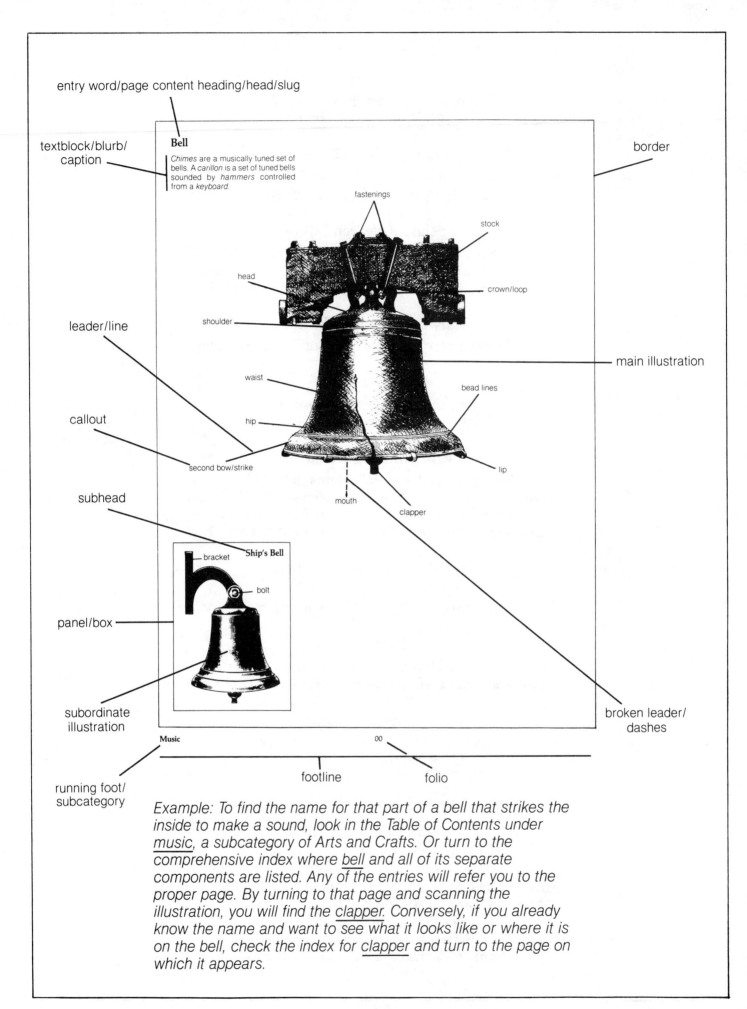

entry word/page content heading/head/slug

textblock/blurb/
caption

border

Bell

Chimes are a musically tuned set of bells. A *carillon* is a set of tuned bells sounded by *hammers* controlled from a *keyboard*.

fastenings

stock

head

crown/loop

leader/line

shoulder

main illustration

waist

bead lines

callout

hip

second bow/strike

lip

subhead

mouth

clapper

broken leader/
dashes

Ship's Bell

bracket

bolt

panel/box

subordinate
illustration

Music

00

footline

folio

running foot/
subcategory

Example: To find the name for that part of a bell that strikes the inside to make a sound, look in the Table of Contents under music, a subcategory of Arts and Crafts. Or turn to the comprehensive index where bell and all of its separate components are listed. Any of the entries will refer you to the proper page. By turning to that page and scanning the illustration, you will find the clapper. Conversely, if you already know the name and want to see what it looks like or where it is on the bell, check the index for clapper and turn to the page on which it appears.

What It Is

Until now, it has been all but impossible to find words you've forgotten or never knew to begin with. The reason for this is obvious: to use a dictionary you need to know the word in order to find it. WHAT'S WHAT provides access to words in an entirely new way—*visually*. Readers can now find words they are seeking by turning to detailed illustrations in which all the visible parts are identified and labeled. This system of visual classification puts within verbal reach of everyone, for the first time, the words used to describe the myriad objects in our everyday world.

The objects chosen for inclusion in WHAT'S WHAT have been selected on the basis of their usefulness to contemporary readers; and although no single volume of this kind can be encyclopedic in its coverage, WHAT'S WHAT is both comprehensive in its scope and practical in its treatment of individual items. Thus, illustrations generally include only the visible parts of objects. However, when it is necessary or desirable to identify part of an item not actually shown, its location is indicated by a broken line. Variations and styles of objects have been presented only when the object's parts make it so distinctive that the item itself has a unique name—lorgnette, for example, which appears on the eyeglasses page. In addition, considerable use has been made of composite illustrations—nonliteral representations combining diverse elements found among similar objects.

How It Works

The book's system of classification is simple and straightforward. Since every object in the physical world is part of a larger whole, the reader can find any detail by locating the larger item. All objects fall naturally into one of the following twelve categories: *The Earth; Living Things; Shelters and Structures; Transportation; Communications; Personal Items; The Home; Sports and Recreation; Arts and Crafts; Machinery, Tools and Weapons; Uniforms, Costumes and Ceremonial Attire;* and *Signs and Symbols.*

To locate an item, turn first to the Table of Contents, where each entry is arranged by category and subcategory according to the object's nature and use. There you will readily determine in what part of the book the item is located. An automobile, for example, is listed under Transportation. An object, or the name of a part, can also be found by consulting the all-inclusive index at the back of the book. A collar stay, for example, can be located by looking under "shirt," "collar," or any other part of a shirt known to the reader, since all these entries will refer to the page on which a shirt is illustrated and all its parts are identified. Rigorous cross-referencing makes the task of finding any item or detail in the book even simpler.

And Why

WHAT'S WHAT is far more than an ordinary reference book. Aided by well-known artists and experts in the visual-arts fields, the editors have made every effort to produce a book that is as engaging as it is informative. Its use, it is hoped, will entertain as well as enlighten.

TABLE OF CONTENTS

THE EARTH – 1

The Planetary System (2–3): the universe
The Earth (4–6): inner world, cartographer's world, wind and ocean currents
Terrains (7–12): land features, mountains, volcano, cave, glacier
Water Systems (13–15): river, wave, shoreline and continental margin
Weather (16–19): clouds, storm systems, weather monitoring equipment, weather map
Maps (20–22): geographic, political, thematic, nautical chart, topographic map

LIVING THINGS – 23

Human Anatomy (24–31): the human body, literary anatomy, skeletal and muscular systems, internal organs, circulatory system and heart, nervous system and brain, sense organs, the extremities
Edible Animals (32–35): cow, lamb, pig, poultry
Domestic Animals (36–38): dog, cat, horse
Wild Animals (39–49): bird, spider, insects, reptiles, dinosaurs, amphibians, fish, marine life, shellfish, ultimate beast
Plants (50–58): tree, root system, leaf, flower, vegetables, fruit, succulents, special plants, grass

SHELTERS AND STRUCTURES – 59

House (60–69): foundation, frame, exterior, house styles, door, window, staircase, fence, building materials, brick wall
Architectural Designs from Other Lands (70–73): international architecture, arch, column
Special Purpose Buildings (74–96): Capitol, White House, prison, skyscraper, elevator, escalator, castle, fortifications, tepee, domed structures, church, temple, courtroom, circus, amusement park, airport, railroad yard
Other Structures (97–104): bridge, tunnel, canal lock, dam, offshore oil rig, supermarket, barn and silo

TRANSPORTATION – 105

Automobile (106–114): exterior, cutaway, car types and body styles, interior, engine, gasoline pump, traffic control devices, highway
Public Transportation (115–119): railroad crossing, railroad, bus, subway
Carriers (120–121): truck, trailer
Emergency Vehicles (122–125): police car, ambulance, fire engine
Public Service Vehicles (126–127): tow truck, street cleaner, garbage truck
Cycles (128–129): bicycle, motorcycle
Recreational Vehicles (130): camper, snowmobile
Carriages (131): stagecoach, hansom cab
Boats and Ships (132–145): nautical terminology, rowboat, sailboat, sail, outboard engine, powerboat, tanker, passenger ship, tugboat and fireboat, hovercraft and hydrofoil
Aircraft (146–151): helicopter, private aircraft, glider, civil aircraft, cockpit, blimp
Spacecraft (152–156): space shuttle, launch pad, flight deck, lunar lander, lunar buggy, flight suit

COMMUNICATIONS – 157

Print Communications (158–171): pen and pencil, correspondence, résumé, typewriter, personal computer, printers, fax machine and copier, typography, printing, book, newspaper, magazine cover, contents page and feature
Visual Communications (172–176): still camera and film, instant cameras, movie camera, projectors, accessories
Aural Communications (177–183): tape recorder, audio equipment, telephone, cellular telephone, answering machine, portable radios and cassette players, transceiver
Audiovisual Communications (184–186): video recorder, television, satellite

TABLE OF CONTENTS *(Continued)*

PERSONAL ITEMS – 187

Men's Apparel (188–194): jacket and vest, shirt, belt and suspenders, pants, neckwear, underwear

Women's Apparel (195–198): foundation garments, jacket and pants, blouse and skirt, dress

Unisex Clothing (199–201): sweater, outerwear

Headwear (202–203): men's hats, women's hats

Footwear (204–207): man's shoe, woman's shoe, boot and sandal, shoe accessories

Fasteners (208–209): pin, zipper, buttons

Hairstyles and Facial Hair (210–214): shavers, men's hair, hair grooming implements, women's hairstyles, hairstyling implements

Cosmetics (215–217): toothbrush, makeup, beauty products

Jewelry (218–219): gemstone, ring, pendant

Timepieces (220): wristwatch, pocket watch

Eyeglasses (221): lens shapes, lorgnette, monocle, contact lens

Bags (222): handbag

Wallet and Currency (223–227): paper money, coin, personal banking, credit card account, traveler's check

Smoking Materials (228–229): cigar, cigarette, pipe

Umbrella (230)

THE HOME – 231

Living Room (232–241): fireplace, clock, chair, lounger, sofa, candelabrum, lamps and lighting, window coverings

Dining Room (242–246): table, side pieces, place setting, dessert setting, carpet

Kitchen (247–269): sink and compactor, stove and microwave oven, refrigerator, dishwasher, openers, coffee makers, toaster, blenders, juicers, knives, pots and pans, mixing and measuring tools, preparation utensils, strainers and drainers, grinders and graters, food ingredients, prepared foods, desserts, snack foods, containers, labeling and packaging

Bedroom (270–272): bed and bedding, dressers

Bathroom (273–275): faucet and sink, bath and shower, toilet

Playroom/Utility Room (276–285): desk, desktop equipment, sewing machine, iron, washer and dryer, broom and mop, vacuum cleaners, fire extinguisher, luggage

Yard (286–288): children's gear and playground equipment, barbecue, chaise longue, hammock

SPORTS AND RECREATION – 289

Team Sports (290–299): baseball, football, ice hockey, basketball, soccer, lacrosse, polo

Competitive Sports (300–319): track and field, running shoe, field events equipment, hurdle, pole vault, gymnastics, trampoline, boxing, golf, tennis, handball and squash, jai alai, fencing, swimming and diving, bowling, shuffleboard and croquet, volleyball and badminton

Table Games (320–321): pool and billiards, ping-pong

Individual Sports (322–334): darts, kites, roller skating and skateboarding, ice skates, skiing, sledding and tobogganing, water skiing, windsurfing and surfing, skin diving, hot air ballooning, parachuting and hang gliding, mountain climbing

Equestrian Sports (335–337): riding equipment, flat and harness racing

Automobile Racing (338–339): Grand Prix, drag racing

Outdoor Sports (340–343): fishing, camping and backpacking

Body Building (344)

Board Games (345): chess and checkers, backgammon and mahjong

Casino Games (346–348): slot machine, roulette wheel, craps table, dice, cards

ARTS AND CRAFTS – 349

Performing Arts (350–351): stage, theater

Music (352–367): bell (see page iv), sheet music, orchestra, violin, woodwinds, brasses, organ, piano, guitar, electric guitar and synthesizer, drums, bagpipe, accordion and folk instruments, musical accessories

Fine Arts (368–379): elements of composition, painting equipment, sculpting tools, potting, woodcut printing, silk screen and scrimshaw, lithography, intaglio and etching, stained glass, framing

Cartooning (380–381)

Fireworks (382–383)

Crafts (384–388): sewing, decorative stitching, knitting, weaving, sewing pattern

TABLE OF CONTENTS *(Continued)*

MACHINERY, TOOLS AND WEAPONS – 389

Power Systems (390–399): wind systems, solar power, nuclear power, particle accelerator, lasers, power line, vacuum tube and transistor, battery, receptacle and plug, meter and fuse box

Climate Control Units (400–404): furnace, hot water heater, air conditioner, heat exchanger, woodburning stove

Engines (405–407): steam engine, internal combustion engine, jet engines

Household Tools (408–426): workbench, vise, nails and screws, nuts and bolts, hammer, screwdriver, pliers, wrench, handsaw, power saw, drills, planing and shaping tools, sander, plumbing tools, electrician's tools, measuring tools, painting tools, Swiss Army knife

Gardening Tools (427–431): hoe and rake, shovel and shears, sprinkler and nozzles, lawn mower, wheelbarrow and seeder, chain saw

Rancher's Equipment (432): lariat, branding iron, barbed wire

Trapping Devices (433): mousetrap, bear trap, lobster trap

Agricultural Tools (434): tractor, hitch and harrow

Construction Equipment (435–436): bulldozer, transit and jackhammer

Computing Tools (437–441): voting booth, computer workstation, computer system, cash register, calculators

Scientific Tools (442–443): microscope, telescope and binoculars

Sensing Devices (444–447): radar and sonar, detectors, laboratory equipment

Medical Tools (448–456): examination equipment, medical tables, treatment aids, supportive devices, dental corrective devices, dental unit, dental equipment, tooth chart

Security Devices (457–460): safe, door locks, key and padlock, hinge and hasp

Chain and Pulley (461)

Execution Devices (462): electric chair, gallows, guillotine

Weapons (463–482): cutting and thrusting weapons, medieval arms, armor, bow and arrow, cannon and catapult, shotgun and rifle, handguns, automatic rifle and machine gun, mortar and bazooka, grenade and land mine, tank, fighting ships, aircraft carrier, submarines and torpedo, combat jet fighter, pilot's instrument panel, missiles

UNIFORMS, COSTUMES AND CEREMONIAL ATTIRE – 483

Royal Vestments (484–485): attire, crown, orb and scepter

Religious Attire (486–487): vestments and ritual items

Wedding Attire (488): bride and groom

Servants' Attire (489): domestic staff

Native Attire (490–491): cowboy and Indian, Arab and Chinese dress

Historical Costumes (492): general, pirate, miser and wizard

Performers' Costumes (493–495): clown, ballet dancer, drum major

Military Attire (496–497): dress and combat

Municipal Uniforms (498–500): policemen, firemen

SIGNS AND SYMBOLS – 501

Flags (502)

Heraldry (503)

Road Signs (504–505)

Public Signs (506)

Gestures (507)

Religious Symbols (508)

Signs of the Zodiac (509)

Symbols of Science, Business and Commerce (510–511)

Sign Alphabet and Braille (512)

Grammatical Symbols (513)

Proofreader's Marks (514)

Graffiti (515)

TOMBSTONE AND COFFIN – 516

The Earth

This section offers various ways of looking at the earth, ranging from showing the earth as a small planet in the larger space it shares with other heavenly bodies to physical features and symbolic depictions illustrating aspects and details of the earth's surface.

Nonliteral renditions, such as the illustration of the universe, condense information visually by pulling together disparate elements for labeling. Cutaway illustrations like the one of the earth's inner layers are used only when elements considered essential to show and identify are not readily visible. The cave illustration, on the other hand, is rendered in cross section in order to show parts and details which might not be apparent in a traditional illustration.

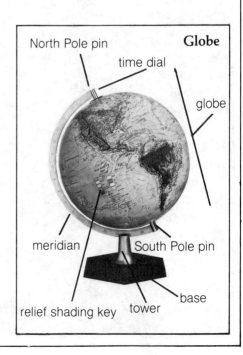

Globe

North Pole pin

time dial

globe

meridian

South Pole pin

relief shading key   tower

base

The Universe

This whimsical creation of the universe includes such bits and pieces of the entire *cosmic mass* as the *solar system*, *local galaxies* and *external galaxies*. Observable *planets* are illuminated by the light of our sun. *Meteors*, or *shooting stars*, are seen as streaks of light in the *sky* as they are vaporized on entering earth's atmosphere.

spiral galaxy

red supergiant star

side

elliptical galaxies

full face

common spiral galaxies

black hole

irregular galaxies

barrel spiral galaxy

asteroids/planetoids

Pluto

nebula/interstellar cloud

Neptune

stars

Uranus

doppler shift

constellation

mystery gas cloud

quark

pulsar

quasar

radiation belt

tail

comet

head/coma

white dwarf star

binary stars/double stars

ion particle cloud

radio waves

supernova

satellite

Cassini division

rings

Saturn

solar flare/solar prominence

Jupiter

Mars

Earth

Venus

Mercury

Titan

moon/satellite

Milky Way Galaxy

Sun

Sun spots

cosmic rays

Earth Core

Geologists divide the earth into three *zones:* the *lithosphere,* containing all solids from the land surface to the earth's center; the *hydrosphere,* all surface water areas; and the *atmosphere,* the layered gaseous envelope surrounding the earth's surface. The moon goes through eight phases every 29.5 days, called a *synodic period,* or *lunar month,* in which parts of it are in dark shadow and not visible from earth.

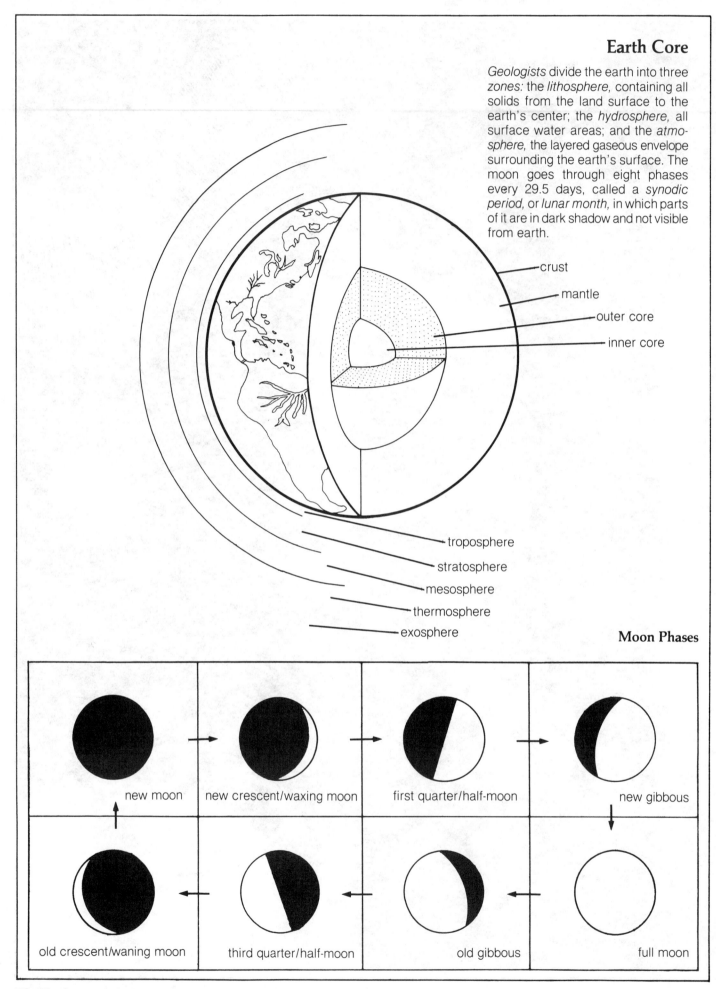

crust

mantle

outer core

inner core

troposphere

stratosphere

mesosphere

thermosphere

exosphere

Moon Phases

| new moon | new crescent/waxing moon | first quarter/half-moon | new gibbous |
| old crescent/waning moon | third quarter/half-moon | old gibbous | full moon |

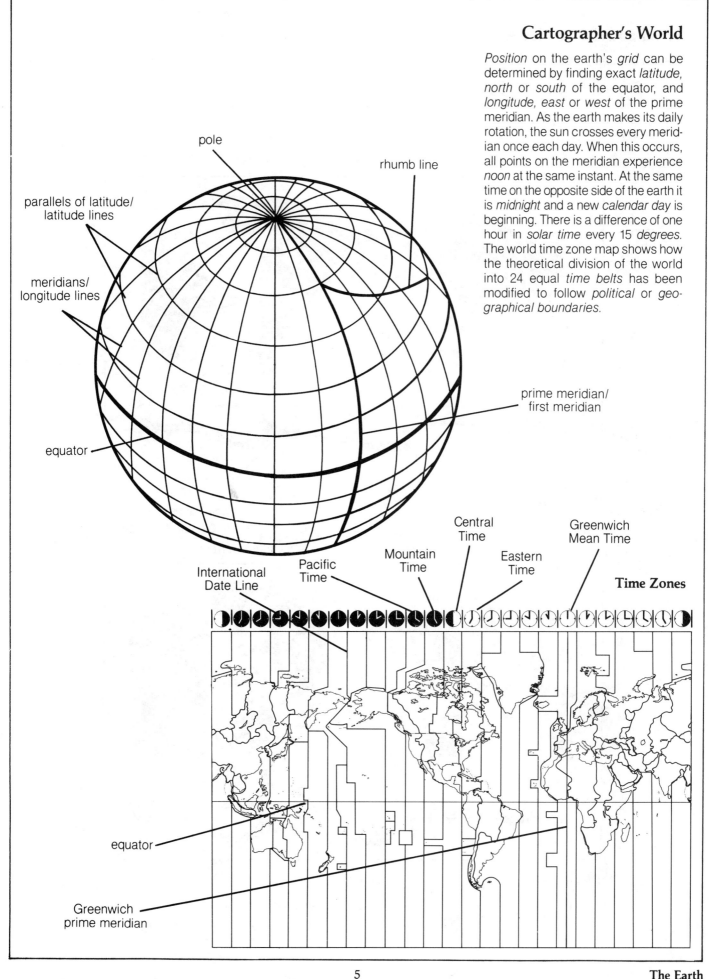

Cartographer's World

Position on the earth's *grid* can be determined by finding exact *latitude, north* or *south* of the equator, and *longitude, east* or *west* of the prime meridian. As the earth makes its daily rotation, the sun crosses every meridian once each day. When this occurs, all points on the meridian experience *noon* at the same instant. At the same time on the opposite side of the earth it is *midnight* and a new *calendar day* is beginning. There is a difference of one hour in *solar time* every 15 *degrees*. The world time zone map shows how the theoretical division of the world into 24 equal *time belts* has been modified to follow *political* or *geographical boundaries*.

pole

rhumb line

parallels of latitude/ latitude lines

meridians/ longitude lines

equator

prime meridian/ first meridian

Central Time

Greenwich Mean Time

Mountain Time

Eastern Time

Pacific Time

Time Zones

International Date Line

equator

Greenwich prime meridian

Wind and Ocean Currents

The *zonal patterns* of wind are displaced northward and southward seasonally. Those shown here prevail in winter. *Seasonal currents* change speed and direction due to seasonal winds, whereas *permanent currents* experience relatively little change.

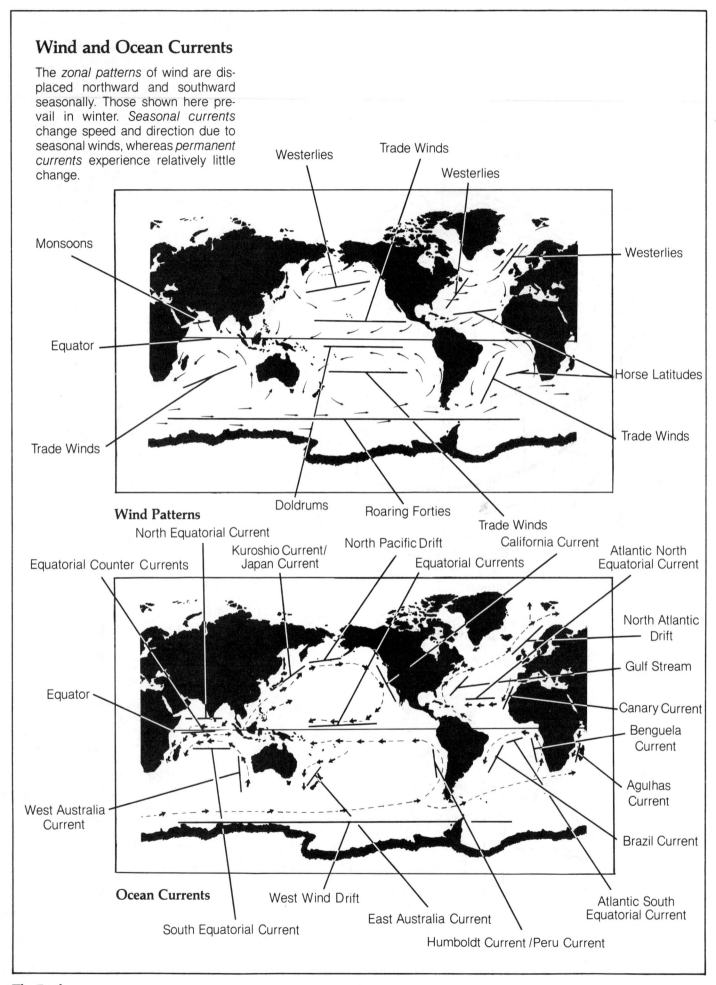

Westerlies

Trade Winds

Westerlies

Westerlies

Monsoons

Equator

Horse Latitudes

Trade Winds

Trade Winds

Wind Patterns

Doldrums

Roaring Forties

Trade Winds

North Equatorial Current

Kuroshio Current/ Japan Current

North Pacific Drift

California Current

Atlantic North Equatorial Current

Equatorial Counter Currents

Equatorial Currents

North Atlantic Drift

Gulf Stream

Equator

Canary Current

Benguela Current

Agulhas Current

West Australia Current

Brazil Current

Ocean Currents

West Wind Drift

Atlantic South Equatorial Current

South Equatorial Current

East Australia Current

Humboldt Current /Peru Current

Land Features

A part of an *ocean* or *sea* extending into the land is a *gulf*. A narrow finger of land extending into the water is a *spit*. A sand or gravel bar connecting an island with the *mainland* or another island is a *tombolo*.

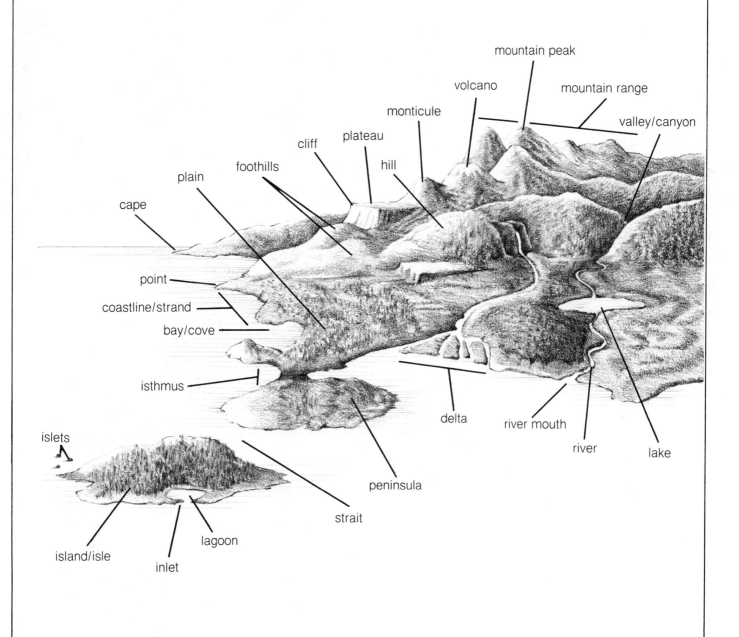

mountain peak

volcano

monticule

mountain range

valley/canyon

cliff

plateau

hill

foothills

plain

cape

point

coastline/strand

bay/cove

isthmus

delta

river mouth

river

lake

islets

peninsula

island/isle

strait

lagoon

inlet

Terrains

Mountains

A series of mountains, such as the Alpine mountains shown here, is a *range*. A circular space in mountains is a *cirque*, or *cwm*. A *kame* is a ridge or material left by a retreating *ice sheet*. An isolated hill or mountain rising abruptly from the surrounding land is a *butte*.

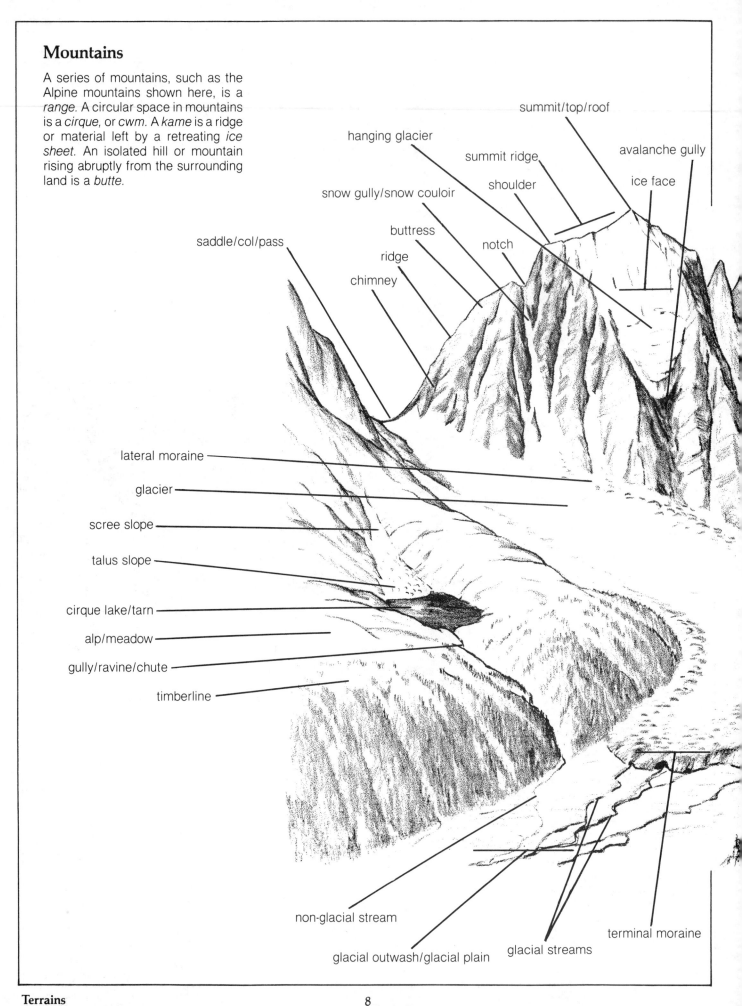

summit/top/roof

hanging glacier

summit ridge

avalanche gully

shoulder

ice face

snow gully/snow couloir

buttress

notch

ridge

saddle/col/pass

chimney

lateral moraine

glacier

scree slope

talus slope

cirque lake/tarn

alp/meadow

gully/ravine/chute

timberline

non-glacial stream

glacial outwash/glacial plain

glacial streams

terminal moraine

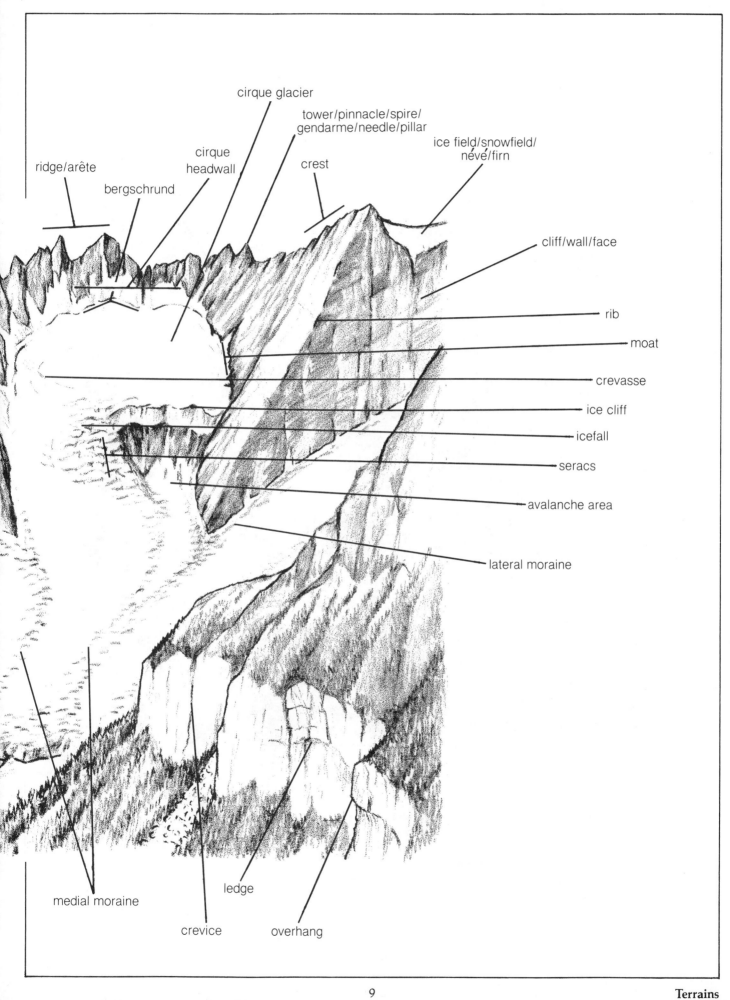

ridge/arête

bergschrund

cirque headwall

cirque glacier

tower/pinnacle/spire/
gendarme/needle/pillar

crest

ice field/snowfield/
névé/firn

cliff/wall/face

rib

moat

crevasse

ice cliff

icefall

seracs

avalanche area

lateral moraine

medial moraine

ledge

crevice

overhang

Terrains

Volcano

In *central-vent volcanoes,* such as the one shown here, material erupts from a single pipe. *Fissure volcanoes* extrude material along extensive *fractures.*

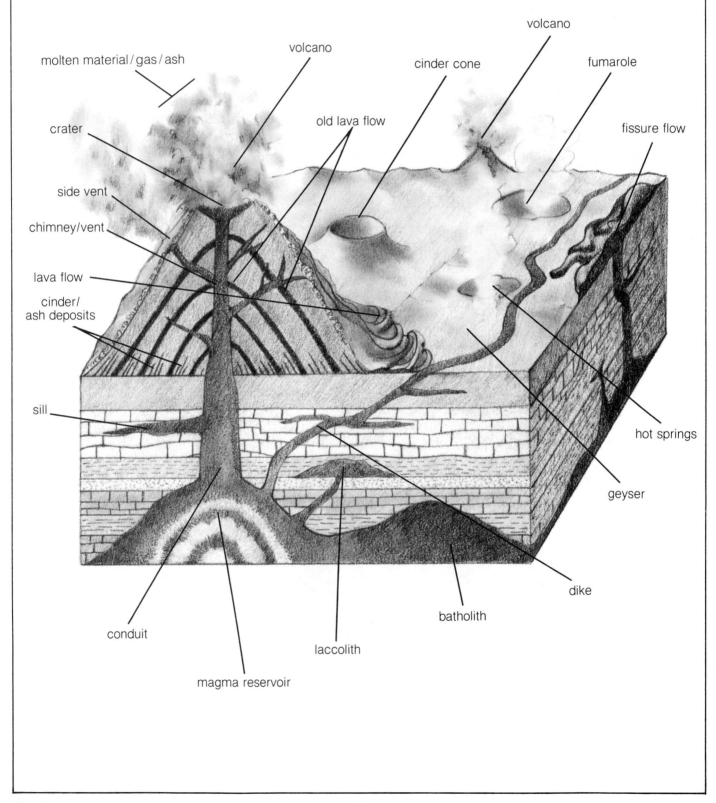

molten material / gas / ash

volcano

volcano

cinder cone

fumarole

crater

old lava flow

fissure flow

side vent

chimney/vent

lava flow

cinder/ ash deposits

sill

hot springs

geyser

dike

conduit

batholith

laccolith

magma reservoir

Cave Cross Section

The exploration of caves, or *caverns* is called *spelunking* or *caving*. The area lighted by daylight just inside a cave entrance is the *twilight zone*. An underground structure containing many *galleries*, *chambers* or *rooms* is a *cave system*. Anything formed inside a cave, *cavern* or *grotto*, by dripping water is *dripstone*. Knobby calcite growths often found on *walls* and *floors* of once-submerged caves are called *cave coral* or *cave popcorn*.

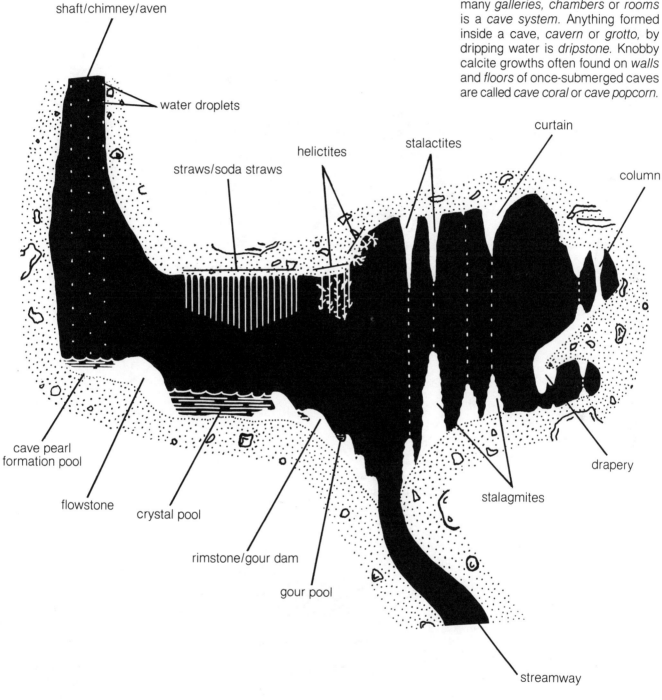

shaft/chimney/aven

water droplets

straws/soda straws

helictites

stalactites

curtain

column

cave pearl formation pool

flowstone

crystal pool

rimstone/gour dam

gour pool

stalagmites

drapery

streamway

Glacier

When a glacier terminates at the water's edge, sections break off, or *calve,* to form icebergs. Icebergs often break apart to form smaller, separate *bergs, bergy bits* or *bitty bergs.* Even smaller sections are called *growlers. Ice packs,* formed when the water surface between floating ice freezes, are called *floes.* Sections that break off are called *floebergs.*

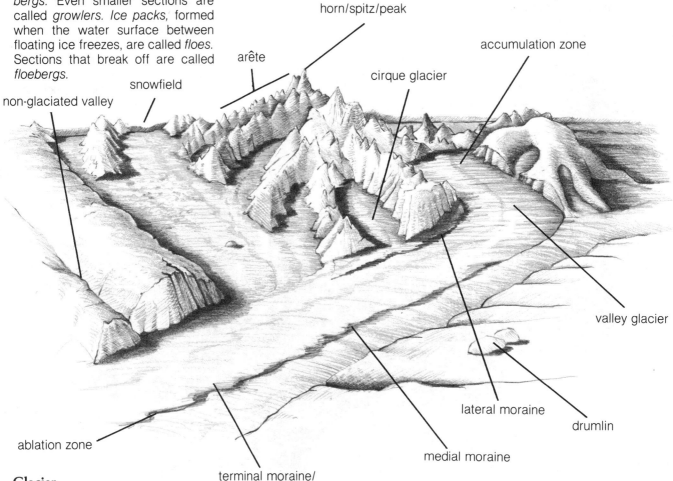

horn/spitz/peak

arête

snowfield

non-glaciated valley

cirque glacier

accumulation zone

valley glacier

lateral moraine

drumlin

medial moraine

ablation zone

terminal moraine/
front/terminus/snout

Glacier

Iceberg

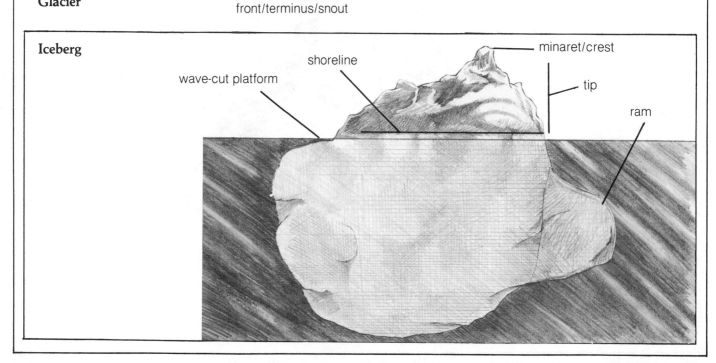

wave-cut platform

shoreline

minaret/crest

tip

ram

River

A *river system* consists of the main river and its tributaries or branches. It drains from a *river basin,* and flows along a *course,* or *watercourse,* cutting a *channel* through the land. A *flood* occurs when it overflows its banks.

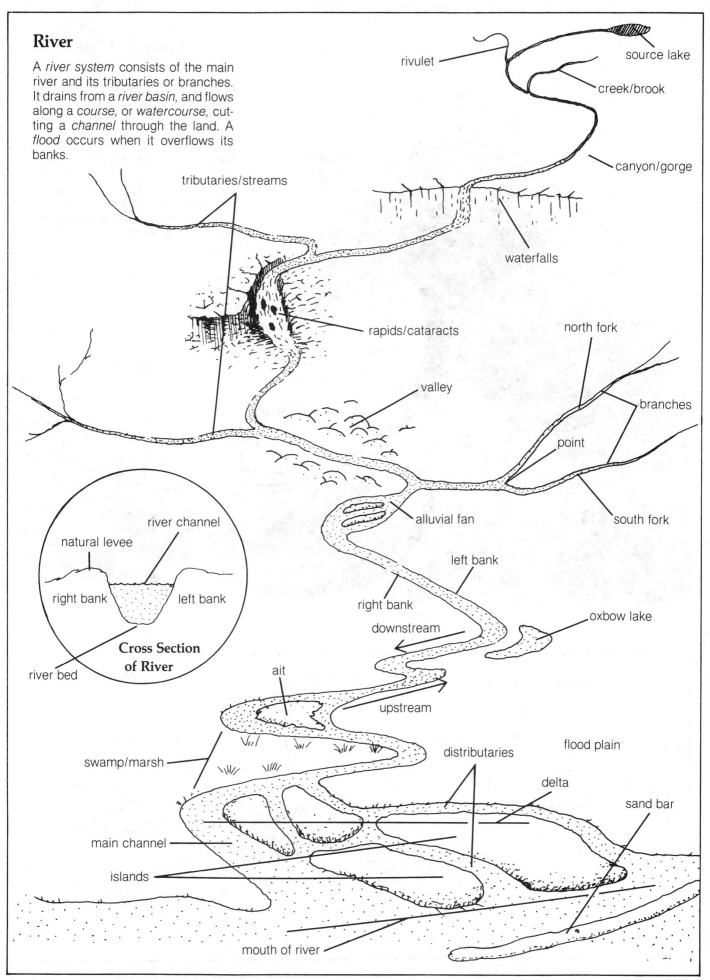

rivulet

source lake

creek/brook

canyon/gorge

tributaries/streams

waterfalls

rapids/cataracts

north fork

branches

valley

point

south fork

left bank

river channel

natural levee

right bank   left bank

Cross Section of River

river bed

alluvial fan

right bank

downstream

oxbow lake

ait

upstream

flood plain

swamp/marsh

distributaries

delta

sand bar

main channel

islands

mouth of river

Water Systems

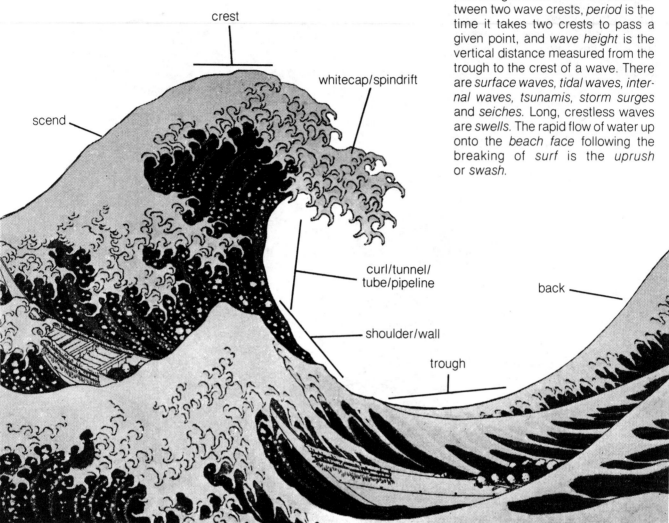

Wave and Shoreline

Wavelength is the linear distance between two wave crests, *period* is the time it takes two crests to pass a given point, and *wave height* is the vertical distance measured from the trough to the crest of a wave. There are *surface waves, tidal waves, internal waves, tsunamis, storm surges* and *seiches*. Long, crestless waves are *swells*. The rapid flow of water up onto the *beach face* following the breaking of *surf* is the *uprush* or *swash*.

crest

whitecap/spindrift

scend

curl/tunnel/
tube/pipeline

back

shoulder/wall

trough

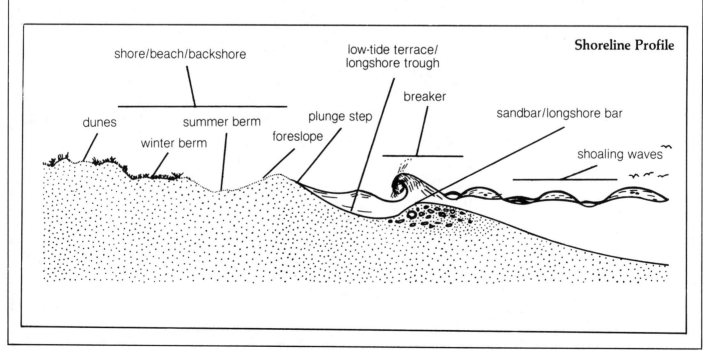

Shoreline Profile

shore/beach/backshore

low-tide terrace/
longshore trough

breaker

dunes

summer berm

plunge step

sandbar/longshore bar

winter berm

foreslope

shoaling waves

Coastline and Continental Margin

The *littoral zone* is that part of the shoreline that lies between *high* and *low tides*. The continental shelf is the submerged border of *landmasses* extending into the *ocean basin*. The *100-fathom curve* has long been used as the outer limit of the continental shelf.

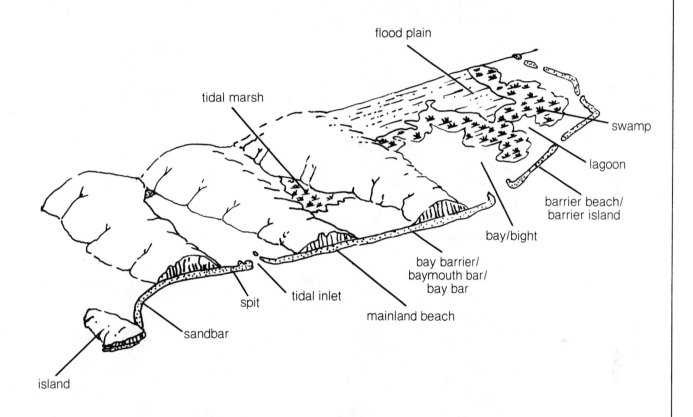

flood plain

tidal marsh

swamp

lagoon

barrier beach/
barrier island

bay/bight

bay barrier/
baymouth bar/
bay bar

spit

tidal inlet

mainland beach

sandbar

island

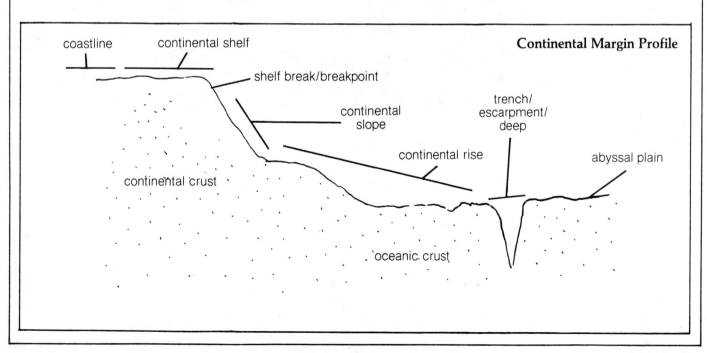

Continental Margin Profile

coastline

continental shelf

shelf break/breakpoint

continental slope

trench/
escarpment/
deep

continental rise

abyssal plain

continental crust

oceanic crust

Water Systems

Clouds

The name of a cloud describes both its appearance and its height above the ground. Clouds are formed from tiny droplets of water or *ice crystals* and continually change shape due to evaporation, wind and *air movements.*

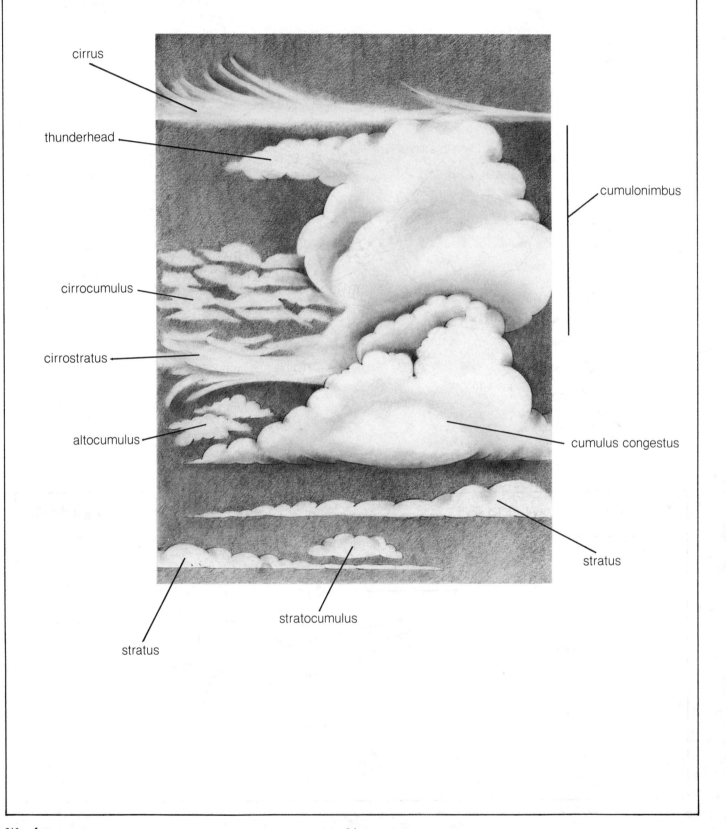

cirrus

thunderhead

cirrocumulus

cirrostratus

altocumulus

cumulonimbus

cumulus congestus

stratus

stratus

stratocumulus

Storm Systems

Thunderstorms carry the same general features: lightning, *thunder*, strong gusts of *wind*, heavy *showers*, and occasionally *hailstones*. When hurricanes occur in the Pacific, they are called *typhoons*. Tornados are also known as *twisters*.

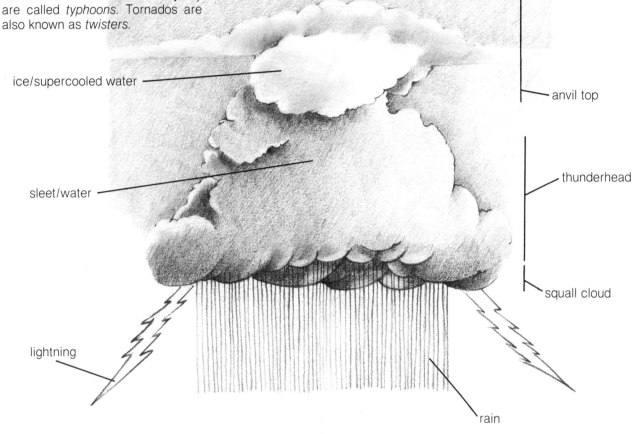

ice/supercooled water

anvil top

sleet/water

thunderhead

squall cloud

lightning

rain

Thunderstorm

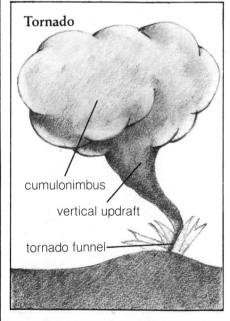

Tornado

cumulonimbus

vertical updraft

tornado funnel

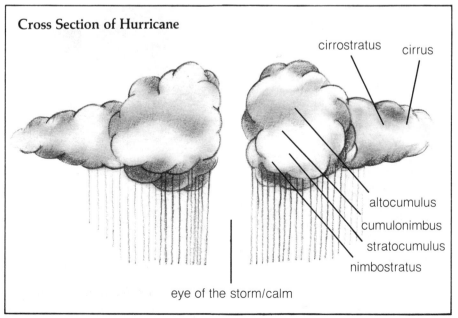

Cross Section of Hurricane

cirrostratus

cirrus

altocumulus

cumulonimbus

stratocumulus

nimbostratus

eye of the storm/calm

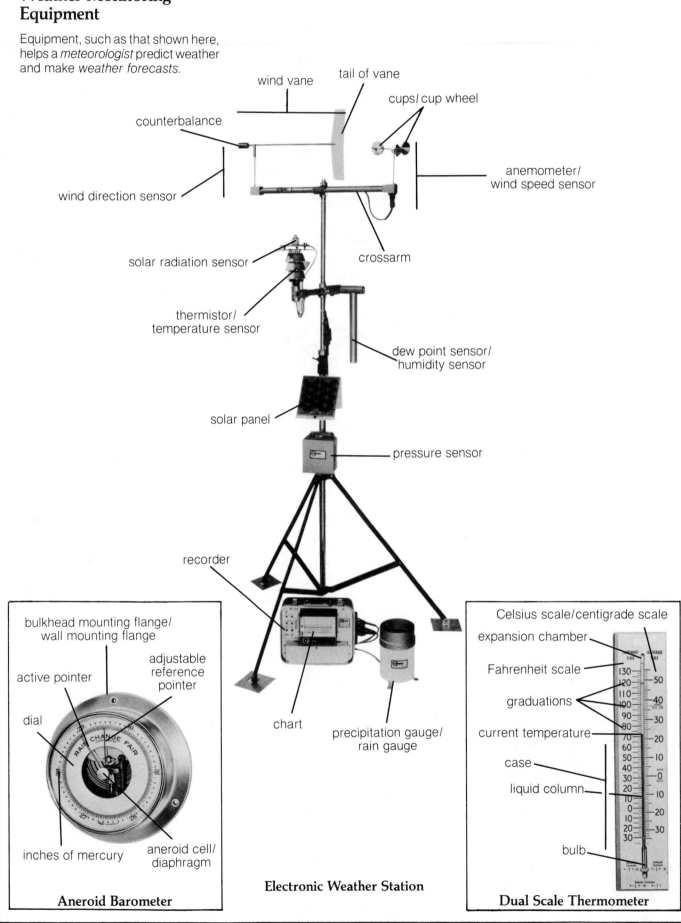

Weather Monitoring Equipment

Equipment, such as that shown here, helps a *meteorologist* predict weather and make *weather forecasts.*

wind vane

tail of vane

cups/cup wheel

counterbalance

anemometer/ wind speed sensor

wind direction sensor

crossarm

solar radiation sensor

thermistor/ temperature sensor

dew point sensor/ humidity sensor

solar panel

pressure sensor

recorder

Aneroid Barometer

bulkhead mounting flange/ wall mounting flange

adjustable reference pointer

active pointer

dial

inches of mercury

aneroid cell/ diaphragm

chart

precipitation gauge/ rain gauge

Electronic Weather Station

Dual Scale Thermometer

Celsius scale/centigrade scale

expansion chamber

Fahrenheit scale

graduations

current temperature

case

liquid column

bulb

Weather Map

This composite weather map, or *synoptic chart,* displays conditions over a broad area. The numbers around the station model indicate *temperature, barometric pressure* and *pressure change.*

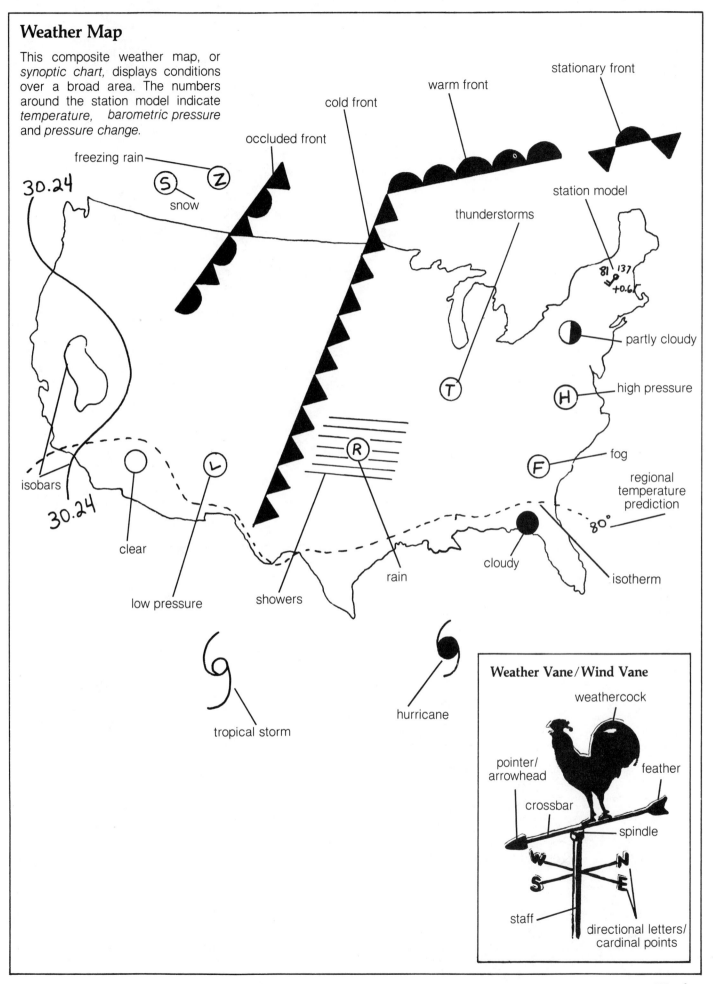

occluded front

freezing rain

snow

cold front

warm front

stationary front

thunderstorms

station model

partly cloudy

high pressure

fog

regional temperature prediction

isotherm

cloudy

rain

showers

low pressure

clear

isobars

30.24

30.24

81 137
+0.6

S

Z

T

H

F

R

L

tropical storm

hurricane

Weather Vane / Wind Vane

weathercock

pointer/arrowhead

feather

crossbar

spindle

staff

directional letters/cardinal points

Map

The science of *mapmaking* is also known as *cartography*. The *projection* of a map is the framework on which its main components, *linework*, point or area symbols and type are placed.

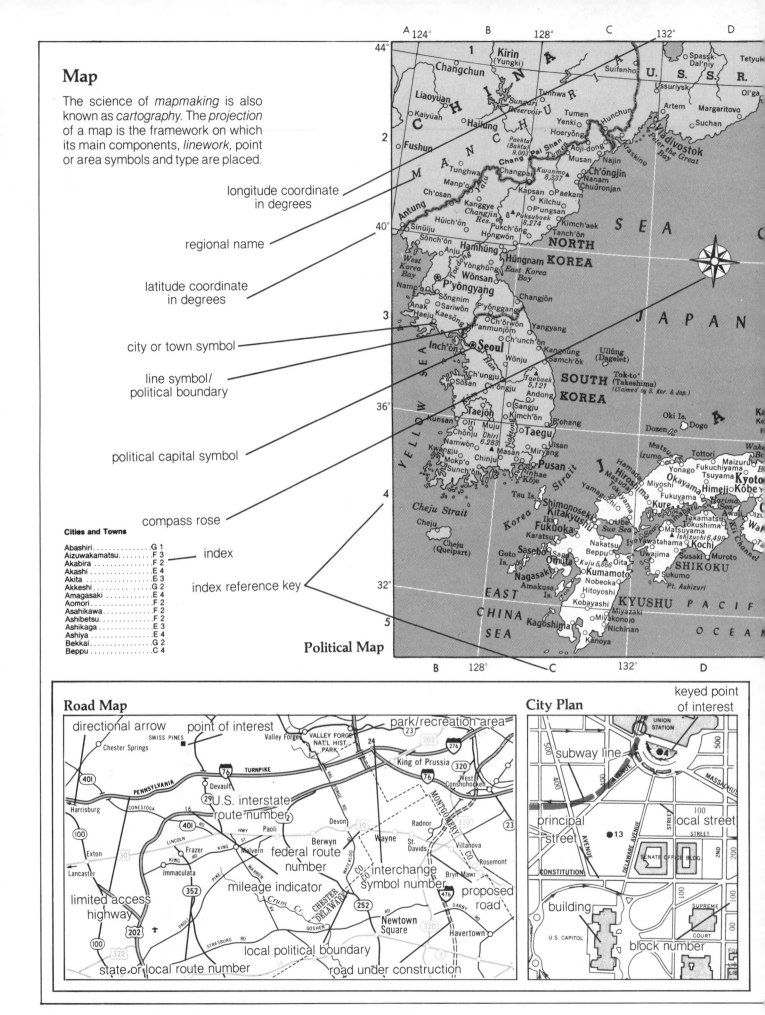

longitude coordinate in degrees

regional name

latitude coordinate in degrees

city or town symbol

line symbol/ political boundary

political capital symbol

compass rose

Cities and Towns

Abashiri	G 1
Aizuwakamatsu	F 3
Akabira	F 2
Akashi	E 4
Akita	E 3
Akkeshi	G 2
Amagasaki	E 4
Aomori	F 2
Asahikawa	F 2
Ashibetsu	F 2
Ashikaga	E 3
Ashiya	E 4
Bekkai	G 2
Beppu	C 4

index

index reference key

Political Map

Road Map

directional arrow
point of interest
park/recreation area
U.S. interstate route number
federal route number
mileage indicator
interchange symbol number
proposed road
limited access highway
local political boundary
state or local route number
road under construction

City Plan

keyed point of interest
subway line
principal street
local street
building
block number

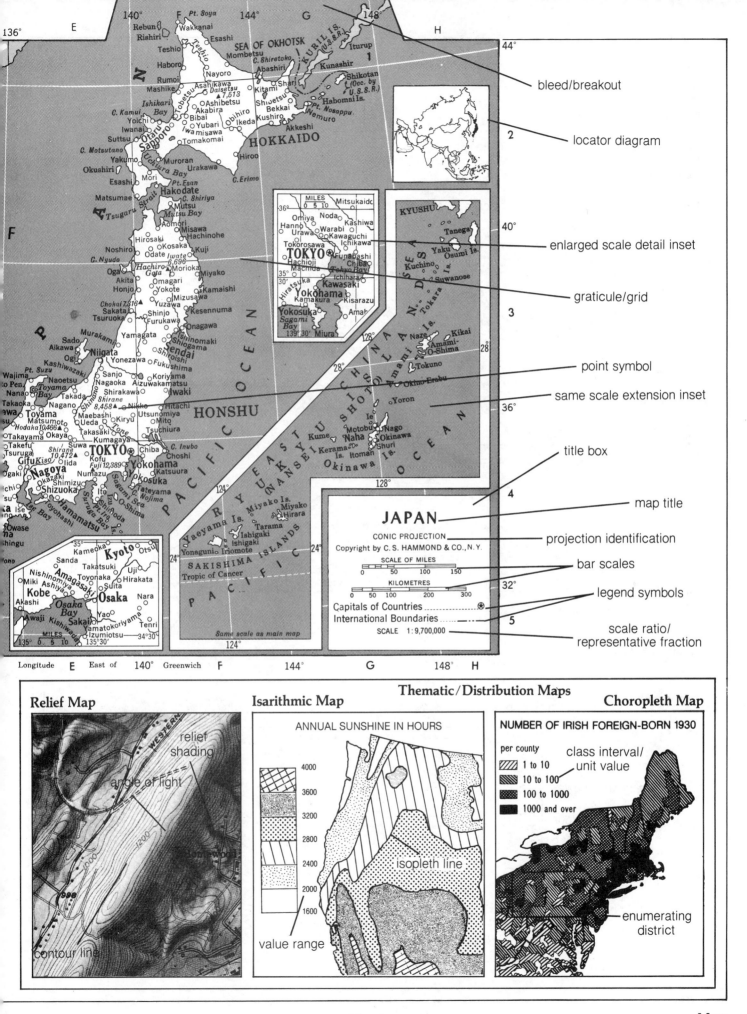

Maps

Nautical Chart and Topographic Map

On nautical charts, *sounding datum reference* is stated in the *chart title*. *Depth conversion scales* are provided to enable the mariner to work in *meters, fathoms,* or *feet*. The space outside a chart or map, used to identify and explain the map, is the *map margin*.

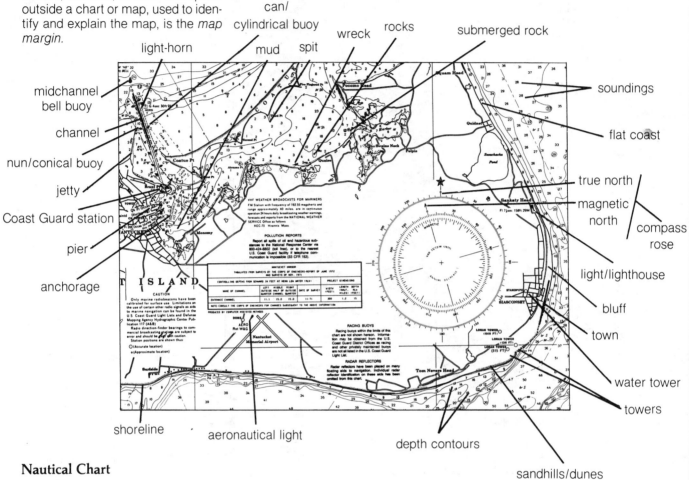

can/cylindrical buoy
wreck
rocks
submerged rock
light-horn
mud
spit
midchannel bell buoy
soundings
channel
flat coast
nun/conical buoy
jetty
Coast Guard station
true north
magnetic north
compass rose
pier
light/lighthouse
anchorage
bluff
town
water tower
towers
shoreline
aeronautical light
depth contours
sandhills/dunes

Nautical Chart

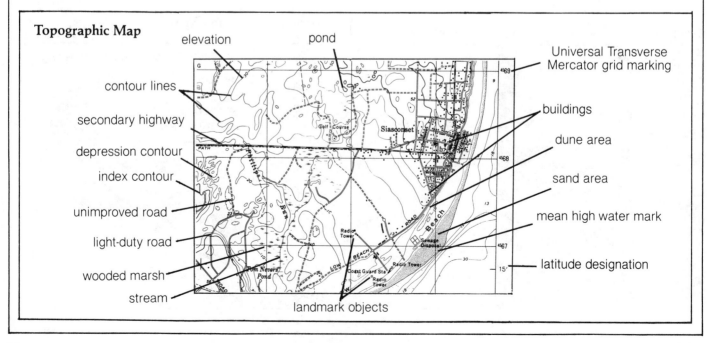

Topographic Map

elevation
pond
Universal Transverse Mercator grid marking
contour lines
buildings
secondary highway
dune area
depression contour
sand area
index contour
mean high water mark
unimproved road
light-duty road
latitude designation
wooded marsh
stream
landmark objects

Living Things

For ease of reference, this section has been divided into five subcategories: man, edible animals, domestic animals, wild animals, and plants. The animals and plants selected for inclusion within each subsection contain most of the parts common to all members of the major families they represent.

With the exception of man, examined more closely than any other subject in this section because of his obvious importance to us, only the external parts of living things have been identified. However, edible animals have been illustrated in such a way as to show those parts which supply our daily food. Domestic and wild animals, some of them grouped by habitat, are represented by single members of a species. But because there are parts which are unique to certain animals, a composite "beast" has been created to illustrate some of them.

The plant kingdom is represented from the roots up, literally, including coverage of parts of a flower, special plants, and edible portions called fruits and vegetables.

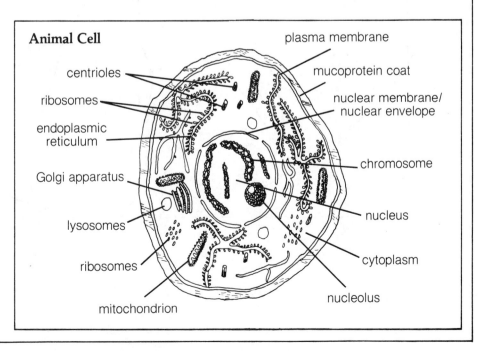

Animal Cell

plasma membrane

centrioles

mucoprotein coat

ribosomes

nuclear membrane/ nuclear envelope

endoplasmic reticulum

chromosome

Golgi apparatus

nucleus

lysosomes

cytoplasm

ribosomes

nucleolus

mitochondrion

The Human Body

The body, less the *head* and *limbs*, is referred to as the *trunk* or *torso*.

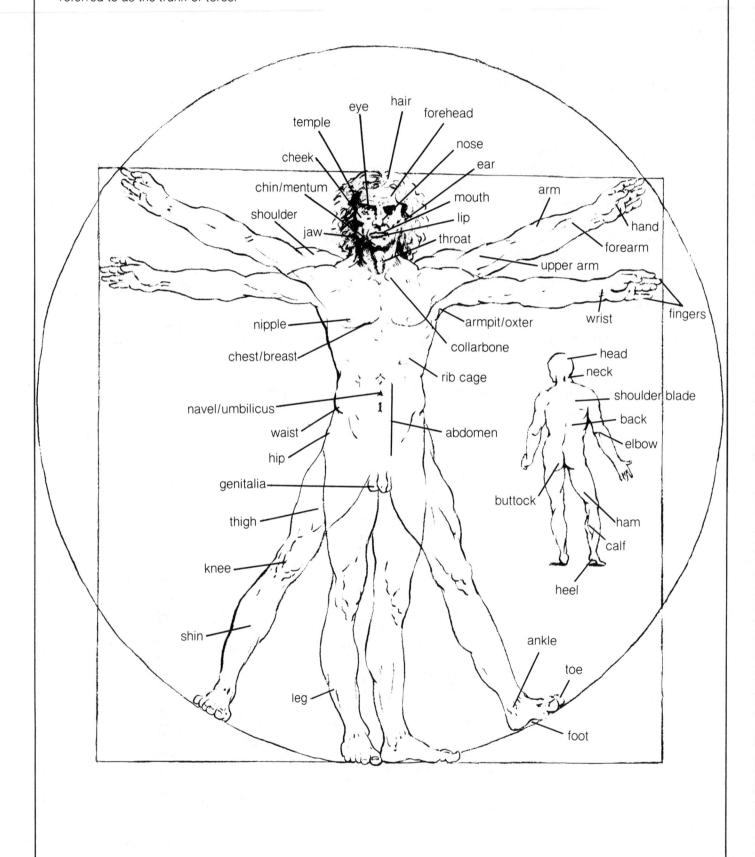

temple
eye
hair
forehead
cheek
nose
chin/mentum
ear
shoulder
mouth
jaw
lip
throat
arm
hand
forearm
upper arm
nipple
armpit/oxter
chest/breast
collarbone
wrist
fingers
rib cage
head
neck
navel/umbilicus
shoulder blade
waist
back
abdomen
elbow
hip
genitalia
thigh
buttock
ham
knee
calf
shin
heel
ankle
toe
leg
foot

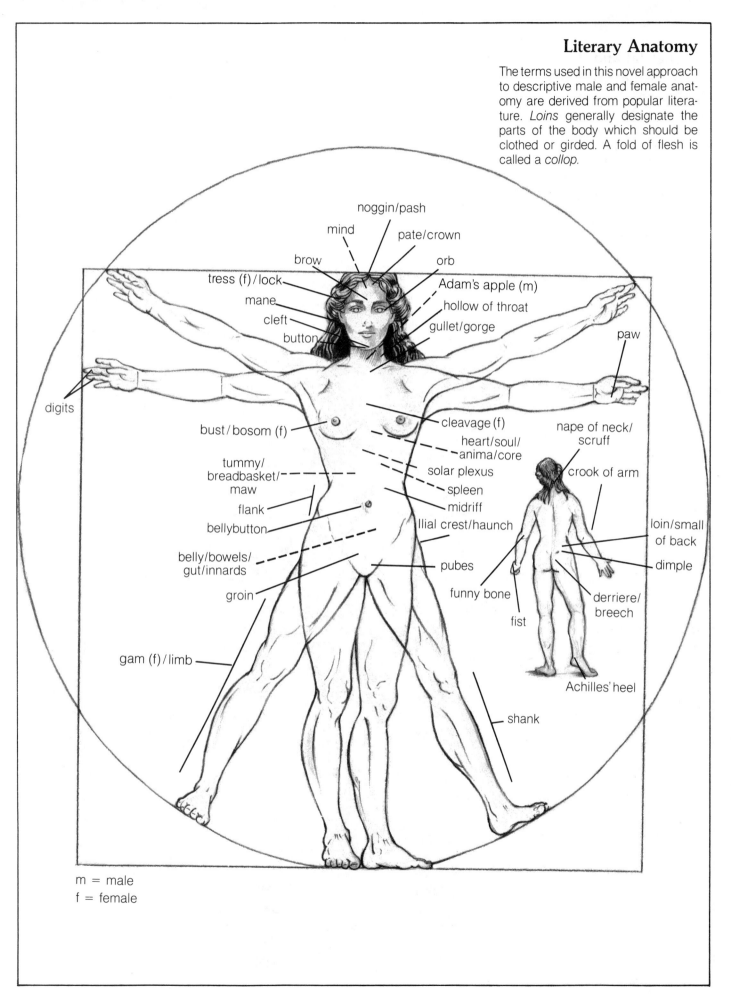

Literary Anatomy

The terms used in this novel approach to descriptive male and female anatomy are derived from popular literature. *Loins* generally designate the parts of the body which should be clothed or girded. A fold of flesh is called a *collop*.

noggin/pash

mind

brow

pate/crown

orb

tress (f)/lock

Adam's apple (m)

mane

hollow of throat

cleft

gullet/gorge

button

paw

digits

bust/bosom (f)

cleavage (f)

nape of neck/
scruff

heart/soul/
anima/core

crook of arm

tummy/
breadbasket/
maw

solar plexus

spleen

midriff

flank

loin/small
of back

bellybutton

Ilial crest/haunch

dimple

belly/bowels/
gut/innards

pubes

derriere/
breech

groin

funny bone

fist

gam (f)/limb

Achilles' heel

shank

m = male
f = female

25

Human Anatomy

Skeletal and Muscular System

Voluntary muscles are subject to or controlled by will, pulling on *bones* of the *skeleton* to produce movement. *Involuntary muscles,* like the heart, act independently of volition. Where one bone meets another is a *joint.* *Cartilage,* or *gristle,* is a flexible type of connective tissue. The bony structure in which the brain is housed is the *cranium.*

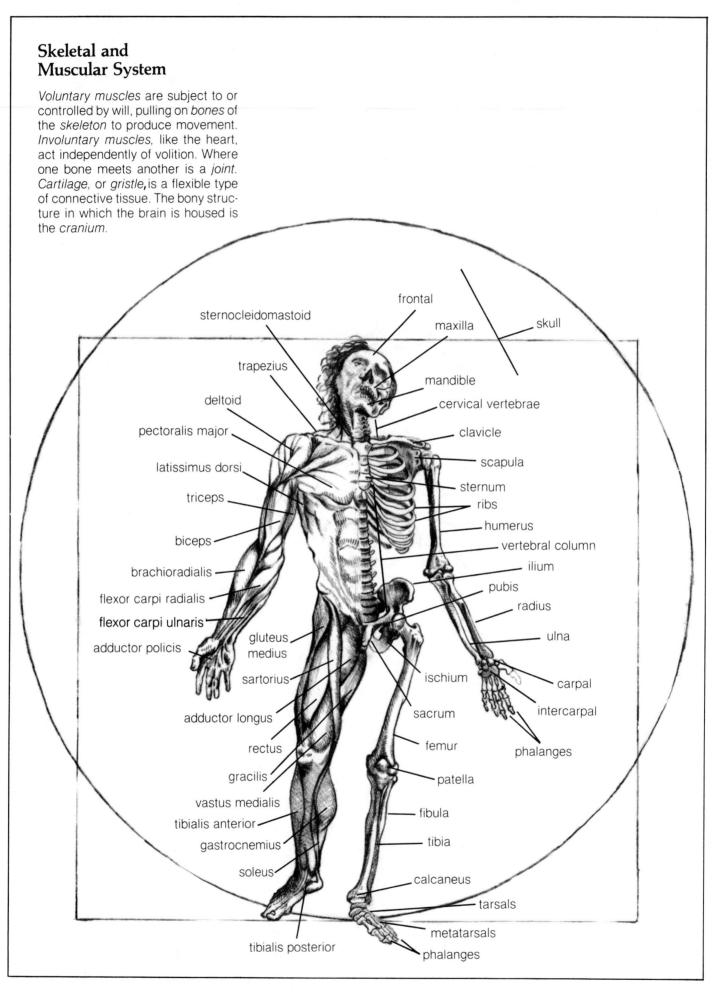

frontal

sternocleidomastoid

maxilla

skull

trapezius

mandible

deltoid

cervical vertebrae

pectoralis major

clavicle

latissimus dorsi

scapula

triceps

sternum

ribs

biceps

humerus

brachioradialis

vertebral column

flexor carpi radialis

ilium

flexor carpi ulnaris

pubis

adductor policis

radius

gluteus medius

ulna

sartorius

ischium

carpal

adductor longus

sacrum

intercarpal

rectus

femur

phalanges

gracilis

patella

vastus medialis

fibula

tibialis anterior

tibia

gastrocnemius

soleus

calcaneus

tarsals

metatarsals

tibialis posterior

phalanges

Internal Organs

The stomach and intestines are the principal organs of the *digestive system*, or *alimentary canal*, and the *pancreas*, liver and *gall bladder* all aid in the nutrition process and the elimination of wastes. The heart is the pump of the *circulatory system*, sending blood through *arteries, veins* and *capillaries*. The lungs are the center of the *respiratory system*.

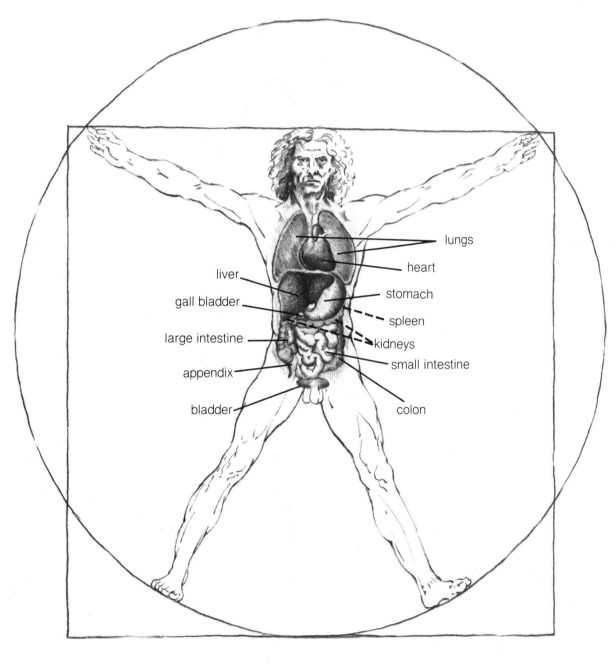

lungs

heart

liver

stomach

gall bladder

spleen

large intestine

kidneys

appendix

small intestine

bladder

colon

Human Anatomy

Circulation System and Heart

The heart pumps oxygenated and nutrient-rich blood throughout the body via arteries and their smaller branches, *arterioles*. Blood flows across body tissue through a network of small vessels, collectively called a *capillary bed*. Deoxygenated blood collects in small vessels called *venules*, which join to form veins.

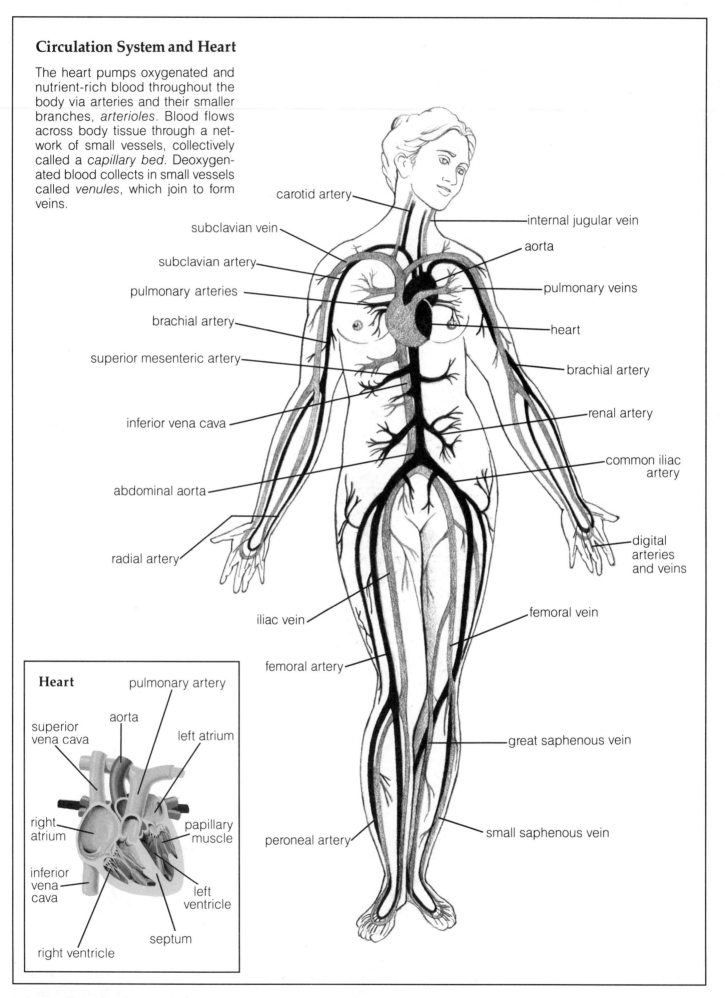

carotid artery

internal jugular vein

subclavian vein

aorta

subclavian artery

pulmonary veins

pulmonary arteries

heart

brachial artery

brachial artery

superior mesenteric artery

renal artery

inferior vena cava

common iliac artery

abdominal aorta

digital arteries and veins

radial artery

iliac vein

femoral vein

femoral artery

great saphenous vein

peroneal artery

small saphenous vein

Heart

pulmonary artery

aorta

superior vena cava

left atrium

right atrium

papillary muscle

inferior vena cava

left ventricle

right ventricle

septum

Nervous System and Brain

Nerve tissue is composed of specialized cells called *neurons*. *Nerves* are composed of *fibers* and accessory *sheaths*. *Sensory*, or *afferent nerves* carry impulses from *receptors* in the *sense organs* to the *central nervous system*. *Motor*, or *efferent nerves* lead in the other direction, out to muscles and other *effectors*.

cerebrum

brain

brain stem

spinal cord

brachial plexus

thoracic nerves

spinal nerves

lumbrosacral plexus

median nerve

ulnar nerve

radial nerve

femoral nerve

sciatic nerve

posterior tibial nerve

common peroneal nerve

sural nerve

tibial nerve

Brain

frontal lobe

cerebral cortex

meninges

parietal lobe

corpus callosum

thalamus

hypothalamus

pituitary gland

pons

temporal lobe

occipital lobe

cerebellum

medulla

Human Anatomy

Sense Organs

The eye, which is located in an *eye socket*, or *orbit*, is covered with a transparent layer called the *cornea*. The angle formed where upper and lower eyelids come together is called the *canthus*. The junction nearest the nose is the *inner canthus*, the other is the *outer canthus*. The tongue rubs against the *palate* at the top of the mouth. The *pharynx* is the beginning of the *throat*, or *gullet*.

Eye

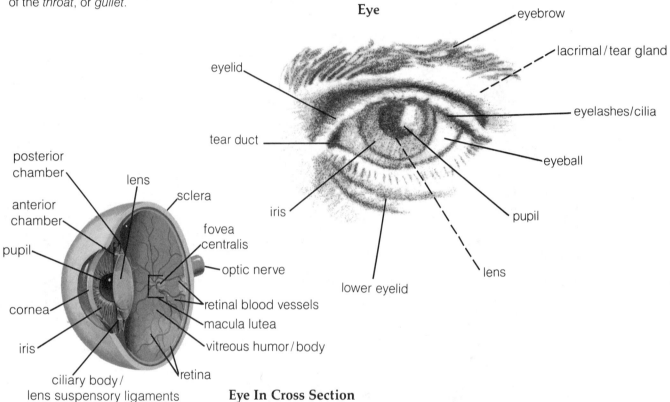

- eyebrow
- lacrimal / tear gland
- eyelid
- eyelashes/cilia
- tear duct
- eyeball
- iris
- pupil
- lower eyelid
- lens

Eye In Cross Section

- posterior chamber
- lens
- sclera
- anterior chamber
- fovea centralis
- pupil
- optic nerve
- cornea
- retinal blood vessels
- macula lutea
- iris
- vitreous humor / body
- ciliary body / lens suspensory ligaments
- retina

Nose and Mouth

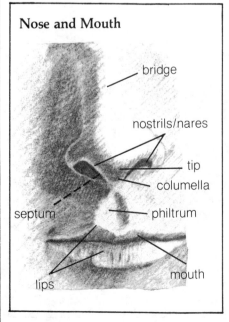

- bridge
- nostrils/nares
- tip
- columella
- septum
- philtrum
- mouth
- lips

Outer Ear / Auricle / Pinna

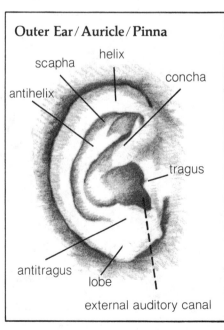

- scapha
- helix
- antihelix
- concha
- tragus
- antitragus
- lobe
- external auditory canal

Tongue

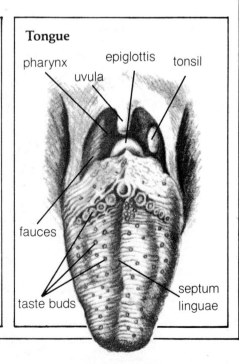

- pharynx
- epiglottis
- tonsil
- uvula
- fauces
- taste buds
- septum linguae

The Extremities

The space between the thumb and extended forefinger is the *purlicue*. A *fingerprint* is an ink impression of the *arches, loops* and *whorls* created by ridges of skin in the finger pad. The *back of the hand* is called the *opisthenar*.

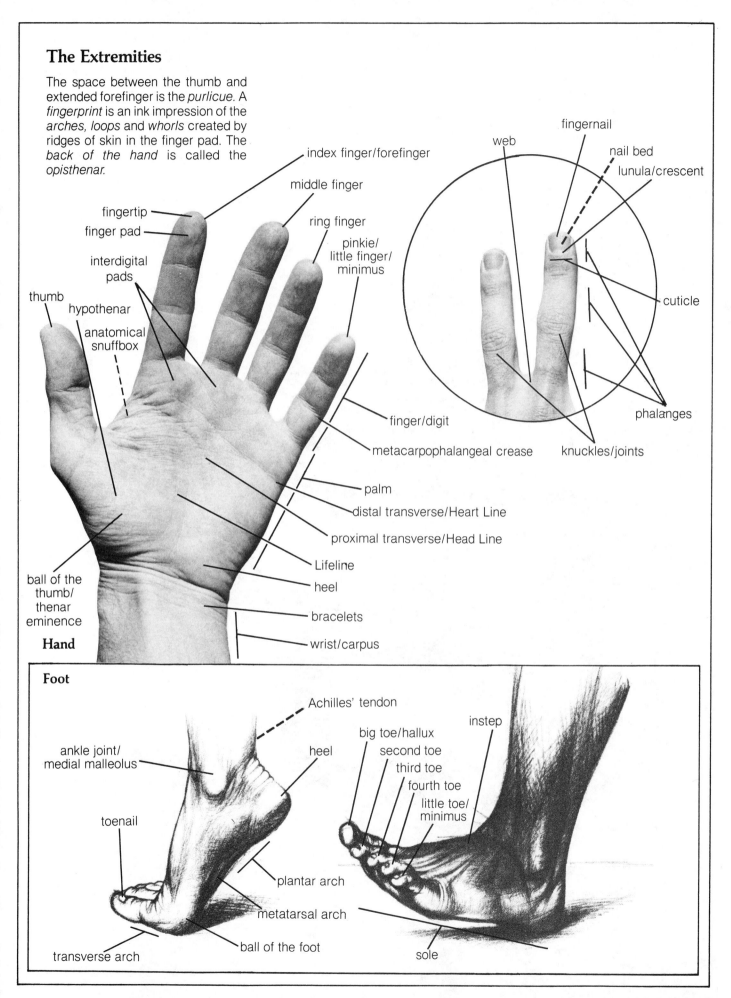

index finger/forefinger

middle finger

fingertip

finger pad

ring finger

pinkie/
little finger/
minimus

interdigital
pads

thumb

hypothenar

anatomical
snuffbox

finger/digit

metacarpophalangeal crease

palm

distal transverse/Heart Line

proximal transverse/Head Line

Lifeline

heel

ball of the
thumb/
thenar
eminence

bracelets

wrist/carpus

Hand

web

fingernail

nail bed

lunula/crescent

cuticle

phalanges

knuckles/joints

Foot

Achilles' tendon

ankle joint/
medial malleolus

heel

big toe/hallux

second toe

third toe

fourth toe

little toe/
minimus

instep

toenail

plantar arch

metatarsal arch

transverse arch

ball of the foot

sole

Human Anatomy

Cow

Young *cattle* are *calves;* females are *heifers* until they give birth and are then cows; males are *bulls.* Castrated males, raised for *beef,* are *steers.* Castrated males, raised as draft animals, are *oxen.* The body, or *torso,* of a cow is known as the *barrel.*

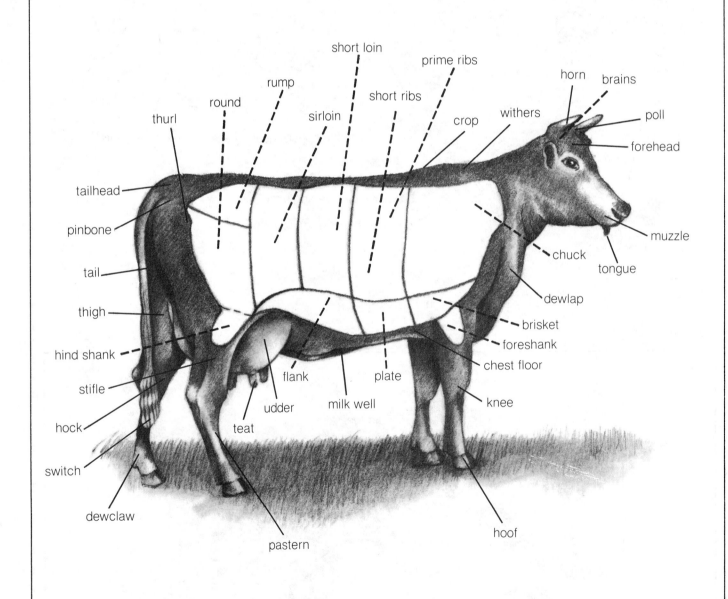

short loin

rump

round

prime ribs

thurl

sirloin

short ribs

horn

brains

crop

withers

poll

forehead

tailhead

pinbone

chuck

muzzle

tongue

tail

dewlap

thigh

brisket

hind shank

foreshank

chest floor

stifle

flank

plate

hock

udder

milk well

knee

switch

teat

dewclaw

pastern

hoof

Sheep

A young sheep is called a *lamb.* An adult male is a *ram;* an adult female is a *ewe.* The meat of a young sheep is called *lamb,* while that of an animal over eighteen months old is called *mutton.*

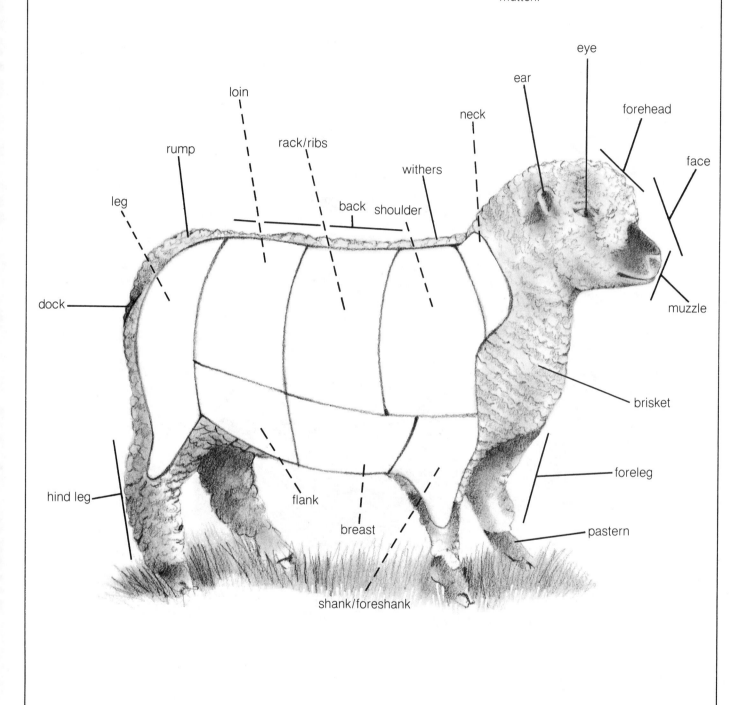

eye

ear

forehead

face

neck

withers

shoulder

back

rack/ribs

loin

rump

leg

dock

muzzle

brisket

foreleg

pastern

flank

breast

hind leg

shank/foreshank

Edible Animals

Pig

Young pigs are called *shoats*. Small or sub-adult domestic animals are *pigs* or *gruntlings*. If they weigh over 120 pounds, they are called *hogs*. Adult males are *boars*. Adult females are *sows*. Pigs, hogs, boars and sows are referred to as *swine*. Pig meat is called *pork*.

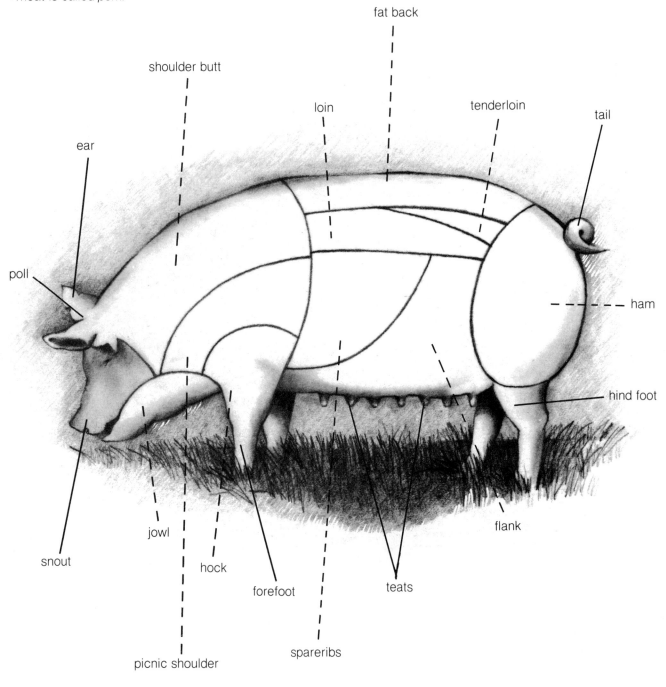

fat back

shoulder butt

loin

tenderloin

tail

ear

poll

ham

snout

jowl

hock

forefoot

teats

flank

hind foot

picnic shoulder

spareribs

Poultry

Chickens, turkeys, *ducks*, *geese* and *pheasants* are known collectively as *fowl* in the wild, as *poultry* if domesticated. A male chicken is a *rooster*; a female is a *hen*. A male turkey is a *tom*. Young chickens are *chicks*; young turkeys are *poults*. A *capon* is a male chicken that has been castrated before sexual maturity. Ducks have *webbed feet* and broad, flat *bills* with small teeth-like ridges. Among the *entrails* of a fowl, the most edible are the *giblets*: the *heart*, the *liver* and the *gizzard*.

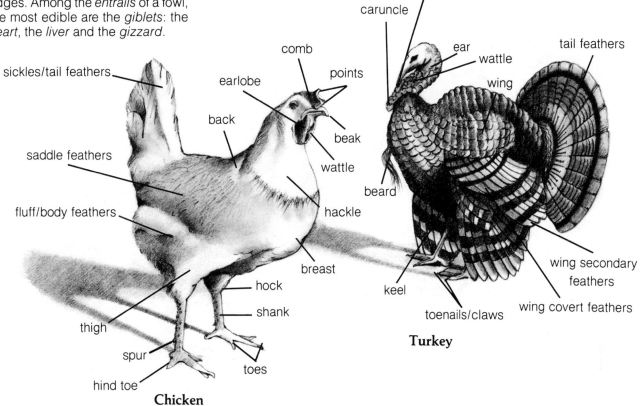

snood/dewbill
caruncle
comb
ear
wattle
tail feathers
earlobe
points
wing
back
beak
wattle
sickles/tail feathers
beard
saddle feathers
hackle
fluff/body feathers
breast
wing secondary feathers
keel
hock
wing covert feathers
shank
toenails/claws
thigh
spur
toes
hind toe

Chicken

Turkey

Poultry Parts

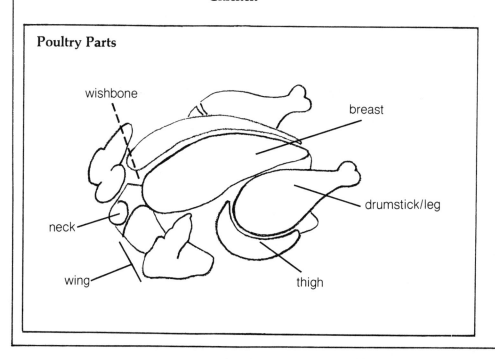

wishbone
breast
neck
drumstick/leg
wing
thigh

Edible Animals

Dog

Dogs are digitigrade animals; they walk on what are anatomically their four *fingertips*, or pads. The fifth finger, or *thumb*, a functionless inner claw, is known as a *dewclaw*, and does not reach the ground. The bushy tail of a rough-coated dog is called a *brush*. A smooth-coated dog's tail is a *stern*.

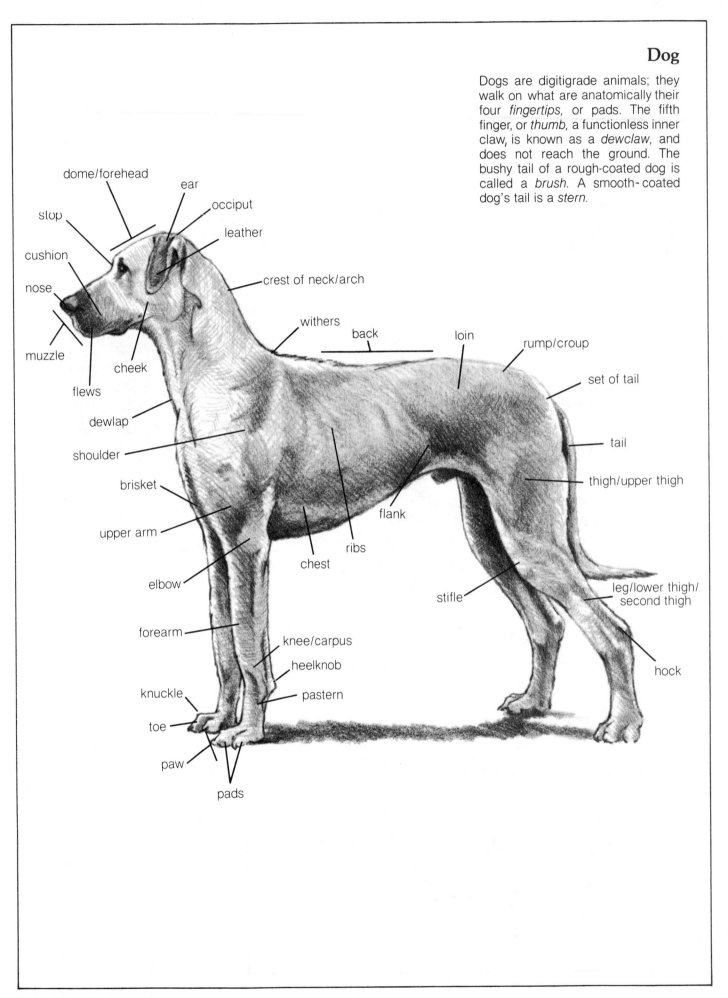

dome/forehead

ear

occiput

stop

leather

cushion

crest of neck/arch

nose

withers

back

loin

rump/croup

muzzle

set of tail

flews

cheek

tail

dewlap

thigh/upper thigh

shoulder

brisket

flank

upper arm

ribs

chest

elbow

stifle

leg/lower thigh/ second thigh

forearm

knee/carpus

hock

heelknob

knuckle

pastern

toe

paw

pads

Cat

Newborn cats are called *kittens*, adult males are *tomcats*, and adult females are *cattas*. Cats are capable of drawing their *toenails*, or *claws*, into *sheaths* located above the *pads* of their feet. A cat's *muzzle* consists of the *nose* and *jaw* sections of its face.

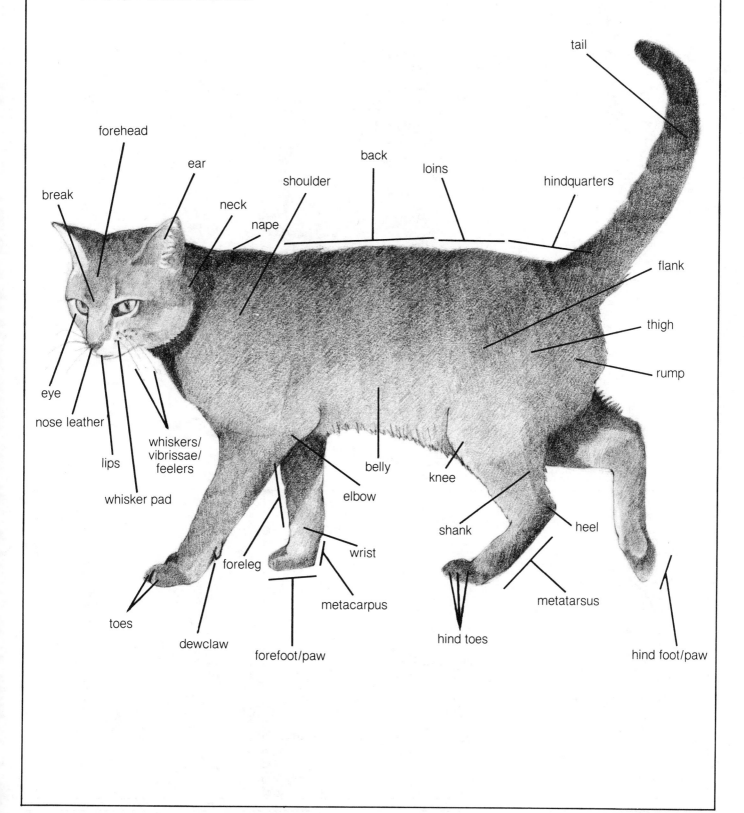

forehead

ear

break

neck

nape

shoulder

back

loins

hindquarters

tail

flank

thigh

rump

eye

nose leather

lips

whiskers/
vibrissae/
feelers

whisker pad

toes

dewclaw

foreleg

forefoot/paw

belly

elbow

wrist

metacarpus

knee

shank

hind toes

heel

metatarsus

hind foot/paw

37

Domestic Animals

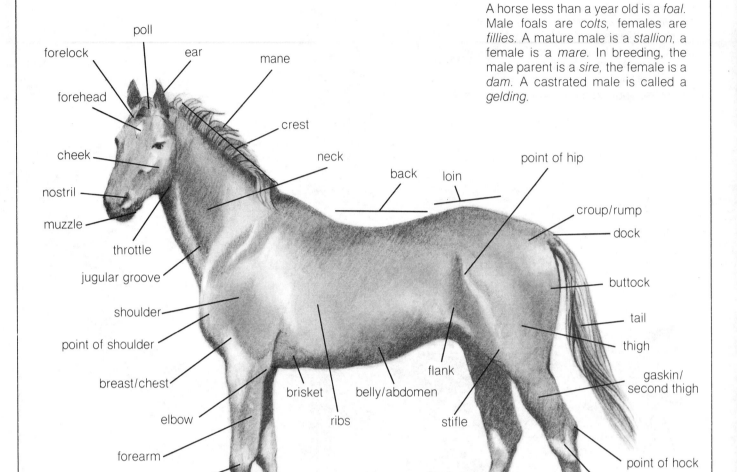

Horse

A horse less than a year old is a *foal*. Male foals are *colts*, females are *fillies*. A mature male is a *stallion*, a female is a *mare*. In breeding, the male parent is a *sire*, the female is a *dam*. A castrated male is called a *gelding*.

poll

forelock

ear

mane

forehead

crest

cheek

neck

nostril

back

loin

point of hip

muzzle

croup/rump

throttle

dock

jugular groove

buttock

shoulder

tail

point of shoulder

thigh

breast/chest

flank

gaskin/ second thigh

elbow

belly/abdomen

brisket

ribs

stifle

point of hock

forearm

hock

knee

heel

fetlock

cannon

coronet

hoof

pastern

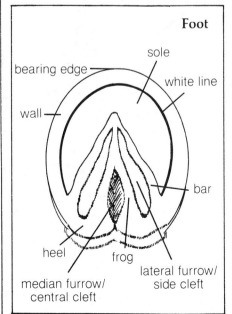

Foot

sole

bearing edge

white line

wall

bar

heel

frog

median furrow/ central cleft

lateral furrow/ side cleft

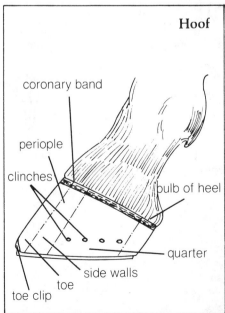

Hoof

coronary band

periople

clinches

bulb of heel

quarter

side walls

toe clip

toe

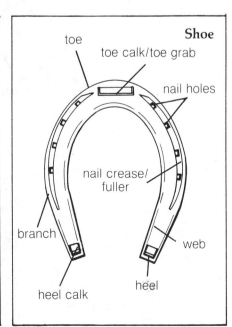

Shoe

toe

toe calk/toe grab

nail holes

nail crease/ fuller

branch

web

heel calk

heel

Bird

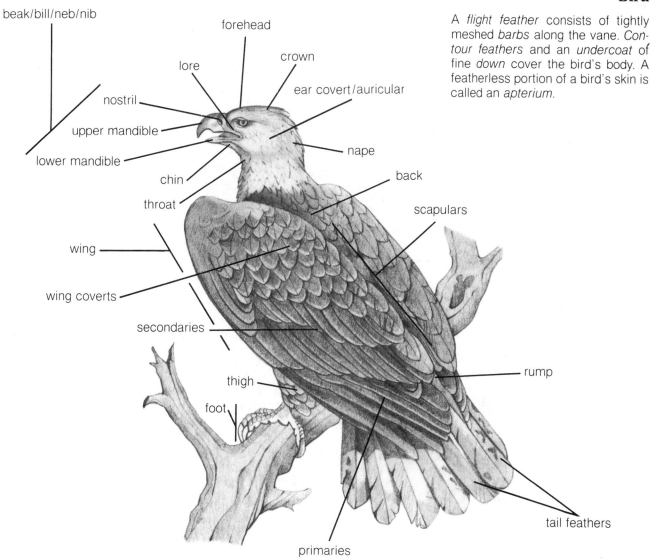

A *flight feather* consists of tightly meshed *barbs* along the vane. *Contour feathers* and an *undercoat* of fine *down* cover the bird's body. A featherless portion of a bird's skin is called an *apterium*.

beak/bill/neb/nib

forehead

lore

crown

ear covert/auricular

nostril

upper mandible

lower mandible

nape

chin

back

throat

scapulars

wing

wing coverts

secondaries

rump

thigh

foot

tail feathers

primaries

Grasping Foot

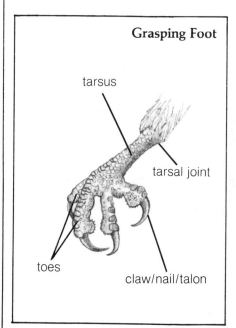

tarsus

tarsal joint

toes

claw/nail/talon

Swimming Foot/Webbed Foot

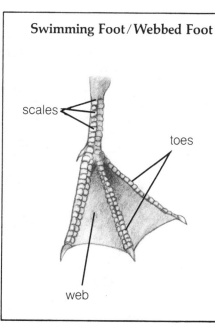

scales

toes

web

Feather

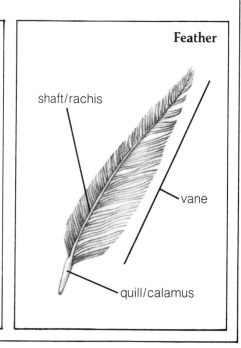

shaft/rachis

vane

quill/calamus

Wild Animals

Spider

Spiders produce *silk threads* which they use to make webs, *nests* or *parachutes* that allow the wind to carry them from one location to another. When a spider spins a web, it first constructs a *bridge* between two supports and fashions an *orb* beneath. A *scaffolding web* of dry thread is then used to lay down a *viscid spiral* of sticky thread.

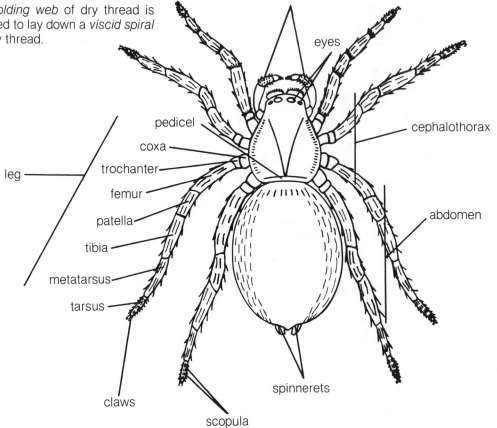

pedipalpi

eyes

pedicel

coxa

trochanter

femur

patella

tibia

metatarsus

tarsus

leg

claws

scopula

spinnerets

cephalothorax

abdomen

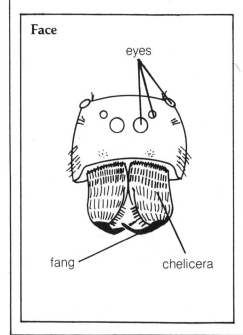

Face

eyes

fang

chelicera

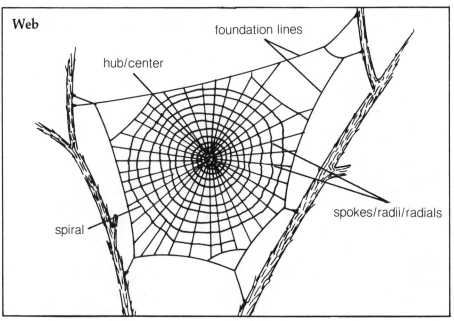

Web

foundation lines

hub/center

spokes/radii/radials

spiral

Insects

Insects have shell-like outer coverings called *exoskeletons*. Most undergo four stages during *metamorphosis:* the *egg*, the *larva*, the *pupa*, and the *adult*.

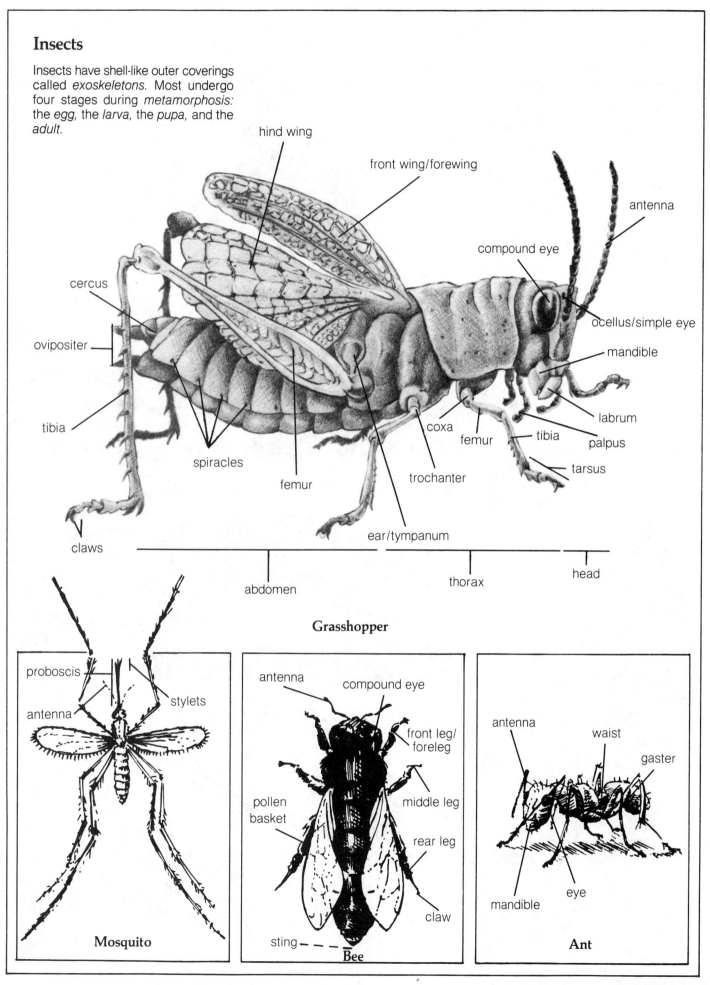

hind wing

front wing/forewing

antenna

compound eye

ocellus/simple eye

mandible

labrum

palpus

tibia

tarsus

femur

coxa

trochanter

ear/tympanum

femur

spiracles

tibia

ovipositer

cercus

claws

abdomen

thorax

head

Grasshopper

proboscis

stylets

antenna

Mosquito

antenna

compound eye

front leg/foreleg

middle leg

rear leg

pollen basket

claw

sting

Bee

antenna

waist

gaster

eye

mandible

Ant

Wild Animals

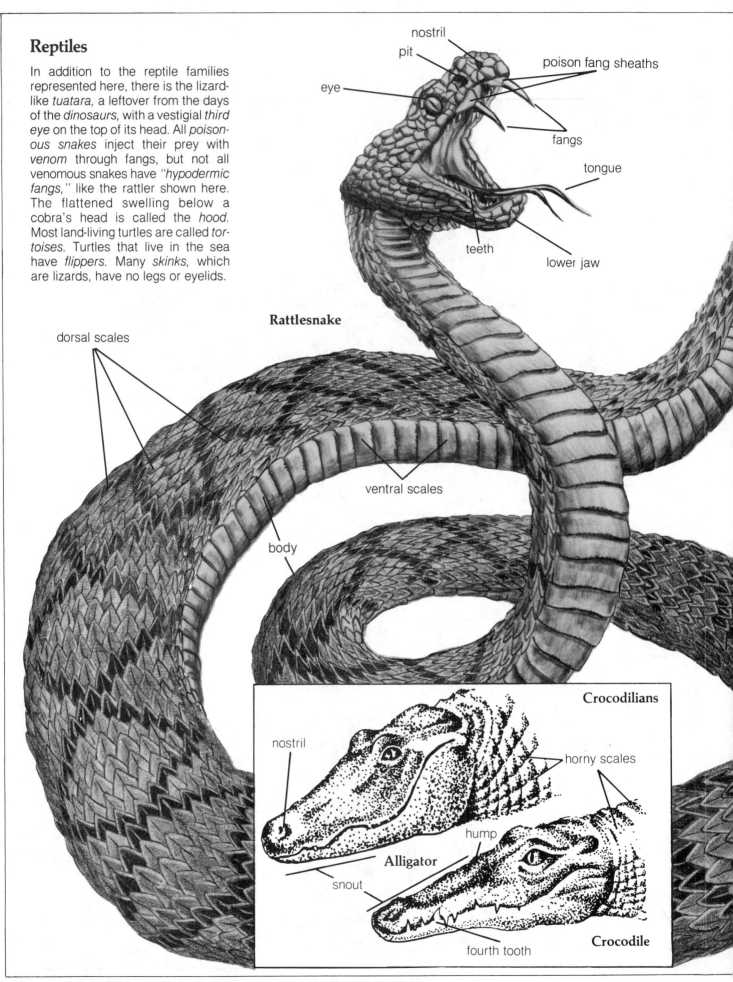

Reptiles

In addition to the reptile families represented here, there is the lizard-like *tuatara*, a leftover from the days of the *dinosaurs*, with a vestigial *third eye* on the top of its head. All *poisonous snakes* inject their prey with *venom* through fangs, but not all venomous snakes have "*hypodermic fangs*," like the rattler shown here. The flattened swelling below a cobra's head is called the *hood*. Most land-living turtles are called *tortoises*. Turtles that live in the sea have *flippers*. Many *skinks*, which are lizards, have no legs or eyelids.

nostril

pit

eye

poison fang sheaths

fangs

tongue

teeth

lower jaw

Rattlesnake

dorsal scales

ventral scales

body

Crocodilians

nostril

horny scales

hump

Alligator

snout

fourth tooth

Crocodile

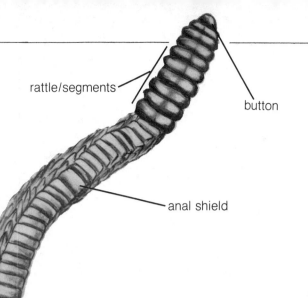

rattle/segments

button

anal shield

Dinosaurs/Extinct Reptiles

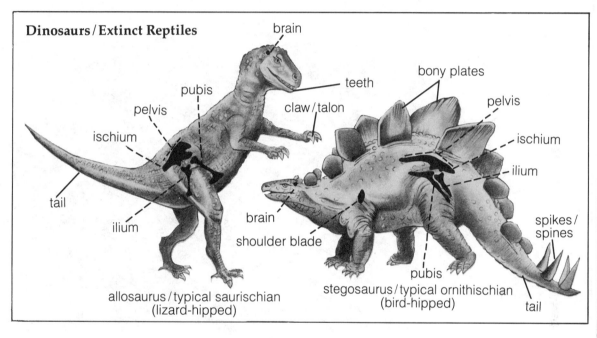

brain

teeth

pubis

claw/talon

pelvis

ischium

bony plates

pelvis

ischium

ilium

tail

ilium

spikes/
spines

brain

shoulder blade

pubis

allosaurus/typical saurischian
(lizard-hipped)

stegosaurus/typical ornithischian
(bird-hipped)

tail

Turtle/Tortoise

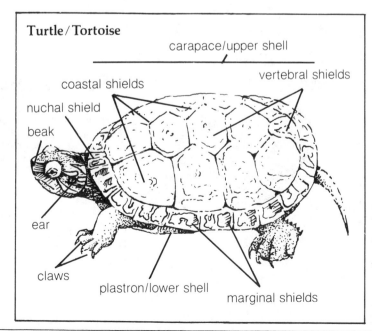

carapace/upper shell

coastal shields

vertebral shields

nuchal shield

beak

ear

claws

plastron/lower shell

marginal shields

Lizard/Iguana

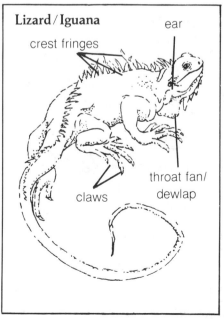

ear

crest fringes

throat fan/
dewlap

claws

Wild Animals

Amphibians

Frogs and toads resemble one another closely, but toads are characteristically more terrestrial and have rougher, drier skin.

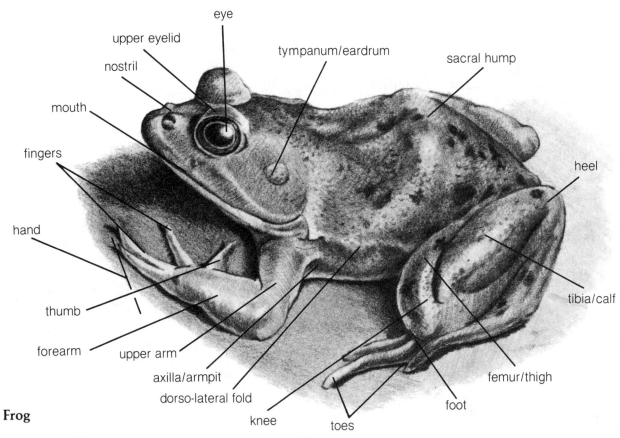

eye

upper eyelid

nostril

tympanum/eardrum

sacral hump

mouth

fingers

heel

hand

thumb

tibia/calf

forearm

upper arm

axilla/armpit

dorso-lateral fold

femur/thigh

knee

foot

toes

Frog

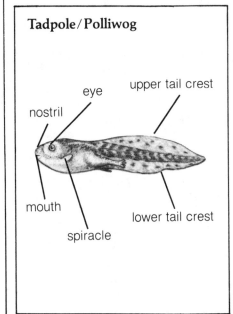

Tadpole/Polliwog

upper tail crest

eye

nostril

mouth

spiracle

lower tail crest

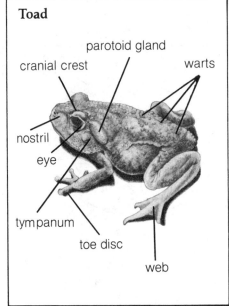

Toad

parotoid gland

cranial crest

warts

nostril

eye

tympanum

toe disc

web

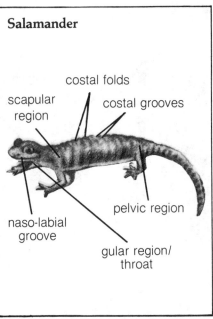

Salamander

costal folds

scapular region

costal grooves

naso-labial groove

pelvic region

gular region/ throat

Marine Life

Fish often swim in groups, called *schools*, and reproduce by depositing eggs, or *spawning*. Recently hatched or small adult fish are called *fry*.

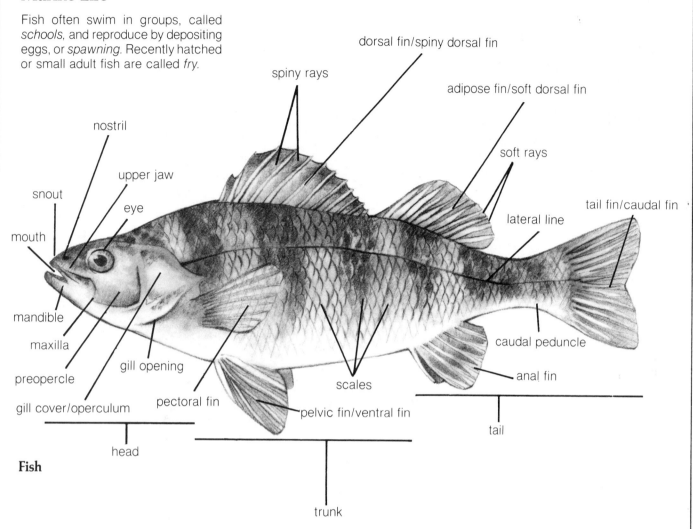

spiny rays

dorsal fin/spiny dorsal fin

adipose fin/soft dorsal fin

soft rays

nostril

upper jaw

snout

eye

tail fin/caudal fin

mouth

lateral line

mandible

maxilla

preopercle

gill opening

gill cover/operculum

pectoral fin

caudal peduncle

anal fin

scales

pelvic fin/ventral fin

head

tail

Fish

trunk

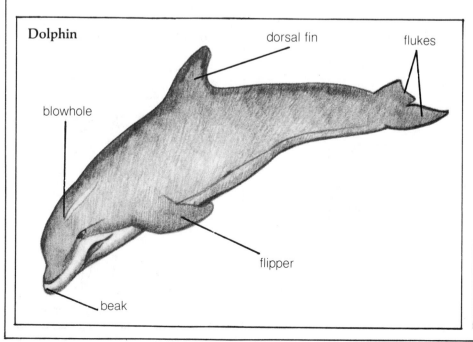

Dolphin

dorsal fin

flukes

blowhole

flipper

beak

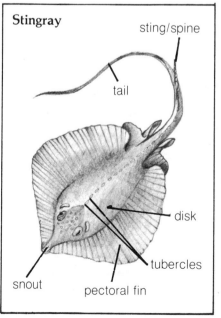

Stingray

sting/spine

tail

disk

tubercles

snout

pectoral fin

Wild Animals

Marine Life

The *mantle* of an octopus is the tough protective wrapper that covers the body and gives it shape. Octopuses and squid have *chromatophores,* or *pigment cells,* which enable them to change color, as well as *ink glands,* or *sacs,* that secrete protective *"ink."* Starfish have *mouths* on their *oral surfaces.* Coral polyps live within limestone *skeletons,* which form the basis for *coral reefs.*

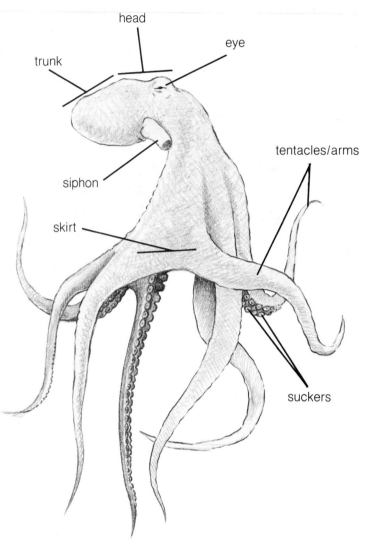

head

eye

trunk

tentacles/arms

siphon

skirt

suckers

Octopus/Devilfish

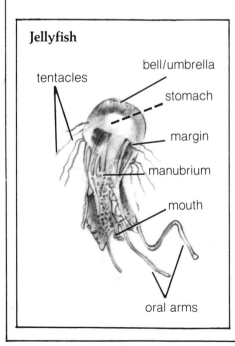

Jellyfish

tentacles

bell/umbrella

stomach

margin

manubrium

mouth

oral arms

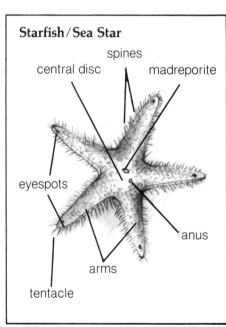

Starfish/Sea Star

spines

central disc

madreporite

eyespots

anus

tentacle

arms

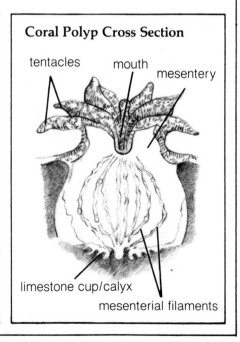

Coral Polyp Cross Section

tentacles

mouth

mesentery

limestone cup/calyx

mesenterial filaments

Shellfish

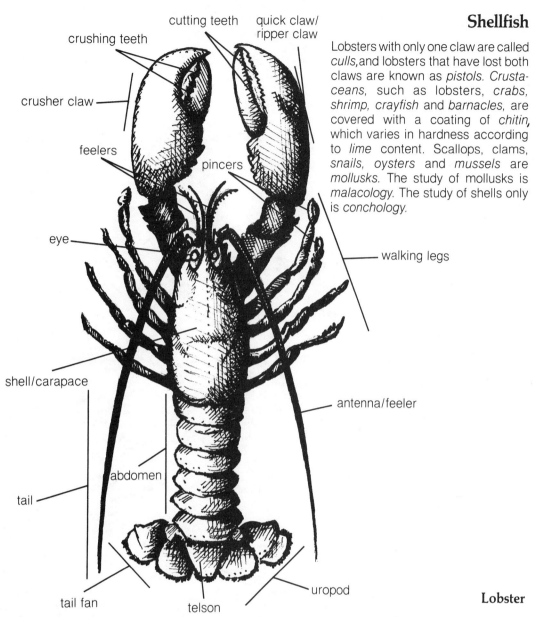

Lobsters with only one claw are called *culls,* and lobsters that have lost both claws are known as *pistols. Crustaceans,* such as lobsters, *crabs, shrimp, crayfish* and *barnacles,* are covered with a coating of *chitin,* which varies in hardness according to *lime* content. Scallops, clams, *snails, oysters* and *mussels* are *mollusks.* The study of mollusks is *malacology.* The study of shells only is *conchology.*

cutting teeth

quick claw/ ripper claw

crushing teeth

crusher claw

feelers

pincers

eye

walking legs

shell/carapace

antenna/feeler

abdomen

tail

tail fan

telson

uropod

Lobster

Univalve Shell/Snail

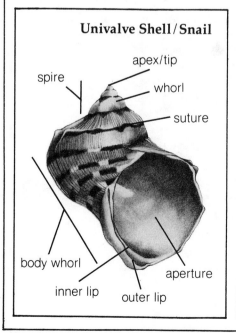

spire

apex/tip

whorl

suture

body whorl

inner lip

outer lip

aperture

Bivalve Shell/Scallop

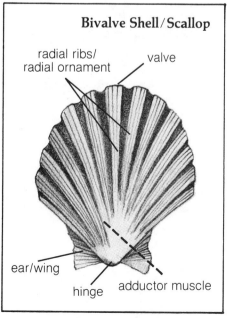

radial ribs/ radial ornament

valve

ear/wing

hinge

adductor muscle

Bivalve Shell/Clam

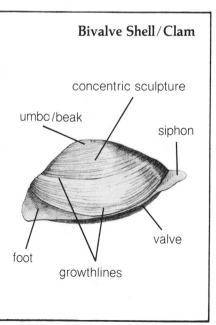

concentric sculpture

umbo/beak

siphon

foot

growthlines

valve

Wild Animals

Ultimate Beast

This remarkable *creature* calls attention to those parts of animals which are distinctive to particular species. Missing are posterior extensions, or *tails,* which vary from long, thin tails that end in a *brush* and have a horny appendage called a *thorn* in the middle, such as a lion's, to brushy fox tails and stubby boar tails. Another composite animal is the legendary *manticore,* which combined the head of a man, the body of a lion, and the tail of a *dragon* or *scorpion.*

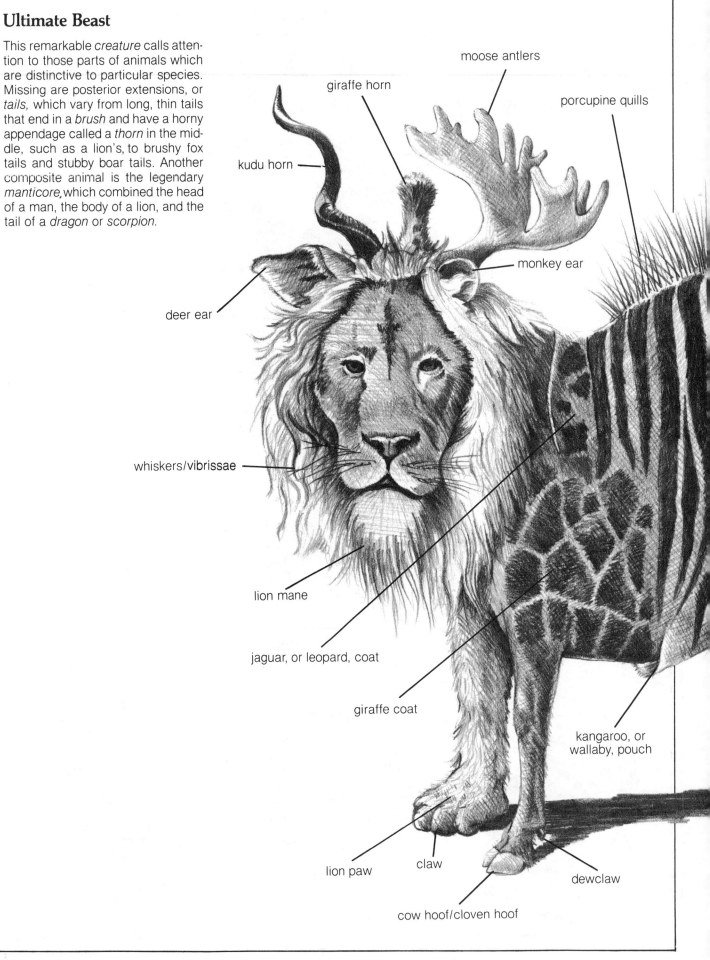

moose antlers

giraffe horn

porcupine quills

kudu horn

monkey ear

deer ear

whiskers/vibrissae

lion mane

jaguar, or leopard, coat

giraffe coat

kangaroo, or wallaby, pouch

lion paw

claw

dewclaw

cow hoof/cloven hoof

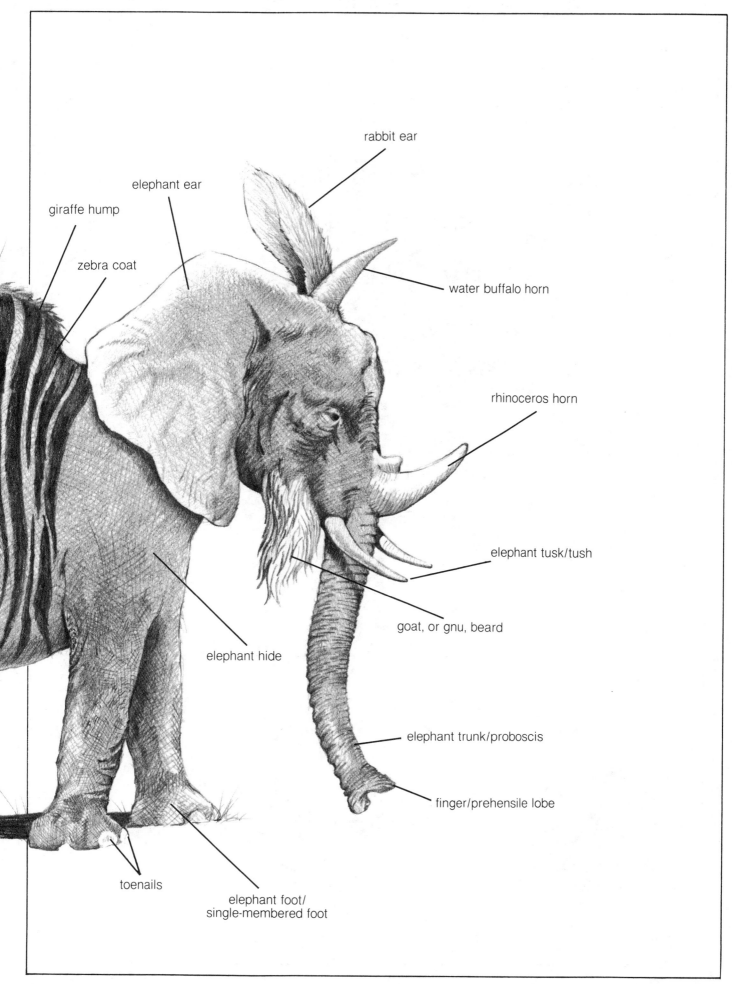

giraffe hump

zebra coat

elephant ear

rabbit ear

water buffalo horn

rhinoceros horn

elephant tusk/tush

goat, or gnu, beard

elephant hide

elephant trunk/proboscis

finger/prehensile lobe

toenails

elephant foot/
single-membered foot

49

Wild Animals

Tree

When a tree is cut down, what remains attached to the *root* is called a *stump*.

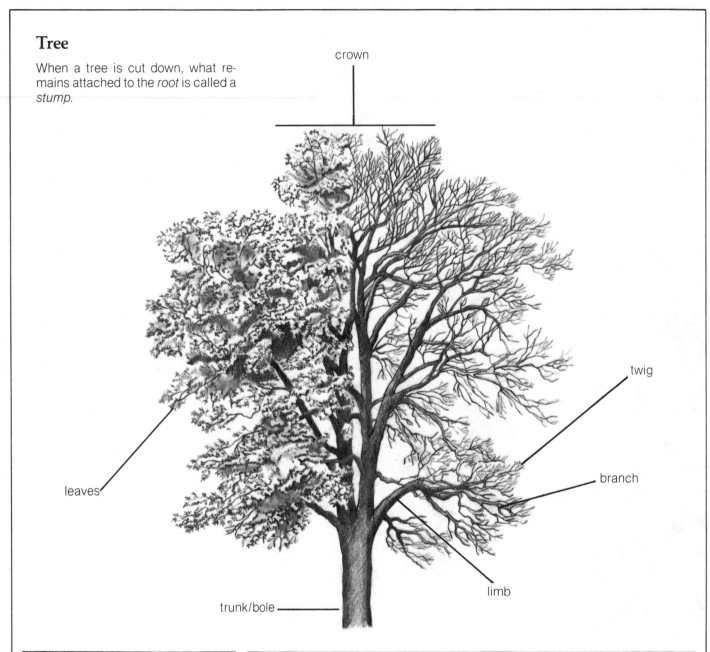

crown

twig

branch

limb

leaves

trunk/bole

Tree Trunk Cross Section

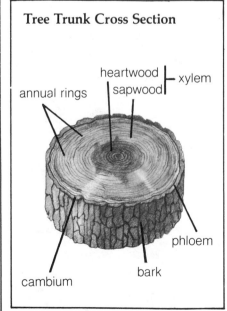

heartwood ⎤
sapwood ⎦ xylem

annual rings

phloem

cambium

bark

Twig

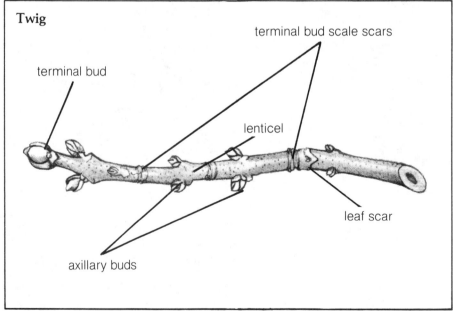

terminal bud scale scars

terminal bud

lenticel

leaf scar

axillary buds

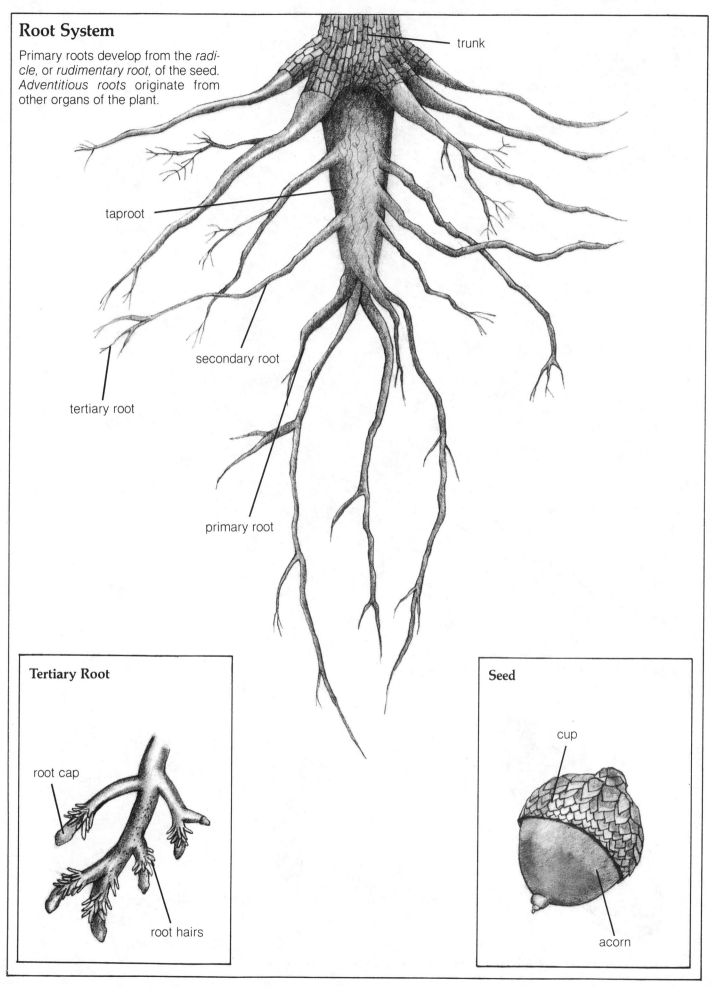

Root System

Primary roots develop from the *radicle,* or *rudimentary root,* of the seed. *Adventitious roots* originate from other organs of the plant.

trunk

taproot

secondary root

tertiary root

primary root

Tertiary Root

root cap

root hairs

Seed

cup

acorn

Plants

Leaf

The waxy layer covering the outer leaf is the *cuticle*. Tiny leaves, spines or growths at the base of a leaf stem are called *stipules*. *Compound leaves* are made up of two or more blades, or *leaflets*. The aggregate of leaves produced by one or more plants is called *foliage*.

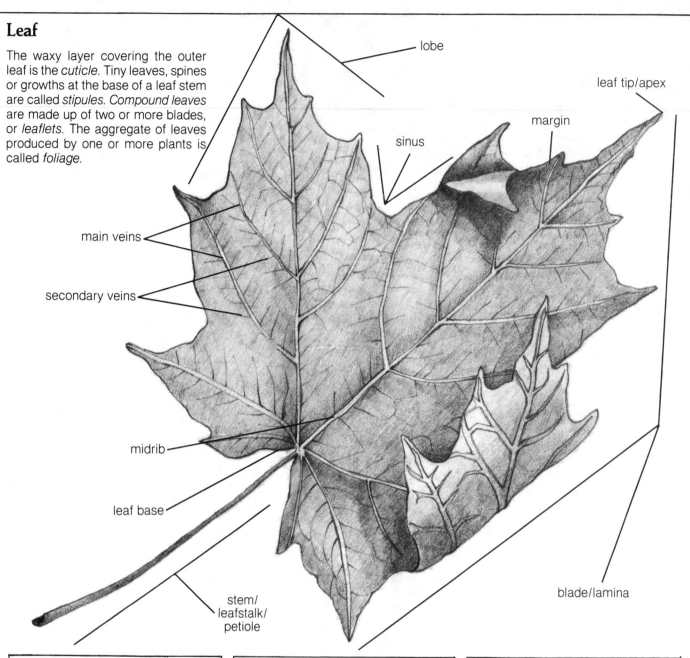

lobe

leaf tip/apex

margin

sinus

main veins

secondary veins

midrib

leaf base

stem/
leafstalk/
petiole

blade/lamina

Pine Cone

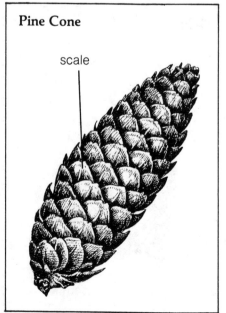

scale

Samara/Key

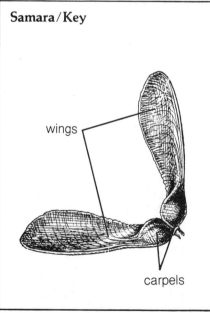

wings

carpels

Palm

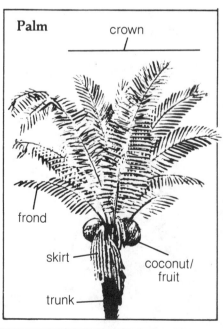

crown

frond

skirt

coconut/
fruit

trunk

Flower

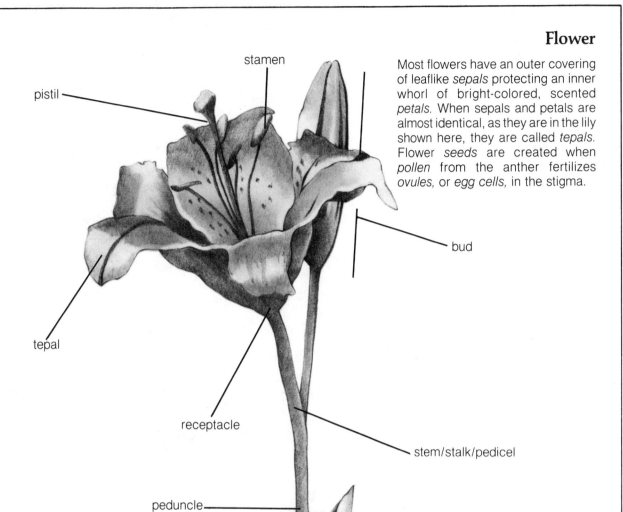

pistil

stamen

Most flowers have an outer covering of leaflike *sepals* protecting an inner whorl of bright-colored, scented *petals*. When sepals and petals are almost identical, as they are in the lily shown here, they are called *tepals*. Flower *seeds* are created when *pollen* from the anther fertilizes *ovules*, or *egg cells*, in the stigma.

bud

tepal

receptacle

stem/stalk/pedicel

peduncle

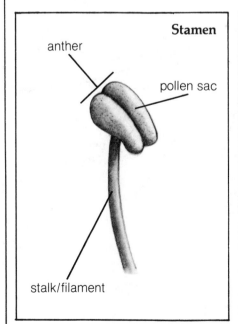

Stamen

anther

pollen sac

stalk/filament

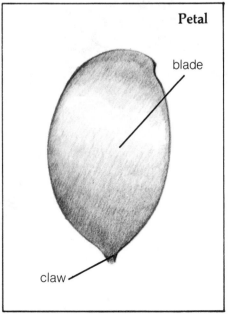

Petal

blade

claw

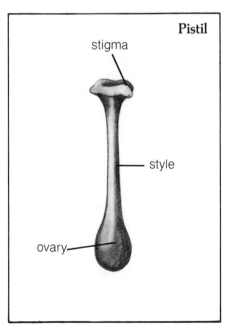

Pistil

stigma

style

ovary

Plants

Vegetables

A vegetable is that part of a plant that can be eaten. The roots of carrots, beets and turnips are edible, as are asparagus stems, potato tubers, leek and onion leaf bases, cabbage, lettuce and spinach leaves, the *immature fruit,* or *ovary,* of cucumbers, peas and summer squash, and the *mature fruit* of tomatoes and winter squash.

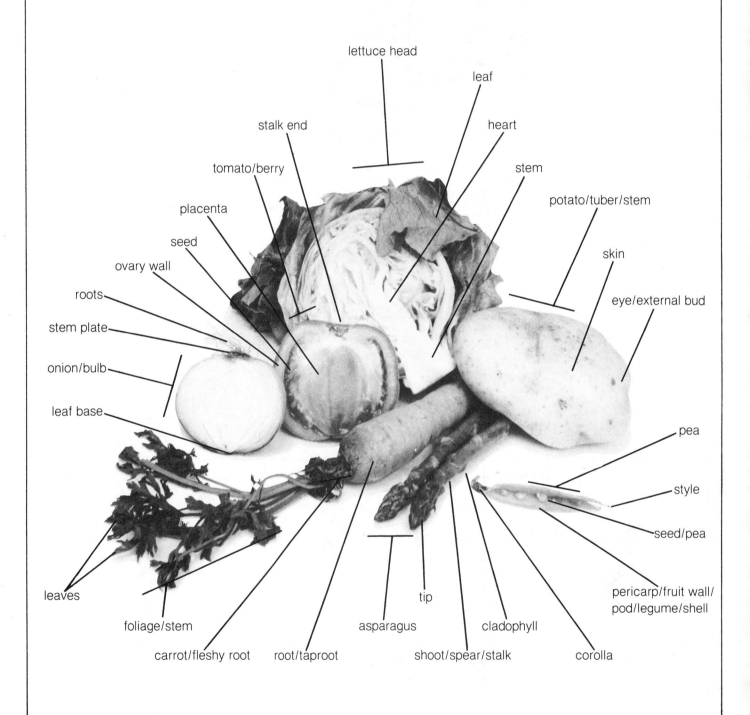

lettuce head

leaf

stalk end

heart

tomato/berry

stem

placenta

potato/tuber/stem

seed

skin

ovary wall

eye/external bud

roots

stem plate

onion/bulb

pea

leaf base

style

seed/pea

pericarp/fruit wall/ pod/legume/shell

leaves

tip

foliage/stem

carrot/fleshy root

root/taproot

asparagus

cladophyll

shoot/spear/stalk

corolla

Nuts and crops commonly referred to as vegetables, such as tomatoes and melons, are actually *vegetable fruits.* Fruits are classed according to the number of ovaries they have: They range from simple fruits, such as peaches, to aggregate fruits, such as strawberries. Each segment of *multiple fruits,* such as pineapples and figs, is edible.

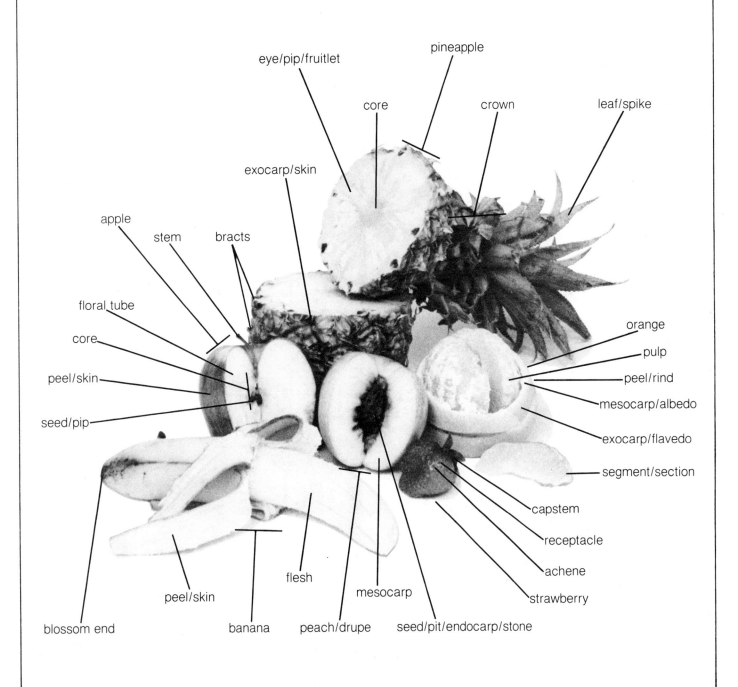

eye/pip/fruitlet

pineapple

core

crown

leaf/spike

exocarp/skin

apple

stem

bracts

floral tube

orange

core

pulp

peel/skin

peel/rind

seed/pip

mesocarp/albedo

exocarp/flavedo

segment/section

capstem

receptacle

achene

strawberry

peel/skin

blossom end

banana

flesh

peach/drupe

mesocarp

seed/pit/endocarp/stone

Plants

Succulents

Succulents are plants with *fleshy tissue* that have the ability to store moisture for long periods of time in their stem. Some cacti have protective *glochidia,* razor-sharp hairlike bristles, in addition to spines and flowers.

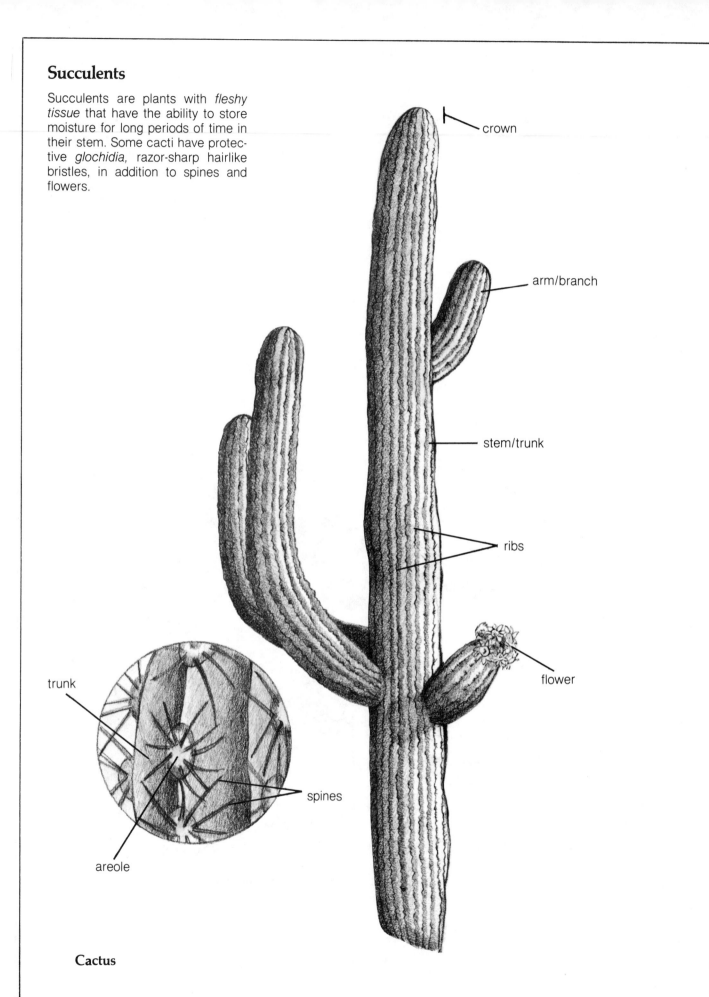

crown

arm/branch

stem/trunk

ribs

flower

trunk

spines

areole

Cactus

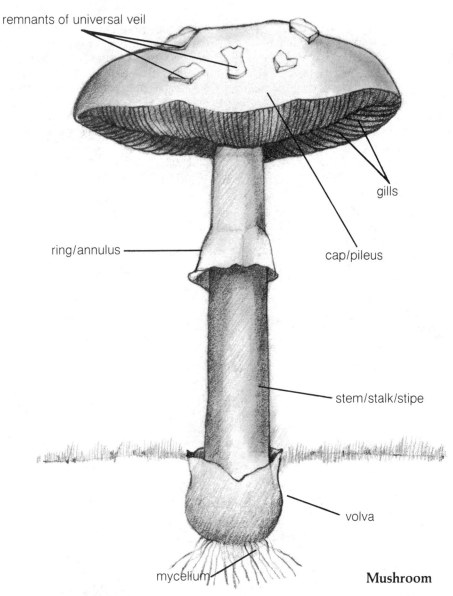

remnants of universal veil

gills

ring/annulus

cap/pileus

stem/stalk/stipe

volva

mycelium

Mushroom

Special Plants

Toadstools are inedible mushrooms, or *fungi*. Flowerless, seedless ferns reproduce by means of *spores* carried in spore cases on the underside of the leaves. Seaweed, such as the *marine algae* shown here, attaches itself to the ocean floor by means of a *holdfast*.

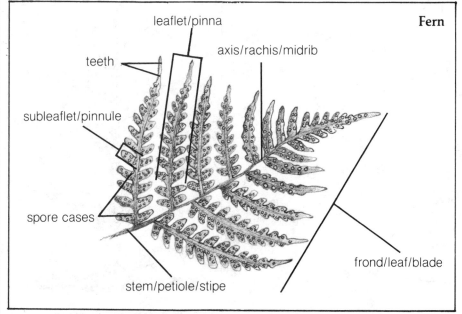

Fern

leaflet/pinna

axis/rachis/midrib

teeth

subleaflet/pinnule

spore cases

stem/petiole/stipe

frond/leaf/blade

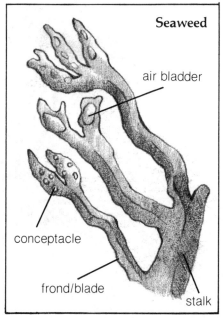

Seaweed

air bladder

conceptacle

frond/blade

stalk

Plants

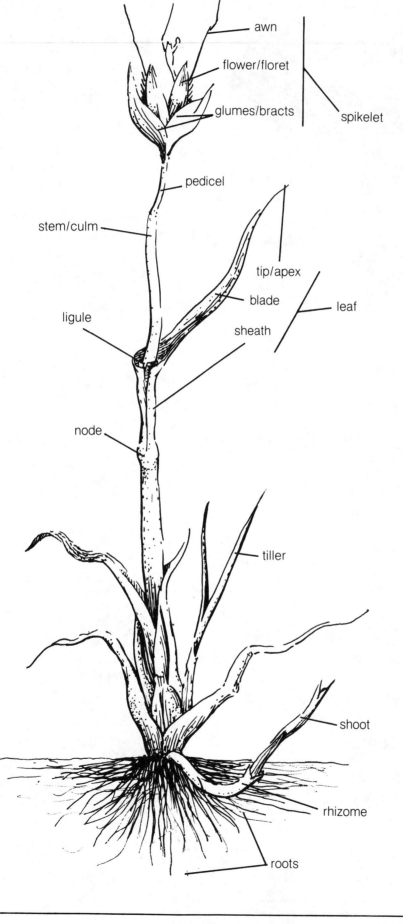

awn

flower/floret

glumes/bracts

spikelet

pedicel

stem/culm

tip/apex

blade

leaf

ligule

sheath

node

tiller

shoot

rhizome

roots

Grass

There are two parts to grass plants, the *vegetable organs* and the *floral organs*. *Cereal grasses*, such as *wheat, oat, barley* and corn, produce edible *fruit, seed* or *kernels*. Rhizomes and *stolons*, or *runners*—above-ground stems—spread out from grass plants to produce new plants. The *inflorescence*, or *flower cluster*, of grasses consists of many spikelets. Grass leaves are *parallel-veined*.

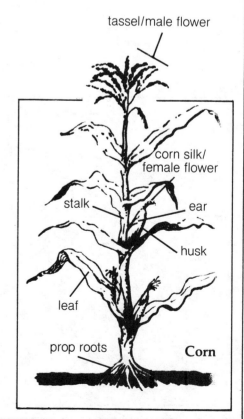

tassel/male flower

corn silk/
female flower

stalk

ear

husk

leaf

prop roots

Corn

Shelters and Structures

Since man's most basic shelter is a house, it is illustrated in a variety of ways, from foundation and frame to windows and walls.

The shelters and structures in the rest of the section are grouped in three subcategories: designs from other lands, which range from pagodas to pyramids; special-purpose buildings such as the Capitol and the White House, skyscrapers and prisons, amusement parks and airports; and other structures which bear on our everyday lives—bridges, tunnels, canals and dams.

The terms for the parts of objects found in most shelter interiors are the same as those found in a house, all of which have been illustrated. But those of a courtroom are sufficiently different to merit coverage, as are the parts of a skyscraper's elevator and escalator. In some cases floor plans and cross-section illustrations have been used to facilitate the reader's access to terms which are unique to a particular structure.

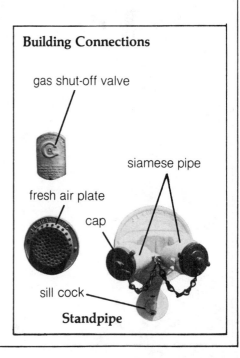

Building Connections

gas shut-off valve

siamese pipe

fresh air plate

cap

sill cock

Standpipe

Foundation

Some houses are built on sunken *posts*, or *piers*. Others are built on concrete floors, or *slabs*. The area of a house built below ground level is the *basement*. Houses without basements usually have an area between the floor joists and the ground called a *crawl space*, through which access is gained to inspect pipes.

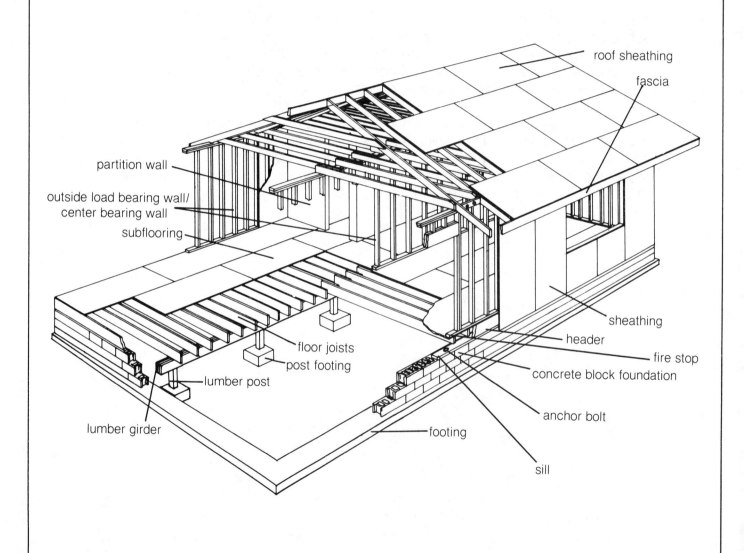

roof sheathing

fascia

partition wall

outside load bearing wall/ center bearing wall

subflooring

sheathing

header

fire stop

concrete block foundation

floor joists

post footing

lumber post

anchor bolt

lumber girder

footing

sill

Frame

Any diagonally placed piece of timber in a frame is a *brace.* A *cat* is a small piece of lumber nailed between studs for reinforcement. *Beams* are squared off pieces of timber, such as *joists,* used to support *floor* or *ceiling,* or *lintels,* horizontal *members* designed to carry loads above openings such as doors and windows.

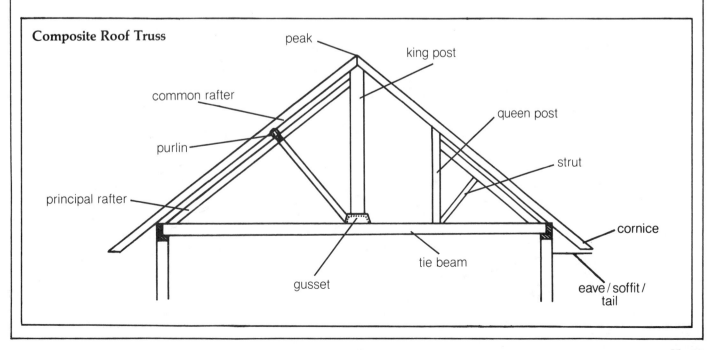

ridgepole/ridgeboard

wood splice

fascia rafter

collar beam

top plate

roof rafter

ceiling joist

cripples

jack stud

fascia

outrigger

header

door bucks

header joist

bottom plate/sole plate

doubling

stud

corner post

anchor bolt

rough sill

sill plate

Composite Roof Truss

peak

king post

common rafter

queen post

purlin

strut

principal rafter

cornice

gusset

tie beam

eave/soffit/tail

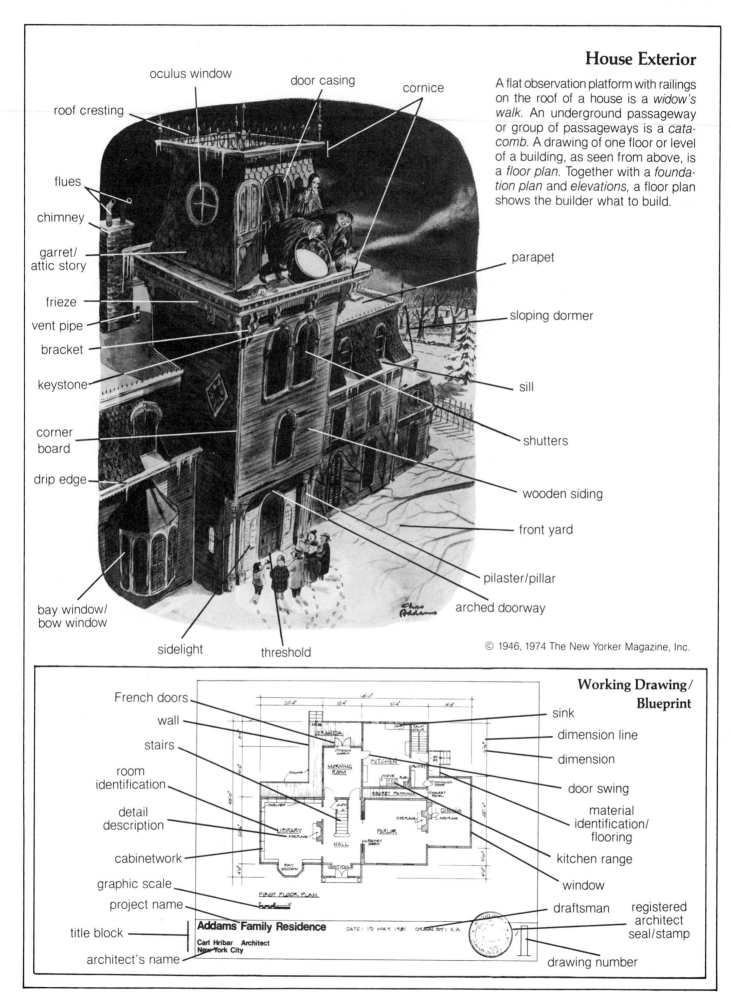

House Exterior

A flat observation platform with railings on the roof of a house is a *widow's walk*. An underground passageway or group of passageways is a *catacomb*. A drawing of one floor or level of a building, as seen from above, is a *floor plan*. Together with a *foundation plan* and *elevations,* a floor plan shows the builder what to build.

oculus window

door casing

cornice

roof cresting

flues

chimney

garret/ attic story

frieze

vent pipe

bracket

keystone

corner board

drip edge

bay window/ bow window

sidelight

threshold

parapet

sloping dormer

sill

shutters

wooden siding

front yard

pilaster/pillar

arched doorway

© 1946, 1974 The New Yorker Magazine, Inc.

Working Drawing/ Blueprint

French doors

wall

stairs

room identification

detail description

cabinetwork

graphic scale

project name

title block

architect's name

sink

dimension line

dimension

door swing

material identification/ flooring

kitchen range

window

draftsman

registered architect seal/stamp

drawing number

FIRST FLOOR PLAN

Addams Family Residence   DATE: 15 MAY 1981   DRAWN BY: K.A.

Carl Hribar   Architect
New York City

VERANDA

FRENCH SUPPLY

MORNING ROOM

KITCHEN

PANTRY

SECRET PASSAGE

STOVE

DINING

FIREPLACE

LIBRARY
FIREPLACE

PARLOR

HALL

BAY WINDOW

VESTIBULE

House Exterior

The room or space under the roof is the *attic*. The lowest story of a house is called the *basement* if it is at least partly below ground or street level. A part of a house projecting on one side or subordinate to the main structure is called a *wing*. Patios, *terraces*, *decks* and *porches* adjoin a house and are used for play or relaxation. An open *gallery* alongside a house with its own roof is a *veranda*.

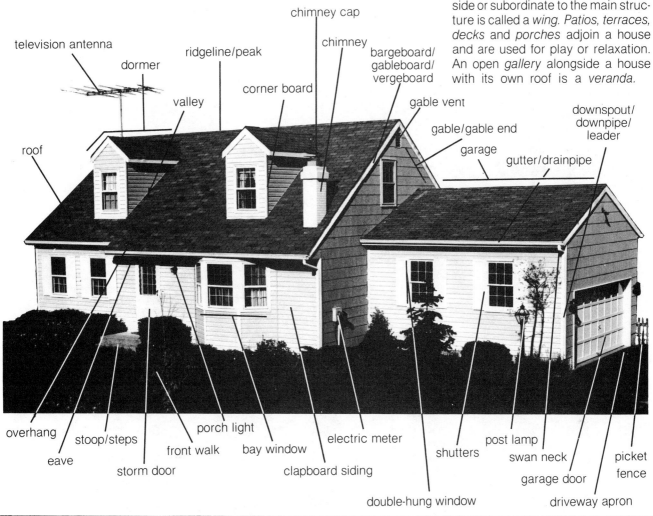

television antenna
dormer
ridgeline/peak
chimney cap
chimney
bargeboard/ gableboard/ vergeboard
valley
corner board
gable vent
gable/gable end
downspout/ downpipe/ leader
roof
garage
gutter/drainpipe

overhang
eave
stoop/steps
storm door
front walk
porch light
bay window
clapboard siding
electric meter
double-hung window
shutters
post lamp
swan neck
garage door
driveway apron
picket fence

House Styles

Federal   Greek Revival   Italianate
Row houses

Second Empire   Contemporary
Detached houses

House

Door

The *sill*, *threshold*, or *saddle* is that part directly beneath the door. Entrance doors are often covered by *screendoors*. A door cut in half horizontally whose two parts can be used independently is called a *Dutch door*. A door having glass panes throughout or nearly throughout its length is a *French door*. The rubber-tipped projection attached to the wall behind an opening door to protect it from the impact is a *doorstop*.

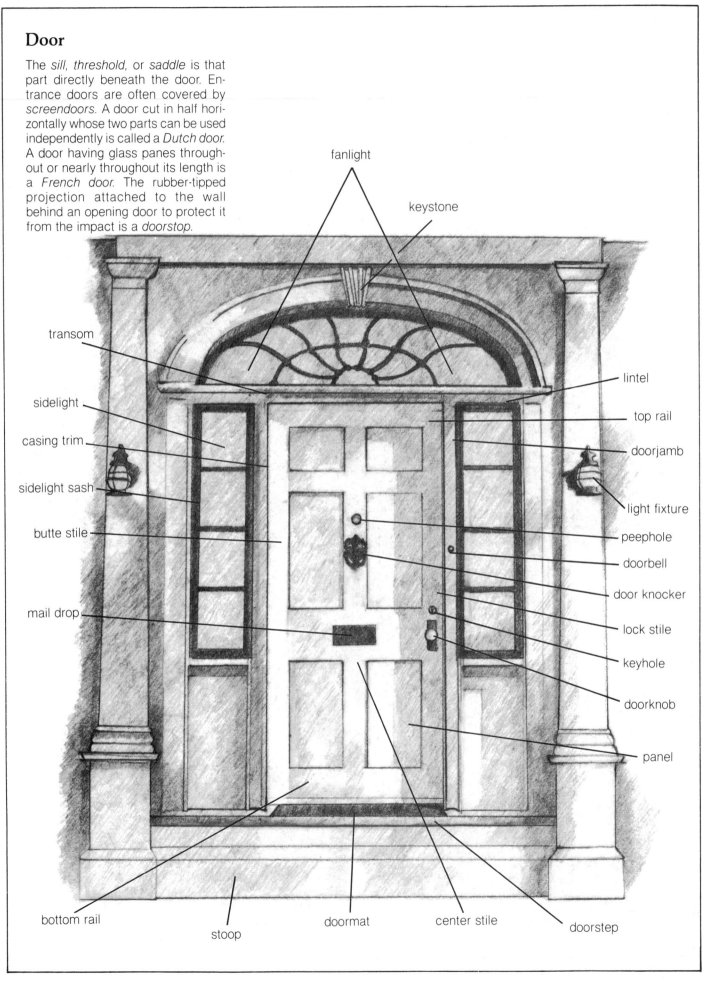

fanlight

keystone

transom

lintel

sidelight

top rail

casing trim

doorjamb

sidelight sash

light fixture

butte stile

peephole

doorbell

door knocker

mail drop

lock stile

keyhole

doorknob

panel

bottom rail

stoop

doormat

center stile

doorstep

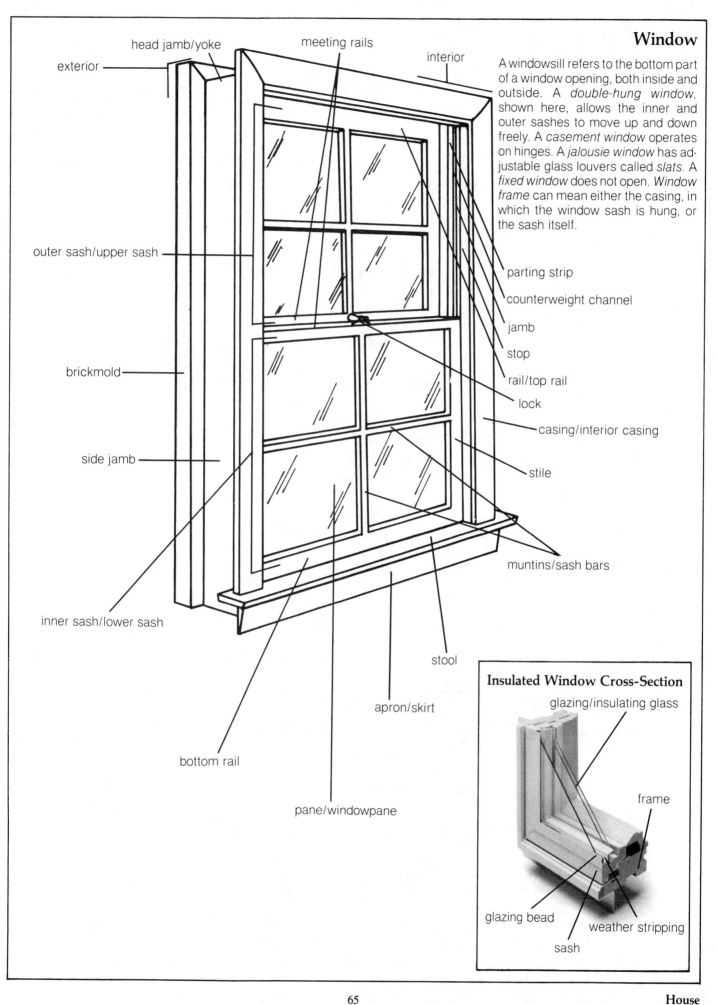

Window

head jamb/yoke

exterior

meeting rails

interior

A windowsill refers to the bottom part of a window opening, both inside and outside. A *double-hung window*, shown here, allows the inner and outer sashes to move up and down freely. A *casement window* operates on hinges. A *jalousie window* has adjustable glass louvers called *slats*. A *fixed window* does not open. *Window frame* can mean either the casing, in which the window sash is hung, or the sash itself.

outer sash/upper sash

parting strip

counterweight channel

jamb

stop

rail/top rail

lock

casing/interior casing

stile

brickmold

side jamb

muntins/sash bars

inner sash/lower sash

stool

apron/skirt

bottom rail

pane/windowpane

Insulated Window Cross-Section

glazing/insulating glass

frame

glazing bead

weather stripping

sash

House

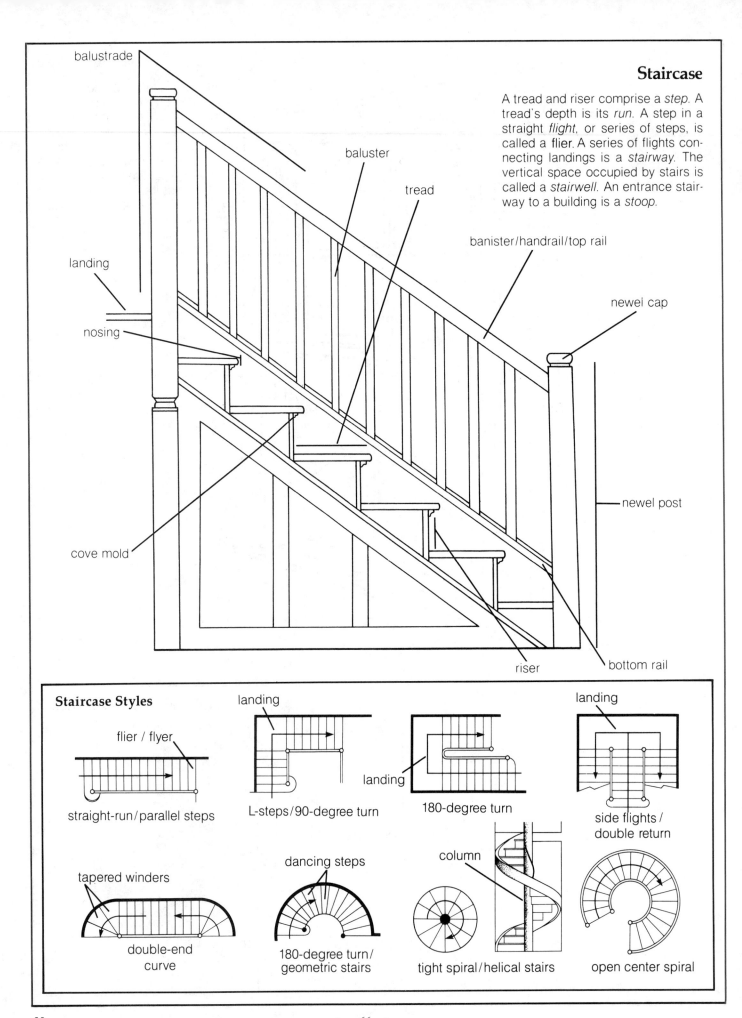

balustrade

baluster

tread

landing

banister/handrail/top rail

Staircase

A tread and riser comprise a *step*. A tread's depth is its *run*. A step in a straight *flight*, or series of steps, is called a **flier**. A series of flights connecting landings is a *stairway*. The vertical space occupied by stairs is called a *stairwell*. An entrance stairway to a building is a *stoop*.

newel cap

nosing

newel post

cove mold

riser

bottom rail

Staircase Styles

flier / flyer

straight-run/parallel steps

landing

L-steps/90-degree turn

landing

landing

180-degree turn

landing

side flights / double return

tapered winders

double-end curve

dancing steps

180-degree turn / geometric stairs

column

tight spiral/helical stairs

open center spiral

Fence

A solid fence can be called a *screen*. If it holds back a slope of ground it is a *retaining wall*. *Supporting members*, or *fence posts*, are anchored in foundation *postholes*. Any material used between posts is *infill*. A *weep hole* in a retaining wall allows water to seep through.

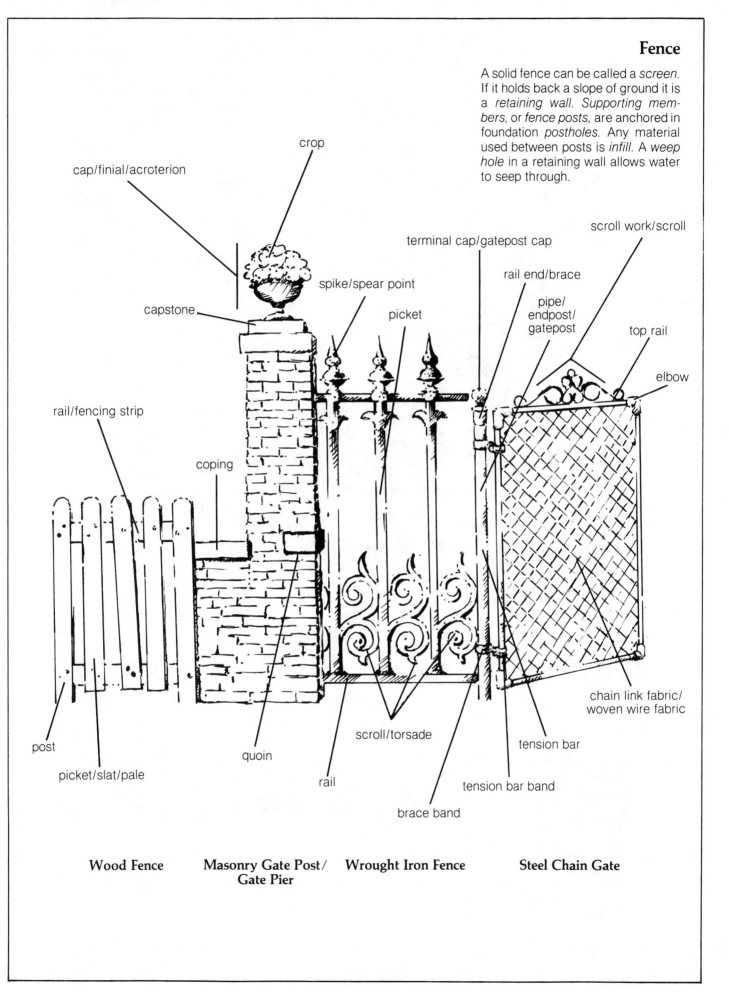

cap/finial/acroterion

crop

capstone

spike/spear point

picket

terminal cap/gatepost cap

rail end/brace

pipe/endpost/gatepost

scroll work/scroll

top rail

elbow

rail/fencing strip

coping

chain link fabric/woven wire fabric

post

picket/slat/pale

quoin

rail

scroll/torsade

brace band

tension bar band

tension bar

Wood Fence   **Masonry Gate Post/Gate Pier**   **Wrought Iron Fence**   **Steel Chain Gate**

House

Building Materials

Boards are *timber,* or lumber, cut in long, flat *slabs.* When used in construction, boards are referred to as *beams,* or *balks.* When they are used to support a pitched roof, they are called *rafters.* A *plank* is thicker than a board. *Shakes* are *wooden shingles,* but cracks in wood caused by wind or frost are also called shakes. A *spall* is a chip or flaking of brick.

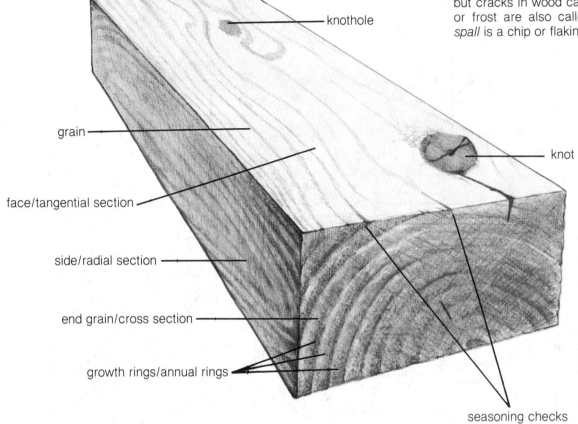

knothole

grain

knot

face/tangential section

side/radial section

end grain/cross section

growth rings/annual rings

seasoning checks

Lumber

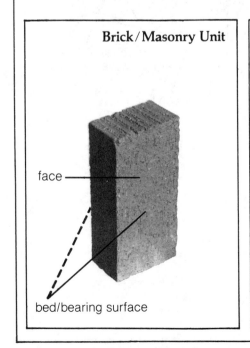

Brick/Masonry Unit

face

bed/bearing surface

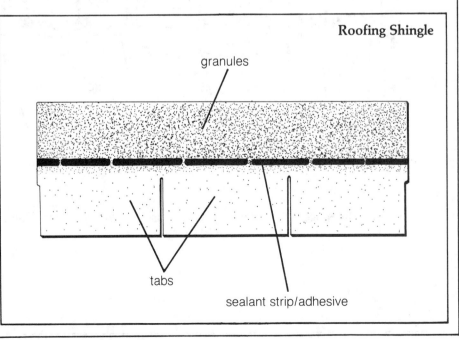

Roofing Shingle

granules

tabs

sealant strip/adhesive

Brick Wall

Bricks and brick faces take on different names, depending on where and how they are used or exposed. Structures built of *stone* or brick are called *masonry.* The pattern in which a wall is laid is its *bond.* The exposed surface is the *face.* A piece of iron or steel used to brace a wall is a *cramp,* while a recess left within for pipes or ducts is a *chase.* A *tie* is any material that holds masonry together.

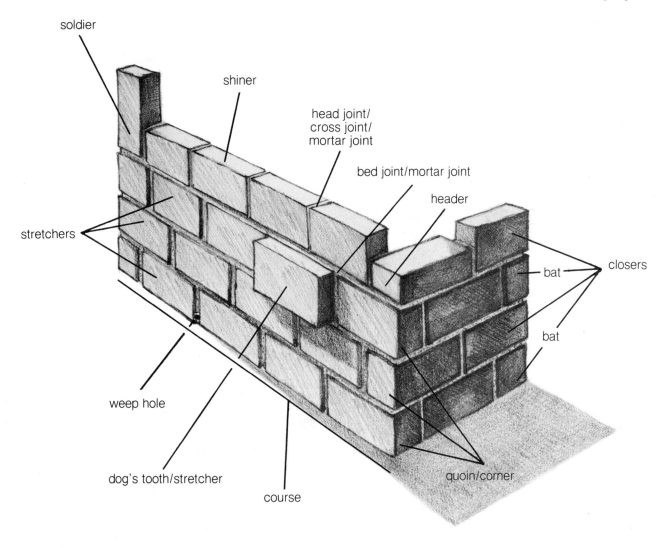

soldier

shiner

head joint/
cross joint/
mortar joint

bed joint/mortar joint

header

stretchers

closers

bat

bat

weep hole

dog's tooth/stretcher

course

quoin/corner

International Architecture

The Japanese developed the *whole-timbered building*, with *interlocking timbered joints*. Minarets, from which *criers*, or *muezzins*, call people to prayer, are normally attached or annexed to a mosque. Obelisks were often surrounded by *pillars*, or stelae, erected in honor of gods. Pyramids, *quadrilateral structures*, were used as tombs or temples. Flat-topped pyramids called *mastabas* were strictly *funerary structures*, while *ziggurats*, stepped pyramids supporting a *shrine*, were used for worship.

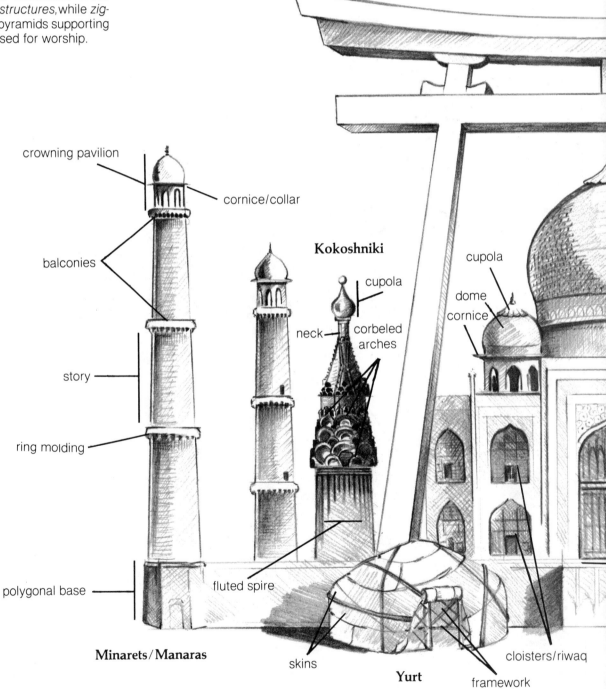

Torii / Shinto Temple Gateway

crowning pavilion

cornice/collar

balconies

Kokoshniki

cupola

neck

corbeled arches

cupola

dome

cornice

story

ring molding

fluted spire

polygonal base

Minarets / Manaras

skins

Yurt

cloisters/riwaq

framework

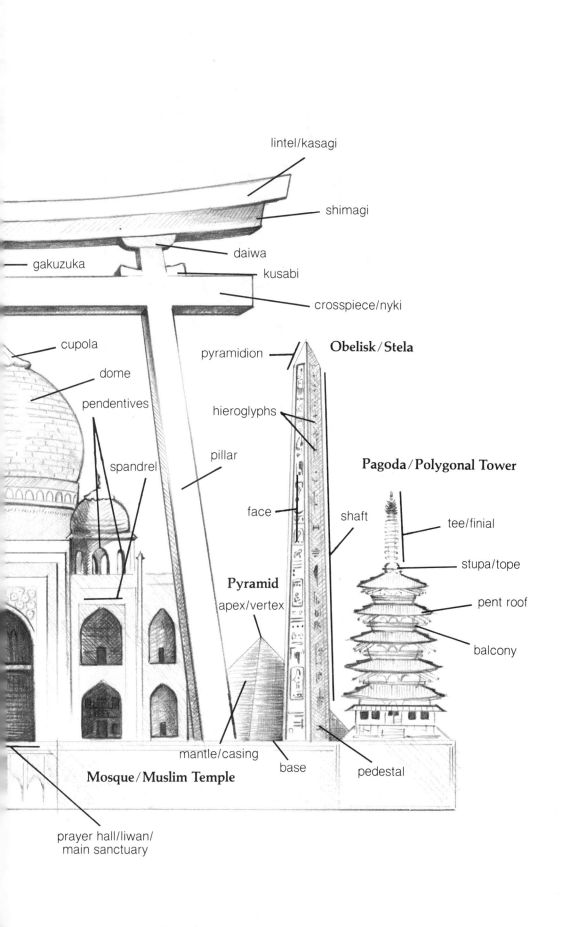

lintel/kasagi

shimagi

gakuzuka

daiwa

kusabi

crosspiece/nyki

Obelisk/Stela

cupola

dome

pendentives

pyramidion

hieroglyphs

Pagoda/Polygonal Tower

spandrel

pillar

shaft

tee/finial

face

stupa/tope

Pyramid

apex/vertex

pent roof

balcony

mantle/casing

base

pedestal

Mosque/Muslim Temple

prayer hall/liwan/
main sanctuary

Arch

The distance between the imposts is called the *span*. The *rise* is the distance between the top of the imposts and the highest point of the intrados. The *crown* is the highest point of the extrados. The area of an arch extending from the crown to the impost is the *haunch,* or *hance.*

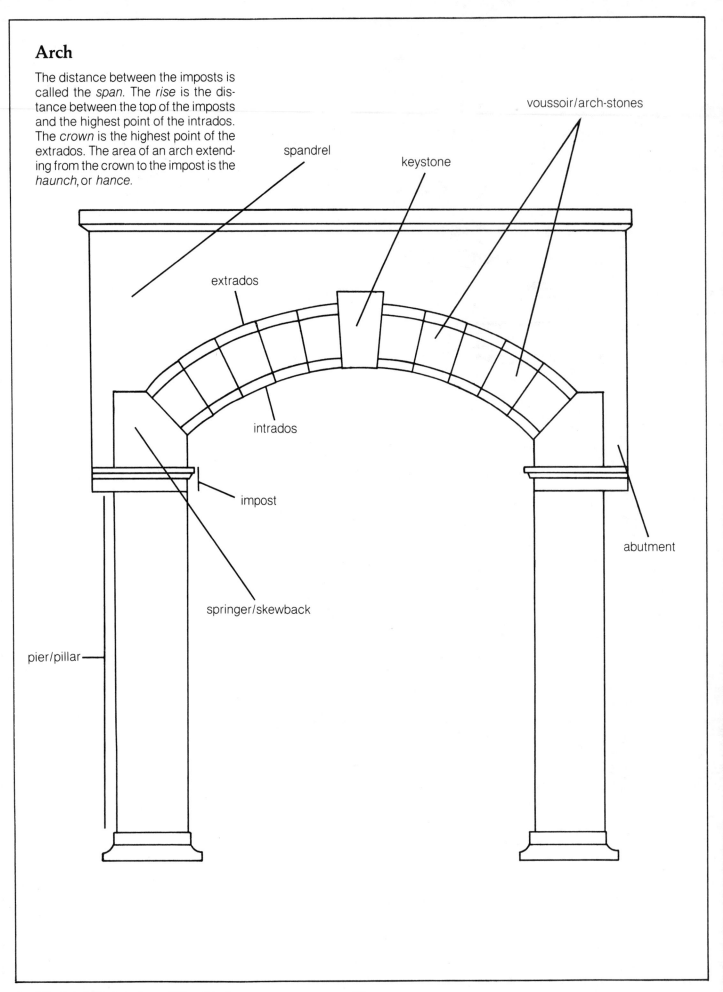

spandrel

voussoir/arch-stones

keystone

extrados

intrados

impost

abutment

springer/skewback

pier/pillar

Column

The clear space between two columns is *intercolumniation*.

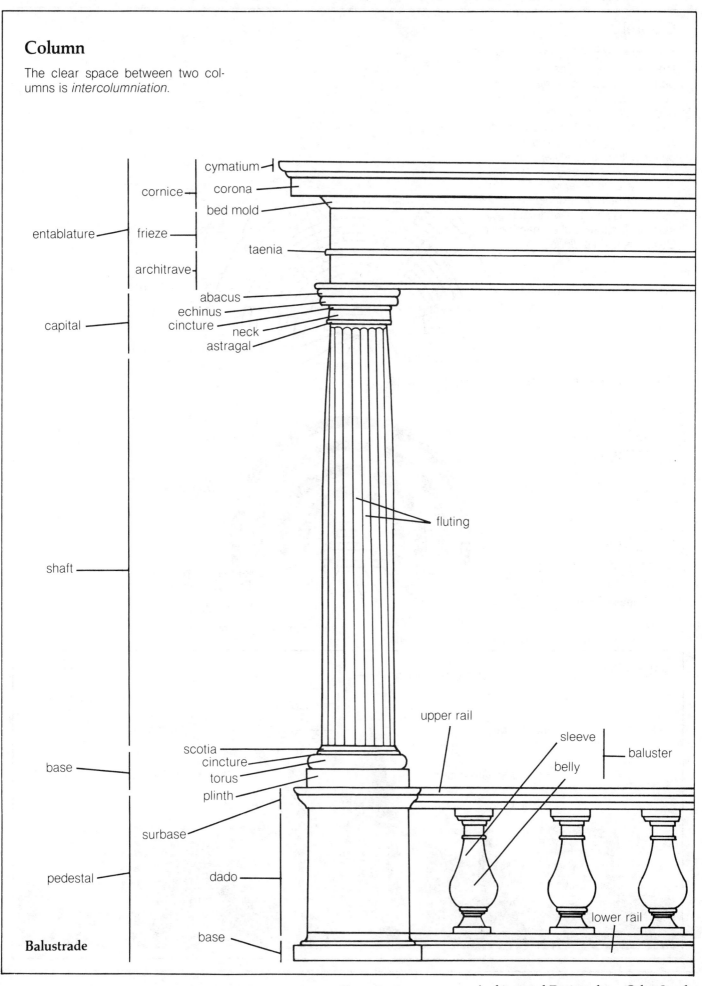

cymatium

cornice

corona

bed mold

entablature

frieze

taenia

architrave

abacus

echinus

capital

cincture

neck

astragal

shaft

fluting

upper rail

sleeve

baluster

belly

scotia

base

cincture

torus

plinth

surbase

pedestal

dado

lower rail

base

Balustrade

Architectural Designs from Other Lands

Capitol

The first floor of the Capitol contains the *Hall of Columns, House* and *Senate corridors, committee rooms, restaurants, transportation offices* and a *post office.* When the House is called to order, the *Mace of the House of Representatives* is placed on a cylindrical *pedestal* to the right of the Speaker's desk. On the Senate side is a *chandelier* with two bulbs below it. The red one indicates an executive session; the white, a regular session. Visitors to the chambers of Congress sit in *galleries.*

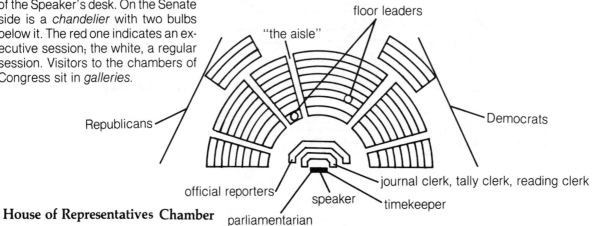

floor leaders

"the aisle"

Republicans

Democrats

official reporters
speaker
parliamentarian
timekeeper
journal clerk, tally clerk, reading clerk

House of Representatives Chamber

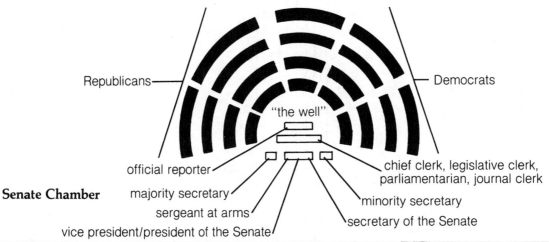

Republicans

Democrats

"the well"

official reporter
majority secretary
sergeant at arms
vice president/president of the Senate
chief clerk, legislative clerk, parliamentarian, journal clerk
minority secretary
secretary of the Senate

Senate Chamber

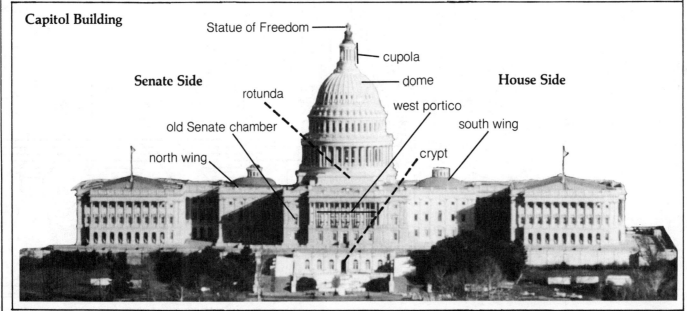

Capitol Building

Statue of Freedom

Senate Side

rotunda

old Senate chamber

north wing

cupola

dome

west portico

crypt

House Side

south wing

White House

The White House, a historic *mansion* that serves as the President's *home* and *office,* contains *portraits, antiques* and *memorabilia.* In addition to the rooms and offices shown here, there is a bombproof *command post* in the cellar and a *helipad* on the south lawn.

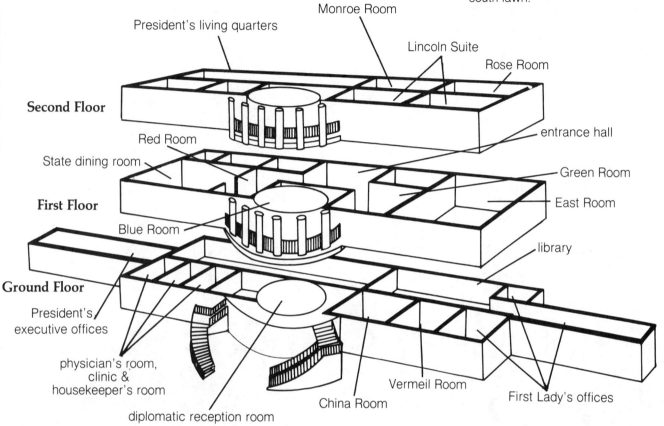

Second Floor

President's living quarters
Monroe Room
Lincoln Suite
Rose Room
entrance hall

First Floor

Red Room
State dining room
Green Room
East Room
Blue Room
library

Ground Floor

President's executive offices
physician's room, clinic & housekeeper's room
diplomatic reception room
China Room
Vermeil Room
First Lady's offices

House Plan

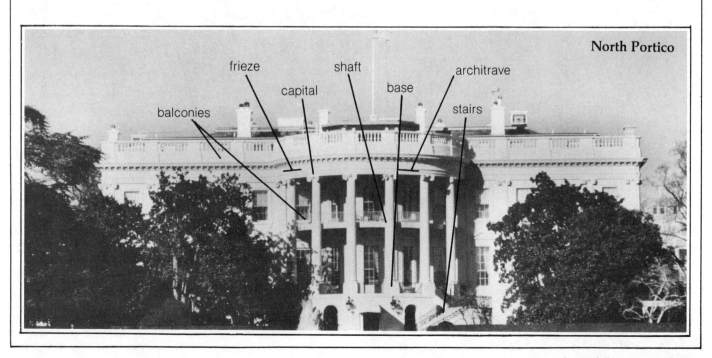

North Portico

frieze
shaft
architrave
capital
base
stairs
balconies

Special Purpose Buildings

Prison

Maximum security prisons, such as the one seen here, are characterized by high *walls*, *armed guards* and *security checkpoints*. *Minimum security prisons* may be surrounded by *chainlink fences* and have *security systems* that are largely electronic, with *doors*, *alarms*, *TV monitors* and *intercoms* monitored by *central computers*. *Prisoners*, or *inmates*, in all *correctional facilities*, including *jails*, live in *cells* with *barred doors*.

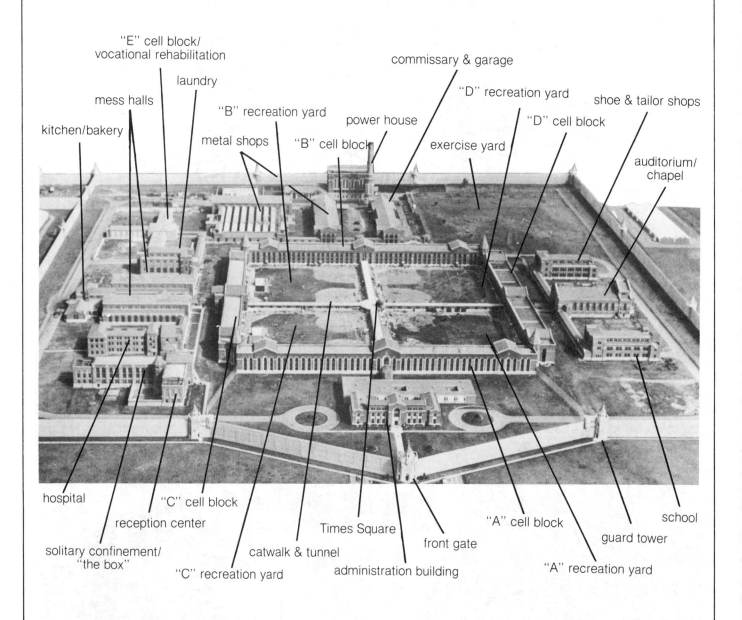

"E" cell block/ vocational rehabilitation

commissary & garage

laundry

"D" recreation yard

mess halls

"B" recreation yard

power house

shoe & tailor shops

"D" cell block

kitchen/bakery

metal shops

"B" cell block

exercise yard

auditorium/ chapel

hospital

"C" cell block

Times Square

"A" cell block

school

reception center

front gate

guard tower

solitary confinement/ "the box"

catwalk & tunnel

"C" recreation yard

administration building

"A" recreation yard

Skyscraper

A skyscraper, or *building* more than twenty stories high, is built on a *foundation* of reinforced concrete *piers* supported by *piles* driven into soil or bedrock. The center of the building, or *core*, usually contains the *elevator bank*. The machinery needed to operate the building's systems is located on the *mechanical floors*. A *cornerstone* is a stone laid at a formal inauguration ceremony.

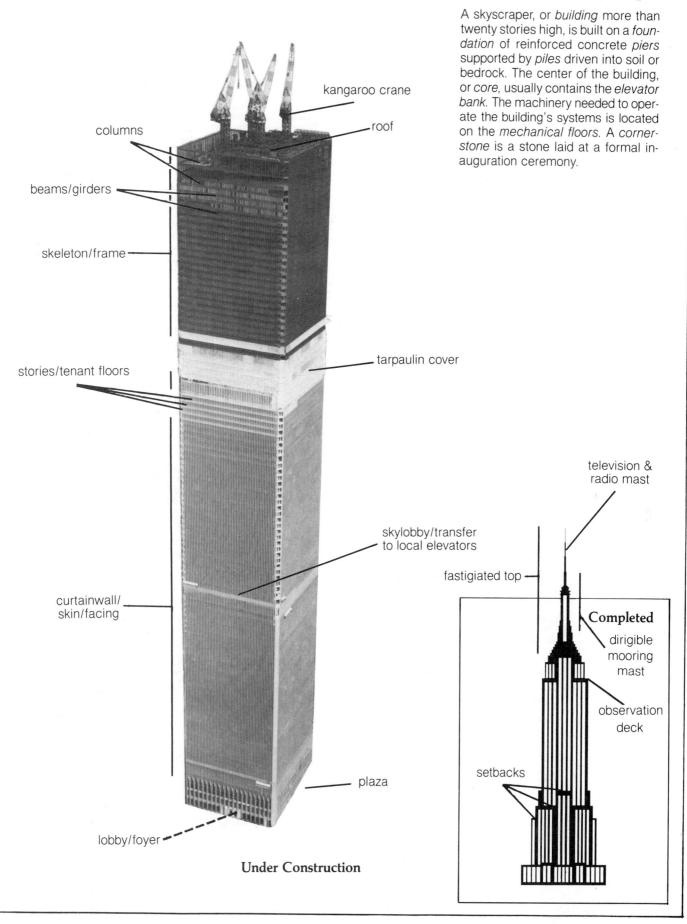

kangaroo crane

columns

roof

beams/girders

skeleton/frame

stories/tenant floors

tarpaulin cover

skylobby/transfer to local elevators

curtainwall/ skin/facing

plaza

lobby/foyer

Under Construction

television & radio mast

fastigiated top

Completed

dirigible mooring mast

observation deck

setbacks

Special Purpose Buildings

Elevator

There is padding which makes up the *safety edges* on the *shafts,* or innermost sides, of elevator doors. Most elevator cars have *emergency top exits* in the *canopy* or real ceiling as well as *service cabinets* which contain *fan switches, light* and *start switches.* An individual who directs people to the next available car in a *bank* of elevators is called a *starter.*

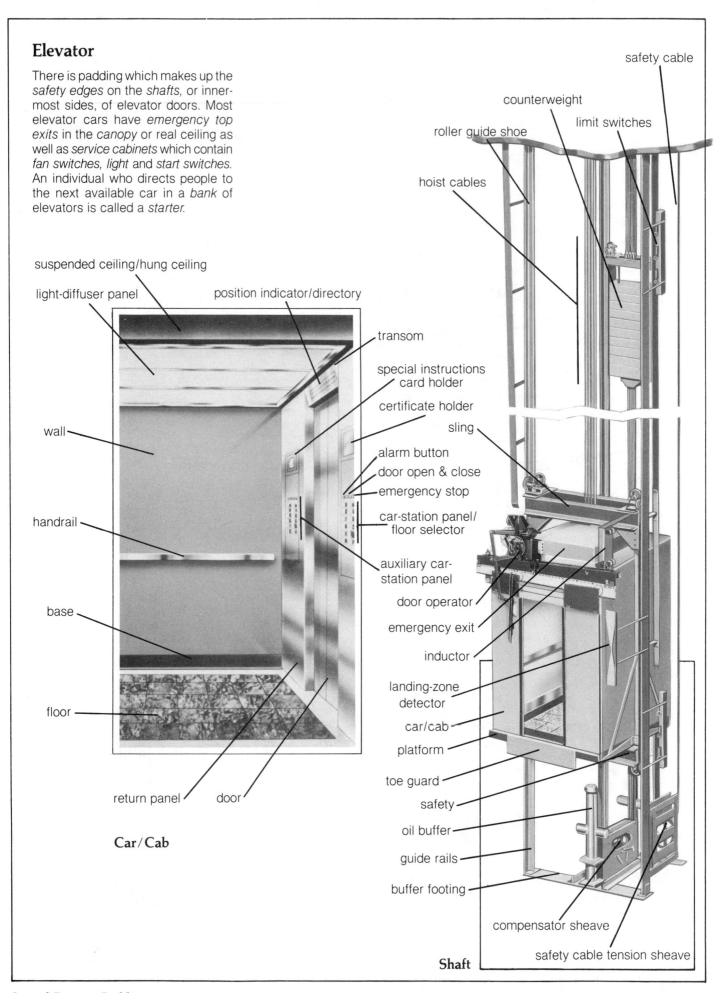

suspended ceiling/hung ceiling

light-diffuser panel

position indicator/directory

transom

special instructions card holder

certificate holder

alarm button

door open & close

emergency stop

car-station panel/ floor selector

auxiliary car-station panel

wall

handrail

base

floor

return panel

door

Car/Cab

safety cable

counterweight

limit switches

roller guide shoe

hoist cables

sling

door operator

emergency exit

inductor

landing-zone detector

car/cab

platform

toe guard

safety

oil buffer

guide rails

buffer footing

compensator sheave

safety cable tension sheave

Shaft

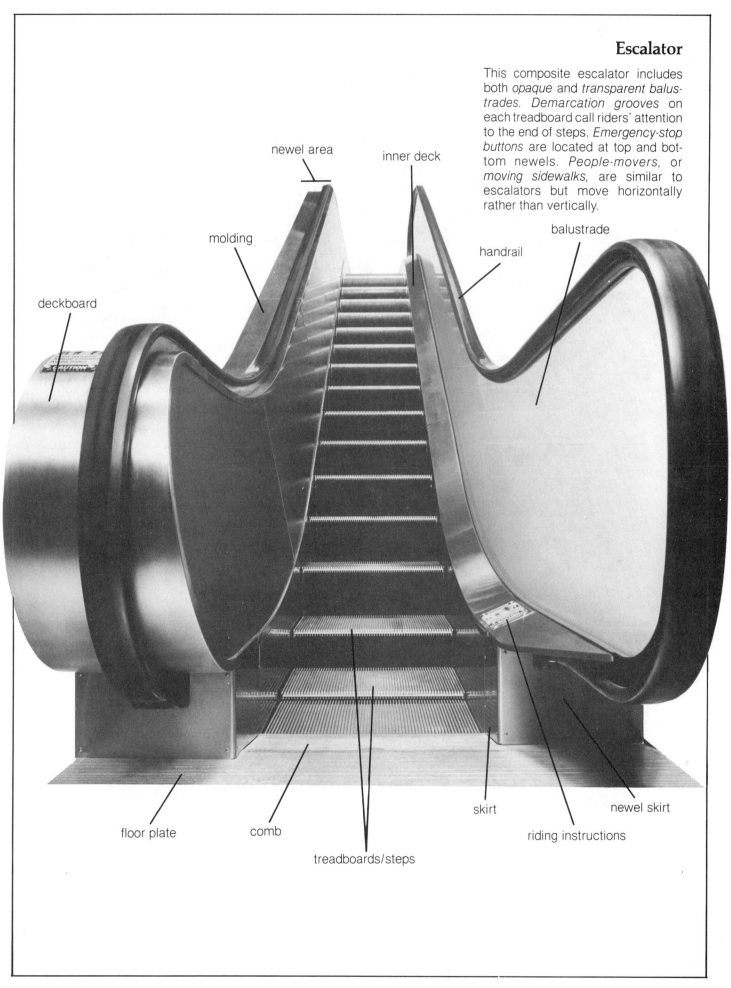

Escalator

This composite escalator includes both *opaque* and *transparent balustrades*. *Demarcation grooves* on each treadboard call riders' attention to the end of steps. *Emergency-stop buttons* are located at top and bottom newels. *People-movers*, or *moving sidewalks*, are similar to escalators but move horizontally rather than vertically.

newel area

inner deck

molding

balustrade

handrail

deckboard

treadboards/steps

floor plate

comb

skirt

newel skirt

riding instructions

Castle

A castle was protected by a moat which could be crossed by a lowered *drawbridge*. Narrow openings in turret or tower floors, used to drop boiling liquids or stones on attackers, were called *machicolations*.

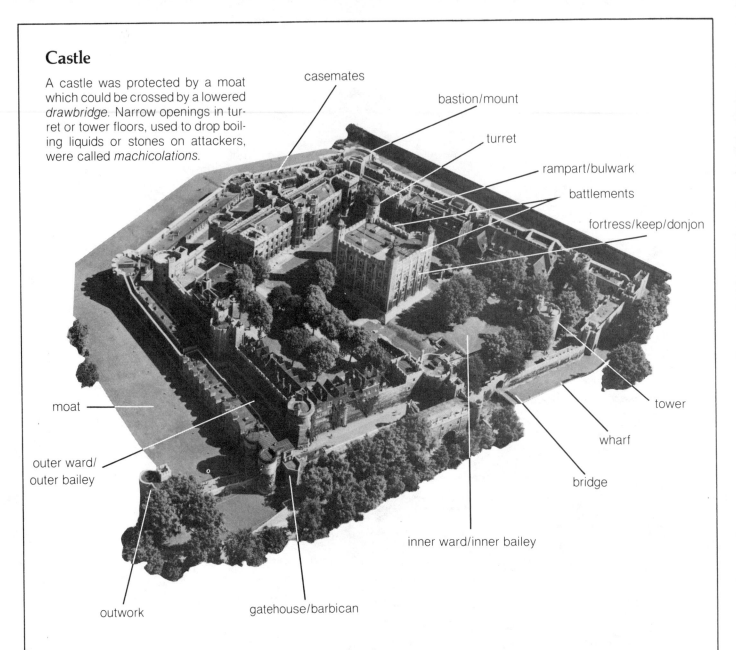

casemates

bastion/mount

turret

rampart/bulwark

battlements

fortress/keep/donjon

tower

wharf

bridge

inner ward/inner bailey

moat

outer ward/ outer bailey

outwork

gatehouse/barbican

Embattled Parapet

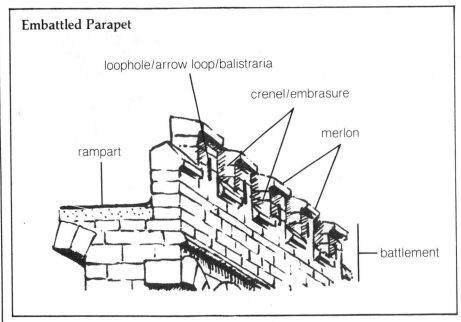

loophole/arrow loop/balistraria

crenel/embrasure

merlon

rampart

battlement

Bartizan/Turret

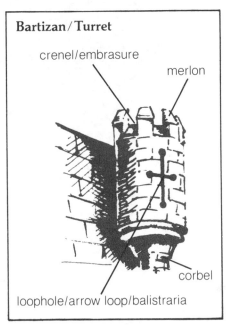

crenel/embrasure

merlon

corbel

loophole/arrow loop/balistraria

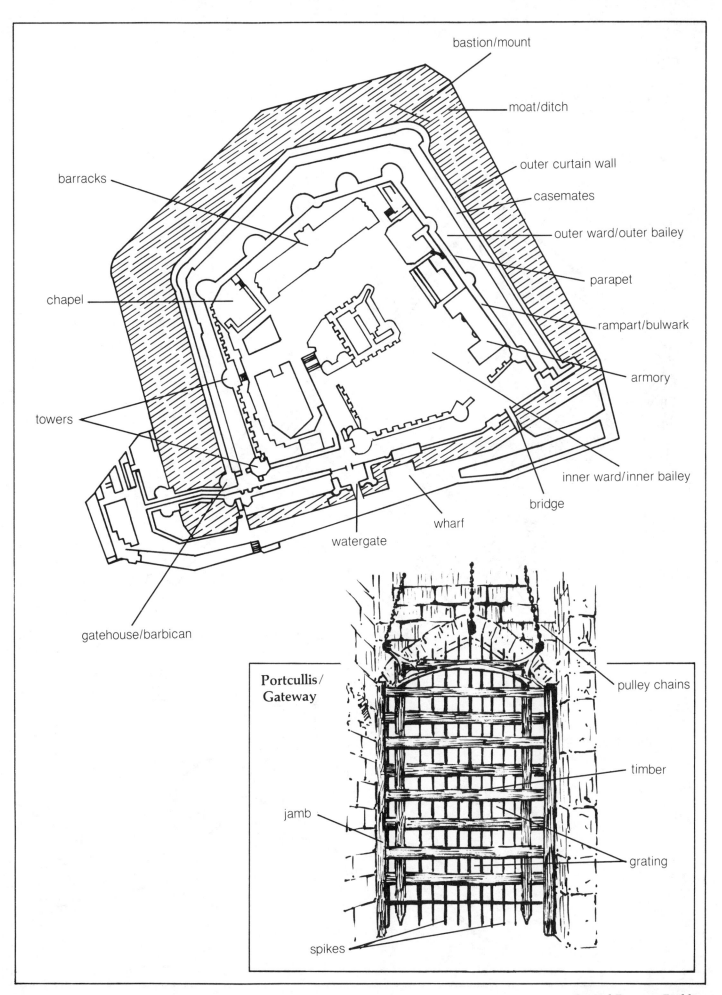

bastion/mount

moat/ditch

outer curtain wall

casemates

outer ward/outer bailey

parapet

rampart/bulwark

armory

barracks

chapel

towers

inner ward/inner bailey

bridge

wharf

watergate

gatehouse/barbican

Portcullis/ Gateway

pulley chains

timber

jamb

grating

spikes

Special Purpose Buildings

Fortifications

This *field fortification* or *trading post* was protected by wooden walls from behind which soldiers could fire on attackers from raised *parapets*. *Powder* and *ammunition* were stored in a building called a *magazine*.

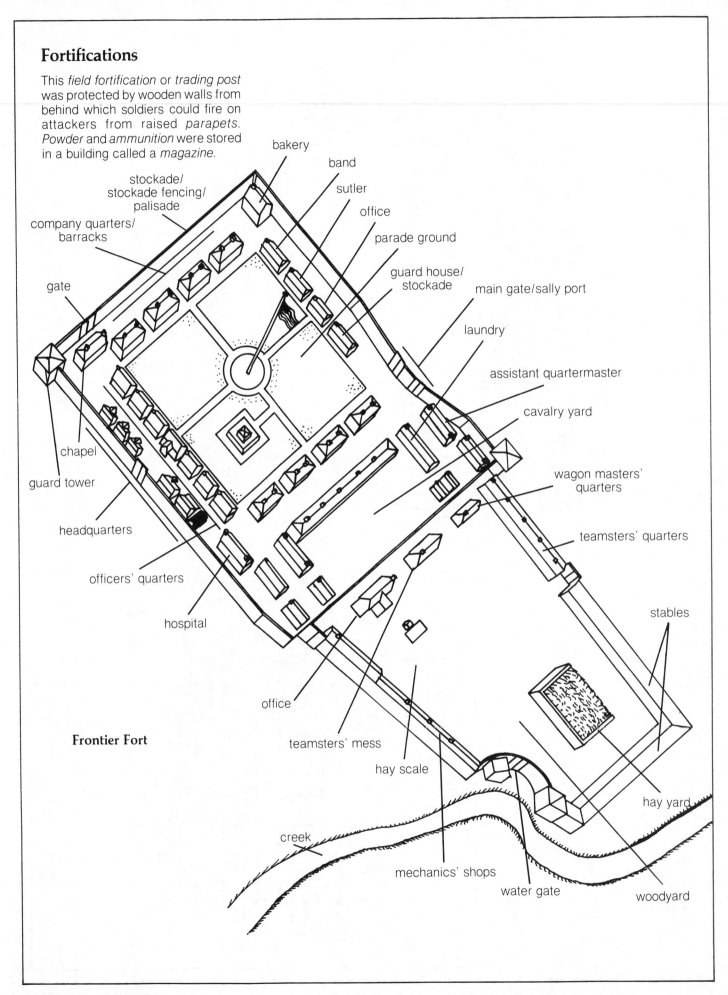

bakery

band

sutler

office

parade ground

guard house/ stockade

main gate/sally port

laundry

assistant quartermaster

cavalry yard

wagon masters' quarters

teamsters' quarters

stables

hay yard

woodyard

water gate

mechanics' shops

hay scale

teamsters' mess

office

hospital

officers' quarters

headquarters

guard tower

chapel

gate

company quarters/ barracks

stockade/ stockade fencing/ palisade

creek

Frontier Fort

Fortifications

Permanent fortifications, such as the *point* of the star fort illustrated here, had *walls* and *slopes* made of *masonry* and earth. They often had *casemates; bombproofs,* walls impervious to explosives; *drawbridges* and *earthen breastworks,* breast-high protection for soldiers.

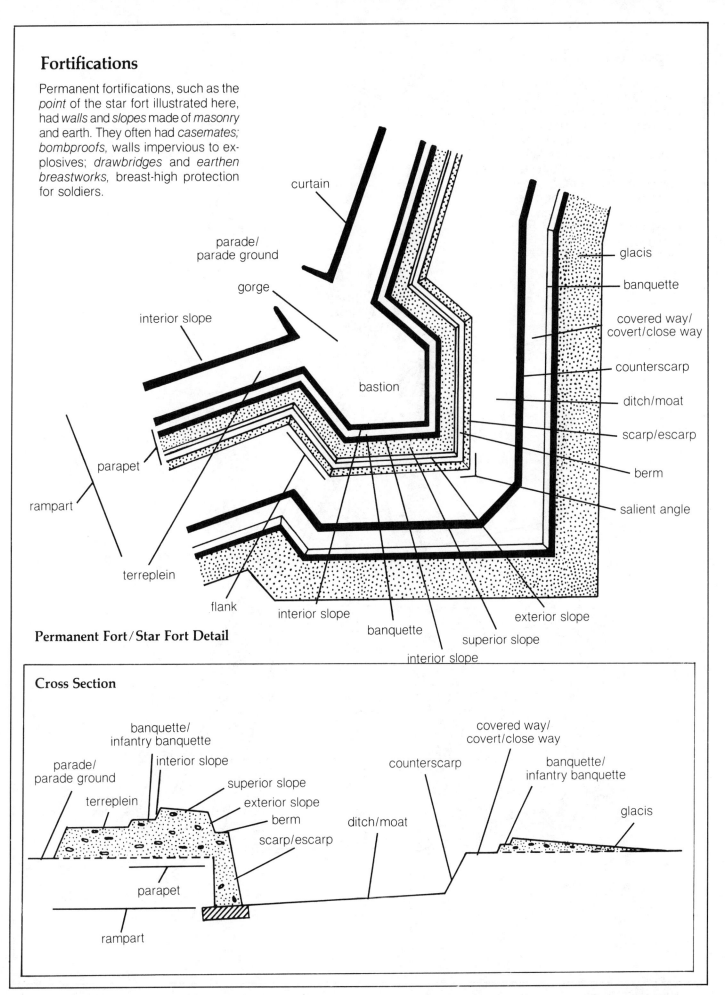

curtain

parade/
parade ground

gorge

interior slope

glacis

banquette

covered way/
covert/close way

counterscarp

bastion

ditch/moat

scarp/escarp

berm

salient angle

parapet

rampart

terreplein

flank

interior slope

banquette

exterior slope

superior slope

interior slope

Permanent Fort/Star Fort Detail

Cross Section

banquette/
infantry banquette

interior slope

covered way/
covert/close way

parade/
parade ground

superior slope

counterscarp

banquette/
infantry banquette

terreplein

exterior slope

berm

scarp/escarp

ditch/moat

glacis

parapet

rampart

Special Purpose Buildings

Tepee / Teepee / Tipi

The *pole frame* of an Indian tepee was held together at the top by a *hide rope*. It was covered with dressed buffalo *skins* and had a *fire pit* on the floor within. Other Indian dwellings included *wigwams*, rounded or oval-shaped lodges formed by poles overlaid with *bark*, *mats* or *skins*; *wickiups*, huts made of *brushwood* or covered with mats; and *hogans*, dwellings constructed of *earth* and *branches* and covered with *mud* or *sod*.

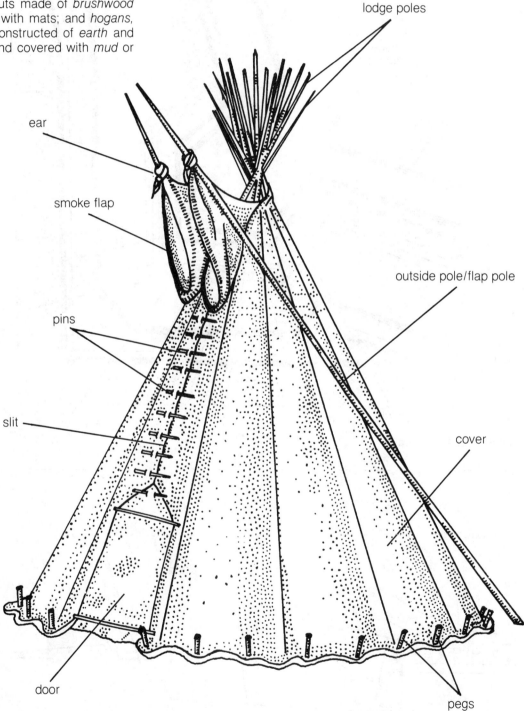

lodge poles

ear

smoke flap

outside pole/flap pole

pins

slit

cover

door

pegs

Domed Structures

Traditionally, a dome is a circular *vault* whose walls exert equal thrust in all directions, resisted by a *tension ring.* The geodesic dome consists of a *grid* of *compression* or *tension members* lying upon *great circles* running in three directions in any given area.

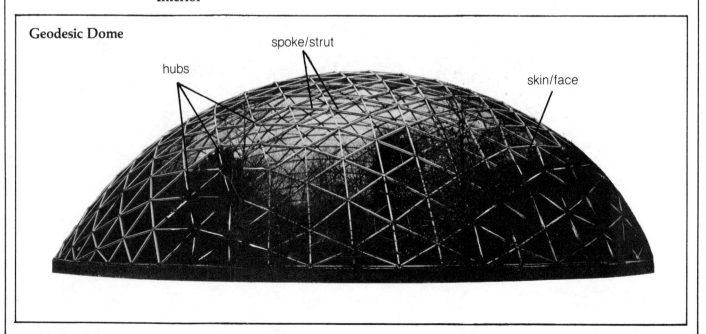

Igloo/Iglu

king block

snow blocks

ice window

storm igloo

air hole

tunnel/tossut

entrance

animal skin

sleeping shelf   entrance

Interior

Geodesic Dome

hubs

spoke/strut

skin/face

Special Purpose Buildings

Church / Cathedral

A small building used for worship is called a *chapel*. Living quarters used by church clergy are the *rectory*. The office in which church business is conducted is the *chancellery*.

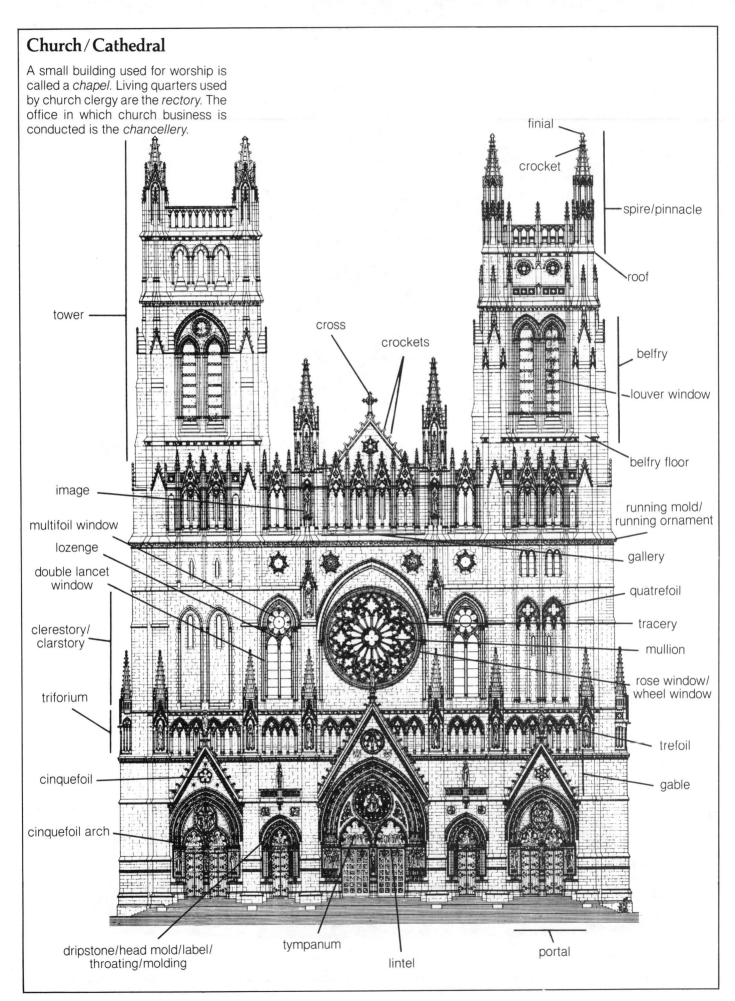

finial

crocket

spire/pinnacle

roof

cross

crockets

belfry

louver window

belfry floor

tower

image

multifoil window

lozenge

double lancet window

clerestory/ clarstory

triforium

cinquefoil

cinquefoil arch

running mold/ running ornament

gallery

quatrefoil

tracery

mullion

rose window/ wheel window

trefoil

gable

dripstone/head mold/label/ throating/molding

tympanum

lintel

portal

Church Interior

That part of a church containing the altar and seats for the clergy and choir is called the *chancel*. A *pulpit* is an elevated platform used in preaching or conducting a worship service. The *tabernacle* is a receptacle for consecrated elements of the Eucharist: the *pix*, the container in which Communion *wafers* are kept; the *paten*, a plate used to hold *Communion bread*; and the *chalice*, or *Communion cup*, used to dispense consecrated *wine*.

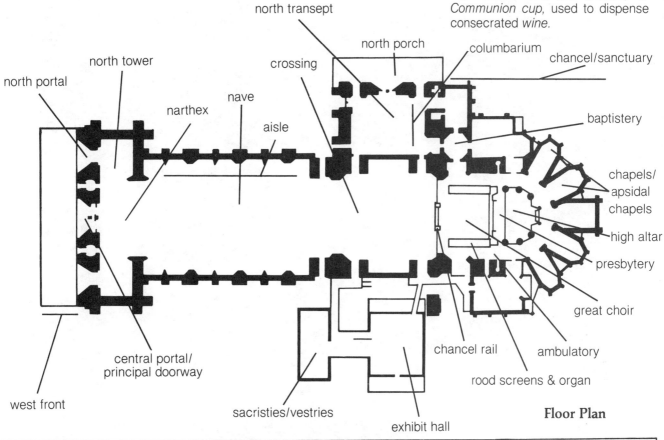

north transept

north porch

columbarium

chancel/sanctuary

crossing

north tower

north portal

nave

narthex

aisle

baptistery

chapels/
apsidal
chapels

high altar

presbytery

great choir

ambulatory

rood screens & organ

chancel rail

central portal/
principal doorway

west front

sacristies/vestries

exhibit hall

Floor Plan

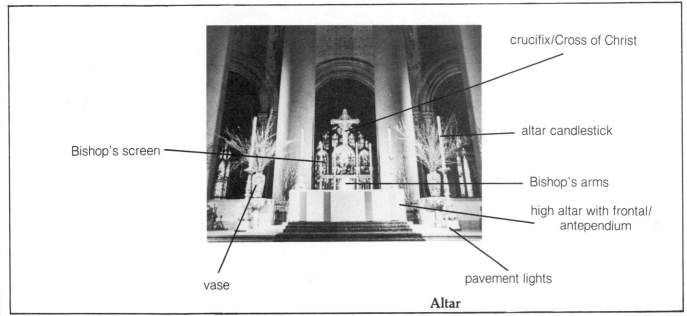

crucifix/Cross of Christ

altar candlestick

Bishop's screen

Bishop's arms

high altar with frontal/
antependium

pavement lights

vase

Altar

Special Purpose Buildings

Synagogue/Temple

The Torah is a parchment or leather *scroll* containing the first five books of the *Scriptures,* or *Pentateuch,* written in Hebrew. It is tied closed with a beltlike *wrapper.*

eternal light/Ner Tamid

Star of David/
Magen David/
Shield of David

ark

menorah

Torah

ark door

pews

pulpit

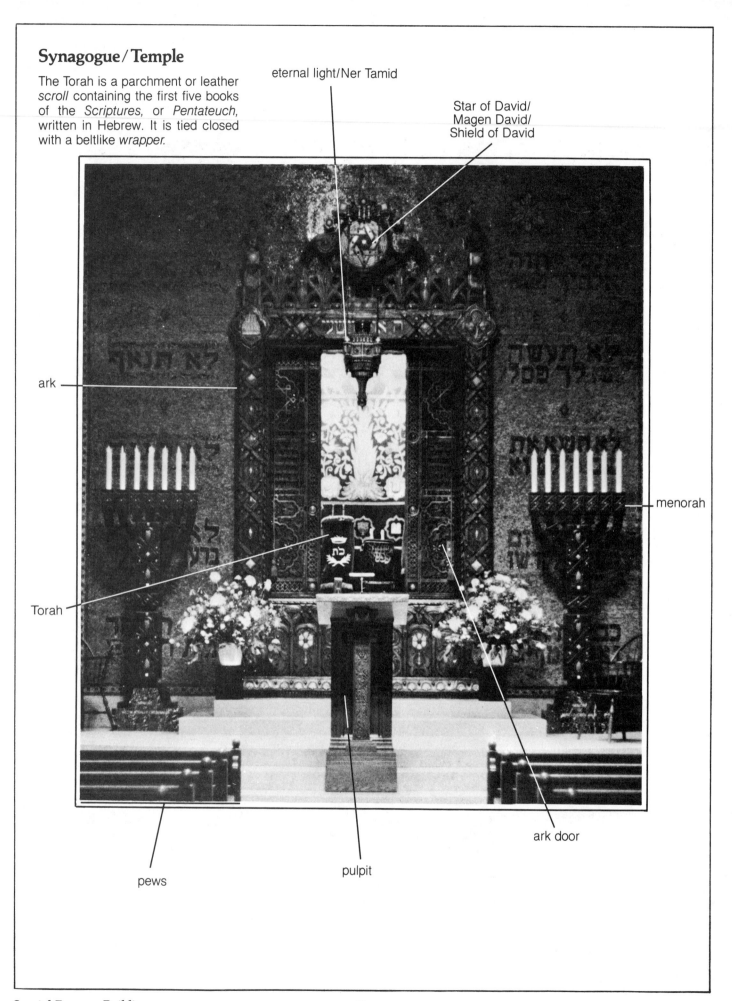

Courtroom

The small anteroom off the courtroom in which the *judge* changes into his *robes* and holds conferences is called the *judge's chambers.* After a *jury* has heard a case, it deliberates in a *jury room.* A judge may sometimes use a malletlike *gavel* during proceedings.

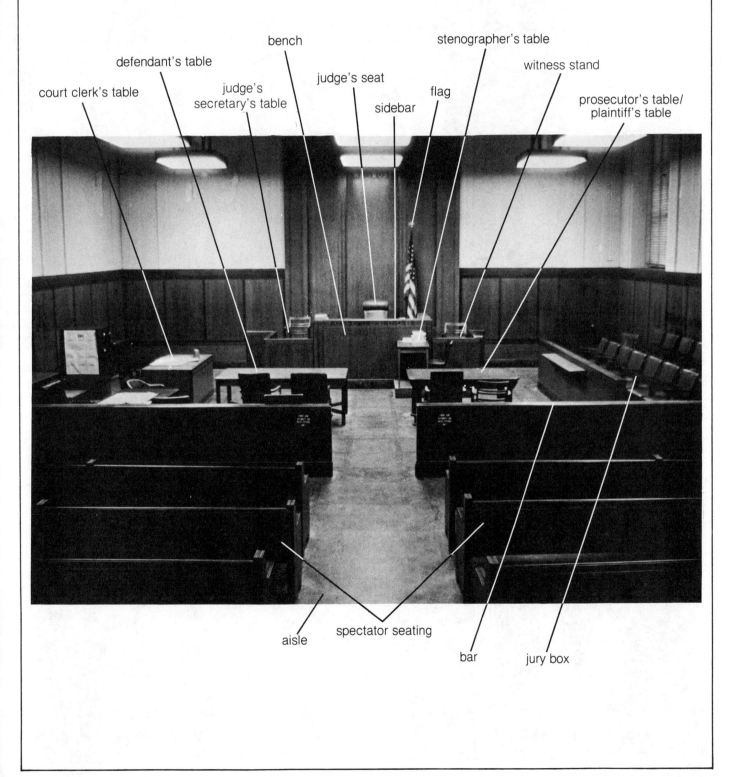

court clerk's table

defendant's table

judge's secretary's table

bench

judge's seat

sidebar

stenographer's table

flag

witness stand

prosecutor's table/ plaintiff's table

aisle

spectator seating

bar

jury box

Special Purpose Buildings

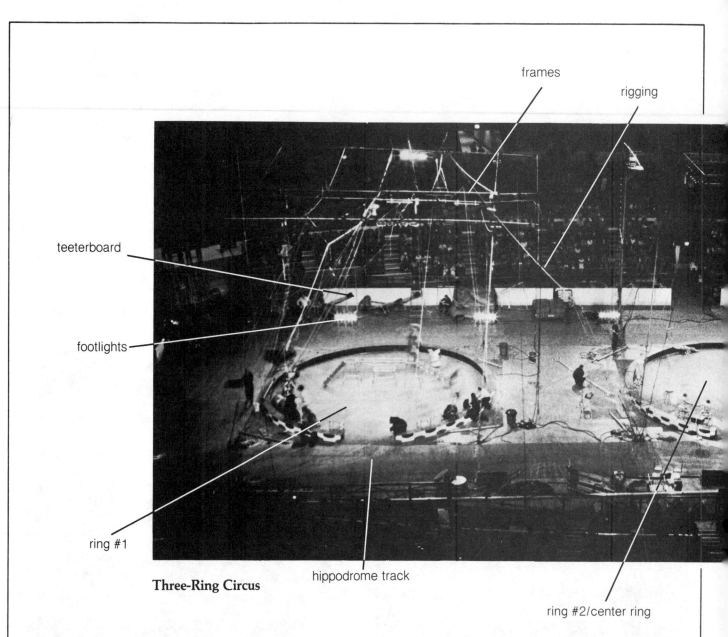

frames

rigging

teeterboard

footlights

ring #1

hippodrome track

Three-Ring Circus

ring #2/center ring

Aerialists/Flyers/Trapeze Artists

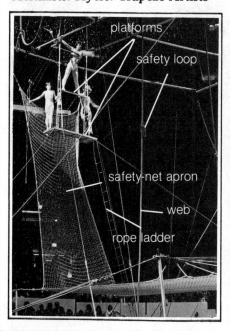

platforms

safety loop

safety-net apron

web

rope ladder

Animal Tamer

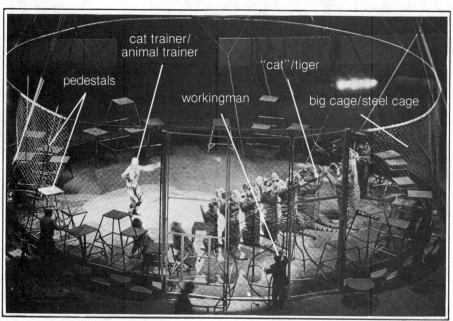

cat trainer/
animal trainer

"cat"/tiger

pedestals

workingman

big cage/steel cage

Circus

Circuses traditionally take place in tents erected by *roustabouts* and begin with a *parade* in which all the performers enter the *arena*. A *ringmaster*, usually clad in *top hat* and *tails*, announces acts, including *animal* and *clown acts; tightrope*, or *high-wire acts;* and *jugglers*. In the past, *sideshows*, which took place in an adjoining tent, featured *tattooed ladies*, *giants*, *midgets*, *swordswallowers* and *fire-eaters*.

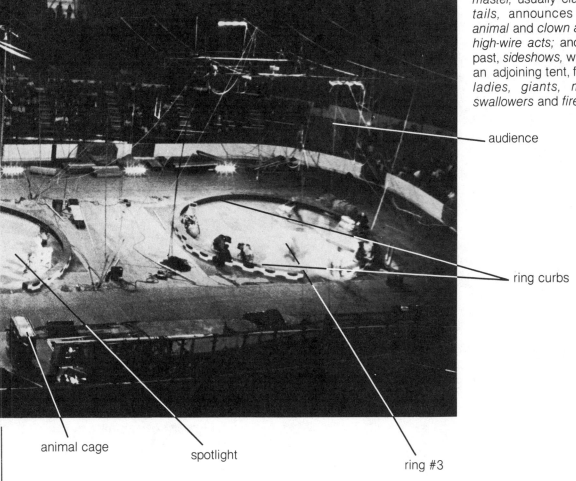

audience

ring curbs

animal cage

spotlight

ring #3

Circus Tent / Big Top / Top

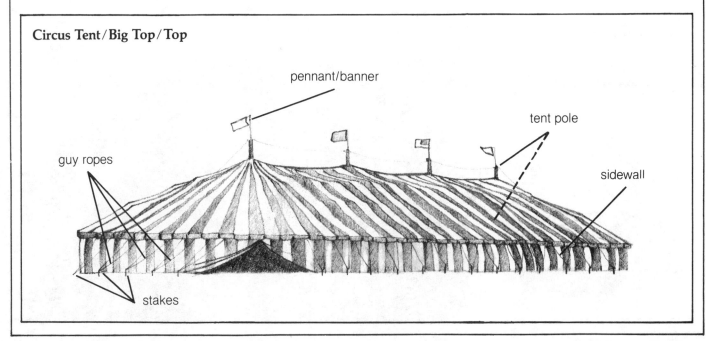

pennant/banner

tent pole

guy ropes

sidewall

stakes

Special Purpose Buildings

Amusement Park

A roller coaster consists of *hills, straightaways* and *loops. Upstop wheels* lock roller-coaster cars to the track, *guide wheels* are used for turns and tractor wheels are used for gliding.

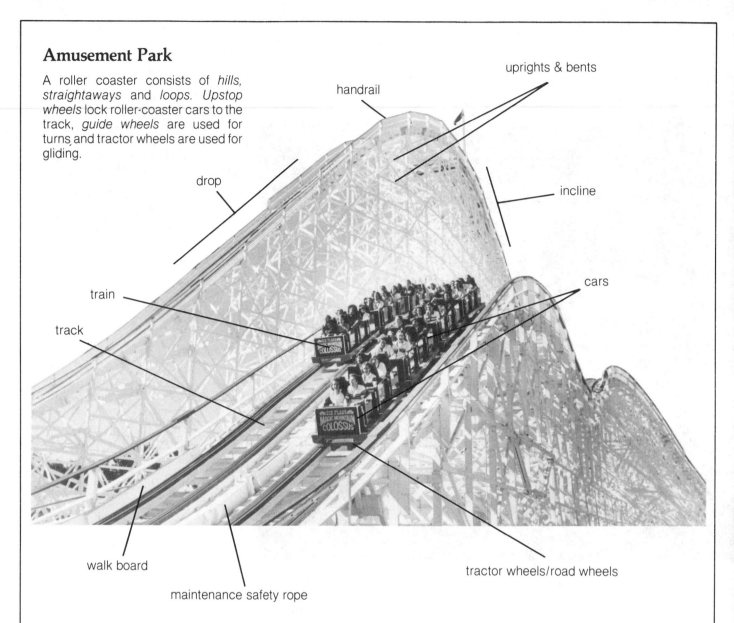

uprights & bents

handrail

drop

incline

train

cars

track

walk board

maintenance safety rope

tractor wheels/road wheels

Roller Coaster

Bumper Car / Scooter Car

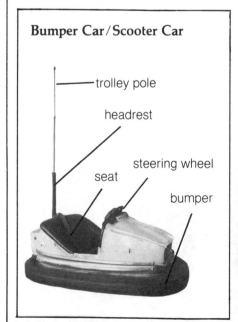

trolley pole

headrest

steering wheel

seat

bumper

Incline Track

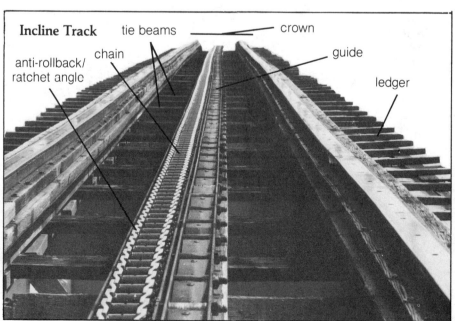

tie beams

crown

chain

guide

anti-rollback/ ratchet angle

ledger

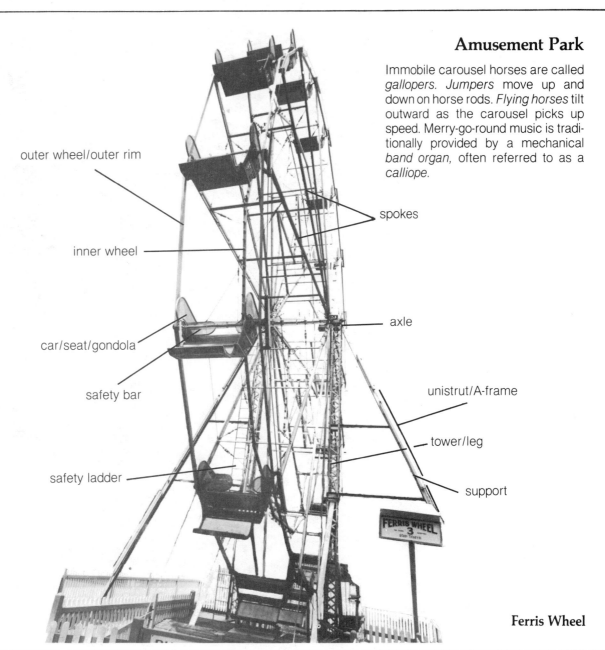

Amusement Park

Immobile carousel horses are called *gallopers*. *Jumpers* move up and down on horse rods. *Flying horses* tilt outward as the carousel picks up speed. Merry-go-round music is traditionally provided by a mechanical *band organ*, often referred to as a *calliope*.

outer wheel/outer rim

inner wheel

spokes

car/seat/gondola

axle

safety bar

unistrut/A-frame

tower/leg

safety ladder

support

FERRIS WHEEL
3

Ferris Wheel

Merry-Go-Round / Carousel

panel painting

rim/rounding board/
cornice/shield

rotating frame

inner cornice

horse rod

horse

gondola/chariot

platform

inside drive

Special Purpose Buildings

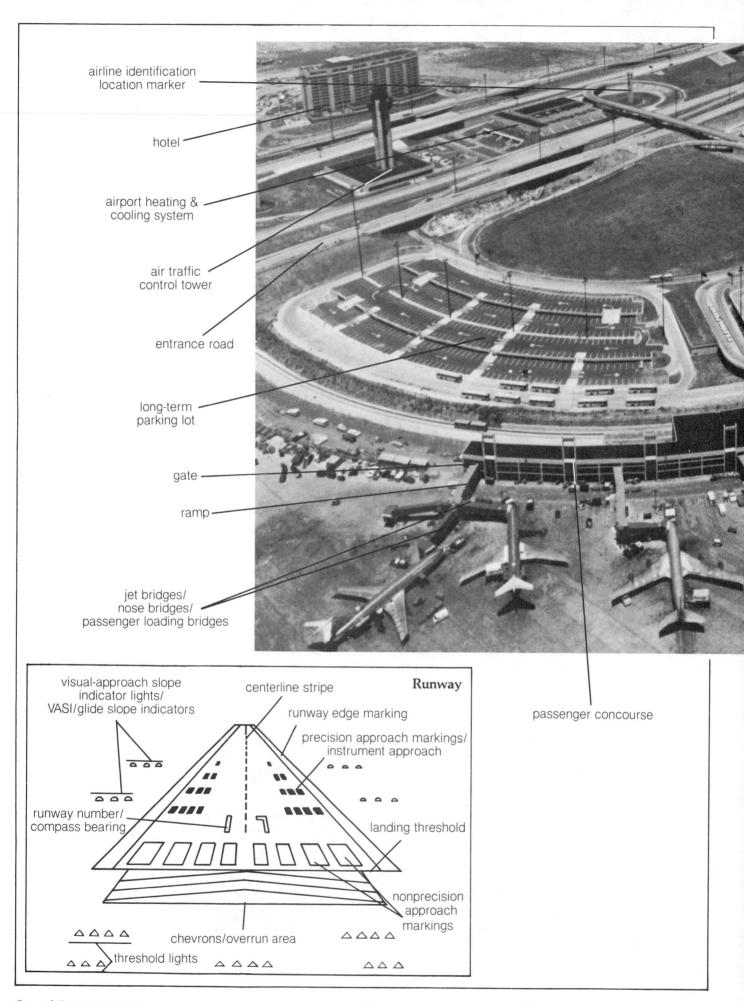

airline identification
location marker

hotel

airport heating &
cooling system

air traffic
control tower

entrance road

long-term
parking lot

gate

ramp

jet bridges/
nose bridges/
passenger loading bridges

passenger concourse

Runway

visual-approach slope
indicator lights/
VASI/glide slope indicators

centerline stripe

runway edge marking

precision approach markings/
instrument approach

runway number/
compass bearing

landing threshold

nonprecision
approach
markings

chevrons/overrun area

threshold lights

Special Purpose Buildings

94

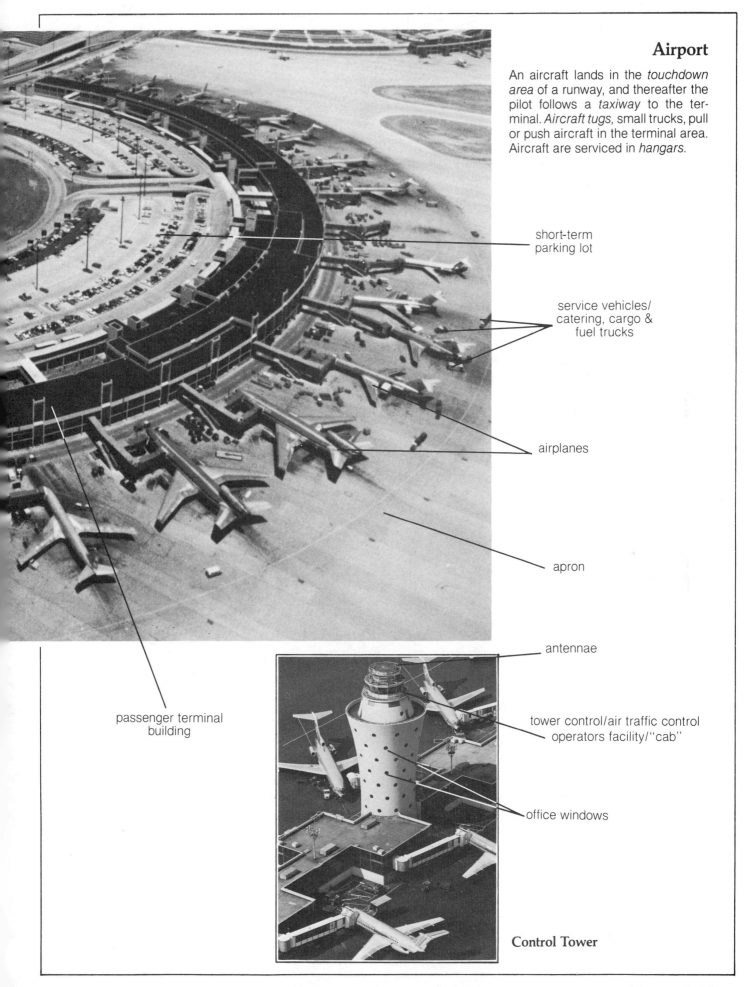

Airport

An aircraft lands in the *touchdown area* of a runway, and thereafter the pilot follows a *taxiway* to the terminal. *Aircraft tugs,* small trucks, pull or push aircraft in the terminal area. Aircraft are serviced in *hangars.*

short-term parking lot

service vehicles/ catering, cargo & fuel trucks

airplanes

apron

passenger terminal building

antennae

tower control/air traffic control operators facility/"cab"

office windows

Control Tower

Special Purpose Buildings

Railroad Yard

A railroad yard, or *marshalling yard*, consists of a system of *parallel tracks*, *crossovers* and *switches* where *cars* are formed into *trains* and where cars, *locomotives* and other *rolling stock* are kept when not in use or awaiting repair. In *hump yards*, freight cars are pushed down a *hump* onto a *siding*, determined by a *yardmaster*, to be coupled to a forming train. *Electropneumatic retarders* control the speed of the cars as they move along the tracks.

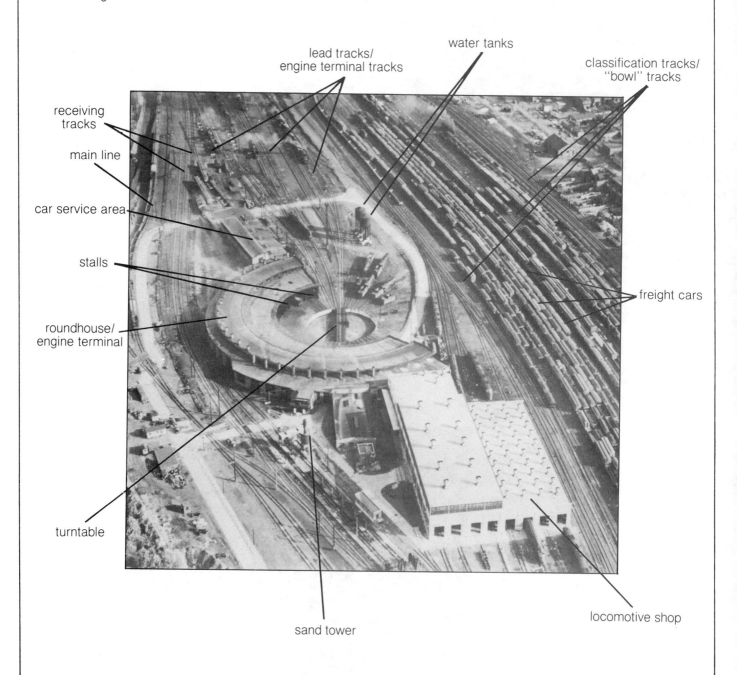

lead tracks/
engine terminal tracks

water tanks

classification tracks/
"bowl" tracks

receiving
tracks

main line

car service area

stalls

roundhouse/
engine terminal

freight cars

turntable

sand tower

locomotive shop

Bridge

A pedestrian walkway on a bridge is a *footpath*. *Fixed bridges* have no moving parts, while *movable bridges*, such as lift bridges, *drawbridges* and *bascule bridges* either lift or swing open. A *pontoon bridge* is built on *floating piers*.

safety rail

window

tower

main cable

stay rope

suspender cables

girder

stiffening trusses

side span

center span

tower leg

pier

Suspension Bridge

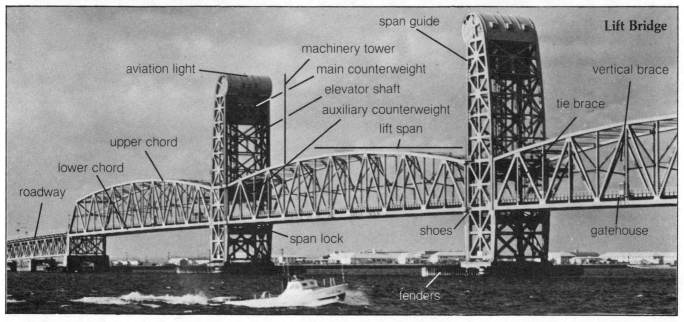

Lift Bridge

span guide

machinery tower

main counterweight

aviation light

elevator shaft

auxiliary counterweight

lift span

vertical brace

tie brace

upper chord

lower chord

roadway

span lock

shoes

gatehouse

fenders

Other Structures

Tunnel

Tunnels that take water to hydroelectric plants or to municipal waterworks and those that remove storm water and sewage are called *conduits*. Tunnels cut through rock frequently require no *lining*. Underwater tunnels can be ventilated by *shafts* leading to the surface or by *exhaust* or *booster fans* at the ends.

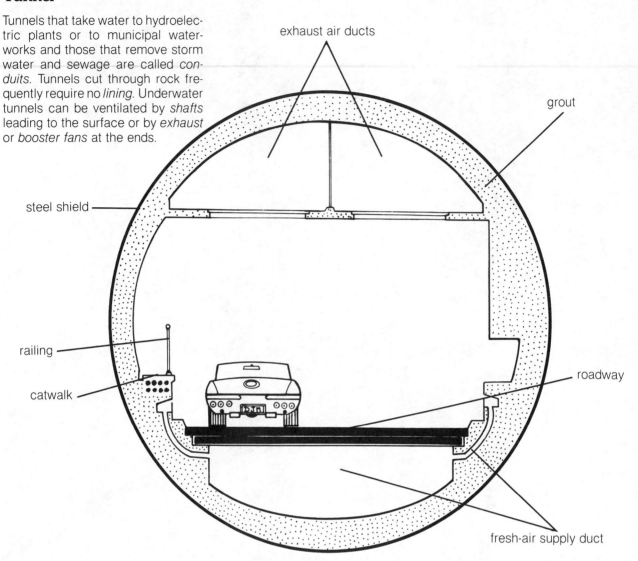

exhaust air ducts

grout

steel shield

railing

catwalk

roadway

fresh-air supply duct

Cross Section

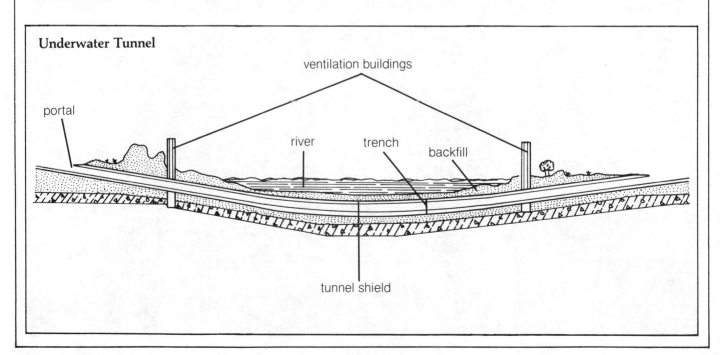

Underwater Tunnel

ventilation buildings

portal

river

trench

backfill

tunnel shield

Other Structures

Canal Lock

The water level in a canal lock is raised or lowered through *sluice gates* in the lock wall or *floor*. *Shipboard lines* or *hawsers* secured to *bollards* along the lockside hold the vessel steady while the lock is in operation. Before *electric locomotives* were used, animals would haul boats through locks following a *towpath*.

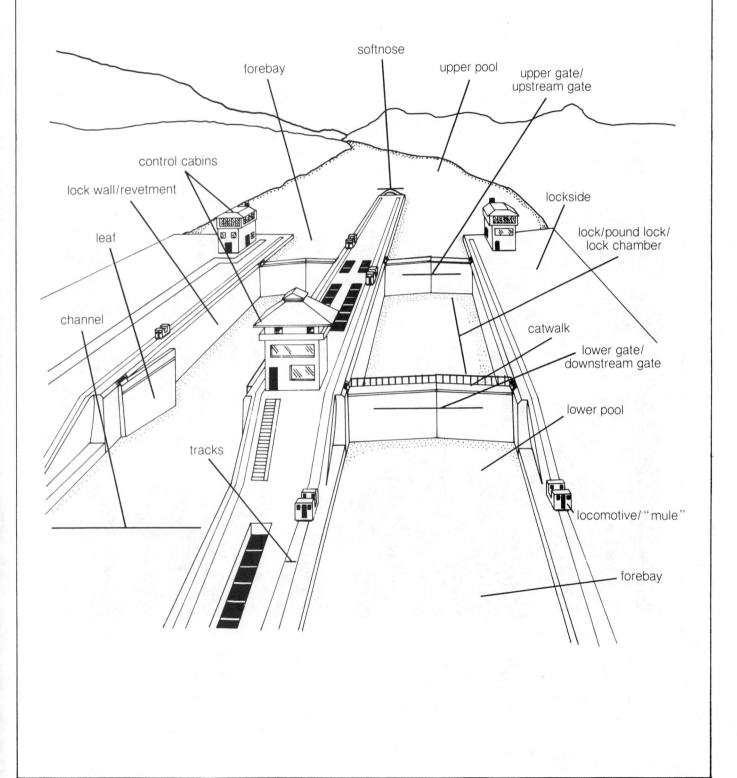

softnose

forebay

upper pool

upper gate/upstream gate

control cabins

lock wall/revetment

lockside

leaf

lock/pound lock/lock chamber

channel

catwalk

lower gate/downstream gate

tracks

lower pool

locomotive/"mule"

forebay

Dam

Many dams have steep channels divided by partitions into pools, called *fishways* or *fish ladders,* that enable fish to swim upriver. Other dams have *log chutes* designed to allow logs to pass through. A *dike,* or *levee,* is an earthwork construction built to block water rather than to regulate its flow.

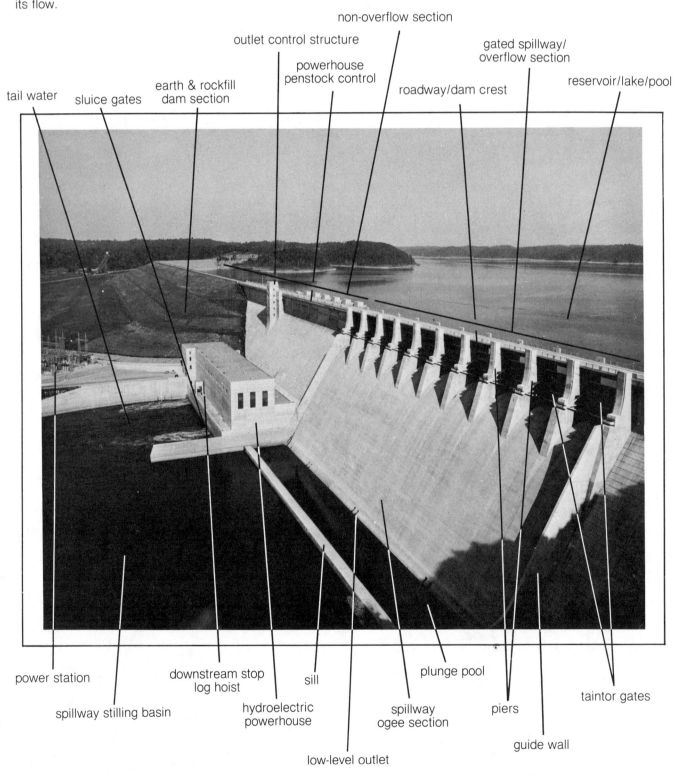

non-overflow section

outlet control structure

powerhouse penstock control

gated spillway/ overflow section

roadway/dam crest

reservoir/lake/pool

tail water

sluice gates

earth & rockfill dam section

power station

downstream stop log hoist

sill

plunge pool

piers

taintor gates

spillway stilling basin

hydroelectric powerhouse

spillway ogee section

guide wall

low-level outlet

Oil Drilling Platform/ Offshore Rig

In shallow water this *semisubmersible* rig drills in the floating position. When drilling at greater depths the motion compensator, a *hydraulic-pneumatic device,* moves up and down as the rig does in the sea to keep the *pipe* stationary in the *hole.* The "driller" controls the *drill, bit* changes and large hydraulic valves, or *blowout preventors.*

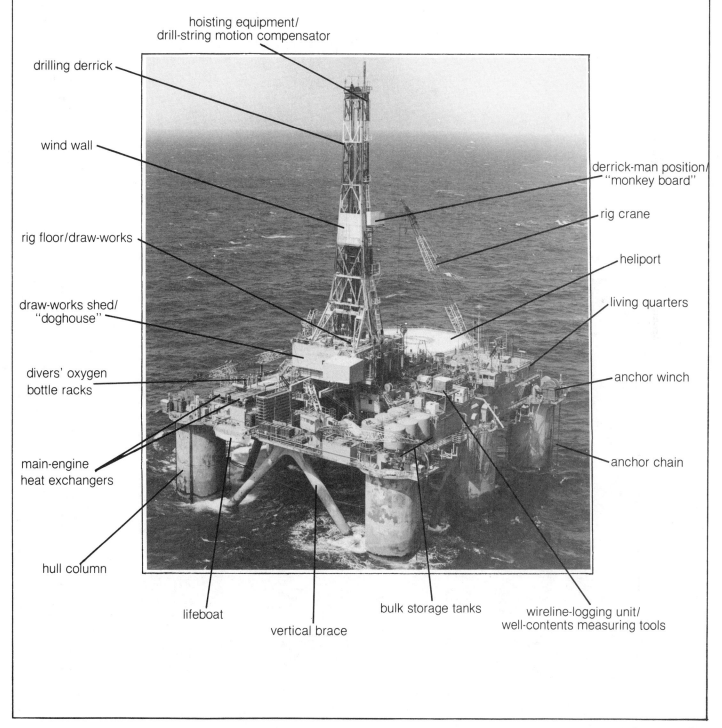

hoisting equipment/ drill-string motion compensator

drilling derrick

wind wall

rig floor/draw-works

draw-works shed/ "doghouse"

divers' oxygen bottle racks

main-engine heat exchangers

hull column

lifeboat

vertical brace

bulk storage tanks

derrick-man position/ "monkey board"

rig crane

heliport

living quarters

anchor winch

anchor chain

wireline-logging unit/ well-contents measuring tools

Other Structures

Supermarket

The representative floor plan shown here is of a typical *superstore*, or *supercombo*, a combination drug store and food store, with emphasis on *perishables* and *preprepared foods*. The supermarkets of the future will be *warehouse stores*, or *hypermarkets*.

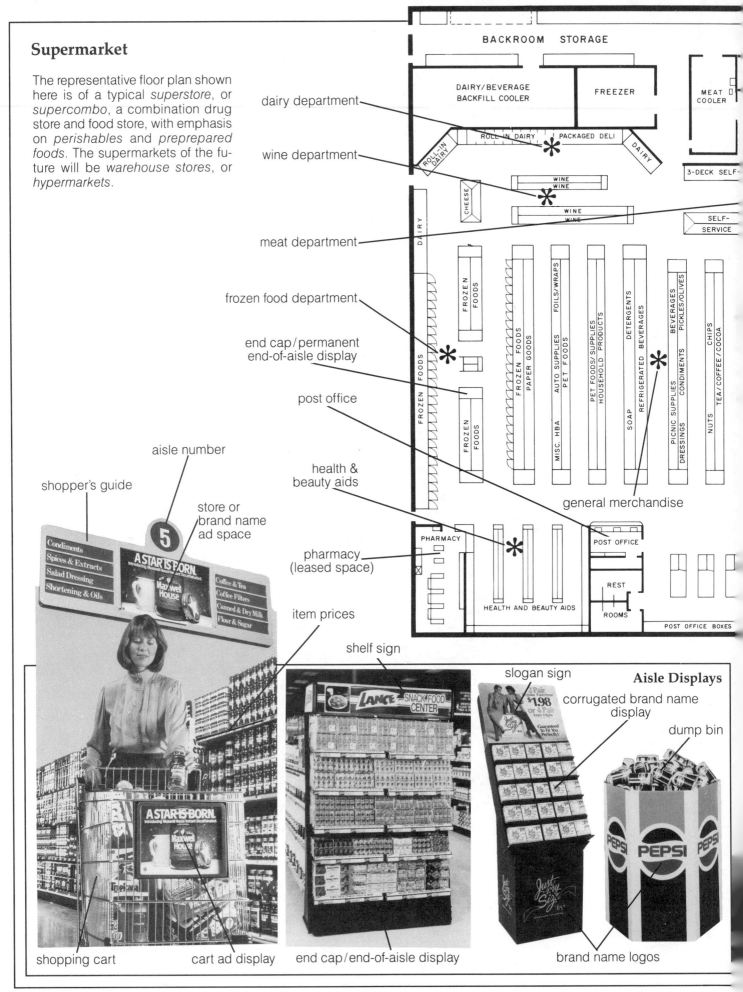

dairy department

wine department

meat department

frozen food department

end cap/permanent end-of-aisle display

post office

health & beauty aids

pharmacy (leased space)

general merchandise

BACKROOM STORAGE

DAIRY/BEVERAGE BACKFILL COOLER

FREEZER

MEAT COOLER

ROLL IN DAIRY

PACKAGED DELI

DAIRY

ROLL-IN DAIRY

3-DECK SELF-

CHEESE

WINE

SELF-SERVICE

DAIRY

FROZEN FOODS

FROZEN FOODS

FROZEN FOODS

PAPER GOODS

FOILS/WRAPS

AUTO SUPPLIES

PET FOODS

PET FOODS/SUPPLIES

HOUSEHOLD PRODUCTS

MISC. HBA

SOAP

DETERGENTS

REFRIGERATED BEVERAGES

BEVERAGES

PICKLES/OLIVES

PICNIC SUPPLIES

CONDIMENTS

DRESSINGS

NUTS

CHIPS

TEA/COFFEE/COCOA

FROZEN FOODS

PHARMACY

POST OFFICE

HEALTH AND BEAUTY AIDS

REST ROOMS

POST OFFICE BOXES

shopper's guide

aisle number

store or brand name ad space

item prices

shelf sign

slogan sign

Aisle Displays

corrugated brand name display

dump bin

Condiments
Spices & Extracts
Salad Dressing
Shortening & Oils

A STAR IS BORN.
Introducing Maxwell House Instant Decaffeinated

Maxwell House

Coffee & Tea
Coffee Filters
Canned & Dry Milk
Flour & Sugar

5

A STAR IS BORN.
Introducing Maxwell House Instant Decaffeinated

Maxwell House

LANCE SNACK FOOD CENTER

$1.98

Just My Size

PEPSI PEPSI PEPSI

shopping cart

cart ad display

end cap/end-of-aisle display

brand name logos

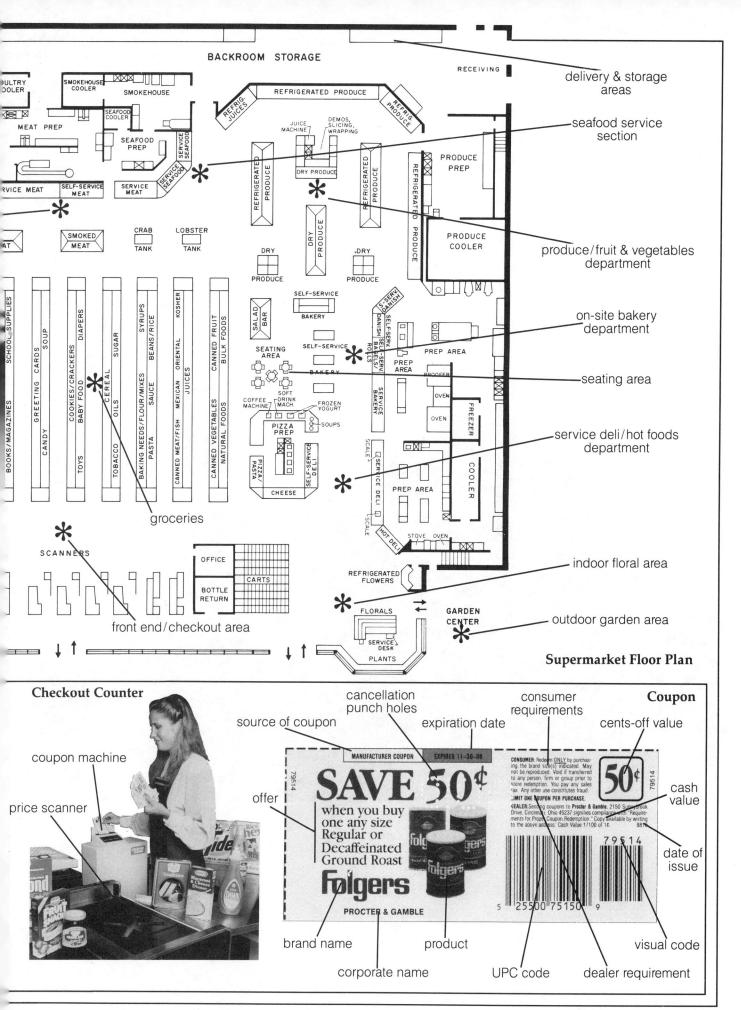

Supermarket Floor Plan

Checkout Counter

Coupon

Other Structures

Barn and Silo

A barn *floor* is divided in the center by a *feed passage* that may be lined with *stanchions* to hold cows. On either side are *manure gutters,* and on each side of these are *mangers, boxes* or *troughs,* from which horses or cattle eat. Hay is stored in a *loft,* a storage room next to the roof. Surrounding a barn is a *yard* with a *manure pit* large enough to back a wagon into. Other barnyard structures, adjoining the main barn or built nearby, include *grain pits,* or *bins; springhouses; smokehouses,* and *pigpens.*

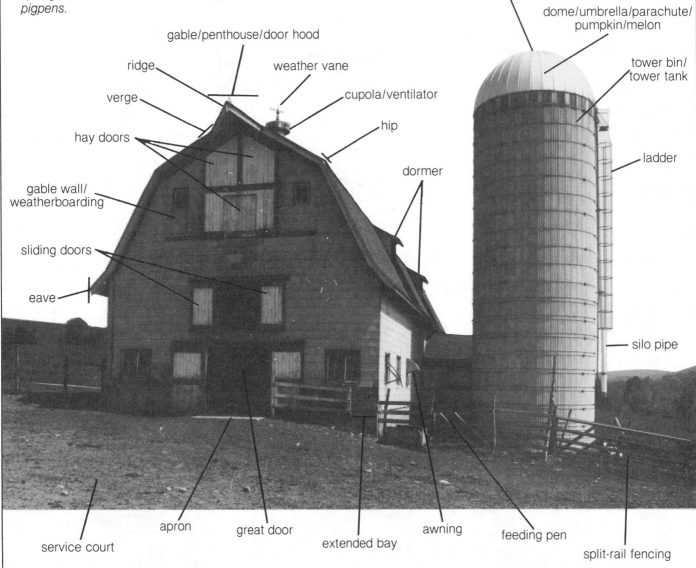

intake

dome/umbrella/parachute/pumpkin/melon

tower bin/tower tank

ladder

gable/penthouse/door hood

weather vane

ridge

cupola/ventilator

verge

hip

dormer

hay doors

gable wall/weatherboarding

sliding doors

eave

silo pipe

apron

great door

awning

feeding pen

service court

extended bay

split-rail fencing

Barn

Silo

Transportation

All the major forms of transportation are incorporated in this section, beginning with the most ubiquitous mode of everyday travel—the automobile. Coverage of the car begins with an illustration of a specially built model displaying all the exterior parts that appear or have appeared on recent designs. Also included is a cutaway drawing that shows the major but often unseen interior components of a car as well as illustrations of a car engine, interior dash and traffic control devices.

The other major subcategories cover public conveyances; emergency, public service and recreational vehicles; boats and ships; aircraft and spacecraft. Vehicles used for military purposes, such as fighting ships and aircraft, are included in this section as well.

Cutaway illustrations have been used to show the reader the interior parts of an ocean liner and the cockpits of a jumbo jet, military fighter and space shuttle.

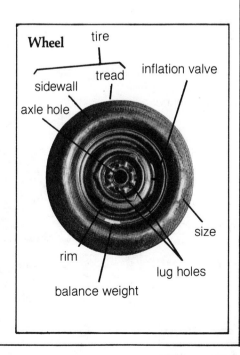

The *body* of this specially designed car, or *customized automobile,* rests on a *chassis* consisting of a *frame* and wheels. Older cars often had *rumble seats* instead of trunks. On *convertibles,* the entire top folds into a compartment called the *boot.* Many contemporary cars have sliding *sun roofs* or *moon roofs.* A *sedan* usually has four doors and full-width front and rear seats. A *coupe* is a smaller version of a sedan, having only two doors. A *station wagon* is a boxlike car with storage space behind the rear seat, which may have *fold-down seats* for additional passenger seating. A high-performance car with a low-slung body is a *sports car.*

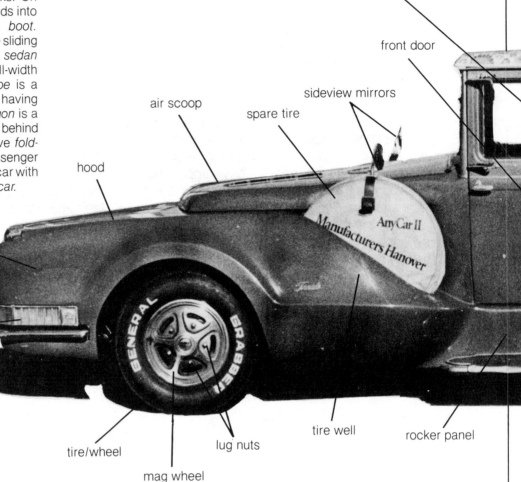

front window/front door window

front door

sideview mirrors

air scoop

spare tire

hood

Manufacturers Hanover

AnyCar II

fender/front quarter panel

signal light/cornering lamp

tire/wheel

mag wheel

lug nuts

tire well

rocker panel

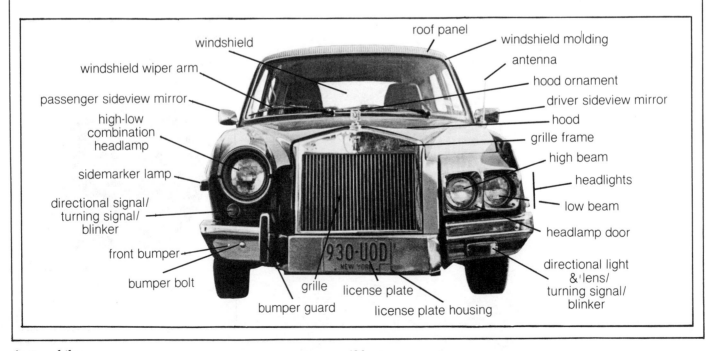

windshield

roof panel

windshield molding

windshield wiper arm

antenna

passenger sideview mirror

hood ornament

high-low combination headlamp

driver sideview mirror

hood

sidemarker lamp

grille frame

high beam

directional signal/turning signal/blinker

headlights

low beam

front bumper

headlamp door

bumper bolt

930-UOD NEW YORK

directional light & lens/turning signal/blinker

grille

license plate

bumper guard

license plate housing

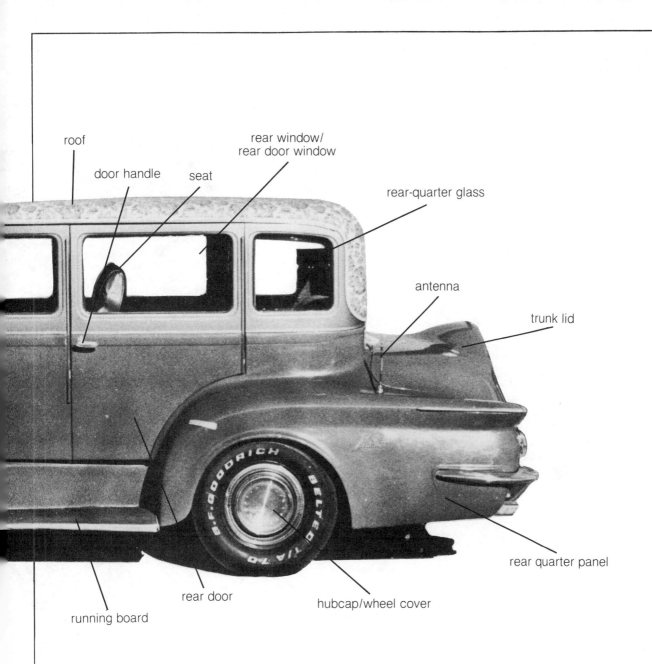

roof

door handle   seat

rear window/
rear door window

rear-quarter glass

antenna

trunk lid

running board

rear door

hubcap/wheel cover

rear quarter panel

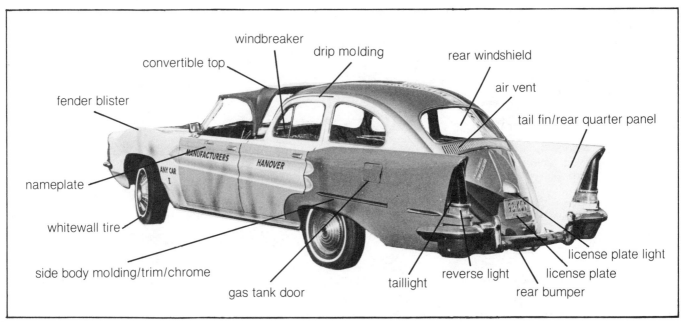

windbreaker

convertible top   drip molding

rear windshield

air vent

fender blister

tail fin/rear quarter panel

nameplate

whitewall tire

side body molding/trim/chrome

gas tank door

taillight   reverse light

license plate light

license plate

rear bumper

Automobile Cutaway

Various systems are incorporated in a car: a *power train,* which consists of *clutch,* transmission, driveshaft and rear axle; a *cooling system* designed to control engine temperature; an *electrical system* to power the engine *starter motor,* accessories and lights; a *suspension system* to provide a smooth ride; and a *braking system.*

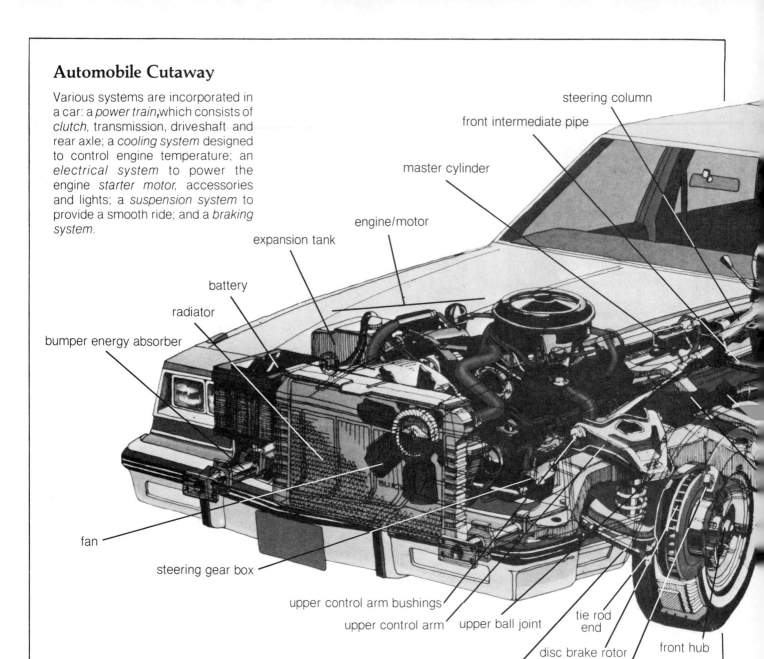

steering column
front intermediate pipe
master cylinder
engine/motor
expansion tank
battery
radiator
bumper energy absorber
fan
steering gear box
upper control arm bushings
upper control arm
upper ball joint
tie rod end
disc brake rotor
lower control arm
disc brake caliper
front hub

Passenger Car Types and Body Styles

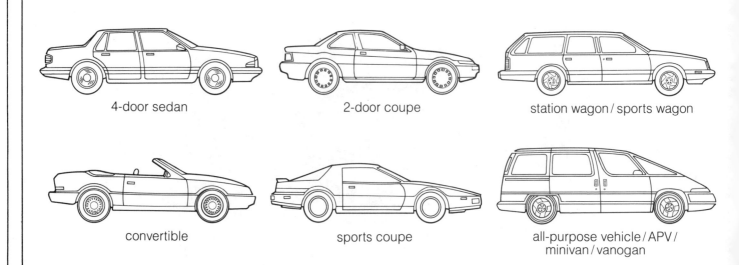

4-door sedan

2-door coupe

station wagon/sports wagon

convertible

sports coupe

all-purpose vehicle/APV/ minivan/vanogan

Automobile

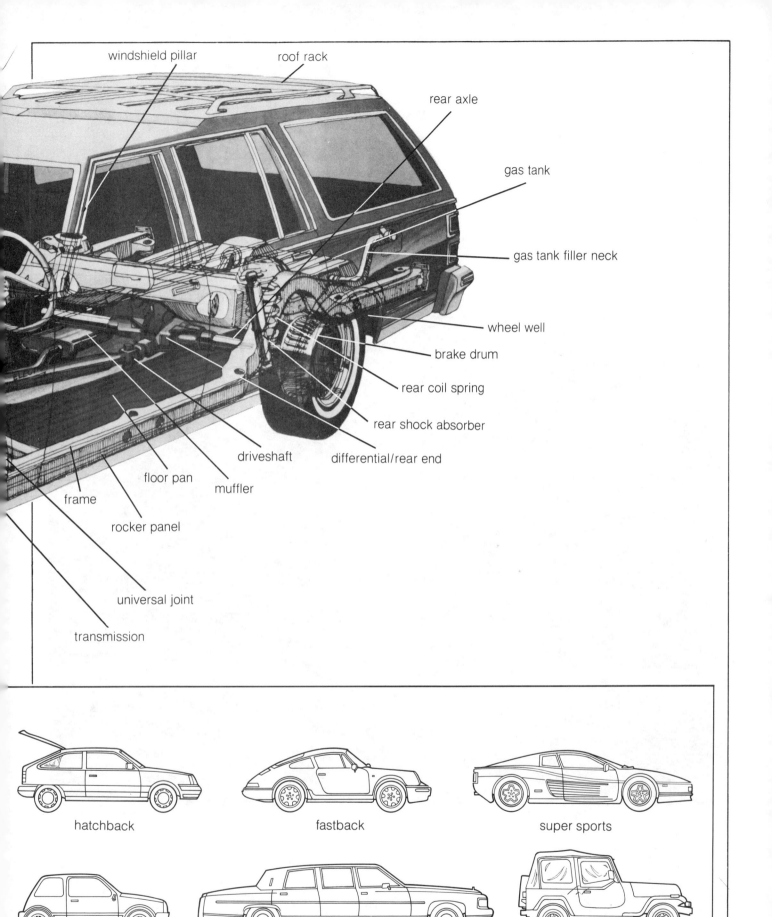

windshield pillar

roof rack

rear axle

gas tank

gas tank filler neck

wheel well

brake drum

rear coil spring

rear shock absorber

differential/rear end

driveshaft

muffler

floor pan

rocker panel

frame

universal joint

transmission

hatchback

fastback

super sports

minicar

limousine/"stretch limo"

recreational vehicle/
4 x 4/"jeep"

Automobile Interior

In addition to parts shown on this *dash,* or *dashboard,* are *headlight* and *warning light controls, hood release, engine choke* and *hand throttle, windshield wiper speed control* and *directional signal switch.* Above the dash, there is usually a *rearview mirror.* Flip-down *sun visors* are located above the windshield. Car seats are equipped with *seat belts* or *safety belts.*

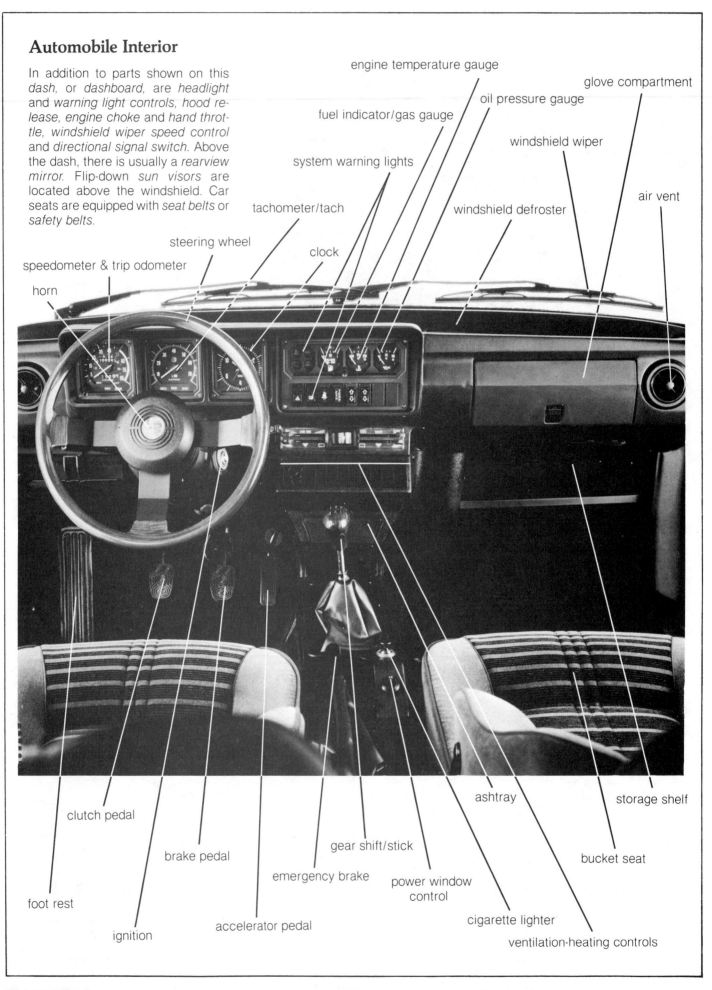

engine temperature gauge

glove compartment

oil pressure gauge

fuel indicator/gas gauge

windshield wiper

system warning lights

air vent

windshield defroster

tachometer/tach

clock

steering wheel

speedometer & trip odometer

horn

clutch pedal

brake pedal

gear shift/stick

ashtray

storage shelf

bucket seat

emergency brake

power window control

foot rest

ignition

accelerator pedal

cigarette lighter

ventilation-heating controls

Automobile Engine

The parts of an engine are fitted into or on the *engine block* or within the *head.* Common engine configurations include the *horizontally opposed,* or *flat four-cylinder;* the *in-line six;* and the *V-8.*

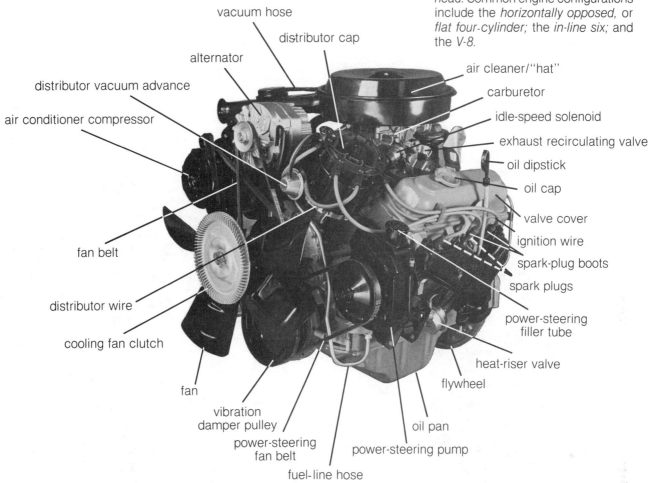

vacuum hose
distributor cap
alternator
distributor vacuum advance
air conditioner compressor
fan belt
distributor wire
cooling fan clutch
fan
vibration damper pulley
power-steering fan belt
fuel-line hose

air cleaner/"hat"
carburetor
idle-speed solenoid
exhaust recirculating valve
oil dipstick
oil cap
valve cover
ignition wire
spark-plug boots
spark plugs
power-steering filler tube
heat-riser valve
flywheel
oil pan
power-steering pump

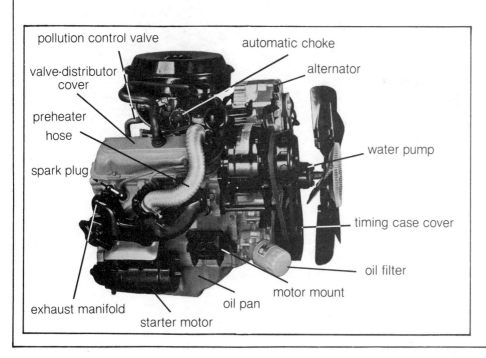

pollution control valve
valve-distributor cover
preheater hose
spark plug
exhaust manifold
starter motor
oil pan
motor mount
automatic choke
alternator
water pump
timing case cover
oil filter

Gasoline Pump

Service station islands can be *self-service* or *full-service*. Gas pumps draw supplies from underground *storage tanks*. Gasoline is purchased in different *grades* determined by *octane number*.

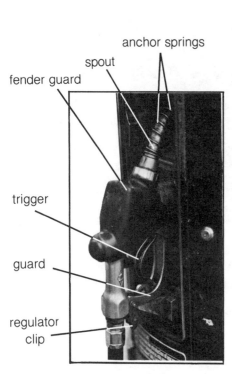

anchor springs

spout

fender guard

trigger

guard

regulator clip

Automatic Nozzle

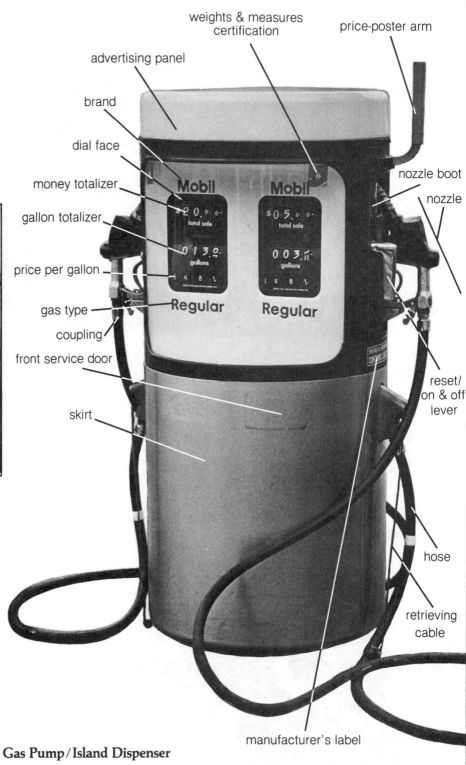

weights & measures certification

price-poster arm

advertising panel

brand

dial face

money totalizer

gallon totalizer

price per gallon

gas type

coupling

front service door

skirt

Mobil

Mobil

$20.₅₀₀·

total sale

$05.₀₀₀·

total sale

013.⁹₇

gallons

003.₁₁

gallons

1 4 8 1

1 4 8 1

Regular

Regular

nozzle boot

nozzle

reset/ on & off lever

hose

retrieving cable

manufacturer's label

Gas Pump/Island Dispenser

Traffic Control Devices

Four-face traffic signals, or lights, are operated manually by a traffic-control official or run automatically by an electric *timer.* Parking meters, set atop *pipe standards,* contain *self-starting timers.* Jammed meters activate a *slot closer* so that additional coins cannot be inserted in the *slot block.* Some meters have a *washer detector* that allows *washers* and *slugs* to pass through without registering time on the *dial.*

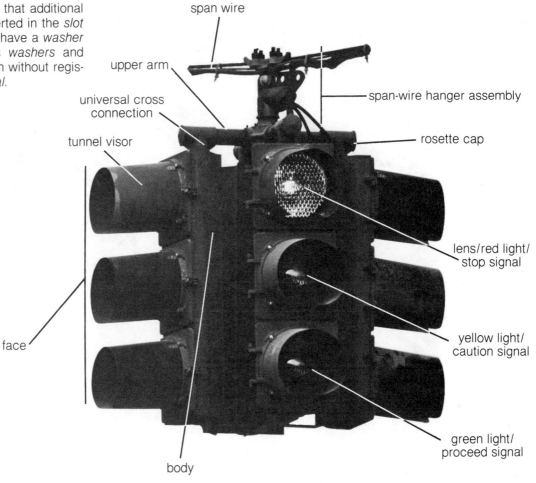

span wire

upper arm

universal cross connection

tunnel visor

span-wire hanger assembly

rosette cap

lens/red light/ stop signal

yellow light/ caution signal

green light/ proceed signal

face

body

Traffic Light

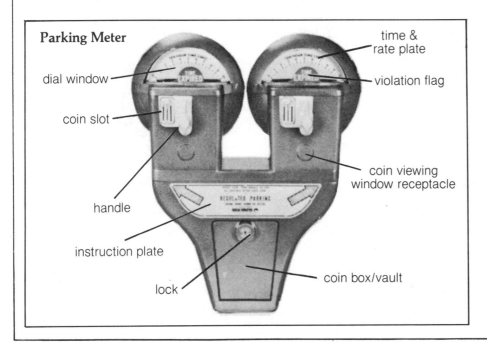

Parking Meter

dial window

coin slot

handle

instruction plate

lock

time & rate plate

violation flag

coin viewing window receptacle

coin box/vault

Highway

Energy absorbing barriers, or impact attenuation devices, are positioned in gore areas to reduce accidents. Some roads are lined with guardrails, or railings. Milestones, or mile markers, provide distance information between specific points. Many expressways, freeways and thruways have rest areas, scenic overlooks and service areas.

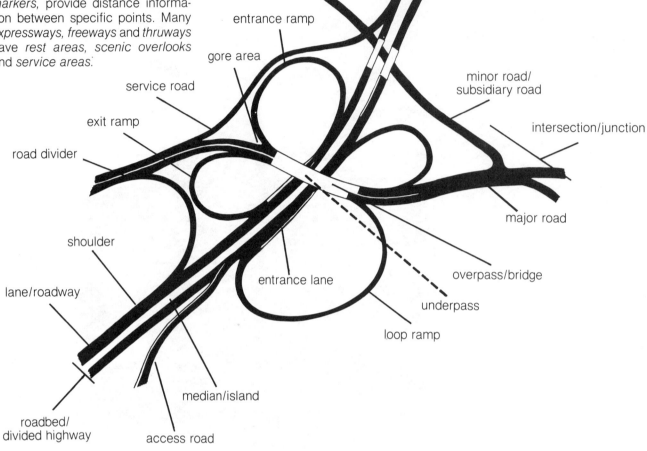

entrance ramp

gore area

service road

exit ramp

road divider

shoulder

lane/roadway

roadbed/
divided highway

access road

median/island

entrance lane

loop ramp

underpass

overpass/bridge

major road

intersection/junction

minor road/
subsidiary road

Cloverleaf / Interchange

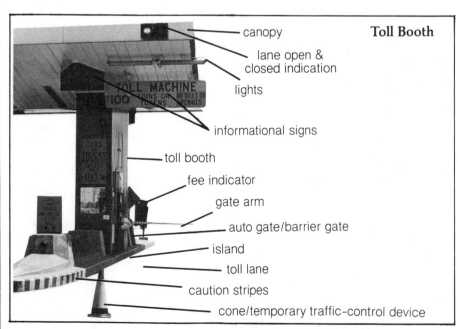

Toll Booth

canopy

lane open &
closed indication

lights

informational signs

toll booth

fee indicator

gate arm

auto gate/barrier gate

island

toll lane

caution stripes

cone/temporary traffic-control device

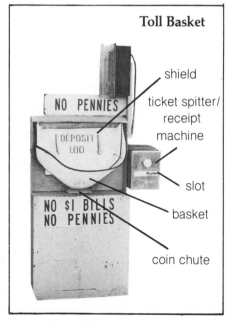

Toll Basket

shield

ticket spitter/
receipt machine

slot

basket

coin chute

NO PENNIES

DEPOSIT 1.00

NO $1 BILLS
NO PENNIES

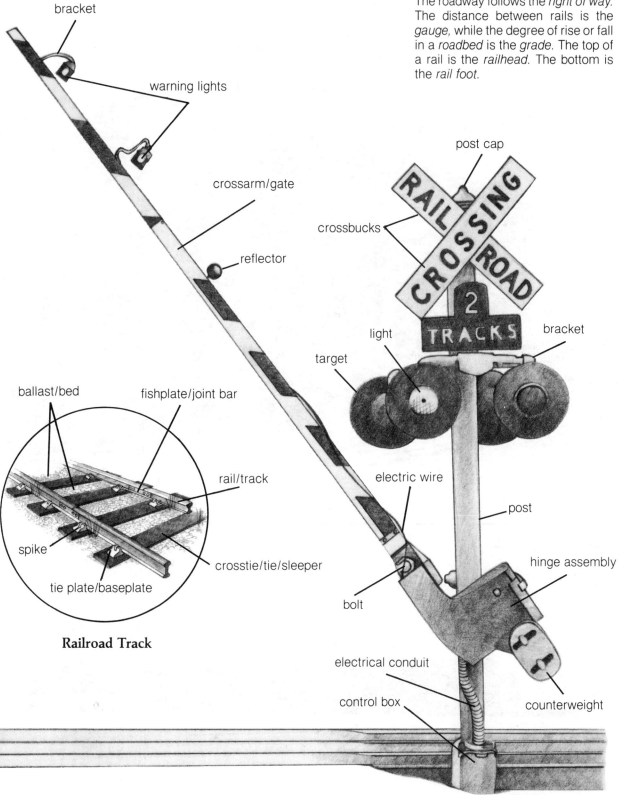

Railroad Crossing

A railroad *roadway* consists of two rails, or tracks, and all their supporting elements, including *railroad bridges, tunnels* and *embankments*. The roadway follows the *right of way*. The distance between rails is the *gauge*, while the degree of rise or fall in a *roadbed* is the *grade*. The top of a rail is the *railhead*. The bottom is the *rail foot*.

bracket

warning lights

crossarm/gate

reflector

ballast/bed

fishplate/joint bar

rail/track

spike

crosstie/tie/sleeper

tie plate/baseplate

Railroad Track

post cap

crossbucks

RAIL ROAD CROSSING

2 TRACKS

light

target

bracket

electric wire

post

bolt

hinge assembly

electrical conduit

control box

counterweight

Crossing Signal

Public Transportation

Railroad

In addition to the locomotives shown here, there are *diesel* and *electric locomotives. Open-top, box* and *flat cars* are the principal types of *freight cars*, while *passenger trains* consist of *coaches, buffet* and *dining cars, sleeping cars, lounge* or *observation cars* and *baggage cars*.

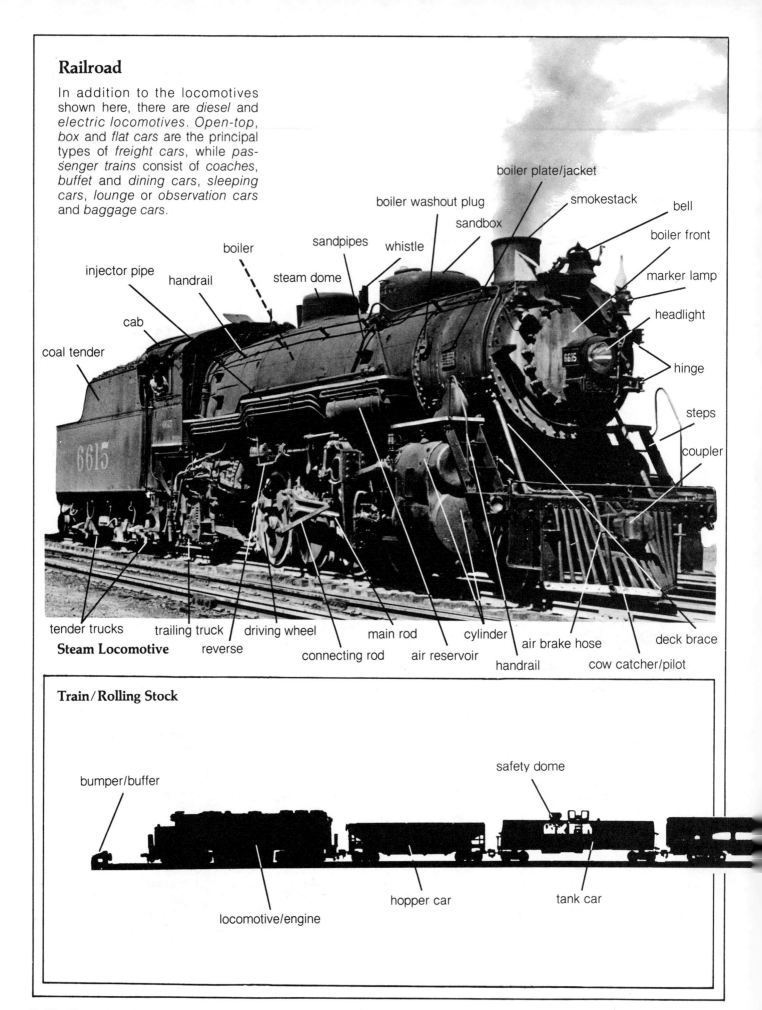

boiler plate/jacket
boiler washout plug
smokestack
bell
sandbox
boiler front
sandpipes
whistle
marker lamp
boiler
steam dome
headlight
injector pipe
handrail
cab
hinge
coal tender
steps
coupler

tender trucks
trailing truck
driving wheel
main rod
cylinder
air brake hose
deck brace
reverse
connecting rod
air reservoir
handrail
cow catcher/pilot

Steam Locomotive

Train/Rolling Stock

safety dome

bumper/buffer

hopper car
tank car

locomotive/engine

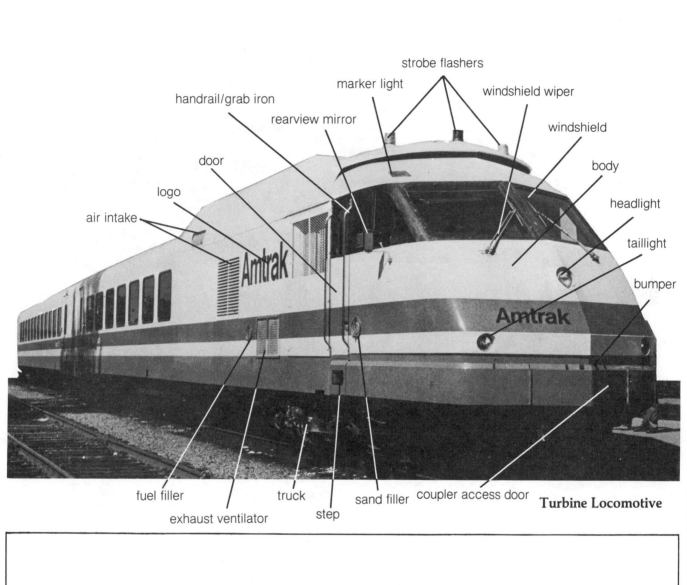

strobe flashers

marker light

windshield wiper

handrail/grab iron

rearview mirror

windshield

body

door

headlight

logo

taillight

air intake

bumper

Amtrak

Amtrak

fuel filler

truck

sand filler

coupler access door

Turbine Locomotive

exhaust ventilator

step

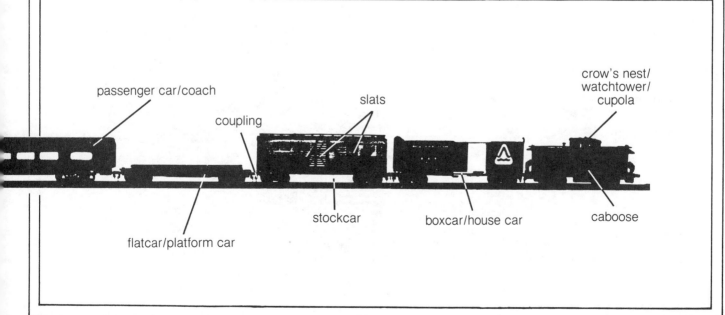

crow's nest/
watchtower/
cupola

passenger car/coach

slats

coupling

stockcar

boxcar/house car

caboose

flatcar/platform car

Bus

Long-distance coaches have airplanelike *reclining seats* with *overhead baggage racks* and *reading lights*. They may also have *lavatories* and *roof ventilation hatches*. *Sightseeing buses* have *transparent roofs*, at least in part, to increase the viewing area.

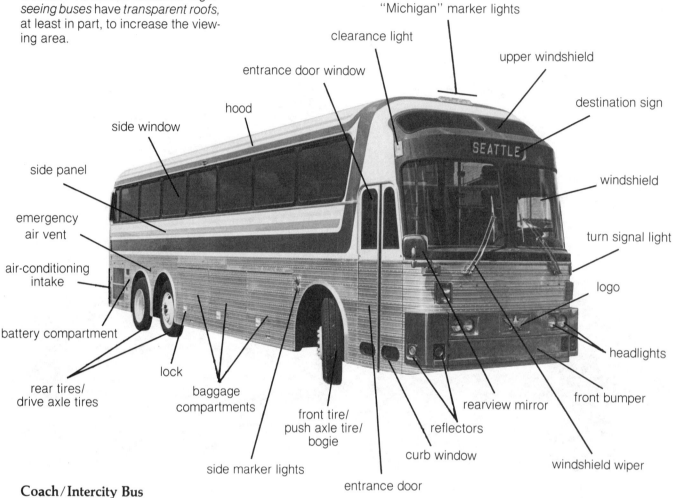

"Michigan" marker lights

clearance light

entrance door window

hood

side window

side panel

emergency air vent

air-conditioning intake

battery compartment

rear tires/ drive axle tires

lock

baggage compartments

side marker lights

front tire/ push axle tire/ bogie

entrance door

curb window

reflectors

rearview mirror

windshield wiper

front bumper

headlights

logo

turn signal light

windshield

destination sign

upper windshield

Coach/Intercity Bus

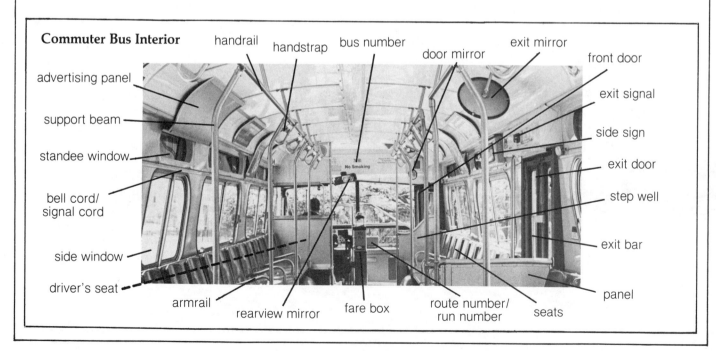

Commuter Bus Interior

advertising panel

support beam

standee window

bell cord/ signal cord

side window

driver's seat

handrail

handstrap

bus number

door mirror

exit mirror

front door

exit signal

side sign

exit door

step well

exit bar

panel

seats

route number/ run number

fare box

rearview mirror

armrail

A subway, or *rapid transit system*, usually consists of a *train* which derives its power from a *third rail*; subterranean *tunnels*, or *tubes*; *elevated tracks*; and *subway stations*, or *stops*, along each *route*.

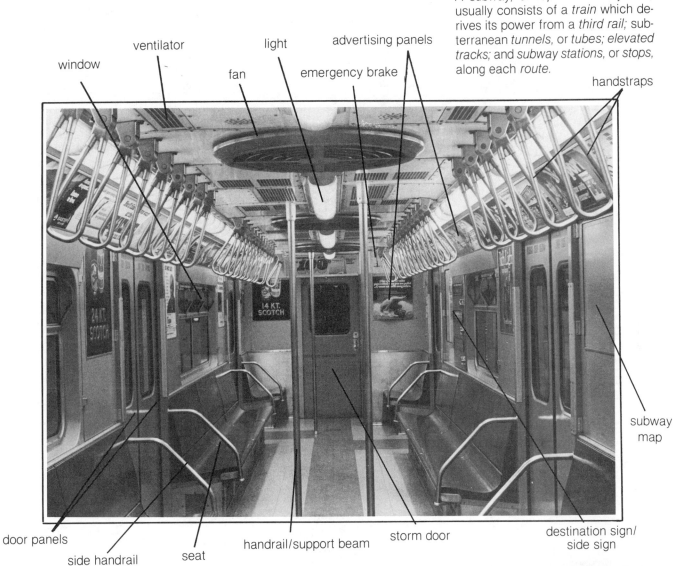

window
ventilator
fan
light
emergency brake
advertising panels
handstraps
subway map
door panels
side handrail
seat
handrail/support beam
storm door
destination sign/ side sign

Taxi Roof Light

off-duty sign
medallion number
signal light

OFF **9F8I** DUTY

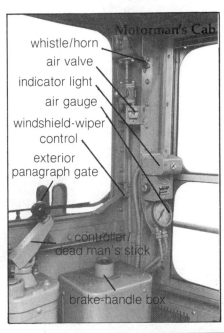

Motorman's Cab
whistle/horn
air valve
indicator light
air gauge
windshield-wiper control
exterior panagraph gate
controller/ dead man's stick
brake-handle box

Truck

A *rig* consists of a tractor *coupled* with or *hooked up* to a trailer. A cab may have a partitioned section within, called a *sleeping box*, for the driver, and a *varashield*, a capelike device designed to deflect air and reduce resistance on the trailer, mounted on the roof. The *refrigeration van*, or *reefer*, shown on the opposite page, is a semi, meaning that the tractor bears some of its weight. A true trailer rests and rides on its own wheels.

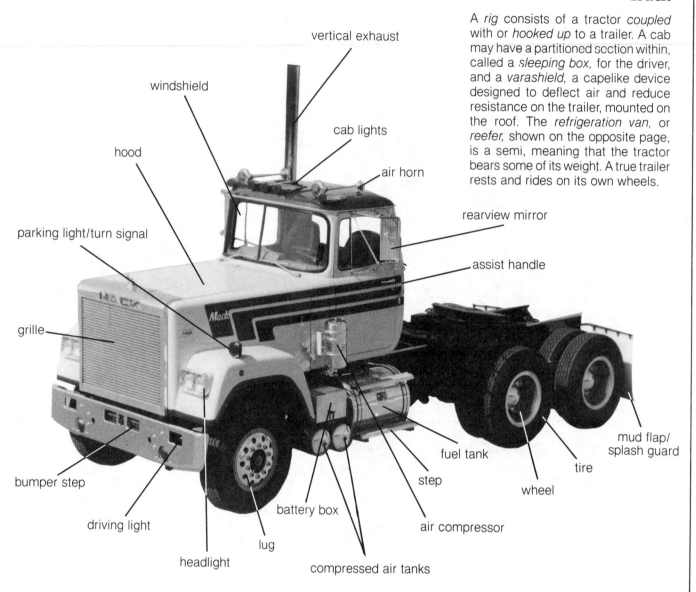

vertical exhaust

windshield

cab lights

air horn

hood

rearview mirror

parking light/turn signal

assist handle

grille

bumper step

fuel tank

mud flap/ splash guard

driving light

step

tire

battery box

air compressor

wheel

headlight

lug

compressed air tanks

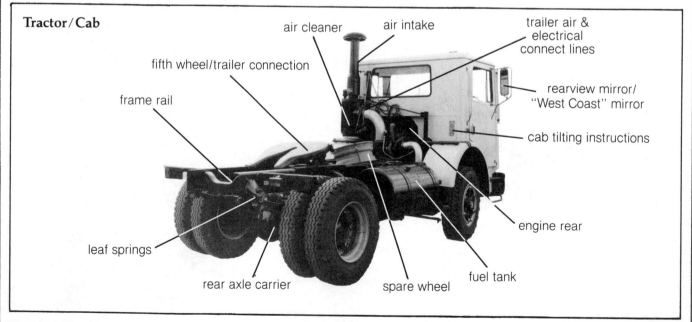

Tractor/Cab

air cleaner

air intake

trailer air & electrical connect lines

fifth wheel/trailer connection

rearview mirror/ "West Coast" mirror

frame rail

cab tilting instructions

engine rear

leaf springs

rear axle carrier

spare wheel

fuel tank

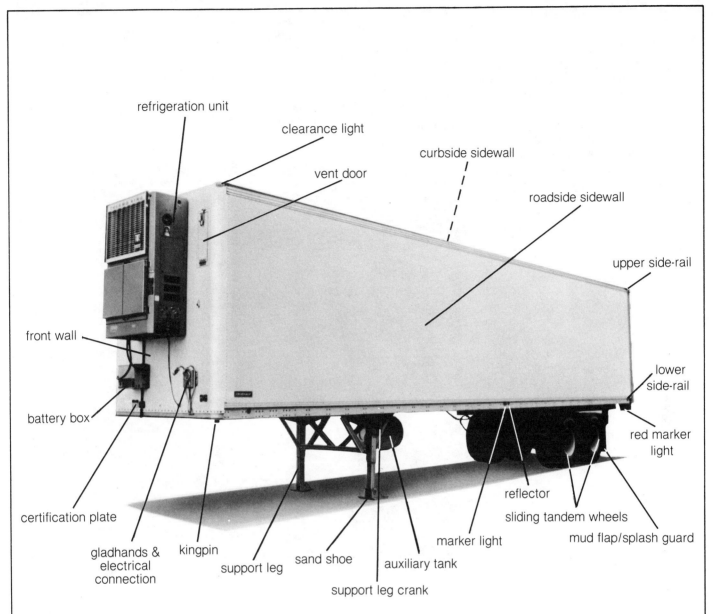

refrigeration unit

clearance light

curbside sidewall

vent door

roadside sidewall

upper side-rail

front wall

lower side-rail

battery box

red marker light

certification plate

reflector

sliding tandem wheels

gladhands & electrical connection

kingpin

support leg

sand shoe

auxiliary tank

marker light

mud flap/splash guard

support leg crank

Semitrailer/Van

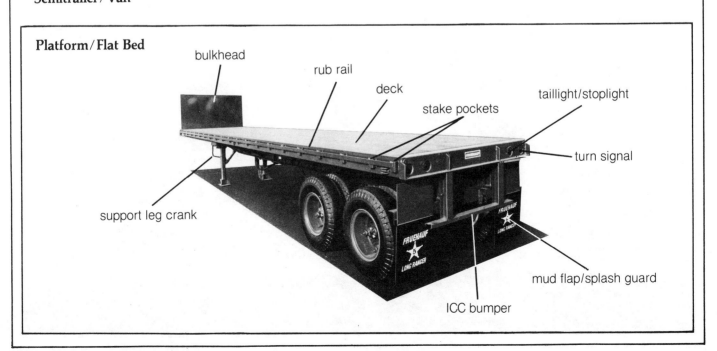

Platform/Flat Bed

bulkhead

rub rail

deck

taillight/stoplight

stake pockets

turn signal

support leg crank

mud flap/splash guard

ICC bumper

Carriers

Police Car

Many police cars have *alley lights*, strong floodlights at either end of the light bar on the roof. A wire screen between the driver's seat and the back seat of the car is called the *cage*. Contained in the trunk of many police cars are a *hurst tool*, or *jaws of life*, a *haligan tool*, an *oxygen unit*, *flares*, a *fire extinguisher*, a *riot gun*, a *first-aid kit*, *blankets* and a *pillow*.

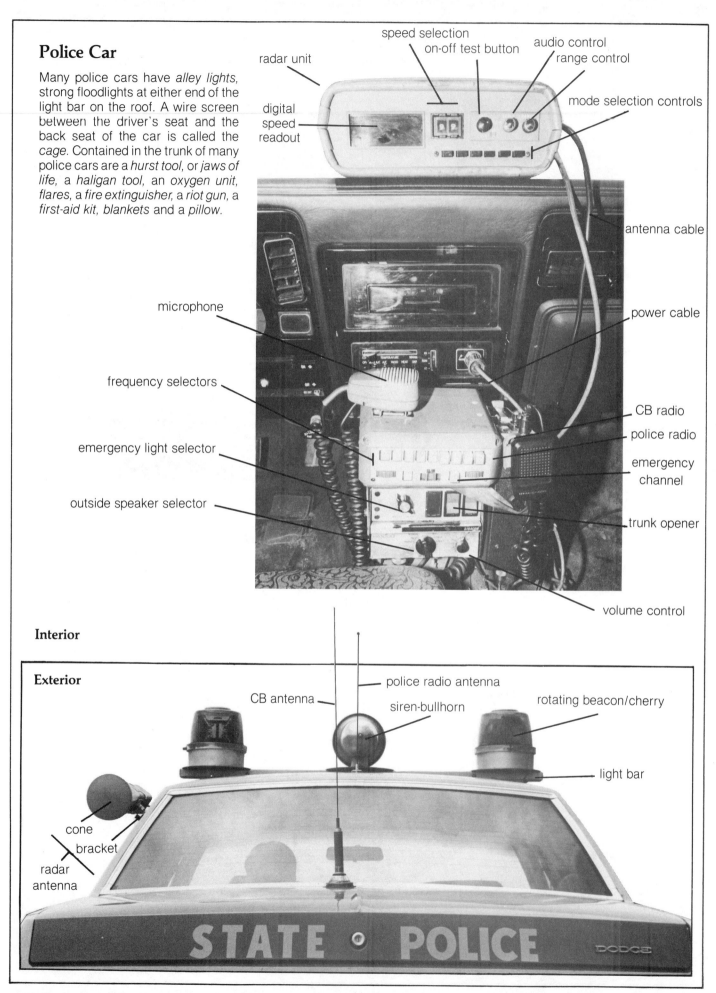

radar unit

speed selection
on-off test button

audio control
range control

mode selection controls

digital speed readout

antenna cable

microphone

power cable

frequency selectors

CB radio

police radio

emergency light selector

emergency channel

outside speaker selector

trunk opener

volume control

Interior

Exterior

CB antenna

police radio antenna

siren-bullhorn

rotating beacon/cherry

light bar

cone

bracket

radar antenna

STATE POLICE

DODGE

Ambulance

Additional equipment carried inside *advanced life-support units,* such as the one shown here, are *burn sheets, gauze, emesis basins, cervical collars, neck rolls, bitee sticks, tongue blades, peroxide* and *alcohol, extension tubes,* additional *oxygen tanks, splints, sandbags* (for traction), *linens,* a *scoop stretcher* and a *carrying chair.*

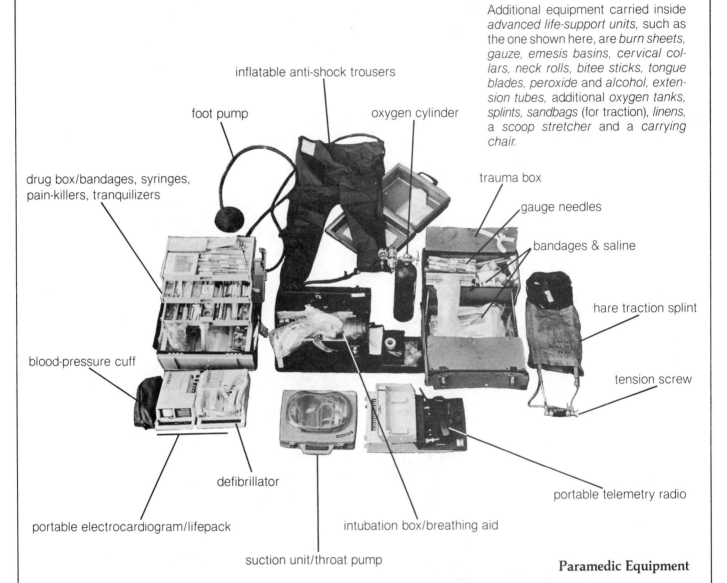

inflatable anti-shock trousers

foot pump

oxygen cylinder

drug box/bandages, syringes, pain-killers, tranquilizers

trauma box

gauge needles

bandages & saline

hare traction splint

blood-pressure cuff

tension screw

defibrillator

portable telemetry radio

portable electrocardiogram/lifepack

intubation box/breathing aid

suction unit/throat pump

Paramedic Equipment

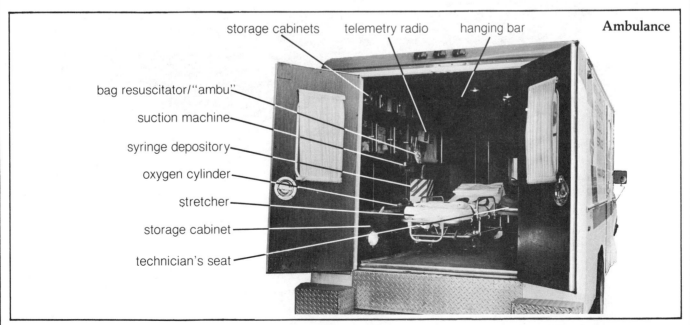

Ambulance

storage cabinets

telemetry radio

hanging bar

bag resuscitator/"ambu"

suction machine

syringe depository

oxygen cylinder

stretcher

storage cabinet

technician's seat

Emergency Vehicles

Fire Engine

On a fire truck, the entire tower ladder and control platform revolve on a *turntable*. Contained within a pumper is a water *booster tank* for fighting small fires, a *booster hose-reel*, for letting out hose line, and an *extension ladder*. Most fire fighting *apparatus* also carry *air tanks, lift-nets, EMT,* or *first aid boxes,* and *smoke ejectors*.

bucket/aerial platform/cherry picker

ladder pipe nozzle/stang

tower ladder

loudspeaker wire

pads

mars lights/marker lights

horn

boom

bell

hydraulic lifter

ladder control platform

bed

chauffeur's cab

stretchers

mount

warning light

steps

tow hook/tow ring

storage compartment

ladder

storage compartments

siren and loudspeaker

tormentor controls

tormentor/stabilizer/outrigger

Tower Ladder / Truck

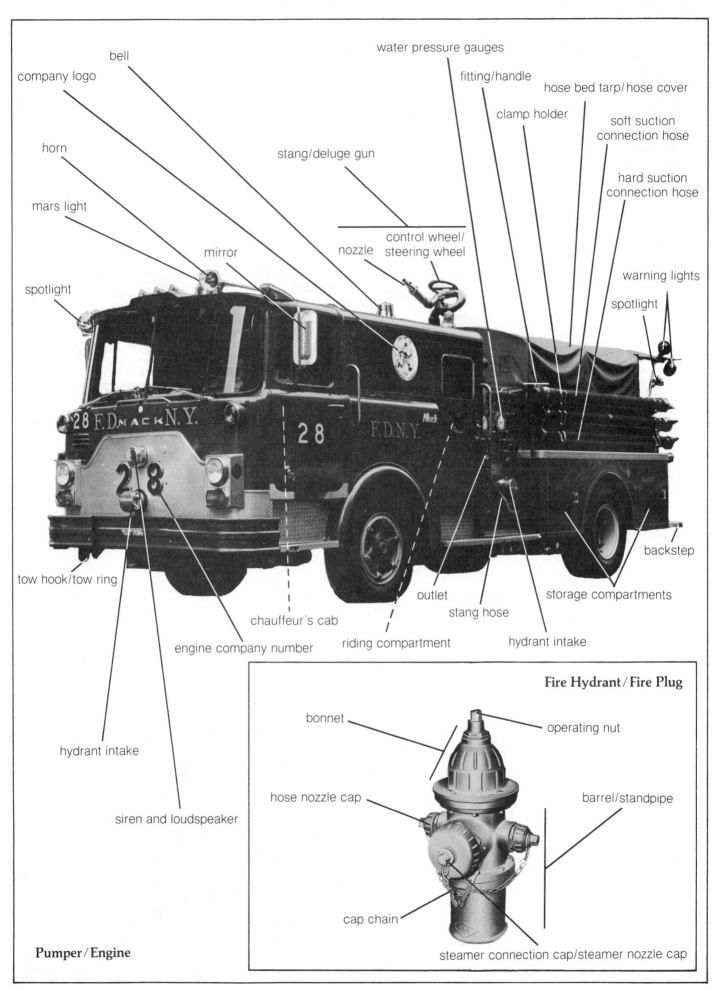

company logo

bell

water pressure gauges

fitting/handle

hose bed tarp/hose cover

clamp holder

soft suction
connection hose

horn

stang/deluge gun

hard suction
connection hose

mars light

nozzle

control wheel/
steering wheel

mirror

warning lights

spotlight

spotlight

28 F.D. MACK N.Y.

28

F.D.N.Y.

backstep

tow hook/tow ring

outlet

storage compartments

stang hose

chauffeur's cab

hydrant intake

engine company number

riding compartment

hydrant intake

hydrant intake

siren and loudspeaker

Fire Hydrant / Fire Plug

bonnet

operating nut

hose nozzle cap

barrel/standpipe

cap chain

steamer connection cap/steamer nozzle cap

Pumper/Engine

Emergency Vehicles

Tow Truck/Wrecker

Tow trucks, or *rigs,* that respond to
accident reports are called "chasers."
A fully-equipped tow truck carries
*fire extinguishers, battery charger,
battery jumper cables,* and a two-
pronged *lockout tool* which enables
the operator to open locked car doors.

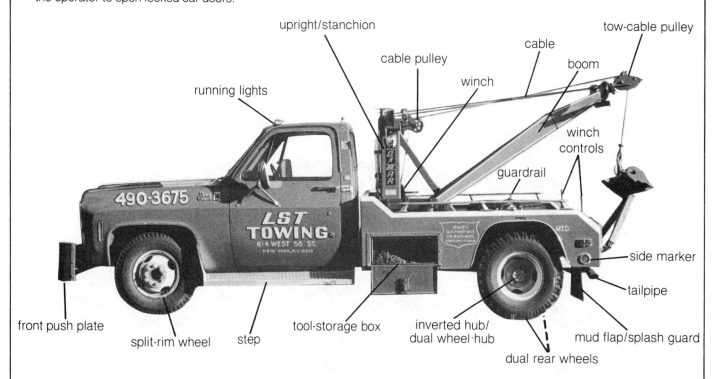

running lights

upright/stanchion

cable pulley

winch

cable

boom

tow-cable pulley

winch
controls

guardrail

side marker

tailpipe

front push plate

split-rim wheel

step

tool-storage box

inverted hub/
dual wheel·hub

dual rear wheels

mud flap/splash guard

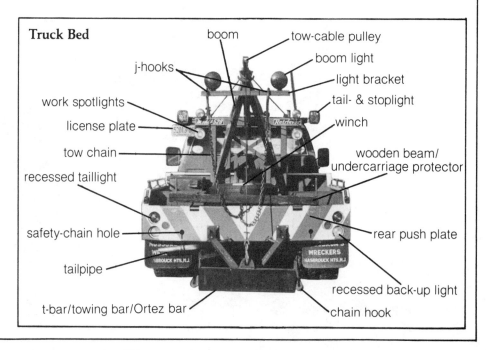

Truck Bed

boom

tow-cable pulley

j-hooks

boom light

light bracket

work spotlights

tail- & stoplight

license plate

winch

tow chain

wooden beam/
undercarriage protector

recessed taillight

safety-chain hole

rear push plate

tailpipe

recessed back-up light

t-bar/towing bar/Ortez bar

chain hook

Sanitation Vehicles

Garbage collectors, sanitation men, or "sanmen," also use a large, water-carrying truck called a flusher to wet down and clean streets.

side-view mirror

air cleaner

engine cover

pedestrian safety mirror

signal lights

sanitation

20L·043   D 2

reflector

bumper

hopper door

water spray bar

side broom balance assembly

gutter broom head

gutter broom

pivot gear housing

dirt shoe

pick-up broom

Mechanical Sweeper/Street Cleaner

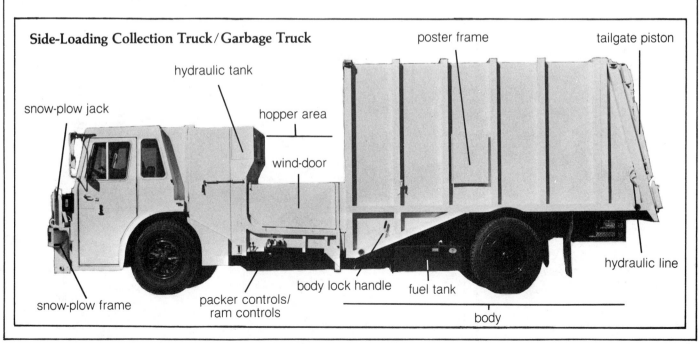

Side-Loading Collection Truck/Garbage Truck

poster frame

tailgate piston

hydraulic tank

snow-plow jack

hopper area

wind-door

hydraulic line

snow-plow frame

packer controls/ram controls

body lock handle

fuel tank

body

Public Service Vehicles

Bicycle

This illustration combines elements from the most popular bicycle styles. The *frame* is the skeleton to which the *wheels* and all other components are attached. A one-wheel cycle is called a *unicycle*. A three-wheeler is a *tricycle*.

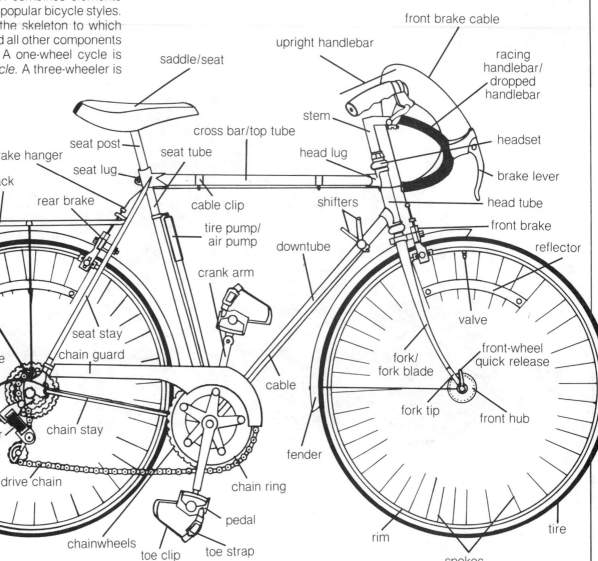

saddle/seat

upright handlebar

front brake cable

racing handlebar/ dropped handlebar

stem

cross bar/top tube

head lug

headset

seat post

seat tube

brake hanger

seat lug

brake lever

rack

rear brake

cable clip

shifters

head tube

reflectors

tire pump/ air pump

downtube

front brake

reflector

crank arm

seat stay

chain guard

derailleur cable

valve

fork/ fork blade

front-wheel quick release

rear derailleur

chain stay

cable

fork tip

front hub

drive chain

chain ring

fender

chainwheels

pedal

rim

tire

toe clip

toe strap

spokes

Rear Section

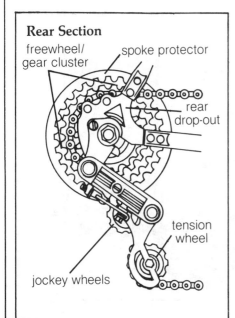

freewheel/ gear cluster

spoke protector

rear drop-out

jockey wheels

tension wheel

Crankset

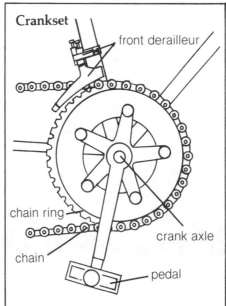

front derailleur

chain ring

chain

crank axle

pedal

Caliper Brake

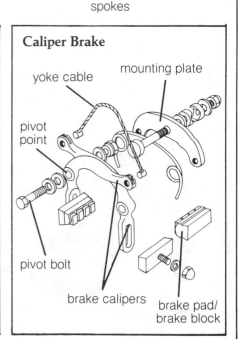

yoke cable

mounting plate

pivot point

pivot bolt

brake calipers

brake pad/ brake block

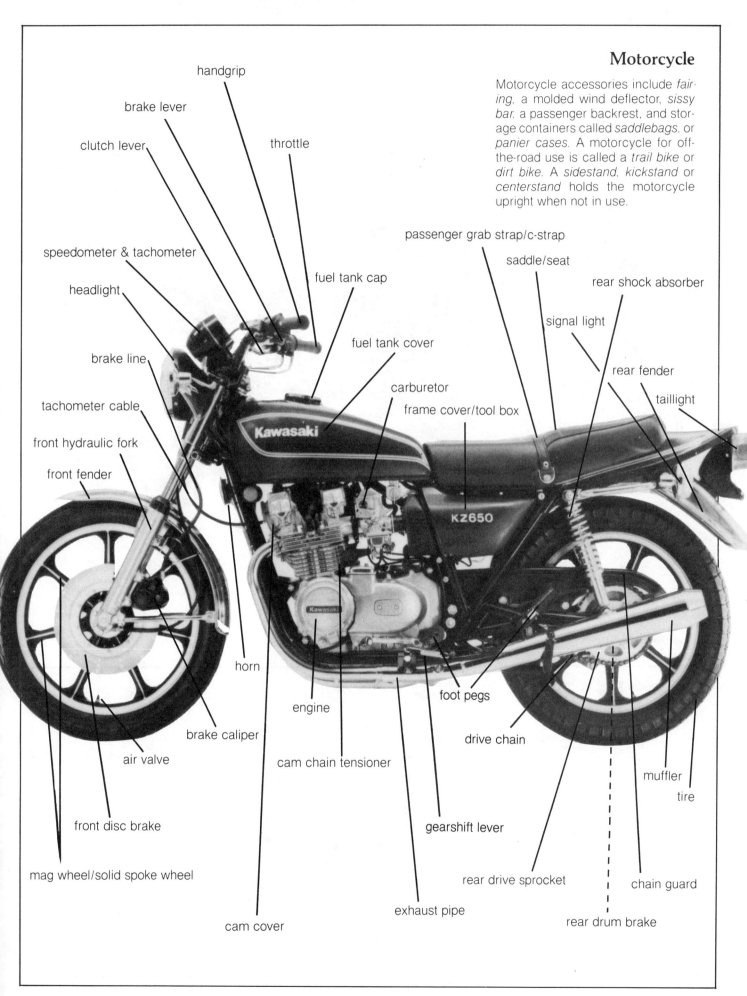

Motorcycle

Motorcycle accessories include *fairing*, a molded wind deflector, *sissy bar*, a passenger backrest, and storage containers called *saddlebags*, or *panier cases*. A motorcycle for off-the-road use is called a *trail bike* or *dirt bike*. A *sidestand*, *kickstand* or *centerstand* holds the motorcycle upright when not in use.

handgrip

brake lever

clutch lever

throttle

passenger grab strap/c-strap

saddle/seat

rear shock absorber

speedometer & tachometer

fuel tank cap

signal light

headlight

fuel tank cover

rear fender

brake line

carburetor

taillight

tachometer cable

frame cover/tool box

front hydraulic fork

front fender

KZ650

horn

brake caliper

air valve

engine

foot pegs

front disc brake

cam chain tensioner

drive chain

mag wheel/solid spoke wheel

gearshift lever

muffler

tire

rear drive sprocket

chain guard

exhaust pipe

rear drum brake

cam cover

Recreational Vehicles

The *heating* and *cooking units* in the rear *coach* of a camper run on *propane gas*. Unlike campers, which run under their own power, *trailers* are hitched behind a vehicle and towed. Other *off-the-road vehicles* include *four-wheel drive jeeps* and *dune buggies*.

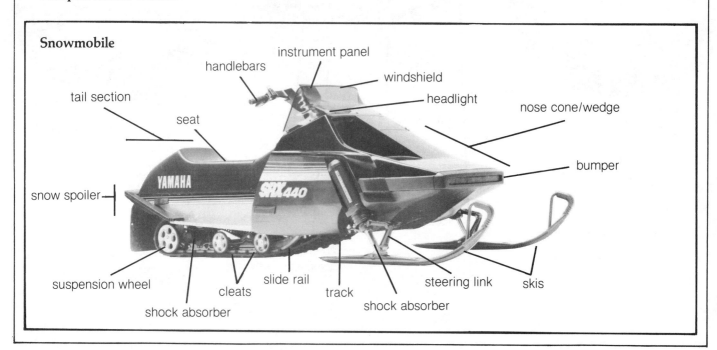

running lights

side window

roof air conditioner

luggage rack

side window

front window

water fill

road light

sewer valve

fuel tank

power-cord compartment

hot water heater

storage compartment

Camper/Motor Home

Snowmobile

instrument panel

handlebars

windshield

tail section

headlight

nose cone/wedge

seat

snow spoiler

bumper

YAMAHA

SRX 440

suspension wheel

cleats

slide rail

track

steering link

skis

shock absorber

shock absorber

Horse-drawn Carriages

Stagecoaches were drawn by teams of horses and commanded by a *driver* called the *whip, Charlie* or *Jehu.* Protection was provided by a *guard*, or *shotgun.* A *buggy* was four-wheeled. A *gig* had two wheels. A *buckboard* had a spring-supported seat attached to a board directly connected to the axles. A *cabriolet* was a *hackney carriage*, or *cab*, with only two wheels and a folding top.

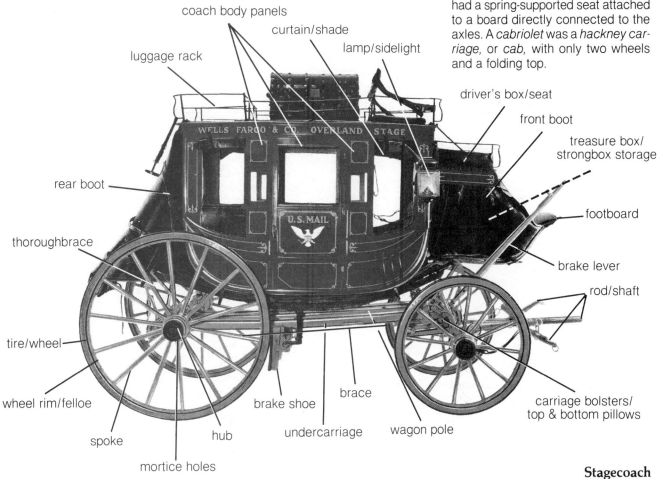

coach body panels
curtain/shade
lamp/sidelight
luggage rack
driver's box/seat
front boot
treasure box/ strongbox storage
rear boot
footboard
thoroughbrace
brake lever
rod/shaft
tire/wheel
carriage bolsters/ top & bottom pillows
wheel rim/felloe
brake shoe
brace
spoke
hub
undercarriage
wagon pole
mortice holes

WELLS FARGO & CO. OVERLAND STAGE
U.S. MAIL

Stagecoach

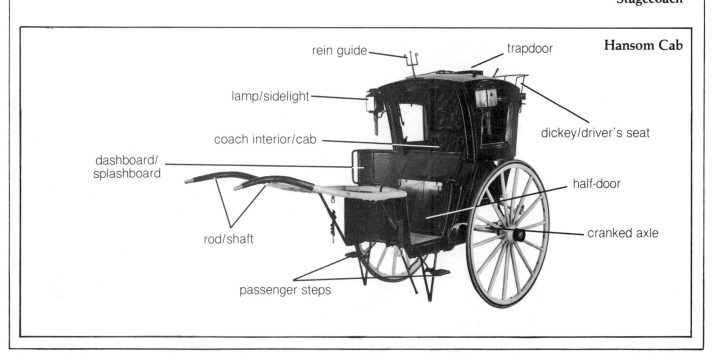

Hansom Cab

rein guide
trapdoor
lamp/sidelight
coach interior/cab
dickey/driver's seat
dashboard/ splashboard
half-door
cranked axle
rod/shaft
passenger steps

Nautical Terminology

The outer shell of a boat is the *hull*. A hull's greatest width is the *beam*. Any line running from one side of a boat to the other is said to run *athwartships*. That part of a boat facing the direction from which the wind is blowing is called the *windward* side. The opposite side is called the *leeward* side.

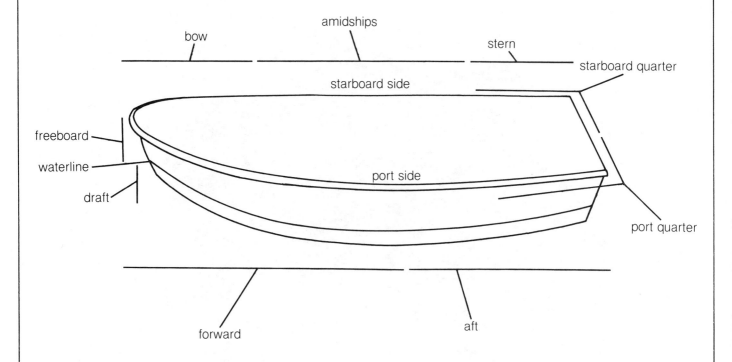

amidships

bow

stern

starboard quarter

starboard side

freeboard

waterline

port side

draft

port quarter

forward

aft

Anchor

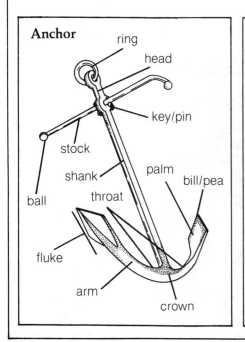

ring

head

key/pin

stock

shank

palm

bill/pea

throat

ball

fluke

arm

crown

Rope / Line

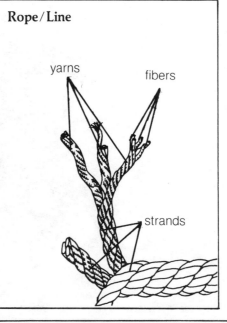

yarns

fibers

strands

Buoy

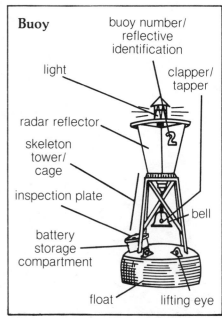

buoy number/ reflective identification

light

clapper/ tapper

radar reflector

skeleton tower/ cage

inspection plate

bell

battery storage compartment

float

lifting eye

Rowboat

Any small *craft,* either *decked* or *open* and propelled by oars, is a rowboat, or *skiff.* If it is used to service a *yacht* or *motor cruiser,* it is called a *dinghy, dink* or *tender.*

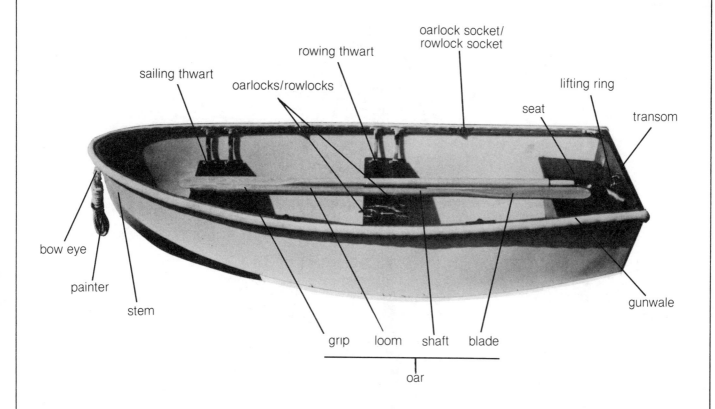

oarlock socket/
rowlock socket

rowing thwart

sailing thwart

oarlocks/rowlocks

lifting ring

seat

transom

bow eye

painter

stem

grip   loom   shaft   blade

oar

gunwale

Inflatable

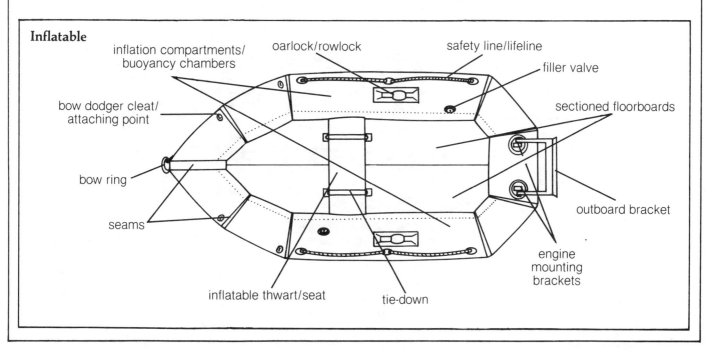

inflation compartments/
buoyancy chambers

oarlock/rowlock

safety line/lifeline

filler valve

bow dodger cleat/
attaching point

sectioned floorboards

bow ring

seams

outboard bracket

engine
mounting
brackets

inflatable thwart/seat

tie-down

Sailboat

Standing rigging, shrouds and stays, keep a sailing vessel's mast, or *spar,* upright. *Halyards* are used to hoist sails and *running rigging,* lines and *sheets,* control them. On some boats a *tiller* is used instead of a wheel to steer.

masthead

mast

forestay

backstay

headstay

mainsail

spreader

shroud

jib/jib topsail/
yankee/jibtop

staysail/club-footed
forestaysail

traveler

boom gallows/gallows frame

gate

staysail boom

companionway

boom

winch

toe rail

cockpit

bow pulpit

stern pulpit/
pushpit

foredeck

taffrail

wheel/helm

plow anchor

counter

bowsprit

rudder

windlass

rudder skeg

hatches

companionway hatch

boot top

keel

stanchion

forefoot

lifeline

mainsheet

ports/portlights

cabin top/
coach roof/
trunk

Sailboat Accommodations

The area between a vessel's cabin sole and its hull is called the *bilge*. Boats with overnight accommodations usually have a *navigator's station*, featuring a *chart table*.

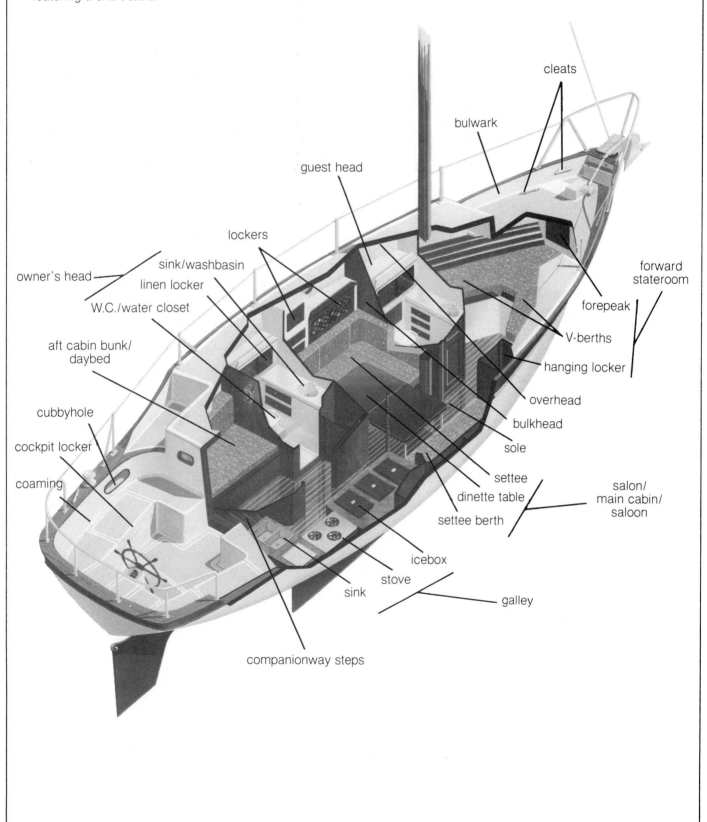

cleats

bulwark

guest head

lockers

sink/washbasin

owner's head

linen locker

W.C./water closet

aft cabin bunk/ daybed

cubbyhole

cockpit locker

coaming

forward stateroom

forepeak

V-berths

hanging locker

overhead

bulkhead

sole

settee

dinette table

settee berth

salon/ main cabin/ saloon

icebox

stove

sink

galley

companionway steps

Sail

Sails fall into two broad categories: *standing sails*, or *suits of sails*, and extras. Standing sails, such as those found on a modern *sloop*, would be mainsail and *headsail*, or *jib*. Extras, set to keep the vessel moving at optimum speed, include *spinnakers*, and, in bad weather, *trysails*. There are two types of compass: the *magnetic compass*, shown below, and the electrically-driven *gyro compass*.

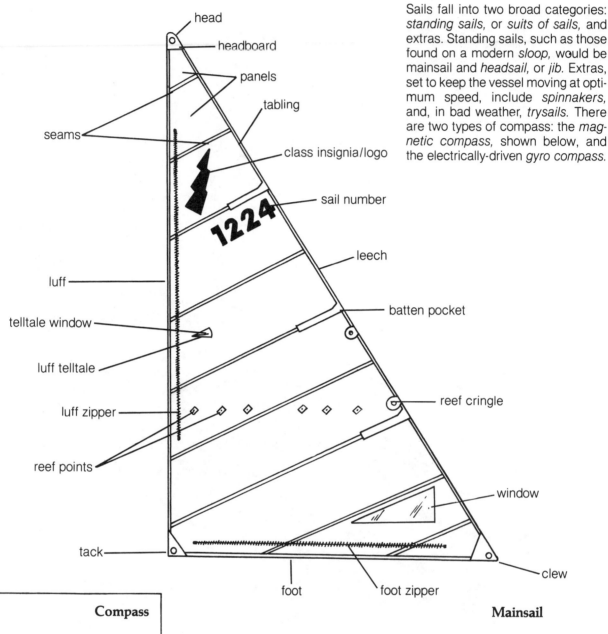

head
headboard
panels
tabling
class insignia/logo
seams
sail number
leech
luff
batten pocket
telltale window
luff telltale
reef cringle
luff zipper
reef points
window
tack
clew
foot
foot zipper

Mainsail

1224

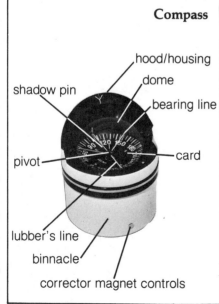

Compass

hood/housing
dome
shadow pin
bearing line
pivot
card
lubber's line
binnacle
corrector magnet controls

Outboard Engine

Three basic types of engines are used to power vessels: outboards, *inboard-outboards,* or *sterndrives,* and *inboards.* A marine sextant, a successor to the *octant* and *quadrant,* is used to measure the angle between a celestial body and the earth's horizon to help mariners determine their position at sea.

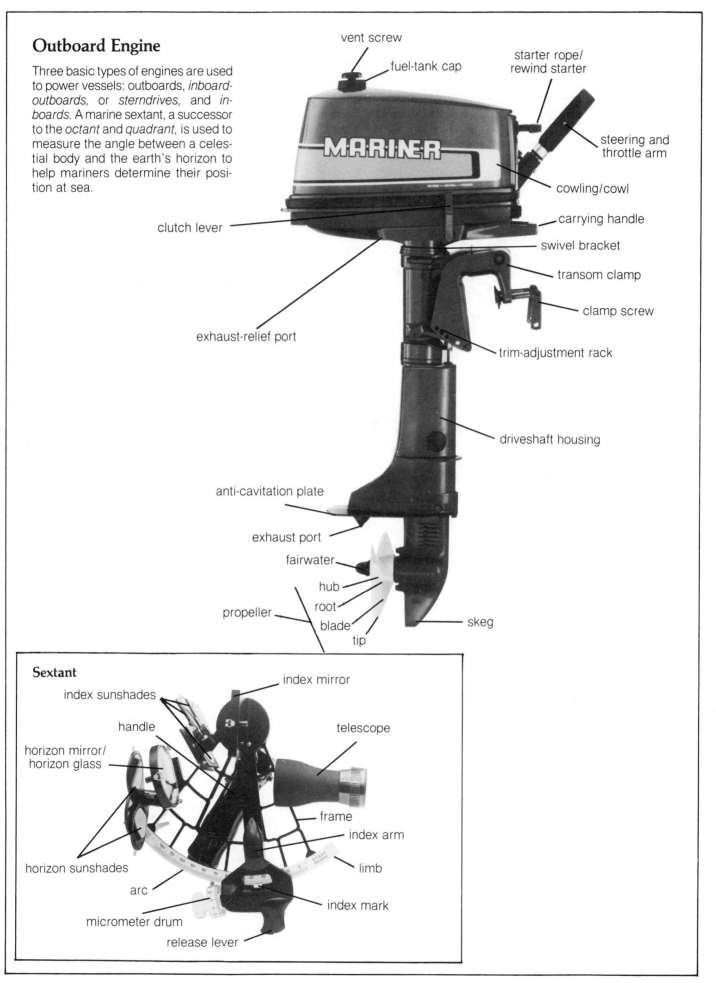

vent screw

fuel-tank cap

starter rope/ rewind starter

steering and throttle arm

cowling/cowl

clutch lever

carrying handle

swivel bracket

transom clamp

clamp screw

exhaust-relief port

trim-adjustment rack

driveshaft housing

anti-cavitation plate

exhaust port

fairwater

hub

root

propeller

blade

tip

skeg

Sextant

index sunshades

index mirror

handle

telescope

horizon mirror/ horizon glass

frame

index arm

limb

horizon sunshades

arc

index mark

micrometer drum

release lever

Boats and Ships

Powerboat

There are basically two kinds of powerboat *hull forms: displacement* and *planing.* Within these categories there are *V-bottom, cathedral, gull-wing, flat-bottom* and *round-bottom* hulls. *Houseboats* are boxlike vessels designed to provide maximum living space aboard. Projecting steel fittings used to hoist and carry a dinghy on a yacht are called *davits.*

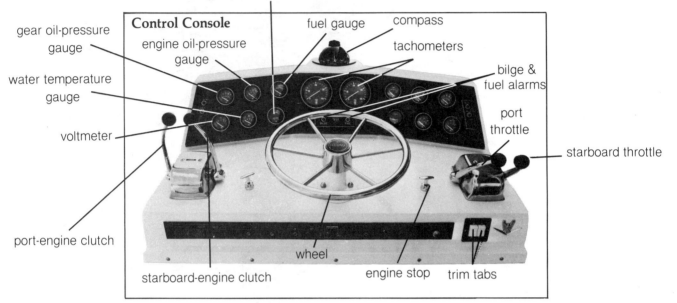

Control Console

engine hour meter

fuel gauge

compass

tachometers

gear oil-pressure gauge

engine oil-pressure gauge

bilge & fuel alarms

water temperature gauge

port throttle

starboard throttle

voltmeter

port-engine clutch

starboard-engine clutch

wheel

engine stop

trim tabs

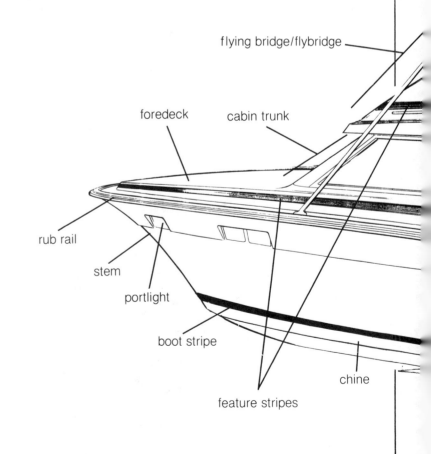

flying bridge/flybridge

foredeck

cabin trunk

rub rail

stem

portlight

boot stripe

chine

feature stripes

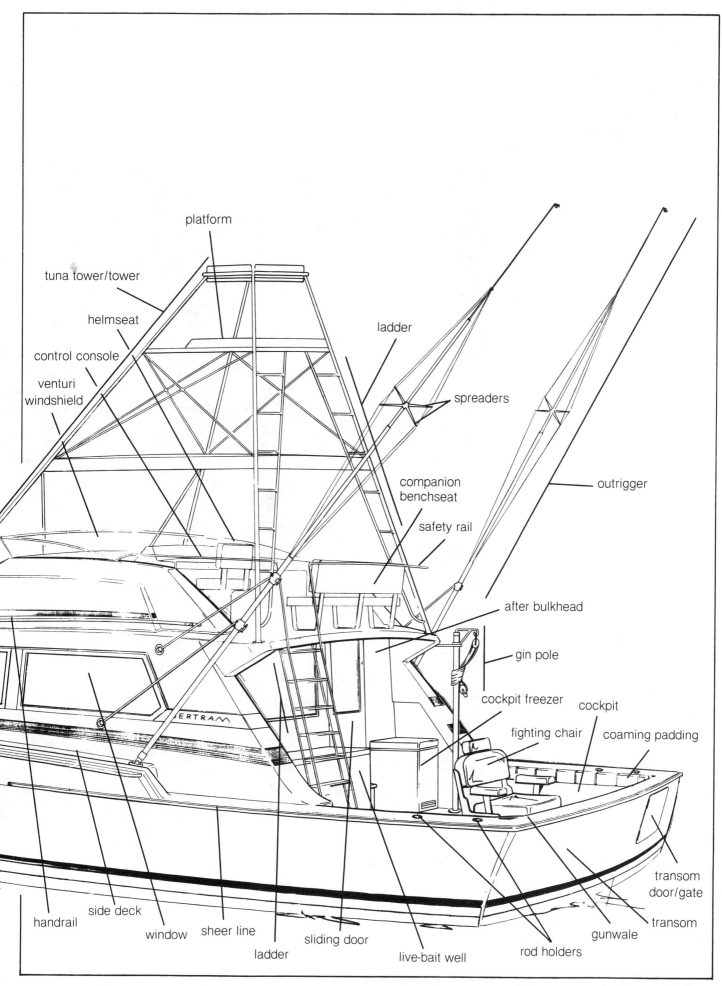

platform

tuna tower/tower

helmseat

control console

venturi
windshield

ladder

spreaders

companion
benchseat

safety rail

outrigger

after bulkhead

gin pole

cockpit freezer   cockpit

fighting chair   coaming padding

transom
door/gate

transom

handrail   side deck

window   sheer line

ladder

sliding door

live-bait well

rod holders

gunwale

139   **Boats and Ships**

Tanker

Cargo ships include *roll on-roll off ships; container ships; barge carriers; pallet ships; refrigerator ships,* or *reefers; dry-bulk carriers;* and *liquid-bulk carriers* such as the *super tanker* seen here. A *merchant ship* carrying *cargo* or *freight* is called a *liner* if it travels on scheduled routes at regular intervals, or a *tramp* if it does not have a fixed or scheduled route.

"catwalk"/
fore & aft gangway

foremast

"crow's nest"/
lookout area

pressure &
vacuum relief valves

belowdeck
storage entrance

anchor windlass &
mooring winch

anchor windlass &
mooring winch

radar mast & radar antennas

bridge/wheelhouse

bridge wing

wireless, telegraph & navigation aerials

king post

lifeboat

hose-handling derrick

"stowed" derrick brackets

aft superstructure/ deckhouse

pressure & vacuum relief valves

deck manifold

tank hatches

rail

foam monitors & fire-fighting stations

gas-vent lines

Passenger Ship/ Ocean Liner

Main bulkheads, steel walls running athwartships on a ship, are normally watertight. A *collision bulkhead* is a *watertight bulkhead* near the bow to prevent flooding in the event of collision. Circular windows aboard ship are called *ports* or *portholes.* A ship is boarded at the pier by a portable stairway, or *gangplank,* which fits in an opening in a ship's *rail* or *bulwark.* A metal shield on *berthing hawsers* to prevent rats from coming aboard is a *ratcatcher.*

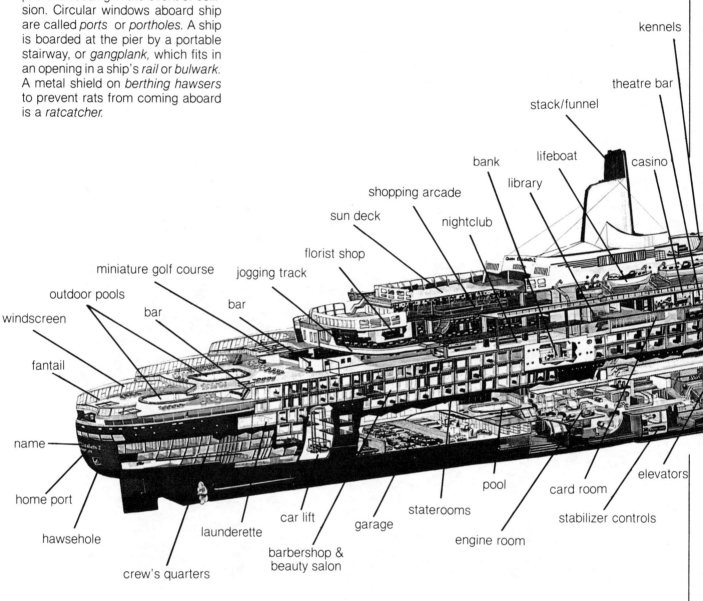

kennels

theatre bar

stack/funnel

bank

lifeboat

casino

shopping arcade

library

sun deck

nightclub

florist shop

miniature golf course

jogging track

outdoor pools

bar

bar

windscreen

fantail

name

home port

hawsehole

crew's quarters

launderette

car lift

barbershop & beauty salon

garage

staterooms

pool

engine room

card room

stabilizer controls

elevators

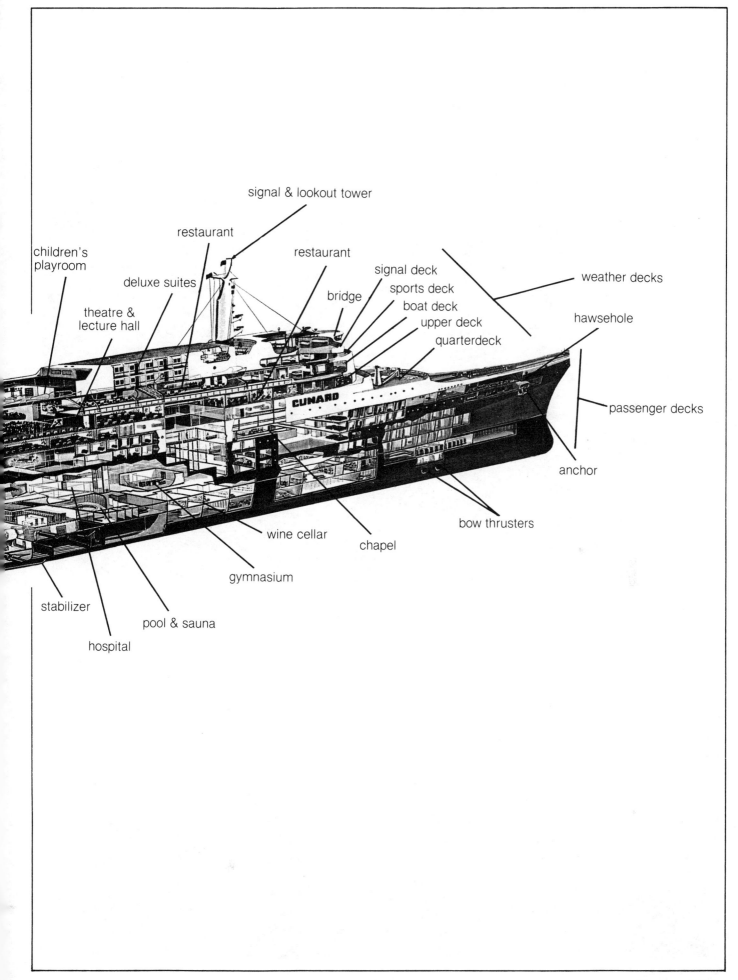

signal & lookout tower

restaurant

restaurant

children's
playroom

signal deck

bridge

sports deck

boat deck

deluxe suites

upper deck

weather decks

theatre &
lecture hall

quarterdeck

hawsehole

CUNARD

passenger decks

anchor

bow thrusters

wine cellar

chapel

gymnasium

stabilizer

pool & sauna

hospital

Tugboat and Fireboat

A *pudding fender* is a large fender made of old rope, formerly fitted to the bow of many *tugs,* or *towboats.* A *pusher tug,* also called a *pushboat,* is specially designed with a high flat bow for *barge cluster* push-towing. A fireboat is usually a tug fitted with such items as *high-pressure pumps, hoses* and *nozzles.*

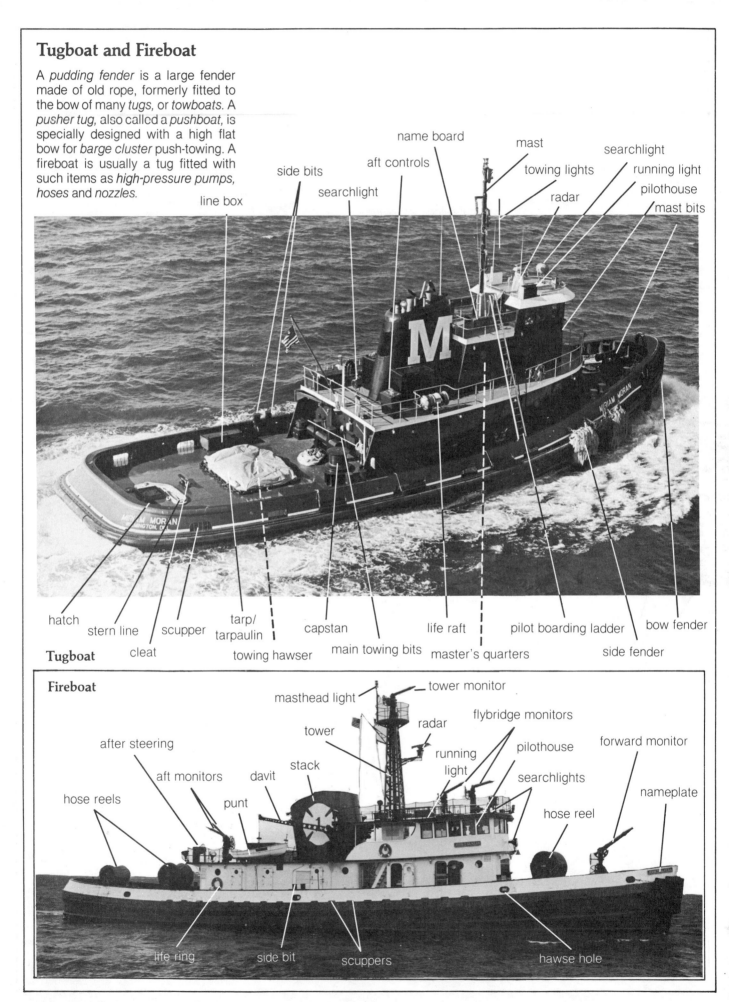

line box

side bits

searchlight

name board

aft controls

mast

towing lights

radar

searchlight

running light

pilothouse

mast bits

hatch

stern line

cleat

scupper

tarp/ tarpaulin

towing hawser

capstan

main towing bits

life raft

master's quarters

pilot boarding ladder

side fender

bow fender

Tugboat

Fireboat

masthead light

tower monitor

tower

radar

flybridge monitors

after steering

running light

pilothouse

forward monitor

aft monitors

davit

stack

searchlights

nameplate

hose reels

punt

hose reel

life ring

side bit

scuppers

hawse hole

Hovercraft and Hydrofoil

Air Cushion Vehicles *(ACV)*, or *ground-effect machines*, are *amphibious vehicles* that ride on a cushion of air blown by *lift fans* through *slots* or *jets* around the underside of the hull. There are four classes of hydrofoils: *ladder, depth-effect, surface-piercing* and *submerged foils.*

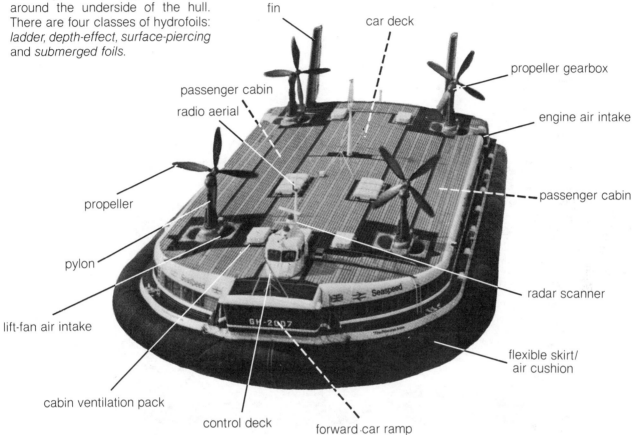

fin

car deck

propeller gearbox

passenger cabin

radio aerial

engine air intake

propeller

passenger cabin

pylon

radar scanner

lift-fan air intake

flexible skirt/ air cushion

cabin ventilation pack

control deck

forward car ramp

Hovercraft / Air Cushion Vehicle

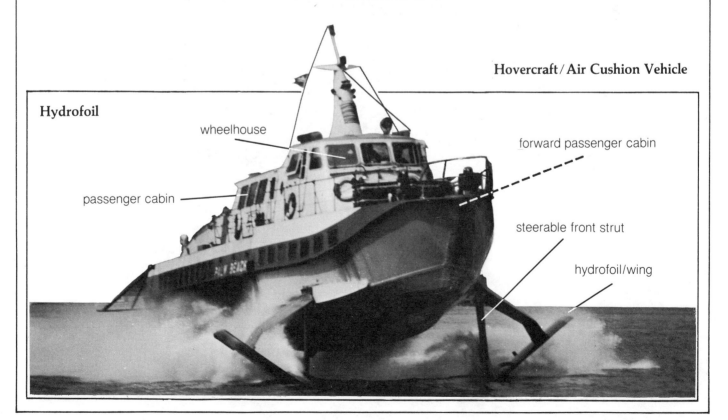

Hydrofoil

wheelhouse

forward passenger cabin

passenger cabin

steerable front strut

hydrofoil/wing

Boats and Ships

Helicopter

The main body of a helicopter, *chopper, whirlybird,* or *eggbeater,* is called the *fuselage.* The rescue helicopter shown here has an *amphibious hull.* Armed military helicopters are called *gunships.*

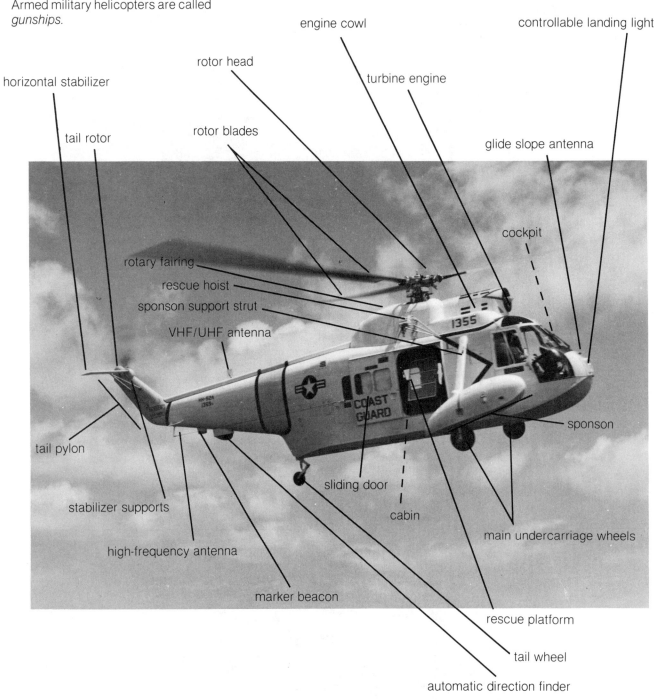

engine cowl

controllable landing light

rotor head

turbine engine

horizontal stabilizer

glide slope antenna

tail rotor

rotor blades

cockpit

rotary fairing

rescue hoist

sponson support strut

VHF/UHF antenna

1355

COAST GUARD

tail pylon

sponson

stabilizer supports

sliding door

cabin

main undercarriage wheels

high-frequency antenna

marker beacon

rescue platform

tail wheel

automatic direction finder

Private Aircraft

An aircraft's central body portion is called the *fuselage*. To land on water, an airplane uses *pontoons*. To become airborne and begin *soaring*, a glider is pulled behind a motor-driven airplane or car by a cable attached to a *tow hook*. A glider lands on either a *landing wheel* or a *skid*.

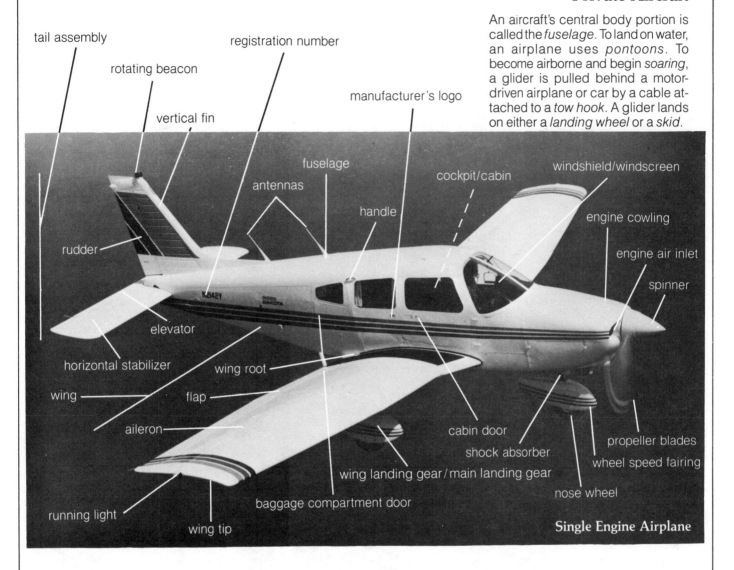

tail assembly

rotating beacon

vertical fin

registration number

manufacturer's logo

fuselage

cockpit/cabin

windshield/windscreen

antennas

handle

engine cowling

engine air inlet

spinner

rudder

elevator

horizontal stabilizer

wing root

wing

flap

aileron

cabin door

shock absorber

propeller blades

wheel speed fairing

wing landing gear / main landing gear

nose wheel

running light

baggage compartment door

wing tip

Single Engine Airplane

Glider / Sailplane

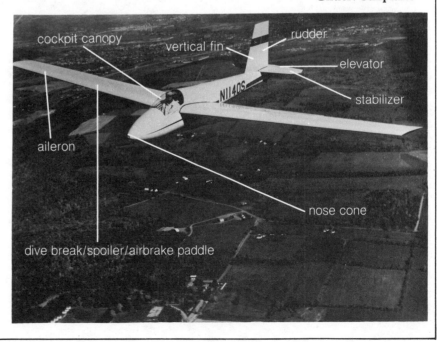

cockpit canopy

vertical fin

rudder

elevator

stabilizer

aileron

nose cone

dive break/spoiler/airbrake paddle

Aircraft

Civil Aircraft

The *trailing edge* of the wings on a *jumbo jet,* such as the one shown here, has small *static discharge wicks* to reduce electrical-charge buildup. Passengers store carry-on belongings in *overhead bins,* or *stowage compartments,* or in front *closets.* Aboard many aircraft, seat cushions double as *flotation devices. Life rafts* are stored in overhead ceiling compartments above the doors, and *emergency escape chutes* are folded inside the doors.

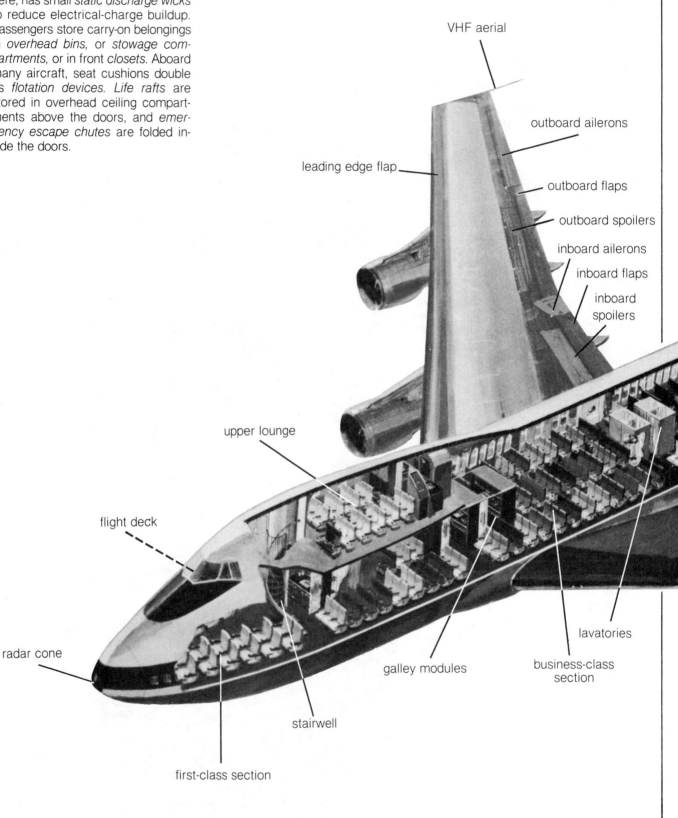

VHF aerial

outboard ailerons

outboard flaps

outboard spoilers

inboard ailerons

inboard flaps

inboard spoilers

leading edge flap

upper lounge

flight deck

radar cone

lavatories

galley modules

business-class section

stairwell

first-class section

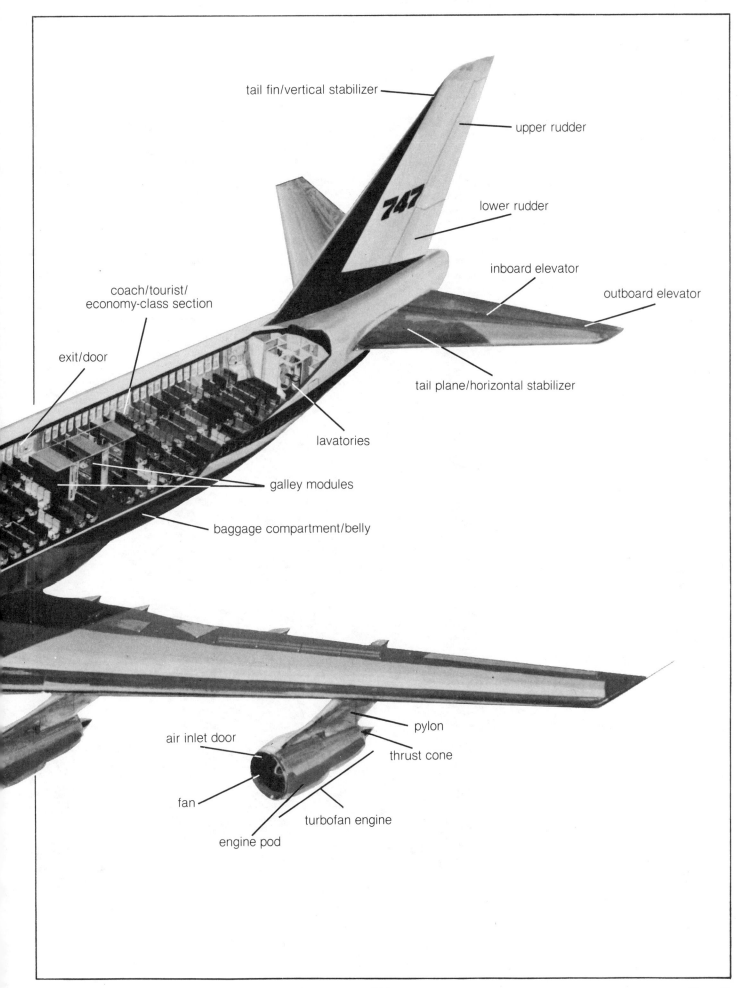

tail fin/vertical stabilizer

upper rudder

lower rudder

inboard elevator

outboard elevator

coach/tourist/
economy-class section

exit/door

tail plane/horizontal stabilizer

lavatories

galley modules

baggage compartment/belly

pylon

air inlet door

thrust cone

fan

turbofan engine

engine pod

149

Aircraft

747 Cockpit

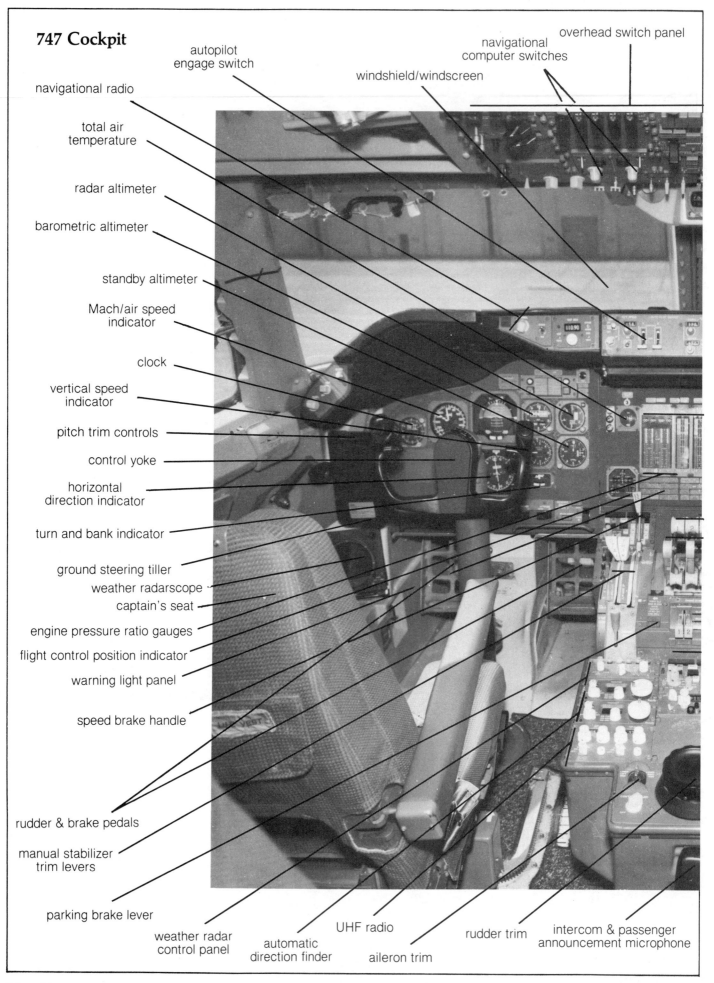

navigational radio

autopilot engage switch

navigational computer switches

overhead switch panel

windshield/windscreen

total air temperature

radar altimeter

barometric altimeter

standby altimeter

Mach/air speed indicator

clock

vertical speed indicator

pitch trim controls

control yoke

horizontal direction indicator

turn and bank indicator

ground steering tiller

weather radarscope

captain's seat

engine pressure ratio gauges

flight control position indicator

warning light panel

speed brake handle

rudder & brake pedals

manual stabilizer trim levers

parking brake lever

weather radar control panel

automatic direction finder

UHF radio

aileron trim

rudder trim

intercom & passenger announcement microphone

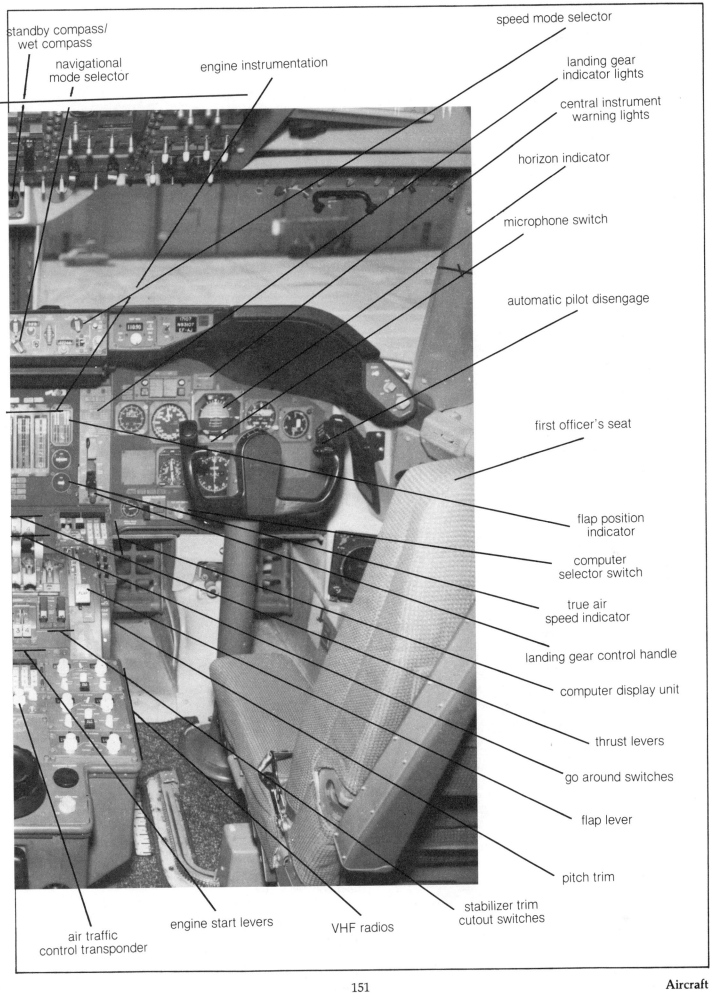

standby compass/
wet compass

navigational
mode selector

engine instrumentation

speed mode selector

landing gear
indicator lights

central instrument
warning lights

horizon indicator

microphone switch

automatic pilot disengage

first officer's seat

flap position
indicator

computer
selector switch

true air
speed indicator

landing gear control handle

computer display unit

thrust levers

go around switches

flap lever

pitch trim

stabilizer trim
cutout switches

air traffic
control transponder

engine start levers

VHF radios

Aircraft

Space Shuttle and Launch Pad

A shuttle has three main components: an orbiter, external tank and two solid-rocket boosters. Many launch pads have *flame buckets* designed to direct *fireballs* and steam away from the pad itself. A gantry is a movable structure used for erecting and servicing a rocket prior to launch.

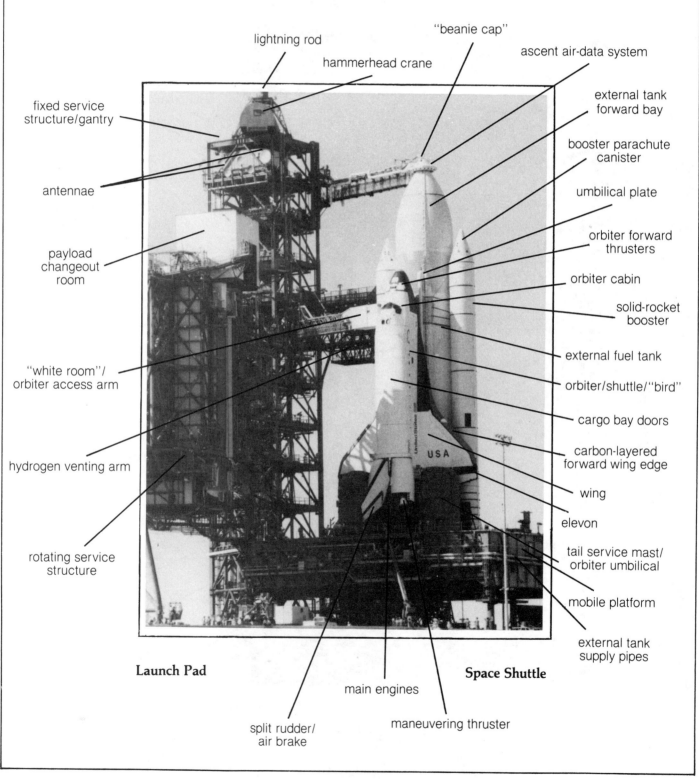

lightning rod

hammerhead crane

"beanie cap"

ascent air-data system

fixed service structure/gantry

external tank forward bay

booster parachute canister

umbilical plate

antennae

orbiter forward thrusters

payload changeout room

orbiter cabin

solid-rocket booster

external fuel tank

orbiter/shuttle/"bird"

"white room"/ orbiter access arm

cargo bay doors

carbon-layered forward wing edge

hydrogen venting arm

wing

elevon

tail service mast/ orbiter umbilical

rotating service structure

mobile platform

external tank supply pipes

Launch Pad

main engines

Space Shuttle

split rudder/ air brake

maneuvering thruster

Space Shuttle Flight Deck

Overhead controls include *circuit breakers*, *environmental monitors* and *fuel cell monitors*. The *orbiter* has work and living quarters for as many as seven people, including two pilots, *mission specialists* and *payload specialists*. It also features a *quad-redundant computer system*, including a fifth computer to arbitrate disputes among the first four.

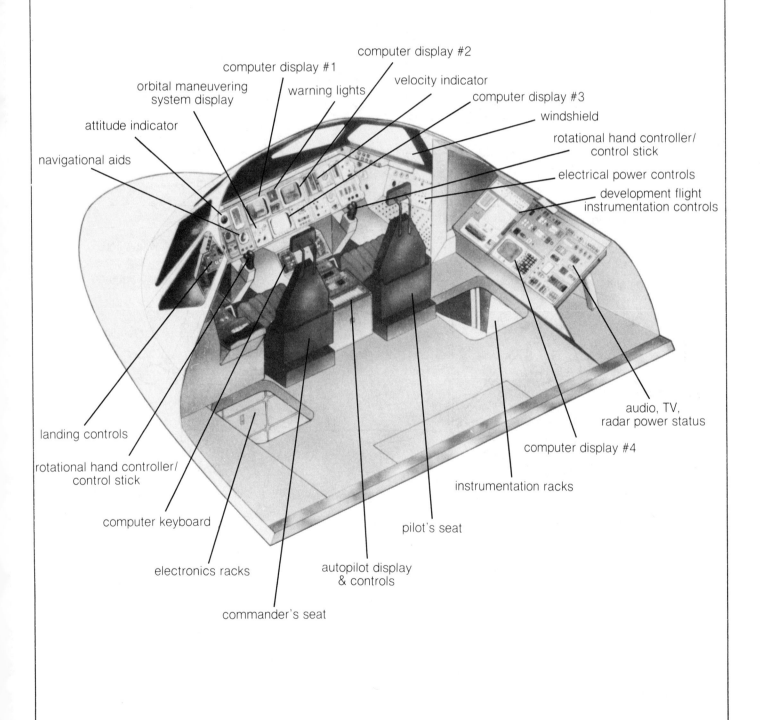

computer display #2

computer display #1

orbital maneuvering system display

warning lights

velocity indicator

computer display #3

attitude indicator

windshield

rotational hand controller/ control stick

navigational aids

electrical power controls

development flight instrumentation controls

landing controls

audio, TV, radar power status

rotational hand controller/ control stick

computer display #4

computer keyboard

instrumentation racks

electronics racks

pilot's seat

autopilot display & controls

commander's seat

Lunar Lander

The *lunar module* consists of a lower *descent stage* which houses the *landing engine, exploration equipment, secondary tanks* and *landing gear.* The *ascent stage* contains *crew compartment* and *controls, equipment compartment, tanks* and *take-off engine,* used to rejoin the *command module.*

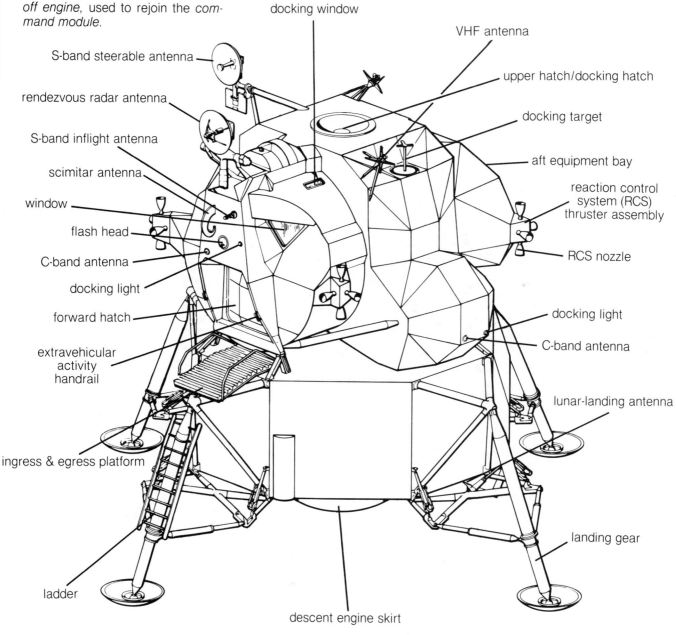

docking window

VHF antenna

S-band steerable antenna

upper hatch/docking hatch

rendezvous radar antenna

docking target

S-band inflight antenna

aft equipment bay

scimitar antenna

reaction control system (RCS) thruster assembly

window

flash head

RCS nozzle

C-band antenna

docking light

docking light

forward hatch

C-band antenna

extravehicular activity handrail

lunar-landing antenna

ingress & egress platform

landing gear

ladder

descent engine skirt

Lunar Rover

Officially called the *Lunar Roving Vehicle*, the *moon buggy* is folded in the Lunar Lander and deployed to transport astronauts and equipment on the lunar surface. The spacesuit, or *integrated thermal meteoroid garment*, is a many-layered structure laced to a *torso limb suit* which consists of an inner cloth *comfort lining*, a *bladder*, and a *restraint layer*.

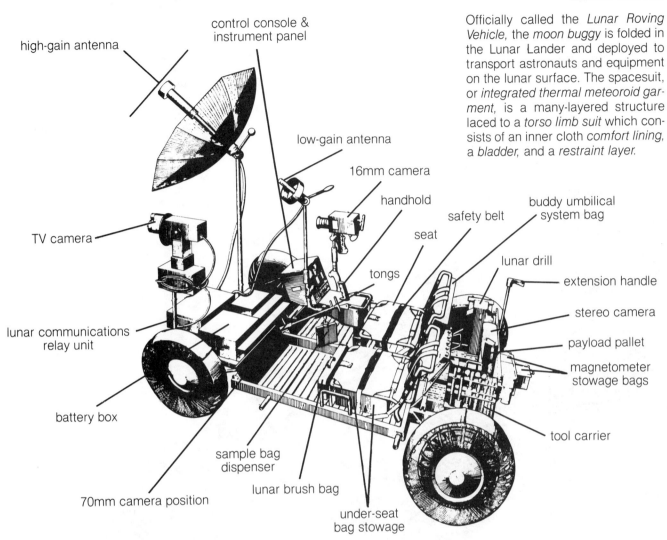

high-gain antenna

control console & instrument panel

low-gain antenna

16mm camera

handhold

safety belt

seat

buddy umbilical system bag

lunar drill

extension handle

stereo camera

payload pallet

magnetometer stowage bags

tool carrier

TV camera

tongs

lunar communications relay unit

battery box

sample bag dispenser

lunar brush bag

under-seat bag stowage

70mm camera position

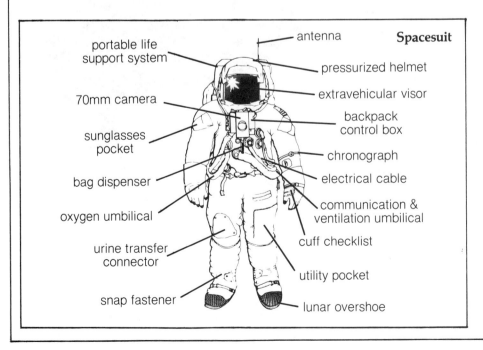

Spacesuit

antenna

portable life support system

pressurized helmet

extravehicular visor

backpack control box

70mm camera

sunglasses pocket

chronograph

electrical cable

bag dispenser

communication & ventilation umbilical

oxygen umbilical

cuff checklist

urine transfer connector

utility pocket

snap fastener

lunar overshoe

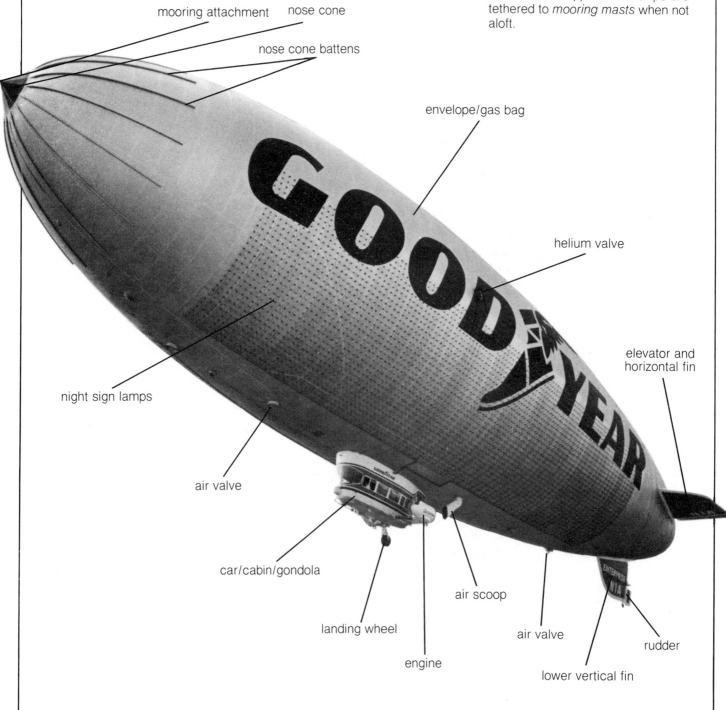

Lighter-than-air Craft

Engine-driven, steerable lighter-than-air craft are called blimps, or dirigibles. They can be *nonrigid* or *semirigid*, dependent on interior *ballonets*, or *air bags*, to maintain their shapes. *Rigid airships*, with metal *frameworks* within their *envelopes*, are referred to as *Zeppelins*. Airships are tethered to *mooring masts* when not aloft.

mooring attachment   nose cone

nose cone battens

envelope/gas bag

helium valve

elevator and horizontal fin

night sign lamps

air valve

car/cabin/gondola

landing wheel

engine

air scoop

air valve

lower vertical fin

rudder

Blimp/Dirigible

Communications

Communications ranks among the fastest-growing areas of modern life. Nevertheless, as this book is meant to demonstrate by providing visual access to language, print communications remains a vital part of the future. Print is therefore examined in some detail, up to and including a close look at the mailing label affixed to periodicals received every day by millions of subscribers.

Space limitations prevent presentation of industrial items such as transmitting stations and microwave towers, sound-recording and television studios and film-processing equipment.

But the devices used in all forms of communications—visual, aural and audiovisual—are represented by objects commonly used in most households. The single exception to this is the satellite which appears at the end of the section. It is included because of the vital role it plays in modern communications of all kinds.

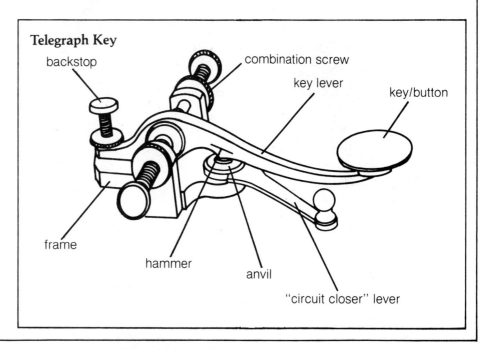

Telegraph Key

backstop

combination screw

key lever

key/button

frame

hammer

anvil

"circuit closer" lever

Pen and Pencil

In refillable *lead pencils* a *barrel cap* is turned in order to push new lead out the tip. Some fountain pens are *cartridge-loaded* but older models have a barrel, *ink reservoir* and *self-filling mechanism. Quills,* or *feather pens,* made from the horny, hollow barrel of bird feathers, were dipped in *ink wells.*

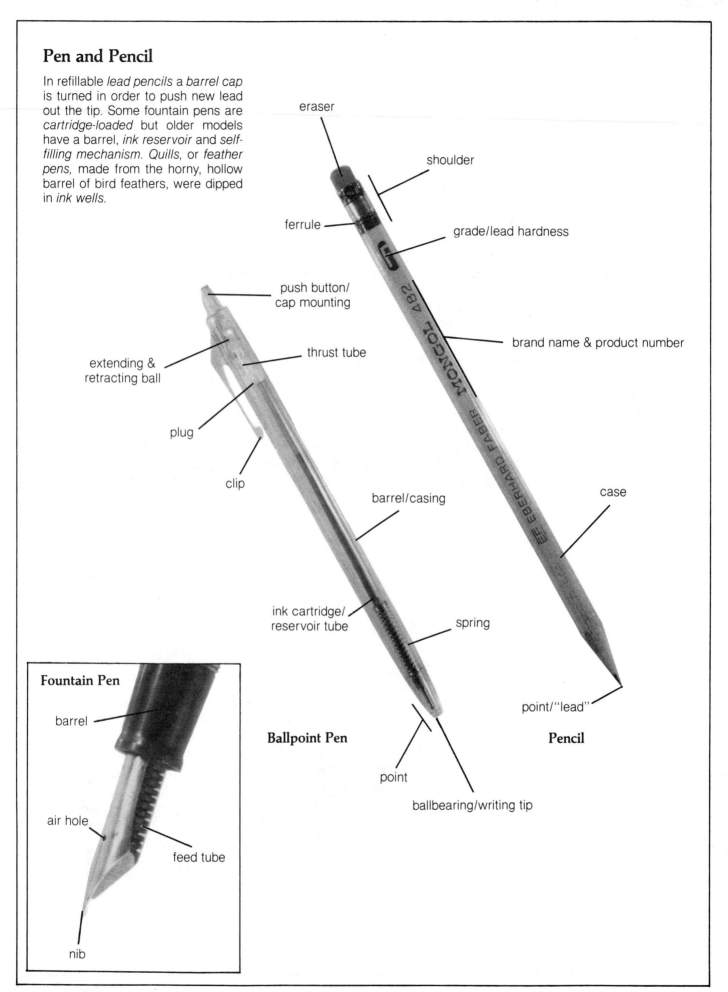

eraser

shoulder

ferrule

grade/lead hardness

push button/ cap mounting

brand name & product number

extending & retracting ball

thrust tube

plug

clip

barrel/casing

case

ink cartridge/ reservoir tube

spring

point/"lead"

Ballpoint Pen

point

Pencil

ballbearing/writing tip

Fountain Pen

barrel

air hole

feed tube

nib

Correspondence

A note appended to a completed letter is called a *postscript,* abbreviated as *P.S.* When items are enclosed with a letter they are indicated by the word *enclosure(s)* or *encl.* The back portion of an envelope which is glued down after a letter has been inserted is the *flap.* Postage stamps can be purchased in *books, strips, blocks, coils* and *sheets,* or *panes.*

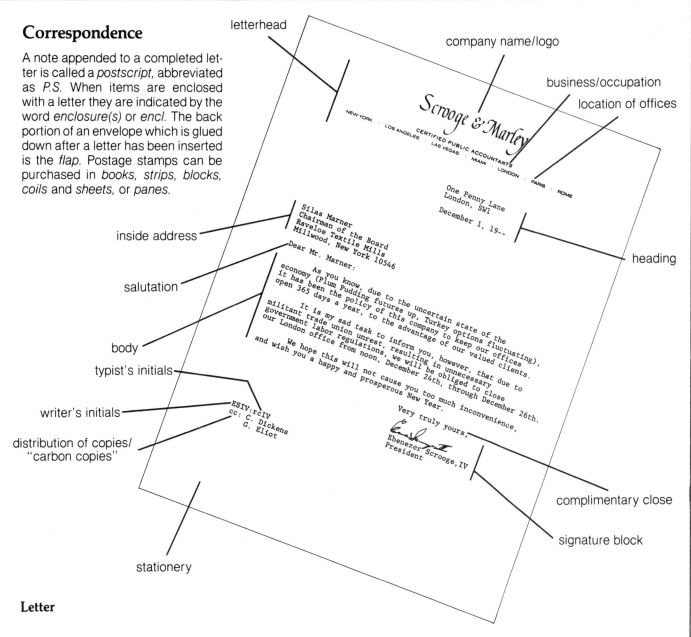

letterhead

company name/logo

business/occupation

location of offices

heading

inside address

salutation

body

typist's initials

writer's initials

distribution of copies/ "carbon copies"

complimentary close

signature block

stationery

Scrooge & Marley
CERTIFIED PUBLIC ACCOUNTANTS
NEW YORK · LOS ANGELES · LAS VEGAS · MIAMI · LONDON · PARIS · ROME

One Penny Lane
London, SW1
December 1, 19--

Silas Marner
Chairman of the Board
Raveloe Textile Mills
Millwood, New York 10546

Dear Mr. Marner:

As you know, due to the uncertain state of the economy (Plum Pudding futures up, Turkey options fluctuating), it has been the policy of this company to keep our offices open 365 days a year, to the advantage of our valued clients.

It is my sad task to inform you, however, that due to militant trade union unrest, resulting in unnecessary government labor regulations, we will be obliged to close our London office from noon, December 24th, through December 26th.

We hope this will not cause you too much inconvenience, and wish you a happy and prosperous New Year.

Very truly yours,

Ebenezer Scrooge, IV
President

ESIV:rcIV
cc: C. Dickens
    G. Eliot

Letter

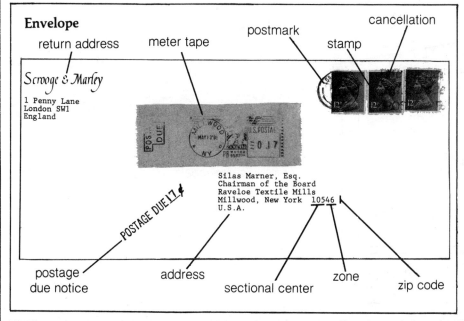

Envelope

return address
meter tape
postmark
stamp
cancellation

Scrooge & Marley
1 Penny Lane
London SW1
England

POSTAGE DUE 17¢

Silas Marner, Esq.
Chairman of the Board
Raveloe Textile Mills
Millwood, New York 10546
U.S.A.

postage due notice

address

sectional center

zone

zip code

Stamp

commemorative subject

issuing government

face value/ denomination

design

cancellation/ postmark

perforation

BICENTENNIAL
EXECUTIVE BRANCH
USA 25

Résumé and Business Card

A summary of a job applicant's background and qualifications is called a résumé or *curriculum vitae*. In addition to brief descriptions of one's education and work experience, it may include *awards* and *honors*, *outside interests* and objectives or goals. Personal references may be listed or made available on request.

name/address

date of birth (optional)

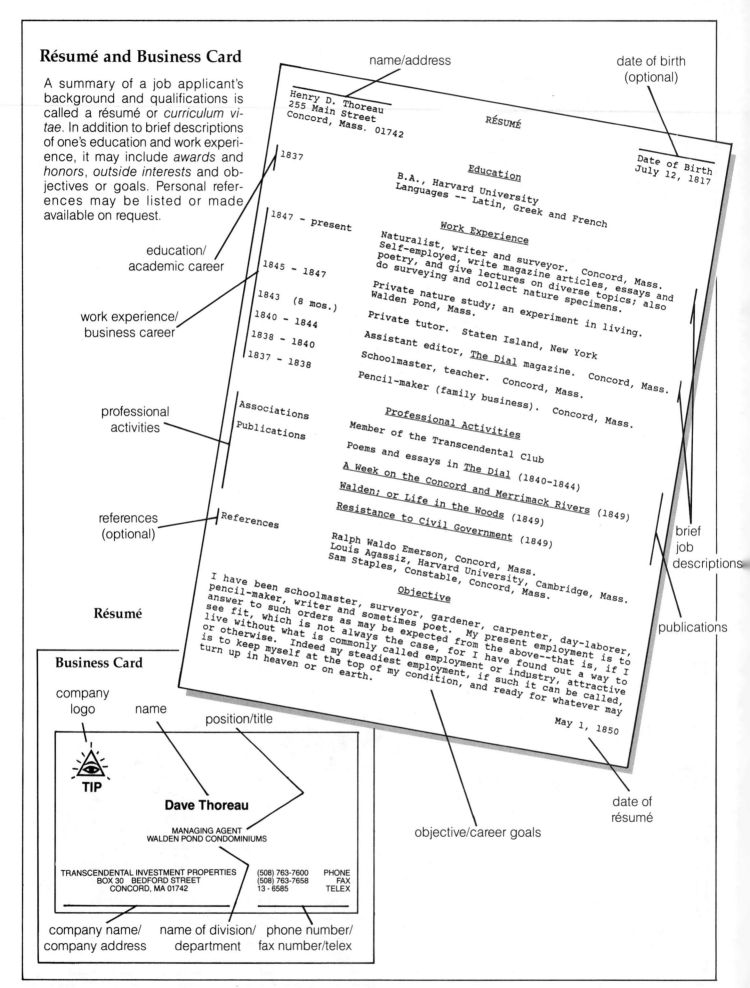

Henry D. Thoreau
255 Main Street
Concord, Mass. 01742

RÉSUMÉ

Date of Birth
July 12, 1817

1837

education/
academic career

Education
B.A., Harvard University
Languages -- Latin, Greek and French

1847 - present

Work Experience
Naturalist, writer and surveyor. Concord, Mass. Self-employed, write magazine articles, essays and poetry, and give lectures on diverse topics; also do surveying and collect nature specimens.

work experience/
business career

1845 - 1847

Private nature study; an experiment in living. Walden Pond, Mass.

1843 (8 mos.)

Private tutor. Staten Island, New York

1840 - 1844

Assistant editor, The Dial magazine. Concord, Mass.

1838 - 1840

Schoolmaster, teacher. Concord, Mass.

1837 - 1838

Pencil-maker (family business). Concord, Mass.

professional
activities

Associations

Publications

Professional Activities
Member of the Transcendental Club

Poems and essays in The Dial (1840-1844)
A Week on the Concord and Merrimack Rivers (1849)
Walden; or Life in the Woods (1849)
Resistance to Civil Government (1849)

brief
job
descriptions

references
(optional)

References

Ralph Waldo Emerson, Concord, Mass.
Louis Agassiz, Harvard University, Cambridge, Mass.
Sam Staples, Constable, Concord, Mass.

Objective
I have been schoolmaster, surveyor, gardener, carpenter, day-laborer, pencil-maker, writer and sometimes poet. My present employment is to answer to such orders as may be expected from the above--that is, if I see fit, which is not always the case, for I have found out a way to live without what is commonly called employment or industry, attractive or otherwise. Indeed my steadiest employment, if such it can be called, is to keep myself at the top of my condition, and ready for whatever may turn up in heaven or on earth.

May 1, 1850

publications

date of
résumé

objective/career goals

Résumé

Business Card

company
logo

name

position/title

TIP

Dave Thoreau

MANAGING AGENT
WALDEN POND CONDOMINIUMS

TRANSCENDENTAL INVESTMENT PROPERTIES
BOX 30 BEDFORD STREET
CONCORD, MA 01742

(508) 763-7600   PHONE
(508) 763-7658   FAX
13 - 6585   TELEX

company name/
company address

name of division/
department

phone number/
fax number/telex

Typewriter

On standard manual or *office type-writers*, lightweight *portables* and older *electrics*, when a key labeled with a *character* is struck, it sends the appropriate type bar toward an inked *ribbon*. On modern electric typewriters type bars in the *type basket* have been replaced with a ball.

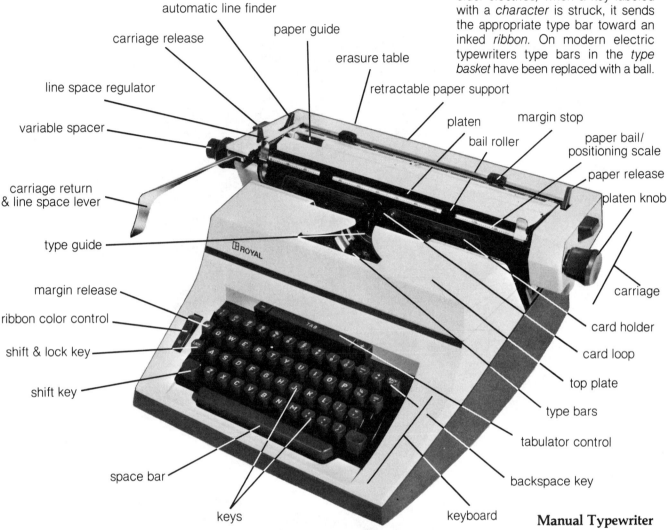

automatic line finder

carriage release

paper guide

erasure table

retractable paper support

line space regulator

variable spacer

platen

margin stop

bail roller

paper bail/positioning scale

carriage return & line space lever

paper release

platen knob

type guide

carriage

margin release

card holder

ribbon color control

card loop

shift & lock key

top plate

shift key

type bars

tabulator control

space bar

backspace key

keys

keyboard

Manual Typewriter

Ribbon Cartridge/Electric Typewriter

ball/core

separator wire

correctable ribbon

element release lever

correction tape

impression control

guide post

roller

typestyle

take-up spool

character

spindle/knob

ribbon end indicator

tape load lever

ribbon load lever

161

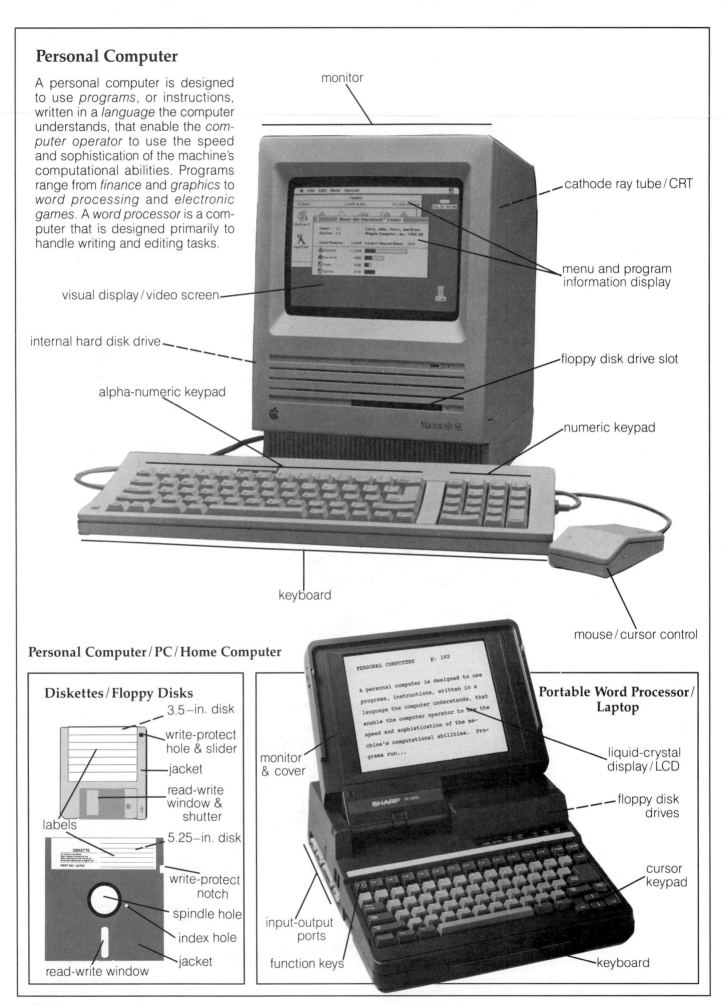

Personal Computer

A personal computer is designed to use *programs*, or instructions, written in a *language* the computer understands, that enable the *computer operator* to use the speed and sophistication of the machine's computational abilities. Programs range from *finance* and *graphics* to *word processing* and *electronic games*. A *word processor* is a computer that is designed primarily to handle writing and editing tasks.

monitor

cathode ray tube / CRT

menu and program information display

visual display / video screen

internal hard disk drive

floppy disk drive slot

alpha-numeric keypad

numeric keypad

Macintosh SE

keyboard

mouse / cursor control

Personal Computer / PC / Home Computer

Diskettes / Floppy Disks

3.5 – in. disk

write-protect hole & slider

jacket

read-write window & shutter

labels

5.25 – in. disk

DISKETTE
PART NO. 34700

write-protect notch

spindle hole

index hole

jacket

read-write window

Portable Word Processor / Laptop

PERSONAL COMPUTERS   p. 162

A personal computer is designed to use programs, instructions, written in a language the computer understands, that enable the computer operator to use the speed and sophistication of the machine's computational abilities. Programs run...

monitor & cover

liquid-crystal display / LCD

floppy disk drives

cursor keypad

input-output ports

function keys

keyboard

Printers

Computer *output* printed on paper is called *hard copy*. The precise form this takes depends on the type of printer used. On dot matrix and laser printers, characters are built out of a series of dots, the laser's being smaller and more closely grouped to produce crisp detail. A *daisy-wheel printer* uses a wheel of type bars, similar to a typewriter's, to produce *"letter quality"* results.

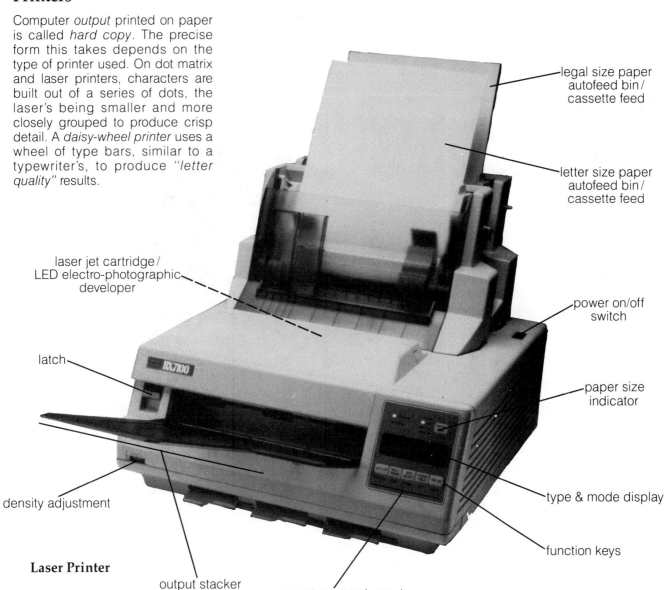

legal size paper autofeed bin/ cassette feed

letter size paper autofeed bin/ cassette feed

laser jet cartridge/ LED electro-photographic developer

power on/off switch

latch

paper size indicator

density adjustment

type & mode display

function keys

Laser Printer

output stacker

operator control panel

Dot Matrix Printer

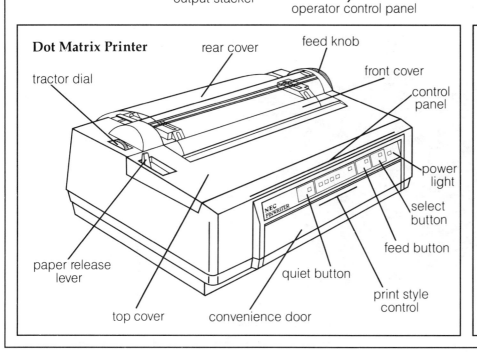

rear cover

feed knob

front cover

tractor dial

control panel

power light

select button

feed button

print style control

paper release lever

top cover

quiet button

convenience door

Print Samples

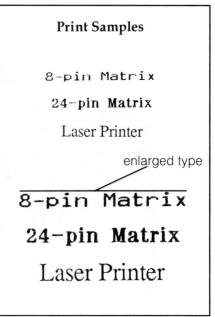

8-pin Matrix

24-pin Matrix

Laser Printer

enlarged type

8-pin Matrix

24-pin Matrix

Laser Printer

Print Communications

Fax Machine and Copier

Fax machines transmit clear, detailed paper *facsimilies* of documents quickly from one *terminal* to another over *telephone lines*. The fax operator may, in addition, couple the transmission with spoken conversation over the telephone handset. Copier, *answering machine, delayed transmission, unattended reception*, memory and automatic dialing capabilities may also be provided.

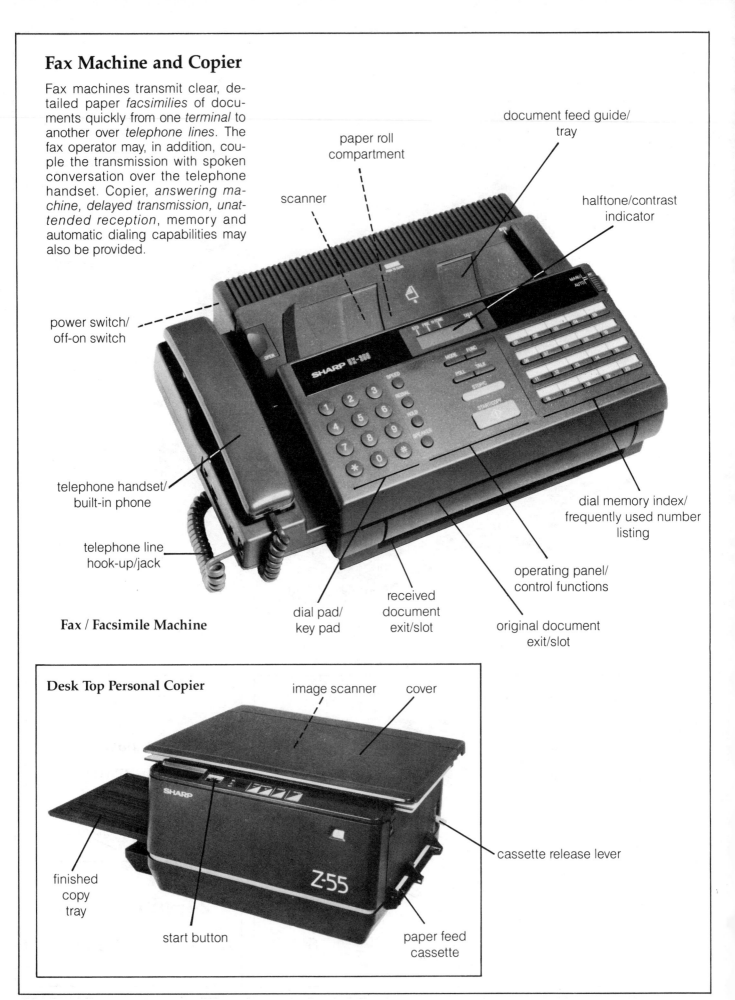

paper roll compartment

document feed guide/ tray

scanner

halftone/contrast indicator

power switch/ off-on switch

telephone handset/ built-in phone

telephone line hook-up/jack

dial memory index/ frequently used number listing

operating panel/ control functions

dial pad/ key pad

received document exit/slot

original document exit/slot

Fax / Facsimile Machine

Desk Top Personal Copier

image scanner

cover

cassette release lever

finished copy tray

start button

paper feed cassette

Type with serifs is called *book type*.
Type without serifs is *sans serif*.

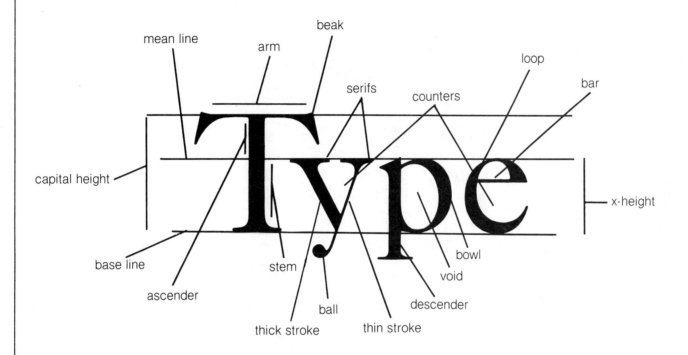

Typeface Composition

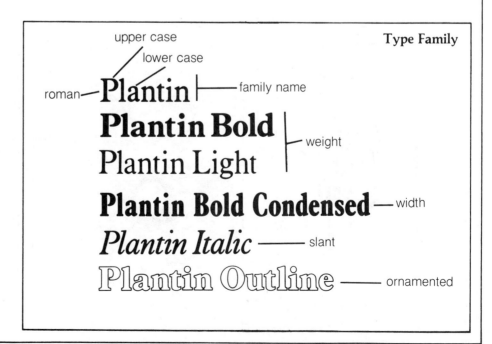

Type Family

Printing Processes

All *metal type* is known collectively as *hot metal*, in contrast to *cold type*, which is produced photographically. The letterpress method of printing uses a raised surface, or *relief*, while gravure uses a depressed surface, or *intaglio*, and lithography uses a *plane*, or *flat surface*. Printing is done on sheets of paper on *sheet-fed presses* or on rolls of paper on *web-fed presses*.

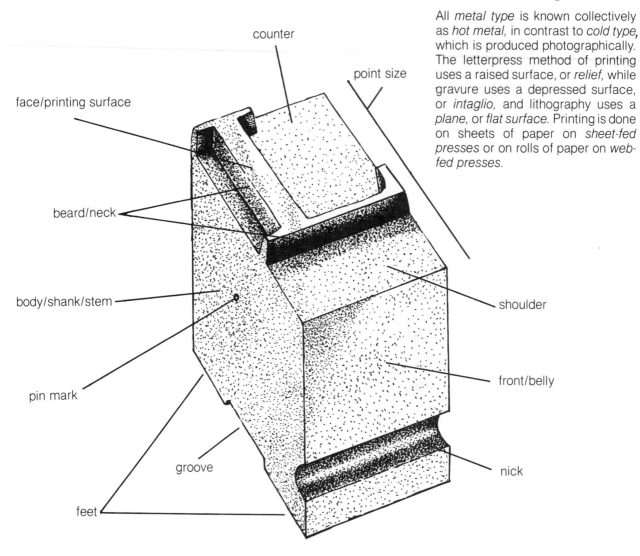

counter

point size

face/printing surface

beard/neck

body/shank/stem

pin mark

groove

feet

shoulder

front/belly

nick

Type

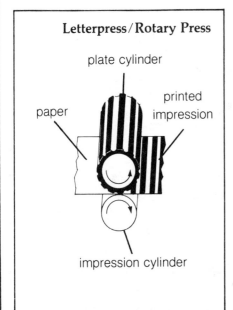

Letterpress/Rotary Press

plate cylinder

paper

printed impression

impression cylinder

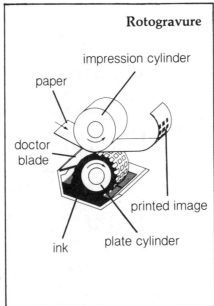

Rotogravure

impression cylinder

paper

doctor blade

ink

plate cylinder

printed image

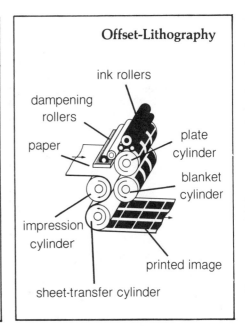

Offset-Lithography

ink rollers

dampening rollers

paper

plate cylinder

blanket cylinder

impression cylinder

printed image

sheet-transfer cylinder

Book

The *body* of a book is made up of *leaves,* each side of which is a *page.* Two facing pages form a *spread.* Pages leading up to the actual *text* are called *preliminaries* or *front matter.* Those pages following the text are *back matter, end matter* or *reference matter.* A box for a book, open at one end, is called a *slipcase* or *forel.*

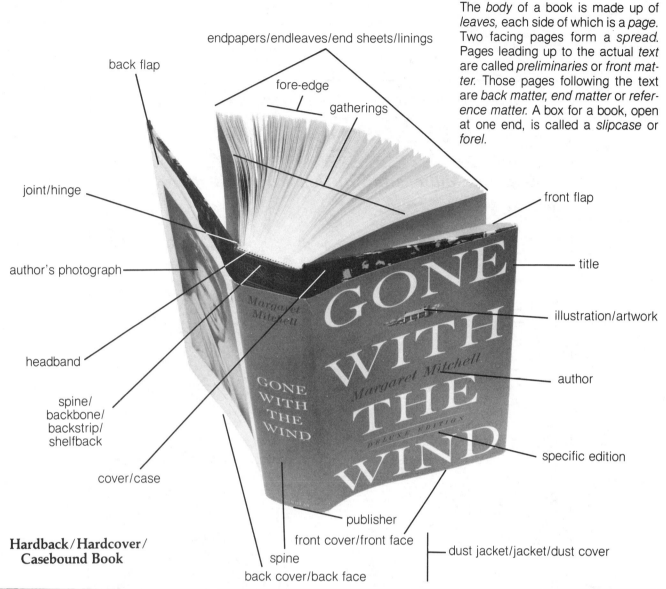

endpapers/endleaves/end sheets/linings

back flap

fore-edge

gatherings

joint/hinge

author's photograph

headband

spine/backbone/backstrip/shelfback

cover/case

spine

back cover/back face

front cover/front face

publisher

front flap

title

illustration/artwork

author

specific edition

dust jacket/jacket/dust cover

Hardback/Hardcover/Casebound Book

Paperback/Softback/Softcover/Softbound Book

covers/wrappers

publisher

colophon/trademark

price

spine

blurb

International Standard Book Number/ISBN

order number/inventory control number

Spread

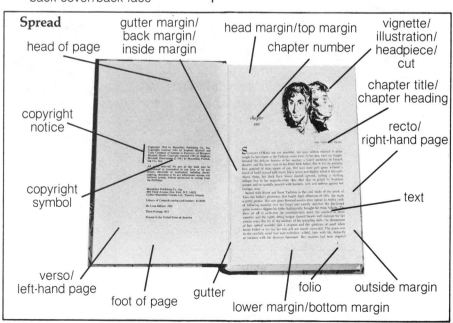

head of page

gutter margin/back margin/inside margin

head margin/top margin

chapter number

vignette/illustration/headpiece/cut

chapter title/chapter heading

copyright notice

copyright symbol

recto/right-hand page

text

verso/left-hand page

foot of page

gutter

folio

lower margin/bottom margin

outside margin

Print Communications

Newspaper

Terms vary from newspaper to newspaper. Those shown here are used at *The New York Times*. Small-size newspapers are called *tabloids*.

Labels (clockwise/positional): nameplate/flag/logo · copyright · issue date · skyline · out-of-town prices · weather ear · price · left ear · volume number · folio line · banner headline · head · deck/bank · bar line · byline · dateline · lead/lede · italic refer · body of story · subhead · jump line · art · hairline rule · index · caption/cut line · credit line · twinned stories · agate line · readout dash · dingbat

TODAY: SIX PAGES OF BICENTENNIAL ARTICLES AND PICTURES

"All the News That's Fit to Print"

The New York Times

LATE CITY EDITION
Weather: Partly cloudy and less humid today through tomorrow. Temperature range: today 64-82; Sunday 63-82. Details on page 20.

VOL. CXXV ... No. 43,262

NEW YORK, MONDAY, JULY 5, 1976

20 CENTS

Nation and Millions in City Joyously Hail Bicentennial

ISRAELIS RETURN WITH 103 RESCUED IN UGANDA RAID

Toll Is Put at 3 Hostages, 7 Hijackers, Army Officer and 20 of Amin's Men

FORD LAUDS OPERATION

Freed Captives Are Received Joyously at Airport After Their 7-Day Ordeal

By TERENCE SMITH

JERUSALEM, July 4—An Israeli commando unit that last night conducted a daring raid on the Entebbe airport in Uganda flew home today with the hostages it released.

PRESIDENT TALKS

Philadelphia Throngs Told U.S. Is Leader— Liberty Bell Rings

By JAMES T. WOOTEN

PANOPLY OF SAILS

Harbor Armada Led by Tall Ships in Salute to Fourth

By RICHARD F. SHEPARD

French Officials See Signs Amin, Hijackers Colluded

By [dateline]

CARTER TO BEGIN TALKS ON TICKET

Will See Muskie Today and Other Possible Running Mates Soon After

By CHARLES MOHR

A Day of Picnics, Pomp, Pageantry and Protest

By JOHN L. HESS

Preceded by a fireboat, the Coast Guard training ship Eagle leads the armada of ships past the Battery up the Hudson for the naval review

Ethnic Diversity Adds Spice to the Holiday

By FRED FERRETTI

O, Say, It Was a Glorious Patchwork Quilt of a Fourth

By McCANDLISH PHILLIPS

President Ford waves to the crowd at Valley Forge, Pa., where he signed a bill making it a national historical site. He stands on a covered wagon that represented Michigan, his home state, in the Bicentennial wagon train.

NEWS INDEX

Magazine Cover and Contents Page

Periodicals may be consumer magazines, intended for the general public; *trade* or *technical magazines,* intended for particular industries and businesses; or *journals,* published for people engaged in professions. *House organs* are distributed within a specific company. Covers may have *cover blurbs* with *selling copy,* describing inside stories, and *cover captions.*

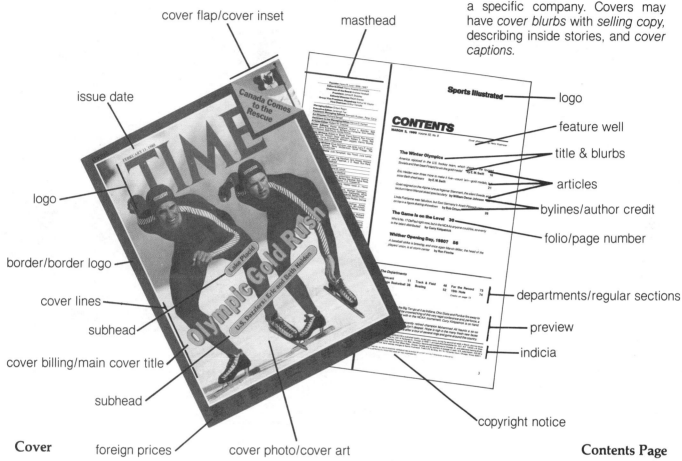

cover flap/cover inset

masthead

issue date

logo

border/border logo

cover lines

subhead

cover billing/main cover title

subhead

Cover

foreign prices

cover photo/cover art

logo

feature well

title & blurbs

articles

bylines/author credit

folio/page number

departments/regular sections

preview

indicia

copyright notice

Contents Page

Mailing Label/Subscriber Label

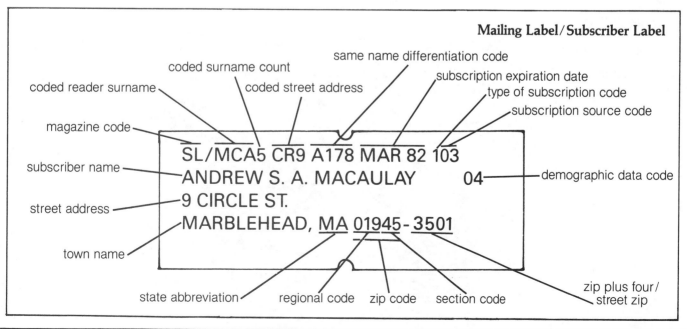

same name differentiation code

coded surname count

subscription expiration date

coded reader surname

coded street address

type of subscription code

subscription source code

magazine code

SL/MCA5 CR9 A178 MAR 82 103

subscriber name

ANDREW S. A. MACAULAY   04

demographic data code

street address

9 CIRCLE ST.

town name

MARBLEHEAD, MA 01945-3501

state abbreviation

regional code

zip code

section code

zip plus four/ street zip

Magazine Feature

The design of a magazine page is called the *layout*. In the feature shown here *dummy type* has been substituted for *text* or *copy*. Two facing pages are called a spread, *double spread,* or *double-truck.* A *sidebar* is a self-contained, boxed *article* bearing on the main feature.

frontispiece/half-title logo

head/headline/title

subhead/pullquote/deck/blurb

byline

dropped initial/set-in cap/
inset initial/descending initial

lead/lede

photo/cut/art

body copy/text

folio

Feature Spread

New York

Open City

"…'You can't be worrying about getting caught,' says Chino. 'You think about getting money. You got to think positive'…"

By Nicholas Pileggi

DEVELOPERS PLAY THEIR PART. ONE TACTIC IS to start off with a fright plan. This shows the dreadful building the developer could put up under existing rules if he was of a mind to. Since almost any other plan would be better, the planners are in the happy position of being able to suggest changes that are bound to be improvements. In the process, they come to identify with the project, sometimes even becoming fierce partisans of it. If community-board people

go up in smoke. The developer will leave town. Construction jobs will be lost. Thus the inviolability of the brutal design for the sides of the Portman Hotel, proposed for the Times Square area. Beneath the great blank slabs of masonry, there would be only a token amount of the retail activity our zoning normally calls for. The walls are, indeed, a virtual declaration of war against the New York street. And the planners went along, ardently.

The anticipation of variances makes them self-fulfilling. The extra bulk, for one thing, gets built into the price of allowing developers, on a case-by-case basis, to put up big-

Raised expectations can do their worst mischief on existing buildings—most particularly, the kind that so enhance their surroundings: Bergdorf-Goodman for example, or the late Bonwit Teller. The problem is the extra bulk that could be built in their place. As rising floor-area ratios increase the bulk, the old building becomes all the more vulnerable. At length, it is decreed obsolete, worth more dead than alive. It is not the impartial workings of the marketplace that have endangered such buildings; it is the New York City Plan-

en my research group found that even at hem would have pre-One reason: no place mental findings, the Commission drew up hese were adopted as cipal provisions in-lationship to the side-walk, more trees, food facilities, and stores on building frontage. Similar standards for residential plazas were adopted in 1977.

By then, however, plazas were old-hat. Planners were pushing *internal* spaces, such as arcades and through-block areas and atriums. These were to be substitute streets. Planners had developed an overriding concern with pedestrian congestion in midtown, and they saw in these spaces the way to relief. They would save people from the crowded streets by enticing them off the sidewalks.

The developer can now plead that he should get the

54   NEW YORK/MARCH 9, 1981

Photographs: top, Cliff Watts; center, Brian Hagiwara

photo credit

Service Articles

scotch rule

art/illustration

oxford rule

head

column rule

special-feature photo treatment

sign-off

"nuts and bolts"

flush-left type

ragged-right type

Reviews

running title

subhead

decorated initial

introduction

breaker

boldface/highlight

column

WINTER PLEASURES
Culture (high and middle and low, too) blooms in the cold.

That's Snow Biz

From now until April, New York's cultural season continues in high gear. We can't guarantee that all the events chronicled below will be wonderful, but they'll certainly be warmer than anything outdoors. (Listings compiled by Ruth Gilbert, Ellen Hopkins, and David Frankel.)

daughter to Joanne Glass's **To Grandmother's House We Go.** The play is set in Wisconsin on Thanksgiving weekend.

The long and lovely Judith Jamison, heretofore seen only in her dancing shoes, will now be starring on Broadway as one of the Sophisticated Ladies. As you might have guessed, the show is based upon the life and songs of Duke Ellington. (February)

Magazine Feature

A page that folds out to twice the size of a regular page is called a *gatefold*. A *jump line*, or *continued line*, at the end of a page refers the reader to the remaining text of a story appearing elsewhere in the magazine. A brief descriptive headline above the main head, designed to attract the reader's attention, is a *kicker, teaser, eyebrow,* or *highline*. Subscription cards bound into a magazine are called *inserts*. Those not physically connected are called *blow-ins*.

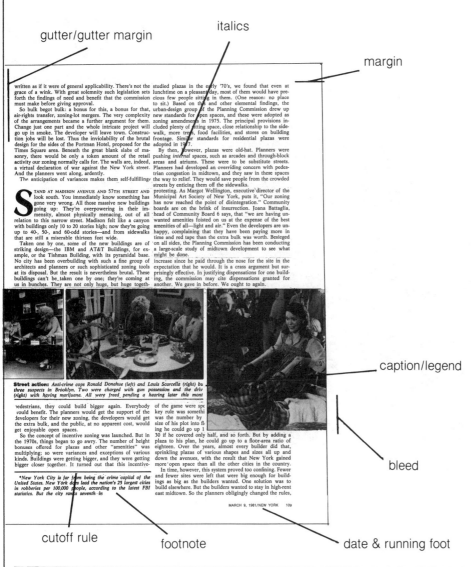

gutter/gutter margin

italics

margin

caption/legend

bleed

cutoff rule

footnote

date & running foot

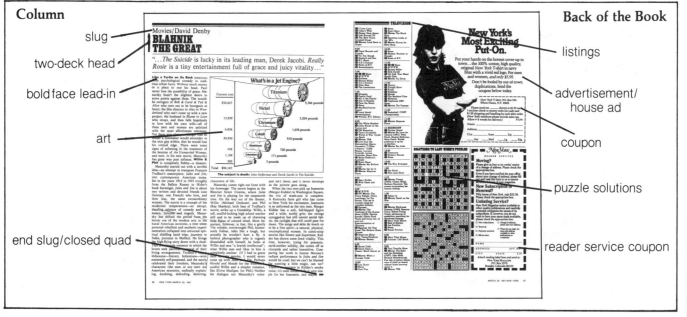

Column

Back of the Book

slug

two-deck head

bold face lead-in

art

end slug/closed quad

listings

advertisement/ house ad

coupon

puzzle solutions

reader service coupon

Print Communications

Still Camera and Film

To focus on an *image*, a photographer looks through the *viewfinder* on the back of the camera. Some cameras have *automatic focus* and *power winder* as in this model shown. Camera accessories include *interchangeable lenses—telephoto, wide-angle, zoom* and *special-purpose—lens caps* and *hoods, filters, focusing screens* and *eyecups.*

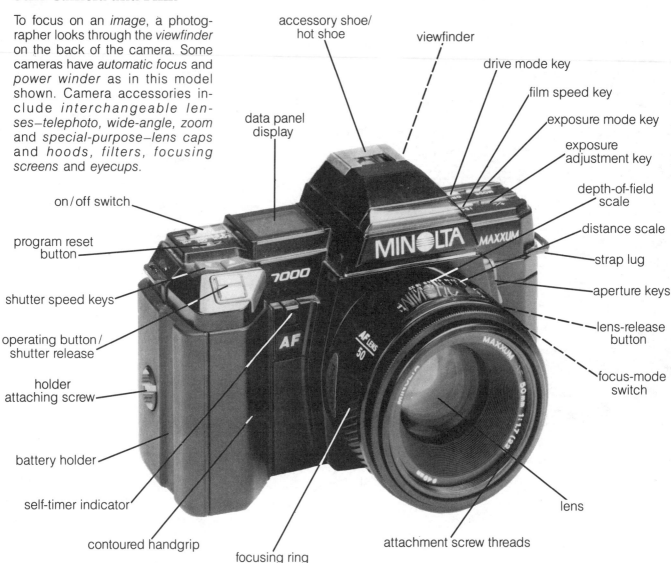

accessory shoe/
hot shoe

viewfinder

drive mode key

film speed key

exposure mode key

exposure
adjustment key

depth-of-field
scale

distance scale

strap lug

aperture keys

lens-release
button

focus-mode
switch

data panel
display

on/off switch

program reset
button

shutter speed keys

operating button/
shutter release

holder
attaching screw

battery holder

self-timer indicator

contoured handgrip

focusing ring

attachment screw threads

lens

Single Lens Reflex/SLR/Autofocus 35 mm Camera

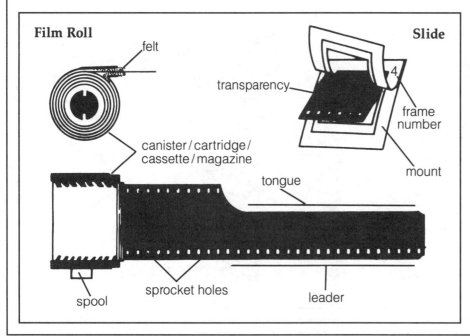

Film Roll

felt

transparency

Slide

frame
number

mount

canister/cartridge/
cassette/magazine

tongue

spool

sprocket holes

leader

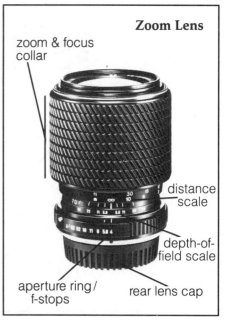

Zoom Lens

zoom & focus
collar

distance
scale

depth-of-
field scale

aperture ring/
f-stops

rear lens cap

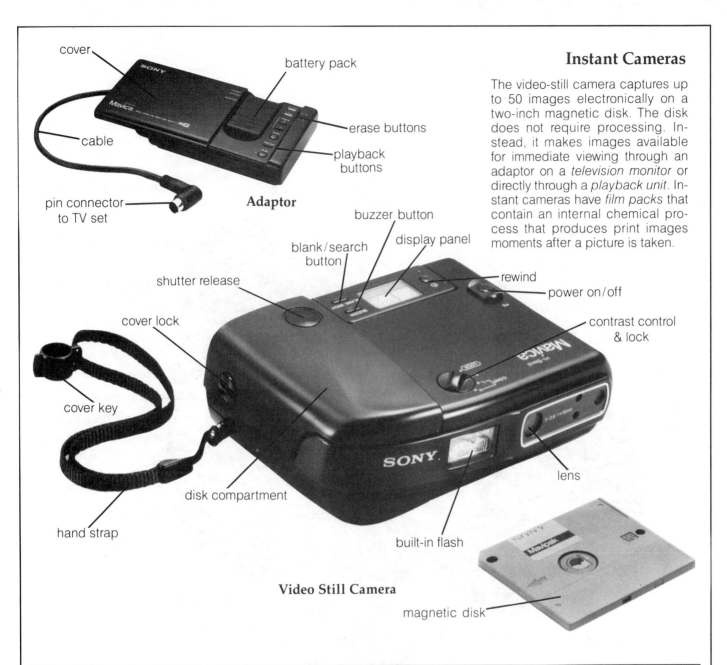

cover

battery pack

cable

erase buttons

pin connector
to TV set

playback
buttons

Adaptor

Instant Cameras

The video-still camera captures up to 50 images electronically on a two-inch magnetic disk. The disk does not require processing. Instead, it makes images available for immediate viewing through an adaptor on a *television monitor* or directly through a *playback unit*. Instant cameras have *film packs* that contain an internal chemical process that produces print images moments after a picture is taken.

buzzer button

blank/search
button

display panel

shutter release

rewind

power on/off

cover lock

contrast control
& lock

cover key

SONY

lens

hand strap

disk compartment

built-in flash

Video Still Camera

magnetic disk

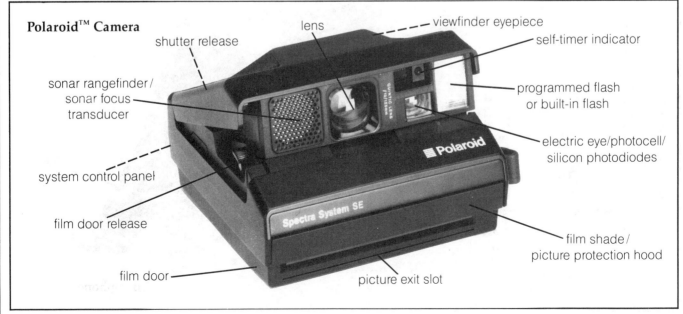

Polaroid™ Camera

lens

viewfinder eyepiece

shutter release

self-timer indicator

sonar rangefinder/
sonar focus
transducer

programmed flash
or built-in flash

electric eye/photocell/
silicon photodiodes

Polaroid

system control panel

Spectra System SE

film door release

film shade/
picture protection hood

film door

picture exit slot

Movie Camera

Home-movie cameras, such as the one shown here, use film contained in *drop-in cartridges*. In large commercial models, *unexposed film* moves through the body from the *supply reel* to the *take-up reel*. The reels in these cameras are often housed in a *blimp,* a soundproof device that fits on top of the body. *Single-system sound cameras* record both *image* and *sound* on the same film. Sound tracks on film may be either *optical* or *magnetic*.

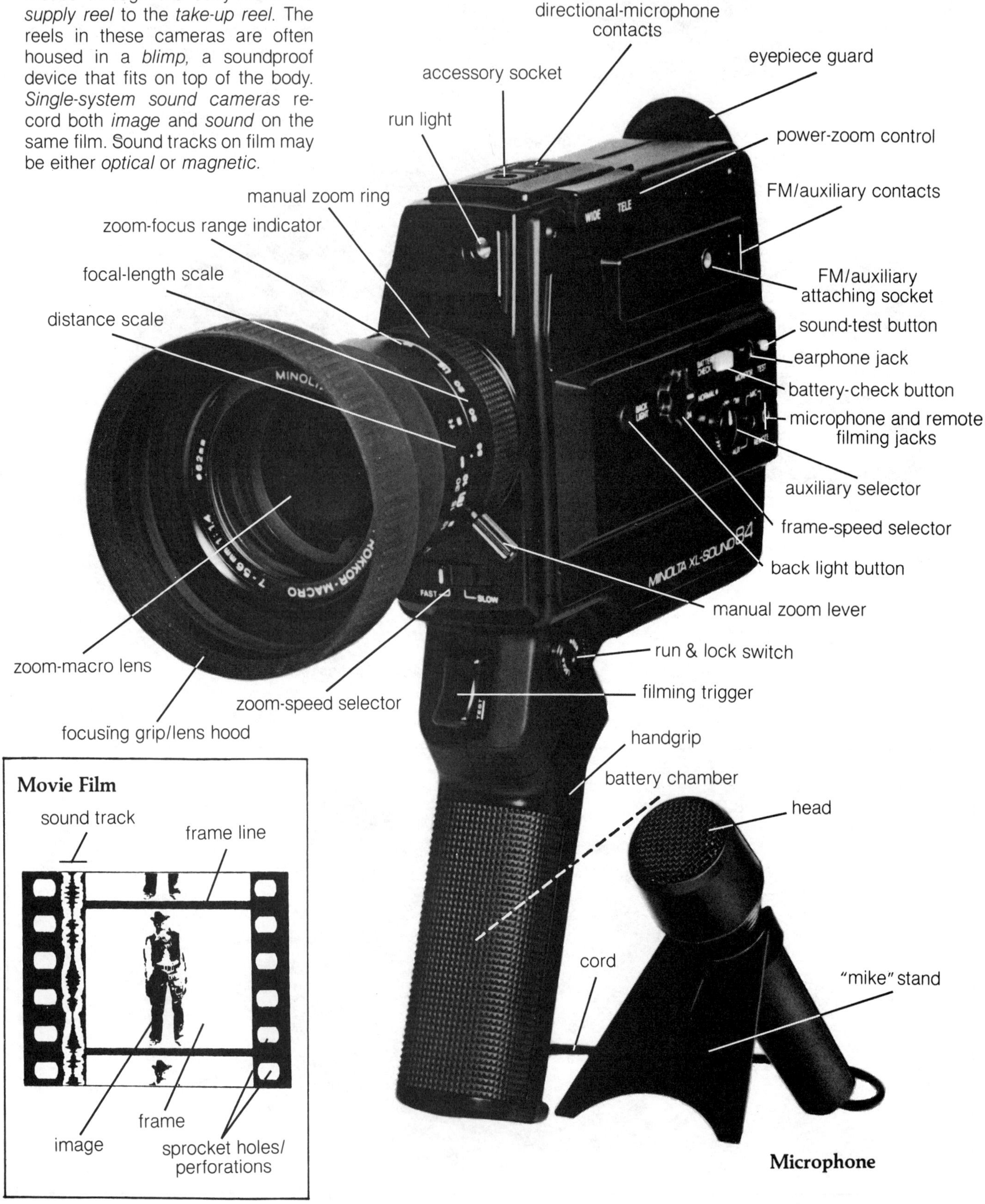

directional-microphone contacts

accessory socket

run light

eyepiece guard

power-zoom control

FM/auxiliary contacts

FM/auxiliary attaching socket

sound-test button

earphone jack

battery-check button

microphone and remote filming jacks

auxiliary selector

frame-speed selector

back light button

manual zoom lever

run & lock switch

filming trigger

handgrip

battery chamber

head

cord

"mike" stand

manual zoom ring

zoom-focus range indicator

focal-length scale

distance scale

zoom-macro lens

focusing grip/lens hood

zoom-speed selector

Movie Film

sound track

frame line

image

frame

sprocket holes/ perforations

Microphone

The film projector shown here is a *self-threading, reel-to-reel model* with a built-in *speaker*. Slide projectors may have circular, or *carousel*, trays, *slide cubes* or *straight trays*.

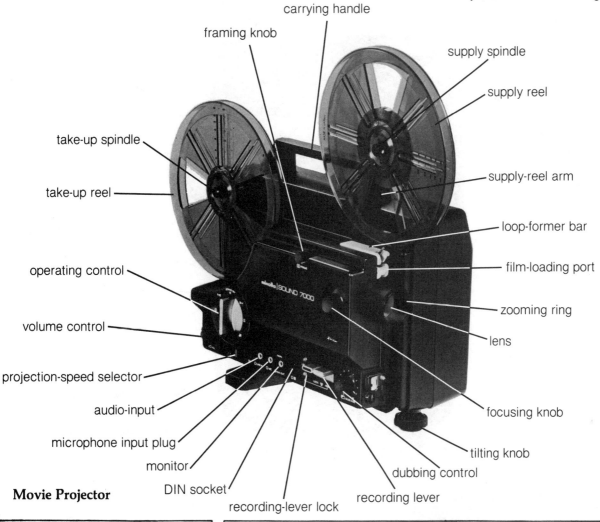

carrying handle

framing knob

supply spindle

supply reel

take-up spindle

supply-reel arm

take-up reel

loop-former bar

film-loading port

operating control

zooming ring

volume control

lens

projection-speed selector

audio-input

focusing knob

microphone input plug

tilting knob

monitor

DIN socket

dubbing control

recording lever

recording-lever lock

Movie Projector

Screen

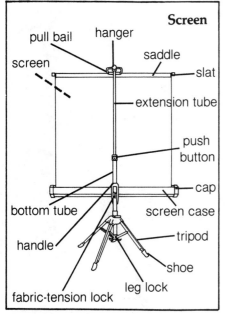

pull bail

hanger

saddle

screen

slat

extension tube

push button

cap

bottom tube

screen case

handle

tripod

shoe

leg lock

fabric-tension lock

Slide Projector

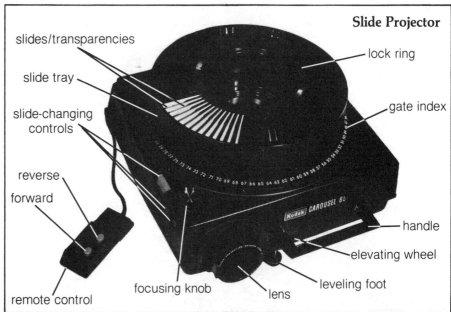

slides/transparencies

lock ring

slide tray

gate index

slide-changing controls

reverse

forward

handle

elevating wheel

leveling foot

focusing knob

lens

remote control

Photographic Accessories

In addition to the accessories shown here, *carrying straps, gadget bags,* and *cleaning supplies* such as *brushes, lens tissue* and *cleaning fluid* are used.

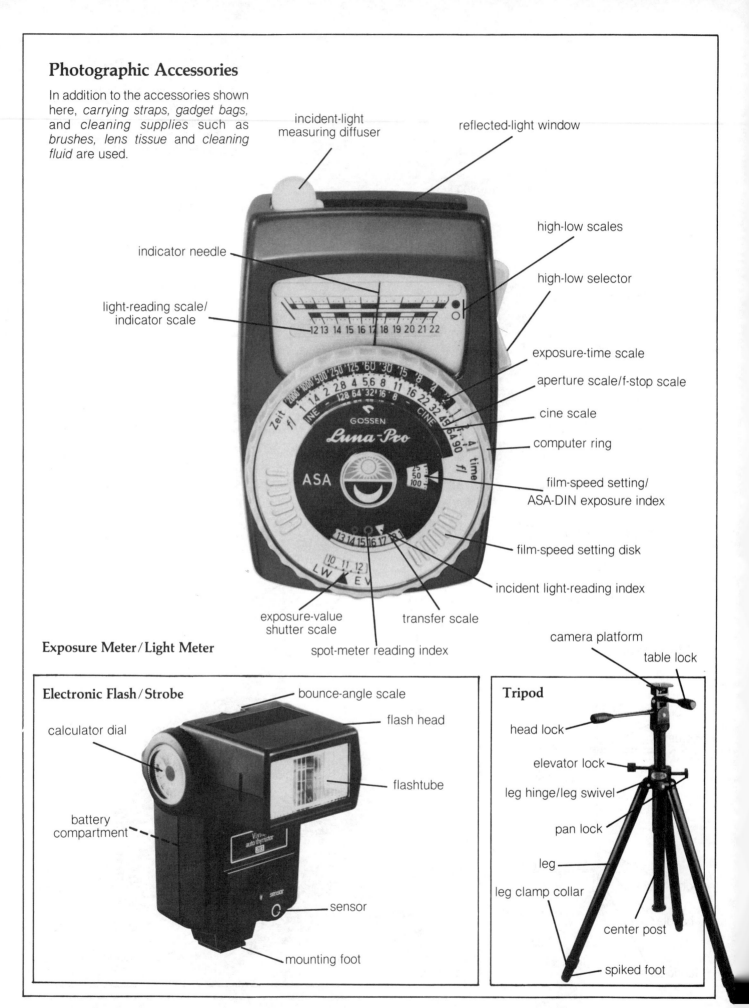

Exposure Meter / Light Meter

- incident-light measuring diffuser
- reflected-light window
- high-low scales
- high-low selector
- indicator needle
- light-reading scale/ indicator scale
- exposure-time scale
- aperture scale/f-stop scale
- cine scale
- computer ring
- film-speed setting/ ASA-DIN exposure index
- film-speed setting disk
- incident light-reading index
- exposure-value shutter scale
- transfer scale
- spot-meter reading index

GOSSEN
Luna-Pro
ASA

Electronic Flash / Strobe

- bounce-angle scale
- flash head
- calculator dial
- flashtube
- battery compartment
- sensor
- mounting foot

Tripod

- camera platform
- table lock
- head lock
- elevator lock
- leg hinge/leg swivel
- pan lock
- leg
- leg clamp collar
- center post
- spiked foot

Tape Recorders

Sound is recorded on *magnetic tape* by passing the tape over a *recording head*. Most cassette recorders have *built-in microphones* but are designed to work with *external mikes* as well. They are *battery-powered*, have *rechargeable battery packs* or *AC power cords*.

monitor switch

speed switch

equalizing switch

bias switch

power button

recording-mode buttons

supply reel

right-channel volume unit meter

front panel

reel lock/keeper

take-up reel

record indicator

direction indicators

left-channel volume unit meter

pause button

pause indicator

record button

headphone jack

play button

microphone jacks

stop button

microphone-recording level control

tape counter

fast-forward button

capstan

fast-rewind button

pinch roller

reset button

pinch roller

line-recording level control

repeat button

play button

pitch-control dial

Reel-to-Reel Recorder and Playback Unit

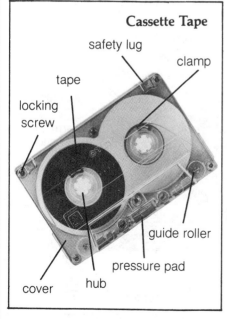

Cassette Tape

safety lug

clamp

tape

locking screw

guide roller

pressure pad

cover

hub

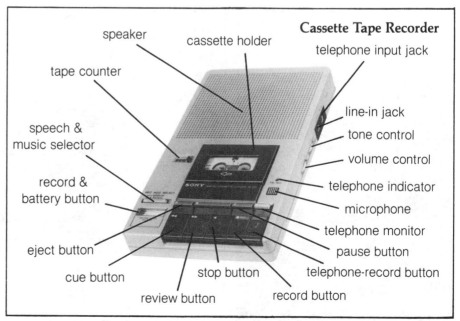

Cassette Tape Recorder

speaker

cassette holder

telephone input jack

tape counter

line-in jack

tone control

speech & music selector

volume control

telephone indicator

record & battery button

microphone

telephone monitor

eject button

pause button

cue button

telephone-record button

review button

stop button

record button

177

Aural Communications

Disc and Record Players

Compact disc players use a *laser tracking system* to play or repeat selections. Multiple albums can be programmed to play in any order on a *CD changer*, while a CD player holds only one album at a time. An optional *monster cable* improves sound by eliminating disc vibration. The amount of information a player can read off a disc is measured in *bits*.

Compact Disc Player/CD Player

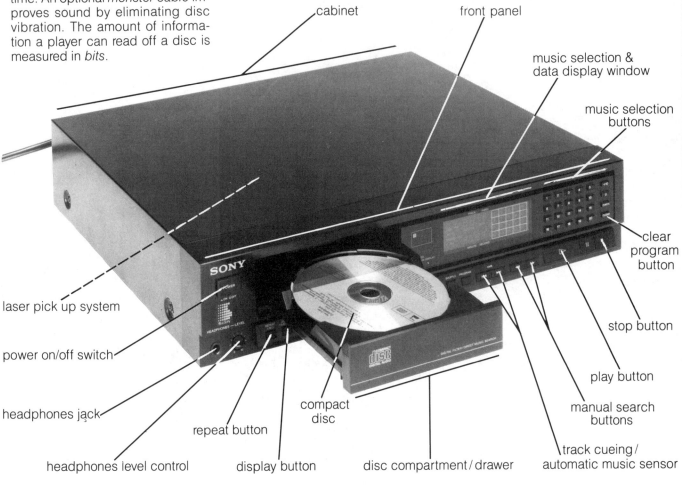

cabinet
front panel
music selection & data display window
music selection buttons
clear program button
stop button
play button
manual search buttons
track cueing/automatic music sensor
disc compartment/drawer
laser pick up system
power on/off switch
headphones jack
repeat button
headphones level control
display button
compact disc

Record/Platter/Disc

lead-in groove
manufacturer
locked groove
record title & artist
grooves/spiral
label
lead-out groove
center hole
master number

Turntable

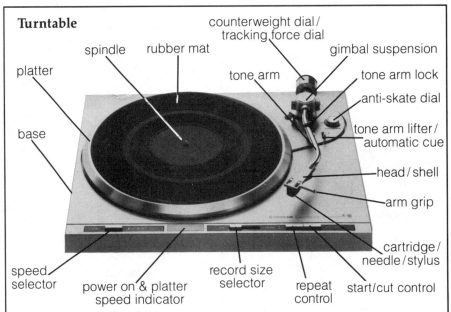

counterweight dial/tracking force dial
gimbal suspension
spindle
rubber mat
tone arm lock
platter
tone arm
anti-skate dial
base
tone arm lifter/automatic cue
head/shell
arm grip
cartridge/needle/stylus
speed selector
power on & platter speed indicator
record size selector
repeat control
start/cut control

Audio Equipment

A home audio system produces minimally distorted sound, or *high fidelity*. It is usually comprised of a *tuner*, a disc or record player, a *pre-amp*, and amplifier and speakers. Its power output is measured in *watts*.

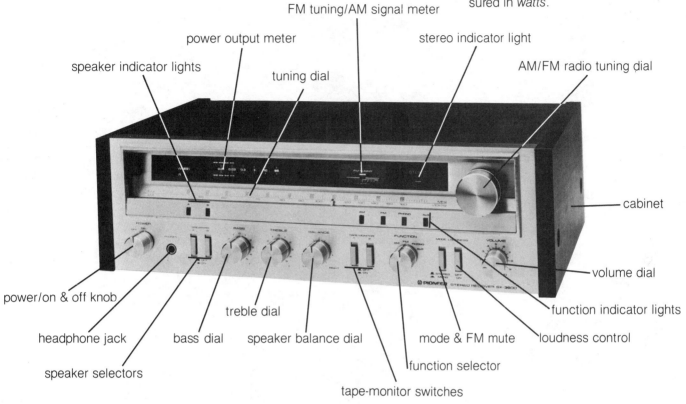

power output meter

FM tuning/AM signal meter

stereo indicator light

speaker indicator lights

tuning dial

AM/FM radio tuning dial

cabinet

power/on & off knob

volume dial

function indicator lights

headphone jack

treble dial

bass dial

speaker balance dial

mode & FM mute

loudness control

speaker selectors

function selector

tape-monitor switches

Receiver / Amplifier

Headphones

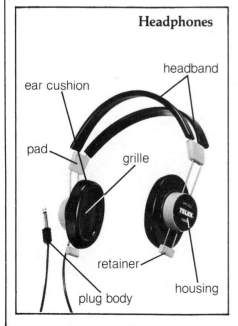

headband

ear cushion

pad

grille

retainer

housing

plug body

Speakers

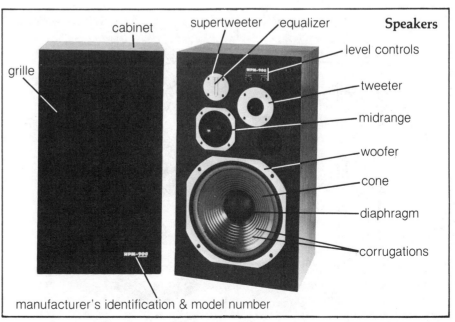

cabinet

supertweeter

equalizer

level controls

grille

tweeter

midrange

woofer

cone

diaphragm

corrugations

manufacturer's identification & model number

179

Aural Communications

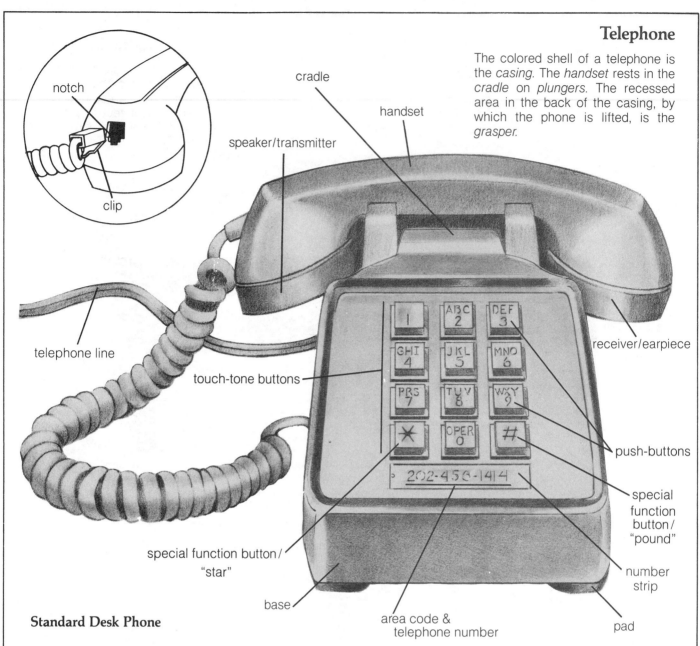

Telephone

The colored shell of a telephone is the *casing*. The *handset* rests in the *cradle* on *plungers*. The recessed area in the back of the casing, by which the phone is lifted, is the *grasper*.

notch

clip

cradle

handset

speaker/transmitter

telephone line

touch-tone buttons

receiver/earpiece

push-buttons

special function button/ "pound"

special function button/ "star"

number strip

base

area code & telephone number

pad

Standard Desk Phone

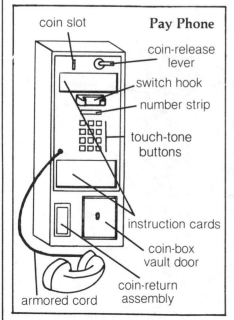

Pay Phone

coin slot

coin-release lever

switch hook

number strip

touch-tone buttons

instruction cards

coin-box vault door

coin-return assembly

armored cord

Trimline Phone

number strip

rotary dial

plunger

finger hole

base

finger stop

bell adjuster

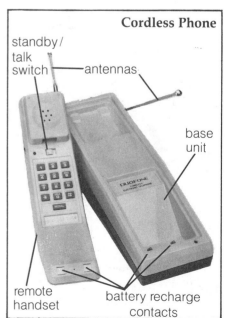

Cordless Phone

standby/ talk switch

antennas

base unit

remote handset

battery recharge contacts

Cellular Telephone

A *cell* is a circular service area of 16 mile radius, and calls are transmitted over radio waves and relayed from cell to cell over telephone wires. Available features include *memory redial* to recall numbers, *hands-off* operation, and an electronic lock to prevent unauthorized use. *Remote operation*, either with a *beeper* or *Touch-tone*™ phone, includes options like message retrieval, or leaving messages or *memos*. Many answering machines allow *call screening*, permitting calls to be heard without being answered.

antenna

liquid crystal display screen/LCD

auto redial

handset

illuminated menu keys

illuminated alpha-numeric keypad

battery pack

signal strength indicator

SIG
01 ABCDEF
1234567890

memory data

Display Screen

carrying handle

number being called

loudspeaker

Cellular Telephone/Mobile Phone

electronic lock

stand/base/case

cord

Answering Machine

message indicator lights

transfer call

telephone handset

play messages button

answer button

alpha-numeric keypad/ telephone push buttons

control buttons

speakerphone

Portable Radios and Cassette Players

A cassette player, or "Walkman"™, may be heard through headphones, a *built-in speaker* or *external speakers*. Portable radios often have detachable speakers. *Auto-reverse*, or *continuous play*, automatically plays both sides of a tape. *Dolby*™ sound reduces tape hiss. Some players with recording capabilities have *high-speed dubbing*, which copies tapes at faster than normal playing speed, and *synchronized dubbing*, which starts the original tape and blank tape simultaneously.

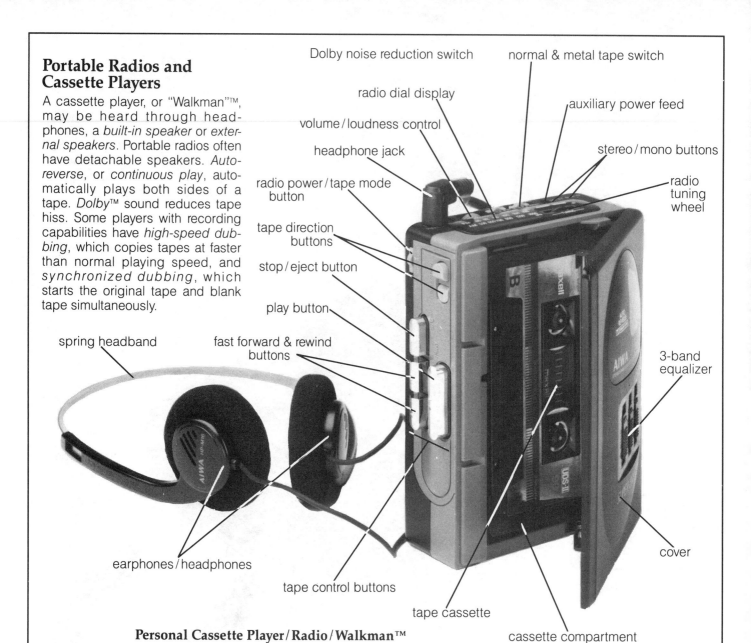

Dolby noise reduction switch

normal & metal tape switch

radio dial display

auxiliary power feed

volume/loudness control

headphone jack

stereo/mono buttons

radio power/tape mode button

radio tuning wheel

tape direction buttons

stop/eject button

play button

spring headband

fast forward & rewind buttons

3-band equalizer

earphones/headphones

cover

tape control buttons

tape cassette

cassette compartment

Personal Cassette Player/Radio/Walkman™

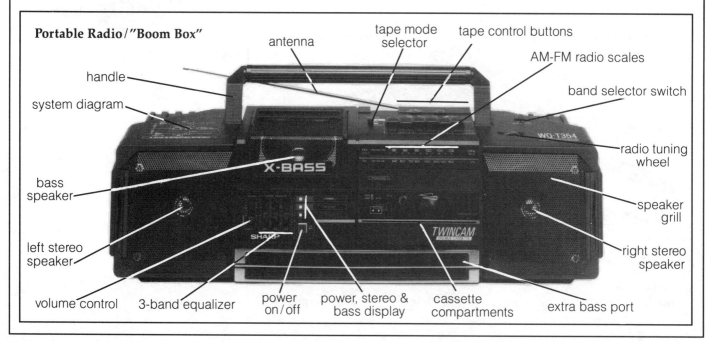

Portable Radio/"Boom Box"

antenna

tape mode selector

tape control buttons

AM-FM radio scales

handle

band selector switch

system diagram

radio tuning wheel

bass speaker

speaker grill

left stereo speaker

right stereo speaker

volume control

3-band equalizer

power on/off

power, stereo & bass display

cassette compartments

extra bass port

Transceiver

A *walkie-talkie* is a hand-held transceiver used to transmit and receive over short distances. *CBs,* or Citizens Band radios, like the one shown here, have greater but still limited range. *Amateur radio operators,* or *"hams,"* use transceivers capable of communicating over vast distances.

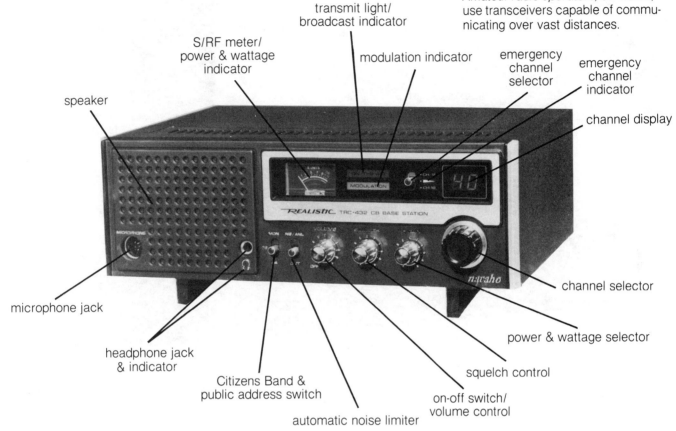

speaker

S/RF meter/ power & wattage indicator

transmit light/ broadcast indicator

modulation indicator

emergency channel selector

emergency channel indicator

channel display

channel selector

microphone jack

headphone jack & indicator

Citizens Band & public address switch

automatic noise limiter

on-off switch/ volume control

squelch control

power & wattage selector

Base Station

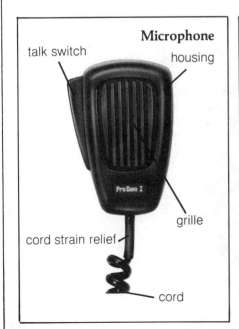

Microphone

talk switch

housing

grille

cord strain relief

cord

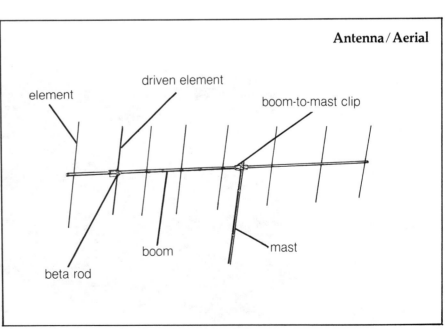

Antenna / Aerial

element

driven element

boom-to-mast clip

boom

mast

beta rod

Aural Communications

Video Recorder

Video recorders are used in conjunction with *television sets*, or *monitors*. They can be operated by hand-size *remote control units*. Some recorders use a grooveless *disc*, others use a *video cassette tape*.

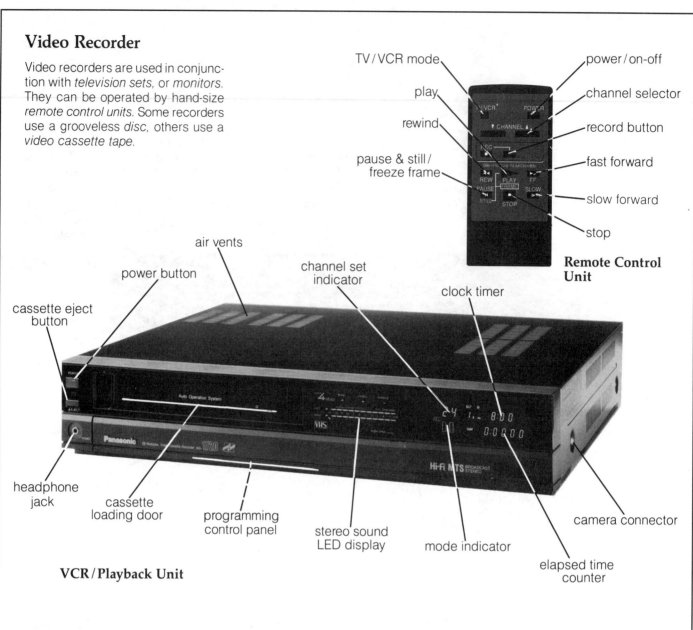

TV/VCR mode

play

rewind

pause & still / freeze frame

power/on-off

channel selector

record button

fast forward

slow forward

stop

Remote Control Unit

air vents

power button

channel set indicator

clock timer

cassette eject button

headphone jack

cassette loading door

programming control panel

stereo sound LED display

mode indicator

elapsed time counter

camera connector

VCR/Playback Unit

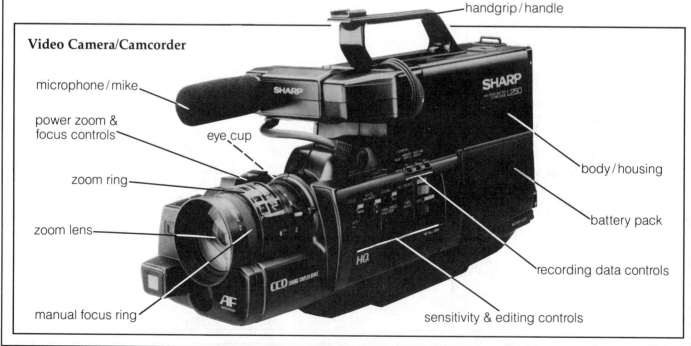

handgrip/handle

Video Camera/Camcorder

microphone/mike

power zoom & focus controls

eye cup

zoom ring

zoom lens

manual focus ring

body/housing

battery pack

recording data controls

sensitivity & editing controls

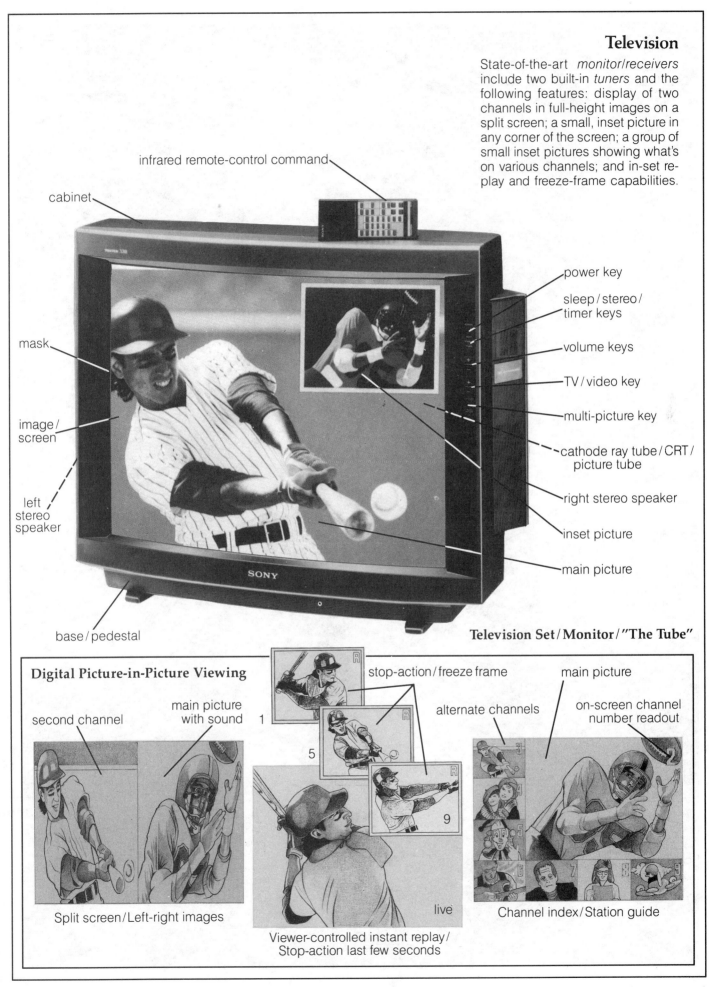

Television

State-of-the-art *monitor/receivers* include two built-in *tuners* and the following features: display of two channels in full-height images on a split screen; a small, inset picture in any corner of the screen; a group of small inset pictures showing what's on various channels; and in-set replay and freeze-frame capabilities.

infrared remote-control command

cabinet

mask

image/ screen

left stereo speaker

base/pedestal

power key

sleep/stereo/ timer keys

volume keys

TV/video key

multi-picture key

cathode ray tube/CRT/ picture tube

right stereo speaker

inset picture

main picture

Television Set/Monitor/"The Tube"

Digital Picture-in-Picture Viewing

second channel

main picture with sound

stop-action/freeze frame

alternate channels

main picture

on-screen channel number readout

Split screen/Left-right images

Viewer-controlled instant replay/ Stop-action last few seconds

live

Channel index/Station guide

Satellite

Active repeater satellites are communications satellites that amplify signals beamed to them for retransmission. *Passive* or *reflector satellites* mirror signals without amplifying them. Satellites used for space exploration, such as the one shown here, make scientific measurements and transmit the information back to earth.

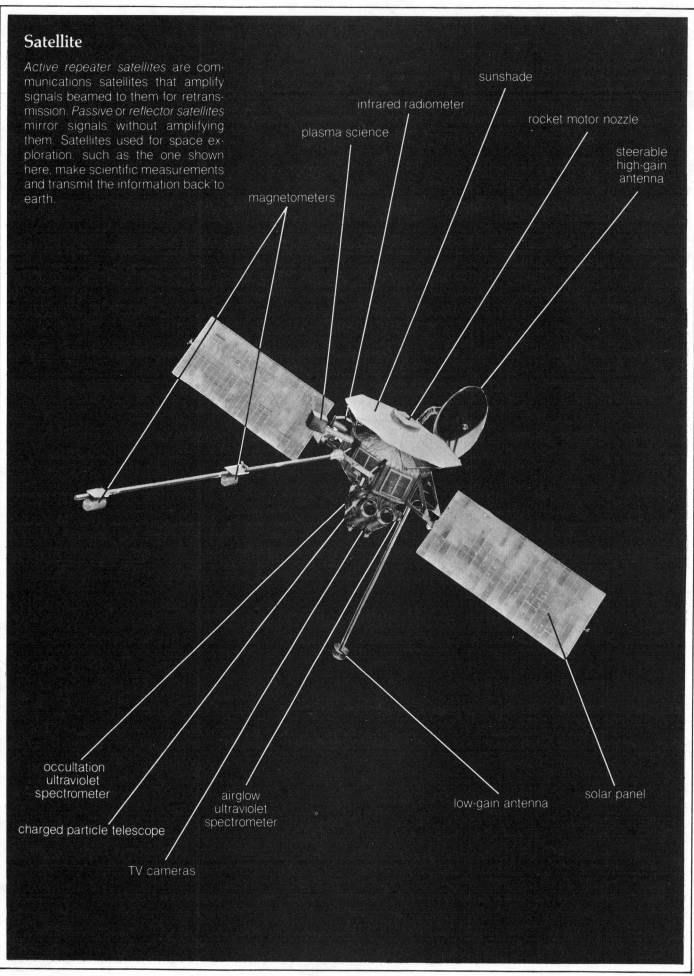

plasma science

magnetometers

infrared radiometer

sunshade

rocket motor nozzle

steerable high-gain antenna

occultation ultraviolet spectrometer

charged particle telescope

airglow ultraviolet spectrometer

TV cameras

low-gain antenna

solar panel

Personal Items

This section includes items people are likely to wear, carry or use in the course of their everyday lives. Thus, coverage includes clothing, hats, shoes, jewelry and money.

Wherever men's and women's apparel differ appreciably, items have been separated. But in the case of items such as sweaters and overcoats, articles worn by both sexes, only one version has been presented. Liberal use has been made to show the variations possible on single objects. However trendy clothing fashions or hairstyles may be, they share the same basic parts and details shown in the illustrations on the pages that follow.

Because cosmetics, grooming, hairstyles and jewelry are an important part of everyday life, they have been included in this section, as have such items as eyeglasses, handbags and wallets, timepieces and smoking materials. And because on rainy days an umbrella is essential to carry, it, too, appears here.

Identification Bracelet

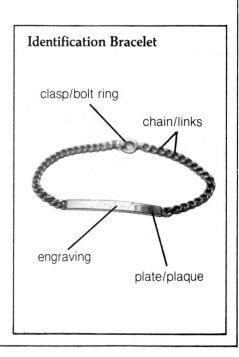

clasp/bolt ring

chain/links

engraving

plate/plaque

187

Jacket and Vest

A jacket, or *coat*, can be *single* or *double-breasted*. A *handkerchief pocket* or *breast pocket* is usually found on the upper left front panel. The pouch-like attachment inside a side pocket is called a *change pocket*. Most jackets have a *vent* or *double vent* cut into the hem in the back panel. Vests have an adjustable *backstrap* in the back.

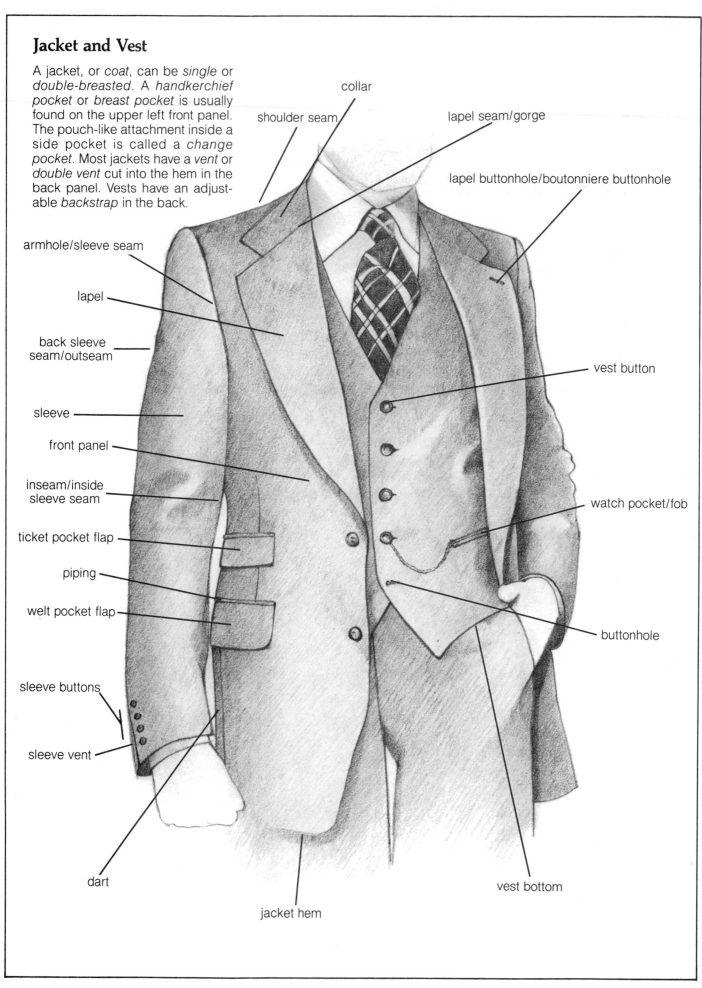

collar

shoulder seam

lapel seam/gorge

lapel buttonhole/boutonniere buttonhole

armhole/sleeve seam

lapel

back sleeve seam/outseam

vest button

sleeve

front panel

inseam/inside sleeve seam

watch pocket/fob

ticket pocket flap

piping

welt pocket flap

buttonhole

sleeve buttons

sleeve vent

dart

vest bottom

jacket hem

Shirt

This illustration combines all the elements found in shirts suitable for casual or formal occasions.

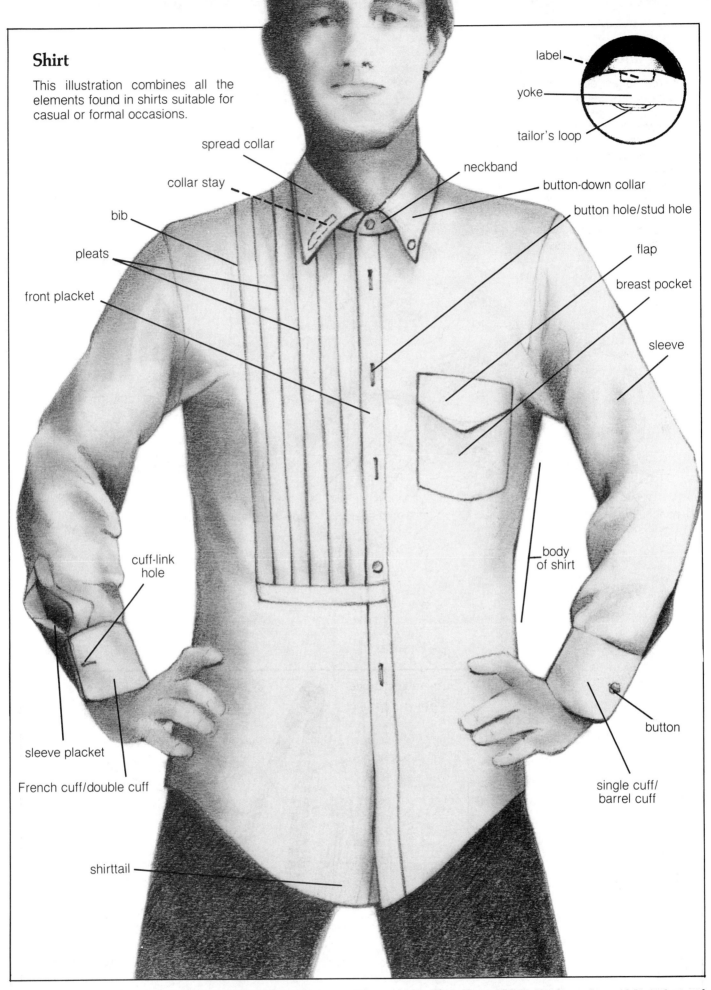

label

yoke

tailor's loop

spread collar

collar stay

bib

pleats

front placket

neckband

button-down collar

button hole/stud hole

flap

breast pocket

sleeve

cuff-link hole

body of shirt

sleeve placket

French cuff/double cuff

button

single cuff/ barrel cuff

shirttail

Men's Apparel

Belt and Suspenders

Large, often elaborately engraved buckles are called *plaque buckles.* *Military buckles,* or *ratchet buckles,* are adjusted by pushing a *tension rod* inside the *frame.* Some belts come with reinforcing *eyelets* in the punch holes. The composite pair of suspenders shown here are *fireman's, policeman's,* or *working man's suspenders.* They all have a single elastic band at the back, whereas *dress suspenders* have crossed bands.

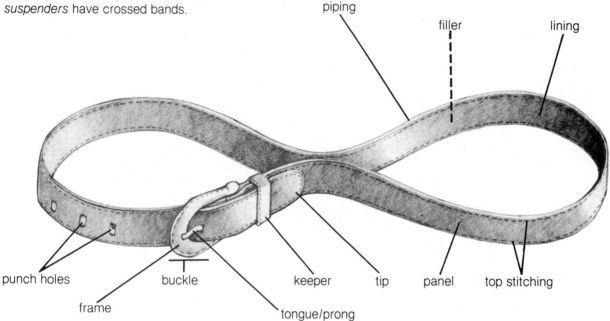

piping

filler

lining

punch holes

frame

buckle

tongue/prong

keeper

tip

panel

top stitching

Belt

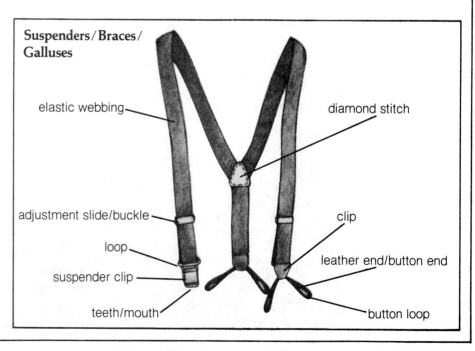

Suspenders/Braces/ Galluses

elastic webbing

diamond stitch

adjustment slide/buckle

clip

loop

leather end/button end

suspender clip

teeth/mouth

button loop

The back of a *pair of pants* is called the *seat*. Mid-thigh or knee length pants are *shorts*. *Jeans* often have pockets and seams reinforced with *rivets*. *Waistband closures* on pants are secured with *button tab closings* or metal *hook and eye closings*.

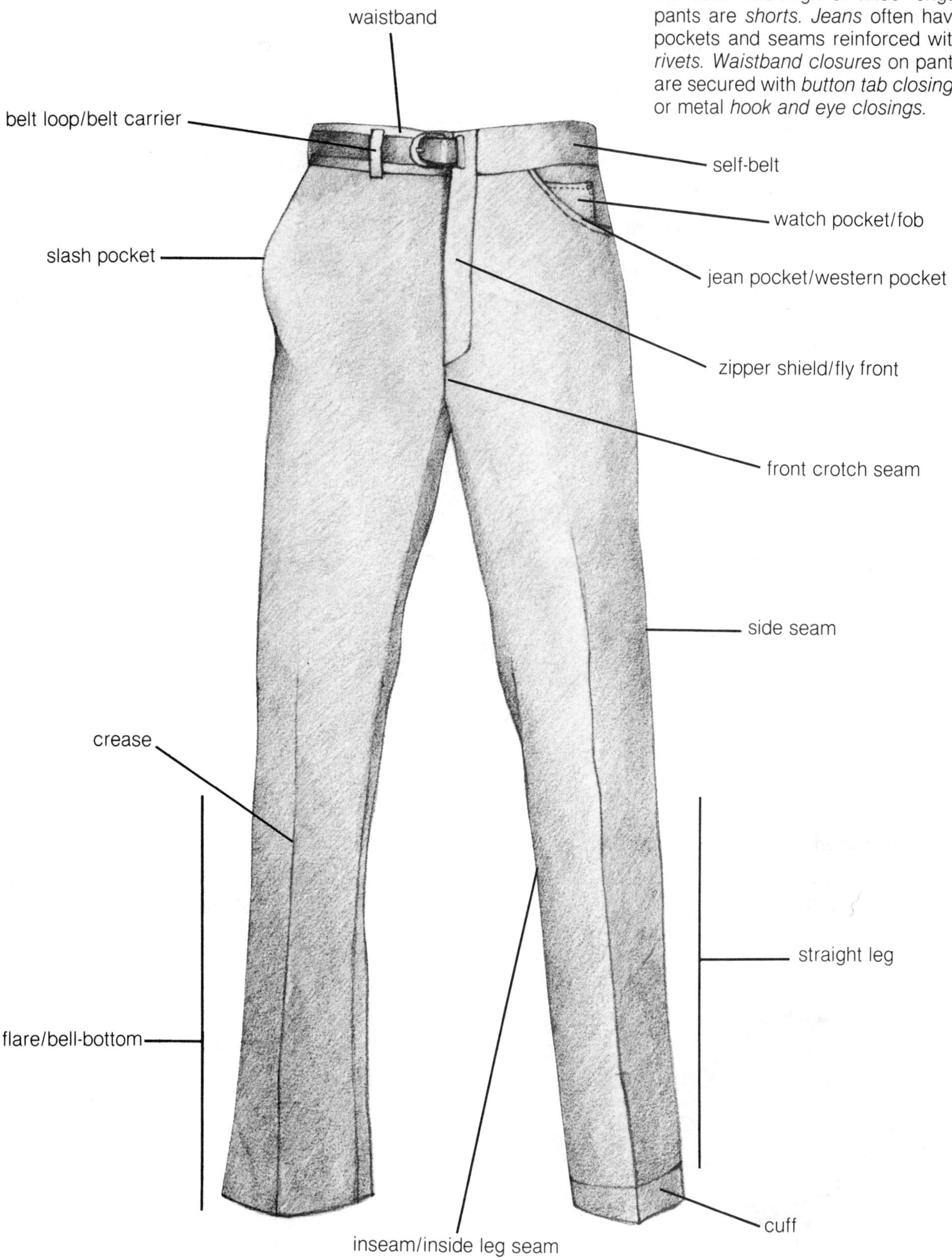

waistband

belt loop/belt carrier

self-belt

watch pocket/fob

slash pocket

jean pocket/western pocket

zipper shield/fly front

front crotch seam

side seam

crease

straight leg

flare/bell-bottom

cuff

inseam/inside leg seam

Trousers/Slacks

Men's Apparel

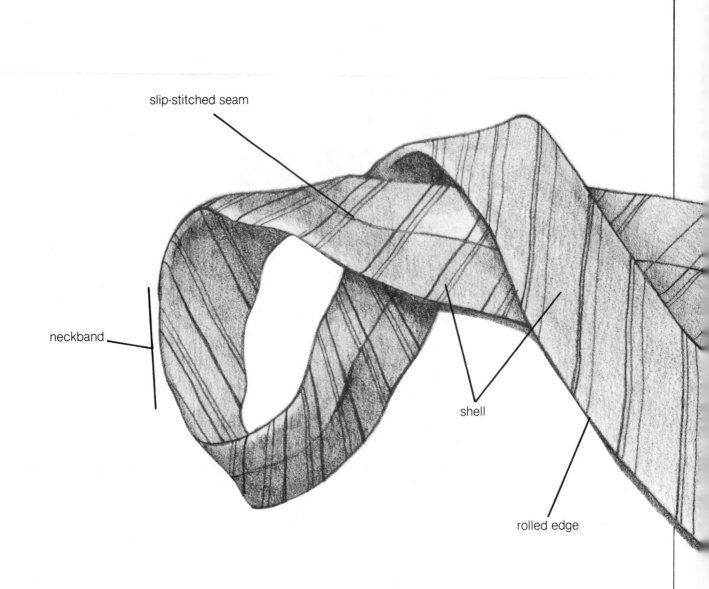

slip-stitched seam

neckband

shell

rolled edge

Necktie/Four-in-Hand

Bow Tie/Butterfly Tie

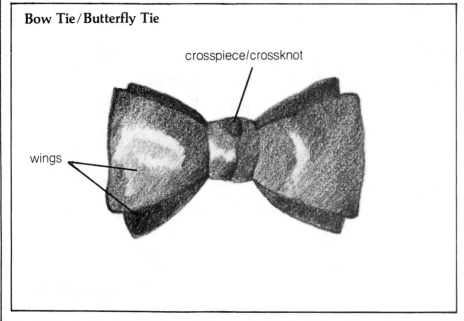

crosspiece/crossknot

wings

String Tie/Bolo Tie

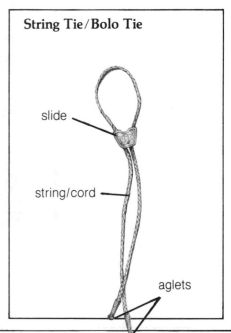

slide

string/cord

aglets

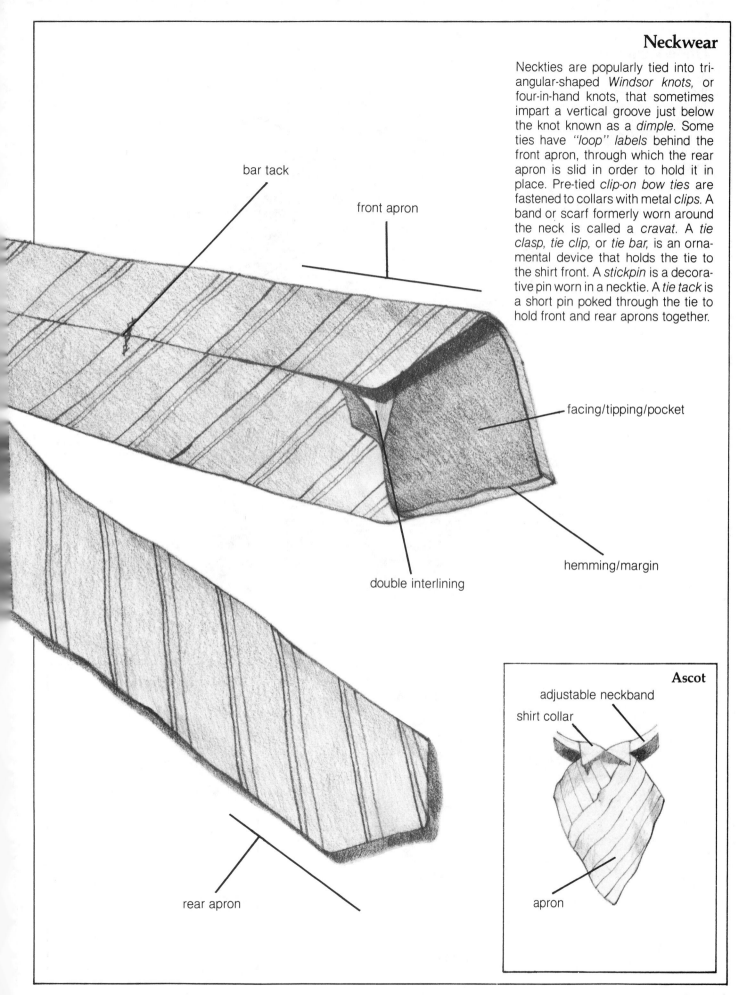

Neckwear

Neckties are popularly tied into tri-angular-shaped *Windsor knots*, or four-in-hand knots, that sometimes impart a vertical groove just below the knot known as a *dimple*. Some ties have *"loop" labels* behind the front apron, through which the rear apron is slid in order to hold it in place. Pre-tied *clip-on bow ties* are fastened to collars with metal *clips*. A band or scarf formerly worn around the neck is called a *cravat*. A *tie clasp*, *tie clip*, or *tie bar*, is an ornamental device that holds the tie to the shirt front. A *stickpin* is a decorative pin worn in a necktie. A *tie tack* is a short pin poked through the tie to hold front and rear aprons together.

bar tack

front apron

facing/tipping/pocket

hemming/margin

double interlining

rear apron

Ascot

adjustable neckband

shirt collar

apron

Underwear

A *T-shirt* has short sleeves rather than shoulder straps. Loose-fitting *boxer shorts* have short, trouserlike legs rather than leg openings. Some athletic supporters, or *jockstraps*, have pockets in the pouch to accommodate rubber-lined *protective cups*.

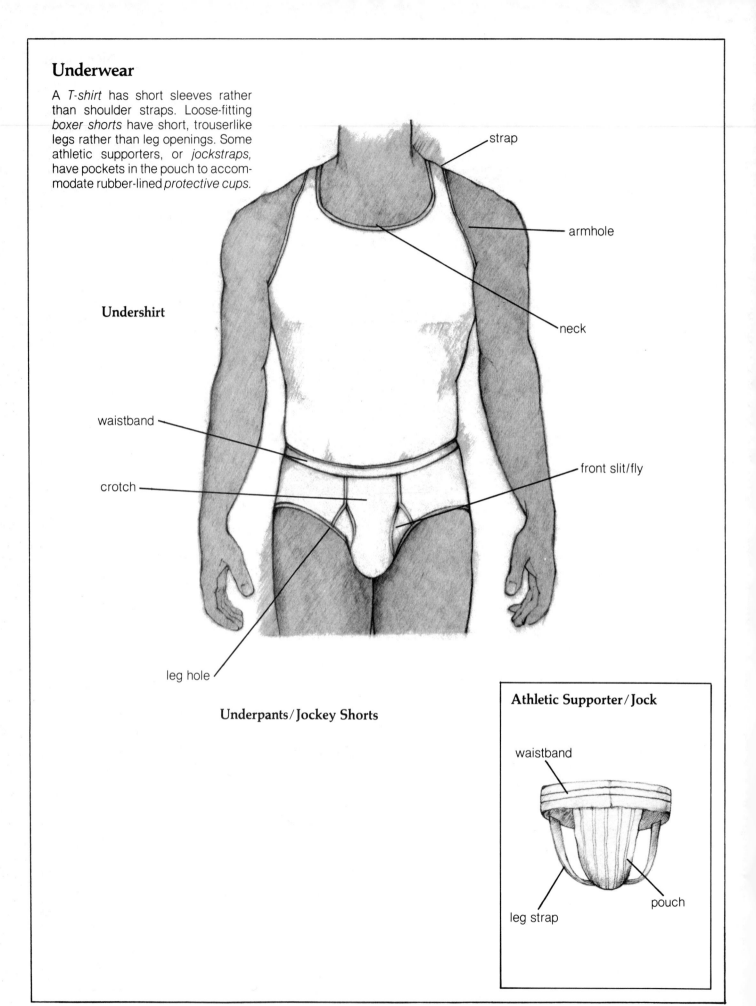

strap

armhole

neck

Undershirt

waistband

crotch

front slit/fly

leg hole

Underpants/Jockey Shorts

Athletic Supporter/Jock

waistband

pouch

leg strap

Foundation Garments

Most *bras* are secured with *hook-and-eye closures* either on a *back-strap* or in the front of the garment. Many have *underwiring* and/or *side-bones* for added support. *Cup padding* is another optional element. Girdles are sometimes stiffened with *spiral bones* or *stays*. *Corsets* are similar to girdles.

Brassiere

Girdle

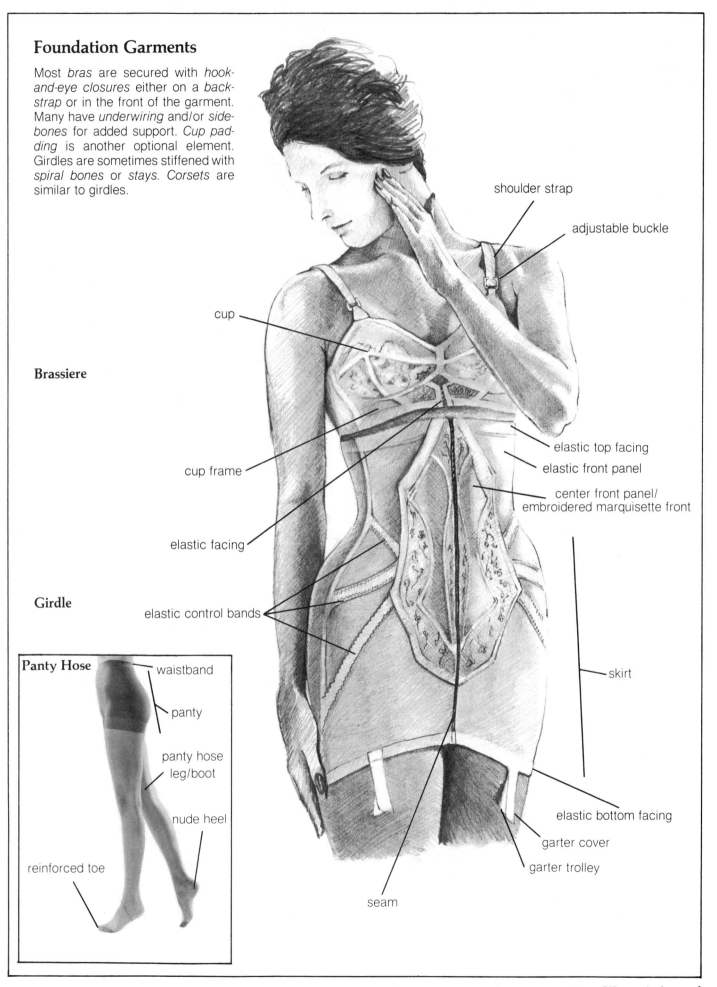

shoulder strap

adjustable buckle

cup

elastic top facing

elastic front panel

center front panel/
embroidered marquisette front

cup frame

elastic facing

elastic control bands

skirt

Panty Hose

waistband

panty

panty hose
leg/boot

nude heel

reinforced toe

elastic bottom facing

garter cover

garter trolley

seam

Jacket and Pants

Facing material is used on the underside of a lapel. *Lining* is used on the inside of a garment to cover up seamwork and provide body. A pair of lined pants has inside material from cuff to waist. In half-lined pants, the material stretches from waist to knee. In unlined garments, *seams* are clean finished with *bias tape,* or bias binding, sewn on a diagonal to provide stretch and support and to protect fabric from raveling.

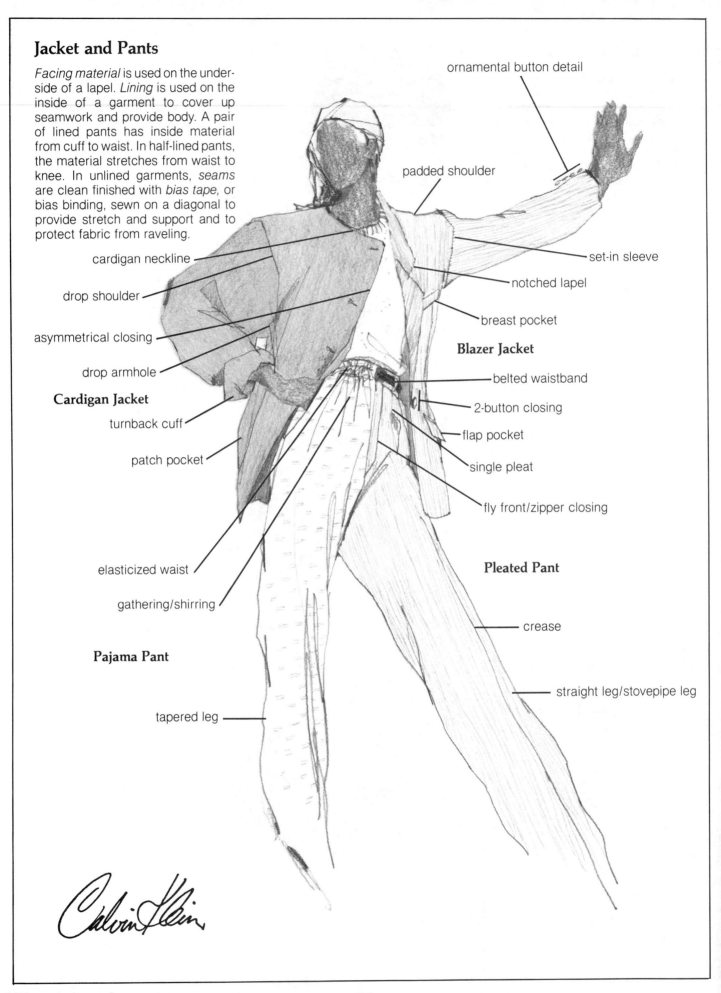

ornamental button detail

padded shoulder

set-in sleeve

cardigan neckline

notched lapel

drop shoulder

breast pocket

asymmetrical closing

Blazer Jacket

drop armhole

belted waistband

Cardigan Jacket

2-button closing

turnback cuff

flap pocket

patch pocket

single pleat

fly front/zipper closing

elasticized waist

Pleated Pant

gathering/shirring

Pajama Pant

crease

tapered leg

straight leg/stovepipe leg

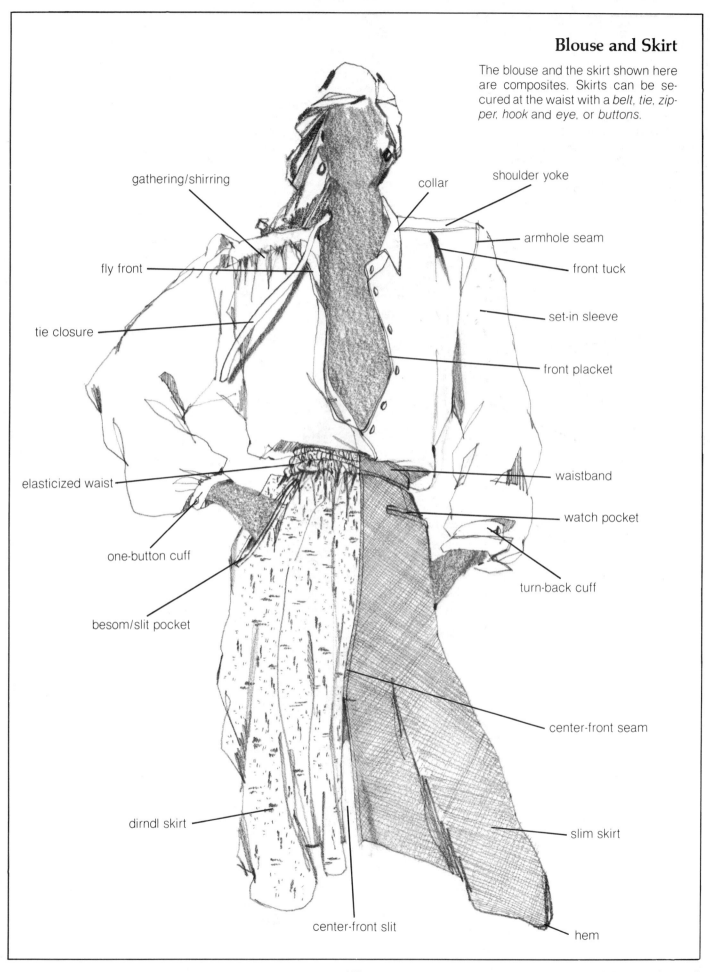

Blouse and Skirt

The blouse and the skirt shown here are composites. Skirts can be secured at the waist with a *belt, tie, zipper, hook* and *eye,* or *buttons.*

gathering/shirring

collar

shoulder yoke

armhole seam

fly front

front tuck

tie closure

set-in sleeve

front placket

elasticized waist

waistband

watch pocket

one-button cuff

turn-back cuff

besom/slit pocket

center-front seam

dirndl skirt

slim skirt

center-front slit

hem

Dress

This composite dress, or *gown*, has a *camisole top*. A dress hanging straight from the shoulders is a *chemise*. Some dresses have a fitted or shaped piece at the shoulder called a *yoke*. *Bratelles* are ornamental suspenderlike straps. Dresses are stored on hangers by means of *keepers*, *carriers*, *riders*, *loops* or *hangers*.

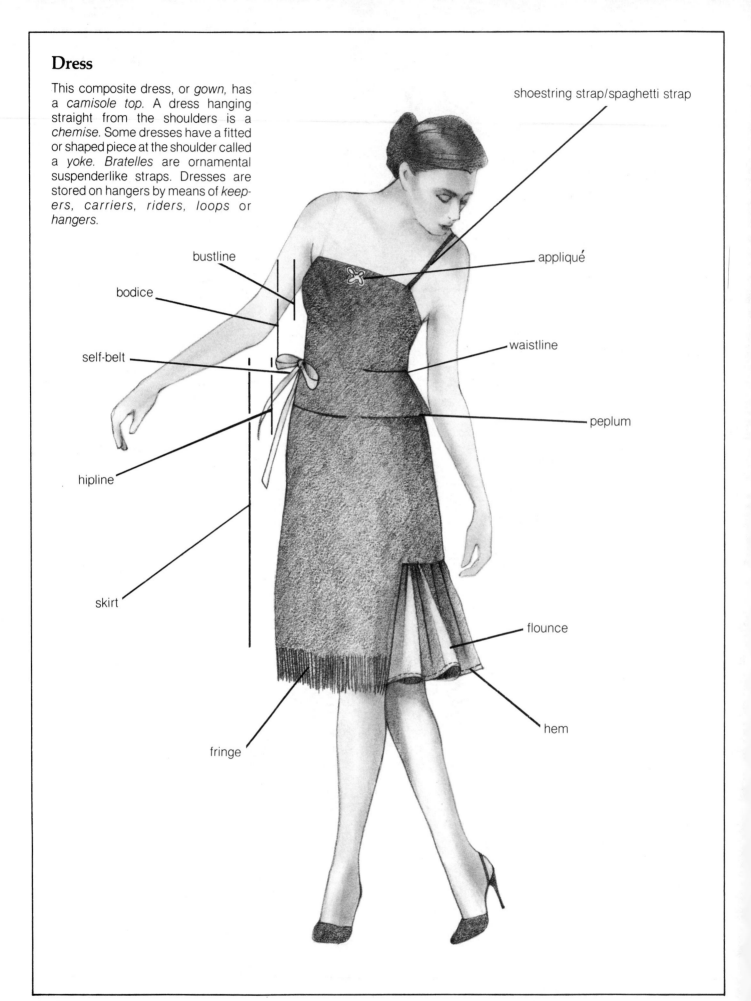

shoestring strap/spaghetti strap

bustline

bodice

appliqué

self-belt

waistline

peplum

hipline

skirt

flounce

hem

fringe

Sweater

A *crew neck sweater* is a pullover with a high, round neck. A *turtleneck* has a high neck that turns back over itself. A sweater with a neck opening that stretches from shoulder to shoulder is a *boat neck,* or *bateau neck.* A sweater without arms is a *vest,* or *knit vest.*

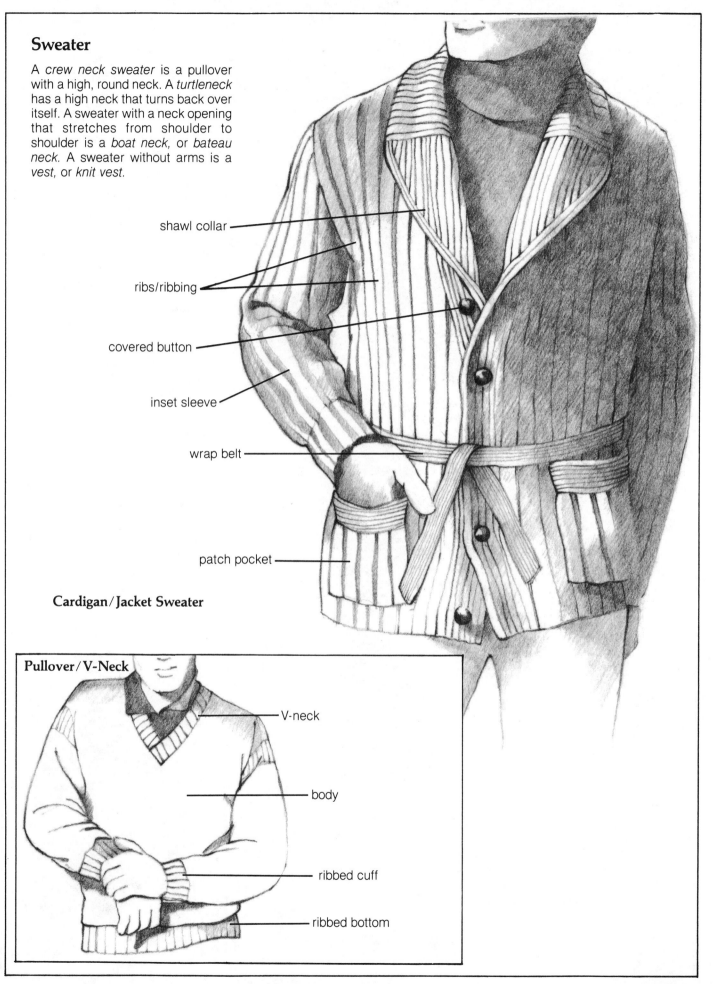

shawl collar

ribs/ribbing

covered button

inset sleeve

wrap belt

patch pocket

Cardigan/Jacket Sweater

Pullover/V-Neck

V-neck

body

ribbed cuff

ribbed bottom

Outerwear

The type of combination *overcoat* and *raincoat* shown here usually has a *button-out* or *zip-out robe lining* which provides warmth in cold weather. It also has a *storm shield* on the back, ornamental *'D' rings* hanging from the back of the belt and sometimes a *throat latch* strap around the collar.

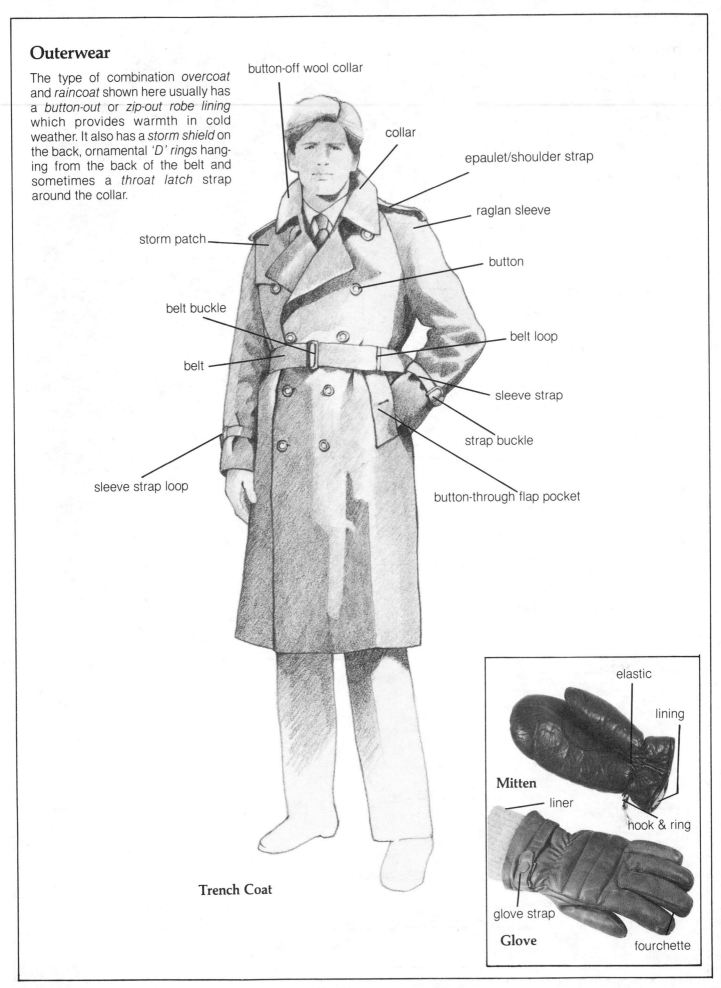

button-off wool collar

collar

epaulet/shoulder strap

raglan sleeve

storm patch

button

belt buckle

belt loop

belt

sleeve strap

strap buckle

sleeve strap loop

button-through flap pocket

Trench Coat

elastic

lining

Mitten

liner

hook & ring

glove strap

Glove

fourchette

Outerwear

Fur pelts used in apparel by *furriers* are first *dressed,* or cleaned, then fleshed, stretched and tanned. The furry parts of a pelt's facial hair are called *gills.*

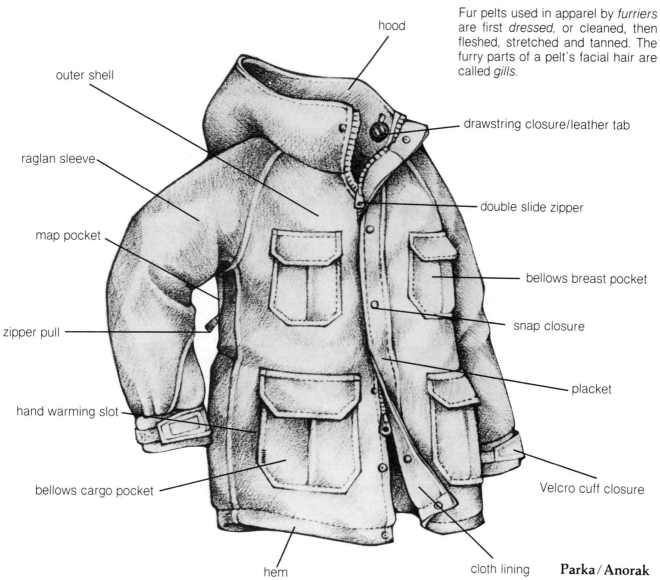

hood

outer shell

raglan sleeve

map pocket

zipper pull

hand warming slot

bellows cargo pocket

hem

drawstring closure/leather tab

double slide zipper

bellows breast pocket

snap closure

placket

Velcro cuff closure

cloth lining

Parka / Anorak

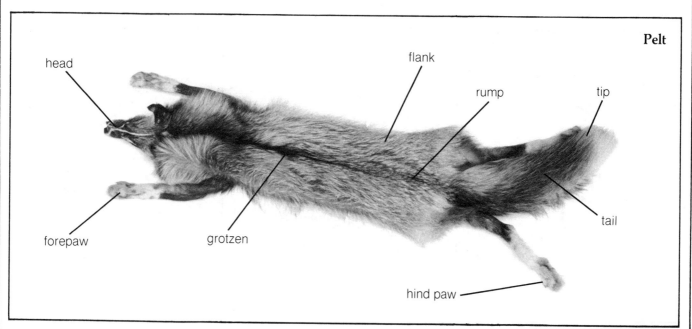

Pelt

head

flank

rump

tip

forepaw

grotzen

tail

hind paw

Unisex Clothing

Men's Hats

Hats are *styled*, or *blocked*, by a *hat-maker* or *hatter*. Hats that have not been creased have an *open crown*. Some hats have *plastic linings*.

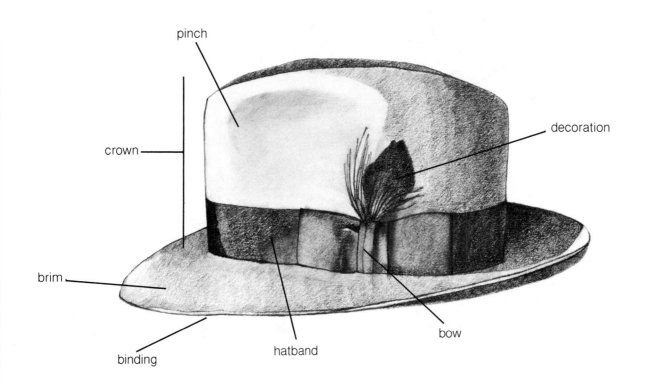

pinch

crown

brim

binding

hatband

bow

decoration

Cowboy Hat / Ten-Gallon Hat

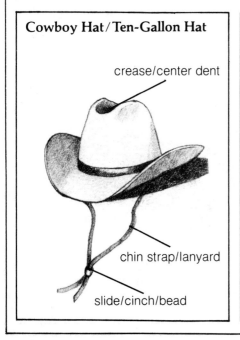

crease/center dent

chin strap/lanyard

slide/cinch/bead

Beret

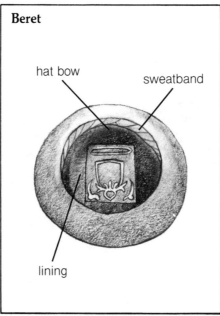

hat bow

sweatband

lining

Cap

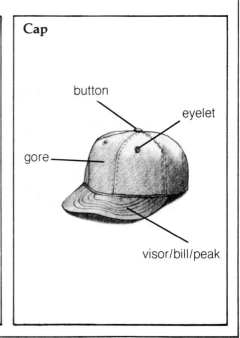

button

eyelet

gore

visor/bill/peak

Women's Hats

Women's hats are designed, made and sold by *milliners. Malines,* or stiff, fine *netting,* is often used as a veil. *Buckles, sequins, plastic fruit, fabric flowers, buttons, tassels* and *braids* are among the many items used as decorative *trimming.* Brimless, close-fitting hats include a *toque,* a *cloche,* and a *turban.* A *picture hat* has a broad flexible brim and is often decorated with trimming. A shallow, round hat with vertical sides is a *pillbox.* A netlike hat or part of a hat or the fabric that holds or covers the back of a woman's hair is a *snood.*

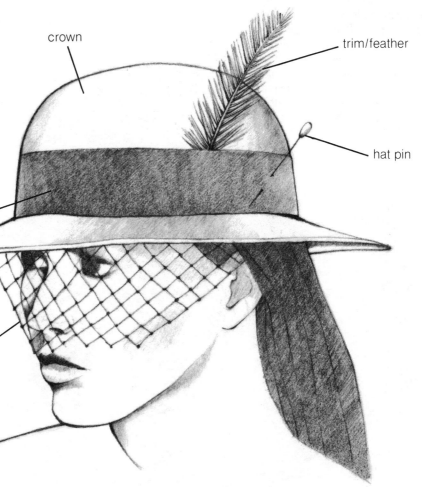

crown

trim/feather

hat pin

hatband

brim

veil

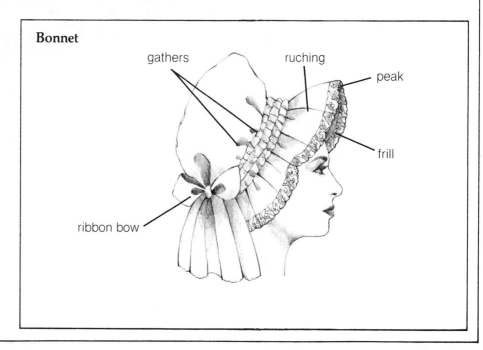

Bonnet

gathers

ruching

peak

frill

ribbon bow

Man's Shoe

A shoe consists of a *bottom,* or heel and sole, an *inner sole,* or *insole,* and an *upper.* Shoes like the one shown here, in which the flaps fold over the tongue or vamp, are *bluchers.* Shoes without this construction are *barrels.* A step-in shoe without laces is a *loafer,* whereas a *moccasin* has neither laces nor a heel. The fringed leather decoration on some shoes that covers the laces is the *kiltie.*

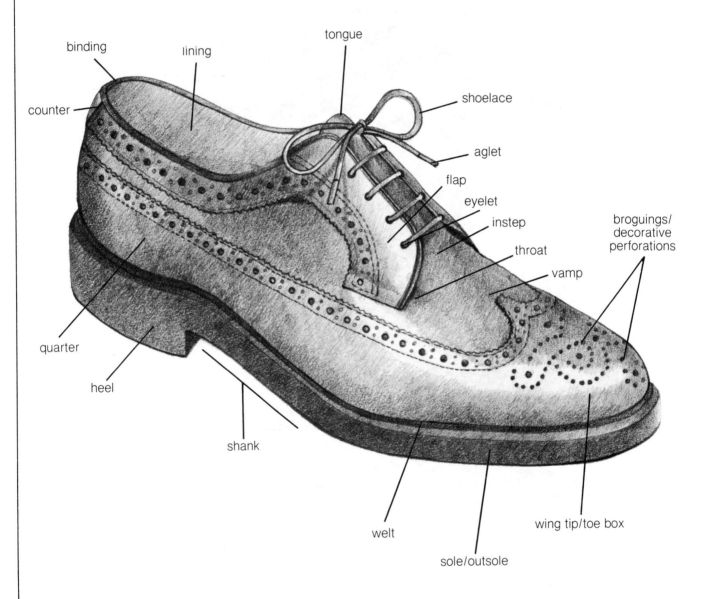

binding

lining

counter

tongue

shoelace

aglet

flap

eyelet

instep

throat

vamp

broguings/ decorative perforations

quarter

heel

shank

welt

sole/outsole

wing tip/toe box

Woman's Shoe

A shoe with an open front is an *open-toed shoe,* whereas a shoe with an open back, held on by a strap, is a *slingback,* or *sling shoe.* The *high-heel shoe* seen here is similar to a *pump* in that it grips both the toe and the heel. A high, thin heel is a *spiked,* or *stiletto, heel.* A shoe with a thick layer between the *inner sole* and the outsole is a *platform.*

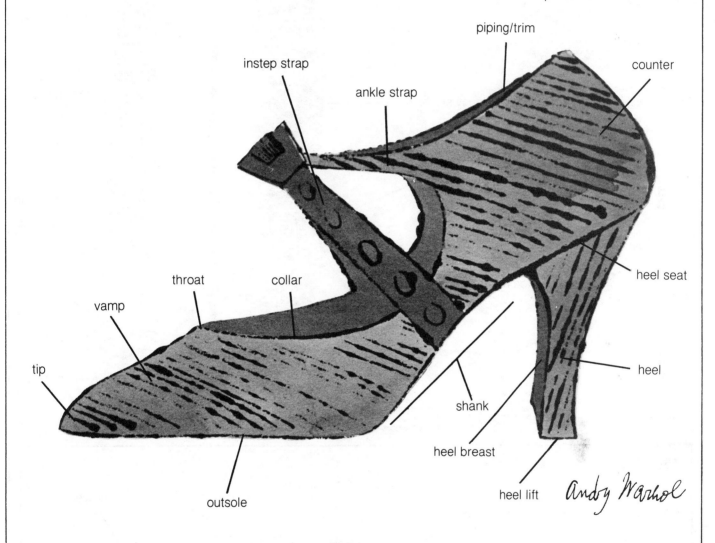

piping/trim

counter

instep strap

ankle strap

throat

collar

vamp

tip

heel seat

shank

heel

heel breast

outsole

heel lift

Andy Warhol

Footwear

Boot and Sandal

The upper section of a boot, called the *shaft*, may extend from ankle to knee. The lower section is called the *foot*. Many boots have a contoured steel *shank*, located between outsole and *insole*, to provide support for the arch area. A *thong* is a type of sandal in which the strap comes up between the big toe and the toe next to it.

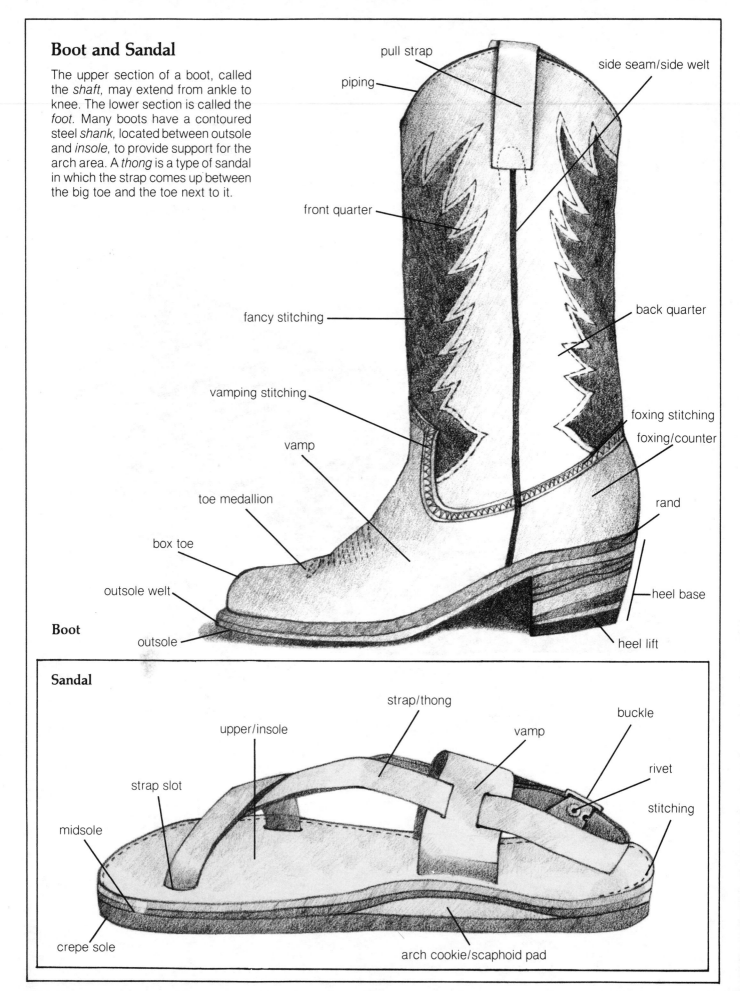

pull strap

piping

side seam/side welt

front quarter

back quarter

fancy stitching

foxing stitching

foxing/counter

vamping stitching

rand

vamp

toe medallion

box toe

heel base

outsole welt

heel lift

Boot

outsole

Sandal

strap/thong

buckle

upper/insole

vamp

strap slot

rivet

stitching

midsole

crepe sole

arch cookie/scaphoid pad

Shoe Accessories

Shoes can be protected in wet weather by *rubbers, rain boots* or *galoshes*. Socks, or *hose*, which extend to the ankle are *ankle socks*, whereas *knee socks* reach to the knee. *Support* hose have a higher *denier*, or mesh count, than regular hose, which provides additional support for the foot and leg. *Peds* are liners that cover the toes, sole and heel. *Boot hooks*, which fit into *boot loops*, help pull boots on, while V-shaped *bootjacks* hold the boot heel for easier removal. *Athletic socks*, or *sweat socks*, absorb perspiration. Shapeless *tube socks* mold to any foot shape.

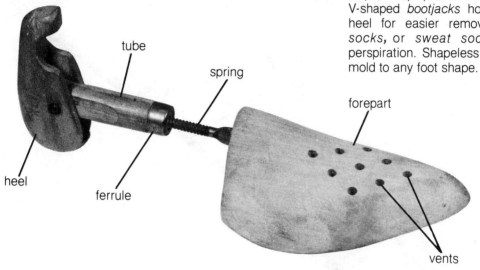

Shoe Tree

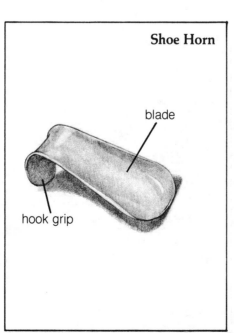

Shoe Horn

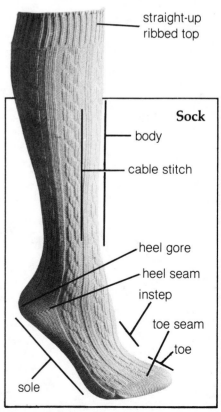

Sock

Fasteners

Heavy-duty hook-and-eye closures are called *hook and bars.* In a *cinch fastener*, a *strap* is pulled through two *rings* then back through the second ring to fasten. A *frog* consists of an intricately knotted *cord loop* through which a button is hooked.

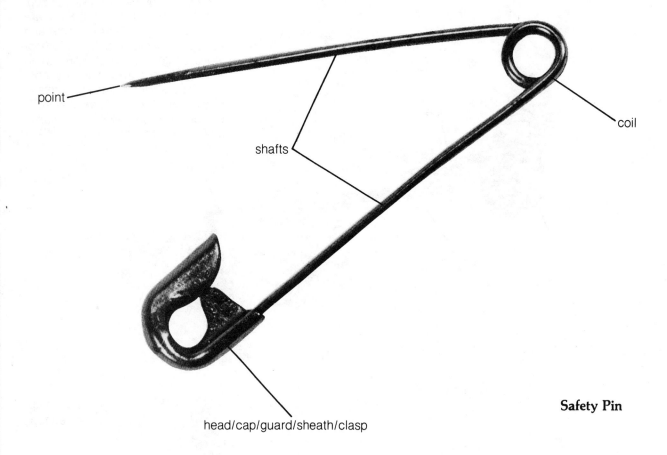

point

shafts

coil

Safety Pin

head/cap/guard/sheath/clasp

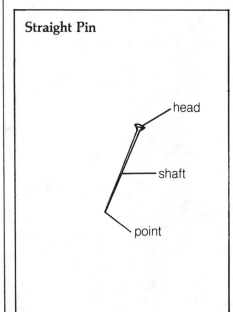

Straight Pin

head

shaft

point

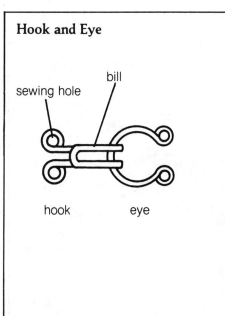

Hook and Eye

sewing hole

bill

hook   eye

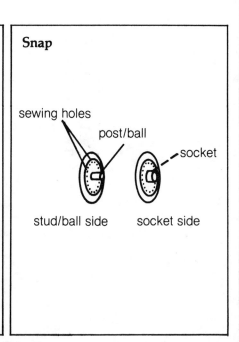

Snap

sewing holes

post/ball

socket

stud/ball side   socket side

Closures

A *divider* within the zipper slide separates teeth when it is moved downward. Some zippers have a *synthetic coil* rather than teeth. A *pull ring* is occasionally attached to the slide for decorative purposes. A *two-way zipper* can be opened from either end, while an *invisible zipper* is concealed when closed and appears to be a *seam*.

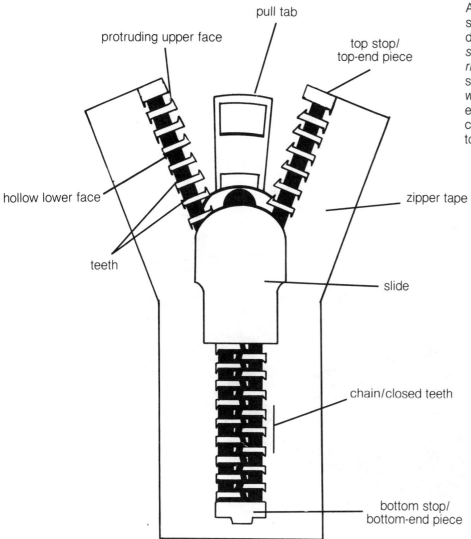

protruding upper face

pull tab

top stop/
top-end piece

hollow lower face

zipper tape

teeth

slide

chain/closed teeth

bottom stop/
bottom-end piece

Zipper/Slide Fastener

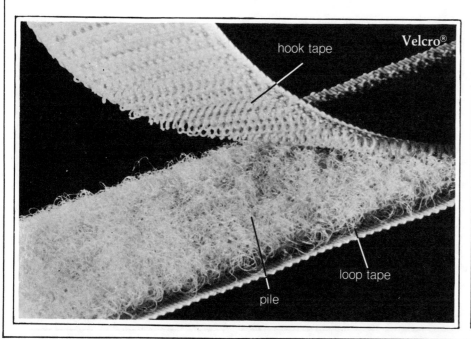

hook tape

Velcro®

loop tape

pile

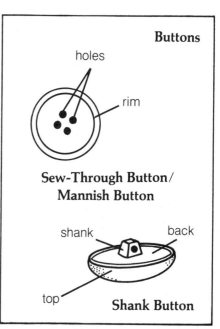

Buttons

holes

rim

**Sew-Through Button/
Mannish Button**

shank

back

top

Shank Button

Fasteners

Shavers

A *straight razor* has a single, long blade which folds into a *handle.* It is sharpened on a long strip of leather called a *strop.* Other, older barbering equipment includes *shaving brushes* and *shaving mugs.* A *safety razor* has two *wings* on the *head* which are opened by a screw at the base of the handle. Bleeding from shaving cuts or nicks can be stopped with a *styptic pencil.*

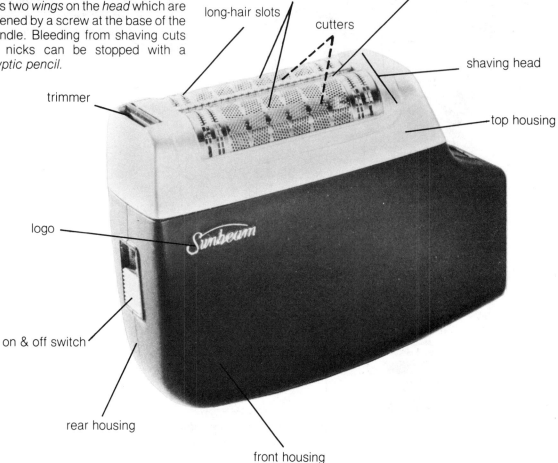

combs

tension bar

long-hair slots

cutters

shaving head

trimmer

top housing

logo

on & off switch

rear housing

front housing

Electric Razor

Razor Blade/Double-Edged Blade

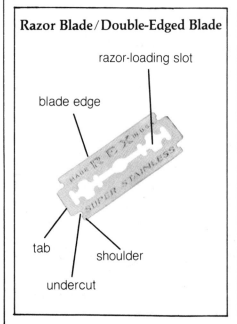

razor-loading slot

blade edge

tab

shoulder

undercut

Blade Injector

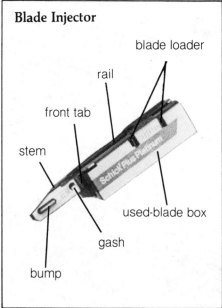

blade loader

rail

front tab

stem

used-blade box

gash

bump

Disposable Razor

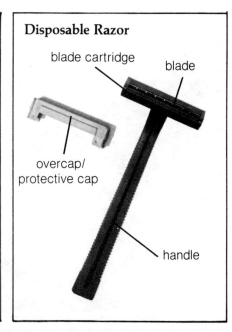

blade cartridge

blade

overcap/ protective cap

handle

Men's Hair

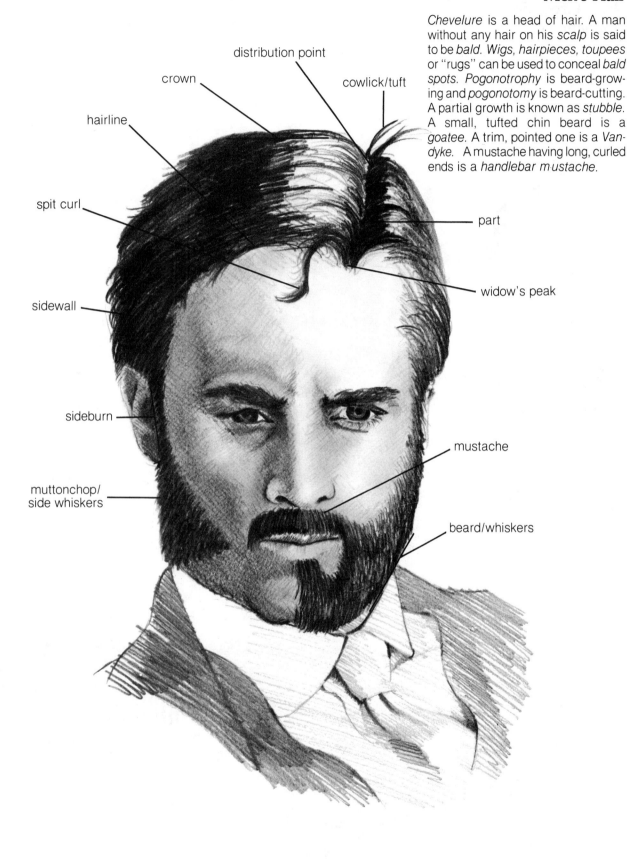

distribution point

crown

cowlick/tuft

hairline

Chevelure is a head of hair. A man without any hair on his *scalp* is said to be *bald*. *Wigs*, *hairpieces*, *toupees* or "rugs" can be used to conceal *bald spots*. *Pogonotrophy* is beard-growing and *pogonotomy* is beard-cutting. A partial growth is known as *stubble*. A small, tufted chin beard is a *goatee*. A trim, pointed one is a *Vandyke*. A mustache having long, curled ends is a *handlebar mustache*.

spit curl

part

sidewall

widow's peak

sideburn

muttonchop/
side whiskers

mustache

beard/whiskers

Hairstyles and Facial Hair

Hair Grooming Implements

Among other attachments available for use with a *pro-style dryer* are combs, brush and an *air-flow nozzle,* to limit the amount of hot air.

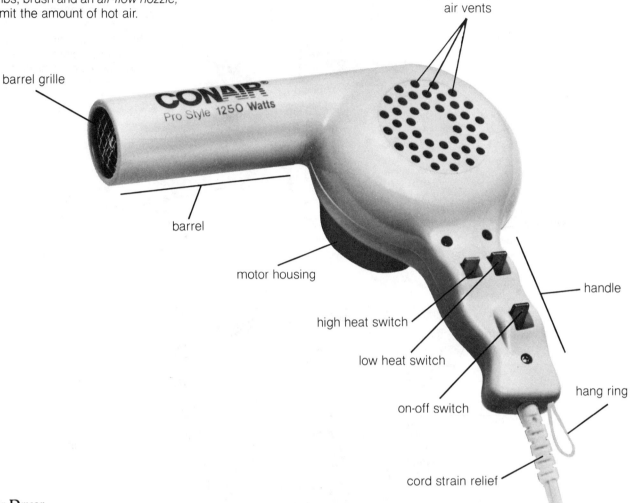

air vents

barrel grille

barrel

motor housing

high heat switch

low heat switch

on-off switch

handle

hang ring

cord strain relief

Hair Dryer

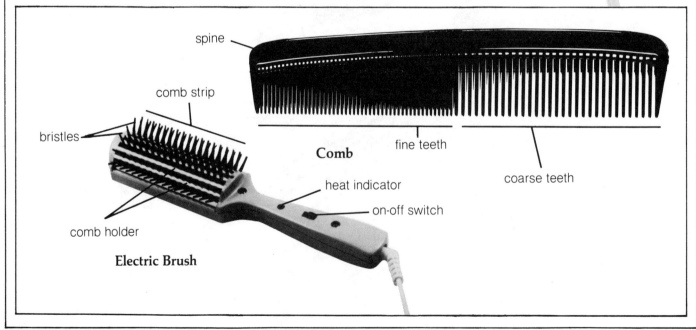

spine

comb strip

bristles

fine teeth

Comb

coarse teeth

heat indicator

on-off switch

comb holder

Electric Brush

Women's Hair

A small portion of hair in a woman's *hairdo,* or *coiffure,* is a *lock. Bouffant* is a puffed-out hairdo. *Teased,* or *back-combed, hair* is achieved by taking hold of a strand and pushing the short hairs toward the scalp with a comb. A braid on the back of the head is a *pigtail.* Hair that turns inward at the end, rather than outward, is a *pageboy.* A long piece of store-bought hair clipped to real hair is a *fall.*

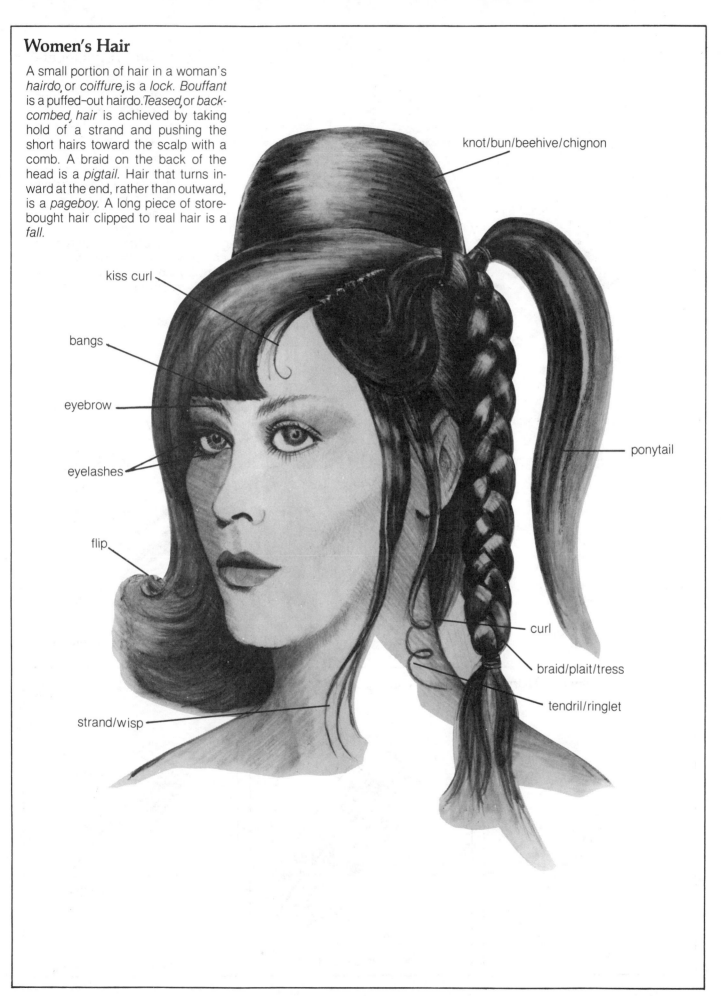

knot/bun/beehive/chignon

kiss curl

bangs

eyebrow

eyelashes

ponytail

flip

curl

braid/plait/tress

tendril/ringlet

strand/wisp

Hairstyles and Facial Hair

Hairstyling Implements

A curling iron is used to curl a *strand* of hair or to straighten it. Hair clips and bobby pins, which may be long or short, can be used to secure a roller while hair is being set. The roller shown here, however, is *self-clasping*. Barrettes, combs, *hair ribbons*, *headbands* and *hair bands* hold hair in place or serve as decorative *hair ornaments*. Professional *hairdressers* use *permanent rods* and *papers*, applicator bottles filled with *permanent lotion, setting lotion, rinse* or *dye*, plastic *caps, dryers* and *infrared lamps* to treat and style *hairdos*.

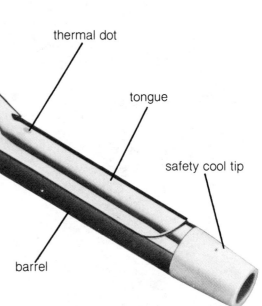

on-off switch

thumb press

power cord

strain relief

thermal dot

tongue

main housing

safety cool tip

stand

barrel

Curling Iron

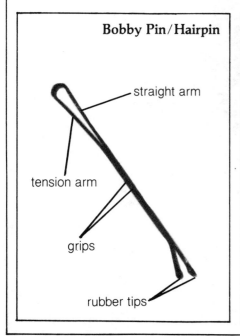

Bobby Pin/Hairpin

straight arm

tension arm

grips

rubber tips

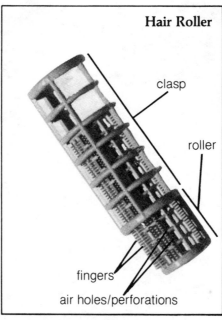

Hair Roller

clasp

roller

fingers

air holes/perforations

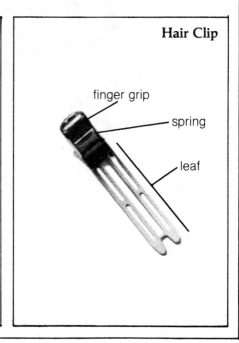

Hair Clip

finger grip

spring

leaf

Toothbrush

The stimulator tip on a toothbrush fits in what is called a *hang-up hole*. Teeth can also be cleaned with *dental floss*, a waxed string, and *high-pressure water-spray units.* Nails can be smoothed with an *emery board*, a cardboard strip covered with *powdered emery*, or a *nail file.*

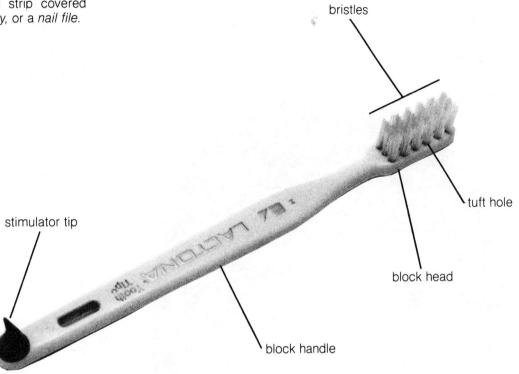

bristles

tuft hole

block head

stimulator tip

block handle

Toothbrush

Tweezers

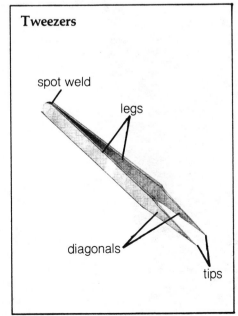

spot weld

legs

diagonals

tips

Nail Clippers

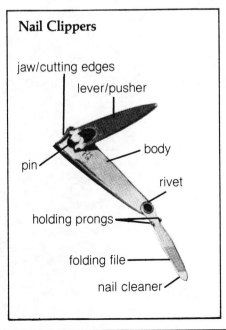

jaw/cutting edges

lever/pusher

body

pin

rivet

holding prongs

folding file

nail cleaner

Makeup

A skin-colored *concealer,* or *coverup,* can be used to cover blemishes or undesirable shadows under the eyes. *Pancake makeup* is a thick face powder used by actors and actresses as a foundation. Makeup can be removed with a *cleansing cream* or *cold cream.*

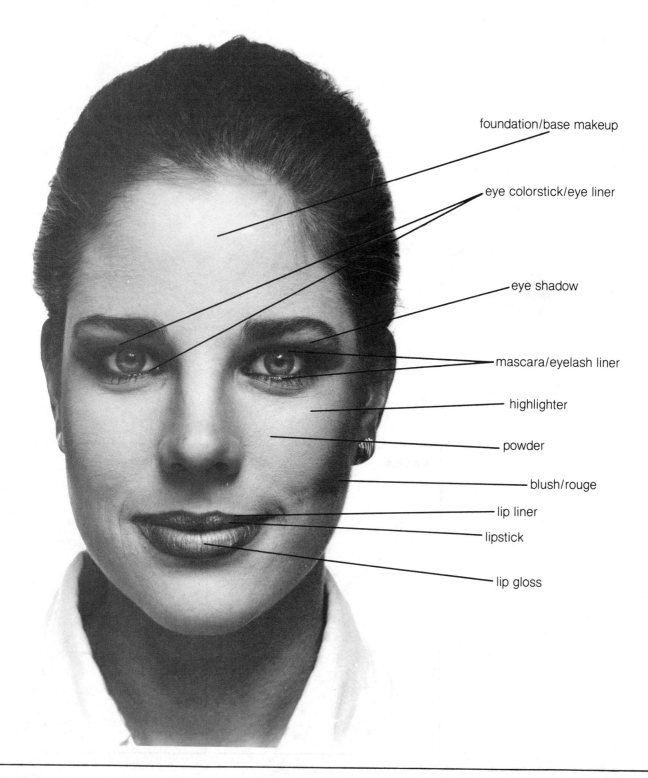

foundation/base makeup

eye colorstick/eye liner

eye shadow

mascara/eyelash liner

highlighter

powder

blush/rouge

lip liner

lipstick

lip gloss

Colored *nail polish* is often used to "paint" fingernails and toenails. In addition to those beauty products shown here, there are *scents,* such as *perfume,* applied by women to *pulse points; bath oils; body oils; moisturizers* and *lotions.* Men use *colognes* or *after-shave lotions.*

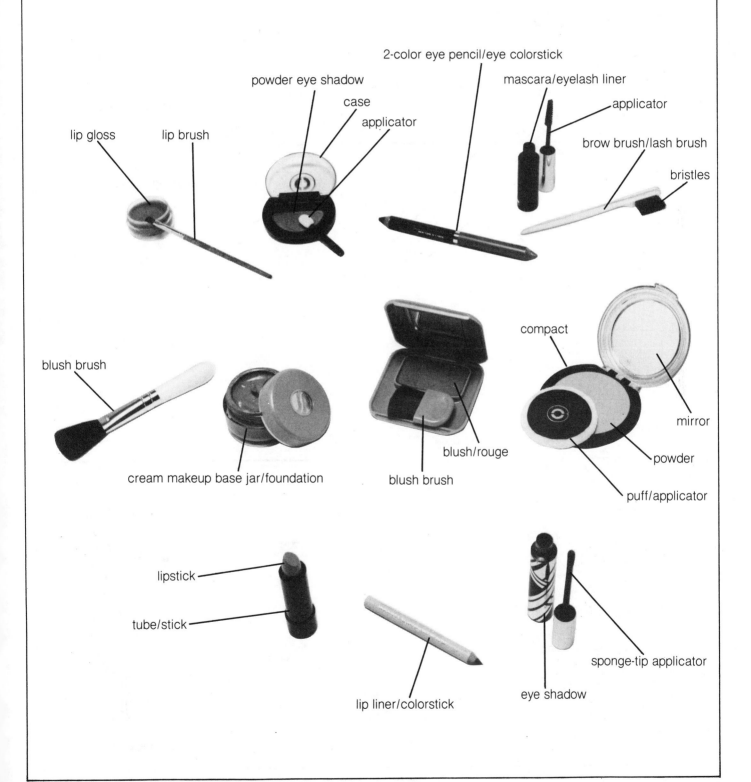

2-color eye pencil/eye colorstick

powder eye shadow

case

applicator

mascara/eyelash liner

applicator

brow brush/lash brush

bristles

lip gloss

lip brush

blush brush

compact

mirror

cream makeup base jar/foundation

blush/rouge

blush brush

powder

puff/applicator

lipstick

tube/stick

lip liner/colorstick

eye shadow

sponge-tip applicator

Gemstone

The shades of color a gemstone gives off are called *fire*. A matched set of jewelry, or *parure,* often includes a necklace, earrings and a *brooch.* A *cameo* is a gem on which a relief carving has been made. Non-precious *costume jewelry* is made to simulate its precious counterparts. The end of a *cuff link* that is passed through the buttonhole and fastened is called a *wing-back,* or *airplane-back.*

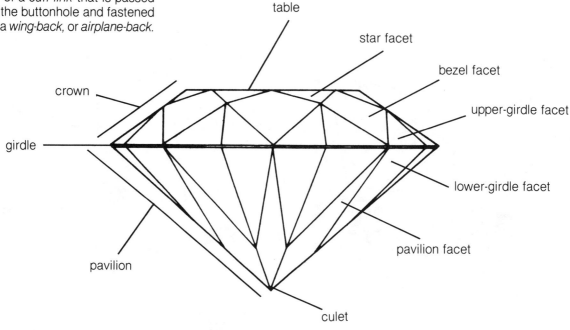

table
star facet
bezel facet
upper-girdle facet
crown
girdle
lower-girdle facet
pavilion facet
pavilion
culet

Cut Gemstone

Findings

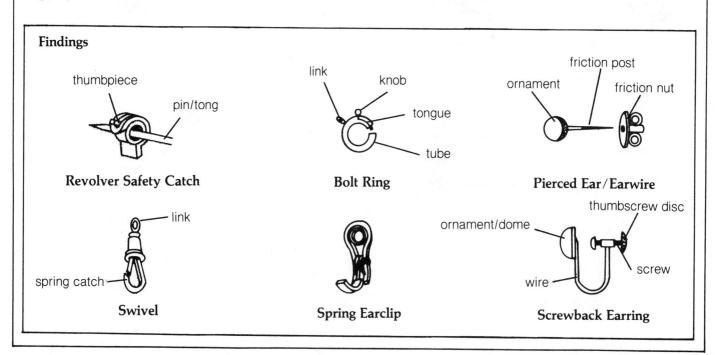

thumbpiece
pin/tong

Revolver Safety Catch

link
knob
tongue
tube

Bolt Ring

friction post
ornament
friction nut

Pierced Ear/Earwire

link
spring catch

Swivel

Spring Earclip

thumbscrew disc
ornament/dome
screw
wire

Screwback Earring

A *lavaliere* is a pendant worn on a chain as a necklace. A *charm* is a trinket worn on a bracelet or necklace, often having personal or symbolic meaning. An *ouch* is a brooch or a setting for a precious stone. *Spangles* are glittering pieces of metal used on clothing for decoration. A *riviere* is a multi-stringed necklace containing many precious stones.

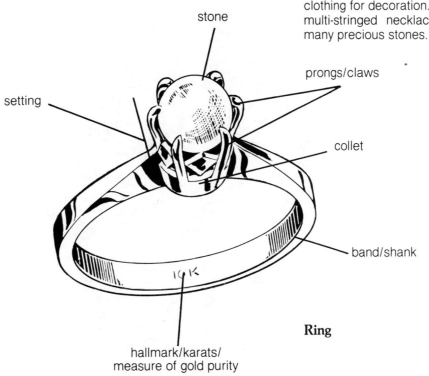

stone

prongs/claws

setting

collet

band/shank

hallmark/karats/
measure of gold purity

Ring

Pendant

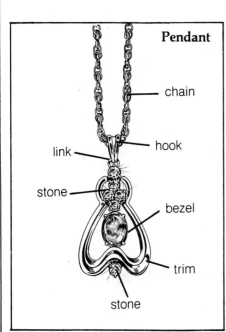

chain

link

hook

stone

bezel

stone

trim

Pieces

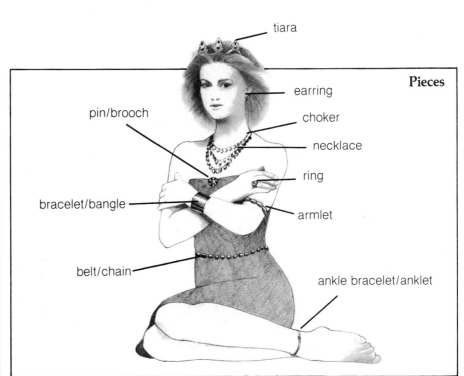

tiara

earring

pin/brooch

choker

necklace

ring

bracelet/bangle

armlet

belt/chain

ankle bracelet/anklet

Watches

The digital display on this watch can indicate date, seconds, time in a different time zone, and it can perform *stopwatch* functions. An extremely accurate timepiece is called a *chronometer*. A watchband, or *strap*, is attached to the case by *push-pins*, or *spring-bars*.

link

watchband/bracelet

zero mark

dial/face

case

minute hand

hour hand

protective shoulder

crown

Liquid Crystal Display (LCD)

LCD second time zone display control

LCD second and date display control

elapsed time bezel

luminous indices/markers

Wristwatch

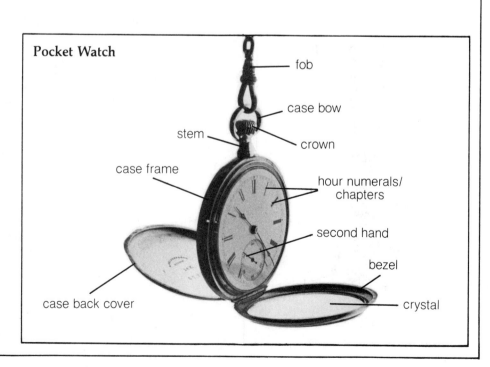

Pocket Watch

fob

case bow

stem

crown

case frame

hour numerals/chapters

second hand

bezel

case back cover

crystal

Eyeglasses

This is a composite pair of eyeglasses, or *spectacles*. The *frame* consists of a *front* and two temples. The front is formed by two *eyewires* which hold the lenses and are connected by a bridge.

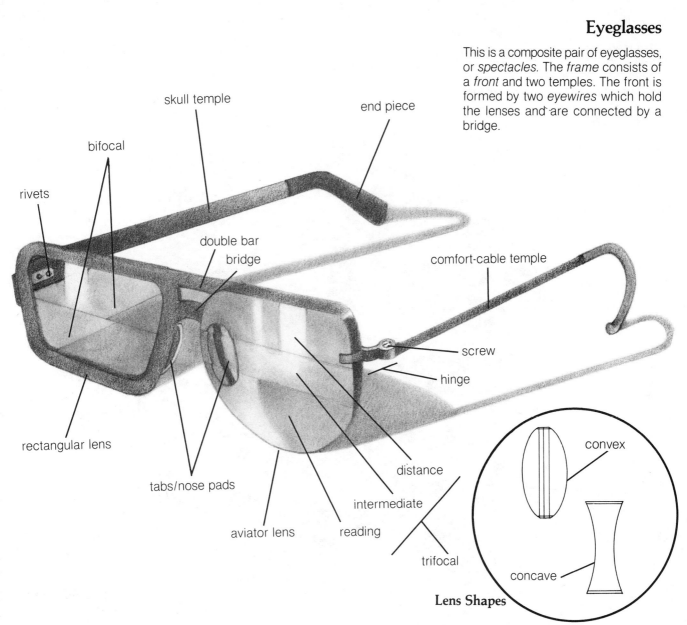

skull temple

end piece

bifocal

rivets

double bar

bridge

comfort-cable temple

screw

hinge

rectangular lens

tabs/nose pads

distance

aviator lens

reading

intermediate

trifocal

convex

concave

Lens Shapes

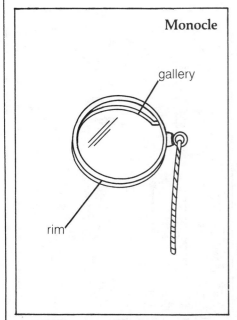

Monocle

gallery

rim

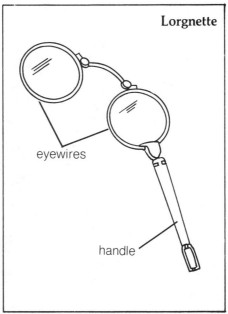

Lorgnette

eyewires

handle

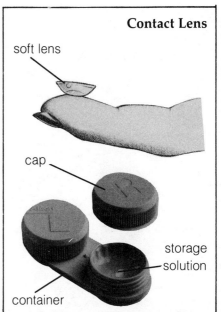

Contact Lens

soft lens

cap

storage
solution

container

Handbag

A handbag can also be referred to as a *pocketbook* or *purse*. A bag with no handles is a *clutch*. *East-west* describes a handbag which is wider than it is long. A *north-south* bag has a long, narrow shape. The metal ornaments and closures on bags are collectively called *hardware* or *fittings*.

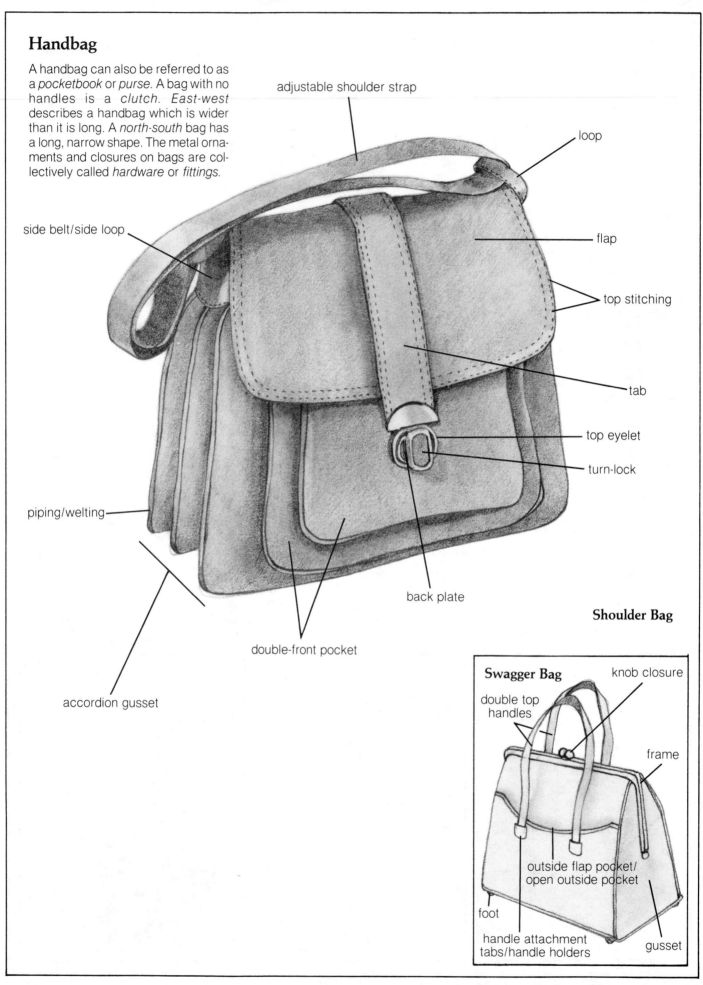

adjustable shoulder strap

loop

flap

top stitching

tab

top eyelet

turn-lock

back plate

double-front pocket

piping/welting

accordion gusset

side belt/side loop

Shoulder Bag

Swagger Bag

double top handles

knob closure

frame

outside flap pocket/ open outside pocket

foot

handle attachment tabs/handle holders

gusset

Wallet / Billfold

A wallet's exterior covering is called the *cover.* Women's wallets often have a *coin purse* within and a *tab closing* on the outside. *Photo holders* that unfold and become a long strip are called *accordion windows.*

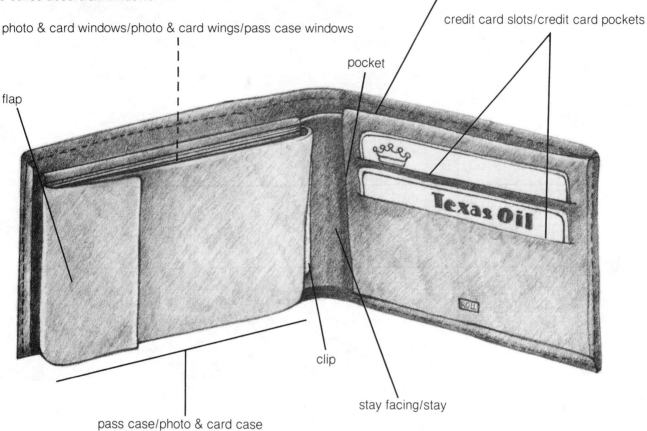

photo & card windows/photo & card wings/pass case windows

flap

bill compartment/currency pocket

credit card slots/credit card pockets

pocket

Texas Oil

pass case/photo & card case

clip

stay facing/stay

Checkbook Clutch

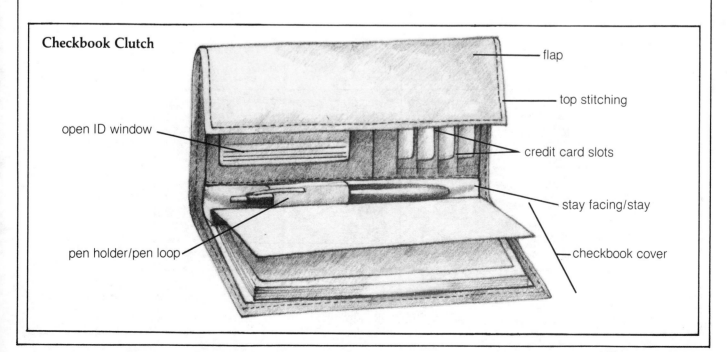

open ID window

flap

top stitching

credit card slots

stay facing/stay

pen holder/pen loop

checkbook cover

Money

United States paper currency in circulation today consists primarily of *Federal Reserve Notes* or "greenbacks" bearing a green seal, and a few *United States Notes* (mainly $100 bills) bearing a red seal. Other types of paper money, such as *Silver Certificates*, have been withdrawn from circulation. *Bills* are printed from *engraved plates* on paper containing colored *fibers*. Notes damaged during printing are replaced by *star notes*. Money printed illegally and passed off as *legal tender* is called *counterfeit money*.

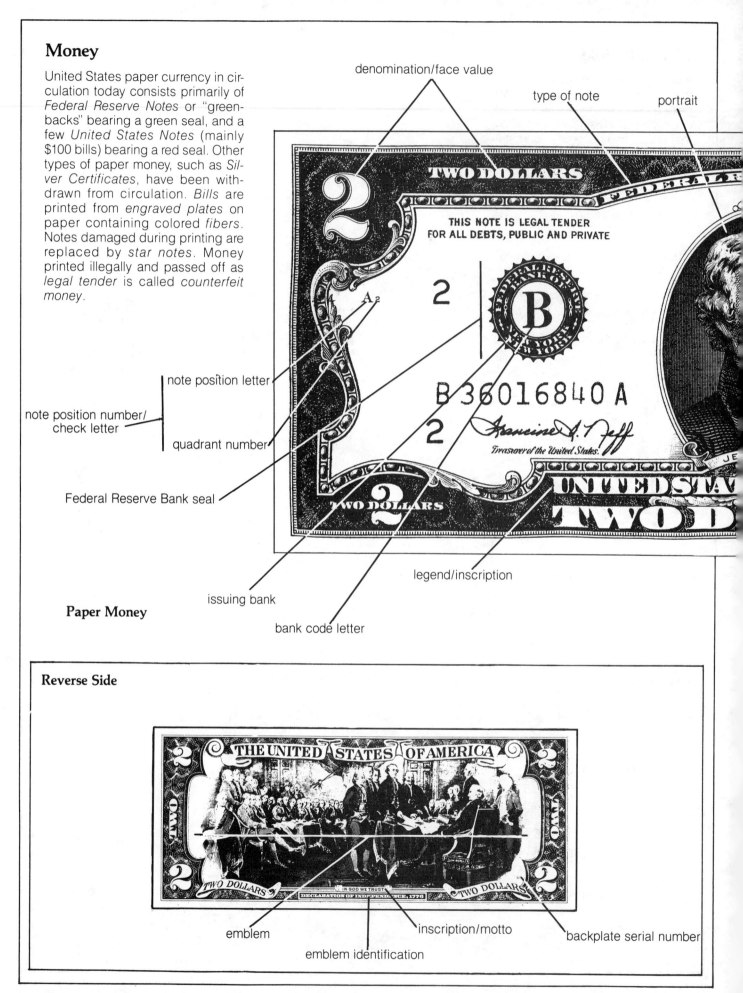

denomination/face value

type of note

portrait

TWO DOLLARS

THIS NOTE IS LEGAL TENDER
FOR ALL DEBTS, PUBLIC AND PRIVATE

A 2

note position letter

note position number/
check letter

quadrant number

Federal Reserve Bank seal

B 36016840 A

Francine I. Neff
Treasurer of the United States.

Paper Money

issuing bank

bank code letter

legend/inscription

Reverse Side

THE UNITED STATES OF AMERICA

IN GOD WE TRUST

DECLARATION OF INDEPENDENCE. 1776

TWO DOLLARS

TWO DOLLARS

emblem

emblem identification

inscription/motto

backplate serial number

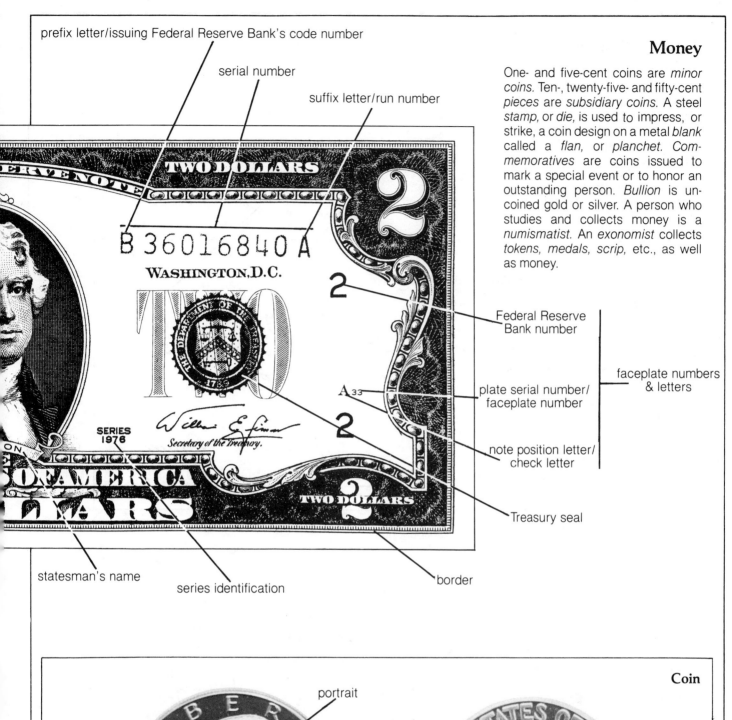

prefix letter/issuing Federal Reserve Bank's code number

serial number

suffix letter/run number

Money

One- and five-cent coins are *minor coins*. Ten-, twenty-five- and fifty-cent *pieces* are *subsidiary coins*. A steel *stamp*, or *die*, is used to impress, or strike, a coin design on a metal *blank* called a *flan*, or *planchet*. *Commemoratives* are coins issued to mark a special event or to honor an outstanding person. *Bullion* is un-coined gold or silver. A person who studies and collects money is a *numismatist*. An *exonomist* collects *tokens, medals, scrip*, etc., as well as money.

Federal Reserve Bank number

faceplate numbers & letters

plate serial number/ faceplate number

note position letter/ check letter

Treasury seal

statesman's name

series identification

border

portrait

inscription

field

mint mark

motto

symbolic date

reeding/milled edge/serrations

Obverse Side/"Heads"/"Face"

Coin

main device

motto

designer's initials

denomination/ face value

Reverse Side/"Tails"/Back

Wallet and Currency

Personal Banking

A check must be signed by the maker, and *endorsed* on the back by the payee to be valid. Banking at an automatic teller machine requires a bank card and a *Personal Identification Number*, or *PIN* number. *Cash machines* allow withdrawals and deposits to be made, while *banking centers* permit most banking functions to be performed.

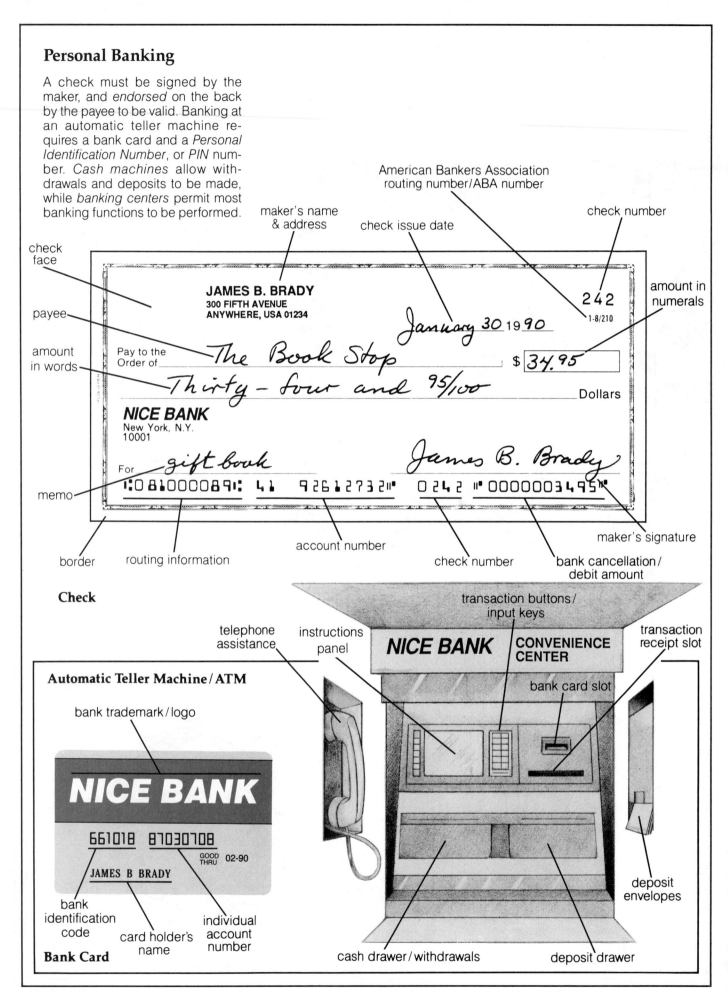

American Bankers Association routing number/ABA number

check issue date

check number

maker's name & address

check face

payee

amount in words

memo

border

routing information

account number

check number

amount in numerals

maker's signature

bank cancellation/ debit amount

JAMES B. BRADY
300 FIFTH AVENUE
ANYWHERE, USA 01234

January 30 19 90

242
1-8/210

Pay to the Order of The Book Stop $ 34.95

Thirty – four and 95/100   Dollars

NICE BANK
New York, N.Y.
10001

For gift book   James B. Brady

⑆081000089⑆ 41 926127321⑈ 0242 ⑈000000349 5⑈

Check

Automatic Teller Machine / ATM

bank trademark/logo

NICE BANK

661018 87030708

GOOD THRU 02-90

JAMES B BRADY

bank identification code

card holder's name

individual account number

Bank Card

telephone assistance

instructions panel

transaction buttons/ input keys

NICE BANK CONVENIENCE CENTER

transaction receipt slot

bank card slot

cash drawer/withdrawals

deposit drawer

deposit envelopes

Credit Card Account

Debts incurred on a *charge card* must be paid in full monthly, while only a minimum payment need be made on a credit card, although interest is charged on the balance. Holograms on the card front make card forgery more difficult. The *magnetic strip* on the back of a card contains the account number, expiration date, name, address, PIN number and service code.

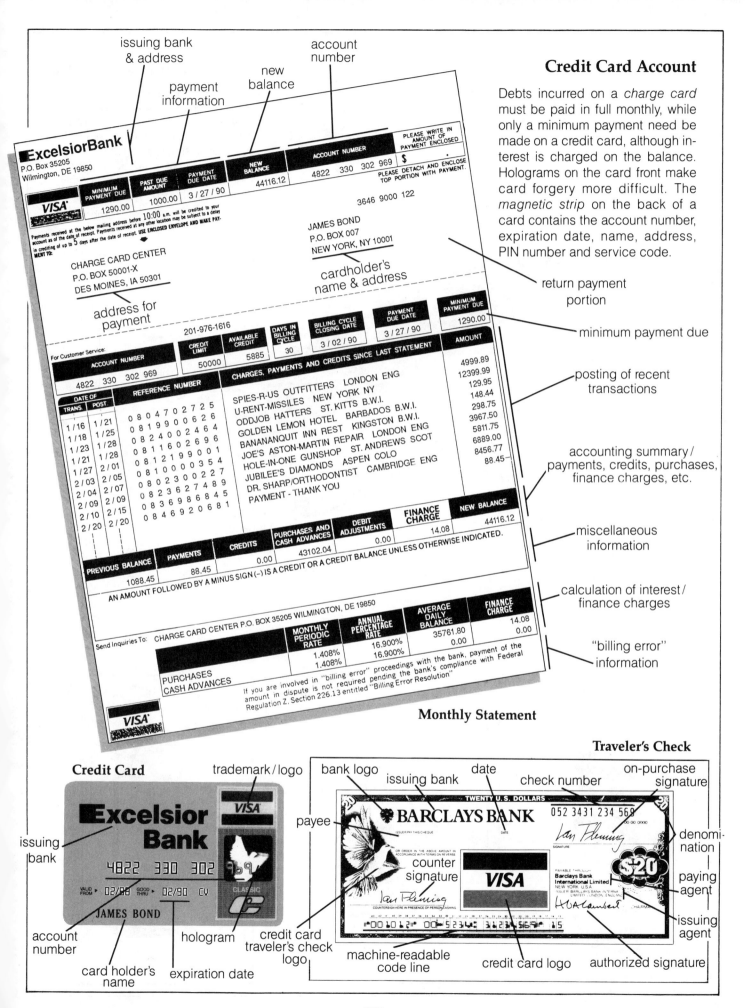

issuing bank & address

payment information

new balance

account number

ExcelsiorBank
P.O. Box 35205
Wilmington, DE 19850

VISA

Payments received at the below mailing address before 10:00 a.m. will be credited to your account as of the date of receipt. Payments received at any other location may be subject to a delay in crediting of up to 5 days after the date of receipt. USE ENCLOSED ENVELOPE AND MAKE PAYMENT TO:

CHARGE CARD CENTER
P.O. BOX 50001-X
DES MOINES, IA 50301

address for payment

PLEASE WRITE IN AMOUNT OF PAYMENT ENCLOSED		
NEW BALANCE	ACCOUNT NUMBER	$.
44116.12	4822 330 302 969	PLEASE DETACH AND ENCLOSE TOP PORTION WITH PAYMENT.

MINIMUM PAYMENT DUE	PAST DUE AMOUNT	PAYMENT DUE DATE
1290.00	1000.00	3/27/90

3646 9000 122

JAMES BOND
P.O. BOX 007
NEW YORK, NY 10001

cardholder's name & address

return payment portion

minimum payment due

201-976-1616

For Customer Service:	ACCOUNT NUMBER	CREDIT LIMIT	AVAILABLE CREDIT	DAYS IN BILLING CYCLE	BILLING CYCLE CLOSING DATE	PAYMENT DUE DATE	MINIMUM PAYMENT DUE
	4822 330 302 969	50000	5885	30	3/02/90	3/27/90	1290.00

DATE OF		REFERENCE NUMBER	CHARGES, PAYMENTS AND CREDITS SINCE LAST STATEMENT	AMOUNT
TRANS.	POST.			
1/16	1/21	0 8 0 4 7 0 2 7 2 5	SPIES-R-US OUTFITTERS LONDON ENG	4999.89
1/18	1/25	0 8 1 9 9 0 0 6 2 6	U-RENT-MISSILES NEW YORK NY	12399.99
1/23	1/28	0 8 2 4 0 0 2 4 6 4	ODDJOB HATTERS ST. KITTS B.W.I.	129.95
1/21	1/28	0 8 1 1 6 0 2 9 6 9	GOLDEN LEMON HOTEL BARBADOS B.W.I.	148.44
1/27	1/28	0 8 1 2 1 9 9 0 0 1	BANANANQUIT INN REST KINGSTON B.W.I.	298.75
2/03	2/01	0 8 1 0 0 0 0 3 5 4	JOE'S ASTON-MARTIN REPAIR LONDON ENG	3967.50
2/04	2/05	0 8 0 2 3 0 0 2 2 7	HOLE-IN-ONE GUNSHOP ST. ANDREWS SCOT	5811.75
2/09	2/07	0 8 2 3 6 2 7 4 8 9	JUBILEE'S DIAMONDS ASPEN COLO	6889.00
2/10	2/09	0 8 3 6 9 8 6 8 4 5	DR. SHARP/ORTHODONTIST CAMBRIDGE ENG	8456.77
2/20	2/15	0 8 4 6 9 2 0 6 8 1	PAYMENT - THANK YOU	88.45−
	2/20			

posting of recent transactions

accounting summary/ payments, credits, purchases, finance charges, etc.

PREVIOUS BALANCE	PAYMENTS	CREDITS	PURCHASES AND CASH ADVANCES	DEBIT ADJUSTMENTS	FINANCE CHARGE	NEW BALANCE
1088.45	88.45	0.00	43102.04	0.00	14.08	44116.12

AN AMOUNT FOLLOWED BY A MINUS SIGN (−) IS A CREDIT OR A CREDIT BALANCE UNLESS OTHERWISE INDICATED.

miscellaneous information

Send Inquiries To: CHARGE CARD CENTER P.O. BOX 35205 WILMINGTON, DE 19850

	MONTHLY PERIODIC RATE	ANNUAL PERCENTAGE RATE	AVERAGE DAILY BALANCE	FINANCE CHARGE
PURCHASES	1.408%	16.900%	35761.80	14.08
CASH ADVANCES	1.408%	16.900%	0.00	0.00

calculation of interest/ finance charges

If you are involved in "billing error" proceedings with the bank, payment of the amount in dispute is not required pending the bank's compliance with Federal Regulation Z, Section 226.13 entitled "Billing Error Resolution"

"billing error" information

VISA

Monthly Statement

Credit Card

trademark/logo

Excelsior Bank

VISA

CLASSIC

issuing bank

4822 330 302 969

VALID FROM ▶ 02/88 GOOD THRU ▶ 02/90 CV

JAMES BOND

account number

card holder's name

hologram

expiration date

Traveler's Check

bank logo

issuing bank

date

check number

on-purchase signature

payee

TWENTY U.S. DOLLARS

BARCLAYS BANK

ISSUER PAY THIS CHEQUE

OR ORDER IN THE ABOVE AMOUNT IN ACCORDANCE WITH TERMS ON REVERSE

052 3431 234 569

00.00 DOLLARS

SIGNATURE

Ian Fleming

counter signature

Ian Fleming

COUNTERSIGN HERE IN PRESENCE OF PERSON CASHING

VISA

PAYABLE THROUGH
Barclays Bank
International Limited
NEW YORK U.S.A.
ISSUER BARCLAYS BANK INTERNATIONAL
LIMITED, LONDON, ENGLAND

$20

HDALambert

CHAIRMAN

denomination

paying agent

issuing agent

credit card traveler's check logo

machine-readable code line

⑈00 ᴸ0 ᴸ2ⅉ⑈ 00⑊5234⑈ 3ᴸ234 5ᴸ5ⅉ⑈ ᴸ5

credit card logo

authorized signature

Cigar and Cigarette

The cigar wrapper, as well as the interior *binder*, is a spirally-rolled *leaf*. Cigars, or *"stogies,"* are stored in *humidors* to insure freshness. The residue of smoked tobacco is *ash*. The remains of a smoked cigar or cigarette is the *butt*. The abrasive striking surface or *friction strip* on which matches are struck is on the *back cover* of a matchbook.

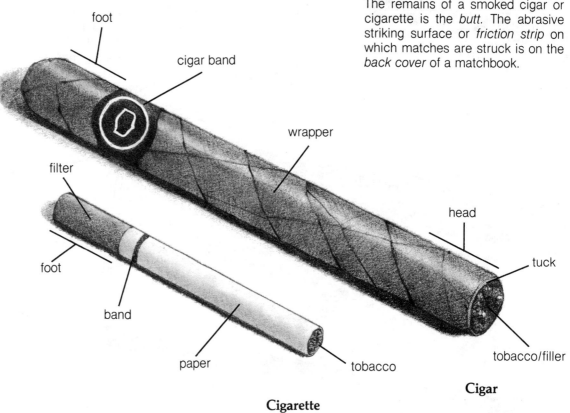

foot

cigar band

wrapper

head

tuck

tobacco/filler

Cigar

filter

foot

band

paper

tobacco

Cigarette

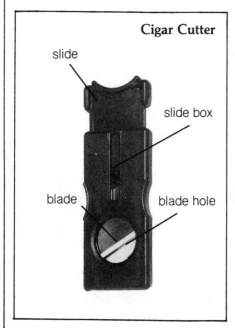

Cigar Cutter

slide

slide box

blade

blade hole

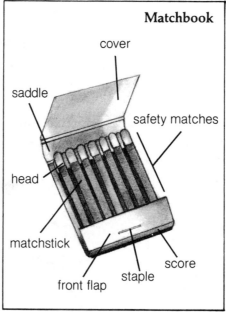

Matchbook

cover

saddle

safety matches

head

matchstick

front flap

staple

score

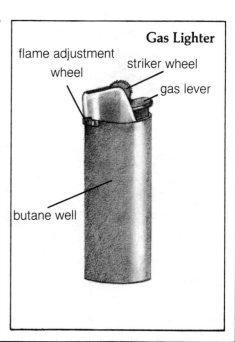

Gas Lighter

flame adjustment wheel

striker wheel

gas lever

butane well

Pipe

Pipe smoke is also called *lunt,* and un-smoked tobacco in the bottom of the bowl after smoking is called *dottle.* The pliable, tufted rod used to clean the inside of a pipe's stem is a *pipe cleaner.* Pipe tobacco is kept in a *pouch.* Some bowls are covered with a *pipe umbrella* or *bowl lid.* An Eastern pipe with a long, flexible tube by which the smoke is drawn through a jar of water and thus cooled is a *water pipe, hookah,* or *hubble-bubble.*

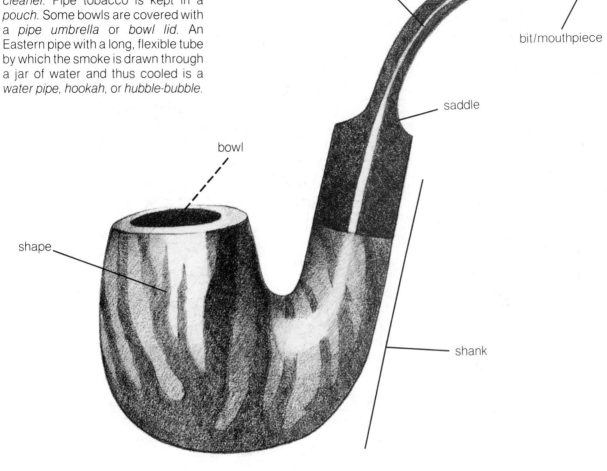

stem

bit/mouthpiece

saddle

bowl

shape

shank

Pipe Tool

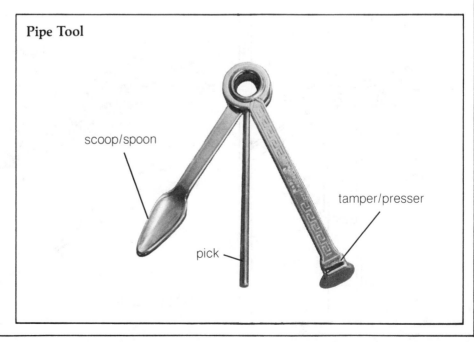

scoop/spoon

pick

tamper/presser

Smoking Materials

Umbrella

An umbrella's water-repellent *fabric* is attached to a *frame,* or *skeleton.* The specific points where the fabric is sewn to the skeleton are called *tacks.*

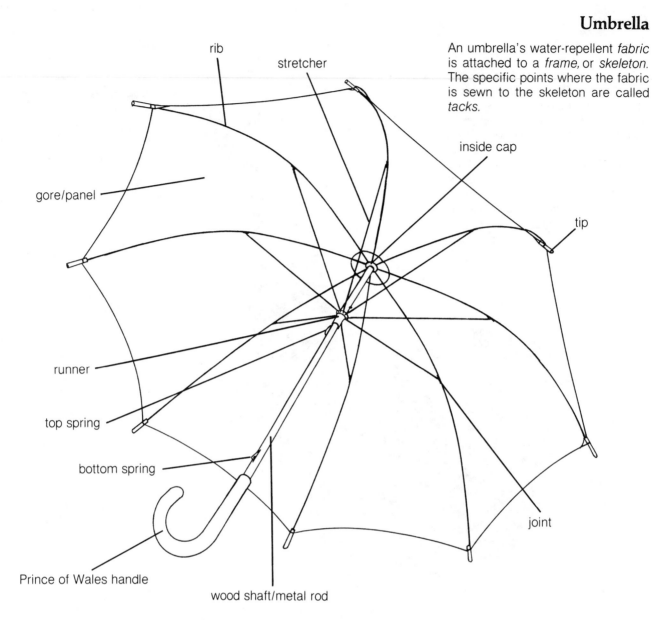

rib

stretcher

inside cap

gore/panel

tip

runner

top spring

bottom spring

joint

Prince of Wales handle

wood shaft/metal rod

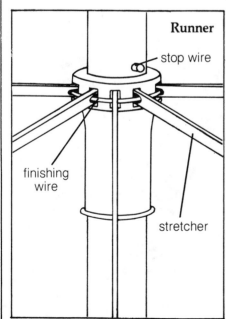

Runner

stop wire

finishing wire

stretcher

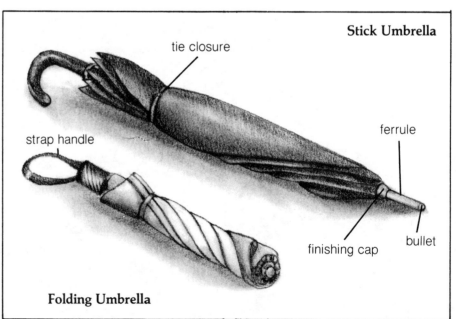

Stick Umbrella

tie closure

strap handle

ferrule

finishing cap

bullet

Folding Umbrella

The Home

To facilitate locating items found in the home, the objects in this section have been grouped according to where they are most likely to be encountered: living room, dining room, kitchen, bedroom, bathroom, playroom, utility room or yard.

The kitchen subsection, for example, includes implements for preparing food as well as appliances that make food preparation easier. In addition to identifying the parts of containers used to bring groceries into the kitchen, coverage includes all the terms used in the designing and packaging of food and kitchenware. Knowing the names for these components will surely change how the reader views his or her cereal box at the breakfast table in the future.

The terms for details of desk equipment, found in the playroom/utility room subsection, apply as well to office furnishings. The seven parts of a paper clip, for example, are valid wherever this unique little device is used.

Although a nursery is not included as a subsection, objects used for or by children—stroller, car seat, playpen, and swings—have been incorporated in the subcategory of yard equipment.

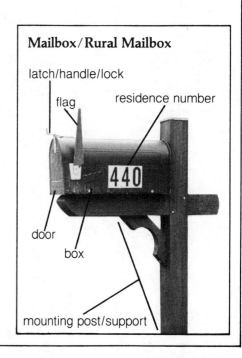

Mailbox/Rural Mailbox

latch/handle/lock

flag

residence number

door

box

mounting post/support

Fireplace

Many fireplaces have glass and metal *fire screens* to prevent heat loss and to keep sparks from flying into the room. Others have a low metal *fender* between the inner and outer hearth. A metal cover, used to shield a banked or dying fire, is called a *curfew*. Fireplace accessories include air-blowing *bellows*, *coal hods* and *wood carriers*, and *grates* or *heat exchangers* which can be used instead of andirons. A *firebrand* is a piece of burning wood.

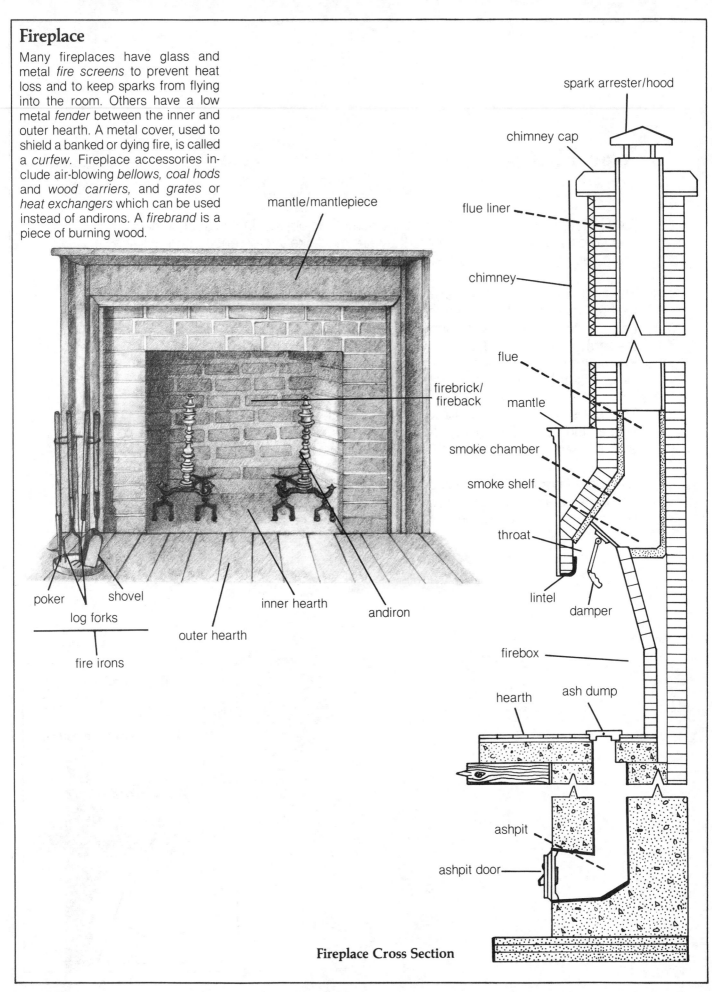

mantle/mantlepiece

firebrick/ fireback

poker

shovel

log forks

fire irons

inner hearth

outer hearth

andiron

spark arrester/hood

chimney cap

flue liner

chimney

flue

mantle

smoke chamber

smoke shelf

throat

lintel

damper

firebox

hearth

ash dump

ashpit

ashpit door

Fireplace Cross Section

Clock

A *pendulum clock* tall enough to stand on the floor, either a grandfather or the shorter *grandmother clock,* is called a *tall-case clock.* The machinery or *movement* within is called the *clockworks.* A *rating,* the length of a pendulum swing, can be adjusted by a *rating nut,* usually found beneath the bob.

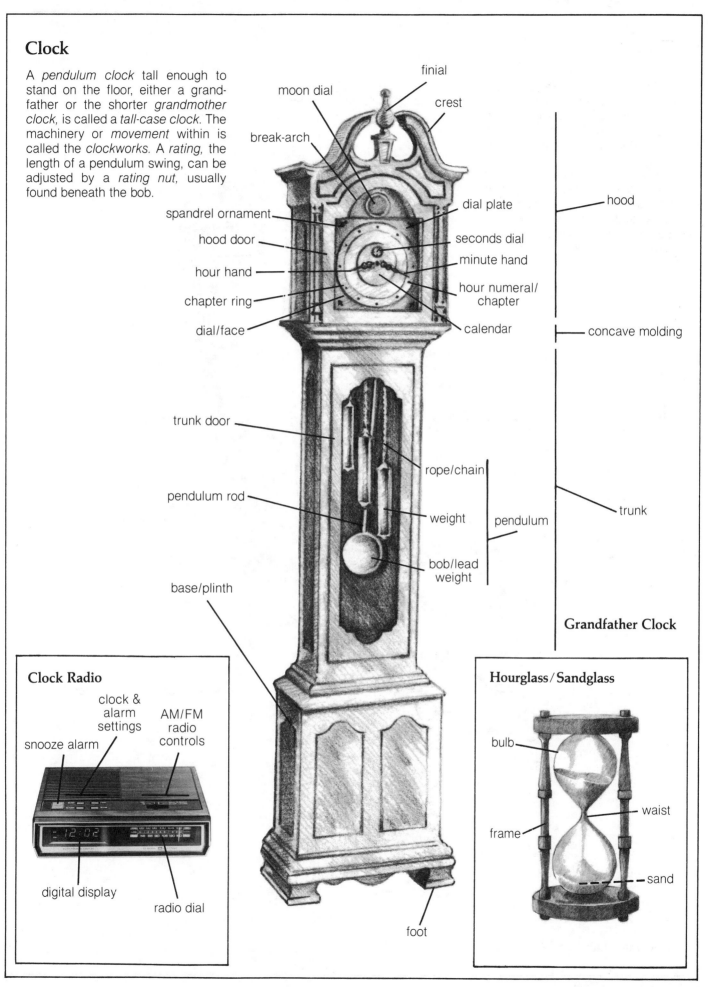

finial

moon dial

crest

break-arch

dial plate

spandrel ornament

seconds dial

hood door

minute hand

hour hand

hour numeral/chapter

chapter ring

dial/face

calendar

hood

concave molding

trunk door

rope/chain

pendulum rod

weight

pendulum

trunk

bob/lead weight

base/plinth

Grandfather Clock

foot

Clock Radio

clock & alarm settings

AM/FM radio controls

snooze alarm

digital display

radio dial

Hourglass/Sandglass

bulb

waist

frame

sand

Chair

A single broad center upright used in place of spindles in a seat back is called a *splat*. Horizontal members across the seat back are called *slats*, or *crosspieces*. *Braces* are two spindles that form a "V" at the back of a chair seat. The crest of a chair may have a shape called a *handgrip, roll top* or *pillow*. A *slip seat* is a seat that is fitted into a molding and can be removed and covered with fabric, then replaced. An extended arm with a flat surface is called a *writing arm*.

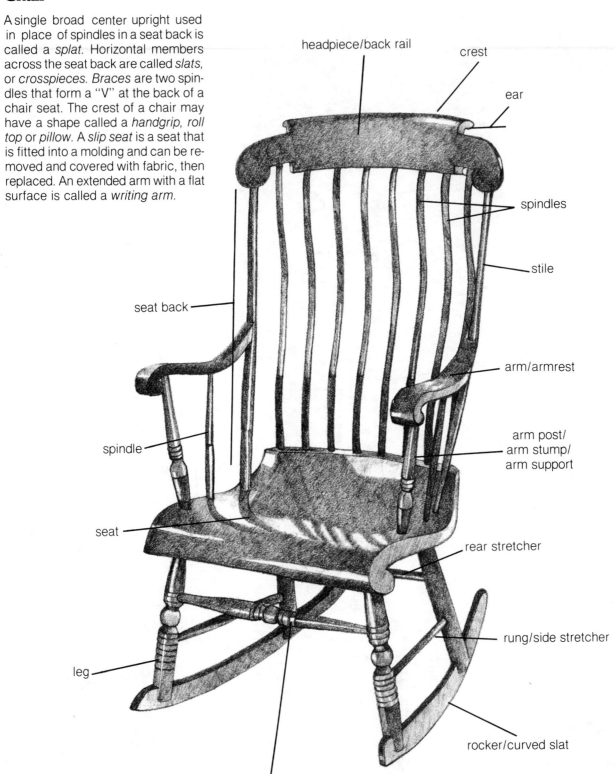

headpiece/back rail

crest

ear

spindles

stile

seat back

arm/armrest

spindle

arm post/
arm stump/
arm support

seat

rear stretcher

rung/side stretcher

leg

rocker/curved slat

front stretcher

Rocking Chair/Rocker

Lounger

When the backrest of this *recliner,* or *Barcalounger,* is pushed back, the *footrest* rises to seat level. The term *ottoman,* or *pouf,* is often used to refer to an overstuffed *footstool.* An *arm pad* on an *easy chair* is also called a *manchette.*

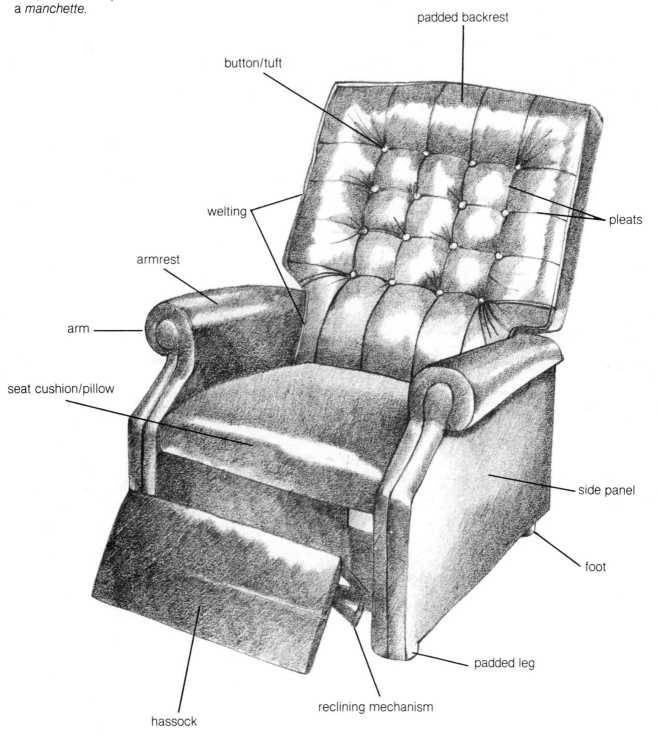

padded backrest

button/tuft

welting

pleats

armrest

arm

seat cushion/pillow

side panel

foot

padded leg

reclining mechanism

hassock

Living Room

Sofa

A sofa is an upholstered *couch* with a back and two arms or raised ends. If it is composed of several independent sections that can be arranged individually or in various combinations, it is a *sectional.* A *davenport* or *convertible* can be converted into a bed for nighttime use, whereas a *divan* is a large couch without back or arms that is often used as a bed. A sofa for two is a *loveseat,* or *courting seat.* Cylindrical pillows, or *bolsters,* and *fitted* or *tailored pillows* or *cushions* are often used on sofas.

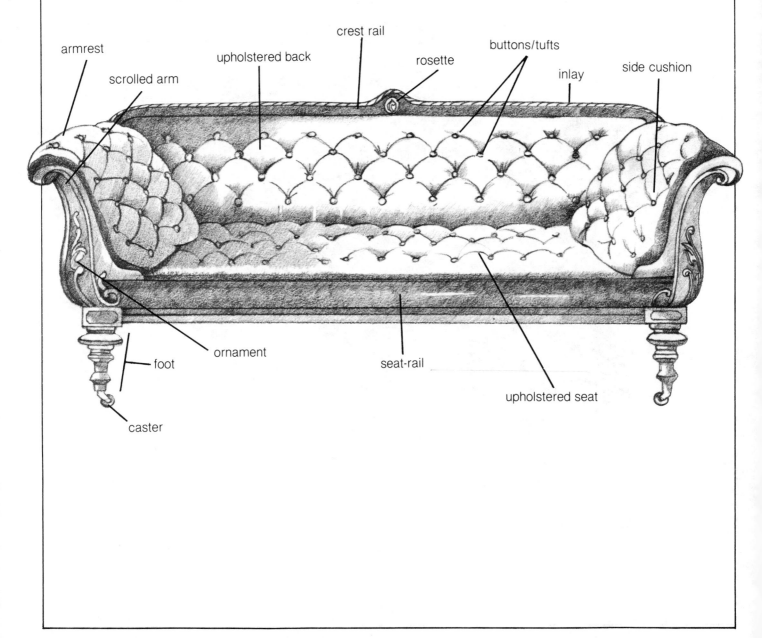

crest rail

buttons/tufts

armrest

upholstered back

rosette

inlay

side cushion

scrolled arm

ornament

foot

seat-rail

upholstered seat

caster

Candle and Candelabrum

Candles, or *tapers*, are made of *tallow, wax* or *paraffin*. Most are *dripless*. A collar placed at the top of a candle is a *burner*. The charred or partly consumed portion of a candlewick, or *snaste*, is the *snuff*, formerly referred to as the *snot*. The remains of a used candle is the *stub*. Many candlesticks have a pointed *pricket* on which a candle is impaled, rather than a socket. Small candles used for religious purposes are called *devotionals* or *votive candles*.

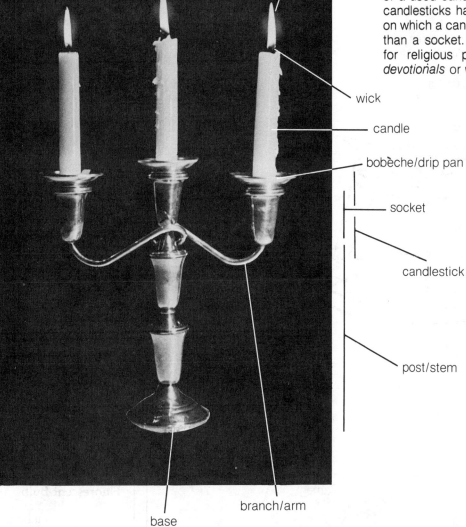

flame

wick

candle

bobèche/drip pan

socket

candlestick

post/stem

branch/arm

base

Candle Snuffer / Extinguisher

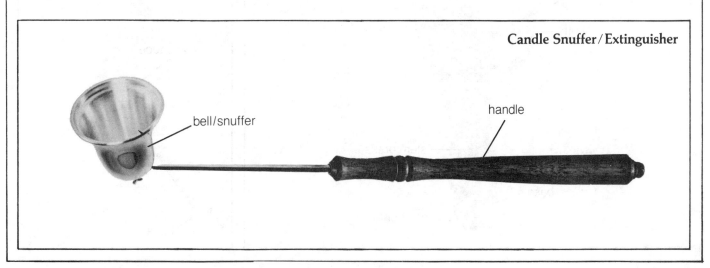

bell/snuffer

handle

Living Room

Lamps and Lighting

Light output, measured in *lumens*, depends on the amount of electricity used by a bulb. *Long-life bulbs* have heavier filaments. *Three-way bulbs* have two filaments, used separately for two of the light levels and together for the third. Two general types of bulb glass are soft, or *lime glass*, and hard, or *heat-resistant glass*. Lamp shades come in *drum, empire* and *bell* shapes. Lighting fixtures suspended from the ceiling are called *chandeliers*. The ceiling cap that covers the *junction box* for hanging lighting fixtures is the *canopy*.

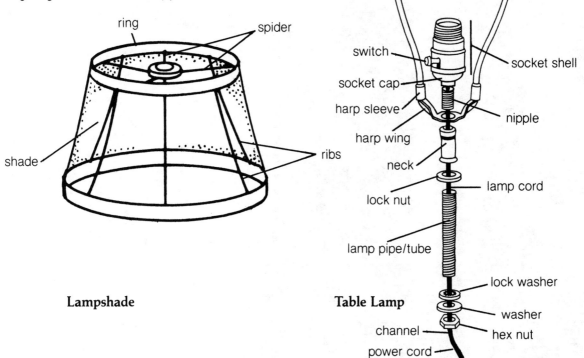

Lampshade

- ring
- spider
- shade
- ribs

Table Lamp

- finial
- harp
- switch
- socket shell
- socket cap
- harp sleeve
- nipple
- harp wing
- neck
- lamp cord
- lock nut
- lamp pipe/tube
- lock washer
- washer
- channel
- hex nut
- power cord

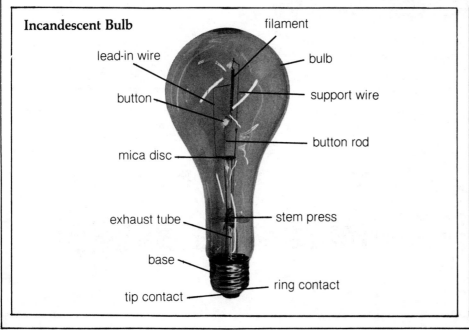

Incandescent Bulb

- filament
- lead-in wire
- bulb
- button
- support wire
- button rod
- mica disc
- exhaust tube
- stem press
- base
- ring contact
- tip contact

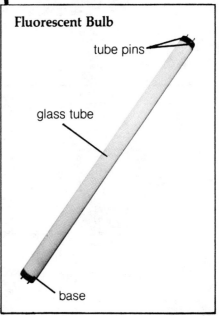

Fluorescent Bulb

- tube pins
- glass tube
- base

Lamps and Lighting

Adjustable lamps, such as the one seen here, have an *inner reflector* around the bulb to help ventilate the shade. *Gooseneck lamps* have flexible shafts which permit the shade to be turned in any direction. *High-intensity* lamps produce a strong beam of light that illuminates only a small area.

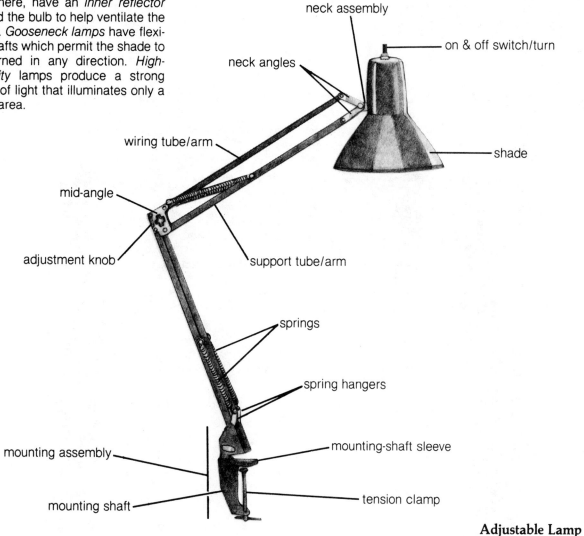

neck assembly

on & off switch/turn

neck angles

wiring tube/arm

mid-angle

adjustment knob

support tube/arm

shade

springs

spring hangers

mounting assembly

mounting-shaft sleeve

mounting shaft

tension clamp

Adjustable Lamp

Track Lighting

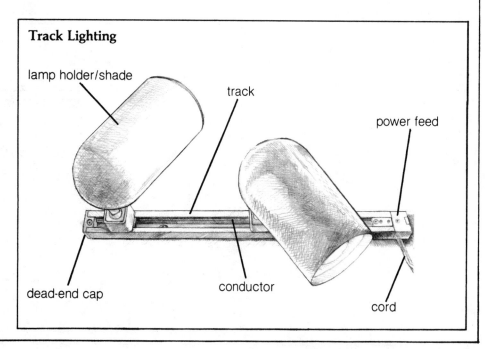

lamp holder/shade

track

power feed

dead-end cap

conductor

cord

Living Room

Window Coverings

The gathering of material at the top of draperies, hidden by the valance in this illustration, is called the *heading*. A *curtain rod* is a simple metal or wooden rod on which curtains are hung and moved by hand, without aid of pulley mechanisms. A curtain *panel* is a vertical section of fabric. *Cafe curtains* are suspended from rings and cover only part of a window.

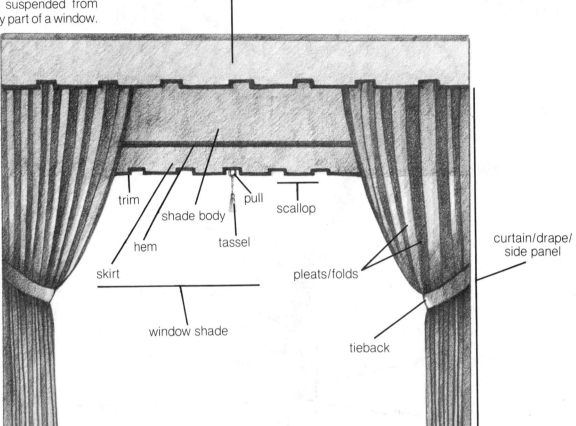

valance/cornice

trim

shade body

pull

scallop

hem

tassel

skirt

pleats/folds

curtain/drape/ side panel

window shade

tieback

Curtains/Draperies and Shade

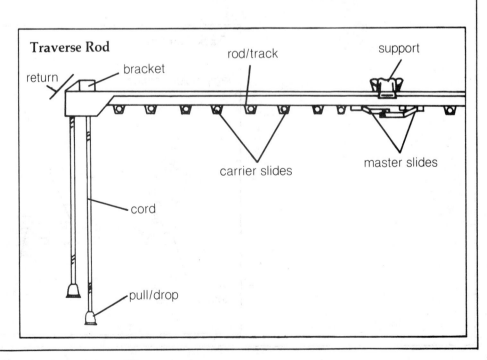

Traverse Rod

rod/track

support

return

bracket

carrier slides

master slides

cord

pull/drop

Window Coverings

Braided ladders are used in place of ladder tapes on some venetian blinds, and tubular wands are sometimes used instead of tilt cords. In roll-up blinds, slat tilt cannot be adjusted. A shutter consists of panels, each one of which contains louvers within a frame.

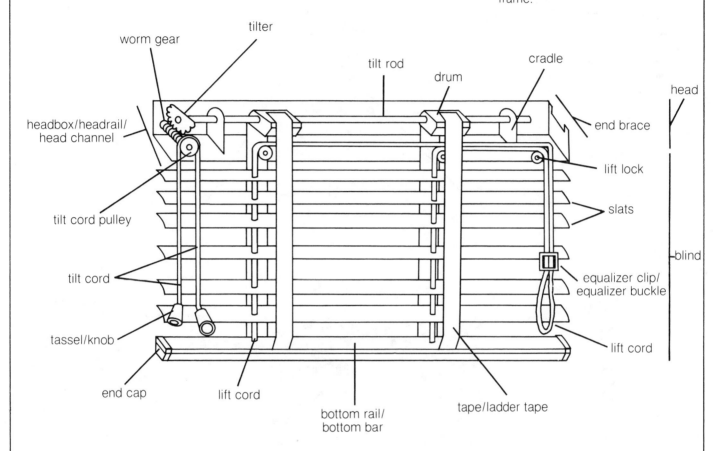

worm gear
tilter
tilt rod
drum
cradle
head
headbox/headrail/ head channel
end brace
lift lock
slats
tilt cord pulley
tilt cord
blind
equalizer clip/ equalizer buckle
tassel/knob
lift cord
end cap
lift cord
bottom rail/ bottom bar
tape/ladder tape

Venetian Blinds

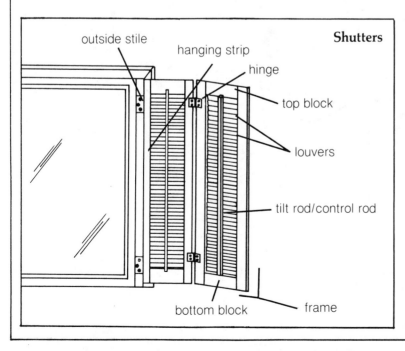

Shutters

outside stile
hanging strip
hinge
top block
louvers
tilt rod/control rod
bottom block
frame

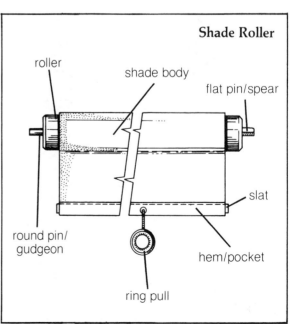

Shade Roller

roller
shade body
flat pin/spear
slat
round pin/ gudgeon
hem/pocket
ring pull

Living Room

Table

A drop-leaf table is any table with a leaf that drops down to the side, such as a *gateleg* or a *butterfly table*. In a butterfly table, which has *splayed legs,* wooden wing-shaped *brackets* support the leaves. *Pedestal tables* rest on a single *base* rather than on legs. Some tables have an *apron,* wooden slats that run along the sides just beneath the top, to provide additional support. *Card tables,* or *bridge tables,* are lightweight, portable tables with folding *frames.*

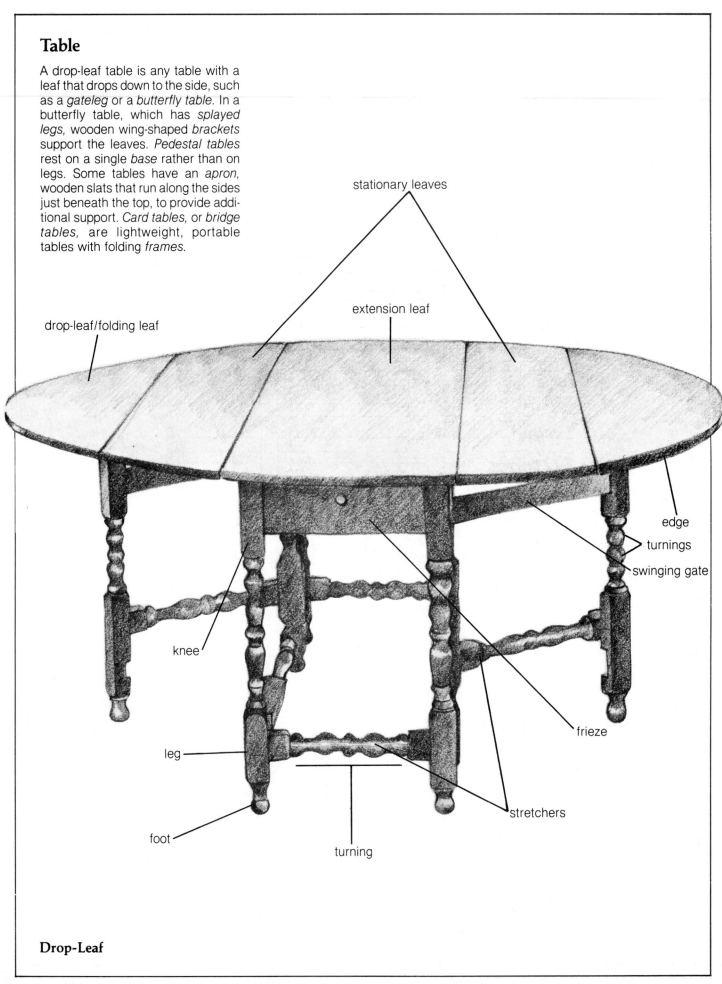

stationary leaves

extension leaf

drop-leaf/folding leaf

edge

turnings

swinging gate

knee

frieze

leg

stretchers

foot

turning

Drop-Leaf

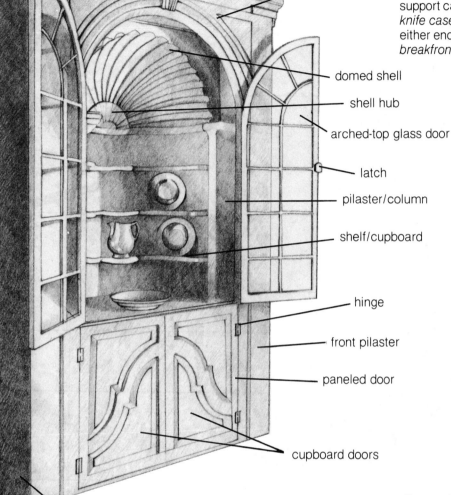

cornice

keystone

rosette

molding

domed shell

shell hub

arched-top glass door

latch

pilaster/column

shelf/cupboard

hinge

front pilaster

paneled door

cupboard doors

return end

Side Pieces

Storage cabinets and receptacles are known as *casework furniture.* Some sideboards have *candle slides,* which are boards that slide out to support candlesticks. *Knife boxes,* or *knife cases,* sit atop the sideboard at either end. Other side pieces include *breakfronts, hutches* and *dry sinks.*

Corner Cupboard / China Cabinet

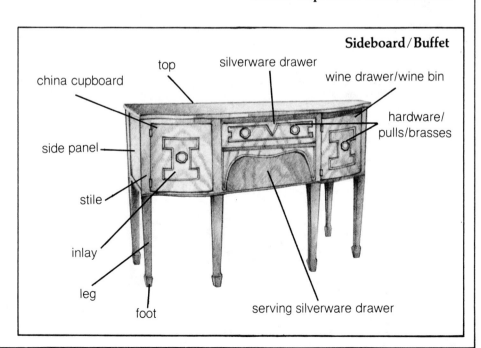

Sideboard / Buffet

china cupboard

top

silverware drawer

wine drawer/wine bin

hardware/ pulls/brasses

side panel

stile

inlay

leg

foot

serving silverware drawer

Dining Room

Place Setting

There is no universally accepted way of setting a table. The elements and their proper position vary. The arrangement shown here is based on that used by the White House on formal occasions.

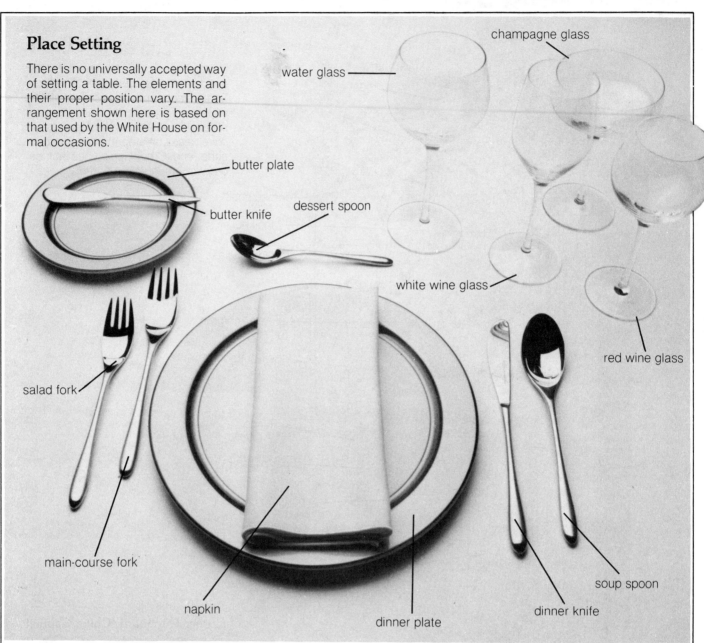

water glass

champagne glass

butter plate

butter knife

dessert spoon

white wine glass

red wine glass

salad fork

main-course fork

napkin

dinner plate

dinner knife

soup spoon

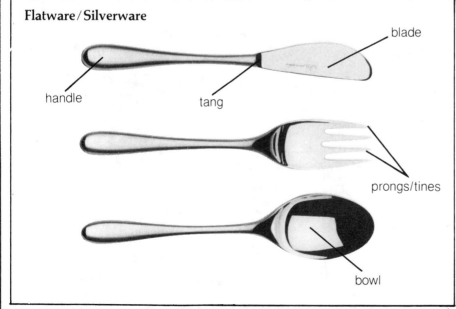

Flatware/Silverware

blade

handle

tang

prongs/tines

bowl

Stemware

rim/lip

head

bowl

stem

foot

Dessert Setting

Among other plates used for serving dessert and sweets are multi-tiered *terrace servers*, *serving trays*, *cake plates*, *fruit bowls* called *centerpieces*, and *compotes*. After-dinner drinks are often poured from ornamental glass bottles called *decanters*.

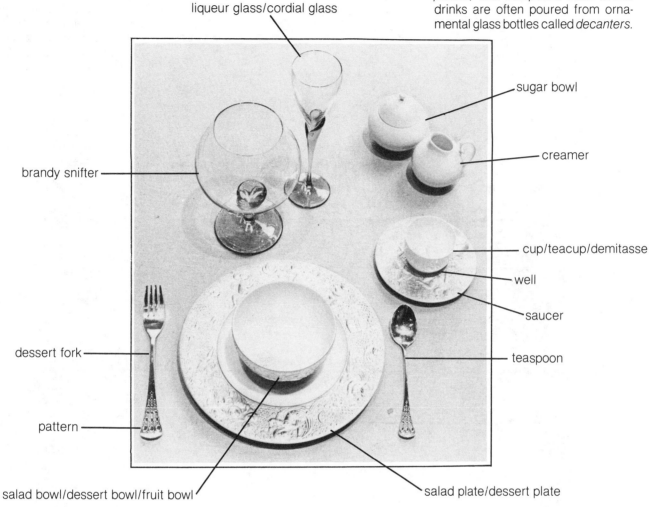

liqueur glass/cordial glass

sugar bowl

creamer

brandy snifter

cup/teacup/demitasse

well

saucer

dessert fork

teaspoon

pattern

salad bowl/dessert bowl/fruit bowl

salad plate/dessert plate

Chafing Dish

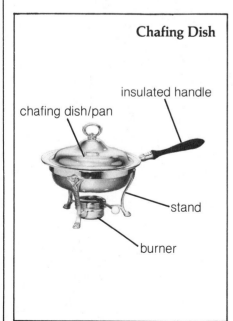

insulated handle

chafing dish/pan

stand

burner

Tea Set/Tea Service and Kettle

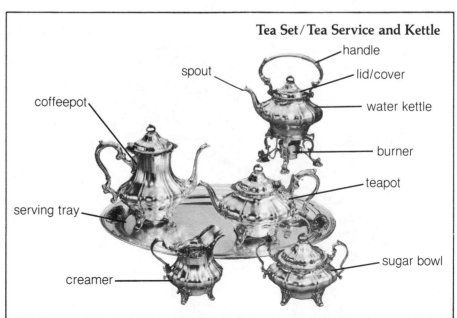

handle

spout

lid/cover

coffeepot

water kettle

burner

teapot

serving tray

sugar bowl

creamer

Carpet

Carpets, or *wall-to-wall carpets,* cover the entire floor of a room, while *rugs, area rugs, throw rugs* and narrow *runners* cover only a part, are not tacked down, and often rest on *rug pads. Tacks* are short nails with flat, broad heads. Much modern *carpeting* is tufted, made by stitching *yarn loops* into a *woven backing.*

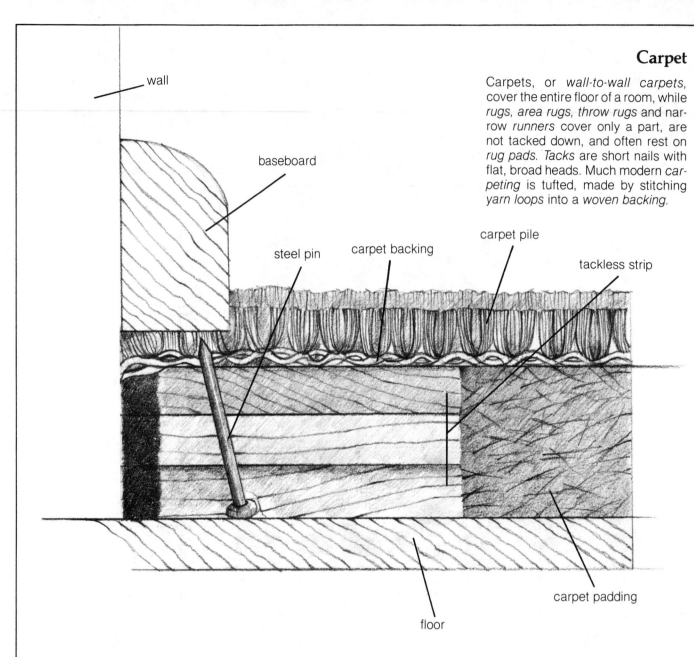

wall

baseboard

steel pin

carpet backing

carpet pile

tackless strip

carpet padding

floor

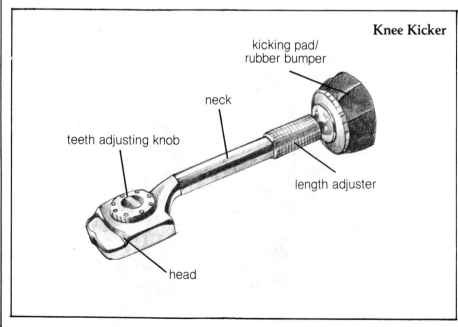

Knee Kicker

kicking pad/ rubber bumper

neck

teeth adjusting knob

length adjuster

head

Sink and Compactor

The hardware in a sink, the faucet handles and spout, are known as *fixtures*. Sink drains usually have perforated *drain baskets* which trap debris but allow water to pass through. Many baskets are two-piece units that form a watertight seal when the *inner basket* is twisted. *Instant hot-water devices* mounted on the spout of some sinks have a constantly heated coil that produces small amounts of hot water on demand.

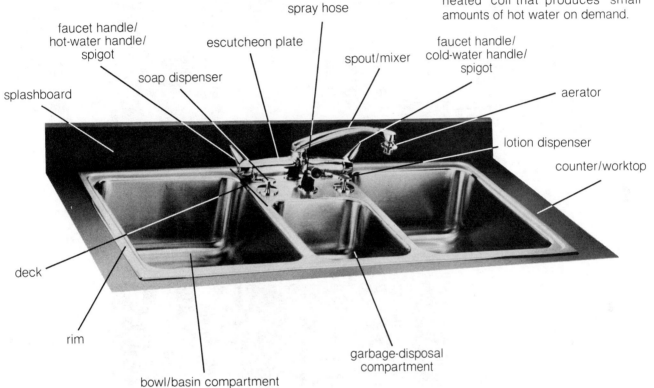

spray hose

faucet handle/
hot-water handle/
spigot

escutcheon plate

soap dispenser

spout/mixer

faucet handle/
cold-water handle/
spigot

splashboard

aerator

lotion dispenser

counter/worktop

deck

rim

garbage-disposal
compartment

bowl/basin compartment

Kitchen Sink

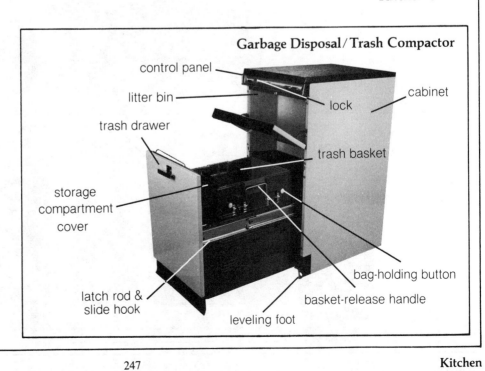

Garbage Disposal / Trash Compactor

control panel

litter bin

lock

cabinet

trash drawer

trash basket

storage
compartment
cover

bag-holding button

latch rod &
slide hook

basket-release handle

leveling foot

Kitchen

Stove/Range

On an *electric range*, *heating elements* connected to *terminal blocks* are used in place of burner grates on a gas model. The permanent flame, used to ignite individual burners on a gas stove, is called a *pilot light*. Some models have an *electric pilot*. The walls of a self-cleaning oven are covered with a heat-resistant porcelain enamel finish.

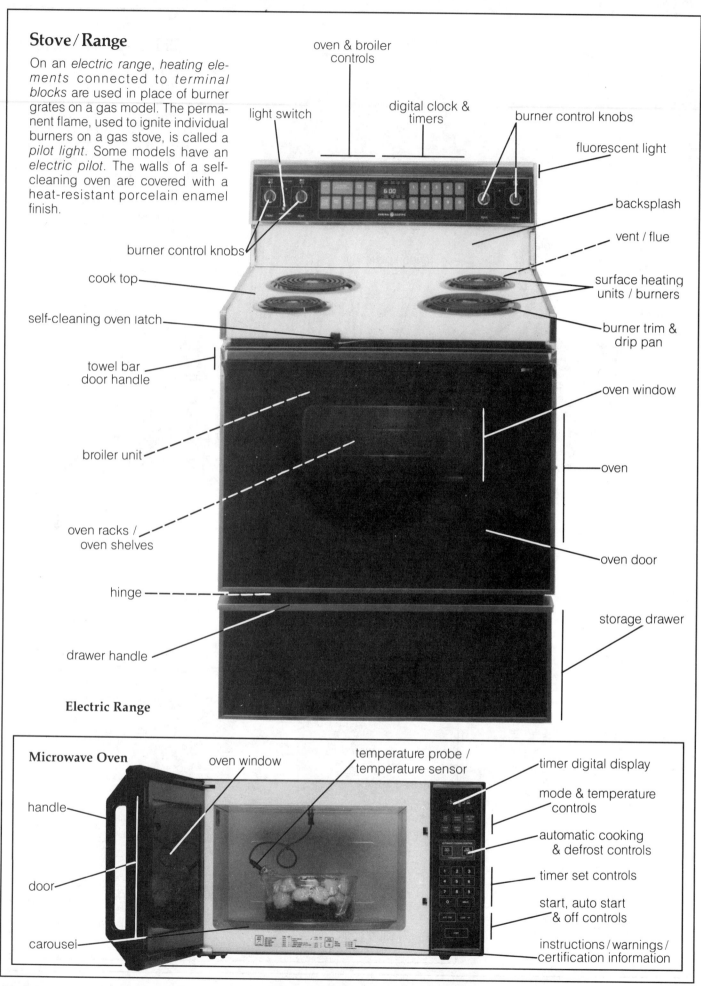

oven & broiler controls

light switch

digital clock & timers

burner control knobs

fluorescent light

burner control knobs

backsplash

vent / flue

cook top

surface heating units / burners

self-cleaning oven latch

burner trim & drip pan

towel bar door handle

oven window

broiler unit

oven

oven racks / oven shelves

oven door

hinge

storage drawer

drawer handle

Electric Range

Microwave Oven

oven window

temperature probe / temperature sensor

timer digital display

handle

mode & temperature controls

automatic cooking & defrost controls

door

timer set controls

start, auto start & off controls

carousel

instructions / warnings / certification information

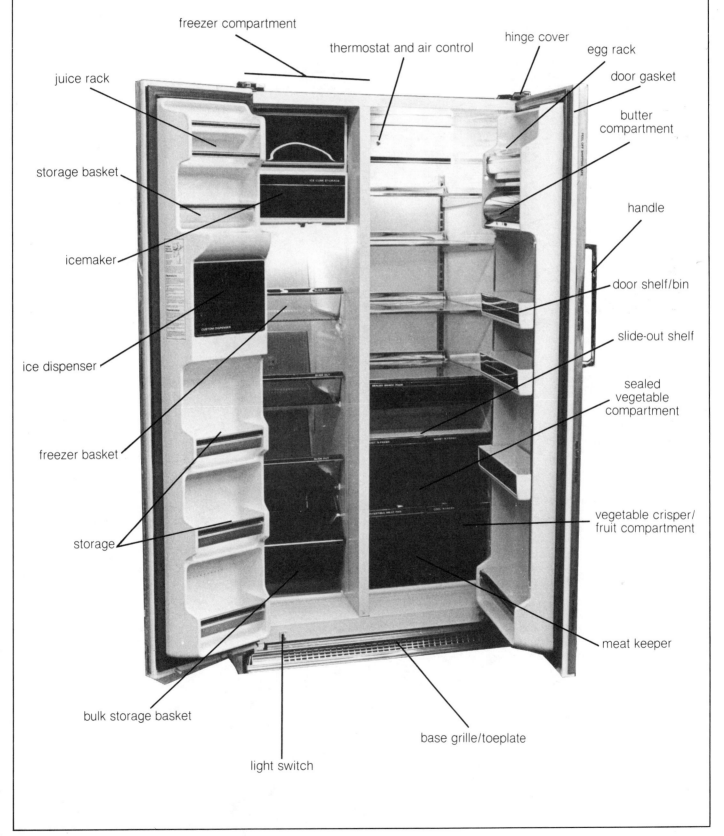

Refrigerator

Some refrigerators, or *iceboxes*, have an *ice dispenser* in the freezer section. Others have *ice trays*. A *frostfree*, or *no-frost*, model does not require defrosting.

freezer compartment

thermostat and air control

hinge cover

egg rack

door gasket

juice rack

butter compartment

storage basket

handle

icemaker

door shelf/bin

slide-out shelf

ice dispenser

sealed vegetable compartment

freezer basket

storage

vegetable crisper/ fruit compartment

meat keeper

bulk storage basket

base grille/toeplate

light switch

Kitchen

Dishwasher

The *cycle-selector control panel* and *timer* are located on the outside of the door of this built-in dishwasher. The machine will operate only when the *external door switch,* or latch, is engaged.

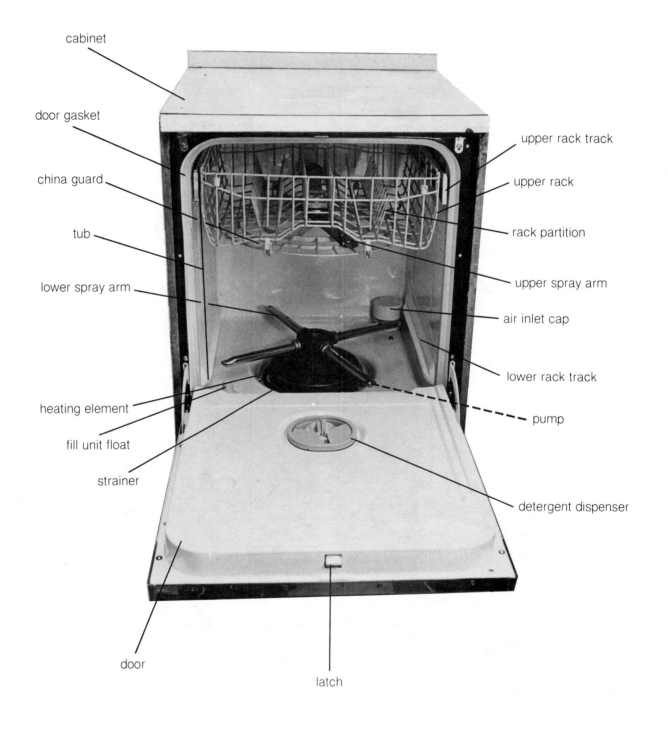

cabinet

door gasket

china guard

tub

lower spray arm

heating element

fill unit float

strainer

door

latch

upper rack track

upper rack

rack partition

upper spray arm

air inlet cap

lower rack track

pump

detergent dispenser

Openers

With manual openers, the can rim is held between a *cutting blade* and a *turning gear,* with pressure applied by squeezing two *handles* and the can rotated with a winged *key.* The blade and handle device used by military personnel to open food ration cans is called a *"John Wayne."* The corkscrew shown below is used by *sommeliers,* or *wine stewards.*

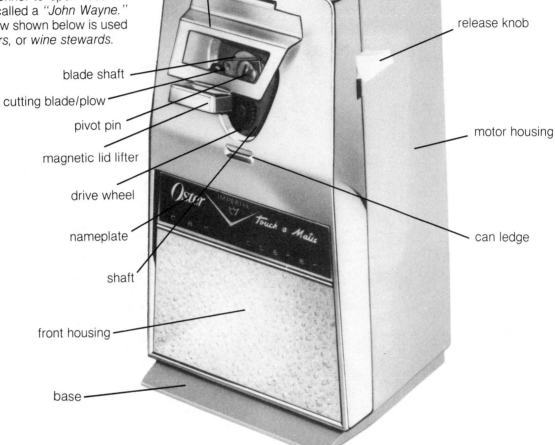

cutting lever

release knob

blade shaft

cutting blade/plow

pivot pin

magnetic lid lifter

drive wheel

motor housing

nameplate

shaft

can ledge

front housing

base

Electric Can Opener

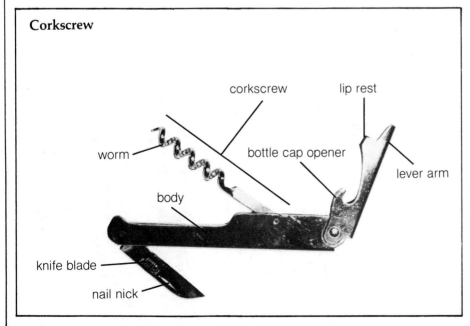

Corkscrew

corkscrew

lip rest

worm

bottle cap opener

lever arm

body

knife blade

nail nick

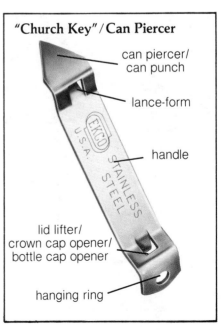

"Church Key"/Can Piercer

can piercer/
can punch

lance-form

handle

lid lifter/
crown cap opener/
bottle cap opener

hanging ring

Kitchen

Coffee Makers

Coffee is *brewed* by passing boiling water through *ground coffee* beans. *Espresso* is brewed by forcing steam through roasted beans. *Cappuccino* consists of espresso and steamed milk.

brew control

fill opening

filter basket

water reservoir

lid

brew starter/automatic timer

handle

on-off switch

carafe/decanter

indicator light/signal light

warming unit/hot plate

cup level scale

Drip Coffee Maker

Percolator

dome

spout

lid

pot/body

plug outlet

brewing & warming element

brew selector

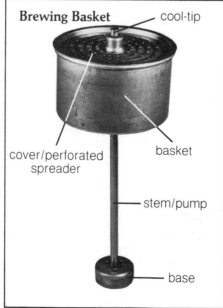

Brewing Basket

cool-tip

cover/perforated spreader

basket

stem/pump

base

Infusion Maker

knob/plunger

lip/spout

rod

frame

beaker/carafe/jug

filter assembly

Many toasters have removable *crumb trays*. The heating elements in toasters are flat *nichrome wires*. Toasters have either a spring-and-cylinder *dash-pot* or a simple spring device to pop toast up once it is browned. Toaster ovens have removable *baking trays*.

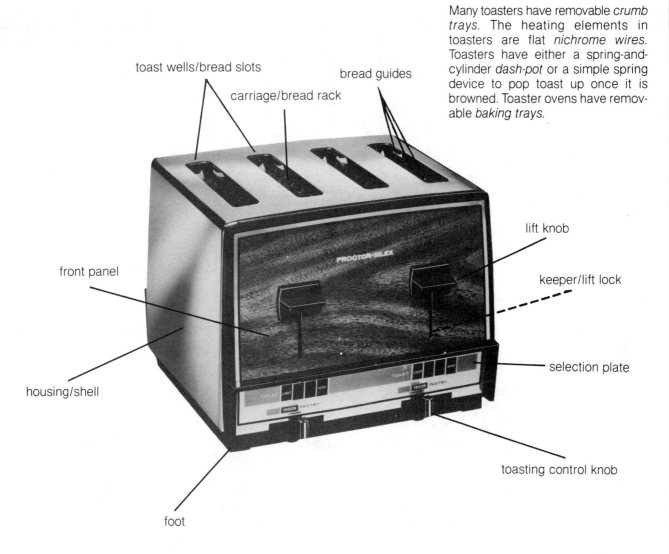

toast wells/bread slots

carriage/bread rack

bread guides

lift knob

keeper/lift lock

front panel

selection plate

housing/shell

toasting control knob

foot

Toaster

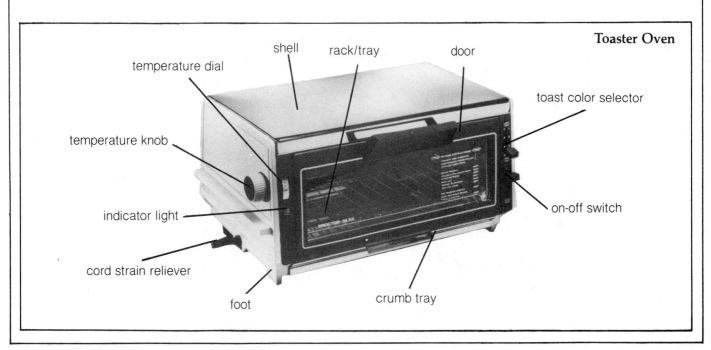

Toaster Oven

shell

rack/tray

door

toast color selector

temperature dial

temperature knob

on-off switch

indicator light

cord strain reliever

foot

crumb tray

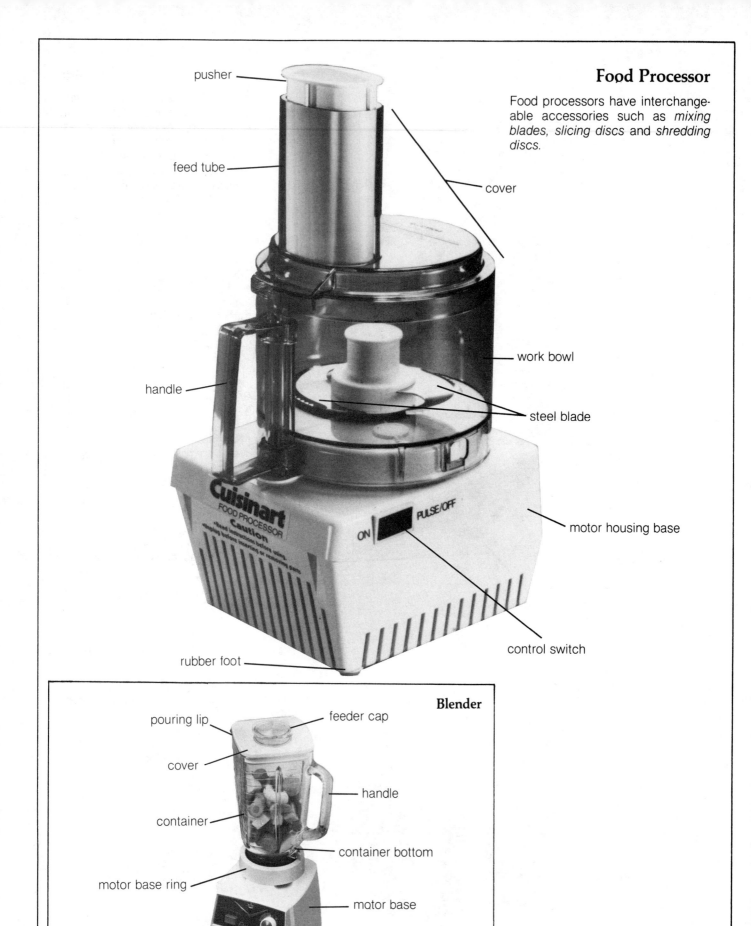

Food Processor

Food processors have interchange-able accessories such as *mixing blades, slicing discs* and *shredding discs.*

pusher

feed tube

cover

work bowl

handle

steel blade

motor housing base

control switch

rubber foot

Blender

pouring lip

feeder cap

cover

handle

container

container bottom

motor base ring

motor base

speed control buttons

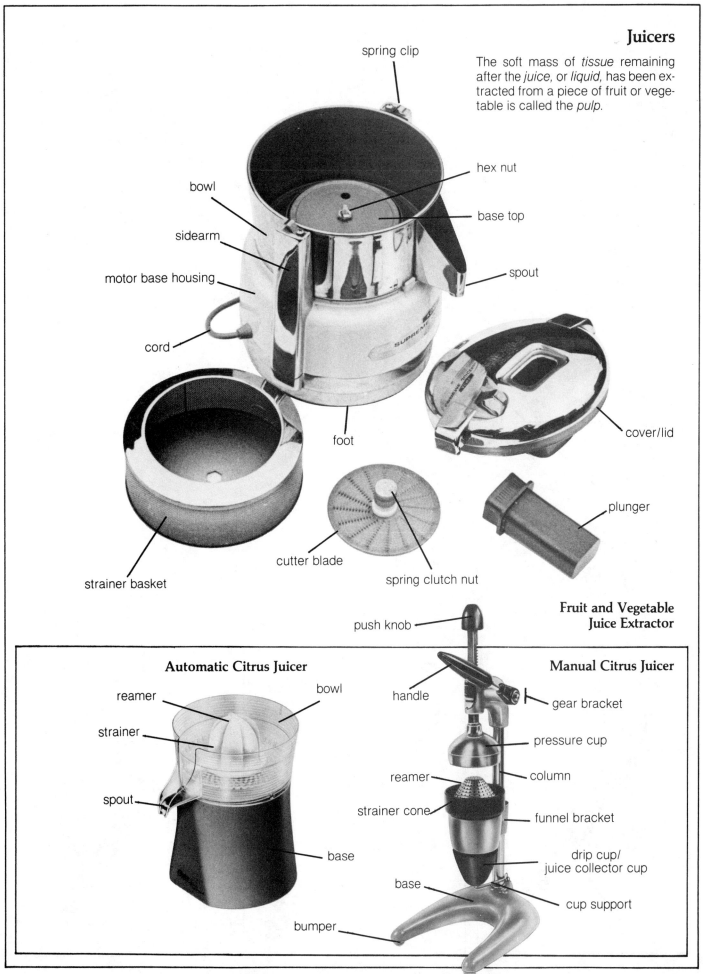

Juicers

The soft mass of *tissue* remaining after the *juice*, or *liquid*, has been extracted from a piece of fruit or vegetable is called the *pulp*.

spring clip

bowl

hex nut

sidearm

base top

motor base housing

spout

cord

cover/lid

foot

strainer basket

cutter blade

spring clutch nut

plunger

Fruit and Vegetable Juice Extractor

push knob

Automatic Citrus Juicer

reamer

bowl

handle

Manual Citrus Juicer

gear bracket

strainer

pressure cup

reamer

column

spout

strainer cone

funnel bracket

base

drip cup/ juice collector cup

base

cup support

bumper

Knife

The part of a knife blade that extends into the handle is called the *tang,* and the blade's formation is known as the *grind.* In a *flat grind,* the sides of the blade are smooth. In a *hollow grind* there is a marked curve or bevel along the length of the blade.

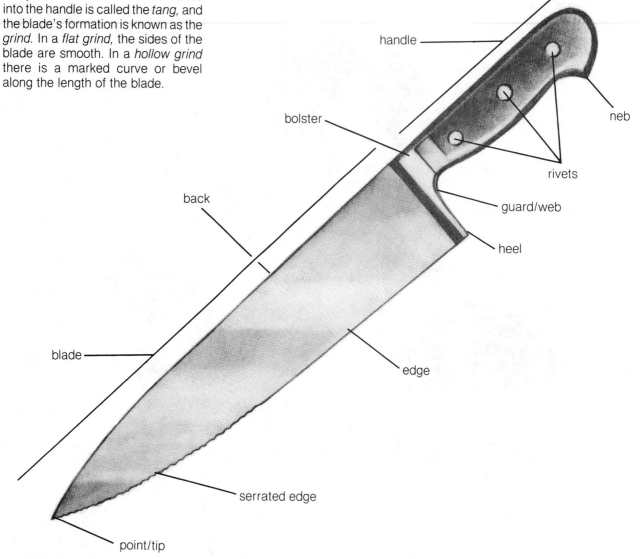

handle

neb

bolster

rivets

guard/web

back

heel

blade

edge

serrated edge

point/tip

Peeler

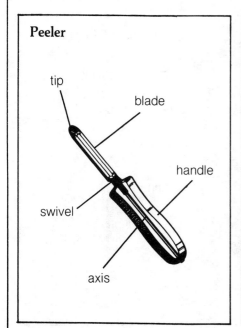

tip

blade

swivel

handle

axis

Sharpening Steel

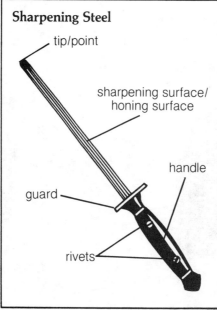

tip/point

sharpening surface/ honing surface

guard

handle

rivets

Cheese Plane/Cheese Slicer

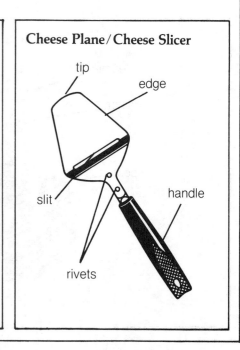

tip

edge

slit

handle

rivets

Pots and Pans

Pots and pans are often described by their function—for example, a *boiler* or *steamer. Crockpots* are pots made of earthenware. *Casseroles* are earthenware, glass or cast-iron pots in which food can be both baked and served. A *pipkin* is a small saucepan with a long handle used to melt butter.

knob

cover/lid

handle

Stock Pot/Stew Pot

rim

Saucepan

lift-out stem

perforated panel

Steamer Basket

leg/foot

side

tang

bottom

hanging ring

handle

Skillet/Frying Pan

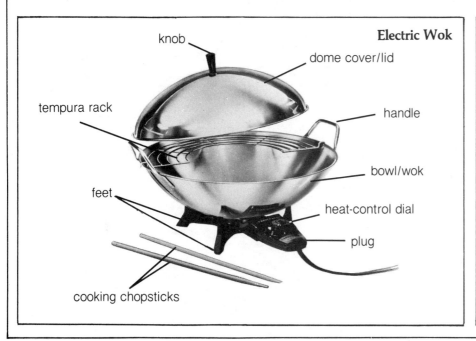

Electric Wok

knob

dome cover/lid

tempura rack

handle

bowl/wok

feet

heat-control dial

plug

cooking chopsticks

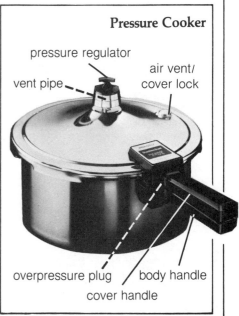

Pressure Cooker

pressure regulator

vent pipe

air vent/ cover lock

overpressure plug

body handle

cover handle

Kitchen

Mixing and Measuring Tools

In addition to the *meat*, or *rapid-response thermometer*, seen here, well-equipped kitchens have *oven* and *freezer thermometers*, *deep-frying thermometers*, *scales* and *funnels*.

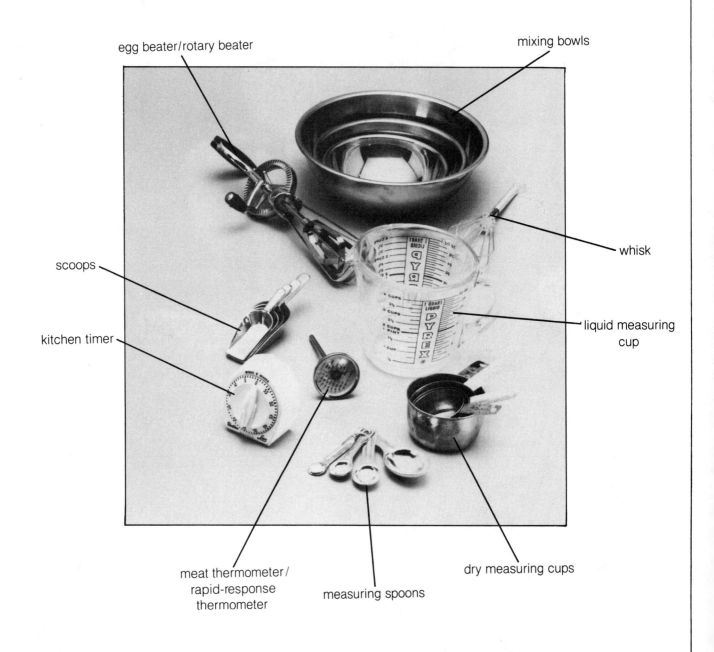

egg beater/rotary beater

mixing bowls

whisk

scoops

liquid measuring cup

kitchen timer

meat thermometer/ rapid-response thermometer

measuring spoons

dry measuring cups

Additional preparation implements include *molding scoops,* for soft foods, wooden *spaghetti spoons* with long *prongs* to wrap pasta and lift it from boiling water, *basting ladles* with an egg-shaped *bowl* for easy pouring, and cylindrical one-piece *pastry pins.*

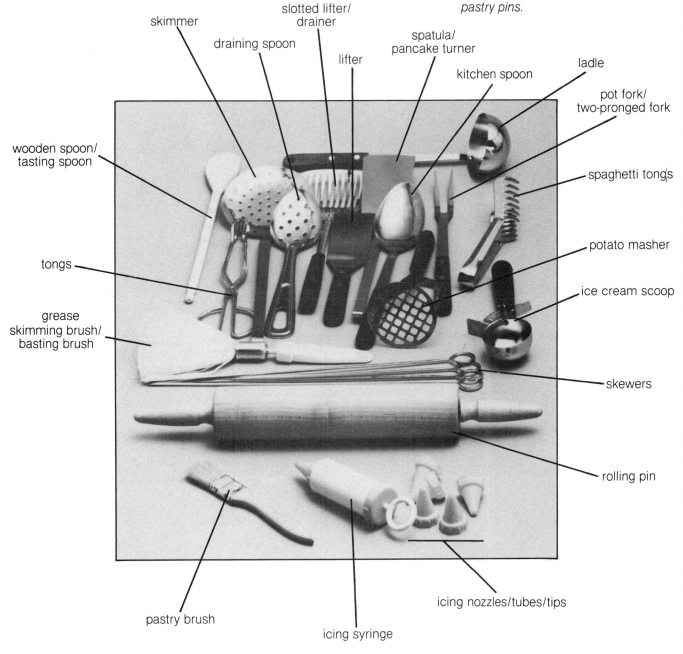

skimmer

slotted lifter/ drainer

draining spoon

lifter

spatula/ pancake turner

kitchen spoon

ladle

pot fork/ two-pronged fork

wooden spoon/ tasting spoon

spaghetti tongs

tongs

potato masher

ice cream scoop

grease skimming brush/ basting brush

skewers

rolling pin

pastry brush

icing syringe

icing nozzles/tubes/tips

Kitchen

Strainers and Drainers

Clean dishes, vegetables and fruits may be left on a *draining rack,* or *dish rack,* to dry. *Cooling racks* are used in conjunction with baked foods. A *sieve* has a mesh bottom for straining. A *food mill,* or *food foley,* is a heavy colander through which food is pressed by means of a flat *plate* attached to a *rotating handle.*

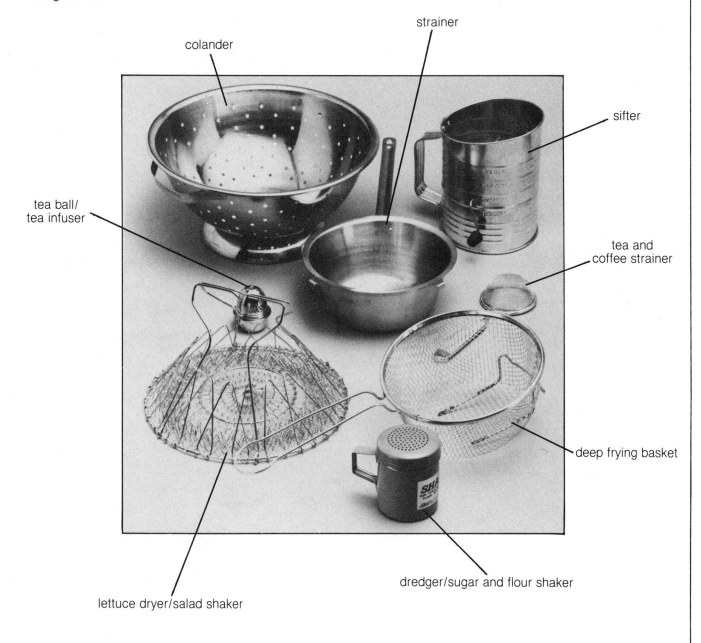

colander

strainer

sifter

tea ball/
tea infuser

tea and
coffee strainer

deep frying basket

lettuce dryer/salad shaker

dredger/sugar and flour shaker

A *potato peeler* has a swivel blade for following contours and a sharp tip for gouging. Hand-cranked *meat grinders* chop meats and other foods. A *zester* is a tool that shaves the thin surface off fruits.

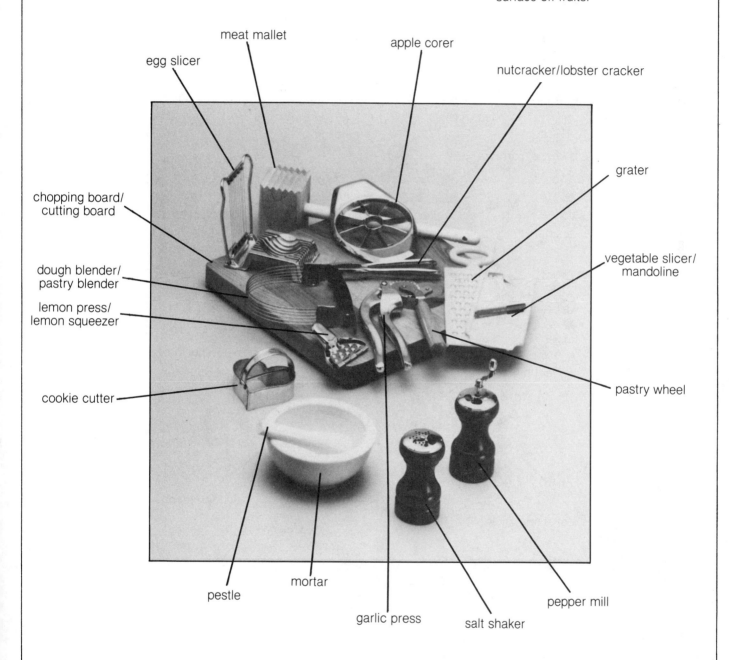

meat mallet

egg slicer

apple corer

nutcracker/lobster cracker

chopping board/ cutting board

grater

dough blender/ pastry blender

vegetable slicer/ mandoline

lemon press/ lemon squeezer

pastry wheel

cookie cutter

pestle

mortar

garlic press

salt shaker

pepper mill

Raw Ingredients

On *lettuce*, the entire mass of leaves is called the *head*, while the center leaves are the *heart*. A small slice of meat is a *collop*. A *peppercorn* is a dried berry of black pepper.

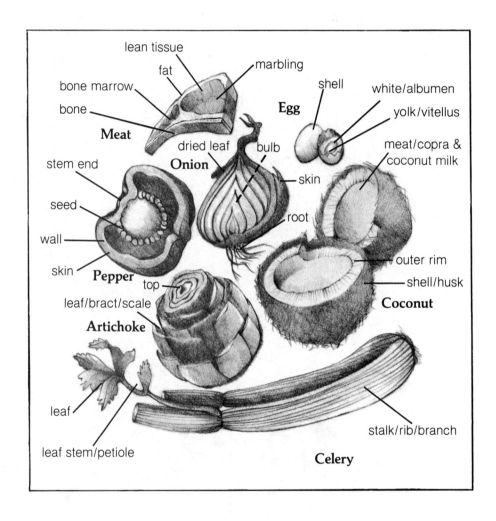

Prepared Foods

Appetizers, or *hors d'oeuvres*, are served before the main *course*, or *entree*. An ingredient, such as a *condiment, spice* or *herb*, added to food for the savor it imparts, is *seasoning*. Cheese is made by separating the *curd*, milk solids, from the *whey*, milk liquids. *Crumb* refers to both the soft inner portion of bread and any tiny piece that flakes off the loaf or a slice.

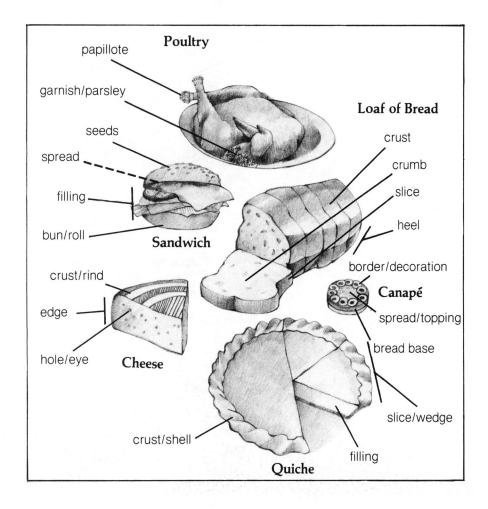

Poultry

papillote

garnish/parsley

seeds

spread

filling

bun/roll

Sandwich

Loaf of Bread

crust

crumb

slice

heel

border/decoration

Canapé

spread/topping

bread base

slice/wedge

crust/rind

edge

hole/eye

Cheese

crust/shell

filling

Quiche

Kitchen

Desserts

Baked desserts, or *sweet goods,* made of dough or having a crust made of enriched dough, such as *pies,* tarts and *turnovers,* are *pastries.* A *parfait* is similar to a sundae but may have layers of fruit and be frozen.

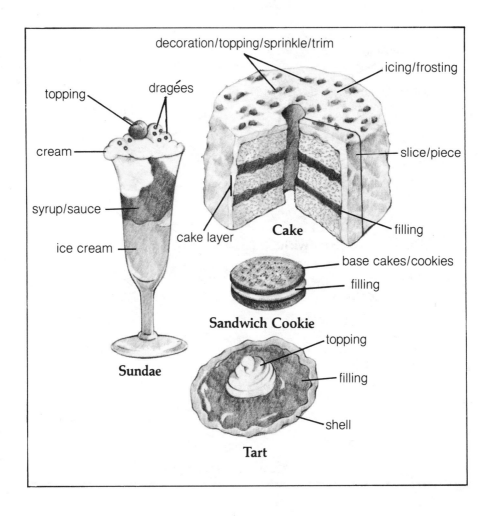

Snack Foods

Ice cream scoops are also put in flat-bottomed *wafer cones* and topped with other *fixings,* including *nuts* and *cherries.* When ice cream melts and drips down the cone, it forms *lickings.* The part of a hot dog roll that remains attached after the roll is sliced is the *hinge. Smoked sausages* are larger than franks and often include additional *seasonings.* Among other pizza toppings are *anchovies, extra cheese, pepperoni* and *onions.*

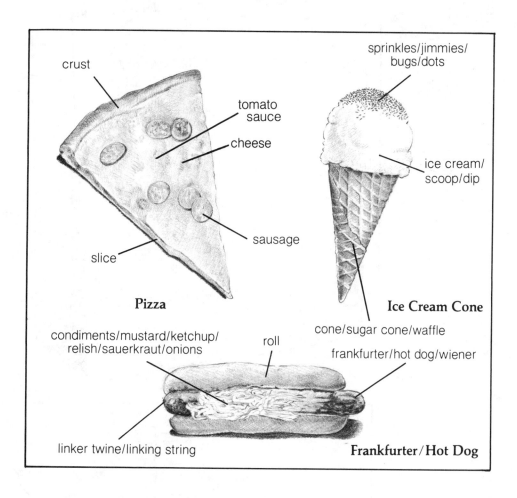

crust

tomato sauce

cheese

sausage

slice

Pizza

sprinkles/jimmies/ bugs/dots

ice cream/ scoop/dip

cone/sugar cone/waffle

Ice Cream Cone

condiments/mustard/ketchup/ relish/sauerkraut/onions

roll

frankfurter/hot dog/wiener

linker twine/linking string

Frankfurter/Hot Dog

Kitchen

Containers

Most baskets are made by weaving individual *strands* or *rods* in front of one *stake* of the *frame* and behind the next. Some baskets have a border, or *foot,* on the bottom, just above the *base,* as well as a *cover,* or *lid,* which often rests on an inside *ledge.* A small, oblong veneer basket with rounded ends, the kind used for mushrooms, is a *climax basket,* and a little wooden paillike container with one stave extending up for a handle is a *piggin.*

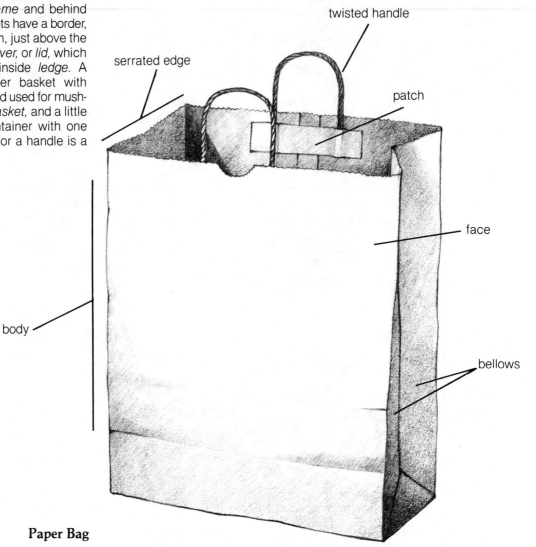

twisted handle

serrated edge

patch

face

body

bellows

Paper Bag

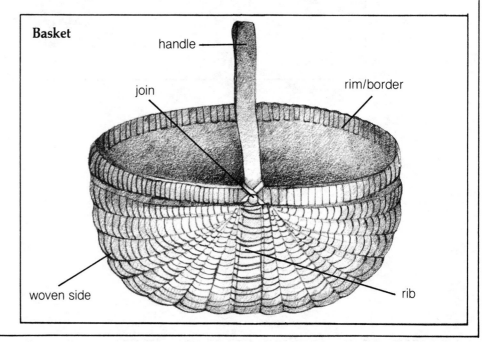

Basket

handle

join

rim/border

woven side

rib

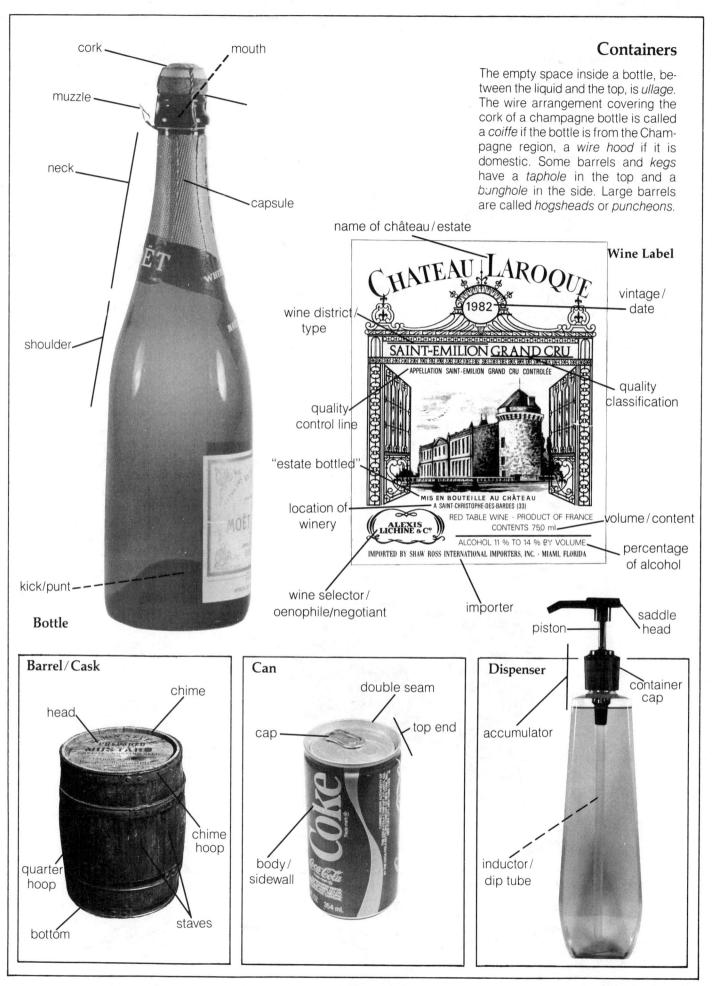

Containers

cork

mouth

muzzle

neck

capsule

shoulder

The empty space inside a bottle, between the liquid and the top, is *ullage*. The wire arrangement covering the cork of a champagne bottle is called a *coiffe* if the bottle is from the Champagne region, a *wire hood* if it is domestic. Some barrels and *kegs* have a *taphole* in the top and a *bunghole* in the side. Large barrels are called *hogsheads* or *puncheons*.

Wine Label

name of château / estate

CHATEAU LAROQUE

1982

SAINT-EMILION GRAND CRU

APPELLATION SAINT-EMILION GRAND CRU CONTROLÉE

wine district / type

vintage / date

quality classification

quality control line

"estate bottled"

location of winery

MIS EN BOUTEILLE AU CHÂTEAU
A SAINT-CHRISTOPHE-DES-BARDES (33)

RED TABLE WINE - PRODUCT OF FRANCE
CONTENTS 750 ml

ALEXIS LICHINE & Cº

ALCOHOL 11 % TO 14 % BY VOLUME

IMPORTED BY SHAW ROSS INTERNATIONAL IMPORTERS, INC. - MIAMI, FLORIDA

volume / content

percentage of alcohol

wine selector / oenophile / negotiant

importer

kick / punt

Bottle

piston

saddle head

container cap

accumulator

Barrel / Cask

chime

head

chime hoop

quarter hoop

bottom

staves

Can

double seam

cap

top end

body / sidewall

Coke

Coca-Cola

354 mL

Dispenser

inductor / dip tube

Kitchen

Labeling and Packaging

Sketches or pictures on labels are called *vignettes*. When letters or vignettes on labels are raised, they are *embossed*. When they are recessed they are *debossed*. A seal of clear plastic that conforms to a product's shape is a *shrinkwrap*. A *promotional*, or *spot label*, often applied over the regular label, is a *tip-on*.

plastic squeeze bottle

threaded neck

hang-card hole

cap/closure

blister

squeeze spout

blister card

die cut

proof-of-purchase seal

VINTAGE YEAR
for fun and knowledge

neck-band label

pull tab/zipper

pour spout

product label

side panel

directions for use

burst

trademark

NEW! easy-to-use

brand designation

register mark

generic/ product name/ logo

ingredients

product blurb

FOR FAST RELIEF OF MISNOMERS
Find any word you want-fast!

graphic device

interrupter

KILLS IMPRECISION ON CONTACT

precautionary statement

CAUTION: KEEP OUT OF REACH OF MUGWUMPS, KNOW-NOTHINGS, FUZZY THINKERS AND MUTTONHEADS. WHATZIT CONTAINS NO WHATCHAMACALLITS, THINGAMAJIGS, WHOOSIWHATSES, DOOHICKEYS, GIZMOS, DINGUSES, WIDGETS OR DOODADS.

inner-liner pouch

net contents

592 FUN-FILLED PAGES

kosher symbol

die cut

PROOF OF PURCHASE

Directions

Ingredients

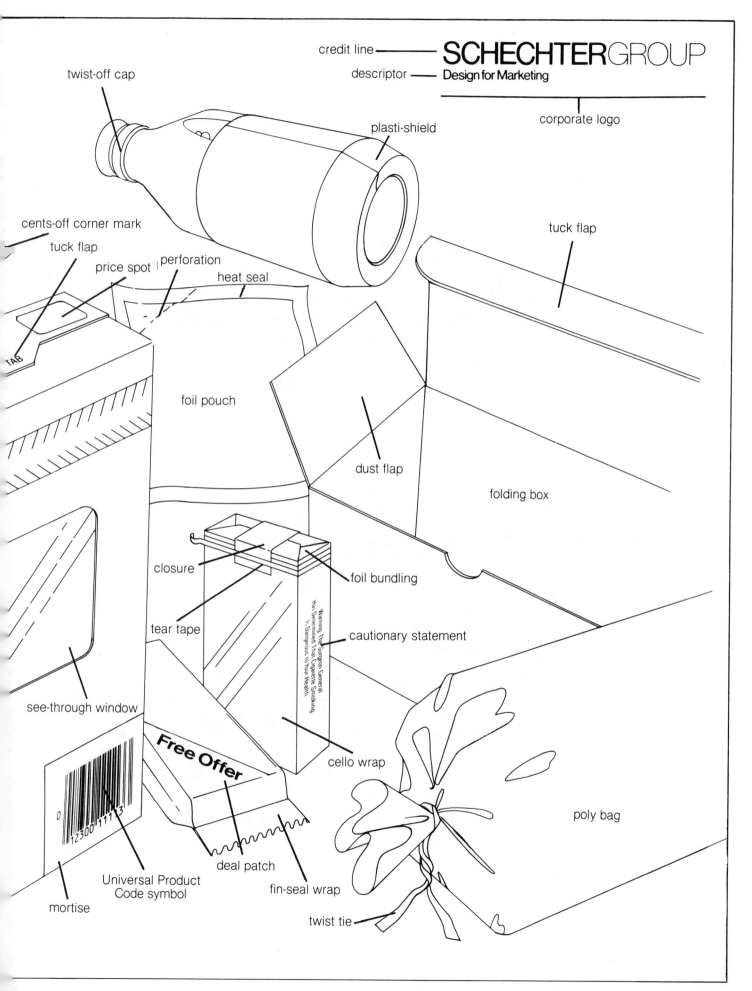

credit line ———

descriptor ———

SCHECHTERGROUP
Design for Marketing

corporate logo

twist-off cap

plasti-shield

tuck flap

cents-off corner mark

tuck flap

price spot

perforation

heat seal

foil pouch

dust flap

folding box

closure

foil bundling

tear tape

cautionary statement

Warning: The Surgeon General Has Determined That Cigarette Smoking Is Dangerous to Your Health.

see-through window

cello wrap

poly bag

Free Offer

0 12300 11113

Universal Product
Code symbol

deal patch

fin-seal wrap

mortise

twist tie

Bed and Bedding

A bedstead or *bed frame* consists of *side rails,* or *bedrails,* which connect the headboard to the *footboard.* A *twin bed* is a single bed, or one of a matching pair or beds, while a *double bed* is large enough to sleep two adults. A *comforter* is a small, thick quilt, while a *throw* is a bedspread with a short *side drop* rather than long *skirts.*

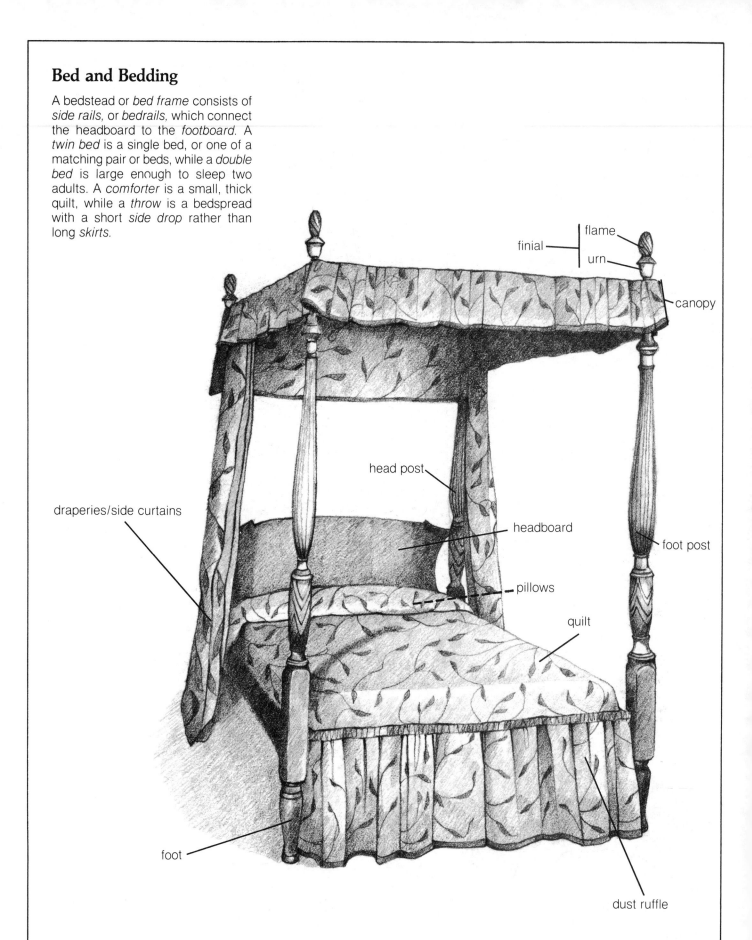

finial

flame

urn

canopy

head post

headboard

foot post

draperies/side curtains

pillows

quilt

foot

dust ruffle

Four-Poster/Canopy Bed

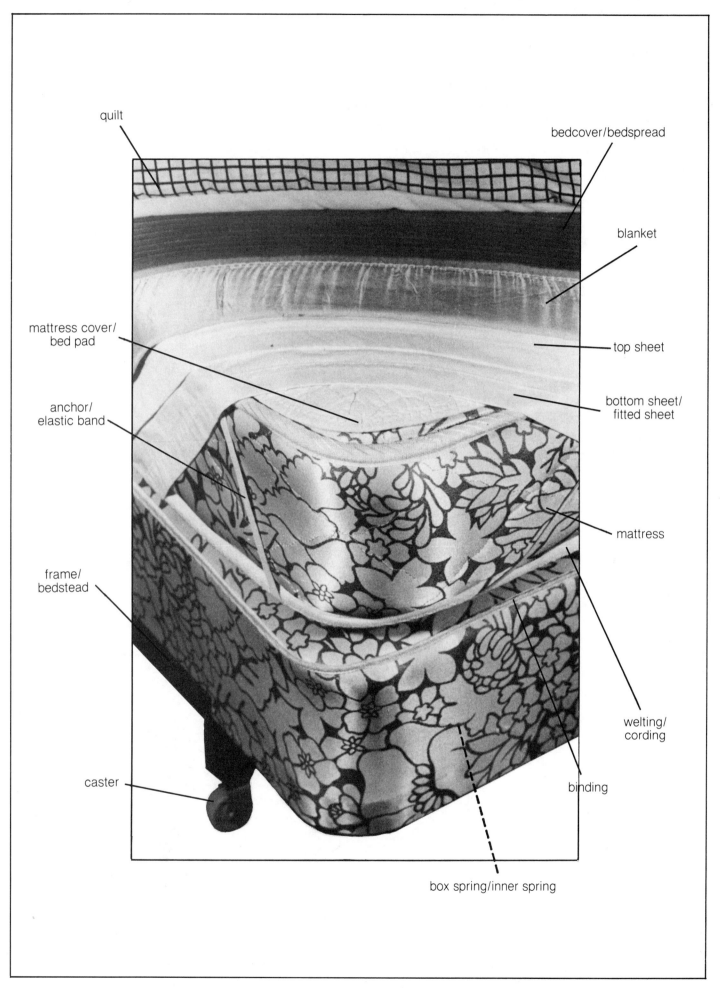

quilt

bedcover/bedspread

blanket

mattress cover/
bed pad

top sheet

bottom sheet/
fitted sheet

anchor/
elastic band

mattress

frame/
bedstead

welting/
cording

caster

binding

box spring/inner spring

Dressers

A dresser without the drawers in it is called the *main body,* or *carcass.* The thin plywood sheets between drawers, to keep *drawer cases* rigid, are *dust panels.* An *armoire,* or *wardrobe,* is a tall, movable closet in which to hang clothes. A *chiffonier* is a high, narrow chest of drawers.

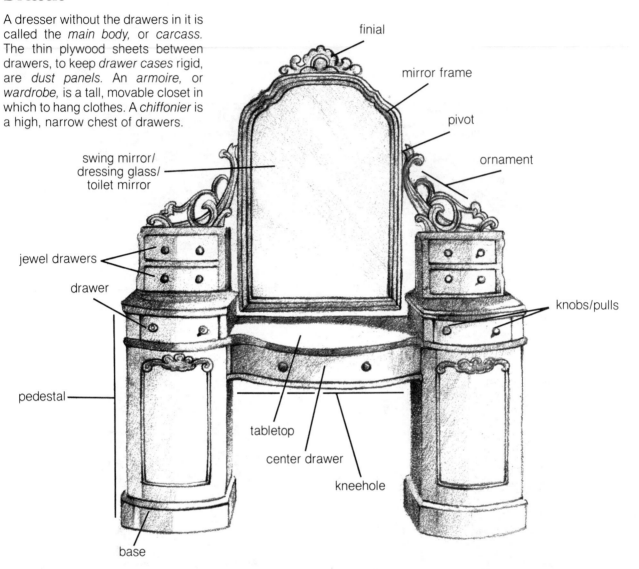

finial

mirror frame

pivot

ornament

swing mirror/ dressing glass/ toilet mirror

jewel drawers

drawer

knobs/pulls

pedestal

tabletop

center drawer

kneehole

base

Dressing Table / Vanity

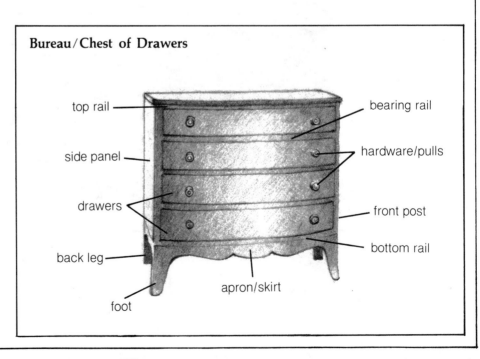

Bureau / Chest of Drawers

top rail

bearing rail

side panel

hardware/pulls

drawers

front post

back leg

bottom rail

foot

apron/skirt

Faucet and Sink

Some basins have *rubber plug* and *chain stoppers* to hold water, and *splash rims* or *lips* to prevent water from overflowing.

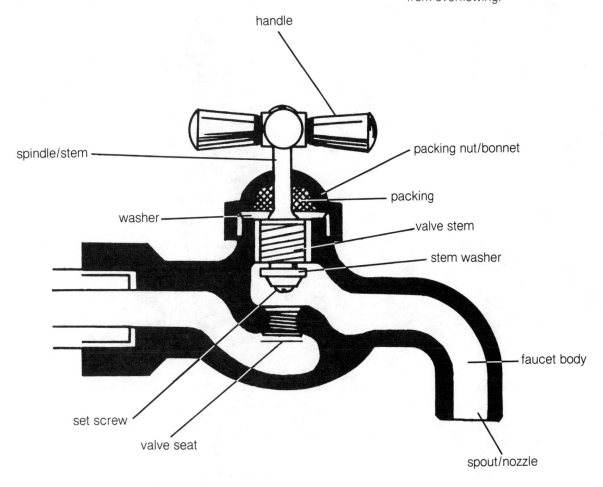

handle

spindle/stem

packing nut/bonnet

packing

washer

valve stem

stem washer

set screw

valve seat

faucet body

spout/nozzle

Faucet / Spigot / Tap / Bibcock

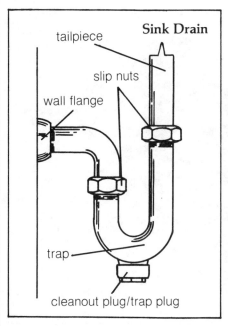

Sink Drain

tailpiece

slip nuts

wall flange

trap

cleanout plug/trap plug

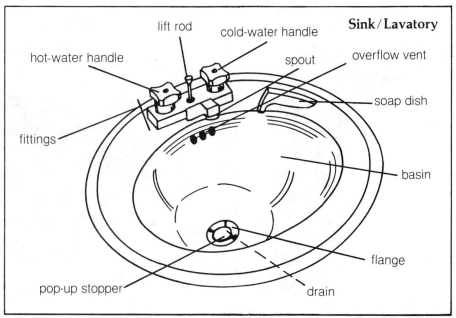

Sink / Lavatory

lift rod

cold-water handle

hot-water handle

spout

overflow vent

soap dish

fittings

basin

flange

pop-up stopper

drain

Bathroom

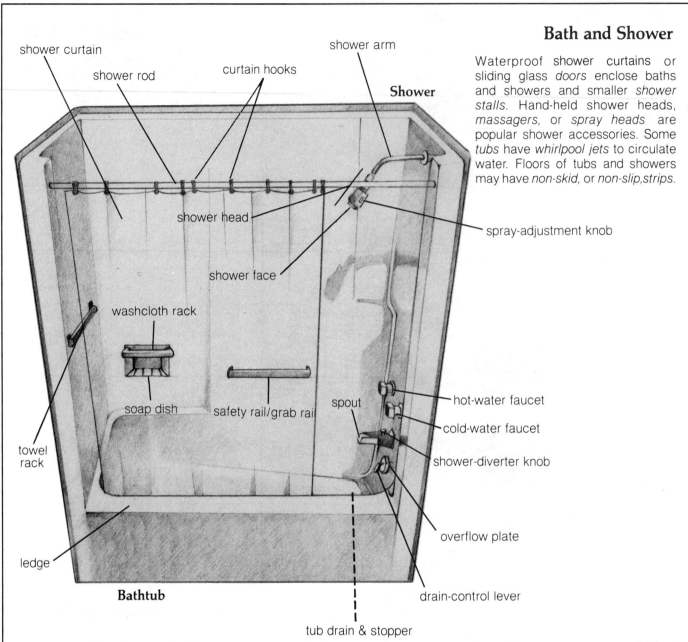

Bath and Shower

Waterproof shower curtains or sliding glass *doors* enclose baths and showers and smaller *shower stalls*. Hand-held shower heads, *massagers*, or *spray heads* are popular shower accessories. Some *tubs* have *whirlpool jets* to circulate water. Floors of tubs and showers may have *non-skid*, or *non-slip,strips*.

shower curtain

shower rod

curtain hooks

shower arm

Shower

shower head

spray-adjustment knob

shower face

washcloth rack

soap dish

safety rail/grab rail

spout

hot-water faucet

cold-water faucet

shower-diverter knob

towel rack

overflow plate

ledge

drain-control lever

Bathtub

tub drain & stopper

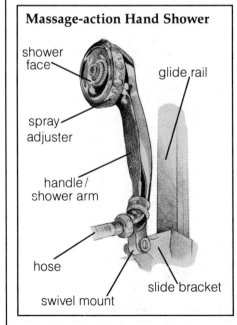

Massage-action Hand Shower

shower face

glide rail

spray adjuster

handle/ shower arm

hose

swivel mount

slide bracket

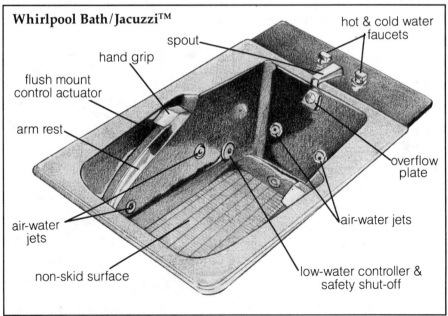

Whirlpool Bath/Jacuzzi™

hot & cold water faucets

spout

hand grip

flush mount control actuator

arm rest

overflow plate

air-water jets

air-water jets

non-skid surface

low-water controller & safety shut-off

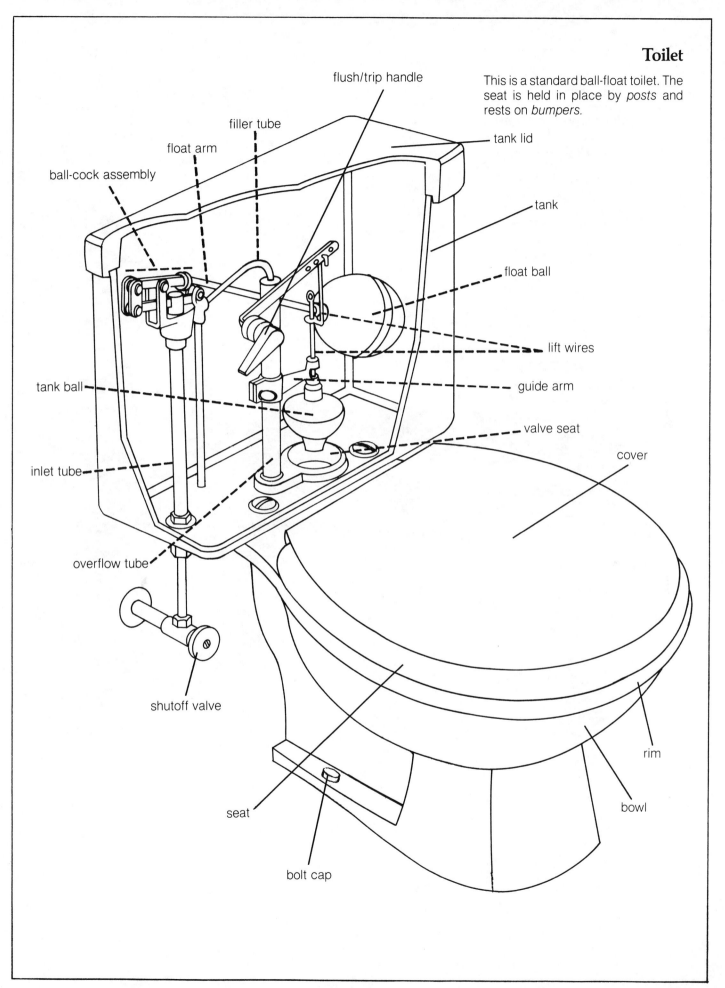

Toilet

This is a standard ball-float toilet. The seat is held in place by *posts* and rests on *bumpers*.

flush/trip handle

filler tube

float arm

ball-cock assembly

tank lid

tank

float ball

lift wires

guide arm

valve seat

tank ball

cover

inlet tube

overflow tube

shutoff valve

seat

bolt cap

rim

bowl

Desk

A *rolltop* or *cylinder desk* has a *sliding cover* that covers the desk's *writing area* when not in use. In *slant-front, falling-front* or *drop-lid desks*, the *front* flips down to offer a writing area which is supported by two *slide-out supports*. Some modern office desks have *elevator platforms* that can be raised and locked in place to hold a business machine, or lowered and closed behind a *cabinet door*.

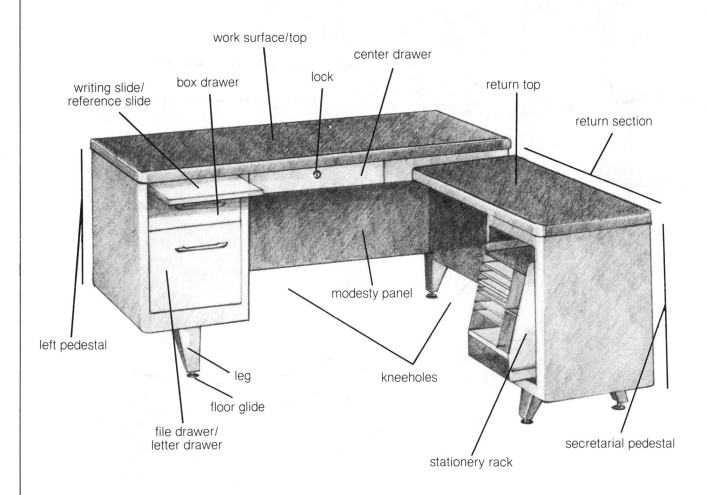

Desktop Equipment

Strips of staples are loaded into a stapler's *channel*. Pencils are sharpened in a *carrier* which holds two grooved cylinders called *cutters*. A paper clip is a piece of bessemer stock wire given three *twists*.

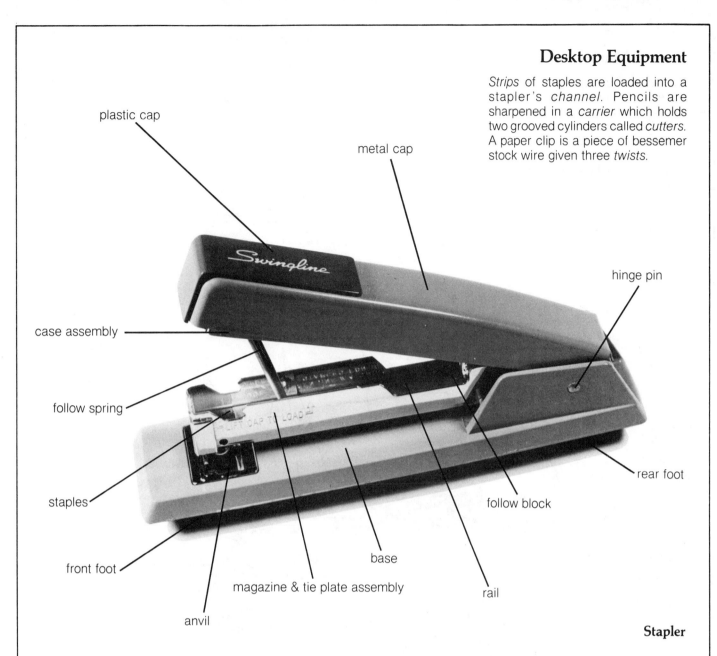

plastic cap

metal cap

hinge pin

case assembly

follow spring

rear foot

staples

follow block

front foot

base

magazine & tie plate assembly

rail

anvil

Stapler

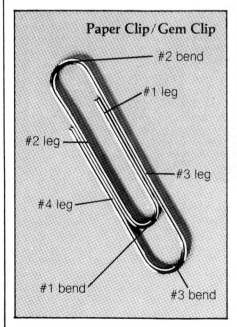

Paper Clip / Gem Clip

#2 bend

#1 leg

#2 leg

#3 leg

#4 leg

#1 bend

#3 bend

Pencil Sharpener

guide spring

crank/handle

aperture

knob

guide

receptacle

stand

actuating lever knob

base/vacuum mount

actuating lever

Sewing Machine

The standard presser foot can be re-placed by a variety of special attach-ments, including a *zipper foot, hem-mer foot* and *roller foot.* Some machines have a *slide plate* as well as a needle plate that opens to pro-vide access to the bobbin case.

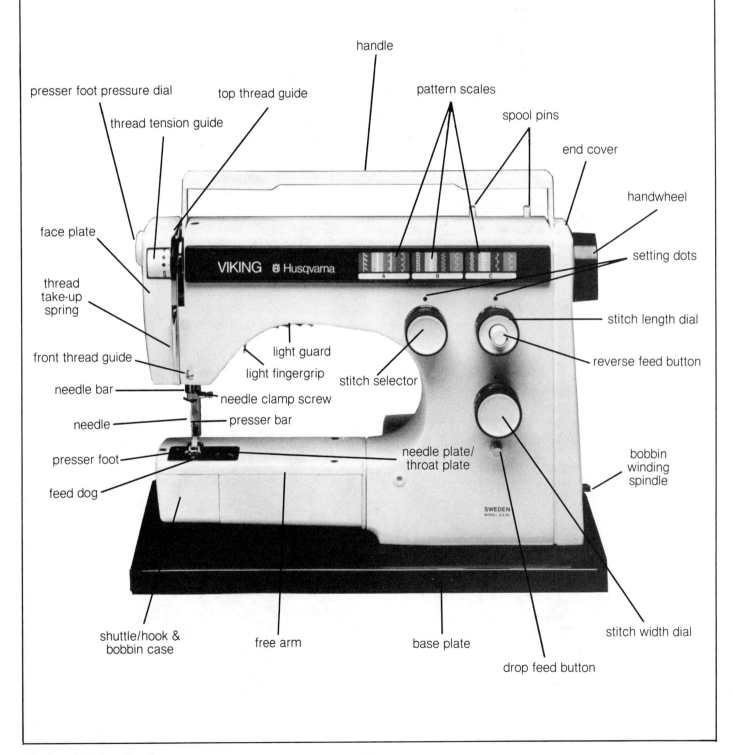

handle

pattern scales

spool pins

end cover

handwheel

presser foot pressure dial

top thread guide

thread tension guide

face plate

setting dots

thread take-up spring

stitch length dial

light guard

light fingergrip

stitch selector

reverse feed button

front thread guide

needle bar

needle clamp screw

needle

presser bar

presser foot

needle plate/ throat plate

bobbin winding spindle

feed dog

VIKING 🅗 Husqvarna

SWEDEN
MODEL 6310

shuttle/hook & bobbin case

free arm

base plate

stitch width dial

drop feed button

Iron

The *steam-and-dry iron,* or *flatiron,* shown here has *steam vents,* or *steam ports,* in the soleplate. Some irons have *front spray nozzles* as well.

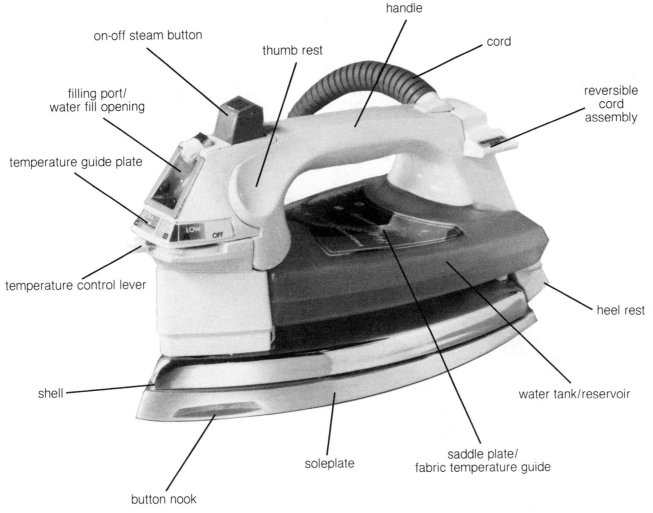

on-off steam button

thumb rest

handle

cord

filling port/
water fill opening

reversible
cord
assembly

temperature guide plate

temperature control lever

shell

heel rest

water tank/reservoir

button nook

soleplate

saddle plate/
fabric temperature guide

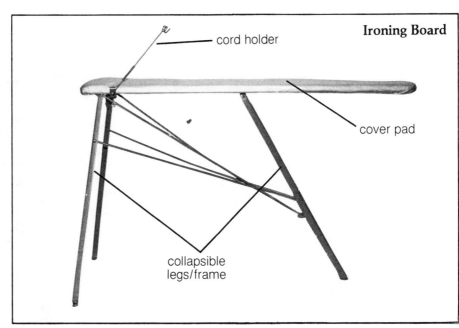

Ironing Board

cord holder

cover pad

collapsible
legs/frame

Playroom/Utility Room

Washing and Drying

Formerly, clothes were washed in a *washtub* with a *scrubboard* and *wringer* before being hung out to dry on *clotheslines,* or *washlines,* with clothespins. Wash-and-wear shirts are still air-dried on hangers. In automatic *top-loading washing machines* and *front-loading washers,* the basket, which has *drain holes* inside it, is contained within a metal *tub.* Some washers and dryers have a *window* in the *door* and a *tub light.*

gripping hole

spring slot

claw end

pinwood

spring

handle

Clothespin

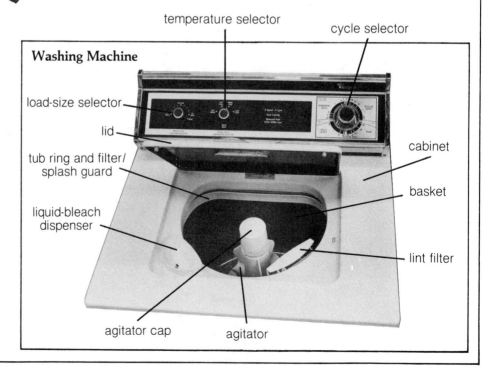

Washing Machine

temperature selector

cycle selector

load-size selector

cabinet

lid

basket

tub ring and filter/ splash guard

liquid-bleach dispenser

lint filter

agitator cap

agitator

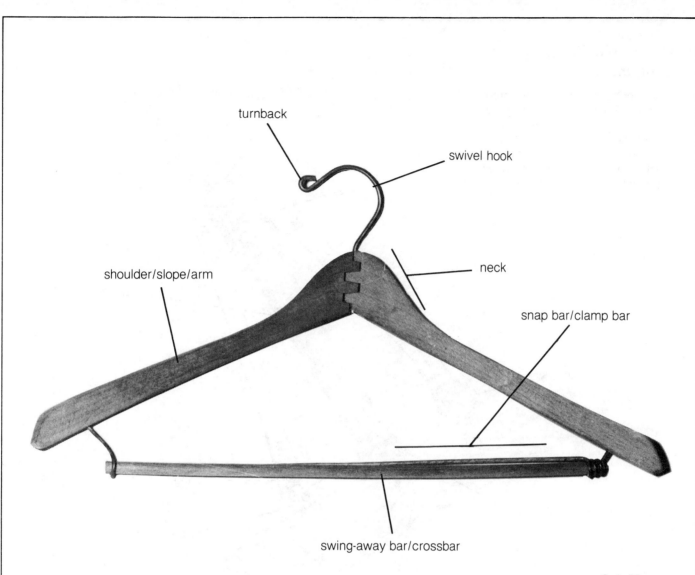

turnback

swivel hook

shoulder/slope/arm

neck

snap bar/clamp bar

swing-away bar/crossbar

Suit Hanger

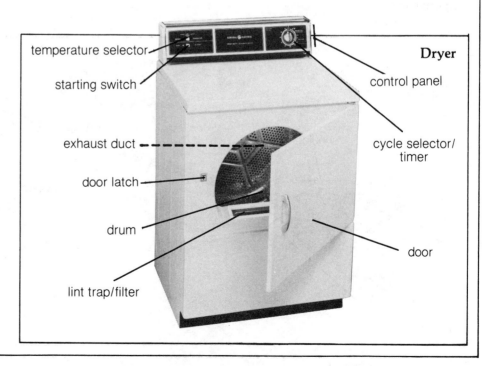

temperature selector

starting switch

Dryer

control panel

exhaust duct

cycle selector/timer

door latch

drum

door

lint trap/filter

Playroom/Utility Room

Household Cleaning Equipment

A conventional mop has absorbent *strands* rather than a sponge. An *electric broom* is a lightweight vacuum cleaner on a handle. A *carpet sweeper* contains two revolving brushes in a box at the end of a pushing handle.

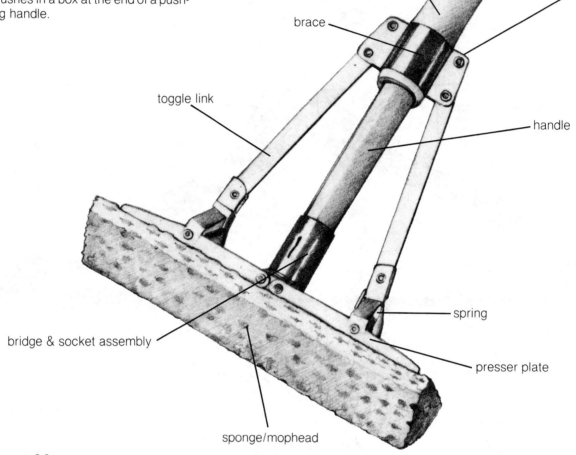

sleeve

brace

rail

toggle link

handle

spring

bridge & socket assembly

presser plate

sponge/mophead

Sponge Mop

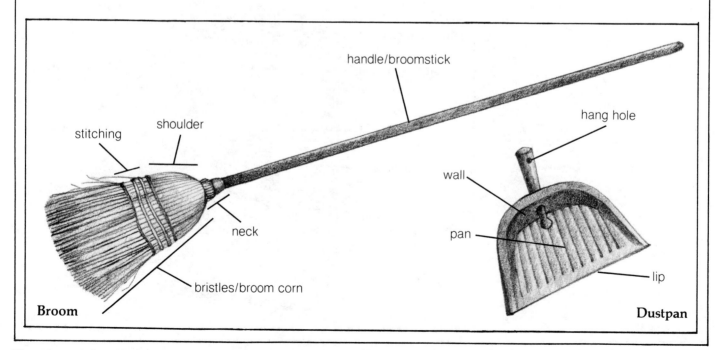

handle/broomstick

shoulder

stitching

hang hole

wall

neck

pan

bristles/broom corn

lip

Broom

Dustpan

Vacuum Cleaners

In an *upright vacuum cleaner,* shown here, *spiral brushes* under the hood and *beater bars* stir up dust and dirt. A *fan* blows these into a *disposable bag.* In a *cylinder model,* all the cleaning components are mounted horizontally. Dirt is sucked directly from the *intake tube* into a *vacuum bag,* or *dust bag.*

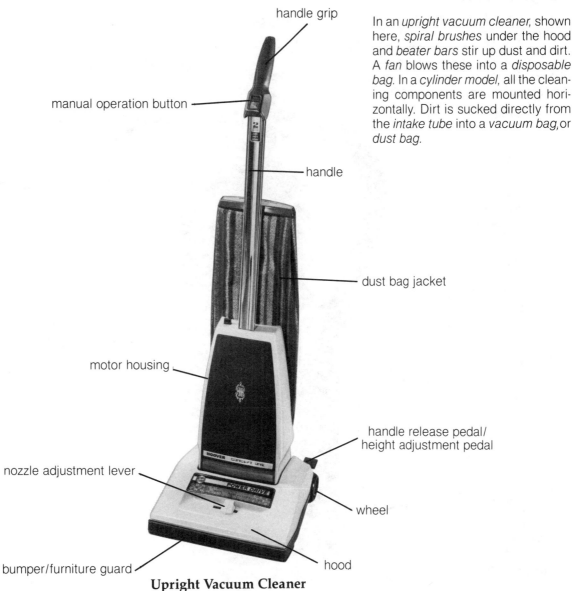

handle grip

manual operation button

handle

dust bag jacket

motor housing

handle release pedal/ height adjustment pedal

nozzle adjustment lever

wheel

bumper/furniture guard

hood

Upright Vacuum Cleaner

Attachments

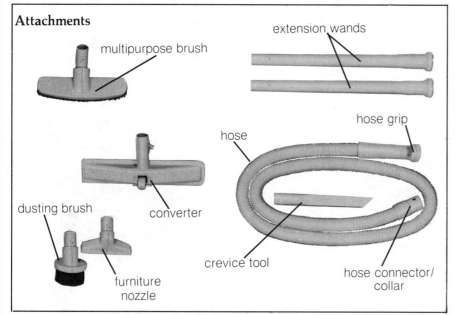

multipurpose brush

extension wands

hose grip

hose

converter

dusting brush

furniture nozzle

crevice tool

hose connector/ collar

Minivacuum

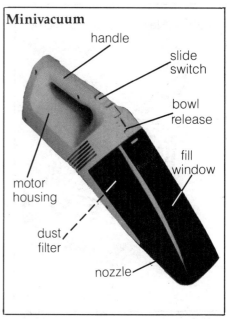

handle

slide switch

bowl release

fill window

motor housing

dust filter

nozzle

Firefighting Devices

Dry chemical extinguishers, containing chemicals and gas under pressure, are activated by squeezing or twisting the handle. *Soda-acid extinguishers,* inverted to mix the contents, produce a smothering *foam.*

pull-pin/locking pin

operating lever

handle

pressure gauge

band

discharge tube/hose

collar

instruction panel

shell/cylinder

horn

Fire Extinguisher

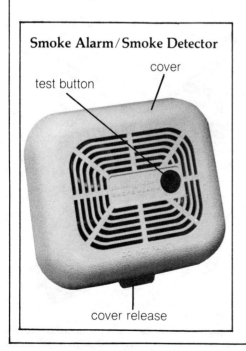

Smoke Alarm/Smoke Detector

cover

test button

cover release

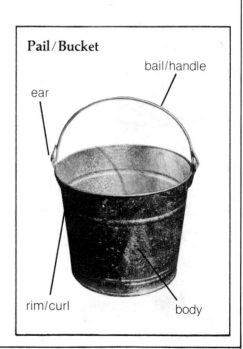

Pail/Bucket

bail/handle

ear

rim/curl

body

Luggage

The exterior parts of a *suitcase* or *bag* are identical to those of an *attaché* case. A suitcase that unfolds to be hung up is called a *garment bag*. Briefcases sometimes have zippered *file folders* or *portfolios* as well as paper storage *pockets*.

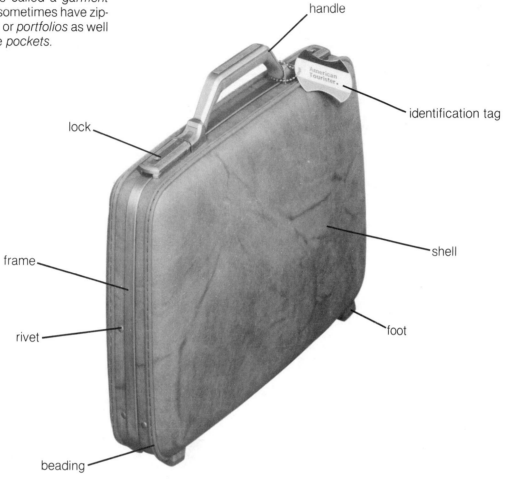

handle

identification tag

lock

shell

frame

rivet

foot

beading

Attaché Case/Briefcase

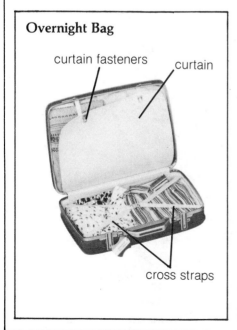

Overnight Bag

curtain fasteners

curtain

cross straps

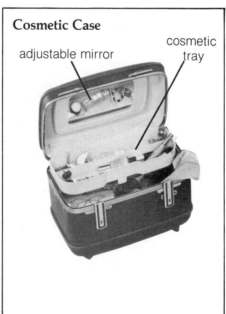

Cosmetic Case

adjustable mirror

cosmetic tray

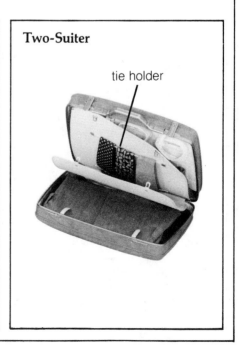

Two-Suiter

tie holder

Playroom/Utility Room

Children's Gear

Modern strollers have largely replaced more elaborate *baby carriages,* or *perambulators.* A portable, basketlike infant bed, often with a *hood* at one end, is called a *bassinet.* An indoor *baby chair,* or *high chair,* has long legs, a *footrest* and a *serving tray.*

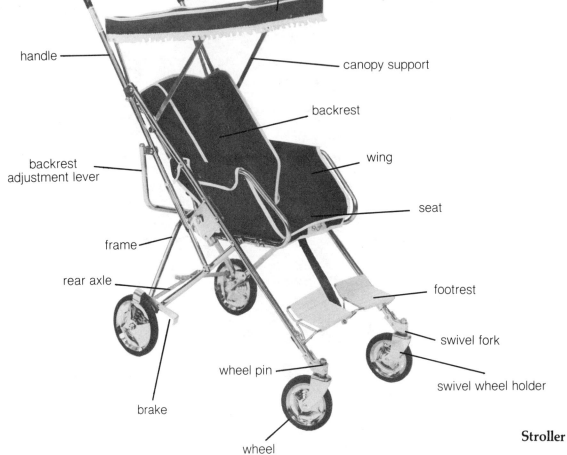

handle grip

canopy

handle

canopy support

backrest

backrest adjustment lever

wing

seat

frame

footrest

rear axle

swivel fork

wheel pin

swivel wheel holder

brake

wheel

Stroller

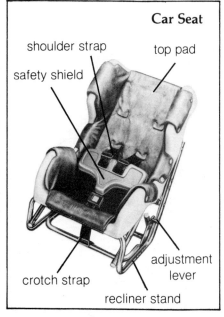

Car Seat

shoulder strap

top pad

safety shield

crotch strap

adjustment lever

recliner stand

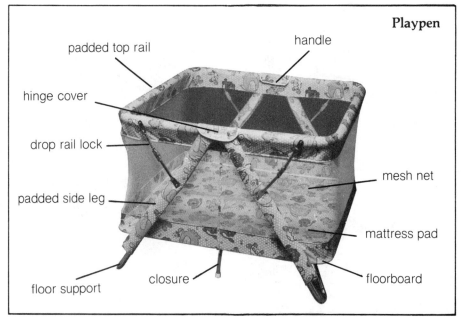

Playpen

padded top rail

handle

hinge cover

drop rail lock

mesh net

padded side leg

mattress pad

floor support

closure

floorboard

Other popular backyard and *play-ground* equipment includes *seesaws,* or *teeter-totters; jungle gyms,* or *monkey bars; climbing nets; over-head ladders* and *sandboxes.*

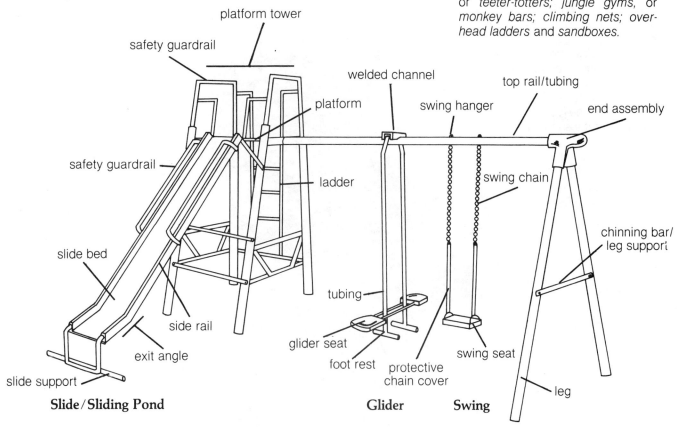

platform tower

safety guardrail

welded channel

top rail/tubing

platform

swing hanger

end assembly

safety guardrail

ladder

swing chain

slide bed

chinning bar/
leg support

tubing

side rail

glider seat

exit angle

swing seat

foot rest

protective
chain cover

slide support

leg

Slide/Sliding Pond

Glider   **Swing**

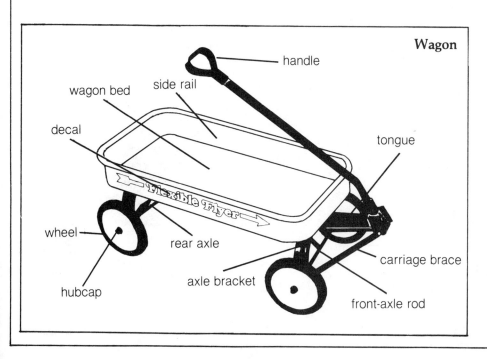

Wagon

handle

side rail

wagon bed

decal

tongue

wheel

rear axle

carriage brace

hubcap

axle bracket

front-axle rod

Patio Accessories

On regular grills and *braziers,* food is cooked over *charcoal briquettes* resting in a *fire bowl,* whereas on gas and electric models food is grilled over *volcanic rock.* Other grills include *hibachis* and *kettle grills* featuring *damper controls, adjustable grills,* and *ash catchers.* On some outdoor lounges and *settees,* small springs, or *helicals,* connect the frame to metal supporting straps.

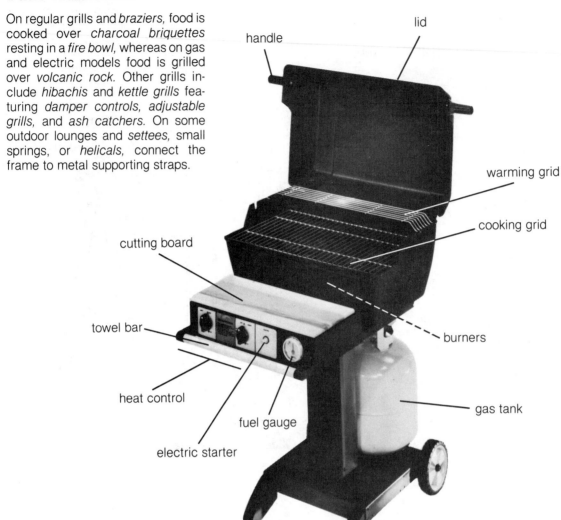

handle

lid

warming grid

cooking grid

cutting board

towel bar

heat control

fuel gauge

electric starter

burners

gas tank

Barbecue Grill/Gas Barbecue

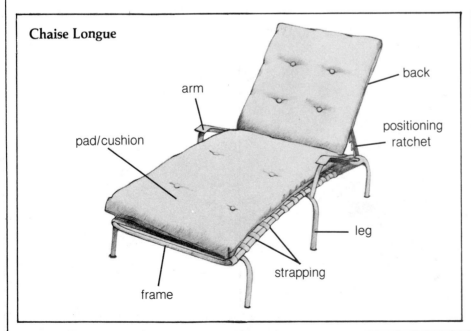

Chaise Longue

back

arm

positioning ratchet

pad/cushion

leg

strapping

frame

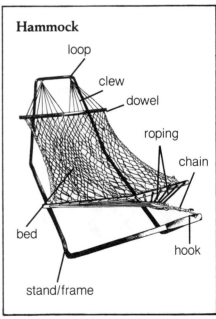

Hammock

loop

clew

dowel

roping

chain

bed

hook

stand/frame

Sports and Recreation

Emphasis in this section is given to major sports and forms of recreational activity which involve gear and equipment. Word and picture games, for example, have been omitted, since the nomenclature involved is so limited.

In order to enable the reader to find particular items quickly, recreational activities have been grouped in the following way: team sports, competitive sports, individual sports, equestrian sports, automobile racing, outdoor sports, bodybuilding, board games and casino games.

Because playing areas involved in team and competitive sports are an integral part of the activity, fields, courts and rinks have been diagramed with all the vital areas, lines and demarcations identified.

And to show the parts of clothing and equipment used by players, real athletes rather than models have been photographed: batter Rod Carew, football running back Bruce Harper, basketball guard Mike Glenn, hockey defenseman Ken Morrow and goalie Billy Smith.

Trophy

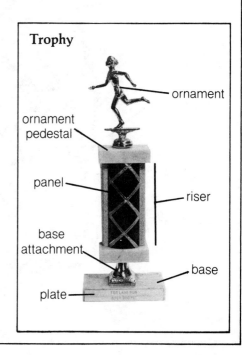

ornament

ornament
pedestal

panel

riser

base
attachment

base

plate

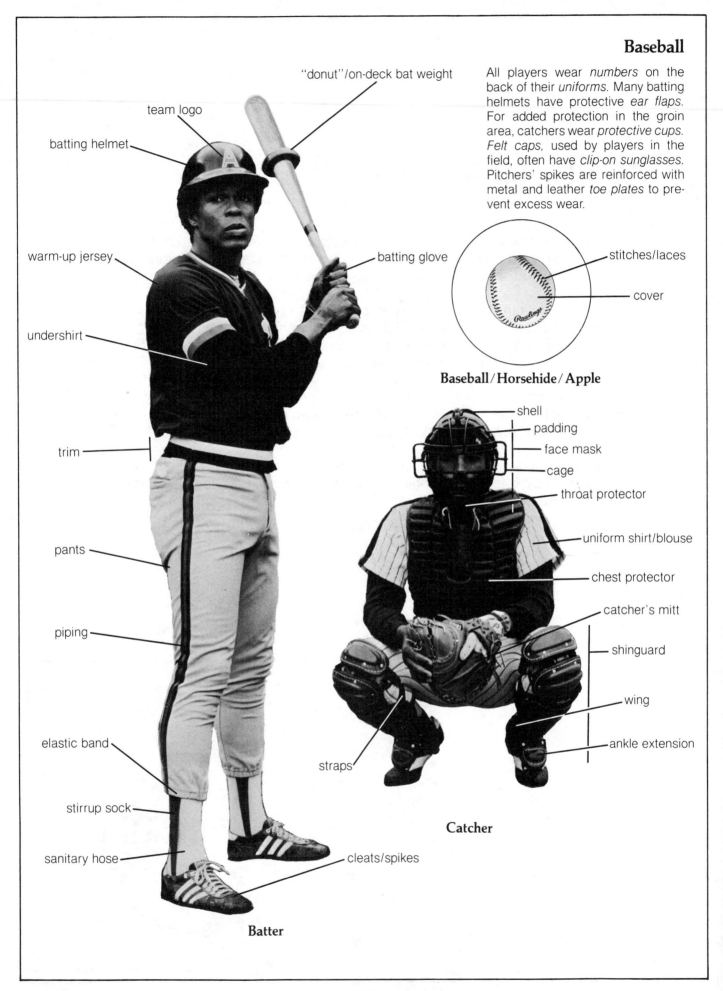

Baseball

"donut"/on-deck bat weight

team logo

batting helmet

warm-up jersey

undershirt

trim

pants

piping

elastic band

stirrup sock

sanitary hose

batting glove

cleats/spikes

Batter

All players wear *numbers* on the back of their *uniforms*. Many batting helmets have protective *ear flaps*. For added protection in the groin area, catchers wear *protective cups*. *Felt caps,* used by players in the field, often have *clip-on sunglasses.* Pitchers' spikes are reinforced with metal and leather *toe plates* to prevent excess wear.

stitches/laces

cover

Baseball/Horsehide/Apple

shell

padding

face mask

cage

throat protector

uniform shirt/blouse

chest protector

catcher's mitt

shinguard

wing

ankle extension

straps

Catcher

Baseball

Artificial turf has replaced natural *grass* in the outfield and certain portions of the infield in many *stadiums,* or *ballparks.*

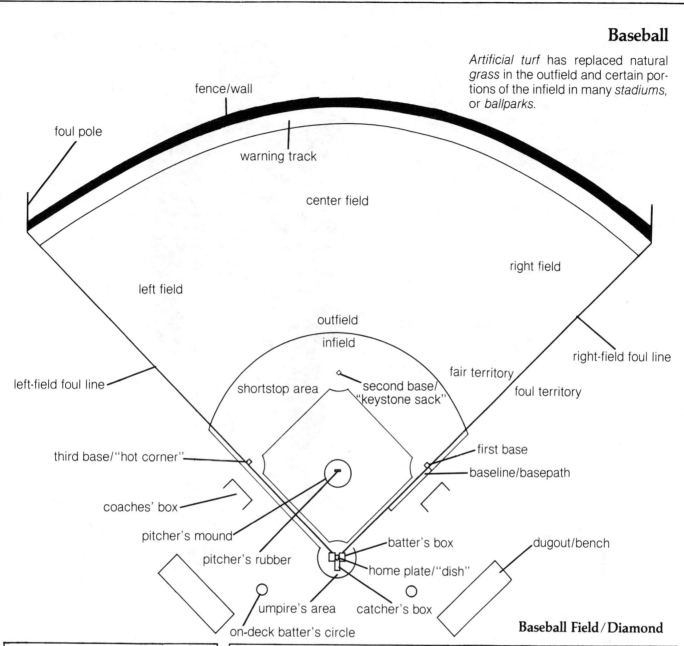

fence/wall

foul pole

warning track

center field

right field

left field

outfield

infield

right-field foul line

fair territory

shortstop area

second base/ "keystone sack"

foul territory

left-field foul line

third base/"hot corner"

first base

baseline/basepath

coaches' box

pitcher's mound

pitcher's rubber

batter's box

dugout/bench

home plate/"dish"

umpire's area

catcher's box

on-deck batter's circle

Baseball Field/Diamond

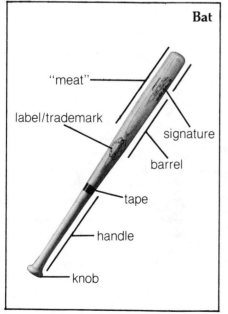

Bat

"meat"

signature

label/trademark

barrel

tape

handle

knob

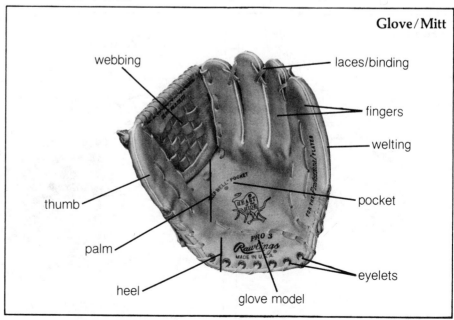

Glove/Mitt

webbing

laces/binding

fingers

welting

thumb

pocket

palm

heel

glove model

eyelets

Team Sports

Football

Protective equipment worn on the upper body is covered with a *numbered jersey*. A *tear-away jersey* is loosely sewn and meant to rip apart when grabbed by an opponent. Helmets are manufactured with different *suspension systems*, some of which are air-inflated. Football covers have a rough *pebble finish* and an air-retaining *bladder* which is filled by inserting an *inflation needle* in the valve.

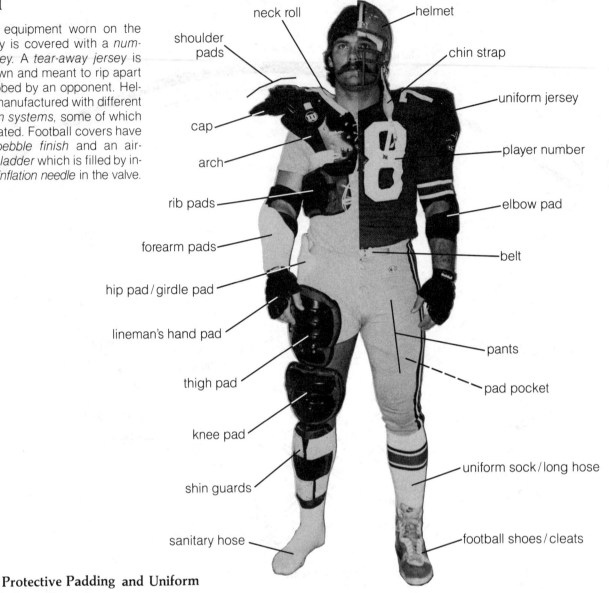

- neck roll
- helmet
- shoulder pads
- chin strap
- cap
- uniform jersey
- arch
- player number
- rib pads
- elbow pad
- forearm pads
- belt
- hip pad / girdle pad
- lineman's hand pad
- thigh pad
- pants
- knee pad
- pad pocket
- shin guards
- uniform sock / long hose
- sanitary hose
- football shoes / cleats

Protective Padding and Uniform

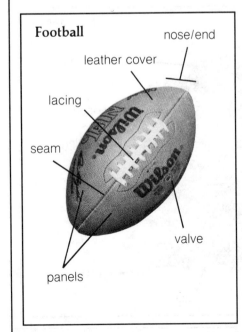

Football

- nose / end
- leather cover
- lacing
- seam
- valve
- panels

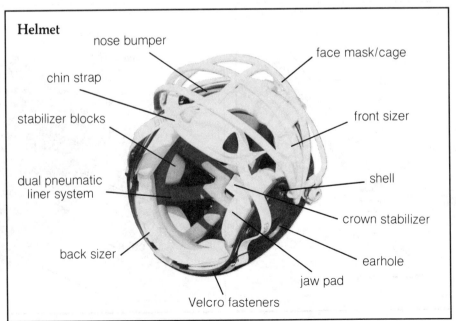

Helmet

- nose bumper
- face mask / cage
- chin strap
- stabilizer blocks
- front sizer
- dual pneumatic liner system
- shell
- crown stabilizer
- back sizer
- earhole
- jaw pad
- Velcro fasteners

Football

A *down marker* is used to mark the exact location of the ball on the field between downs. The *flip chart* at the top of the down marker has *flip panels* to indicate what down is about to be played. Yard lines cross the field every five yards. *Flags* are located at the junction of the goal line and sideline to mark in bounds. Small, rubber inverted V-shaped *yard markers* are placed at five-yard intervals along the sidelines.

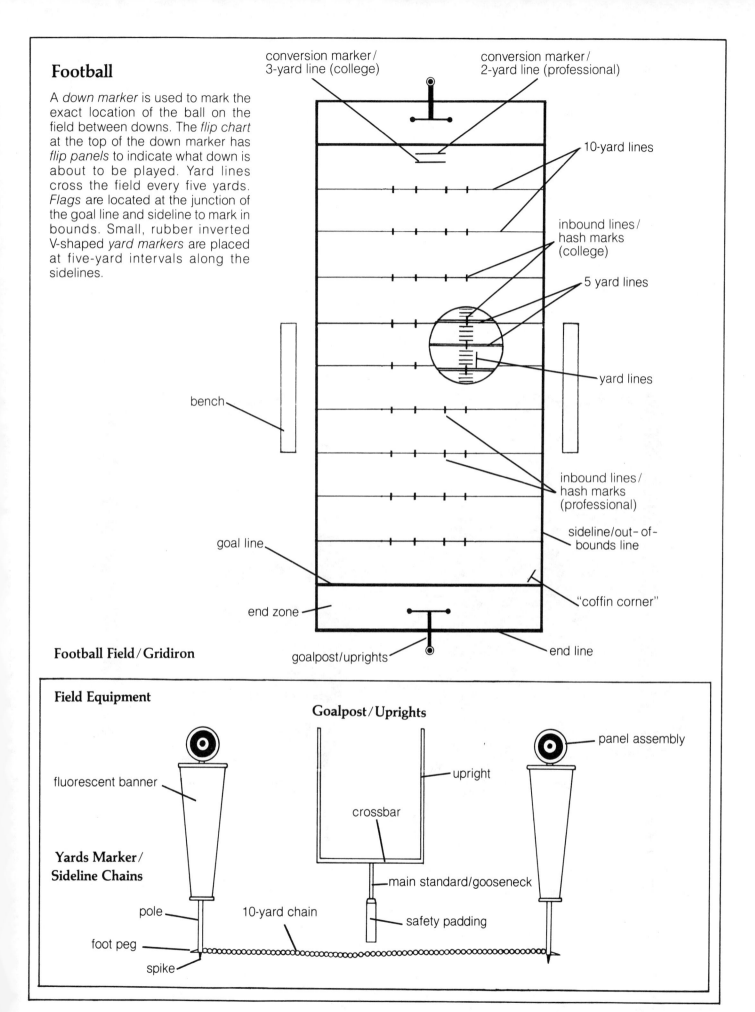

conversion marker/ 3-yard line (college)

conversion marker/ 2-yard line (professional)

10-yard lines

inbound lines/ hash marks (college)

5 yard lines

yard lines

bench

inbound lines/ hash marks (professional)

sideline/out-of-bounds line

goal line

"coffin corner"

end zone

goalpost/uprights

end line

Football Field/Gridiron

Field Equipment

Goalpost/Uprights

fluorescent banner

panel assembly

upright

crossbar

Yards Marker/ Sideline Chains

main standard/gooseneck

pole

10-yard chain

safety padding

foot peg

spike

Team Sports

Ice Hockey

Hockey players' pants are held up by *suspenders*. Socks are attached to a *garter belt*. The angle between the shaft of a hockey stick and the blade is called the *lie*. The game is played with a black vulcanized rubber *puck*. A blinking *red light* atop the goal judge's box indicates a goal.

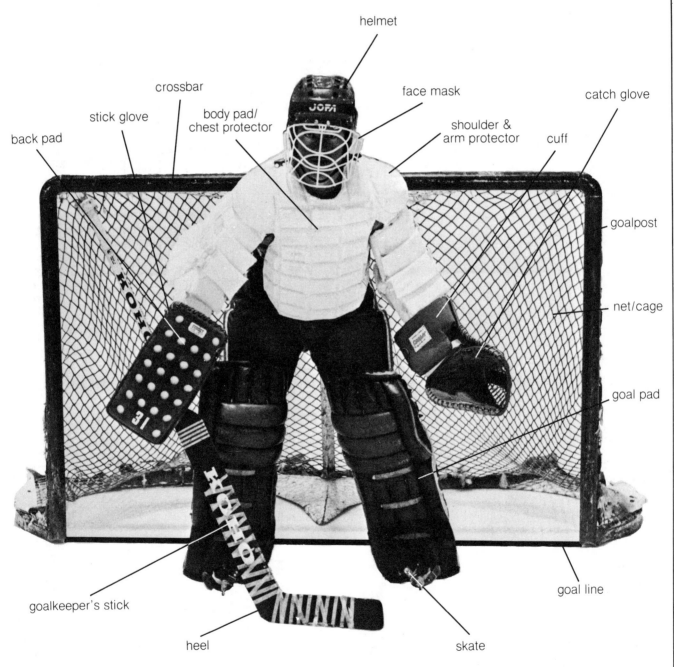

helmet

crossbar

face mask

stick glove

catch glove

body pad/ chest protector

shoulder & arm protector

cuff

back pad

goalpost

net/cage

goal pad

goalkeeper's stick

goal line

heel

skate

Goal and Goalie/Goalkeeper/Goaler

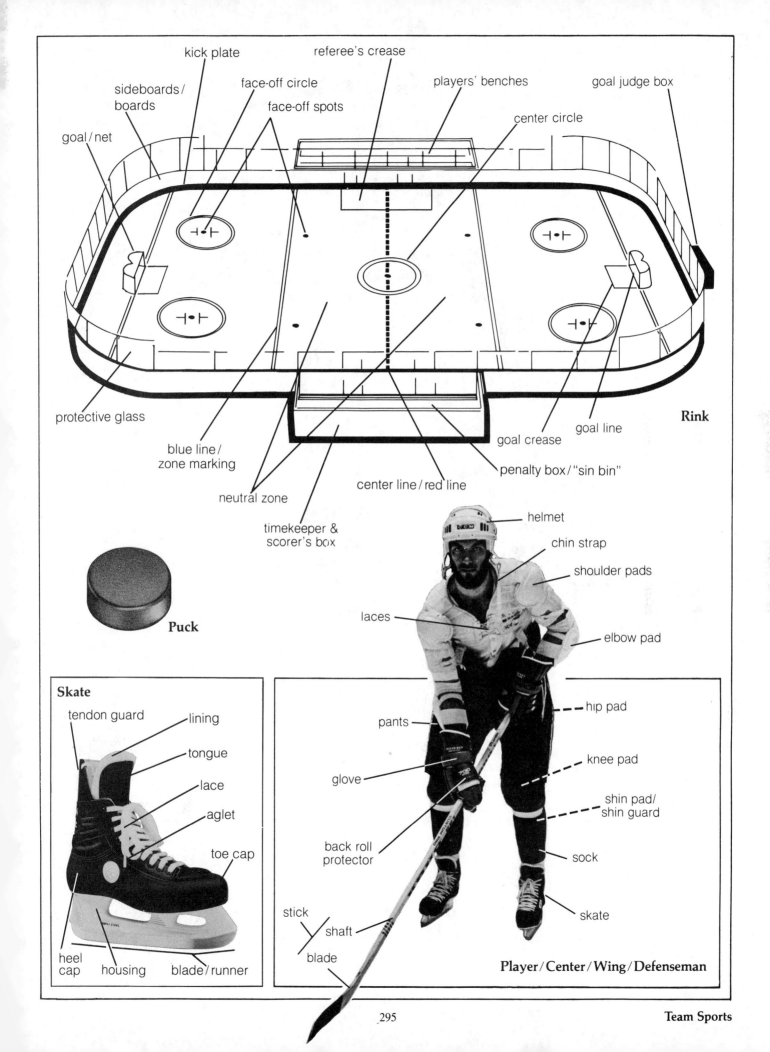

kick plate

referee's crease

players' benches

goal judge box

face-off circle

center circle

sideboards/
boards

face-off spots

goal/net

protective glass

blue line/
zone marking

neutral zone

timekeeper &
scorer's box

center line/red line

goal crease

goal line

penalty box/"sin bin"

Rink

Puck

helmet

chin strap

shoulder pads

laces

elbow pad

hip pad

Skate

tendon guard

lining

tongue

lace

aglet

toe cap

pants

glove

knee pad

shin pad/
shin guard

back roll
protector

sock

heel
cap

housing

blade/runner

stick

shaft

blade

skate

Player/Center/Wing/Defenseman

Team Sports

Basketball

The offensive team advances from its own *backcourt* into the *forecourt*. The area at the top of the free-throw lane, usually patrolled by the *center* (as opposed to one of two *guards* or two *forwards*), is called the *pivot*. Many players wear *kneepads* and *elbow pads* for protection, and *warm-up suits* prior to games.

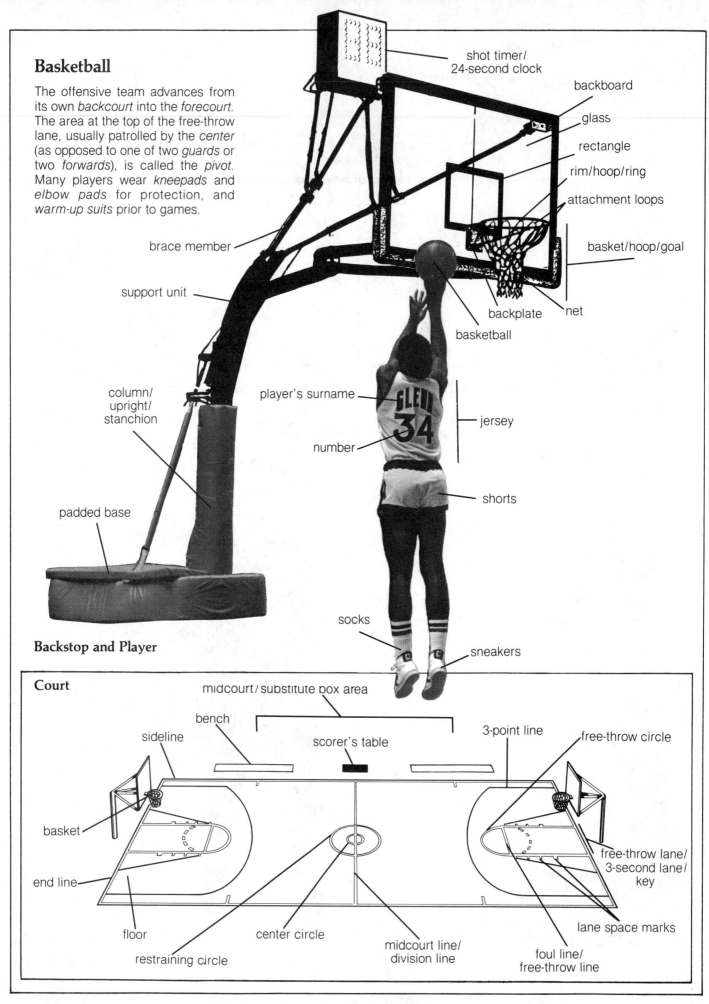

shot timer/
24-second clock

backboard

glass

rectangle

rim/hoop/ring

attachment loops

basket/hoop/goal

net

backplate

basketball

brace member

support unit

column/
upright/
stanchion

padded base

player's surname

jersey

number

shorts

socks

sneakers

Backstop and Player

Court

midcourt/substitute box area

bench

scorer's table

3-point line

free-throw circle

sideline

basket

end line

floor

center circle

restraining circle

midcourt line/
division line

free-throw lane/
3-second lane/
key

lane space marks

foul line/
free-throw line

Soccer

Football, or *association football*, as soccer is known in most of the world, is played by two teams of 11 players. If a *match* is tied after two 45-minute *halves*, the game is decided by a *sudden-death overtime*, in which the first team to score wins, or a *shootout*, in which each team is given several free kicks.

Footballers/Players

jersey/shirt

wristband

team/club insignia

shorts

sock/stocking

shin pad

player number

shoe/boot

color panel

Ball

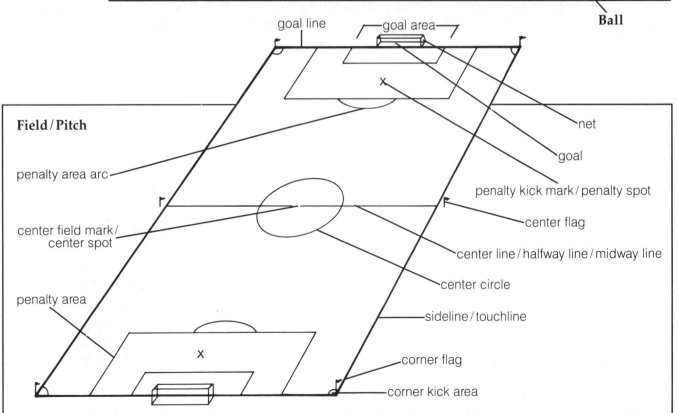

Field/Pitch

goal line

goal area

net

goal

penalty area arc

penalty kick mark/penalty spot

center flag

center field mark/center spot

center line/halfway line/midway line

center circle

penalty area

sideline/touchline

corner flag

corner kick area

Team Sports

Lacrosse

Lacrosse is a *contact sport*, meaning that *blocking* and other physical contact is legal. Defensive players use their sticks or bodies to *check* a *possession player* carrying the ball. Illegal body checks or slashing players with a stick are *personal fouls*; the offending player is sent to a penalty box for 1 to 3 minutes.

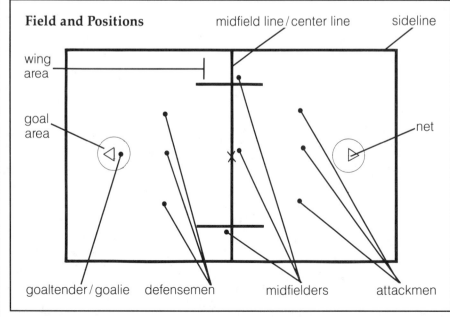

head
top lip
scoop
guard/wall
pocket/face
bridge
throat
shaft/handle
knob/end/buttend

Stick/Crosse

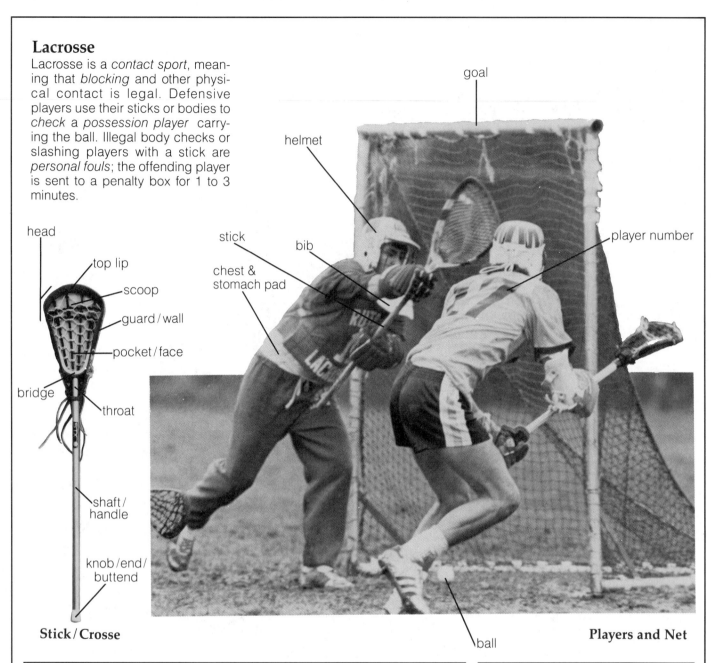

goal
helmet
stick
bib
chest & stomach pad
player number
ball

Players and Net

Field and Positions

wing area
goal area
midfield line/center line
sideline
net
goaltender/goalie
defensemen
midfielders
attackmen

Glove

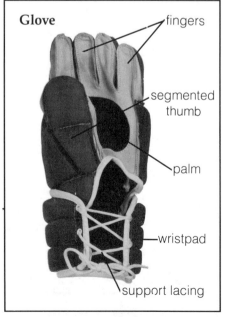

fingers
segmented thumb
palm
wristpad
support lacing

Polo

Polo is played on horseback by two teams of four players each. A *match* consists of eight seven-minute periods, or *chukkas*. Players ride a *string*, or several ponies, during play. The match is officiated by two mounted *umpires* and a *referee* on the sideline.

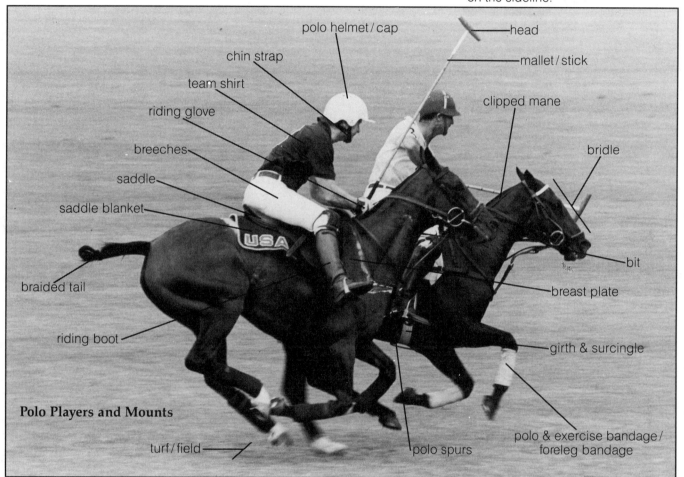

polo helmet/cap
head
chin strap
mallet/stick
team shirt
clipped mane
riding glove
bridle
breeches
saddle
saddle blanket
bit
braided tail
breast plate
riding boot
girth & surcingle
Polo Players and Mounts
polo & exercise bandage/
foreleg bandage
turf/field
polo spurs

Polo Grounds and Positions

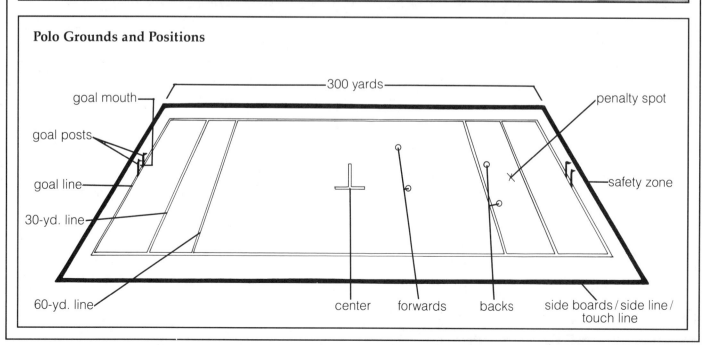

300 yards
goal mouth
penalty spot
goal posts
goal line
safety zone
30-yd. line
60-yd. line
center
forwards
backs
side boards/side line/
touch line

299

Track and Field

Track-and-field events take place on a *running track* and the enclosed *field* within. Besides *jumping events* and *throwing events,* there are *footraces,* including *walking races, hurdle races, steeplechase, relay races, medley relays, runs* and the *marathon.* The *decathlon* is a ten-event contest, while the *pentathlon* consists of five events.

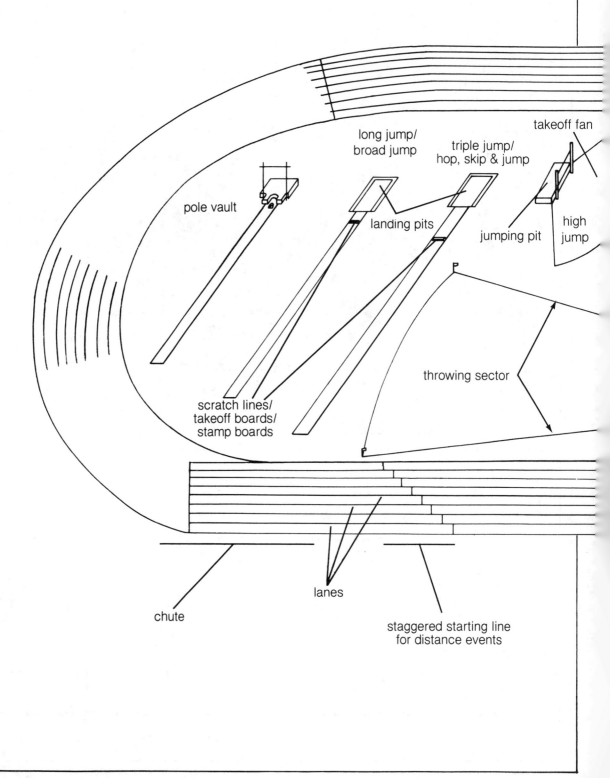

pole vault

long jump/ broad jump

triple jump/ hop, skip & jump

takeoff fan

landing pits

jumping pit

high jump

throwing sector

scratch lines/ takeoff boards/ stamp boards

lanes

chute

staggered starting line for distance events

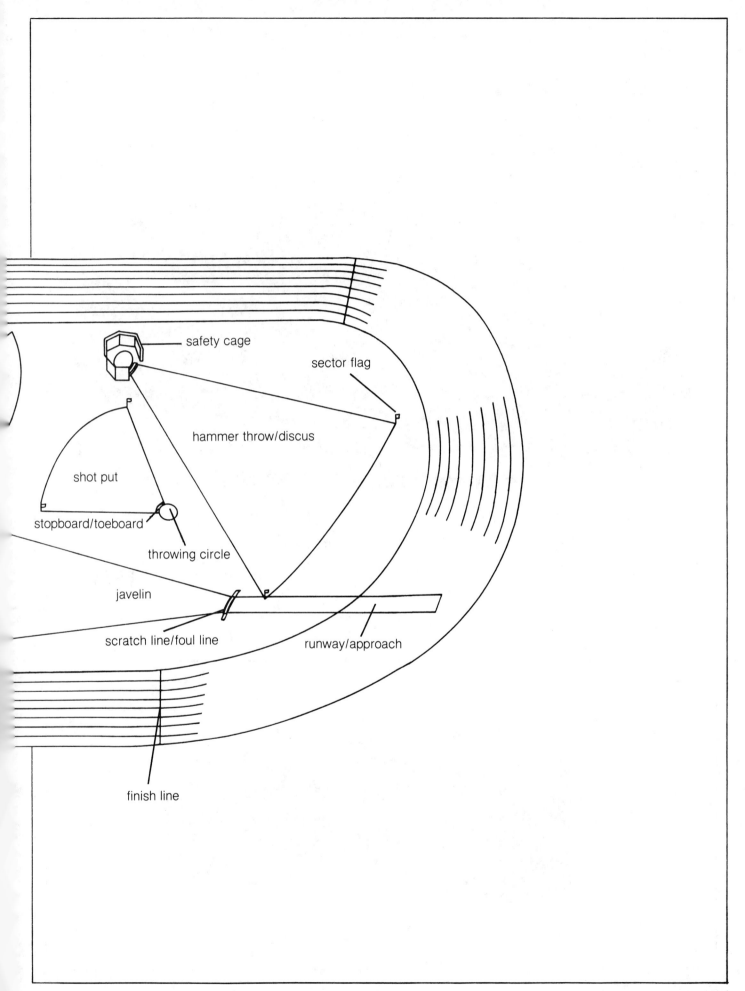

safety cage

sector flag

hammer throw/discus

shot put

stopboard/toeboard

throwing circle

javelin

scratch line/foul line

runway/approach

finish line

Running Shoe

These *training shoes*, or *trainers*, are more durable than lighter-weight *racing flats*. Lightweight running shoes are worn by *joggers* or *distance runners* in long races such as *marathons*. *Track shoes*, shoes with *spikes*, are used for most track-and-field events.

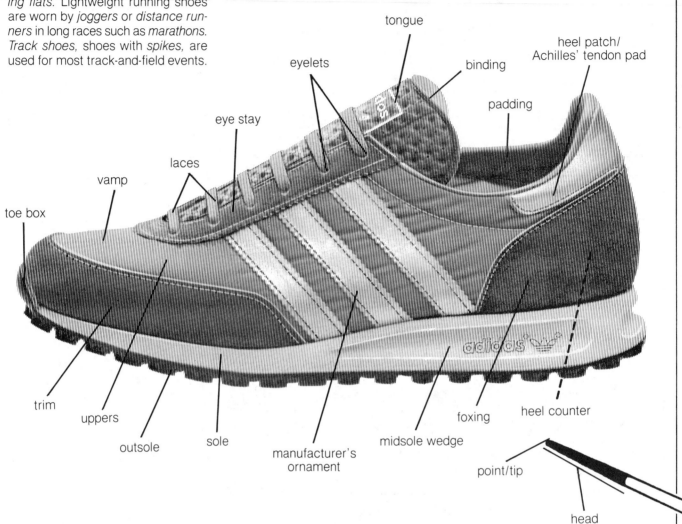

tongue

heel patch/
Achilles' tendon pad

eyelets

binding

padding

eye stay

laces

vamp

toe box

trim

uppers

outsole

sole

manufacturer's
ornament

midsole wedge

foxing

heel counter

point/tip

head

Tread

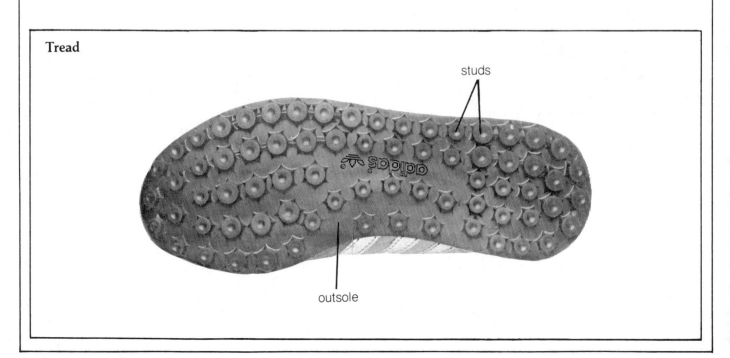

studs

outsole

Field Events Equipment

In addition to the equipment shown here, a round metal ball called a *shot put*, or *shot*, is also used in field events. Hammer throwers often wear *gloves* with padded palms.

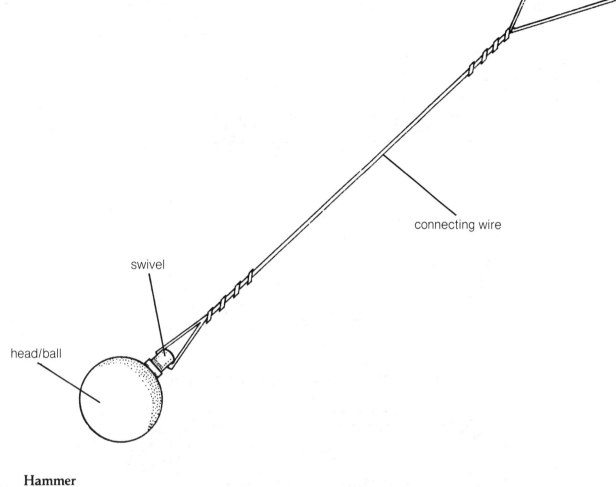

grip

handle

connecting wire

swivel

head/ball

Hammer

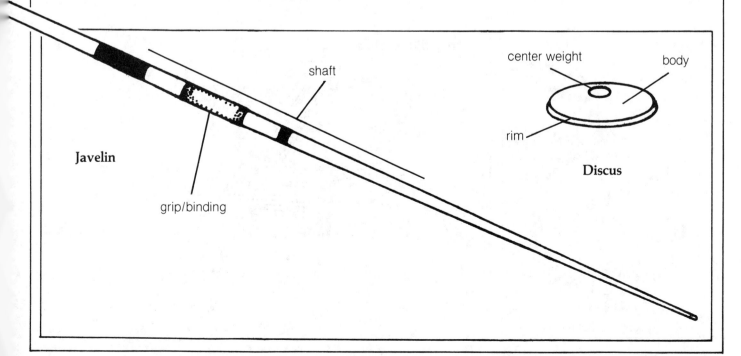

shaft

center weight

body

rim

Javelin

grip/binding

Discus

Competitive Sports

Hurdle

The height of hurdles can be adjusted for use in *high, intermediate* and *low hurdle* events. Base weights can also be adjusted to provide the proper *pullover,* or *flipover,* the force required to knock them over. *Fixed hurdles* are used in a *steeplechase race,* an event that includes *water hazards.* Roller, or notched *lever locks* permit runners to adjust the slant on starting blocks, and a *plunger snap lock* allows them to position the blocks individually on the rail.

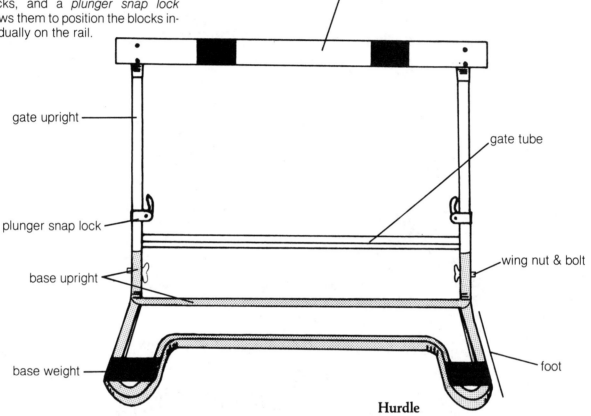

gatebar/top bar

gate upright

gate tube

plunger snap lock

base upright

wing nut & bolt

base weight

foot

Hurdle

Stopwatch

lanyard

bow

crown/start & stop button

reset button

minute hand

60

55

5

50

10

45

15

40

20

35

25

30

second bits

CHESTERFIELD DOLMY 1/5

bezel

second hand

Starting Block/Blocks

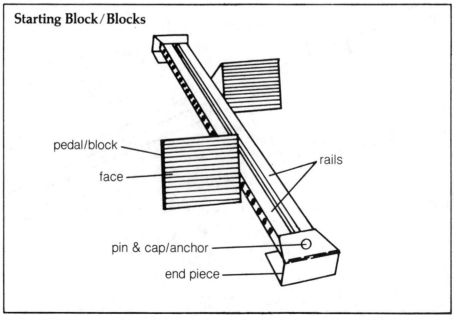

pedal/block

face

rails

pin & cap/anchor

end piece

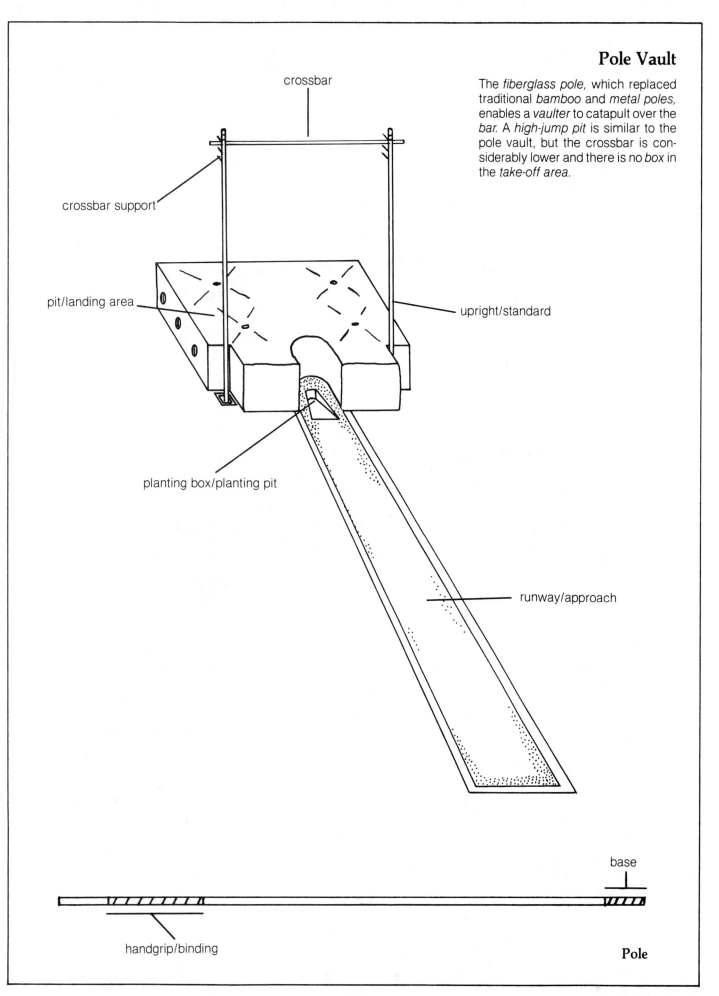

crossbar

Pole Vault

The *fiberglass pole*, which replaced traditional *bamboo* and *metal poles*, enables a *vaulter* to catapult over the *bar*. A *high-jump pit* is similar to the pole vault, but the crossbar is considerably lower and there is no *box* in the *take-off area*.

crossbar support

pit/landing area

upright/standard

planting box/planting pit

runway/approach

base

handgrip/binding

Pole

Competitive Sports

Gymnastics

Protective *landing mats* are placed around each piece of gymnastic equipment when it is in use. In addition, during practice sessions, assistants called *spotters* stand by to aid the *gymnast*. Gymnastic competition called *floor exercises* takes place on lined *floor exercise mats*.

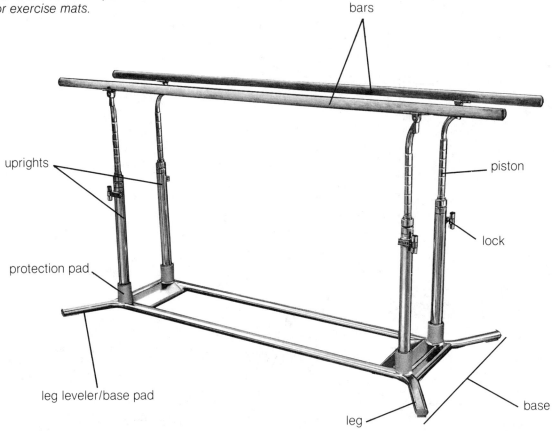

bars

uprights

piston

lock

protection pad

leg leveler/base pad

leg

base

Parallel Bars

Horizontal Bar/High Bar

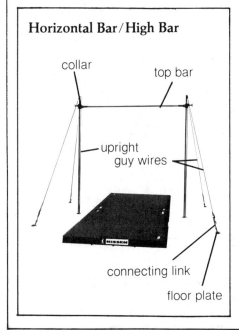

collar

top bar

upright
guy wires

connecting link

floor plate

Uneven Parallel Bars

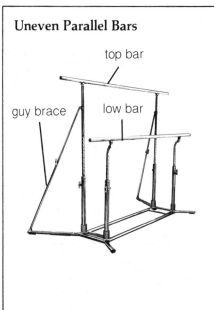

top bar

guy brace

low bar

Balance Beam

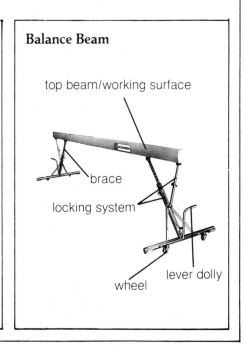

top beam/working surface

brace

locking system

wheel

lever dolly

Gymnastics

Some pommel horses, or *side horses*, can be converted into *vaulting*, or *long, horses* by removing the pommels and plugging the holes they fit in. *Vaulting boards*, or *springboards*, are used by *vaulters* to gain height when mounting the apparatus.

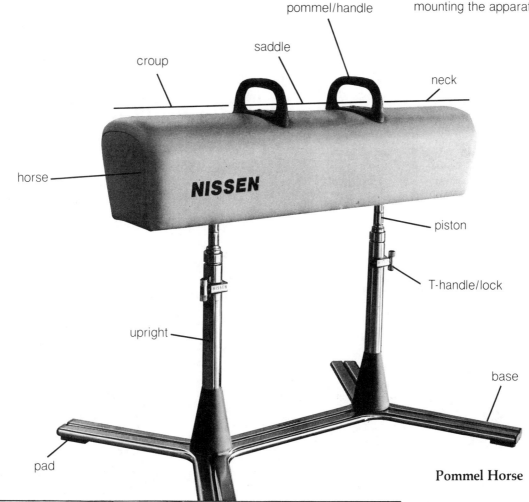

croup

saddle

pommel/handle

neck

horse

NISSEN

piston

T-handle/lock

upright

base

pad

Pommel Horse

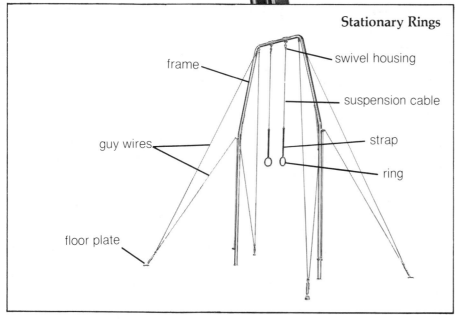

Stationary Rings

frame

swivel housing

suspension cable

guy wires

strap

ring

floor plate

Trampoline

Trampolining, trampoline tumbling, or *rebound tumbling* is performed on the canvas or elastic-webbing bed. Smaller *trampolets* are often used as *springboards* for mounting gymnastic apparatus.

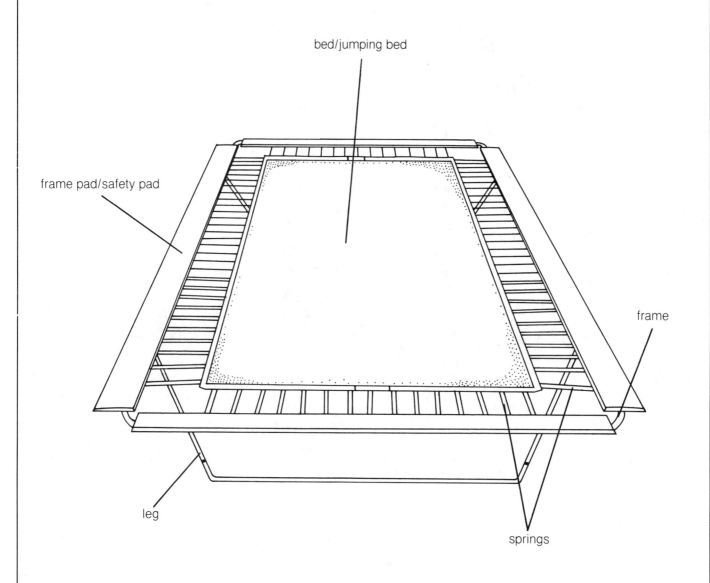

bed/jumping bed

frame pad/safety pad

frame

leg

springs

Boxing

In addition to the *sparring,* or practice, equipment shown here, *boxers* use a *mouthpiece* or *mouthguard* for protection of teeth. A *bell* at *ringside* is used to indicate the beginning and end of each *round.* Boxers rest on *stools* placed in their corners by assistants, or *handlers,* between rounds. Corners not used by fighters during these periods are called *neutral corners.*

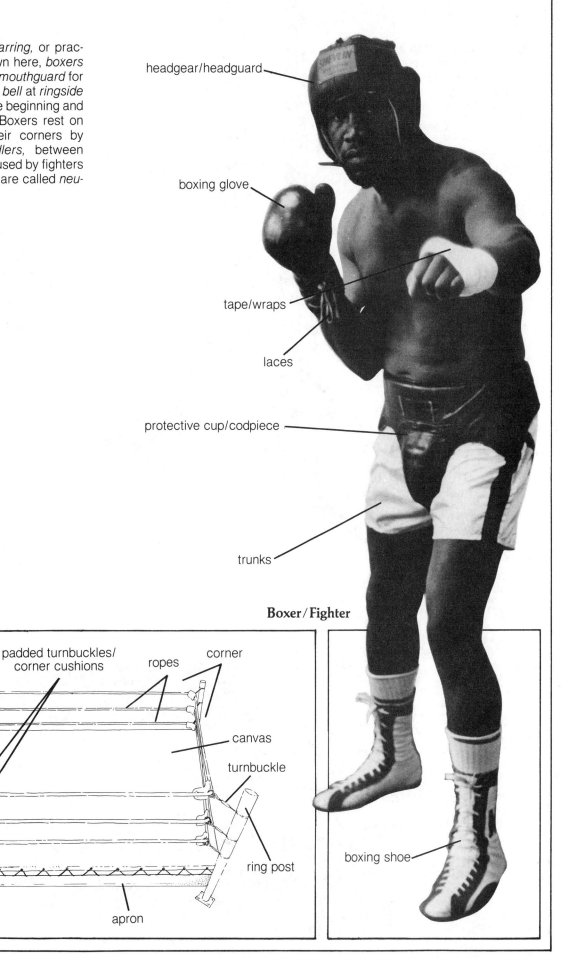

headgear/headguard

boxing glove

tape/wraps

laces

protective cup/codpiece

trunks

Boxer/Fighter

Boxing Ring

padded turnbuckles/ corner cushions

ropes

corner

canvas

turnbuckle

ring post

apron

boxing shoe

Golf

Clubs are numbered in order of increasing *loft,* the angle of the clubface from the vertical, with woods numbered from one to five and the irons numbered two through nine. A *golfer* may also carry a *pitching wedge,* a *sand wedge* and a putter. The spot where the ball lands after being hit is called the *lie.*

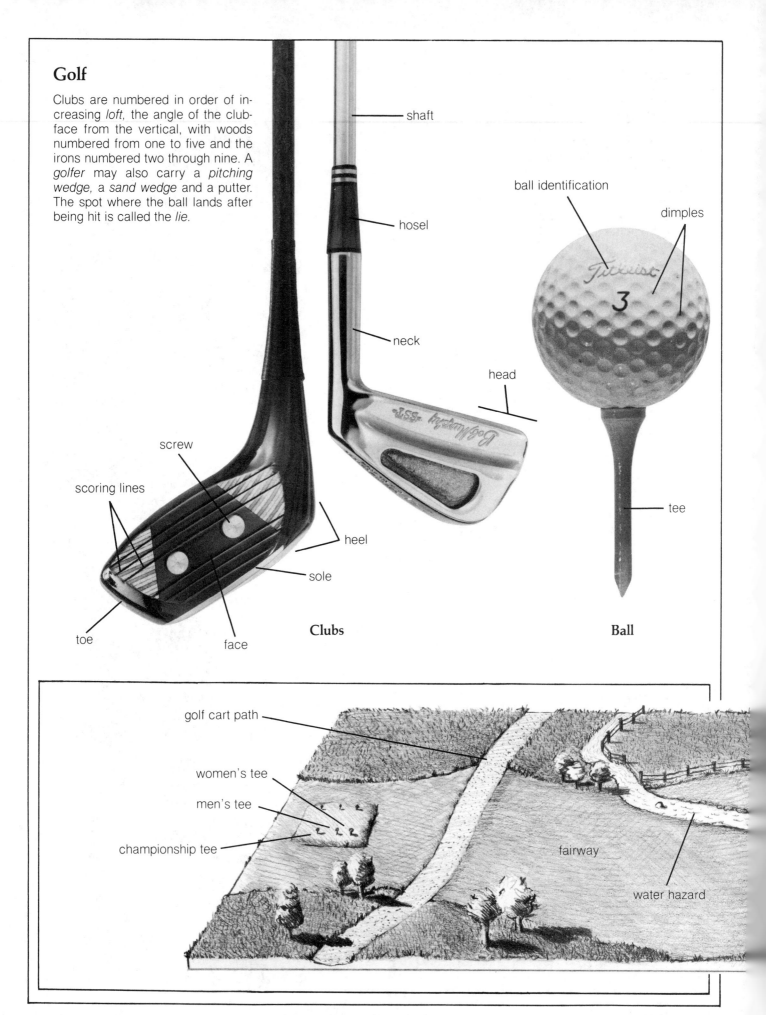

shaft

hosel

neck

head

ball identification

dimples

tee

screw

scoring lines

heel

sole

toe

face

Clubs

Ball

golf cart path

women's tee

men's tee

championship tee

fairway

water hazard

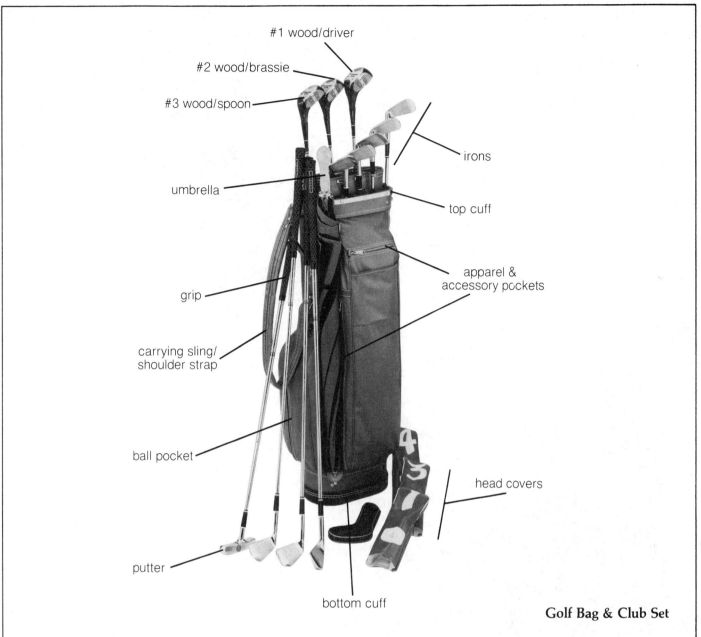

#1 wood/driver

#2 wood/brassie

#3 wood/spoon

irons

umbrella

top cuff

grip

apparel &
accessory pockets

carrying sling/
shoulder strap

ball pocket

head covers

putter

bottom cuff

Golf Bag & Club Set

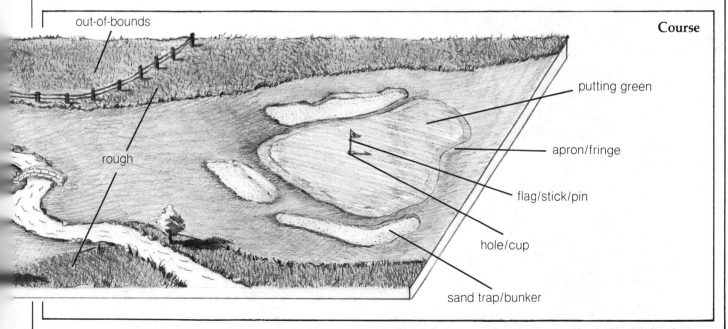

out-of-bounds

Course

putting green

apron/fringe

rough

flag/stick/pin

hole/cup

sand trap/bunker

Tennis

Some rackets have an interchangeable handle, or *pallet*, and a replaceable *throatpiece*, or *yoke*. The "sweet spot" is the prime hitting area of a racket *face*.

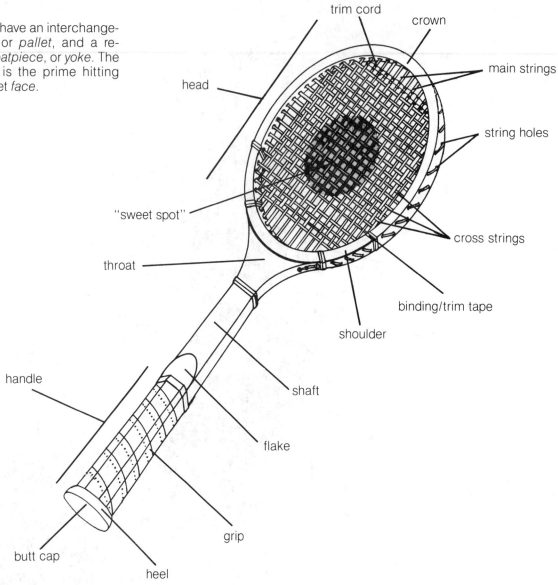

trim cord

crown

main strings

head

string holes

"sweet spot"

cross strings

throat

binding/trim tape

shoulder

handle

shaft

flake

grip

butt cap

heel

Racket

Court

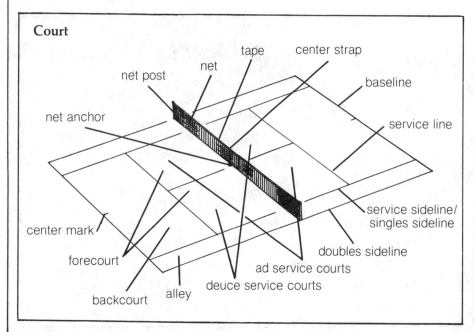

tape

center strap

net post

net

baseline

net anchor

service line

center mark

service sideline/
singles sideline

forecourt

doubles sideline

backcourt

alley

deuce service courts

ad service courts

Ball

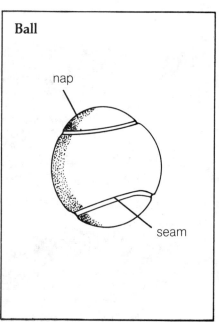

nap

seam

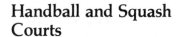

Handball and Squash Courts

The composite court shown here includes both handball and squash rackets terms. In each case, the court is entered through a small *door* in the *back wall*. In handball, players alternately hit a hard black *ball* with their hands, whereas in squash a soft rubber ball is hit with a *racket*.

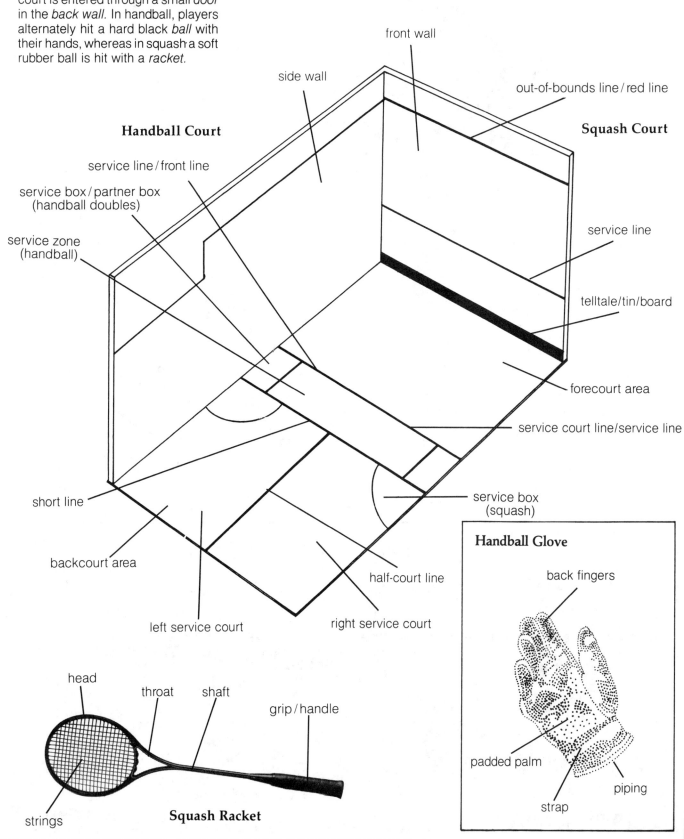

front wall

side wall

out-of-bounds line / red line

Squash Court

Handball Court

service line / front line

service box / partner box (handball doubles)

service zone (handball)

service line

telltale / tin / board

forecourt area

service court line / service line

short line

service box (squash)

backcourt area

half-court line

left service court

right service court

Handball Glove

back fingers

padded palm

piping

strap

head

throat

shaft

grip / handle

strings

Squash Racket

Competitive Sports

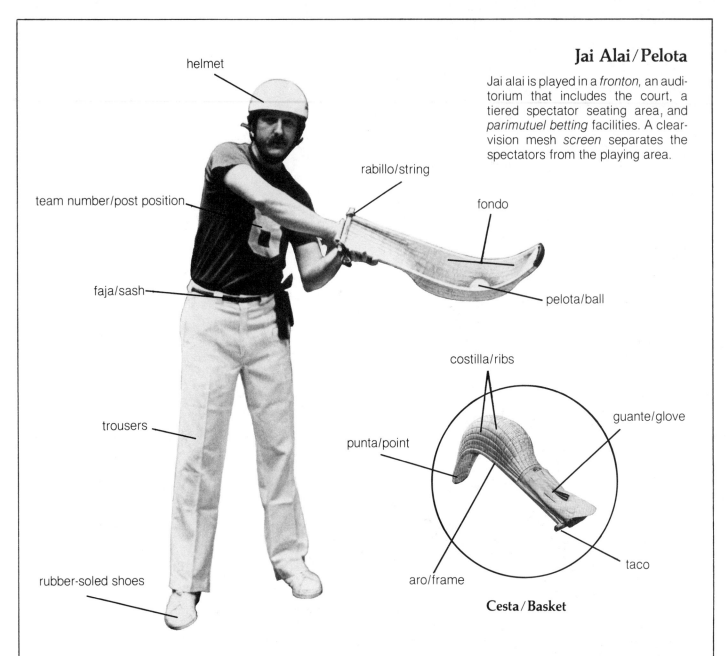

Jai Alai/Pelota

Jai alai is played in a *fronton,* an auditorium that includes the court, a tiered spectator seating area, and *parimutuel betting* facilities. A clear-vision mesh *screen* separates the spectators from the playing area.

helmet

rabillo/string

fondo

team number/post position

pelota/ball

faja/sash

costilla/ribs

trousers

guante/glove

punta/point

rubber-soled shoes

aro/frame

taco

Cesta/Basket

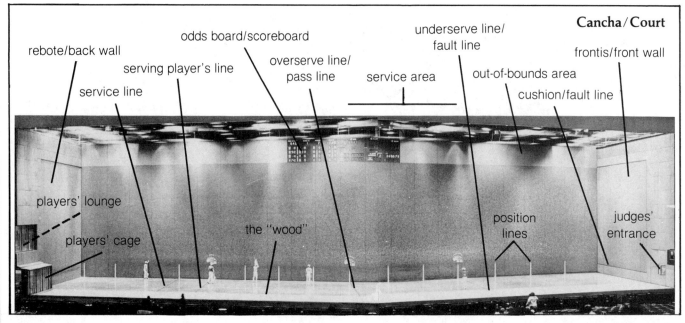

Cancha/Court

odds board/scoreboard

underserve line/fault line

rebote/back wall

frontis/front wall

serving player's line

overserve line/pass line

out-of-bounds area

service line

service area

cushion/fault line

players' lounge

players' cage

the "wood"

position lines

judges' entrance

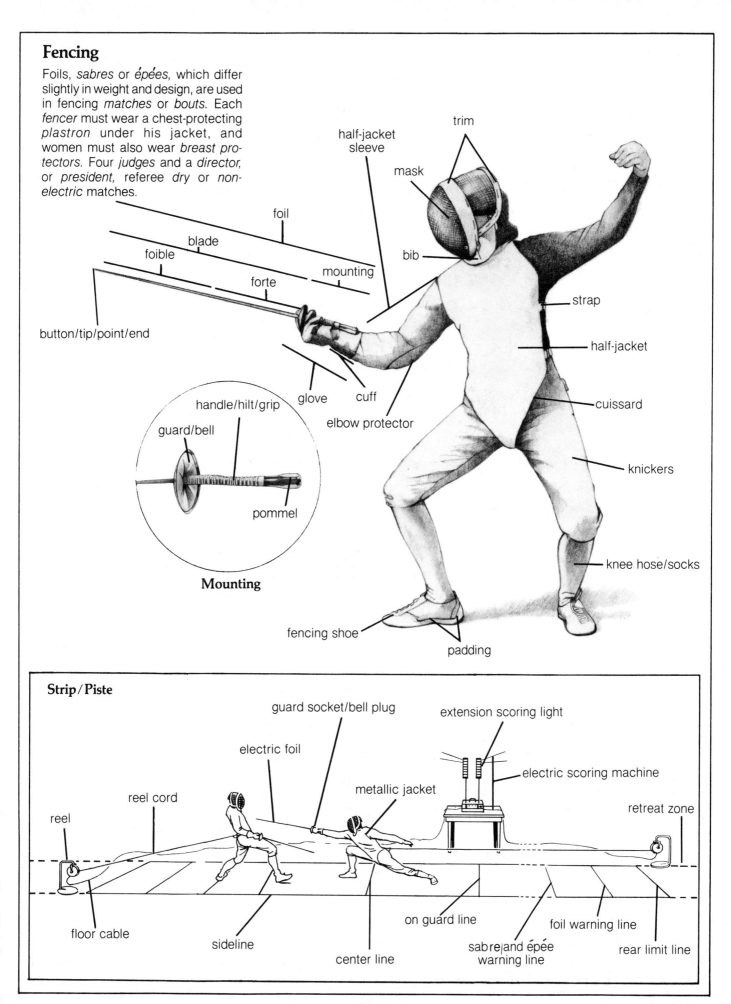

Fencing

Foils, *sabres* or *épées,* which differ slightly in weight and design, are used in fencing *matches* or *bouts.* Each *fencer* must wear a chest-protecting *plastron* under his jacket, and women must also wear *breast protectors.* Four *judges* and a *director,* or *president,* referee *dry* or *non-electric* matches.

trim

half-jacket
sleeve

mask

bib

foil

blade

foible

mounting

forte

button/tip/point/end

strap

half-jacket

glove

cuff

elbow protector

cuissard

knickers

knee hose/socks

handle/hilt/grip

guard/bell

pommel

Mounting

fencing shoe

padding

Strip / Piste

guard socket/bell plug

extension scoring light

electric foil

electric scoring machine

reel cord

metallic jacket

retreat zone

reel

floor cable

sideline

center line

on guard line

sabre and épée
warning line

foil warning line

rear limit line

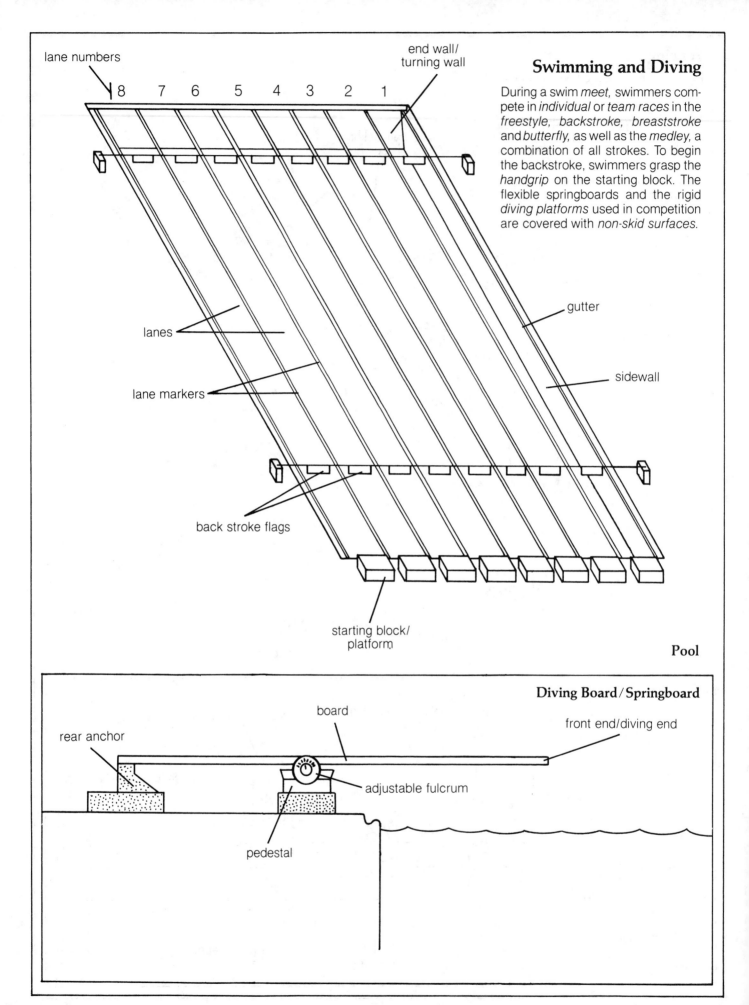

Swimming and Diving

During a swim *meet,* swimmers compete in *individual* or *team races* in the *freestyle, backstroke, breaststroke* and *butterfly,* as well as the *medley,* a combination of all strokes. To begin the backstroke, swimmers grasp the *handgrip* on the starting block. The flexible springboards and the rigid *diving platforms* used in competition are covered with *non-skid surfaces.*

lane numbers

end wall/
turning wall

8 7 6 5 4 3 2 1

lanes

lane markers

gutter

sidewall

back stroke flags

starting block/
platform

Pool

Diving Board / Springboard

board

front end/diving end

rear anchor

adjustable fulcrum

pedestal

Bowling

The strike pocket opposite to the hand delivering the ball is called the *Brooklyn pocket* or *Jersey pocket*. Pins are reset by a mechanical *pinsetter* or *pinspotter*. *Duckpins* and *candlepins* are forms of bowling in which differently shaped pins and lighter, smaller balls are used.

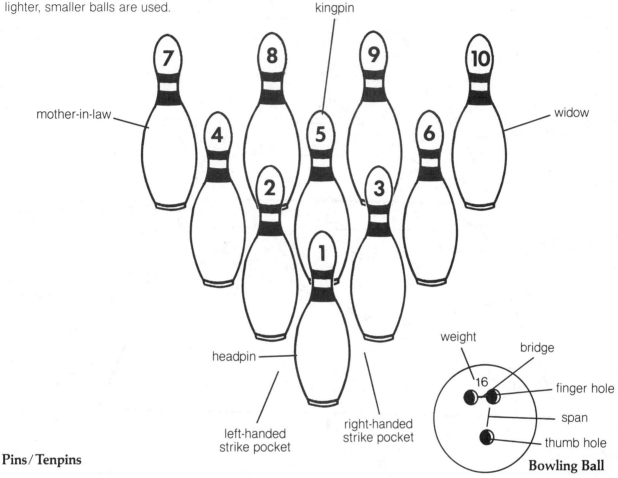

kingpin

mother-in-law

widow

headpin

weight

bridge

finger hole

span

thumb hole

left-handed strike pocket

right-handed strike pocket

Pins/Tenpins

Bowling Ball

Lane/Alley

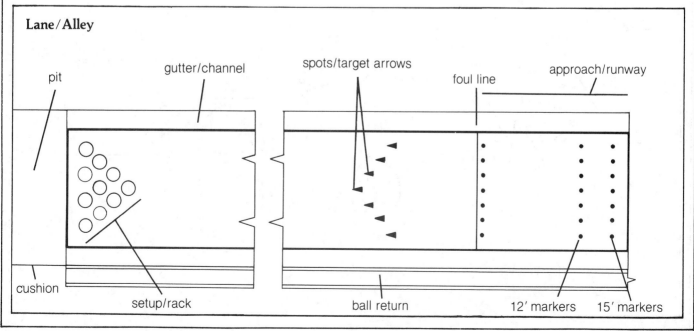

pit

gutter/channel

spots/target arrows

foul line

approach/runway

cushion

setup/rack

ball return

12' markers

15' markers

Competitive Sports

Shuffleboard and Croquet

A shuffleboard game may begin at either end of a *court*. That end is designated the *head*. The opposite end is the *foot*. In croquet, *strikers* start at the *home stake* and return to it after going through wickets and hitting the *turning stake*.

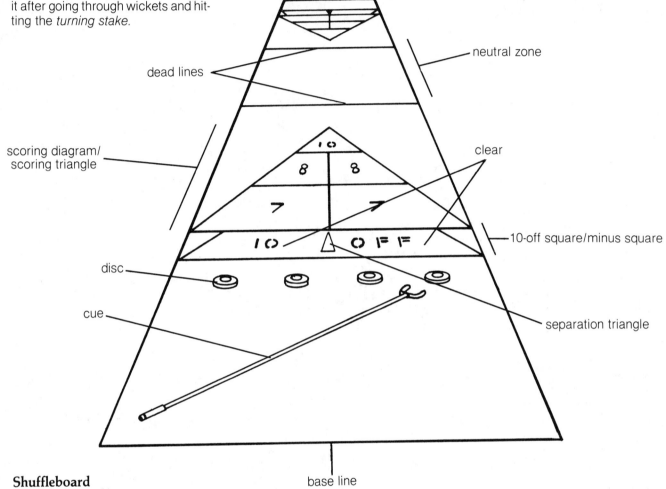

dead lines

neutral zone

scoring diagram/
scoring triangle

clear

10

8   8

7   7

10   O F F

10-off square/minus square

disc

cue

separation triangle

Shuffleboard

base line

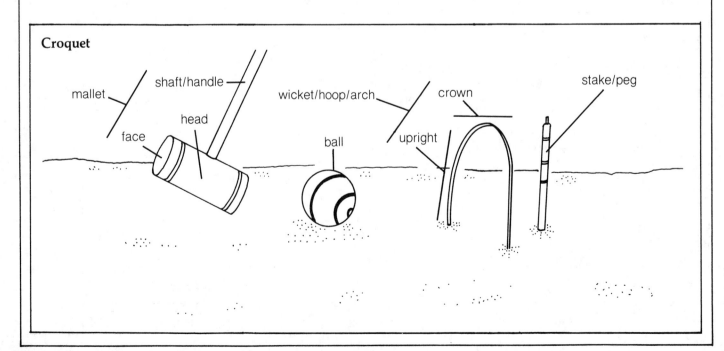

Croquet

mallet

shaft/handle

head

face

wicket/hoop/arch

crown

stake/peg

ball

upright

Volleyball and Badminton

In volleyball, an inflated ball hit sharply is called a *spike* or *kill*. Badminton is played with a *racket* or *bat* whose parts are similar to those of a tennis racket. Some badminton shuttles have nylon *skirts* rather than feathers.

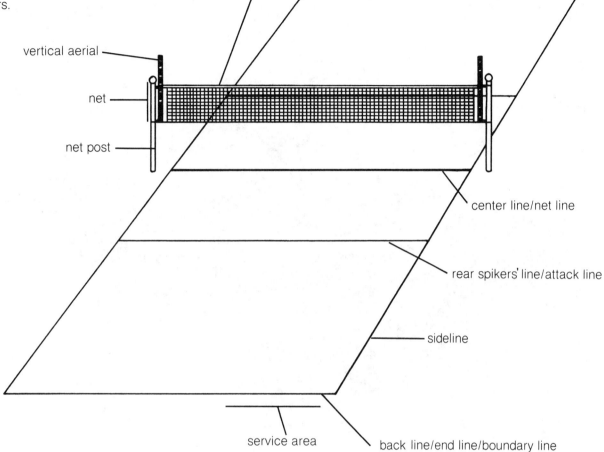

tape

vertical aerial

net

net post

center line/net line

rear spikers' line/attack line

sideline

service area

back line/end line/boundary line

Volleyball Court

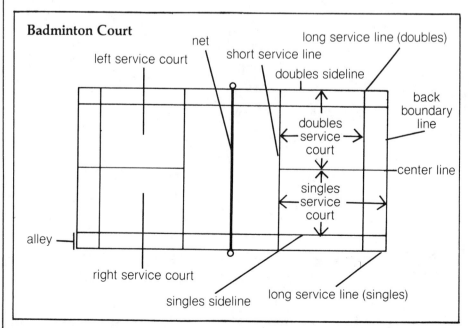

Badminton Court

net

left service court

short service line

long service line (doubles)

doubles sideline

doubles service court

back boundary line

center line

singles service court

alley

right service court

singles sideline

long service line (singles)

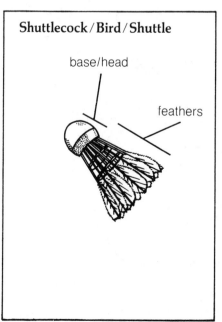

Shuttlecock/Bird/Shuttle

base/head

feathers

Competitive Sports

Billiards and Pool

Billiard and pool tables are usually covered with a dark green cloth called *felt,* or *bed cloth.* A triangular *rack* is used to position object balls at the beginning of a pool or *snooker* game. *Chalk* is used on cue tips. A point scored in billiards is called a *carom.*

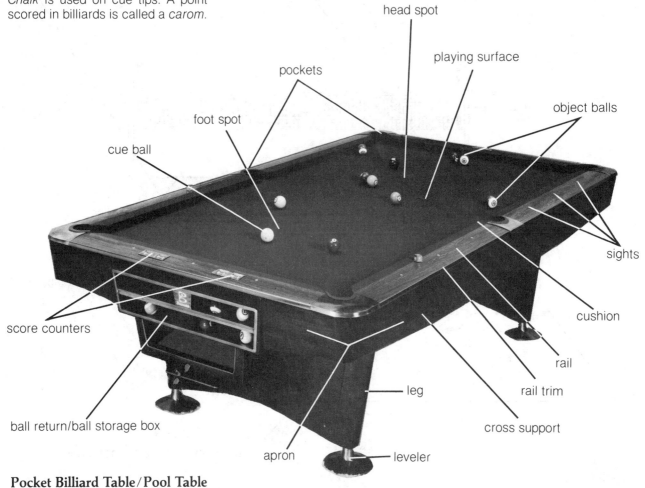

head spot

playing surface

pockets

object balls

foot spot

cue ball

sights

cushion

score counters

rail

rail trim

ball return/ball storage box

leg

cross support

apron

leveler

Pocket Billiard Table/Pool Table

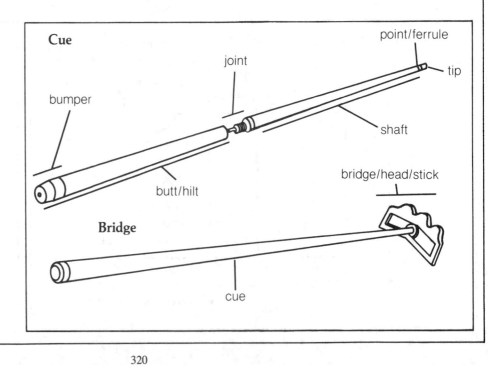

Cue

point/ferrule

joint

tip

bumper

shaft

butt/hilt

bridge/head/stick

Bridge

cue

Ping-Pong/Table Tennis

Paddles have two types of grips, *shake-hands grips* and *penhold grips*, and two types of faces, *rubber* and *sponge*. The game is played with a ping-pong *ball*.

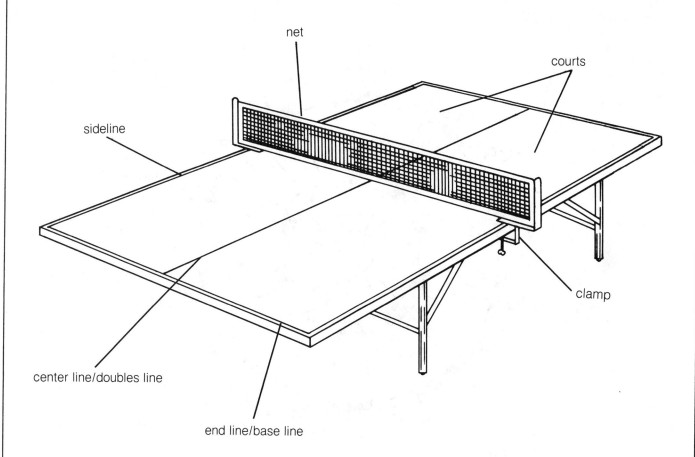

net

courts

sideline

clamp

center line/doubles line

end line/base line

Ping-Pong Table

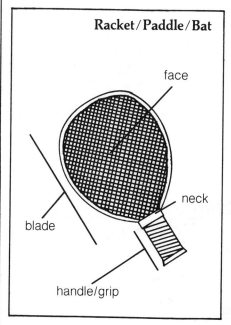

Racket/Paddle/Bat

face

blade

neck

handle/grip

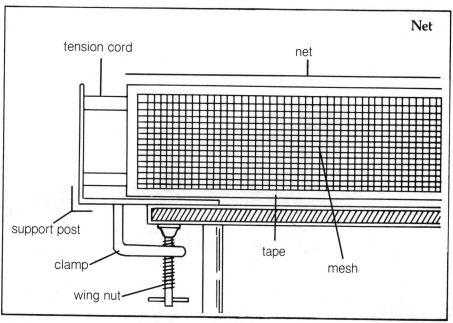

Net

tension cord

net

support post

clamp

wing nut

tape

mesh

Table Games

Darts

Darts, or *darting*, is played by two *dartists* or teams of from two to eight. Darts are scored on *point of entry* on the board *face*. Of the *clock-face games*, *tournament darts* is the most popular. Other games include *round-the-clock, all-fives, baseball, high score, cricket, 51-in-5's, 14-stop, killer, Mulligan, 301, sudden death,* and *Shanghai.*

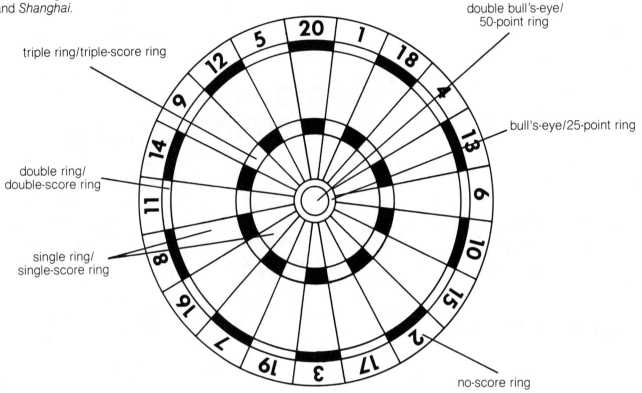

triple ring/triple-score ring

double ring/ double-score ring

single ring/ single-score ring

double bull's-eye/ 50-point ring

bull's-eye/25-point ring

no-score ring

Dart Board/English Clock

Dart

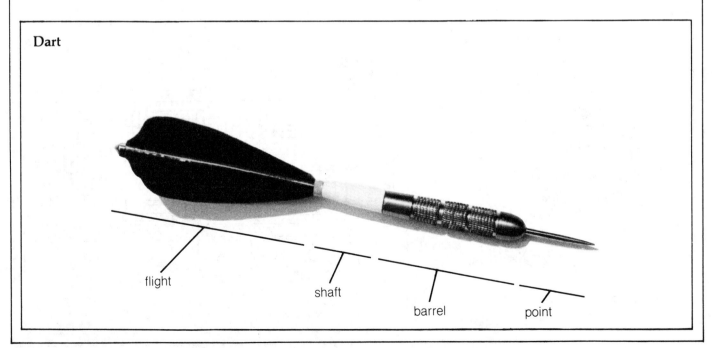

flight

shaft

barrel

point

Kites

Bridle lines are attached to the spine through holes in the front cover. They are shown here on the rear of the kite only for illustrative purposes. Among the limitless varieties of kites, there are six major categories: flat, *plane,* or *two-stick kites; bowed kites,* sometimes known by their classic example, the *Eddy;* box, or *cellular,* kites; *compound kites,* represented by the *Conyne kite; semiflexible kites,* such as *delta-keels;* and *Rogallos,* or *flexible,* kites. *Fighting kites* have two flying lines.

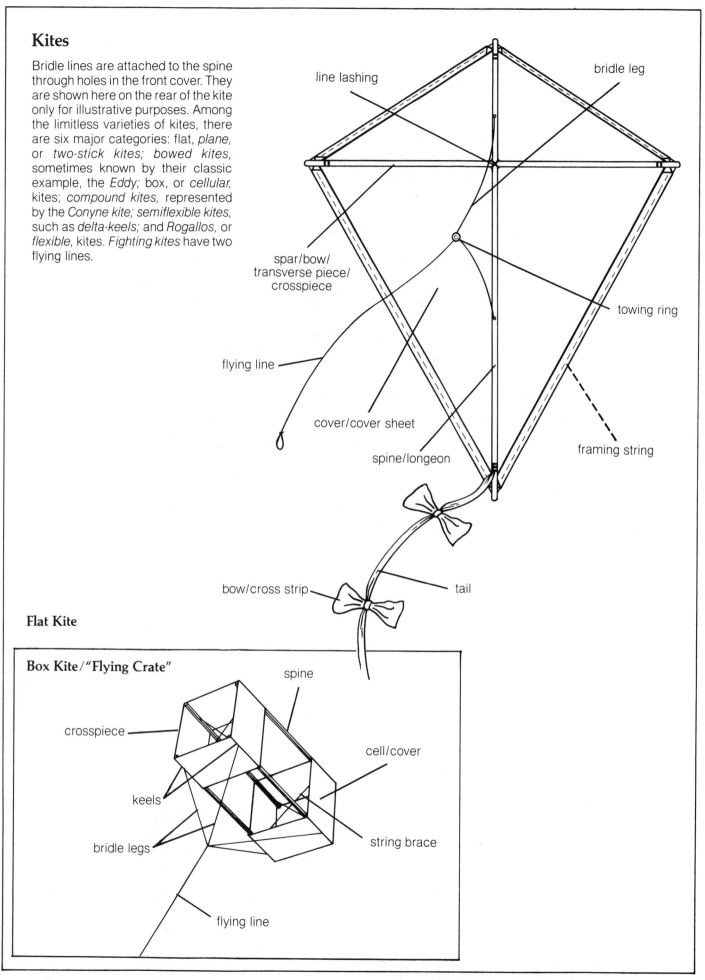

line lashing

bridle leg

spar/bow/transverse piece/crosspiece

towing ring

flying line

cover/cover sheet

spine/longeon

framing string

bow/cross strip

tail

Flat Kite

Box Kite/"Flying Crate"

spine

crosspiece

cell/cover

keels

string brace

bridle legs

flying line

Individual Sports

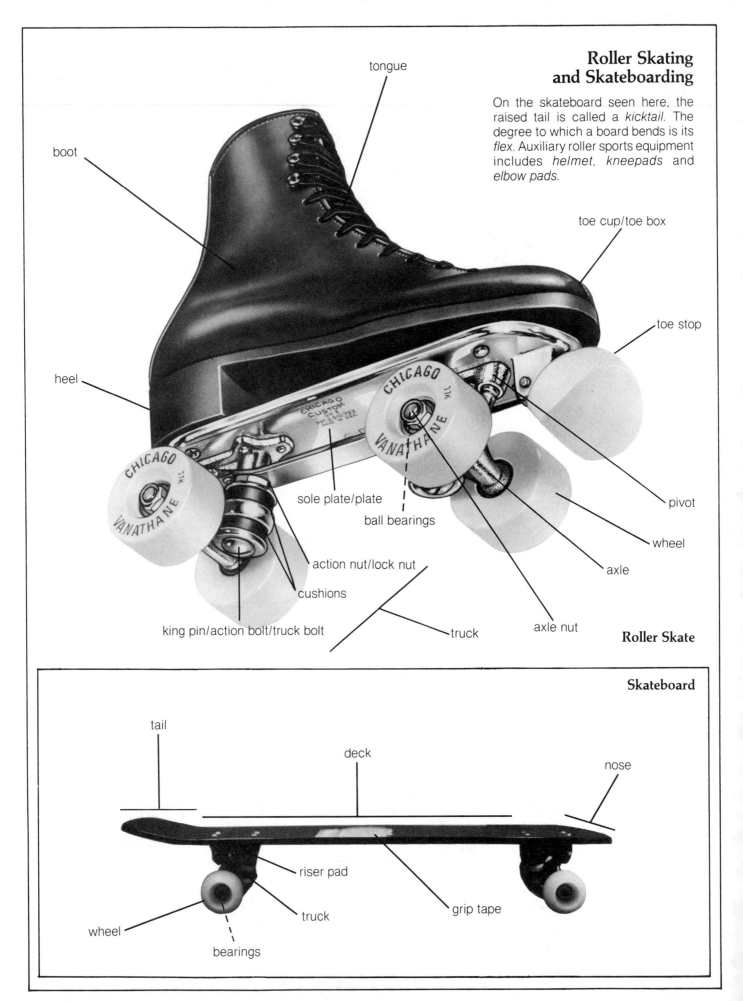

Roller Skating and Skateboarding

On the skateboard seen here, the raised tail is called a *kicktail*. The degree to which a board bends is its *flex*. Auxiliary roller sports equipment includes *helmet*, *kneepads* and *elbow pads*.

tongue

boot

toe cup/toe box

toe stop

heel

pivot

sole plate/plate

ball bearings

wheel

action nut/lock nut

axle

cushions

axle nut

king pin/action bolt/truck bolt

truck

Roller Skate

Skateboard

tail

deck

nose

riser pad

grip tape

truck

wheel

bearings

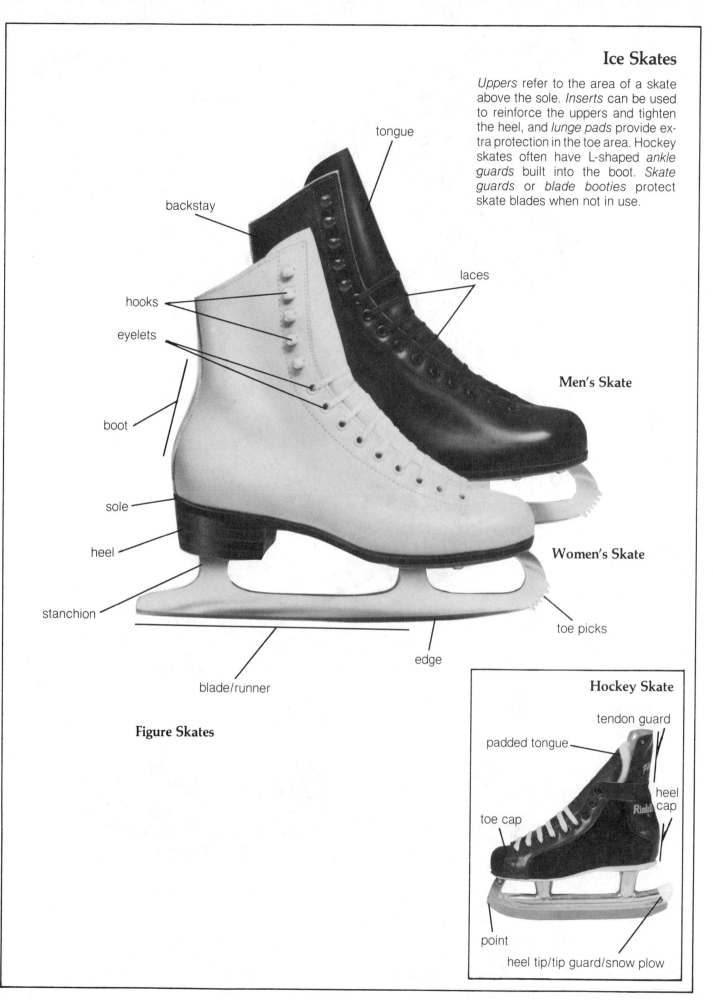

Ice Skates

Uppers refer to the area of a skate above the sole. *Inserts* can be used to reinforce the uppers and tighten the heel, and *lunge pads* provide extra protection in the toe area. Hockey skates often have L-shaped *ankle guards* built into the boot. *Skate guards* or *blade booties* protect skate blades when not in use.

tongue

backstay

laces

hooks

eyelets

Men's Skate

boot

sole

heel

Women's Skate

stanchion

toe picks

edge

blade/runner

Figure Skates

Hockey Skate

tendon guard

padded tongue

heel cap

toe cap

point

heel tip/tip guard/snow plow

Individual Sports

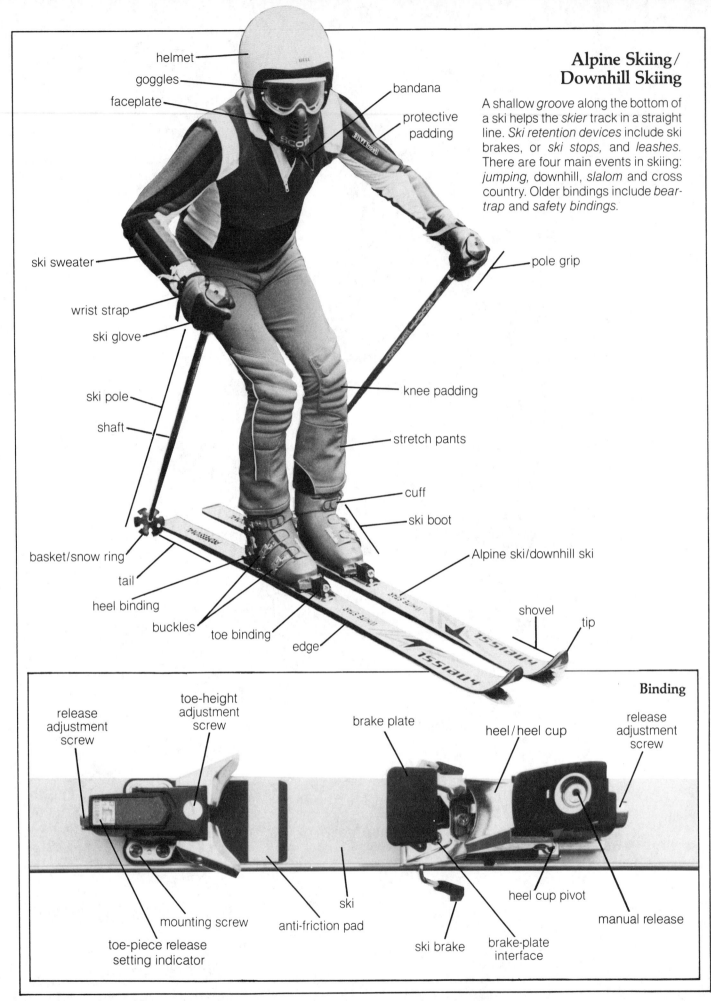

helmet

goggles

faceplate

bandana

protective padding

Alpine Skiing/ Downhill Skiing

A shallow *groove* along the bottom of a ski helps the *skier* track in a straight line. *Ski retention devices* include ski brakes, or *ski stops,* and *leashes.* There are four main events in skiing: *jumping,* downhill, *slalom* and cross country. Older bindings include *bear-trap* and *safety bindings.*

ski sweater

wrist strap

ski glove

ski pole

shaft

basket/snow ring

tail

heel binding

buckles

toe binding

edge

pole grip

knee padding

stretch pants

cuff

ski boot

Alpine ski/downhill ski

shovel

tip

Binding

release adjustment screw

toe-height adjustment screw

brake plate

heel/heel cup

release adjustment screw

mounting screw

toe-piece release setting indicator

anti-friction pad

ski

ski brake

brake-plate interface

heel cup pivot

manual release

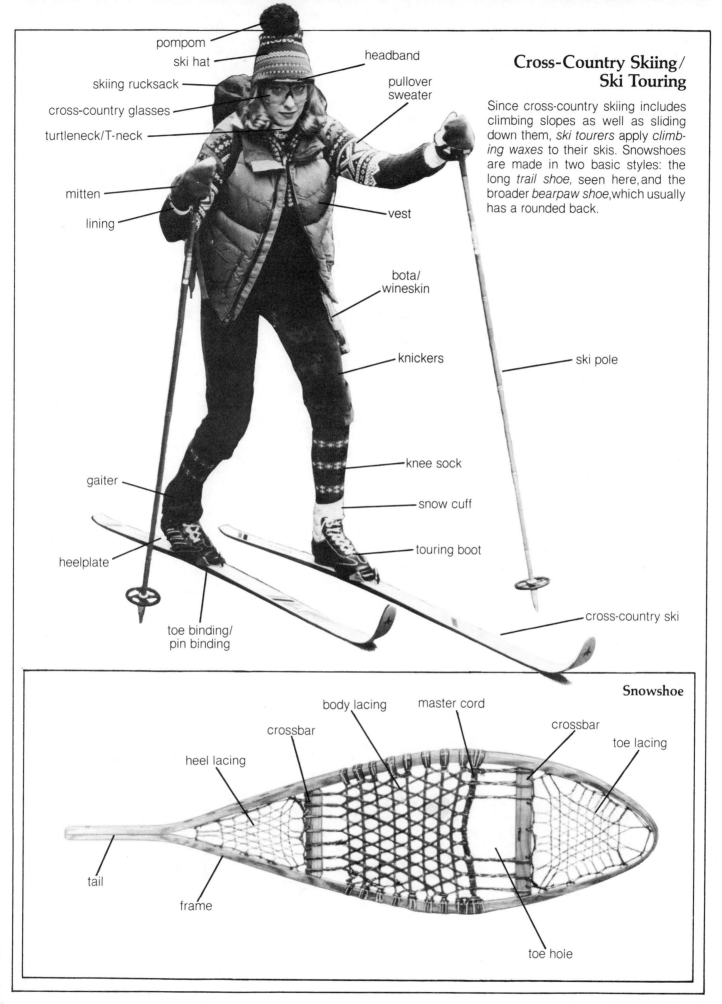

pompom

ski hat

skiing rucksack

cross-country glasses

turtleneck/T-neck

mitten

lining

headband

pullover sweater

vest

bota/ wineskin

knickers

knee sock

snow cuff

touring boot

gaiter

heelplate

toe binding/ pin binding

ski pole

cross-country ski

Cross-Country Skiing/ Ski Touring

Since cross-country skiing includes climbing slopes as well as sliding down them, *ski tourers* apply *climbing waxes* to their skis. Snowshoes are made in two basic styles: the long *trail shoe,* seen here, and the broader *bearpaw shoe,* which usually has a rounded back.

Snowshoe

body lacing

master cord

crossbar

crossbar

toe lacing

heel lacing

tail

frame

toe hole

Sledding and Tobogganing

Bobsleds, driven by two- or four-man crews, have a racing *cowl* and toothed metal *brake.* Small racing sleds called *luges* are controlled by reclining drivers using their feet and *hand ropes.*

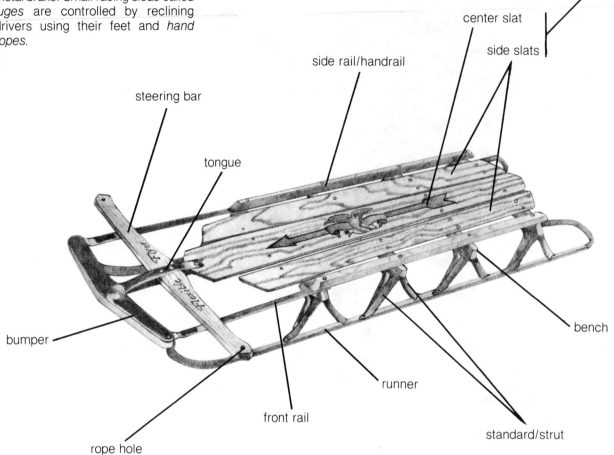

deck

center slat

side slats

side rail/handrail

steering bar

tongue

bumper

front rail

rope hole

runner

standard/strut

bench

Sled

Toboggan

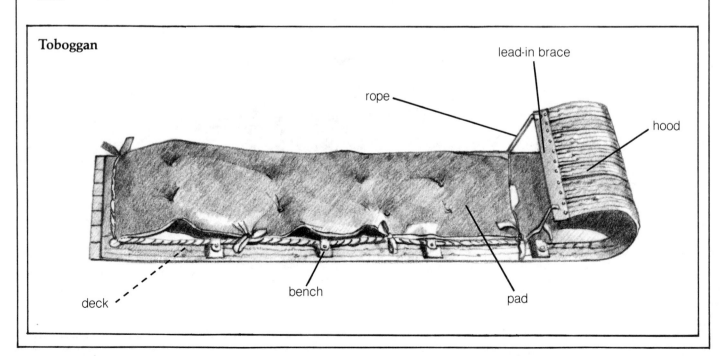

lead-in brace

rope

hood

deck

bench

pad

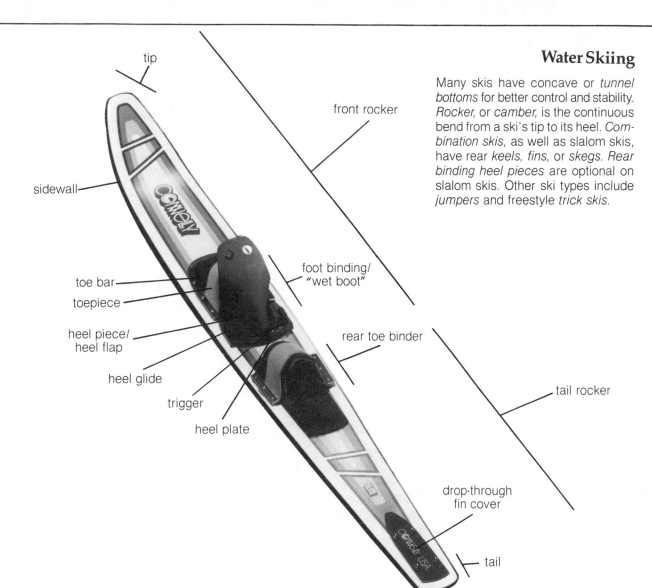

tip

front rocker

Water Skiing

Many skis have concave or *tunnel bottoms* for better control and stability. *Rocker,* or *camber,* is the continuous bend from a ski's tip to its heel. *Combination skis,* as well as slalom skis, have rear *keels, fins,* or *skegs. Rear binding heel pieces* are optional on slalom skis. Other ski types include *jumpers* and freestyle *trick skis.*

sidewall

toe bar

toepiece

heel piece/
heel flap

heel glide

trigger

heel plate

foot binding/
"wet boot"

rear toe binder

tail rocker

drop-through
fin cover

tail

Slalom Ski

Ski Vest/Safety Jacket

reinforced shoulder

strap/belt

buckle

snap

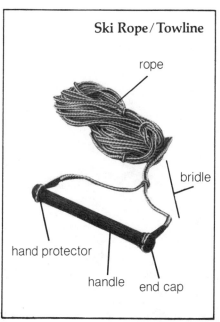

Ski Rope/Towline

rope

bridle

hand protector

handle

end cap

Individual Sports

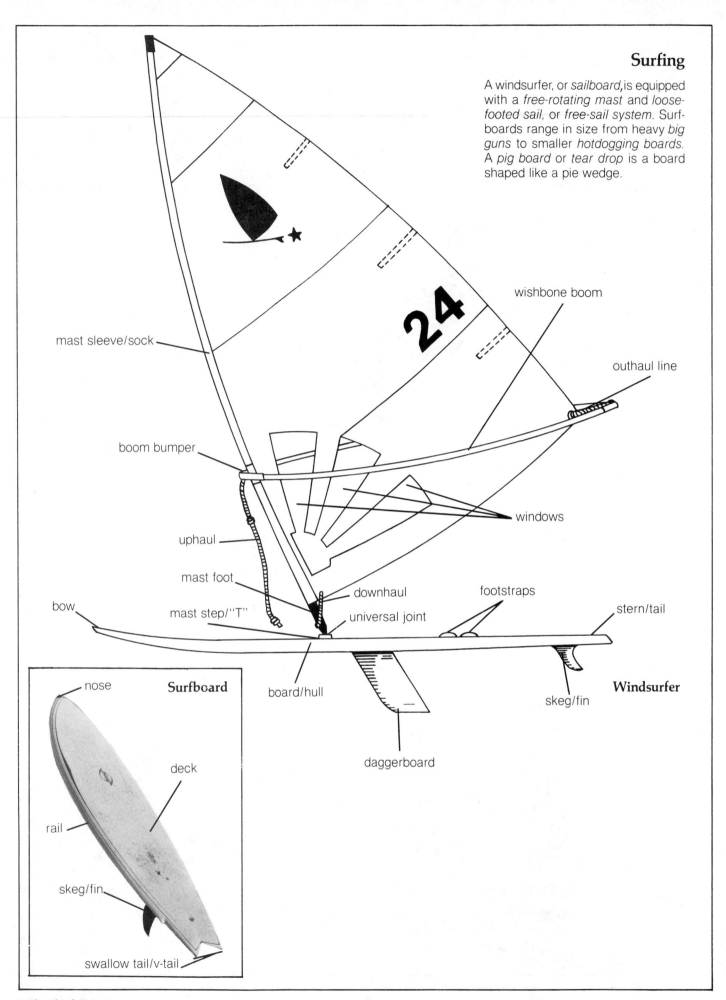

Surfing

A windsurfer, or *sailboard*, is equipped with a *free-rotating mast* and *loose-footed sail*, or *free-sail system*. Surfboards range in size from heavy *big guns* to smaller *hotdogging boards*. A *pig board* or *tear drop* is a board shaped like a pie wedge.

wishbone boom

outhaul line

mast sleeve/sock

boom bumper

windows

uphaul

mast foot

downhaul

footstraps

stern/tail

bow

mast step/"T"

universal joint

Windsurfer

board/hull

skeg/fin

daggerboard

nose

Surfboard

deck

rail

skeg/fin

swallow tail/v-tail

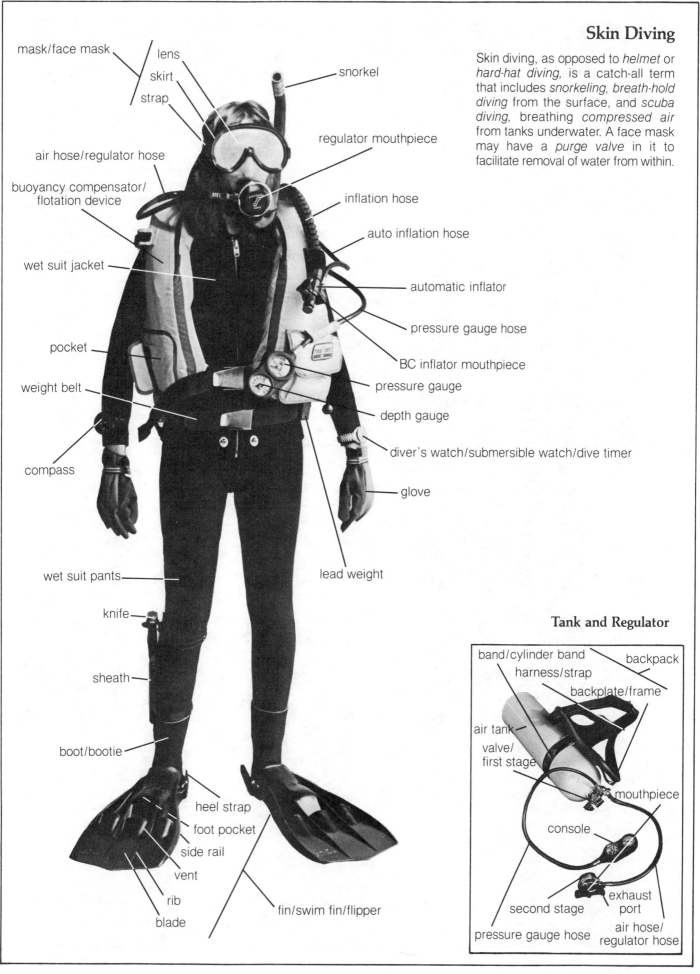

Skin Diving

Skin diving, as opposed to *helmet* or *hard-hat diving*, is a catch-all term that includes *snorkeling, breath-hold diving* from the surface, and *scuba diving*, breathing *compressed air* from tanks underwater. A face mask may have a *purge valve* in it to facilitate removal of water from within.

mask/face mask

lens

skirt

strap

snorkel

air hose/regulator hose

regulator mouthpiece

buoyancy compensator/ flotation device

inflation hose

auto inflation hose

automatic inflator

wet suit jacket

pressure gauge hose

BC inflator mouthpiece

pocket

pressure gauge

weight belt

depth gauge

diver's watch/submersible watch/dive timer

compass

glove

lead weight

wet suit pants

knife

sheath

boot/bootie

heel strap

foot pocket

side rail

vent

rib

blade

fin/swim fin/flipper

Tank and Regulator

band/cylinder band

backpack

harness/strap

backplate/frame

air tank

valve/ first stage

mouthpiece

console

second stage

exhaust port

pressure gauge hose

air hose/ regulator hose

Individual Sports

Hot Air Balloon

A balloon, or *montgolfier*, rises when *ballast*, usually water or *sandbags*, is jettisoned. A *drag*, or *trail rope*, hangs from the balloon to give it stability in flight and slow it down upon landing. To deflate the balloon a *ripping panel*, or *rip panel*, near the top is opened.

parachute valve/
parachute vent

envelope/bag

registration number/
"N" number

envelope
graphic

panel seams

gore seams

load cords

panels

bottom girdle

skirt

skirt band

burner

suspension rope

load ring

padding

basket handle

mouth

valve line

burner support

basket/carriage

scuff leather

tether line

Parachuting and Hang Gliding

Unless attached to a *static line*, which automatically opens a *chute* once a *jumper* has cleared the *jump plane*, a *sky diver* can *free-fall* before pulling his *rip cord*.

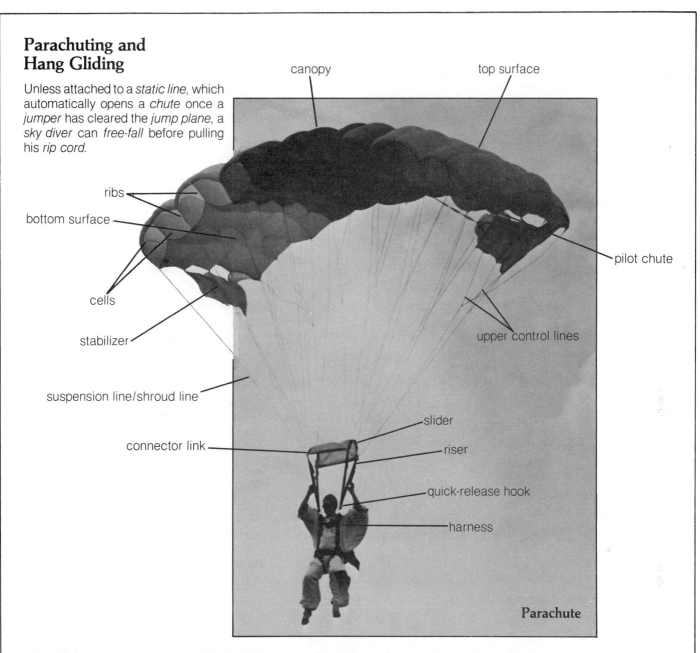

canopy

top surface

ribs

bottom surface

cells

stabilizer

pilot chute

upper control lines

suspension line/shroud line

slider

connector link

riser

quick-release hook

harness

Parachute

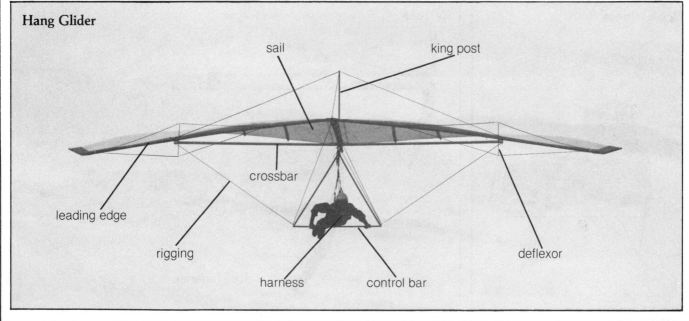

Hang Glider

sail

king post

crossbar

leading edge

rigging

harness

control bar

deflexor

Individual Sports

Mountain Climbing

Mountaineers use nylon webbing for *shoulder slings* and *swami belts*. Carabiners, either oval- or D-shaped, have spring-loaded *gates* for connecting various pieces of climbing equipment. Unlike *pitons*, which are hammered into cracks, nuts are wedged into cracks and easily removed. *Icescrews*, ring-topped threaded tubes, are actually screwed into the ice for protection.

hardware sling

carabiners

climbing harness

tape

rand

smooth-soled climbing shoe/
klettershoe/PA

chocks & nuts

climbing rope

Ice Climbing Boot

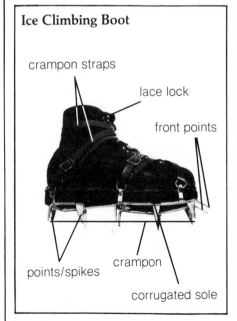

crampon straps

lace lock

front points

points/spikes

crampon

corrugated sole

Ice Tools

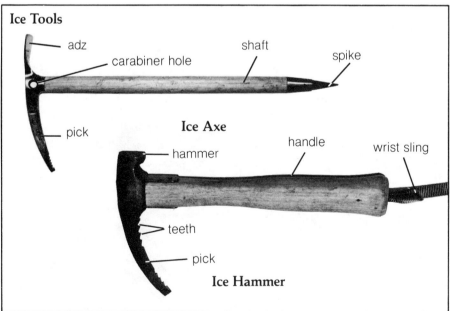

adz

shaft

carabiner hole

spike

pick

Ice Axe

hammer

handle

wrist sling

teeth

pick

Ice Hammer

Riding Equipment

A saddle is built on a frame called a *saddle tree.* A *saddle blanket* or *saddle pad* is placed between horse and saddle. Metal stirrups, or *stirrup irons,* are attached to the saddle by *stirrup leathers. Saddlebags* fit over the back of the saddle.

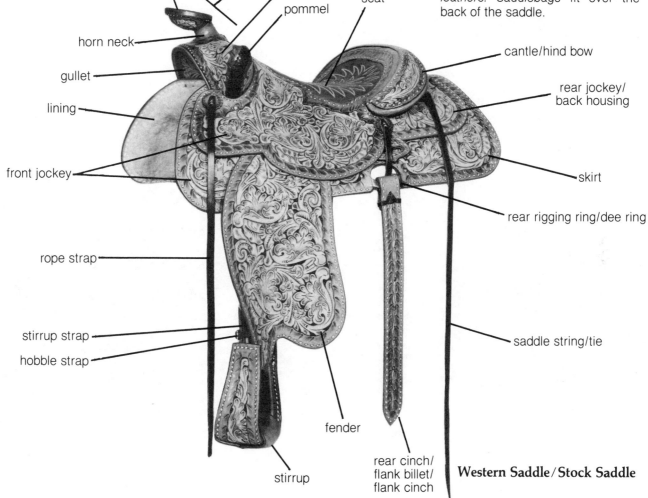

horn cap

horn

fork/swell

pommel

seat

horn neck

gullet

lining

front jockey

rope strap

stirrup strap

hobble strap

cantle/hind bow

rear jockey/ back housing

skirt

rear rigging ring/dee ring

saddle string/tie

fender

rear cinch/ flank billet/ flank cinch

stirrup

Western Saddle/Stock Saddle

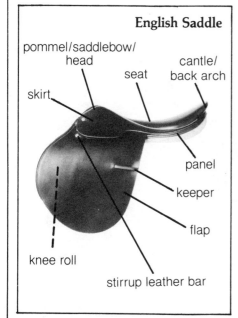

English Saddle

pommel/saddlebow/ head

cantle/ back arch

seat

skirt

panel

keeper

flap

knee roll

stirrup leather bar

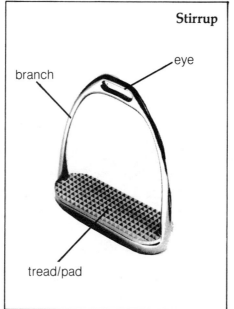

Stirrup

branch

eye

tread/pad

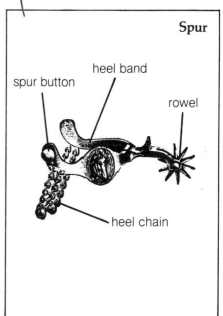

Spur

spur button

heel band

rowel

heel chain

Equestrian Sports

Flat Racing

The equipment used on a racehorse is called the *tack*. *Thoroughbreds* start from a fixed *starting gate*, while harness racers start from a car-pulled *moving gate*. The most desirable *post position* in a race is gate number one, the *pole position* closest to the *rail*. Bettors pick horses to finish first, second and third, or *win, place* and *show*. Picking all three finishers in the right order is called a *trifecta*.

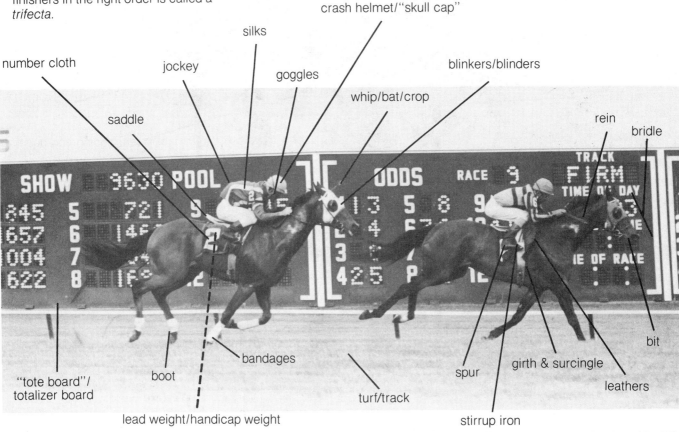

crash helmet/"skull cap"

silks

number cloth

jockey

goggles

blinkers/blinders

whip/bat/crop

rein

bridle

saddle

bandages

"tote board"/ totalizer board

boot

turf/track

spur

girth & surcingle

bit

leathers

lead weight/handicap weight

stirrup iron

Racing Program Entry

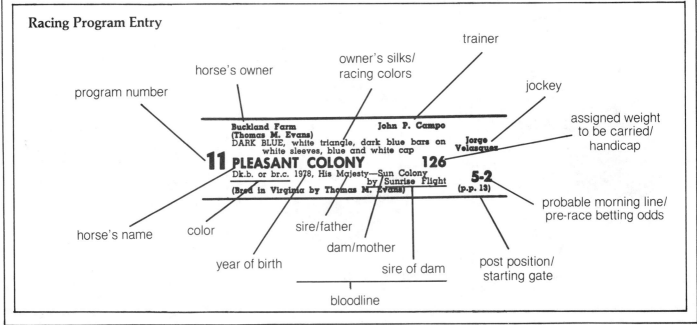

trainer

owner's silks/ racing colors

horse's owner

jockey

program number

assigned weight to be carried/ handicap

Buckland Farm
(Thomas M. Evans)   John P. Campo
DARK BLUE, white triangle, dark blue bars on
white sleeves, blue and white cap   Jorge Velasquez

11 PLEASANT COLONY   **126**

Dk.b. or br.c. 1978, His Majesty—Sun Colony
by Sunrise Flight   **5-2**
(Bred in Virginia by Thomas M. Evans)   (p.p. 13)

probable morning line/ pre-race betting odds

horse's name

color

sire/father

dam/mother

year of birth

sire of dam

post position/ starting gate

bloodline

Harness Racing

Trotters and pacers race in *harness.* Trotters move front and opposing rear legs in unison, *laterally gaited,* while pacers move front and rear legs on the same side in unison, *diagonally gaited.* Horses are assembled, saddled and paraded in the *paddock area.*

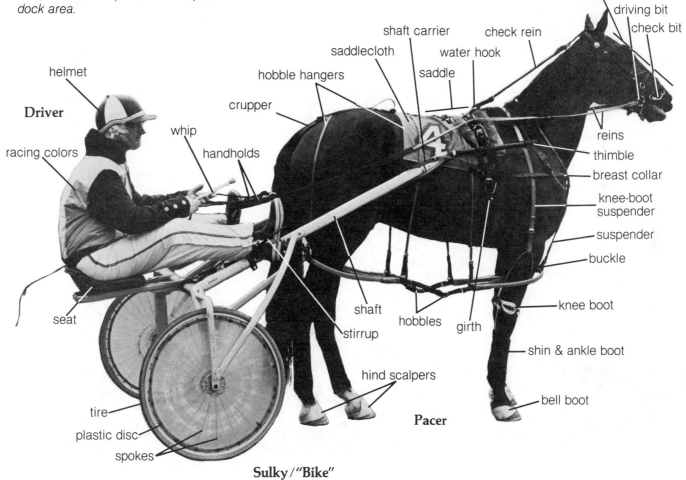

Driver

helmet
racing colors
whip
handholds
seat
tire
plastic disc
spokes
shaft
stirrup
crupper
hobble hangers
saddlecloth
shaft carrier
water hook
saddle
hobbles
girth
hind scalpers

Sulky/"Bike"

bridle
driving bit
check bit
check rein
reins
thimble
breast collar
knee-boot suspender
suspender
buckle
knee boot
shin & ankle boot
bell boot

Pacer

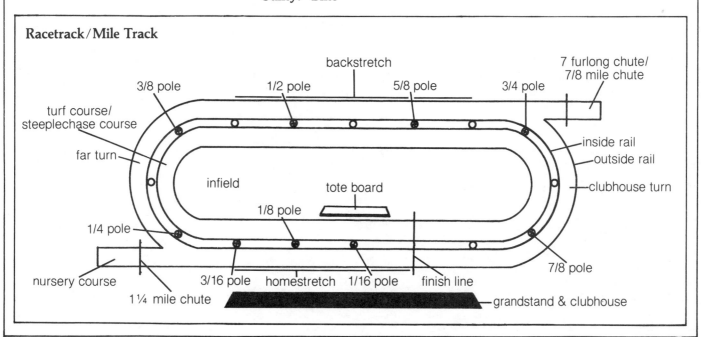

Racetrack/Mile Track

backstretch
7 furlong chute/ 7/8 mile chute
3/8 pole
1/2 pole
5/8 pole
3/4 pole
turf course/ steeplechase course
far turn
inside rail
outside rail
infield
tote board
clubhouse turn
1/4 pole
1/8 pole
7/8 pole
nursery course
3/16 pole
homestretch
1/16 pole
finish line
1¼ mile chute
grandstand & clubhouse

337

Equestrian Sports

Grand Prix Racing

International *road racing* takes place on *closed-circuit tracks* laid out through the countryside, as opposed to *speedway racing,* which takes place on banked, oval-shaped *race tracks. Formulas* primarily limit engine size and car weight, and range from *Super-Vee* to *Formula One,* used in Grand Prix racing.

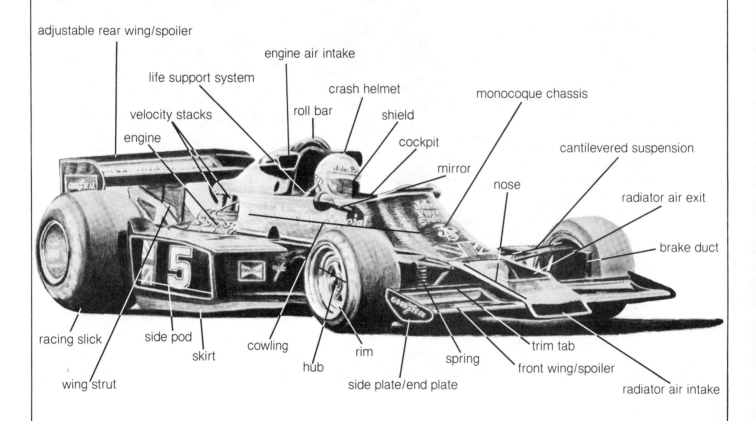

adjustable rear wing/spoiler
engine air intake
life support system
crash helmet
velocity stacks
roll bar
shield
monocoque chassis
engine
cockpit
cantilevered suspension
mirror
nose
radiator air exit
brake duct
racing slick
side pod
cowling
rim
trim tab
skirt
spring
front wing/spoiler
hub
radiator air intake
wing strut
side plate/end plate

Formula One Racing Car

Drag Racing

Each drag racing *event,* or *acceleration contest,* involves two-car *heats,* the winner of which is deemed the *eliminator.* Vehicles include *slingshot dragsters* and *funny cars* whose mismatched bodies, or *"hulls,"* and *chassis* give them an unusual appearance. The Christmas Tree is situated in the middle of a divided, two-lane *straight-line course, drag strip* or *dragway. Elapsed time,* or *"ET,"* is computed from the moment a car breaks a *light beam* at the *starting line* until it breaks a similar beam at the *finish.* A car leaving the starting line prematurely, in either *handicap* or *heads-up racing,* is said to be *"red-lighting."*

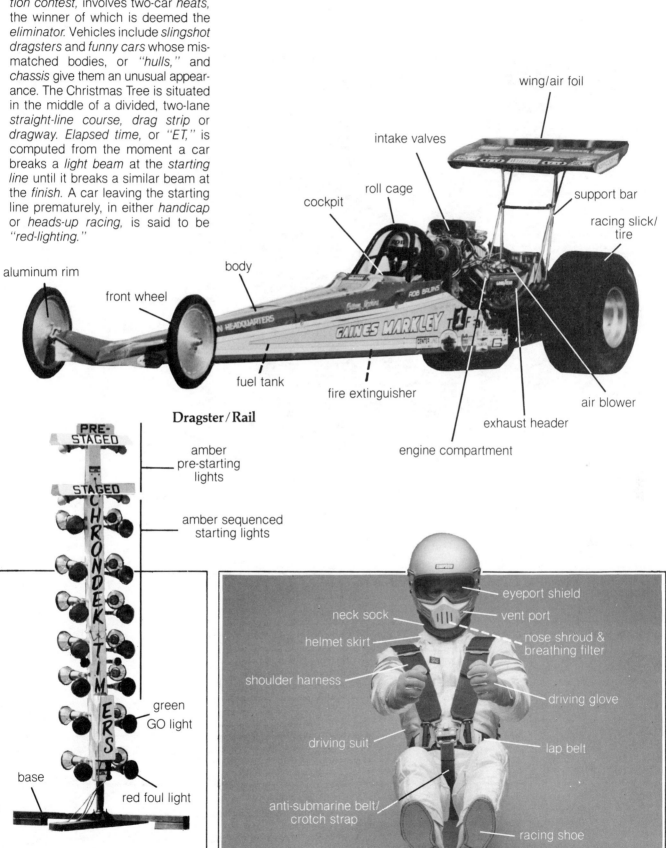

wing/air foil

intake valves

roll cage

cockpit

support bar

racing slick/tire

aluminum rim

body

front wheel

fuel tank

fire extinguisher

air blower

exhaust header

engine compartment

Dragster / Rail

amber pre-starting lights

amber sequenced starting lights

green GO light

base

red foul light

Starting Lights / Christmas Tree

eyeport shield

neck sock

vent port

helmet skirt

nose shroud & breathing filter

shoulder harness

driving glove

driving suit

lap belt

anti-submarine belt/ crotch strap

racing shoe

Driver's Fire Suit

handle

foot/pole mount

leg/reel stem

crank handle

bail/pick-up arm

trip/dog

spool skirt

spool

anti-reverse lever

rear bearing

PENN
750 SS

3 BALL BEARINGS
SKIRTED SPOOL

gear housing

bearing cover

silent
anti-reverse
housing

line roller/line guide

drag-adjustment knob/
drag knob

Reel/Spinning Reel

Rod/Spinning Rod

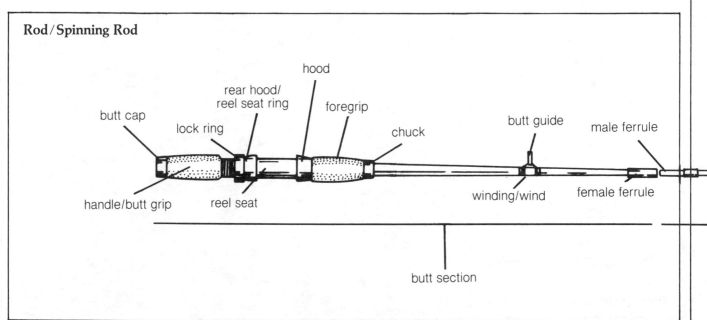

hood

rear hood/
reel seat ring

foregrip

butt cap

lock ring

chuck

butt guide

male ferrule

handle/butt grip

reel seat

winding/wind

female ferrule

butt section

Fishing

Fishermen, or *anglers*, use a variety of *tackle*, from simple *cane rods*, or *bank rods*, to sophisticated *fly rods* and *trolling gear*. *Sinkers* hold bait underwater, while *floats*, or *bobbers*, keep it suspended from the surface. A *gaff* or *landing net* is used to land fish.

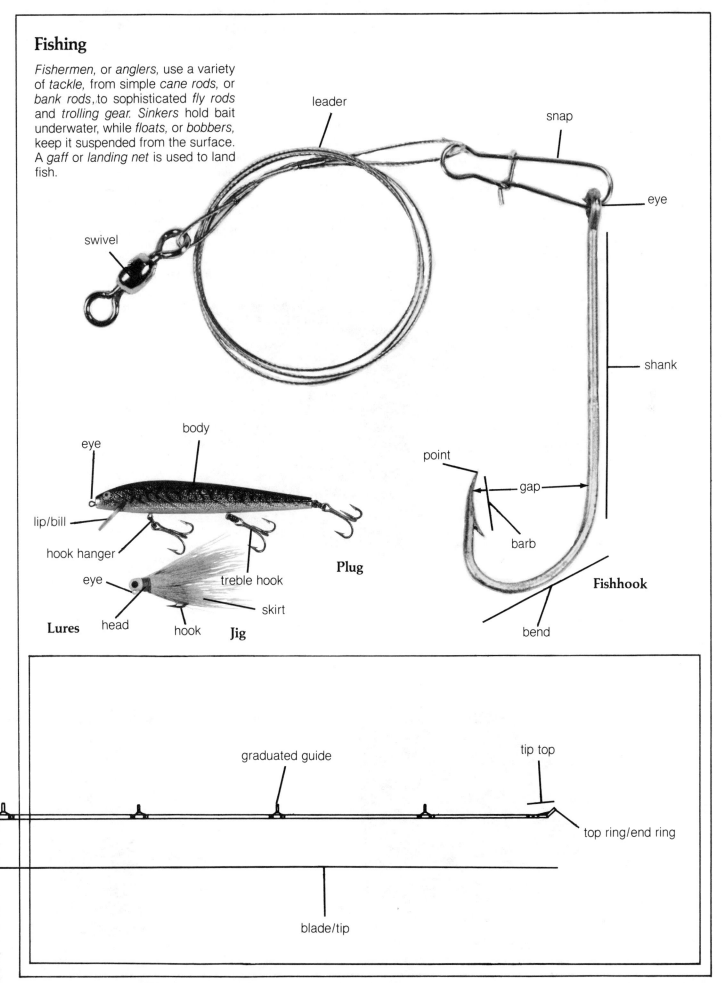

leader

snap

swivel

eye

shank

point

gap

barb

Fishhook

bend

body

eye

lip/bill

hook hanger

eye

head

hook

treble hook

skirt

Plug

Lures

Jig

graduated guide

tip top

top ring/end ring

blade/tip

Camping

Wall tents and pup tents are held up by tent poles. Many modern tents have *exterior frame* construction. Features in all the above-mentioned tents include *lap-felled* or *French seams,* which provide four layers for keeping out water, webbed–tape *backing* and pressed-on *grommets* or sewn-in *rings* for *ropes* secured to the ground with *pegs* or *stakes,* and sewn-in *flooring.* A lantern is primed by pumping the *pump valve* and lit by a match placed in the *lighting hole.*

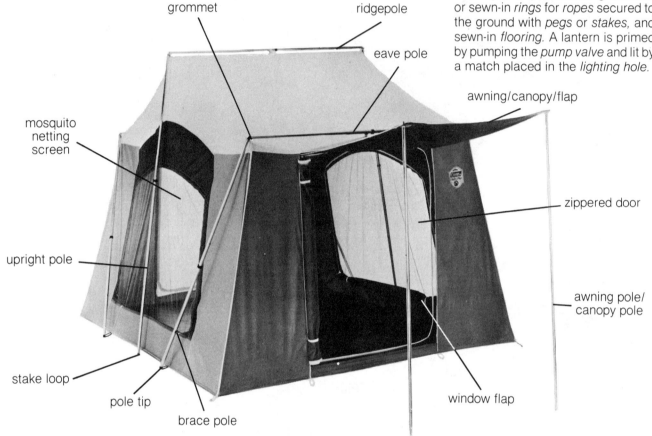

grommet

ridgepole

eave pole

awning/canopy/flap

mosquito netting screen

zippered door

upright pole

awning pole/ canopy pole

stake loop

pole tip

brace pole

window flap

Tent

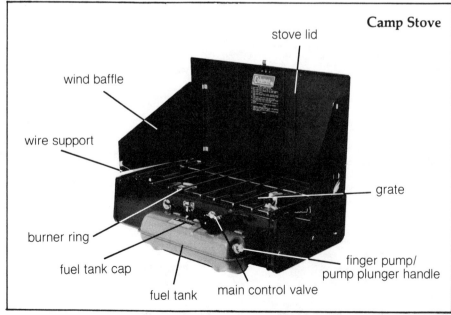

Camp Stove

stove lid

wind baffle

wire support

grate

burner ring

fuel tank cap

finger pump/ pump plunger handle

fuel tank

main control valve

Lantern

ventilator

bail

mantle

globe

heat shield

fuel valve

base rest

tank/fount

fuel cap

Backpacking

Loft is the trade term for fluffiness in sleeping bags. *Bonded insulation filling* eliminates the need for *quilting* and reduces "cold spots." The various pockets of backpacks, *knapsacks* or *rucksacks,* are called *local organizers.* Small camping items are packed in *stuffsacks,* which are then put inside a hiker's *pack.*

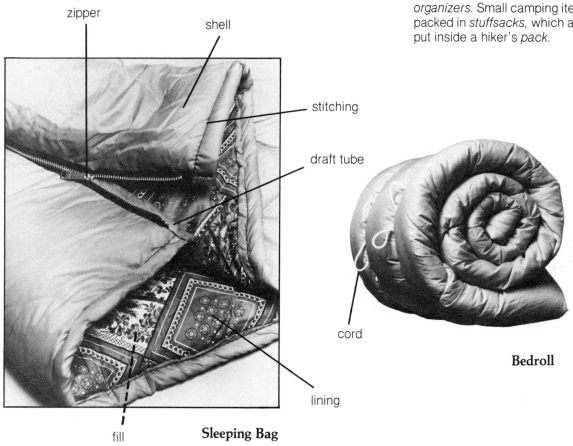

zipper

shell

stitching

draft tube

lining

fill

Sleeping Bag

cord

Bedroll

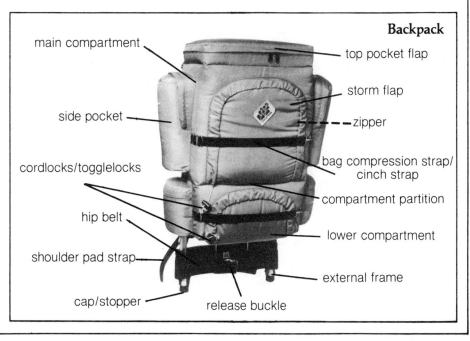

Backpack

main compartment

top pocket flap

storm flap

side pocket

zipper

cordlocks/togglelocks

bag compression strap/
cinch strap

compartment partition

hip belt

lower compartment

shoulder pad strap

external frame

cap/stopper

release buckle

Body Building

Among other *stations* in the universal gym, designed to improve muscle development through *isotonic exercises*, are *dead lift* and *low pulley*. Muscle-building and toning equipment includes *dumbbells, hand grips,* or *hand flexors, scissor grips, tone-up wheels, power twisters, exercise bikes, neck developers, ankle* and *wrist weights, triceps exercisers* and *waist trimmers.*

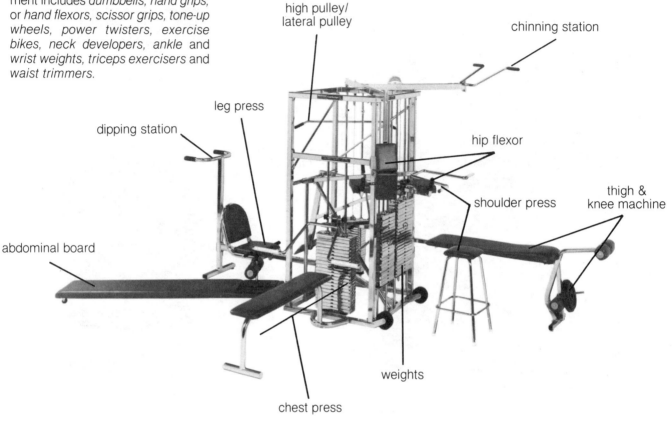

high pulley/
lateral pulley

chinning station

leg press

dipping station

hip flexor

shoulder press

thigh &
knee machine

abdominal board

weights

chest press

Universal Gym

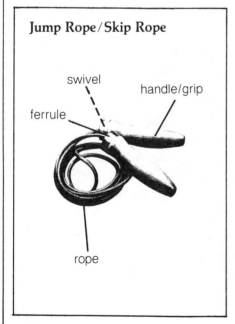

Jump Rope/Skip Rope

swivel

handle/grip

ferrule

rope

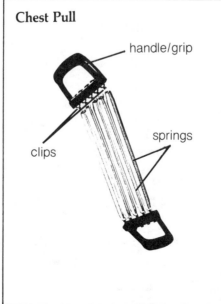

Chest Pull

handle/grip

clips

springs

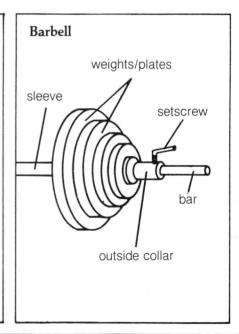

Barbell

weights/plates

sleeve

setscrew

bar

outside collar

Chess, Checkers, Backgammon and Tile Games

When chessmen and checkers are arranged at the start of a game, they are positioned in a *setup.* A chessboard's horizontal rows are called *ranks.* Vertical rows are *files.* In backgammon, a player increases the stakes by turning a dicelike *doubling cube.* A single backgammon piece on a point is called a *blot.* Two or more on a point make a *block.* In dominos, pieces with identical numbers on both ends are called *doubles* or *spinners.* Dominos that have been played form a *layout.* In mah-jongg, tiles are arranged in a *wall* to begin a game.

double corner

white square

checkers/checker men

king

single corner

king row

black square

chessmen/ chess pieces

queen rook/ queen castle

queen rook pawn/ queen castle pawn

queen knight

queen bishop pawn

queen bishop

queen knight pawn

queen pawn

queen

king pawn

king

king bishop pawn

king bishop

king knight

king knight pawn

king rook/ king castle

king rook pawn/ king castle pawn

Chessboard/Checkerboard

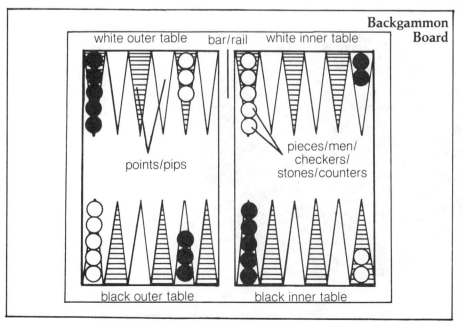

Backgammon Board

white outer table   bar/rail   white inner table

points/pips

pieces/men/ checkers/ stones/counters

black outer table   black inner table

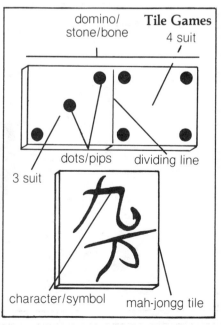

domino/ stone/bone

Tile Games

4 suit

3 suit

dots/pips   dividing line

character/symbol   mah-jongg tile

Gambling Equipment

A roulette wheel is operated by a *croupier*. Bets are placed on a *layout*. Slots are divided into *red* and *black* for betting purposes. Dice players bet either with the person rolling the dice, the *shooter*, or with the casino, or *house*. The blackjack dealer pushes money won by the house into a double-locked *drop box* below the betting table. Other casino games include *baccarat, chemin de fer, wheel of fortune,* and *chuck-a-luck,* a game played with three dice.

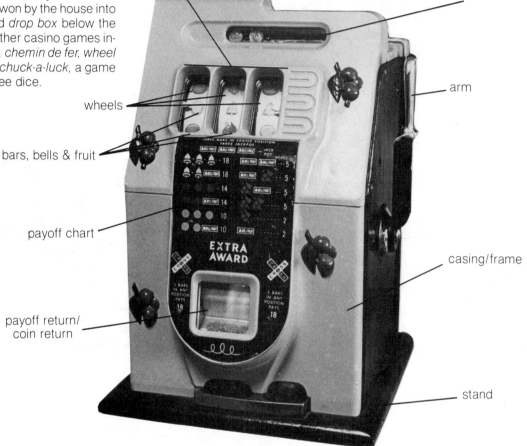

coin slot

face

coin viewer/window

arm

wheels

bars, bells & fruit

payoff chart

EXTRA AWARD

casing/frame

payoff return/ coin return

stand

Slot Machine/One-Arm Bandit

Roulette Wheel

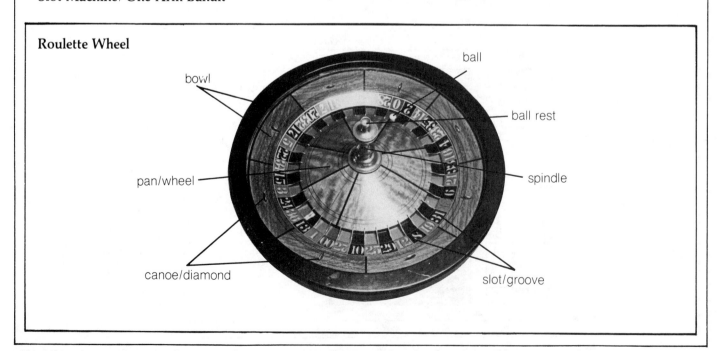

bowl

ball

ball rest

pan/wheel

spindle

canoe/diamond

slot/groove

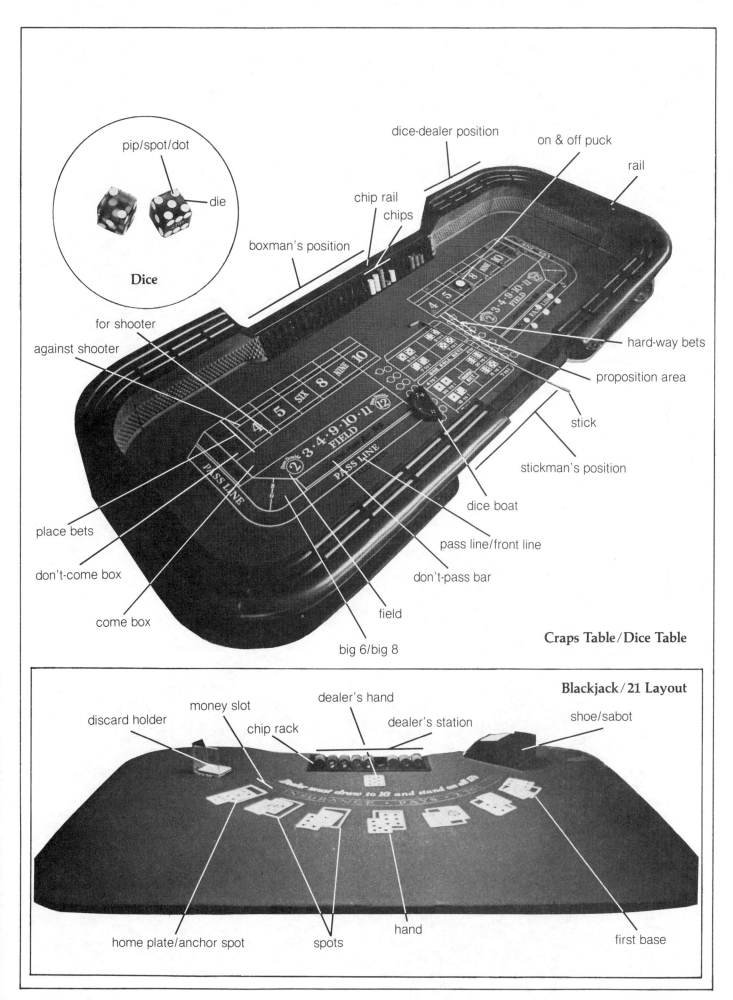

pip/spot/dot

die

Dice

dice-dealer position

on & off puck

rail

chip rail

chips

boxman's position

hard-way bets

for shooter

against shooter

proposition area

stick

stickman's position

place bets

don't-come box

dice boat

come box

pass line/front line

don't-pass bar

field

big 6/big 8

Craps Table/Dice Table

PASS LINE

PASS LINE

NINE 10

SIX 8

4 5

3·4·9·10·11 FIELD

Double 2

Double 12

BIG

4 5 6 8 10

3·4·9·10·11 FIELD

PASS LINE

Blackjack/21 Layout

discard holder

money slot

dealer's hand

chip rack

dealer's station

shoe/sabot

home plate/anchor spot

spots

hand

first base

Casino Games

Playing Cards

There are 52 cards in a *deck* or *pack*. The *aces*, shown below, and cards numbered two through ten, are called *spot cards* or *pip cards*. An additional card, the *joker*, or *mistigris*, is used in *card games* requiring a *wild card*. A *marked deck* is one in which the card *backs* have been altered slightly to allow a player to read their *values* illegally.

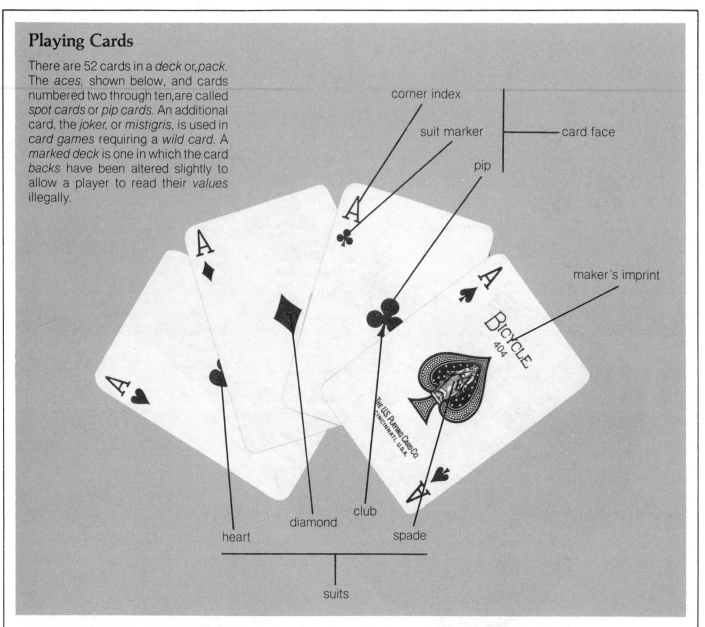

corner index

suit marker

card face

pip

maker's imprint

heart

diamond

club

spade

suits

Picture Cards / Court Cards / Face Cards

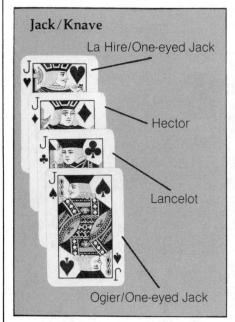

Jack/Knave

La Hire/One-eyed Jack

Hector

Lancelot

Ogier/One-eyed Jack

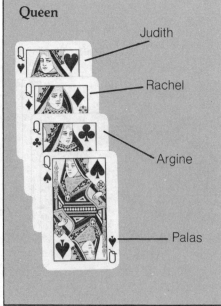

Queen

Judith

Rachel

Argine

Palas

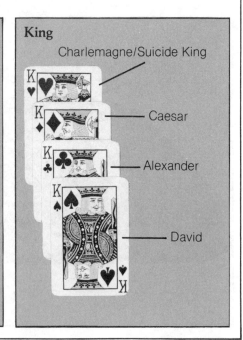

King

Charlemagne/Suicide King

Caesar

Alexander

David

Arts and Crafts

The main subsections here include the platforms on which the performing arts take place; coverage of the music field, ranging from the symbols that appear on sheet music to the parts of various musical instruments; the fine arts and crafts.

In the fine arts subsection an effort has been made to identify the terms for elements of style, rather than to cover styles themselves. The equipment used in everything from painting and sculpting to relief arts and stained glass are also illustrated and their parts labeled. The crafts subsection covers decorative stitching, knitting and weaving, and also includes the terms used to identify a sewing pattern.

Cartooning has a subsection all to itself. Here, for the first time, the reader will be able to identify everything from the beads of fear on a comic character (plewds) to the meaning of double XX's on a cartoon bottle (boozex). In addition the reader will henceforth be able to recognize the difference between a thought balloon, a speech balloon and an idea balloon in a cartoon panel.

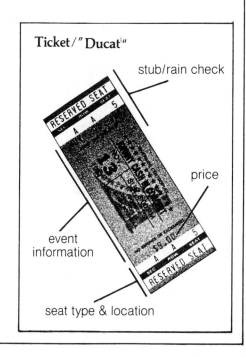

Ticket/"Ducat"

stub/rain check

price

event information

seat type & location

Stage

Also found on many stages are *tormentors,* or *legs* which frame the stage to narrow the acting area, a *trapdoor,* or *scruto,* an *elevator,* and a fabric backdrop, or *scrim.* Everything used on stages, or *boards,* are *props,* or *properties.* The arrangement of scenery, furniture and properties is called a set.

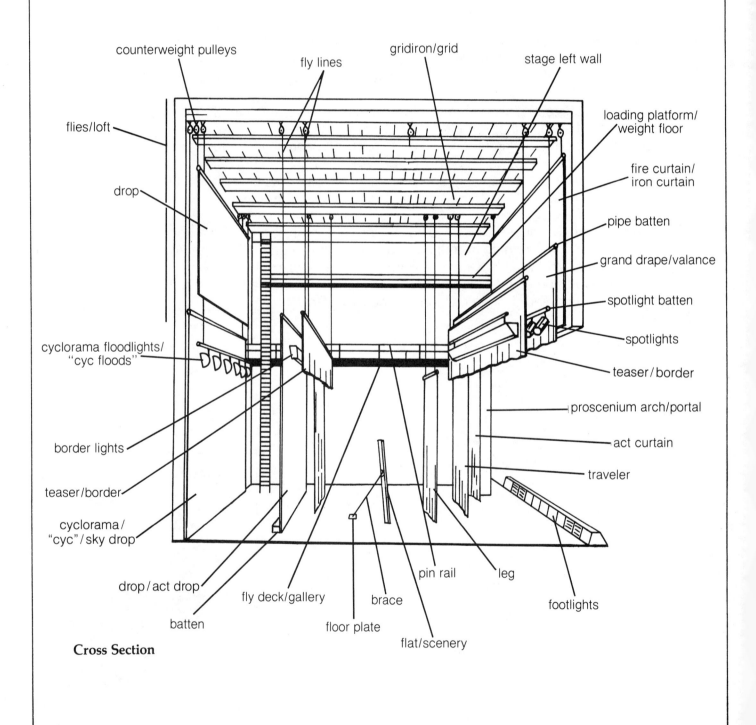

counterweight pulleys

fly lines

gridiron/grid

stage left wall

flies/loft

loading platform/ weight floor

drop

fire curtain/ iron curtain

pipe batten

grand drape/valance

spotlight batten

cyclorama floodlights/ "cyc floods"

spotlights

teaser/border

border lights

proscenium arch/portal

act curtain

teaser/border

traveler

cyclorama/ "cyc"/sky drop

drop/act drop

fly deck/gallery

brace

pin rail

leg

footlights

batten

floor plate

flat/scenery

Cross Section

Theater

In a *performance hall*, the orchestra sits in a sunken *orchestra pit* between the audience and the stage. For some shows a *runway*, or *ramp*, extends from the stage into the *center aisle*. The seating area above the orchestra is the *balcony*. In theaters with more than one balcony, the lowest one is the *mezzanine*, the front section of which is the loge.

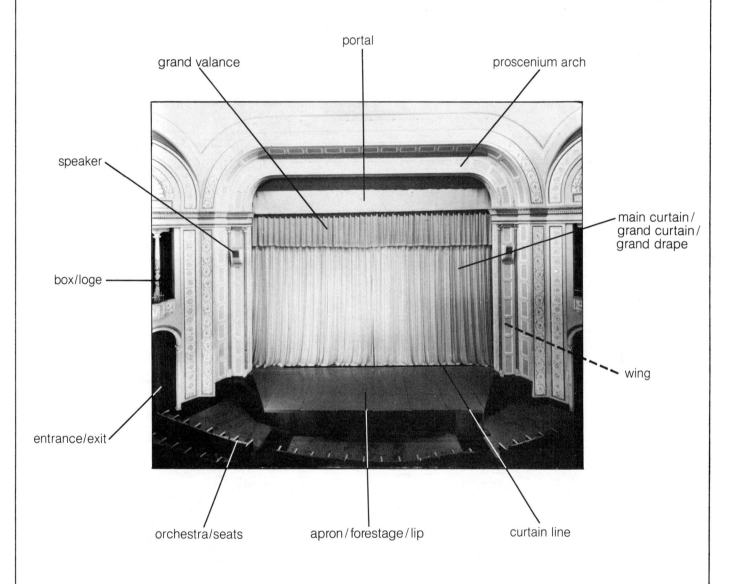

portal

grand valance

proscenium arch

speaker

main curtain /
grand curtain /
grand drape

box / loge

wing

entrance / exit

orchestra / seats

apron / forestage / lip

curtain line

Sheet Music Notations

Words to be sung, or *lyrics,* appear below the staff on sheet music. The notation ' is a *breath mark* indicating that the singer or musician should briefly pause. A combination of tones that blend harmoniously is a *chord.* Sharps, flats and naturals appearing directly in front of specific notes are called *accidentals.* A *quasihemi-demisemiquaver* is a 128th note.

Lines and Spaces/Staff Degrees

Orchestra

In symphony orchestras, string, woodwind and brass parts are performed by many *musicians*. In *chamber music ensembles,* each part is usually played by a single *player. Bands* do not normally include stringed instruments. *Marching bands* generally use no oboes or bassoons, and flutes are replaced with piccolos or *fifes. Dance bands* and *jazz bands* are loosely structured.

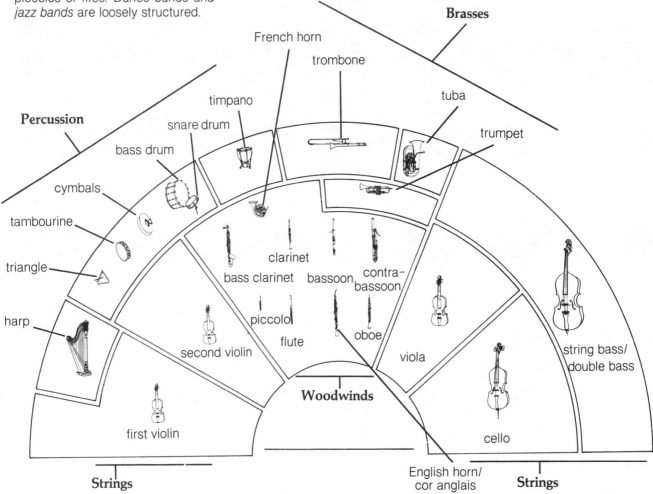

Brasses

French horn

trombone

tuba

trumpet

Percussion

timpano

snare drum

bass drum

cymbals

tambourine

triangle

harp

clarinet

bass clarinet

bassoon

contra-bassoon

piccolo

oboe

viola

string bass/ double bass

second violin

flute

Woodwinds

cello

first violin

English horn/ cor anglais

Strings

Strings

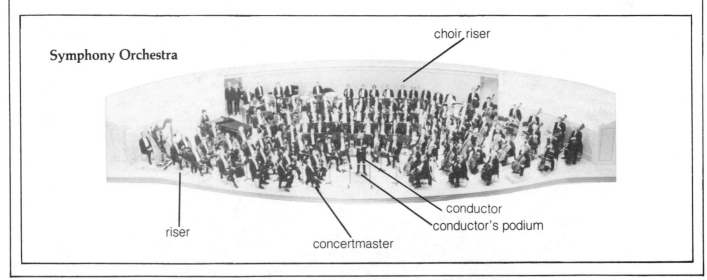

Symphony Orchestra

choir riser

conductor

conductor's podium

riser

concertmaster

Violin

Stringed instruments produce tones when a bow is drawn across the strings (*arco*) or they are finger-plucked (*pizzicato*). The sympathetic vibration produced between the instrument's belly and *back* adds *resonance* and *volume* to the sound.

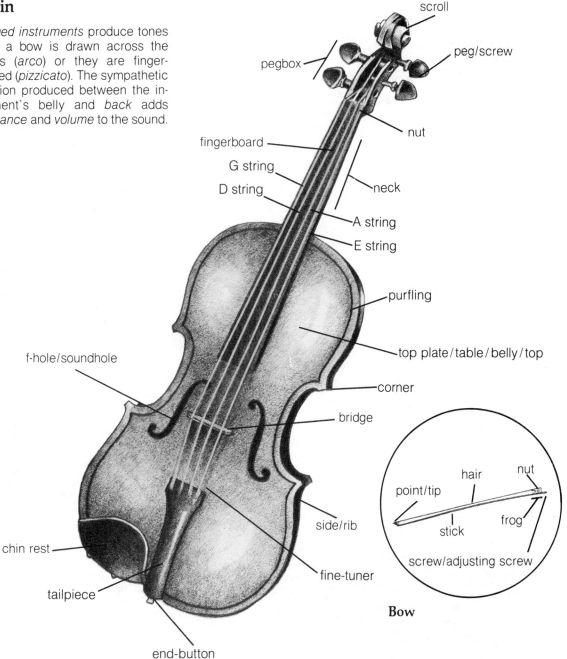

scroll

peg/screw

pegbox

nut

fingerboard

G string

D string

neck

A string

E string

purfling

top plate / table / belly / top

f-hole/soundhole

corner

bridge

side/rib

chin rest

fine-tuner

tailpiece

end-button

point/tip

hair

nut

stick

frog

screw/adjusting screw

Bow

Viola da Gamba

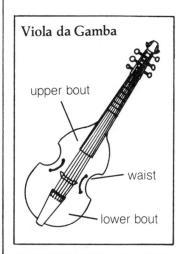

upper bout

waist

lower bout

Cello / Violoncello

endpin

Lyre

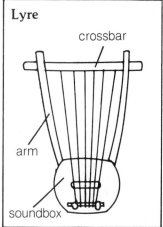

crossbar

arm

soundbox

Double Bass / Bass / Bass Fiddle

E string

A string

D string

G string

Woodwinds

Woodwinds produce *tones* by the vibration of one or two reeds of pliant cane in the mouthpiece or by the passing of air across a blow hole.

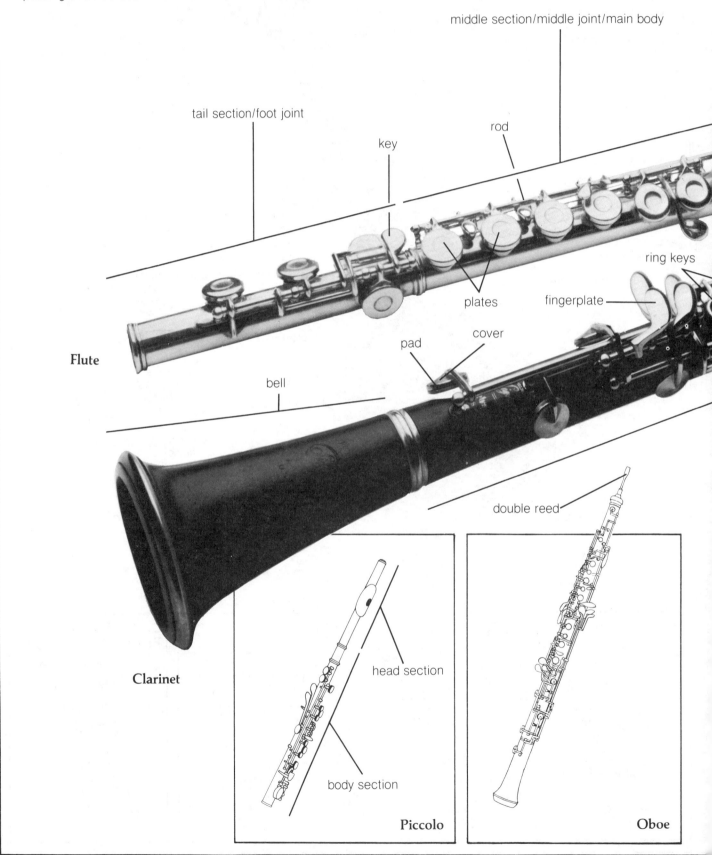

middle section/middle joint/main body

tail section/foot joint

key

rod

ring keys

plates

fingerplate

cover

pad

Flute

bell

double reed

Clarinet

head section

body section

Piccolo

Oboe

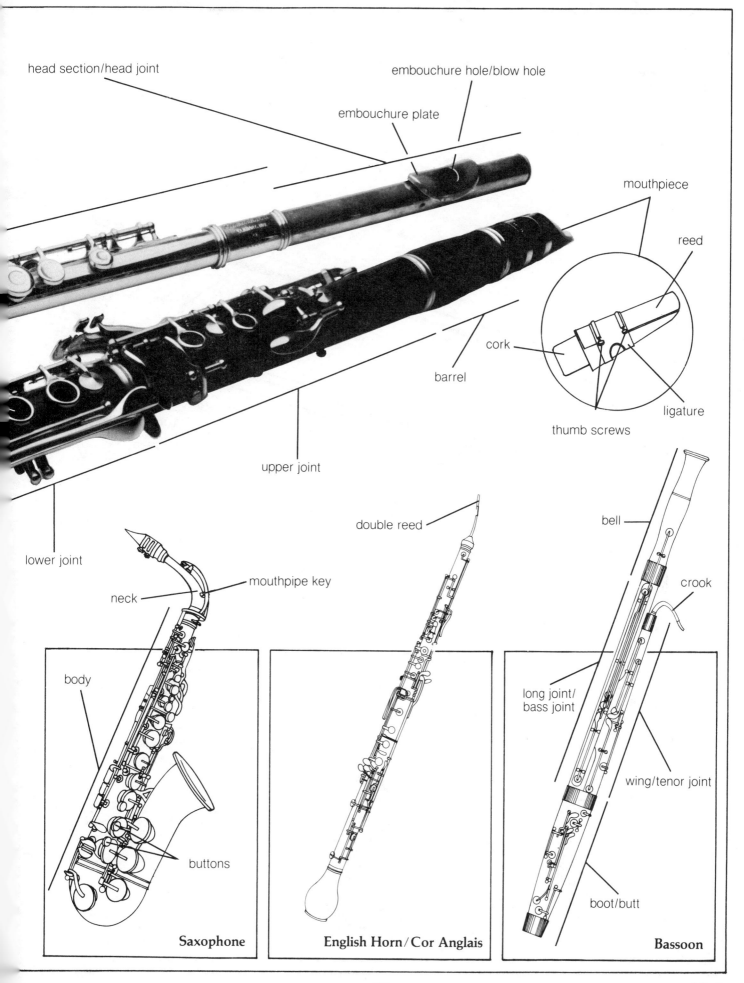

head section/head joint

embouchure hole/blow hole

embouchure plate

mouthpiece

reed

cork

barrel

ligature

thumb screws

upper joint

double reed

bell

crook

lower joint

neck

mouthpipe key

long joint/
bass joint

body

wing/tenor joint

buttons

boot/butt

Saxophone

English Horn/Cor Anglais

Bassoon

Music

Brasses

Brasses are *wind instruments* that produce *tones* when lips are buzzed against the mouthpiece. The range of brass instruments is increased by added lengths of tubing called *crooks* or *shanks*.

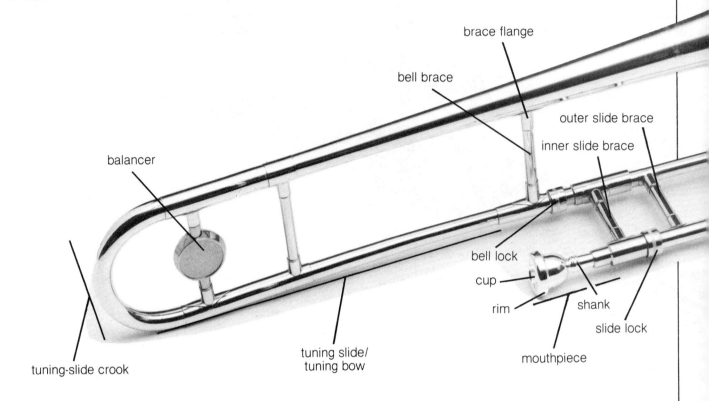

brace flange

bell brace

outer slide brace

inner slide brace

balancer

bell lock

cup

rim

shank

slide lock

tuning-slide crook

tuning slide/ tuning bow

mouthpiece

Trombone

Sousaphone

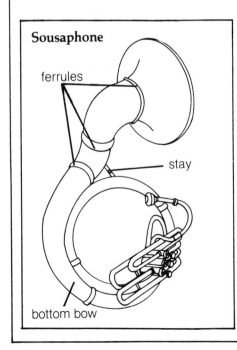

ferrules

stay

bottom bow

Tuba

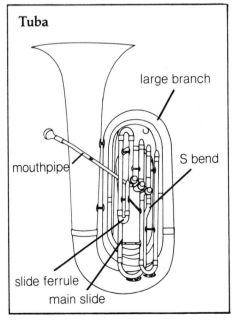

large branch

mouthpipe

S bend

slide ferrule

main slide

French Horn

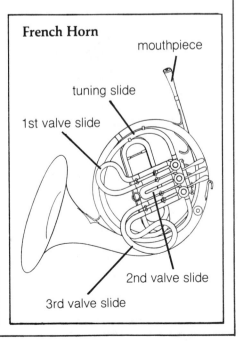

mouthpiece

tuning slide

1st valve slide

2nd valve slide

3rd valve slide

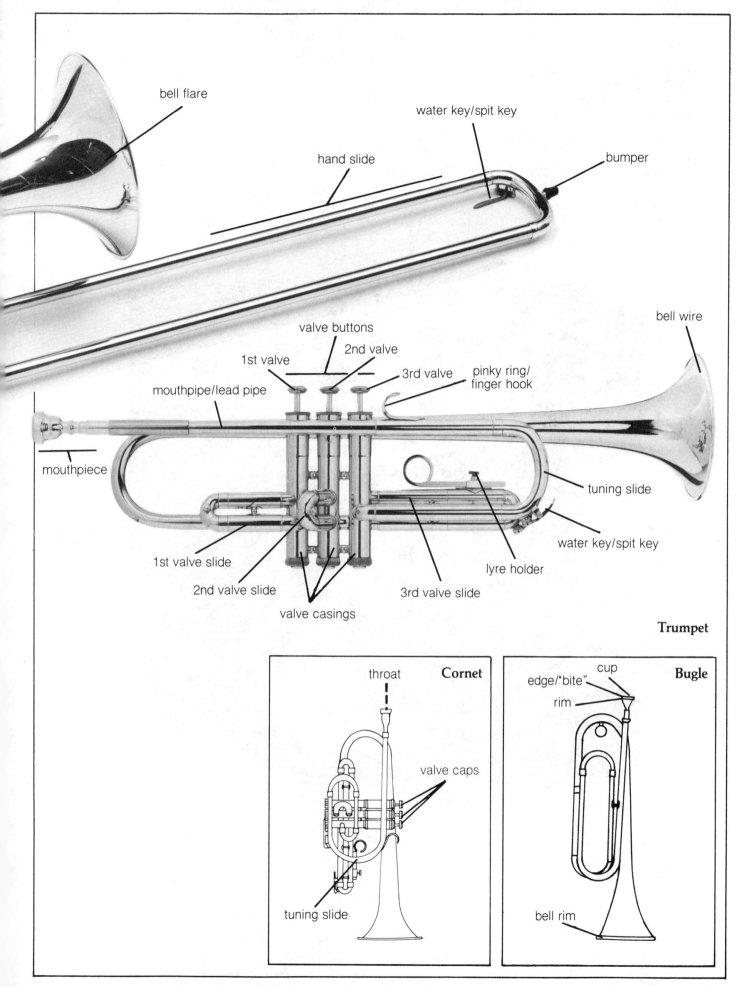

bell flare

water key/spit key

hand slide

bumper

bell wire

valve buttons

2nd valve

1st valve

3rd valve

pinky ring/
finger hook

mouthpipe/lead pipe

mouthpiece

tuning slide

1st valve slide

water key/spit key

2nd valve slide

lyre holder

3rd valve slide

valve casings

Trumpet

throat

Cornet

cup

edge/"bite"

Bugle

rim

valve caps

tuning slide

bell rim

Organ

The keyboards, or *manuals*, and pedal board, contained in a *console* or *keydesk*, as shown here, together with a number of *organ pipes,* separate from the console, comprise a pipe organ. Music is produced when air, sent into a *wind chest* by *bellows*, is directed into a selection of the organ's many pipes. An *electric organ* produces tones mechanically; an *electronic organ* uses integrated circuits and speakers to make *sounds*.

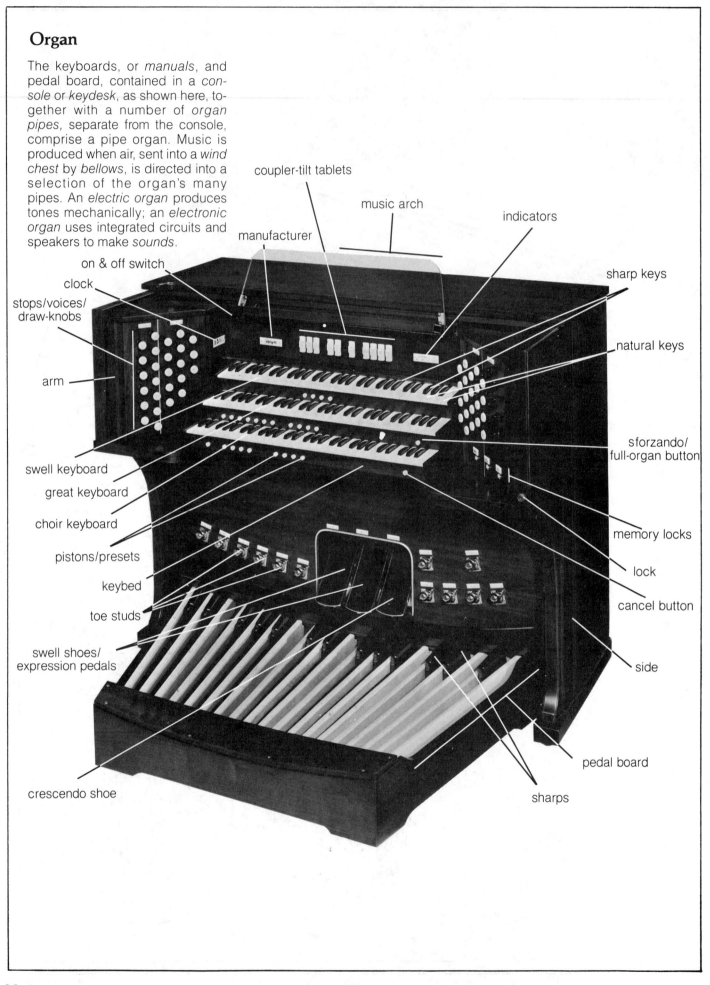

coupler-tilt tablets

music arch

indicators

manufacturer

on & off switch

clock

stops/voices/draw-knobs

arm

sharp keys

natural keys

swell keyboard

great keyboard

choir keyboard

sforzando/full-organ button

pistons/presets

keybed

toe studs

memory locks

lock

cancel button

swell shoes/expression pedals

side

pedal board

crescendo shoe

sharps

Piano

A piano is made up of a *structural unit,* a *tone unit* and a *mechanical unit.* The keys activate a mechanism that throws felt-covered *hammers* against the strings in the piano *case.* A *digitorium* is a silent machine for piano practice.

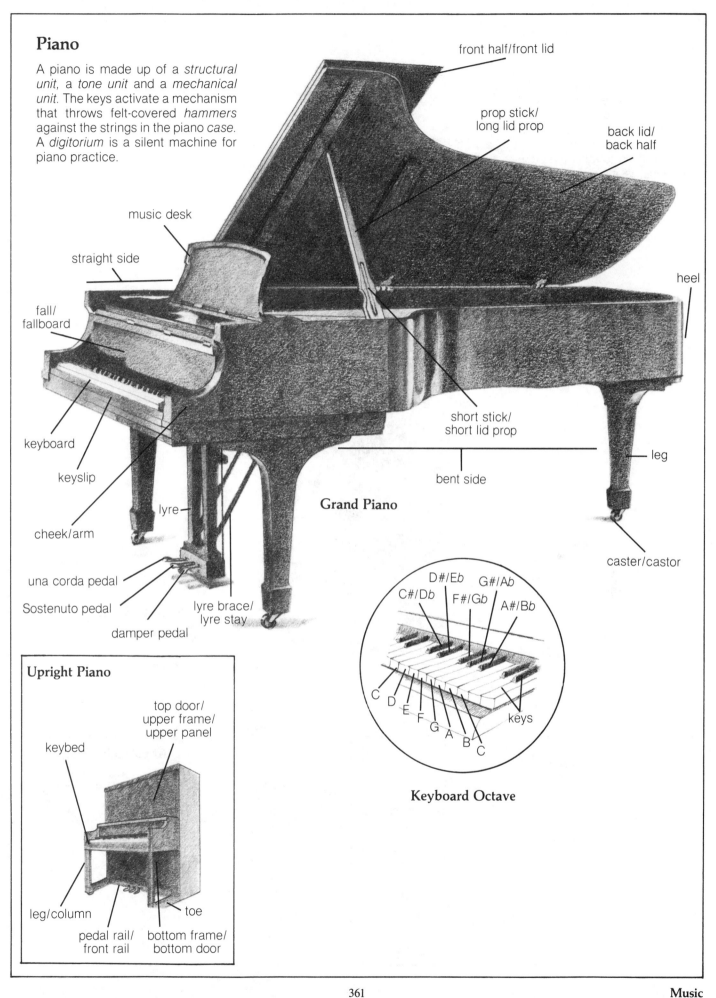

front half/front lid

prop stick/
long lid prop

back lid/
back half

music desk

straight side

heel

fall/
fallboard

keyboard

keyslip

short stick/
short lid prop

leg

cheek/arm

bent side

Grand Piano

lyre

una corda pedal

Sostenuto pedal

damper pedal

lyre brace/
lyre stay

caster/castor

C#/Db

D#/Eb

F#/Gb

G#/Ab

A#/Bb

C
D
E
F
G
A
B
C

keys

Keyboard Octave

Upright Piano

top door/
upper frame/
upper panel

keybed

leg/column

toe

pedal rail/
front rail

bottom frame/
bottom door

Guitar

These *chordophones,* or *stringed instruments,* are members of the lute family. They are played by plucking or strumming the strings with the fingers or with a stiff *plectrum* or *pick.* A movable device attached to a guitar neck, used to raise the pitch of the strings, is a *capo.* There are *sympathetic strings* inside the hollow neck of a sitar that vibrate in response to the drone or melody strings.

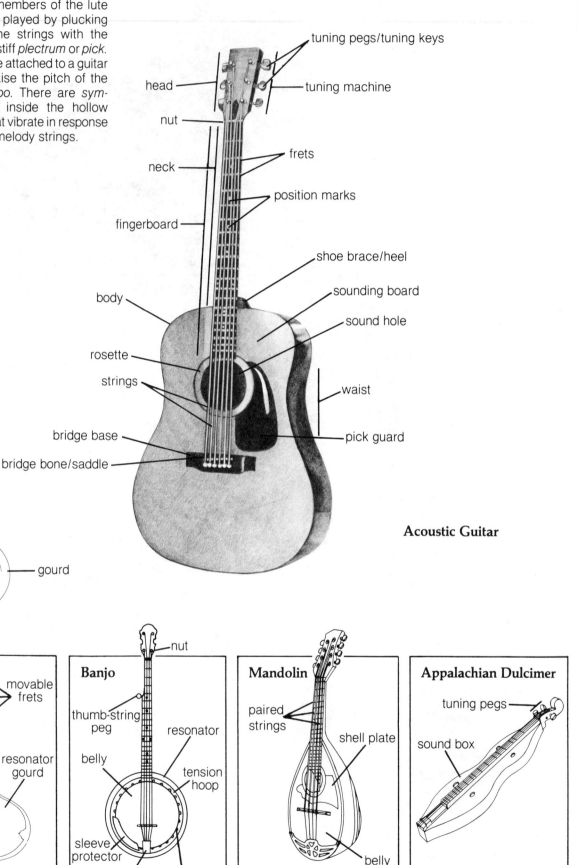

tuning pegs/tuning keys

head

tuning machine

nut

frets

neck

position marks

fingerboard

shoe brace/heel

sounding board

body

sound hole

rosette

strings

waist

bridge base

pick guard

bridge bone/saddle

Acoustic Guitar

tuning pegs

gourd

Sitar

movable frets

drone strings

melody strings

resonator gourd

Banjo

nut

thumb-string peg

resonator

belly

tension hoop

sleeve protector

tailpiece

tension screw

Mandolin

paired strings

shell plate

belly

Appalachian Dulcimer

tuning pegs

sound box

Electric Guitar and Synthesizer

The electric guitar has a *solid body* rather than the *hollow* or *semi-hollow body* of an acoustic guitar. *Special-effects pedals,* among them *fuzz, fuzz-phaser, wah-wah* and *distortion,* can be linked to the amplifier. *Pre-amplifiers,* which serve to magnify weak signals, can also be hooked up to the amplifier.

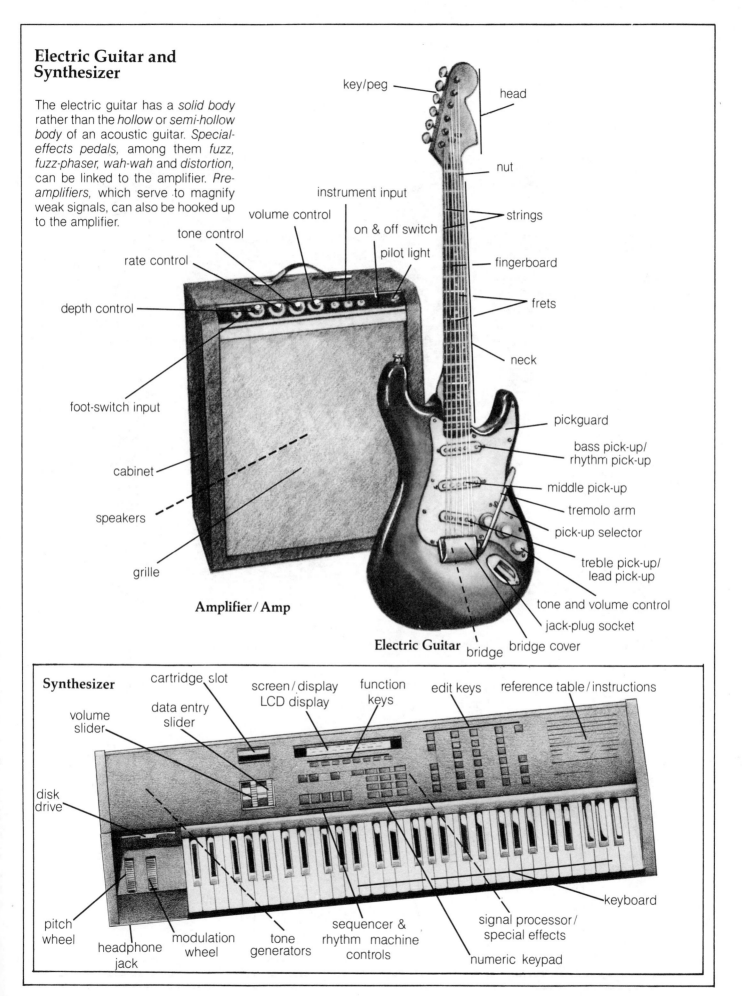

key/peg

head

nut

instrument input

volume control

on & off switch

tone control

pilot light

rate control

strings

depth control

fingerboard

frets

neck

foot-switch input

pickguard

bass pick-up/ rhythm pick-up

middle pick-up

tremolo arm

cabinet

pick-up selector

treble pick-up/ lead pick-up

speakers

grille

tone and volume control

jack-plug socket

Amplifier / Amp

Electric Guitar

bridge cover

bridge

Synthesizer

cartridge slot

screen / display LCD display

function keys

edit keys

reference table / instructions

volume slider

data entry slider

disk drive

pitch wheel

headphone jack

modulation wheel

tone generators

sequencer & rhythm machine controls

signal processor / special effects

numeric keypad

keyboard

Drums

Drums, or *membranophones,* in a *drum set* such as the one shown here, are played with *drumsticks, mallets* or *brushes.* A *gong* is struck with a *beater.* Adjustable metal, nylon or gut strings, called *snares,* are stretched across the bottom head, or *snare head,* of a snare drum. Timpani can be adjusted by screws or pedals to produce sounds of different pitches.

bell

bow

edge

Cymbal

Aerial Tom-Toms

tom-tom holder

lugs

Hi-Hat Cymbal

batter head

cymbal stand

lock

tension control knob

lug

shell

shell

counterhoop

head

tom-tom leg

counterhoop

foot

foot pedal

tension rod

beater

pedal

Snare Drum/Side Drum

Bass Drum

Floor Tom-Tom/Tenor Drum

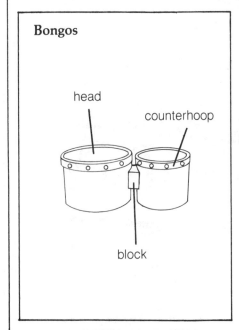

Bongos

head

counterhoop

block

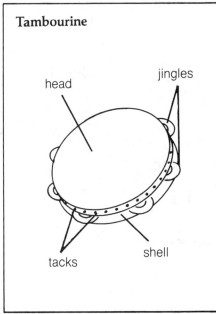

Tambourine

jingles

head

tacks

shell

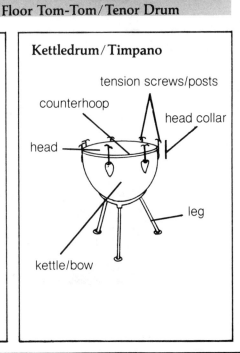

Kettledrum/Timpano

tension screws/posts

counterhoop

head collar

head

leg

kettle/bow

Bagpipe

A *drone reed*, or *double-reed*, held inside the chanter by a *tenon*, creates music when air is blown into the *pipes* by a *bagpiper* or by pumping *bellows* strapped to the *piper's* body. The melody is played on the eight *open holes* in the chanter. The *leather bag* is usually covered with a decorative *bag cover*.

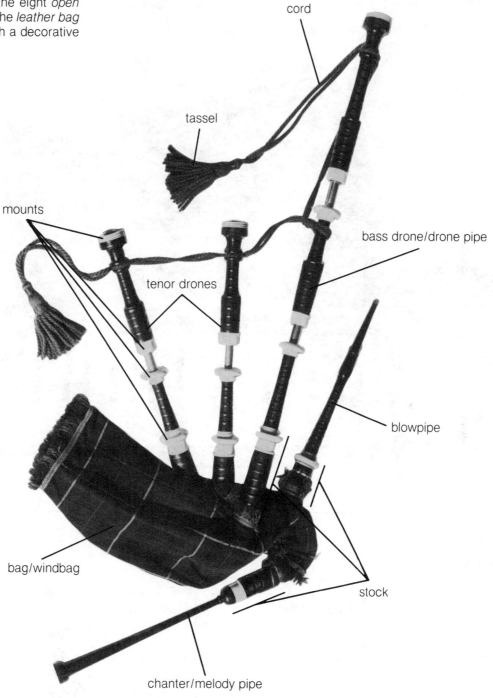

cord

tassel

mounts

tenor drones

bass drone/drone pipe

blowpipe

bag/windbag

stock

chanter/melody pipe

Folk Instruments

Like the harmonica, the accordion, or *piano-accordion,* is a *free-reed instrument.* Many accordions have *treble* and *bass register buttons* which allow the *accordionist* to change the tone of the instrument.

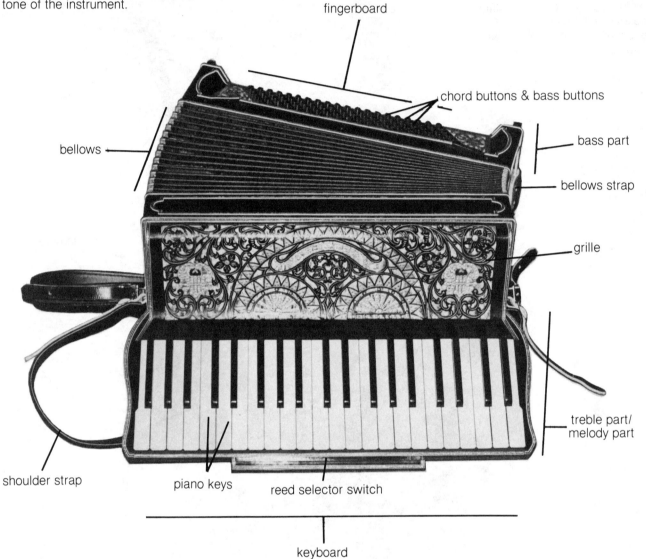

fingerboard

chord buttons & bass buttons

bass part

bellows

bellows strap

grille

treble part/ melody part

shoulder strap

piano keys

reed selector switch

keyboard

Accordion

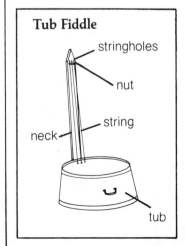

Tub Fiddle

stringholes

nut

neck

string

tub

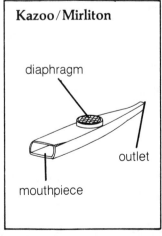

Kazoo/Mirliton

diaphragm

outlet

mouthpiece

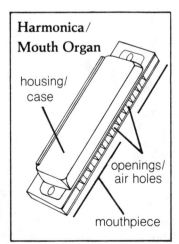

Harmonica/ Mouth Organ

housing/ case

openings/ air holes

mouthpiece

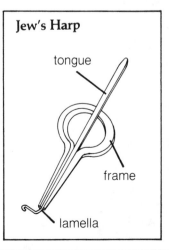

Jew's Harp

tongue

frame

lamella

Musical Accessories

A metronome, used to find the correct speed for music in beats per minute, can be spring wound or electric. A tuning fork is constructed and tempered so as to give a pure *tone* when caused to vibrate. It can be used in conjunction with a *resonance box* to amplify its sound.

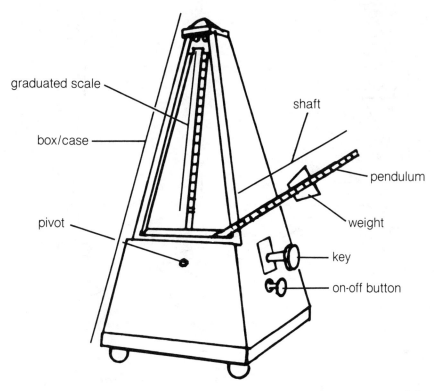

graduated scale

shaft

box/case

pendulum

weight

pivot

key

on-off button

Metronome

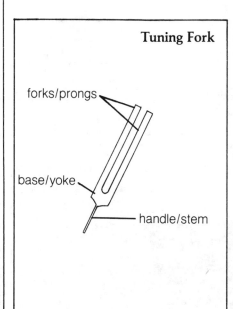

Tuning Fork

forks/prongs

base/yoke

handle/stem

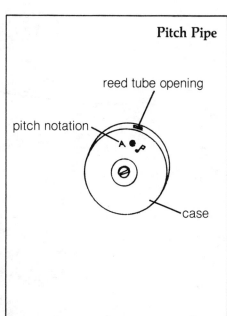

Pitch Pipe

reed tube opening

pitch notation

case

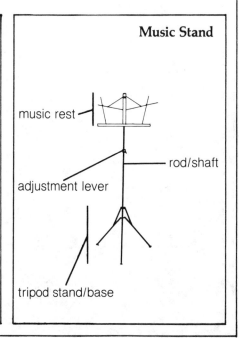

Music Stand

music rest

rod/shaft

adjustment lever

tripod stand/base

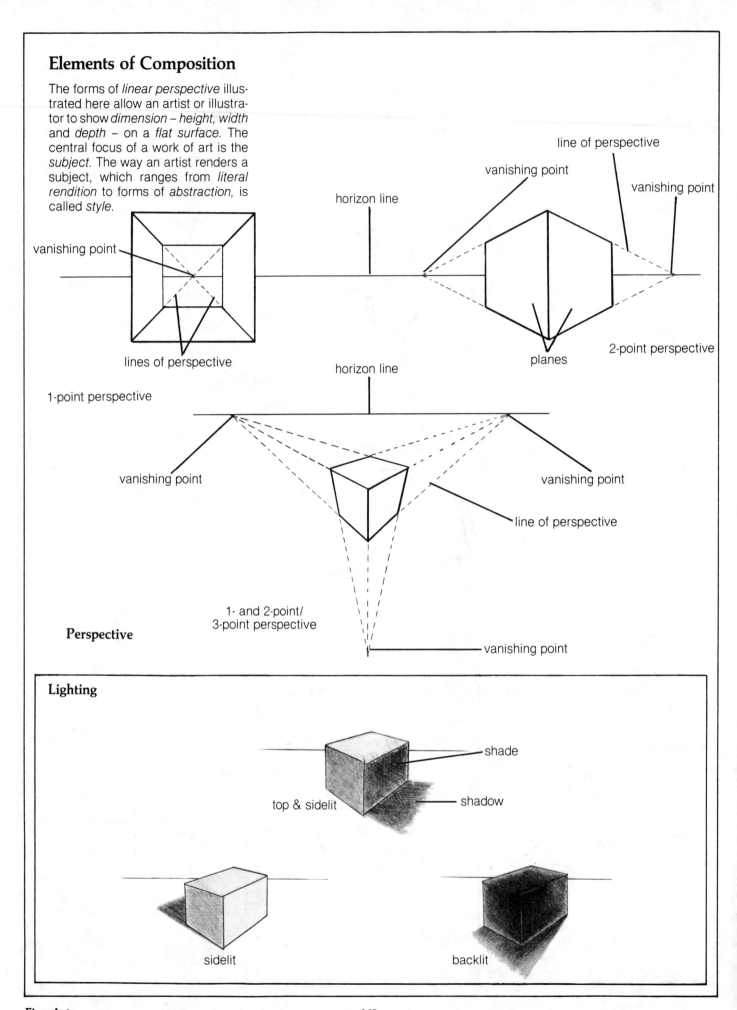

Elements of Composition

The forms of *linear perspective* illustrated here allow an artist or illustrator to show *dimension – height, width* and *depth* – on a *flat surface.* The central focus of a work of art is the *subject.* The way an artist renders a subject, which ranges from *literal rendition* to forms of *abstraction,* is called *style.*

horizon line

vanishing point

vanishing point

line of perspective

vanishing point

vanishing point

lines of perspective

planes

2-point perspective

1-point perspective

horizon line

vanishing point

vanishing point

line of perspective

1- and 2-point/ 3-point perspective

Perspective

vanishing point

Lighting

shade

shadow

top & sidelit

sidelit

backlit

Composition

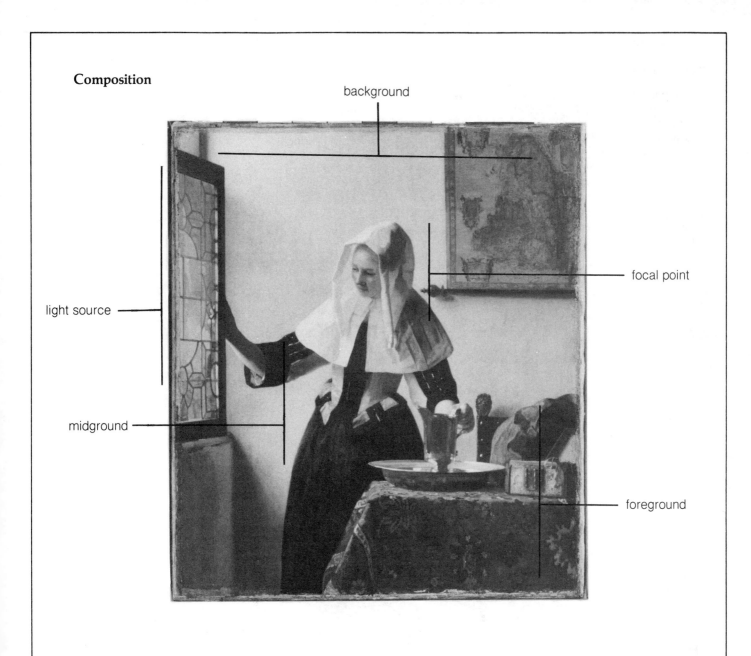

background

light source

focal point

midground

foreground

Texture

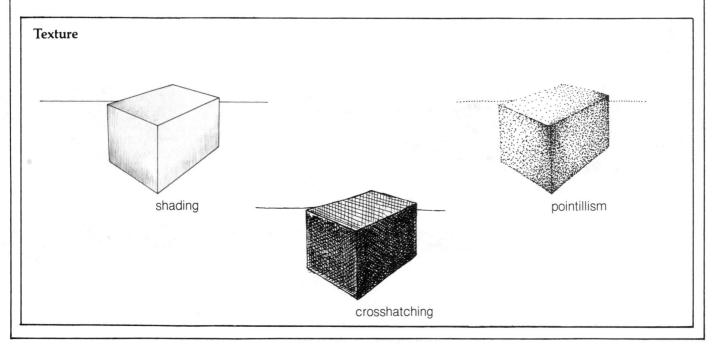

shading

crosshatching

pointillism

Painting

Before paint is applied to a *canvas* it must be drawn taut on a *stretcher* and the surface coated with *primer,* usually a substance called *gesso.* The *artist,* or *painter,* chooses a type of paint, or *medium,* in which to work, the most common of which are *tempera, acrylic* and *oil.* A thin blade set in a handle, used for mixing colors or applying them to a canvas, is a palette knife.

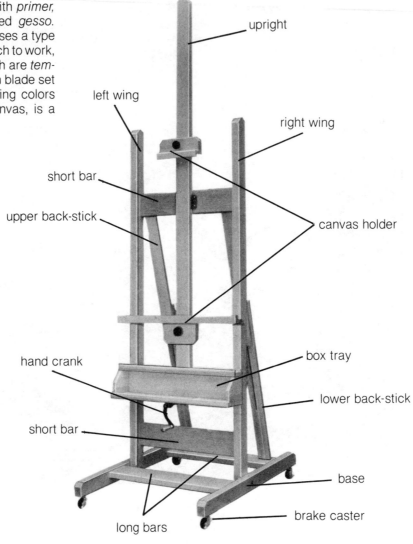

upright

left wing

right wing

short bar

canvas holder

upper back-stick

hand crank

box tray

lower back-stick

short bar

base

long bars

brake caster

Easel

Brushes

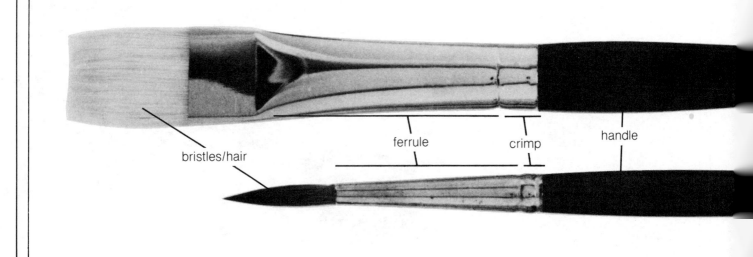

bristles/hair

ferrule

crimp

handle

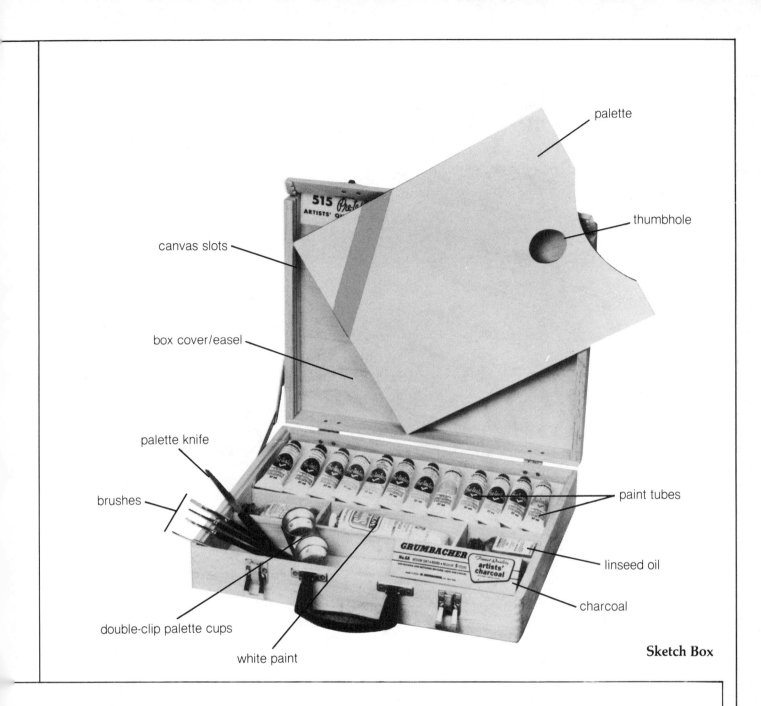

palette

thumbhole

canvas slots

box cover/easel

palette knife

brushes

paint tubes

linseed oil

charcoal

GRUMBACHER
No. 6A
artists' charcoal

double-clip palette cups

white paint

Sketch Box

7 M. GRUMBACHER N.Y. 127-B U.S.A.

brush size

manufacturer

series number

5 M. GRUMBACHER N.Y. 977 U.S.A.

Sculpting Tools

In stone sculpture, a *subtractive process,* forms or objects are created in *three dimensions* or in *relief.* Works may be carved or built up from some flexible material. Whenever a pliant material is used, it may be laid upon an inner skeleton, or *armature.* To make the finished product more durable, it may be fired or cast.

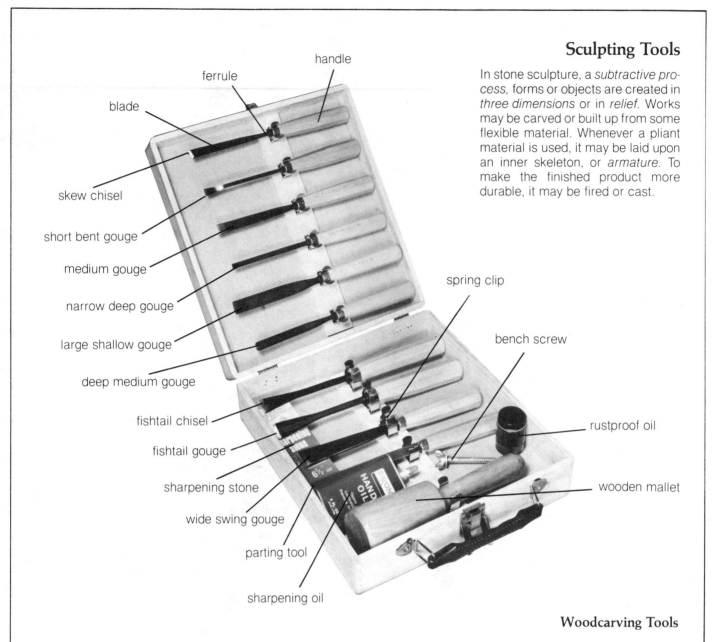

handle
ferrule
blade
skew chisel
short bent gouge
medium gouge
narrow deep gouge
large shallow gouge
deep medium gouge
fishtail chisel
fishtail gouge
sharpening stone
wide swing gouge
parting tool
sharpening oil
spring clip
bench screw
rustproof oil
wooden mallet

HAND OIL
6½ oz

Woodcarving Tools

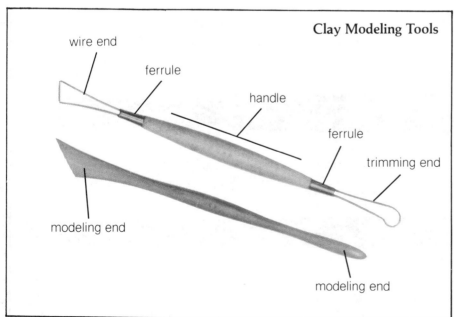

Clay Modeling Tools

wire end
ferrule
handle
ferrule
trimming end
modeling end
modeling end

Stonecutting Tools

flat chisel
point chisel
round-end chisel
toothed chisel
cape/splitting tool
stone carving hammer

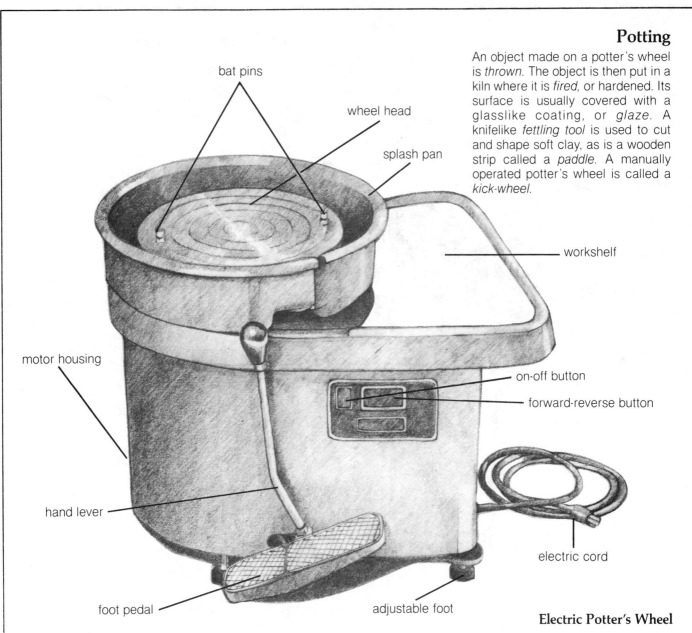

Potting

An object made on a potter's wheel is *thrown*. The object is then put in a kiln where it is *fired*, or hardened. Its surface is usually covered with a glasslike coating, or *glaze*. A knifelike *fettling tool* is used to cut and shape soft clay, as is a wooden strip called a *paddle*. A manually operated potter's wheel is called a *kick-wheel*.

bat pins

wheel head

splash pan

works;helf

motor housing

on-off button

forward-reverse button

electric cord

hand lever

foot pedal

adjustable foot

Electric Potter's Wheel

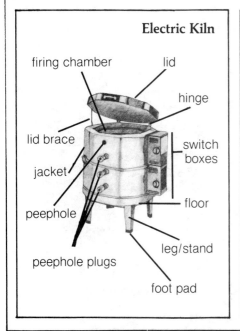

Electric Kiln

firing chamber

lid

hinge

lid brace

switch boxes

jacket

peephole

floor

peephole plugs

leg/stand

foot pad

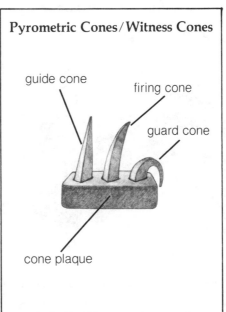

Pyrometric Cones / Witness Cones

guide cone

firing cone

guard cone

cone plaque

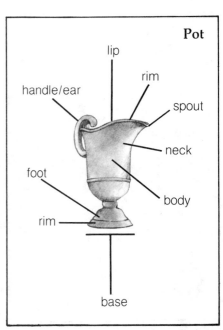

Pot

lip

rim

handle/ear

spout

neck

foot

body

rim

base

Fine Arts

The art of making *engravings* with wooden blocks is *xylography,* and the tools used to create the designs are called *gravers.*

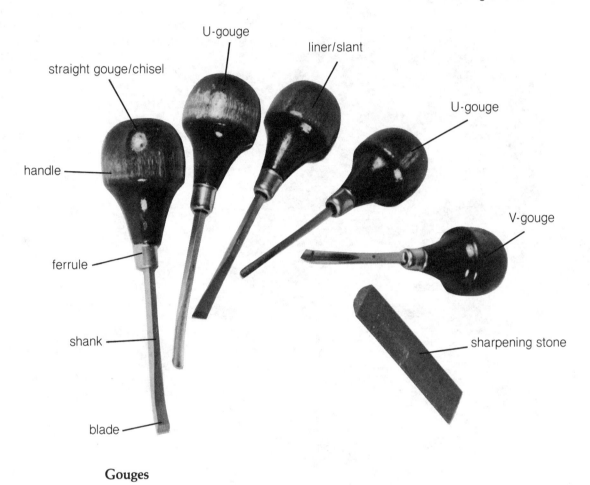

U-gouge

liner/slant

straight gouge/chisel

U-gouge

handle

V-gouge

ferrule

shank

sharpening stone

blade

Gouges

Wood Block

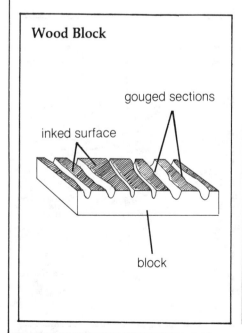

gouged sections

inked surface

block

Brayer/Roller

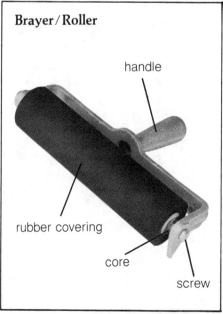

handle

rubber covering

core

screw

Baren

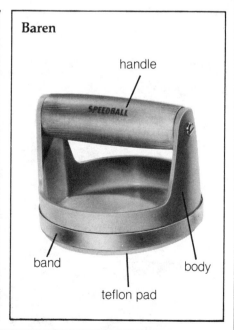

handle

band

body

teflon pad

Silk Screen and Scrimshaw

The *silk-screen printmaking process* is called *serigraphy*. A *stopping medium,* called a *resist,* blocks out or *masks* an area of the screen. Ink or paint passes through the unprotected areas of the screen to become the print. A person who does *decorative engravings* or *carvings* in *ivory* or *whalebone* is called a *scrimshander.*

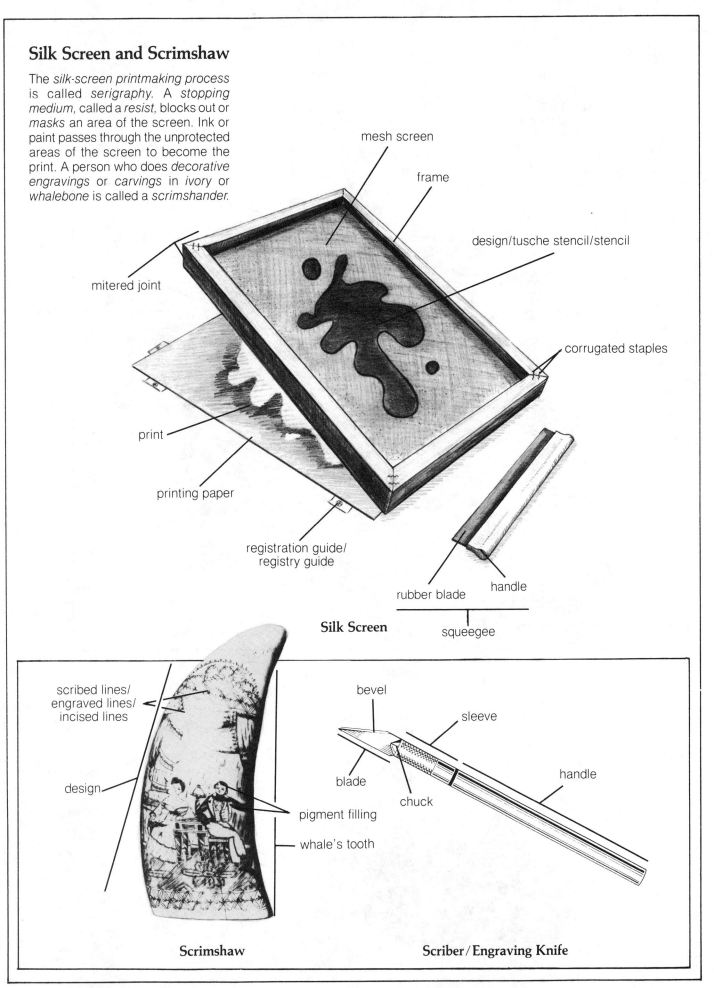

mesh screen

frame

design/tusche stencil/stencil

mitered joint

corrugated staples

print

printing paper

registration guide/
registry guide

rubber blade

handle

squeegee

Silk Screen

scribed lines/
engraved lines/
incised lines

design

pigment filling

whale's tooth

bevel

sleeve

blade

chuck

handle

Scrimshaw

Scriber / Engraving Knife

Fine Arts

Lithography

Lithography is a form of *plano-graphic printing*. The design is made on a stone, prepared, or "grained," by spinning the levigator over its surface, or on a metal *plate* with a *lithographic crayon, lithographic pencil, rubbing ink* or *asphaltum*.

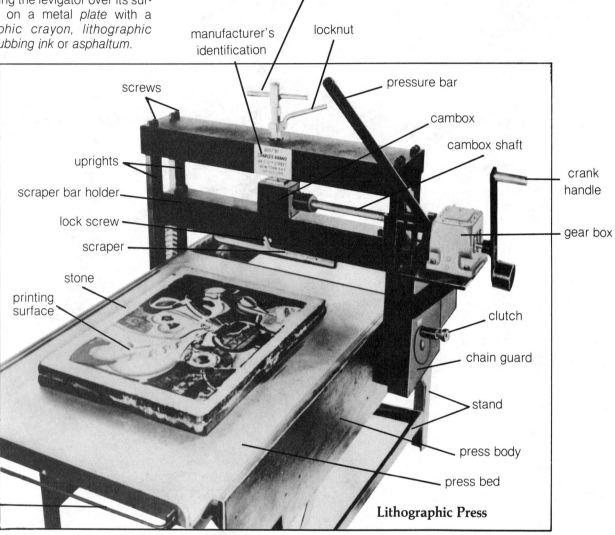

adjustment screw

manufacturer's identification

locknut

pressure bar

screws

cambox

cambox shaft

uprights

crank handle

scraper bar holder

gear box

lock screw

scraper

stone

printing surface

clutch

chain guard

stand

press body

press bed

bed handle

Lithographic Press

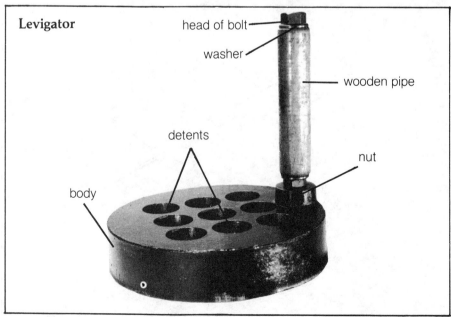

Levigator

head of bolt

washer

wooden pipe

detents

nut

body

Intaglio and Etching

Intaglio, or *incised printing,* is a type of *printmaking* in which a design is cut into a *plate* by techniques such as etching, *engraving, soft ground* or *aquatint.* A person who engraves metal is called a *chaser.*

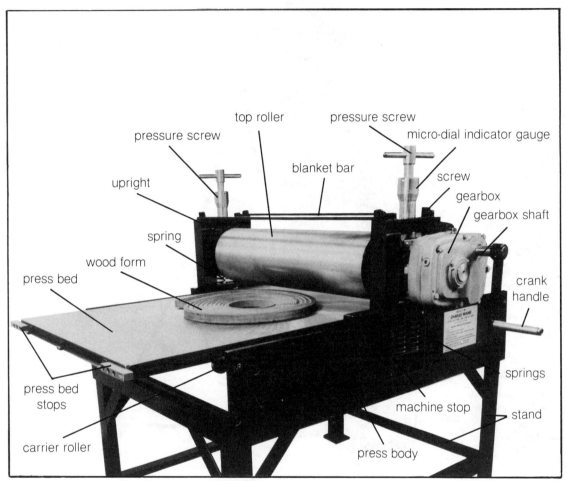

top roller

pressure screw

pressure screw

micro-dial indicator gauge

blanket bar

screw

upright

gearbox

gearbox shaft

spring

wood form

crank handle

press bed

springs

press bed stops

machine stop

stand

carrier roller

press body

Etching Press

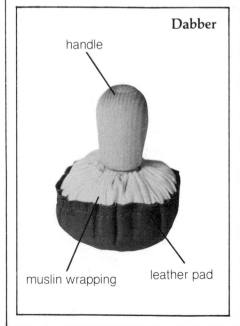

Dabber

handle

muslin wrapping

leather pad

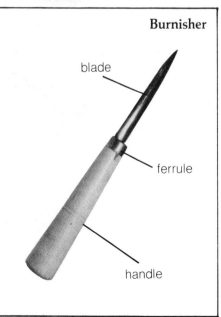

Burnisher

blade

ferrule

handle

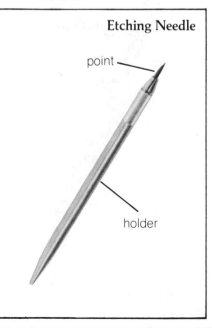

Etching Needle

point

holder

Fine Arts

Stained Glass

Cut sections of *colored glass* are separated by *breakers. Grozing pliers* are used to grind or bite away irregular glass edges.

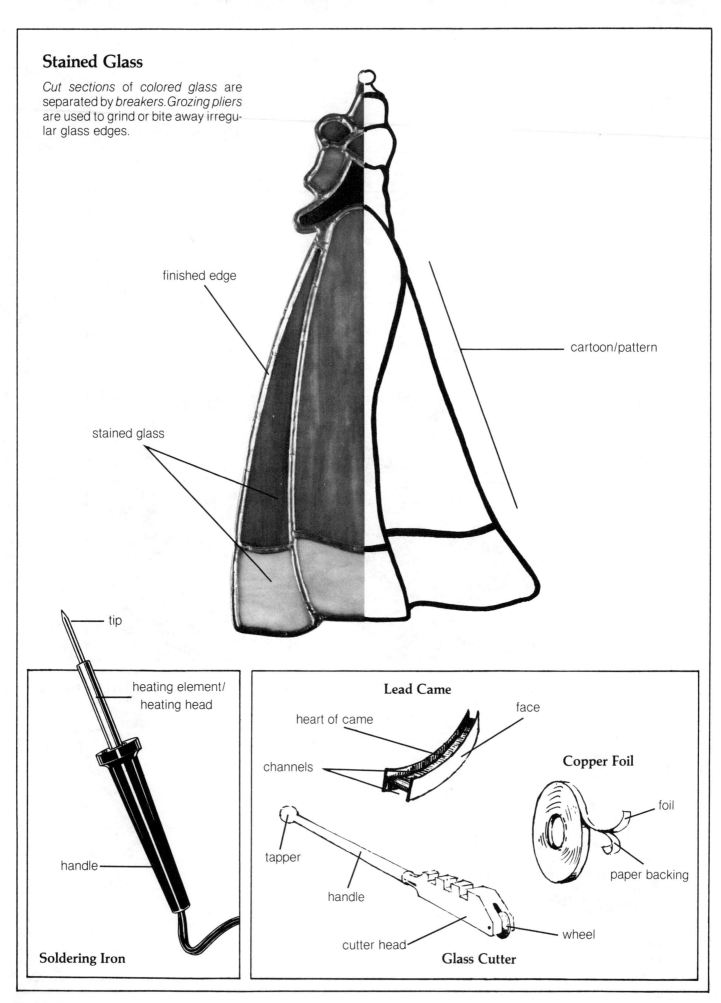

finished edge

cartoon/pattern

stained glass

tip

heating element/ heating head

handle

Soldering Iron

Lead Came

heart of came

face

channels

tapper

handle

cutter head

Glass Cutter

Copper Foil

foil

paper backing

wheel

Frame

The frame shown here is a long-lasting *archival frame*. The area cut out of the mat to reveal the artwork is the *mat window*. A wire hanger can be attached to L-shaped *shoulder hooks*, *picture hooks* or *nails* as well as to screw eyes. The process of permanently affixing artwork to a backing is called *mounting*. A *free-standing easel-back* or *piano frame* consists of an easel, backing and an angled support *stand*. In *passe-partout*, the framing elements are held together by strips of cloth or paper pasted over the edges.

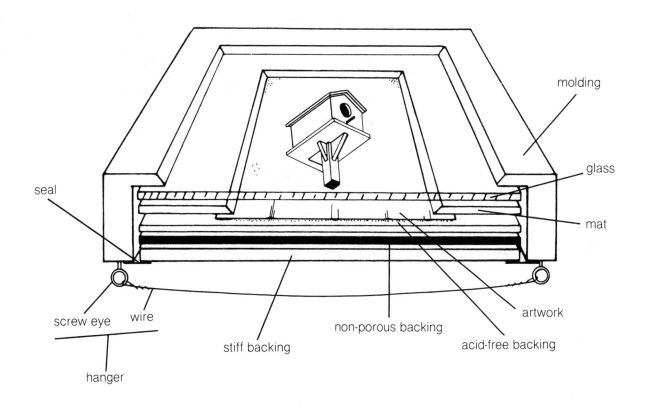

molding

glass

mat

artwork

acid-free backing

non-porous backing

stiff backing

seal

screw eye

wire

hanger

Fine Arts

Cartooning

Many one-panel cartoons use *captions* or *labels* below the *illustration* for dialogue or explanation. Those appearing on the editorial pages of newspapers are called *editorial* or *political cartoons* and usually feature an exaggerated likeness, or *caricature*, of some well-known figure, as the main *character*. *Comics*, or *comic books*, use cartooning throughout. A complete *sphericasia*, or *swalloop*, is used by a *cartoonist* to depict a complete swing at an object, be it a golf ball or another person.

brick symbolia

thought balloon

agitrons

onomatopoeia

dites

lucaflect

staggeration

hites

briffit

vites

artist's signature

cross-hatching

Comic Strip

strip title

cartoonist

beetle bailey by mort walker

DOES ANYONE KNOW WHERE I LEFT MY...MY, UH...

cartoon panel/frame

border

...WHERE I LEFT MY, UH...

speech balloon

...THINGAMAJIG?

Fireworks

Fireworks makers, *pyrotechnists*, work in concrete block buildings called *magazines*. *Display rockets*, *aerial bombs*, *pin wheels* or *Catherine wheels*, and *fountains* derive their explosive force from a combination of *saltpeter*, *sulfur* and *charcoal*. Explosive *M-80s* and *cherry bombs* are now banned.

chrysanthemums

aerial flash

titanium salute

firing smoke

Grand Finale

twice-changing chrysanthemum

star shell

tails

palm trees

electric sparks

octopus

magnesium star shells

peonies

Crystal Palace set piece

lasers

flitter candles

flare

jetting fire crescendo

fountains

Aerial Shells

bare match end

fuse / black match

twine ties

outside wrap / shell wrap

label

lift section wrap

Exterior case

fuse

shell fuse

fuse for lifting charge

washer

quick match / communications fuse

lifting charge / gunpowder

stars / metallic salts

shell case

bursting charge / gunpowder

Interior assembly

Rocket

cap

shell / papier-mâché case

bursting charge

stars

propellant

clay choke / plug

stick

fuse

Fireworks

Sewing

Each in-and-out movement of a threaded needle produces a *stitch*. A scissor's *bite* is the distance it cuts into a fabric on a single stroke. A small cushion into which pins or most-used needles are stuck until needed is called a *pincushion*.

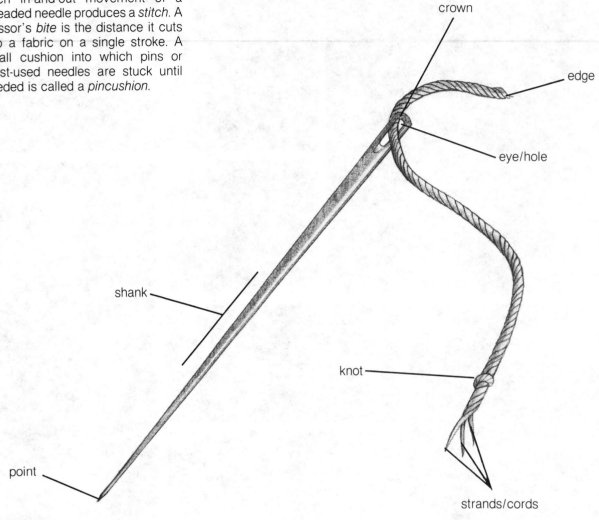

crown

edge

eye/hole

shank

knot

point

strands/cords

Needle and Thread

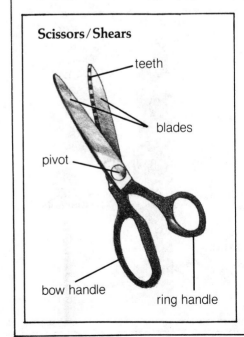

Scissors/Shears

teeth

blades

pivot

bow handle

ring handle

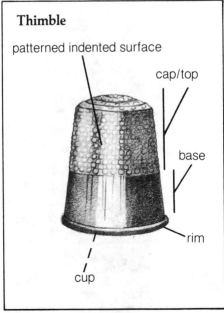

Thimble

patterned indented surface

cap/top

base

rim

cup

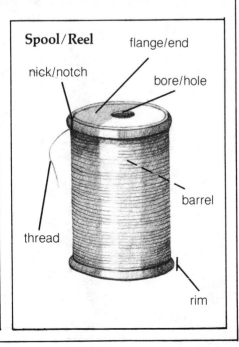

Spool/Reel

flange/end

nick/notch

bore/hole

thread

barrel

rim

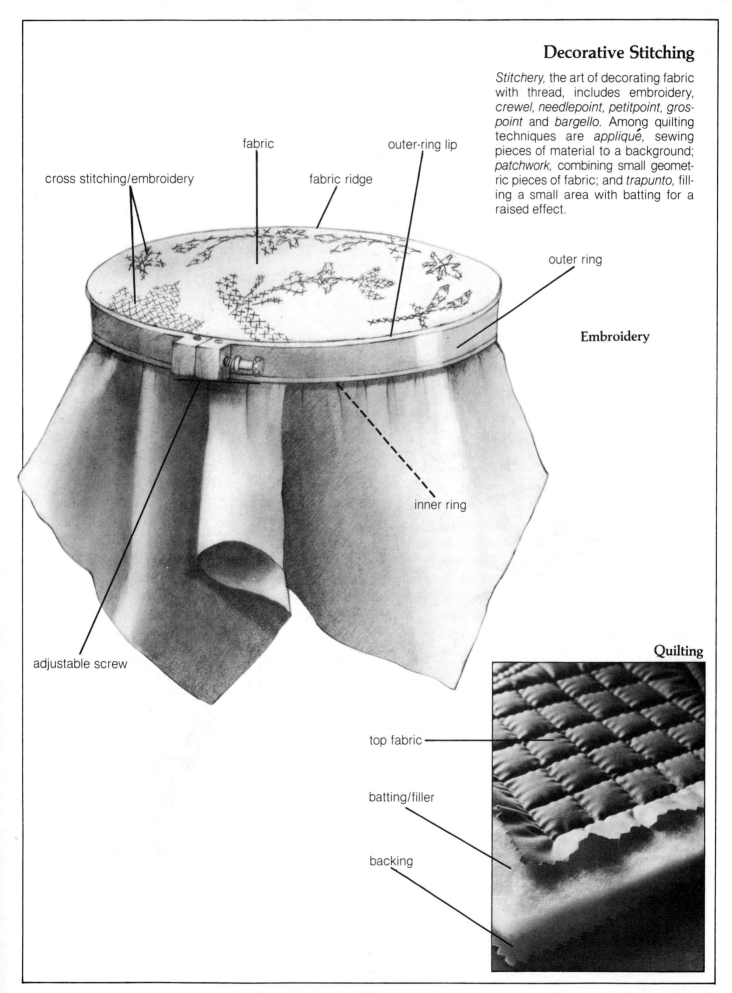

Decorative Stitching

Stitchery, the art of decorating fabric with thread, includes embroidery, *crewel*, *needlepoint*, *petitpoint*, *grospoint* and *bargello*. Among quilting techniques are *appliqué*, sewing pieces of material to a background; *patchwork*, combining small geometric pieces of fabric; and *trapunto*, filling a small area with batting for a raised effect.

cross stitching/embroidery

fabric

fabric ridge

outer-ring lip

outer ring

Embroidery

inner ring

adjustable screw

Quilting

top fabric

batting/filler

backing

Crafts

Knitting

Knitting is the interlacing of *loops*. The main stitches are the *knit stitch*, or *stitch*, and the *purl stitch*, or *purl*. *Crocheting* is a form of *needlework* done by looping thread with a *crochet needle*. *Macrame* is knotting, and *tatting* is done by looping and knotting with a single cotton thread and a small shuttle.

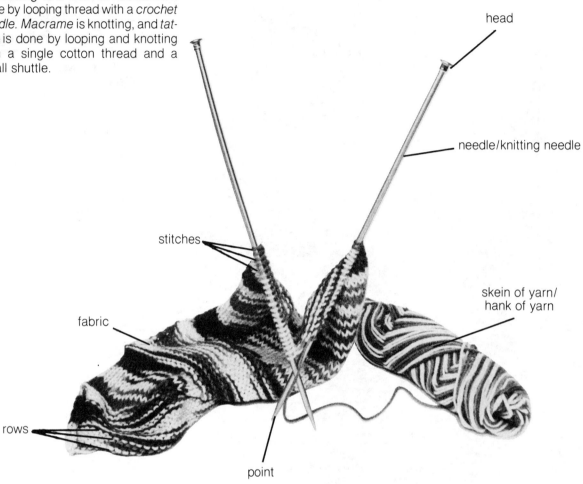

head

needle/knitting needle

skein of yarn/
hank of yarn

stitches

fabric

rows

point

Hand Knitting

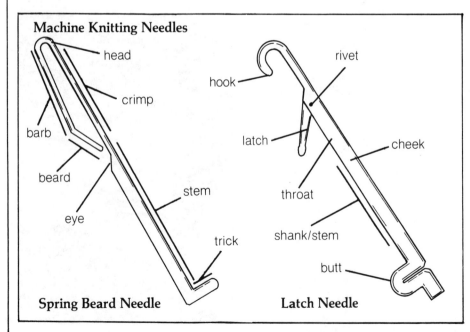

Machine Knitting Needles

head

crimp

barb

beard

eye

stem

trick

Spring Beard Needle

hook

rivet

latch

cheek

throat

shank/stem

butt

Latch Needle

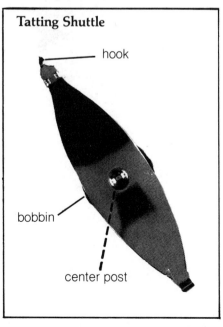

Tatting Shuttle

hook

bobbin

center post

Weaving

The lengthwise (front to back) *yarn* or *threads* on a loom are called the warp. Threads taken together which run from side to side, or from *selvage* to selvage, are called the *weft*. The weft is also often called the *woof*, although more correctly, the woof is the same as the *web*, or finished *fabric*.

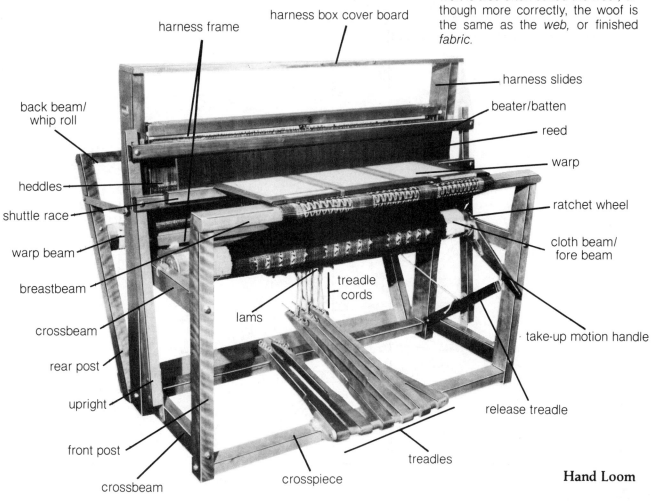

harness frame

harness box cover board

harness slides

back beam/ whip roll

beater/batten

reed

warp

heddles

shuttle race

ratchet wheel

warp beam

cloth beam/ fore beam

breastbeam

treadle cords

crossbeam

lams

rear post

take-up motion handle

upright

front post

release treadle

crossbeam

crosspiece

treadles

Hand Loom

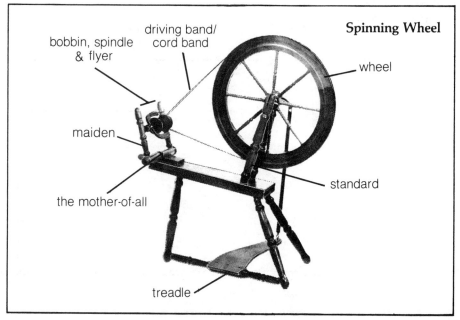

Spinning Wheel

driving band/ cord band

bobbin, spindle & flyer

wheel

maiden

the mother-of-all

standard

treadle

Crafts

Sewing Pattern

A roll of fabric of a specified length is called a *bolt*. A sample of a fabric is a *swatch*. Fabrics sold at lengths specified by the customer are called *piece goods* or *yard goods*.

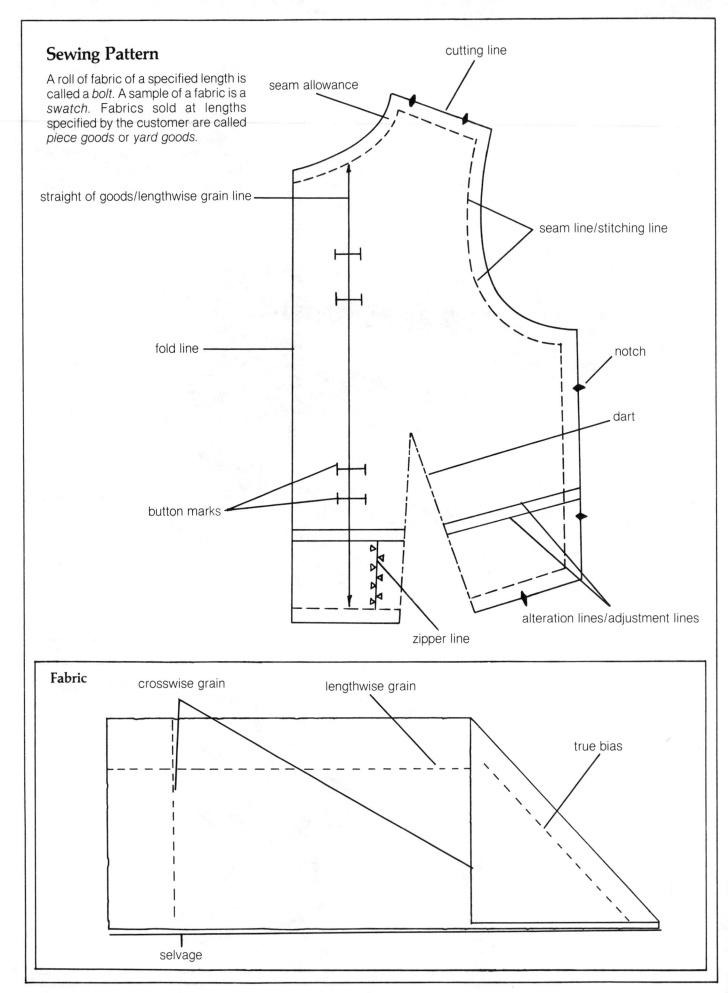

cutting line

seam allowance

straight of goods/lengthwise grain line

seam line/stitching line

fold line

notch

dart

button marks

alteration lines/adjustment lines

zipper line

Fabric

crosswise grain

lengthwise grain

true bias

selvage

Machinery, Tools and Weapons

Except for office and industrial equipment, which is outside the scope of this book, this section covers all the man-made equipment one is likely to encounter in everyday life, daily reading or classroom learning. It includes basic power systems and offshoots, everything from a nuclear power plant to an electrical plug, equipment used to control temperature in a house, and components of various engines.

Considerable space has been devoted to illustrating the parts of tools used around the home and in the yard while not ignoring the basic gear used by ranchers, trappers, farmers, scientists and doctors. Even penal equipment used for capital punishment has been included.

The weaponry subsection traces the names and parts of articles used in warfare from medieval times to objects used today. Thus, a student reading about King Arthur for the first time will be able to identify the parts of a sword as easily as a newspaper reader is able to identify the parts of a modern missile.

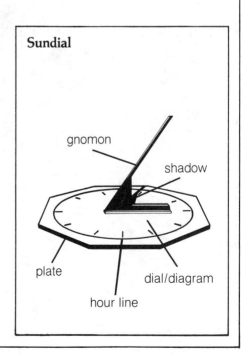

Sundial

gnomon

shadow

plate

hour line

dial/diagram

Wind Systems

The cloth sail on this *smock mill* is in a *first reef,* or *curled,* position, as opposed to *sword point, dagger point* or *full sail.* Sails or *shutters* on a fantail are called *vanes.* Some mills have *petticoats,* or vertical boards, below the cap, to provide protection where cap and tower meet, and *beards,* or decorated boards behind the cannister.

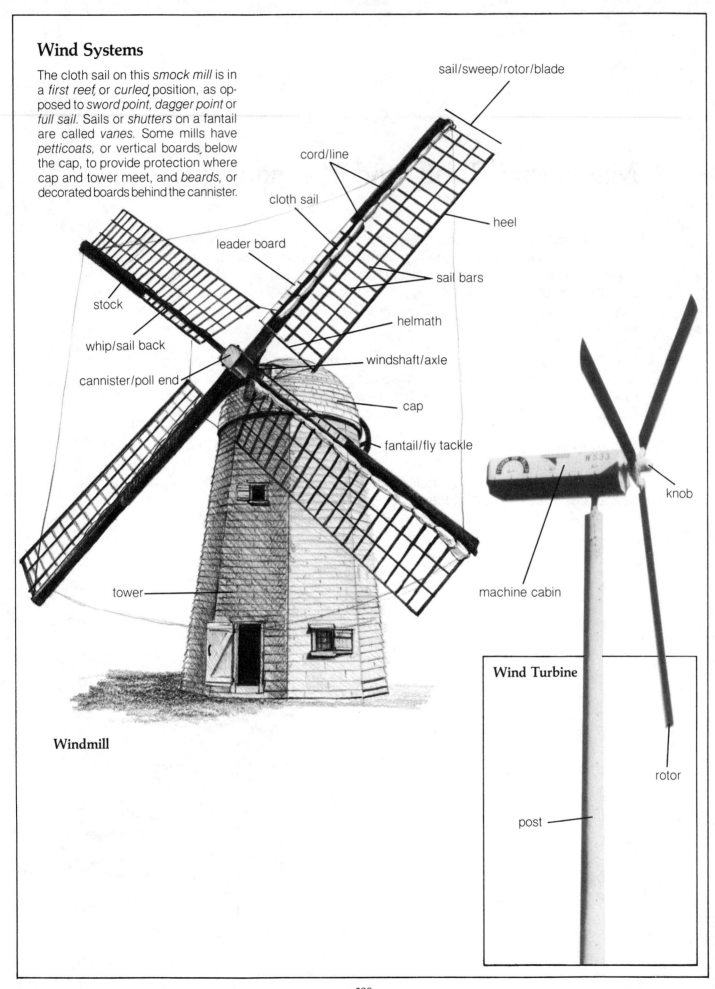

sail/sweep/rotor/blade

cord/line

cloth sail

heel

leader board

sail bars

stock

helmath

whip/sail back

windshaft/axle

cannister/poll end

cap

fantail/fly tackle

tower

knob

machine cabin

Windmill

Wind Turbine

rotor

post

Solar Power System

Solar energy can be collected by systems such as the one shown here, which operate like *radiators* working in reverse to produce hot water. The sun's energy can also be converted directly into *electricity* by *solar cells*. *Concentrating solar collectors* use *lenses* or *reflecting sufaces* to direct sunlight on a trough-type collector to produce large amounts of heat which can be converted into electricity.

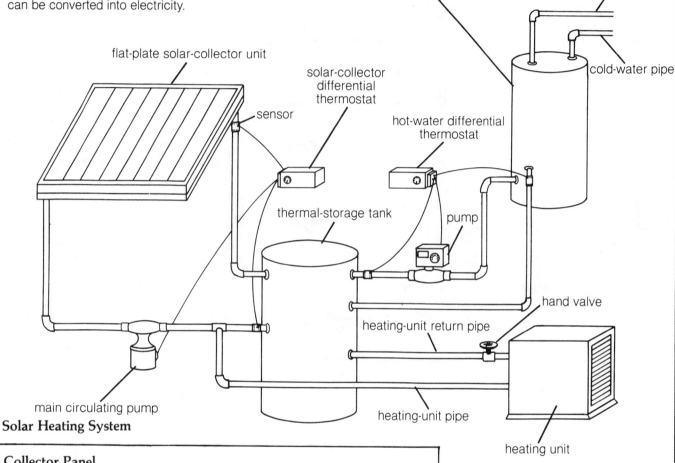

flat-plate solar-collector unit

solar-collector differential thermostat

sensor

domestic hot-water tank

hot-water pipe

cold-water pipe

hot-water differential thermostat

thermal-storage tank

pump

hand valve

heating-unit return pipe

heating-unit pipe

heating unit

main circulating pump

Solar Heating System

Collector Panel

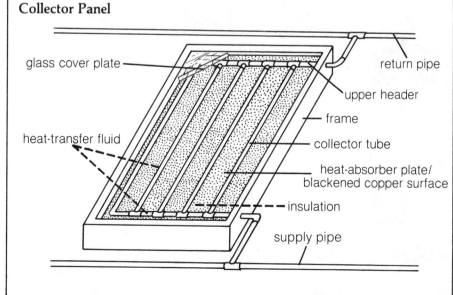

glass cover plate

return pipe

upper header

frame

collector tube

heat-absorber plate/ blackened copper surface

heat-transfer fluid

insulation

supply pipe

Power Systems

Nuclear Power Reactor

In order to generate *electricity* by using the heat produced by *fission,* the *chain reaction* must be slowed down and controlled. To control the reaction rate in a reactor, or *pile,* *rods* of neutron-absorbing material are moved in and out as required. The smallest amount of *fissionable material* in which fission is self-sustaining is called the *critical mass.* If more fissionable material is produced than consumed, the reactor is called a *breeder reactor.*

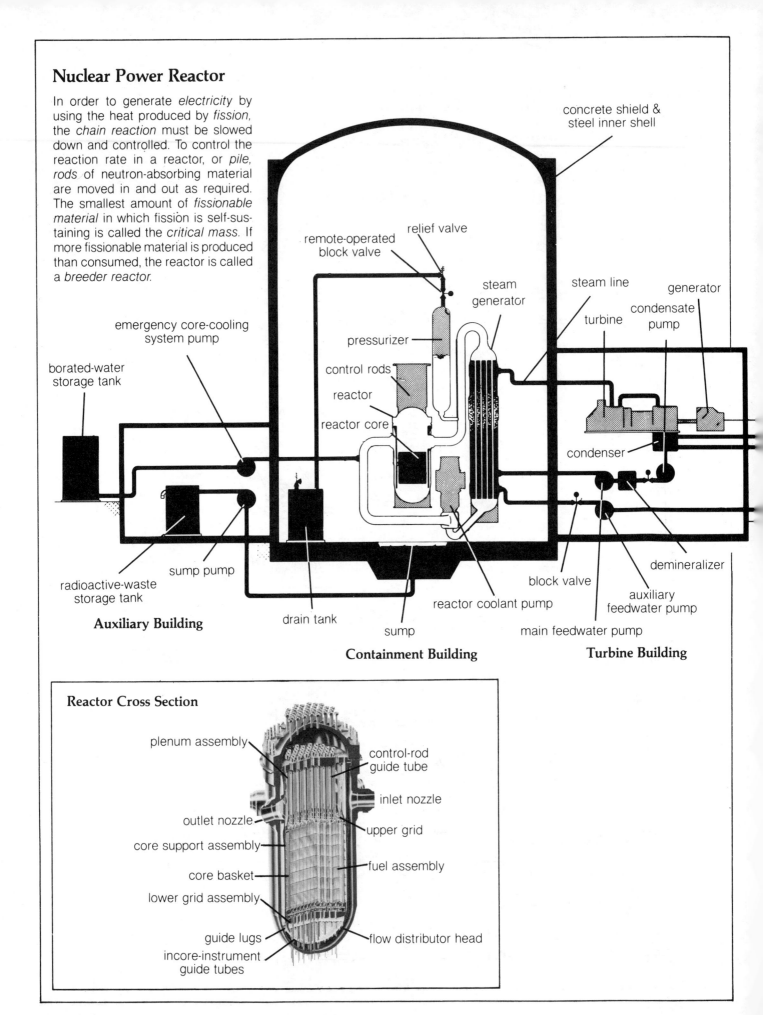

concrete shield & steel inner shell

relief valve

remote-operated block valve

steam generator

steam line

turbine

generator

condensate pump

pressurizer

control rods

reactor

reactor core

emergency core-cooling system pump

borated-water storage tank

condenser

radioactive-waste storage tank

sump pump

drain tank

sump

reactor coolant pump

block valve

main feedwater pump

auxiliary feedwater pump

demineralizer

Auxiliary Building

Containment Building

Turbine Building

Reactor Cross Section

plenum assembly

control-rod guide tube

inlet nozzle

outlet nozzle

upper grid

core support assembly

core basket

fuel assembly

lower grid assembly

guide lugs

incore-instrument guide tubes

flow distributor head

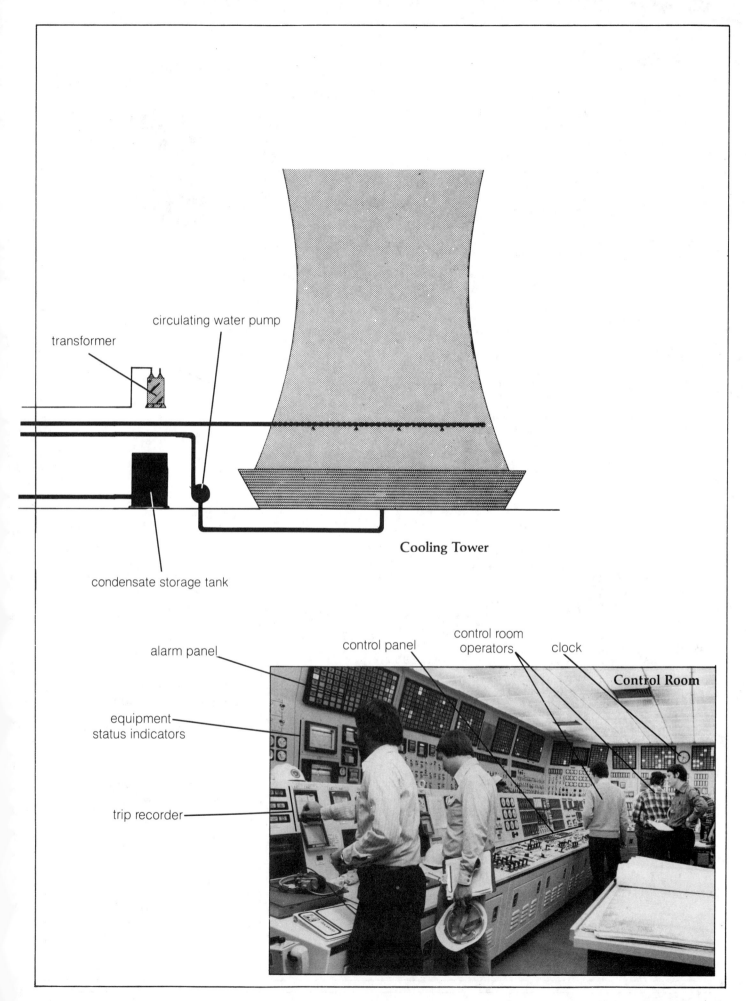

transformer

circulating water pump

Cooling Tower

condensate storage tank

alarm panel

control panel

control room operators

clock

Control Room

equipment status indicators

trip recorder

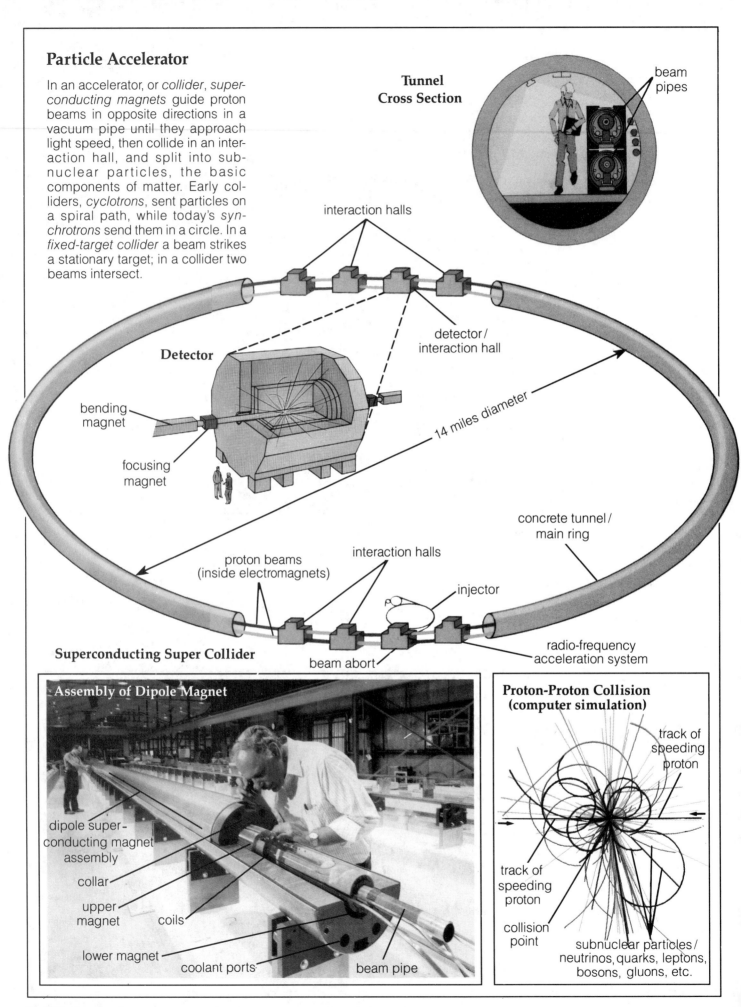

Particle Accelerator

In an accelerator, or *collider*, *superconducting magnets* guide proton beams in opposite directions in a vacuum pipe until they approach light speed, then collide in an interaction hall, and split into subnuclear particles, the basic components of matter. Early colliders, *cyclotrons*, sent particles on a spiral path, while today's *synchrotrons* send them in a circle. In a *fixed-target collider* a beam strikes a stationary target; in a collider two beams intersect.

Tunnel Cross Section

beam pipes

interaction halls

detector / interaction hall

Detector

bending magnet

focusing magnet

14 miles diameter

concrete tunnel / main ring

proton beams (inside electromagnets)

interaction halls

injector

beam abort

radio-frequency acceleration system

Superconducting Super Collider

Assembly of Dipole Magnet

dipole superconducting magnet assembly

collar

upper magnet

coils

lower magnet

coolant ports

beam pipe

Proton-Proton Collision (computer simulation)

track of speeding proton

track of speeding proton

collision point

subnuclear particles / neutrinos, quarks, leptons, bosons, gluons, etc.

Lasers and Holography

Laser, an acronym for Light Amplification by Stimulated Emission of Radiation, is a device that produces intense light from a laser tube, or *resonator*. Photons in a laser light race along a narrow, "coherent" *beam* in which all the rays are vibrating together, on exactly the same *wavelength* and at exactly the same phase. In holography, a laser's beam is split in two, the object beam, which lights the subject, and the reference beam, which goes to a film plate. In the resulting hologram, the image appears to be *three-dimensional*.

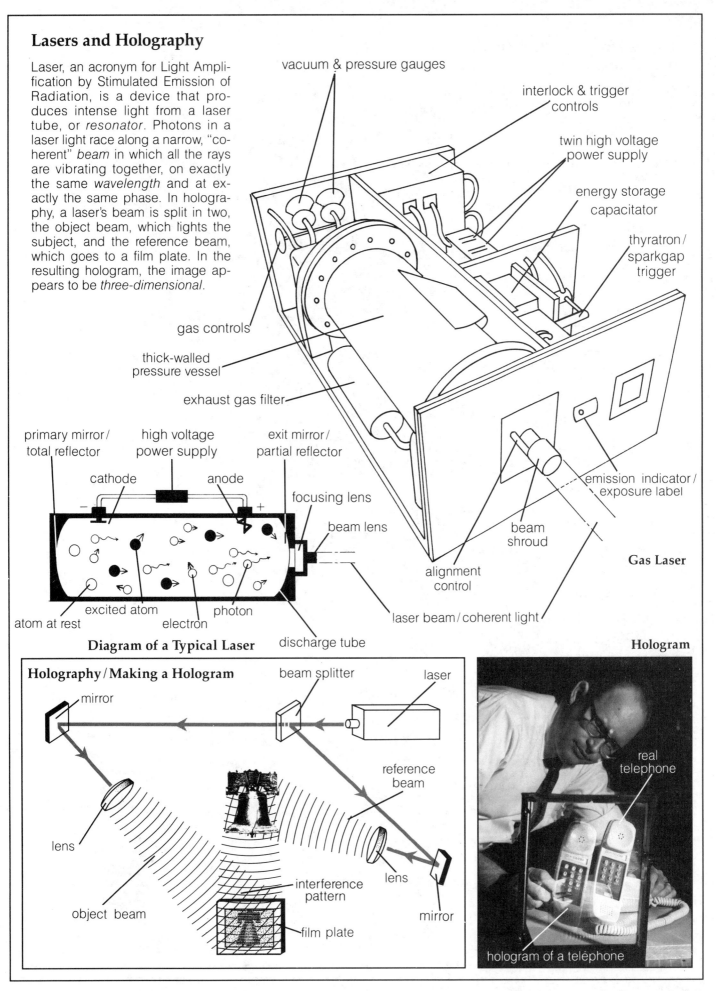

vacuum & pressure gauges

interlock & trigger controls

twin high voltage power supply

energy storage capacitator

thyratron / sparkgap trigger

gas controls

thick-walled pressure vessel

exhaust gas filter

emission indicator / exposure label

beam shroud

alignment control

Gas Laser

primary mirror / total reflector

high voltage power supply

exit mirror / partial reflector

cathode

anode

focusing lens

beam lens

excited atom

photon

atom at rest

electron

laser beam / coherent light

Diagram of a Typical Laser

discharge tube

Hologram

Holography / Making a Hologram

beam splitter

laser

mirror

reference beam

lens

real telephone

interference pattern

object beam

lens

mirror

film plate

hologram of a telephone

Power Line, Vacuum Tube and Transistor

An *overhead line support, lattice-work tower* or *double-circuit tower* transmits high-voltage electrical power from *generating plants* to various parts of a *power network*. A transistor consists of a small block of a *semiconductor* with at least three *electrodes*.

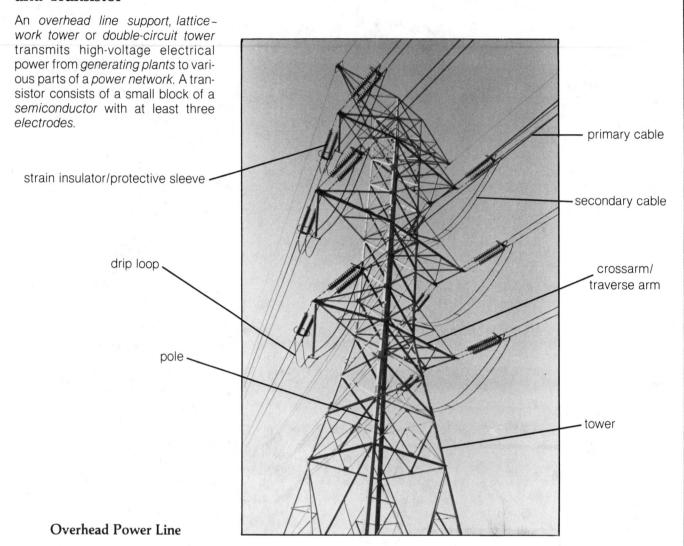

strain insulator/protective sleeve

drip loop

pole

primary cable

secondary cable

crossarm/
traverse arm

tower

Overhead Power Line

Transistor Chip

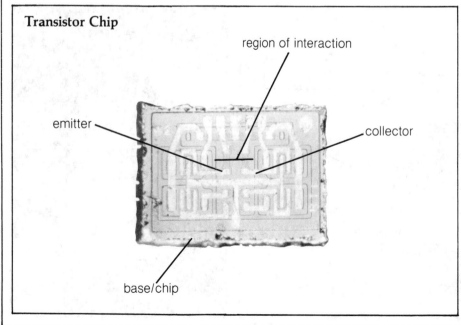

region of interaction

emitter

collector

base/chip

Vacuum Tube/Electron Tube

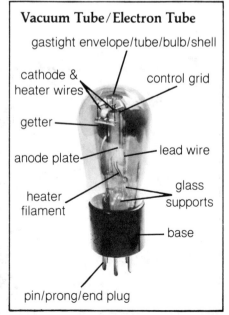

gastight envelope/tube/bulb/shell

cathode &
heater wires

control grid

getter

anode plate

lead wire

glass
supports

heater
filament

base

pin/prong/end plug

Battery

Batteries are marked with *polarity symbols*, + identifying the positive terminal, − the negative. *Secondary cells* can be recharged, while *primary cells* cannot.

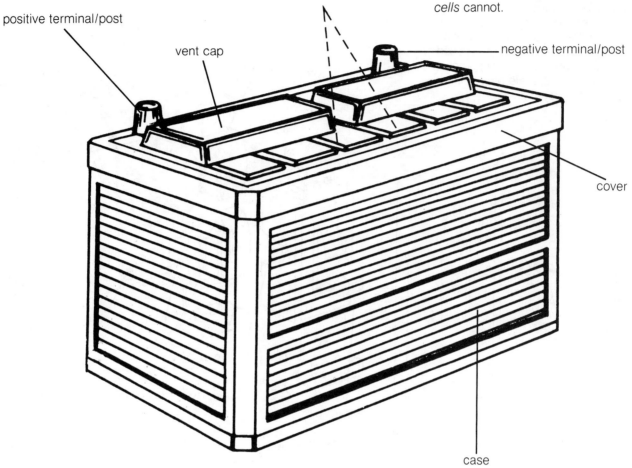

cell compartments

positive terminal/post

vent cap

negative terminal/post

cover

case

Lead Acid Battery

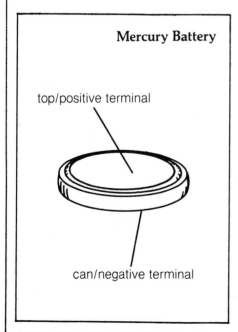

Mercury Battery

top/positive terminal

can/negative terminal

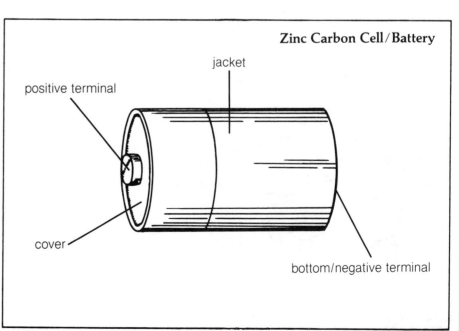

Zinc Carbon Cell / Battery

jacket

positive terminal

cover

bottom/negative terminal

Switch, Receptacle and Plug

A wall switch conducts *electrical current* only when it is in the up, or *on position,* as opposed to the down, or *off position. Ground wires* are located inside the junction box. *Attachment plugs,* or *"dead front" plugs,* such as the one shown here, have no exposed current-carrying parts except prongs, blades or *pins.* A *male plug* is fitted into a *female receptacle.*

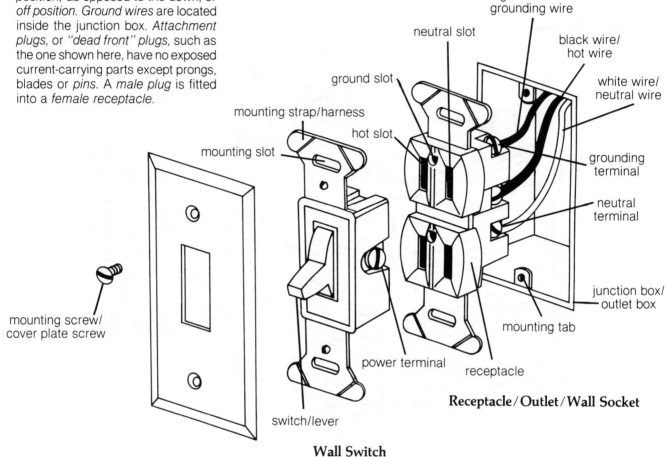

Cover Plate/Switch Plate

Wall Switch

Receptacle/Outlet/Wall Socket

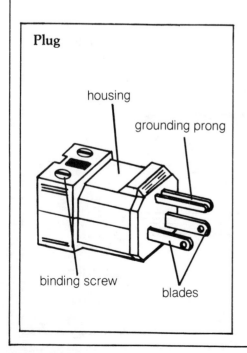

Plug

Meter and Fuse Box

Fuses "blow" and circuit breakers "trip" when there is too much current in the wires of a particular *circuit*. The fuse or circuit breaker acts as a safety device to keep fire from starting by heat caused by an *overload* or by a *short circuit*.

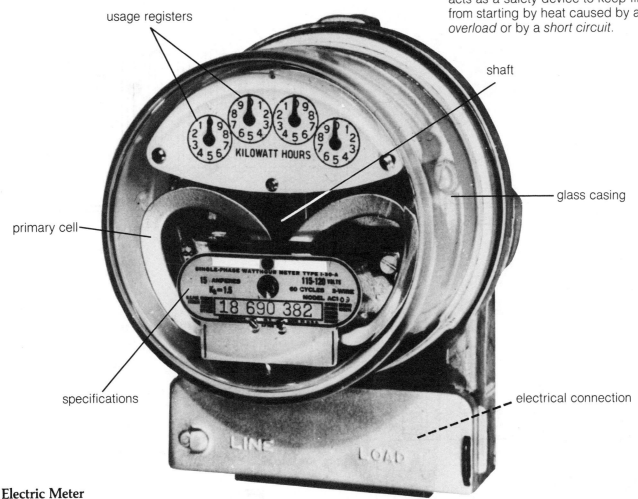

usage registers

shaft

glass casing

primary cell

KILOWATT HOURS

SINGLE-PHASE WATTHOUR METER TYPE I-30-A
15 AMPERES   115-120 VOLTS
$K_h = 1.5$ 60 CYCLES 3-WIRE
MODEL AC10.9

18 690 382

specifications

electrical connection

LINE   LOAD

Electric Meter

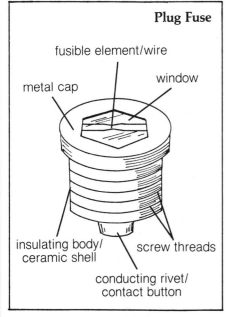

Plug Fuse

fusible element/wire

window

metal cap

insulating body/
ceramic shell

screw threads

conducting rivet/
contact button

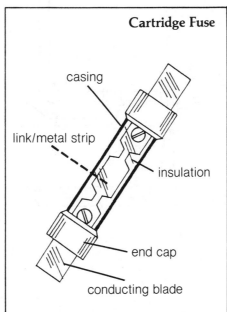

Cartridge Fuse

casing

link/metal strip

insulation

end cap

conducting blade

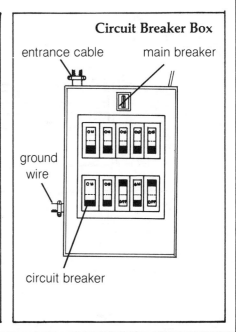

Circuit Breaker Box

entrance cable

main breaker

ground
wire

circuit breaker

Power Systems

Furnace

The furnace shown in this schematic illustration provides *steam heat* to radiators located in various parts of a building.

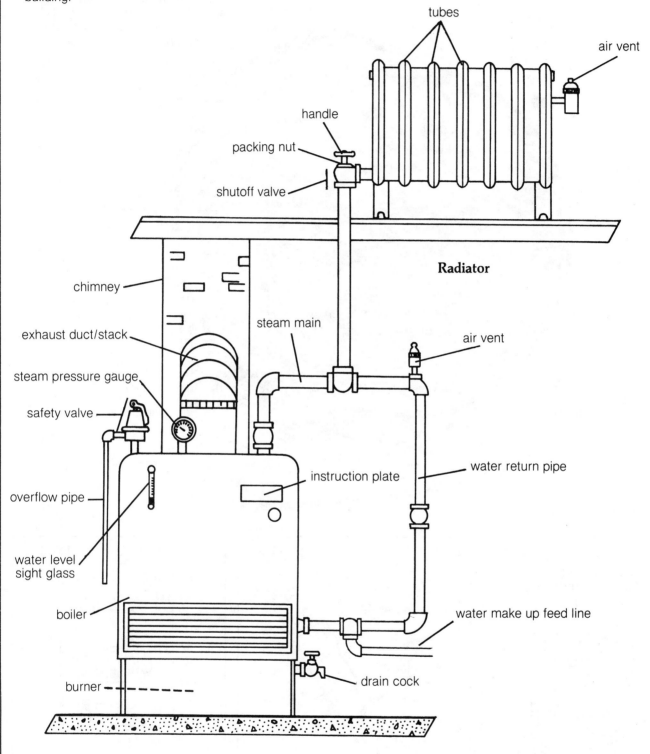

tubes

air vent

handle

packing nut

shutoff valve

Radiator

chimney

steam main

exhaust duct/stack

air vent

steam pressure gauge

safety valve

instruction plate

water return pipe

overflow pipe

water level
sight glass

boiler

water make up feed line

burner

drain cock

Furnace

Hot Water Heater

The unit shown here is *gas-fired.*
Other models include *electric water
heaters* and *oil water heaters.*

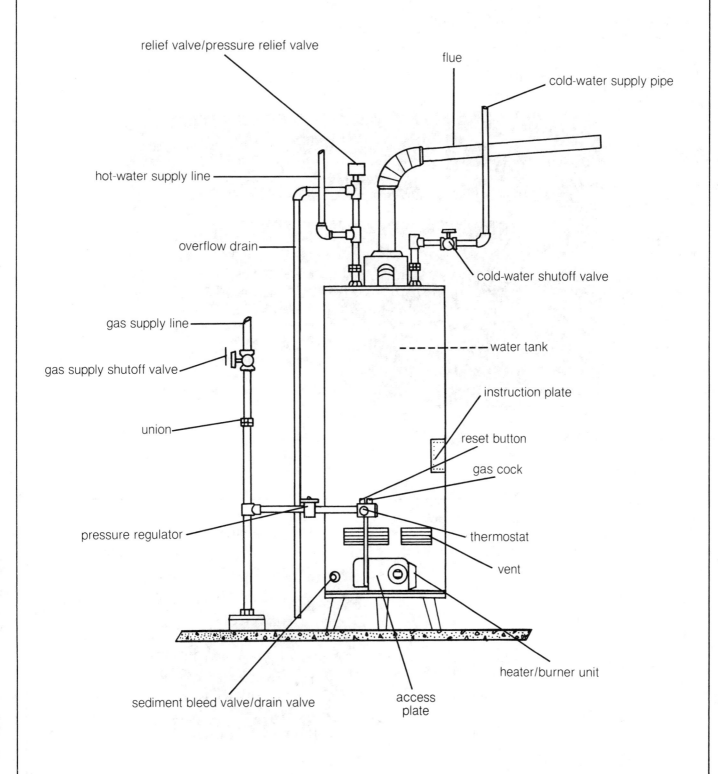

relief valve/pressure relief valve

flue

cold-water supply pipe

hot-water supply line

overflow drain

cold-water shutoff valve

gas supply line

water tank

gas supply shutoff valve

instruction plate

reset button

gas cock

union

pressure regulator

thermostat

vent

heater/burner unit

sediment bleed valve/drain valve

access
plate

Climate Control Units

Air Conditioning

An air conditioner's *front grille* has *louvers* which allow cooled air to be directed to any part of a room. *Condenser coils* in the rear of the unit discharge heat outdoors. Hand-held *folding fans, overhead fans* and *rotary fans* circulate air without actually cooling it. A *dehumidifier* removes moisture from the air, whereas a humidifier adds moisture to it.

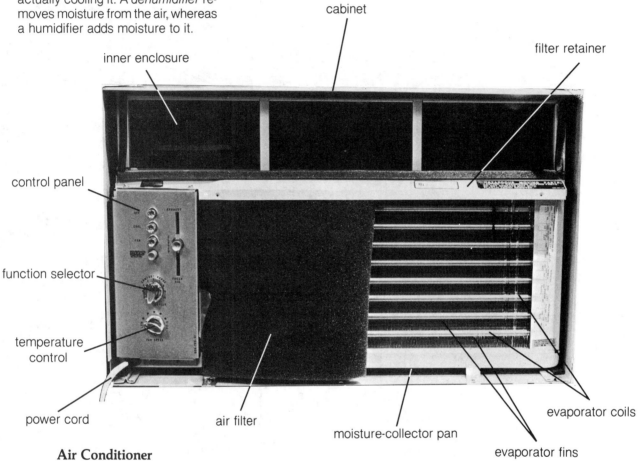

cabinet

filter retainer

inner enclosure

control panel

function selector

temperature control

power cord

air filter

moisture-collector pan

evaporator fins

evaporator coils

Air Conditioner

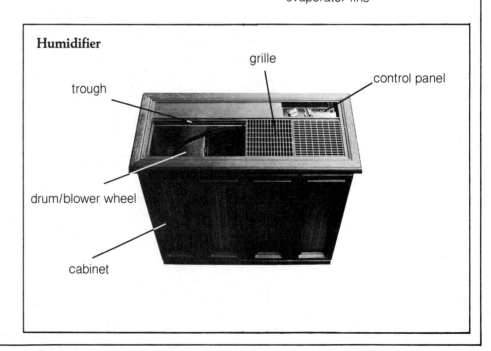

Humidifier

grille

control panel

trough

drum/blower wheel

cabinet

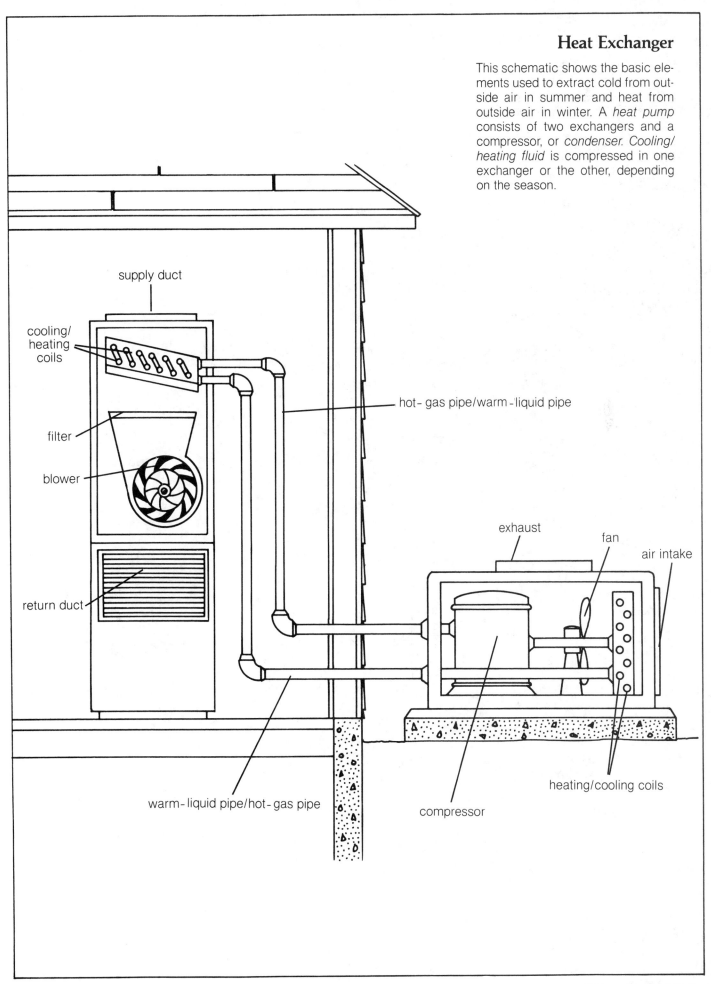

Heat Exchanger

This schematic shows the basic elements used to extract cold from outside air in summer and heat from outside air in winter. A *heat pump* consists of two exchangers and a compressor, or *condenser. Cooling/ heating fluid* is compressed in one exchanger or the other, depending on the season.

supply duct

cooling/ heating coils

filter

blower

return duct

hot- gas pipe/warm -liquid pipe

exhaust

fan

air intake

heating/cooling coils

compressor

warm- liquid pipe/hot- gas pipe

Climate Control Units

Woodburning Stove

When the *stove damper* is closed, interior *baffles* direct air into the *secondary combustion chamber,* then through the *smoke path* until it exits through the flue collar. A stovepipe led through a wall is attached to a *thimble*. The original *Franklin stove* was built into the wall, but three sides extended into the room to radiate heat.

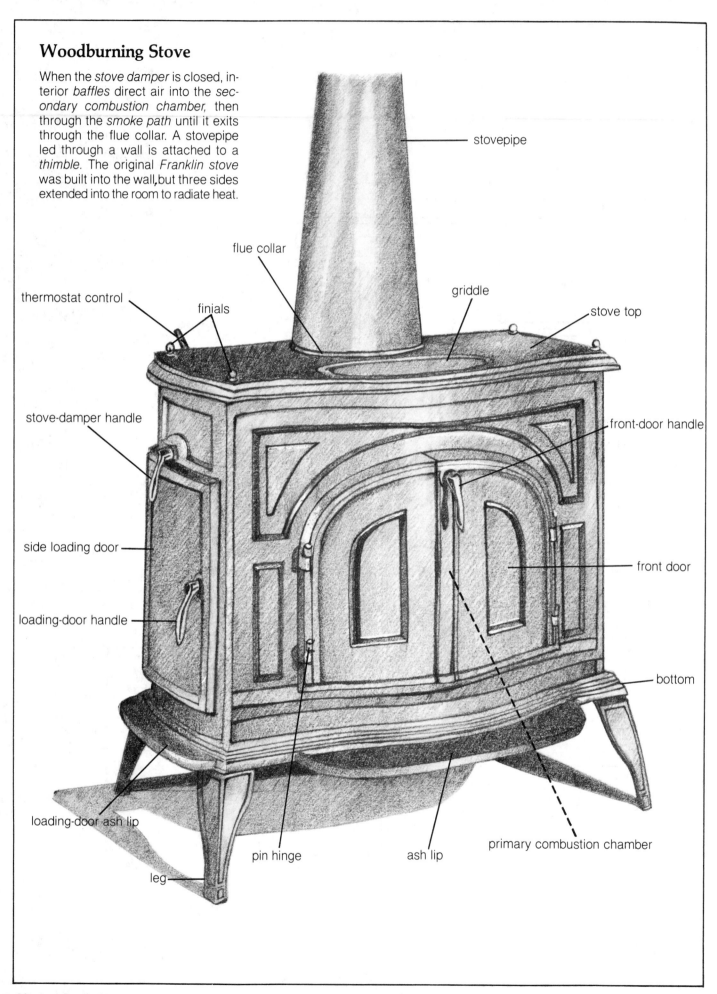

stovepipe

flue collar

griddle

thermostat control

finials

stove top

stove-damper handle

front-door handle

side loading door

front door

loading-door handle

bottom

loading-door ash lip

pin hinge

ash lip

primary combustion chamber

leg

Steam Engine

The steam engine was used to generate *mechanical power* from *thermal energy*. A *piston* inside the steam cylinder, or *engine cylinder*, was driven by *high-pressure steam*. It moved the crankshaft to provide *rotational motion*.

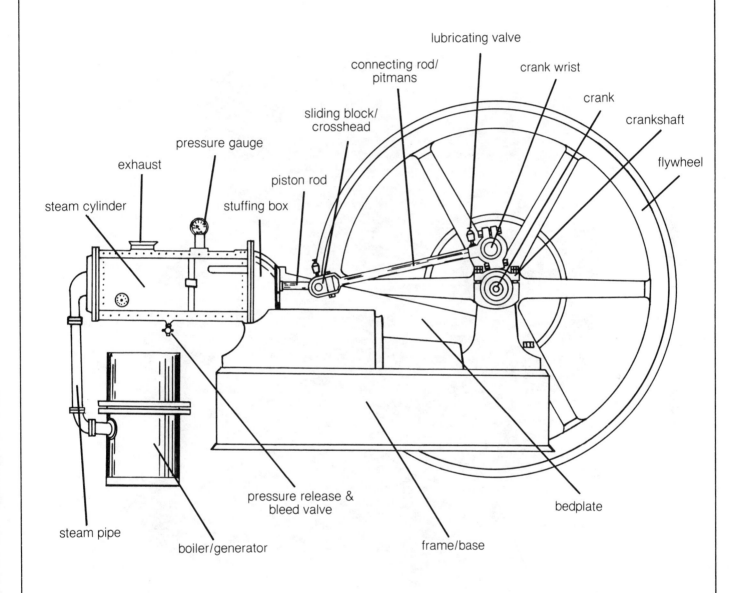

lubricating valve

connecting rod/
pitmans

crank wrist

crank

crankshaft

sliding block/
crosshead

flywheel

pressure gauge

exhaust

piston rod

steam cylinder

stuffing box

steam pipe

pressure release &
bleed valve

boiler/generator

frame/base

bedplate

Internal Combustion Engine

The internal combustion engine is one in which combustion of fuel takes place within the *cylinder*, the product of which is measured in *horsepower*. Engines are *two-cycle*, *four-cycle*, or *Otto cycle*; *gas-* or *diesel-fueled*; *air-cooled* or *liquid-cooled*.

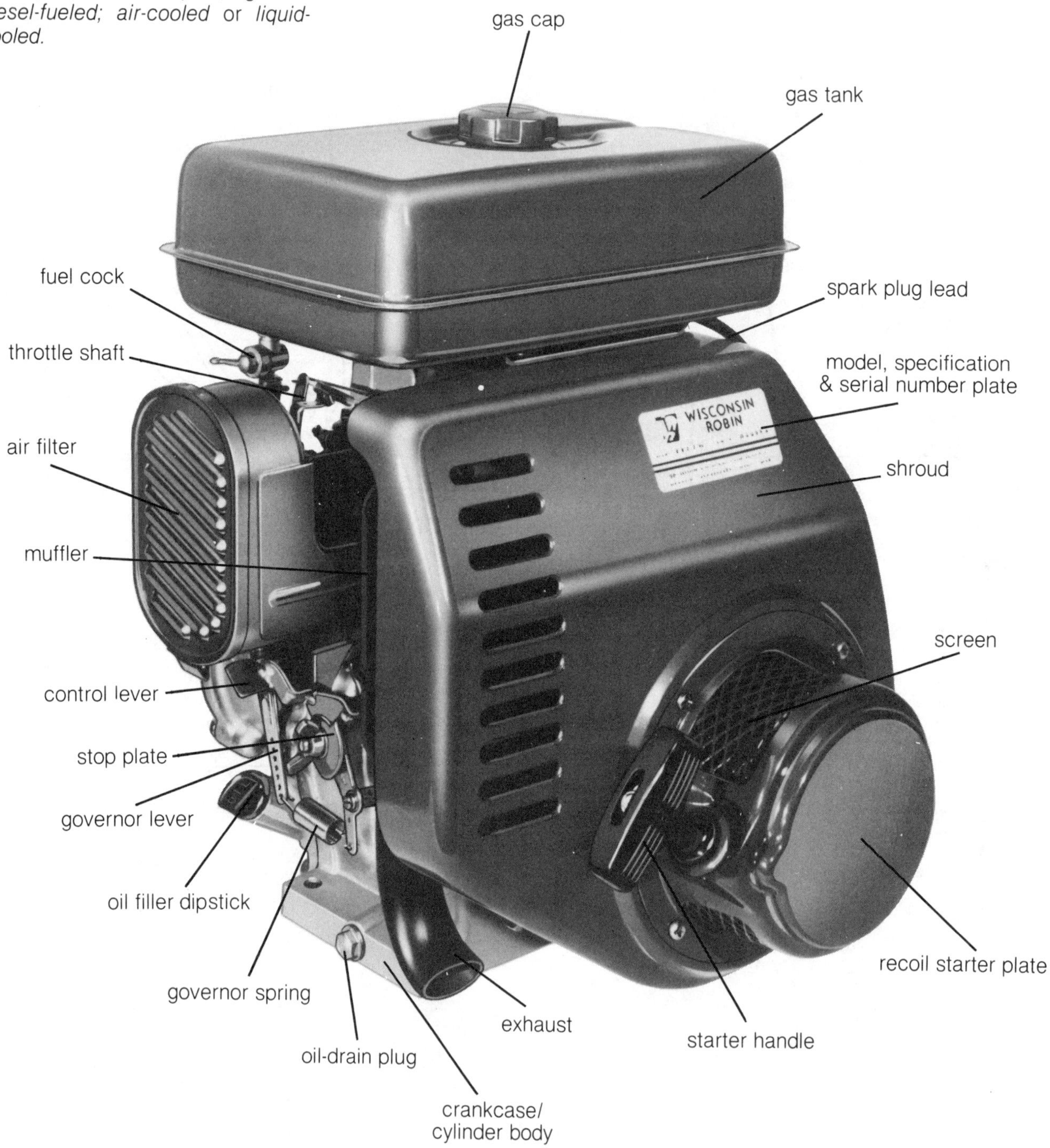
gas cap
gas tank
fuel cock
spark plug lead
throttle shaft
model, specification & serial number plate
WISCONSIN ROBIN
air filter
shroud
muffler
screen
control lever
stop plate
governor lever
oil filler dipstick
recoil starter plate
governor spring
exhaust
starter handle
oil-drain plug
crankcase/ cylinder body

Jet Engines

A *turboprop engine* is like a combustion jet engine or *turbofan jet,* except that its turbine wheel is attached to a *crankshaft* that turns a *propeller.* Unlike a rocket, a *ramjet,* or *flying stovepipe,* combines compressed incoming air with fuel injection and ignition for propulsion.

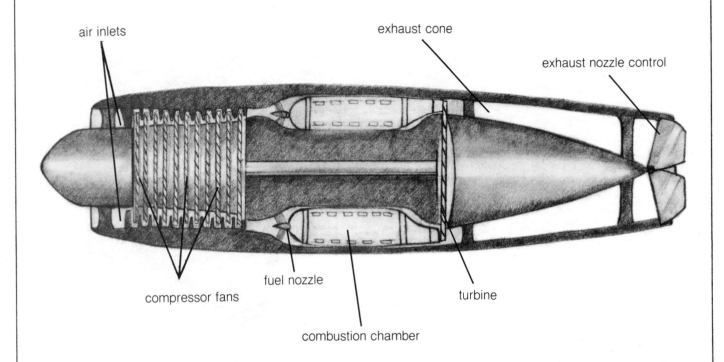

air inlets

exhaust cone

exhaust nozzle control

compressor fans

fuel nozzle

combustion chamber

turbine

Combustion Jet Engine

Rocket

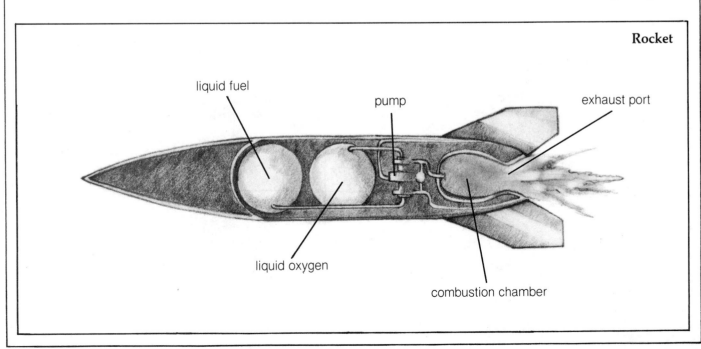

liquid fuel

pump

exhaust port

liquid oxygen

combustion chamber

Engines

Workbench

A *machinist's vise* has two parallel iron *jaws* with a wide *throat opening* to allow as much working room as possible. A *vise dog* is a steel pin in a vise which can be raised to hold materials between the vise and the bench dogs. A *backstop* is a raised portion at the rear of a workbench.

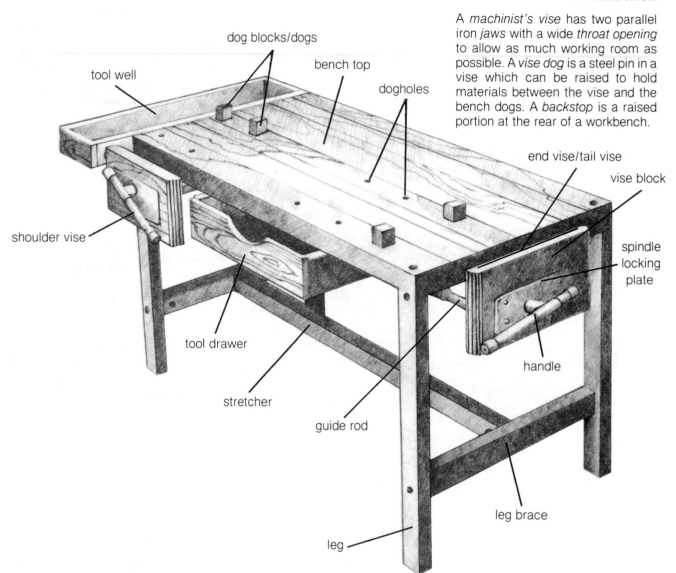

dog blocks/dogs

tool well

bench top

dogholes

end vise/tail vise

vise block

shoulder vise

spindle

locking plate

tool drawer

handle

stretcher

guide rod

leg brace

leg

Sawhorse / Sawbuck

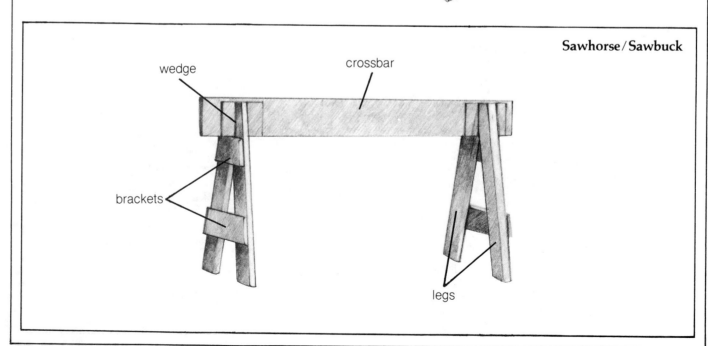

wedge

crossbar

brackets

legs

Clamps

In addition to the *holding tools* shown here, there are *hand screws, bar clamps, miter clamps, band clamps* and *spring clamps*. A *woodworking vise* is similar to a *metalworking vise* except that its jaws are padded in order to hold lumber without marring it. In wood clamps, the steel screws operate through *pivots* so that the jaws can be set at any required angle. *Adjustable C-clamps*, also known as *short bar clamps*, have an adjustable jaw that slides along a flat metal bar to the desired position.

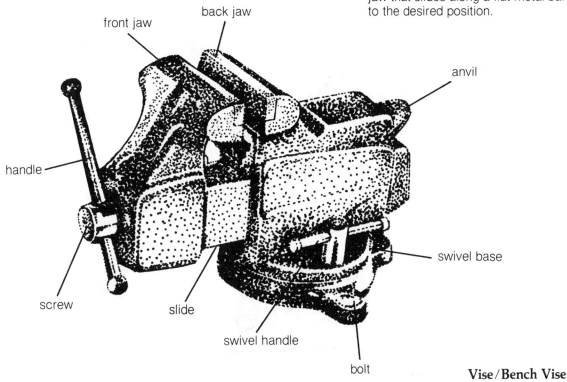

front jaw

back jaw

anvil

handle

screw

slide

swivel handle

swivel base

bolt

Vise/Bench Vise

Hand-Screw Clamp/ Wood Clamp

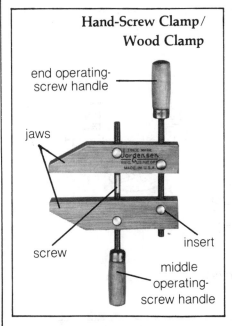

end operating-screw handle

jaws

screw

insert

middle operating-screw handle

C-Clamp

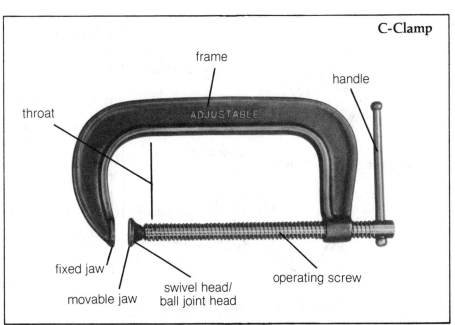

frame

throat

handle

fixed jaw

movable jaw

swivel head/ ball joint head

operating screw

Nails and Screws

A nail is measured in *penny sizes*. A *brad* is a thin *finishing nail* with a tiny *nailhead* used mainly in cabinetwork. *Spikes* are large, heavy nails. The small hole drilled prior to driving a screw is called a *pilot hole*.

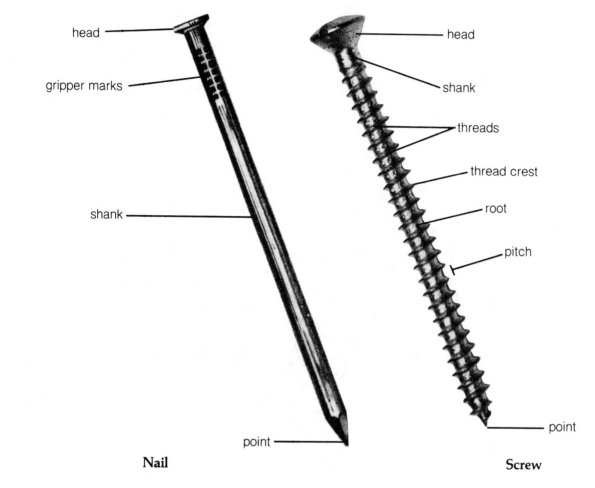

Nail

Screw

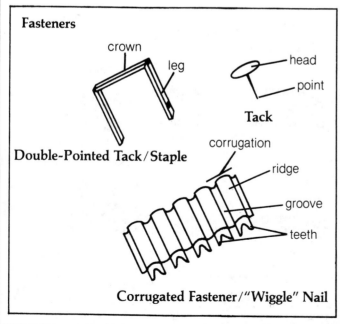

Fasteners

crown

leg

head

point

Tack

Double-Pointed Tack/Staple

corrugation

ridge

groove

teeth

Corrugated Fastener/"Wiggle" Nail

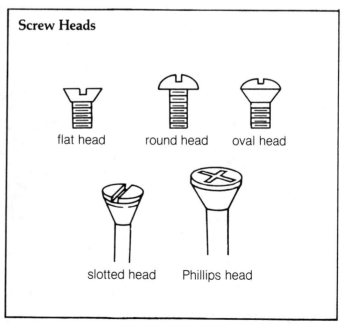

Screw Heads

flat head

round head

oval head

slotted head

Phillips head

Nuts and Bolts

Some bolts have small *collars* below the head to prevent them from turning in a piece of wood. *Washers,* flat discs with a hole in the center, are used to prevent nutheads or bolts from digging into wooden surfaces. *Eyebolts* have rounded tops that enable them to anchor string or rope.

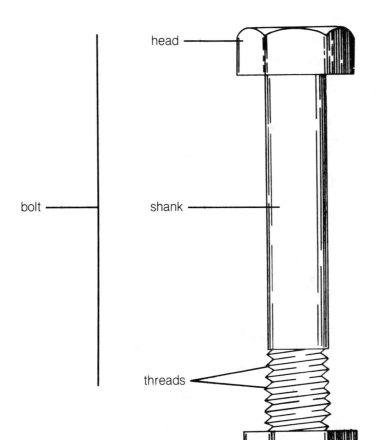

head

bolt

shank

threads

nut

Nuts

acorn nut/cap nut

hex nut/full nut

square nut

wing nut/butterfly nut

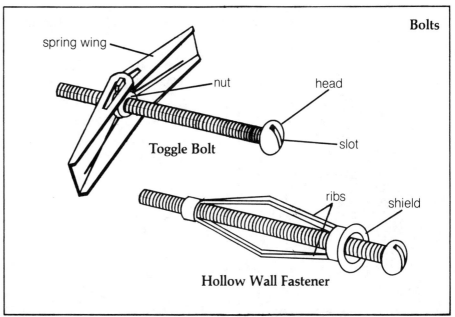

Bolts

spring wing

nut

head

slot

Toggle Bolt

ribs

shield

Hollow Wall Fastener

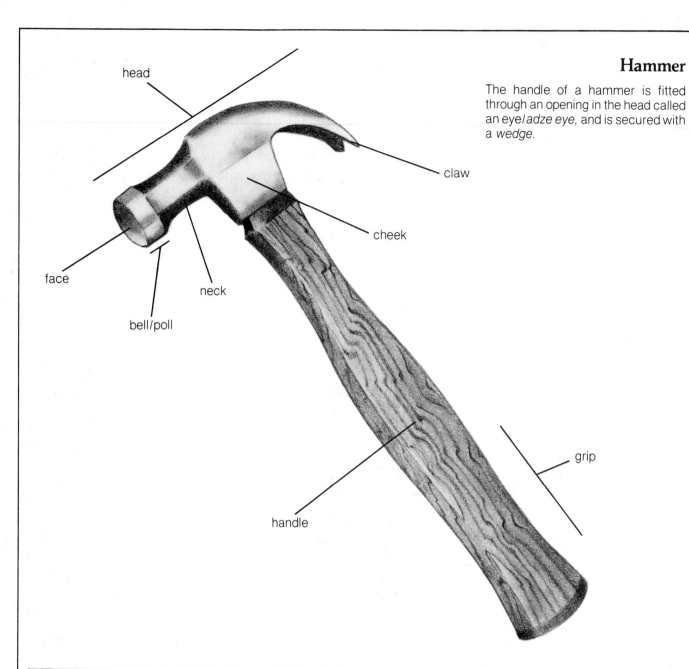

Hammer

The handle of a hammer is fitted through an opening in the head called an eye/*adze eye*, and is secured with a *wedge*.

head

claw

cheek

face

neck

bell/poll

grip

handle

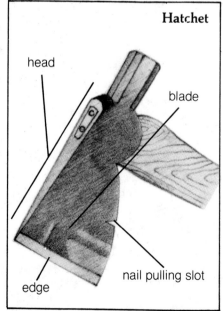

Hatchet

head

blade

edge

nail pulling slot

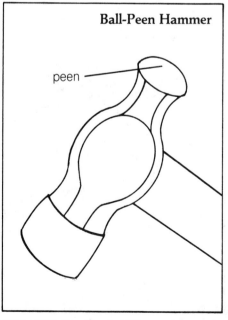

Ball-Peen Hammer

peen

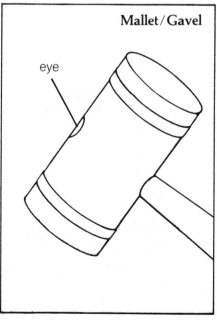

Mallet/Gavel

eye

Screwdriver

Screwdrivers are specified by the length of the blade and the width of the tip. Some have a *ferrule* where the blade meets the handle. *Offset screwdrivers* are used when working in tight areas where a regular screwdriver will not fit. The *standard ratchet screwdriver* is the predecessor to the spiral ratchet screwdriver. It has a *ratcheting mechanism* in the handle.

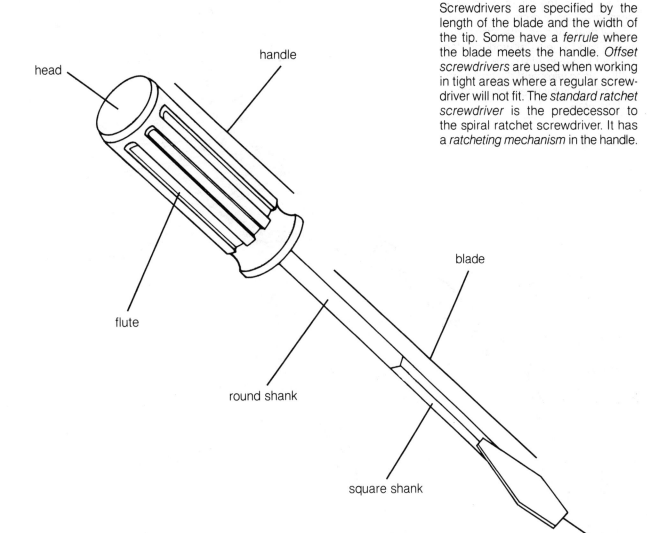

head

handle

flute

round shank

blade

square shank

tip

Spiral Ratchet Screwdriver

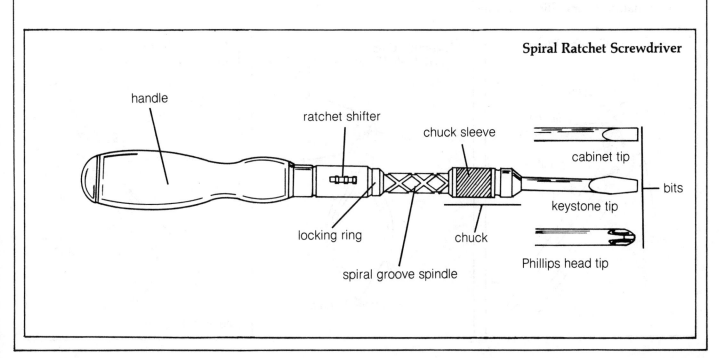

handle

ratchet shifter

chuck sleeve

locking ring

spiral groove spindle

chuck

cabinet tip

bits

keystone tip

Phillips head tip

Household Tools

Pliers

In addition to the pliers seen here, there are heavy-duty *bolt cutters; midget pliers* and *needle-nose pliers,* often used for jewelry work or electrical jobs; *music wire pliers,* used for cutting piano wire; and *duckbill pliers,* used primarily by telephone workers and weavers.

nose

curved jaw

straight jaw

teeth

nest

wire cutter

slip joint/pivot

handle

Combination Pliers / Slip-Joint Pliers

Tongue-and-Groove Pliers

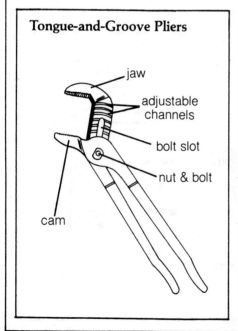

jaw

adjustable channels

bolt slot

nut & bolt

cam

Lineman's Pliers / Electrician's Pliers

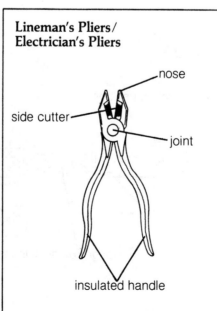

nose

side cutter

joint

insulated handle

Locking Pliers / Lever-Wrench Pliers

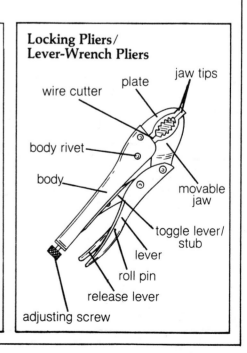

wire cutter

plate

jaw tips

body rivet

body

movable jaw

toggle lever/ stub

lever

roll pin

release lever

adjusting screw

Wrench

Adjustable wrenches come in two styles, locking and non-locking. A "cheater" is a handle extension used to increase leverage. Some wrenches have offset handles to provide clearance over obstructions. Socket wrenches combine an offset handle with a male drive piece which has a spring-loaded bearing to lock on various sized sockets. Many socket wrenches also have a ratchet handle so that reversing is possible.

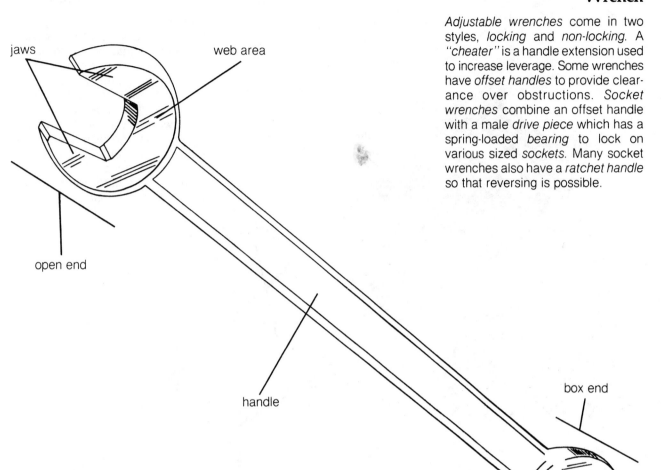

jaws

web area

open end

handle

box end

web area

points

box

Combination Wrench

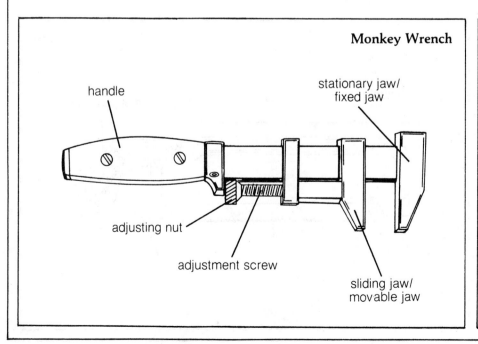

Monkey Wrench

handle

stationary jaw/ fixed jaw

adjusting nut

adjustment screw

sliding jaw/ movable jaw

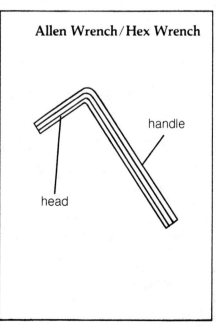

Allen Wrench/Hex Wrench

handle

head

Handsaws

The cut or incision made by a saw blade is the *kerf*. The carpenter's saw, shown here, occurs in two major varieties, the *ripsaw* (used for cutting with the grain) and the *crosscut saw* (for cutting across the grain). A *skewback handsaw* has an inwardly curved back. On a coping saw, the distance from the blade to the frame is the *throat* or *throat clearance*. A coping saw with a particularly long throat is called a *deep throat*.

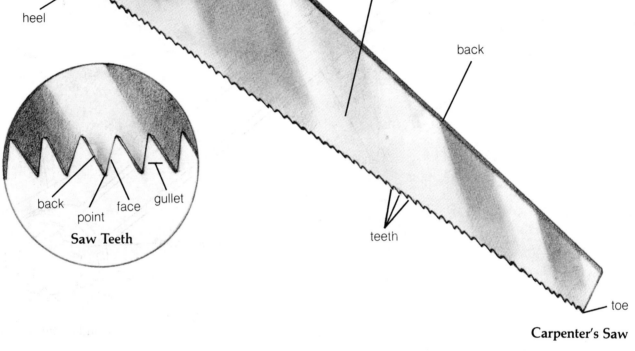

handle

fittings

heel

blade

back

teeth

toe

Carpenter's Saw

back

point

face

gullet

Saw Teeth

Coping Saw

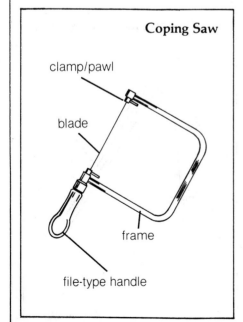

clamp/pawl

blade

frame

file-type handle

Hacksaw

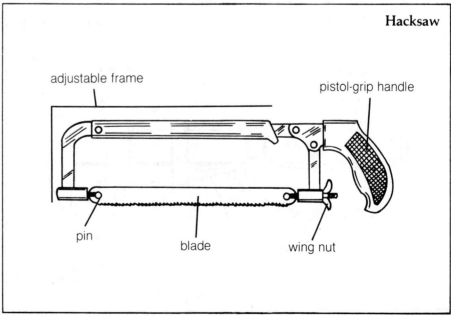

adjustable frame

pistol-grip handle

pin

blade

wing nut

Power Saw

The round blades used in table and circular saws have either *crosscut teeth* or *rip teeth.* Circular saws can be equipped with a *rip guide* and an *ejector chute,* which routes sawdust to the rear or side. Saber units include *variable-speed controls* and a *roller support* behind the blade. The *band saw* derives its name from the fact that its blade is a continuous band revolving on two wheels.

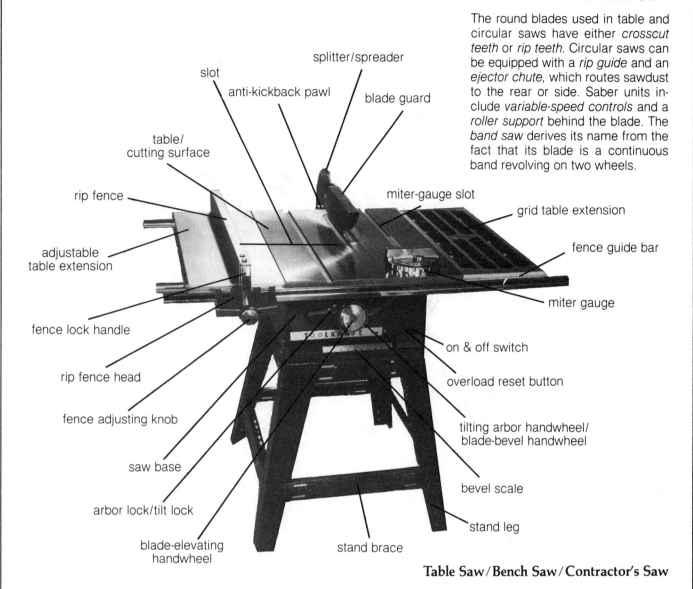

slot

splitter/spreader

anti-kickback pawl

blade guard

table/ cutting surface

miter-gauge slot

rip fence

grid table extension

adjustable table extension

fence guide bar

fence lock handle

miter gauge

rip fence head

on & off switch

fence adjusting knob

overload reset button

saw base

tilting arbor handwheel/ blade-bevel handwheel

arbor lock/tilt lock

bevel scale

blade-elevating handwheel

stand leg

stand brace

Table Saw/Bench Saw/Contractor's Saw

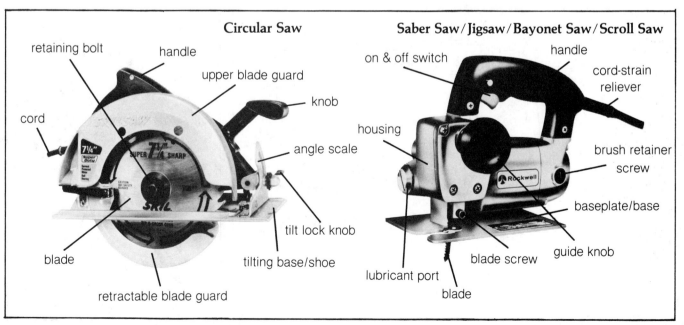

Circular Saw

Saber Saw/Jigsaw/Bayonet Saw/Scroll Saw

retaining bolt

handle

on & off switch

handle

upper blade guard

cord-strain reliever

knob

cord

housing

angle scale

brush retainer screw

baseplate/base

tilt lock knob

blade

guide knob

tilting base/shoe

blade screw

retractable blade guard

lubricant port

blade

Household Tools

Manual Drill

Drilling accessories include a *bit gage, reamer, auger bits, dowel bits, expanding bits, screwdriver bits, countersink bits, twist drill bits, spade bits* and *power bore bits.* The circle described by turning the handle of a brace is called the *sweep.*

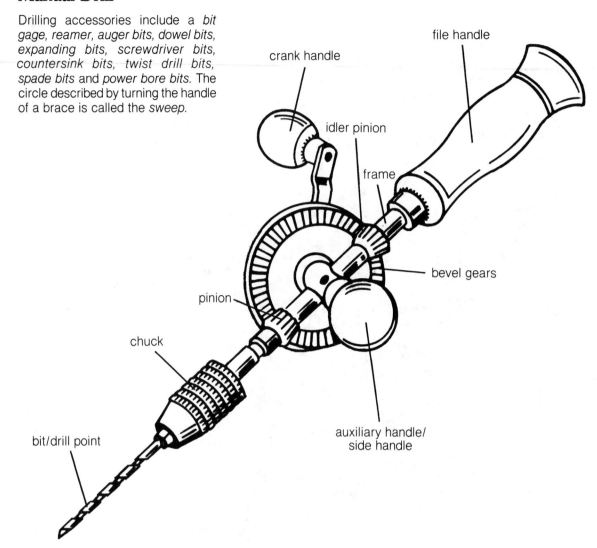

crank handle

file handle

idler pinion

frame

bevel gears

pinion

chuck

bit/drill point

auxiliary handle/
side handle

Hand Drill

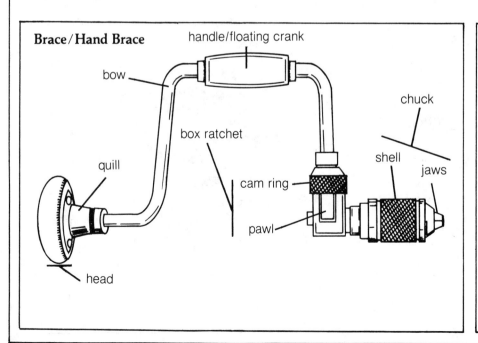

Brace/Hand Brace

handle/floating crank

bow

box ratchet

chuck

quill

cam ring

shell

jaws

pawl

head

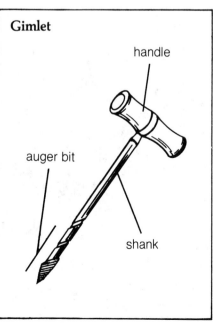

Gimlet

handle

auger bit

shank

Power Drills

A regular bit, or *drill,* consists of a *point, body* and shank. Some bits have specially configured *tangs* at the end of the shank. If a drill has a *geared key chuck,* the bit is locked in place with a key. Holes can be drilled to predetermined depths by clamping an *adjustable bit gauge* to the bit shank. A drill is classified by the largest bit its chuck will accept. Some drills have *reversible motors.*

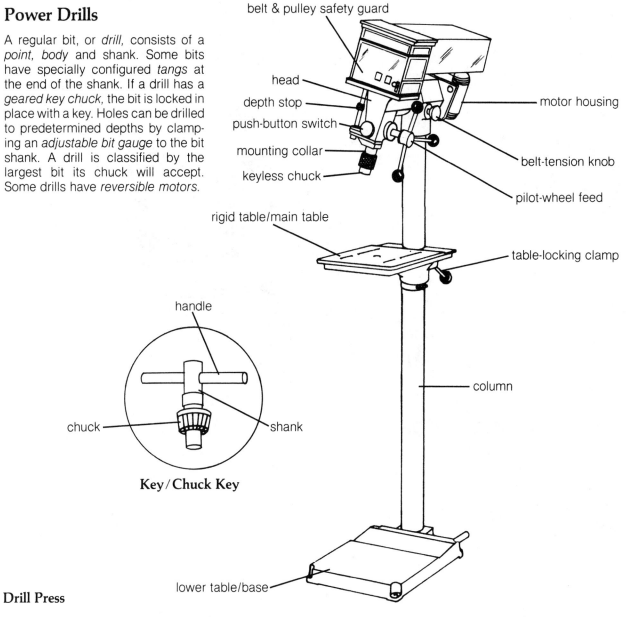

belt & pulley safety guard
head
depth stop
push-button switch
mounting collar
keyless chuck
motor housing
belt-tension knob
pilot-wheel feed
rigid table/main table
table-locking clamp
column

handle
chuck
shank

Key / Chuck Key

lower table/base

Drill Press

Hand Drill and Bits

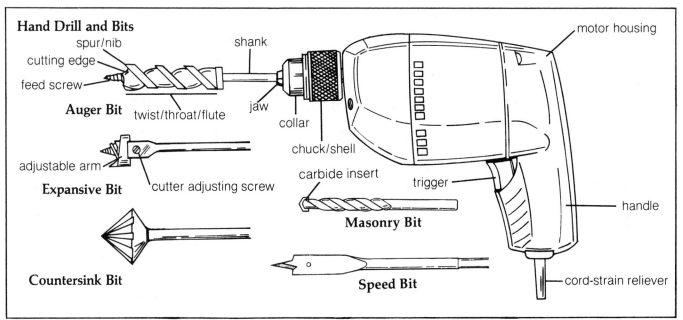

spur/nib
cutting edge
feed screw
Auger Bit
twist/throat/flute
shank
jaw
collar
chuck/shell
motor housing

adjustable arm
Expansive Bit
cutter adjusting screw
carbide insert
Masonry Bit
trigger
handle

Countersink Bit
Speed Bit
cord-strain reliever

Household Tools

Planing and Shaping Tools

The body of a plane is the *frame*. The angle of the blade is the *pitch*. The flat side of a chisel is its *back*. *Cold chisels* are designed to cut metal and have no handles. *Gouges* are either *in-cannel*, with the bevel ground on the inside of the curved blade, or *out-cannel*, with the bevel ground on the outside. The rough side of a rasp or file is the *face*. The smooth side is called the *"safe" side*.

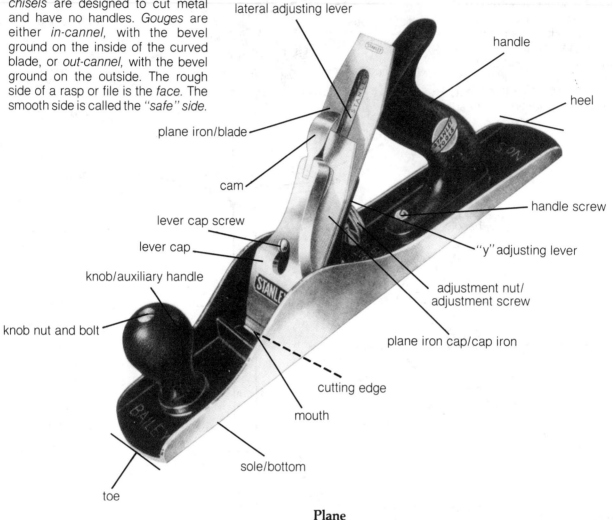

lateral adjusting lever

handle

heel

plane iron/blade

cam

handle screw

lever cap screw

lever cap

"y" adjusting lever

knob/auxiliary handle

adjustment nut/ adjustment screw

knob nut and bolt

plane iron cap/cap iron

cutting edge

mouth

sole/bottom

toe

Plane

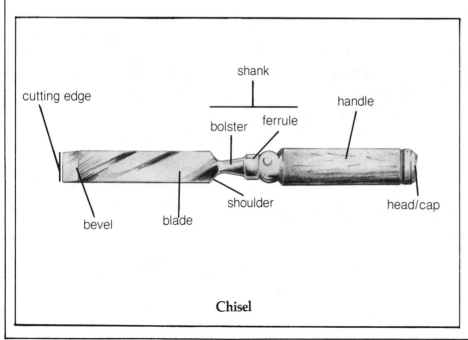

cutting edge

shank

handle

bolster

ferrule

shoulder

head/cap

bevel

blade

Chisel

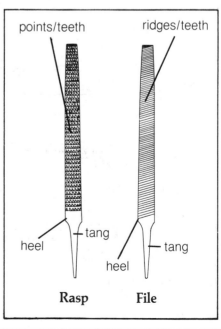

points/teeth

ridges/teeth

heel

tang

heel

tang

heel

Rasp   **File**

Sander

In a finishing, or *straight-line*, sander, the pad moves back and forth, whereas in the similar-looking *orbital sander*, the pad moves in a small orbital pattern. *Belt sanders* use a continuous *belt* of either *natural* or *artificial abrasive material*, and are available with or without *dust bags*. Sandpaper has either an *open* or *closed coat*, depending on spacing between *grains*.

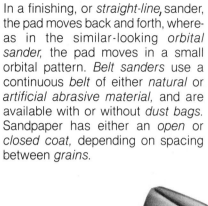

handle

cord strain reliever

front handle

trigger switch

paper clamp

upper housing

lower housing

shoe

paper clamp

pad

Finishing Sander

Sandpaper

grit/abrasive coating

36

grit number

backing

Belt Sander

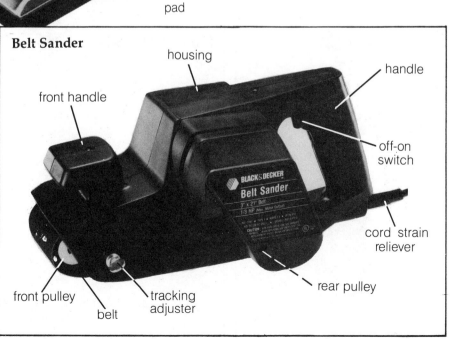

housing

front handle

handle

off-on switch

BLACK&DECKER
Belt Sander
3" x 21" Belt
1/3 HP Max. Motor Output

cord strain reliever

front pulley

belt

tracking adjuster

rear pulley

Plumbing Tools

In addition to the basic plumbing tools shown here, there are *tubing,* or *pipe cutters,* some of which have built-in *polishers; reamers* for removing *burrs* inside cut *pipe;* and *flaring tools,* used to spread the ends of copper *tubing* for *flare fittings.* In *sweat soldering, flux* and *solder* are used. When working with *threaded pipe,* a *pipe threader* (which consists of a *die, diestock* and *handles*) and *joint-sealing tape* or *compound* are used. Other basic plumbing tools are *hacksaws* and *pipe wrenches.*

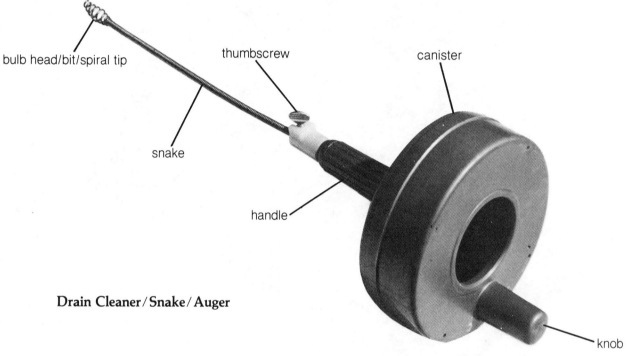

bulb head/bit/spiral tip

thumbscrew

canister

snake

handle

knob

Drain Cleaner / Snake / Auger

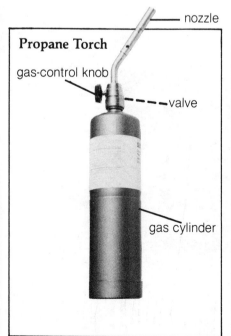

nozzle

Propane Torch

gas-control knob

valve

gas cylinder

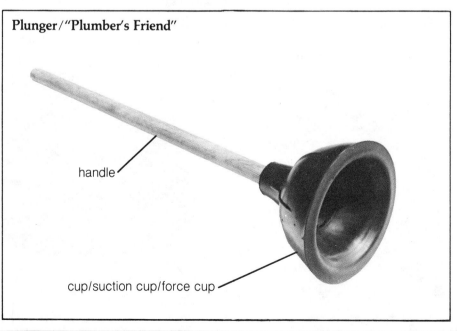

Plunger / "Plumber's Friend"

handle

cup/suction cup/force cup

Electrician's Tools

A volt-ohm meter, also known as a *multimeter* or *volt-ohm-milliammeter*, is used with test *leads* and *jacks* attached to needle-type *probes* or *alligator clips*. The markings on the sheath of a wire describe *wire size*, number of *conductors*, the existence of a ground wire and cable type.

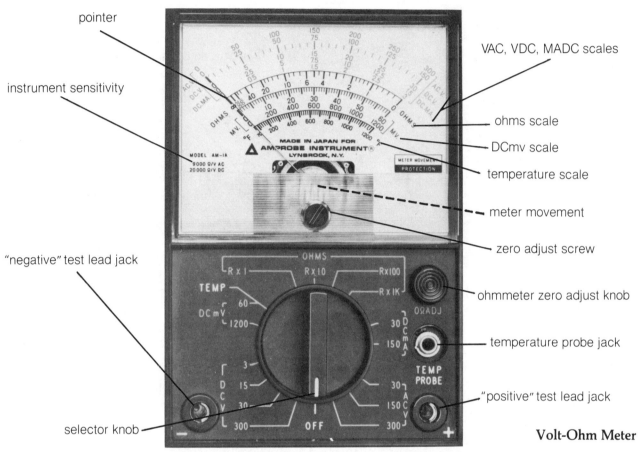

pointer

instrument sensitivity

VAC, VDC, MADC scales

ohms scale

DCmv scale

temperature scale

meter movement

zero adjust screw

MADE IN JAPAN FOR AMPROBE INSTRUMENT® LYNBROOK, N.Y.

MODEL AM-1A
9000 Ω/V AC
20000 Ω/V DC

METER MOVEMENT
PROTECTION

"negative" test lead jack

OHMS
R x 1   R x 10   R x 100
R x 1K

TEMP
60
DC mV
1200

3
D 15
C 30
V
L 300

OFF

30
150
DCmA

30
150
300
ACV

Ω ADJ

TEMP PROBE

ohmmeter zero adjust knob

temperature probe jack

"positive" test lead jack

selector knob

Volt-Ohm Meter

Wire Stripper and Crimper/Multipurpose Tool

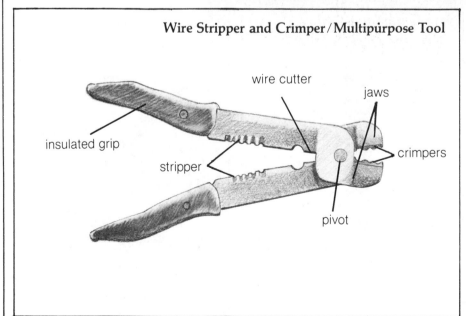

insulated grip

wire cutter

jaws

crimpers

stripper

pivot

Wire/Cable/Cord

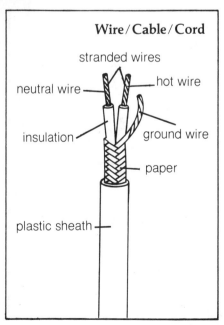

stranded wires

neutral wire

hot wire

insulation

ground wire

paper

plastic sheath

Household Tools

Measuring Tools

The basic measuring tool is the one-piece *bench rule,* or *ruler.* Tape measures also come in *reels* which can be manually rewound. An *L-shaped square* has two *arms* set at right angles. The longer arm is the *blade,* the shorter one is the *tongue.* They meet at the *heel.* A *combination square* substitutes for *try squares, depth gauges* and *marking gauges.* When the *air bubble* in a monovial stops between *marks,* the level is on the desired *plane.*

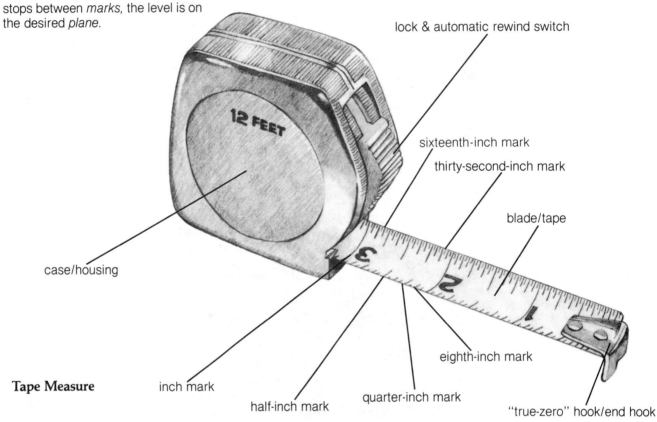

lock & automatic rewind switch

sixteenth-inch mark

thirty-second-inch mark

blade/tape

case/housing

eighth-inch mark

Tape Measure

inch mark

half-inch mark

quarter-inch mark

"true-zero" hook/end hook

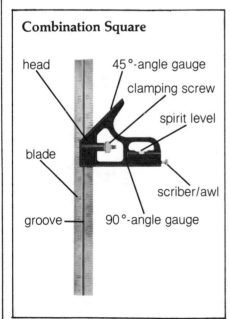

Combination Square

head

45°-angle gauge

clamping screw

spirit level

blade

scriber/awl

groove

90°-angle gauge

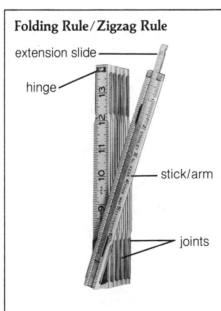

Folding Rule/Zigzag Rule

extension slide

hinge

stick/arm

joints

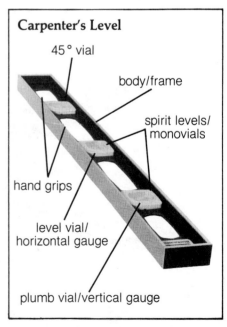

Carpenter's Level

45° vial

body/frame

spirit levels/monovials

hand grips

level vial/horizontal gauge

plumb vial/vertical gauge

Painting Tools

A regular *paint brush* has *bristles* with *split,* or *flagged,* *ends.* The *heel* section of a brush is where the *butt ends* of bristles fit into a *ferrule* attached to the handle. Other paint-application tools include *pressure brushes, foam brushes* and *pad applicators.* Accessories include *pot* and *brush holders* and *brush spinners.* Paint rollers may have *threaded handles* to accommodate *extenders. Tack cloth* is used to clean surfaces to be painted, and a *drop cloth* protects objects and areas against paint spills.

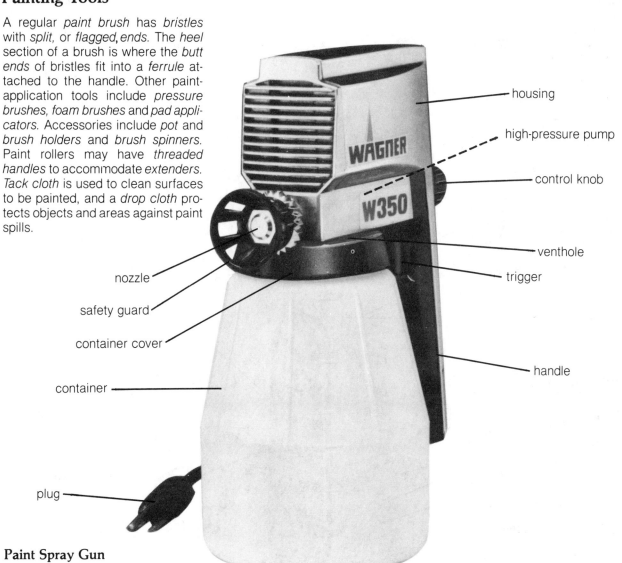

housing

high-pressure pump

control knob

venthole

trigger

handle

nozzle

safety guard

container cover

container

plug

Paint Spray Gun

Tray and Roller

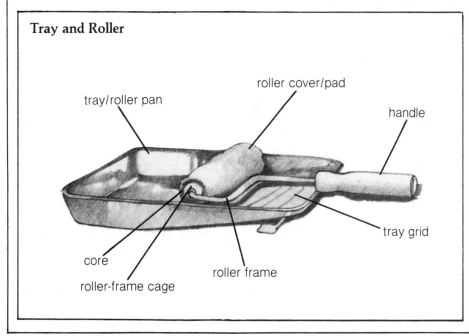

tray/roller pan

roller cover/pad

handle

core

roller-frame cage

roller frame

tray grid

Ladder/Stepladder

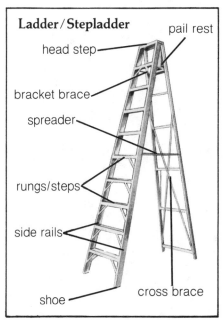

pail rest

head step

bracket brace

spreader

rungs/steps

side rails

shoe

cross brace

Household Tools

Swiss Army Knife

The *dividers* in the *handle* of a *jack-knife*, pocketknife or *camping knife* keep each blade or *tool* separate.

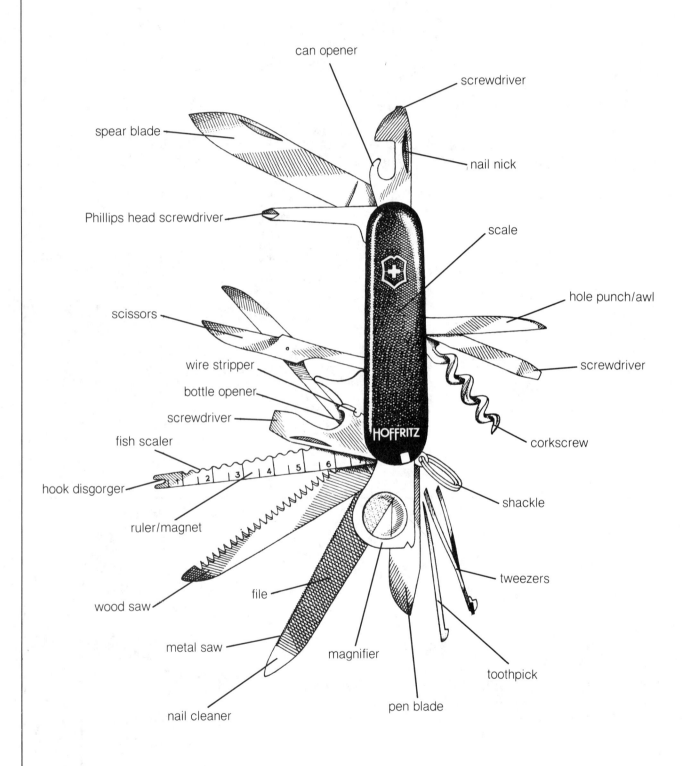

can opener

screwdriver

spear blade

nail nick

Phillips head screwdriver

scale

scissors

hole punch/awl

wire stripper

screwdriver

bottle opener

screwdriver

corkscrew

fish scaler

hook disgorger

shackle

ruler/magnet

tweezers

wood saw

file

metal saw

magnifier

toothpick

nail cleaner

pen blade

HOFFRITZ

Gardening Implements

A hand tool with a small scooped blade used for potting and planting is a *trowel.* A *spading fork* is used for turning soil. Shears are generally of two types: *anvil,* in which a blade cuts through a branch and stops against an anvil, and *by-pass,* which uses a shearing action to cut.

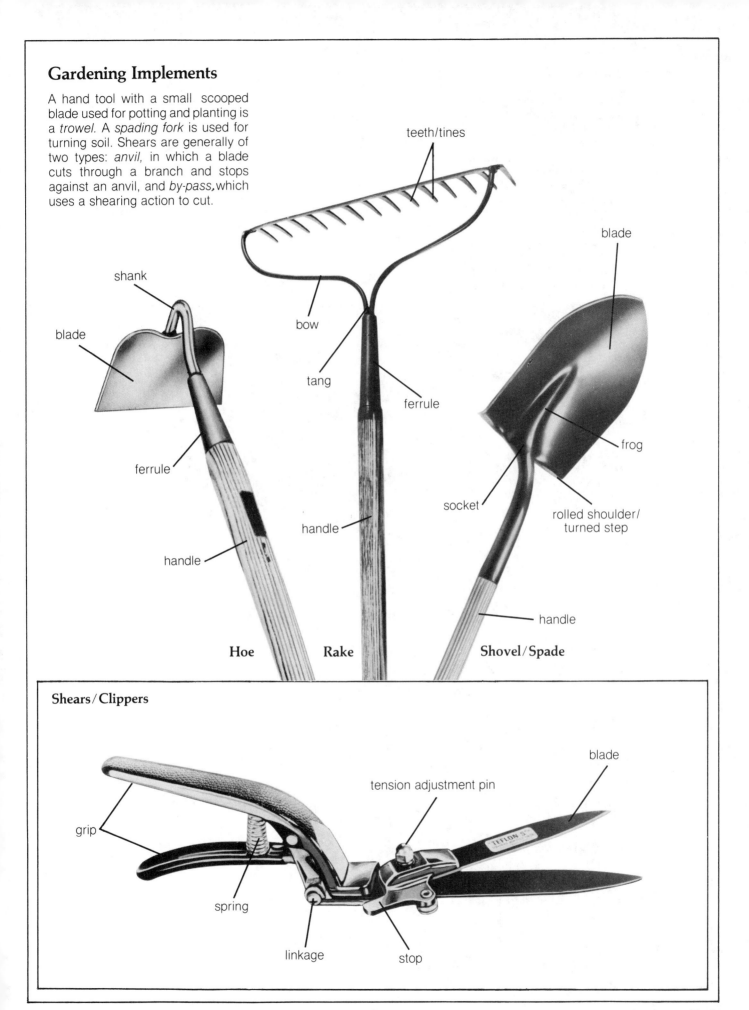

teeth/tines

blade

shank

bow

blade

tang

ferrule

ferrule

frog

handle

handle

socket

rolled shoulder/
turned step

handle

Hoe   **Rake**   **Shovel/Spade**

Shears/Clippers

blade

tension adjustment pin

grip

spring

linkage   stop

Sprinkler and Nozzles

Revolving sprinklers have rotating *arms* that spray water through nozzles at each end. An inverted Y-shaped *coupling,* or *siamese,* makes it possible to connect two *hoses* to a single *faucet.* In making a *hose connection,* the larger *female coupling* is fitted over the *male coupling* and turned until the connection is made fast. *Washers* inside couplings make seals watertight.

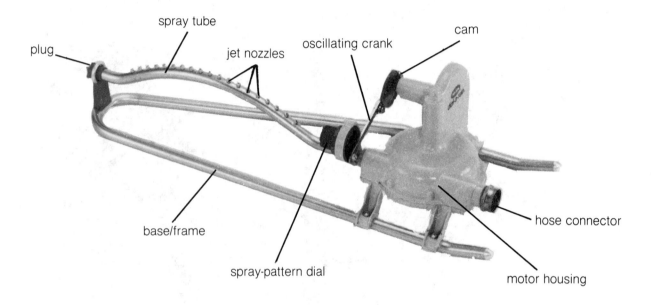

plug

spray tube

jet nozzles

oscillating crank

cam

base/frame

spray-pattern dial

hose connector

motor housing

Oscillating Lawn Sprinkler

Hose Nozzle

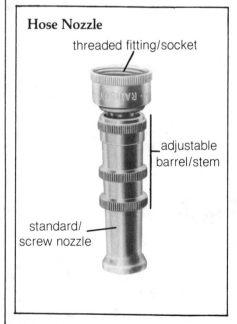

threaded fitting/socket

adjustable barrel/stem

standard/ screw nozzle

Pistol Nozzle

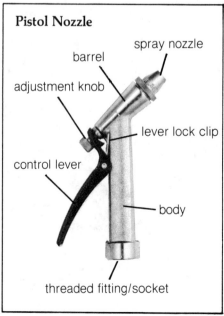

barrel

spray nozzle

adjustment knob

lever lock clip

control lever

body

threaded fitting/socket

Lawn Mower

Rotary mowers, such as the one shown here, use a single *blade* to slice off grass, as does a *scythe*. *Reel mowers*, such as the *sickle-bar mower*, use multiple blades, called a *reel*, to push grass against a stationary *bed knife* at the base of the mower. Cut grass is contained in a bag called a *grass-catcher*. With a *mulching mower*, bagging is unnecessary. A *lawn sweeper* uses a rotating sweeping action to pick up cuttings and leaves. *Lawn edgers* and *trimmers* are used to cut grass in areas where mowers cannot.

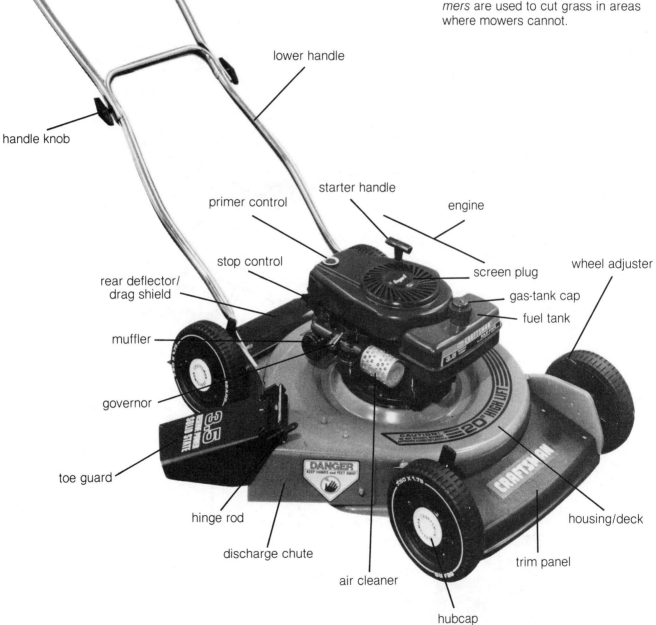

upper handle

lower handle

handle knob

starter handle

primer control

engine

stop control

screen plug

wheel adjuster

rear deflector/ drag shield

gas-tank cap

fuel tank

muffler

governor

toe guard

hinge rod

discharge chute

air cleaner

hubcap

trim panel

housing/deck

DANGER
KEEP HANDS and FEET AWAY

Power Mower

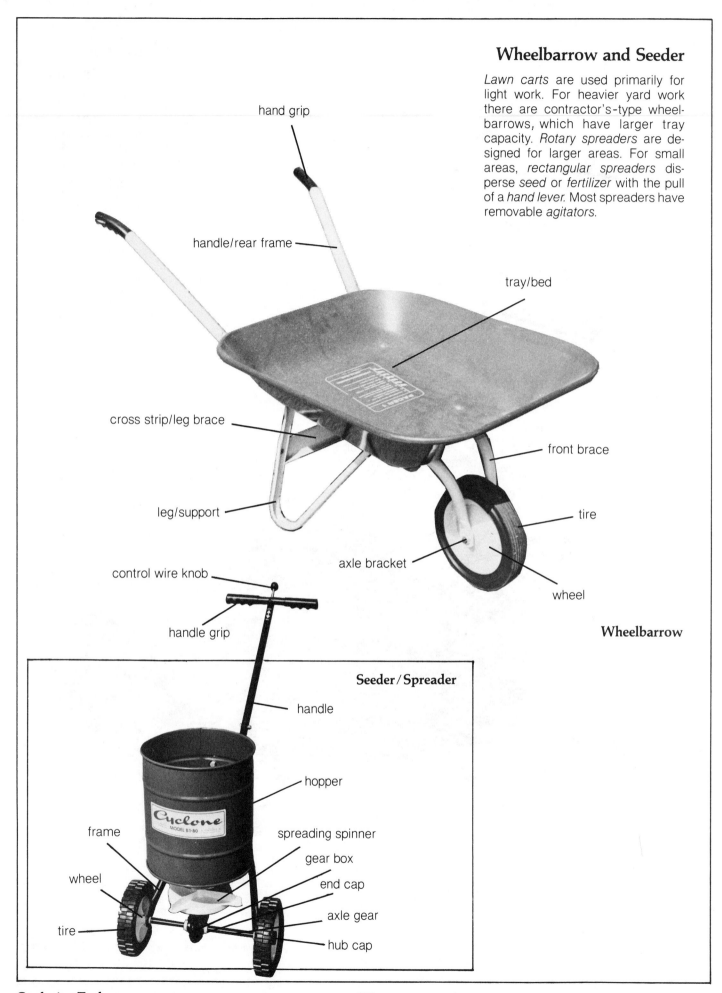

Wheelbarrow and Seeder

Lawn carts are used primarily for light work. For heavier yard work there are contractor's-type wheelbarrows, which have larger tray capacity. *Rotary spreaders* are designed for larger areas. For small areas, *rectangular spreaders* disperse *seed* or *fertilizer* with the pull of a *hand lever.* Most spreaders have removable *agitators.*

hand grip

handle/rear frame

tray/bed

cross strip/leg brace

front brace

leg/support

tire

axle bracket

wheel

control wire knob

handle grip

Wheelbarrow

Seeder/Spreader

handle

hopper

frame

spreading spinner

gear box

wheel

end cap

tire

axle gear

hub cap

Chain Saw

Chain saws are either gasoline- or electric-powered. Power output is measured in cubic inches of *piston displacement* in the *power head* rather than in horsepower. The *cutting head* may be *direct drive* or *gear drive*. A *sprocket-tip cutting bar* increases cutting speed because it eliminates most of the friction around the *bar tip*. Safety devices include a *chain brake* intended to stop the moving chain when the saw begins to kick back, *throttle latches* for safer starting, *safety triggers* to prevent accidental acceleration, *muffler shields*, and *chain catchers* designed to protect the operator from a broken or slipped chain.

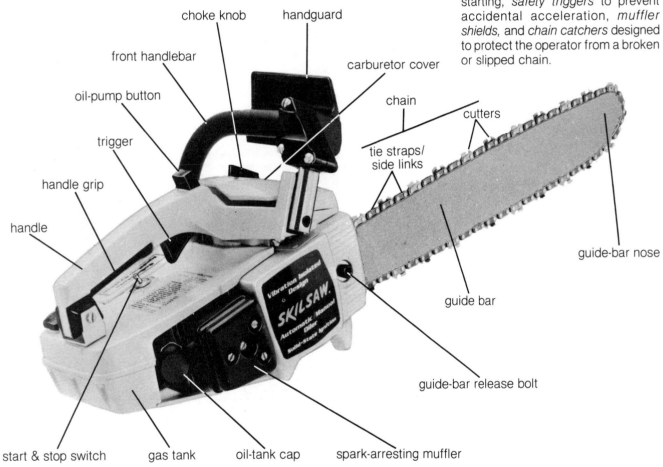

choke knob

handguard

front handlebar

carburetor cover

oil-pump button

chain

cutters

trigger

tie straps/
side links

handle grip

handle

guide-bar nose

guide bar

start & stop switch

gas tank

oil-tank cap

spark-arresting muffler

guide-bar release bolt

Vibration Isolated Design

SKILSAW.

Automatic/Manual
Oiler

Solid-State Ignition

Gardening Tools

Ranching Gear

In the days of cattle ranching, *ketch hands* would rope *calves,* or "critters," an *iron man* would brand them, and, in some instances, a *knife man* would cut an additional identifying notch, or *earmark,* in their ears. A *tally man* would record the operation.

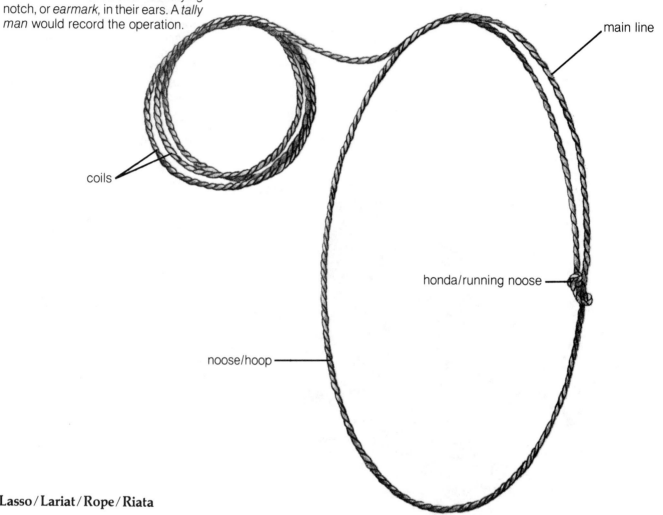

coils

main line

honda/running noose

noose/hoop

Lasso/Lariat/Rope/Riata

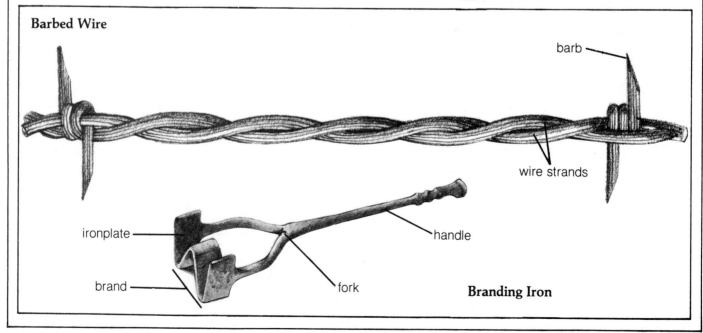

Barbed Wire

barb

wire strands

ironplate

handle

brand

fork

Branding Iron

Traps

Enclosing traps catch animals without hurting them. *Arresting traps,* such as the bear trap shown here, catch and hold animals in their teeth. *Killing traps* destroy animals and rodents.

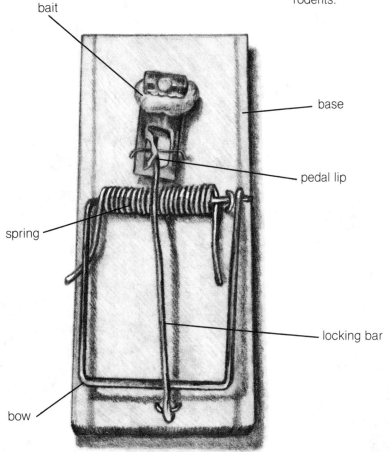

bait

base

pedal lip

spring

locking bar

bow

Mousetrap

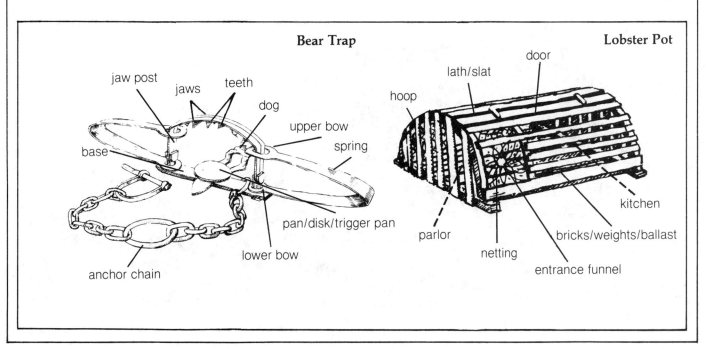

Bear Trap

jaw post

jaws

teeth

dog

upper bow

base

spring

pan/disk/trigger pan

lower bow

anchor chain

Lobster Pot

door

lath/slat

hoop

kitchen

parlor

netting

bricks/weights/ballast

entrance funnel

Trapping Devices

Tractor

Plows, reapers, cultivators, like the harrow seen here, and various *planting machines* are coupled to a tractor to work the land. The operating speed of attachments is controlled by a *power takeoff*. Optional *outboard planetaries* with *adjustable wheel treads* and *add-on segment weights* help boost traction.

front windows

cab

muffler

warning light

headlamp/ headlight

hood

air filter

grille

fender

front-end weights

rear axle

adapter plate

frame

wide tire

side panel

steps

Hitch and Harrow

parking stand

SMV (slow-moving vehicle) symbol

lift link

top link

lower links

universal drive joint

flywheel

drive yoke and rocker

tine bars

tines

crumble roller

depth adjusting screw

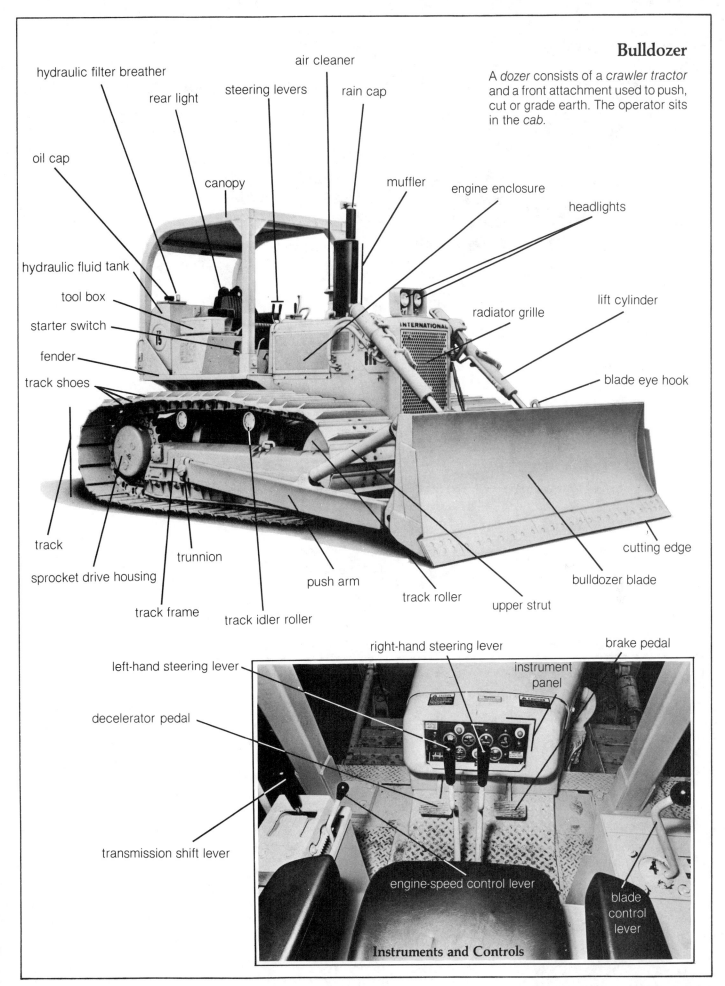

Bulldozer

A *dozer* consists of a *crawler tractor* and a front attachment used to push, cut or grade earth. The operator sits in the *cab*.

hydraulic filter breather

air cleaner

rear light

steering levers

rain cap

oil cap

canopy

muffler

engine enclosure

headlights

hydraulic fluid tank

tool box

starter switch

radiator grille

lift cylinder

fender

blade eye hook

track shoes

track

sprocket drive housing

trunnion

track frame

track idler roller

push arm

track roller

upper strut

cutting edge

bulldozer blade

left-hand steering lever

right-hand steering lever

brake pedal

decelerator pedal

instrument panel

transmission shift lever

engine-speed control lever

blade control lever

Instruments and Controls

Construction Equipment

Transit and Jackhammer

A transit is used by *engineers* and *surveyors* to determine *angles, bearings* and *levels.* It is mounted on a three-legged stand called a *tripod.* A weight, known as a *plumb* or *plumb bob,* is suspended directly below the telescope to determine *true vertical.*

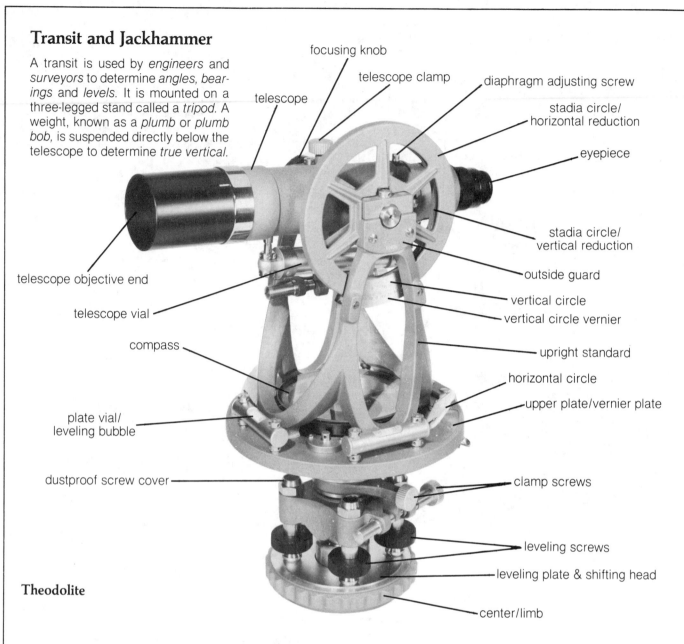

focusing knob

telescope clamp

diaphragm adjusting screw

stadia circle/ horizontal reduction

eyepiece

telescope

stadia circle/ vertical reduction

telescope objective end

outside guard

vertical circle

telescope vial

vertical circle vernier

compass

upright standard

horizontal circle

plate vial/ leveling bubble

upper plate/vernier plate

dustproof screw cover

clamp screws

leveling screws

leveling plate & shifting head

Theodolite

center/limb

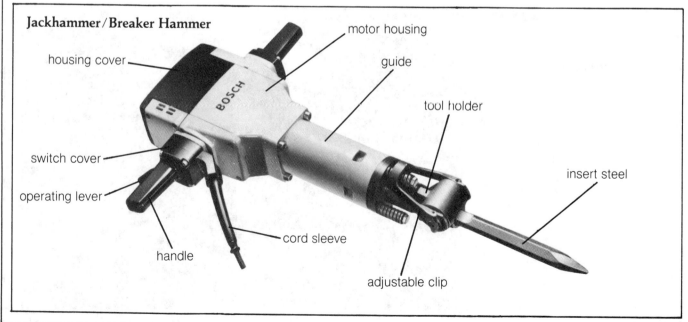

Jackhammer/Breaker Hammer

motor housing

housing cover

guide

tool holder

BOSCH

insert steel

switch cover

operating lever

cord sleeve

handle

adjustable clip

Voting Booth

Voting booths, or *mechanized voting machines,* are located at *polling places,* or *polls.* An *x-indication* appears next to a candidate's name when a lever is pressed. When a *voter* presses levers for every candidate of a single political party, it is called voting a *straight ticket.* Any variation is a *split ballot.*

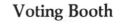

light

question index column

office index column

candidate's name column

selection levers/ individual voting levers

curtain

personal choice/ write-in

voter handle

ballot/face

custodian's seal

officer's lock & seal

poll's open & closed indicator

Mechanical Voting Booth

Electronic Voting System

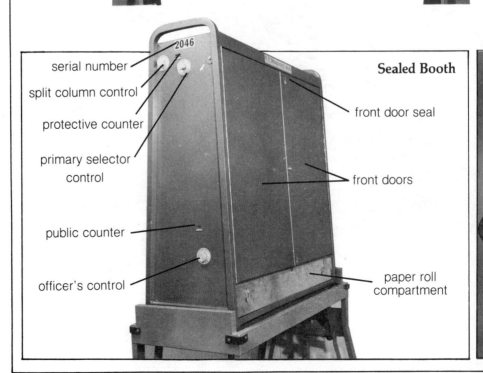

Sealed Booth

serial number

split column control

protective counter

primary selector control

public counter

officer's control

front door seal

front doors

paper roll compartment

ballot layout

privacy curtain

electronic touch button voting positions

console door

Computing Tools

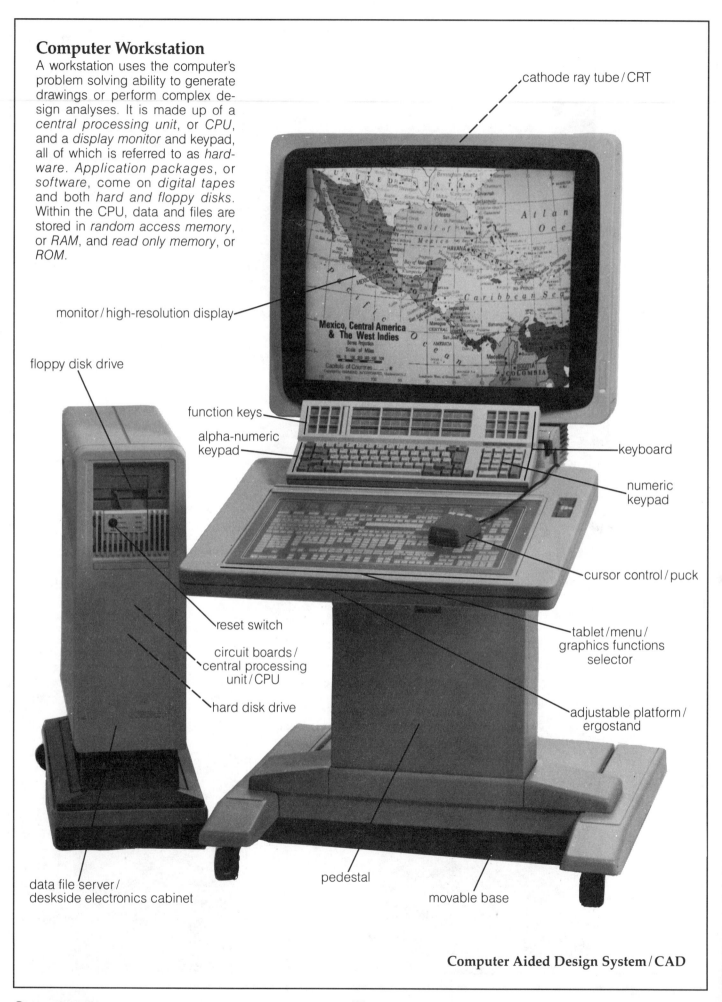

Computer Workstation

A workstation uses the computer's problem solving ability to generate drawings or perform complex design analyses. It is made up of a *central processing unit*, or *CPU*, and a *display monitor* and keypad, all of which is referred to as *hardware*. *Application packages*, or *software*, come on *digital tapes* and both *hard and floppy disks*. Within the CPU, data and files are stored in *random access memory*, or *RAM*, and *read only memory*, or *ROM*.

cathode ray tube / CRT

monitor / high-resolution display

Mexico, Central America & The West Indies

floppy disk drive

function keys

alpha-numeric keypad

keyboard

numeric keypad

cursor control / puck

reset switch

circuit boards / central processing unit / CPU

hard disk drive

tablet / menu / graphics functions selector

adjustable platform / ergostand

data file server / deskside electronics cabinet

pedestal

movable base

Computer Aided Design System / CAD

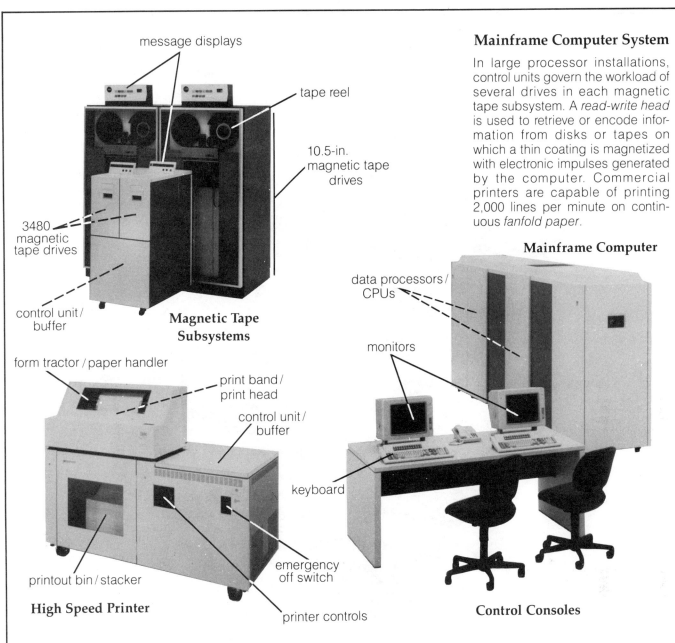

message displays

tape reel

10.5-in.
magnetic tape
drives

3480
magnetic
tape drives

control unit /
buffer

**Magnetic Tape
Subsystems**

Mainframe Computer System

In large processor installations, control units govern the workload of several drives in each magnetic tape subsystem. A *read-write head* is used to retrieve or encode information from disks or tapes on which a thin coating is magnetized with electronic impulses generated by the computer. Commercial printers are capable of printing 2,000 lines per minute on continuous *fanfold paper*.

Mainframe Computer

data processors /
CPUs

monitors

keyboard

Control Consoles

form tractor / paper handler

print band /
print head

control unit /
buffer

emergency
off switch

printout bin / stacker

High Speed Printer

printer controls

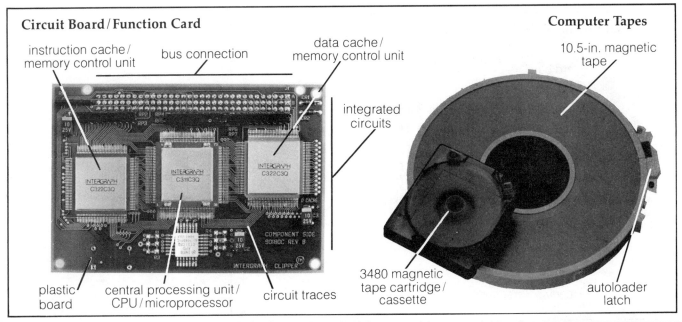

Circuit Board / Function Card

instruction cache /
memory control unit

bus connection

data cache /
memory control unit

integrated
circuits

plastic
board

central processing unit /
CPU / microprocessor

circuit traces

Computer Tapes

10.5-in. magnetic
tape

3480 magnetic
tape cartridge /
cassette

autoloader
latch

Computing Tools

Cash Register

The money drawer of a cash register is the *cash box,* or *till.* A roll of coins put up in paper is a *rouleau.* A *checkout center,* such as the one shown here, is sometimes equipped with a penlike optical *scanner* that translates information on the Universal Product Code, or *UPC label,* into a *cash register receipt* or *item-by-item tape.* It can also feed data to a *central inventory control unit.*

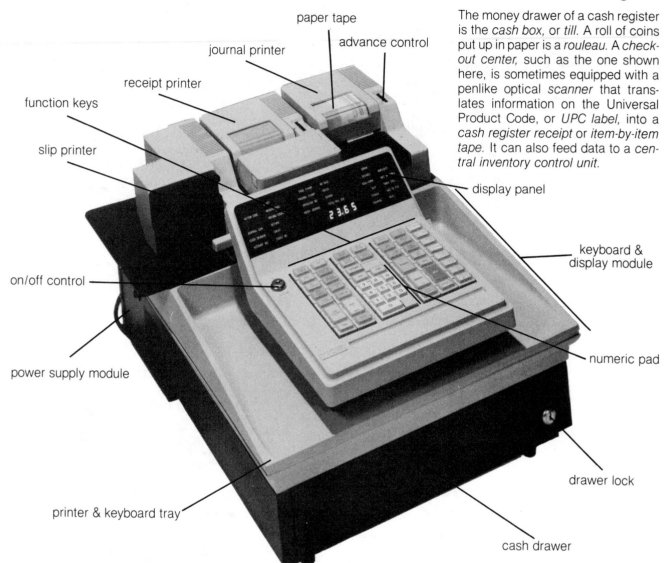

paper tape

journal printer

advance control

receipt printer

function keys

slip printer

display panel

keyboard & display module

on/off control

power supply module

numeric pad

drawer lock

printer & keyboard tray

cash drawer

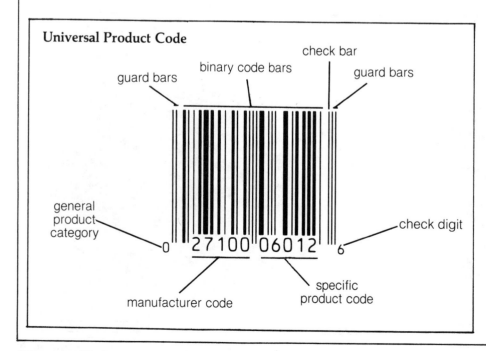

Universal Product Code

guard bars

binary code bars

check bar

guard bars

general product category

check digit

0 27100 06012 6

manufacturer code

specific product code

Calculators

The electronic calculator has generally replaced the *adding machine* today. The linear slide rule, seen here, often has scales on both sides. A *circular slide rule* can only be used for *multiplication* and *division*. A *cylindrical slide rule* is a series of long scales wound around a cylinder like a screw thread. The abacus is an ancient calculator used for solving problems of *addition*, *subtraction*, *multiplication* and *division*, all by the movement of beads. Other early devices include *counting rods*, or "*bones*."

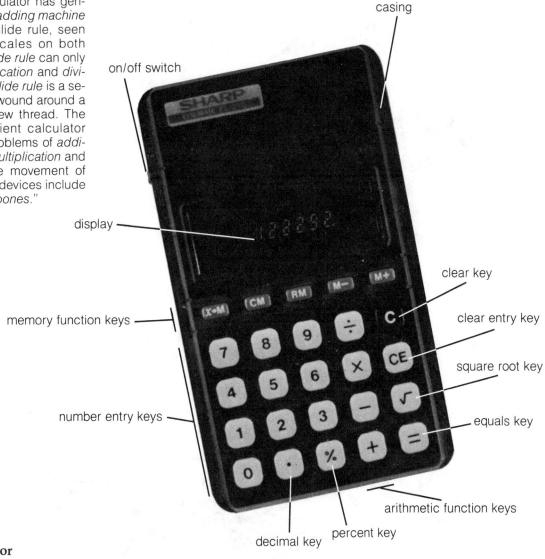

casing

on/off switch

display

memory function keys

number entry keys

clear key

clear entry key

square root key

equals key

arithmetic function keys

decimal key

percent key

Electronic Calculator

Linear Slide Rule

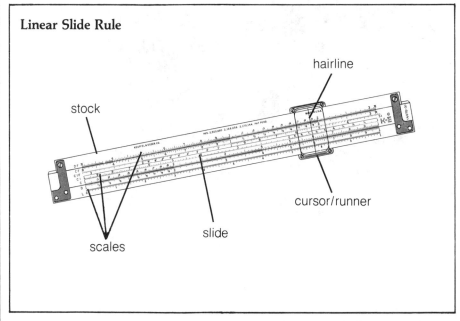

hairline

stock

cursor/runner

scales

slide

Abacus

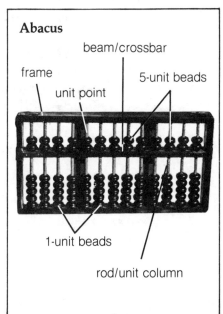

beam/crossbar

frame

unit point

5-unit beads

1-unit beads

rod/unit column

Computing Tools

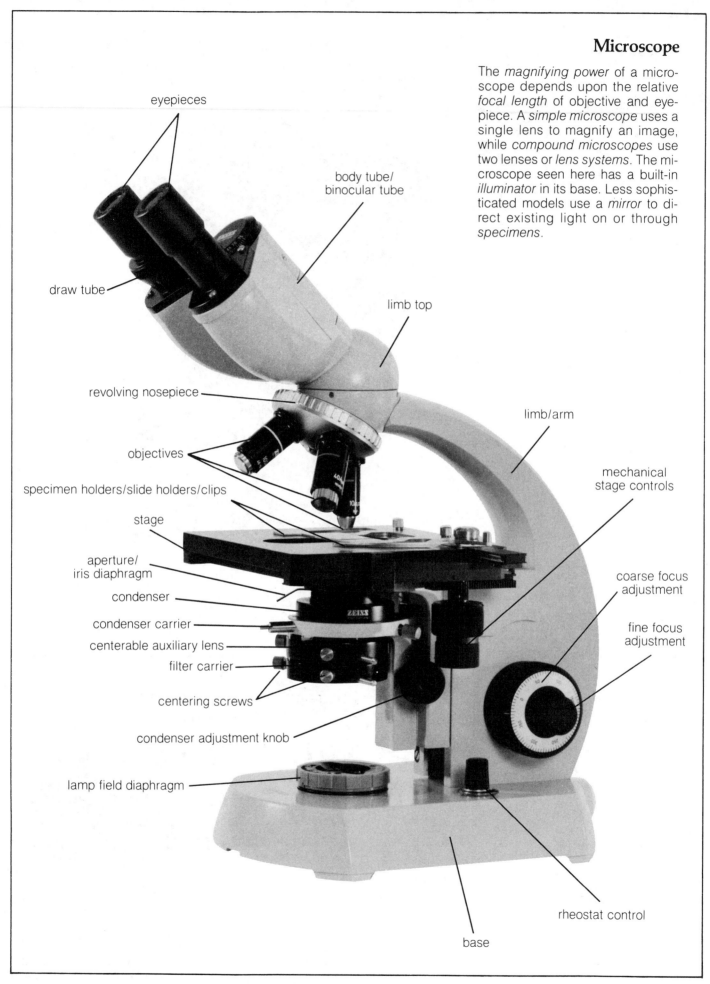

Microscope

The *magnifying power* of a microscope depends upon the relative *focal length* of objective and eyepiece. A *simple microscope* uses a single lens to magnify an image, while *compound microscopes* use two lenses or *lens systems*. The microscope seen here has a built-in *illuminator* in its base. Less sophisticated models use a *mirror* to direct existing light on or through *specimens*.

eyepieces

body tube/
binocular tube

draw tube

limb top

revolving nosepiece

limb/arm

objectives

specimen holders/slide holders/clips

mechanical
stage controls

stage

aperture/
iris diaphragm

condenser

condenser carrier

centerable auxiliary lens

coarse focus
adjustment

fine focus
adjustment

filter carrier

centering screws

condenser adjustment knob

lamp field diaphragm

rheostat control

base

Telescope & Binoculars

A *refracting telescope,* such as the one seen here, relies on the objective lens to concentrate incoming light. A *reflecting telescope* employs a *concave mirror* to do the same task. Binoculars are composed of two similar telescopes, one for each eye. *Field glasses* are lightweight binoculars that employ *erecting telescopes* of the *spyglass* type, while *opera glasses,* designed for use inside, use *Galilean telescopes.*

objective outer cell

objective lens

telescope maintube

dewcap/sunshade

UNITRON

cradle

altitude coarse-motion clamp

viewfinder/guide scope

slow-motion control knobs

viewfinder collimating screw

azimuth coarse-motion clamp

eyepiece

focus knob

altazimuth mounting

star diagonal

fine focus sleeve

drawtube

eyepiece holder

tripod leg

tripod accessories shelf

shelf mount

Telescope

Binoculars   central focusing drive

eyecup

eyepiece

ocular lens

hinge

body/frame

objective lens

Scientific Tools

Radar and Sonar

The cursor on a radar display unit is used to determine the *relative bearings* of *targets*. Most units come with a *viewing hood* and *magnifying lens*. Sonar, formerly known as *asdic*, uses a trainable *transducer* housed in a *soundome* beneath a vessel's hull.

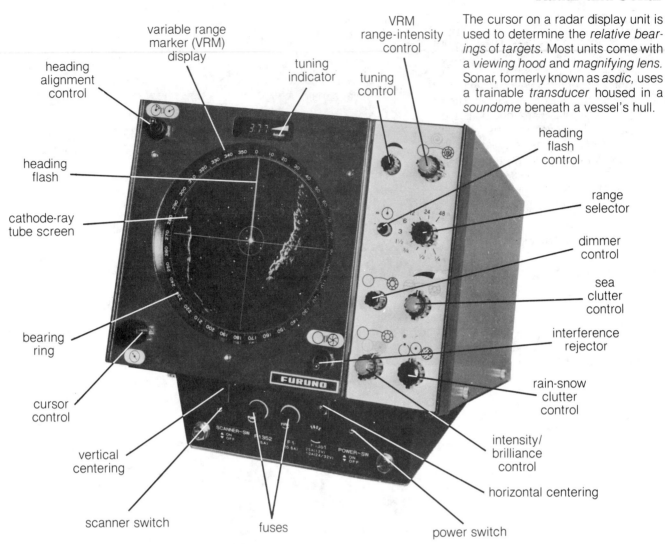

heading alignment control

variable range marker (VRM) display

tuning indicator

VRM range-intensity control

tuning control

heading flash control

heading flash

cathode-ray tube screen

range selector

dimmer control

sea clutter control

interference rejector

bearing ring

rain-snow clutter control

cursor control

intensity/ brilliance control

vertical centering

horizontal centering

scanner switch

fuses

power switch

Radar Display Unit

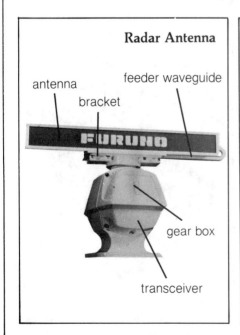

Radar Antenna

antenna

bracket

feeder waveguide

gear box

transceiver

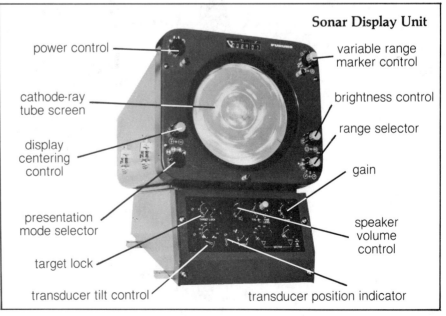

Sonar Display Unit

power control

variable range marker control

cathode-ray tube screen

brightness control

range selector

display centering control

gain

presentation mode selector

speaker volume control

target lock

transducer tilt control

transducer position indicator

Detectors

A *metal locator* works by subtracting a frequency produced by an *oscillator* from a frequency produced by internal circuitry. When the *search coil* is near a metal object, this produces an audio frequency in the speaker or headphones.

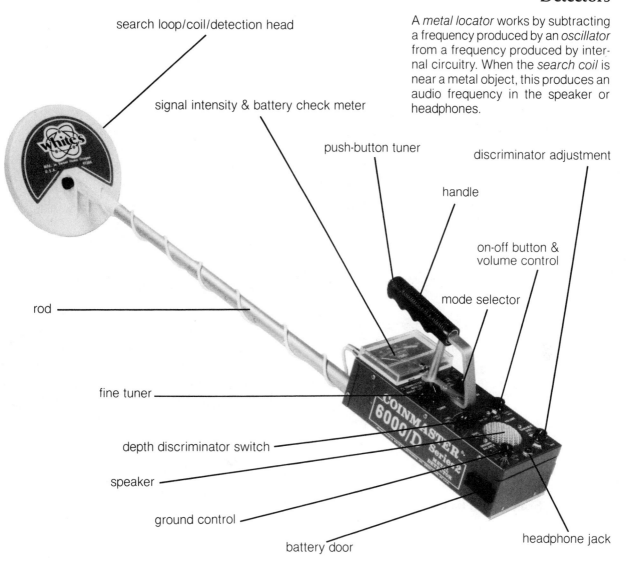

search loop/coil/detection head

signal intensity & battery check meter

push-button tuner

discriminator adjustment

handle

on-off button & volume control

mode selector

rod

fine tuner

depth discriminator switch

speaker

ground control

battery door

headphone jack

Metal and Mineral Detector

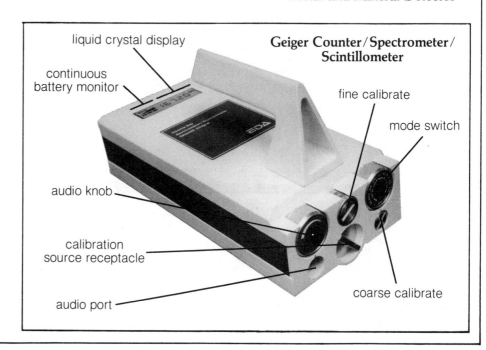

liquid crystal display

Geiger Counter/Spectrometer/ Scintillometer

continuous battery monitor

fine calibrate

mode switch

audio knob

calibration source receptacle

coarse calibrate

audio port

Sensing Devices

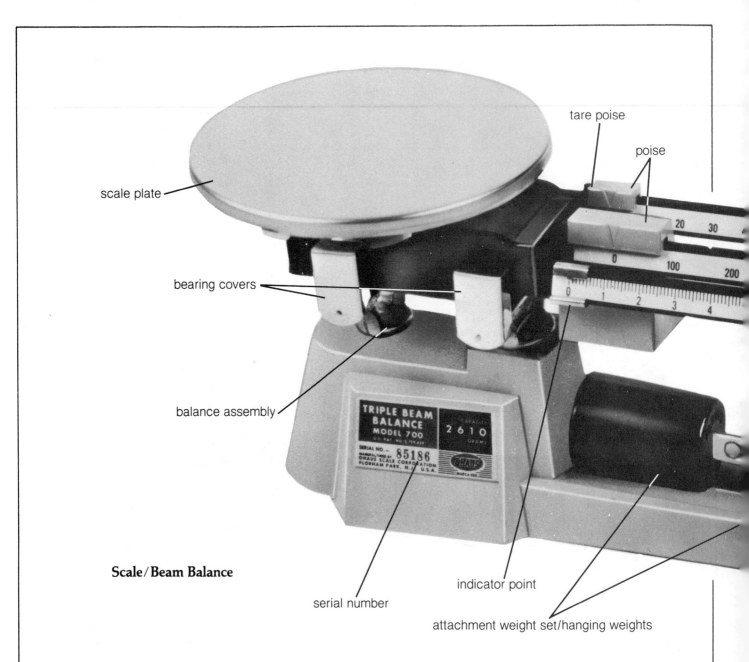

scale plate

tare poise

poise

20   30

0   100   200

bearing covers

0   1   2   3   4

balance assembly

TRIPLE BEAM
BALANCE
MODEL 700

CAPACITY
2610
GRAMS

SERIAL NO... 85186
MANUFACTURED BY
OHAUS SCALE CORPORATION
FLORHAM PARK, N.J. U.S.A.

OHAUS
MARCA REG.

Scale/Beam Balance

indicator point

serial number

attachment weight set/hanging weights

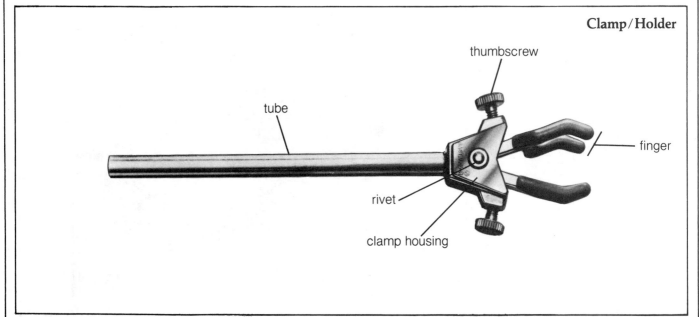

Clamp/Holder

thumbscrew

tube

finger

rivet

clamp housing

Other laboratory equipment includes *ring stands,* to hold various cylinders, *flasks, laboratory thermometers, burettes,* for measuring the volume of liquids, *hydrometers, vacuum jars, microscopes* and *slides, adjustable stands* and *distilling equipment.*

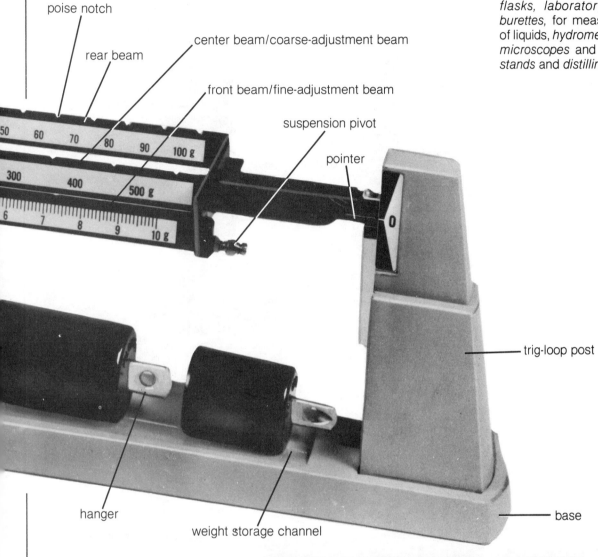

poise notch

rear beam

center beam/coarse-adjustment beam

front beam/fine-adjustment beam

suspension pivot

pointer

50 60 70 80 90 100 g

300 400 500 g

6 7 8 9 10 g

0

trig-loop post

hanger

weight storage channel

base

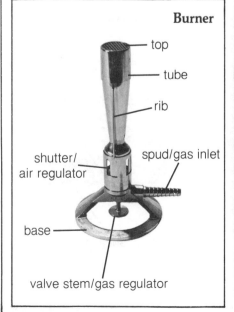

Burner

top

tube

rib

shutter/
air regulator

spud/gas inlet

base

valve stem/gas regulator

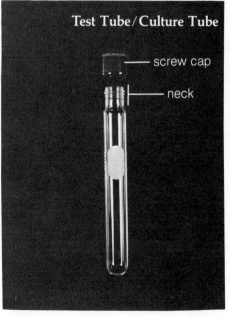

Test Tube/Culture Tube

screw cap

neck

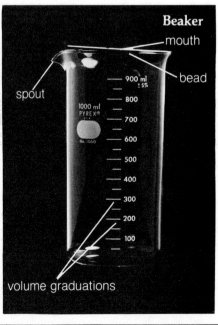

Beaker

mouth

bead

spout

900 ml ±5%

800

1000 ml
PYREX®

700

600

No. 1000

500

400

300

200

100

volume graduations

Sensing Devices

Examination Equipment

The scopes seen below are used by *Eye, Ear, Nose and Throat Doctors,* or *EENT specialists.* The speculum is used by *gynecologists* and *obstetricians. Headlights* mounted on headbands provide a light source for doctors.

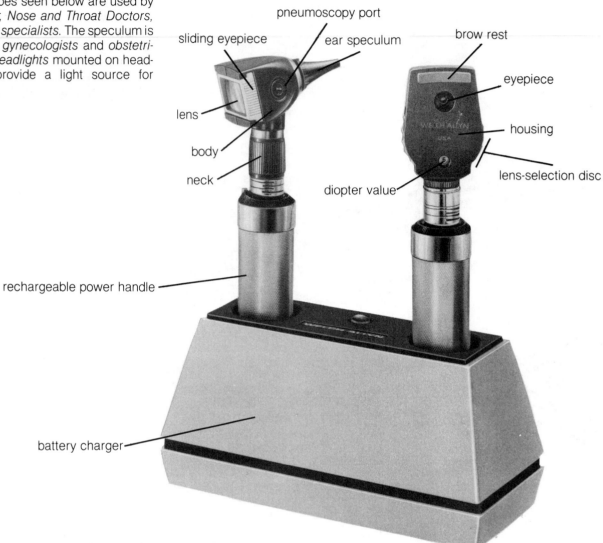

pneumoscopy port

sliding eyepiece

ear speculum

brow rest

eyepiece

housing

lens

lens-selection disc

body

diopter value

neck

rechargeable power handle

battery charger

Ear Scope / Otoscope

Eye Scope / Ophthalmoscope

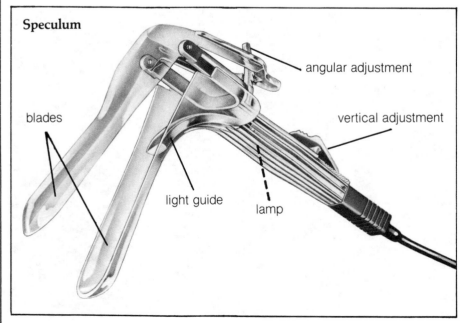

Speculum

angular adjustment

vertical adjustment

blades

light guide

lamp

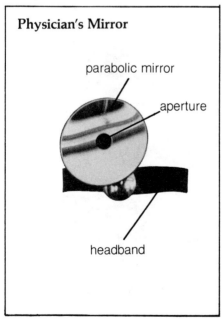

Physician's Mirror

parabolic mirror

aperture

headband

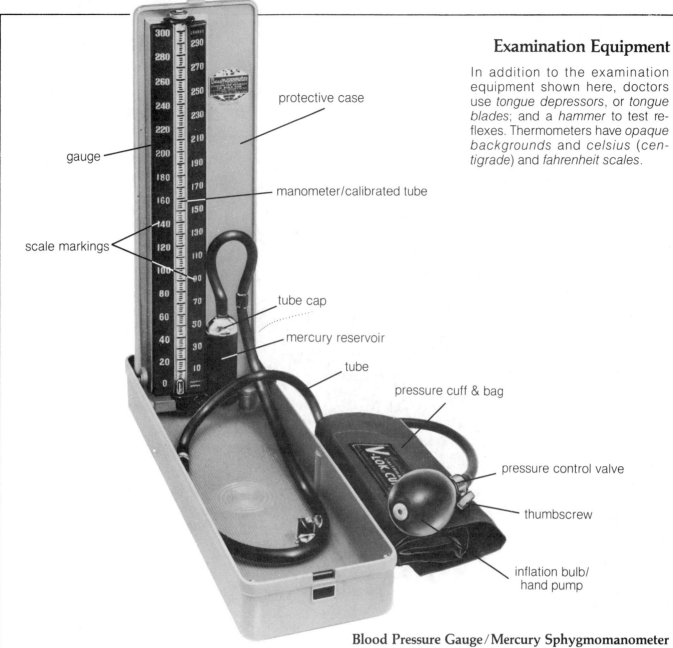

Examination Equipment

In addition to the examination equipment shown here, doctors use *tongue depressors*, or *tongue blades*; and a *hammer* to test reflexes. Thermometers have *opaque backgrounds* and *celsius* (*centigrade*) and *fahrenheit scales*.

gauge

protective case

manometer/calibrated tube

scale markings

tube cap

mercury reservoir

tube

pressure cuff & bag

pressure control valve

thumbscrew

inflation bulb/ hand pump

Blood Pressure Gauge/Mercury Sphygmomanometer

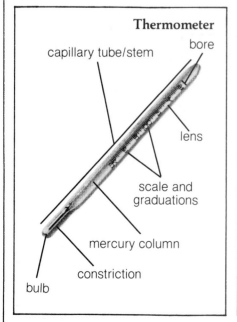

Thermometer

capillary tube/stem

bore

lens

scale and graduations

mercury column

constriction

bulb

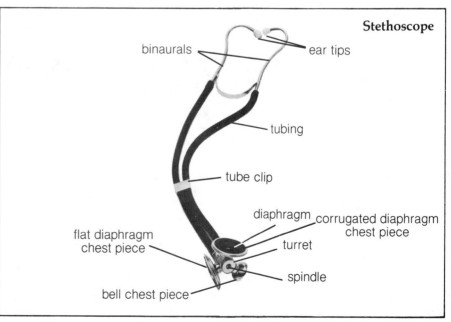

Stethoscope

binaurals

ear tips

tubing

tube clip

diaphragm

corrugated diaphragm chest piece

flat diaphragm chest piece

turret

spindle

bell chest piece

Medical Tools

Surgical, or *operating room, tables,* have built-in *channels* for holding *x-ray cassettes.* Among the accessories that can be attached to them are *intravenous,* or *IV, equipment, arm-* and *footboard extensions, crutch sockets* for holding legs in position, and buckle-type *body-restraint straps.*

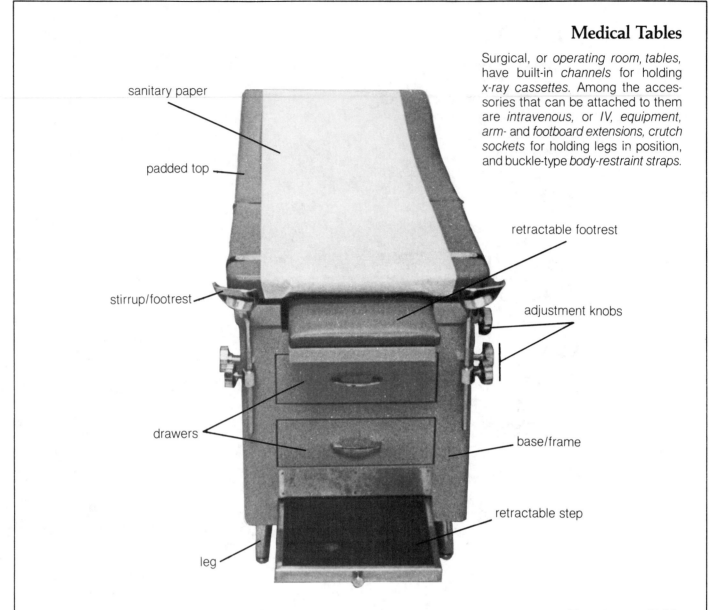

sanitary paper

padded top

retractable footrest

stirrup/footrest

adjustment knobs

drawers

base/frame

retractable step

leg

Examination Table

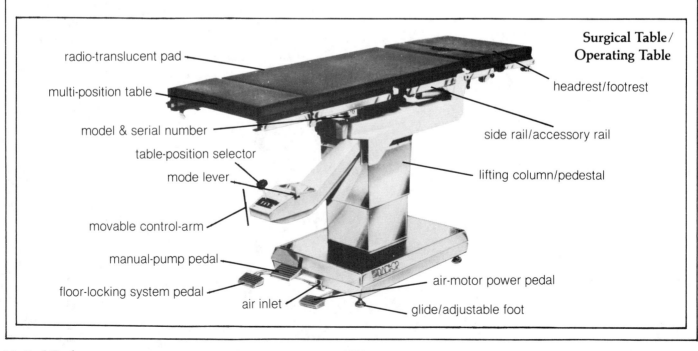

**Surgical Table/
Operating Table**

radio-translucent pad

multi-position table

headrest/footrest

model & serial number

side rail/accessory rail

table-position selector

mode lever

movable control-arm

lifting column/pedestal

manual-pump pedal

floor-locking system pedal

air-motor power pedal

air inlet

glide/adjustable foot

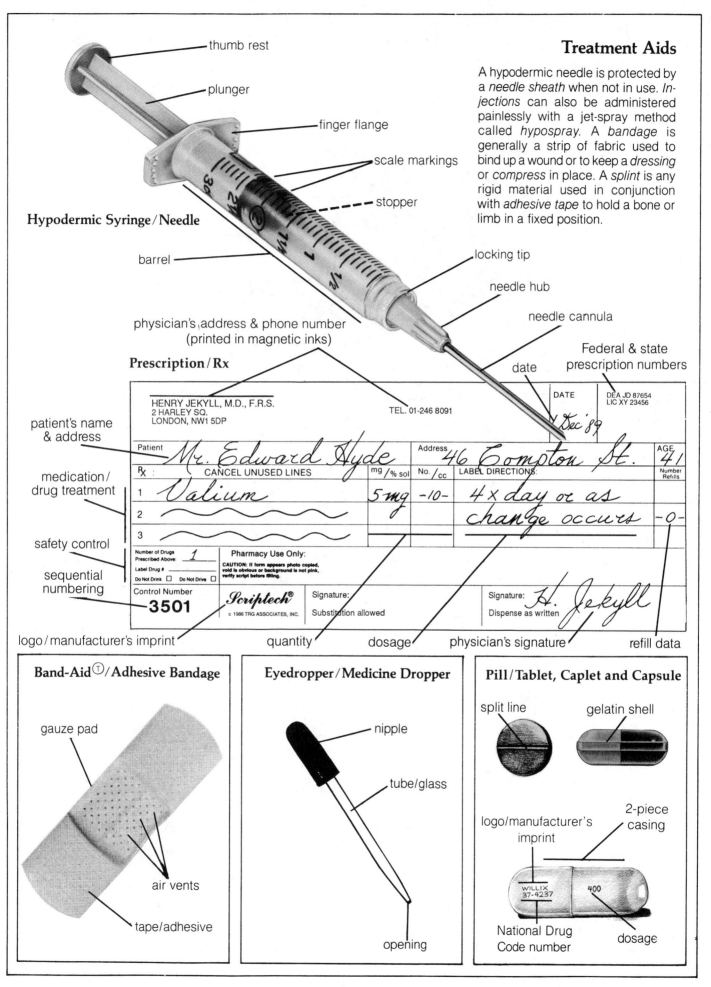

thumb rest

plunger

finger flange

scale markings

stopper

Hypodermic Syringe/Needle

barrel

locking tip

needle hub

needle cannula

date

Federal & state
prescription numbers

physician's address & phone number
(printed in magnetic inks)

Prescription/Rx

Treatment Aids

A hypodermic needle is protected by a *needle sheath* when not in use. *Injections* can also be administered painlessly with a jet-spray method called *hypospray*. A *bandage* is generally a strip of fabric used to bind up a wound or to keep a *dressing* or *compress* in place. A *splint* is any rigid material used in conjunction with *adhesive tape* to hold a bone or limb in a fixed position.

HENRY JEKYLL, M.D., F.R.S.
2 HARLEY SQ.
LONDON, NW1 5DP

TEL. 01-246 8091

DATE

DEA JD 87654
LIC XY 23456

patient's name
& address

medication/
drug treatment

safety control

sequential
numbering

Patient	Mr. Edward Hyde		Address	46 Compton St.	AGE 41
Rx :	CANCEL UNUSED LINES	mg/% sol	No./cc	LABEL DIRECTIONS:	Number Refills
1	Valium	5 mg	-10-	4 x day or as	
2				change occurs	-0-
3					

4 Dec '89

Number of Drugs
Prescribed Above: **1**

Label Drug #

Do Not Drink ☐   Do Not Drive ☐

Pharmacy Use Only:

CAUTION: If form appears photo copied, void is obvious or background is not pink, verify script before filling.

Control Number
3501

Scriptech®
© 1986 TRG ASSOCIATES, INC.

Signature:
Substitution allowed

Signature: *H. Jekyll*
Dispense as written

logo/manufacturer's imprint

quantity

dosage

physician's signature

refill data

Band-Aid①/Adhesive Bandage

gauze pad

air vents

tape/adhesive

Eyedropper/Medicine Dropper

nipple

tube/glass

opening

Pill/Tablet, Caplet and Capsule

split line

gelatin shell

logo/manufacturer's
imprint

2-piece
casing

WILLIX
37-4237

400

National Drug
Code number

dosage

Supportive Devices

Battery-powered *electric chairs* provide mobility for totally handicapped people. For minor leg and foot injuries, a *cane*, or *walking stick*, is used. Other supportive devices include *dialysis machines, iron lungs, oxygen tents, decompression chambers,* and *braces* of various kinds.

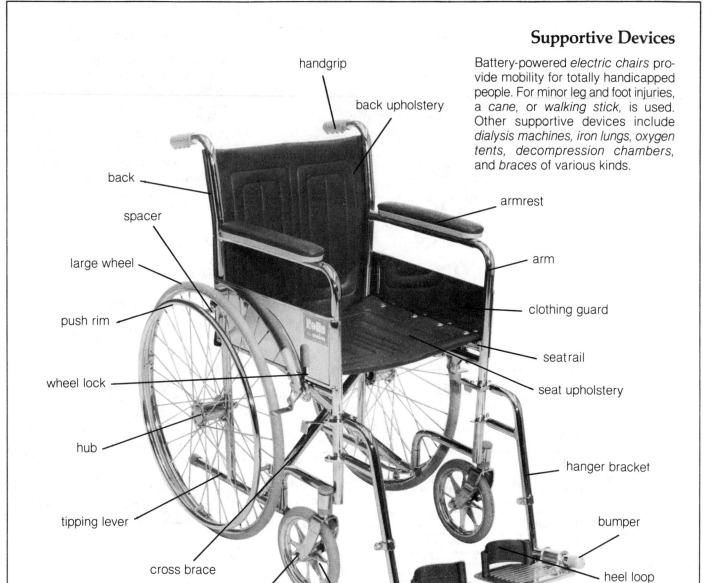

handgrip

back upholstery

back

spacer

large wheel

push rim

wheel lock

hub

tipping lever

cross brace

caster

axle bolt

footplate

armrest

arm

clothing guard

seat rail

seat upholstery

hanger bracket

bumper

heel loop

Wheelchair

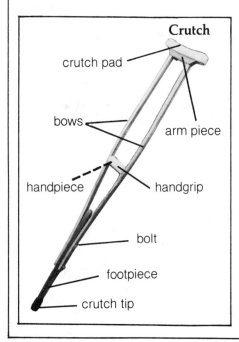

Crutch

crutch pad

bows

arm piece

handpiece

handgrip

bolt

footpiece

crutch tip

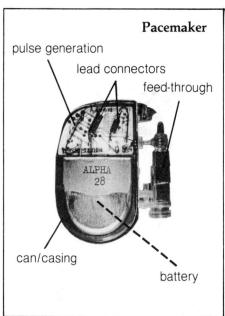

Pacemaker

pulse generation

lead connectors

feed-through

ALPHA 28

can/casing

battery

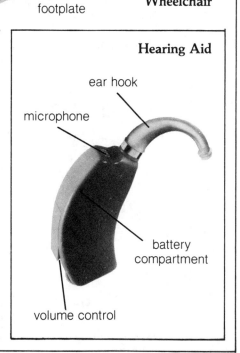

Hearing Aid

ear hook

microphone

battery compartment

volume control

Dental Corrective Devices

A *bridge* consists of one or more false teeth anchored between abutment teeth. The portion of the bridge that actually replaces the missing tooth or teeth is the *pontic*. A *crown* or *jacket crown* covers that part of the tooth normally protected by enamel. In *orthodontia*, the correction of the position of teeth, a *band* or *wire* is inserted in the slot and held in place by *rubber bands* looped over the tie wings.

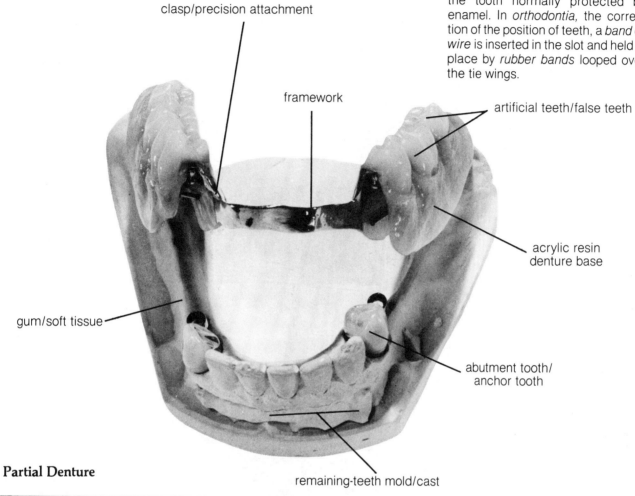

clasp/precision attachment

framework

artificial teeth/false teeth

acrylic resin denture base

gum/soft tissue

abutment tooth/ anchor tooth

remaining-teeth mold/cast

Partial Denture

Full Denture

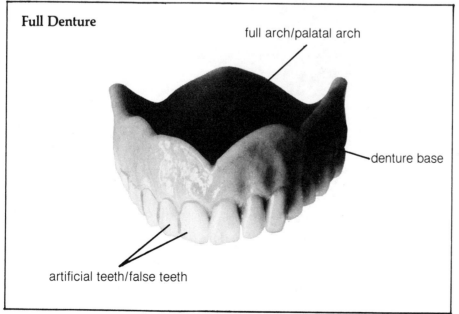

full arch/palatal arch

denture base

artificial teeth/false teeth

Braces/Orthodontic Bracket

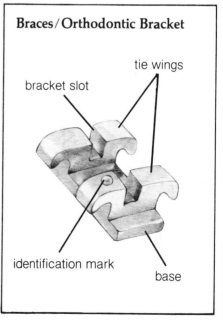

tie wings

bracket slot

identification mark

base

Medical Tools

Dental Unit

A high-intensity *dental light* is usually attached to a dental unit, or *dental island.* Instrument trays may be attached to a *drift-free arm,* such as the one shown here, or to a *post-mounted arm.*

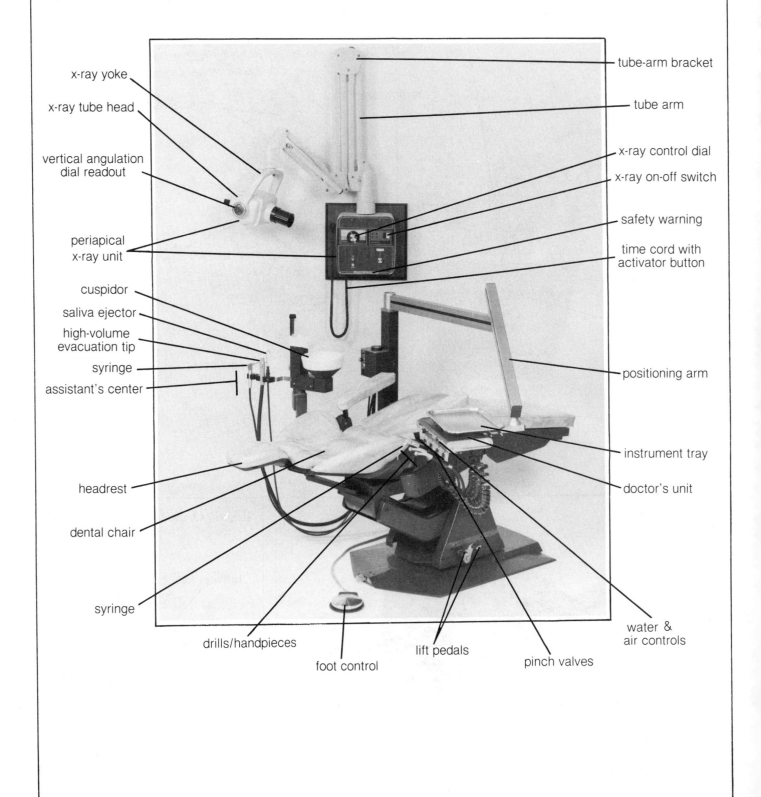

x-ray yoke

x-ray tube head

vertical angulation dial readout

periapical x-ray unit

cuspidor

saliva ejector

high-volume evacuation tip

syringe

assistant's center

headrest

dental chair

syringe

drills/handpieces

foot control

lift pedals

pinch valves

tube-arm bracket

tube arm

x-ray control dial

x-ray on-off switch

safety warning

time cord with activator button

positioning arm

instrument tray

doctor's unit

water & air controls

Dental Equipment

Fillings of *silver amalgam* or *inlays,* *cast restorations* of *gold, synthetic porcelain* or *acrylic resins,* are used to fill *cavities.* Teeth can also be fitted with *crowns* or *caps.*

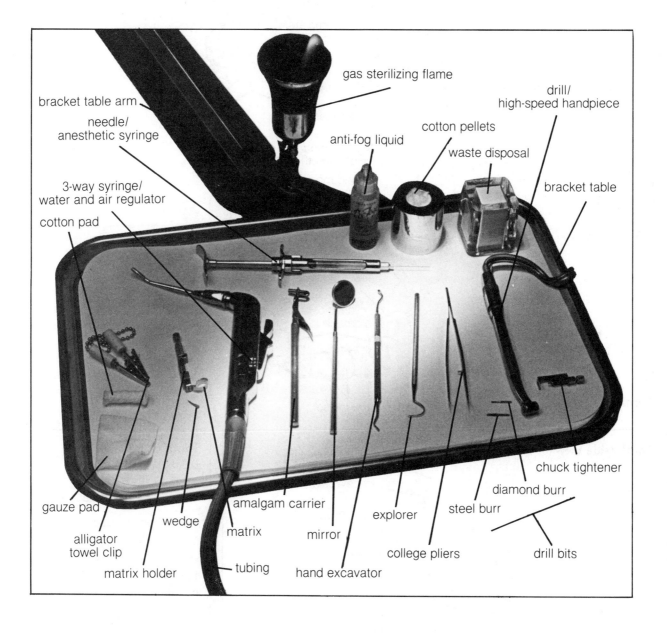

gas sterilizing flame

bracket table arm

needle/ anesthetic syringe

3-way syringe/ water and air regulator

cotton pad

anti-fog liquid

cotton pellets

waste disposal

drill/ high-speed handpiece

bracket table

gauze pad

alligator towel clip

wedge

matrix holder

matrix

tubing

amalgam carrier

mirror

hand excavator

explorer

college pliers

steel burr

diamond burr

chuck tightener

drill bits

Teeth

Each tooth has one or two *neighbors* and a biting *partner* in the opposite jaw. Teeth fit into *sockets*. The first set of teeth are *baby teeth*, or *milk teeth*, replaced in time by permanent teeth. A person with a fondness for sugary edibles is said to have a *sweet tooth*.

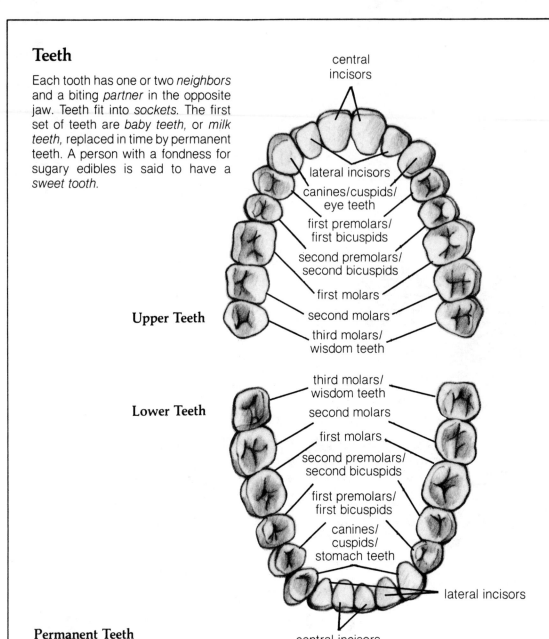

Upper Teeth

central incisors
lateral incisors
canines/cuspids/ eye teeth
first premolars/ first bicuspids
second premolars/ second bicuspids
first molars
second molars
third molars/ wisdom teeth

Lower Teeth

third molars/ wisdom teeth
second molars
first molars
second premolars/ second bicuspids
first premolars/ first bicuspids
canines/ cuspids/ stomach teeth
lateral incisors
central incisors

Permanent Teeth

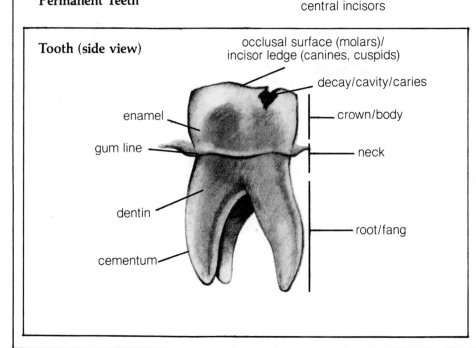

Tooth (side view)

occlusal surface (molars)/ incisor ledge (canines, cuspids)
decay/cavity/caries
enamel
crown/body
gum line
neck
dentin
root/fang
cementum

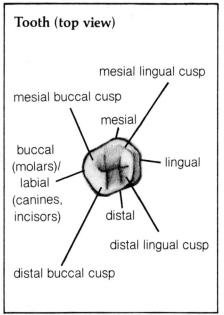

Tooth (top view)

mesial lingual cusp
mesial buccal cusp
mesial
buccal (molars)/ labial (canines, incisors)
lingual
distal
distal lingual cusp
distal buccal cusp

Vault and Safe

Vaults are connected to *alarm systems*, which include *bells* and *silent alarms*. *Time locks* open safes or vaults at a predetermined time and prevent their being opened otherwise. A *strongbox* is a stoutly made box or chest for preserving valuable possessions. Most safes are insulated to protect against fire as well as theft. A home *money box, coin bank* or *piggy bank* is opened at the bottom or with a hammer.

door jamb

architrave

door hinge

bolt-retracting gears

primary combination dial

vault door

locking bolts

door handle

bolt-activating gear rings

bolt guide ring

dust cover/ bolt cover

safe deposit boxes

day gate

bolt holes

vestibule

bridge

timelock/movement dial

bolt linkage

Vault

recessed door

body wall

Safe

escutcheon plate

hinge

handle

combination lock

serial number

Security Devices

Door Locks

Many mortise locks have two *buttons* below the latch bolt which allow the *outside knob* to be independently locked or unlocked. Bolts fit into a *striker plate,* attached to the door frame. A *latch* is a device which holds a door closed, but cannot be locked. A *catch* holds lightweight doors, such as cabinet doors, closed. A *lockset* has the features of a lock and a catch.

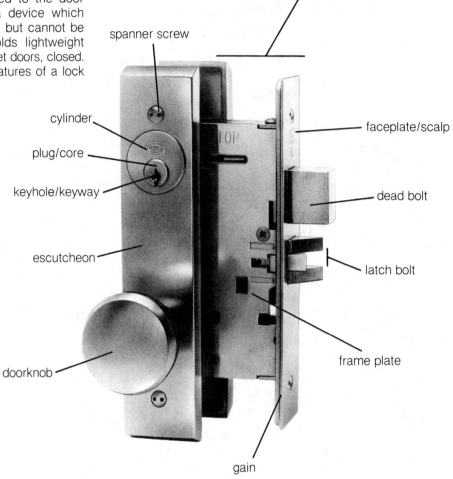

latch assembly

spanner screw

cylinder

plug/core

keyhole/keyway

escutcheon

doorknob

faceplate/scalp

dead bolt

latch bolt

frame plate

gain

Mortise Lock

Chain Lock/Door Bolt

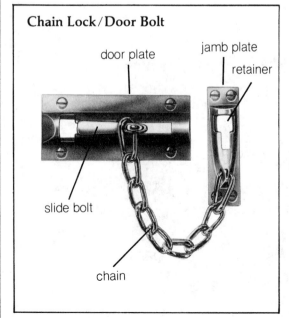

door plate

jamb plate

retainer

slide bolt

chain

Inter-grip Rim Lock

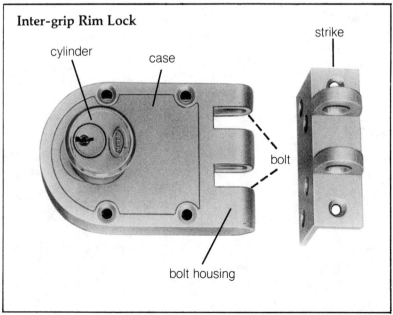

cylinder

case

strike

bolt

bolt housing

Key and Padlock

A key is inserted into a lock's cylinder via a *keyway*. The angled serrations, or *cuts*, on a key blade correspond to different sized *pin-tumblers*, or *pins*, within the lock cylinder. A key that has not yet been configured to any particular lock is a *blank*. A key used to open many common locks is a *skeleton key*.

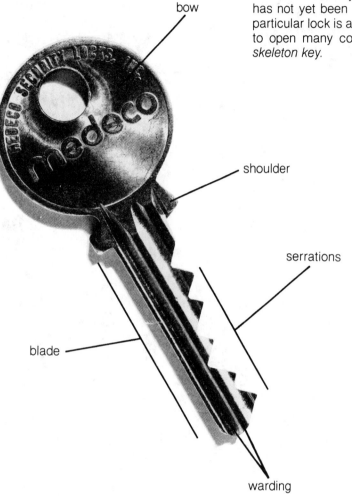

bow

shoulder

serrations

blade

warding

Key

Padlock

shackle

medeco

cylinder/plug

case/body

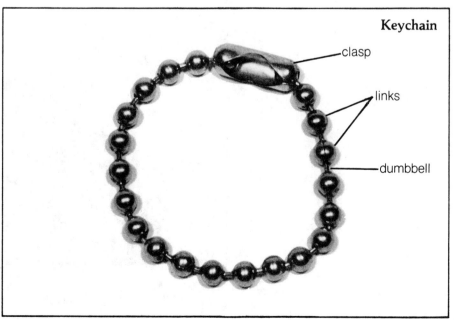

Keychain

clasp

links

dumbbell

Security Devices

Hinge and Hasp

In addition to the *butt hinge,* seen here, there are *pivot hinges, full-surface hinges, half-surface hinges, spring hinges, strap hinges* and *continuous hinges.* Hinge pivot pins or *fixed pins,* used on smaller hinges, are available in a variety of ornamental *heads,* or *caps,* such as the ball tip seen here. A *safety hasp* is secured with a padlock or pin.

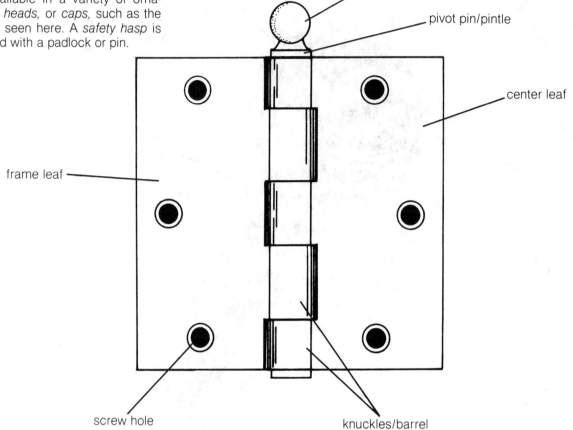

ball tip head

pivot pin/pintle

center leaf

frame leaf

screw hole

knuckles/barrel

Hinge

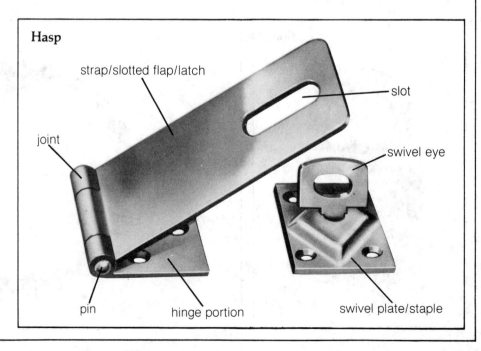

Hasp

strap/slotted flap/latch

slot

joint

swivel eye

pin

hinge portion

swivel plate/staple

Chain and Pulley

When a rope is reeved, or passed through the block, it fits into a narrow groove, or *score,* around the circumference of the sheave. That part of the rope used to apply power or hoist is the *fall.* The lower, or *choke,end* of a common wood block is the *arse.*

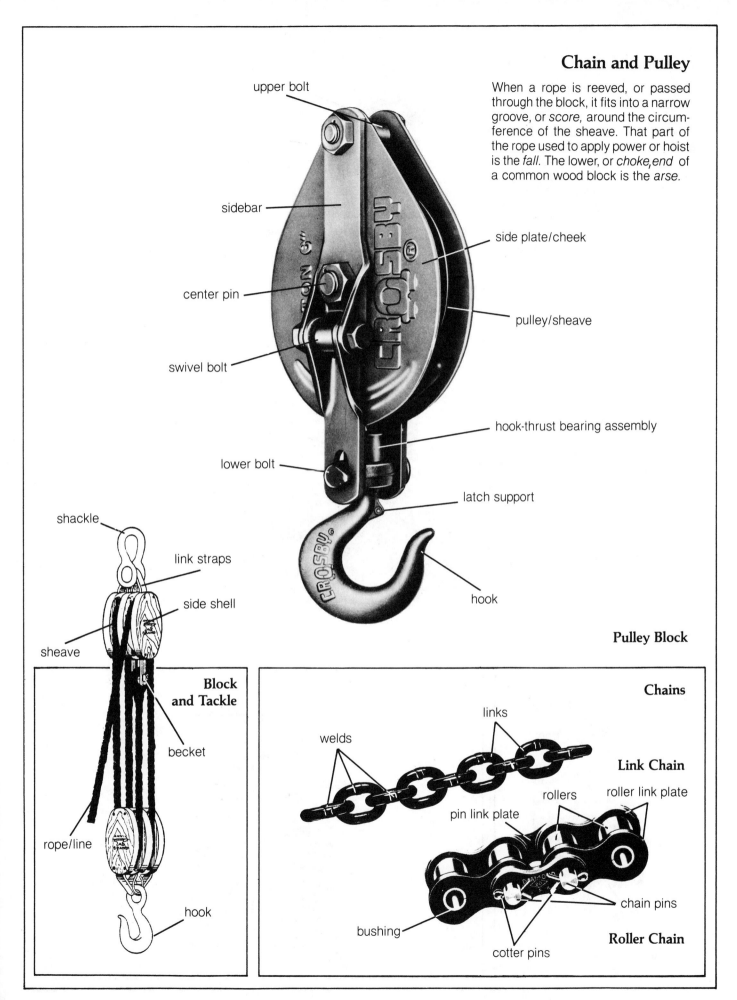

upper bolt

sidebar

center pin

swivel bolt

side plate/cheek

pulley/sheave

hook-thrust bearing assembly

lower bolt

latch support

hook

Pulley Block

shackle

link straps

side shell

sheave

Block and Tackle

becket

rope/line

hook

Chains

links

welds

Link Chain

rollers

roller link plate

pin link plate

chain pins

bushing

cotter pins

Roller Chain

Chain and Pulley

Execution Devices

The blade on the guillotine is released by a *release cord* or *release button*. The Italian *mannaia* and the Scottish *maiden* were variations of the French guillotine. A *gibbet,* similar to a gallows, has a single, horizontal arm from which the noose was hung. On an electric chair, electrodes are attached to the prisoner's head and leg to complete the circuit. A *tumbrel* is any vehicle used to bring condemned people to the place of execution.

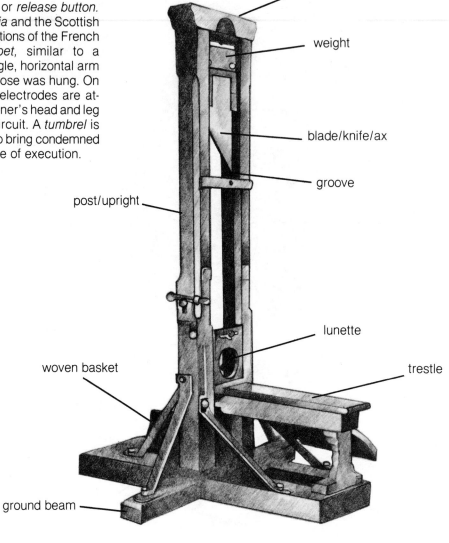

crossbeam

weight

blade/knife/ax

groove

post/upright

lunette

woven basket

trestle

ground beam

Guillotine

Gallows

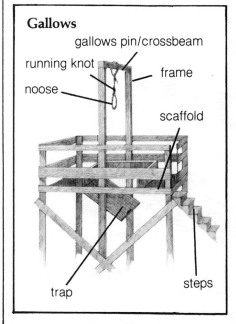

gallows pin/crossbeam

running knot

frame

noose

scaffold

trap

steps

Electric Chair

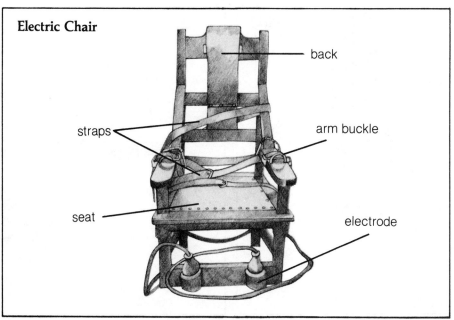

back

straps

arm buckle

seat

electrode

A knife or sword is stored in a *sheath*. The handle fits over the *tang*, a projection from the upper end of the blade.

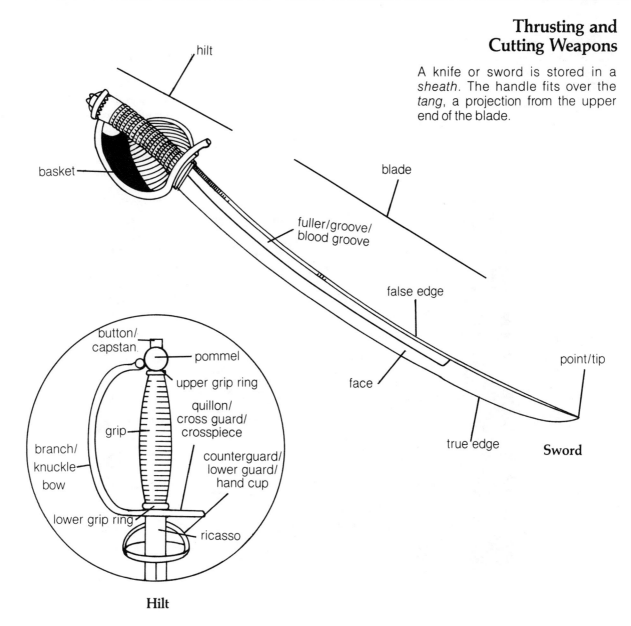

hilt

basket

blade

fuller/groove/
blood groove

false edge

point/tip

face

true edge

Sword

button/
capstan

pommel

upper grip ring

grip

quillon/
cross guard/
crosspiece

branch/
knuckle
bow

counterguard/
lower guard/
hand cup

lower grip ring

ricasso

Hilt

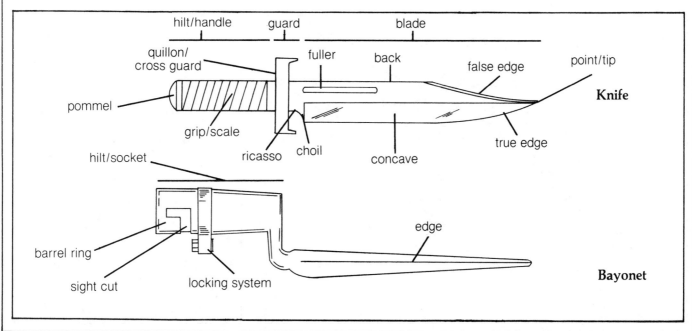

hilt/handle   guard   blade

quillon/
cross guard

fuller

back

false edge

point/tip

pommel

Knife

grip/scale

ricasso   choil

concave

true edge

hilt/socket

barrel ring

edge

sight cut   locking system

Bayonet

Medieval Arms

A round shield held at arm's length is called a *buckler*, while a shield held across the body by straps or handles called *enarmes* is a *target*. A shield offering protection during a siege is a *pavise*. Cutouts on the sides of a shield for holding spears to be thrown are called *bouches*. A shafted weapon having a *spear blade* and a pair of curved *lobes* at the base of the *spearhead* is a *partisan*.

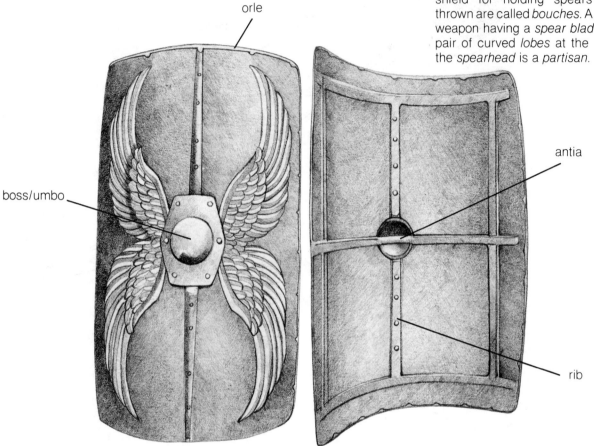

orle

boss/umbo

antia

rib

Shield

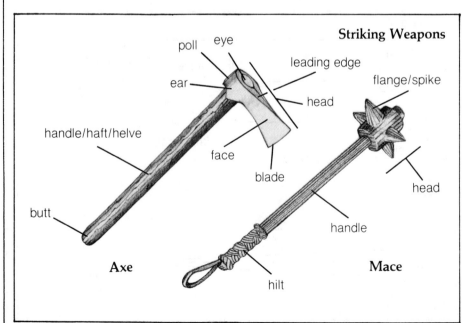

Striking Weapons

poll

eye

ear

leading edge

head

handle/haft/helve

flange/spike

face

blade

butt

hilt

handle

head

Axe

Mace

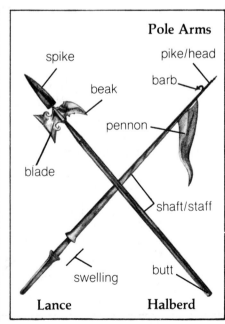

Pole Arms

spike

pike/head

beak

barb

pennon

blade

shaft/staff

swelling

butt

Lance

Halberd

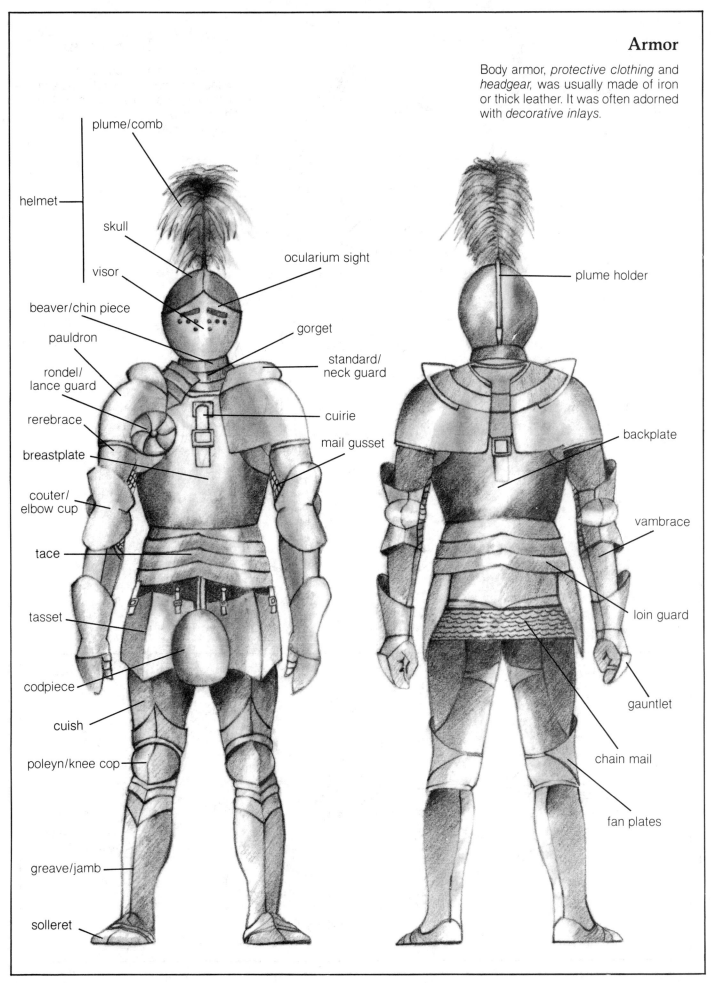

Armor

Body armor, *protective clothing* and *headgear*, was usually made of iron or thick leather. It was often adorned with *decorative inlays*.

plume/comb

helmet

skull

visor

beaver/chin piece

pauldron

rondel/lance guard

rerebrace

breastplate

couter/elbow cup

tace

tasset

codpiece

cuish

poleyn/knee cop

greave/jamb

solleret

ocularium sight

gorget

standard/neck guard

cuirie

mail gusset

plume holder

backplate

vambrace

loin guard

gauntlet

chain mail

fan plates

Weapons

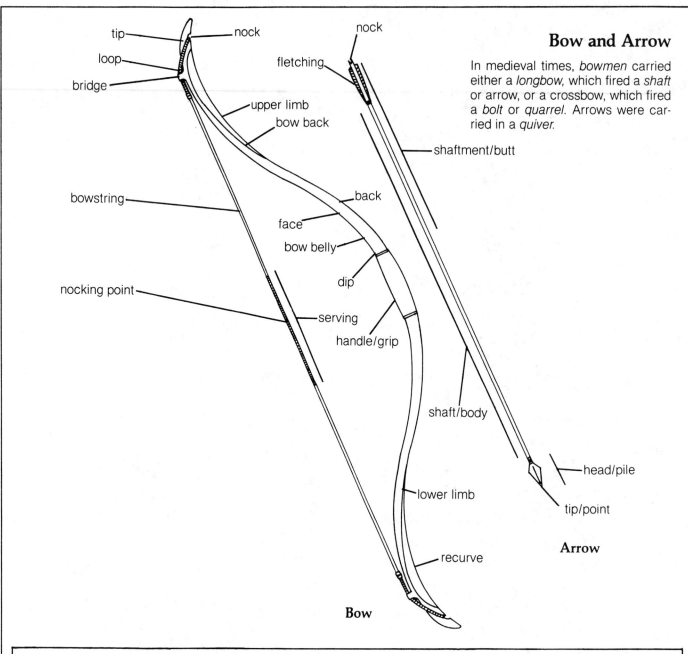

Bow and Arrow

In medieval times, *bowmen* carried either a *longbow*, which fired a *shaft* or arrow, or a *crossbow*, which fired a *bolt* or *quarrel*. Arrows were carried in a *quiver*.

tip
nock
loop
bridge
nock
fletching
upper limb
bow back
shaftment/butt
bowstring
back
face
bow belly
dip
nocking point
serving
handle/grip
shaft/body
head/pile
lower limb
tip/point

Arrow

recurve

Bow

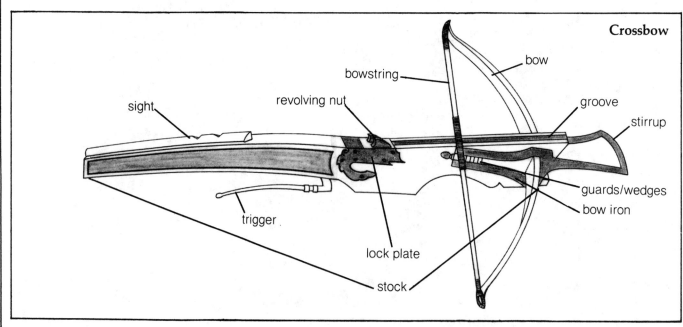

Crossbow

bowstring
revolving nut
bow
sight
groove
stirrup
trigger
guards/wedges
bow iron
lock plate
stock

Cannon and Catapult

Cannonballs fired by *muzzle-loaders* were transported in *caissons* and stacked in trays called *monkeys*. *Loaders* used a *swab* or *sponge* to get rid of residue, a *worm* to remove obstructions, and a *rammer* to drive the *projectile* into the *bore* at the muzzle, or *mouth*, of the cannon. Catapults were used to fire javelinlike shafts a quarter of a mile or more. Ballistas, using the same system of hurling, were employed to heave heavy stones short distances.

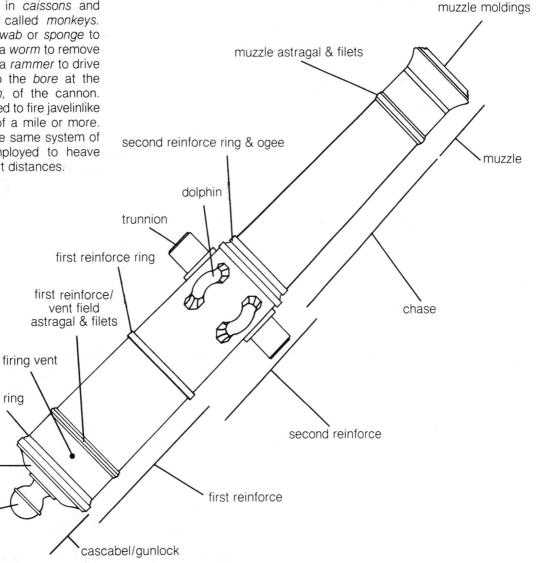

Cannon Barrel

muzzle moldings

muzzle astragal & filets

muzzle

second reinforce ring & ogee

dolphin

trunnion

first reinforce ring

first reinforce/ vent field astragal & filets

chase

firing vent

base ring

second reinforce

breech

button/knob

first reinforce

cascabel/gunlock

Carriage

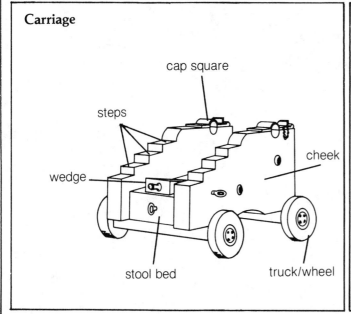

cap square

steps

cheek

wedge

stool bed

truck/wheel

Ballista

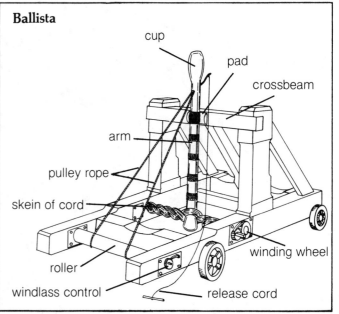

cup

pad

crossbeam

arm

pulley rope

skein of cord

winding wheel

roller

windlass control

release cord

Shotgun and Rifle

A shotgun fires small *pellets* through a *smooth bore,* while a rifle fires *bullets* through a *rifled barrel.* Shotgun barrels are usually tapered, or *choked,* to constrict the *shot pattern.* Rifles may be carried across the shoulder on a beltlike *sling* connected to the weapon by *sling swivels* and adjusted with bucklelike *claws.*

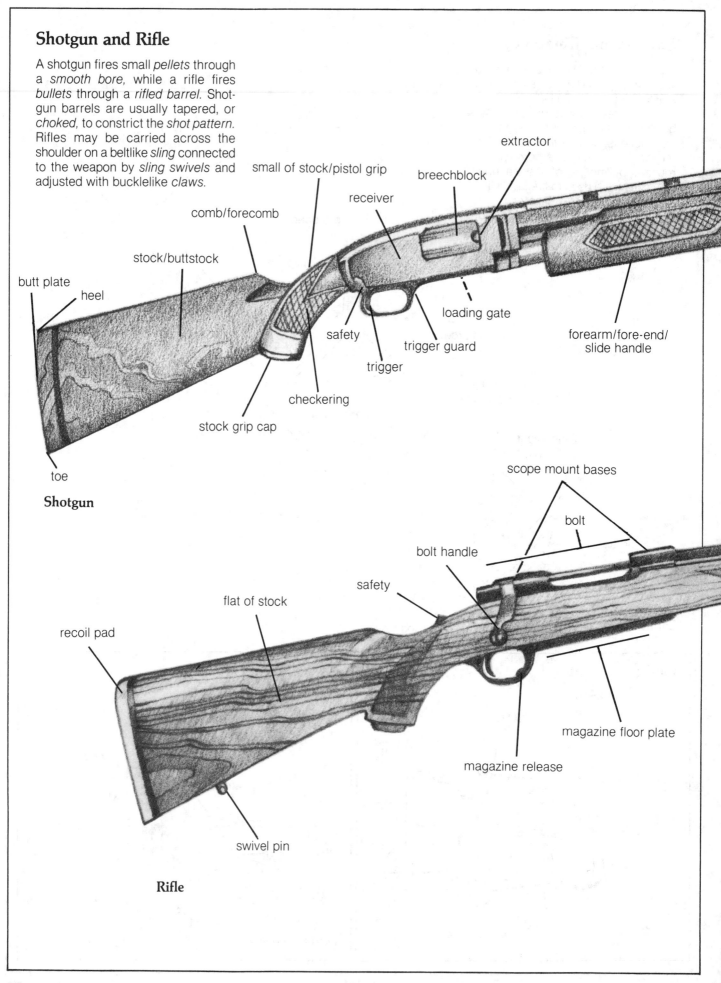

extractor

small of stock/pistol grip

breechblock

receiver

comb/forecomb

stock/buttstock

butt plate

heel

safety

trigger guard

loading gate

trigger

forearm/fore-end/ slide handle

checkering

stock grip cap

toe

Shotgun

scope mount bases

bolt

bolt handle

safety

flat of stock

recoil pad

magazine floor plate

magazine release

swivel pin

Rifle

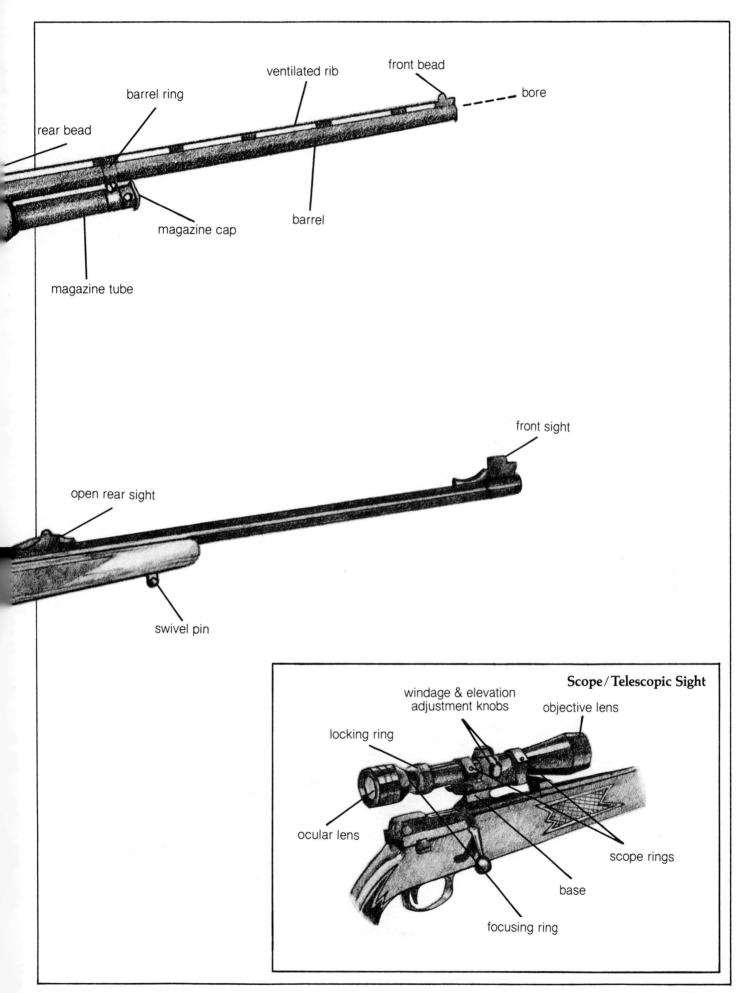

rear bead

barrel ring

ventilated rib

front bead

bore

magazine cap

barrel

magazine tube

front sight

open rear sight

swivel pin

Scope/Telescopic Sight

windage & elevation
adjustment knobs

objective lens

locking ring

ocular lens

scope rings

base

focusing ring

469

Weapons

Handguns

A *gun,* or *side arm,* is *fired* when a *firing pin* in the *breech* strikes the cartridge primer. A *silencer* dampens the sound of a gun's *discharge.* Grooves in the barrel, called *rifling,* cause a fired bullet to spiral for stability in flight. Cartridges are measured in *calibers,* their diameters in hundredths or thousandths of an inch written in a decimal fraction, or in *millimeters.* Handguns are carried in *holsters.*

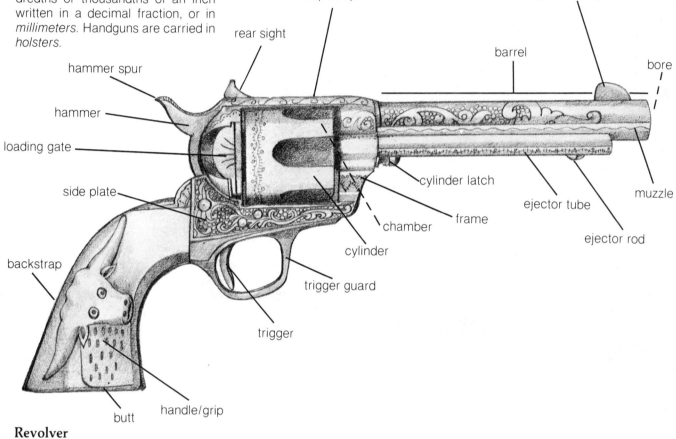

top strap

rear sight

front sight/front sight blade

barrel

bore

hammer spur

hammer

loading gate

side plate

backstrap

cylinder latch

frame

chamber

cylinder

ejector tube

muzzle

ejector rod

trigger guard

trigger

butt

handle/grip

Revolver

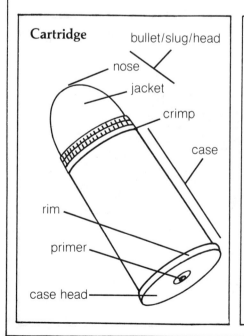

Cartridge

bullet/slug/head

nose

jacket

crimp

case

rim

primer

case head

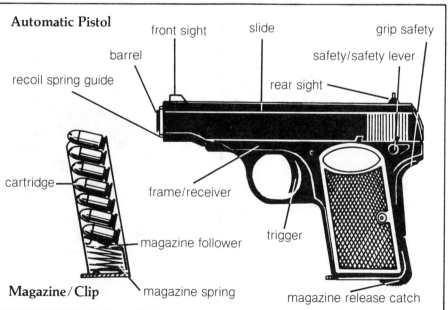

Automatic Pistol

front sight

slide

grip safety

barrel

safety/safety lever

recoil spring guide

rear sight

cartridge

frame/receiver

magazine follower

trigger

Magazine/Clip

magazine spring

magazine release catch

Automatic Weapons

Multi-shot automatic weapons are grouped by weight: light, medium and heavy. The *air-cooled,* medium-weight machine gun shown here can be handled by one man on the ground or on a vehicle when mounted on *pintle mounts.* The light, hand-held automatic rifle is also able to deliver a rapid burst of continuous fire as long as the trigger is depressed. *Ammunition* is fed to it from *handle clips* or *banana clips.*

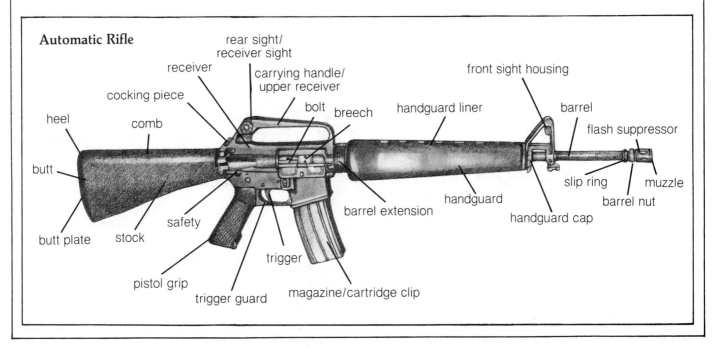

front sight
flash suppressor
forearm
barrel
cocking handle
chassis plate
carrying handle
rear sight
grips
feed plate
trigger/firing lever
operating rod
tripod/tripod mount
height adjustment control

cartridge
feed belt
cartridge box

Machine Gun

Ammunition Can

Automatic Rifle

rear sight/
receiver sight
receiver
carrying handle/
upper receiver
front sight housing
cocking piece
bolt
breech
handguard liner
barrel
heel
comb
flash suppressor
butt
safety
barrel extension
handguard
muzzle
slip ring
butt plate
stock
handguard cap
barrel nut
trigger
pistol grip
magazine/cartridge clip
trigger guard

Mortar and Bazooka

A mortar is a *muzzle-loading cannon*, or *midget howitzer*, used to throw *finned projectiles* at high angles. A bazooka is a portable shoulder weapon with an *open-breech smoothbore firing tube* that fires several types of *rockets*.

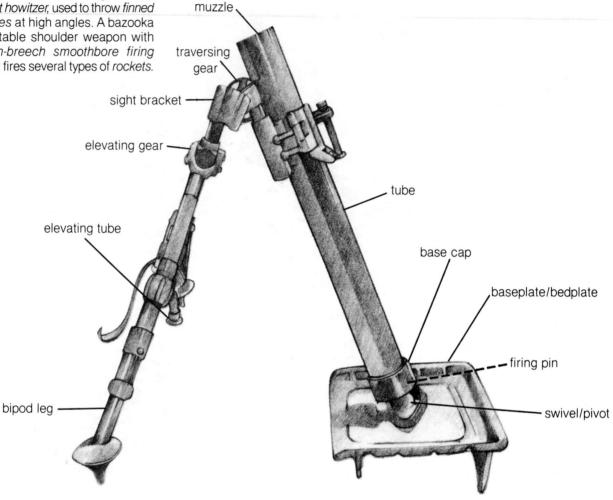

muzzle

traversing gear

sight bracket

elevating gear

elevating tube

tube

base cap

baseplate/bedplate

firing pin

bipod leg

swivel/pivot

Mortar

Bazooka / Rocket Launcher

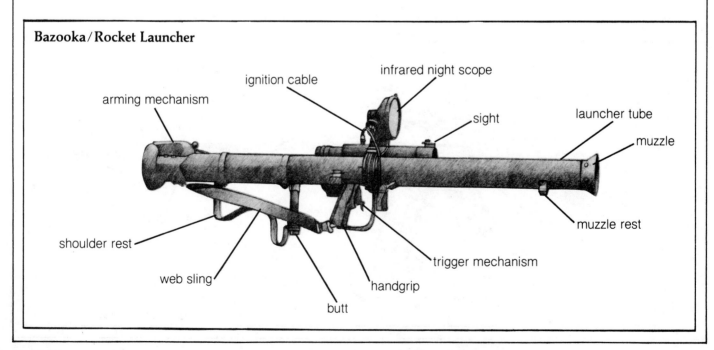

arming mechanism

ignition cable

infrared night scope

sight

launcher tube

muzzle

shoulder rest

web sling

butt

handgrip

trigger mechanism

muzzle rest

Grenade and Mine

When the type of grenade shown here is detonated, it bursts into numerous metal fragments called *shrapnel*. Other types of grenades include *smoke grenades* and *concussion grenades*. Streamlined *rifle grenades* have rear *fins* to provide stability in flight. A "*Molotov cocktail*," a crude grenade often thrown at tanks to set them on fire, consists of a gasoline-filled bottle with a lighted *wick* at the top.

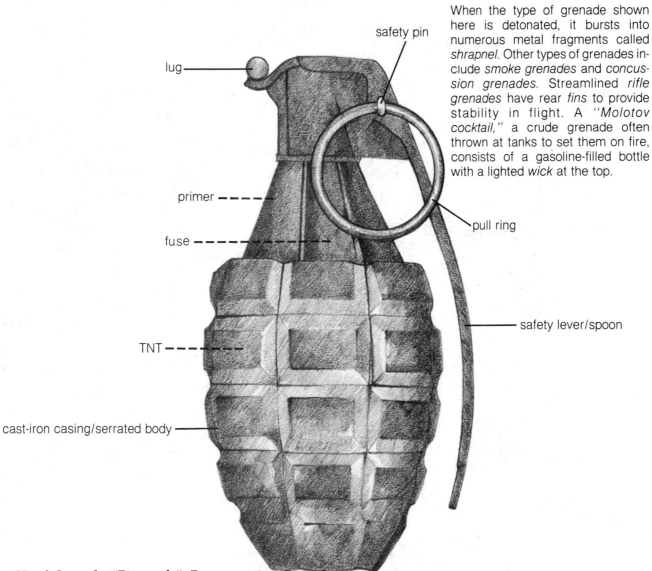

lug
safety pin
primer
fuse
TNT
cast-iron casing/serrated body
pull ring
safety lever/spoon

Hand Grenade/"Pineapple"/Fragmentation Grenade

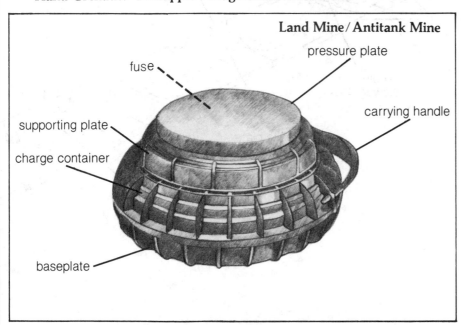

Land Mine/Antitank Mine

fuse
pressure plate
carrying handle
supporting plate
charge container
baseplate

Weapons

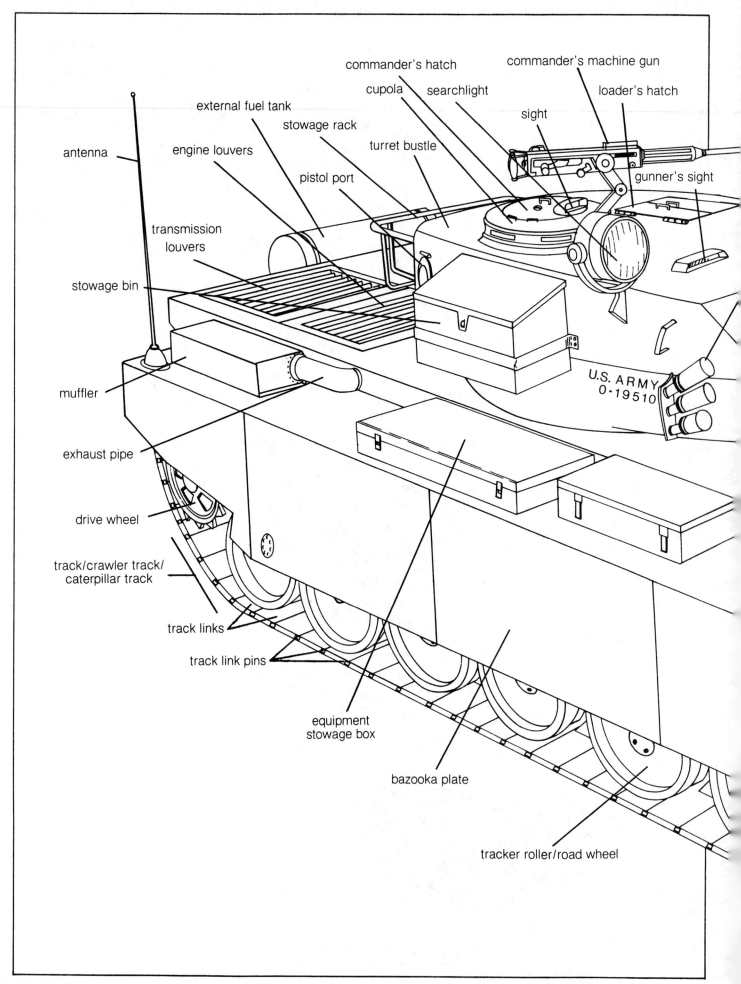

commander's hatch

commander's machine gun

cupola   searchlight

loader's hatch

external fuel tank

sight

stowage rack

turret bustle

antenna

engine louvers

pistol port

gunner's sight

transmission
louvers

stowage bin

U.S. ARMY
0-19510

muffler

exhaust pipe

drive wheel

track/crawler track/
caterpillar track

track links

track link pins

equipment
stowage box

bazooka plate

tracker roller/road wheel

Tank

A tank, such as the composite shown here, is an *armor-plated* vehicle consisting of a revolving *turret* set atop a tracked *hull*. Track links are sometimes covered with vulcanized rubber *pads*.

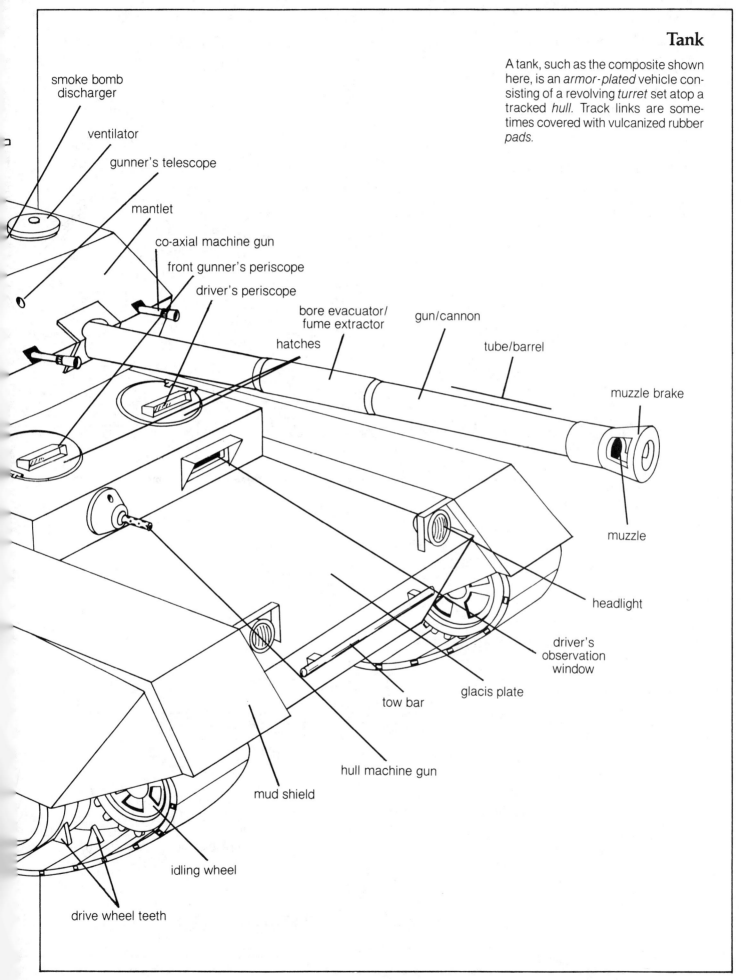

smoke bomb discharger

ventilator

gunner's telescope

mantlet

co-axial machine gun

front gunner's periscope

driver's periscope

bore evacuator/ fume extractor

gun/cannon

hatches

tube/barrel

muzzle brake

muzzle

headlight

driver's observation window

glacis plate

tow bar

hull machine gun

mud shield

idling wheel

drive wheel teeth

Surface Fighting Ship

Beginning with *dreadnoughts*, or *battleships*, modern surface *warships*, such as this *destroyer*, or *tin can*, have the capability to protect *shipping lanes*, deter invasions or support military operations on land. Today military vessels carry *surface-to-air missiles* and *surface-to-surface missiles*, as well as a range of *defensive guided weapons*. Many are *nuclear-powered*.

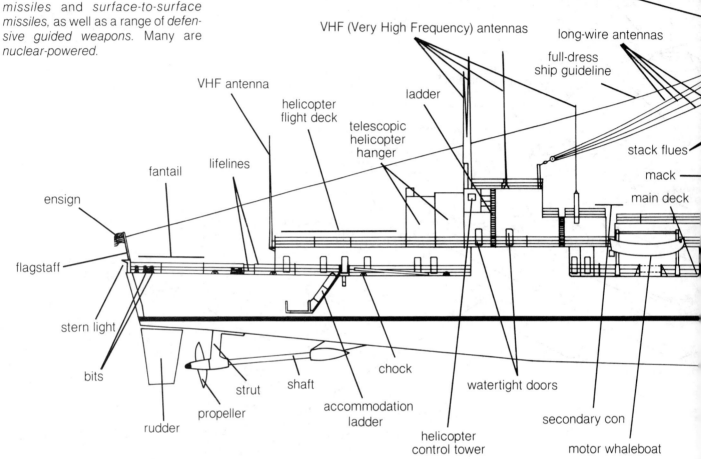

TACAN antenna

VHF (Very High Frequency) antennas

long-wire antennas

full-dress ship guideline

stack flues

mack

main deck

VHF antenna

helicopter flight deck

telescopic helicopter hanger

ladder

fantail

lifelines

ensign

flagstaff

stern light

bits

rudder

propeller

strut

shaft

accommodation ladder

chock

helicopter control tower

watertight doors

secondary con

motor whaleboat

Fighting Ship Types

scale 1:2,600

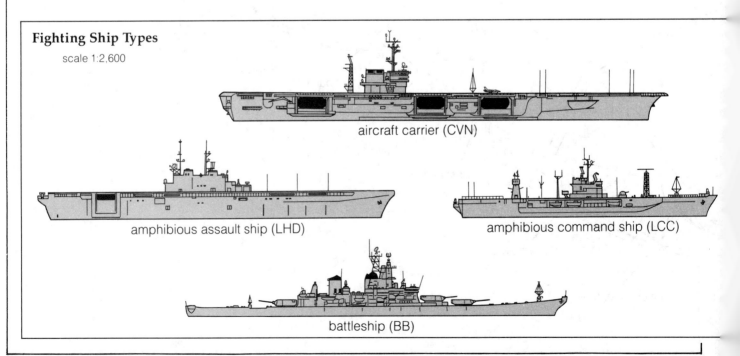

aircraft carrier (CVN)

amphibious assault ship (LHD)

amphibious command ship (LCC)

battleship (BB)

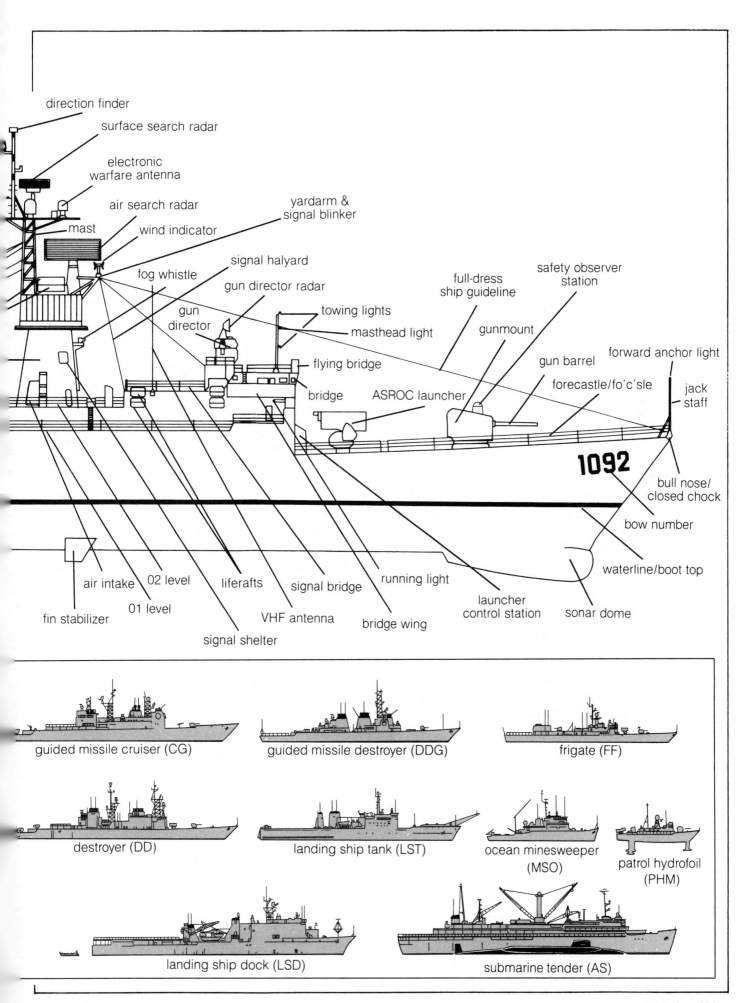

direction finder

surface search radar

electronic
warfare antenna

air search radar

mast

wind indicator

yardarm &
signal blinker

fog whistle

signal halyard

gun director radar

gun
director

towing lights

masthead light

flying bridge

bridge

full-dress
ship guideline

safety observer
station

gunmount

gun barrel

forecastle/fo'c'sle

forward anchor light

jack
staff

ASROC launcher

1092

bull nose/
closed chock

bow number

waterline/boot top

air intake

02 level

liferafts

signal bridge

running light

launcher
control station

sonar dome

fin stabilizer

01 level

VHF antenna

bridge wing

signal shelter

guided missile cruiser (CG)

guided missile destroyer (DDG)

frigate (FF)

destroyer (DD)

landing ship tank (LST)

ocean minesweeper
(MSO)

patrol hydrofoil
(PHM)

landing ship dock (LSD)

submarine tender (AS)

Fighting Ships

Aircraft Carrier

The superstructure on an aircraft carrier, or *flattop,* is called the *island.* On take-off, aircraft are assisted by steam-driven catapults located on the *flight deck* or *angled deck.*

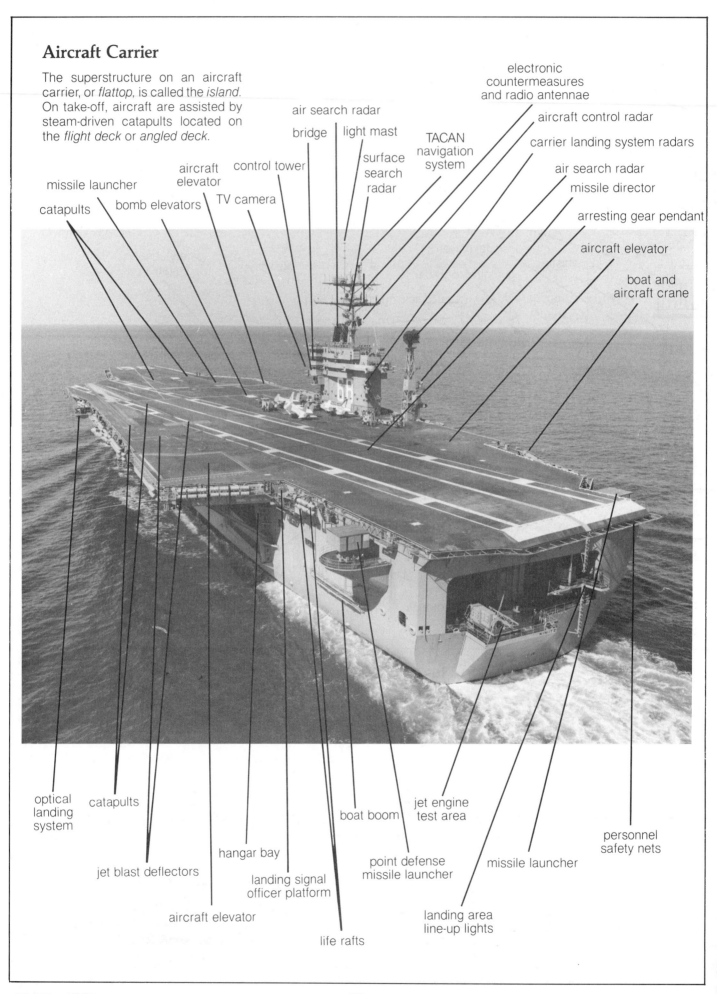

air search radar

bridge | light mast

control tower

TV camera

surface search radar

TACAN navigation system

electronic countermeasures and radio antennae

aircraft control radar

carrier landing system radars

air search radar

missile director

arresting gear pendant

aircraft elevator

boat and aircraft crane

missile launcher

catapults

aircraft elevator

bomb elevators

optical landing system

catapults

jet blast deflectors

hangar bay

landing signal officer platform

aircraft elevator

life rafts

boat boom

jet engine test area

point defense missile launcher

landing area line-up lights

missile launcher

personnel safety nets

Submarine

Submarines, formerly called *U-boats* or *pigboats,* have thick inner *pressure hulls* and lighter *outer hulls*. The space between hulls is divided into several *ballast tanks,* used to control the vessel's buoyancy and trim. The conning tower contains *radio* and *radar antennas* and various *periscopes,* used for observation and navigation. In older submarines the sail also contained a *snorkel tube.* Navigation underwater is accomplished by means of an *inertial guidance system.* In addition to missiles, submarines can carry *torpedoes.*

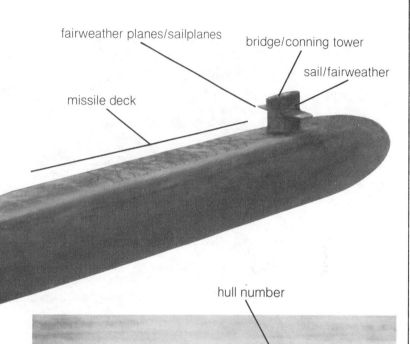

fairweather planes/sailplanes

bridge/conning tower

sail/fairweather

missile deck

rudder

propeller

diving plane

Fleet Ballistic Missile Submarine

hull number

Nuclear-Powered Attack Submarine

Torpedo

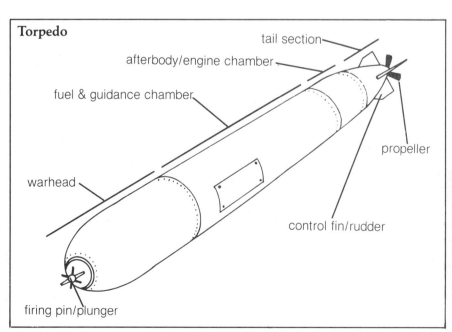

tail section

afterbody/engine chamber

fuel & guidance chamber

propeller

warhead

control fin/rudder

firing pin/plunger

Ballistic Missiles Launch Deck

hatch covers

launch tubes/silos

Combat Aircraft

A fighter, such as the one shown here, has an advanced *airframe* with a *variable sweep wing* and a *long-range weapon system*. It is flown at speeds in excess of the speed of sound, or *mach speeds*.

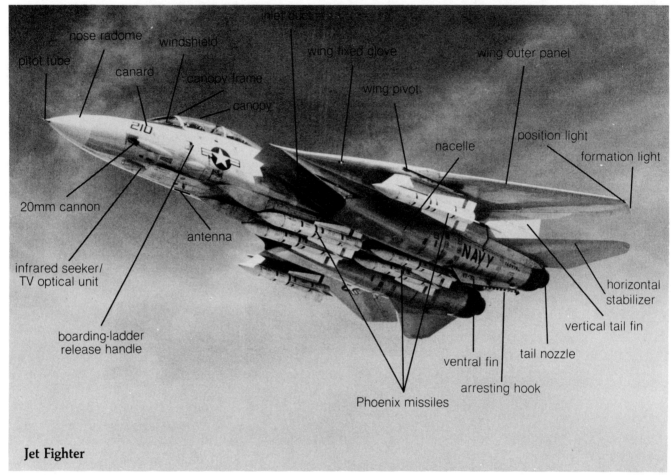

pilot tube

nose radome

canard

windshield

canopy frame

canopy

inlet duct

wing fixed glove

wing pivot

wing outer panel

position light

formation light

nacelle

20mm cannon

antenna

infrared seeker/ TV optical unit

boarding-ladder release handle

Phoenix missiles

ventral fin

arresting hook

tail nozzle

vertical tail fin

horizontal stabilizer

Jet Fighter

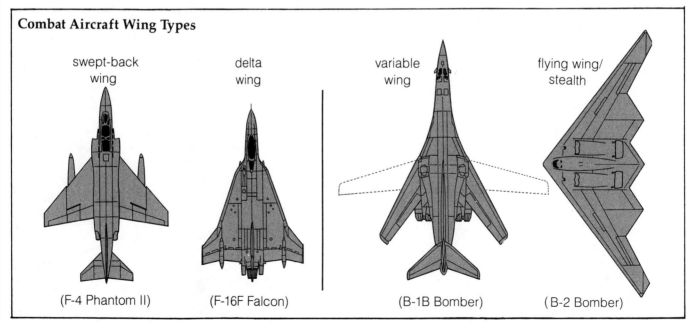

Combat Aircraft Wing Types

swept-back wing

delta wing

variable wing

flying wing/ stealth

(F-4 Phantom II)

(F-16F Falcon)

(B-1B Bomber)

(B-2 Bomber)

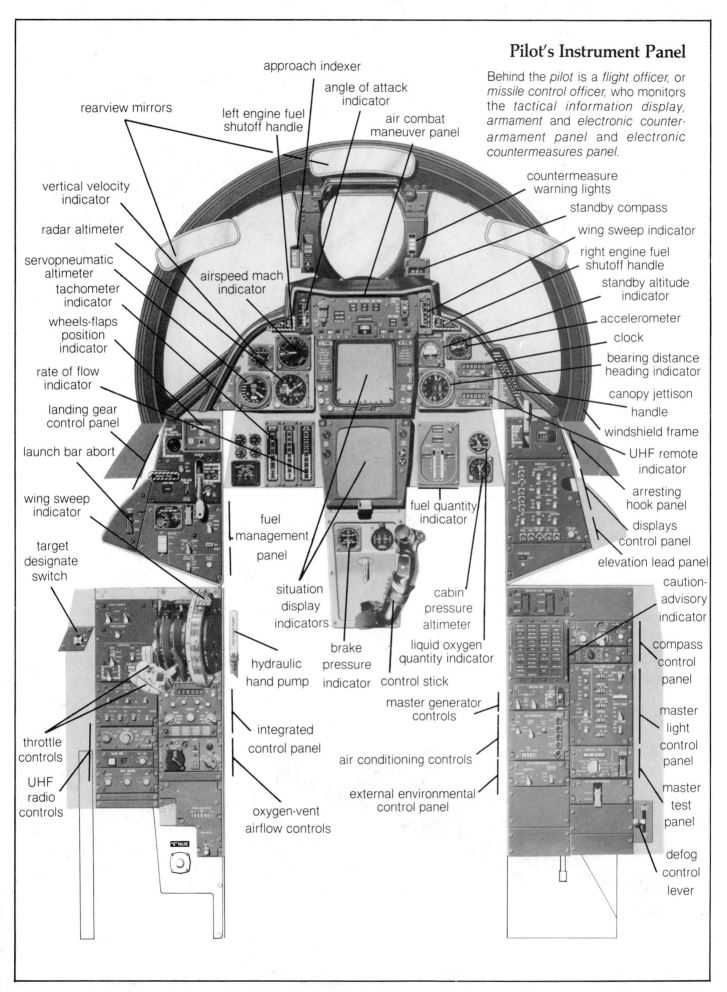

Pilot's Instrument Panel

Behind the *pilot* is a *flight officer*, or *missile control officer*, who monitors the *tactical information display*, *armament* and *electronic counter-armament panel* and *electronic countermeasures panel*.

approach indexer

angle of attack indicator

air combat maneuver panel

left engine fuel shutoff handle

rearview mirrors

vertical velocity indicator

radar altimeter

servopneumatic altimeter

tachometer indicator

wheels-flaps position indicator

rate of flow indicator

landing gear control panel

launch bar abort

wing sweep indicator

target designate switch

throttle controls

UHF radio controls

airspeed mach indicator

fuel management panel

situation display indicators

hydraulic hand pump

integrated control panel

oxygen-vent airflow controls

brake pressure indicator

control stick

master generator controls

air conditioning controls

external environmental control panel

fuel quantity indicator

cabin pressure altimeter

liquid oxygen quantity indicator

countermeasure warning lights

standby compass

wing sweep indicator

right engine fuel shutoff handle

standby altitude indicator

accelerometer

clock

bearing distance heading indicator

canopy jettison handle

windshield frame

UHF remote indicator

arresting hook panel

displays control panel

elevation lead panel

caution-advisory indicator

compass control panel

master light control panel

master test panel

defog control lever

481   **Combat Aircraft**

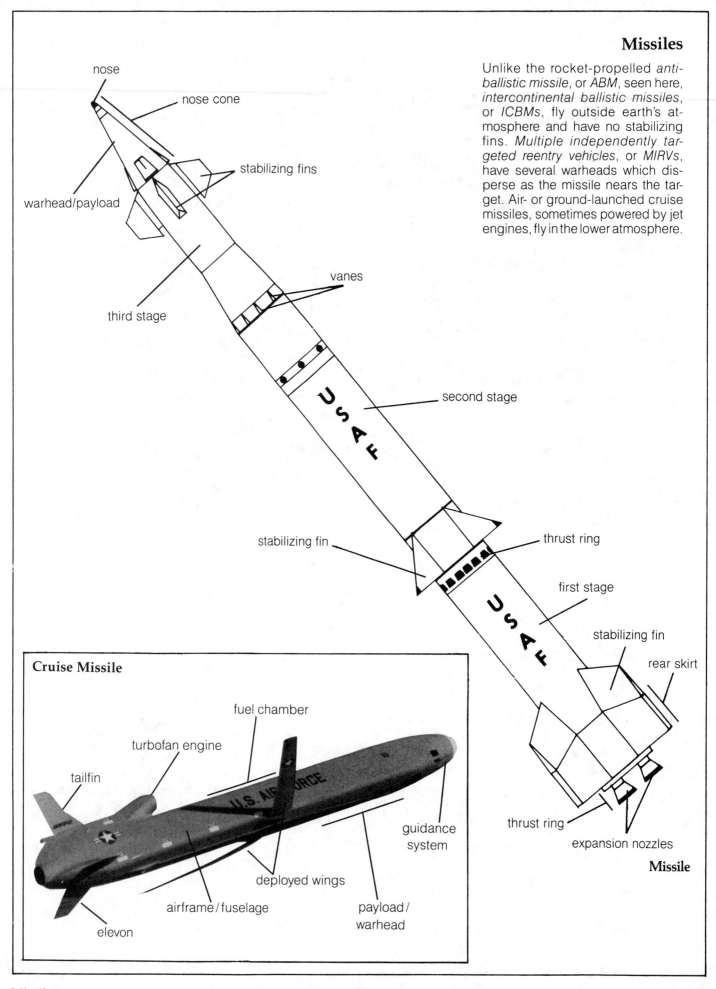

Missiles

Unlike the rocket-propelled *anti-ballistic missile*, or *ABM*, seen here, *intercontinental ballistic missiles*, or *ICBMs*, fly outside earth's atmosphere and have no stabilizing fins. *Multiple independently targeted reentry vehicles*, or *MIRVs*, have several warheads which disperse as the missile nears the target. Air- or ground-launched cruise missiles, sometimes powered by jet engines, fly in the lower atmosphere.

nose

nose cone

stabilizing fins

warhead/payload

vanes

third stage

second stage

stabilizing fin

thrust ring

first stage

stabilizing fin

rear skirt

USAF

USAF

Cruise Missile

fuel chamber

turbofan engine

tailfin

U.S. AIR FORCE

guidance system

elevon

deployed wings

airframe/fuselage

payload/warhead

thrust ring

expansion nozzles

Missile

Uniforms, Costumes and Ceremonial Attire

The attire presented in this section ranges from vestments and formal dress used on special occasions to dress of distinctive design or fashion worn by members of particular groups. The parts of military or municipal attire, for example, serve to identify not only branch of service but rank and distinction as well.

Garb can be highly stylized or informal. Manchu Court dress, for example, was worn only on formal occasions, whereas the clothes commonly worn by cowboys, dictated by the demands of the profession, was casual.

In addition to the trappings that have come to typify characters in history— a general, pirate, miser, magician—this section also includes clothing used by performers such as clowns, ballet dancers and drum majorettes.

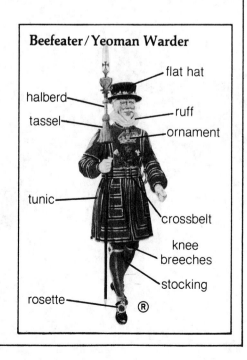

Beefeater / Yeoman Warder

halberd

tassel

tunic

rosette

flat hat

ruff

ornament

crossbelt

knee breeches

stocking

483

Royal Regalia

In coronations and investitures, a king wears a blunted sword called a *curtein* on his sash. Among a queen's foundation garments, or *underpinnings,* are a *corset, corselet, chemise* and *pantaloons.*

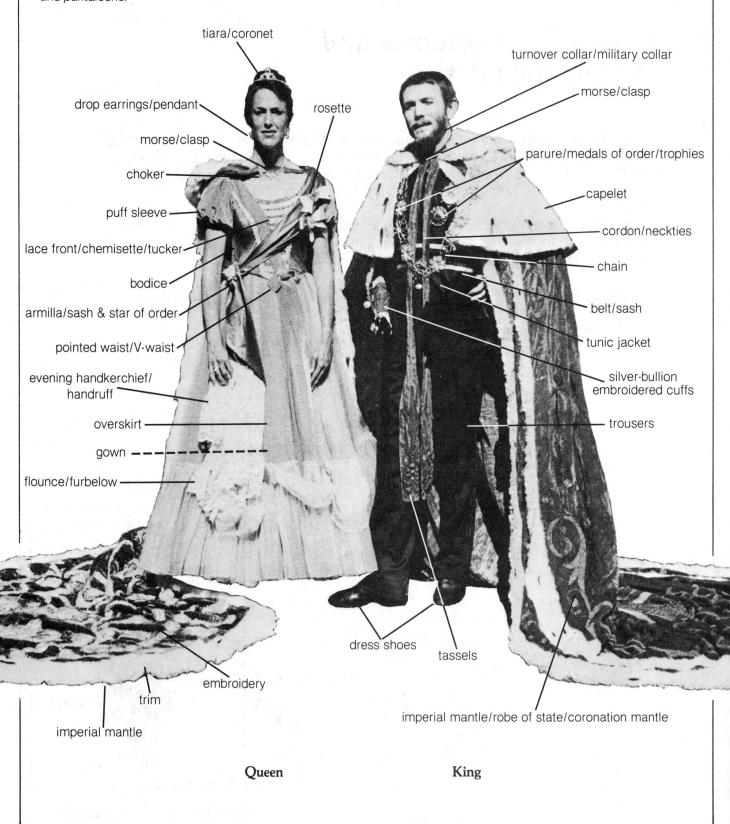

tiara/coronet

drop earrings/pendant

rosette

morse/clasp

choker

puff sleeve

lace front/chemisette/tucker

bodice

armilla/sash & star of order

pointed waist/V-waist

evening handkerchief/ handruff

overskirt

gown

flounce/furbelow

embroidery

trim

imperial mantle

turnover collar/military collar

morse/clasp

parure/medals of order/trophies

capelet

cordon/neckties

chain

belt/sash

tunic jacket

silver-bullion embroidered cuffs

trousers

dress shoes

tassels

imperial mantle/robe of state/coronation mantle

Queen

King

Royal Regalia

A *coronet* is a small crown worn by royalty ranking below the reigning monarch. A *tiara* is a royal head-piece, usually consisting of a *diadem,* or band, tied around the forehead, supporting several tiers of ornaments. A wreath, or circlet of leaves, worn as a crown or collar is a *garland.*

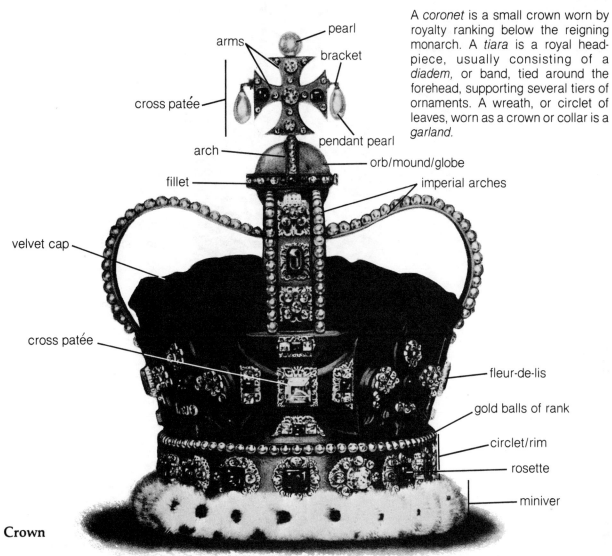

arms
pearl
bracket
cross patée
pendant pearl
arch
orb/mound/globe
fillet
imperial arches
velvet cap
cross patée
fleur-de-lis
gold balls of rank
circlet/rim
rosette
miniver

Crown

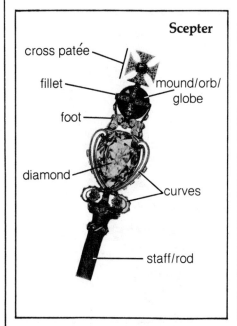

Scepter

cross patée
fillet
mound/orb/globe
foot
diamond
curves
staff/rod

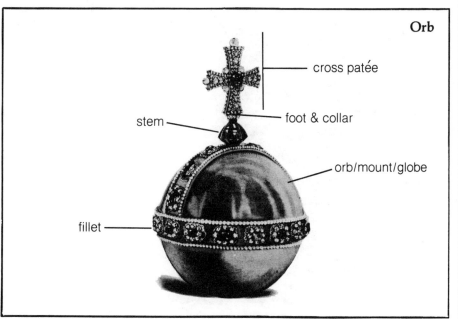

Orb

cross patée
stem
foot & collar
orb/mount/globe
fillet

Royal Vestments

Jewish Ritual Items

During regular service in a *Temple,* or *Synagogue,* excerpts are read by the *Rabbi,* who is assisted in leading the service by a *Cantor,* who sings the liturgy. Their vestments are the same as the rest of the congregation. During morning prayer, a *shel rosh,* similar to the tefillin, is worn on the forehead. Some Jews hang a *mezuzah,* a decorative box containing passages from the Torah, on the doorpost of their homes.

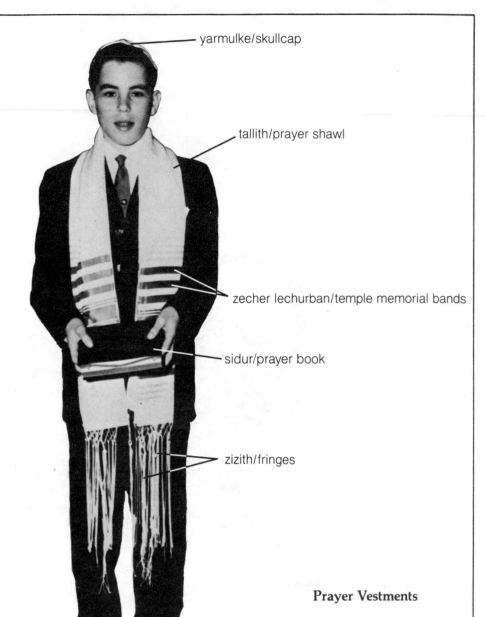

yarmulke/skullcap

tallith/prayer shawl

zecher lechurban/temple memorial bands

sidur/prayer book

zizith/fringes

Prayer Vestments

Ner Tamid/eternal light

Torah

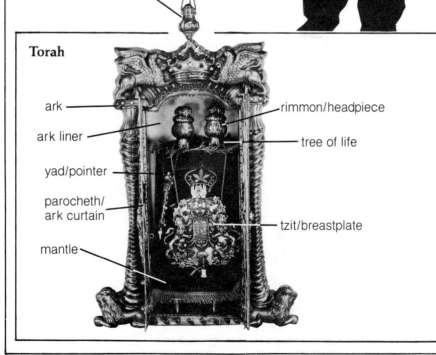

ark

ark liner

yad/pointer

parocheth/ark curtain

mantle

rimmon/headpiece

tree of life

tzit/breastplate

Tefillin/Phylacteries

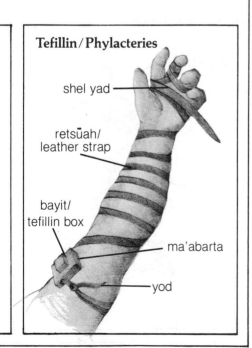

shel yad

retsūah/leather strap

bayit/tefillin box

ma'abarta

yod

Religious Vestments

The small square cap with three corners worn by Roman Catholic clergy is a *biretta*. Ropes, belts or sashes used to keep vestments closed are *cinctures*. Traditionally, the white band worn by nuns to encircle their faces is a *wimple*, while the wide cloth worn below it to cover their necks and shoulders is a *guimpe*. The ring worn by the Pope is the *Ring of the Fisherman*.

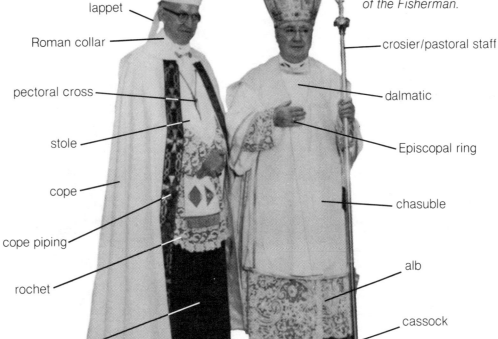

simple miter

precious miter

lappet

Roman collar

pectoral cross

stole

cope

cope piping

rochet

cassock

crosier/pastoral staff

dalmatic

Episcopal ring

chasuble

alb

cassock

Bishop   **Cardinal**

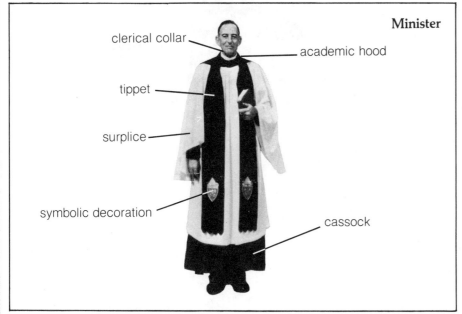

Minister

clerical collar

academic hood

tippet

surplice

symbolic decoration

cassock

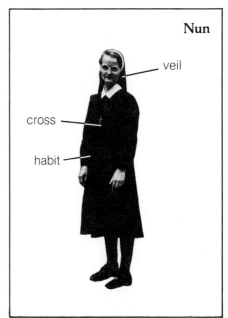

Nun

veil

cross

habit

487

Religious Attire

Bride and Groom

The bride, wearing white to symbolize purity, and a veil, symbol of modesty, is carrying a fan rather than the more traditional *wedding,* or *bridal, bouquet,* or *nosegay.* Some grooms wear semiformal evening dress at weddings: *tuxedos,* or *tuxes,* which are worn with *cummerbunds,* broad *waistbands, pleated* or *ruffled shirts* with *studs,* and *bow ties.*

picture hat/Gainsborough

veil

appliquéd lace/point d'appliqué

attached bertha/cascade collar/jabot

fan

princess waistline

modified leg-of-mutton sleeve/ modified bishop sleeve

fitted cuff

lace glove

train

scalloped hem

pumps

standing collar

white tie

boutonniere

formal shirt

cutaway coat/ morning coat

waistcoat/vest

French cuff

trousers

tail

Bridal Dress/Gown

Men's Formal Attire

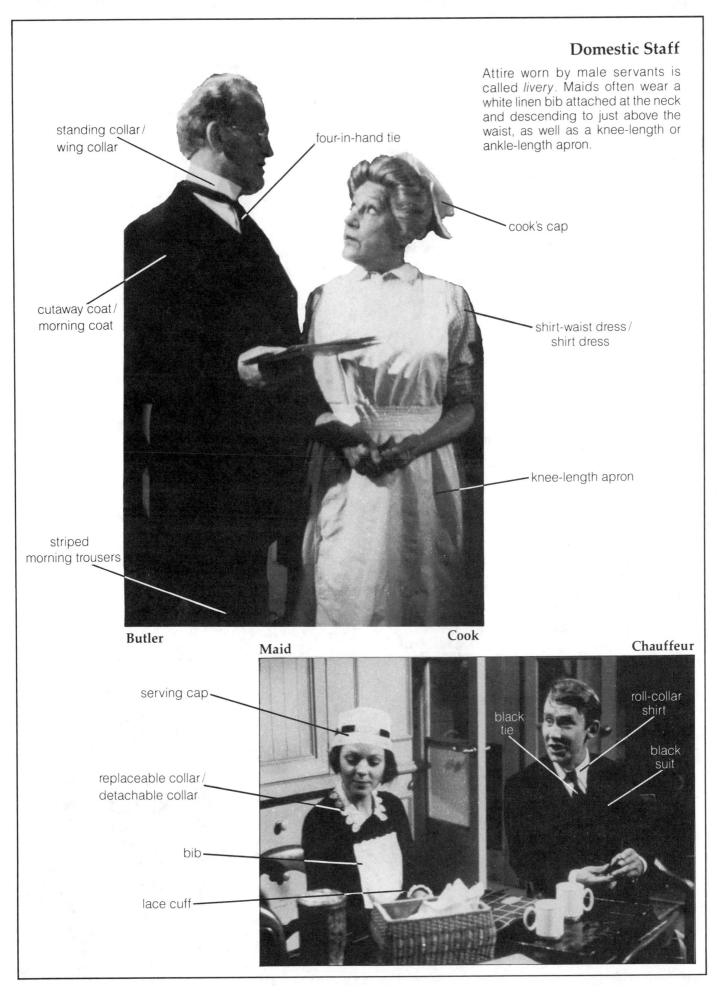

Domestic Staff

Attire worn by male servants is called *livery*. Maids often wear a white linen bib attached at the neck and descending to just above the waist, as well as a knee-length or ankle-length apron.

standing collar / wing collar

four-in-hand tie

cook's cap

cutaway coat / morning coat

shirt-waist dress / shirt dress

knee-length apron

striped morning trousers

Butler

Cook

Maid

Chauffeur

serving cap

replaceable collar / detachable collar

bib

lace cuff

black tie

roll-collar shirt

black suit

Servants' Attire

Cowboy and Indian

On the range, cowboys, *cow punchers*, or *buckaroos*, carried *oilskin slickers*, a *tarp*, and heavy cotton or wool quilts to make up a *bedroll, crumb incubator, shakedown*, or *fleatrap*. Bullets, carried in *loops* on *cartridge belts*, were known as *blue whistlers* or *lead plums*. A cowboy's *ten-gallon hat* was held in place in a wind by buckskin thongs known as *bonnet strings*.

Members of most Indian tribes wore *leggings* and *moccasins*. Many decorated their faces with *war paint* prior to battle. Indians in the East shaved their heads except for a ridge of hair in the middle called a *roach*.

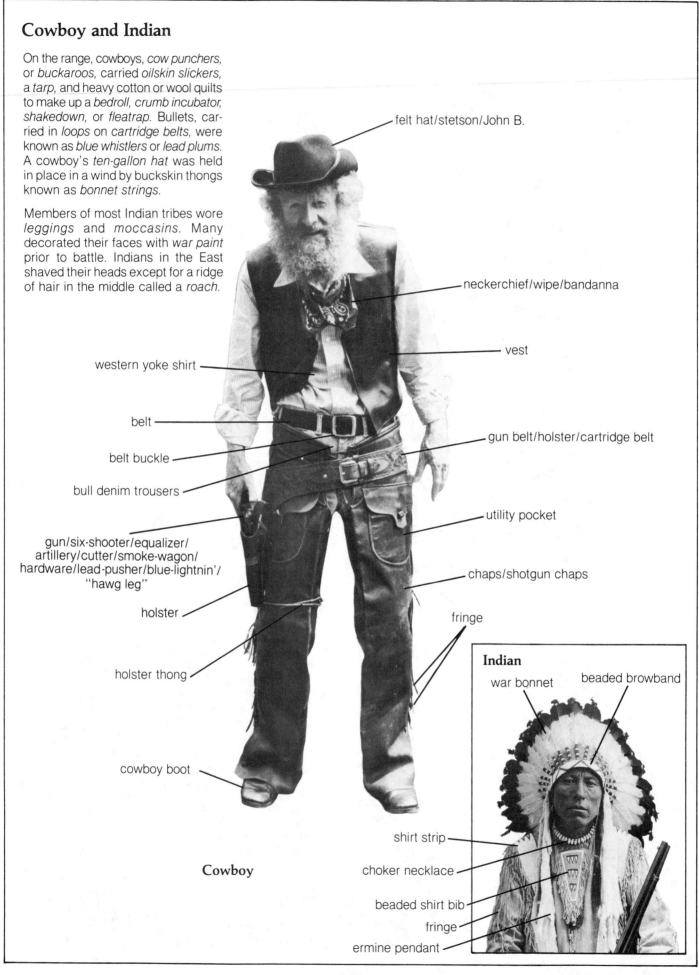

felt hat/stetson/John B.

neckerchief/wipe/bandanna

vest

western yoke shirt

belt

belt buckle

bull denim trousers

gun/six-shooter/equalizer/
artillery/cutter/smoke-wagon/
hardware/lead-pusher/blue-lightnin'/
"hawg leg"

holster

holster thong

cowboy boot

gun belt/holster/cartridge belt

utility pocket

chaps/shotgun chaps

fringe

Cowboy

Indian

war bonnet

beaded browband

shirt strip

choker necklace

beaded shirt bib

fringe

ermine pendant

Native Dress

Romans wore full-length, loose-fitting robes called *togas*. East Indian women wear *sarongs*, but Indian (Hindu) women wear *saris*. An ankle-length Middle East garment with long sleeves and a waist sash is called a *caftan*. The loose-fitting, sleeveless robes worn by Arabs are called *abas*.

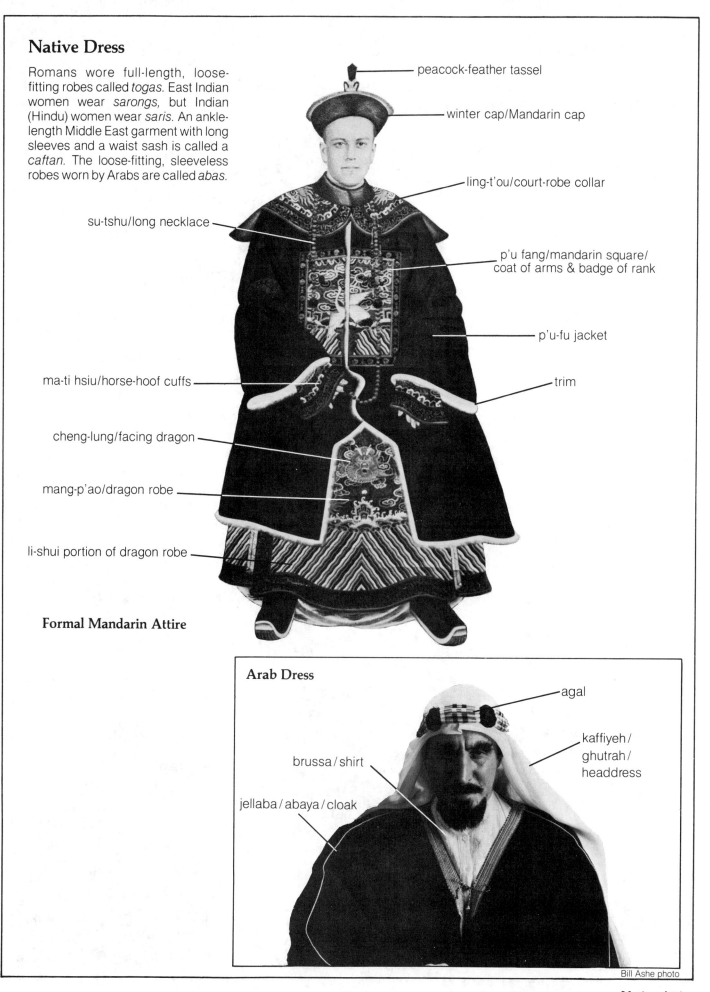

peacock-feather tassel

winter cap/Mandarin cap

ling-t'ou/court-robe collar

su-tshu/long necklace

p'u fang/mandarin square/ coat of arms & badge of rank

p'u-fu jacket

ma-ti hsiu/horse-hoof cuffs

trim

cheng-lung/facing dragon

mang-p'ao/dragon robe

li-shui portion of dragon robe

Formal Mandarin Attire

Arab Dress

agal

kaffiyeh/ ghutrah/ headdress

brussa/shirt

jellaba/abaya/cloak

Bill Ashe photo

Native Attire

Historical Costumes

Many characters in popular lore and history have become identified or associated with the clothing they wear. Other military attire worn by *Revolutionary* officers included a tunic, a plain jacket with a stiff collar, and a particularly heavy overcoat called a *greatcoat*.

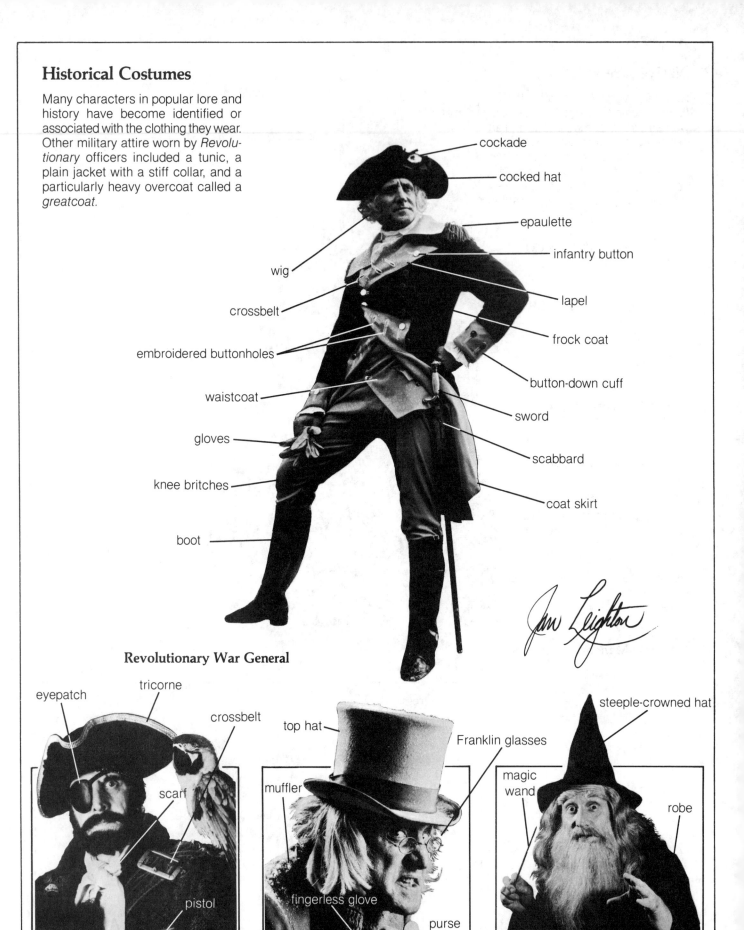

cockade

cocked hat

epaulette

infantry button

lapel

frock coat

button-down cuff

sword

scabbard

coat skirt

wig

crossbelt

embroidered buttonholes

waistcoat

gloves

knee britches

boot

Revolutionary War General

eyepatch

tricorne

crossbelt

scarf

pistol

Pirate

top hat

muffler

Franklin glasses

fingerless glove

purse

Miser

steeple-crowned hat

magic wand

robe

Wizard

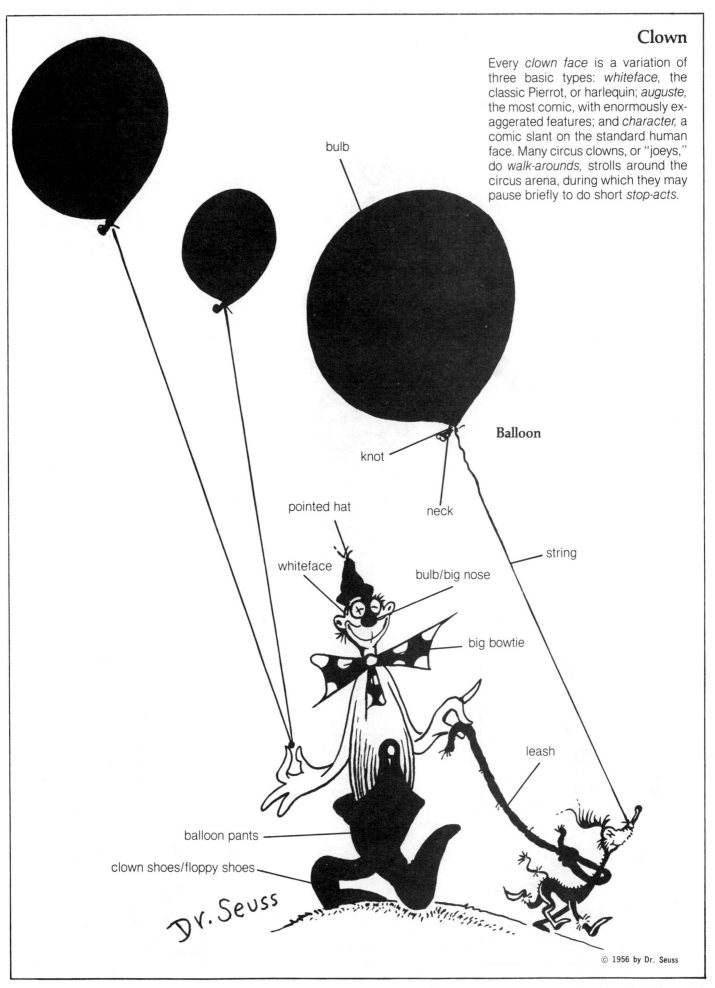

Clown

Every *clown face* is a variation of three basic types: *whiteface,* the classic Pierrot, or harlequin; *auguste,* the most comic, with enormously exaggerated features; and *character,* a comic slant on the standard human face. Many circus clowns, or "joeys," do *walk-arounds,* strolls around the circus arena, during which they may pause briefly to do short *stop-acts.*

bulb

Balloon

knot

neck

string

pointed hat

whiteface

bulb/big nose

big bowtie

leash

balloon pants

clown shoes/floppy shoes

Dr. Seuss

Performers' Costumes

Ballet Dancer

The toeshoes worn by this *ballerina* are satin covered. Cloth mache has replaced wooden box toes. A short skirt of layered net often worn by female dancers is called a *tutu*.

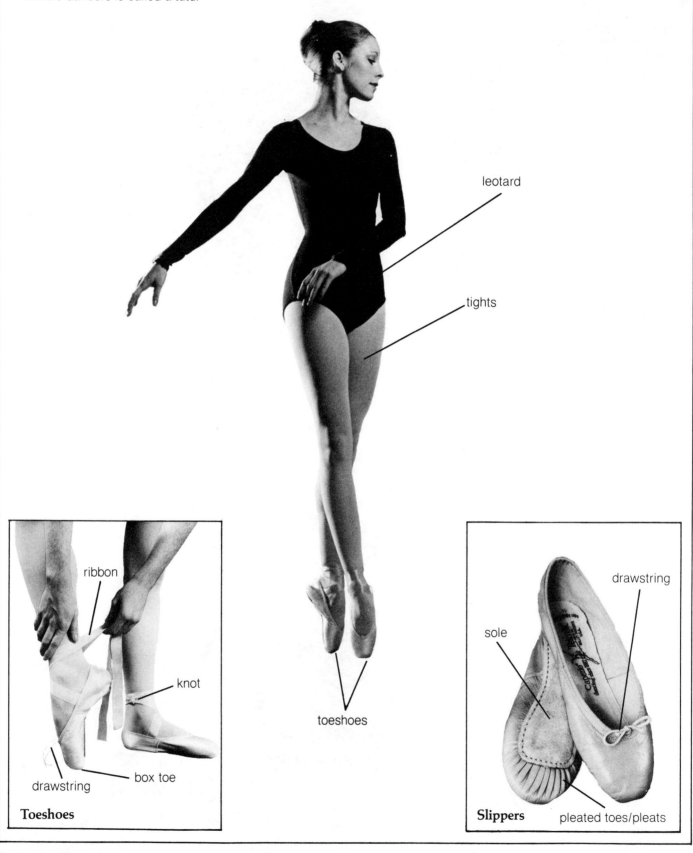

leotard

tights

ribbon

knot

drawstring

box toe

Toeshoes

toeshoes

sole

drawstring

Slippers

pleated toes/pleats

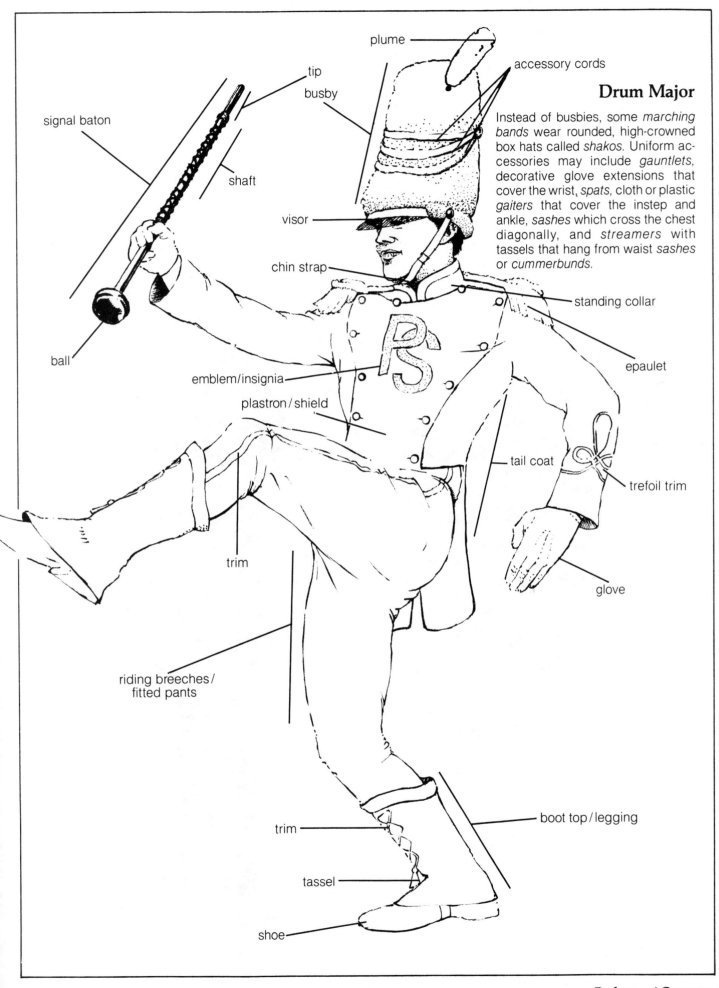

signal baton

tip

busby

plume

accessory cords

shaft

Drum Major

Instead of busbies, some *marching bands* wear rounded, high-crowned box hats called *shakos*. Uniform accessories may include *gauntlets*, decorative glove extensions that cover the wrist, *spats*, cloth or plastic *gaiters* that cover the instep and ankle, *sashes* which cross the chest diagonally, and *streamers* with tassels that hang from waist *sashes* or *cummerbunds*.

visor

chin strap

standing collar

ball

epaulet

emblem/insignia

plastron/shield

tail coat

trefoil trim

glove

trim

riding breeches/
fitted pants

boot top/legging

trim

tassel

shoe

Performers' Costumes

Military Uniforms

The *uniform of the day* is worn for the season, day or occasion. A cloth band worn around the arm above the elbow, such as the one worn by *Military Police,* or *MPs,* is a *brassard.* A leather belt for a dress uniform is a *Sam Browne, or garrison, belt.* Service ribbons are worn on a *ribbon bar.* The only *neck decoration* awarded to members of the armed services is the *Medal of Honor.*

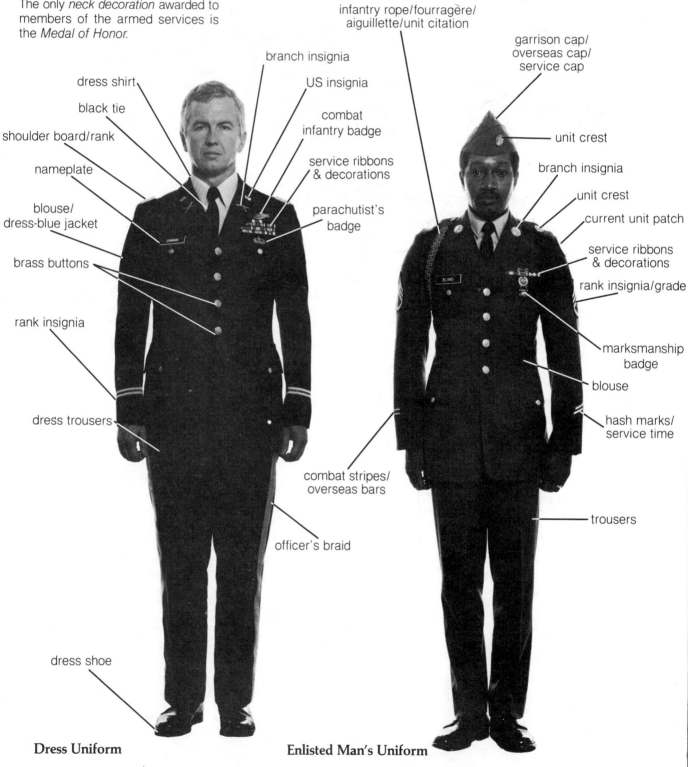

infantry rope/fourragère/
aiguillette/unit citation

branch insignia

US insignia

combat
infantry badge

service ribbons
& decorations

parachutist's
badge

dress shirt

black tie

shoulder board/rank

nameplate

blouse/
dress-blue jacket

brass buttons

rank insignia

dress trousers

combat stripes/
overseas bars

officer's braid

dress shoe

garrison cap/
overseas cap/
service cap

unit crest

branch insignia

unit crest

current unit patch

service ribbons
& decorations

rank insignia/grade

marksmanship
badge

blouse

hash marks/
service time

trousers

Dress Uniform

Enlisted Man's Uniform

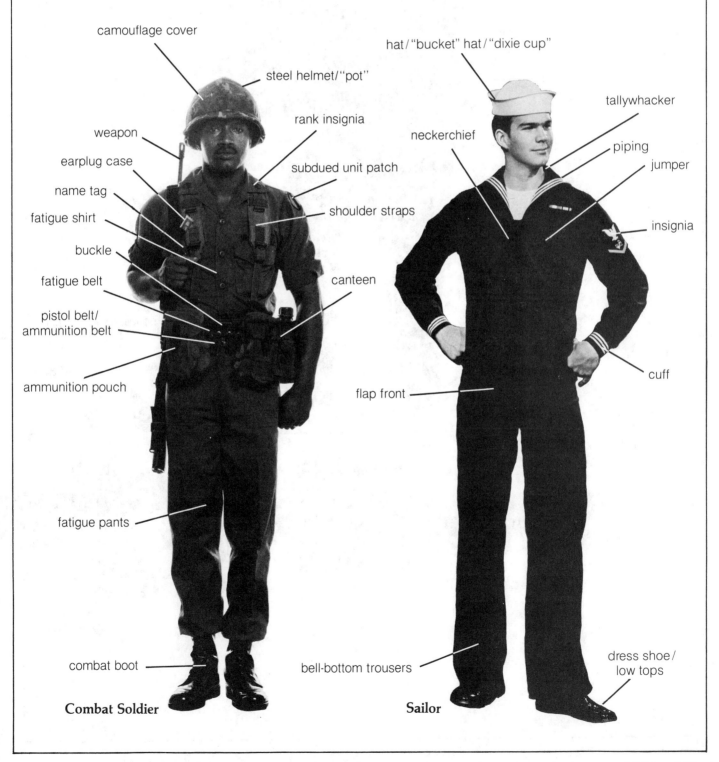

Military Uniforms

An *infantryman*, or "grunt," carries a *rain poncho* on his ammunition belt. A sailor, "swab," or " gob," may wear a *watch cap, leggings* and a *jersey* instead of a jumper. Sailors aboard ship keep their clothing in *seabags*.

Combat Soldier labels:
- camouflage cover
- steel helmet/"pot"
- weapon
- rank insignia
- earplug case
- subdued unit patch
- name tag
- shoulder straps
- fatigue shirt
- buckle
- fatigue belt
- canteen
- pistol belt/ ammunition belt
- ammunition pouch
- fatigue pants
- combat boot

Sailor labels:
- hat/"bucket" hat/"dixie cup"
- tallywhacker
- neckerchief
- piping
- jumper
- insignia
- cuff
- flap front
- bell-bottom trousers
- dress shoe/ low tops

Combat Soldier

Sailor

Military Attire

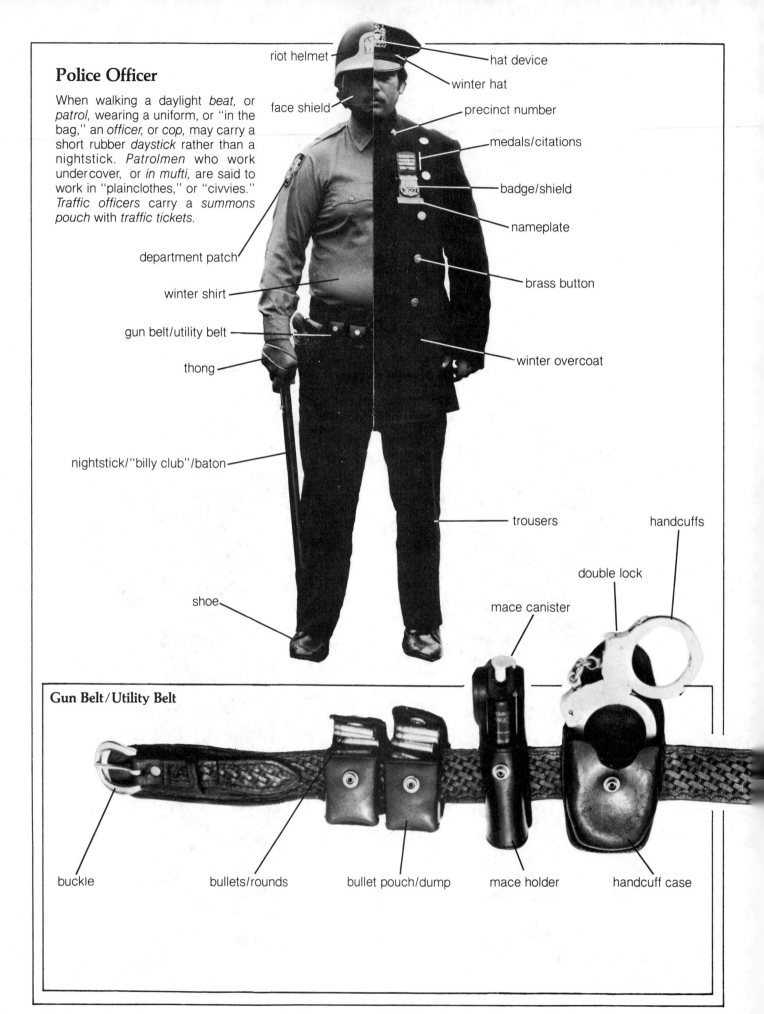

Police Officer

When walking a daylight *beat,* or *patrol,* wearing a uniform, or "in the bag," an *officer,* or *cop,* may carry a short rubber *daystick* rather than a nightstick. *Patrolmen* who work undercover, or *in mufti,* are said to work in "plainclothes," or "civvies." *Traffic officers* carry a *summons pouch* with *traffic tickets.*

riot helmet

hat device

winter hat

face shield

precinct number

medals/citations

badge/shield

nameplate

department patch

brass button

winter shirt

gun belt/utility belt

winter overcoat

thong

nightstick/"billy club"/baton

trousers

handcuffs

double lock

mace canister

shoe

Gun Belt/Utility Belt

buckle

bullets/rounds

bullet pouch/dump

mace holder

handcuff case

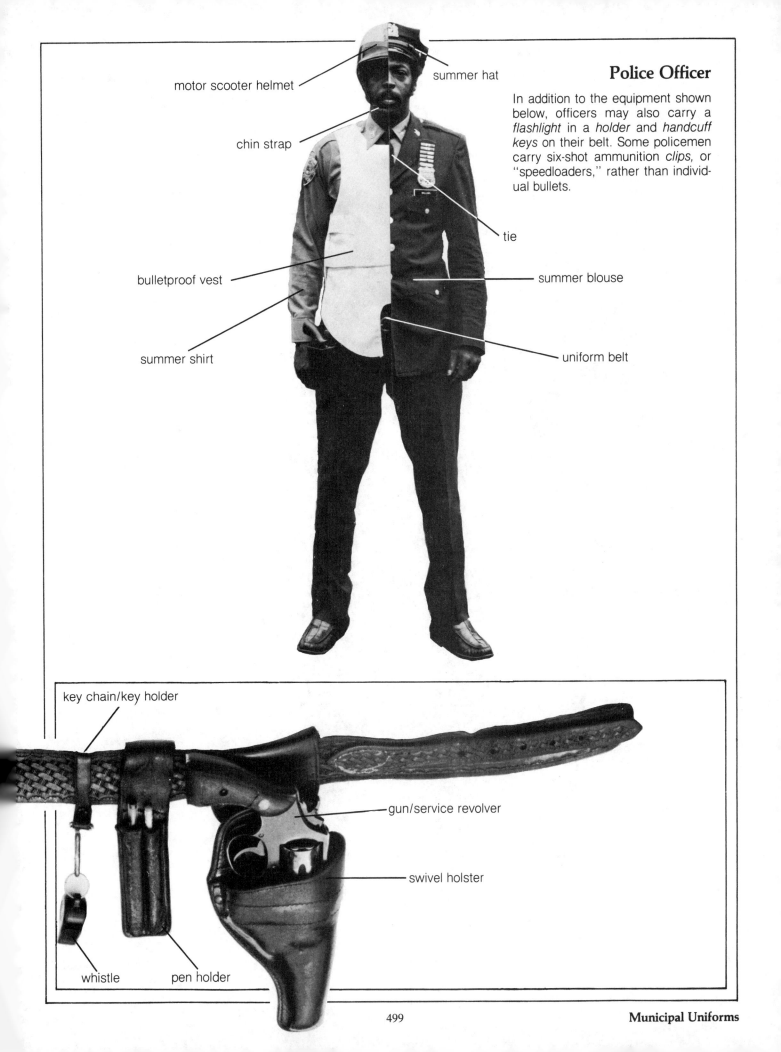

motor scooter helmet

summer hat

chin strap

Police Officer

In addition to the equipment shown below, officers may also carry a *flashlight* in a *holder* and *handcuff keys* on their belt. Some policemen carry six-shot ammunition *clips,* or "speedloaders," rather than individual bullets.

tie

bulletproof vest

summer blouse

summer shirt

uniform belt

key chain/key holder

gun/service revolver

swivel holster

whistle   pen holder

Municipal Uniforms

Fireman

A fireman's working uniform is called his *turnouts*.

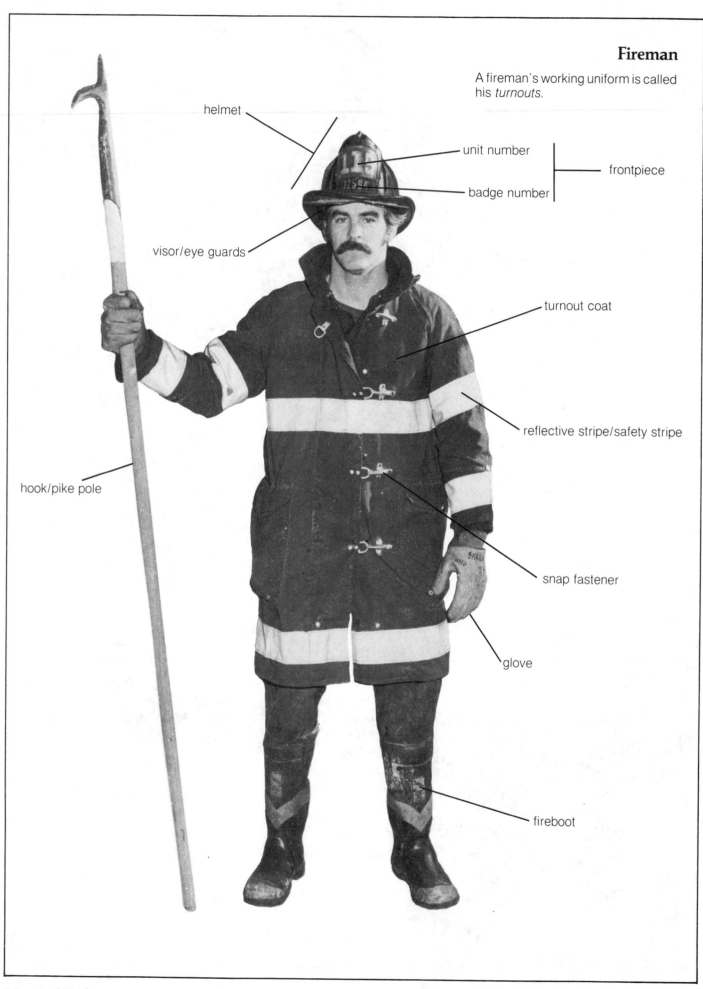

helmet

unit number

badge number

frontpiece

visor/eye guards

turnout coat

reflective stripe/safety stripe

hook/pike pole

snap fastener

glove

fireboot

Signs and Symbols

While signs and symbols take the place of language or are used to represent meaning, either by suggestion, relationship or association, many have parts for which there are proper names. A flag is used as a sign of a nation, for example, or as a symbol of patriotism, yet it has distinctive components which are identifiable.

Other signs, such as editing and proofreading marks, also included in this section, are used to convey instructions, while sign language is a set of gestures used as a substitute for words or letters.

The fields of science, business and industry have all devised signs whose meanings have legal as well as instructional implications, and the world of transportation is largely controlled by traffic signs. Even hobos, whose pictographs appear here, use pictorial signs instead of written language to communicate messages.

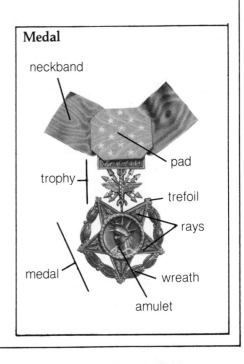

Medal

neckband

pad

trophy

trefoil

rays

medal

wreath

amulet

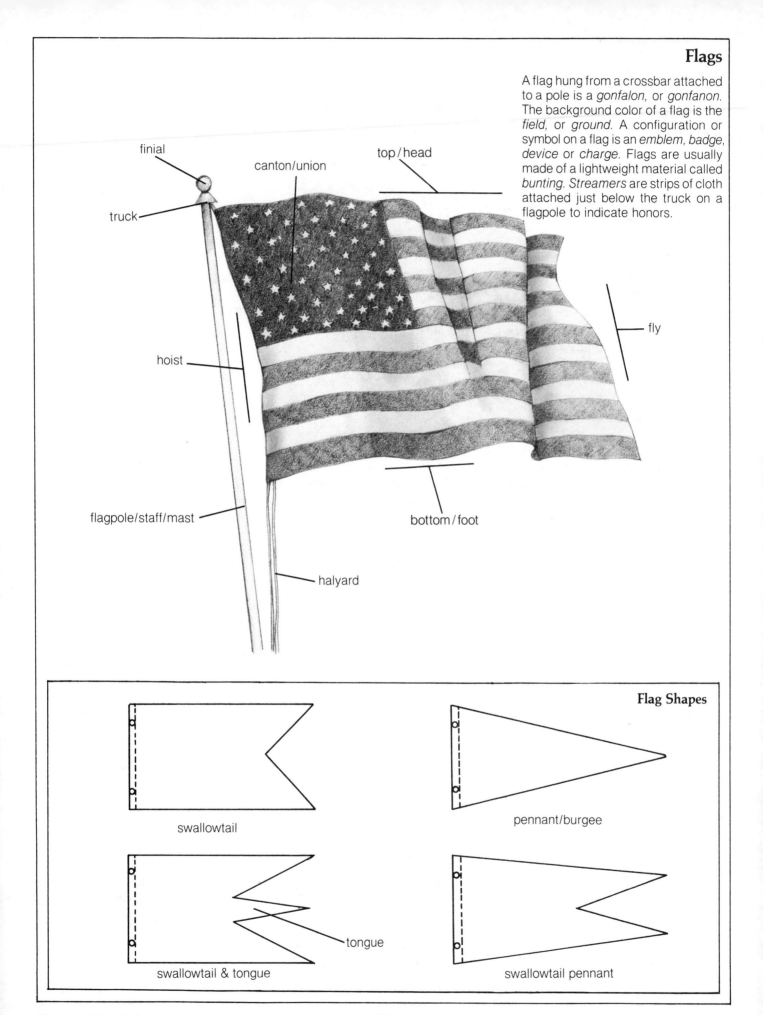

Flags

finial

canton/union

top/head

truck

A flag hung from a crossbar attached to a pole is a *gonfalon,* or *gonfanon.* The background color of a flag is the *field,* or *ground.* A configuration or symbol on a flag is an *emblem, badge, device* or *charge.* Flags are usually made of a lightweight material called *bunting. Streamers* are strips of cloth attached just below the truck on a flagpole to indicate honors.

hoist

fly

flagpole/staff/mast

bottom/foot

halyard

Flag Shapes

swallowtail

pennant/burgee

tongue

swallowtail & tongue

swallowtail pennant

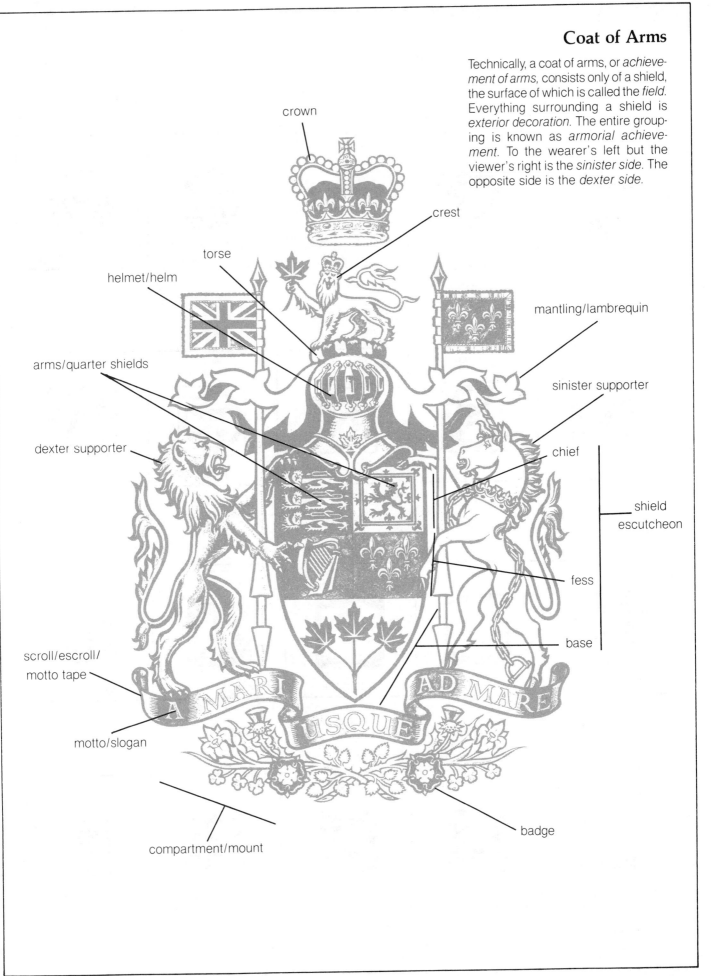

Coat of Arms

Technically, a coat of arms, or *achievement of arms,* consists only of a shield, the surface of which is called the *field.* Everything surrounding a shield is *exterior decoration.* The entire grouping is known as *armorial achievement.* To the wearer's left but the viewer's right is the *sinister side.* The opposite side is the *dexter side.*

crown

crest

torse

helmet/helm

mantling/lambrequin

arms/quarter shields

sinister supporter

dexter supporter

chief

shield
escutcheon

fess

base

scroll/escroll/
motto tape

A MARI USQUE AD MARE

motto/slogan

badge

compartment/mount

stop	yield	one way	one-way traffic/ do not enter	railroad crossing

no bicycles	no trucks	no U turn	no right turn	no left turn

interstate route	U.S. route	state route	trail	bike route

picnic area	camping	trailer park	hospital	telephone

Road Signs

With the exception of *route signs*, which are different shapes and colors, road signs are color-coded: red signs are *prohibit movement signs;* yellow are *warning signs;* white are *regulatory signs;* orange are *construction signs;* blue are *service signs;* green are *guide signs.* Octagonal red signs are used exclusively for *stop signs.* Rectangular signs with white letters on a green background are *destination signs.*

signal ahead	two-way traffic	no-passing zone	divided highway ends	merge

merge left	winding road	slippery when wet	hill	school crossing

pedestrian crossing	bicycle crossing	farm machinery	cattle crossing	deer crossing

Signs and Symbols

Public Signs

Pasigraphy is a universal written language that uses signs and symbols rather than words, whereas *pictographs* can represent an object as well as a thought. A symbol or character that represents a word, syllable or phoneme is a *phonogram*. A symbolic representation of an idea rather than a word is an *ideogram* or *ideograph*.

first aid

information

handicapped

hotel/motel

restaurant

coffee shop

bar

no smoking

toilets

taxi stand

bus transportation

air transportation

car rental

rail transportation

elevator

baggage check-in

baggage claim

customs

lost and found

telephone

mail

gas station

no parking

parking

mechanic

picnic area

campfires

bicycle trail

hiking trail

playground

launching ramp

horse trail

no entry

Signs and Symbols

Gestures

A gesture, the movement of the head, arm, hand or body to express reaction, emotion, opinion or a concept, can be one of friendship (as in a kiss, a hug, nose rubbing, back slapping) or one of anger (with a clenched fist or a raised middle finger).

approval disapproval

everything's OK / perfection

you're out / hitch-hiking

for good luck

the end / cut it / "throat-cutting"

blunder / faux pas

close escape / close call

no money

money / "pay up"

good luck / knock-on-wood

beckoning / come here

excessive talk / "yackety-yak"

self-congratulation

close relationship

derision / mockery

victory / V-sign

odd / foolish / "crazy"

annoyance / exasperation

Signs and Symbols

Religious Symbols

The symbols shown here represent beliefs and religions such as Christianity, Judaism, Islam, Shinto, as well as Chinese philosophy. The ankh was an ancient Egyptian *symbol of life,* and the gammadion was an eon-old Oriental and Indian *good luck symbol.*

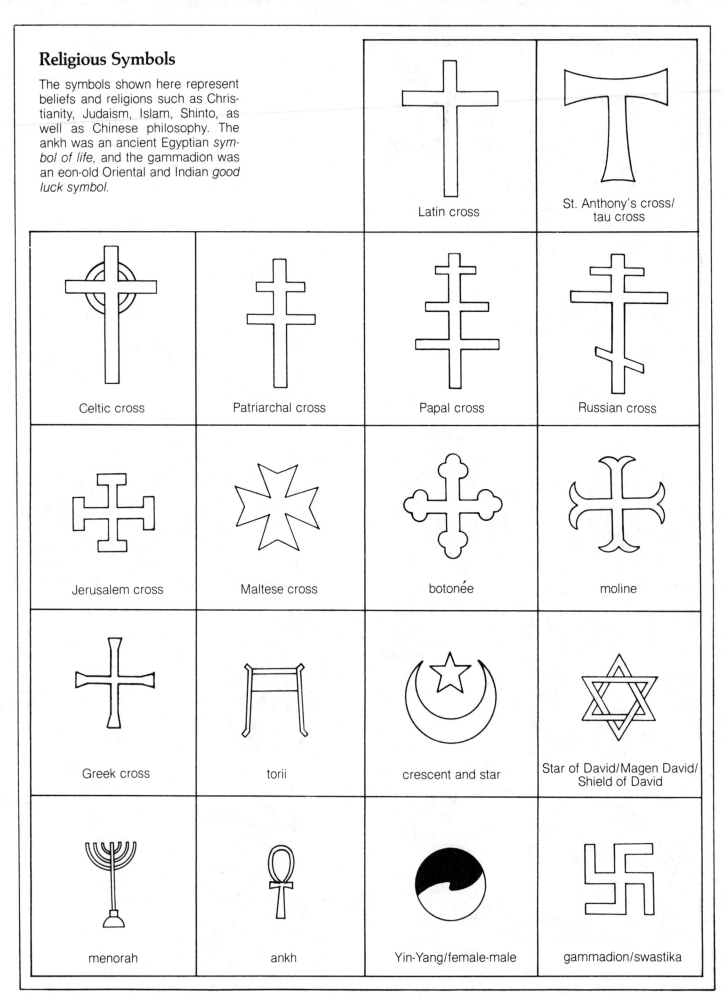

Latin cross

St. Anthony's cross/ tau cross

Celtic cross

Patriarchal cross

Papal cross

Russian cross

Jerusalem cross

Maltese cross

botonée

moline

Greek cross

torii

crescent and star

Star of David/Magen David/ Shield of David

menorah

ankh

Yin-Yang/female-male

gammadion/swastika

Signs of the Zodiac

The *zodiac* is an imaginary belt in the heavens divided into twelve parts named for constellations, called *houses*. A *horoscope*, drawn by an *astrologer*, foretells the influence of these heavenly bodies on human affairs.

Spring Signs

Aries — The Ram
March 21—April 20

Taurus — The Bull
April 21—May 21

Gemini — The Twins
May 22—June 21

Summer Signs

Cancer — The Crab
June 22—July 22

Leo — The Lion
July 23—August 23

Virgo — The Virgin
August 24—September 23

Autumn Signs

Libra — The Balance
September 24—October 23

Scorpio — The Scorpion
October 24—November 22

Sagittarius — The Archer
November 23—December 21

Winter Signs

Capricorn — The Goat
December 22—January 20

Aquarius — The Water Bearer
January 21—February 19

Pisces — The Fish
February 20—March 20

Signs and Symbols

Symbols of Science, Business and Commerce

The symbols shown here are used in the medical and pharmaceutical fields, in chemistry, engineering and electronics, in mathematics and business, and by currency-exchange centers and banks. Also included are miscellaneous symbols used in other walks of life.

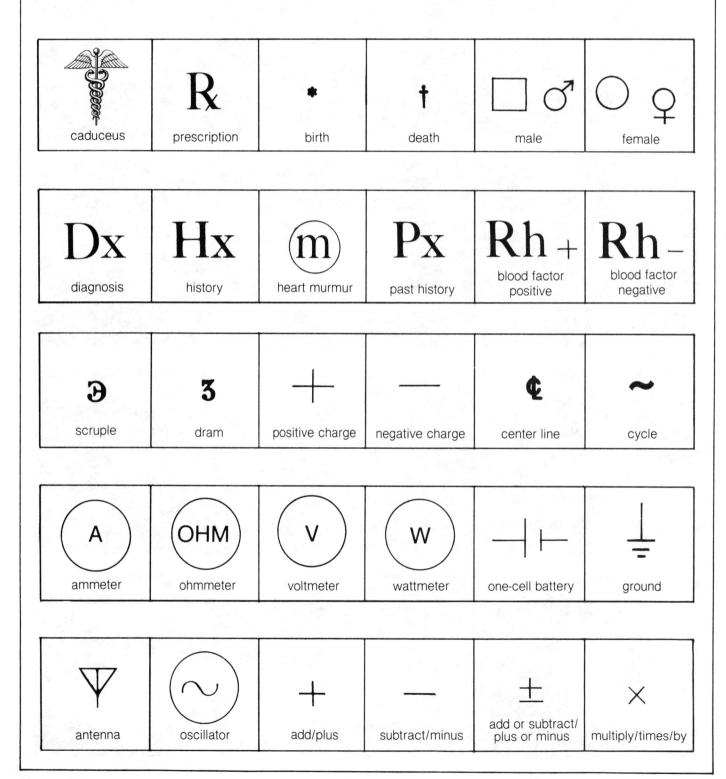

caduceus	prescription	birth	death	male	female
diagnosis	history	heart murmur	past history	blood factor positive	blood factor negative
scruple	dram	positive charge	negative charge	center line	cycle
ammeter	ohmmeter	voltmeter	wattmeter	one-cell battery	ground
antenna	oscillator	add/plus	subtract/minus	add or subtract/ plus or minus	multiply/times/by

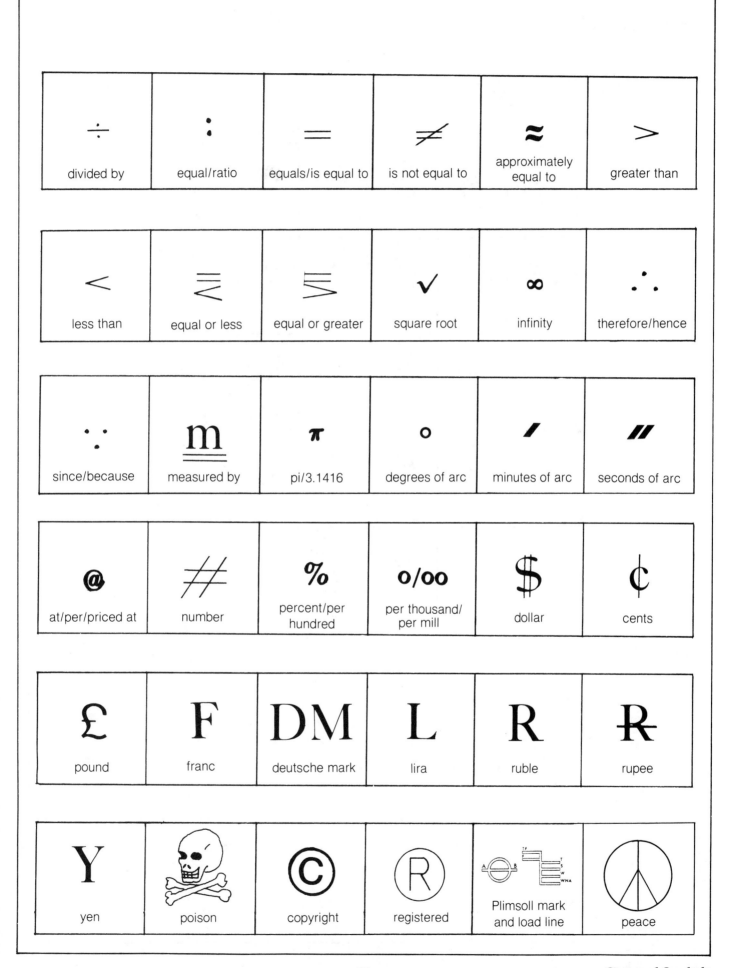

÷	:	=	≠	≈	>
divided by	equal/ratio	equals/is equal to	is not equal to	approximately equal to	greater than

<	≦	≧	√	∞	∴
less than	equal or less	equal or greater	square root	infinity	therefore/hence

∵	m̲	π	°	′	″
since/because	measured by	pi/3.1416	degrees of arc	minutes of arc	seconds of arc

@	#	%	o/oo	$	¢
at/per/priced at	number	percent/per hundred	per thousand/ per mill	dollar	cents

£	F	DM	L	R	₨
pound	franc	deutsche mark	lira	ruble	rupee

Y		©	®		
yen	poison	copyright	registered	Plimsoll mark and load line	peace

Signs and Symbols

Symbolic Language

Sign language, used by deaf-mutes, substitutes *gestures* for spoken words. Embossed *dots* are used by blind people to read by touch. *Semaphore* and *wigwag* are systems of signalling by hand-held flags.

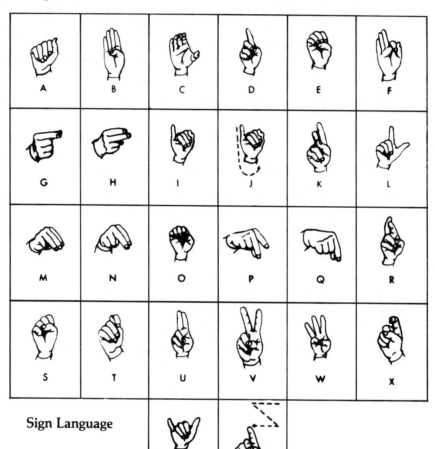

Sign Language

Braille

a	b	c	d	e	f	g	h	i	j	k	l	m

n	o	p	q	r	s	t	u	v	w	x	y	z

Grammatical Symbols

In addition to these *punctuation*, *diacritic* and *pronunciation symbols*, there are *phonetic symbols*, *abbreviations* and *contractions*.

'a' single quotation marks	"a" quotation marks	' foot/minute/prime	" inch/second/ double prime	a' apostrophe
(a) parentheses	[a] brackets/crotchets	a-a hyphen	a—a dash	a/a virgule/ slant/slash
, comma	; semicolon	: colon	& ampersand	* asterisk
• period/full point	• • • ellipsis/marks of omission	! exclamation point/ bang/ecphoneme	? question mark/ eroteme	‽ interrobang/ interabang
a̲ underline/ underscore	ſh ligature	é acute accent	à grave accent	â circumflex accent/ doghouse
ñ tilde	ç cedilla	ā macron	ă breve	äi dieresis/umlaut

Signs and Symbols

Proofreader's Marks

The marks illustrated below are used for the purpose of standardizing the transmittal of corrections and queries between *editors* and/or *proofreaders* and *typesetters* and/or *printers*. When the corrected *copy* is set in *type* it is *proved,* or *proofed,* and additional marks are then made on the *galley proofs.* The first *impressions* of the corrected galleys are called *page proofs.*

Mark	Symbol	Meaning

Mark

Enter HAMLET.

¶ ₐ <u>Ham.</u> To be, or not to be: that is the question:

Whether (᾿t is) nobler in the mind to suffer

The slings ⌢ and arrows of outrageous fortune

]Or to take arms against a˙sea of troubles,

And ⸨end \by opposing⸩ them? To die: to sleep:

No ₥ore; and by a sleep to say we end

The heart-ache and the (1000) natural shocks

That flesh is heir to ₐ't is a consummation

Devoutly˅to˅be ˅ wish'd.˙To˅die,˅ to sleep;

⌈To sleep: perchance to dream: ay, there's

□□□ ⟵————————————⌈the rub;

For in that sleep of death what dreams ⌐may come⌐

When we have (shuffled off) this mortal coil,

Must give us pause. There's the res⌢pect

That makes calamity of so₰ long life;

For who would bear|the whips and scorns of time,

The oppressor's wrong, the ₚroud mar|s contumely,

The p⟋ngs of disprized love, the law's delay,

The ⁱns°lence of office, and the spurns

That patient (merit) of the unworthy takes,

When he himself might ⌣his quietus make

With a bare bodkin ₐ who would fardels bear,

t̲o grunt and sweat under a weary life,

But that the dread of something ₐ death,

Symbol — **Meaning**

ital ———— set in italics

¶ ———— begin a paragraph

(G?) ———— grammar?

⊞ ———— close up partly/ less space/ take out space

] ———— move right/ flush left

tr — transpose

lc ———— set in lower case

(sp) — spell out

↱ ———— insert comma

eq. # ———— equalize space

[———— move left/square up

[———— move left – indent 3 ems

⊔ ———— move down

au? ———— query author

⌒ ———— close up completely/ take out space

ꝯ ——— delete

———— insert space/insert lead

⸒ ———— insert apostrophe

a/ ———— substitute letter

⹀ ——— straighten type horizontally

rom ———— set in roman type

stet ———— let it stand

? ———— insert question mark

cap ———— set in capitals

after —— insert/insert omitted matter

Symbols, inscriptions, phrases and signatures drawn in public places are collectively called graffiti. Those shown here are used among tramps and vagrants.

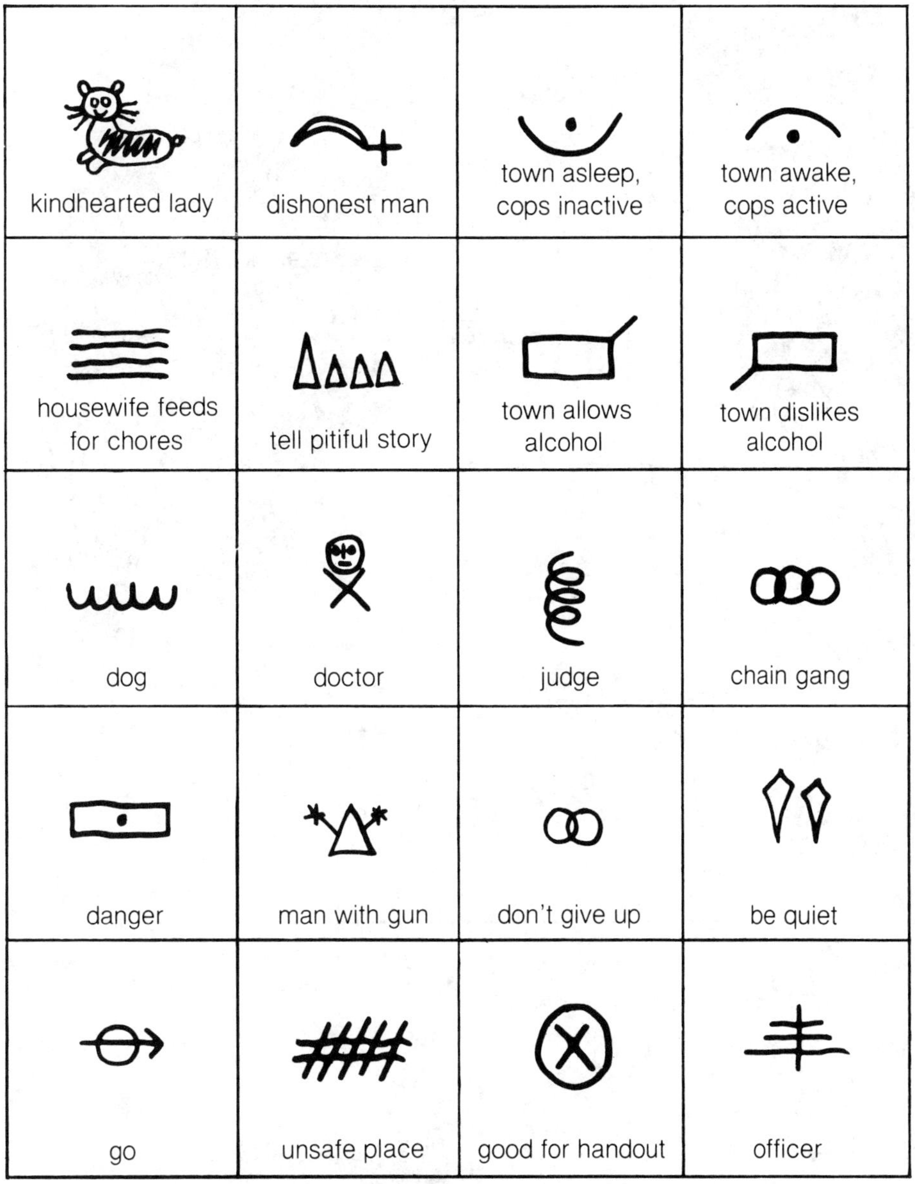

kindhearted lady	dishonest man	town asleep, cops inactive	town awake, cops active
housewife feeds for chores	tell pitiful story	town allows alcohol	town dislikes alcohol
dog	doctor	judge	chain gang
danger	man with gun	don't give up	be quiet
go	unsafe place	good for handout	officer

Signs and Symbols

Tombstone and Coffin

A stone placed at the foot of a grave is a *footstone*. *Crypts*, or *vaults*, are wholly or partly underground *burial chambers*. *Mausoleums* are large aboveground *tombs*.

ornament/carving

floral carving

inscription

year of birth

epitaph

base

tombstone/memorial/ monument/tablet/ gravestone/headstone

year of death

wreath

easel

grave/plot

J.SMITH

1803 – 1875

I TOLD THE DOCTOR I WAS SICK

MORT WALKER

Coffin/Casket

interior panel

pillow

drop

bed/mattress

arm

handle

bridge

overlay

lid panel

fishtail

end handle

lug

Index

A

A: braille, 512; piano keyboard octave, 361; sheet music notation, 353; sign language, 512
aba, Arab robe, 491
abacus, 441; column, 73
ABA number, check, 226
abaya, Arab dress, 491
abbreviation: grammatical symbol, 513; magazine mailing label, 169
abdomen: grasshopper, 41; horse, 38; human, 24; lobster, 47; spider, 40
abdominal aorta, human, 28
abdominal board, universal gym, 344
ablation zone, glacier, 12
ABM, 482
abort, pilot's instrument panel, 481
abrasive material, sander, 421
abstraction, work of art, 368
abutment, arch, 72
abutment tooth, partial denture, 453
abyssal plain, continental margin, 15
academic career, résumé, 160
academic hood, minister, 487
acceleration contest, drag racing, 339
accelerator, 394
accelerator pedal, car, 110
accelerometer, pilot's instrument panel, 481
accent, grammatical symbol, 513
access arm, launch pad, 152
access door, turbine locomotive coupler, 117
accessory shoe, camera, 172
accessories: musical, 367; patio, 288; photographic, 176
accessories shelf, telescope, 443
accessory cords, drum major's busby, 495
accessory rail, surgical table, 450
accessory socket, movie camera, 174
access plate, water heater, 401
access road, highway cloverleaf, 114
accidental, music notation, 352
accommodation, sailboat, 135
accommodation ladder, destroyer, 476
accordion, 366
accordion gusset, shoulder bag, 222
accordion windows, wallet, 223
accounting summary, monthly statement, 227
account number: bank card, 226; check, 226; credit card, 227; monthly statement, 227
accumulation zone, glacier, 12
accumulator, dispenser, 267
ace, playing card, 348
A cell block, prison, 76
achene, strawberry, 55

achievement of arms, 503
Achilles' heel, 25
Achilles' tendon, 31; pad, running shoe, 302
acid-free backing, frame, 379
acorn, seed, 51
acorn nut, 411
acoustic guitar, 356
AC power cord, tape recorder, 177
acroterion, masonry gate post, 67
acrylic, painting medium, 370
acrylic resin, dental, 453, 455
act, circus, 90
act curtain, stage, 350
act drop, stage, 350
action bolt, roller skate, 324
action nut, roller skate, 324
activating lever, pencil sharpener, 277
activator button, dental x-ray, 454
active pointer, aneroid barometer, 18
active repeater satellite, 186
acute accent, grammatical symbol, 513
ACV, 145
Adam's apple, human, 25
adapter plate, tractor, 434
add, symbol, 510
adding machine, 441
addition, with abacus, 441
add-on segment weight, tractor planetary, 434
add or subtract, symbol, 510
address: check, 226; envelope, 159; letter, 159; magazine mailing label, 169; résumé, 160
adductor longus, human, 26
adductor muscle, scallop, 47
adductor policis, human, 26
adhesive: Band-aid, 451; roofing shingle, 68
adhesive tape, 451
adipose fin, fish, 45
adjustable arm, expansive bit, 419
adjustable barrel, hose nozzle, 428
adjustable bit gauge, drill, 419
adjustable buckle, brassiere, 195
adjustable channel, pliers, 414
adjustable C-clamp, 409
adjustable clip, jackhammer, 436
adjustable foot: potter's wheel, 373; surgical table, 450
adjustable frame, hacksaw, 416
adjustable fulcrum, diving board, 316
adjustable grill, patio accessory, 288
adjustable lamp, 239
adjustable mirror, cosmetic case, 285
adjustable neckband, ascot, 193
adjustable platform, computer workstation, 438
adjustable rear wing, racing car, 338
adjustable reference pointer, barometer, 18

adjustable screw, embroidery ring, 385
adjustable shoulder strap, bag, 222
adjustable stand, laboratory, 447
adjustable table extension, saw, 417
adjustable wheel tread, tractor planetary, 434
adjustable wrench, 415
adjuster, power mower wheel, 429
adjusting knob: knee kicker, 246; saw, 417
adjusting lever, plane, 420
adjusting nut, monkey wrench, 415
adjusting screw: expansive bit, 419; hitch and harrow, 434; pliers, 414; theodolite, 436; violin bow, 355
adjust knob, volt-ohm meter, 423
adjustment: microscope focus, 442; speculum, 448
adjustment control, machine gun, 471
adjustment knob: lamp, 239; medical examination table, 450; microscope, 442; nozzle, 428; rifle scope, 469
adjustment lever: child's car seat, 286; stroller, 286
adjustment lines, sewing pattern, 388
adjustment nut, plane, 420
adjustment screw: lithographic press, 376; monkey wrench, 415; plane, 420; volt-ohm meter, 423
administration building, prison, 76
ad service courts, tennis, 312
adult, insect, 41
advance control, cash register, 440
advanced life-support unit, ambulance, 123
adventitious root, 51
advertisement, magazine, 171
advertising panel: bus, 118; gas pump, 112; subway car, 119
adz, ice axe, 334
adze eye, hammer, 412
aerator, kitchen sink, 247
aerial: CB radio, 183; hovercraft, 145; jumbo jet, 148; tanker, 141
aerial displays, 382-383
aerial flash, fireworks, 382
aerialist, circus, 90
aerial platform, tower ladder, 124
aerial shell, 383
aerial tom-tom, 364
aeronautical light, nautical chart, 22
A flat, piano keyboard octave, 361
A-frame, Ferris wheel, 93
aft, boat, 132
aft cabin bunk, sailboat, 135
aft controls, tugboat, 144
aft equipment bay, lunar lander, 154

afterbody, torpedo, 479
after bulkhead, powerboat, 139
after-shave lotion, 217
after steering, fireboat, 144
aft monitor, fireboat, 144
aft superstructure, tanker, 141
against shooter, craps table, 347
agal, Arab dress, 491
agate line, newspaper, 168
agitator: spreader, 430; washing machine, 280
agitron, cartoon, 380
aglet: shoelace, 204; skate, 295; stringtie, 192
Agulhas Current, ocean, 6
aid: hearing, 452; public sign, 506; space shuttle navigation, 153
aiguillette, enlisted man's uniform, 496
aileron: glider, 147; jumbo jet, 148; single engine airplane, 147
aileron trim, 747 cockpit, 150
air bags, blimp, 156
air bladder, seaweed, 57
air blower, drag racing dragster, 339
air brake, shuttle, 152
airbrake hose, locomotive, 116
airbrake paddle, glider, 147
air bubble, monorail, 424
air cleaner: automobile engine, 107; bulldozer, 435; mechanical sweeper, 127; mower, 429; truck, 120
air combat maneuver panel, pilot's instrument panel, 481
air compressor, truck, 120
air conditioner, 402; camper, 130
air conditioner compressor, automobile engine, 111
air conditioning: control, pilot's instrument panel, 481; intake, bus, 118
air connect lines, truck, 120
air control: dental unit, 454; refrigerator, 249
air-cooled engine, 406
air-cooled machine gun, 471
aircraft: airport, 95; civil, 148-149; combat, 480; instrument panel, 481; 747 cockpit, 150; single engine, 147
aircraft carrier, 476, 478
aircraft tug, 95
air cushion vehicle (ACV), 145
air-data system, space shuttle, 152
air ducts, tunnel, 98
air filter: engine, 406; tractor, 434
airflow control, pilot's instrument panel, 481
airflow nozzle, hair dryer, 212
air foil, drag racing dragster, 339
airframe: cruise missile, 482; jet fighter, 480
air gauge, subway motorman's cab, 119
airglow ultraviolet spectrometer, satellite, 186
air hole: fountain pen, 158;

hair roller, 214; harmonica, 366; igloo, 85
air horn, truck, 120
air hose, skin diving, 331
air inlet: aircraft, 147, 149, 407; dishwasher, 250; surgical table, 450
air intake: destroyer, 477; heat exchanger, 403; hovercraft, 145; locomotive, 117; racing car, 338; truck, 120
air jet, Jacuzzi, 274
airline identification location marker, airport, 94
air-motor power pedal, surgical table, 450
air movement, cloud, 16
airplane, see aircraft
airplane-back, cufflink, 218
air plate, standpipe, 59
airport, 94-95
air pump, bicycle, 128
air regulator: dental, 455; laboratory burner, 437
air reservoir, locomotive, 116
air scoop: automobile, 106; blimp, 156
air search radar: aircraft carrier, 478; destroyer, 477
airship, 156
air speed indicator, 747 cockpit, 150, 151
airspeed mach indicator, pilot's instrument panel, 481
airtank: fire engine, 124; skin diving, 331
air temperature, 747 cockpit, 150
air traffic control: operator facility, 95; tower, 94; transporter, 747 cockpit, 151
air transportation, public sign, 506
air valve: blimp, 156; motorcycle, 129; subway motorman's cab, 119
air vent: automobile, 107, 110; Band-Aid, 451; furnace, 400; hair dryer, 212; intercity bus, 118; pressure cooker, 257; radiator, 400; VCR, 184
aisle: church, 87; courtroom, 89; House of Representatives, 74; theatre, 351
aisle display, 102
aisle number, supermarket, 102
ait, river, 13
alarm: clock radio, 233; elevator car button, 78; powerboat, 138; prison, 76; vault, 457
alarm panel, nuclear reactor control room, 393
alb, cardinal, 487
albedo, orange, 55
albumen, egg, 262
alcohol, ambulance, 123
alcohol percentage, wine label, 267
Alexander, playing card king, 348
algae, marine, 57
alignment control: gas laser, 395; radar, 444
alimentary canal, human, 27
Allen wrench, 415
alley: badminton court, 319; bowling, 317; tennis court, 312
alley light, police car, 122
all-fives, darts, 322
alligator, 42
alligator clip: dental towel, 455; and volt-ohm meter, 423
allosaurus, 43

all-purpose vehicle, 108
alluvial fan, river, 13
alp, mountain, 8
alpha-numeric keypad: answering machine, 181; cellular telephone, 181; computer workstation, 438; personal computer, 162
Alpine skiing, 326
altar, church, 87
altazimuth mounting, telescope, 453
alteration lines, sewing pattern, 388
alternate channel, picture-in-picture viewing, 185
alternator, automobile engine, 111
altimeter: pilot's instrument panel, 481; 747 cockpit, 150
altitude coarse-motion clamp, telescope, 443
altitude indicator, pilot's instrument panel, 481
altocumulus cloud, 16, 17
aluminum rim, drag racing dragster, 339
amalgam carrier, dental, 455
amateur radio operator, 183
amber starting light, drag racing, 339
ambu, ambulance, 123
ambulance, 123
ambulatory, church, 87
American Bankers Association routing number, check, 226
AM/FM controls, clock radio, 233
AM-FM radio scale, portable radio/cassette player, 182
AM/FM radio tuning dial, audio receiver, 179
amidships, boat, 132
ammeter, symbol, 510
ammunition: automatic weapon, 471; combat soldier, 497; fort, 82
amount: check, 226
amp, electric guitar, 363
amperage rating, circuit breaker box, 399
ampersand, grammatical symbol, 513
amphibian, 44
amphibious assault ship, 476
amphibious command ship, 476
amphibious hull, helicopter, 146
amphibious vehicle, 145
amplifier: guitar, 363; phonograph, 179
AM signal meter, phonograph, 179
amulet, medal, 501
amusement park, 92-93
anal fin, fish, 45
anal shield, snake, 43
anatomical snuffbox, human hand, 31
anatomy, literary, 25
anchor: boar, 132; diving board, 316; mattress cover, 271; passenger ship, 143; sailboat, 134; starting block, 304; tennis net, 312
anchorage, nautical chart, 22
anchor bolt, house, 60, 61
anchor chain: bear trap, 433; oil drilling platform, 101
anchor light, destroyer, 477
anchor spot, blackjack, 347
anchor spring, gas pump nozzle, 112
anchor tooth, denture, 453
anchor winch, oil drilling platform, 101

anchor windlass, tanker, 140
anchovies, pizza, 265
andiron, fireplace, 232
anemometer, weather station, 18
aneroid barometer, 18
anesthetic syringe, dental, 455
angle: fort, 83; incline track, 92; lamp, 239; slide, 287; transit, 436
angled deck, aircraft carrier, 478
angle of attack indicator, pilot's instrument panel, 481
angle of light, relief map, 21
angler, fishing, 341
angle scale, circular saw, 417
angular adjustment, speculum, 448
angulation dial readout, dental x-ray unit, 454
anima, human, 25
animal: cell, 23; circus, 90, 91; composite, 48-49
animal trainer, 90
animal skin, igloo, 85
ankh, symbol, 508
ankle, human, 24, 31
ankle boot, harness racing pacer, 337
ankle bracelet, 219
ankle extension, baseball catcher's shinguard, 290
ankle guard, hockey skate, 325
ankle sock, 207
ankle strap, woman's shoe, 205
anklet, 219
ankle weight, body building, 344; announcement microphone, 747 cockpit, 150
annoyance, gesture, 507
annual ring: lumber, 68; tree, 50
annulus, mushroom, 57
anode, laser, 395
anode plate, vacuum tube, 396
anorak, 201
answer button, answering machine, 181
answering machine, 181
answering machine capability, fax machine, 164
ant, 41
antenna: aircraft carrier, 478; airport control tower, 95; automobile, 106, 107; CB radio, 183; cellular telephone, 181; cordless phone, 180; destroyer, 476, 477; helicopter, 146; house, 63; insect, 41; jet fighter, 480; launch pad, 152; lobster, 47; lunar lander, 154; lunar rover, 155; police car, 122; portable radio/cassette player, 182; radar, 444; satellite, 186; single engine airplane, 147; spacesuit, 155; submarine, 479; symbol, 510; tank, 474; tanker, 141
antependium, church, 87
anterior chamber, eye, 30
anther, flower stamen, 53
antia, shield, 464
anti-ballistic missile (ABM), 482
anti-cavitation plate, outboard engine, 137
anti-fog liquid, dental, 455
anti-friction pad, ski binding, 326
antihelix, outer ear, 30
anti-kickback panel, saw, 417
antique, White House, 75

anti-reverse housing, fishing reel, 340
anti-rollback, incline track, 92
anti-shock trousers, paramedic equipment, 123
anti-skate dial, phonograph, 178
anti-submarine belt, drag racing driver, 339
antitank mine, 473
antitragus, outer ear, 30
antlers, ultimate beast, 48
anus, starfish, 46
anvil: stapler, 277; telegraph key, 157; vise, 409
anvil shears, gardening, 427
anvil toe, thundercloud, 17
aorta, heart, 28
aperture: microscope, 442; pencil sharpener, 277; physician's mirror, 448; univalve shell, 47
aperture key, camera, 172
aperture ring, zoom lens, 172
aperture scale: light meter, 176
apex: grass, 58; leaf, 52; pyramid, 71; univalve shell, 47
apostrophe: grammatical symbol, 513; proofreader's mark, 514
Appalachian dulcimer, 362
apparatus, animal cell, 23
apparel pocket, golf bag, 311
appendix, human, 27
appetizer, 263
apple, 55; baseball, 290; corer, 261
application package, computer, 438
applicator, beauty product, 217
applicator bottle, hair styling lotion, 214
appliqué: dress, 198; quilting, 385
appliquéd lace, bridal gown, 488
approach: airport runway, 94; bowling lane, 317; javelin throw, 301; pole vault, 305
approach indexer, pilot's instrument panel, 481
approval, gesture, 507
approximately equal to, symbol, 511
apron: airport, 95; ascot, 193; barn, 104; boxing ring, 309; bureau, 272; circus aerialist, 90; cook, 489; golf course, 311; house driveway, 63; necktie, 193; pool table, 320; table, 242; theatre, 351; window, 65
apsidal chapel, church, 87
apterium, bird, 39
APV, passenger car, 108
Aquarius, zodiac, 509
aquatint, printmaking, 377
Arab dress, 491
arbor lock, table saw, 417
arc: sextant, 137; Torah, 486
arcade, passengership, 142
arch, 72; church, 86; croquet, 318; denture, 453; dog, 36; football uniform, 292; house doorway, 62; human fingertip, 31; human foot, 31; kokoshniki, 70; organ, 360; royal crown, 485; saddle, 335; stage, 350, 351
arch cookie, sandal, 206
arched-top glass door, corner cabinet, 243
archer, zodiac, 509
architect, house blueprint, 62
architecture, international, 70-71
architrave: column entablature,

73; vault, **457**; White House, **75**
archival frame, **379**
arch-stones, arch, **72**
arco, stringed instrument, **355**
area code, telephone, **180**
area rug, **246**
A recreation yard, prison, **76**
arena, circus, **90**
areole, cactus, **56**
arête: glacier, **12**; mountain, **9**
Argine, playing card queen, **348**
Aries, zodiac, **509**
arithmetic function key calculator, **441**
ark, synagogue, **88**
arm: anchor, **132**; automobile, **161**, **166**; ballista, **467**; bobby pin, **214**; cactus, **56**; candelabrum, **237**; chaise longue, **288**; clothes hanger, **281**; coffin, **516**; corkscrew, **251**; dental, **454**, **455**; dishwasher, **250**; dog, **36**; drill bit, **419**; fishing reel, **340**; folding rule, **424**; frog, **44**; gas pump price-poster, **112**; guitar, **363**; hand shower, **274**; human, **24**, **25**; jellyfish, **46**; lamp, **239**; launch pad, **152**; lounger, **235**; L-shaped square, **424**; lyre, **355**; microscope, **442**; movie projector, **175**; octopus, **46**; outboard engine, **137**; organ, **360**; overhead power line, **396**; phonograph turntable, **178**; piano, **361**; revolving sprinkler, **428**; rocking chair, **234**; sewing machine, **278**; sextant, **137**; shower, **274**; slot machine, **346**; sofa, **236**; starfish, **46**; toilet, **275**; toll booth gate, **114**; traffic light, **113**; type, **165**; wheelchair, **452**; *see also* arms
armament countermeasure panel, **481**
armament panel, pilot's, **481**
armature, sculpture, **372**
armboard extension, operating table, **450**
arm buckle, electric chair, **462**
armed guard, prison, **76**
arm grip, phonograph turntable, **178**
armhole: jacket, **188**, **196**; undershirt, **194**
armhole seam, blouse, **197**
armilla, queen's regalia, **484**
arming mechanism, bazooka, **472**
armlet, jewelry, **219**
armoire, **272**
armor, **465**
armored cord, pay phone, **180**
armorial achievement, coat of arms, **503**
armor-plated vehicle, **474-475**
armory, castle, **81**
arm pad, lounger, **235**
arm piece, crutch, **452**
arm post, rocking chair, **234**
arm protector, ice hockey goalie, **294**
armrail, commuter bus, **118**
armrest: Jacuzzi, **274**; lounger, **235**; rocking chair, **234**; sofa, **236**; wheelchair, **452**
arms: church, **87**; coat of, **503**; Manchu coat dress, **491**; medieval, **464**; royal crown, **485**; *see also* arm
aro, jai alai cesta, **314**
arrester, fireplace sparks, **232**

arresting gear pendant, aircraft carrier, **478**
arresting hook, jet fighter, **480**
arresting hook panel, pilot's instrument panel, **481**
arresting trap, **433**
arrow, **466**; bowling lane, **317**; road map, **20**
arrowhead, weather vane, **19**
arrow loop, castle, **80**
arse, wood block, **461**
art: book jacket, **167**; composition, **368-369**; in frame, **379**; magazine, **169**, **170**, **171**; newspaper, **168**
arteriole, human, **28**
artery, human; **27**, **28**
article, magazine, **169**, **170**
artificial abrasive material, sander, **421**
artificial teeth, denture, **453**
artificial turf, baseball field, **291**
artillery, cowboy, **490**
artist: cartoon, **380**; circus, **90**; painting, **370**; phonograph record, **178**
ASA-DIN exposure index, light meter, **176**
ascender, type, **165**
ascent air-data system, space shuttle, **152**
ascent stage, lunar lander, **154**
ascot, **193**
asdic, **444**
ash: cigar and cigarette, **228**; volcano, **10**
A sharp, piano keyboard octave, **361**
ash catcher, grill, **288**
ash dump, fireplace, **232**
ash lip, woodburning stove, **404**
ashpit, fireplace, **232**
ashtray, car, **110**
asparagus, **54**
asphaltum, **376**
ASROC launcher, destroyer, **477**
assembly: backyard equipment, **287**; lamp, **239**; pulley block, **461**; scale, **446**
assigned weight, flat racing entry, **336**
assistance telephone, automatic teller machine, **226**
assistant quartermaster, frontier fort, **82**
assistant's center, dental unit, **454**
assist handle, truck tractor, **120**
association football, **297**
asterisk, grammatical symbol, **513**
asteroid, Milky Way, **2**
astragal: cannon barrel, **467**; column, **73**
A string, double bass, **355**
astrologer, **509**
asymmetrical closing, jacket, **196**
at, symbol, **511**
athletic sock, **207**
athletic supporter, **194**
athwartships, boat, **132**
Atlantic Drift, ocean, **6**
Atlantic North Equatorial Current, ocean, **6**
Atlantic South Equatorial Current, ocean, **6**
ATM, **226**
atmosphere, earth, **4**
atom smasher, **394**
attaché case, **285**
attached bertha, bridal gown, **488**

attaching point, inflatable, **133**
attaching socket, movie camera, **174**
attachment: denture, **453**; vacuum cleaner, **283**
attachment loop, basketball backstop, **296**
attachment plug, electrical, **398**
attachment screw thread, camera, **172**
attachment weight set, scale, **446**
attack indicator, pilot's instrument panel, **481**
attack line, volleyball court, **319**
attackman, lacrosse position, **298**
attic, house, **62**, **63**
attitude indicator, space shuttle, **153**
audience, circus, **91**
audio control, police car, **122**
audio-input, movie projector, **175**
audio knob, Geiger counter, **445**
audio port, Geiger counter, **445**
audio power status, space shuttle, **153**
audio system, **179**
auditorium, prison, **76**
auditory canal, **30**
auger, **422**
auger bit, drill, **418**, **419**
auguste face, clown, **493**
auricle, **30**
auricular, bird, **39**
author: book, **167**; magazine, **169**; music, **352**
authorized signature, traveler's check, **227**
autofeed bin, laser printer, **163**
autofocus 35 mm camera, **172**
auto gate, toll booth, **114**
auto inflation, hose, skin diving, **331**
autoloader latch, computer tape, **439**
automatic choke, automobile, **111**
automatic citrus juicer, **255**
automatic cue, phonograph turntable, **178**
automatic direction finder: helicopter, **146**; 747 cockpit, **150**
automatic inflator, skin diving, **331**
automatic line finder, typewriter, **161**
automatic music sensor, compact disc player, **178**
automatic noise limiter, CB radio, **183**
automatic nozzle, gas pump, **112**
automatic pilot disengage, 747 cockpit, **151**
automatic pistol, **470**
automatic rewind switch, tape measure, **424**
automatic rifle, **471**
automatic teller machine, **226**
automatic teller machine card, **226**
automatic temperature probe, microwave oven, **248**
automatic timer, coffee maker, **252**
automatic weapons, **471**
automobile: cutaway, **108-109**; drag racing, **339**; engine, **111**; exterior, **106-107**; Grand Prix racer, **338**; interior, **110**; police, **122**; *see also* car

autopilot display, space shuttle, **153**
autopilot engage switch, 747 cockpit, **150**
auto redial, cellular telephone, **181**
auto-reverse, portable radio/cassette player, **182**
auxiliary attaching socket, movie camera, **174**
auxiliary building, nuclear reactor, **392**
auxiliary car-station panel, elevator car, **78**
auxiliary contact, movie camera, **174**
auxiliary counterweight, lift bridge, **97**
auxiliary feedwater pump, nuclear reactor, **392**
auxiliary handle: hand drill, **418**; plane, **420**
auxiliary instruments arm, dental, **454**
auxiliary lens, microscope, **442**
auxiliary power feed, Walkman, **182**
auxiliary selector, movie camera, **174**
auxiliary tank, truck, **121**
avalanche area, mountain, **9**
aven, cave, **11**
aviation light, bridge, **97**
aviation lens, eyeglasses, **221**
awards, résumé, **160**
awl: combination square, **424**; knife, **426**
awn, grass, **58**
awning: barn, **104**; tent, **342**
ax: guillotine, **462**; ice climbing, **334**; medieval, **464**
axilla, frog, **44**
axillary bud, tree, **50**
axis: fern, **57**; peeler, **256**
axle: automobile, **109**; bicycle, **128**; child's wagon, **287**; Ferris wheel, **93**; Hansom cab, **131**; roller skate, **324**; stroller, **286**; tractor, **434**; wheelbarrow, **430**; wheelchair, **452**; windmill, **390**
axle gear, seeder, **430**
axle hole, tire, **105**
azimuth coarse-motion clamp, telescope, **443**

B

B: braille, **512**; music notation, **353**; piano keyboard octave, **361**; sign language, **512**
B-1B Bomber, **480**
B-2 Bomber, **480**
baby carriage, **286**
baby chair, **286**
baby teeth, **456**
baccarat, **346**
back: bird, **39**; bow, **466**; carpenter's saw, **416**; cat, **37**; chaise longue, **288**; chicken, **35**; chisel, **420**; coin, **225**; dog, **36**; easel, **370**; electric chair, **462**; horse, **38**; human, **24**, **25**; knife, **256**, **463**; playing card, **348**; polo position, **299**; rocking chair, **234**; saw tooth, **416**; shank button, **209**; sheep, **33**; sofa, **236**; stringed instrument, **355**; wave, **14** wheelchair, **452**
back arch, English saddle, **335**
back beam, hand loom, **387**
backboard, basketball backstop, **296**
backbone, hardback book, **167**
back boundary line, badminton court, **319**

backcombed hair, woman's, 213
backcourt: basketball, 296; handball, 313; squash, 313; tennis, 312
back cover: hardback book, 167; matchbook, 228
back face, hardback book, 167
backfill, underwater tunnel, 98
back finger, handball glove, 313
back flap, book jacket, 167
backgammon, 345
background, composition, 369
back guard, stove, 248
back half, piano, 361
back housing, saddle, 335
backing: carpet, 246; frame, 379; quilting, 385; sandpaper, 421; tent, 342
back jaw, vise, 409
back leg, bureau, 272
back lid, grand piano, 361
back light button, movie camera, 174
back line, volleyball court, 319
backlit composition, 368
back margin, book page, 167
back matter, book, 167
back of book, magazine, 171
back of hand, human, 31
backpack, 343; skin diving tank, 331
backpack control box, spacesuit, 155
backpacking, 343
back pad, ice hockey goalie, 294
back panel, man's jacket, 188
backplate: armor, 465; basketball backstop, 296; shoulder bag, 222; skin diving tank, 331
backplate serial number, paper money, 224
back quarter, boot, 206
back rail, rocking chair, 234
backrest: lounger, 235; stroller, 286
back roll protector, ice hockey player, 295
backshore, shoreline, 14
back sizer, football helmet, 292
back sleeve seam, jacket, 188
backspace key, typewriter, 161
backstay: ice skates, 325; sailboat, 134
backstep, pumper, 125
back-stick, easel, 370
backstop: basketball, 296; telegraph key, 157; workbench, 408
backstrap: brassiere, 195; revolver, 470; vest, 188
backstretch, harness racetrack, 337
backstrip, hardback book, 167
backstroke swimming race, 316
back upholstery, wheelchair, 452
back-up light, tow truck bed, 126
back wall: handball and squash courts, 313; jai alai cancha, 314
badge: coat of arms, 503; fireman's helmet, 500; flag, 502; military, 496; police, 498
badge of rank, Manchu court dress, 491
badminton, 319
baffle, stove, 342, 404
bag: backpacking, 343; bagpipe, 365; blood pressure gauge, 449; golf, 311; hot air balloon, 332; luggage, 285;

lunar rover, 155; packaging, 269; paper, 266; photographic, 176; vacuum cleaner, 283
bag compression strap, backpack, 343
bag dispenser, spacesuit, 155
baggage car, passenger train, 116
baggage check-in, public sign, 506
baggage claim, public sign, 506
baggage compartment: bus, 118; jumbo jet, 149; single engine airplane, 147
baggage rack, intercity bus, 118
bag-holding button, garbage disposal, 247
bagpipe, 365
bag resuscitator, ambulance, 123
bag stowage, lunar rover, 155
bail: fishing reel, 340; lantern, 342; pail, 284; screen, 175; typewriter, 161
bailey, castle, 80, 81
bail roller, typewriter, 161
bait, mousetrap, 433
baked dessert, 264
bakery: frontier fort, 82; prison, 76
bakery department, supermarket, 103
baking tray, toaster oven, 253
balance: laboratory, 446-447; monthly statement, 227; zodiac, 509
balance beam, gymnastics, 306
balance dial, phonograph, 179
balancer, trombone, 358
balance weight, tire, 105
balcony: minaret, 70; pagoda, 71; theatre, 351; White House, 75
bald spot, 211
balistraria, castle, 80
balk, lumber, 68
ball: anchor, 132; ballpoint pen, 158; baseball, 290; bowling, 317; croquet, 318; door, 64; drum major's baton, 495; field events hammer, 303; foot, 31; golf, 310; handball, 313; jai alai, 314; lacrosse, 298; Ping-Pong, 321; pool table, 320; roulette wheel, 346; shower fitting, 274; snap fastener, 208; soccer, 297; tea, 260; tennis, 312; thumb, 31; toilet tank, 275; type, 165; typewriter, 161
ballast: hot air balloon, 332; lobster pot, 433; railroad track, 115
ballast tank, submarine, 479
ball bearing: ballpoint pen, 158; roller skate, 324
ball-cock assembly, toilet, 275
ballet dancer, 494
ballista, 467
ballistic missile, 482; submarine, 479
ballistic missile launch deck, submarine, 479
ball joint, automobile, 108
ball joint head, C-clamp, 409
ball of rank royal crown, 485
ballonets, blimp, 156
balloon: cartoon, 380, 381; clown, 493; hot air, 332
balloon pants, clown, 493
balloon pointer, comic strip, 381
ballot, voting booth, 437

ballot layout, electronic voting system, 437
ballpark, 291
ball-peen hammer, 412
ball pocket, golf bag, 311
ballpoint pen, 158
ball rest, roulette wheel, 346
ball return: bowling lane, 317; pool table, 320
ball side, snap fastener, 208
ball storage box, pool table, 320
ball tip head, hinge, 460
baluster: column, 73; staircase, 66
balustrade: column, 73; escalator, 79; staircase, 66
bamboo pole, pole vault, 305
banana, 55
banana clip, automatic rifle, 471
band: baren, 374; baseball uniform, 290; cigar, 228; cigarette, 228; dance, 354; dental, 453; fire extinguisher, 284; frontier fort, 82; girdle, 195; horse's hoof, 38; hot air balloon, 332; Jewish prayer shawl, 486; marching, 271; ring, 219; skin diving tank, 331; spinning wheel, 387; spur, 335; woman's hat, 203; wristwatch, 220
bandage, 451; paramedic equipment, 123; polo, 299; racehorse, 336
Band-Aid, 451
bandanna: cowboy, 490; skier's, 326
band clamp, 409
band organ, merry-go-round, 93
band saw, 417
band switch, portable radio/cassette player, 182
bang: grammatical symbol, 513; woman's hair, 213
bangle, jewelry, 219
banister, staircase, 66
banjo, 362
bank: check, 226; elevator, 77, 78; name and address, 226; newspaper, 168; paper money, 224; passenger ship, 142; river, 13; vault, 457
bank card, 226
bank card slot, automatic teller machine, 226
bank indicator, 747 cockpit, 150
bank logo, traveler's check, 227
bank rod, fishing, 341
banner: circus tent, 91; football field, 293; newspaper headline, 168
banquette, permanent fort, 83
baptistery, church, 87
bar: backgammon board, 345; backyard equipment, 287; barbell, 344; barbecue grill, 288; bicycle, 128; chain saw, 431; commuter bus, 118; courtroom, 89; craps table, 347; drag racing dragster, 339; easel, 370; electric razor, 210; etching press, 377; fastener, 208; Ferris wheel, 93; Grand Prix racer, 338; hang glider, 333; hurdle, 304; hitch and harrow, 434; horizontal bar, 306; horse's foot, 38; lithographic press, 376; military uniform, 496; mousetrap, 433; movie

projector, 175; music, 352, 353; necktie, 192; parallel bars, 306; passenger ship, 142; public sign, 506; railroad track, 115; saddle, 335; shoreline, 14; slalom water ski, 329; slot machine, 346; suit hanger, 281; table saw, 417; tank, 475; tow truck bed, 126; type, 165; typewriter, 161
barb: barbed wire, 432; bird, 39; fishhook, 341; lance, 464; spring beard needle, 386
barbed wire, 432
barbell, body building, 344
barbecue grill, 288
barbershop, passenger ship, 142
barbican, castle, 80, 81
Barcalounger, 235
bar clamp, 409
bare match end, aerial shell, 383
baren, woodcut printing, 374
bargeboard, house, 63
barge carrier, 140
barge cluster, pushboat, 144
bargello stitchery, 385
bark, wigwam, 84
barley, 58
bar line: music, 352; newspaper, 168
barn, 104
barnacle, 47
barometer, aneroid, 18
barometric altimeter, 747 cockpit, 150
barrack: castle, 81; frontier fort, 82
barred door, prison, 76
barrel, 267; automatic weapons, 468, 469, 470, 471; baseball bat, 291; cannon, 467; clarinet, 357; cow, 32; curling iron, 214; dart, 322; destroyer gun, 477; fire hydrant, 125; hair dryer, 212; hinge, 460; hypodermic syringe, 451; man's shoe, 204; pen, 158; shirt cuff, 189; spool, 384; tank gun, 475
barrel cap, lead pencil, 158
barrel grille, hair dryer, 212
barrel ring: bayonet, 463; shotgun, 469
barrel spiral galaxy, 2
barrette, 214
barrier, highway, 114
barrier beach, 15
barrier gate, toll booth, 114
barrier island, 15
bar scale, political map, 21
bar tack, necktie, 193
bar tip, chair saw, 431
bartizan, castle, 80
bascule bridge, 97
base: acoustic guitar, 362; badminton shuttlecock, 319; baseball field, 291; basket, 266; basketball backstop, 296; bear trap, 433; blackjack, 347; blender, 254; canapé, 263; candelabrum, 237; cannon barrel ring, 467; can opener, 251; CB radio station, 183; cellular telephone, 181; citrus juicer, 255; coat of arms, 503; column, 73; computer workstation, 438; dental brace, 453; denture, 453; drag racing starting lights, 339; dressing table, 272; drill press, 419; easel, 370; elevator car, 78; food processor, 254; globe, 1; grandfather clock, 233;

hurdle, 304; juice extractor, 255; laboratory burner, 447; laboratory scale, 447; lantern, 342; lawn sprinkler, 428; leaf, 52; light bulb, 238; makeup, 216; medical examination table, 450; microscope, 442; minaret, 70; mortar cap, 472; mousetrap, 433; music stand, 367; onion, 54; parallel bars, 306; pedestal table, 242; pencil sharpener, 277; percolator brewing basket, 252; phonograph turntable, 178; pole vault pole, 305; pommel horse, 307; pot, 373; power saw, 417; pyramid, 71; refrigerator grille, 249; rifle scope, 468, 469; sandwich cookie, 264; stapler, 277; steam engine, 405; telephone, 180; television, 185; thimble, 384; tombstone, 516; transistor chip, 396; trimline phone, 180; trophy, 289; tuning fork, 367; vacuum tube, 396; vise, 409; White House, 75

baseball, 290-291; darts, 322

baseboard, and carpet, 246

baseline: baseball field, 291; Ping-Pong table, 321; shuffleboard court, 319; tennis court, 312; type, 165

basement, house, 60, 63

basepath, baseball field, 291

baseplate: land mine, 473; mortar, 472; railroad track, 115; saber saw, 417; sewing machine, 278

base unit, cordless phone, 180

basin: ambulance, 123; dam, 100; river, 13; sink, 273

basin compartment, sink, 247

basket: basketball, 296; bee, 41; coffee maker, 252; container, 266; deep frying, 260; garbage disposal, 247; guillotine, 462; hot air balloon, 332; jai alai, 314; juice extractor, 255; refrigerator, 249; sink, 247; ski pole, 326; sword, 463; toll booth, 114; typewriter type, 161; washing machine, 280

basketball, 296

basket-release handle, garbage disposal, 247

bass: accordion, 366; bagpipe drone, 365; bassoon joint, 357; fiddle, 354, 355; guitar, 363; music clef, 353; phonograph dial, 179

bass and guitar, double-neck, 363

bass clarinet, 354

bass display, portable radio/cassette player, 182

bass drum, 354, 364

bass fiddle, 354, 355

bassinet, 286

bass neck, double-neck bass and guitar, 363

bassoon, 354, 357

bass speaker, portable radio/cassette player, 182

basting brush, 259

basting ladle, 259

bastion: castle, 80, 81; permanent fort, 83

bat: badminton, 319; baseball, 291; brick wall, 69; flat racing, 336; Ping-Pong, 321

bateau neck, sweater, 199

bath, 274

bath oil, 217

batholith, volcano, 10

bathtub, 274

baton: drum major, 495; police, 498

bat pin, potter's wheel, 373

batten: hand loom, 387; stage, 350

batten pocket, mainsail, 136

batter, baseball, 290

batter head, snare drum, 364

batter's box, baseball, 291

batter's circle, baseball, 291

battery, 397; automobile, 108; buoy, 132; electronic flash, 176; Geiger counter, 445; hearing aid, 452; intercity bus, 118; lunar rover, 155; metal detector, 445; movie camera, 174; pacemaker, 452; tape recorder, 177; truck, 120, 121

battery charger: medical examination equipment, 448; tow truck, 126

battery holder, camera, 172

battery jumper cable, tow truck, 126

battery pack: cellular telephone, 181; video camera, 184; video-still camera adaptor, 173

battery-powered tape recorder, 177

battery recharge contact, cordless phone, 180

batting, quilting, 385

batting glove, baseball, 290

batting helmet, baseball, 290

battlement, castle, 80

battleship, 476

bat weight, baseball, 290

bay: aircraft carrier, 478; barn, 104; coastline, 7, 15; space shuttle, 152

bay bar, 15

bay barrier, 15

bayit, tefillin, 486

baymouth, bar, 15

bayonet, 463

bayonet saw, 417

bay window, house, 62, 63

bazooka, 472

bazooka plate, tank, 474

B cell block, prison, 76

BC inflator mouthpiece, skin diving, 331

beach, 14, 15

beacon: helicopter, 146; police car, 122; single engine airplane, 147

bead: abacus, 441; beaker, 447; cowboy hat, 202; shotgun, 469

beading: attaché case, 285; Indian attire, 490

bead line, bell, iv

beak: bird, 39; chicken, 35; clam, 47; dolphin, 45; halberd, 464; turtle, 43; type, 165

beaker: coffee maker, 252; laboratory, 447

beam: abacus, 441; automobile, 106; boat, 132; bus, 118; drag racing, 339; guillotine, 462; gymnastic, 306; hand loom, 387; house, 61; incline track, 92; laboratory scale, 447; laser, 395; lumber, 68; skyscraper, 77; subway car, 119; tow truck bed, 126

beam abort, super collider, 394

beam balance, laboratory, 446-447

beam lens, laser, 395

beam pipe, super collider, 394

beam shroud, gas laser, 395

beam splitter, holography, 395

beanie cap, space shuttle, 152

beard: man's, 211; spring beard needle, 386; turkey, 35; type, 166; ultimate beast, 49; windmill, 390

bearing: airport runway, 94; fishing reel, 340; laboratory scale, 446; radar, 444; roller skate, 324; skateboard, 324; socket wrench, 415; transit, 436

bearing distance heading indicator, pilot's instrument panel, 481

bearing edge, horse's foot, 38

bearing line, compass, 136

bearing rail, bureau, 272

bearing ring, radar, 444

bearing surface, brick, 68

bearpaw shoe, snowshoe, 327

bear trap, 433

bear trap binding, ski, 326

beat, police, 498

beater: bass drum, 364; kitchen tool, 258; vacuum cleaner, 283

beauty products, 217

beauty salon, passenger ship, 142

beaver, armor, 465

because, symbol, 511

becket, block and tackle, 461

beckoning, gesture, 507

bed, 270-271; brick, 68; cannon carriage, 467; child's wagon, 287; coffin, 516; etching press, 377; hammock, 288; highway, 114; lithographic press, 376; railroad track, 115; river, 13; slide, 287; tower, ladder, 124; trampoline, 308; wheelbarrow, 430

bed cloth, pool table, 320

bedcover, 271

bedding, 270-271

bed handle, lithographic press, 376

bed joint, brick wall, 69

bed knife, sickle-bar mower, 429

bed mold, column entablature, 73

bedplate: mortar, 472; steam engine, 405

bedrail, 270

bedroll: backpacking, 343; cowboy, 490

bedspread, 271

bee, 41

beef, 32

Beefeater, 483

beehive, woman's hair, 213

begin paragraph, proofreader's mark, 514

belfry, church, 86

bell, iv; bassoon, 357; boxing, 309; buoy, 132; candle snuffer, 237; clarinet, 356; cymbal, 364; fire engine, 124, 125; foil mounting, 315; hammer, 412; jellyfish, 46; slot machine, 346; steam locomotive, 116; telephone, 180; trombone, 358, 359; vault, 457

bell boot, harness racing pacer 337

bell-bottom trousers, 191, 497

bell brace, trombone, 358

bell buoy, nautical chart, 22

bell chest piece, stethoscope, 449

bell cord, commuter bus, 118

bellows: accordion, 366; bagpipe, 365; fireplace, 232; organ, 360; paper bag, 266

bellows pocket, parka, 201

bellows strap, accordion, 366

bell plug, fencing foil, 315

bell rim, bugle, 359

bell shade, lamp, 238

bell wire, trumpet, 359

belly: baluster, 73; banjo, 362; cat, 37; horse, 38; human, 25; jumbo jet, 149; mandolin, 362; type, 166; violin, 355

bellybutton, 25

belowdeck storage entrance, tanker, 140

belt: automobile engine, 111; backpack, 343; belt sander, 421; cardigan sweater, 199; cowboy, 490; drag racing driver, 339; dress, 198; football uniform, 292; ice hockey player, 294; jewelry, 219; king's regalia, 484; machine gun ammunition, 471; man's, 190; military, 496, 497; Milky Way, 3; mountain climbing, 334; police, 498-499; sander, 421; shoulder bag, 222; skirt, 197; time, 5; trench coat, 200; trousers, 191; waterskiing vest, 329

belt carrier, trousers, 191

belted waistband, woman's pants, 196

belt safety guard, drill press, 419

belt sander, 421

belt-tension knob, drill press, 419

bench: baseball field, 291; basketball court, 296; courtroom, 89; football field, 293; ice hockey rink, 295; sled, 328; toboggan, 328

bench rule, 424

bench saw, 417

benchseat, powerboat, 139

bench screw, woodcarving, 372

bench top, workbench, 408

bench vise, 409

bend: fishhook, 341; paper clip, 277; tuba, 358

bending magnet, super collider, 394

Benguela Current, ocean, 6

bent, roller coaster, 92

bent gouge, woodcarving, 372

bent side, grand piano, 361

beret, 202

berg, glacier, 12

bergschrund, mountain, 9

bergy bit, glacier, 12

berm: permanent fort, 83; shoreline, 14

berry, tomato, 54

berth, sailboat, 135

berta, bridal gown, 488

berthing hawser, passenger ship, 142

besom, skirt, 197

beta rod, radio antenna, 183

betting: jai alai, 314; odds, flat racing, 336

bevel: chisel, 420; scriber, 375

bevel gear, hand drill, 418

bevel scale, table saw, 417

bezel: pendant, 219; watch, 220, 304

bezel facet, cut gemstone, 218

B flat, piano keyboard octave, 361

bias, fabric, 388

bias switch, tape recorder, 177

bias tape, garment seam, 196

bib: fencing mask, 315; Indian

521

shirt, 490; lacrosse uniform, 298; maid's uniform, 489; man's shirt, 189
bibcock, 273
biceps, human, 26
bicuspid, 456
bicycle, 128; body building, 344
bicycle crossing, road sign, 505
bicycle trail, public sign, 506
bifocal eyeglasses, 221
big bowtie, clown, 493
big cage, circus, 90
big 8, craps table, 347
big guns, surfboard, 330
big nose, clown, 493
bight, coastline, 15
big 6, craps table, 347
big toe, human foot, 31
big top, circus, 90
bike: body building, 344; harness racing, 337
bike route, road sign, 504
bilge, sailboat, 135
bilge alarm, powerboat, 138
bill: anchor, 132; bird, 39; duck, 35; fishing plug, 341; hook and eye, 208; man's cap, 202; paper money, 224
bill compartment, wallet, 223
billet, saddle, 335
billfold, 223
billiard table, 320
billing, magazine cover, 169
billing error information, monthly statement, 227
billy club, police, 498
bin: garbage disposal, 247; jumbo jet, 148; refrigerator, 249; sideboard, 243; silo, 104; tank, 474
binary code bars, Universal Product Code, 440
binary star, 3
binaural, stethoscope, 449
binder: cigar, 228; water ski, 329
binding: baseball glove, 291; hat, 202; javelin, 303; mattress, 271; pole vault pole, 305; shoe, 204, 302; ski, 326, 327, 329; tennis racket, 312
binding screw, electric plug, 398
binnacle, compass, 136
binoculars, 443
binocular tube, microscope, 442
bipod leg, mortar, 472
bird, 39; badminton, 319; space shuttle, 152
biretta, clergy, 487
birth: racing entry, 336; symbol, 510
birth date, résumé, 160
bishop: chess, 345; vestments, 487
bishop pawn, chess, 345
bishop's arms, church, 87
bishop sleeve, bridal gown, 488
bishop's screen, church, 87
bit: dental, 455; destroyer, 476; drain cleaner, 422; fireboat, 144; flat racing, 336; gimlet, 418; glacier, 12; hand drill, 418, 419; harness racing, 337; oil drilling, 101; pipe, 229; polo, 299; screwdriver, 413; stopwatch, 304; tugboat, 144
bite: bugle, 359; scissors, 384
bitee stick, ambulance, 123
bit gauge, drill, 418, 419
bitty berg, glacier, 12
bivalve shell, 47

blackened copper surface, solar collector panel, 391
black hole, 2
black inner table, backgammon, 345
blackjack, 347
black match, aerial shell, 383
black outer table, backgammon, 345
black slot, roulette, 376
black square, chessboard, 345
black suit, chauffeur, 489
black tie: chauffeur, 489; military uniform, 496
black wire, electrical receptacle, 398
bladder: football, 292; human, 27; seeweed, 57; spacesuit, 155
blade: airplane propeller, 147; ambulance, 123; ax, 464; bicycle, 128; booties, ice skates, 325; bulldozer, 435; burnisher, 377; can opener, 251; cartridge fuse, 399; chisel, 420; cigar cutter, 228; combination square, 424; corkscrew, 251; electric plug, 398; fencing foil, 315; fern, 57; fishing rod, 341; flower petal, 53; food processor, 254; gardening shears, 427; gouge, 374; grass, 58; guillotine, 462; halberd, 464; hatchet, 412; helicopter rotor, 146; hoe, 427; ice hockey stick, 295; ice skates, 325; juice extractor, 255; key, 459; knife, 244, 256, 426, 463; lawn mower, 429; leaf, 52; L-shaped square, 424; outboard engine, 137; partisan, 464; peeler, 256; Ping-Pong racket, 321; plane, 420; razor, 210; rotogravure, 166; rowboat oar, 133; saw, 416, 417; scissors, 384; screwdriver, 413; scriber, 375; seaweed, 57; shoe horn, 207; shovel, 427; silk screen squeegee, 375; skate, 295; skin diving fin, 331; speculum, 448; sword, 463; tape measure, 424; windmill, 390; woodcarving tool, 372
blade-bevel handwheel, table saw, 417
blade cartridge, razor, 210
blade control lever, bulldozer, 435
blade-elevating handwheel, saw, 417
blade eye hook, bulldozer, 435
blade guard, power saw, 417
blade hole, cigar cutter, 228
blade injector, shaver, 210
blade screw, saw, 417
blade shaft, can opener, 251
blank: coin, 225; key, 459
blanket: bedding, 271; police car, 122; saddle, 335
blanket bar, etching press, 377
blanket cylinder, offset press, 166
blank/search button, video-still camera, 173
blazer jacket, woman's, 196
bleach dispenser, washing machine, 280
bleed: magazine, 171; political map, 21
bleed valve, steam engine, 405
blender, 254; pastry, 261
blimp, 156; camera, 174
blind, window, 241
blinder, flat racing, 336
blinker: automobile, 106;

destroyer, 477; flat racing, 336
blister: automobile fender, 107; packaging, 268
block: automobile engine, 111; backgammon, 345; bongo drum, 364; football helmet, 292; igloo, 85; letter, 159; postage stamps, 159; pulley, 461; racing, 304; stapler, 277; steam engine, swimming pool, 316; and tackle, 461; toothbrush, 215; window shutters, 241; woodcut printing, 374; workbench, 408
blocked man's hat, 202
blocking, lacrosse, 298
block number, city plan, 20
block valve, nuclear reactor, 392
blood factor symbols, 510
blood groove, sword, 463
bloodline, flat racing entry, 336
blood-pressure cuff, 123
blood-pressure gauge, 449
blossom end, banana, 55
blot, backgammon, 345
blouse: baseball catcher, 290; military, 496; police, 499; woman's, 197
blower: drag racing dragster, 339; heat exchanger, 403
blow wheel, humidifier, 402
blowhole: dolphin, 45; flute, 357
blow-in, magazine, 171
blowpipe, bagpipe, 365
blowout preventor, oil drilling, 101
blucher, man's shoe, 204
blue lightnin', cowboy, 490
blue line, ice hockey rink, 295
blueprint, house, 62
Blue Room, White House, 75
blue whistler, cowboy, 490
bluff, nautical chart, 22
blunder, gesture, 507
blurb: book, iv, 167; label, 268; magazine, 169, 170
blurgit, cartoon, 381
blush, makeup, 216, 217
boar, 34
board: backgammon, 345; barbecue grill, 288; darts, 322; diving, 316; guitar, 362; hand loom, 387; horseracing, 336, 337; ice hockey rink, 295; jai alai cancha, 314; kitchen tool, 261; merry-go-round, 93; military uniform, 496; organ, 360; roller coaster, 92; squash court, 313; stage, 350; track and field, 300; universal gym, 344; windsurfer, 330
boarding, barn, 104
boarding ladder: combat aircraft, 480; tugboat, 144
boat, 132; craps table, 347
boat boom, aircraft carrier, 478
boat deck, passenger ship, 143
boat neck, sweater, 199
bob, clock pendulum, 233
bobber, fishing, 341
bobbin: sewing machine, 278; spinning wheel, 387; tatting shuttle, 386
bobby pin, 214
bobêche, candelabrum, 237
bobsled, 328
bodice: dress, 198; queen's regalia, 484
body: arrow, 466; automobile, 106; baren, 374; binoculars, 443; book, 167; can, 267;

carpenter's level, 424; discus, 303; drag racing dragster, 339; drill bit, 419; ear scope, 448; faucet, 273; fishing plug, 341; garbage truck, 127; guitar, 362, 363; hand grenade, 473; human, 24-31; internal combustion engine, 406; letter, 159; levigator, 376; locking pliers, 414; locomotive, 117; nail clippers, 215; newspaper story, 168; padlock, 459; pail, 284; paper bag, 266; percolator, 252; pistol nozzle, 428; phonograph headphone, 179; piccolo, 356; pot, 373; printing press, 376, 377; saxophone, 357; shirt, 189; snake, 42; sock, 207; sweater, 199; tooth, 456; traffic light, 113; type, 166; video camera, 184; window shade, 240, 241
body building, 344
body case, rocket, 383
body feather, chicken, 35
body handle, pressure cooker, 257
body lacing, snowshoe, 327
body lock handle, garbage truck, 127
body molding, automobile, 107
body oil, 217
body pad, ice hockey goalie, 294
body panel, stagecoach, 131
body-restraint strap, operating table, 450
body rivet, pliers, 414
body tube, microscope, 442
body wall, safe, 457
body whorl, univalve shell, 47
bogie, bus, 118
boiler: furnace, 400; locomotive, 116; pot, 257; steam engine, 405
bold face type, 165; magazine, 170, 171
bole, tree, 50
bollard, canal lock, 99
bolo tie, 192
bolster: chisel, 420; knife, 256; sofa, 236; stagecoach, 131
bolt, 411; bicycle, 128; saw, 417, 431; crossbow, 466; crutch, 452; door, 458; fabric, 388; house, 61; hurdle, 304; levigator, 376; lock, 458; plane knob, 420; pliers, 414; pulley block, 461; railroad crossing signal, 115; rifle, 468, 471; roller skate, 324; ship's bell, iv; vault, 457; vise, 409; wheelchair, 452
bolt-activating gear ring, vault, 457
bolt cap, toilet, 275
bolt cutter, 414
bolt ring, 218; identification bracelet, 187
bolt-retracting gear, vault, 457
bomb elevators, aircraft carrier, 478
bombproof, permanent fort, 83
bond, wall, 69
bonded insulation filling, sleeping bag, 343
bone: acoustic guitar, 362; early calculator, 441; girdle, 195; human, 25, 26; meat, 262; tile games, 345
bone marrow, meat, 262
bongos, 364
bonnet, 203; faucet, 273; fire hydrant, 125; Indian, 490

bonnet string, cowboy, 490
bony plate, stegosaurus, 43
book, 167; postage stamps, 159; sample page, **iv**; type, 165
boom: aircraft carrier, 478; radio antenna, 183; sailboat, 134; tower ladder, 124; tow truck, 126; windsurfer, 330
boom box, 182
boom bumper, windsurfer, 330
boom gallows, sailboat, 134
boom light, truck bed, 126
boom-to-mast clip, CB radio antenna, 183
booster, space shuttle, 152
booster fan, underwater tunnel, 98
booster hose-reel, pumper, 124
booster parachute canister, space shuttle, 152
booster tank, pumper, 124
boot, 206; automobile, 106; bassoon, 357; cowboy, 490; fireman, 500; harness racing pacer, 337; ice climbing, 334; ice skate, 325; panty hose, 195; polo, 299; race horse, 336; rain, 207; Revolutionary War general, 492; roller skate, 324; soccer, 297; skin diving, 331; skiing, 327, 329; soldier's, 497; spark plug, 111; stagecoach, 131
booth, voting, 437
boot hook, 207
bootie, skin diving, 331
bootjack, 207
boot stripe, power boat, 138
boot top: destroyer, 477; drum major's shoe, 495; sailboat, 134
boozex, cartoon, 381
borated-water storage tank, nuclear reactor, 392
border: basket, 266; book page, **iv**; canapé, 263; check, 226; comic strip, 380; magazine cover, 169; paper money, 225; stage, 350
bore: spool, 384; thermometer, 449; weapons, 467, 468, 469, 470
bore evacuator, tank gun, 475
bosom, human, 25
boson, 394
boss, shield, 464
bota, ski clothes, 327
botonee, symbol, 508
bottle, 267, 268; hair lotion applicator, 214; opener, 251, 426
bottle rack, oil drilling platform, 101
bottom: barrel, 267; book page, 167; flag, 502; girdle, 195; golf bag, 311; man's shoe, 204; parachute, 333; piano, 361; plane, 420; screen, 175; skillet, 257; stove, 404; sweater, 199; vest, 188; waterski, 329; window shutter, 241; zinc carbon cell, 397; zipper, 209
bottom bow, sousaphone, 358
bottom girdle, hot air balloon, 332
bottom pillow, stage coach, 131
bottom plate, house, 61
bottom rail: bureau, 272; door, 64; staircase, 66; venetian blind, 241; window, 65
bottom sheet, bedding, 271
bottom spring, 230
bouffant hairdo, woman's, 213
bounce-angle scale, electronic flash, 176

bouche, shield, 464
boundaries, map, 5, 20
boundary line, volleyball court, 319
bouquet, bridal, 488
bout: fencing, 315; viola, 355
boutonniere, jacket, 188, 488
bow, 466; bear trap, 433; bell, **iv**; beret, 202; boat, 132, 133, 144; bonnet, 203; brace, 418; crutch, 452; cymbal, 364; kettledrum, 364; key, 459; kite, 323; man's hat, 202; mousetrap, 433; rake, 427; saddle, 335; scissors, 384; sousaphone, 358; sword hilt, 463; trombone, 358; violin, 355; watch, 220, 304; windsurfer, 330
bowel, human, 25
bowl: basting ladle, 259; brazier, 288; dessert setting, 245; electric wok, 257; food processor, 254; juice extractor, 255; kitchen sink, 247; mixing, 258; pipe, 229; roulette wheel, 346; spoon, 244; stemware, 244; toilet, 275; type, 165
bowling, 317
bowl release, minivacuum, 283
bowl track, railroad yard, 96
bowmen, 466
bow numbers, destroyer, 477
bow pulpit, sailboat, 134
bowsprit, sailboat, 134
bowstring, 466
bow thruster, passenger ship, 143
bow tie, 192; clown, 493; man's formal attire, 488
bow window, house, 62
box: automobile steering gear, 108; ballet toeshoes, 494; barn, 104; baseball field, 291; blackjack table, 346; book page, **iv**; boot, 206; bus, 118; cigar cutter, 228; circuit breaker, 399; courtroom, 89; craps table, 347; dulcimer, 362; easel, 370; electrical receptacle, 398; handball court, 313; ice hockey rink, 295; light fixture, 238; lithographic press, 376; machine gun cartridge, 471; mail, 231; map, 21; metronome, 367; money, 457; packaging, 269; paramedic equipment, 123; parking meter, 113; pole vault, 305; pool table, 320; prison, 76; radar antenna, 444; railroad crossing signal, 115; razor blade injector, 210; resonance, 367; running shoe, 302; seeder, 430; sideboard, 243; sketch, 371; stagecoach, 131; steam engine, 405; subway motorman's cab, 119; tank, 474; tefillin, 486; theatre, 351; tow truck, 126; tugboat, 144; vault, 457; wrench, 415
boxcar, train, 117
box drawer, desk, 276
boxer, pugilist, 309
boxer shorts, 194
boxing, 309
box kit, 323
boxman, craps table, 347
box ratchet, brace, 418
box spring, bed, 271
bra, 195
brace, 418; balance beam, 306; basketball backstop, 296; bridge, 97; child's wagon, 287; dental, 453; fence gate,

69; guitar, 362; house, 61; kiln, 373; kite, 323; ladder, 425; locomotive, 116; man's, 190; oil drilling platform, 101; parallel bars, 306; rocking chair, 234; sponge mop, 283; stage, 350; stagecoach, 131; supportive, 452; table saw, 417; toboggan, 328; trombone, 358; venetian blind, 241; wheelbarrow, 430; wheelchair, 452; workbench, 408
brace flange, trombone, 358
bracelet: human hand, 31; identification, 187; jewelry, 219; wristwatch, 220
brace pole, tent, 342
brachial artery, human, 28
brachial plexus, human, 29
brachioradialis, human, 26
bracket: butterfly table, 242; child's wagon, 287; citrus juicer, 255; dental unit, 454; grammatical symbol, 513; house, 62; inflatable, 133; ladder, 425; mortar, 472; orthodontic, 453; outboard engine, 137; police car, 122; radar antenna, 444; railroad crossing signal, 115; royal crown, 485; sawhorse, 408; ship's bell, 115; tanker, 141; tow truck bed, 126; traverse rod, 240; wheelbarrow, 430; wheelchair, 452
bracket slot, dental braces, 453
bracket table, dental, 455
bract: grass, 58; lettuce, 262; pineapple, 55
brad, 410
braid: military uniform, 496; venetian blind, 241; woman's hair, 213; woman's hat, 203
braided tail, polo pony, 299
braille, 512
brain: allosaurus, 43; human, 29; stegosaurus, 43
brains, beef, 32
brain stem, human, 29
brake: bicycle, 128; bobsled, 328; bulldozer, 435; car, 108, 110; chain saw, 431; locomotive, 116; motorcycle, 129; 747 cockpit, 150; ski binding, 326; space shuttle, 152; stagecoach, 131; stroller, 286; subway car, 119; tank gun muzzle, 475
brake caliper: automobile, 108; bicycle, 128; motorcycle, 129
brake caster, easel, 370
brake drum, automobile, 109
brake duct, racing car, 338
brake handle: 747 cockpit, 150; subway motorman's cab, 119
brake plate, ski binding, 326
brake pressure indicator, pilot's instrument panel, 481
branch: cactus, 56; candelabrum, 237; celery, 262; hogan, 84; horseshoe, 38; military insignia, 496; river, 13; stirrup, 335; sword hilt, 463; tree, 50; tuba, 358
brand: branding iron, 432; gas pump, 112; label, 268; pencil, 158
branding iron, 432
brand name, coupon, 103
brand name ad space, supermarket, 102
brand name logo, aisle display, 102
brandy snifter, 245

brass: musical instruments, 354, 358-359; sideboard, 243
brassard, military police, 496
brass button: military, 496; police, 498
brassie, golf club, 311
brassiere, 195
bratelles, dress, 198
brayer, woodcut printing, 374
brazier, patio, 288
Brazil Current, ocean, 6
bread: canapé base, 263; Communion, 87; loaf, 157
breadbasket, human, 25
bread rack, toaster, 253
break, cat, 37
break-arch, grandfather clock, 233
breaker: circuit, 399; magazine, 170; shoreline, 14; stained glass, 378
breaker hammer, 436
breakfront, 243
breakout, political map, 21
breakpoint, continental margin, 15
breakfast: chicken, 35; horse, 38; human, 24; lamb, 33; poultry, 35; woman's shoe heel, 205
breastbeam, hand loom, 387
breast collar, harness racing, 337
breastplate: armor, 465; polo, 299; Torah, 486
breast pocket: men's jacket, 188; parka, 201; shirt, 189; woman's jacket, 196
breast protector, fencing, 315
breaststroke swimming race, 316
breastworks, permanent fort, 83
breath-hold diving, 331
breathing aid, paramedic, 123
breathing filter, drag racing fire suit, 339
breath mark, music, 352
B recreation yard, prison, 76
breech: human, 25; weapons, 467, 470, 471
breechblock, shotgun, 468
breeches, see trousers
breeches, polo, 299
breeder reactor, nuclear power, 392
breve, grammatical symbol, 513
brewed coffee, 252
brick: building material, 68; lobster pot, 433
brickmold, window, 65
brick symbolia, cartoon, 380
brick wall, 69
bridal dress, 488
bridge, 97; aircraft carrier, 478; airport, 94; billiards, 320; bow, 466; bowling ball, 317; castle, 80, 81; coffin, 516; dental, 453; destroyer, 477; eyeglasses, 221; guitar, 362; highway cloverleaf, 114; lacrosse stick, 298; nose, 30; passenger ship, 143; railroad, 115; spider web, 40; submarine, 479; tanker, 141; vault, 457; violin, 355
bridge and socket assembly, sponge mop, 282
bridge cover, guitar, 363
bridge table, 242
bridle: horseracing, 336, 337; kite leg, 323; polo, 299; waterskiing towline, 329
briefcase, 285
briffit, cartoon, 380
brightness control, sonar, 444
brilliance control, radar, 444

brim, hat, 202, 203
briquette, charcoal, 288
brisket: beef, 32; dog, 36; horse, 38; sheep, 33
bristle: broom, 282; brow brush, 217; hairbrush, 212; painting brush, 370; paint brush, 425; toothbrush, 215
broadcast indicator, CB radio, 183
broad jump, 300
broguings, man's shoe, 204
broiler unit, stove, 248
broken leader, book page, iv
brooch, 218, 219
brook, 13
Brooklyn pocket, bowling, 317
broom, 282; mechanical sweeper, 127
brow, human, 25
browband, Indian, 490
brow brush, beauty product, 217
brow rest, eye scope, 448
brush: beauty product, 217; cooking utensil, 229; dog, 36; drum, 364; electric, 212; house painting, 425; painting, 370, 371; photographic supplies, 176; shaving, 210; ultimate beast's tail, 48; vacuum cleaner, 283
brush bag, lunar rover, 155
brush retainer screw, saber saw, 417
brushwood, wickiup, 84
brussa, Arab dress, 491
bubble: monovial, 424; theodolite, 436
buccal, tooth, 456
buccal cusp, tooth, 456
buckaroo, 490
buckboard, 131
bucket, 284; launch pad, 152; tower-ladder, 124
bucket hat, sailor, 497
bucket seat, car, 110
buckle: backpack, 343; brassiere, 195; combat soldier, 497; cowboy belt, 490; electric chair, 462; harness racing, 337; man's, 190; police gun belt, 498; sandal, 206; ski boot, 326; trench coat, 200; venetian blind, 241; waterskiing vest, 329; woman's hat, 203
buckler, medieval shield, 464
bud: flower, 53; potato, 54; taste, 30; tree, 50
buddy umbilical system bag, lunar rover, 155
buffalo horn, ultimate beast, 49
buffer: elevator shaft, 78; high-speed printer, 439; magnetic tape subsystem, 439; train track, 116
buffet, 243
buffet car, passenger train, 116
bug, ice cream cone, 265
buggy, horse-drawn, 131
bugle, 359
building, 77; city plan, 20; topographic map, 22; whole-timbered, 70
building material, 68
built-in flash: Polaroid, 173; video-still camera, 173
built-in microphone, tape recorder, 177
built-in phone, fax machine, 164
built-in speaker, personal cassette player, 182
bulb: balloon, 493; blood pressure gauge, 449; clown,

493; hourglass, 233; light, 238; onion, 54, 262; thermometer, 18, 449; vacuum tube, 396
bulb head, drain cleaner, 422
bulb of heel, horse, 38
bulkhead: passenger ship, 142; powerboat, 139; sailboat, 135; truck platform, 121
bulkhead mounting flange, aneroid barometer, 18
bulk storage: oil drilling platform, 101; refrigerator, 249
bull, 32; zodiac, 509
bull denim trousers, cowboy, 490
bulldozer, 435
bullet: cartridge, 470; police gun belt, 498; stick umbrella, 230
bulletproof vest, 499
bullhorn, police car, 122
bullion, 225
bull nose, destroyer, 477
bull's-eye, dart board, 322
bulwark: castle, 80, 81; passenger ship, 142; sailboat, 135
bump, razor blade injector, 210
bumper: automobile, 106, 107, 108; billiard cue, 320; bus, 118; citrus juicer, 255; football helmet, 292; knee kicker, 246; locomotive, 117; mechanical sweeper, 127; sled, 328; snowmobile, 130; toilet, 275; train track, 116; trombone, 359; vacuum cleaner, 283; wheelchair, 452; windsurfer, 330
bumper car, amusement park, 92
bumper steps, truck tractor, 120
bun: sandwich, 263; woman's hair, 213
bundling, package, 269
bunghole, keg, 267
bunk, sailboat, 135
bunker, golf course, 405
bunting, flag, 502
buoy, 132; nautical chart, 22
buoyancy chamber, inflatable, 133
buoyancy compensator, skin diving, 331
bureau, dresser, 272
burette, laboratory, 447
burgee, flag, 502
burial chamber, 516
burner: barbecue grill, 288; camper stove, 342; candle, 237; chafing dish, 245; furnace, 400; hot air balloon, 332; laboratory, 447; stove, 248; tea kettle, 245; water heater, 401
burnisher, 377
burn sheet, ambulance, 123
burr: dental, 455; pipe, 422
burst, label, 268
bursting charge, aerial shell, 383
bus, 118
busby, drum major, 495
bus connection, circuit board, 439
bushing: automobile, 108; roller chain, 461
business, letter, 159
business card, 160
business career, résumé, 160
business-class section, jumbo jet, 148
bust, human, 25
bustle, tank, 474

bustline, dress, 198
bus transportation, public sign, 506
butane well, gas cigarette lighter, 228
butler, 489
butt: arrow, 466; ax, 464; bassoon, 357; bazooka, 472; billiard cue, 320; cigar, 228; cigarette, 228; fishing rod, 340; halberd, 464; latch needle, 386; pork, 34; revolver, 470; rifle, 471
butt cap: fishing rod, 340; tennis racket, 312
butte, mountain, 8
butt end, lacrosse stick, 298; paint brush bristle, 425
butter compartment, refrigerator, 249
butterfly net, 411
butterfly swimming race, 316
butterfly table, 242
butterfly tie, 192
butter knife, 244
butter plate, 244
butter stile, door, 64
butt hinge, 460
buttock: horse, 38; human, 24
button, 209; accordion, 366; answering machine, 181; ballpoint pen, 158; blender, 254; camera, 172; cannon barrel, 467; cardigan sweater, 199; chain saw, 431; compact disc player, 178; copier, 164; dental unit, 454; door lock, 458; elevator car, 78; escalator, 79; fencing foil, 315; garbage disposal, 247; guillotine, 462; human, 25; incandescent bulb, 238; jacket, 188, 196; lounger, 235; man's cap, 202; metronome, 367; military uniform, 496; movie camera, 174; organ, 360; plug fuse, 399; police car, 122; police uniform, 498; portable radio/cassette player, 182; potter's wheel, 373; remote control unit, 184; Revolutionary War general, 492; saxophone, 357; screen, 175; sewing machine, 278; skirt, 197; snake rattle, 43; sofa, 236; spur, 335; stopwatch, 304; suspenders, 190; sword hilt, 463; table saw, 417; tape recorder, 177; telegraph key, 157; trench coat, 200; trumpet, 359; vacuum cleaner, 283; vest, 188; Walkman, 182; woman's hat, 203
button-down collar, shirt, 189
button-down cuff, Revolutionary War general, 492
buttonhole: jacket, 188; Revolutionary War general, 492; shirt, 189; vest, 188
button mark, sewing pattern, 388
button nook, iron, 279
button-off collar, trench coat, 200
button-out robe lining, overcoat, 200
button rod, incandescent bulb, 238
button tab closings, pants, 191
button-through pocket, trench coat, 200
butt plate: rifle, 471; shotgun, 468
buttress, mountain, 8
butt section, fishing rod, 340

buttstock, shotgun, 468
buzzer button, video-still camera, 173
by, symbol, 510
byline: magazine, 169, 170; newspaper, 168
by-pass shears, gardening, 427

C

C: braille, 512; piano keyboard octave, 361; music notation, 353; sign language, 512
cab: airport control tower, 95; bulldozer, 435; elevator, 78; fire engine, 124, 125; horse-drawn, 131; locomotive, 116; subway, 119; tractor, 434; truck, 120
cabin: aircraft, 146, 147, 156; hovercraft, 145; sailboat, 134, 135; space shuttle, 152
cabinet: air conditioner, 402; ambulance, 123; china, 243; desk, 276; dishwasher, 250; elevator, 78; garbage disposal, 247; guitar amplifier, 363; humidifier, 402; phonograph, 179; television, 185; washing machine, 280
cabinet tip, screwdriver, 413
cabinetwork, house blueprint, 62
cabin pressure altimeter, pilot's instrument panel, 481
cabin trunk, powerboat, 138
cable: bazooka, 472; bicycle, 128; bridge, 97; circuit breaker box, 399; electrician's, 423; elevator shaft, 78; fencing strip, 315; gas pump, 112; motorcycle, 129; police car, 122; power line, 396; space suit, 155; stationary rings, 307; tow truck, 126; video-still camera adaptor, 173
cable stitch, sock, 207
caboose, train, 117
cabriolet, 131
caftan, 491
cactus, 56
CAD, 438
caduceus, symbol, 510
Caesar, playing card king, 348
cafe curtain, 240
cage: baseball catcher's, 290; buoy, 132; circus, 91; drag racing dragster, 339; football helmet, 292; hammer throw, 301; ice hockey goal, 294; jai alai cancha, 314; police car, 122
caisson, cannon, 467
cake, 264
cake plate, 245
calamus, bird feather, 39
calcaneus, human, 26
calculator, 441
calculator dial, electronic flash, 176
calendar, grandfather clock, 233
calendar day, globe, 5
calf, 32, 432; frog, 44; human, 24
caliber, cartridge, 470
calibration: blood pressure gauge, 449; Geiger counter, 445
California Current, ocean, 6
caliper: automobile disc brake, 108; bicycle, 128; motorcycle, 129
calk, horseshoe, 38
calliope, merry-go-round, 93
callount, book page, iv
calm, hurricane, 17

calving, glacier, 12
calyx, coral polyp, 46
cam: lawn sprinkler, 428;
    motorcycle, 129; plane, 420;
    pliers, 414
camber, skiing, 329
cambium, tree, 50
cambox, lithographic press,
    376
camcorder, 184
came, lead, 378
cameo, 218
camera, 173; lunar rover, 155;
    satellite, 186; spacesuit, 155
camera connector, VCR, 184
camera platform, tripod, 176
camisole top, dress, 198
camouflage cover, soldier's
    helmet, 497
camper, 130
campfire, public sign, 506
camping, 342; road sign, 504
cam ring, brace, 418
can, 267; ammunition, 471;
    mercury battery, 397;
    nautical chart, 22;
    pacemaker, 452
canal lock, 99
canapé, 263
canard, jet fighter, 480
Canary Current, ocean, 6
cancel button, organ, 360
cancellation, envelope, 159
Cancer, zodiac, 509
cancha, jai alai, 314
candelabrum, 237
candidate's name column,
    voting booth, 437
candle, 237
candlepin, bowling, 317
candle slide, sideboard, 243
candlestick, 237; church, 87
cane, supportive device, 452
cane rod, fishing, 341
canine teeth, 456
canister: drain cleaner, 422;
    film roll, 172; police gun
    belt, 498; space shuttle, 152;
    windmill, 390
can ledge, can opener, 251
cannon, 467; horse, 38; jet
    fighter, 480; muzzle-loading,
    472; tank, 475
cannonball, 467
cannula, hypodermic syringe,
    451
canoe, roulette wheel, 346
can opener, 251; pocket knife,
    426
canopy: bed, 270; bulldozer,
    435; elevator, 78; glider
    cockpit, 147; jet fighter, 480;
    light fixture, 238; parachute,
    333; stroller, 286; tent, 342;
    toll booth, 114
canopy jettison handle, pilot's
    instrument panel, 481
canteen, soldier's, 497
canthus, eye, 30
cantilevered suspension,
    racing car, 338
cantle, saddle, 335
canton, flag, 502
cantor, synagogue, 486
canvas: boxing ring, 309;
    painting, 370
canvas holder, easel, 370
canvas slot, sketch box, 371
canyon, 7, 13
cap: backpack, 343; baseball,
    290; blender, 254; blood
    pressure gauge, 449; bottle,
    268, 269; bulldozer, 435;
    can, 267; cartridge fuse, 399;
    chimney, 63, 232; chisel,
    420; contact lens container,
    221; cornet, 359; dental, 455;
    dishwasher, 250; dispenser,

267; engine, 111, 137, 406;
fence gate, 67; fire hydrant,
125; fishing rod, 340;
football, 292; hair styling,
214; hinge pin, 460; hockey
skate, 325; lamp, 238;
lantern, 342; magazine, 170;
Manchu court dress, 491;
man's, 202; military, 496,
497; mortar, 472;
motorcycle, 129; mower,
429; mushroom, 57; pencil,
158; pin, 208; plane, 420;
plug fuse, 399; polo, 299;
racing, 336; razor, 210;
railroad crossing signal, 115;
rifle, 471; rocket, 383; royal
crown, 485; saddle, 335;
saw, 431; screen, 175;
seeder, 430; shotgun, 468,
469; space shuttle, 152;
standpipe, 59; stapler, 277;
starting block, 304; stove,
342; tennis racket, 312; test
tube, 447; thimble, 384;
toilet, 275; track lighting,
239; traffic light, 113;
umbrella, 230; venetian
blind, 241; washing
machine, 280; waterskiing
towline, 329; windmill, 390
cape: land feature, 7;
    stonecutting, 342
capelet, king's, 484
capillary, human, 27
capillary bed, human, 28
capillary tube, thermometer,
    449
capital: column, 73; political
    map symbol, 20;
    proofreader's mark, 514;
    type height, 165; White
    House, 75
Capitol building, 74
caplet, medicinal, 451
cap mounting, ballpoint pen,
    158
cap nut, 411
capo, guitar, 362
capon, 35
cap opener, corkscrew, 251
cappuccino, 252
Capricorn, zodiac, 509
cap square, carriage, 467
capstan: sword hilt, 463; tape
    recorder, 177; tugboat, 144
capstem, strawberry, 55
capstone, gate post, 67
capsule: bottle, 267; medicinal,
    451
captain's seat, 747 cockpit, 150
caption: book page, iv;
    cartoon, 380; magazine, 169,
    171; newspaper, 168
car: amusement park ride, 92,
    93; blimp, 156; drag racing,
    339; elevator, 78; subway,
    119; train, 96, 116, 117; see
    also automobile
carabiner, mountain climbing,
    334
carapace, turtle, 43
carbide insert, masonry bit,
    419
carbiner hole, ice ax, 242
carafe, coffee maker, 252
carapace, lobster, 47
carbon copy, letter, 159
carbon-layered forward wing
    edge, space shuttle, 152
carburetor: automobile, 111;
    chain saw, 431; motorcycle,
    129
carcass, furniture, 272
card: automatic teller machine,
    226; blister, 268; compass,
    136; playing, 348
card case, wallet, 223

car deck, hovercraft, 145
card holder: bank card, 226;
    elevator car, 78; typewriter,
    161
cardholder's address, monthly
    statement, 227
cardholder's name, monthly
    statement, 227
cardigan: jacket, 196; sweater,
    199
cardinal, religious vestments,
    487
cardinal points, weather vane,
    19
card loop, typewriter, 161
card room, passenger ship,
    142
card table, 242
card window, wallet, 223
career goal, résumé, 160
cargo, merchant ship, 140
cargo bay door, space shuttle,
    152
cargo pocket, parka, 201
cargo ship, 140
cargo truck, airport, 95
caricature, cartooning, 380
caries, tooth, 456
carillon, iv
car lift, passenger ship, 142
carom, billiards, 320
carotid artery, human, 28
carousel: amusement park, 93;
    microwave oven, 248
carousel tray, slide projector,
    175
carpal, human, 26
carpels, samara, 52
carpenter's level, 424
carpenter's saw, 416
carpet, 246; sweeper, 282; tack,
    246
carpus: dog, 36; human hand,
    31
car ramp, hovercraft, 145
car rental, public sign, 506
carriage: baby, 286; cannon,
    467; horse-drawn, 131; hot
    air balloon; toaster, 253;
    typewriter, 161
carriage bolster, stagecoach,
    131
carriage brace, child's wagon,
    287
carrier: aircraft, 478; dental,
    455; dress, 198; etching
    press roller, 377; fireplace
    wood, 232; harness racing,
    337; microscope, 442; pencil
    sharpener, 277; traverse rod,
    240
carrot, 54
carrying chair, ambulance, 123
carrying handle: golf bag, 311;
    landmine, 473; machine
    gun, 471; movie projector,
    175; outboard engine, 137;
    photographic bag, 176; rifle,
    471
car seat, child's, 286
car service area, railroad yard,
    96
car-station panel, elevator, 78
art, lawn, 430
cart ad display, supermarket,
    102
cartilage, human, 26
cartography, 5, 20
cartoon, stained glass, 378
cartooning, 380-381
cartridge: cowboy, belt, 490;
    film, 172, 174; laser printer,
    163; pen, 158; phonograph
    turntable, 178; weapons,
    470, 471
cartridge fuse, 399
cartridge slot, synthesizer, 363
caruncle, turkey, 35

carving: scrimshaw, 375;
    tombstone, 516
carving hammer, stonecutting,
    342
cascable, cannon, 467
cascade collar, bridal gown,
    488
case: attaché, 285; battery, 397;
    beauty product, 217; blood
    pressure gauge, 449; cellular
    telephone, 181; cosmetic,
    285; handgun cartridge, 470;
    hardback book, 167;
    harmonica, 366; lock, 458;
    luggage, 288; metronome,
    367; padlock, 459; pencil,
    158; pitch pipe, 367; police
    gun belt, 499; screen, 175;
    sideboard, 243; stapler, 277;
    tape measure, 424;
    thermometer, 18; wallet,
    223; watch, 220
casebound book, 167
casemate: castle, 80, 81;
    permanent fort, 89
casement window, 65
casework furniture, 243
cash drawer, automatic teller
    machine, 226
cash machine, 226
cash register, 440
cash value, coupon, 103
casing: calculator, 441;
    cartridge fuse, 399; door, 62,
    64; electric meter, 399; hand
    grenade, 473; pacemaker,
    452; pen, 158; pill, 451;
    pyramid, 71; slot machine,
    346; telephone, 180; trumpet
    valve, 359; window, 65
casino, passenger ship, 142
cask, 267
casket, 516
casserole, 257
cassette: film, 172; operating
    table, 450; recorder, 177;
    tape, 177; Walkman, 182
cassette compartment,
    portable radio/cassette
    player, 182; Walkman, 182
cassette eject button, VCR,
    184
cassette feed, laser printer, 163
cassette loading door, VCR,
    184
cassette player, 182
cassette release lever, copier,
    164
Cassini division, Saturn's
    rings, 3
cassock, 487
cast, denture, 453
caster: bed, 271; piano, 361;
    sofa, 236; wheelchair, 452
cast-iron casing, hand
    grenade, 473
castle, 80-81; chess, 345
castle pawn, chess, 345
castor, grand piano, 361
cast restoration, dental, 455
cat, 37; house, 61; circus, 90
catacomb, house, 62
catapult, 467; aircraft carrier,
    478
cataract, river, 13
catch: door, 458; pistol, 470;
    swivel, 218
catcher: baseball, 290, 291;
    grill, 288; saw, 431
catch glove, ice hockey goalie,
    294
catering truck, airport, 95
caterpillar track, tank, 474
cathedral, 86
cathedral hull, powerboat, 138
cathode, laser, 395
cathode ray tube: computer
    workstation, 438; personal

computer, 162; television, 185
cathode-ray tube screen, radar and sonar, 444
cathode wire, vacuum tube, 396
catta, 37
cattle, 32
cattle crossing, road sign, 505
cat trainer, circus, 90
catwalk: canal lock, 99; prison, 76; tanker, 140; tunnel, 98
caudal fin, fish, 45
caudal peduncle, fish, 45
caution signal: pilot's instrument panel, 481; toll booth, 114; traffic light, 113
cautionary statement, label, 269
cavalry yard, frontier fort, 82
cave, 11
cavern, 11
cavity, tooth, 455, 456
C-band antenna, lunar lander, 154
CB radio, 183; police car, 122
C cell block, prison, 76
C-clamp, 409
CD, compact disc player, 178
CD player, 178
cedilla, grammatical symbol, 513
ceiling: elevator car, 78; house, 61
celery, 262
cell: animal, 23; barometer, 18; battery, 397; electric meter, 399; flower, 53; kite, 323; octopus, 46; parachute, 333; prison, 76; solar power system, 391; telescope, 443
cellar, passenger ship, 143
cello, 354, 355
cello wrap, packaging, 269
cellular kite, 323
cellular telephone, 181
Celsius scale, thermometer; 18, 449
Celtic cross, symbol, 508
cementum, tooth, 456
cent, symbol, 511
center: basketball, 296; envelope, 159; ice hockey, 295; polo, 299; spider web, 40; theodolite, 436
centerable lens, microscope, 442
center aisle, theatre, 351
center beam, laboratory scale, 447
center bearing wall, house, 60
center circle: basketball court, 296; ice hockey rink, 295; soccer field, 297
center dent, cowboy hat, 202
center drawer: desk, 276; dressing table, 272
center field, baseball, 291
center field mark, soccer field, 297
center flag, soccer field, 297
center front panel, girdle, 195
center-front seam, skirt, 197
center hole, phonograph record, 178
centering: radar, 444; sonar, 444
centering screw, microscope, 442
center leaf, hinge, 460
center line: airport runway, 94; badminton court, 319; fencing strip, 315; ice hockey rink, 295; lacrosse field, 298; Ping-Pong table, 321; soccer field, 297; symbol, 510; volleyball court, 319

center mark, tennis court, 312
centerpiece, dessert setting, 245
center pin, pulley block, 461
center post: camera tripod, 176; tatting shuttle, 386
center ring, circus, 90-91
center slat, sled, 328
center span, bridge, 97
center spot, soccer field, 297
center stand, motorcycle, 129
center stile, door, 64
center strap, tennis net, 312
center weight, discus, 303
centigrade scale, thermometer, 18, 449
central cleft, horse's foot, 38
central computer, prison, 76
central disc, starfish, 46
central focusing drive, binoculars, 443
central incisor, tooth, 456
central instrument warning light, 747 cockpit, 151
central inventory control unit, cash register, 440
central nervous system, human, 29
central portal, church, 87
central processing unit, 438
Central Time, 5
central-vent volcano, 10
centriole, animal cell, 23
cents-off corner mark, label, 269
cents-off value, coupon, 103
cephalothorax, spider, 40
ceramic shell, plug fuse, 399
cerebellum, brain, 29
cerebral cortex, brain, 29
cerebrum, brain, 29
cereal grass, 38
cercus, grasshopper, 41
certificate holder, elevator car, 78
certification, gas pump, 112
certification plate, truck van, 121
cervical collar, ambulance, 123
cervical vertebrae, human, 26
cesta, jai alai, 314
chafing dish, 245
chain, 461; bear trap, 433; bicycle, 128; castle portcullis, 81; chain saw, 431; fire hydrant, 125; football sidelines, 293; gun belt, 499; grandfather clock, 233; hammock, 288; identification bracelet, 187; incline track, 92; jewelry, 219; king's regalia, 484; lock, 458; oil drilling platform, 101; spur, 335; swing, 287; tow truck bed, 126; zipper, 209
chain guard: bicycle, 128; lithographic press, 376; motorcycle, 129
chainlink fence, 67; prison, 76
chain lock, 458
chain mail, armor, 465
chain pin, roller chain, 461
chain reaction, nuclear reactor, 392
chain saw, 431
chain stopper, sink, 273
chair: ambulance, 123; dental, 454; electric, 462; powerboat, 139; reclining, 235; rocking, 234; wheeled, 452
chaise longue, 288
chalice, 87
chalk, billiards, 320
chamber: burial, 516; camera, 174; cave, 11; Capitol, 74; combustion jet engine, 407; decompession, 452;

fireplace, 232; revolver, 470; rocket, 407; stove, 404
chamber music ensemble, 354
champagne glass, 244
championship tee, golf course, 310
chancel, church, 87
chancellery, 86
chandelier: light fixture, 238; Senate, 74
changeout room, launch pad, 152
change pocket, jacket, 188
channel: backyard glider, 287; bowling lane, 317; canal lock, 99; CB radio, 183; laboratory scale, 447; lamp, 238; lead came, 378; nautical chart, 22; operating room table, 450; pliers, 414; police radio, 122; river, 13; stapler, 277; window, 65
channel index, picture-in-picture viewing, 185
channel number readout, picture-in-picture viewing, 185
channel selector, remote control unit, 184
channel set indicator, VCR, 184
chanter, bagpipe, 365
chapel: castle, 81; church, 86, 87; frontier fort, 82; passenger ship, 143; prison, 76
chaps, cowboy, 490
chapter: book, 167; grandfather clock, 233; pocket watch, 220
character: cartooning, 380; clown face, 493; mah-jongg tile, 345; typewriter, 161
charcoal: briquette, 288; sketch box, 371
charge, flag, 502
charge card, 227
charge container, land mine, 473
charged particle telescope, satellite, 186
charger, tow truck, 126
chariot, merry-go-round, 93
Charlemagne, playing card king, 348
Charlie, stagecoach, 131
charm, jewelry, 219
chart: electronic weather station, 18; nautical, 22
chart table, sailboat, 135
chase: cannon barrel, 467; wall, 69
chaser, engraving, 377
chassis: automobile, 106; racing car, 338-339; machine gun, 471
chasuble, cardinal, 487
château name, wine label, 267
chauffeur, 489
chauffeur's cab, fire engine, 124, 125
cheater, wrench, 415
check, 226; lacrosse, 298; lumber, 68; ticket, 349
check bars, Universal Product Code, 440
check bit, harness racing, 337
checkbook clutch, 223
check digit, bank card, 226
checker, 345
checkerboard, 345
checkering, shotgun, 468
check-in, public sign, 506
check issue date, 226
check letter, paper money, 224, 225

checkout area, supermarket, 103
checkout center, 440
checkout counter, 103
checkpoint, prison, 76
check rein, harness racing, 337
cheek: cannon carriage, 467; dog, 36; horse, 38; hammer, 412; human, 24; latch needle, 386; piano, 361; pulley block, 461
cheese, 263; pizza, 265; slicer, 256
chelicera, spider, 40
chemin de fer, 346
chemise: dress, 198; queen's underpinnings, 484
cheng-lung, Manchu court dress, 491
cherry: ice cream cone, 265; police car, 122
cherry picker, tower ladder, 124
chess, 345
chest: dog, 36; horse, 38; human, 24; organ, 360
chest and stomach pad, lacrosse uniform, 298
chest floor, cow, 32
chest of drawers, 272
chest piece, stethoscope, 449
chest press, universal gym, 344
chest protector: baseball catcher, 290; ice hockey goalie, 294
chest pull, body building, 344
chevelure, 211
chevron, airport runway, 94
chicken, 35
chief, coat of arms, 503
chief clerk, Senate, 74
chiffonier, 272
chignon, woman's hair, 213
children: backyard equipment, 286-287; gear, 286; playroom, passenger ship, 143
chime: barrel, 267; bell, iv
chimney: cave, 11; fireplace, 232; furnace, 400; house, 62, 63; mountain, 8; volcano, 10
chin: bird, 39; human, 24
china cabinet, 243
china guard, dishwasher, 244
China Room, White House, 75
chine, powerboat, 138
chinning bar, backyard, 287
chinning station, universal gym, 344
chin piece, armor, 465
chin rest, violin, 355
chin strap: cowboy hat, 202; drum major's busby, 495; football helmet, 292; ice hockey player, 295; police helmet, 499; polo, 299
chip: blackjack, 347; craps table, 347; transistor, 396
chisel, 372, 374, 420
chitin, crustacean, 47
chock: destroyer, 476, 477; mountain climbing, 334
choil, knife, 463
choir, church, 87
choir keyboard, organ, 360
choir riser, orchestra, 354
choke, car, 110, 111
choked barrel, shotgun, 468
choke end, wood block, 461
choke knob, chain saw, 431
choker necklace, 219; Indian, 490; queen's, 484
chopper, helicopter, 261
chopping board, 261
chopsticks, electric wok, 257
chord: lift bridge, 97; music, 352

526

chord buttons, accordion, 366
chordophone, 362
choropleth map, 21
Christmas tree, drag racing starting lights, 339
chromatophore, octopus, 46
chrome, automobile, 107
chronograph, spacesuit, 155
chronometer, 220
chromosome, cell, 23
chrysanthemum, fireworks, 382
chuck: beef, 32; brace, 418; drill, 418, 419; fishing rod, 340; screwdriver, 413; scriber, 375
chuck-a-luck, 346
chuck tightener, dental, 455
chukka, polo, 299
church, 86-87
church key, can opener, 251
chute: dam, 100; jumbo jet, 148; mountain, 8; mower, 429; parachuting, 333; racetrack, 337; running track, 300; saw, 417; toll basket, 114
cigar, 228
cigarette, 228
cigarette lighter, 228; car, 110
cilia, eye, 30
ciliary body, eye, 30
cinch: backpack strap, 343; cowboy hat, 202; fastener, 208; saddle, 335
cincture: column, 73; religious vestments, 487
cinder, volcano, 10
cine scale, light meter, 176
cinquefoil, church, 86
circle: baseball field, 291; basketball court, 296; geodesic dome, 85; ice hockey rink, 295; shot put, 301; theodolite, 436
circlet, royal crown, 485
circuit, electric, 399
circuit board, 439
circuit breaker, 399; space shuttle, 153
circuit closer lever, telegraph key, 157
circuit traces, circuit board, 439
circular saw, 417
circular slide rule, 441
circulating pump, solar heating system, 391
circulating water pump, nuclear reactor, 393
circulatory system, human, 27, 28
circumflex accent, grammatical symbol, 513
circus, 90-91
cirque, mountain, 8
cirque glacier, 9, 12
cirrocumulus cloud, 16
cirrostratus cloud, 16, 17
cirrus cloud, 16, 17
citation: enlisted man, 496; police, 498
Citizen's Band radio, 183
citrus juicer, 255
city plan, map, 20
city symbol, political map, 20
civil aircraft, 148-149
cladophyll, asparagus, 54
clam, 47
clamp, 409; cassette tape, 177; drill press, 419; finishing sander, 421; laboratory, 446; lamp, 239; outboard engine, 137; Ping-Pong net, 321; paw, 416; telescope, 443; theodolite, 436
clamp bar, suit hanger, 281
clamp collar, camera tripod, 176

clamp holder, pumper, 125
clamp screw: combination square, 424; outboard engine, 137; sewing machine, 278; theodolite, 436
clapboard siding, house, 63
clapper: bell, iv; buoy, 132
clarinet, 354, 356-357
clarstory, church, 86
clasp: denture, 453; hair roller, 214; identification bracelet, 187; keychain, 459; necktie, 192; pin, 208; royal regalia, 484
classification track, railroad yard, 96
class insignia, mainsail, 136
class interval, thematic map, 21
clavicle, human, 26
clavier, organ, 360
claw: allosaurus, 43; bee, 41; bird, 39; cat, 37; clothespin, 280; flower petal, 53; grasshopper, 41; hammer, 412; lizard, 43; lobster, 47; rifle sling, 468; ring, 219; spider, 40; turkey, 35; turtle, 43; ultimate beast, 48
clay choke, rocket, 383
cleaner: automobile engine, 111; mower, 429; nail clippers, 215; pipe, 229
cleaning supplies, photographic, 176
cleanout plug, sink drain, 273
cleansing cream, 216
clear: shuffleboard court, 318; weather map, 19
clearance light: bus, 118; truck, 121
clear key, calculator, 441
clear program button, compact disc player, 178
cleat: baseball, 290; football, 292; sailboat, 135; snowmobile, 130; tugboat, 144
cleavage, human, 25
clef, music, 352, 353
cleft: horse's foot, 38; human, 25
clerical collar, minister, 487
clerestory, church, 86
clerk, Congress, 74
clerk's table, courtroom, 89
clew: hammock, 288; mainsail, 136
cliff, 7, 9
climax basket, 266
climbing, mountain, 334
climbing net, backyard, 287
climbing wax, ski, 327
clinch, horse's hoof, 38
clinic, White House, 75
clip: ammunition, 499; bicycle, 128; bow tie, 192; CB radio antenna, 183; chest pull, 344; dental, 455; hair, 214; jackhammer, 436; juice extractor, 255; microscope, 442; pen, 158; pistol, 470; pistol nozzle, 428; rifle, 471; stethoscope, 449; suspenders, 190; telephone, 180; venetian blinds, 241; and volt-ohm meter, 423; wallet, 223; woodcarving, 372
clip-on bow tie, 192
clip-on sunglasses, 290
clipped mane, polo pony, 299
clippers, gardening, 427
cloche, 203
clock, 233; basketball backstop, 296; car, 110; darts, 322; nuclear reactor

control room, 393; organ, 360; pilot's instrument panel, 481; 747 cockpit, 150; stove, 248
clock timer, VCR, 184
cloister, mosque, 70
close, letter, 159
close call, gesture, 507
closed chock, destroyer, 477
closed-circuit track, road racing, 338
closed coat, sandpaper, 421
closed quad, magazine, 171
closed teeth, zipper, 209
close escape, gesture, 507
closer, brick wall, 69
close relationship, gesture, 507
closet, jumbo jet, 148
close up, proofreader's mark, 514
close way, permanent fort, 83
closure, 209; brassiere, 195; parka, 201; package, 268, 269; playpen, 286; swagger bag, 222; trousers, 191; woman's jacket and pants, 196
cloth: flat racing, 336; pool table, 320
cloth beam, hand loom, 387
clothes dryer, 281
clothesline, 280
clothespin, 280
clothing guard, wheelchair, 452
cloth lining, parka, 201
cloth said, windmill, 390
cloud, 2, 3, 16
cloudy, weather map, 19
cloven hoof, ultimate beast, 48
cloverleaf, highway, 114
clown, 493; circus act, 90
club: golf, 310, 311; playing cards, 348; police, 498
club-footed forestaysail, sailboat, 134
clubhouse, racetrack, 337
clubhouse turn, racetrack, 337
club insignia, soccer uniform, 297
clutch: automobile, 108, 110, 111; checkbook, 223; handbag, 222; lithographic press, 376; powerboat, 138
clutch lever: motorcycle, 129; outboard engine, 137
clutch nut, juice extractor, 255
clutter control, radar, 444
coach: bus, 118; horse-drawn, 131; passenger train, 116; recreational vehicle, 130
coaches' box, baseball field, 291
coach roof, sailboat, 134
coach section, jumbo jet, 149
coal hod, fireplace, 232
coal tender, steam locomotive, 116
coaming, sailboat, 135
coaming padding, powerboat, 139
coarse-adjustment beam, laboratory scale, 447
coarse calibrate, Geiger counter, 445
coarse focus adjustment, microscope, 442
coarse-motion clamp, telescope, 443
coarse teeth, hair comb, 212
coast, nautical chart, 22
coastal shield, turtle, 43
Coast Guard station, nautical chart, 22
coastline, 7, 15
coat: animal cell, 23; butler, 489; drum major, 495; fireman, 500; man, 188, 488;

Revolutionary War general, 492; sandpaper, 421; ultimate beast, 48, 49
coating, sandpaper, 421
coat of arms, 503; Manchu court dress, 491
co-axial machine gun, tank, 475
cock: furnace, 400; internal combustion engine, 406; standpipe, 121
cockade, 492
cocked hat, 492
cocking handle, machine gun, 471
cocking piece, rifle, 471
cockpit: aircraft, 146, 147, 150-151; powerboat, 139; racing car, 338-339; sailboat, 134
coconut, 262; palm, 52
coda sign, music, 353
code: envelope, 159; magazine mailing label, 169; paper money, 224
codpiece: armor, 465; boxing, 309
coffeepot, tea set, 245
coffee shop, public sign, 506
coffee strainer, 260
coffin, 516
coffin corner, football field, 293
coherent light, laser, 395
coiffe, champagne cork, 267
coiffure, 213
coil: air conditioner, 402; automobile spring, 109; dipole magnet, 394; heat exchanger, 403; lasso, 432; metal detector, 445; postage stamps, 159; safety pin, 208; zipper, 209
coin, money, 225
coin bank, 457
coin box: parking meter, 113; pay phone, 180
coin chute, toll basket, 114
coin purse, wallet, 223
coin return: pay phone, 180; slot machine, 346
coin slot: parking meter, 113; pay phone, 180; slot machine, 346
col, mountain, 8
colander, 260
cold chisel, 420
cold cream, 216
cold front, 19
cold type, 166
cold-water faucet: bathtub, 274; Jacuzzi, 274; sink, 247, 273
cold-water pipe: solar heating system, 391; water heater, 401
collapsible legs, ironing board, 279
collar: ambulance, 123; ascot, 193; barbell, 344; bishop, 487; blouse, 197; bolt, 411; bridal gown, 488; camera tripod, 176; cardigan sweater, 199; dipole magnet, 394; drum major's coat, 495; fire extinguisher, 284; harness racing gear, 337; horizontal bar, 306; house beam, 61; jacket, 188, 488; kettledrum, 364; king's regalia, 484; Manchu court dress, 491; minaret, 70; minister, 487; power drill, 419; royal orb, 485; shirt, 189; shoe, 205; stove, 404; trench coat, 200; vacuum cleaner hose, 283
collarbone, human, 24

527

collection pan, air conditioner, 402
collector: solar panel, 391; transistor chip, 396
college pliers, dental, 455
collet, ring, 219
collider, 394
collimating screw, telescope, 443
collision bulkhead, passenger ship, 142
collop: human, 25; meat, 262
cologne, 217
colon: grammatical symbol, 513; human, 27
colophon, book, 167
color(s): horseracing, 336, 337; typewriter ribbon, 161
colored glass, 378
color panel, soccer ball, 297
color selector, toaster oven, 253
colorstick, makeup, 216, 217
colt, 38
columbarium, church, 87
columella, nose, 30
column, 73; abacus, 441; basketball backstop, 296; cave, 11; citrus juicer, 255; cupboard, 243; drill press, 419; magazine, 170, 171; oil drilling platform, 101; piano, 361; skyscraper, 77; surgical table, 450; thermometer, 449; voting booth, 437
coma, comet, 3
comb: armor, 465; chicken, 35; escalator, 79; hair, 212; razor, 210; rifle, 471; shotgun, 468
combat aircraft, 480
combat infantry badge, 496
combat maneuver panel, pilot's instrument panel, 481
combat soldier's uniform, 497
comb holder, electric hairbrush, 212
combination dial, vault, 457
combination headlamp, automobile, 106
combination lock, safe, 457
combination pliers, 414
combination screw, telegraph key, 157
combination square, 424
combination water ski, 329
combination wrench, 415
comb strip, electric hairbrush, 212
combustion chamber: engine, 407; rocket, 407; stove, 404
combustion jet engine, 407
come box, craps table, 347
come here, gesture, 507
comet, 3
comfort-cable temple, eyeglasses, 221
comforter, bedding, 270
comfort lining, spacesuit, 155
comic book, 380
comic strip, 380-381
comma: grammatical symbol, 513; proofreader's mark, 514
commander's hatch, tank, 474
commander's seat, space shuttle, 153
command module, lunar lander, 154
command post, White House, 75
commemorative, coin, 215
commemorative subject, stamp, 159
commissary, prison, 76
commissure, horse's foot, 38
committee, room, Capitol, 74
common iliac artery, human, 28

common peroneal nerve, human, 29
common rafter, house, 61
common spiral galaxy, 2
communication fuse, rocket, 383
communication umbilical, spacesuit, 155
Communion bread, 87
Communion cup, 87
commuter bus, 118
compact, beauty product, 217
compact disc, compact disc player, 178
compact disc player, 178
compactor, trash, 247
companion benchseat, powerboat, 139
companionway, sailboat, 134, 135
company address, business card, 160
company logo: business card, 160; pumper, 125
company name: business card, 160; letter, 159
company quarters, frontier fort, 82
compartment: backpack, 343; bus, 118; camper, 130; coat of arms, 503; drag racing dragster, 339; electronic flash, 176; garbage disposal, 247; hearing aid, 452; jumbo jet, 148, 149; refrigerator, 249; sealed voting booth, 437; sink, 247; wallet, 223
compass, 136; airplane, 151, 481; powerboat, 138; skin diving, 331; theodolite, 436
compass bearing, airport runway, 94
compass rose: nautical chart, 22; political map, 20
compensator sheave, elevator shaft, 78
complimentary close, letter, 159
composition: art, 368-369; typeface, 165
compote dish, 245
compound eye: bee, 41; grasshopper, 41
compound kite, 323
compound leaves, 52
compound microscope, 442
compress, medicinal, 451
compressed air: skin diving, 331; truck tractor, 120
compression member, geodesic dome, 85
compression strap, backpack, 343
compressor: automobile engine, 111; heat exchanger, 403
compressor fan, combustion engine, 407
computer, 162, 438, 439; prison, 76; 747 cockpit, 150, 151; space shuttle, 153
computer aided design system, 438
computer ring, light meter, 176
computer system, 439
computer tape, 439
computer workstation, 438
concave knife, 463
concave lens, 221
concave mirror, telescope, 443
concave molding, grandfather clock, 233
concealer, makeup, 216
concentrating solar collector, 391
concentric sculpture, clam shell, 47
conceptacle, seaweed, 57

concertmaster, orchestra, 354
concha, outer ear, 30
conchology, 47
concourse, airport, 94
concrete block foundation, house, 60
concrete shield, nuclear reactor, 392
concrete tunnel, super collider, 394
concussion grenade, 473
condensed type, 165
condenser: heat pump, 403; microscope, 442; nuclear reactor, 392
condenser coil, air conditioner, 402
condiment, 263, 265
conducting blade, cartridge fuse, 399
conducting rivet, plug fuse, 399
conductor: electrician's wire, 423; track lighting, 239
conductor's podium, orchestra, 354
conduit, 98; railroad crossing signal, 115; volcano, 10
cone: blimp, 156; citrus juicer, 255; combustion jet engine, 407; ice cream, 265; jumbo jet, 148, 149; missile, 482; phonograph receiver, 179; pine, 52; police car, 122; potting, 373; toll booth, 114; volcano, 10
Congress, 74
conical buoy, nautical chart, 22
connecting link, horizontal bar, 306
connecting rod: steam engine, 405; steam locomotive, 116
connecting wire, field events hammer, 303
connection: electric meter, 399; pacemaker, 452; parachute harness, 333; pumper, 125; sprinkler, 428
conning tower, submarine, 479
console: computer system, 439; lunar rover, 155; organ, 360; powerboat, 138, 139; skin diving tank, 331
console door, electronic voting system, 437
constellation, 2
constriction, thermometer, 449
construction, road map, 20
construction sign, road, 505
consumer requirements, coupon, 103
contact: incandescent bulb, 238; movie camera, 174; plugfuse, 399
contact lens, 221
contact sport, 298
container, 266-267; blender, 254; contact lens, 221; land mine, 473; paint spray gun, 425
container ship, 140
containment building, nuclear reactor, 392
contemporary, house style, 63
content: label, 268; wine label, 267
content heading, book page, 12
contents page, magazine, 169
contest, drag racing, 339
continental margin, 15
continued line, magazine, 171
continuous battery monitor, Geiger counter, 445
continuous hinge, 460
contour: nautical chart, 22; topographic map, 22

contoured handgrip, camera, 172
contour feathers, bird, 39
contour line, map, 21, 22
contra-bassoon, 354
contraction, grammatical symbol, 513
contractor's saw, 417
contrast control, video-still camera, 173
contrast indicator, fax machine, 164
control: air conditioner, 402; aircraft, 150, 151, 481; automobile, 108, 110; ballista, 467; barbecue grill, 288; blender, 254; blood pressure gauge, 449; bulldozer, 435; camera, 174; canal lock, 99; cash register, 440; CB radio, 183; clock radio, 233; clothes dryer, 281; compass, 136; dam, 100; dental unit, 454; dishwasher, 250; drum, 364; engine, 406, 407; fire engine, 124, 125; food processor, 254; garbage disposal, 247; garbage truck, 127; girdle, 195; guitar, 363; hand glider, 333; hearing aid, 452; high-speed printer, 439; hovercraft, 145; humidifier, 402; iron, 279; lunar lander, 154; lunar rover, 155; machine gun height, 471; metal detector, 445; microscope, 442; microwave oven, 248; mower, 429; nozzle, 428; nuclear reactor, 392; paint spray gun, 425; parachute, 333; passenger ship, 142; phonograph, 178, 179; police car, 122; powerboat, 138, 139; projector, 175; radar, 444; railroad crossing signal, 115; saber saw, 417; sealed voting booth, 437; seeder, 430; sonar, 444; space shuttle, 153; spacesuit, 155; stove, 248, 342, 404; subway, 119; surgical table, 450; synthesizer, 363; telescope, 443; toaster, 253; toll booth, 114; tow truck, 126; tugboat, 144; typewriter, 161; vacuum tube, 396; video camera, 184; wristwatch, 220
control button, answering machine, 181
control console, computer, 439
control functions, fax machine, 164
controllable landing light, helicopter, 146
control panel: dot matrix printer, 163; nuclear reactor control room, 393
control rod, window shutters, 241
control-rod guide tube, nuclear reactor, 392
control room, nuclear reactor, 393
control room operator, nuclear reactor, 393
control station, destroyer launcher, 477
control structure, dam, 100
control tower: aircraft carrier, 478; airport, 94, 95; destroyer, 476
control unit: high-speed printer, 439; magnetic tape subsystem, 439
conversion marker, football field, 293

conversion scale, nautical chart, 22
converter, vacuum cleaner, 283
convertible, 108; automobile, 106, 107
convertible sofa, 236
convenience door, dot matrix printer, 163
convex lens, 221
Conyne kite, 323
cook, 489
cookie, 264
cookie cutter, 261
cooking chopsticks, 257
cooking grid, barbecue grill, 288
cooking unit, camper, 130
cook's cap, 489
cook top, stove, 248
coolant port, dipole magnet, 394
coolant pump, nuclear reactor, 392
cooling fan clutch, automobile engine, 111
cooling/heating coils, heat exchanger, 403
cooling rack, kitchen, 260
cooling system: airport, 94; automobile, 108
cooling tower, nuclear reactor, 393
cool tip: curling iron, 214; percolator basket, 252
cop, police, 498
cope, bishop, 487
copier, 164
coping, masonry gate post, 67
coping saw, 416
copper foil, 378
copper surface, solar collector panel, 391
copra, 262
copy: letter, 159; magazine cover, 169
copyist, music, 353;
copyright: book, 167; magazine, 169; music, 353; newspaper, 168; symbol, 511
coral, cave, 11
coral polyp, 46
coral reef, 46
cor anglais, 354, 357
corbel, castle, 80
corbeled arch, kokoshniki, 70
cord: air conditioner, 402; bagpipe, 365; ballista, 467; bedroll, 343; bus, 118; CB radio, 183; cellular telephone, 181; curling iron, 214; dental X-ray unit, 454; electrician's, 423; fastener, 208; fencing strip, 315; guillotine, 462; hand loom, 387; hot air balloon, 332; iron, 279; jackhammer, 436; juice extractor, 255; lamp, 238; movie camera microphone, 174; parachute, 333; Ping-Pong net, 321; saw, 417; snowshoe, 334; spinning wheel, 387; string tie, 192; tape recorder, 177; telephone, 180; thread, 384; track lighting, 239; traverse rod, 240; venetian blind, 241; windmill, 390
cord holder, ironing board, 279
cordial glass, 245
cording, mattress, 271
cordless phone, 180
cordlock, backpack, 343
cordon, king's regalia, 484
cord strain relief: CB radio microphone, 183; finishing sander, 421; hair dryer, 212;

hand drill, 419; saber saw, 417; toaster oven, 253
core: apple, 55; brayer, 374; earth, 4; human, 25; mortise lock, 458; nuclear reactor, 392; paint roller, 425; pineapple, 55; skyscraper, 77; typewriter, 161
core basket, nuclear reactor, 392
corer, apple, 261
core support assembly, nuclear reactor, 392
cork: bottle, 267; clarinet mouthpiece, 357
corkscrew, 251; pocket knife, 426
corn, 58
cornea, eye, 30
corner: boxing ring, 309; brick wall, 69; chessboard, 345; football field, 293; house, 62, 63; skyscraper, 77; violin, 355
corner cupboard, 243
corner cushion, boxing ring, 309
corner flag, soccer field, 297
corner index, playing cards, 348
cornering lamp, automobile, 106
corner kick area, soccer field, 297
corner mark, label, 269
corner post, house, 61
cornerstone, skyscraper, 77
cornet, 359
cornice: column entablature, 73; cupboard, 243; curtain, 240; house, 61, 62; merry-go-round, 93; minaret, 70; mosque, 70
cornsilk, 58
corolla, pea, 54
corona, column entablature, 73
coronary band, horse's hoof, 38
coronation mantle, king, 484
coronet: horse, 38; queen, 484; royal headpiece, 485
corpus callosum, human, 29
correctable ribbon, typewriter, 161
correctional facility, 76
correction tape, typewriter, 161
corrective device, dental, 453
corrector magnet control, compass, 136
correspondence, 159
corridor, Capitol building, 74
corrugated brand name display, supermarket, 102
corrugated diaphragm chest piece, stethoscope, 449
corrugated fastener, 410
corrugated sole, ice climbing boot, 334
corrugated staple, silk screen, 375
corrugation: fastener, 410; speaker, 179
corselet, queen's, 484
corset, 195; queen's, 484
cosmetic case, 285
cosmic mass, 2
cosmic rays, 3
costal fold, salamander, 44
costal groove, salamander, 44
costilla, jai alai cesta, 314
costume, historical, 492
costume jewelry, 218
cotter pin, roller chain, 461
cotton, dental, 455
couch, upholstered, 236
couloir, mountain, 8

count, magazine mailing label, 169
counter: backgammon, 345; footware, 204, 205, 206, 302; pool table, 320; sink, 247; sailboat, 134; sealed voting booth, 437; tape recorder, 177; type, 165, 166
counterbalance, electronic weather station, 18
counter current, ocean, 6
counterfeit money, 224
counterguard, sword hilt, 463
counter hoop, drum, 364
countermeasures antenna, aircraft carrier, 478
countermeasure warning, pilot's instrument panel, 481
counterscarp, permanent fort, 83
countersink bit, drill, 418, 419
counterweight: elevator shaft, 78; lift bridge, 97; phonograph turntable, 178; railroad crossing signal, 115; stage pulley, 350; window, 65
counting rod, 441
coupe, automobile, 106
coupled truck, 120
coupler, locomotive, 116, 117
coupler-tilt tablet, organ, 360
coupling: gas pump, 112; hose, 428; train, 117
coupon, 103; magazine, 171
coupon machine, checkout counter, 103
course: brick wall, 69; drag racing, 339; harness racetrack, 337; meal, 263; river, 13
court: badminton, 319; barn, 104; basketball, 296; handball, 313; jai alai, 314; Ping-Pong table, 321; shuffleboard, 318; squash, 313; tennis, 312; volleyball, 319
court cards, 348
court clerk's table, courtroom, 89
court dress, Manchu, 491
courting seat, 236
courtroom, 89
couter, armor, 465
cove, 7
cove mold, staircase, 66
cover: automobile, 107, 111; bagpipe, 365; baseball, 290; basket, 266; battery, 397; blender, 254; book, 167; brayer, 374; cassette tape, 177; chain saw, 431; clarinet pad, 356; combat helmet, 497; copier, 164; desk, 276; fishing reel, 340; food processor, 247; football, 292; garbage disposal, 247; girdle, 195; hand loom, 387; ironing board, 279; jackhammer, 436; juice extractor, 255; kite, 323; laboratory scale, 446; magazine, 169; matchbook, 228; mattress, 271; motorcycle, 129; paint spray gun, 425; percolator basket, 252; pocket watch, 220; portable word processor, 162; pots and pans, 257; sewing machine, 278; sketch box, 371; skyscraper, 77; smoke alarm, 284; swing, 287; tea kettle, 245; tepee, 84; theodolite, 436; toilet, 275; vault, 457; video-still camera adaptor, 173; Walkman, 182; wallet,

223; water ski, 329; window, 241
covered button cardigan sweater, 199
covered way, permanent fort, 83
cover key, video-still camera, 173
cover lock, video-still camera, 173
cover plate: electrical, 344; solar panel, 391
cover sheet, kite, 323
covert: bird, 39; permanent fort, 83; turkey, 35
coverup, makeup, 216
cow, 32
cowboy, 490; hat, 202
cowcatcher, locomotive, 116
cow hoof, ultimate beast, 48
cowl: bobsled, 328; helicopter, 146; outboard engine, 137
cowlick, 211
cowling: airplane, 147; outboard engine, 137; racing car, 338
cow puncher, 490
coxa: grasshopper, 41; spider, 40
CPU, 438; circuit board, 439; mainframe, 439
crab, 47; zodiac, 509
cracker, nut, 261
cradle, telephone, 180; telescope, 443; venetian blind, 241
craft, 132, 133
cramp, wall, 69
crampon, ice climbing, 334
crane: aircraft carrier, 478; launch pad, 152; oil drilling platform, 101; sky-scraper, 77
cranial crest, toad, 44
cranium, human, 26
crank: brace, 418; drill, 418; easel, 370; engine, 405, 406, 407; fishing reel, 340; lawn sprinkler, 428; pencil sharpener, 277; printing press, 376, 377; truck platform, 121
crank arm, bicycle, 128
cranked axle, Hansom cab, 131
crankset, bicycle, 128
craps table, 347
crash helmet, 336, 338
crater, volcano, 10
cravat, 192
crawler track, tank, 474
crawler tractor, bulldozer, 435
crawl space, house, 60
crayfish, 47
crayon, lithographic, 376
crazy, gesture, 507
cream: makeup, 216, 217; sundae, 264
creamer, tea set, 245
crease: cowboy hat, 202; human hand, 31; ice hockey rink, 295; trousers, 191; woman's pants, 196
C recreation yard, prison, 76
credit, magazine, 169, 171
credit card, 227
credit card account, 227
credit card logo, traveler's check, 227
credit card slots, wallet, 223
credit line, newspaper, 168
creek: frontier fort, 82; river, 13
crenel, castle, 80
crepe sole, sandal, 206
crescendo, music, 352
crescendo, shoe, organ, 360
crescent, fingernail, 31
crescent and star, symbol, 508

crescent moon, 4
crest: coat of arms, 503; dam, 100; dog, 36; enlisted men's uniform, 496; grandfather clock, 233; horse, 38; human, 25; iceberg, 12; mountain, 9; rocking chair, 234; screw thread, 410; wave, 14
crest fringe, lizard, 43
crest rail, sofa, 236
crevasse, mountain, 9
crevice, mountain, 9
crevice tool, vacuum cleaner, 283
crew compartment, lunar lander, 154
crewel, stitchery, 385
crew neck sweater, 199
crew's quarters, passenger ship, 142
cricket, darts, 322
crier, and minaret, 70
crimp: cartridge, 470; painting brush, 370; spring board needle, 386
crimper, electrician's wire stripper, 423
cringle, mainsail, 136
cripples, house, 61
crisper, refrigerator, 249
critical mass, nuclear power, 392
crocheting, 386
crocket, church, 86
crockpot, 257
crocodile, 42
crocodilians, 42
crook: of arm, 25; bassoon, 357; brasses, 358, 359
crop: cow, 32; flat racing, 336; masonry gate post, 67
croquet, 318
crosier, cardinal, 487
cross, 86, 487; symbol, 508
crossarm: power line, 396; railroad crossing signal, 115; weather station, 18
crossbar: abacus, 441; bicycle, 128; football goalpost, 293; hand glider, 333; ice hockey goal, 294; lyre, 355; pole vault, 305; sawhorse, 408; snowshoe, 327; suit hanger, 281; weather vane, 19
crossbeam: ballista, 467; gallows, 462; guillotine, 462; hand loom, 387
crossbelt, 483, 492
crossbow, 466
cross brace: ladder, 47; wheelchair, 452
crossbuck, railroad crossing signal, 115
cross-country skiing, 327
crosscut saw, 416, 417
crosse, 298
cross guard, knife, 463
crosshatching: cartoon, 380; and texture, composition, 369
crosshead, steam engine, 405
crossing: church, 87; railroad, 115
cross joint, brick wall, 69
crossknot, bow tie, 192
Cross of Christ, church, 87
crossover, railroad yard, 96
cross patée, royal regalia, 485
crosspiece: bow tie, 192; hand loom, 387; kite, 323; rocking chair, 234; sword hilt, 463; torii, 71
cross section: cave, 11; coral polyp, 46; fireplace, 232; frame, 379; hurricane, 17; insulated window, 65; lumber, 68; permanent fort,

83; river, 13; stage, 350; tree trunk, 50; tunnel, 98; volcano, 10
cross stitching, 385
cross straps, overnight bag, 285
cross strings, tennis racket, 312
cross strip: kite, 323; wheelbarrow, 430
cross support, pool table, 320
crosstie, railroad track, 115
crosswise grain, fabric, 388
crotch: underpants, 194; trousers, 191
crotchet: grammatical symbol, 513; music, 352
crotch strap: child's car seat, 286; drag racing driver's belt, 339
croup: dog, 36; horse, 38; pommel horse, 307
croupier, roulette, 346
crown: anchor, 132; arch, 72; bell, iv; bird, 39; cactus, 56; coat of arms, 503; croquet wicket, 318; cut gemstone, 218; human, 25; incline track, 92; man's hat, 211; palm, 52; pineapple, 55; royal, 485; staple, 410; tennis racket, 312; tooth, 453, 455, 456; tree, 50; watch, 220, 304; woman's hat, 203
crown cap opener, 251
crowning pavilion, minaret, 70
crown stabilizer, football helmet, 292
crow's nest: tanker, 140; train caboose, 117
CRT: computer workstation, 438; personal computer, 162; television, 185
crucifix, church, 87
cruise missile, 482
crumb, bread, 263
crumb incubator, cowboy's, 490
crumble roller, hitch and harrow, 434
crumb tray, toaster, 253
crupper, harness racing, 337
crusher claw, lobster, 47
crust: earth, 4; prepared food, 263, 265
crustacean, 47
crutch, 452
crutch socket, operating table, 450
crypt: burial chamber, 516; Capitol, 74
crystal, watch, 220
Crystal Palace set piece, fireworks, 383
crystal pool, cave, 11
C sharp, piano keyboard octave, 361
C-strap, motorcycle, 129
cubbyhole, sailboat, 135
cube: backgammon, 345; slide projector, 175
cucumber, 54
cue: billiards, 320; cassette tape recorder, button, 177; phonograph turntable, 178; shuffleboard, 318
cuff: blood pressure gauge, 449; blouse, 197; bridal gown, 488; fencing glove, 315; golf bag, 311; ice hockey goalie's glove, 294; jacket, 196; king's regalia, 484; Manchu court dress, 491; paramedic, 123; parka, 201; Revolutionary War general, 492; sailor, 497; shirt, 189, 488; ski boot, 326,

327; sweater, 199; trousers, 191
cuff checklist, spacesuit, 155
cuff link, 218
cuirie, armor, 465
cuish, armor, 465
cuissard, fencing, 315
culet, cut gemstone, 218
cull, lobster, 47
culm, grass, 58
cultivator, 434
culture tube, laboratory, 447
cummerbund, 488, 495
cumulonimbus cloud, 16, 17
cumulus congestus cloud, 16
cup: armor, 465; athletic supporter, 194; ballista, 467; baseball catcher, 290; brassiere, 195; bugle, 359; citrus juicer, 255; Communion, 87; coral polyp, 46; golf course, 311; measuring, 258; plumber's plunger, 422; seed, 51; sketch box, 371; table setting, 245; thimble, 384; trombone, 358; weather station, 18
cupboard, 243
cup level scale, coffee maker, 252
cupola: barn, 104; Capitol, 74; kokoshniki, 70; mosque, 70, 71; tank, 474; train caboose, 117
curbside sidewall, truck van, 121
curb window, bus, 118
curd, cheese, 263
curfew, fireplace, 232
curl: pail, 284; wave, 14; woman's hair, 213
curled position, windmill, 390
curling iron, 214
currency pocket, wallet, 223
current: electrical, 398; ocean, 6
current temperature, thermometer, 18
current unit patch, enlisted man's uniform, 496
curriculum vitae, 160
cursor: linear slide rule, 441; radar, 441
cursor control: computer workstation, 438; personal computer, 162
cursor keypad, portable word processor, 162
curtain: cave, 11; four-poster bed, 270; living room, 240; overnight bag, 285; permanent fort, 83; shower, 274; stage, 350; stagecoach, 131; theatre, 351; Torah, 486; voting booth, 437
curtain rod, 240
curtain wall: castle, 81; skyscraper, 77
curtein, king's regalia, 484
curve, royal scepter, 485
curved jaw, combination pliers, 414
curved slat, rocking chair, 234
cushion: bowling lane, 320; boxing ring, 309; chaise longue, 288; dog, 36; jai alai cancha, 314; lounger, 235; phonograph headphone, 179; pool table, 320; roller skate, 324; sofa, 236
cusp, tooth, 456
cuspid, 456
cuspidor, dental unit, 454
custodian's seal, voting booth, 437
customized automobile, 106-107

customs, public sign, 506
cut: book, 167; key blade, 459; label, 268; magazine, 170
cutaway coat: butler's uniform, 489; man's formal attire, 488
cut gemstone, 218
cuticle: human fingernail, 31; leaf, 52
cut it, gesture, 507
cut line, newspaper, 168
cutoff rule, magazine, 171
cutout switch, 747 cockpit, 151
cut section, stained glass, 378
cutter: can opener, 251; chain saw chain, 431; cigar, 228; cowboy, 490; electric razor, 210; glass, 378; juice extractor, 255; kitchen tool, 261; pencil sharpener, 277; pliers, 414; wirestripper, 423
cutter adjusting-screw, expansive bit, 419
cutting board, 261; barbecue grill, 288
cutting edge: auger bit, 419; bulldozer, 435; chisel, 420; nail clippers, 215; plane, 420
cutting line, sewing pattern, 388
cutting surface, table saw, 417
cutting teeth, lobster, 47
cwm, mountain, 8
cyc, stage, 350
cyc flood, stage, 350
cycle: internal combustion engine, 406; symbol, 510
cycle selector: clothes dryer, 281; dishwasher, 250; washing machine, 280
cyclorama, stage, 350
cyclorama floodlight, stage, 350
cyclotron, 394
cylinder: ambulance, 123; automobile, 108, 111; fire extinguisher, 284; internal combustion engine, 406; letterpress, 166; lock, 458; locomotive, 116; offset-lithography, 166; padlock, 459; propane torch, 422; revolver, 470; rotogravure, 166; skin diving, 331; steam engine, 405
cylinder desk, 276
cylinder model, vacuum cleaner, 283
cylindrical buoy, nautical chart, 22
cylindrical slide rule, 441
cymatium, column entablature, 73
cymbal, 354, 364
cytoplasm, animal cell, 23

D

D: braille, 512; music notation, 353; piano keyboard octave, 341; sign language, 512
dabber, 377
dado, column pedestal, 73
daggerboard, windsurfer, 330
dagger point position, windmill, 390
dairy department, supermarket, 102
daisy-wheel printer, 163
daiwa, torii, 71
dalmatic, cardinal, 487
dal segno sign, music, 353
dam, 100; cave, 11; horse, 38, 336
dampening roller, offset-lithography, 166
damper: fireplace, 232; grill, 288; woodburning stove, 404

damper pedal, grand piano, 361

dance band, 354

dancing step, staircase, 66

dart: jacket, 188; sewing pattern, 388

dart board, 322

darts, 322

dash: book page, iv; car, 110; grammatical symbol, 513

dashboard: car, 110; Hansom cab, 131

dash-pot, toaster, 253

data display window, compact disc player, 178

data cache, circuit board, 439

data code, magazine mailing label, 169

data entry slider, synthesizer, 363

data file server, computer workstation, 438

data panel display, camera, 172

data processor, mainframe, 439

date: coin, 225; magazine, 169, 171; newspaper, 168; résumé, 160; traveler's check, 227; wine label, 267

date display control, wristwatch, 220

dateline: map, 5; newspaper, 168

date of issue, coupon, 103

davenport, 236

David, playing card king, 348

davit: fireboat, 144; powerboat, 138

day, globe, 5

daybed, sailboat, 135

day gate, vault, 457

daystick, police, 498

D cell block, prison, 76

DCmv scale, volt-ohm meter, 423

dead bolt, mortise lock, 458

dead-end cap, track lighting, 239

dead front plug, electrical, 398

dead lift, universal gym, 344

dead line, shuffle board court, 318

dead man's stick, subway motorman's cab, 119

dealer, blackjack, 347

dealer requirements, coupon, 103

deal patch, label, 269

death, darts, 322; symbol, 510

debit amount, check, 226

debossed label, 268

decal, child's wagon, 287

decanter, 245; coffee maker, 252

decathlon, 300

decay, tooth, 456

decelerator pedal, bulldozer, 435

decimal key, electronic calculator, 441

deck: aircraft carrier, 478; destroyer, 476; escalator, 79; fleet ballistic missile submarine, 479; house, 63; hovercraft, 145; jumbo jet, 148; kitchen sink, 247; magazine, 170; newspaper, 168; passenger ship, 142, 143; playing cards, 348; power mower, 429; powerboat, 138, 139; skateboard, 324; skyscraper, 77; sled, 328; stage, 350; surfboard, 330; toboggan, 328; truck platform, 121

deck brace, steam locomotive, 116

decked craft, 133

deckhouse, tanker, 141

deck manifold, tanker, 141

decompression chamber, 452

decorated initial, magazine, 170

decoration: cake, 264; canapé, 263; man's hat, 202; military uniform, 496; minister, 487

decorative engravings, scrimshaw, 375

decorative inlays, armor, 465

decorative perforations, man's shoe, 204

decorative stitching, 385

deep, continental margin, 15

deep-frying basket, 260

deep-frying thermometer, 258

deep gouge, woodcarving, 372

deep medium gouge, woodcarving, 372

deep throat, coping paw, 416

deer crossing, road sign, 505

deer ear, ultimate beast, 48

dee ring, Western saddle, 335

defendant's table, courtroom, 89

defenseman: ice hockey, 295; lacrosse, 298

defensive guided weapons, 476

defibrillator, paramedic equipment, 123

deflector: aircraft carrier, 478; power mower, 429

deflexor, hang glider, 333

defog control lever, pilot's instrument panel, 481

defroster, car windshield, 110

degree: longitude, 5; music notation, 353; political map, 20

degrees of arc, symbol, 511

dehumidifier, 402

delayed transmission capability, fax machine, 164

delete, proofreader's mark, 514

deli, supermarket, 103

delivery area, supermarket, 102

delta, 7, 13

delta-keel, kite, 323

delta wing, combat aircraft, 480

deltoid, human, 26

deluge gun, pumper, 125

deluxe suite, passenger ship, 143

demarcation groove, escalator, 79

demineralizer, nuclear reactor, 392

demisemiquaver, music, 353

demitasse cup, 245

Democrat, Congress, 74

demographic data code, magazine mailing label, 169

denier, support base, 207

denim trousers, cowboy, 490

denomination: money, 225; stamp, 159; traveler's check, 227

density adjustment, laser printer, 163

dental corrective devices, 453

dental equipment, 455

dental floss, 215

dental unit, 454

dentin, tooth, 456

denture, 453

department: business card, 160; magazine, 169

department patch, police, 498

deployed wing, cruise missile, 482

deposit box, vault, 457

deposit drawer, automatic teller machine, 226

deposit envelopes, automatic teller machine, 226

depository, ambulance, 123

depression contour, topographic map, 22

depth adjusting screw, hitch and harrow, 434

depth: nautical chart, 22; and perspective, 368

depth control, guitar amplifier, 363

depth discriminator switch, metal detector, 445

depth-effect hydrofoil, 145

depth gauge: 424; skin diving, 331

depth-of-field scale, camera, 172; zoom lens, 172

depth stop, drill press, 419

derailleur, bicycle, 128

derision, gesture, 507

derrick: oil drilling platform, 101; tanker, 141

derrière, human, 25

descender, type, 165

descending initial, magazine, 170

descent stage, lunar lander, 154

design: scrimshaw, 375; silk screen, 375; stamp, 159

designation: label, 268; topographic map, 22

designer's initials, coin, 225

desk, 276; grand piano, 361

desk phone, 180

deskside electronics cabinet, computer workstation, 438

desk top personal copier, 164

dessert, 264

dessert setting, 244, 245

destination sign: bus, 118; road, 505; subway car, 119

destroyer, 476, 477

detachable collar, maid's uniform, 489

detached house, 63

detail: house blueprint, 62; political map, 21; woman's jacket, 196

detection head, metal detector, 445

detector: elevator shaft, 78; metal, 445; super collider, 394

detent, levigator, 376

detergent dispenser, dishwasher, 250

deuce service courts, tennis, 312

deutsche mark, symbol, 511

development flight instrumentation control, space shuttle, 153

device: coin, 225; execution, 462; flag, 502; label, 268; police uniform, 498; supportive, 452

devilfish, 46

devotional candle, 237

dewbill, turkey, 35

dewcap, telescope, 443

dewclaw: cat, 37; cow, 32; dog, 36; ultimate beast, 48

dewlap: cow, 32; dog, 36; lizard, 43

dew point sensor, weather station, 18

dexter supporter, coat of arms, 503

D flat, piano keyboard octave, 361

diacritic grammatical symbol, 513

diadem, tiara, 485

diagnosis, symbol, 510

diagonal: telescope, 443; tweezers, 215

diagonally gaited pacer, 337

diagram: political map, 21; shuffleboard, 318; sundial, 389

dial: aneroid barometer, 18; clock radio, 233; dental unit, 454; electronic flash, 176; electric wok, 257; gas pump, 112; globe, 1; grandfather clock, 233; lawn sprinkler, 428; parking meter, 113; phonograph, 178, 179; sewing machine, 278; sundial, 389; tape recorder, 177; telephone, 180; toaster oven, 253; vault, 457; wristwatch, 220

dial memory index, fax machine, 164

dialogue, comic strip, 381

dial pad, fax machine, 164

dialysis machine, 452

diamond: baseball, 291; dental burr, 455; playing card, 348; roulette wheel, 346; royal scepter, 485

diamond stitch, suspenders, 190

diaphragm: aneroid barometer, 18; kazoo, 366; microscope, 442; speaker, 179; stethoscope, 449

diaphragm adjusting screw, theodolite, 436

dice, 347

dice boat, craps table, 347

dice table, 347

dickey, Hansom cab, 131

die: 347; coin, 225; pipe threader, 422

die cut, label, 268

dieresis, grammatical symbol, 513

diesel-fueled internal combustion engine, 406

diesel locomotive, 116

diestock, pipe threader, 422

differential, automobile, 109

differential thermostat, solar heating system, 391

differentiation code, magazine mailing label, 169

diffuser, light meter, 176

digestive system, human, 27

digit, human, 25, 31

digital artery, human, 28

digital display, clock radio, 233

digital speed readout, police car, 122

digital tape, computer workstation, 438

digital vein, human, 28

digiton, cartoon, 381

digitorium, piano, 361

dike, 100; volcano, 10

dimension: house blueprint, 62; and perspective, 368

diminuendo, music, 352

dimmer control, radar, 444

dimple: golf ball, 310; human, 25; necktie, 192

dinette table, sailboat, 135

dingbat, newspaper, 168

dinghy, 133

dining car, passenger train, 116

dining room, White House, 75

DIN socket, movie projector, 175

dink, 133

dinner knife, 244

dinner plate, 244

dinosaur, 43

diopter value, eye scope, 448

dip: bow, 466; ice cream cone, 265

dipping station, universal gym, 344
diplomatic reception room, White House, 75
dipole magnet, super collider, 394
dipole superconducting magnet assembly, 394
dipstick, 111, 406
dip tube, dispenser, 267
direct drive, chain saw, 431
directional arrow, road map, 20
directional letter, weather vane, 19
directional light, automobile, 106
directional-microphone contact, movie camera, 174
directional signal, automobile, 106, 110
direction finder: destroyer, 477; helicopter, 146; 747 cockpit, 150
direction indicator: tape recorder, 177; 747 cockpit, 150
directions for use, package, 268
director, fencing match, 315
directory, elevator car, 78
dirigible, 156
dirigible mooring mast, skyscraper, 77
dirndl skirt, 197
dirt bike, 129
dirt shoe, mechanical sweeper, 127
disapproval, gesture, 507
disc, see disk
discard holder, blackjack, 347
disc brake: automobile, 108; motorcycle, 129
disc compartment, compact disc player, 178
discharge chute, power mower, 429
discharge tube: fire extinguisher, 284; laser, 395
discriminator adjustment, metal detector, 445
discus, 301, 303
dish: bathtub, 274; chafing, 245; table setting, 244-245
dish rack, 260
dishwasher, 250
disk: bear trap, 433; eye scope, 448; harness racing sulky, 337; incandescent bulb, 238; light meter, 176; phonograph, 178; screwback earring, 218; shuffleboard, 318; starfish, 46; stingray, 45; video recorder, 184; video-still camera, 173
disk compartment, video-still camera, 173
disk drive, synthesizer, 363
diskette, personal computer, 162
dispenser: dishwasher, 250; kitchen sink, 247; washing machine, 280
displacement, chain saw, 431
displacement hull, powerboat, 138
display: calculator, 441; cash register, 440; CB radio, 183; radar, 444; space shuttle, 153
display button, compact disc player, 178
display control: pilot's instrument panel, 481; sonar, 444; wristwatch, 220
display panel, video-still camera, 173
display screen, cellular telephone, 181

disposable bag, vacuum cleaner, 283
disposable razor, 210
distal, tooth, 456
distal transverse, human hand, 31
distance event, track and field, 300
distance heading indicator, pilot's instrument panel, 481
distance lens, eyeglasses, 221
distance runner, shoe, 302
distance scale, camera, 172, 174; zoom lens, 172
distilling equipment, laboratory, 447
distortion pedal, guitar, 363
distributary, river, 13
distribution map, 21
distribution of copies, letter, 159
distribution point, man's hair, 211
distributor, automobile engine, 111
district, thematic map, 21
ditch: castle, 81; permanent fort, 83
dite, cartoon, 380
divan, 236
dive break, glider, 147
divers' oxygen bottle rack, oil drilling platform, 101
diver's watch, skin diving, 331
dive timer, skin diving, 331
divided by, symbol, 511
divided highway, 114
divided highway ends, road sign, 505
divider: highway, 114; pocket knife, 426; zipper, 209
dividing line, domino, 345
diving board, 316
diving plane, submarine, 479
diving platform, 316
division: business card, 160; thematic map, 21; with slide rule, 441
division line, basketball court, 296
dixie cup, sailor, 497
dock: horse, 38; sheep, 33
doctor blade, rotogravure, 166
doctor's unit, dental, 144
document feed guide, fax machine, 164
document feed tray, fax machine, 164
dodger cleat, inflatable, 133
dog, 36; bear trap, 433; fishing reel, 340; snack food, 265; workbench, 408
doghouse: grammatical symbol, 513; oil drilling platform, 101
dog's tooth, brick wall, 69
Dolby, portable radio/cassette player, 182
Dolby switch, Walkman, 182
doldrums, wind, 6
dollar, symbol, 511
dolly, balance beam, 306
dome: Capitol, 74; compass, 136; destroyer, 477; dog, 36; locomotive, 116; mosque, 70, 71; percolator, 252; screwback earring, 218; silo, 104
dome cover, wok, 257
domed shell, cupboard, 243
domed structures, 85
domestic hot-water tank, solar heating system, 391
domestic staff, 489
domino, 345
donjon, castle, 80
do not enter, road sign, 504

don't-come box, craps table, 347
don't-pass bar, craps table, 347
donut, baseball bat, 290
door: 64; automobile, 106, 107; barn, 104; bath and shower, 274; bolt, 458; bus, 118; church, 87; clothes dryer, 281; cupboard, 243; destroyer, 476; dishwasher, 250; elevator car, 78; fireplace ashpit, 292; garage, 63; garbage truck, 127; grandfather clock, 233; handball and squash courts, 313; helicopter, 146; house, 61, 62, 63; jumbo jet, 149; lobster pot, 433; lock, 458; locomotive, 117; mailbox, 231; mechanical sweeper, 127; microwave oven, 248; piano, 361; powerboat, 139; prison, 76; refrigerator, 249; safe, 457; sealed voting booth, 437; single engine airplane, 147; space shuttle, 152; stove, 248, 404; subway car, 119; synagogue ark, 88; tent, 342; tepee, 84; toaster oven, 253; vault, 457; washing machine, 280
doorknob, 64, 458
doormat, 64
door mirror, bus, 118
doppler shift, 2
dormer: barn, 104; house, 62, 63
dorsal fin, fish, 45
dorsal scale, snake, 42
dorso-lateral fold, frog, 44
dosage, pill, 451
dosage, prescription, 451
dot: braille, 512; curling iron, 214; dice, 347; domino, 345; ice cream cone, 265; music notation, 353; sewing machine, 278
dot matrix printer, 163
dotted half note, music, 352
dottle, pipe, 229
double, dominos, 345
double bar, music, 353
double bar bridge, eyeglasses, 221
double bass, 354, 355
double bed, 270
double-breasted jacket, 188
double bull's eye, dart board, 322
double-circuit tower, power network, 396
double-clip palette cup, sketch box, 371
double corner, chessboard, 345
double cuff shirt, 189
double-edged blade, shaver, 210
double-end curve, staircase, 66
double-front pocket, shoulder bag, 222
double-hung window, 63, 67
double interlining, necktie, 193
double lancet window, church, 86
double lock, police gun belt, 498
double-pointed tack, 410
double prime, grammatical symbol, 513
double reed: bagpipe, 365; English horn, 357; oboe, 356
double return, staircase, 66
double ring, dart board, 322
double-score ring, dart board, 322
double seam, can, 267
double slide zipper, parka, 201

doubles line, Ping-Pong table, 321
double spread, magazine, 170
doubles service court, badminton, 319
doubles sideline: badminton court, 319; tennis court, 312
double star, 3
double top handles, swagger bag, 222
double-truck, magazine, 170
double vent, jacket, 188
doubling, house, 61
doubling cube, backgammon, 345
dough blender, 261
dowel, hammock, 288
dowel bit, manual drill, 418
down, bird, 39
down haul, windsurfer, 330
downhill skiing, 326
down marker, football field, 293
downpipe, house, 63
downspout, house, 63
downstream, river, 13
downstream gate, canal lock, 99
downstream stop log hoist, dam, 100
downtube, bicycle, 128
dozer, 435
draft, boat, 132
draftsman, house blueprint, 62
draft tube, sleeping bag, 343
dragee, sundae, 264
drag, hot air balloon, 332
drag knob, fishing reel, 340
dragon, 48; Manchu court dress, 491
drag racing, 339
drag shield, power mower, 429
dragster, drag racing, 339
drain: bathtub, 274 cleaner, 422; sink, 247, 273; washing machine basket, 280; water heater, 401
drain cock, furnace, 400
drainer, kitchen tool, 259, 260
draining rack, kitchen, 260
draining spoon, kitchen utensil, 259
drainpipe, house, 63
drain tank, nuclear reactor, 392
dram, symbol, 510
drape: curtain, 240; stage, 350, 351
drapery, 240; cave, 4; four-poster bed, 270
drawbridge, 97; castle, 80; permanent fort, 83
drawer: bureau, 272; cash register, 440; compact disc player, 178; desk, 276; dressing table, 272; garbage disposal, 247; medical examination table, 450; sideboard, 243; workbench, 408
drawer case, furniture, 272
drawing, house, 62
draw-knob, organ, 360
drawstring: ballet slippers, 494; parka, 201
drawtube: microscope, 442; telescope, 443
draw-works, oil drilling platform, 101
dreadnought, 476
D recreation yard, prison, 76
dredger, kitchen tool, 260
dress, 198; cook, 489; native, 491
dress-blue jacket, military, 496
dressed pelt, 201
dresser, 272
dressing medicinal, 451

dressing table, 272
dress shoe: king's, 484; military, 496; sailor, 497
dress suspenders, 190
dress uniform, military, 496
dried leaf, onion, 262
drift, ocean, 6
drift-free arm, dental unit, 454
drill: dental, 454, 455; hand, 418, 419; oil drilling platform, 101
drilling platform, oil, 101
drill press, 419
D-ring, trenchcoat, 200
drip coffee maker, 252
drip cup, citrus juicer, 255
drip edge, house, 62
drip hoop, overhead power line, 396
drip molding, automobile, 107
dripless candle, 237
drip pan, candelabrum, 237; stove, 248
dripstone, cave, 11; church, 86
drive: chain saw, 431; merry-go-round, 93
drive axle tire, bus, 118
drive chain: bicycle, 128; motorcycle, 129
drive joint, hitch and harrow, 434
drive mode key, camera, 172
driven element, CB radio antenna, 183
drive piece, socket wrench, 415
driver: golf club, 311; harness racing, 337; stagecoach, 131
driver's box, stagecoach, 131
driver's fire suit, drag racing, 339
driver sideview mirror, automobile, 106
driver's observation window, tank, 475
driver's seat: bus, 118; Hansom cab, 131
driveshaft: automobile, 109; outboard engine, 137
driveway apron, house, 63
drive wheel: can opener, 251; locomotive, 116; tank, 474, 475
drive yoke, hitch and harrow, 434
driving band, spinning wheel, 387
driving bit, harness racing, 337
driving glove, drag racing, 339
driving light, truck tractor, 120
driving suit, drag racing, 339
drone, bagpipe, 365
drone string, sitar, 362
drop: coffin, 516; roller coaster, 92; stage, 350; traverse rod, 240
drop armhole, woman's jacket, 196
drop box, blackjack, 346
drop cloth, painting, 425
drop earrings, queen's regalia, 484
drop feed button, sewing machine, 278
drop-in cartridge, movie film, 174
drop-leaf table, 242
drop-lid desk, 276
drop-out, bicycle, 128
dropped handlebar, bicycle, 128
dropped initial, magazine, 170
drop rail lock, playpen, 286
drop shoulder, woman's jacket, 196
drop-through fin cover, slalom water ski, 329
drug box, paramedic, 123

drug treatment, prescription, 451
drum, 354, 364; automobile brake, 109; clothes dryer, 281; humidifier, 402; sextant, 137; venetian blind, 241
drum brake, motorcycle, 129
drumlin, glacier, 12
drum major, 495
drum set, 364
drum shade, lamp, 238
drumstick: drum, 364; poultry, 35
drupe, peach, 55
dry-bulk carrier, 140
dry chemical fire extinguisher, 284
dryer: clothes, 281; hair, 214; lettuce, 260
dry fencing match, 315
drying, laundry, 280
dry measuring cup, 258
dry sink, 243
d.s., music notation, 353
D sharp, piano keyboard octave, 361
D string, double bass, 355
dual pneumatic liner system, football helmet, 292
dual rear wheel, tow truck, 126
dual scale thermometer, 18
dual wheel hub, tow truck, 126
dubbing control, movie projector, 175
ducat, 349
duck, 35
duckbill pliers, 414
duckpin, 317
duct: clothes dryer, 281; eye, 30; furnace, 400; heat exchanger, 403; jet fighter, 480; racing car, 338
dugout, baseball field, 291
dulcimer, Appalachian, 362
dumbbell: body building, 344; keychain, 459
dummy type, magazine, 170
dump: fireplace ashes, 232; police gun belt, 498
dump bin, aisle display, 102
dune: nautical chart, 22; shoreline, 14; topographic map, 22
dune buggy, 130
dust bag: sander, 421; vacuum cleaner, 283
dust cover: hardback book, 167; vault, 457
dust filter, minivacuum, 283
dust flap, folding box, 269
dustproof screw cover, theodolite, 436
dusting brush, vacuum cleaner, 283
dust jacket, hardback book, 167
dustpan, 282
dust panel, furniture, 272
dust ruffle, bedding, 270
Dutch door, 64
dwarf star, 3
dye, hair, 214
dynamic marking, music, 352
dynamic positioning equipment, oil drilling platform, 101

E

E: braille, 512; music notation, 353; piano keyboard octave, 361; sign language, 512
ear: ax, 464; cat, 37; corn, 58; dog, 36; grasshopper, 41; horse, 38; human, 24, 30; lizard, 43; pail, 284; pig, 34; pot, 373; rocking chair, 234;
scallop, 47; sheep, 33; tepee, 84; turkey, 35; turtle, 43; ultimate beast, 48
earclip, spring, 218
ear covert, bird, 39
ear cushion, audio headphone, 179
ear doctor, examination equipment, 448
eardrum, frog, 44
ear flap, baseball batting helmet, 290
earhole, football helmet, 292
ear hook, hearing aid, 452
earlobe, chicken, 35
earmark, cattle, 432
earphone jack, movie camera, 174
earphones, Walkman, 182
earpiece, desk, 180
earplug case, combat soldier's uniform, 497
earring, 219; findings, 218; queen's regalia, 484
ear scope, 448
earth, 3; core, 4; hogan, 84
earth dam section, dam, 100
earthen breastwork, permanent fort, 83
ear tip, stethoscope, 449
ear wire, findings, 218
easel: painting, 370, 371; tombstone, 516
East Australia Current, ocean, 6
Eastern Time, 5
east longitude, 5
East Room, White House, 75
east-west handbag, 222
easy chair, 235
eave: barn, 104; house, 61, 63
eave pole, tent, 342
E cell block, prison, 76
eachinus, column, 73
ecphoneme, grammatical symbol, 513
economy-class section, jumbo jet, 149
Eddy, kite, 323
edge: auger bit, 419; ax, 464; bayonet, 463; bugle, 359; cheese, 263; cheese plane, 256; coin, 225; cymbal, 364; drop-leaf table, 242; hang glider, 333; hatchet, 412; horse's foot, 38; ice skates, 325; knife, 256, 463; necktie, 192; paper bag, 266; razor blade, 210; ski, 326; space shuttle wing, 152; sword, 463
edge flap, jumbo jet, 148
edge marking, airport runway, 94
edger, lawn, 429
editing control, video camera, 184
edition, book, 167
editorial cartoon, 380
education, résumé, 160
EENT specialist, 448
E flat, piano keyboard octave, 361
effector, nervous system, 29
efferent nerve, human, 29
egg, 262; insect, 41
eggbeater: helicopter, 146; kitchen tool, 258
egg cell, flower, 53
egg rack, refrigerator, 249
egg slicer, 261
eighth-inch mark, tape measure, 424
eighth-mile pole, harness racetrack, 337
eighth note, music, 352
eighth rest, music, 352

eight pin, bowling, 317
eject button, cassette tape recorder, 177; Walkman, 182
ejector, dental unit, 454
ejector chute, circular saw, 417
ejector rod, revolver, 470
elapsed time, drag racing, 339
elapsed time bezel, wristwatch, 220
elapsed time indicator, VCR, 184
elastic, mitten, 200
elastic band: baseball uniform, 290; mattress cover, 271
elastic facing: brassiere, 195; girdle, 195
elasticized waist: shirt, 197; woman's pants, 196
elastic webbing, suspenders, 190
elbow: cat, 37; dog, 36; fence gate, 67; horse, 38; human, 24
elbow cup, armor, 465
elbow pad: basketball, 296; football, 292; ice hockey, 295; rollerskating, 324
elbow protector, fencing, 315
electrical cable, spacesuit, 155
electrical conduit, railroad crossing signal, 115
electrical connection: meter, 399; truck, 120, 121
electrical current, switch, 398
electrical power control, space shuttle, 153
electrical system, automobile, 108
electric broom, 282
electric can opener, 251
electric chair, 462
electric cord, potter's wheel, 373
electric eye, Polaroid, 173
electric foil, fencing strip, 315
electric guitar, 363
electric hair brush, 212
electrician's pliers, 414
electrician's tools, 423
electricity: nuclear reactor, 392; solar power system, 391
electric kiln, 373
electric locomotive, 116; canal lock, 99
electric meter, 399; house, 63
electric organ, 360
electric pilot, stove, 248
electric potter's wheel, 373
electric range, 248
electric razor, 210
electric scoring machine, fencing strip, 315
electric sparks, fireworks, 383
electric starter, barbecue grill, 288
electric typewriter, 161
electric water heater, 401
electric wheelchair, 432
electric wire, railroad crossing signal, 115
electric wok, 257
electrocardiogram, 123
electrode: electric chair, 462; transistor, 396
electronic calculator, 441
electronic countermeasures antenna, aircraft carrier, 478
electronic countermeasure warning light, pilot's instrument panel, 481
electronic flash, photographic, 176
electronic game program, personal computer, 162
electronic lock, cellular telephone, 181
electronic organ, 360

electronics rack, space shuttle, 153
electronic touch button voting position, electronic voting system, 437
electronic warfare antenna, destroyer, 477
electronic weather station, 18
electron tube, 396
electropneumatic retarder, railroad yard, 96
element, CB radio antenna, 183; dishwasher, 250
element release lever, typewriter, 161
elephant, ultimate beast, 49
elevated track, subway, 119
elevating tube, mortar, 472
elevating wheel, slide projector, 175
elevation: house, 62; topographic map, 22
elevation adjustment knob, rifle scope, 469
elevation lead panel, pilot's instrument panel, 481
elevator, 78; aircraft carrier, 478; airplane, 147; blimp, 156; glider, 147; jumbo jet, 149; passenger ship, 142; public sign, 506; skyscraper, 77; stage, 350
elevator lock, camera tripod, 176
elevator platforms, desk, 276
elevator shaft, lift bridge, 97
elevon: cruise missile, 482; space shuttle, 152
eliminator, drag racing, 339
ellipsis, grammatical symbol, 513
elliptical galaxy, 2
embankment, railroad, 115
embattled parapet, castle, 80
emblem: drum major's coat, 495; flag, 502; paper money, 224
embossed label, 268
embouchure hole, flute, 357
embrasure, castle, 80
embroidered buttonhole, Revolutionary War general, 492
embroider cuff, king, 484
embroidered marquisette front, girdle, 195
embroidery, 385; queen's regalia, 484
emergency air vent, bus, 118
emergency brake: car, 110; subway car, 119
emergency channel: CB radio, 183; police radio, 122
emergency core-cooling system pump, nuclear reactor, 392
emergency escape chute, jumbo jet, 148
emergency exit, elevator shaft, 78
emergency light selector, police car, 122
emergency off switch, high-speed printer, 439
emergency stop: elevator car, 78; escalator, 79
emery board, 215
emesis basin, ambulance, 123
emission indicator, gas laser, 395
emitter, transistor chip, 396
empire shade, lamp, 238
EMT, fire engine, 124
enamel, tooth, 456
enarme, shield, 464
enclosing trap, 433
enclosure: air conditioner, 402; letter, 159

end: banana, 55; can, 267; clay modeling tool, 372; clothespin, 280; cupboard, 243; diving board, 316; domino, 345; fencing foil, 315; football, 292; lacrosse stick, 298; music, 353; spool, 384; suspenders, 190; theodolite, 436; tomato, 54; wrench, 415
end assembly, backyard equipment, 287
end-button, violin, 355
end cap: aisle display, 102; cartridge fuse, 399; seeder, 430; venetian blind, 241; waterskiing towline, 329
end cover, sewing machine, 278
end grain, lumber, 68
end handle, coffin, 516
end hook, tape measure, 424
endleaves, hardback book, 167
end line: basketball court, 296; football field, 293; Ping Pong table, 321; volleyball court, 319
end matter, book, 167
endocarp, peach, 55
end operating-screw handle, hand-screw clamp, 409
endoplasmic reticulum, animal cell, 23
endpapers, hardback book, 167
end piece: eyeglasses, 221; starting block, 304; zipper, 209
end pin, cello, 355
end plate, racing car, 338
end plug, vacuum tube, 396
endpost, fence gate, 67
end ring, fishing rod, 341
end slug, magazine, 171
end vise, workbench, 408
end wall, swimming pool, 316
end zone, football field, 293
energy: solar, 391; steam engine, 405
energy absorber: automobile bumper, 108; highway barrier, 114
energy storage capacitor, gas laser, 395
engage switch, 747 cockpit, 150
engine: automobile, 108, 110, 111; blimp, 156; bulldozer, 435; cruise missile, 482; fire fighter, 125; helicopter, 146; hovercraft, 145; internal combustion, 406; jet, 149, 407; lunar lander, 154; mechanical sweeper, 127; motorcycle, 129; outboard, 137; power mower, 429; racing car, 338, 339; single engine airplane, 147; space shuttle, 152; steam, 405; train, 116; truck tractor, 120
engine chamber, torpedo, 479
engine company number, pumper, 125
engineer, and transit, 436
engine fuel shutoff handle, pilot's instrument panel, 481
engine hour meter, powerboat, 138
engine instrumentation, 747 cockpit, 150, 151
engine louvers, tank, 474
engine mounting brackets inflatable, 133
engine oil-pressure gauge, powerboat, 138
engine room, passenger ship, 142

engine terminal, railroad yard, 96
engine test area, aircraft carrier, 478
English clock, darts, 322
English horn, 354, 357
English saddle, 335
engraved line, scrimshaw, 375
engraved plate, paper money, 224
engraving: identification bracelet, 187; knife, 375; and printing, 374, 377
enlarged scale detail inset, political map, 21
enlisted man's uniform, 496
ensemble, chamber music, 354
ensign, destroyer, 476
entablature, column, 73
entrance: airport, 94; bus, 118; circuit breaker box, 399; highway cloverleaf, 114; igloo, 85; jai alai cancha, 314; lobster pot, 433; tanker belowdeck storage, 140; theatre, 351; White House, 75
entrée, meal, 263
entry, darts, 322
entry word, book page, iv
enumerating district, thematic map, 21
envelope, 159; animal cell, 23; hot air balloon, 332; vacuum tube, 396; Zeppelin, 156
environmental control, pilot's instrument panel, 481
environmental monitor, space shuttle, 153
epaulet: drum major's coat, 495; Revolutionary War general,; 492; trench coat, 200
épée, 315
epiglottis, tongue, 30
Episcopal ring, cardinal, 487
epitaph, tombstone, 516
equal, symbol, 511
equalizer: audio speaker, 179, 182; cowboy, 490
equalizer buckle, venetian blind, 241
equalize space, proofreader's mark, 514
equalizing switch, tape recorder, 177
equal or greater, symbol, 511
equal or less, symbol, 511
equals: calculator key, 441; symbol, 511
equator, 5, 6
equatorial counter current, ocean, 6
equatorial current, ocean, 6
equipment bay, lunar lander, 154
equipment status indicator, nuclear reactor control room, 393
equipment stowage box, tank, 474
erase button, video-still camera adaptor, 173
eraser, pencil, 158
erasure table, typewriter, 161
erecting telescope, field glasses, 443
ergostand, computer workstation, 438
ermine pendant, Indian, 490
eroteme, grammatical symbol, 513
escalator, 79
escape chute, jumbo jet, 148
escarp, permanent fort, 83
escarpment, continental margin, 15

escroll, coat of arms, 503
escutcheon: coat of arms, 503; mortise lock, 458
escutcheon plate: kitchen sink, 247; safe, 457
espresso coffee, 252
estate bottled, wine label, 267
estate name, wine label, 267
E string, double bass, 355
ET, drag racing, 339
etching, 377
eternal light: synagogue, 88; Torah, 486
evacuation tip, dental unit, 454
evaporator coil, air conditioner, 402
evening handkerchief, queen's regalia, 484
event: drag racing, 339; information, ticket, 349; track and field, 300
everything's OK, gesture, 507
ewe, 33
examination equipment, medical, 449
examination table, medical, 450
exasperation, gesture, 507
excavator, dental, 455
excessive talk, gesture, 507
exchanger, fireplace heat, 232
exclamation point, grammatical symbol, 506
execution device, 462
executive office, White House, 75
exercise, body building, 344
exercise yard, prison, 76
exhaust: automobile engine, 111; combustion jet engine, 407; drag racing dragster, 339; heat exchanger, 403; internal combustion engine, 406; locomotive, 117; motorcycle, 129; steam engine, 405; tank, 474; truck tractor, 120
exhaust duct: clothes dryer, 281; furnace, 400; tunnel, 98
exhaust line gas filter, gas laser, 395
exhaust port, outboard engine, 137; rocket, 407; skin diving tank, 331
exhaust tube, incandescent bulb, 238
exhibit hall, church, 87
exit: elevator, 78; jumbo jet, 149; theatre, 351
exit angle, slide, 287
exit bar, bus, 118
exit door, bus, 118
exit mirror, laser, 395
exit ramp, highway cloverleaf, 114
exocarp: orange, 55; pineapple, 55
exonomist, 225
exoskeleton, insect, 41
exosphere, earth, 4
expanding bit, drill, 418
expansion chamber, thermometer, 18
expansion nozzle, missile, 456
expansion tank, automobile, 108
expansive bit, drill, 419
expiration date: coupon, 103; credit card, 227; magazine mailing label, 169
exploration equipment, lunar lander, 154
explorer, dental, 455
exposure adjustment key, camera, 172
exposure index, light meter, 176
exposure label, gas laser, 395

exposure meter, 176
exposure mode key, camera, 172
expression pedal, organ, 360
expressway, 114
extended bay, barn, 104
extender, paint roller, 425
extending ball, pen, 158
extension: automatic rifle barrel, 471; baseball catcher's shinguard, 290; dropleaf table, 242; folding rule, 424; operating table, 450; political map, 21; table saw, 417; vacuum cleaner, 283
extension handle, lunar rover, 155
extension ladder, pumper, 124
extension scoring light, fencing strip, 315
extension tube: ambulance, 123; screen, 175
exterior, window, 65
exterior decoration, coat of arms, 503
exterior frame, tent, 342
exterior panagraph gate, subway motorman's cab, 119
exterior slope, permanent fort, 89
external auditory canal, ear, 30
external bud, potato, 54
external door switch, dishwasher, 250
external environmental control, pilot's instrument panel, 481
external frame, 343
external fuel tank, space shuttle, 152; tank, 474
external galaxy, 2
external microphone, cassette tape recorder, 177
external speaker, personal cassette player, 182
external tank forward bay, space shuttle, 152
extinct reptiles, 43
extinguisher: candle, 237; drag racing dragster, 339
extra bass port, portable radio/cassette player, 182
extra cheese, pizza, 265
extractor: juice, 255; shotgun, 468
extrados, arch, 72
extravehicular activity handrail, lunar lander, 154
extravehicular visor, spacesuit, 155
extremities, human, 31
eye: ant, 41; ax, 464; bee, 41; cat, 37; cheese, 263; fish, 45; fishhook, 341; fishing jig, 341; frame, 379; frog, 44; grasshopper, 41; hammer, 412; hasp, 460; hook and eye, 208; human, 24, 30; hurricane, 17; lobster, 47; mallet, 412; needle, 384; octopus, 46; pineapple, 55; potato, 54; sheep, 33; snake, 42; spider, 40; spring beard needle, 386; stirrup, 335; tadpole, 44; toad, 44
eyeball, 30
eyebolt, 411
eyebrow, 30; magazine, 171; woman's, 213
eye colorstick, 216, 217
eyecup: binoculars, 443; video camera, 184
eye doctor, examination equipment, 448
eyedropper, 451
eyeglasses, 221

eye guards, fireman's helmet, 500
eyelashes, 30, 213; liner, 216, 217
eyelet: baseball glove, 291; ice skates, 325; man's belt, 190; cap, 202; man's shoe, 204; running shoe, 302; shoulder bag, 222
eyelid: frog, 44; human, 30
eyeliner, makeup, 216
eyepatch, pirate, 492
eye pencil, 217
eyepiece: binoculars, 443; camera, 174; ear scope, 448; eye scope, 448; microscope, 442; Polaroid, 173; telescope, 443; theodolite, 436
eyeport shield, drag racing driver, 339
eye scope, 448
eye shadow, 217
eye socket, 30
eyespot, starfish, 46
eyestay, running shoe, 302
eye teeth, 456
eyewires, eyeglasses, 221

F

F: braille, 512; music notation, 353; piano keyboard octave, 361; sign language, 512
F-4 Phantom II, 480
F-16F Falcon, 480
fabric, 388; embroidery, 385; hand knitting, quilting, 385; umbrella, 230; weaving, 387
fabric flowers, woman's hat, 203
fabric ridge, embroidery ring, 385
fabric temperature guide, iron, 279
fabric-tension lock, screen, 175
face: ax, 464; bow, 466; brick, 68; check, 226; clown, 493; coin, 225; croquet mallet, 318; dart board, 322; elliptical galaxy, 2; file, 420; gas pump, 112; geodesic dome, 85; golf club, 310; grandfather clock, 233; hammer, 412; hand shower, 274; lacrosse stick, 298; lead came, 378; lumber, 68; mountain, 8, 9; obelisk, 71; paper bag, 266; Ping-Pong racket, 321; playing cards, 348; rasp, 420; saw tooth, 416; sheep, 33; shower, 274; slot machine, 346; spider, 40; starting block, 304; sword, 463; tennis racket, 312; traffic light, 113; type, 166; voting booth, 437; wall, 69; wristwatch, 220; zipper, 209
face cards, 348
face mask: baseball catcher, 290; football helmet, 292; ice hockey goalie, 294; skin diving, 331
face-off circle, ice hockey rink, 295
faceplate: mortise lock, 458; paper money, 225; sewing machine, 278; ski helmet, 326
face shield, police, 498
facet, cut gemstone, 218
face value: money, 224, 225; stamp, 159
facing: brassiere, 195; girdle, 195; necktie, 193; skyscraper, 77; woman's jacket, 196
facing dragon, Manchu court dress, 491

facsimile, fax machine, 164
Fahrenheit scale, thermometer, 18, 449
fairing, helicopter, 146; motorcycle, 129
fair territory, baseball field, 291
fairwater, outboard engine, 137
fairway, golf course, 310
fairweather, submarine, 479
faja, jai alai player, 314
fall: grand piano, 361; pulley block rope, 461; woman's hair, 213
falling front desk, 276
false edge, knife, 463
false teeth, 453
family name, typeface, 165
fan: air circulating, 402; automobile, 108, 111; bridal costume, 488; combustion jet engine, 407; heat exchanger, 403; high jump, 300; hovercraft, 145; jumbo jet, 149; lobster tail, 47; subway car, 119; underwater tunnel, 98; vacuum cleaner, 283
fan belt, 111
fan clutch, 111
fancy stitching, boot, 206
fanfold paper, computer, 439
fang: snake, 42; spider, 40; tooth, 456
fanlight, door, 64
fan plate, armor, 465
fan switch, elevator, 78
fantail: destroyer, 476; passenger ship, 142; windmill, 390
fare box, commuter bus, 118
farm machinery, road sign, 505
far turn, harness racetrack, 337
fascia, house, 60, 61
fastback, passenger car, 109
fastener, 208; corrugated, 410; football helmet, 292; hollow wall, 411; overnight bag, 285; spacesuit, 155
fastening, bell, iv
fast forward: remote control unit, 184; tape recorder, 177
fast forward button, Walkman, 182
fastigiated top, skyscraper, 77
fast-rewind button, tape recorder, 177
fat, meat, 262
fat back, pork, 34
father, flat racing entry, 336
fathom, nautical chart, 22
fatigue belt, 497
fatigue pants, 497
fatigue shirt, 497
fauces, tongue, 30
faucet, 273; bathtub, 274; hose coupling, 428; Jacuzzi, 274; kitchen sink, 247
fault line, jai alai cancha, 314
fax machine, 164
fax number, business card, 160
F clef, music, 353
feather: badminton shuttlecock, 319; bird, 39; chicken, 35; turkey, 35; weather vane, 19; woman's hat, 203
feather pen, 158
feature spread, magazine, 170-171
feature stripes, powerboat, 138
feature well, magazine, 169
Federal, house style, 63
federal prescription number, prescription, 451

Federal Reserve Bank seal, paper money, 224
Federal Reserve note, 224
federal route number, road map, 20
feed: drill press, 419; machine gun ammunition, 471; track lighting, 239
feed dog, sewing machine, 278
feeder cap, blender, 254
feeder waveguide, radar antenna, 444
feeding pen, barnyard, 104
feed knob, dot matrix printer, 163
feed line, furnace, 400
feed passage, barn, 104
feed plate, machine gun, 471
feed screw, auger bit, 419
feed-through, pacemaker, 452
feed tube: food processor, 254; fountain pen, 158
feedwater pump, nuclear reactor, 392
fee indicator, toll booth, 114
feeler: cat, 37; lobster, 47
feet: nautical chart, 22; type, 166
felloe, stagecoach, 131
felt: film roll, 172; pool table, 320
felt cap, baseball gear, 290
felt hat, cowboy, 490
female, symbol, 510
female coupling, hose connection, 428
female ferrule, fishing rod, 340
female flower, corn, 58
female-male, symbol, 508
female receptacle, electrical, 398
femoral artery, human, 28
femoral nerve, human, 29
femoral vein, human, 28
femur: frog, 44; grasshopper, 41; human, 26; spider, 40
fence: 67; baseball field, 291; house, 63; prison, 76; table saw, 417
fence posts, 67
fencing, 315; barnyard, 104
fencing shoe, 315
fencing strip, wood fence, 67
fender: automobile, 106, 107; bicycle, 128; bulldozer, 435; fireplace, 232; lift bridge, 97; motorcycle, 129; saddle, 335; tractor, 434; tugboat, 144
fender guard, gas pump automatic nozzle, 112
fermata, music, 352
fern, 57
Ferris wheel, 93
ferrule: billiard cue, 320; burnisher, 377; clay modeling tool, 372; chisel, 420; fishing rod, 340; gouge, 374; hoe, 427; jump rope, 344; paint brush, 425; painting brush, 370; pencil, 158; rake, 427; screwdriver, 413; shoe tree, 207; sousaphone, 358; stick umbrella, 230; tuba, 358; woodcarving tool, 372
fertilizer, 430
fess, coat of arms, 503
fetlock, horse, 38
fettling tool, potter's wheel, 373
F-hole, violin, 355
fiber: nerve, 29; paper money, 224; rope, 132
fiberglass pole, pole vaulting, 305
fibula, human, 26
fiddle: bass, 355; tub, 366
field: baseball, 291; coat of

arms, **503**; coin, **225**; craps table, **347**; flag, **502**; football, **293**; lacrosse, **298**; mountain, **9**; polo, **299**; soccer, **297**; track and field, **300-301**
field events equipment, **303**
field fortification, **82**
fieldglasses, **443**
fife, marching band, **354**
15' marker, bowling lane, **317**
fifth wheel, truck trailer, **120**
51-in-5's, darts, **322**
50-point ring, dart board, **322**
50-yard line, football field, **293**
fighter, jet aircraft, **480**
fighting chair, powerboat, **139**
fighting kite, **323**
fighting ship, surface, **476-477**
figure skates, **325**
filament: coral polyp, **46**; flower stamen, **53**; incandescent bulb, **238**; vacuum tube, **396**
file, **420**; briefcase, **285**; chessboard, **345**; desk, **276**; nail, **215**; pocket knife, **426**
file handle, drill, **418**
filet, cannon barrel, **467**
file-type handle, coping saw, **416**
fill, sleeping bag, **343**
filler: cigar, **228**; inflatable, **133**; locomotive, **117**; man's belt, **190**; quilting, **385**
filler neck, automobile gas tank, **109**
filler tube: automobile engine power steering, **111**; toilet, **275**
fillet, royal regalia, **485**
filling, dental, **455**; dessert, **264**; quiche, **263**; sandwich, **263**; scrimshaw, **375**; sleeping bag, **343**
filling port, iron, **279**
fill opening, coffee maker, **252**
fill unit float, dishwasher, **250**
fill window, minivacuum, **283**
filly, horse, **38**
film, **172**; camera, **174**
film door, Polaroid, **173**
film door release, Polaroid, **173**
filming trigger, movie camera, **174**
film-loading port, movie projector, **175**
film pack, instant camera, **173**
film plate, **395**
film projector, **175**
film roll, **172**
film shade, Polaroid, **173**
film speed, lightmeter, **176**
film speed key, camera, **172**
filter: air conditioner, **402**; cigarette, **228**; dryer, **281**; coffee maker, **252**; drag racing driver's fire suit, **339**; engine, **111**, **406**; heat exchanger, **403**; tractor, **434**; washing machine, **280**
filter carrier, microscope, **442**
fin: air conditioner, **402**; automobile, **107**; blimp, **156**; fish, **45**; glider, **147**; hovercraft, **145**; jet fighter, **480**; jumbo jet, **149**; missile, **482**; rifle grenade, **473**; single engine airplane, **147**; skin diving, **331**; stingray, **45**; surfboard, **330**; waterskiing, **329**; windsurfer, **330**
finance program, personal computer, **162**
fin cover, slalom water ski, **329**
findings, jewelry, **218**
fine-adjustment beam, laboratory scale, **447**

fine calibrate, Geiger counter, **445**
fine focus: microscope, **442**; telescope, **443**
fine tooth, hair comb, **212**
fine tuner: metal detector, **445**; violin, **355**
finger: baseball glove, **291**; frog, **44**; hair roller, **214**; handball glove, **313**; human, **24**, **31**; laboratory clamp, **446**; lacrosse glove, **298**; ultimate beast, **49**
fingerboard: accordion, **366**; guitar, **362**, **363**; violin, **355**
finger flange, hypodermic syringe, **451**
fingerless glove, miser, **492**
finger grip: hair clip, **214**; sewing machine, **278**
finger hole: bowling ball, **317**; desk phone, **180**
finger hook, trumpet, **359**
fingernail, **31**
finger pad, **31**
fingerplate, clarinet, **356**
fingerprint, human, **31**
finger pump, camp stove, **342**
finger stop, desk phone, **180**
fingertip: dog, **36**; human, **31**
finial: church, **86**; dressing table, **272**; flagpole, **502**; four-poster bed, **270**; gate post, **67**; grandfather clock, **233**; lamp, **238**; pagoda, **71**; woodburning stove, **404**
finish: drag racing, **339**; football, **292**; stained glass, **378**
finished copy tray, copier, **164**
finishing cap, umbrella, **230**
finishing nail, **410**
finishing sander, **421**
finishing wire, umbrella runner, **230**
finish line: harness racetrack, **337**; running track, **301**
finned projectile, mortar, **472**
fin-seal wrap, package, **269**
fin stabilizer, destroyer, **477**
fire, gemstone, **218**
fireback, fireplace, **232**
fireball, launch pad, **152**
fireboat, **144**
fireboot, **500**
fire bowl, brazier, **288**
firebox, fireplace, **232**
fire curtain, stage, **350**
fired handguns, **470**
fired pot, **373**
fire-eater, circus, **90**
fire engine, **124-125**
fire extinguisher, **284**; drag racing dragster, **339**; police car, **122**; tow truck, **126**
fire-fighting station, tanker, **141**
fire hydrant, **125**
fire irons, fireplace, **232**
fireman, **500**; suspenders, **190**
fire pit, tepee, **84**
fireplace, **232**
fire plug, **125**
fire screen, fireplace, **232**
fire stop, house, **60**
fire suit, drag racing driver's, **339**
fireworks, **382-383**
firing chamber, kiln, **373**
firing cone, potting, **373**
firing lever, machine gun, **471**
firing pin, torpedo, **479**
firing tube, bazooka, **472**
firing vent, cannon barrel, **467**
firn, mountain, **9**
first aid, public sign, **506**
first-aid box, fire engine, **124**
first-aid kit, police car, **122**

first base: baseball field, **291**; blackjack, **347**
first baseman's mitt, **291**
first bicuspid, **456**
first-class section, jumbo jet, **148**
first floor, White House, **75**
First Lady's office, White House, **75**
first meridian, globe, **5**
first molar, **456**
first officer's seat, 747 cockpit, **151**
first premolar, **456**
first quarter moon, **4**
first reef position, windmill, **390**
first reinforce, cannon barrel, **467**
first stage: missile, **482**; skin diving tank, **331**
first valve, trumpet, **359**
first valve slide: French horn, **358**; trumpet, **359**
first violin, **354**
fish, **45**; zodiac, **509**
fishing, **340-341**
fish ladder, dam, **100**
fishplate, railroad track, **115**
fish scaler, pocket knife, **426**
fish tail, coffin, **516**
fishtail chisel, woodcarving, **372**
fishtail gouge, woodcarving, **372**
fishway, dam, **100**
fission, nuclear reactor, **392**
fissure volcano, **10**
fist, human, **25**
fitted cuff, bridal gown, **488**
fitted pants, drum major, **495**
fitted pillow, sofa, **236**
fitted sheet, bedding, **271**
fitting: nozzle, **428**; pumper, **125**; saw, **416**; shoulder bag, **222**; shower, **274**; sink, **273**
five pin, bowling, **317**
5/8 pole, harness racetrack, **337**
5.25-inch disk format, diskette, **162**
five-unit beads, abacus, **441**
5 yard line, football field, **293**
fixed bridge, **97**
fixed glove, jet fighter, **480**
fixed hurdle, **304**
fixed jaw: C-clamp, **409**; monkey wrench, **415**
fixed pin, hinge, **460**
fixed service structure, launch pad, **152**
fixed-target collider, **394**
fixed window, **65**
fixings, ice cream, **265**
fixture, sink, **247**
flag, **502**; courtroom, **89**; football field, **293**; golf course, **311**; mailbox, **231**; music note, **353**; newspaper, **168**; parking meter, **113**; soccer field, **297**; swimming pool, **316**; track and field, **301**
flagged end, paint brush bristle, **425**
flagpole, **502**
flagstaff, destroyer, **476**
flake, tennis racket, **312**
flame: candle, **237**; dental, **455**; four-poster bed, **270**
flame bucket, launch pad, **152**
flame adjustment wheel, gas cigarette lighter, **228**
flan, coin, **225**
flange: barometer, **18**; hypodermic syringe, **451**; mace, **464**; sink, **273**; spool, **384**; trombone, **358**

flank: beef, **32**; cat, **37**; dog, **36**; horse, **38**; human, **25**; lamb, **33**; pelt, **201**; permanent fort, **83**; pork, **34**
flank billet, Western saddle, **335**
flap: backpack, **343**; baseball helmet, **290**; checkbook clutch, **223**; envelope, **159**; hasp, **460**; jumbo jet, **148**; magazine cover, **169**; man's shoe, **204**; matchbook, **228**; package, **269**; pocket, **188**, **189**, **196**, **200**; saddle, **335**; sailor's uniform, **497**; shoulder bag, **222**; single engine airplane, **147**; slalom water ski, **329**; tent, **342**; tepee, **84**; tow truck, **126**; wallet, **223**
flap lever, 747 cockpit, **151**
flare: police car, **122**; solar, **3**; trombone, **359**; trousers, **191**
flare fitting, plumbing, **422**
flaring tool, plumbing, **422**
flash: electronic, **176**; radar, **444**
flasher, locomotive, **117**
flash head: electronic flash, **176**; lunar lander, **154**
flashlight, police, **499**
flash suppressor, automatic weapon, **471**
flask, laboratory, **447**
flat: music, **352**; stage, **350**
flat bed, truck, **121**
flat-bottom hull, powerboat, **138**
flatcar, train, **117**
flat chisel, stonecutting, **372**
flat coast, nautical chart, **22**
flat diaphragm chest piece, stethoscope, **449**
flat four-cylinder automobile engine, **111**
flat grind, knife, **256**
flat hat, Beefeater, **483**
flat head, screw, **410**
flatiron, **279**
flat kite, **323**
flat of stock, rifle, **468**
flat pin, window shade roller, **241**
flat plate, solar heating system collector unit, **391**
flat racing, **336**
flat surface: perspective, **368**; printing, **166**
flattop, **478**
flatware, **244**
flavedo, orange, **55**
fleatrap, cowboy, **490**
fleet ballistic missile submarine, **479**
flesh, banana, **55**
fleshy root, carrot, **54**
fleshy tissue, succulent, **56**
fletching, arrow, **466**
fleur-de-lis, royal crown, **485**
flews, dog, **36**
flex, skateboard, **324**
flexible kite, **323**
flexible skirt, hovercraft, **145**
flexor, universal gym, **344**
flexor carpi radialis, human, **26**
flexor carpi ulnaris, human, **26**
flier, staircase, **66**
flies, stage, **350**
flight: dart, **322**; of steps, **66**
flight control position indicator, 747 cockpit, **150**
flight deck: aircraft carrier, **478**; destroyer, **476**; jumbo jet, **148**
flight feather, bird, **39**
flight instrumentation control, space shuttle, **153**
flight officer, airplane, **481**

flip, woman's hair, 213
flip chart, football down marker, 293
flipover, hurdle, 304
flip panel, football down marker, 293
flipper: dolphin, 45; skin diving, 331; turtle, 42
flitter candle, fireworks, 383
float: buoy, 132; dishwasher, 250; fishing, 341; toilet, 275
floating crank, brace, 418
floating pier, pontoon bridge, 97
floating position, oil drilling platform, 101
floe, glacier, 12
floeberg, glacier, 12
flood: river, 13; stage, 350
flood plain, 13, 15
floodlight, stage, 350
floor: barn, 104; basketball court, 296; canal lock, 99; and carpet, 246; cave, 11; church, 118; elevator car, 78; house, 60, 61, 62; kiln, 373; oil drilling platform, 101; skyscraper, 77; stage, 350; White House, 75
floorboards: inflatable, 133; playpen, 286
floor cable, fencing strip, 315
floor exercise, gymnastics, 306
floor glide, desk, 276
flooring, tent, 342
floor leader, House of Representatives, 74
floor-locking system pedal, surgical table, 450
floor pan, automobile, 109
floor plan: church, 87; house, 62
floor plate: escalator, 79; horizontal bar, 306; rifle, 468; stage, 350; stationary rings, 307
floor selector, elevator car, 78
floor support, playpen, 286
floor tom-tom, 364
floppy disk: computer, 438; personal computer, 162
floppy disk drive: computer workstation, 438; portable word processor, 162
floppy disk drive slot, personal computer, 162
floppy shoe, clown, 493
floral carving, tombstone, 516
floral organs, grass, 58
floral tube, apple, 55
floret, grass, 58
florist shop, passenger ship, 142
flotation device: skin diving, 331; jumbo jet, 148
flounce: dress, 198; queen's regalia, 484
flour shaker, 260
flow, volcano, 10
flow distributor head, nuclear reactor, 392
flower, 53; cactus, 56; corn, 58; grass, 58; woman's hat, 203
flow indicator, pilot's instrument panel, 481
flowstone, cave, 11
flue: destroyer, 476; fireplace, 232; house, 62; stove, 248, 404; water heater, 401
fluff, chicken, 35
fluid, solar collector panel, 391
fluke: anchor, 132; dolphin, 45
fluorescent banner, football field, 293
fluorescent bulb, lighting, 238
fluorescent light, oven, 248
flush, toilet, 275
flusher, sanitation vehicle, 127

flush left, proofreader's mark, 514
flush-left type, 170
flush-mount control actuator, Jacuzzi, 274
flute, 354, 356-357; auger bit, 419; screwdriver, 413
fluted spire, kokoshniki, 70
fluting, column, 73
flux, plumbing, 422
fly: flag, 502; man's underpants, 194
flybridge: powerboat, 138
flybridge monitor, fireboat, 144
fly deck, stage, 350
flyer: circus, 90; spinning wheel, 387; staircase, 66
fly front: blouse, 197; trousers, 191; woman's pants, 196
flying bridge: destroyer, 477; powerboat, 138
flying crate, kite, 323
flying horse, merry-go-round, 93
flying line, kite, 323
flying stovepipe, jet engine, 407
flying wing, combat aircraft, 480
fly line, stage, 350
fly rod, fishing, 341
fly tackle, windmill, 390
flywheel: automobile engine, 111; hitch and harrow, 434; steam engine, 405
FM: movie camera, 174; receiver, 179
foal, horse, 38
foam, fire extinguisher, 284
foam brush, house painting, 425
foam monitor, tanker, 141
fob: pocket watch, 220; trousers, 191; vest, 188
focal length: microscope, 442; movie camera, 174
focal point, composition, 369
fo'c'sle, destroyer, 477
focus: binoculars, 443; camera, 174; microscope, 442; projector, 175; rifle scope, 469; telescope, 443; theodolite, 436
focus collar, zoom lens, 172
focus control, video camera, 184
focusing lens, laser, 395
focusing magnet, super collider, 394
focusing ring, camera, 172
focus mode switch, camera, 172
fog, weather map, 19
fog whistle, destroyer, 477
foible, fencing foil, 315
foil: copper, 378; drag racing dragster, 339; electric, 315; fencing, 315; package, 269
fold: curtain, 240; frog, 44; salamander, 44
fold-down seat, automobile, 106
folder, briefcase, 285
folding box, package, 269
folding fan, 402
folding file, nail clippers, 215
folding leaf, drop-leaf table, 242
folding rule, 424
folding umbrella, 230
fold line, sewing pattern, 388
foley, 260
foliage, 52; carrot, 54
folio: book page, iv, 167; magazine, 169, 170; newspaper, 168
folk instruments, 366
follow block, stapler, 277

follower, magazine, 470
follow spring, stapler, 277
fondo, jai alai cesta, 314
food: desserts, 264; prepared, 263; raw, 262
food mill, 260
food processor, 254
foolish, gesture, 507
foot: attaché case, 285; basket, 266; bed, 270; bird, 39; book page, 167; boot, 206; bureau, 272; camera tripod, 176; cat, 37; cigar, 228; cigarette, 228; clam, 47; cymbal, 364; drop-leaf table, 242; electronic flash, 176; fishing reel, 340; flag, 502; food processor, 254; frog, 44; garbage disposal, 247; grammatical symbol, 506; grandfather clock, 233; horse, 38; human, 24, 31; hurdle, 304; juice extractor, 255; lounger, 235; mainsail, 136; pig, 34; pot, 373; potter's wheel, 373; rail, 115; royal regalia, 485; sewing machine, 278; shoulder bag, 222; shuffleboard court, 318; sideboard, 243; slide projector, 175; sofa, 236; stapler, 277; steamer basket, 257; stemware, 244; surgical table, 450; toaster, 253; ultimate beast, 49; windsurfer mast, 330; wok, 257
football, 292-293; association, 297
footballer, 297
foot binding, slalom water ski, 329
footboard: bed, 270; stagecoach, 131; operating table, 450
foot control, dental unit, 454
foothills, 7
footing: elevator shaft, 78; house, 60
foot joint, flute, 356
footline, book page, iv
footnote, magazine, 171
foot pad, kiln, 373
footpath, bridge, 97
foot peg: football field, 293; motorcycle, 129
footpiece, crutch, 452
footplate, wheelchair, 452
foot pocket, skin diving fin, 331
foot pump, paramedic equipment, 123
footrace, 300
footrest: baby's high chair, 286; car, 110; glider, 287; lounger, 235; medical examination table, 450; stroller, 286
foot spot, pool table, 320
footstool, 235
foot-switch input, guitar amplifier, 363
footstraps, windsurfer, 330
foot zipper, mainsail, 136
force cup, plumber's plunger, 422
fore and aft gangway, tanker, 140
forearm: dog, 36; frog, 44; horse, 38; human, 24; machine gun, 471; shotgun, 468
forearm pad, football uniform, 292
forebay, canal lock, 99
fore beam, hand loom, 387
forecast, weather, 18

forecastle, destroyer, 477
forecomb, shotgun, 468
forecourt: basketball, 296; handball, 313; squash, 313; tennis, 312
foredeck: powerboat, 138; sailboat, 134
fore-edge, book, 167
forefinger, hand, 31
forefoot: cat, 37; pig, 34; sailboat, 134
foregrip, fishing rod, 340
forehead: bird, 39; cat, 37; cow, 32; dog, 36; horse, 38; human, 24; sheep, 33
foreign price, magazine, 169
forel, book, 167
foreleg: bee, 41; cat, 37; sheep, 33
foreleg bandage, polo, 299
forelock, horse, 38
foremast, tanker, 140
forepart, shoe tree, 207
forepaw, pelt, 201
forepeak, sailboat, 135
foreshank: beef, 32; lamb, 33
foreslope, shoreline, 14
forestage, theatre, 351
forestay, sailboat, 134
forestaysail, sailboat, 134
forewing, grasshopper, 41
for good luck, gesture, 507
fork: bicycle, 128; branding iron, 432; fireplace logs, 232; kitchen utensil, 259; motorcycle, 129; river, 13; saddle, 335; spading, 427; stroller, 286; table setting, 244, 245; tuning, 367
form, etching press, 377
formal Mandarin attire, 491
formal shirt, man's, 488
formation light, jet fighter, 480
form tractor, high-speed printer, 439
Formula One racing car, 338
for shooter, craps table, 347
fort, frontier, 82
forte: fencing foil, 315; music notation, 352
fortification, 82, 83
fortress, castle, 80
45°-angle gauge, combination square, 424
45° vial, carpenter's level, 424
forward: basketball, 296; boat, 132; destroyer, 477; fireboat, 144; hovercraft, 145; lunar lander, 154; polo, 299; sailboat, 135; slide projector, 175; space shuttle, 152
forward-reverse button, potter's wheel, 373
foul light, drag racing, 339
foul line: baseball field, 291; basketball court, 296; bowling lane, 317; javelin throw, 301
foundation: beauty product, 216, 217; house, 60; skyscraper, 77; undergarment, 195
foundation lines, spider web, 40
foundation plan, house, 62
fount, lantern, 342
fountain, fireworks, 383
fountain pen, 158
4x4, passenger vehicle, 109
fourchette, glove, 200
four-cycle internal combustion engine, 406
four-cylinder automobile engine, 111
4-door sedan, 108
four-face traffic signals, 113
four-in-hand tie, 192-193
four-poster bed, 270

four pin, bowling, 317
fourragère, enlisted man's uniform, 496
four suit, domino, 345
14-stop, darts, 322
fourth toe, human foot, 31
fourth tooth, crocodile, 42
four-wheel drive jeep, 130
fovea centralis, eye, 30
fowl, 35
foxing: boot, 206; running shoe, 302
foyer, skyscraper, 77
fraction, political map, 21
fracture, volcano, 10
fragmentation grenade, 473
frame: 379; abacus, 441; attaché case, 285; automobile, 106, 109; automatic pistol, 470; backpack, 343; basket, 266; bed, 270, 271; bicycle, 128; binoculars, 443; brassiere, 195; card table, 347; carpenter's level, 424; C-clamp, 409; chaise longue, 288; circus, 90; coffee maker, 252; comic strip, 380; drill, 418; dressing table mirror, 272; eyeglasses, 221; film, 174; gallows, 462; garbage truck, 127; hammock, 288; hand loom, 387; hourglass, 233; house, 61; ironing board, 279; jai alai cesta, 314; jet fighter canopy, 480; Jew's harp, 366; lawn sprinkler, 428; man's belt buckle, 190; medical examination table, 450; paint roller, 425; piano, 361; pilot's instrument panel, 481; plane, 420; pocket watch, 220; revolver, 470; sailboat, 134; saw, 416; seeder, 430; sextant, 137; shutters, 241; silk screen, 375; skin diving tank, 331; skyscraper, 77; slot machine, 346; snowshoe, 327; solar collector panel, 391; stationary rings, 307; steam engine, 405; stroller, 286; swagger bag, 222; telegraph key, 157; tent, 342; tepee, 84; tractor, 434; trampoline, 308; umbrella, 230; wheelbarrow, 430; window, 65
frame cover, motorcycle, 129
frame leaf, hinge, 460
frame plate, mortise lock, 458
frame rail, truck tractor, 120
framework: denture, 453; yurt, 70; Zeppelin, 156
framing string, kite, 323
framing knob, movie projector, 175
franc, symbol, 511
frankfurter, 265
Franklin glasses, miser, 492
Franklin stove, 404
free arm, sewing machine, 278
freeboard, boat, 132
free-fall, parachuting, 333
free-reed instrument, 366
free-rotating mast, windsurfer, 330
free-sail system, windsurfer, 330
free-standing easel-back frame, 379
freestyle swimming race, 316
free-throw circle, basketball court, 296
freeway, 114
freewheel, bicycle, 128

freeze frame, picture-in-picture viewing, 185
freeze frame button, remote control unit, 184
freezer: powerboat, 139; refrigerator, 249; thermometer, 258
freezing rain, weather map, 19
freight, merchant ship, 140
freight car: railroad yard, 96; train, 116-117
French cuff, shirt, 189, 488
French door, 62, 64
French horn, 354, 358
French seam, tent, 342
frequency selector, police car, 122
frequently-used number listing, fax machine, 164
fresh air plate, standpipe, 59
fresh-air supply duct, tunnel, 98
fret: guitar, 362, 363; sitar, 362
friction post, jewelry findings, 218
frieze: column entablature, 73; drop-leaf table, 242; house, 62; White House, 75
frigate, 477
frill, bonnet, 203
fringe: cowboy, 490; dress, 198; golf course, 311; Indian, 490; Jewish prayer shawl, 486
frock coat, Revolutionary War general, 492
frog, 44; fastener, 208; horse's foot, 38; shovel, 427; violin bow, 355
from the sign, music notation, 353
frond: fern, 57; palm, 52; seaweed, 57
front: church, 87; desk, 276; eyeglasses, 221; glacier, 12; queen's regalia, 484; sailor's uniform, 497; steam locomotive boiler, 116; type, 166; weather map, 19; woman's pants, 196
frontal, church high altar, 87
frontal bone, human, 26
frontal lobe, brain, 29
front apron, 193
front-axle rod, child's wagon, 287
front bead, shotgun, 469
front beam, laboratory scale, 447
front boot, stagecoach, 131
front brace, wheelbarrow, 430
front brake, bicycle, 128
front bumper: automobile, 106; bus, 118
front cover: book, 167; dot matrix printer, 163
front crotch seam, trousers, 191
front derailleur, bicycle, 128
front disc brake, motorcycle, 129
front door: automobile, 106; bus, 118; sealed voting booth, 437; woodburning stove, 404
front end: diving board, 316; supermarket, 103
front end weight, tractor, 434
front face, book, 167
front fender, motorcycle, 129
front flap: book jacket, 167; matchbook, 228
front foot, stapler, 277
front gate, prison, 76
front grille, air conditioner, 402
front gunner's periscope, tank, 475

front half, grand piano, 361
front handle, sander, 421
front handlebar, chain saw, 431
front housing: can opener, 251; electric razor, 210
front hub: automobile, 108; bicycle, 128
front hydraulic fork, motorcycle, 129
frontier fort, 82
frontis, jai alai cancha, 314
frontispiece, magazine, 170
front jaw, vise, 409
front jockey, saddle, 335
front leg, bee, 41
front lid, grand piano, 361
front line: craps table, 347; handball, 313; squash, 313
front-loading washing machine, 280
front matter, book, 167
fronton, jai alai, 314
frontpiece: compact disc player, 178; jacket, 188; tape recorder, 177; toaster, 253
frontpiece, fireman's helmet, 500
front pilaster, cupboard, 243
front placket: blouse, 197; shirt, 189
front point, ice climbing boot, 334
front post: bureau, 272; hand loom, 387
front pulley, belt sander, 421
front-push plate, tow truck, 126
front quarter: automobile, 106; boot, 206 •
front rail: piano, 361; sled, 328
front rocker, slalom water ski, 329
front service door, gas pump, 112
front sight, weapon, 469, 470, 471
front sizer, football helmet, 292
front slit, man's underpants, 194
front spray nozzle, iron, 279
front stretcher, rocking chair, 234
front strut, hydrofoil, 145
front tab, razor blade injector, 210
front thread guide, sewing machine, 278
front tire, bus, 118
front tuck, blouse, 197
front walk, house, 62
front wall: jai alai cancha, 314; squash, 313; truck van, 121
front wheel: bicycle, 128; drag racing dragster, 339
front window: automobile, 106; camper, 130; tractor, 434
front wing: grasshopper, 41; racing car, 338
front yard, house, 62
frosting, cake, 264
frostfree refrigerator, 249
frozen food department, supermarket, 102
fruit, 55; grass, 58; palm, 52; slot machine, 346; woman's hat, 203
fruit & vegetable department, supermarket, 103
fruit bowl, 245
fruit compartment, refrigerator, 249
fruit juice extractor, 255
fruitlet, pineapple, 55
fruit wall, pea, 54
fry, fish, 45

frying basket, 260
frying pan, 257
F sharp, piano keyboard octave, 361
f-stop, zoom lens, 172
f-stop scale, light meter, 176
fuel, rocket, 407
fuel alarm, powerboat, 138
fuel assembly, nuclear reactor, 392
fuel cap, lantern, 342
fuel cell monitor, space shuttle, 153
fuel chamber: cruise missile, 482; torpedo, 479
fuel cock, internal combustion engine, 312
fuel filler, locomotive, 117
fuel gauge: barbecue grill, 288; powerboat, 138
fuel indicator, car, 110
fuel-line hose, automobile engine, 111
fuel management panel, pilot's instrument panel, 481
fuel nozzle, combustion jet engine, 407
fuel tank: camper, 130; camp stove, 342; drag racing dragster, 339; garbage truck, 127; motorcycle, 129; mower, 429; outboard engine, 137; space shuttle, 152; tank, 474; truck tractor, 120
fuel truck, airport, 95
fuel valve, lantern, 342
fulcrum, diving board, 316
full denture, 453
full-dress ship guideline, destroyer, 476, 477
fuller: horseshoe, 38; knife, 463; sword, 463
full face, elliptical galaxy, 2
full moon, 4
full nut, 411
full-organ button, organ, 360
full point, grammatical symbol, 513
full sail position, windmill, 390
full-service island, service station, 112
full-surface hinge, 460
fumarole, volcano, 10
fume extractor, tank gun, 475
function board, 439
function control, synthesizer, 363
function indicator: phonograph receiver, 179
function key: cash register, 440; computer workstation, 438; laser printer, 163; portable word processor, 162; synthesizer, 363
function selector: air conditioner, 402; phonograph receiver, 179
funerary structure, pyramid, 70
fungi, 57
funnel: citrus juicer, 255; kitchen, 258; lobster pot, 433; passenger ship, 142; tornado, 17
funny bone, 25
funny car, drag racing, 339
furbelow, queen's regalia, 484
furnace, 400
furniture guard, vacuum cleaner, 283
furniture nozzle, vacuum cleaner, 283
furrier, 201
furrow, horse's foot, 38
fuse: aerial shell, 383; cartridge, 399; hand

grenade, 473; land mine, 473; plug, 399; radar, 444
fuselage: cruise missile, 482; helicopter, 146; single engine airplane, 147
fusible element, plug fuse, 399
fuzz pedal, electric guitar, 363

G

G: braille, 512; music notation, 353; piano keyboard octave, 361; sign language, 512
gable: barn, 104; church, 86; house, 63
gadget bag, photographic, 176
gaff, fishing, 341
gage, drill, 418
gain: mortise lock, 458; sonar, 444
Gainsborough, bride's hat, 488
gaited horse, 337
gaiter: drum major, 495; ski clothes, 327
gakuzuka, torii, 70, 71
galaxy, Milky Way, 2, 3
Galilean telescopes, opera glasses, 443
gall bladder, human, 27
gallery: cave, 11; church, 86; Congress, 74; house, 63; monocle, 221; stage, 350
galley, sailboat, 135
galley module, jumbo jet, 148, 149
gallon totalizer, gas pump, 112
galloper, merry-go-round, 93
gallows, 464; sailboat, 134
galluses, man's, 190
galoshes, 207
gam, human, 25
gambling equipment, 346, 347
gammadion, symbol, 508
gangplank: passenger ship, 142; tanker, 140
gantry, launch pad, 152
gap, fishhook, 341
garage: house, 63; passenger ship, 142; prison, 76
garbage disposal, 247
garbage truck, 127
gardening implement, 427
garland, royal regalia, 485
garlic press, 261
garment bag, 285
garnish, poultry, 263
garret, house, 62
garrison belt, 496
garrison cap, 496
garter belt, ice hockey player, 294
garter trolley, girdle, 195
gas, volcano, 10
gas bag, blimp, 156
gas barbecue, 288
gas cap, internal combustion engine, 406
gas cigarette lighter, 228
gas cloud, 3
gas cock, water heater, 401
gas control, laser, 395
gas cylinder, plumber's torch, 422
gas-fired water heater, 401
gas-fueled internal combustion engine, 406
gas gauge, car, 110
gas inlet, laboratory burner, 447
gash, razor blade injector, 210
gasket: dishwasher, 250; refrigerator, 249
gaskin, horse, 38
gas laser, holography, 395
gasoline pump, 112
gas regulator, laboratory burner, 447
gas shutoff valve, standpipe, 59

gas station, public sign, 506
gas sterilizing flame, dental, 455
gas supply line, water heater, 401
gas tank: automobile, 107, 109; barbecue grill, 288; chain saw, 431; internal combustion engine, 406; mower, 429
gaster, ant, 41
gastight envelope, vacuum tube, 396
gastrocnemius, human, 26
gas-vent line, tanker, 141
gate: airport, 94; canal lock, 99; dam, 100; dropleaf table, 242; flat racing, 336; frontier fort, 82; hurdle, 304; mountain climbing carabiner, 334; powerboat, 139; prison, 76; railroad crossing signal, 115; sailboat, 134; shotgun, 468; subway motorman's cab, 119; toll booth, 114; vault, 457
gatebar, hurdle, 304
gated spillway, dam, 100
gatefold, magazine, 171
gatehouse: castle, 80, 81; lift bridge, 97
gate index, slide projector, 175
gateleg table, 242
gate pier, fence, 67
gatepost, steel chain fence, 67
gateway: castle, 81; Shinto temple, 70, 71
gather, bonnet, 203
gathering: blouse, 197; hardback book, 167; woman's pants, 196
gauge: barbecue grill, 288; blood pressure, 449; car, 110; carpenter's level, 424; combination square, 424; drill, 419; etching press, 377; fire extinguisher, 284; furnace, 388; powerboat, 138; pumper, 125; railroad, 115; 747 cockpit, 150; skin diving, 331; steam engine, 405; subway motorman's cab, 119; table saw, 417; weather station, 18
gauge needle, paramedic equipment, 123
gauntlet: armor, 465; drum major, 495
gauze, 123, 451, 455
gavel, 89, 412
G clef, music, 352, 353
gear: can opener, 251; fishing, 341; hand drill, 418; mortar, 472; seeder, 430; single engine airplane, 147; vault, 457; venetian blinds, 241
gearbox, automobile, 108; etching press, 377; hovercraft propeller, 145; lithographic press, 376; radar antenna, 444; seeder, 430
gear bracket, citrus juicer, 255
gear cluster, bicycle, 128
gear drive, chain saw, 431
geared key chuck, power drill, 419
gear housing, fishing reel, 340
gear oil-pressure gauge, powerboat, 138
gear ring, vault, 457
gearshift: car, 110; motorcycle, 129
Geiger counter, 445
gelatin casing, pill, 451
gelatin shell, caplet, 451
gelding, horse, 38

gem clip, 277
Gemini, zodiac, 509
gemstone, 218
gendarme, mountain, 9
general, Revolutionary War, 492
general merchandise, supermarket, 102
general product category, Universal Product Code, 440
generating plant, power network, 396
generation, pacemaker, 452
generator: nuclear reactor, 392; steam engine, 405
generator control, pilot's instrument panel, 481
generic name, label, 268
genitalia, human, 24
geodesic dome, 85
geographical boundaries, world, 5
geologist, 4
geometric stairs, staircase, 66
gesso, 370
gesture, 507
gestures, sign language, 512
getter, vacuum tube, 396
geyser, volcano, 10
G flat, piano keyboard octave, 361
ghutrah, Arab dress, 491
giant, circus, 90
gibbet, 462
gibbous moon, 4
giblets, fowl, 35
gig, horse-drawn carriage, 131
gill: fish, 45; mushroom, 57; pelt, 201
gimbal suspension, phonograph turntable, 178
gimlet, 418
gin pole, powerboat, 139
giraffe, ultimate beast, 48
girder: house, 60; skyscraper, 77; suspension bridge, 97
girdle, 195; cut gemstone, 218; hot air balloon, 332
girdle pad, football uniform, 292
girth, racing, 336, 337
girth & surcingle, polo, 299
gizzard, fowl, 35
glacial plain, mountain, 8
glacier, 8, 9, 12
glacis, permanent fort, 83
glacis plate, tank, 475
gladhand, truck van, 121
gland, octopus, 46
glass: basketball backboard, 296; cupboard door, 243; dressing table, 272; eye dropper, 451; electric meter casing, 399; fluorescent bulb tube, 238; frame, 379; light bulb, 238; sextant, 137; solar panel cover plate, 391; stained, 378; table setting, 244, 245
glass cutter, 378
glasses: field, 443; miser, 492; ski touring, 327
glass support, vacuum tube, 396
glaze, pot, 373
glazing, window, 67
glide: desk, 276; slalom water ski, 329; surgical table, 450
glider, 147; backyard, 287; hang, 333
glide slope antenna, helicopter, 146
glide slope indicator, airport runway, 94
globe, 1, 5; lantern, 342; royal regalia, 485
glochidia, cactus, 56
gloss, makeup, 216

glove, 200; baseball, 290, 291; boxing, 309; bridal costume, 488; drag racing driver's, 339; drum major, 495; fencing, 315; fireman, 500; hammer thrower, 303; handball, 313; ice hockey player, 294, 295; jai alai cesta, 314; jet fighter, 480; lacrosse, 298; miser, 492; Revolutionary War general, 492; skiing, 326; skin diving, 331
glove compartment, car, 110
glume, grass, 58
gluon, 394
gluteus medius, human, 26
gnomon, sundial, 389
gnu beard, ultimate beast, 49
goal: basketball, 296; football, 293; ice hockey, 294, 295; lacrosse, 298; soccer, 297
goalie, lacrosse position, 298
goal line, polo grounds, 299; soccer, 297
goal mouth, polo grounds, 299
goal post, polo grounds, 299
goaltender, lacrosse position, 298
go around switch, 747 cockpit, 151
goat, zodiac, 509
goat beard, ultimate beast, 49
goatee, men's beard, 211
goggles: flat racing, 336; ski helmet, 326
gold: dental, 455; ring, 219
gold ball of rank, royal crown, 485
golf ball, 310
golf club, 310, 311
golf course, 310, 311; passenger ship, 142
Golgi apparatus, animal cell, 23
GO light, drag racing, 339
gondola: blimp, 156; Ferris wheel, 93; merry-go-round, 93
gonfalon, 502
gonfanon, 502
gong, drums, 364
good luck, gesture, 507
good luck symbol, 508
goose, 35
gooseneck: football goalpost, 293; lamp, 239
gore: hot air balloon, 332; man's cap, 202; sock, 207; umbrella, 230
gore area, highway cloverleaf, 114
gorge: human, 25; jacket, 188; permanent fort, 83; river, 13
gorget, armor, 465
gouge, 374, 420; woodcarving, 372
gouged sections, wood block, 374
gourd, sitar, 362
gour dam, cave, 11
governor: internal combustion engine, 406; power mower, 429
governor-rope tension sheave, elevator shaft, 78
gown, 198; queen's regalia, 484
grab iron, locomotive, 117
grab rail, bathtub, 274
grab strap, motorcycle, 129
gracilis, human, 26
grade: enlisted man's uniform, 496; gasoline, 112; pencil, 158; railroad crossing, 115
graduated guide, fishing rod, 341

graduated scale, metronome, 367
graduation: beaker, 447; thermometer, 18, 449
grain: fabric, 388; lumber, 68; sandpaper, 421
grain pit, barnyard, 104
grammar, proofreader's mark, 514
grammatical symbol, 513
grand curtain, theater, 351
grand drape, stage, 350, 351
grand finale, fireworks, 382
grand valance, theater, 351
grandfather clock, 233
grandmother clock, 233
grand piano, 361
Grand Prix racing, 338
grandstand, harness racetrack, 337
granule, roofing shingle, 68
graphic, hot air balloon, 332
graphic device, label, 268
graphic scale, house blueprint, 62
graphics function selector, computer workstation, 438
graphics program, personal computer, 162
grasper, desk phone, 180
grasping foot, bird, 39
grass, 58; baseball field, 291
grass-catcher, lawn mower, 429
grasshopper, 41
grate: fireplace, 232; stove, 342
grater, kitchen tool, 261
graticule, political map, 21
grating, castle portcullis, 81
grave, 516
grave accent, grammatical symbol, 513
gravure, printing, 166, 374
grawlix, cartoon, 381
grease skimming brush, 259
great choir, church, 87
great circle, geodesic dome, 85
greatcoat, Revolutionary officer, 492
great door, barn, 104
greater than, symbol, 511
great keyboard, organ, 360
great saphenous vein, human, 28
greave, armor, 465
Greek cross, symbol, 508
Greek Revival, house style, 63
green, golf course, 311
greenback, paper money, 224
green light: drag racing, 339; traffic, 113
Green Room, White House, 75
Greenwich Mean Time, 5
Greenwich prime meridian, 5
green wire, electrical receptacle, 398
grenade, 473
grid: barbecue grill, 288; earth, 5; geodesic dome, 85; paint tray, 425; political map, 21; stage, 350; vacuum tube, 396
griddle, stove, 248, 404
gridiron, 293; stage, 350
grid marking, topographic map, 22
grid table extension, saw, 417
grill, barbecue, 288
grille: accordion, 366; air conditioner, 402; automobile, 106; CB radio antenna, 183; guitar amplifier, 363; hair dryer, 212; humidifier, 402; phonograph, 179; refrigerator, 249; tractor, 434; truck, 120
grind, knife, 256
grinder, kitchen tool, 261

grip: automatic weapon, 471; bobby pin, 214; bow, 466; carpenter's level, 424; chain saw, 431; chest pull, 344; field events hammer, 303; fishing rod, 340; foil mounting, 315; gardening shears, 427; golf club, 311; hair clip, 214; hammer, 412; javelin, 303; jump rope, 344; knife, 463; movie camera, 174; Ping-Pong racket, 321; revolver, 470; rowboat car, 133; seeder, 430; shoe horn, 207; shotgun, 468; ski pole, 326; squash racket, 313; stroller, 286; sword hilt, 463; tennis racket, 312; wheelbarrow, 430; wire stripper, 423
grip cap, shotgun, 468
gripper mark, nail, 410
gripping hole, clothespin, 280
grip safety, pistol, 470 grip tape, skateboard, 324
gristle, human, 26
grit, sandpaper, 421
groceries, supermarket, 103
groin, human, 25
grommet, tent, 342
groove: combination square, 424; corrugated fastener, 410; crossbow, 466; escalator, 79; guillotine, 462; horse, 38; phonograph record, 178; roulette wheel, 346; salamander, 44; ski, 326; sword, 463; type, 166
grospoint, stitchery, 385
grotto, 11
grotzen, pelt, 201
ground: flag, 502; symbol, 510
ground beam, guillotine, 462
ground coffee, 252
ground control, metal detector, 445
ground-effect machine, amphibious, 145
ground floor, White House, 75
grounding prong, electric plug, 344
grounding terminal, electrical receptacle, 398
ground steering tiller, 747 cockpit, 150
ground wire: circuit breaker box, 399; electrician's, 423; electrical receptacle junction box, 398
grout, tunnel, 98
growler, glacier, 12
growthline, clam shell, 47
growth ring, lumber, 68
grozing pliers, for stained glass, 378
grunting, 34
G sharp, piano keyboard octave, 361
G string, double bass, 355
guante, jai alai cesta, 314
guard: armor, 465; basketball, 296; crossbow, 466; dishwasher, 250; drill press, 419; elevator shaft, 78; foil mounting, 315; gas pump automatic nozzle, 112; guitar, 362, 363; ice hockey player, 295; knife, 256, 463; lacrosse stick, 298; lithographic press, 376; movie camera eyepiece, 174; mower, 429; prison, 76; revolver, 470; rifle, 471; safety pin, 208; saw, 417; sharpening steel, 256; shotgun trigger, 468; stagecoach, 131; sword hilt, 463; theodolite, 436; tow

truck, 126; washing machine, 280; wheelchair, 452
guard bars, Universal Product Code, 440
guard cone, potting, 373
guard house, frontier fort, 82
guardrail, highway, 114; slide, 287; tow truck, 126
guard socket, fencing foil, 315
guard tower, frontier fort, 82; prison, 76
gudgeon, window shade roller, 241
guest head, sailboat, 135
guidance chamber, torpedo, 479
guidance system: cruise missile, 482; submarine, 479
guide: fishing reel, 340; fishing rod, 340, 341; Hansom cab rein, 131; incline track, 92; jackhammer, 436; pencil sharpener, 277; power saw, 417; silk screen, 375; speculum, 448; toaster, 253
guide arm, toilet, 275
guide bar, saw, 417, 431
guide cone, potting, 373
guided missile cruiser, 477
guided missile destroyer, 477
guided weapons, defensive, 476
guideline, destroyer, 476, 477
guide lugs, nuclear reactor, 392
guide post, typewriter, 161
guide rail, elevator shaft, 78
guide ring, vault, 457
guide rod, workbench, 408
guide roller, cassette tape, 177
guide scope, telescope, 443
guide shoe, elevator shaft, 78
guide sign, road, 505
guide spring, pencil sharpener, 277
guide wall, dam, 100
guide wheel, roller coaster, 92
guillotine, 462
guimpe, nun, 487
guitar, 362, 363
gular region, salamander, 44
gulf, 7
Gulf Stream, ocean, 6
gullet, 25, 30; saddle, 335; saw teeth, 416
gull-wing hull, powerboat, 138
gully, mountain, 8
gum, and denture, 453
gum line, tooth, 456
gun, 470; cowboy, 490; jet fighter, 480; machine, 471; police, 499; police car, 122; pumper, 125; tank, 474, 475
gun barrel, destroyer, 477
gun belt: cowboy, 490; police, 498-499
gun director, destroyer, 477
gunlock, cannon barrel, 467
gunmount, destroyer, 477
gunner's periscope, tank, 475
gunship, helicopter, 146
gunwale: powerboat, 139; rowboat, 133
gusset: armor, 465; handbag, 222; house, 61
gut, human, 25
gutter: barn, 104; book, 167; bowling lane, 317; house, 63; magazine, 171; swimming pool, 316; gutter broom, mechanical sweeper, 127
gutter margin, book page, 167
guy brace, uneven parallel bars, 306
guy rope, circus tent, 91

guy wire: horizontal bar, 306; stationary rings, 307
gym, universal, 344
gymnasium, passenger ship, 143
gymnastics, 306-307
gynecologist, examination equipment, 448
gyro compass, 136

H

H: braille, 512; sign language, 512
habit, nun, 487
hackle, chicken, 35
hackney carriage, 131
hacksaw, 416, 422
haft, ax, 464
hailstone, 17
hair: human, 24, 211, 213; painting brush, 370; violin bow, 355
hair band, 214
hairbrush, electric, 212
hair clip, 214
hairdo, 214
hair dryer, 212
hairline: linear slide rule, 441; man's, 211; newspaper, 168
hairpiece, man's, 211
hairpin, 214
halberd: Beefeater, 483; medieval, 464
half, soccer, 297
half-court line, handball, 313
half-door, Hansom cab, 131
half-inch mark, tape measure, 424
half-jacket, fencing, 315
half-mile pole, harness racetrack, 337
half-moon, 4
half note, music, 352
half note rest, music, 352
half-surface hinge, 460
half-title logo, magazine, 170
halftone indicator, fax machine, 164
halfway line, soccer field, 297
haligan tool, police car, 122
hall: church, 87; mosque, 70-71; theatre, 351; White House, 75
hallmark, ring, 219
Hall of Columns, Capitol, 74
hallux, human foot, 20
halyard: destroyer, 477; flag, 502; sailboat, 134
ham, 34; human, 24; radio operator, 183
hammer: ball-peen, 412; carillon, iv; field events, 303; ice climbing, 334; jackhammer, 436; piano, 361; revolver, 470; stonecutting, 372; for testing reflexes, 449; telegraph key, 157
hammerhead crane, launch pad, 152
hammer throw, track and field, 301
hammock, 288
hance, arch, 72
hand: blackjack, 347; cattle ranch, 432; frog, 44; grandfather clock, 233; human, 24, 31; pocket watch, 220; stopwatch, 304; wristwatch, 220
handbag, 222
handball court, 313
hand brace, 418
hand controller, space shuttle, 153
hand crank, easel, 370
handcuff, police gun belt, 498
hand cup, sword hilt, 463

hand drill, 418, 419
hand excavator, dental, 455
hand flexor, body building, 344
hand grenade, 473
handgrip: bazooka, 472; body building, 344; carpenter's level, 424; crutch, 452; Jacuzzi, 274; motorcycle, 129; movie camera, 174; pole vault pole, 305; rocking chair, 234; swimming pool, 316; video camera, 184; wheelbarrow, 430; wheelchair, 452
handguard, automatic rifle, 471; chain saw, 431
handgun, 470
handhold: harness racing driver, 337; lunar rover, 155
handicap: drag racing, 339; flat racing entry, 336
handicapped, public sign, 506
handkerchief, queen's regalia, 484
handkerchief pocket, jacket, 188
hand knitting, 386
handle: attaché case, 285; automobile door, 107; ax, 464; barbecue grill, 288; baren, 374; baseball bat, 291; basket, 266; blender, 254; bow, 466; brace, 418; branding iron, 432; brayer, 374; broom, 282; burnisher, 377; candle snuffer, 237; can opener, 251; C-clamp, 409; cellular telephone, 181; chafing dish, 245; cheese plane, 256; chest pull, 344; child's wagon, 287; chisel, 420; citrus juicer, 255; clay modeling tool, 372; clothespin, 280; coffee maker, 252; coffin, 516; croquet mallet, 318; dabber, 377; drain cleaner, 422; drill, 418, 419; ear scope, 448; etching press, 377; faucet, 273; field events hammer, 303; finishing sander, 421; fire engine, 125; fire extinguisher, 284; fishing reel, 340; fishing rod, 340; foil mounting, 315; food mill, 260; food processor, 254; garbage disposal, 247; garbage truck, 127; gimlet, 418; glass cutter, 378; gouge, 374; hair dryer, 212; hammer, 412; handbag, 222; hand loom, 387; hand shower, 274; hoe, 427, hot air balloon, 332; ice hammer, 334; internal combustion engine, 406; iron, 279; jackhammer, 436; jet fighter, 480; jump rope, 344; knife, 244, 256, 463; lacrosse stick, 298; land mine, 473; lithographic press, 376; lorgnette, 221; mace, 464; mailbox, 231; metal detector, 445; microwave oven, 248; mower, 429; outboard engine, 137; pail, 284; painting brush, 370; paint roller, 425; paint spray gun, 425; paper bag, 266; parking meter, 113; peeler, 256; pencil sharpener, 277; pilot's instrument panel, 481; Ping-Pong racket, 321; plane, 420; playpen, 286; pliers, 414; plumber's plunger, 422; pocket knife,

426; pommel horse, 307; portable radio/cassette player, 182; pots and pans, 257; projector, 175; radiator, 400; rake, 427; razor, 210; refrigerator door, 249; revolver, 470; rifle, 471; safe, 457; scissors, 384; saw, 416, 417, 431; screen, 175; screwdriver, 413; scriber, 375; seeder, 430; 747 cockpit, 150, 151; sewing machine, 278; sextant, 137; sharpening steel, 256; shaver, 210; shotgun, 468; shovel, 427; silk screen squeegee, 375; single engine airplane, 147; sink, 247, 273; soldering iron, 378; sponge mop, 282; squash racket, 313; stove, 342, 248, 404; stroller, 286; tea kettle, 245; tennis racket, 312; thrown pot, 373; toilet, 275; toothbrush, 215; tuning fork, 367; umbrella, 230; vacuum cleaner, 283; vault, 457; video camera, 184; vise, 408, 409; voting booth, 437; waterskiing towline, 329; wheelbarrow, 430; woodcarving tool, 372; wrench, 415
handlebar: bicycle, 128; chain saw, 431; snowmobile, 130
handlebar mustache, 211
handle grip: chain saw, 431; seeder, 430; stroller, 286; vacuum cleaner, 283
handler, boxing, 309
handle release pedal, vacuum cleaner, 283
handle screw, plane, 420
hand lever: potter's wheel, 373; spreader, 430
hand loom, 387
hand pad, football uniform, 292
handpiece: crutch, 452; dental, 454, 455
hand protector, waterskiing towline, 329
hand pump: blood pressure gauge, 449; pilot's instrument panel, 481
handrail: bus, 118; elevator car, 78; escalator, 79; locomotive, 116, 117; lunar lander, 154; powerboat, 139; roller coaster, 92; sled, 328; staircase, 66; subway car, 119
hand rope, racing sled, 328
handruff, queen's regalia, 484
handsaw, 416
hand screw, 409
handset, desk phone, 180; cellular telephone, 181
hand shower, 274
hand slide, trombone, 359
handstrap: bus, 118; subway car, 119; video-still camera, 173
hand throttle, car, 110
hand valve, solar heating system, 391
hand warming slot, parka, 201
handwheel: sewing machine, 278; table saw, 417
hangar, airport, 95
hangar bay, aircraft carrier, 478
hanger: dress, 198; fishing plug, 341; frame, 379; harness racing, 337; laboratory scale weight, 447; lamp, 239; screen, 175; swing, 287

hanger bracket, wheelchair, 452
hang glider, 333
hang hole: blister card, 268; dustpan, 282
hanging glacier, mountain, 8
hanging locker, sailboat, 135
hanging ring: can opener, 251; skillet, 359
hanging strip, window shutters, 241
hanging weight, laboratory scale, 446
hang ring, hair dryer, 212
hang-up hole, toothbrush, 215
hank, knitting yarn, 386
Hansom cab, 131
hardback book, 167
hard copy, computer printer, 163
hardcover book, 167
hard disk, computer, 438
hard-hat diving, 331
hardness, pencil lead, 158
hard suction connection hose, pumper, 125
hardware: bureau, 272; computer workstation, 438; cowboy, 490; shoulder bag, 222; sideboard, 243
hardware sling, mountain climbing, 334
hard-way bets, craps table, 347
hare traction splint, paramedic equipment, 123
harmonica, 366
harness: drag racing driver, 339; electrical wall switch, 398; hang glider, 333; harness racing, 337; mountain climbing, 334; parachute, 333; skin diving tank, 331
harness frame, hand loom, 387
harness racing, 336, 337
harp: orchestra, 354; table lamp, 238
harrow, tractor, 434
hash mark: enlisted man's uniform, 496; football field, 293
hassock, lounger, 235
hasp, 460
hat: automobile engine, 111; Beefeater, 483; circus ringmaster, 90; clown, 493; cowboy, 490; miser, 492; pirate, 492; police, 498, 499; Revolutionary War general, 492; sailor, 497; skiing, 327; wizard, 492; woman's, 203
hatband, 202, 203
hat bow, beret, 202
hatch: bus, 118; fireboat, 144; lunar lander, 154; sailboat, 134; tank, 474, 475; tanker, 141; tugboat, 144
hatchback, passenger car, 109
hatch cover, ballistic missile launch deck, 479
hatchet, 412
hatmaker, 202
hat pin, woman's hat, 203
hatter, men's hats, 202
haunch: arch, 72; human, 25
hawg leg, cowboy, 490
hawsehole: fireboat, 144; passenger ship, 142, 143
hawser: and canal lock, 99; passenger ship, 142; tugboat, 144
hay door, barn, 104
hay scale, frontier fort, 82
hay yard, frontier fort, 82
hazard, golf course, 310-311
head: Allen wrench, 415; anchor, 132; arrow, 466; automobile engine, 111; ax,

464; badminton shuttlecock, 319; barrel, 267; bell, iv; billiard bridge, 320; bolt, 411; book page, iv, 167; bowling lane, 317; brace, 418; cartridge, 470; C-clamp, 409; chain saw, 431; chisel, 420; cigar, 228; coin, 225; combination square, 424; comet, 3; croquet mallet, 318; dental x-ray tube, 454; dispenser, 267; drain cleaner, 422; drill press, 419; drum, 364; electric razor, 210; electronic flash, 176; field events hammer, 303; fish, 45; fishing jig, 341; flag, 502; golf club, 310; grasshopper, 41; guitar, 362, 363; hammer, 412; hatchet, 412; helicopter rotor, 146; hinge fixed pin, 460; human, 24; javelin, 302; knee kicker, 246; knitting needle, 386; lacrosse stick, 298; lance, 464; lettuce, 262; levigator bolt, 376; mace, 464; magazine, 170, 171; mainsail, 136; match, 228; mechanical sweeper gutter broom, 127; movie camera microphone, 174; music note, 353; nail, 410; newspaper, 168; octopus, 46; pelt, 201; pin, 208; polo mallet, 299; saddle, 335; sailboat, 135; screw, 410; screwdriver, 413; shower, 274; shuffleboard court, 318; soldering iron, 378; spring beard needle, 386; squash racket, 313; stemware, 244; tambourine, 364; table saw, 417; tack, 410; tape recorder, 177; tennis racket, 312; theodolite, 436; toothbrush, 215; venetian blinds, 241
headband: hair ornament, 214; hardback book, 167; headphone, 179, 182; physician's mirror, 448; ski hat, 327
headboard: four-poster bed, 270; mainsail, 136
head box, venetian blind, 241
head channel, venetian blind, 241
head collar, kettledrum, 364
head cover, golf club, 311
headdress, Arab dress, 491
header: brick wall, 69; drag racing dragster, 339; house, 60, 61; solar collector panel, 391
headgear: armor, 465; boxing, 309
headguard, boxing, 309
heading: book page, iv; draperies, 240; letter, 159; radar, 444
heading alignment control, radar, 444
head jamb, window, 65
head joint: brick wall, 69; flute, 357
headlight: automobile, 106; bulldozer, 435; bus, 118; locomotive, 116, 117; medical examination equipment, 448; motorcycle, 129; snowmobile, 130; tank, 475; tractor, 434; truck, 120
headlight controls, car, 110
headline: human hand, 31; magazine, 170; newspaper, 168
head lock, camera tripod, 176
head lug, bicycle, 128

head margin, book page, 167
head mold, church, 86
head piece: book, 167; rocking chair, 234
headphone, audio, 179, 182
headphone jack: CB radio, 183; compact disc player, 178; metal detector, 445; receiver, 179; tape recorder, 177; VCR, 184; Walkman, 182
headphone level control, compact disc player, 178
headphones, Walkman, 182
headpiece, Torah, 486
headpin, bowling, 317
head post, four-poster bed, 270
headquarters, frontier fort, 82
headrail, venetian blind, 241
headrest: bumper car, 92; dental unit, 454; surgical table, 450
headsail, 136
head section: flute, 357; piccolo, 356
headset, bicycle, 128
headshell, phonograph turntable, 178
head spot, pool table, 320
headstay, sailboat, 134
head step, ladder, 425
headstone, grave, 516
heads-up, drag racing, 339
head tube, bicycle, 128
headwall, mountain, 9
health & beauty aids, supermarket, 102
hearing aid, 452
heart: fowl, 35; human, 25, 27, 28; lettuce, 262; playing cards, 348
hearth, fireplace, 232
heart line, human hand, 31
heart murmur, symbol, 510
heart of came, lead came, 378
heartwood, tree, 50
heat, drag racing, 339
heat-absorber plate, solar collector panel, 391
heat control: barbecue grill, 288; electric wok, 257
heater: camper, 130; water, 401
heater filament, vacuum tube, 396
heater wire, vacuum tube, 396
heat exchanger: 403; fireplace, 232; oil drilling platform, 101
heat indicator, electric hair brush, 212
heating controls, car, 110
heating/cooling coils, heat exchanger, 403
heating element: dishwasher, 250; soldering iron, 378; stove, 248
heating system, airport, 94
heating unit: camper, 130; solar heating system, 391
heat pump, 403
heat-resistant glass, light bulb, 238
heat-riser valve, automobile engine, 111
heat seal, foil pouch, 269
heat shield, lantern, 342
heat switch, hair dryer, 212
heat-transfer fluid, solar collector panel, 391
Hector, playing card jack, 348
heddle, hand loom, 387
heel: Achilles', 25; automatic rifle, 471; baseball glove, 291; boot, 206; bread, 263; carpenter's saw, 416; cat, 37; file, 420; frog, 44; golf club, 310; grand piano, 361; guitar, 362; horse, 38;

horseshoe, 38; human foot, 24, 31; human hand, 31; ice hockey goalkeeper's stick, 294; ice skate, 325; knife, 256; L-shaped square, 424; man's shoe, 204; paint brush, 425; panty hose, 195; plane, 420; rasp, 420; roller skate, 324; shoe tree, 207; shotgun, 468; ski binding, 326; tennis racket, 312; windmill, 390; woman's shoe, 205
heel band, spur, 335
heel binding, ski, 326
heel breast, woman's shoe, 205
heel cap: hockey skate, 325; skate, 295
heel chain, spur, 335
heel counter, running shoe, 302
heel cup, ski binding, 326
heel cup pivot, ski binding, 326
heel glide, slalom water ski, 329
heel gore, sock, 207
heelknob, dog, 36
heel lacing, snowshoe, 327
heel lift: boot, 206; woman's shoe, 205
heel loop, wheelchair, 452
heel patch, running shoe, 302
heel piece, slalom water ski, 329
heelplate, ski, 327, 329
heel rest, iron, 279
heel seam, sock, 207
heel seat, woman's shoe, 205
heel strap, skin diving fin, 331
heel tip, hockey skate, 325
heifer, 32
height: and perspective, 368; wave, 14
height adjustment: machine gun, 471; ski binding, 326; vacuum cleaner, 283
helical, settee, 288; staircase, 66
helicopter, 146
helicopter flight deck, destroyer, 476
helictite, cave, 11
helipad, White House, 75
heliport, oil drilling platform, 101
helium valve, blimp, 156
helix, outer ear, 30
helm: coat of arms, 503; sailboat, 134
helmath, windmill, 390
helmet: armor, 465; baseball batter, 290; coat of arms, 503; combat soldier, 497; downhill skiing, 326; drag racing driver's fire suit, 339; fireman, 500; flat racing, 336; football uniform, 292; Grand Prix racing, 338; harness racing, 337; ice hockey, 295; jai alai, 314; lacrosse, 298; police, 498, 499; polo, 299; roller skating, 324; spacesuit, 155
helmet diving, 331
helmet skirt, drag racing driver's fire suit, 339
helmseat, powerboat, 139
helve, axe, 464
hem: bridal gown, 488; dress, 198; jacket, 188; parka, 201; skirt, 197; window shade, 240, 241
hemmer foot, sewing machine, 278
hemming, necktie, 193
hen, 35
hence, symbol, 511

herb, prepared foods, 263
hex nut, 411; juice extractor, 255; table lamp, 238
hex wrench, 415
hibachi, 288
hide, ultimate beast, 49
hide rope, tepee, 84
hieroglyph, obelisk, 71
high altar, church, 87
high bar, gymnastics, 306
high beam, automobile, 106
high chair, 286
high fidelity phonograph, 179
high-frequency antenna, helicopter, 146
high-gain antenna, lunar rover, 155
high heat switch, hair dryer, 212
high-heel woman's shoe, 205
high hurdle, 304
high intensity lamp, 239
high jump, 300, 305
highlight, magazine, 170
highlighter, makeup, 216
highline, magazine, 171
high-low combination headlamp, automobile, 106
high-low scale, light meter, 176
high pressure, weather map, 19
high-pressure pump: fireboat, 144; paint spray gun, 425
high-pressure steam, steam engine, 405
high pressure water spray, tooth cleaner, 215
high pulley, universal gym, 344
high-resolution display, computer workstation, 438
high score, darts, 322
high-speed dubbing, portable radio/cassette player, 182
high-speed handpiece, dental, 455
high-speed printer, 439
high tide, 15
high-voltage power supply, gas laser, 395
high-volume evacuation tip, dental, 454
high water mark, topographic map, 22
highway, 114; map, 20, 22
high-wire act, circus, 90
hi-hat cymbal, 364
hiking trail, public sign, 506
hill, 7; road sign, 505; roller coaster, 92
hilt: bayonet, 463; billiard cue, 320; foil mounting, 315; knife, 463; mace, 464; sword, 463
hind bow, saddle, 335
hind foot: cat, 37; pig, 34; sheep, 33
hind paw, pelt, 201
hindquarters, 37
hind scalper, harness racing pacer, 337
hind shank, beef, 32
hind toe: cat, 37; chicken, 35
hind wing, grasshopper, 41
hinge, 460; binoculars, 443; book, 167; camera tripod, 176; cupboard, 243; eyeglasses, 221; folding rule, 424; hot dog roll, 265; kiln, 373; locomotive, 116; railroad signal, 115; safe, 457; scallop shell, 47; stapler, 277; stove oven door, 248; vault, 457; window shutters, 39; woodburning stove, 404

hinge cover: playpen, 286; refrigerator, 249
hinge portion, hasp, 460
hinge rod, power mower, 429
hip: barn, 104; bell, iv; horse, 38; human, 24
hip belt, backpack, 39
hip flexor, universal gym, 344
hipline, dress, 198
hip pad: football, 292; ice hockey, 295
hippodrome track, circus, 90
historical costumes, 492
history, symbol, 510
hitch, tractor, 434
hitch-hiking, gesture, 507
hite, cartoon, 380
hobble, harness racing gear, 337
hobble strap, saddle, 335
hock: chicken, 3; cow, 32; dog, 36; horse, 38; jet fighter, 480; pork, 34
hockey, ice, 294, 295
hockey skate, 325
hod, fireplace coal, 232
hoe, 427
hog, 34
hogan, 84
hogshead, 267
hoist: dam, 100; flag, 502; helicopter, 146
hoist cable, elevator shaft, 78
hoisting equipment, oil drilling platform, 101
hold, music notation, 352
holder: blackjack, 347; cassette tape recorder, 177; dental, 455; easel, 370; elevator car, 78; etching needle, 377; jackhammer, 436; laboratory, 446; lithographic press, 376; microscope slide, 442; police uniform, 498, 499; stroller, 286; telescope, 443; tom-tom, 364; track lighting, 239; two-suiter, 285
holder attaching screw, camera, 172
holdfast, seaweed, 57
holding prong, nail clippers, 215
holding tools, 409
hole: bagpipe, 365; blister card, 268; bowling ball, 317; button, 209; cheese, 263; cigar cutter blade, 228; clothespin, 280; film, 172, 174; fireboat, 144; fountain pen, 158; golf course, 311; guitar, 362; hair roller, 214; hinge, 460; hook and eye, 208; horseshoe, 38; ice axe, 334; igloo, 85; lantern, 342; man's belt, 190; man's underwear, 194; Milky Way, 2; needle, 384; oil drilling platform, 101; phonograph record, 178; snap fastener, 208; snowshoe, 327; spool, 384; stagecoach, 131; telephone, 180; tire, 105; tow truck bed, 126; vault, 457
hole punch, pocket knife, 426
hollow body, acoustic guitar, 363
hollow grind, knife, 256
hollow lower face, zipper, 209
hollow of throat, human, 25
hollow wall fastener, 411
hologram, 395; credit card, 227
holster, 470, 490, 499
home, White House, 75
home plate: baseball field, 291; blackjack, 347
home port, passenger ship, 142

home stake, croquet, 318
homestretch, harness
  racetrack, 337
honda, lasso, 432
honing surface, sharpening
  steel, 256
honors, résumé, 160
hood: automobile, 106; barn,
  104; bassinet, 286; bus, 118;
  camera lens, 174; cobra, 42;
  compass, 136; fireplace, 232;
  fishing rod, 340; grandfather
  clock, 233; minister, 487;
  parka, 201; radar, 444;
  toboggan, 328; tractor, 434;
  truck, 120; vacuum cleaner,
  283
hood door, grandfather clock,
  233
hood release, car, 110
hoof: cow, 32; horse, 38;
  ultimate beast, 48
hook: block and tackle, 461;
  boot, 207; bulldozer, 435;
  fire engine, 124, 125;
  fireman, 500; fishing jig,
  341; fishing plug, 341;
  frame, 379; garbage
  disposal, 247; hammock,
  288; harness racing gear,
  337; hearing aid, 452; ice
  skates, 325; latch needle,
  386; parachute, 333;
  pendant, 219; pulley block,
  461; shower curtain, 274;
  suit hanger, 281; tape
  measure, 424; tatting
  shuttle, 386; tow truck bed,
  126; trumpet, 359; see also
  hook and eye
hookah, 229
hook and bar, fastener, 208
hook and bobbin case, sewing
  machine, 278
hook and eye: brassiere, 195;
  fastener, 208; pants, 191;
  skirt, 197; see also hook
hook and ring, mitten, 200
hook disgorger, pocket knife,
  426
hooked-up truck, 120
hook grip, shoe horn, 207
hook panel, pilot's instrument
  panel, 481
hook tape, Velcro, 209
hook-thrust bearing assembly,
  pulley block, 461
hoop: banjo, 362; barrel, 267;
  basketball backstop, 296;
  croquet, 318; lasso, 432;
  lobster pot, 433
hopper: garbage truck, 127;
  mechanical sweeper, 127;
  seeder, 430
hopper car, train, 116
hop, skip, and jump, track and
  field, 300
horizontal bar, gymnastics,
  306
horizontal centering, radar,
  444
horizontal circle, theodolite,
  436
horizontal direction indicator,
  747 cockpit, 150
horizontal fin, blimp,
  156
horizontal gauge, carpenter's
  level, 424
horizontally opposed
  automobile engine, 111
horizontal reduction,
  theodolite, 436
horizontal stabilizer:
  helicopter, 146; jet fighter,
  480; jumbo jet, 149; single
  engine airplane, 147
horizon glass, sextant, 137

horizon indicator, 747 cockpit,
  151
horizon line, perspective, 368
horizon mirror, sextant, 137
horizon sunshade, sextant, 137
horn: car, 110; cow, 32; fire
  engine, 124, 125; fire
  extinguisher, 284; French,
  358; glacier, 12; motorcycle,
  129; orchestra, 354; saddle,
  335; shoe, 207; subway
  motorman's cab, 119; truck
  tractor, 120; ultimate beast,
  48
horny scale: alligator, 42;
  crocodile, 42
horoscope, 509
hors d'oeuvre, 263
horse, 38; flat racing entry,
  336; merry-go-round, 93;
  pommel, 307
horse-drawn carriage, 131
horsehide, baseball, 290
horse-hoof cuff, Manchu court
  dress, 491
horse latitudes, wind, 6
horsepower, internal
  combustion engine, 406
horseracing, 336-337
horse rod, merry-go-round, 93
horse shoe, 38
horse trail, public sign, 506
hose, 207; automobile engine,
  111; baseball batter, 290;
  fireboat, 144; fire
  extinguisher, 284; gas pump,
  112; hand shower, 274;
  kitchen sink, 247; lawn
  sprinkler, 428; locomotive,
  116; panty, 195; pumper,
  125; skin diving, 331;
  vacuum cleaner, 283
hose-handling derrick, tanker,
  141
hosel, golf club, 310
hose nozzle, 428; fire hydrant,
  125
hose reel: fireboat, 144; tower
  ladder, 124
hospital: frontier fort, 82;
  passenger ship, 143; prison,
  76; road sign, 504
hot air balloon, 332
hot corner, baseball field, 291
hot dog, 265
hotdogging board, surfboard,
  330
hotel, airport, 94
hotel/motel, public sign, 506
hot foods department,
  supermarket, 103
hot gas pipe, heat exchanger,
  403
hot metal, printing, 166
hot plate, coffee maker, 252
hot shoe, camera, 172
hot slot, electrical receptacle,
  398
hot springs, volcano, 10
hot type, printing, 166
hot-water differential
  thermostat, solar heating
  system, 391
hot-water device, sink, 247
hot-water faucet: bathtub, 274;
  Jacuzzi, 274
hot water handle, sink, 247,
  273
hot-water heater, 401; camper,
  130
hot-water tank, solar heating
  system, 391
hot wire: electrical receptacle,
  398; electrician's, 423
hourglass, 233
hour hand: clock, 233; watch,
  220
hour line, sundial, 389

hour meter, powerboat engine,
  138
house, craps, 346; foundation,
  60; exterior, 62-63; frame,
  61; roof truss, 61; zodiac,
  509
house ad, magazine, 171
houseboat, 138
house car, train, 117
House corridor, Capitol, 74
housekeeper's room, White
  House, 75
House of Representatives
  chamber, Capitol, 74
house organ magazine, 169
house plan, White House, 75
house styles, 63
housing: automatic rifle, 471;
  automobile license plate,
  106; belt sander, 421; CB
  radio microphone, 183;
  compass, 136; curling iron,
  214; drill, 419; electric plug,
  398; eye scope, 448;
  finishing sander, 421; fishing
  reel, 340; hair dryer, 212;
  harmonica, 366;
  jackhammer, 436; juice
  extractor, 255; laboratory
  clamp, 446; lawn sprinkler,
  428; mechanical sweeper,
  127; outboard engine, 137;
  paint spray gun, 425;
  phonograph headphone,
  179; potter's wheel, 373;
  power mower, 429; razor,
  210; saber saw, 417; saddle,
  335; skate, 295; stationary
  rings, 424; tape measure,
  424; toaster, 253; video
  camera, 184
hovercraft, 145
howitzer, midget, 472
hub: automobile, 108; bicycle,
  128; cassette tape, 177;
  cupboard, 243; geodesic
  dome, 85; hypodermic
  syringe, 451; outboard
  engine, 137; racing car, 338;
  spider web, 40; stagecoach,
  131; tow truck, 126;
  wheelchair, 452
hubble-bubble, 229
hubcap: automobile, 107
hubcap: child's wagon, 287;
  power mower, 429; seeder,
  430
hull: boat, 132; drag racing,
  339; helicopter, 146;
  submarine, 479; tank, 475;
  windsurfer, 330
hull column, oil drilling
  platform, 101
hull form, powerboat, 138
hull machine gun, tank, 475
hull number: mainsail, 136;
  submarine, 479
human body, 24-31
Humboldt Current, ocean, 6
humerus, human, 26
humidifier, 402
humidity sensor, weather
  station, 18
humidor, cigar, 228
hump: frog, 44; crocodile, 42;
  railroad yard, 96; ultimate
  beast, 49
hump yard, railroad, 96
hung ceiling, elevator car, 78
hurdle, 304
hurdle race, track and field,
  300
hurricane, 17; weather map,
  19
hurst tool, police car, 122
husk: coconut, 262; corn, 58
hutch, side piece, 243
hydrant intake, pumper, 125

hydraulic filter breather,
  bulldozer, 435
hydraulic fluid tank, bulldozer,
  435
hydraulic fork, motorcycle, 129
hydraulic hand pump, pilot's
  instrument panel, 481
hydraulic lifter, tower ladder,
  124
hydraulic line, garbage truck,
  127
hydraulic-pneumatic device,
  oil drilling platform, 101
hydraulic tank, garbage truck,
  127
hydroelectric powerhouse,
  dam, 100
hydrofoil, 145
hydrogen venting arm, launch
  pad, 152
hydrometer, laboratory, 447
hypermarket, 102
hyphen, grammatical symbol,
  513
hypodermic fang, snake, 42
hypodermic needle, 451
hypodermic syringe, 451
hydrosphere, earth, 4
hypospray, 451
hypothalamus, human, 29
hypothenar, human hand, 31

I

I: braille, 512; sign language,
  512
ICBM, 482
ICC bumper, truck platform,
  121
ice, thundercloud, 17
ice ax, mountain climbing, 334
iceberg, glacier, 12
icebox, 249; sailboat, 135
ice cliff, mountain, 9
ice climbing boot, 334
ice cream: cone, 265; scoop,
  259; sundae, 264
ice crystal, clouds, 16
ice dispenser, refrigerator, 249
ice face, mountain, 8
icefall, mountain, 9
ice field, mountain, 9
ice hammer, mountain
  climbing, 334
ice hockey, 294-295
icemaker, refrigerator, 249
ice pack, 12
ice screw, mountain climbing,
  334
ice sheet, 8
ice skates, 325
ice tray, refrigerator, 249
ice window, igloo, 85
icing, cake, 264
icing nozzle, 259
icing syringe, 259
idea balloon, cartoon, 381
identification: golf ball, 310;
  paper money, 224, 225;
  political map, 21
identification bracelet, 187
identification code, bank card,
  226
identification mark, dental
  braces, 453
identification number,
  phonograph speaker, 121
identification tags, attaché
  case, 285
ideogram, public sign, 506
ideograph, public sign, 506
idler pinion, hand drill, 418
idle-speed, solenoid,
  automobile engine, 111
idling wheel, tank, 475
ID window, checkbook clutch,
  223
igloo, 85
ignition, car, 110

ignition cable, bazooka, **472**
ignition wire, automobile engine, **111**
iguana, **43**
iliac artery, human, **28**
ilial crest, human, **25**
ilium: allosaurus, **43**; human, **26**; stegosaurus, **43**
illuminator, microscope, **442**
illustration: book jacket, **167**; book page, **iv**, **167**; cartooning, **380**; magazine, **170**
image: church, **86**; movie film, **174**; offset-lithography, **166**; rotogravure, **166**; television, **185**
image scanner, copier, **164**
immature fruit, cucumber, **54**
impact attenuation device, highway, **114**
imperial arch, royal crown, **485**
imperial mantle, royal regalia, **484**
importer, wine label, **267**
impost, arch, **72**
impression, letterpress, **166**
impression control, typewriter, **161**
impression cylinder, printing press, **166**
inboard aileron, jumbo jet, **148**
inboard elevator, jumbo jet, **149**
inboard engine, **137**
inboard-outboard engine, **137**
inboard spoiler, jumbo jet, **148**
inbound line, football field, **293**
incandescent bulb, lighting, **238**
in-cannel, gouge, **420**
inch, grammatical symbol, **513**
inches of mercury, aneroid barometer, **18**
inch mark, tape measure, **424**
incident-light index, light meter, **176**
incised line, scrimshaw, **375**
incised printing, **377**
incisor, tooth, **456**
incline, roller coaster, **92**
incline track, amusement park, **9**
incore-instrument guide tube, nuclear reactor, **392**
indent, proofreader's mark, **514**
indented surface, thimble, **384**
index: light meter, **176**; newspaper, **168**; playing card, **348**; political map, **20**; slide projector, **175**; wristwatch, **220**
index arm, sextant, **137**
index column, voting booth, **437**
index contour, topographic map, **22**
indexer, pilot's instrument panel, **153**
index finger, human hand, **31**
index hole, diskette, **162**
index mark, sextant, **137**
index mirror, sextant, **137**
index reference key, political map, **20**
index sunshade, sextant, **137**
Indian, **490**
indicator: CB radio, **183**; destroyer, **477**; laboratory scale, **446**; light meter, **176**; organ, **360**; phonograph turntable, **178**; pilot's instrument panel, **481**; roadmap, **20**; 747 cockpit, **150**, **151**; ski binding, **326**; space shuttle, **153**; tape

recorder, **177**; toll booth fee, **114**; voting booth, **437**
indicator light: airport runway, **94**; coffee maker, **252**; phonograph receiver, **179**; 747 cockpit, **151**; subway motorman's cab, **119**; toaster oven, **253**
indicia, magazine, **169**
individual race, swimming pool, **316**
individual lever, voting booth, **437**
indoor floral department, supermarket, **103**
inductor: dispenser, **267**; elevator shaft, **78**
inertial guidance system, submarine, **479**
infantry badge, military uniform, **496**
infantry banquette, permanent fort, **83**
infantry button, Revolutionary War general, **492**
infantryman, uniform, **496**, **497**
infantry rope, uniform, **496**
infield: baseball, **291**; harness racetrack, **337**
infinity, symbol, **511**
inflatable anti-shock trousers, paramedic equipment, **123**
inflation bulb, blood pressure gauge, **449**
inflation needle, football, **292**
infill, fence, **67**
inflatable, **133**
inflation hose, skin, diving, **331**
inflation valve, tire, **105**
inflator, skin diving, **331**
inflorescence, grass, **58**
information: ticket, **349**; toll booth, **114**
information display, pilot's instrument panel, **481**
infrared lamp, hair styling, **214**
infrared night scope, bazooka, **472**
infrared radiometer, satellite, **186**
infrared remote-control command, television, **185**
infrared seeker, jet fighter, **480**
infuser, tea, **260**
infusion coffee maker, **252**
ingredient, package, **268**
ingress and egress platform, lunar lander, **154**
initial: letter, **159**; magazine, **170**
injection, hypodermic syringe, **451**
injector, razor blade, **210**; super collider, **394**
injector pipe, locomotive, **116**
ink: octopus, **46**; pen, **158**; rotogravure, **166**; rubbing, **376**; well, **158**
inked surface, wood block, **374**
ink roller, offset-lithography, **166**
inlay: armor, **465**; dental, **455**; sideboard, **243**; sofa, **236**
inlet: coastline, **15**; combustion jet engine, **407**; jet fighter, **480**; laboratory burner, **447**; surgical table, **450**; toilet, **275**
inlet nozzle, nuclear reactor, **392**
in-line six automobile engine, **111**
inmate, prison, **76**
in mufti, police, **498**
innards, human, **25**
inner bailey, castle, **80**, **81**

inner basket, sink, **247**
inner canthus, eye, **30**
inner cornice, merry-go-round, **93**
inner core, earth, **4**
inner deck, escalator, **79**
inner enclosure, air conditioner, **402**
inner hearth, fireplace, **232**
inner-liner pouch, package, **268**
inner lip, univalve shell, **47**
inner reflector, adjustable lamp, **239**
inner ring, embroidery, **385**
inner sash, window, **65**
inner shell, nuclear reactor, **392**
inner slide brace, trombone, **358-359**
inner sole, shoe, **204**, **205**
inner spring, bed, **271**
inner table, backgammon board, **345**
inner ward, castle, **80**, **81**
inner wheel, Ferris wheel, **93**
input, guitar amplifier, **363**
input jack, cassette tape recorder, **177**
input key, automatic teller machine, **226**
input-output port, portable word processor, **162**
input plug, movie projector, **175**
inscription: money, **224**; tombstone, **516**
inseam: jacket, **188**; trousers, **191**
insect, **41**
insert: clamp, **409**; ice skates, **325**; magazine, **171**; proofreader's mark, **514**
insert steel, jackhammer, **436**
inset: magazine, **169**, **170**; political map, **21**
inset picture, television, **185**
inset sleeve, cardigan sweater, **199**
inside address, letter, **159**
inside cap, umbrella, **230**
inside drive, merry-go-round, **93**
inside leg seam, trousers, **191**
inside margin, book page, **167**
inside rail, harness racetrack, **337**
inside sleeve seam, jacket, **188**
insignia: drum major's coat, **495**; mainsail, **136**; military uniform, **496**, **497**
insole: boot, **206**; man's shoe, **204**; sandal, **206**
inspection plate, buoy, **132**
instant camera, **173**
instant hot-water device, sink, **247**
instant replay, picture-in-picture viewing, **185**
instep: human foot, **31**; shoe, **204**, **205**; sock, **207**
instruction cache, circuit board, **439**
instruction panel, automatic teller machine, **226**
instructions: fire extinguisher, **284**; furnace, **400**; microwave oven, **248**; parking meter, **113**; pay telephone, **180**; sheet music, **352**; synthesizer, **363**; water heater, **401**
instrument, musical, **354-366**
instrument approach, airport runway, **94**
instrumentation, 747 engine, **151**

instrumentation control, space shuttle, **153**
instrument input, guitar amplifier, **363**
instrument panel: airplane, **481**; bulldozer, **435**; lunar rover, **155**; snowmobile, **130**
instrument sensitivity, volt-ohm meter, **423**
instrument tray, dental unit, **454**
instrument warning light, 747 cockpit, **151**
insulated grip, wire stripper, **423**
insulated handle: chafing dish, **245**; lineman's pliers, **414**
insulated window, **65**
insulating body, plug fuse, **399**
insulating glass, window, **65**
insulation: cartridge fuse, **399**; electrician's wire, **423**; solar collector panel, **391**
insulator, overhead power line, **396**
intaglio: and etching, **377**; printing, **166**
intake: bus, **118**; destroyer, **477**; racing car, **338**, **339**; silo, **104**; turbine locomotive, **117**; vacuum cleaner, **283**
integrated circuit, circuit board, **439**
integrated control panel, pilot's instrument panel, **481**
integrated thermal meteoroid garment, **155**
intensity control, radar, **444**
interabang, grammatical symbol, **513**
interaction hall, super collider, **394**
interaction region, transistor chip, **396**
intercarpal, human, **26**
interchange, highway, **114**
interchange symbol number, road map, **20**
intercity bus, **118**
intercolumniation, **73**
intercom: prison, **76**; 747 cockpit, **150**
intercontinental ballistic missile (ICBM), **482**
interdigital pad, human hand, **31**
interest, monthly statement, **227**
interface, ski binding, **326**
interference rejector, radar, **444**
inter-grip rim lock, **458**
interlining, necktie, **193**
interlocking timbered joint, Japanese architecture, **70**
interior: Hansom cab, **131**; window, **65**
interior panel, coffin, **516**
interior slope, permanent fort, **83**
interlock control, gas laser, **395**
intermediate hurdle, **304**
intermediate lens, eyeglasses, **221**
intermediate pipe, automobile, **108**
internal combustion engine, **406**
internal hard disk drive, personal computer, **162**
internal jugular vein, human, **28**
internal organs, human, **27**
internal wave, **14**
international architecture, **70-71**
International Date Line, **5**

International Standard Book Number, 167
interrobang, grammatical symbol, 513
interrupter, label, 268
intersection, highway, 114
interstate route: road map, 20; road sign, 504
interstellar cloud, 2
interval, thematic map, 21
intestine, human, 27
intrados, arch, 72
intravenous equipment, operating room table, 450
introduction, magazine, 170
intubation box, paramedic equipment, 123
inventory control number, paperback book, 167
inverted hub, two truck, 126
invisible zipper, 209
involuntary muscle, human, 26
ion particle cloud, 3
iris, eye, 30
iris diaphragm, microscope, 442
iron, 279; branding, 432; crossbow, 466; fireplace, 232; flat racing, 336; golf club, 311; hair styling, 214; plane, 420
iron curtain, stage, 350
ironing board, 279
iron lung, 452
iron man, cattle ranch, 432
irregular galaxy, 2
isarithmic map, 21
ISBN, book, 167
ischium: allosaurus, 43; human, 26; stegosaurus, 43
is equal to, symbol, 511
island, 7, 15; aircraft carrier, 478; dental, 454; highway, 114; river, 13; service station, 112; toll booth, 114
isle, 7
islet, 7
is not equal to, symbol, 511
isobar, weather map, 19
isopleth line, thematic map, 21
isotherm, weather map, 19
isotonic exercises, body building, 344
issue date: magazine, 169; newspaper, 168
issuer, paper money, 224; traveler's check, 227
issuing bank: credit card, 227; monthly statement, 227; traveler's check, 227
issuing country, stamp, 159
issuing Federal Reserve Bank's code number, paper money, 225
isthmus, 7
Italianate, house style, 63
italic: proofreader's mark, 514; type, 165
italic refer, newspaper, 168
item-by-item tape, cash register, 440
IV equipment, operating room table, 450
ivory carving, scrimshaw, 375

J

J: braille, 512; sign language, 512
jabot, bridal gown, 488
jack: CB radio, 183; garbage truck, 127; metal detector, 445; movie camera, 174; phonograph receiver, 179; playing cards, 348; tape recorder, 177; volt-ohm meter, 423
jacket: cartridge, 470; diskette, 162; fencing, 315; hardback book, 167; kiln, 373; king's regalia, 484; locomotive, 116; Manchu court dress, 491; man's, 188; military uniform, 496; skin diving, 331; sweater, 199; vacuum cleaner dust bag, 283; waterskiing, 329; woman's, 196; zinc carbon cell, 397
jacket crown, dental, 453
jackhammer, 436
jack knife, 426
jack-plug socket, electric guitar, 363
jack staff, destroyer, 477
jack stud, house, 61
Jacuzzi, 274
jaguar coat, ultimate beast, 48
jail, 76
jai alai, 314
jalousie window, 65
jamb: arrow, 465; castle portcullis, 81; door, 64; vault, 457; window, 65
jamb plate, chain lock, 458
Japan Current, ocean, 6
jar: beauty product, 217; laboratory, 447
jarn, cartoon, 381
javelin, 301, 303
jaw: bear trap, 433; brace chuck, 418; cat, 37; clamp, 409; drill, 419; fish, 45; human, 24; nail clippers, 215; pliers, 414; snake, 42; vise, 408, 409; wire stripper, 423; wrench, 415
jaw pad, football helmet, 292
jaws of life, police car, 122
jazz band, 354
jean pocket, trousers, 191
jeans, 191
jeep, 109, 130
Jehu, stagecoach, 131
jellaba, Arab dress, 491
jellyfish, 46
jersey: basketball, 296; football, 292; sailor, 497; soccer, 297
Jersey pocket, bowling, 317
Jerusalem cross, symbol, 508
jet: bath, 274; engine, 407; fighter, 480; hovercraft, 145; jumbo, 148
jet blast deflector, aircraft carrier, 478
jet bridge, airport, 94
jet engine test area, aircraft carrier, 478
jet nozzle, lawn sprinkler, 428
jetting fire crescendo, fireworks, 383
jettison handle, pilot's instrument panel, 481
jetty, nautical chart, 22
jewel drawer, dressing table, 272
Jewish ritual items, 486
Jew's harp, 366
j-hook, tow truck bed, 126
jib: sail, 136; sailboat, 134
jibtop, 134
jib topsail, 134
jig, fishing, 341
jigsaw, 417
jingle, tambourine, 364
job descriptions, résumé, 160
jock, 194
jockey: flat racing, 336; saddle, 335
jockey shorts, 194
jockstrap, 194
jockey wheel, bicycle, 128
jogger, running shoe, 302
jogging track, passenger ship, 142
John B., cowboy hat, 490
'John Wayne,' can opener, 251

join, basket, 266
joint: automobile, 109; billiard cue, 320; brick wall, 69; folding rule, 424; hardback book, 167; hasp, 460; hitch and harrow, 434; human, 26, 31; oil drilling platform, 101; pliers, 414; silkscreen, 375; timbered, 70; umbrella, 230; windsurfer, 330
joint bar, railroad track, 115
joint-sealing compound, plumbing, 422
joist, house, 60, 61
joker, playing cards, 348
journal, 169
journal clerk, Congress, 12
journal printer, cash register, 440
jowl, pork, 34
judge, 89; fencing match, 315
judge's box, ice hockey rink, 295
judge's chambers, 89
judge's entrance, jai alai cancha, 314
judge's seat, courtroom, 89
judge's secretary's table, courtroom, 89
Judith, playing card queen, 348
jug, infusion coffee maker, 252
juggler, circus, 90
jugular groove, horse, 38
jugular vein, human, 28
juice extractor, 255
juicer, 255
juice rack, refrigerator, 249
jumbo jet, 148-149
jump, track and field, 300
jumper: merry-go-round, 93; parachuting, 333; sailor's uniform, 497; waterskiing, 329
jumper cable, tow truck, 126
jumping: ski, 326; track and field, 300
jumping bed, trampoline, 308
jumping pit, high jump, 300
jump line: magazine, 171; newspaper, 168
jump plane, parachuting, 333
jump rope, body building, 344
junction, highway, 114
junction box: electrical receptacle, 398; light fixture, 238
jungle gym, backyard, 287
Jupiter, planet, 3
jury box, courtroom, 89
juryroom, 89

K

K: braille, 512; sign language, 512
kaffiyeh, Arab dress, 491
kame, mountain, 8
kangaroo crane, skyscraper, 77
kangaroo pouch, ultimate beast, 48
karat, ring, 219
kasagi, torii, 70-71
kazoo, 366
keel: box kite, 323; sailboard, 134; turkey, 35; waterskiing, 329
keep, castle, 80
keeper: dress, 198; man's belt, 190; saddle, 335; tape recorder, 177; toaster, 253
keg, 267
kennel, passenger ship, 142
kerf, saw, 416
kernel, grass, 58
ketch hand, cattle ranch, 432
ketchup, and frankfurter, 265
kettle, tea service, 245
kettledrum, 354, 364
kettle grill, 288

key, 459; accordion, 366; anchor, 132; basketball court, 296; calculator, 441; camera, 172; can opener, 251; cash register, 440; clarinet, 356; computer workstation, 438; drill press, 419; flute, 356; fruit, 52; globe, 1; guitar, 362, 363; metronome, 367; organ, 360; piano, 361; political map, 20; saw, 411; saxophone, 357; synthesizer, 363; telegraph key, 157; television, 185; trombone, 359; trumpet, 359; typewriter, 161
keyboard: accordion, 366; carillon, iv; cash register, 440; computer, 439; computer workstation, 438; organ, 360; personal computer, 162; piano, 361; portable word processor, 162; space shuttle computer, 153; synthesizer, 363; typewriter, 161
keychain, 459; police gun belt, 499
key chuck, power drill, 419
keydesk, pipe organ, 360
keyed point of interest, city plan, 20
keyhold, mortise lock, 458
key holder, police gun belt, 498
keyhole, door, 64
keyless chuck, drill press, 419
key lever, telegraph, 157
keypad: computer workstation, 438; fax machine, 164; personal computer, 162
key signature, music, 352
keyslip, grand piano, 361
keystone: arch, 72; arched window, 62; cupboard, 243; door, 64
keystone tip, screwdriver, 413
keyway, lock, 458, 459
kick, bottle, 267
kicker, magazine, 171
kicking pad, knee kicker, 246
kick plate, ice hockey rink, 295
kickstand, motorcycle, 129
kicktail, skateboard, 324
kick-wheel, potter's wheel, 373
kidney, human, 27
kill, volleyball, 319
killer, darts, 322
killing trap, 433
kiln, 373
kiltie, man's shoe, 204
king: checkers, 345; chess, 345; playing cards, 348; royal regalia, 484
king block, igloo, 85
kingpin: bowling, 317; roller skate, 324; truck van, 121
king post: hang glider, 333; house, 61; tanker, 141
king row, checkers, 345
kingside men, chess, 345
kiss curl, woman's hair, 213
kitchen: lobster pot, 433; prison, 76
kitchen range, house blueprint, 62
kitchen sink, 247
kitchen spoon, 259
kitchen timer, 258
kite, 323
kitten, 37
klettershoe, mountain climbing, 334
knapsack, 343
knave, playing cards, 348
knee: cat, 37; cow, 32; dog, 36;

drop-leaf table, 242; frog, 44; horse, 38; human, 24
knee boot, harness racing, 337
knee breeches: Beefeater, 483; Revolutionary War general, 492
knee cup, armor, 465
kneehole: desk, 276; dressing table, 272
knee hose, fencing, 315
knee kicker, for carpet laying, 246
knee-length apron, cook's uniform, 489
knee machine, universal gym, 344
kneepad: basketball, 296; football, 292; ice hockey, 295; rollerskating, 324; ski pants, 326
knee roll, saddle, 335
knee sock, 207; ski clothes, 327
knickers: fencing, 315; ski clothes, 327
knife: corkscrew, 251; engraving, 375; guillotine, 462; kitchen, 256; mower, 429; painting, 370; pocket, 426; skin diving, 331; Swiss army, 426; table, 244; thrusting and cutting weapon, 463
knife box, sideboard, 243
knife case, sideboard, 243
knife man, cattle ranch, 432
knight, chess, 345
knight pawn, chess, 345
knitting needle, 386
knit vest, 199
knob: baseball bat, 291; bathtub, 274; bolt ring, 218; cannon barrel, 467; can opener, 251; chain saw, 431; citrus juicer, 255; coffee maker, 252; door, 64, 458; drain cleaner, 422; dressing table, 272; drill press, 419; drum, 364; fishing reel, 340; handbag, 222; knee kicker, 246; lacrosse stick, 298; lamp, 239; medical examination table, 450; microscope, 442; mower, 429; paint spray gun, 425; pencil sharpener, 277; phonograph receiver, 179; plane, 420; pots and pans, 257; projector, 175; propane torch, 422; rifle scope, 469; saw, 417; seeder, 430; telescope, 443; theodolite, 436; toaster, 253; typewriter, 161; venetian blind, 241; volt-ohm meter, 423; wind turbine, 390
knob nut and bolt, plane, 420
knocker, door, 64
knock-on-wood, gesture, 507
knot: ballet toeshoes, 494; balloon, 493; gallows, 462; lumber, 68; thread, 384; woman's hair, 213
knothole, lumber, 6
knuckle: dog, 36; hinge, 460; human hand, 31
knuckle bow, sword hilt, 463
kokoshniki, architecture, 70
kosher symbol, label, 268
kudu horn, ultimate beast, 48
Kuroshio Current, ocean, 6
kusabi, torii, 71

L

L: braille, 512; sign language, 512
label: baseball bat, 291; cartooning, 380; church, 86; diskette, 162; gas pump,

112; magazine, 169; necktie, 192; package, 268-269; phonograph record, 178; shirt, 189; wine bottle, 267
labeling, 268-269
labial, tooth, 456
laboratory equipment, 446-447
labrum, grasshopper, 41
laccolith, volcano, 10
lace: baseball, 290; baseball glove, 291; boxing glove, 309; bridal gown, 488; ice hockey, 295; ice skates, 325; man's shoe, 204; queen's regalia, 484; running shoe, 302; skate, 295
lace cuff, maid's uniform, 489
lace lock, ice climbing boot, 334
lacing: football, 292; lacrosse glove, 298; snowshoe, 327
lacrimal, eye, 30
lacrosse, 298
lacrosse field, 298
ladder, 425; circus aerialist, 90; destroyer, 476; Ferris wheel, 93; hydrofoil, 145; lunar lander, 154; powerboat, 139; silo, 104; slide, 287; tower ladder, 124; tugboat, 144; venetian blind, 241
ladle, 259
lagoon, 7, 15
La Hire, playing card jack, 348
lake, 7, 13; dam, 100; mountain, 8
lam, hand loom, 387
lamb, 33
lambrequin, coat of arms, 503
lamella, Jew's harp, 366
lamina, leaf, 52
lamp, 238; adjustable, 239; automobile, 106; blimp, 156; hair styling, 214; Hansom cab, 131; house, 63; locomotive, 116; speculum, 448; stagecoach, 131; track lighting, 239
lamp field diaphragm, microscope, 442
lampshade, 238
lance, medieval, 464
lance guard, armor, 465
Lancelot, playing card jack, 348
lancet window, church, 86
land feature, 7
landing, staircase, 66
landing area: aircraft carrier, 478; pole vault, 305
landing control, space shuttle, 153
landing gear, lunar lander, 154
landing gear controls: pilot's instrument panel, 481; 747 cockpit, 151
landing light, helicopter, 146
landing mat, gymnastics, 306
landing net, fishing, 341
landing pit, track and field, 300
landing ship dock, 477
landing ship tank, 477
landing system, aircraft carrier, 478
landing threshold, airport runway, 94
landing wheel: blimp, 156; glider, 147
landing-zone detector, elevator shaft, 78
landmark object, topographic map, 22
landmass, and continental shelf, 15
land mine, 473
lane: basketball court, 296; bowling, 317; highway, 114;

running track, 300; swimming pool, 316; toll booth, 114
language, personal computer, 162
language, symbolic, 512
lantern, camping, 342
lanyard: cowboy hat, 202; stopwatch, 304
lap belt, drag racing driver, 339
lapel: jacket, 188, 196; Revolutionary War general, 492
lap-felled seam, tent, 342
lappet, bishop, 487
laptop, 162
large branch, tuba, 358
large intestine, human, 27
large shallow gouge, woodcarving, 372
large wheel, wheelchair, 452
lariat, ranching gear, 432
larva, insect, 41
laser, 395
laser and flares, fireworks, 383
laser beam, holography, 395
laser jet cartridge, laser printer, 163
laser pickup system, compact disc player, 178
laser printer, 163
lash brush, beauty product, 217
lashing, flat kite, 323
lasso, 432
latch: chain saw, 431; clothes dryer, 281; cupboard, 243; dishwasher, 250; door, 458; garbage disposal, 247; hasp, 460; laser printer, 163; mailbox, 231; mortise lock, 458; needle, 386; oven, 248; revolver, 470; trenchcoat, 200
latch needle, 386
latch support, pulley block, 461
lateral adjusting lever, plane, 420
lateral furrow, horse's foot, 38
lateral incisor, tooth, 456
lateral line, fish, 45
laterally gaited trotter, 337
lateral moraine, 8, 9, 12
lateral pulley, universal gym, 344
lath, lobster pot, 433
Latin cross, symbol, 508
latissimus dorsi, human, 26
latitude, parallel of, 5, 20
latticework tower, power network, 396
launch bar abort, pilot's instrument panel, 481
launch deck, submarine, 479
launcher: aircraft carrier, 478; destroyer, 477; rocket, 472
launcher tube, bazooka, 472
launching ramp, public sign, 506
launch pad, space shuttle, 152
launch tube, ballistic missile launch deck, 479
laundry: frontier fort, 82; passenger ship, 142; prison, 76
lava flow, volcano, 10
lavaliere, 219
lavatory, 273; bus, 118; jumbo jet, 148, 149
lawn cart, 430
lawn mower, 429
lawn sprinkler, 428
layout: dominos, 345; magazine, 170; roulette, 376
LCD: cellular telephone, 181;

portable word processor, 162; wristwatch, 220
LCD display, synthesizer, 363
lead: internal combustion engine, 406; magazine, 170; newspaper, 168; pencil, 158; proofreader's mark, 514; and volt-ohm meter, 423
lead acid battery, 397
lead came, 378
lead connector, pacemaker, 452
leader: book page, iv; film, 172; fishhook, 341; house, 63; House of Representatives, 74
leader board, windmill, 390
leader-pusher, cowboy, 490
lead-in, magazine, 171
lead-in brace, toboggan, 328
leading edge: ax, 464; hang glider, 333; jumbo jet, 148
lead-in groove, phonograph record, 178
lead-in wire, bulb, 239
lead-out groove, phonograph record, 178
lead pencil, 158
lead pick-up, guitar, 363
lead pipe, trumpet, 359
lead plum, cowboy, 490
lead pusher, cowboy, 490
lead track, railroad yard, 96
lead weight: flat racing, 336; grandfather clock pendulum, 233; skin diving, 331
lead wire, vacuum tube, 396
leaf, 52; book, 167; canal lock, 99; carrot, 54; celery, 262; cigar, 228; corn, 58; fern, 57; grass, 58; hair clip, 214; hinge, 460; lettuce, 262; onion, 54, 262; pineapple, 55; table, 242; tree, 50
leaf springs, truck tractor, 120
lean tissue, meat, 262
leash: clown, 493; ski, 326
leather: bagpipe bag, 365; dabber pad, 377; dog, 36; flat racing, 336; football, 292; hot air balloon, 332; parka tab, 201; saddle bar, 335; stirrup, 335; suspenders, 190; tefillin strap, 486
lechurban, Jewish prayer shawl, 486
lecture hall, passenger ship, 143
lede: magazine, 170; newspaper, 168
LED electro-photographic developer, laser printer, 163
ledge: basket, 266; bathtub, 274; can opener, 251; mountain, 9
ledger, incline track, 92
ledger line, music, 353
leech, mainsail, 136
leeward side, boat, 132
left atrium, heart, 28
left bank, river, 13
left-channel volume unit meter, tape recorder, 177
left ear, newspaper, 168
left engine fuel shutoff handle, pilot's instrument panel, 481
left field, baseball, 291
left-handed strike pocket, bowling, 317
left-hand page, book, 167
left-hand steering lever, bulldozer, 435
left image, picture-in-picture viewing, 185
left pedestal, desk, 276
left service court: badminton, 319; handball, 313

546

left stereo speaker: portable radio/cassette player, 182; television, 185
left ventricle, heart, 28
left wing, easel, 370
leg: backyard equipment, 287; bee, 41; bridge, 97; bureau, 272; camera tripod, 176; cat, 37; chaise longue, 288; dog, 36; desk, 276; Ferris wheel, 93; fishing reel, 340; human, 24; ironing board, 279; kettledrum, 364; kiln, 373; kite, 323; lamb, 33; lobster, 47; lounger, 235; medical examination table, 450; mortar, 472; panty hose, 195; paper clip, 277; parallel bars, 306; piano, 361; playpen, 286; pool table, 320; poultry, 35; rocking chair, 234; sawhorse, 408; sheep, 33; sideboard, 243; stage, 350; staple, 410; steamer basket, 257; stove, 404; table, 242; table saw, 417; telescope, 443; tom-tom, 364; trampoline, 308; trousers, 191; tweezers, 215; wheelbarrow, 430; woman's pants, 196; workbench, 408; see also limb
legal tender, paper money, 224
leg brace: wheelbarrow, 430; workbench, 408
legend: magazine, 171; money, 224; political map, 21
legging: drum major's shoe, 495; Indian, 490; sailor, 497
leg hole, man's underpants, 194
legislative clerk, Senate, 74
leg leveler, parallel bars, 306
leg lock, screen, 175
leg-of-mutton sleeve, bridal gown, 488
leg press, universal gym, 344
leg strap, athletic supporter, 194
leg support, backyard equipment, 287
legume, pea, 54
lemon press, 261
lemon squeezer, 261
length adjuster, knee kicker, 246
lengthwise grain, fabric, 388
lengthwise grain line, sewing pattern, 388
lens: automobile, 106; binoculars, 443; camera, 172; ear scope, 448; eye, 30; eyeglasses, 221; holography, 395; microscope, 442; movie camera, 174; Polaroid, 173; projector, 175; radar, 444; rifle scope, 469; shapes, 221; skin diving mask, 331; solar power system, 391; telescope, 443; thermometer, 449; traffic light, 113; video camera, 184; video-still camera, 173
lens release button, camera, 172
lens-selection disc, eye scope, 448
lens suspensory ligament, eye, 30
lens tissue, photographic, 176
lenticel, tree, 50
Leo, zodiac, 509
leopard coat, ultimate beast, 48
leotard, ballet dancer, 494
lepton, 394

less space, proofreader's mark, 514
less than, symbol, 511
let it stand, proofreader's mark, 514
letter, 159; paper money, 224, 225; weather vane, 19
letter drawer, desk, 276
letterhead, 159
letterpress printing, 166
lettuce, 54, 262
lettuce dryer, 260
levee, 100; river, 13
level: carpenter's, 424; combination square, 424; transit, 436
level control, phonograph speaker, 179
leveler: parallel bars, 306; pool table, 320
leveling bubble, theodolite, 436
leveling foot: garbage disposal, 247; slide projector, 175
lever: bathtub, 274; bicycle, 128; bulldozer, 435; can opener, 251; child's car seat, 286; guitar, 363; electrical wall switch, 398; fire extinguisher, 284; fishing reel, 340; gas cigarette lighter, 228; gas pump, 112; hand grenade, 473; internal combustion engine, 406; iron, 279; jackhammer, 436; machine gun, 471; motorcycle, 129; movie projector, 175; nail clippers, 215; outboard engine, 137; pay phone, 180; pencil sharpener, 277; pilot's instrument panel, 481; pistol nozzle, 428; plane, 420; pliers, 414; potter's wheel, 373; 747 cockpit, 150, 151; sextant, 137; spreader, 430; stagecoach, 131; stroller, 286; surgical table, 450; telegraph key, 157; typewriter, 161; voting booth, 437; wheelchair, 452
lever arm, corkscrew, 251
lever cap, plane, 420
lever dolly, balance beam, 306
lever knob, pencil sharpener, 277
lever lock: pistol nozzle, 428; starting block, 304
lever-wrench pliers, 414
levigator, lithography, 376
Libra, zodiac, 509
library: passenger ship, 142; White House, 75
license plate: automobile, 106, 107; tow truck bed, 126
lickings, ice cream cone, 265
lid: automobile trunk, 107; barbecue grill, 288; basket, 266; camp stove, 342; can opener, 251; coffee maker, 252; coffin, 516; juice extractor, 255; kiln, 373; percolator, 252; piano, 361; pipe bowl, 229; pots and pans, 257; tea kettle, 245; toilet, 275; washing machine, 280
lie: golf, 310; ice hockey stick, 294
life, symbol of, 508
lifeboat: destroyer, 477; oil drilling platform, 101; passenger ship, 142; tanker, 141
life jacket, waterskiing, 329
lifeline: destroyer, 476; human hand, 31; inflatable, 133; sailboat, 134

lifepack, paramedic equipment, 123
life raft: aircraft carrier, 478; jumbo jet, 148; tugboat, 144
life ring, fireboat, 144
life-support system: ambulance, 123; racing car, 338; spacesuit, 155
lift: body building, 344; boot, 206; passenger ship, 142
lift bridge, 97
lift cord, venetian blind, 241
lift cylinder, bulldozer, 435
lifter: can opener, 251; kitchen utensil, 259; phonograph, 178; tower ladder, 124
lift fan, hovercraft, 145
lifting charge, aerial shell, 383
lifting column, surgical table, 450
lifting eye, buoy, 132
lifting ring, rowboat, 133
lift knob, toaster, 253
lift link, hitch and harrow, 434
lift lock: toaster, 253; venetian blind, 241
lift-net, tower ladder, 124
lift pedal, dental unit, 454
lift-out stem, steamer basket, 257
lift rod, sink, 273
lift section wrap, aerial shell, 383
lift span, bridge, 97
lift wires, toilet, 275
ligament, eye, 30
ligature: clarinet mouthpiece, 357; grammatical symbol, 513
light: aircraft carrier, 478; airport runway, 94; automobile, 106, 107; bulldozer, 435; buoy, 132; bus, 118; camera, 174; camper, 130; CB radio, 183; church, 87; coffee maker, 252; dental unit, 454; destroyer, 476, 477; door, 64; drag racing, 339; fencing strip, 315; fireboat, 144; fire engine, 124, 125; guitar amplifier, 363; helicopter, 146; house, 63; ice hockey, 294; jet fighter, 480; lift bridge, 97; locomotive, 117; lunar lander, 154; mechanical sweeper, 127; motorcycle, 129; nautical chart, 22; phonograph receiver, 179; pilot's instrument panel, 481; police car, 122; powerboat, 138; railroad crossing signal, 115; relief map, 21; sailboat, 134; 747 cockpit, 150, 151; sewing machine, 278; single engine airplane, 147; space shuttle, 153; speculum, 448; stage, 350; subway car, 119; synagogue, 88; taxi roof, 119; toaster oven, 253; toll booth, 114; Torah, 486; tow truck, 126; tractor, 434; traffic, 113; truck, 120, 121; tugboat, 144; voting booth, 437; washing machine, 280
light control, pilot's instrument panel, 481
light-diffuser panel, elevator car, 78
light-duty road, topographic map, 22
lighter, cigarette, 228
light-horn, nautical chart, 22
lighthouse, nautical chart, 22
lighting: and composition, 368; track, 239
lighting hole, lantern, 342

light mast, aircraft carrier, 478
light meter, photographic, 176
lightning, 17
lightning rod, launch pad, 152
light-reading index, light meter, 176
light selector, police car, 122
light source, composition, 369
light switch: elevator, 78; refrigerator, 249; stove oven, 248
light type, 169
ligule, grass, 58
limb: bow, 466; human, 24, 25; microscope, 442; sextant, 137; theodolite, 436; tree, 50; see also leg
limb top, microscope, 442
lime, crustacean chitin, 47
lime glass, light bulb, 238
limestone cup, coral polyp, 46
limited access highway, road map, 20
limiter, CB radio noise, 183
limit line, fencing strip, 315
limit switch, elevator shaft, 78
limousine, 109
Lincoln Suite, White House, 75
line: badminton court, 319; basketball court, 296; bell, iv; block and tackle, 461; boat, 132; book page, iv; bowling lane, 317; compass, 136; craps table, 347; drag racing, 339; fencing strip, 315; flat racing entry, 336; football field, 293; garbage truck, 127; globe, 5; handball court, 313; harness racetrack, 337; horse's foot, 38; hot air balloon, 332; ice hockey, 294, 295; jai alai cancha, 314; kite, 323; lasso, 432; magazine, 169, 171; map, 20, 21; movie film, 174; music notation, 352, 353; newspaper, 168; nuclear reactor, 392; parachute, 333; perspective, 368; power, 396; powerboat, 139; scrimshaw, 375; shuffleboard court, 318; squash court, 313; spider web, 40; stage, 350; sundial, 389; tanker, 141; telephone, 180; theatre, 351; track and field, 300, 301; tugboat, 144; volleyball court, 319; windmill, 390; windsurfer, 330
linear perspective, and composition, 368
linear slide rule, 441
line box, tugboat, 144
line finder, typewriter, 161
line guide, fishing reel, 340
line-in jack, tape recorder, 177
line lashing, kite, 323
lineman's pliers, 414
linen, ambulance, 123
linen locker, sailboat, 135
line of perspective, 368
liner: automatic rifle handguard, 471; fireplace flue, 232; football helmet, 292; glove, 200; gouge, 374; makeup, 216; ship, 140, 142; Torah, 486
line-recording level control, tape recorder, 177
line roller, fishing rod, 340
line space lever, typewriter, 161
line support, power network, 396
line symbol, political, map, 20
line-up light, aircraft carrier, 478

linework, map, 20
ling-t'ou, Manchu court dress, **491**
lingual, tooth, **456**
lingual cusp, tooth, **456**
lining: beret, **202**; garment, **196**; hardback book, **167**; man's belt, **190**; man's shoe, **204**; mitten, **200**; parka, **201**; saddle, **335**; skate, **295**; ski clothes, **327**; sleeping bag, **343**; trenchcoat, **200**; tunnel, **98**
link: bolt ring, **218**; cartridge fuse, **399**; chain, **461**; chain saw chain, **431**; hitch and harrow, **434**; horizontal bar, **306**; identification bracelet, **187**; keychain, **459**; parachute harness, **333**; pendant, **219**; sponge mop, **282**; swivel, **218**; tank track, **474**; wristwatch band, **220**
linkage: gardening shears, **427**; vault, **457**
link chain, **461**
linking string, frankfurter, **265**
link strap, block and tackle, **461**
linseed oil, sketch, **371**
lintel: church, **86**; door, **64**; fireplace, **232**; house, **61**; torii, **70-71**
lint filter, washing machine, **280**
lint trap, clothes dryer, **281**
lion: ultimate beast, **48**; zodiac, **509**
lip: bell, **iv**; blender, **254**; bottle, **267**; cat, **37**; coffee maker, **252**; dustpan, **282**; embroidery ring, **385**; fishing plug, **341**; human, **24**; mousetrap, **433**; mouth, **30**; pot, **373**; sink, **273**; stemware, **244**; stove, **404**; theater, **351**; univalve shell, **47**
lip brush, **217**
lip gloss, **216, 217**
lip liner, **216, 217**
lip rest, corkscrew, **251**
lipstick, **216, 217**
liqueur glass, **245**
liquid: dental, **455**; fruit, **255**
liquid-bleach dispenser, washing machine, **280**
liquid-bulk carrier, **140**
liquid column, dual scale thermometer, **18**
liquid-cooled internal combustion engine, **406**
liquid crystal display: cellular telephone, **181**; Geiger counter, **445**; portable word processor, **162**; wristwatch, **220**
liquid fuel, rocket, **407**
liquid measuring cup, **258**
liquid oxygen: pilot's instrument panel indicator, **481**; rocket, **407**
lira, symbol, **511**
li-shui portion of dragon robe, Manchu court attire, **491**
listed number, telephone, **180**
listing, magazine, **171**
literal rendition, work of art, **368**
literary anatomy, **25**
lithographic crayon, **376**
lithographic pencil, **376**
lithographic press, **376**
lithography, **166, 376**
lithosphere, **4**
litter, bin, **247**
little finger, human hand, **31**
little toe, human foot, **31**

littoral zone, coastline, **15**
live-bait well, powerboat, **139**
liver: fowl, **35**; human, **27**
living quarters: oil drilling platform, **101**; White House, **75**
liwan, mosque, **70-71**
lizard, **43**
load bearing wall, house, **60**
load cord, hot air balloon, **332**
loader: cannon, **467**; razor blade, **210**
loader's hatch, tank, **474**
loading bridge, airport, **94**
loading door, stove, **404**
loading gate: revolver, **470**; shotgun, **468**
loading platform, stage, **350**
loading slot, razor blade, **210**
load lever, typewriter, **161**
load line, symbol, **511**
load ring, hot air balloon, **332**
load-size selector, washing machine, **280**
loaf, bread, **263**
loafer, man's shoe, **204**
lobby, skyscraper, **77**
lobe: leaf, **52**; outer ear, **30**; partisan, **464**; ultimate beast, **49**
lobster, **47**
lobster cracker, **261**
lobster pot, **433**
local elevator, skyscraper, **77**
local galaxy, **2**
local organizer, backpack, **343**
local political boundary, road map, **20**
local route number, road map, **20**
local street, city plan, **20**
location marker, airport, **94**
location of office, letter, **159**
location of winery, wine label, **267**
locator diagram, political map, **21**
lock: attaché case, **285**; bus, **118**; canal lock, **99**; cash register, **440**; cymbal stand, **364**; desk, **276**; garbage disposal, **247**; garbage truck, **127**; handbag, **222**; human, **25**; hurdle, **304**; ice climbing boot lace, **334**; lift bridge, **97**; mailbox, **231**; movie projector, **175**; organ, **360**; parallel bars, **306**; parking meter, **113**; phonograph tone arm, **178**; playpen, **286**; police gun belt, **498**; pommel horse, **307**; pressure cooker, **257**; safe, **457**; screen, **175**; sonar, **444**; starting block, **304**; tape recorder, **177**; table saw, **417**; toaster, **253**; tripod, **176**; trombone, **358**; vault, **457**; venetian blinds, **241**; voting booth, **437**; wheelchair, **452**; window, **65**
locked groove, phonograph record, **178**
locker, sailboat, **135**
locking bar, mousetrap, **433**
locking bolt, vault, **457**
locking pin, fire extinguisher, **284**
locking plate, workbench vise, **408**
locking pliers, **414**
locking ring: rifle scope, **469**; screwdriver, **413**
locking screw, cassette tape, **176**
locking system: balance beam, **306**; bayonet, **463**

locking tip, hypodermic syringe, **451**
locking adjustable wrench, **415**
lock key, typewriter shift, **161**
locknut: lamp, **238**; lithographic press, **376**; roller skate, **324**
lockout tool, tow truck, **126**
lock plate, crossbow, **466**
lock ring: fishing rod, **340**; slide projector, **175**
lock screw, lithographic press, **376**
lock set, door, **458**
lockside, canal lock, **99**
lock stile, door, **64**
lock switch: movie camera, **174**; tape measure, **424**; video-still camera, **173**
lock wall, canal lock, **99**
lock washer, lamp, **238**
locomotive: canal lock, **99**; railroad yard, **96**; train, **116-117**
lodge pole, tepee, **84**
loft: barn, **104**; golf clubs, **310**; sleeping bag, **343**; stage, **350**
log chute, dam, **100**
loge, theatre, **351**
log fork, fire iron, **232**
log hoist, dam, **100**
logo: aisle display, **102**; bank card, **226**; baseball team, **290**; bus, **118**; credit card, **227**; electric razor, **210**; fire engine, **125**; label, **268**; letter, **159**; locomotive, **117**; magazine, **169, 170**; mainsail, **136**; newspaper, **168**; pill, **451**; prescription, **451**; single engine airplane, **147**
loin: beef, **32**; lamb, **33**; pork, **34**
loin guard, armor, **465**
loins: cat, **37**; dog, **36**; horse, **38**; human, **25**
long bar, easel, **370**
longbow, **466**
longeon, flat kite, **323**
long-hair slot, electric razor, **210**
long horse, gymnastics, **307**
longitude, meridian of, **5, 20, 22**
long joint, bassoon, **357**
long jump, track and field, **300**
long hose, football uniform, **292**
long lid prop, grand piano, **361**
long-life light bulb, **238**
long necklace, Manchu court dress, **491**
long-range weapon system, jet fighter, **480**
long service line, badminton court, **319**
longshore bar, **14**
longshore trough, **14**
long-term parking lot, airport, **94**
long-wire antenna, destroyer, **476**
lookout area, tanker, **140**
lookout tower, passenger ship, **143**
loom: rowboat oar, **133**; weaving, **387**
loop: basketball backstop, **296**; bell, **iv**; book, **207**; bow, **466**; carpet, **246**; checkbook clutch, **223**; circus aerialist, **90**; cowboy cartridge belt, **490**; dress, **198**; fastener, **208**; hammock, **288**; handbag, **222**; human fingertip, **31**; knitting, **386**;

overhead power line, **396**; roller coaster, **92**; suspenders, **190**; tent, **342**; trench coat, **200**; type, **165**; wheelchair, **452**
loop-former bar, movie projector, **175**
loophole, castle, **80**
loop label, necktie, **192**
loop ramp, highway cloverleaf, **114**
loop tape, Velcro, **209**
loosefooted sail, windsurfer, **330**
lore, bird, **39**
lorgnette, **221**
lost and found, public sign, **506**
lotion, beauty product, **214, 217**
lotion dispenser, kitchen sink, **247**
loud, music notation, **352**
loudness control, phonograph receiver, **179**
loudspeaker: cellular telephone, **181**; fire engine, **124, 125**
lounge: jai alai cancha, **314**; jumbo jet, **148**; passenger train, **116**
lounger, **235**
louver: air conditioner, **402**; church window, **86**; tank, **474**; window shutters, **241**
loveseat, **236**
low bar, uneven parallel bars, **306**
low beam, automobile, **106**
lower back-stick, easel, **370**
lower bolt, pulley block, **461**
lower bout, viola, **355**
lower bow, bear trap, **433**
lower case: proofreader's mark, **514**; type, **165**
lower chord, lift bridge, **97**
lower compartment, backpack, **343**
lower control arm, automobile, **108**
lower eyelid, **30**
lower face, zipper, **209**
lower gate, canal lock, **99**
lower-girdle facet, cut gemstone, **218**
lower grid assembly, nuclear reactor, **392**
lower grip ring, sword hilt, **463**
lower guard, sword hilt, **463**
lower handle, power mower, **429**
lower housing, finishing sander, **421**
lower jaw, snake, **42**
lower joint, clarinet, **357**
lower limb, bow, **466**
lower link, hitch and harrow, **434**
lower magnet, dipole magnet, **394**
lower mandible, bird, **39**
lower margin, book page, **167**
lower pool, canal lock, **99**
lower rack track, dishwasher, **250**
lower rail, balustrade, **73**
lower rudder, jumbo jet, **149**
lower sash, window, **65**
lower shell, turtle, **43**
lower side-rail, truck van, **121**
lower spray arm, dishwasher, **250**
lower table, drill press, **419**
lower tail crest, tadpole, **44**
lower teeth, **456**
lower thigh, dog, **36**
lower vertical fin, blimp, **156**

low-gain antenna: lunar rover, 155; satellite, 186
low heat switch, hair dryer, 212
low hurdle, 304
low-level outlet, dam, 100
low pressure, weather map, 19
low pulley, universal gym, 344
low tide, 15
low-tide terrace, 14
low tops, sailor, 497
low water controller, Jacuzzi, 274
lozenge, church, 86
L-shaped square, 424
L-steps, staircase, 66
lubber's line, compass, 136
lubricant port, saber saw, 417
lubricating valve, steam engine, 405
lucaflect, cartoon, 380
luff, mainsail, 136
lug: bicycle, 128; cassette tape, 177; coffin, 516; drum, 364; hand grenade, 473; nuclear reactor, 393; truck tractor, 120
luge, 328
luggage, 288
luggage rack: camper, 130; stagecoach, 131
lug hole, tire, 105
lug nuts, automobile, 106
lumber, building material, 68
lumber girder, 60
lumber post, 60
lumbrosacral plexus, human, 29
lumen, light, 238
luminous indices, wristwatch, 220
lunar lander, 154
lunar module, 154
lunar month, 4
lunar overshoe, spacesuit, 155
lunar rover, 155
lunette, guillotine, 462
lung: human, 27; iron, 452
lunge pads, ice skates, 325
lunt, pipe, 229
lunula, human fingernail, 31
lure, fishing, 341
lyre, 355; grand piano, 361
lyre holder, trumpet lyrics, music, 352
lysosome, animal cell, 23

M

M: braille, 512; sign language, 512
ma'abarta, tefellin, 486
mace: House of Representatives, 74; medieval, 464
mace canister, police gun belt, 498
machicolations, castle, 80
mach indicator: pilot's instrument panel, 481; 747 cockpit, 150
machine: acoustic guitar, 362; ambulance, 123; dialysis, 452; planting, 434; toll basket, 114; voting, 437
machine cabin, wind turbine, 390
machine gun, 471; tank, 474, 475
machine knitting needle, 386
machine-readable codeline, traveler's check, 227
machinery tower, lift bridge, 97
machine stop, etching press, 377
machinist's vise, workbench, 408
mach speed, jet fighter, 480

mack, destroyer, 476
macrame, 386
macron, grammatical symbol, 513
macula lutea, eye, 30
MADC scale, volt-ohm meter, 423
madreporite, starfish, 46
magazine: cover and contents page, 169; feature spread, 170, 171; film, 172; fort, 82; pistol, 470; rifle, 468, 471; shotgun, 469; stapler, 277
Magen David, 88, 508
magic wand, wizard, 492
magma reservoir, volcano, 10
magnesium star shell, fireworks, 383
magnet: pocket knife, 426; super collider, 394
magnetic compass, 136
magnetic disk, video-still camera, 173
magnetic lid lifter, can opener, 251
magnetic north, compass rose, 22
magnetic sound track, movie film, 174
magnetic strip, credit card, 227
magnetic tape, 177
magnetometer, satellite, 186
magnetometer stowage bags, lunar rover, 155
magnifier, pocket knife, 426
magnifying lens, radar, 444
magnifying power, microscope, 442
mag wheel: automobile, 106; motorcycle, 129
mah-jongg tile, 345
maid, 489
maiden: execution device, 462; spinning wheel, 387
mail: armor, 465; public sign, 506
mailbox, 231
mail drop, door, 64
mailing label, magazine, 169
main, furnace, 400
main body: flute, 356; furniture, 272
main breaker, circuit breaker box, 399
main bulkhead, passenger ship, 142
main cabin, sailboat, 135
main cable, suspension bridge, 97
main channel, river, 13
main circulating pump, solar heating system, 391
main compartment, backpack, 343
main control valve, camp stove, 342
main counterweight, lift bridge, 97
main-course table fork, 244
main cover title, magazine, 169
main curtain, theater, 351
main deck, destroyer, 476
main device, coin, 225
main engine, space shuttle, 152
main-engine heat exchanger, oil drilling platform, 101
main feedwater pump, nuclear reactor, 392
mainframe computer, 439
main gate, frontier fort, 82
main housing, curling iron, 214
main illustration, book page, iv
mainland, 7
mainland beach, 15

main landing gear, single engine airplane, 147
main line: lasso, 432; railroad yard, 96
main picture: picture-in-picture viewing, 185; television, 185
main ring, super collider, 394
main rod, steam locomotive, 116
mainsail, 136; sailboat, 134
main sanctuary, mosque, 70, 71
mainsheet, sailboat, 134
main slide, tuba, 358
main standard, football goalpost, 293
main strings, tennis racket, 312
main table, drill press, 419
maintenance safety rope, roller coaster, 92
main towing bit, tugboat, 144
maintube, telescope, 443
main undercarriage wheel, helicopter, 146
main vein, leaf, 52
majority secretary, Senate, 74
major road, 114
maker's imprint, playing cards, 348
maker's signature, check, 226
makeup, 216, 217
malacology, 47
maladicta balloon, cartoon, 381
malar, human, 24
male, symbol, 496
male coupling, hose connection, 428
male ferrule, fishing rod, 340
male flower, corn, 58
male plug, electrical, 398
maline, woman's hat, 203
malleolus, human foot, 31
mallet, 412; croquet, 318; drums, 364; kitchen tool, 261; polo, 299; woodcarving, 372
Maltese cross, symbol, 508
man: backgammon, 345; chess, 345; ranching, 432
manara, architecture, 70
manchete, lounger, 235
Manchu court dress, 491
mandible: ant, 41; bird, 39; fish, 45; grasshopper, 41; human, 26
mandolin, 362
mandoline, kitchen cutter, 261
mane: horse, 38; human, 25; polo pony, 299; ultimate beast, 48
maneuvering system, space shuttle, 152, 153
manger, barn, 104
mang-p'ao, Manchu court dress, 491
manifold: automobile engine, 111; tanker, 141
mannaia, execution device, 462
mannish button, 209
manometer, blood pressure gauge, 449
man's formal attire, 488
man's hair, 211
man's hat, 202
mansion, White House, 75
man's shirt, 189
man's shoe, 204
man's skate, 325
man's underwear, 92
manticore, legendary beast, 48
mantle: earth, 4; fireplace, 232; lantern, 342; octopus, 46; pyramid, 71; royal regalia, 484; Torah, 486
mantlepiece, fireplace, 232

mantlet, tank, 475
mantling, coat of arms, 503
manual, organ, 360
manual citrus juicer, 255
manual drill, 418
manual focusing, video camera, 184
manual operation button, vacuum cleaner, 283
manual-pump pedal, surgical table, 450
manual release, ski binding, 326
manual search button, compact disc player, 178
manual stabilizer trim lever, 747 cockpit, 150
manual typewriter, 161
manual zoom lever, movie camera, 174
manubrium, jellyfish, 46
manufacturer: gas pump, 112; lithographic press, 376; organ, 360; painting brush, 371; phonograph record, 178; phonograph speaker, 179; running shoe, 302; single engine airplane, 147; Universal Product Code, 440
manufacturer's imprint, prescription, 451
manure gutter, barn, 104
manure pit, barnyard, 104
map, 5, 20-22; subway car, 119
map pocket, parka, 201
marathon, 300; running shoe, 302
marbling, meat, 262
marching band, 354, 495
mare, 38
margin; book page, 167; jellyfish, 46; leaf, 52; magazine page, 171; map, 22; necktie, 193
marginal shield, turtle, 43
margin stop, typewriter, 161
marine algae, 57
marine life, 46
mark: basketball court, 296; coin, 225; dental braces, 453; grammatical symbol, 513; guitar, 362; label, 268, 269; military uniform, 496; monovial, 424; music notation, 352; nail, 410; proofreader's, 514; sextant, 137; tape measure, 424; topographic map, 22; type, 166
marked deck, playing card, 348
marker: airport, 84; bowling lane, 317; football field, 293; swimming pool lane, 316; tow truck, 126; wristwatch, 220
marker beacon, helicopter, 146
marker control, sonar, 444
marker lamp, locomotive, 116
marker light: bus, 118; fire engine, 124; locomotive, 117; truck van, 121
marking: airport runway, 94; blood pressure gauge, 449; hypodermic syringe, 451; music, 352; topographic map, 22
marking gauge, measuring tool, 424
mark of omission, grammatical symbol, 513
marksmanship badge, military uniform, 496
marrow, meat bone, 262
Mars, planet, 3
marsh: coastline, 15; river, 13; topographic map, 22
marshalling yard, railroad, 96

mars light, fire engine, 124, 125
mascara, 216, 217
masher kitchen utensil, 259
mask: baseball catcher, 290; fencing, 315; football helmet, 292; ice hockey goalie, 294; silk screen, 375; skin diving, 331; television, 185
masonry: building material, 68; permanent fort, 83; wall, 69
masonry bit, drill, 419
masonry gate post, fence, 67
mass: cosmic, 2; nuclear reactor, 392
massage-action hand shower, 274
massager shower, 274
mast: aircraft carrier, 478; CB radio antenna, 183; destroyer, 477; flag, 502; sailboat, 134; skyscraper, 77; space shuttle, 152; tanker, 140, 141; tugboat, 144; windsurfer, 330
mastabe, pyramid, 70
master control, pilot's instrument panel, 481
master cord, snowshoe, 327
master cylinder, automobile, 108
master number, phonograph record, 178
master slide, traverse rod, 240
master's quarters, tugboat, 144
masthead: magazine, 169; sailboat, 134
masthead light: destroyer, 477; fireboat, 144
mat: in frame, 379; gymnastics, 306; phonograph turntable, 178; wigwam, 84
match, 228; fencing, 315; polo, 299; soccer, 297
matchbook, 228
material identification, house blueprint, 62
match, soccer, 297
ma-ti hsiu, Manchu court dress, 491
matrix, dental, 455
mattress, 271; coffin, 516; playpen pad, 286
mature fruit, tomato, 54
mat window, frame, 379
mausoleum, 516
maw, human, 25
maxilla: fish, 45; human, 26
maximum security prison, 76
meadow, mountain, 8
mean high water mark, topographic map, 22
mean line, type, 165
mean time, 5
measure, music, 352; tape, 424
measured by, symbol, 511
measure of gold purity, ring, 219
measuring cup, 258
measuring diffuser, light meter, 176
measuring spoon, 258
measuring tool, 424; kitchen, 258; oil drilling platform, 101
meat: baseball bat, 291; beef, 32; coconut, 262; lamb, 33; pork, 34; poultry, 35; raw, 262
meat department, supermarket, 102
meat grinder, 261
meat keeper, refrigerator, 249
meat mallet, 261
meat thermometer, 258

mechanic, public sign, 506
mechanical floor, skyscraper, 77
mechanical power, steam engine, 405
mechanical stage control, microscope, 442
mechanical sweeper, 127
mechanical unit, piano, 361
mechanic's shops, frontier fort, 82
mechanism: bazooka, 472; fountain pen, 158; recliner, 235
mechanized voting machine, 437
medal, 501; collector, 225; military, 496; police, 498
Medal of Honor, 496
medal of order, king's regalia, 484
medial malleolus, human foot, 31
medial moraine, 9, 12
median, highway, 114
median furrow, horse, 38
median nerve, human, 29
medical examination equipment, 448
medical table, 450
medical treatment aids, 451
medication, 451; prescription, 451
medicine dropper, 451
medieval arms, 464
medium, painting, 370
medium gouge, woodcarving, 372
medley relay, track and field, 300
medley swimming race, 316
medulla, brain, 29
meeting rails, window, 65
melody part, accordion, 366
melody pipe, bagpipe, 365
melody string, sitar, 362
melon, silo, 104
member: basketball backstop, 296; geodesic dome, 85; house, 61
membrane, animal cell, 23
membranophone, 364
memo, check, 226
memorabilia, White House, 75
memorial, tombstone, 516
memorial band, Jewish prayer vestment, 486
memory control unit, circuit board, 439
memory data, cellular telephone, 181
memory function key, electronic calculator, 441
memory lock, organ, 360
meninges, brain, 29
menorah: symbol, 508; synagogue, 88
men's tee, golf course, 310
mentum, human, 24
menu: computer workstation, 438; personal computer, 162
menu key, cellular telephone, 181
Mercator grid, map, 22
merchant ship, 140
mercury: barometer, 18; battery, 397; blood pressure gauge, 449; planet, 3; thermometer, 449
mercury sphygmomanometer, 449
merge, road sign, 505
merge left, road sign, 505
meridian of longitude, 1, 5
merlon, castle, 80
merry-go-round, 93

mesentery, coral polyp, 46
mesh: Ping-Pong net, 321; playpen net, 286; silk screen, 375
mesial, tooth, 456
mesial buccal cusp, 456
mesial lingual cusp, 456
mesocarp: orange, 55; peach, 55
mesophere, earth, 4
mess, frontier fort, 82
message display, magnetic tape subsystem, 439
message indicator light, answering machine, 181
mess hall, prison, 76
metacarpopalangeal crease, human hand, 31
metacarpus, cat, 37
metal: fuse cap, 399; vaulting pole, 305; printing type, 166; stapler cap, 277; umbrella rod, 230
metal detector, 445
metallic jacket, fencing, 315
metallic salts, aerial shell, 383
metal locator, 445
metal saw, pocket knife, 426
metal shop, prison, 76
metalworking vise, 409
metamorphosis, insect, 41
metatarsal arch, human foot, 31
metatarsals, human, 26
metatarsus: cat, 37; spider, 40
meteor, 2
meteorologist, weather monitoring equipment, 18
meter: CB radio, 183; and fuse box, 399; house, 63; nautical chart, 22; parking, 113; phonograph receiver, 179; powerboat, 138; tape recorder, 177; volt-ohm, 423
meter tape, envelope, 159
metronome, 367
mezuzah, Jewish ritual item, 486
mezzanine, theatre, 351
mezzo forte, music notation, 352
M-51 gun, jet fighter, 480
mica disc, incandescent bulb, 238
Michigan marker light, bus, 118
micro-dial indicator gauge, etching press, 377
micrometer drum, sextant, 137
microphone: CB radio, 183; hearing aid, 452; movie camera, 174; police car, 122; 747 cockpit, 150; tape recorder, 177; video camera, 184
microphone input plug, movie projector, 175
microphone jack: CB radio, 183; movie camera, 174; tape recorder, 177
microprocessor, circuit board, 439
microscope, 442, 447
microwave oven, 248
mid-angle, lamp, 239
midchannel nautical chart, 22
midcourt, basketball court, 296
midcourt line, basketball court, 296
middle finger, human hand, 31
middle joint, flute, 356
middle leg, bee, 41
middle operating-screw handle, clamp, 409
middle pick-up, guitar, 363
middle section, flute, 356
midfielder, lacrosse, 298

midfield line, lacrosse field, 298
midget, circus, 90
midget howitzer, 472
midget pliers, 414
midground, composition, 369
midnight, globe, 5
midrange audio speaker, 179
midrib; fern, 57; leaf, 52
midriff, human, 25
midsole: running shoe, 302; sandal, 206
midway line, soccer field, 297
mike stand, movie camera, 174
mike, video camera, 184
mileage indicator, road map, 20
milestone, highway, 114
mile track, harness racing, 337
military buckle, man's belt, 190
military collar, king's regalia, 484
military uniform, 496-497
milk, coconut, 262
milk teeth, 456
milk well, cow, 32
Milky Way galaxy, 2-3
mill, pepper grinder, 261
milled edge, coin, 225
millimeters, cartridge, 470
milliner, 203
minaret: architecture, 70; iceberg, 12
mind, human, 25
mine, 473
mineral detector, 445
miniature golf course, passenger ship, 142
minicar, 109
minim, music notation, 352
minimum payment, monthly statement, 227
minimum security prison, 76
minimus: foot, 31; hand, 31
minister, religious vestments, 487
minivacuum, 283
minivan, 108
miniver, royal crown, 485
minor coin, 225
minor road, highway, 114
minority secretary, Senate, 74
mint mark, coin, 225
minus, symbol, 510
minus square, shuffleboard court, 318
minute, grammatical symbol, 513
minute hand: grandfather clock, 233; stopwatch, 304; wristwatch, 220
minutes of arc, symbol, 511
mirliton, 366
mirror, 217; automobile, 106, 110; bus, 118; cosmetic case, 288; dental, 455; dressing table, 272; fire engine, 125; holography, 395; locomotive, 117; mechanical sweeper, 127; microscope, 442; physician's, 448; pilot's instrument panel, 481; racing car, 338; sextant, 137; telescope, 443; truck tractor, 120
MIRV, 482
miscellaneous information, monthly statement, 227
miser, costume, 492
missile, 482; jet fighter, 480; surface-to-air, 476; surface-to-surface, 476
missile control officer, and pilot's instrument panel, 481
missile deck, submarine, 479

missile launcher, aircraft carrier, 478
mission specialist, space shuttle, 153
mistigris, playing cards, 348
miter: bishop, 487; cardinal, 487
miter clamp, 409
mitered joint, silk screen, 375
miter gauge, table saw, 417
mitochondrion, animal cell, 23
mitt, baseball, 290, 291
mitten, 200; ski clothes, 327
mixer, kitchen sink, 247
mixing blades, food processor, 254
mixing bowl, 258
mixing tools, kitchen, 258
moat: castle, 80, 81; mountain, 9; permanent fort, 83
mobile platform, space shuttle, 152
moccasin: Indian, 490; man's shoe, 204
mockery, gesture, 507
mode control, microwave oven, 248
mode display window, laser printer, 163
mode indicator, VCR, 184
model: baseball glove, 291; internal combustion engine, 406
mode lever, surgical table, 450
modeling end, clay modeling tool, 372
model number: phonograph speaker, 179; surgical table, 450
mode mute, phonograph receiver, 179
moderately loud, music, 352
mode selection control, police car, 122
mode selector: metal detector, 445; 747 cockpit, 151; sonar, 444
modesty panel, desk, 276
mode switch, Geiger counter, 445
modified bishop sleeve, bridal gown, 488
modified leg-of-mutton sleeve, bridal gown, 488
modulation indicator, CB radio, 183
modulation wheel, synthesizer, 363
module, jumbo jet gallery, 148; 149
moisture collector pan, air conditioner, 402
moisturizer, beauty product, 217
molar, tooth, 456
mold: church, 86; denture, 453
molding: automobile, 106, 107; church, 86; cupboard, 243; escalator, 79; frame, 379; grandfather clock, 233; minaret, 70
molding scoop, cooking utensil, 259
moline, symbol, 508
Molotov cocktail, 473
molten material, volcano, 10
money, 224-225; gesture, 507
money box, 457
money slot, blackjack, 347
money totalizer, gas pump, 112
monitor, 184; computer, 439; computer workstation, 438; fireboat, 144; movie projector, 175; personal computer, 162; portable word processor, 162; prison, 76; space shuttle, 153;

tanker, 141; tape recorder, 177; television, 185
monkey, caisson, 467
monkey bars, backyard equipment, 287
monkey board, oil drilling platform, 101
monkey ear, ultimate beast, 48
monkey wrench, 415
monocle, 221
monocoque chassis, racing car, 338
monorial, carpenter's level, 424
Monroe Room, White House, 75
monsoon, 6
montgolfier hot air balloon, 332
month, lunar, 4
monthly statement, credit card, 227
monticule, 7
monument, tombstone, 516
moon, 3; phases, 4
moon buggy, 155
moon dial, grandfather clock, 233
moon roof, automobile, 106
mooring mast: airship, 156; skyscraper, 77
mooring winch, tanker, 140
moose antler, ultimate beast, 48
mop, 282
moraine, 8, 9, 12
morning coat: butler's uniform, 489; man's formal attire, 488
morning line, flat racing entry, 336
morse, royal regalia, 484
mortar, 472; kitchen tool, 261
mortar joint, brick wall, 69
mortice hole, stagecoach, 131
mortise, label, 269
mortise lock, 458
mosque, 70
mosquito, 41
mosquito netting screen, tent, 342
mother, flat racing entry, 336
mother-in-law, bowling pin, 317
mother-of-all, spinning wheel, 387
motion, steam engine, 405
motion compensator, oil drilling platform, 101
motor: automobile, 108; automobile engine starter, 111; power drill, 419
motor cruiser, 133
motorcycle, 129
motor home, 130
motor housing: blender, 254; can opener, 251; food processor, 254; hair dryer, 212; jackhammer, 436; juice extractor, 255; lawn sprinkler, 428; potter's wheel, 373; power drill, 419; vacuum cleaner, 283
motorman's cab, subway, 119
motor mount, automobile engine, 111
motor nerve, human, 29
motor scooter helmet, police, 498
motor whaleboat, destroyer, 476
motto: coat of arms, 503; money, 224
mound: baseball field, 291; royal regalia, 485
mount: automobile engine, 111; bagpipe, 365; castle, 80, 81; coat of arms, 503; film

slide, 172; fire engine, 124; fishing reel, 340; machine gun tripod, 471; pencil sharpener, 277; polo, 299
mountain, 8-9; peak, 7
mountain climbing, 334
Mountain Time, 5
mount base, rifle scope, 468
mounting: ballpoint pen, 158; bicycle caliper brake, 128; drill press, 419; electrical receptacle, 398; electrical wall switch, 398; electronic flash, 176; fencing foil, 315; frame, 379; lamp, 239; mailbox, 231; ski binding, 326; telescope, 443
mouse, personal computer, 162
mousetrap, 433
mouth: beaker, 447; bell, iv; bottle, 267; cannon, 467; coral polyp, 46; fish, 45; frog, 44; hot air balloon, 332; human, 24, 30; jellyfish, 46; plane, 420; river, 7, 13; starfish, 46; suspenders, 190; tadpole, 44
mouth organ, 366
mouthpiece: boxing, 309; clarinet, 357; French horn, 358; harmonica, 366; kazoo, 366; pipe, 229; skin diving, 331; trombone, 358; trumpet, 359; tuba, 358
mouthpiece key, saxophone, 357
movable base, computer workstation, 438
movable bridge, 97
movable control-arm, surgical table, 450
movable fret, sitar, 362
movable jaw: C-clamp, 409; locking pliers, 414; monkey wrench, 415
move down, proofreader's mark, 514
move left, proofreader's mark, 514
movement, clock, 233
movement dial, vault, 457
move right, proofreader's mark, 514
movie camera, 174
movie projector, 174
movie film, 174
moving gate, racing, 336
moving sidewalk, 79
mower, lawn, 429
MP, uniform, 496
mucoprotein coat, animal cell, 23
mud: hogan, 84; nautical chart, 22
mud flap, truck, 120, 121, 126
mud shield, tank, 475
muezzin, and minaret, 70
muffler: automobile, 109; bulldozer, 435; internal combustion engine, 406; miser, 492; motorcycle, 129; power mower, 429; tank, 474; tractor, 434
muffler shield, chain saw, 431
mufti, police, 498
mug, shaving, 210
mulching lawn mower, 429
mule, canal lock, 99
Mulligan, darts, 322
mullion, church, 86
multifoil window, church, 86
multimeter, 423
multi-picture key, television, 185
multiple fruit, 55
multiple independently

targeted reentry vehicle (MIRV), 482
multiplication, with slide rule, 441
multiply, symbol, 510
multi-position surgical table, 450
multipurpose electrician's tool, 423
multipurpose vacuum cleaner brush, 283
muntins, window, 65
muscle: human, 26; scallop, 47
mushroom, 57
music: accessories, 367; notation, 352
music arch, organ, 360
music desk, grand piano, 361
music ensemble, 354
musician, orchestra, 354
music selection button, compact disc player, 178
music selection window, compact disc player, 178
music selector, tape recorder, 177
music stand, 367
music wire pliers, 414
Muslim temple, 70-71
muslin wrapping, dabber, 377
mussel, 47
mustache, 211
mustard, and frankfurter, 265
mute, phonograph receiver, 179
mutton, 33
muttonchop whiskers, 211
muzzle: automatic rifle, 471; bazooka, 472; cannon barrel, 467; cat, 37; cow, 32; dog, 36; horse, 38; mortar, 472; neck, 267; revolver, 470; sheep, 33; tank gun, 475
muzzle-loading cannon, 472
mycelium, mushroom, 57
mystery gas cloud, Milky Way, 3

N

N: braille, 512; sign language, 512
nacelle, jet fighter, 480
nail, 410; bird, 39; frame, 379; human hand, 31
nail cleaner: clippers, 215; pocket knife, 426
nail clippers, 215
nail crease, horseshoe, 38
nail file, 215
nail hole, horseshoe, 38
nail nick: corkscrew, 251; pocket knife, 426
nail polish, 217
nail pulling slot, hatchet, 412
name: business card, 160; credit card, 227; flat racing entry, 336; label, 268; letter, 159; magazine mailing label, 169; paper money, 225; passenger ship, 142; pencil brand, 158; political map, 20; résumé, 160; tugboat, 144
name column, voting booth, 437
nameplate: automobile, 107; can opener, 251; fireboat, 144; military uniform, 496; newspaper, 168; police uniform, 498
name tag, soldier's uniform, 497
nap, tennis ball, 312
nape: bird, 39; cat, 37; human, 25
napkin, 244
nare, nose, 30

narrow deep gouge, woodcarving, 372
narthex, church, 87
naso-labial groove, salamander, 44
native dress, 491
natural, music notation, 352
natural abrasive material, sander, 421
natural key, organ, 360
natural lever, river, 13
nautical chart, 22
nautical terminology, 132
nave, church, 87
navel, human, 24
navigation aerial, tanker, 141
navigational aid, space shuttle, 153
navigational instruments, 747 cockpit, 150, 151
navigation system, aircraft carrier, 478
navigator's station, sailboat, 135
neb: bird, 39; knife, 256
nebula, Milky Way, 2
neck: balloon, 493; bottle, 267, 268; broom, 282; cat, 37; column, 73; ear scope, 448; golf club, 310; guitar, 362; hammer, 412; horse, 38; human, 24, 25; knee kicker, 246; kokoshniki, 70; lamb, 33; lamp, 238; Ping-Pong racket, 321; pommel horse, 307; pot, 373; poultry, 35; saddle, 335; saxophone, 357; suit hangar, 281; sweater, 199; test tube, 447; tooth, 456; tub fiddle, 366; type, 166; undershirt, 194; violin, 355
neckband: ascot, 193; medal, 501; necktie, 192; shirt, 189
neckband label, 268
neck decoration, military uniform, 496
neck developer, body building, 344
neckerchief: cowboy, 490; sailor, 497
neck guard, armor, 465
necklace: Indian, 490; jewelry, 219; Manchu court dress, 491
neckline, woman's sweater, 196
neck roll: ambulance, 123; football uniform, 292
neck sock, drag racing driver, 339
necktie, 192-193; king's regalia, 484
needle: crochet, 386; dental, 455; etching, 377; football, 292; hypodermic, 451; knitting, 386; latch, 386; light meter, 176; mountain, 9; paramedic, 123; phonograph, 178; sewing, 384; sewing machine, 278; spring board, 386
needle-nose pliers, 414
needlepoint, 385
needlework, 386
negative charge, symbol, 510
negative terminal, battery, 397
negative test lead jack, volt-ohm meter, 423
neighbor, teeth, 456
Neptune, planet, 2
Ner Tamid, 88, 486
nerve, human, 29
nerve tissue, human, 29
nervous system, human, 29
nest: pliers, 414; spider, 40
net: aircraft carrier, 478; backyard equipment, 287;

badminton court, 319; basketball backstop, 296; circus aerialist, 90; fishing, 341; ice hockey goal, 294; ice hockey rink, 295; lacrosse, 298; Ping-Pong, 321; playpen, 286; soccer, 297; tennis, 312; volleyball court, 319
net contents, label, 268
netting: lobster pot, 433; woman's hat, 203
netting screen, tent, 342
network, power, 396
neuron, human, 29
neutral corner, boxing ring, 309
neutral terminal, electrical receptacle, 398
neutral wire: electrical receptacle, 398; electrician's, 423
neutral zone: ice hockey rink, 295; shuffleboard court, 318
neutrino, 394
neve, mountain, 9
new balance, monthly statement, 227
new crescent moon, 4
newel post, staircase, 66
newel skirt, escalator, 79
new gibbous moon, 4
new moon, 4
newspaper, 168
nib: auger bit, 419; bird, 39; fountain pen, 158
nichrome wire, toaster, 253
nick: corkscrew, 251; spool, 384; type, 166
nightclub, passenger ship, 142
night scope, bazooka, 472
night sign lamps, blimp, 156
nightstick, police, 498
nimbostratus cloud, 17
90 degree gauge, combination square, 424
90-degree turn, staircase, 66
nine pin, bowling, 317
nipple: eyedropper, 451; human, 24; lamp, 238
nittle, cartoon, 381
N number, hot air balloon, 332
no bicycles, road sign, 504
nock, bow and arrow, 466
node, grass, 58
no entry, public sign, 506
no-frost refrigerator, 249
noggin, human, 25
noise limiter, CB radio, 183
no left turn, road sign, 504
no money, gesture, 507
nonelectric fencing match, 315
non-glacial stream, mountain, 8
non-glaciated valley, 12
non-locking adjustable wrench, 415
non-overflow section dam, 100
non-porous backing, frame, 379
nonprecision approach marking, airport runway, 94
nonrigid lighter-than-air craft, 156
non-skid strip, bath and shower, 274
non-skid surface: diving platform, 316; Jacuzzi, 274
noon, 5
noose: gallows, 462; lasso, 432
no parking, public sign, 506
no-passing zone, road sign, 505
no right turn, road sign, 504
normal/metal tape switch, Walkman, 182
north, compass rose, 22

North Atlantic Drift, ocean, 6
North Equatorial Current, ocean, 6
north fork, river, 13
north latitude, globe, 5
North Pacific Drift, ocean, 6
North Pole pin, globe, 1
north porch, church, 87
north portal, church, 87
north portico, White House, 75
north-south handbag, 222
north tower, church, 87
north transept, church, 87
north wing, Capitol, 74
no-score ring, dart board, 322
nose: cartridge, 470; cat, 37; chain saw guide bar, 431; clown, 493; destroyer, 477; dog, 36; football, 292; human, 24, 30; missile, 482; pliers, 414; racing car, 338; skateboard, 324; surfboard, 330
nose bridge, airport, 94
nose bumper, football helmet, 292
nose cone: blimp, 156; glider, 147; missile, 482; snowmobile, 130
nose doctor, examination equipment, 448
nosegay, bride, 488
nose leather, cat, 37
nose pads, eyeglasses, 221
nosepiece, microscope, 442
nose radome, jet fighter, 480
nose shroud, drag racing driver's fire suit, 339
nose wheel, single engine airplane, 147
nosing, staircase, 66
no smoking, public sign, 506
nostril: alligator, 42; bird, 39; fish, 45; frog, 44; horse, 38; human, 30; snake, 42; tadpole, 44; toad, 44
notation: music, 352; pitch pipe, 367
notch: laboratory scale, 447; mountain, 8; sewing pattern, 388; spool, 384; telephone, 180; woman's jacket lapel, 196
note, music, 352, 353
not equal to, symbol, 511
note position letter and number, paper money, 224, 225
notice: envelope, 159; magazine, 169; sheet music, 353
no trucks, road sign, 504
no U turn, road sign, 504
nozzle: combustion jet engine, 407; faucet, 273; fireboat, 144; fire engine, 124, 125; gas pump, 112; icing syringe, 259; iron, 279; jet fighter, 480; lawn sprinkler, 428; lunar lander, 154; minivacuum, 283; missile, 482; paint spray gun, 425; propane plumber's torch, 422; satellite, 186; sprinkler, 428; vacuum cleaner, 283
nuchal shield, turtle, 43
nuclear envelope, animal cell, 23
nuclear membrane, animal cell, 23
nuclear-powered attack submarine, 479
nuclear-powered ship, 476-477
nuclear power reactor, 392-393
nucleolus, animal cell, 23
nucleus, animal cell, 23
nude heel, panty hose, 195

number: airport runway, 94; baseball uniform, 290; basketball player, 296; bus, 118; check, 226; destroyer, 477; envelope, 159; film slide, 172; football jersey, 292; hot air balloon, 332; laboratory scale, 446; lacrosse uniform, 298; magazine page, 169; mailbox, 231; mainsail, 136; map, 20; painting brush, 371; paper money, 224, 225; pencil, 158; phonograph record, 178; phonograph speaker, 179; police uniform, 498; racing program entry, 336; safe, 457; sealed voting booth, 437; soccer uniform, 297; submarine, 479; surgical table, 450; swimming pool lane, 316; symbol, 511; taxi, 119; telephone, 180; traveler's check, 227
number cloth, flat racing, 336
number entry keys, electronic calculator, 441
number plate: internal combustion engine, 406
number strip, telephone, 180
one bend, paper clip, 277
one leg, paper clip, 277
#1 wood, golf club, 311
two bend, paper clip, 277
two leg, paper clip, 277
#2 wood, golf club, 311
three bend, paper clip, 277
three leg, paper clip, 277
#3 wood, golf club, 311
four leg, paper clip, 277
numerals, pocket watch, 220
numeric keypad: computer workstation, 438; personal computer, 162; synthesizer, 363
numeric pad, cash register, 440
numismatist, 225
nun, religious vestments, 487
nun buoy, nautical chart, 22
nursery course, harness racetrack, 337
nut: automobile, 106; banjo, 362; crossbow, 466; faucet, 273; fire hydrant, 125; food, 55; guitar, 362, 363; hacksaw, 416; hurdle, 304; ice cream cone, 265; jewelry findings, 218; juice extractor, 255; lamp, 238; levigator, 376; monkey wrench, 415; mountain climbing, 334; nuts and bolts, 411; pendulum clock, 233; Ping-Pong net, 321; plane, 420; pliers, 414; radiator, 400; rifle, 471; roller skate, 324; sink drain, 273; tub fiddle, 366; violin and bow, 355
nutcracker, 261
nuts and bolts, 411; magazine article, 170
nyki, torii, 71

O

O: braille, 512; sign language, 512
oar, rowboat, 133
oarlock: inflatable, 133; rowboat, 133
oat, 58
obelisk, 71
object ball, pool table, 320
object beam, holography, 395
objective, microscope, 442; résumé, 160
objective end, theodolite, 436

objective lens: binoculars, **443**; rifle scope, **469**; telescope, **443**
objective outer cell, telescope, **443**
oboe, **354**, **356**
observation car, passenger train, **116**
observation deck, skyscraper, **77**
observation window, tank, **475**
observer station, destroyer, **477**
obstetrician, examination equipment, **448**
obverse side, coin, **225**
occipital lobe, brain, **29**
occiput, dog, **36**
occluded front, weather map, **19**
occlusal surface, tooth, **456**
occultation ultraviolet spectrometer, satellite, **186**
occupation, letter, **159**
ocean, **7**; basin, **15**; currents, **6**
oceanic crust, **15**
ocean liner, **142-143**
ocean minesweeper, **477**
ocellus, grasshopper, **41**
octane number, gasoline, **112**
octant, **137**
octave, piano, **361**
octopus, **46**; fireworks, **383**
oculama, cartoon, **381**
ocularium sight, armor, **465**
ocular lens: binoculars, **443**; rifle scope, **469**
oculus window, house, **62**
odd, gesture, **507**
odds, flat racing entry, **336**
odds board, jai alai cancha, **314**
odometer, car, **110**
oenophile negotiant, wine label, **267**
off-duty sign, taxi, **119**
offer, coupon, **103**
office: frontier fort, **82**; White House, **75**
office index column, voting booth, **437**
office location, letter, **159**
officer: airplane, **481**; police, **498**
officer's braid, military uniform, **496**
officer's lock and seal, voting booth, **437**
officers' quarters, frontier fort, **82**
office typewriter, **161**
office window, airport control tower, **95**
official reporter, Congress, **74**
off position, electrical wall switch, **398**
offset handle, wrench, **415**
offset-lithography, printing, **166**
offset screwdriver, **413**
offshore rig, oil drilling, **101**
off-the-road vehicle, **130**
ogee, cannon barrel, **467**
ogee section, dam, **100**
Ogier, playing card jack, **348**
ohmmeter, symbol, **510**
ohms scale, volt-ohm meter, **423**
oil: beauty product, **217**; painting medium, **370**; sketch box, **371**; woodcarving, **372**
oil buffer, elevator shaft, **78**
oil cap: automobile, engine, **111**; bulldozer, **435**
oil dipstick, engine, **111**, **406**
oil-drain plug, engine, **406**
oil drilling platform, **101**
oil filter, **111**

oil pan, **111**
oil pressure gauge: car, **110**; powerboat, **138**
oil-pump button, chain saw, **431**
oilskin slicker, cowboy, **490**
oil-tank cap, chain saw, **431**
oil water heater, **401**
old crescent moon, **4**
old gibbous moon, **4**
old lava flow, volcano, **10**
old Senate chamber, Capitol, **74**
omission, grammatical symbol, **513**
on and off lever, gas pump, **112**
on and off puck, craps table, **347**
on-deck batter's circle, baseball field, **291**
on-deck bat weight, baseball bat, **290**
1 1/4 mile chute, harness racetrack, **337**
one-arm bandit, **346**
one-button cuff, blouse, **197**
one-cell battery, symbol, **510**
1/8 pole, harness racetrack, **337**
one-eyed jack, playing card, **348**
1/2 pole, harness racetrack, **337**
180-degree turn, staircase, **66**
100-fathom curve, continental shelf, **15**
one pin, bowling, **317**
one-point perspective, **368**
1/4 pole, harness racetrack, **337**
1/16 pole, harness racetrack, **337**
one-unit beads, abacus, **441**
one way, road sign, **504**
one-way traffic, road sign, **504**
on guard line, fencing strip, **315**
onion, **262**, **265**
on-off button: iron, **279**; metal detector, **445**; metronome, **367**; police car, **122**; potter's wheel, **373**; remote control unit, **184**
on-off control, cash register, **440**
on-off switch: belt sander, **421**; camera, **172**; CB radio, **183**; coffee maker, **252**; compact disc player, **178**; curling iron, **214**; dental unit, **454**; electric hairbrush, **212**; electronic calculator, **441**; fax machine, **164**; guitar amplifier, **363**; hair dryer, **212**; lamp, **239**; laser printer, **163**; organ, **360**; phonograph receiver, **179**; portable radio/cassette player, **182**; power saw, **417**; razor, **210**; toaster oven, **253**; video-still camera, **173**
onomatopoeia, cartoon, **380**
on position, electrical wall switch, **398**
on-purchase signature, traveler's check, **227**
on-site bakery department, supermarket, **103**
01 level, destroyer, **477**
opaque background, thermometer, **449**
opaque balustrade, escalator, **79**
open and close: elevator car, **78**; voting booth, **437**
open-breech smoothbore firing tube, bazooka, **472**

open center spiral, staircase, **66**
open coat, sandpaper, **421**
open craft, **133**
open crown, man's hat, **202**
open end, wrench, **415**
opener, kitchen tool, **251**
open hole, bagpipe, **365**
open ID window, checkbook clutch, **223**
opening: eyedropper, **451**; harmonica, **366**; machinist's vise, **408**; pitch pipe, **367**
open outside pocket, shoulder bag, **222**
open rear sight, rifle, **469**
open-toed woman's shoe, **205**
open-top freight car, **116**
opera glasses, **443**
operating button, camera, **172**
operating control, movie projector, **175**
operating lever: fire extinguisher, **284**; jackhammer, **436**
operating nut, fire hydrant, **125**
operating panel, fax machine, **164**
operating rod, machine gun, **471**
operating room table, **450**
operating screw, clamp, **409**
operating table, **450**
operator: computer, **162**; radio, **183**
operator control panel, laser printer, **163**
operators facility, airport control tower, **95**
operculum, fish, **45**
ophthalmoscope, **448**
opisthenar, human hand, **31**
optical landing system, aircraft carrier, **478**
optical sound track, movie film, **174**
optical unit, jet fighter, **480**
optic nerve, eye, **30**
oral arm, jellyfish, **46**
oral surface, starfish, **46**
orange, **55**
orb: human, **25**; royal regalia, **485**; spider web, **40**
orbit, eye, **30**
orbital sander, **421**
orbiter, space shuttle, **152**, **153**
orchestra, **354**; theatre, **351**
orchestra pit, theatre, **351**
order number, paperback book, **167**
organ, **360**; church, **87**; merry-go-round, **93**
organizer, backpack, **343**
original document exit, fax machine, **164**
orle, shield, **464**
ornament: automobile hood, **106**; Beefeater, **483**; church, **86**; dressing table, **272**; earring, **218**; grandfather clock, **233**; running shoe, **302**; scallop shell, **47**; sofa, **236**; tombstone, **516**; trophy, **289**; woman's jacket, **196**
ornamented type, **165**
ornament pedestal, trophy, **289**
ornithischian, dinosaur, **43**
Ortez bar, tow truck bed, **126**
orthodontia, **453**
orthodontic bracket, **453**
oscillating lawn sprinkler, **428**
oscillator: metal detector, **445**; symbol, **510**
otoscope, **448**
Otto cycle internal combustion engine, **406**

ottoman, **235**
02 level, destroyer, **477**
ouch, jewelry, **219**
outboard aileron, jumbo jet, **148**
outboard bracket, inflatable, **133**
outboard elevator, jumbo jet, **149**
outboard engine, **137**
outboard flap, jumbo jet, **148**
outboard planetaries, tractor, **434**
outboard spoiler, jumbo jet, **148**
out-cannel, gouge, **420**
outdoor garden area, supermarket, **103**
outdoor pool, passenger ship, **142**
outer bailey, castle, **80**, **81**
outer canthus, eye, **30**
outer cell, telescope, **443**
outer core, earth, **4**
outer curtain wall, castle, **81**
outer ear, **30**
outer hearth, fireplace, **232**
outer hull, submarine, **479**
outer lip, univalve shell, **47**
outer panel, jet fighter, **480**
outer rim: coconut, **262**; Ferris wheel, **93**
outer ring, embroidery, **385**
outer sash, window, **65**
outer shell, parka, **201**
outer slide brace, trombone, **358**
outer table, backgammon, **345**
outer ward, castle, **80**, **81**
outerwear, **200**
outer wheel, Ferris wheel, **93**
outfield, baseball, **291**
outhaul line, windsurfer, **330**
outlet: dam, **100**; electrical, **398**; fire engine, **125**; kazoo, **366**
outlet nozzle, nuclear reactor, **392**
outline type, **165**
out of bounds: football field, **293**; golf course, **310-311**; jai alai cancha, **314**; squash, **313**
out-of-town prices, newspaper, **168**
output, computer, **163**
output meter, phonograph, **179**
output stacker, laser printer, **163**
outrigger: fire engine, **124**; house, **61**; powerboat, **139**
outseam, jacket, **188**
outside collar, barbell, **344**
outside flap pocket, shoulder bag, **222**
outside guard, theodolite, **436**
outside interests, résumé, **160**
outside knob, door, **458**
outside load bearing wall, house, **60**
outside margin, book page, **167**
outside pole, tepee, **84**
outside rail, harness racetrack, **337**
outside stile, window shutters, **241**
outside speaker selector, police car, **122**
outside wrap, aerial shell, **383**
outsole: boot, **206**; man's shoe, **204**; running shoe, **302**; woman's shoe, **205**
outwash, mountain, **8**
outwork, castle, **80**
oval head, screw, **410**
ovary: cucumber, **54**; flower pistil, **53**

ovary wall, tomato, 54
oven: stove, 248; toaster, 253
oven thermometer, 258
overcap, disposable razor, 210
overcoat, 200; police uniform, 498
overflow drain, water heater, 401
overflow pipe, furnace, 400
overflow plate: bathtub, 274; Jacuzzi, 274
overflow section, dam, 100
overflow tube, toilet, 275
overflow vent, sink, 273
overhang: house, 63; mountain, 9
overhead, sailboat, 135
overhead baggage rack, bus, 118
overhead bin, jumbo jet, 148
overhead fan, 402
overhead ladder, backyard equipment, 287
overhead power line, 396
overhead switch panel, 747 cockpit, 150
overlay, coffin, 516
overload, fuse box, 399
overload reset button, table saw, 417
overlook highway, 114
overpass, highway cloverleaf, 114
overpressure plug, pressure cooker, 257
overrun area, airport runway, 94
overseas bars, military uniform, 496
overseas cap, military uniform, 496
overserve line, jai alai cancha, 314
overshoe, spacesuit, 155
overskirt, queen's regalia, 484
ovipositer, grasshopper, 41
ovule, flower, 53
owner, racing entry, 336
owner's head, sailboat, 135
owner's silks, racing entry, 336
oxbow lake, river, 13
oxen, 32
oxford rule, magazine, 170
oxter, human, 24
oxygen, rocket, 407
oxygen bottle rack, oil drilling platform, 101
oxygen cylinder, ambulance, 123
oxygen quantity indicator, pilot's instrument panel, 481
oxygen tank, ambulance, 123
oxygen tent, 452
oxygen umbilical, spacesuit, 155
oxygen unit, police car, 122
oyster, 47

P

P: braille, 512; sign language, 512
PA, mountain climbing, 334
pacemaker, 452
pacer, harness racing, 337
Pacific Drift, ocean, 6
Pacific Time, 5
pack: backpacking, 343; glacier, 12; playing cards, 348
packaging, 268-269
packer controls, garbage truck, 127
packing, faucet, 273
packing nut: faucet, 273; radiator, 400
pad: ballista, 467; Band-Aid, 451; baren, 374; basketball, 296; bed, 271; cassette tape,

177; cat, 37; chaise longue, 288; child's car seat, 286; clarinet, 356; crutch, 452; dabber, 377; dental, 455; dog, 36; fire engine, 124; football uniform, 292; handball glove, 313; human hand, 31; ice hockey player, 294, 295; kiln, 373; knee kicker, 246; launch, 152; lounger, 235; medal, 501; medical examination table, 450; paint roller, 425; parallel bars, 306; phonograph headphone, 179; playpen, 286; pommel horse, 307; rifle, 468; roller skate, 324; rug, 246; running shoe, 302; saddle, 335; sandal, 206; sander, 421; ski binding, 326; stirrup, 335; surgical table, 450; tank, 475; telephone, 180; toboggan, 328; trampoline, 308
pad applicators, house painting, 425
padded turnbuckles, boxing ring, 309
padding: baseball catcher's mask, 290; brassiere, 195; carpet, 246; fencing shoe, 315; football goalpost, 293; hockey skate, 325; hot air balloon, 332; playpen, 286; powerboat, 139; running shoe, 302; ski clothes, 326; woman's jacket, 196
paddle: glider airbrake, 147; for potting, 373; Ping-Pong, 321
paddock area, harness racetrack, 337
padlock, 459
pad pocket, football uniform, 292
page: book, iv, 167; magazine, 169
pageboy, woman's hair, 213
pagoda, 71
pail, 284
pail rest, ladder, 425
pain-killer, paramedic equipment, 123
paint: Indian, 490; sketch box, 371
paint brush, 425
painter, 370; rowboat, 133
painting, 370-371; merry-go-round, 93; tools, 425
paired string, mandolin, 362
pair of pants, 191
pajama pants, woman's, 196
Palas, playing card queen, 348
palatal arch, denture, 453
palate, mouth, 30
pale, wood fence, 67
palette, sketch box, 371
palette knife, 370, 371
palisade, frontier fort, 82
pallet, tennis racket, 312
pallet ship, 140
palm: anchor, 132; baseball glove, 397; handball glove, 313; human hand, 31; lacrosse glove, 298; tree, 52
palm tree, fireworks, 383
palpus, grasshopper, 41
pan: air conditioner, 402; automobile, 109, 111; bear trap, 433; candelabrum, 237; chafing dish, 245; dustpan, 282; kitchen, 257; potter's wheel, 373; roulette wheel, 346
panagraph gate, subway motorman's cab, 119

pancake makeup, 216
pancake turner, 259
pancreas, human, 27
pane: postage stamps, 159; window, 65
panel: air conditioner, 402; automobile, 106, 107, 109; book page, iv; bureau, 272; bus, 118; cartoon, 39; clothes dryer, 281; coffin, 516; cupboard door, 243; curtain, 240; desk, 276; dishwasher, 250; door, 64; elevator car, 78; football, 292; football down marker, 293; garbage disposal, 247; girdle, 195; hot air balloon, 332; humidifier, 402; jacket, 188; jet fighter, 480; lounger, 235; mainsail, 136; man's belt, 190; mower, 429; package, 268; piano, 361; pilot's instruments, 481; satellite, 186; saddle, 335; 747 cockpit, 150; sideboard, 243; snowmobile, 130; solar collector, 391; stagecoach, 131; steamer basket, 257; subway car, 119; tape recorder, 177; toaster, 253; tractor, 434; trophy, 289; umbrella, 230; window shutter, 241
panel assembly, football field, 293
panel painting, merry-go-round, 93
panier cases, motorcycle, 129
pan lock, camera tripod, 176
pantaloons, queen's underpinnings, 484
pants, 191; baseball batter, 290; clown, 493; combat soldier, 497; football, 292; ice hockey, 295; skiing, 326; skin diving, 331; woman's, 196; see also trousers
panty hose, 195
Papal cross, symbol, 508
paper: cigarette, 228; copper foil backing, 378; electrician's wire, 423; hair styling, 214; medical examination table, 450; printing, 166; silkscreen, 375
paperback book, 167
paper bag, 266
paper bail, typewriter, 161
paper clamp, finishing sander, 421
paper clip, 277
paper feed cassette, copier, 164
paper guide, typewriter, 161
paper handler, high-speed printer, 439
paper money, 224-225
paper release lever, dot matrix printer, 163
paper roll compartment: fax machine, 164; sealed voting booth, 437
paper size indicator, laser printer, 163
paper tape, cash register, 440
papillary muscle, heart, 28
papillote, poultry, 263
parabolic mirror, physician's, 448
parachute, 333; silo, 104; spider, 40
parachute canister, space shuttle, 152
parachute vent, hot air balloon, 332
parachutist's badge, military uniform, 496
parade: circus, 90; fort, 83
parade ground, fort, 82, 83

paraffin, candle, 237
paragraph, proofreader's mark, 514
parallel, staircase, 66
parallel bars, 306
parallel of latitude, 5
parallel tracks, railroad yard, 96
parallel-veined leaves, grass, 58
paramedic equipment, 123
parapet: castle, 80, 81; fort, 82, 83; house, 62
parenthesis, grammatical symbol, 513
parfait, dessert, 264
parietal lobe, brain, 29
parimutual betting, jai alai, 314
park: amusement, 92-93; road map, 20
parka, 201
parking, public sign, 506
parking brake lever, 747 cockpit, 150
parking light, truck tractor, 120
parking lot, airport, 94, 95
parking meter, 113
parking stand, hitch and harrow, 434
parliamentarian, Congress, 74
parlor, lobster pot, 433
parocheth, Torah, 486
parotoid gland, toad, 44
parsley, and poultry, 263
part: man's hair, 211; poultry, 35
partial denture, 453
partial reflector, laser, 395
particle accelerator, 394
parting strip, window, 65
parting tool, woodcarving, 372
partisan, medieval weapon, 464
partition: backpack, 343; dishwasher, 250; house, 60
partly cloudy, weather map, 19
partner, teeth, 456
partner box, handball, 313
parure: jewelry, 218; king's regalia, 484
pash, human, 25
pasigraphy, 506
pass, mountain, 8
passage, barn, 104
pass case, wallet, 223
passenger cabin: hovercraft, 145; hydrofoil, 145
passenger car, train, 117
passenger concourse, airport, 94
passenger deck, ship, 143
passenger grab strap, motorcycle, 129
passenger loading bridge, airport, 94
passenger ship 142-143
passenger sideview mirror, automobile, 106
passenger steps, Hansom cab, 131
passenger terminal building, airport, 95
passenger train, 116
passe-partout, 379
passive satellite, 186
pass line: craps table, 347; jai alai cancha, 314
pastern: cow, 32; dog, 36; horse, 38; sheep, 33
past history, symbol, 510
pastoral staff, cardinal, 487
pastry, 264
pastry blender, 261
pastry brush, 259
pastry pin, 259

pastry wheel, 261
patch: label, 269; military uniform, 496, 497; paper bag, 266; police uniform, 498; running shoe, 302
patch pocket: cardigan, 199; woman's jacket, 196
patchwork quilting, 385
pate, human, 25
patella: human, 26; spider, 40
paten, for Communion bread, 87
path, golf course, 310
patient's address, prescription, 451
patient's name, prescription, 451
patio, 63; accessories, 288
Patriarchal cross, symbol, 508
patrol, police, 498
patrol hydrofoil, 477
patrolman, police, 498
pattern: sewing, 400; stained glass, 378; table setting, 245; wind, 6
patterned indented surface, thimble, 384
pattern scale, sewing machine, 276
pauldron, armor, 465
pause button: remote control unit, 184; tape recorder, 177
pavement light, church, 87
pavilion: cut gemstone, 218; minaret, 70
pavise, medieval shield, 464
paw: cat 37; dog, 36; human, 25; ultimate beast, 48
pawl: brace, 418; saw, 416, 417
pawn, chess, 345
payee: check, 226; traveler's check, 227
paying agent, traveler's check, 227
payload, missile, 482
payload changeout room, launch pad, 152
payload pallet, lunar rover, 155
payload specialist, space shuttle, 153
payment address, monthly statement, 227
payment information, monthly statement, 227
payoff chart, slot machine, 346
payoff return, slot machine, 346
pay phone, 180
pay up, gesture, 507
pea, 54; anchor, 132
peace, symbol, 511
peach, 55
peacock-feather tassel, Manchu court dress, 491
peak: bonnet, 203; glacier, 12; house, 61, 63; man's cap, 202; mountain, 7
pearl: cave, 11; royal crown, 485
pebble finish, football, 292
pectoral cross, bishop, 487
pectoral fin: fish, 45; stingray, 45
pectoralis major, human, 26
ped, 210
pedal: brass drum, 364; bicycle, 128; bulldozer, 435; car, 110; dental unit, 454; organ, 360; piano, 361; potter's wheel, 373; 747 cockpit, 150; starting block, 304; surgical table, 450; vacuum cleaner, 283
petal lip, mousetrap, 433
pedestal: animal tamer, 90; column, 73; computer workstation, 438; desk, 276;

diving board, 316; dressing table, 272; House of Representatives, 74; obelisk, 71; surgical table, 450; television, 185; trophy, 289
pedestal table, 242
pedestrian crossing, road sign, 505
pedestrian safety mirror, mechanical sweeper, 127
pedicel: flower, 53; grass, 58; spider, 40
pedipalpi, spider, 40
peduncle, flower, 53
peel, fruit, 55
peeler, 256, 261
peen, hammer, 412
peephole: door, 64; kiln, 373
peg: banjo, 362; croquet, 318; dulcimer, 362, guitar, 362, 363; sitar, 362; tent, 342; tepee, 84; violin, 355
pegbox, violin, 355
pellet: dental, 455; shotgun, 468
pelota, jai alai, 314
pelt, 201
pelvic fin, fish, 45
pelvic region, salamander, 44
pelvis: allosaurus, 43; stegosaurus, 43
pen: barnyard, 104; writing tool, 158
penalty area, soccer field, 297
penalty box: ice hockey rink, 295
penalty kick mark, soccer field, 297
penalty spot: polo grounds, 299; soccer field, 297
pen blade, pocket knife, 426
pencil: beauty product, 217; lithographic, 376; styptic, 210; writing tool, 158
pencil sharpener, 277
pendant: aircraft carrier, 478; Indian, 490; jewelry, 219; queen's regalia, 484
pendant pearl, royal crown, 485
pendentive, mosque, 71
pendulum: clock, 233; metronome, 367
pen holder: checkbook clutch, 223; police gun belt, 499
penhold grip, Ping-Pong, 321
pen loop, checkbook clutch, 223
pennant, 502; circus tent, 91
pennon, lance, 464
penny size, nail, 410
penstock control, dam, 100
Pentateuch, Torah, 88
pentathlon, track and field, 300
penthouse, barn, 104
pent roof, pagoda, 71
peonies, fireworks, 383
people-mover, 79
peplum, dress, 198
pepper, raw, 262
peppercorn, 262
pepper mill, 261
pepperoni, pizza, 265
per, symbol, 511
perambulator, 286
percent key, electronic calculator, 441
percolator, 252
percussion, orchestra, 354
perfection, gesture, 507
perforated panel, steamer basket, 257
perforated spreader, percolator brewing basket, 252
perforation: envelope, 159; foil pouch, 269; hair roller, 214;

man's shoe, 204; movie film, 174; stamp, 159
performance hall, theatre, 351
performance instruction, music, 352
performing rights organization, music, 353
perfume, 217
per hundred, symbol, 511
periapical dental x-ray unit, 454
pericarp, pea, 54
period: grammatical symbol, 513; wave, 14
periodical, 169
periople, horse's hoof, 38
periscope: submarine, 479; tank, 475
perishables, supermarket, 102
permanent current, ocean, 6
permanent end-of-aisle display, supermarket, 102
permanent fort, 83
permanent lotion, hair styling, 214
permanent rod, hair styling, 214
permanent teeth, 456
per mill, symbol, 511
peroneal artery, human, 28
peroxide, ambulance, 123
personal cassette player/radio, 182
personal choice, voting booth, 437
personal computer, 162
personal foul, lacrosse, 298
personal identification number, ATM card, 226
personnel safety net, aircraft carrier, 478
perspective, and composition, 368
per thousand, symbol, 511
Peru Current, ocean, 6
pestle, kitchen tool, 261
petal, flower, 53
petiole: celery, 262; fern, 57; leaf, 52
petitpoint, stitchery, 385
petticoat, windmill, 390
pew, synagogue, 88
phalanges, human, 26, 31
pharmacy, supermarket, 102
pharynx, mouth, 30
phase of moon, 4
pheasant, 35
Phillips head, screw, 410
Phillips head screwdriver, pocket knife, 426
Phillips head tip, screwdriver, 413
philtrum, face, 30
phloem, tree, 50
Phoenix missile, jet fighter, 480
phone, 180
phone number, business card, 160
phonetic symbol, grammatical, 513
phonogram, public sign, 506
photo, magazine, 169, 170
photo and card case, wallet, 223
photocell, Polaroid, 173
photograph, book jacket, 167
photographic accessories, 176
photo holder, wallet, 223
phyllacteries, Jewish ritual items, 486
physician's address, prescription, 451
physician's mirror, 448
physician's name, prescription, 451
physician's phone number, prescription, 451

physician's room, White House, 75
physician's signature, prescription, 451
pi, symbol, 511
pianissimo, music notation, 353
piano, 361; music notation, 352
piano-accordion, 366
piano frame, 379
piccolo, 354, 356
pick: figure skates, 325; ice ax, 334; ice hammer, 334; pipe tool, 229; stringed instrument, 362
picket fence, 63, 67
pick guard, guitar, 362, 363
pick-up, guitar, 363
pick-up arm, fishing reel, 340
pick-up broom, mechanical sweeper, 127
pick-up selector, guitar, 363
picnic area: public sign, 506; road sign, 504
picnic shoulder, pork, 34
pictograph, public sign, 506
picture card, 348
picture exit slot, Polaroid, 173
picture frame, 379
picture hat, 203; bride's, 488
picture hook, 379
picture-in-picture viewing, 185
picture protection hood, Polaroid, 173
picture tube, television, 185
pie, 264
piece: backgammon, 345; cake, 264; chess, 345; coin, 225; crutch, 452; jewelry, 219; kite, 323; rifle, 471; slalom water ski, 329
piece goods, fabric, 388
pier: arch, 72; bridge, 97; dam, 100; house, 60; nautical chart, 22; skyscraper, 77
pierced ear findings, 218
piercer, can opener, 251
pierum assembly, nuclear reactor, 392
pig, 34
pig board, windsurfer, 330
pigboat, 479
piggin, container, 266
piggy bank, 457
pigment cell, octopus, 46
pigment filling, scrimshaw, 375
pigpen, 104
pigtail, woman's hair, 213
pike, lance, 464
pike pole, fireman, 500
pilaster: cupboard, 243; house, 62
pile: arrow, 484; carpet, 246; nuclear, 392; skyscraper, 77; Velcro, 209
pileus, mushroom, 57
pill, medicinal, 451
pillar: arch, 72; automobile windshield, 109; house, 62; mountain, 9; and obelisk, 70; torii, 71
pillbox, woman's hat, 203
pillow: bedding, 270; coffin, 516; lounger, 235; police car, 122; rocking chair, 234; sofa, 236; stagecoach, 131
pilot: airplane, 481; locomotive, 116
pilot boarding ladder, tugboat, 144
pilot chute, 333
pilot hole, screw, 410
pilothouse: fireboat, 144; tugboat, 144
pilot light: guitar amplifier, 363; stove, 248
pilot's seat, space shuttle, 153

pilot-wheel feed, drill press, **419**

pin: anchor, **132**; attachment plug, **398**; bowling, **317**; can opener, **251**; and carpet, **246**; compass, **136**; fastener, **208**; fire extinguisher, **284**; fluorescent bulb, **238**; gallows, **462**; gardening shears, **427**; globe, **1**; golf course, **311**; hacksaw, **416**; hair, **214**; hand grenade, **473**; hasp, **460**; jewelry, **219**; kitchen utensil, **259**; lock cylinder, **459**; mortar, **472**; nail clippers, **215**; pliers, **414**; potter's wheel, **373**; pulley block, **461**; revolver safety catch, **218**; rifle, **468**, **469**; roller chain, **461**; roller skate, **324**; sewing machine, **278**; stapler, **277**; starting block, **304**; stroller, **286**; tepee, **84**; track link, **474**; vacuum tube, **396**; window shade roller, **241**; woman's hat, **203**

pin binding, ski, **327**
pinbone, cow, **32**
pincer, lobster, **47**
pinch, man's hat, **202**
pinch roller, tape recorder, **177**
pinch valve, dental unit, **454**
pin connector, video-still camera adaptor, **173**
pincushion, **384**
pineapple, **55**; grenade, **473**
pine cone, **52**
Ping-Pong, **321**
pin hinge, stove, **404**
pinion, hand drill, **418**
pinkie, human hand, **31**
pinky ring, trumpet, **359**
pin link plate, roller chain, **461**
pin mark, type, **166**
pinna, **30**; fern, **57**
pinnacle: church, **86**; mountain, **9**
pinnule, fern, **57**
PIN number, ATM card, **226**
pin rail, stage, **350**
pinsetter, bowling, **317**
pinspotter, bowling, **317**
pintle, hinge, **460**
pintle mount, machine gun, **471**
pin-tumbler, lock cylinder, **459**
pinwood, clothespin, **280**
pip: apple, **55**; backgammon board, **345**; dice, **347**; domino, **345**; pineapple, **55**; playing card, **348**
pip card, **348**
pipe: automobile, **108**; bagpipe, **365**; furnace, **400**; heat exchanger, **403**; lamp, **238**; levigator, **376**; locomotive, **116**; motorcycle, **129**; oil drilling platform, **101**; organ, **360**; pitch, **367**; plumbing, **422**; pressure cooker, **257**; silo, **104**; smoking, **229**; solar heating system, **391**; space shuttle, **152**; standpipe, **59**; steam engine, **405**; steel chain fence gate, **67**; super collider, **394**; tank **474**; trumpet, **359**; water heater, **401**

pipe batten, stage, **350**
pipe cleaner, **229**
pipe cutter, plumbing, **422**
pipe-holding jaw, vise, **409**
pipeline, wave, **15**
pipe nozzle, fire engine, **124**
piper, bagpipe, **365**

pipe standard, parking meter, **113**
pipe threader, **422**
pipe tool, **229**
pipe umbrella, **229**
pipe wrench, plumbing, **422**
piping: baseball uniform, **290**; bishop's cope, **487**; boot, **206**; handball glove, **313**; jacket, **188**; man's belt, **190**; shoulder bag, **222**; woman's shoe, **205**

pipkin, **257**
pirate, costume, **492**
Pisces, zodiac, **509**
piste, fencing, **315**
pistil, flower, **53**
pistol, **470**; lobster, **47**; pirate, **492**
pistol belt, soldier, **497**
pistol grip: hacksaw, **416**; rifle, **471**; shotgun, **468**
pistol nozzle, **428**
pistol port, tank, **474**
piston: garbage truck, **127**; dispenser, **267**; organ, **360**; parallel bars, **306**; pommel horse, **316**; steam engine, **405**

piston displacement, chain saw, **431**
piston rod, steam engine, **405**
pit: barnyard, **104**; bowling lane, **317**; high jump, **305**; peach, **55**; pole vault, **305**; snake, **42**; theatre, **351**
pitch: plane blade, **420**; screw, **410**; soccer, **297**
pitch-control dial, tape recorder, **177**
pitcher's mound, baseball field, **291**
pitcher's rubber, baseball field, **291**
pitching wedge, golf club, **310**
pitch pipe, **367**
pitch trim, 747 cockpit, **151**
pitch wheel, synthesizer, **363**
pitmans, steam engine, **405**
piton, mountain climbing, **334**
pitot tube, jet fighter, **480**
pituitary gland, human, **29**
pivot: basketball, **296**; clamp, **409**; compass, **136**; dressing table mirror, **272**; jet fighter wing, **480**; laboratory, scale, **447**; metronome, **367**; mortar, **472**; pliers, **414**; roller skate, **428**; scissors, **384**; ski binding, **326**; wire stripper, **423**

pivot bolt, bicycle caliper brake, **128**
pivot gear housing, mechanical sweeper, **127**
pivot hinge, **460**
pivot pin: can opener, **251**; hinge, **460**
pivot point, bicycle caliper brake, **128**
pix, church, **87**
pizza, **265**
pizzicato, stringed instruments, **355**
place, flat racing, **336**
place bets, craps table, **347**
placenta, tomato, **54**
place setting, **244**
placket: blouse, **197**; parka, **201**; shirt, **189**
plain, **7**, **8**, **15**
plaintiff's table, courtroom, **89**
plait, woman's hair, **213**
plan: church, **87**; White House, **75**
planchet, coin, **225**
plane, **420**; monorail, **424**; perspective, **368**

plane iron, **420**
plane kite, **323**
plane surface, printing, **166**
planet, **2**, **3**
planetary, tractor, **434**
planetoid, **2**
planing hull, powerboat, **138**
plank, lumber, **68**
planographic printing, **376**
plant power network, **396**
plantar arch, human foot, **31**
Plantin typeface, **165**
planting box, pole vault, **305**
planting machine, **434**
planting pit, pole vault, **305**
plaque: identification bracelet, **187**; man's belt buckle, **190**; pyrometric cone, **373**
plasma membrane, animal cell, **23**
plasma science, satellite, **186**
plastic board, circuit board, **439**
plastic cap, stapler, **277**
plastic disc, harness racing sulky, **337**
plastic fruit, woman's hat, **203**
plastic lining, man's hat, **202**
plastic sheath, electrician's wire, **423**
plastic squeeze, bottle, **268**
plasti-shield, bottle, **269**
plastron: drum major's coat, **495**; fencing, **315**; turtle, **43**
plate: armor, **465**; automatic weapon, **471**; barbell, **344**; baseball field, **291**; baseball pitcher's spikes, **290**; bathtub, **274**; blackjack, **347**; beef, **32**; bicycle, **245**; chain lock, **458**; crossbow, **466**; escalator, **79**; flute, **356**; food mill, **260**; furnace, **400**; hasp, **460**; horizontal bar, **306**; house, **61**; identification bracelet, **187**; intaglio, **377**; internal combustion engine, **406**; iron, **279**; kitchen sink, **247**; laboratory scale, **446**; land mine, **473**; lithographic, **376**; locomotive, **116**; mandolin, **362**; mortise lock, **458**; onion, **54**; outboard engine, **137**; paper money, **224**; parking meter, **113**; pliers, **414**; pulley block, **461**; railroad track, **115**; rifle, **468**; roller chain, **461**; roller skate, **324**; safe, **457**; sewing machine, **278**; shotgun butt, **468**; ski binding, **326**; slalom water ski, **329**; solar collector panel, **391**; space shuttle, **152**; sponge mop, **282**; stage, **350**; standpipe, **59**; stationary rings, **307**; sundial, **389**; table setting, **244**, **245**; tank, **474**, **475**; theodolite, **436**; toaster, **253**; tow truck, **126**; tractor, **434**; trophy, **289**; typewriter, **161**; vacuum tube, **396**; vise, **408**

plate number: envelope, **159**; paper money, **225**
plate vial, theodolite, **436**
plateau, **7**
plate cylinder, printing, **166**
platen, typewriter, **161**
platform: aircraft carrier, **478**; camera tripod, **176**; circus aerialist, **90**; diving, **316**; elevator shaft, **78**; fire engine, **124**; helicopter, **146**; iceberg, **12**; lunar lander, **154**; merry-go-round, **93**; powerboat, **139**; slide, **287**; space shuttle, **152**; stage,

350; swimming pool, **316**; truck, **121**
platform car, train, **117**
platform shoe, woman's, **214**
platform tower, slide, **287**
platter, phonograph, **178**
playback control, video-still camera adaptor, **173**
playback unit, **184**; tape recorder, **177**; video-still camera, **173**
play button: answering machine, **181**; compact disc player, **178**; remote control unit, **184**; tape recorder, **177**; Walkman, **182**
player: basketball, **296**; ice hockey, **295**; jai alai cancha, **314**; lacrosse, **298**; orchestra, **354**; polo, **299**; soccer, **297**
player number, football uniform, **292**
playground: equipment, **287**; public signs, **506**
playing cards, **348**
playing surface, pool table, **320**
playpen, child's, **286**
playroom, passenger ship, **143**
plaza, skyscraper, **77**
pleat: ballet slippers, **494**; curtain, **240**; lounger, **235**; shirt, **189**; woman's pants, **196**
pleated pants, woman's, **196**
pleated ruffled shirt, man's, **488**
plectrum, stringed instrument, **362**
plenum assembly, nuclear reactor, **405**
plewd, cartoon, **381**
plexus, human, **25**
pliers, **414**; dental, **455**; stained glass, **378**
Plimsoll mark, symbol, **511**
plinth: column, **73**; grandfather clock, **233**
plot, grave, **516**
plow, **434**; can opener, **251**
plow anchor, sailboat, **134**
plug: ballpoint pen, **158**; electric, **398**; fishing, **341**; internal combustion engine, **406**; kiln, **373**; lawn sprinkler, **428**; locomotive boiler, **116**; mortise lock, **458**; movie projector, **175**; mower, **429**; padlock, **459**; paint spray gun, **425**; percolator, **252**; pots and pans, **257**; rocket, **383**; vacuum tube, **396**
plug body, phonograph headphone, **179**
plug fuse, **399**
plum, cowboy bullet, **490**
plumb, transit, **436**
plumber's friend, **422**
plumber's tool, **422**
plumbing tool, **422**
plumb vial, carpenter's level, **424**
plume: armor, **465**; drum major's busby, **495**
plunge pool, dam, **100**
plunger: coffee maker, **252**; hypodermic syringe, **451**; juice extractor, **255**; plumbing tool, **422**; telephone, **180**; torpedo, **479**
plunger handle, camp stove, **342**
plunger snap lock, starting block, **304**
plunge step, shoreline, **14**
plus, symbol, **510**
plus or minus, symbol, **510**
Pluto, planet, **2**

pneumatic liner system, football helmet, 292
pneumoscopy port, ear scope, 448
pocket: backpack, 343; baseball glove, 291; bowling, 337; briefcase, 285; cardigan sweater, 199; cowboy, 490; football uniform, 292; golf bag, 311; handbag, 222; jacket, 188; lacrosse stick, 298; mainsail, 136; necktie, 193; parka, 201; pool table, 320; shirt, 189; skin diving gear, 331; skirt, 197; spacesuit, 155; trench coat, 200; trousers, 191; wallet, 223; woman's jacket and pants, 196; window shade, 241
pocket billiard table, 320
pocketbook, 222
pocket flap, backpack, 343
pocketknife, 426
pocket watch, 220
pod: jumbo jet engine, 149; pea, 54; racing car, 338
podium, symphony orchestra, 354
pogonotomy, 211
pogonotrophy, 211
point: arrow, 466; backgammon board, 345; ballpoint pen, 158; billiard cue, 320; chicken comb, 35; clown's hat, 493; dart, 322; drill bit, 419; etching needle, 377; fencing foil, 315; fish hook, 341; grammatical symbol, 513; hockey skate, 325; ice climbing boot, 334; jai alai cesta, 314; javelin, 302; knife, 256, 463; knitting needle, 386; laboratory scale, 446; land, 7; mainsail, 136; nail, 410; needle, 384; pencil, 158; pin, 208; rasp, 420; river, 13; saw tooth, 416; screw, 410; sharpening steel, 256; star fort, 83; sword, 463; tack, 410; violin bow, 355; weather vane, 19; wrench, 415; wrought iron fence, 67
point chisel, stonecutting, 372
point d'appliqué, bridal gown, 488
point defense missile launcher, aircraft carrier, 478
pointed waist, queen's regalia, 484
pointer: barometer, 18; comic strip, 381; laboratory scale, 447; Torah, 486; volt-ohm meter, 423; weather vane, 19
pointillism and texture, composition, 369
point of entry, darts, 322
point of hip, horse, 38
point of hock, horse, 38
point of interest, city plan, 20
point of shoulder, horse, 38
point ring, darts, 322
point size, type, 166
point symbol, political map, 21
poise, laboratory scale, 446
poison, symbol, 511
poisonous snake, 42
poker, fire iron, 232
polarity symbol, battery, 397
Polaroid, 173
pole: baseball field, 291; bumper car, 92; circus tent, 91; football field, 293; globe, 5; harness racetrack, 337; overhead power line, 396; pole vaulting, 305; powerboat, 139; skiing, 326,

327; stagecoach, 131; tent, 342; tepee, 84
pole arms, medieval, 464
pole grip, ski pole, 326
pole mount, fishing reel, 340
pole position, flat racing, 336
pole vault, 300, 305
poleyn, armor, 465
police car, 122
policeman's suspenders, 190
police officer, 498-499
polish, beauty product, 217
polisher, pipe cutter, 422
political boundary, map, 5, 20
political capital symbol, map, 20
political cartoon, 380
political map, 20-21
poll(s): ax, 464; cow, 32; hammer, 412; horse, 38; pig, 34; voting, 437
pollen, flower, 53
pollen basket, bee, 41
poll end, windmill, 390
pollen sac, flower stamen, 53
polling place, 437
polliwog, 44
pollution control valve, automobile engine, 111
polo, 299
polo & exercise bandage, polo, 299
polo grounds, 299
poly bag, packaging, 269
polygonal base, minaret, 70
polygonal tower, architecture, 71
polyp, coral, 46
pommel: foil mounting, 315; knife, 463; pommel horse, 307; saddle, 335; sword hilt, 463
pommel horse, 307
pompom, ski hat, 327
poncho, infantryman's uniform, 497
pond, topographic map, 22
pons, brain, 29
pontic, dental bridge, 453
pontoon, single engine airplane, 147
pontoon bridge, 97
ponytail, woman's hair, 213
pool, 320; canal lock, 99; cave, 11; dam, 100; passenger ship, 142, 143; swimming, 316
pool table, 320
popcorn, cave, 11
pop-up stopper, sink, 273
porcelain, dental, 455
porch: church, 87; house, 63
porcupine, ultimate beast, 48
pork, 34
port: drag racing driver's fire suit, 339; ear scope, 448; movie projector, 175; outboard; engine, 137; passenger ship, 142; rocket, 407; saber saw, 417; sailboat, 134; tank, 474
portable electrocardiogram, paramedic equipment, 123
portable life support system, spacesuit, 155
portable radio/cassette player, 182
portable telemetry radio, paramedic equipment, 123
portable typewriter, 161
portable word processor, 162
portal: church, 86-87; stage, 350, 351; underwater tunnel, 98
portcullis, castle, 81
port-engine clutch, powerboat, 138
portfolio, briefcase, 285

porthole, passenger ship, 142
portico: Capitol, 74; White House, 75
portlight: powerboat, 138; sailboat, 134
port quarter, boat, 132
portrait: money, 225; White House, 75
port side, boat, 132
port throttle, powerboat, 138
position: business card, 160; flat racing, 336; globe, 5
position indicator: elevator car, 78; 747 cockpit, 150; sonar, 444
positioning arm, dental unit, 454
positioning ratchet, chaise longue, 288
positioning scale, typewriter, 161
position letter, paper money, 224, 225
position light, jet fighter, 480
position lines, jai alai cancha, 314
position mark, guitar, 362
position number, paper money, 224
positive charge, symbol, 510
positive terminal, battery, 397
positive test lead jack, volt-ohm meter, 423
possession player, lacrosse, 298
post: battery, 397; bear trap, 433; bed, 270; bicycle, 128; boxing ring, 309; bureau, 272; camera tripod, 176; candelabrum, 237; fence, 67; guillotine, 462; hand loom, 387; hang glider, 333; house, 60, 61; jewelry findings, 218; kettledrum, 364; laboratory scale, 447; mailbox, 231; Ping-Pong net, 321; railroad crossing signal, 115; rocking chair, 208; snap fastener, 234; tanker, 141; tatting shuttle, 386; toilet, 275; typewriter guide, 161; wind turbine, 390
postage due notice, envelope, 159
post cap, railroad crossing signal, 115
poster arm, gas pump, 112
poster frame, garbage truck, 127
posterior chamber, eye, 30
posterior tibial nerve, human, 29
post footing, house, 60
posthole, fence, 67
post lamp, house, 63
postmark, envelope, 159
post-mounted arm, dental unit, 454
post office, Capitol, 74; supermarket, 102
post position: flat racing, 336; jai alai player, 314
postscript, letter, 159
pot, 373; combat soldier's helmet, 497; kitchen, 257; percolator, 252; tea set, 245
potato, 54; masher, 259; peeler, 261
pot fork, 259
pot holder, house painting, 425
potter's wheel, 373
pouch: athletic supporter, 194; combat soldier's uniform, 497; package, 268, 269; police gun belt, 498; tobacco, 259; ultimate beast, 48

pouf, footstool, 235
poult, turkey, 35
poultry, 35, 263
pound, symbol, 511
pound button, telephone, 180
pound lock, 99
pouring lip, blender, 254
pour spout, package, 268
powder: fortification, 82; makeup, 216, 217
powdered emery, nail file, 215
powder eye shadow, 217
power, steam engine, 405
powerboat, 138-139
power bore bit, drill, 418
power button: remote control unit, 184; tape recorder, 177; VCR, 184
power cable, police car, 122
power control: sonar, 444; space shuttle, 153
power cord: air conditioner, 402; camper, 130; curling iron, 214; lamp, 238; tape recorder, 177
power display, portable radio/cassette player, 182
power drill, 419
power feed, track lighting, 239
power handle, ear scope, 448
power head, chain saw, 431
powerhouse: dam, 100; prison, 76
power indicator, CB radio, 183
power key, television, 185
power knob, phonograph receiver, 179
power lawn mower, 429
power light, dot matrix printer, 163
power line, overhead, 396
power network, 396
power on indicator, phonograph turntable, 178
power output meter, phonograph receiver, 179
power pedal, surgical table, 450
power saw, 417
power station, dam, 100
power status, space shuttle, 153
power steering, automobile engine, 111
power supply module, cash register, 440
power switch: fax machine, 164; laser printer, 163; radar, 444
power takeoff, tractor, 434
power terminal, electrical wall switch, 344
power train, automobile, 108
power twister, body building, 344
power window control, car, 110
power-zoom control, camera, 174
prayer book, Jewish, 486
prayer hall, mosque, 70-71
prayer shawl, Jewish, 486
prayer vestment, Jewish, 486
pre-amp, phonograph, 179
preamplifier, guitar, 363
precautionary statement, label, 268
precinct number, police uniform, 498
precious miter, cardinal, 487
precipitation gauge, weather station, 18
precision approach marking, runway, 94
precision attachment, denture, 453
prediction, weather map, 19
prefix letter, paper money, 225

preheater hose, automobile engine, 111
prehensile lobe, ultimate beast, 49
preliminaries, book, 167
premolar, 456
preparation utensils, cooking, 259
prepared foods, 263
prepercle, fish, 45
pre-prepared food, supermarket, 102
pre-race betting odds, flat racing entry, 336
presbytery, church, 87
prescription, 451
prescription, symbol, 510
prescription number, prescription, 451
presentation mode selector, sonar, 444
preset, organ, 360
president: fencing match, 315; Senate, 74
President's executive office, White House, 75
President's living quarters, White House, 75
press: curling iron, 21; etching, 377; incandescent bulb, 238; kitchen tool, 261; lithographic, 376; printing, 166; universal gym, 344
presser, pipe tool, 229
presser foot, sewing machine, 278
presser plate, sponge mop, 282
pressure, weather map, 19
pressure altimeter, pilot's instrument panel, 481
pressure brush, house painting, 425
pressure cooker, 257
pressure cup, citrus juicer, 255
pressure cuff, blood pressure gauge, 449
pressure dial, sewing machine presser foot, 278
pressure gauge: fire extinguisher, 284; furnace, 400; gas laser, 395; skin diving, 331; steam engine, 405
pressure hull, submarine, 479
pressure indicator, pilot's instrument panel, 481
pressure pad, cassette tape, 177
pressure plate: key punch, 430; land mine, 473
pressure ratio gauge, 747 cockpit, 150
pressure regulator: pressure cooker, 257; steam engine, 405; water heater, 401
pressure relief valve: tanker, 140, 141; water heater, 401
pressure screw, etching press, 377
pressure sensor, weather station, 18
pressurized helmet, spacesuit, 155
pressurizer, nuclear reactor, 392
pre-starting light, drag racing, 339
preview, magazine, 169
price: book, 167; gas pump, 112; magazine, 169; newspaper, 168; ticket, 349
priced at, symbol, 511
price scanner, checkout counter, 103
price spot, label, 269
pricket, candlestick, 237
primary, bird, 39

primary cable, overhead power line, 396
primary cell: battery, 397; electric meter, 399
primary combination dial, vault, 457
primary combustion chamber, woodburning stove, 404
primary mirror, laser, 395
primary root, 51
primary selector control, sealed voting booth, 437
prime, grammatical symbol, 513
prime meridian, 5
primer: cartridge, 470; hand grenade, 473; painting, 370; rocket, 383
primer control, mower, 429
prime ribs, beef, 32
Prince of Wales handle, umbrella, 230
princess waistline, bridal gown, 488
principal doorway, church, 87
principal rafter, house, 61
principal street, city plan, 20
print, silk screen, 375
print band, high-speed printer, 439
printed image, 166
printed impression, 166
printer: cash register, 440; computer, 163
print head, high-speed printer, 439
printing: incised, 377; planographic, 376; processes, 166; silk screen, 273; woodcut, 374
printing surface: lithographic press, 376; type, 166
printmaking, 377; silk screen, 375
print-out bin, high-speed printer, 439
print sample: dot matrix printer, 163; laser printer, 163
print style control, dot matrix printer, 163
prison, 76
privacy curtain, electronic voting system, 437
probable morning line, flat racing, 336
probe jack, volt-ohm meter, 423
proboscis: mosquito, 41; ultimate beast, 49
proceed signal, traffic light, 113
produce department, supermarket, 103
product, coupon, 103
product label, 268
product number, pencil, 158
professional activities, résumé, 160
profile, shoreline, 14, 15
program, personal computer, 162
program information display, personal computer, 162
programmed flash, Polaroid, 173
program number, flat racing entry, 336
program reset button, camera, 172
prohibit movement sign, road, 505
projectile: cannon, 467; mortar, 472
projection, map, 20, 21
projection speed selector, movie projector, 175

project name, house blueprint, 62
projector, 175
prominence, solar, 2-3
promotional label, 268
prong: electric plug, 398; fork, 244, 259; man's belt, 190; nail clippers, 215; ring, 219; tuning fork, 367; vacuum tube, 396
pronunciation symbol, 513
proof-of-purchase seal, package, 268
proofreader's marks, 514
prop: grand piano, 361; stage, 350
propane gas, camper, 130
propane plumber's torch, 422
propellant, rocket, 383
propeller: destroyer, 476; hovercraft, 145; outboard engine, 137; single engine airplane, 147; submarine, 479; turboprop jet engine, 407
property, stage, 350
proposed road, road map, 20
proposition area, craps table, 347
prop root, corn, 58
prop stick, grand piano, 361
proscenium arch, stage, 350, 351
prosecutor's table, courtroom, 89
pro-style hair dryer, 212
protection pad, parallel bars, 306
protective cap, razor, 210
protective case, blood pressure gauge, 449
protective chain cover, swing, 287
protective clothing, armor, 465
protective counter, sealed voting booth, 437
protective cup: athletic supporter, 194; baseball catcher, 290; boxing, 309
protective glass, ice hockey rink, 295
protective padding, ski clothes, 326
protective shoulder, wristwatch, 220
protective sleeve, overhead power line, 396
protector: banjo, 362; baseball catcher, 290; ice hockey player, 294, 295; tow truck bed, 126; waterskiing towline, 329
proton, 394
proton-proton collision, 394
protruding upper face, zipper, 209
proximal transverse, human hand, 31
pubes, human, 25
pubis: allosaurus, 43; human, 26; stegosaurus, 43
public address switch, CB radio, 183
publications, résumé, 160
public counter, sealed voting booth, 437
public sign, 506
publisher, book, 167
puck: computer workstation, 438; craps table, 347; ice hockey, 294, 295
pudding fender, tugboat, 144
p'u fang, Manchu court dress, 491
puff, beauty product, 217
puff sleeve, queen's regalia, 484

p'u-fu, Manchu court dress, 491
pull: bureau, 272; dressing table, 272; sideboard, 243; traverse rod, 240; window shade, 240, 241
pull bail, screen, 175
pulley, 461; automobile engine, 111; belt sander, 421; block and tackle, 461; stage, 350; tow truck, 126; universal gym, 344; venetian blind, 241
pulley block, 461
pulley chain, castle portcullis, 81
pulley rope, ballista, 467
pulley safety guard, drill press, 419
pullover: hurdle, 304; sweater, 199, 327
pull-pin, fire extinguisher, 284
pullquote, magazine, 170
pull ring: hand grenade, 473; zipper slide, 209
pull strap, boot, 206
pull tab: package, 268; zipper, 209
pulmonary artery, human, 28
pulmonary vein, human, 28
pulp, fruit, 55, 255
pulpit: church, 87; sailboat, 134; synagogue, 88
pulsar, 3
pulse generation, pacemaker, 452
pulse point, and perfume, 217
pump: automobile engine, 111; bicycle, 128; blood pressure gauge, 449; dishwasher, 250; fireboat, 144; gas, 112; nuclear reactor, 392; paint spray gun, 425; paramedic equipment, 123; percolator brewing basket, 252; pilot's instrument panel, 481; rocket, 407; solar heating system, 391; woman's shoe, 205, 488
pumper, fire engine, 125
pumpkin, silo, 104
pump plunger handle, camp stove, 342
pump valve, lantern, 342
puncheon, 267
punch hole, man's belt, 190
punch line, comic strip, 381
punctuation, grammatical symbol, 513
punt: bottle, 267; fireboat, 144
punta, jai alai cesta, 314
pupa, insect, 41
pupil, eye, 30
pup tent, 342
purfling, violin, 355
purge valve, skin diving face mask, 331
purl, knitting, 386
purlicue, human hand, 31
purlin, house, 61
purl stitch, knitting, 386
purse, 222; miser, 492
push arm, bulldozer, 435
push axle tire, bus, 118
pushboat, 144
pushbutton: ballpoint pen, 158; drill press, 419; metal detector, 445; screen, 175; telephone, 180
pusher: food processor, 254; nail clippers, 215
pusher tug, 144
push knob, citrus juicer, 25
push-pin, wristwatch, 220
pushpit, sailboat, 134
push plate, tow truck bed, 126
push rim, wheelchair, 432
putter, golf club, 311

putting green, 311
puzzle solution, magazine, 171
pylon: helicopter, 146; hovercraft, 145; jumbo jet, 149
pyramid, 71
pyramidion, obelisk, 71
pyrometric cones, potting, 373

Q

Q: braille, 512; sign language, 512
quad, magazine column, 171
quadrant, 137
quadrant number, paper money, 224
quadredundant computer system, space shuttle, 153
quadrilateral structure, pyramid, 70
quality classification, wine label, 267
quality control line, wine label, 267
quantity, prescription, 451
quantity indicator, pilot's instrument panel, 481
quark, 3, 394
quarrel, crossbow, 466
quarter: boat, 206; horse's hoof, 38; man's shoe, 204
quarterdeck, passenger ship, 143
quarter glass, automobile, 107
quarter hoop, barrel, 267
quarter-inch mark, tape measure, 424
quartermaster, frontier fort, 82
quarter-mile pole, harness racetrack, 337
quarter moon, 4
quarter note, music, 352
quarter panel, automobile, 106, 107
quarter rest, music, 353
quarters: frontier fort, 82; oil drilling platform, 101; passenger ship, 142; tugboat, 144; White House, 75
quarter shield, coat of arms, 503
quasar, 3
quasihemidemisemiquaver, music, 352
quatrefoil, church, 86
quaver, music, 352
queen: chess, 345; playing cards, 348; royal regalia, 484
queen post, house, 61
queenside men, chess, 345
query author, proofreader's mark, 514
question index column, voting booth, 437
question mark: grammatical symbol, 513; proofreader's mark, 514
quiche, 263
quick claw, lobster, 47
quick match, rocket, 383
quick-release hook, parachute, 333
quiet button, dot matrix printer, 163
quill: bird feather, 39; brace, 418; pen, 158; ultimate beast, 48
quillon: knife, 463; sword hilt, 463
quilt, 270, 271
quilting, sleeping bag, 343
quimp, cartoon, 381
quiver, arrow, 466
quoin: brick wall, 69; masonry gate post, 67
quotation mark, 513

R

R: braille, 512; sign language, 512
rabbi, 486
rabbit ear, ultimate beast, 49
rabillo, jai alai cesta, 314
race: hand loom, 387; swimming, 316; track and field, 300
race track: Grand Prix, 338; harness, 337
Rachel, playing card queen, 348
rachis: bird feather, 39; fern, 57
racing: drag, 339; flat, 336; Grand Prix, 338; harness, 337; starting block, 304
racing colors, flat racing entry, 336
racing flat, 302
racing handlebar, bicycle, 128
racing slick, 338, 339
rack: automobile, 109; bathtub, 274; bicycle, 128; billiards, 320; blackjack, 320; bowling lane, 317; bus, 118; camper, 130; desk, 276; dishwasher, 250; kitchen tool, 260; lamb, 33; oil drilling platform, 101; outboard engine, 137; space shuttle, 153; stagecoach, 131; tank, 474; toaster, 253; wok, 257
racket: badminton, 319; Ping-Pong, 321; squash, 313; tennis, 312
radar, 444; aircraft carrier, 478; buoy, 132; destroyer, 477; fireboat, 144; hovercraft, 145; jumbo jet, 148; pilot's instrument panel, 481; police car, 122; 747 cockpit, 150; space shuttle, 153; submarine, 479; tanker, 141; tugboat, 144
radial: lumber, 68; scallop shell, 47; spider web, 40
radial artery, human, 28
radial nerve, human, 29
radiation belt, Milky Way, 3
radiator, 400; automobile, 108; bulldozer, 435; racing car, 338; solar power system, 391
radicle, root system, 51
radii, spider web, 40
radio: aircraft carrier, 478; ambulance, 123; Citizens Band, 183; clock, 233; hovercraft, 145; pilot's instrument panel, 481; police car, 122; 747 cockpit, 150; submarine, 479
radioactive-waste storage tank, nuclear reactor, 392
radio display, Walkman, 182
radio frequency acceleration system, super collider, 394
radio mast, skyscraper, 77
radiometer, satellite, 186
radio operator, 183
radio/tape mode switch, Walkman, 182
radio-translucent pad, surgical table, 450
radio tuning dial, phonograph receiver, 179
radio tuning wheel: portable radio/cassette player, 182; Walkman, 182
radio wave, 2-3
radius, human, 26
radome, jet fighter, 480
raft: aircraft carrier, 478; jumbo jet, 148; tugboat, 144
rafter: house, 61; lumber, 68

ragged-right type, magazine, 170
raglan sleeve: parka, 201; trench coat, 200
rail: backgammon board, 345; backyard equipment, 287; balustrade, 73; bathtub, 274; bed, 270; bridge, 97; bureau, 272; child's wagon, 287; church, 87; craps table, 347; door, 64; drag racing, 339; escalator, 79; fence, 67; flat racing, 336; harness racetrack, 337; ladder, 425; passenger ship, 142, 361; playpen, 286; pool table, 320; powerboat, 138, 139; railroad, 115; razor blade injector, 210; rocking chair, 134; sailboat, 134; skin diving fin, 331; sled, 328; slide, 287; snowmobile, 130; sofa, 236; sponge mop, 282; stage, 350; staircase, 66; stapler, 277; starting block, 304; subway, 119; surfboard, 330; surgical table, 450; tanker, 141; truck, 120, 121; venetian blind, 241; wheelchair, 452; window, 65
railing: highway, 114; tunnel, 98
railroad, 116-117
railroad crossing, 115; road sign, 504
railroad track, 115
railroad yard, 96
rail transportation, public sign, 506
rain, 17, 19
rain boot, 207
rain cap, bulldozer, 435
rain check, ticket, 349
raincoat, 200
rain gauge, weather station, 18
rain poncho, infantryman's uniform, 497
rain-snow clutter control, radar, 444
rake, 427
RAM, computer, 438
ram, 33; iceberg, 11; zodiac, 509
ram control, garbage truck, 127
ramjet, 407
rammer, cannon, 467
ramp: airport, 94; highway cloverleaf, 114; hovercraft, 145; theatre stage, 351
rampart: castle, 80, 81; fort, 83
ranching gear, 432
rand: boot, 206; mountain climbing, 334
random access memory, computer, 438
range: kitchen, 237; mountain, 7, 8; thematic map, 21
range control: police car, 122; radar, 444; sonar, 444
range indicator, movie camera, 174
rank: chessboard, 345; military uniform, 496, 497
rank badge, Manchu court dress, 491
rapid-response thermometer, 258
rapids, river, 13
rapid transit system, 119
rasp, 427
ratcatcher, passenger ship, 142
ratchet: brace, 418; chaise lounge, 288; screwdriver, 413
ratchet angle, incline track, 92
ratchet buckle, man's belt, 190

ratchet handle, socket wrench, 415
ratchet wheel, hand loom, 387
rate control, guitar amplifier, 363
rate of flow indicator, pilot's instrument panel, 481
rate plate, parking meter, 113
rating, clock, 233
ratio: political map, 21; symbol, 511
rattle, snake, 43
rattlesnake, 42-43
ravine, mountain, 8
raw ingredients, food, 262
ray: fish, 45; medal, 501; Milky Way, 3
razor, 210
razor blade, 210
RCS nozzle, lunar lander, 154
reaction, nuclear power, 392
reaction control system (RCS) thruster assembly, lunar lander, 154
reactor, nuclear, 392
reader service coupon, magazine, 171
reader surname, magazine mailing label, 169
reading clerk, House of Representatives, 74
reading lens, eyeglasses, 221
reading light, bus, 118
read only memory, computer, 438
readout, dental unit, 454
readout dash, newspaper, 168
read-write head, computer, 439
read-write window, diskette, 162
read-write window & shutter, diskette, 162
reamer: citrus juicer, 255; drill, 418; plumbing, 422
reaper, 434
rear anchor, diving board, 316
rear apron, necktie, 193
rear axle: automobile, 109; stroller, 286; tractor, 434; truck, 120; wagon, 287
rear bead, shotgun, 469
rear beam, laboratory scale, 447
rear bearing, fishing reel, 340
rear binding heel piece, slalom water ski, 329
rear boot, stagecoach, 131
rear brake, bicycle, 128
rear bumper, automobile, 107
rear cinch, saddle, 315
rear coil spring, automobile, 109
rear cover, dot matrix printer, 163
rear deflector, mower, 429
rear derailleur, bicycle, 128
rear door, automobile, 107
rear drive sprocket, motorcycle, 129
rear drop-out, bicycle, 128
rear drum brake, motorcycle, 129
rear end, automobile, 109
rear fender, motorcycle, 129
rear foot, stapler, 277
rear frame, wheelbarrow, 430
rear hood, fishing rod, 340
rear housing, razor, 210
rear jockey, saddle, 335
rear leg, bee, 41
rear lens cap, zoom lens, 172
rear light, bulldozer, 435
rear limit line, fencing strip, 315
rear post, hand loom, 387
rear quarter panel, automobile, 107

rear pulley, belt sander, 421
rear push plate, tow truck bed, 126
rear rigging ring, saddle, 335
rear section, bicycle, 128
rear shock absorber: automobile, 109; motorcycle, 129
rear sight, weapon, 469, 470, 471
rear skirt, missile, 482
rear spikers' line, volleyball court, 319
rear stretcher, rocking chair, 234
rear tire, bus, 118
rear wing, racing car, 338
rear toe binder, slalom water ski, 329
rearview mirror: bus, 118; car, 110; locomotive, 117; pilot's instrument panel, 481; truck, 120
rear wheel, tow truck, 126
rear window, automobile, 107
rear windshield, automobile, 107
rebote, jai alai cancha, 314
rebound tumbling, trampoline, 308
receipt: cash register, 440; toll booth, 114
received document exit, fax machine, 164
received document slot, fax machine, 164
receiver: automatic weapon, 470, 471; phonograph, 179; shotgun, 468; telephone, 180; television, 185
receiving track, railroad yard, 96
recent transactions, monthly statement, 227
receptacle: electrical, 398; flower, 53; pencil sharpener, 277; strawberry, 55
reception center, prison, 76
reception room, White House, 75
receptor, nervous system, 29
recessed back-up light, tow truck bed, 126
recessed door, safe, 457
recessed taillight, tow truck bed, 126
rechargeable battery pack, tape recorder, 177
rechargeable power handle, ear scope, 448
recirculating valve, automobile engine, 111
recliner, 235
recliner stand, child's car seat, 286
reclining seat, bus, 118
recoil pad, rifle, 468
recoil spring guide, automatic pistol, 470
recoil starter plate, internal combustion engine, 406
record: phonograph, 178
record button: remote control unit, 184; tape recorder, 177
recorder: tape, 177; weather station, 18
recording data control, video camera, 184
recording lever, movie projector, 175
recording phonograph, 178
red light, ice hockey, 294
red line: ice hockey, 295; squash, 313
record meter, tape recorder, 177
record size selector, phonograph turntable, 178

recreational vehicle, 109, 130
recreation area, road map, 20
recreation yard, prison, 76
rectangle, basketball backstop, 296
rectangular lens, eyeglasses, 221
rectangular spreader, 430
recto, book page, 167
rectory, 86
rectus, human, 26
recurve, bow, 466
red foul light, drag racing, 339
red light, traffic light, 113
red lighting, drag racing, 339
red line, squash court, 313
red marker light, truck van, 121
Red Room, White House, 75
red slot, roulette, 376
red supergiant star, 2
reduction, theodolite, 436
red wine glass, 244
reed: bagpipe, 365; clarinet, 357; English horn, 357; hand loom, 387; oboe, 356
reeding, coin, 225
reed selector switch, accordion, 366
reed tube opening, pitch pipe, 367
reef, coral, 46
reef cringle, mainsail, 136
reefer: refrigerator ship, 140; truck, 120
reef point, mainsail, 136
reel: fencing strip, 315; fireboat, 144; fishing, 340; movie camera, 174; movie projector, 175; mower, 429; tape measure, 424; tape recorder, 177; thread, 384
reel lawn mower, 429
reel seat, fishing rod, 340
referee, polo, 299
referee's crease, ice hockey rink, 295
reference beam, holography, 395
reference key, political map, 20
reference matter, book, 167
references, résumé, 160
reference slide, desk, 276
reference table, synthesizer, 363
refill data, prescription, 451
reflected-light window, light meter, 176
reflecting surface, solar power system, 391
reflecting telescope, 443
reflective identification, buoy, 132
reflective stripe, fireman's coat, 500
reflector: bicycle, 128; bus, 118; lamp, 239; mechanical sweeper, 127; railroad crossing signal, 115; truck van, 121
reflector satellite, 186
refracting telescope, 443
refrigeration van, truck, 120, 121
refrigerator, 249
refrigerator ship, 140
regalia, royal, 485
regional code, magazine mailing label, 169
regional name, political map, 20
regional temperature prediction, weather map, 19
region of interaction, transistor chip, 396
register, electric meter, 399

register buttons, accordion, 366
registered, symbol, 511
registered architect seal, house blueprint, 62
register mark, label, 268
registration guide, silk screen, 375
registration number, hot air balloon, 332
registration number, single engine airplane, 147
registry guide, silk screen, 375
regular section, magazine, 169
regulator: dental, 455; gas pump automatic nozzle, 112; laboratory burner, 447; pressure cooker, 257; skin diving, 331
regulatory sign, road, 505
rehabilitation, prison, 76
rehearsal marking, music, 352
rein, horseracing, 336, 337
reinforce, cannon barrel, 467
reinforced shoulder, waterskiing vest, 329
reinforced toe, panty hose, 195
reinforce ring, cannon barrel, 467
rein guide, Hansom cab, 131
relative bearing, radar, 444
relay race, track and field, 300
relay unit, lunar rover, 155
release: backpack, 343; ballista, 467; can opener, 251; chain saw, 431; guillotine, 462; hand loom, 387; jet fighter, 480; pistol, 470; pliers, 414; rifle, 468; sextant, 137; ski binding, 326; steam engine, 405; typewriter, 161
relief: printing, 166; stone sculpture, 372
relief map, 21
relief shading key, globe, 1
relief valve: nuclear reactor, 392; tanker, 140, 141; water heater, 401
reliever, saber saw, 417
religious symbol, 508
religious vestment, 487
relish, and frankfurter, 265
remaining-teeth mold, denture, 453
remnants of universal veil, mushroom, 57
remote control: slide projector, 175; television, 185
remote control unit, VCR, 184
remote filming jack, movie camera, 174
remote handset, cordless phone, 180
remote-operated block valve, nuclear reactor, 392
rendezvous radar antenna, lunar lander, 154
rendition, work of art, 368
repeat button: compact disc player, 178; tape recorder, 177
repeat control, phonograph turntable, 178
repeat sign, music, 352
replaceable collar, maid's uniform, 489
reporter, Congress, 74
representative fraction, political map, 21
reptiles, 42-43
Republican, Congress, 74
rerebrace, armor, 465
rescue, hoist, helicopter, 146
rescue platform, helicopter, 146
reservoir: blood pressure gauge, 449; dam, 100; iron,

279; locomotive, 116; pen, 158
reset: gas pump, 112; stopwatch, 304; table saw, 417; tape recorder, 177; water heater, 401
residence number, mailbox, 231
resin, dental, 453, 455
resist, silk screen, 375
resonance, stringed instruments, 355
resonance box, tuning fork, 367
resonator: banjo, 362; laser, 395; sitar, 362
respiratory system, human, 27
rest: bazooka, 472; child's glider, 287; corkscrew, 251; eye scope, 499; hypodermic syringe, 451; lantern, 342; music notation, 352, 353; music stand, 367
rest area, highway, 114
restaurant: Capitol, 74; passenger ship, 143; public sign, 506
restoration, dental, 455
restraining circle, basketball court, 296
restraint layer, spacesuit, 155
résumé, 160
resuscitator, ambulance, 123
retainer: air conditioner, 402; chain lock, 458; phonograph headphone, 179; saw, 417
retaining wall fence, 67
retarder, railroad yard, 96
retention device, ski, 326
reticulum, animal cell, 23
retina, eye, 30
retinal blood vessel, eye, 30
retractable blade guard, circular saw, 417
retractable footrest, medical examination table, 450
retractable paper support, typewriter, 161
retractable step, medical examination table, 450
retracting ball, pen, 158
retreat zone, fencing strip, 315
retrieving cable, gas pump, 112
retsüah, tefillin, 486
return: bowling lane, 317; traverse rod, 240
return address, envelope, 159
return duct, heat exchanger, 403
return end, cupboard, 243
return panel, elevator car, 78
return payment portion, monthly statement, 227
return pipe: furnace, 400; solar heating system, 391
return section, desk, 276
return top, desk, 276
reverse: locomotive, 116; money, 225; sewing machine, 278; slide projector, 175
reverse light, automobile, 107
reversible cord assembly, iron, 279
reversible motor, power drill, 419
revetment, canal lock, 99
review, magazine, 170
review button, tape recorder, 177
Revolutionary War general, costume, 492
revolver, 470, police gun belt, 499
revolver safety catch, jewelry findings, 218

560

revolving nosepiece, microscope, **442**
revolving nut, crossbow, **466**
revolving sprinkler, **428**
rewind button: remote control unit, **184**; tape recorder, **177**; video-still camera, **173**; Walkman, **182**
rewind starter, outboard engine, **137**
rewind switch, tape measure, **424**
rheostat control, microscope, **442**
rhinoceros horn, ultimate beast, **49**
rhizome, grass, **58**
rhumb line, globe, **5**
rhythm pick-up, guitar, **363**
riata, **432**
rib: basket, **266**; beef, **32**; cactus, **56**; celery, **262**; dog, **36**; hollow wall fastener, **411**; horse, **38**; human, **26**; jai alai cesta, **314**; laboratory burner, **447**; lamb, **33**; lampshade, **238**; mountain, **9**; parachute, **333**; scallop shell, **47**; shield, **464**; shotgun, **469**; skin diving fin, **331**; sock, **207**; sweater, **199**; umbrella, **230**; violin, **355**
ribbon: ballet toeshoe, **386**; bonnet, **203**; hair ornament, **214**; military uniform, **496**
ribbon cartridge typewriter, **161**
rib cage, human, **24**
ribosome, animal cell, **23**
rib pad, football uniform, **292**
ricasso: knife, **463**; sword hilt, **463**
rider, dress, **198**
ridge: barn, **104**; corrugated fastener, **410**; embroidery ring, **385**; file, **420**; mountain, **8, 9**
ridgeboard, house, **61**
ridgeline, house, **63**
ridgepole, house, **61**; tent, **342**
riding boot, polo, **299**
riding breeches, drum major, **495**
riding compartment, pumper, **125**
riding equipment, **335**
riding glove, polo, **299**
riding instructions, escalator, **79**
rifle, **468-469**; automatic, **471**
rifle grenade, **473**
rifle, gun, **470**
rig, **120**; oil drilling, **101**; wrecker, **126**
rigging: circus, **90**; hang glider, **333**; sailboat, **134**
rigging ring, saddle, **335**
right atrium, heart, **28**
right bank, river, **13**
right-channel volume unit meter, tape recorder, **177**
right engine fuel shutoff handle, pilot's instrument panel, **481**
right field, baseball, **291**
right-handed strike pocket, bowling, **317**
right-hand page, book, **167**
right-hand steering lever, bulldozer, **435**
right image, picture-in-picture viewing, **185**
right of way, railroad, **115**
right service court: badminton, **319**; handball, **313**
right stereo speaker: portable

radio/cassette player, **182**; television, **185**
right ventricle, heart, **28**
right wing, easel, **370**
rigid airships, **156**
rigid table, dull press, **419**
rim: basket, **266**; basketball backstop, **296**; bicycle wheel, **128**; bugle, **359**; button, **209**; cartridge, **470**; coconut, **262**; discus, **303**; Ferris wheel, **93**; merry-go-round, **93**; monocle, **221**; pail, **284**; pot, **373**; racing car, **338, 339**; royal crown, **485**; saucepan, **359**; sink, **247**; spool, **384**; stagecoach wheel, **131**; stemware, **244**; thimble, **384**; tire, **105**; toilet, **275**; trombone, **358**; wheelchair, **452**
rimmon, Torah, **486**
rimstone, cave, **11**
rind: cheese, **263**; orange, **55**
ring: anchor, **132**; basketball backstop, **296**; bayonet, **463**; bicycle, **128**; blender, **254**; boxing, **309**; brace, **418**; cannon barrel, **467**; can opener, **251**; cardinal, **487**; cinch fastener, **208**; circus, **90, 91**; clock, **233**; dart board, **322**; domed structure, **85**; embroidery, **385**; fire engine, **124, 125**; fishing rod, **340, 341**; grenade, **473**; hair dryer, **212**; hot air balloon, **332**; jewelry, **219**; kite, **323**; lampshade, **238**; light meter, **176**; lumber, **68**; missile, **482**; mitten, **200**; mushroom, **57**; projector, **175**; radar, **444**; rifle, **469, 471**; rowboat, **133**; saddle, **335**; Saturn, **3**; screwdriver, **413**; shotgun barrel, **469**; skillet, **359**; ski pole, **326**; stationary rings, **307**; stove, **342**; sword hilt, **463**; tent, **342**; tree, **50**; trumpet, **359**; vault, **457**; window shade pull, **241**
ring contact, incandescent bulb, **247**
ring finger, human hand, **31**
ring handle, scissors, **384**
ring key, clarinet, **356**
ringlet, woman's hair, **213**
ringmaster, circus, **90**
ring molding, minaret, **70**
Ring of the Fisherman, Pope, **487**
ringside, boxing, **309**
ring stand, laboratory, **447**
rink, ice hockey, **295**
riot gun, police car, **122**
riot helmet, police, **498**
rip cord, parachute, **333**
rip fence, saw, **417**
rip guide, saw, **417**
rip panel, hot air balloon, **332**
rip teeth, saw, **417**
ripper claw, lobster, **47**
ripping panel, hot air balloon, **332**
ripsaw, **416**
rise: arch, **72**; continental, **15**
riser: orchestra, **354**; parachute, **333**; staircase, **66**; trophy, **289**
riser pad, skateboard, **324**
ritard, music notation, **352**
ritual item, Jewish, **486**
river, **7, 13**; and underwater tunnel, **98**
rivet: attaché case, **285**; cheese plane, **256**; eyeglasses, **221**; jeans, **191**; knife, **256**; latch

needle, **386**; laboratory clamp, **446**; nail clippers, **215**; pliers, **414**; plug fuse, **399**; sandal, **206**; sharpening steel, **256**
rivière, jewelry, **219**
rivulet, **13**
riwaq, mosque, **70**
roach, Indian, **490**
road: airport, **94**; highway, **114**; topographic map, **22**
roadbed: highway, **114**; railroad, **115**
road light, camper, **130**
road map, **20**
road racing, **338**
roadside sidewall, truck, **121**
road sign, **504-505**
road under construction, map, **20**
roadway: bridge, **97**; dam, **100**; highway, **114**; railroad, **115**; tunnel, **98**
road wheel: roller coaster, **92**; tank, **474**
roaring forties, wind, **6**
robe: judge, **89**; Manchu court dress, **491**; wizard, **492**
robe of state, king's regalia, **484**
rochet, bishop, **487**
rock: brazier, **288**; nautical chart, **22**
rocker: rocking chair, **234**; hitch and harrow, **434**; waterski, **329**
rocker panel, automobile, **106, 109**
rocket, **383, 407**; bazooka, **472**
rocket launcher, **472**
rocket motor nozzle, satellite, **186**
rockfill section, dam, **100**
rocking chair, **234**
rod: abacus, **441**; basket, **266**; belt buckle, **190**; CB radio antenna, **183**; child's wagon, **287**; coffee maker, **252**; drum, **364**; fishing, **340-341**; flute, **356**; garbage disposal, **247**; grandfather clock, **233**; hair styling, **214**; Hansom cab, **131**; incandescent bulb, **238**; launch pad, **152**; locomotive, **116**; machine gun, **471**; merry-go-round, **93**; metal detector, **445**; mower, **429**; music stand, **367**; nuclear reactor, **392**; powerboat, **139**; royal scepter, **485**; shower, **274**; stagecoach, **131**; steam engine, **405**; traverse, **240**; umbrella, **230**; window shutter, **277**; workbench, **408**
Rogallo kite, **323**
roll: ambulance, **123**; football uniform, **292**; frankfurter, **265**; hand loom, **387**; saddle, **335**; sandwich, **263**
roll bag, racing car, **338**
roll cage, drag racer, **339**
roll-collar shirt, chauffeur, **489**
rolled edge, necktie, **192**
rolled shoulder, shovel, **427**
roller: ballista, **467**; bulldozer, **435**; cassette tape, **177**; chain, **461**; etching press, **377**; fishing reel, **340**; hair, **214**; hitch and harrow, **434**; offset-lithography, **166**; painting, **425**; tank, **474**; tape recorder, **177**; typewriter, **161**; window shade, **241**; roller, woodcut printing, **374**
roller-coaster, **92**

roller guide shoe, elevator shaft, **78**
roller link plate, chain, **461**
roller foot, sewing machine, **278**
roller skate, **324**
roller support, saw, **417**
rolling pin, **259**
rolling stock, railroad, **96, 116-117**
roll on-roll off ship, **140**
roll pin, pliers, **414**
roll top, rocking chair, **234**
rolltop desk, **276**
roll-up blind, window, **241**
ROM, computer, **438**
Roman collar, bishop, **487**
roman type, **165**; proofreader's mark, **514**
rondel, armor, **465**
rood screen, church, **87**
roof: automobile, **106, 107, 109**; bus, **118**; church, **86**; house, **60, 61, 62, 63**; mountain, **8**; pagoda, **71**; skyscraper, **77**
roof air conditioner, camper, **130**
roofing shingle, **68**
roof light, subway, **119**
roof seam, tent, **342**
rook, chess, **345**
rook pawn, chess, **345**
room: cave, **11**; house blueprint, **62**; launch pad, **152**; White House, **75**
rooster, **35**
root: carrot, **54**; corn, **58**; grass, **58**; onion, **262**; outboard engine, **137**; screw, **410**; tertiary, **51**; tooth, **456**; tree, **50**
rope: **132**; ballista, **467**; block and tackle, **461**; boxing ring, **309**; bridge, **97**; circus tent, **91**; elevator shaft, **78**; military uniform, **496**; grandfather clock, **233**; hot air balloon, **332**; jump rope, **344**; mountain climbing, **334**; outboard engine, **137**; ranching gear, **432**; roller coaster, **92**; tent, **342**; tepee, **84**; toboggan, **328**; waterskiing towline, **329**
rope hole, sled, **328**
rope ladder, circus aerialist, **90**
rope strap, saddle, **335**
roping, hammock, **288**
Rose Room, White House, **75**
rosette: Beefeater, **483**; cupboard, **243**; guitar, **362**; queen's regalia, **484**; royal crown, **485**; sofa, **236**
rosette cap, traffic light, **113**
rose window, church, **86**
rotary beater, kitchen, **258**
rotary dial, telephone, **180**
rotary fairing, helicopter, **146**
rotary fan, **402**
rotary lawn mower, **429**
rotary press, printing, **166**
rotary spreader, **430**
rotating beacon: police car, **122**; single engine airplane, **147**
rotating frame, merry-go-round, **93**
rotating handle, food mill, **260**
rotating mast, windsurfer, **330**
rotating service structure, launch pad, **152**
rotational hand controller, space shuttle, **153**
rotational motion, steam engine, **405**
rotogravure, printing, **166**
rotor: automobile disc brake,

108; helicopter, 146; windmill, 390; wind turbine, 390
rotunda, Capitol, 74
rouge, 216, 217
rough, golf course, 310-311
roughneck, oil drilling, 101
rough sill, house, 61
rouleau, 440
roulette wheel, 346
round: beef, 32; boxing, 309; police ammunition, 498
round-bottom hull, powerboat, 138
round-end chisel, stonecutting, 372
round head, screw, 410
roundhouse, railroad yard, 96
rounding board, merry-go-round, 93
round pin, window shade roller, 241
round shank, screwdriver, 413
round-the-clock, darts, 322
roustabout, circus, 90
route: bus, 118; road map, 20; subway, 119
route sign, road, 505
routing number, check, 226
row, hand knitting, 386
rowboat, 133
rowel, spur, 335
row house, 63
royal regalia, 484-485
rubber: baseball pitcher, 291; shoe accessory, 207
rubber band, dental, 453
rubber blade, silkscreen squeegee, 375
rubber bumper, knee kicker, 246
rubber covering, brayer, 374
rubber face, Ping-Pong racket, 321
rubber foot, food processor, 254
rubber mat, phonograph turntable, 178
rubber plug, sink, 273
rubber-soled shoe, jai alai player, 314
rubber tip, bobby pin, 214
rubbing ink, 376
ruble, symbol, 511
rub rail: powerboat, 138; truck platform, 121
ruching, bonnet, 203
rucksack: backpacking, 343; ski touring, 327
rudder: blimp, 156; destroyer, 476; glider, 147; jumbo jet, 149; sailboat, 134; single engine airplane, 147; space shuttle, 152; submarine, 479
rudder pedal, 747 cockpit, 150
rudimentary root, 51
ruff, Beefeater, 483
ruffled shirt, man's, 488
rug, 246; hairpiece, 211
rule: magazine, 170, 171; measuring, 424
ruler, 424; pocket knife, 426
rumble seat, automobile, 106
rump: beef, 134; bird, 39; cat, 37; dog, 36; horse, 38; pelt, 201; sheep, 33
run: step tread, 66; track and field, 300
run and lock switch, movie camera, 174
rung: ladder, 425; rocking chair, 234
run light, movie camera, 174
runner: grass, 58; ice skates, 325; rug, 246; running shoe, 302; skate, 295; sled, 328; slide rule, 441; umbrella, 230

running board, automobile, 107
running foot: book page, iv; magazine, 171
running knot, gallows, 462
running light: camper, 130; destroyer, 477; fireboat, 144; single engine airplane, 147; tow truck, 126; tugboat, 144
running mold, church, 86
running noose, lasso, 432
running ornament, church, 86
running rigging, sailboat, 134
running shoe, 302
running title, magazine, 170
running track, 300
run number: bus, 118; paper money, 225
runway: airport, 94; bowling lane, 317; javelin throw, 301; pole vault, 305; stage, 351
rupee, symbol, 511
rural mailbox, 231
Russian Cross, symbol, 508
rustproof oil, woodcarving, 372
Rx, prescription symbol, 451

S: braille, 512; sign language, 512
saber saw, 417
sabot, blackjack, 347
sabre, 315
sabre and épée warning line, fencing strip, 315
sac: flower stamen, 53; octopus, 46
sacral hump, frog, 44
sacristy, church, 87
sacrum, human, 26
saddle: bicycle, 128; door, 64; guitar, 362; horse, 335, 336, 337; matchbook, 228; motorcycle, 129; mountain, 8; pipe, 229; polo, 299; pommel horse, 307; screen, 175
saddlebag: 335; motorcycle, 129
saddle blanket, polo, 299
saddle feather, chicken, 35
saddle head, dispenser, 267
saddle plate, iron, 279
safe, 457
safe deposit box, 457
safe side, file, 420
safety: elevator shaft, 78; weapon, 468, 470, 471
safety bar, Ferris wheel, 93
safety belt: car, 110; lunar rover, 155
safety binding, ski, 326
safety cable, elevator, 78
safety cable tension sheave, elevator, 78
safety cage, hammer throw, 301
safety catch, revolver, 218
safety-chain hole, tow truck bed, 126
safety control data, prescription, 451
safety cool tip, curling iron, 214
safety dome, train tank car, 116
safety edge, elevator door, 78
safety guard: drill press, 419; paint spray gun, 425
safety guardrail, slide, 287
safety hasp, 460
safety jacket, waterskiing, 329
safety ladder, Ferris wheel, 93
safety lever: hand grenade, 473; pistol, 470
safety line, inflatable, 133
safety loop, circus aerialist, 90

safety lug, cassette tape, 177
safety matches, 228
safety mirror, mechanical sweeper, 127
safety net: aircraft carrier, 478; circus aerialist, 90
safety observer station, destroyer, 477
safety pad, trampoline, 308
safety padding, football goalpost, 293
safety pin, 208; hand grenade, 473
safety rail: bathtub, 274; bridge, 97; powerboat, 139
safety razor, 300
safety rope, roller coaster, 92
safety shield, child's car seat, 286
safety shut-off, Jacuzzi, 274
safety stripe, fireman's coat, 500
safety trigger, chain saw, 431
safety valve, furnace, 400
safety warning, dental x-ray unit, 454
safety zone, polo grounds, 299
Sagittarius, zodiac, 509
sail, 134, 136; hang glider, 333; submarine, 479; windmill, 390; windsurfer, 330
sailboard, 330
sailboat, 134-135
sailing thwart, rowboat, 133
sailor, uniform, 497
sailplane, 147; submarine, 479
St. Anthony's cross, symbol, 508
salad bowl, 245
salad fork, 244
salad plate, 245
salad shaker, 260
salamander, 44
salient angle. 83
saline, paramedic equipment, 123
saliva ejector, dental unit, 454
sally port, frontier fort, 82
salon, sailboat, 135
salt shaker, 261
salutation, letter, 159
samara, 52
Sam Browne belt, 496
same name differentiation code, magazine mailing label, 169
same scale extension inset, political map, 21
sample bag dispenser, lunar rover, 155
sanctuary: church, 87; mosque, 70-71
sand, hourglass, 233
sandal, 206
sand area, topographic map, 22
sandbag: ambulance, 123; hot air balloon, 332
sandbar: coastline, 14, 15; river, 13
sandbox: backyard, 287; locomotive, 116, 117
sander, 421
sandglass, 233
sandhill, nautical chart, 22
sandpaper, 421
sand shoe, truck van, 121
sand tower, railroad yard, 96
sand trap, golf course, 311
sand wedge, golf club, 310
sandwich, 263
sandwich cookie, 264
sanitary hose: baseball, 290; football uniform, 292
sanitary paper, medical examination table, 450
sanitation vehicle, 127
sanman, 127

sans serif type, 165
sapwood, tree, 50
sari, 491
sarong, 491
sartorius, human, 26
sash: drum major, 495; jai alai player, 314; royal regalia, 484; window, 65
satellite, 3, 186
Saturn, planet, 3
sauce, sundae, 264
saucepan, 257
saucer, 245
sauerkraut, and frankfurter, 265
sauna, passenger ship, 143
saurischian, dinosaur, 43
sausage, pizza, 265
saw, 416, 417; pocket knife, 426
sawbuck, 408
sawhorse, 408
saxophone, 357
S-band antenna, lunar lander, 154
S bend, tuba, 358
scabbard, Revolutionary War general, 492
scaffold, gallows, 462
scaffolding web, spider, 40
scale: bird foot, 39; blood pressure gauge, 449; camera, 174; coffee maker, 252; electronic flash, 176; fish, 45; frontier fort, 82; house blueprint, 62; hypodermic syringe, 451; kitchen, 258; knife, 426, 463; laboratory, 446-447; lettuce, 262; light meter, 176; metronome, 367; nautical chart, 22; pine cone, 52; political map, 21; saw, 417; sewing machine, 278; slide rule, 441; snake, 42; thermometer, 18, 449; typewriter, 161; volt-ohm meter, 423
scallop, 47; bridal gown hem, 488; curtain, 240
scalp, 211; mortise lock, 458
scalper, harness racing pacer, 337
scanner: cash register, 440; fax machine, 164; hovercraft, 145; radar, 444
scapha, outer ear, 30
scaphoid pad, sandal, 206
scapula, human, 26
scapular, bird, 39
scapular region, salamander, 44
scarf, pirate, 492
scarp, fort, 83
scend, wave, 14
scenery, stage, 350
scenic overlook, highway, 114
scent, 217
scepter, royal, 485
school: fish, 45; prison, 76
school crossing, road sign, 505
sciatic nerve, human, 29
scimitar antenna, lunar lander, 154
scintillometer, 445
scissor grip, body building, 344
scissors, 384; pocket knife, 426
sclera, eye, 30
scoop: ice cream cone, 265; kitchen tool, 258, 259; lacrosse stick, 298; pipe tool, 229
scoop stretcher, ambulance, 123
scooter car, amusement park, 92
scooter helmet, police, 499

scope: bazooka, 472; rifle, 469; telescope, 443
scopula, spider, 40
score: matchbook, 228; pulley block, 461
scoreboard, jai alai cancha, 314
score counter, pool table, 320
scorer's box, ice hockey rink, 295
scorer's table: basketball court, 296
scoring diagram, shuffleboard court, 318
scoring lines, golf club, 310
scoring machine, fencing strip, 315
scoring triangle, shuffleboard court, 318
Scorpio, zodiac, 509
scorpion, 48; zodiac, 509
scotch rule, magazine, 170
scotia, column, 73
scraper, lithographic press, 376
scratch line, track and field, 300, 301
screen: case, 175; church, 87; fireplace, 232; internal combustion engine, 406; jai alai cancha, 314; projector, 175; radar, 444; silk, 375; sonar, 444; television, 185; tent, 342
screendoor, 64
screen fence, 67
screen plug, mower, 429
scree slope, mountain, 8
screw, 410; banjo, 362; brayer, 374; cassette tape, 177; clamp, 409; combination square, 424; drill bit, 419; earring, 218; electric plug, 398; embroidery ring, 385; etching press, 377; eyeglasses, 221; faucet, 273; golf club, 310; hitch and harrow, 434; kettledrum, 364; lithographic press, 376; lock, 458; microscope, 442; outboard engine, 137; paramedic equipment, 123; plane, 420; pliers, 414; saw, 417; sewing machine, 278; ski binding, 326; telegraph key, 157; telescope, 443; theodolite, 436; violin, 355; violin bow, 355; vise, 409; volt-ohm meter, 423; woodcarving, 372; wrench, 415
screwback earring findings, 218
screw cap, test tube, 447
screwdriver, 413; pocket knife, 426
screwdriver bit, drill, 418
screw eye, frame, 379
screw hole, hinge, 460
screw nozzle, 428
screw thread, plug fuse, 399
scribed line, scrimshaw, 375
scriber, 375; combination square, 424
scrim, stage, 350
scrimshander, 375
scrimshaw, 375
scrip, collector, 225
Scripture, Torah, 88
scroll: coat of arms, 503; fence, 67; Torah, 88; violin, 355
scrolled arm, sofa, 236
scroll saw, 417
scrubboard, 280
scruff, human, 25
scruple, symbol, 510
scruto, stage, 350
scuba diving, 331

scuff leather, hot air balloon, 332
sculpting tools, 372
scupper: fireboat, 144; tugboat, 144
scythe, 429
sea, 7
seabag, 497
sea clutter control, radar, 444
seafood service section, supermarket, 103
seal: frame, 379; house architect, 62; package, 268-269; paper money, 224; voting booth, 437
sealant strip, roofing shingle, 68
sealed voting booth, 437
sealed vegetable compartment, refrigerator, 249
seam: blouse, 197; boot, 206; can, 267; football, 292; garment, 196; girdle, 195; hot air balloon, 332; inflatable, 133; jacket, 188; mainsail, 136; necktie, 192; sewing pattern, 388; skirt, 197; sock, 207; tennis ball, 312; tent, 342; trousers, 191; and zipper, 209
search coil, metal detector, 445
searchlight: fireboat, 144; tank, 474; tugboat, 144
search loop, metal detector, 445
seasonal current, ocean, 6
seasoning: frankfurter, 265; prepared food, 263
seasoning check, lumber, 68
sea star, 46
seat: ambulance, 123; automobile, 106, 107, 110, 286; backyard glider, 287; bicycle, 128; bumper car, 92; bus, 118; courtroom, 89; electric chair, 462; Ferris wheel, 93; fishing rod, 340; harness racing sulky, 335; inflatable, 133; lounger, 235; lunar rover, 155; motorcycle, 129; pants, 191; rocking chair, 234; rowboat, 133; saddle, 335; 747 cockpit, 150, 151; snowmobile, 130; sofa, 236; space shuttle, 153; stagecoach, 131; stroller, 286; subway car, 119; swing, 287; theatre, 351; toilet, 275; wheelchair, 452; woman's shoe heel, 205
seat belt, car, 110
seating area, supermarket, 103
seat location, ticket, 349
seaweed, 57
second, grammatical symbol, 513
secondary cable, overhead power line, 396
secondary cell, battery, 397
secondary combustion chamber, stove, 404
secondary con, destroyer, 476
secondary feather, 35, 39
secondary highway, 22
secondary root, 51
secondary tank, lunar lander, 154
secondary vein, leaf, 52
second base, baseball, 291
second bicuspid, 456
second bow, bell, iv
second channel, picture-in-picture viewing, 185
Second Empire, house style, 63
second floor, White House, 75
second hand, watch, 220, 304

second molar, 456
second premolar, 456
second reinforce, cannon barrel, 467
seconds bit, stopwatch, 304
seconds dial, grandfather clock, 233
seconds of arc, symbol, 511
second stage: missile, 482; skin diving tank, 331
second thigh: dog, 36; horse, 38
second toe, human foot, 31
second valve slide: French horn, 358; trumpet, 359
second violin, orchestra, 354
secretarial pedestal, desk, 276
secretary, Senate, 74
secretary's table, courtroom, 89
section: dam, 100; fishing rod, 340; jumbo jet, 148, 149; lumber, 68; magazine, 169; orange, 55; theatre, 351
sectional center, envelope, 159
sectional sofa, 236
section code, magazine mailing label, 169
sectioned floorboard, inflatable, 133
sector, track and field, 300
sector flag, hammer throw, 301
security system, prison, 76
sedan, automobile, 106
sediment bleed valve, water heater, 401
seed: 51; apple, 55; flower, 53; gardening, 430; grass, 58; pea, 54; peach, 55; pepper, 262; sandwich, 263; tomato, 54
seeder, gardening, 430
seeker, jet fighter, 480
seesaw, 287
see-through window, package, 269
segment: orange, 55; snake rattle, 42
segmented thumb, lacrosse glove, 298
seiche, 14
select button, dot matrix printer, 163
selection lever, voting booth, 437
selection plate, toaster, 253
selector: accordion, 366; air conditioner, 402; camera, 174; CB radio, 183; clothes dryer, 281; light meter, 176; movie projector, 175; phonograph, 178, 179; radar, 444; surgical table, 450; toaster oven, 253; volt-ohm meter, 423; washing machine, 280
selector control, sealed voting booth, 437
self-belt: dress, 198; trousers, 191
self-clasping hair roller, 214
self-cleaning oven, 248
self-congratulation, gesture, 507
self-filling mechanism, pen, 158
self-service gas station island, 112
self-starting timer, parking meter, 113
self-threading projector, 175
self-timer, camera, 172
self-timer indicator, camera, 172; Polaroid, 173
selling copy, magazine cover, 169
selvage: fabric, 388; weaving, 387

semaphore, 512
semibreve, music, 352
semicolon, grammatical symbol, 513
semiconductor, transistor, 396
semiflexible kite, 323
semi-hollow body, guitar, 363
semiquaver, music, 352
semirigid lighter-than-air craft, 156
semisubmersible design, oil drilling platform, 101
semitrailer, truck, 121
Senate side, Capitol, 74
sense organs, 30
sensitivity, volt-ohm meter, 423
sensitivity control, video camera, 184
sensor: electronic flash, 176; solar heating system, 391; weather station, 18
sensory nerve, human, 29
sepals, flower, 53
separation triangle, shuffleboard court, 318
separator wire, typewriter, 161
septum: nose, 30; heart, 28
septum linguae, tongue, 30
sequenced starting light, drag racing, 339
sequencer control, synthesizer, 363
sequins, woman's hat, 203
serac, mountain, 9
sergeant at arms, Senate, 74
serial number: internal combustion engine, 406; laboratory scale, 446; paper money, 224, 225; safe, 457; sealed voting booth, 437; surgical table, 450
series identification, paper money, 225
series number, painting brush, 371
serif, type, 165
serigraphy, 375
serrated body, hand grenade, 473
serrated edge: knife, 256; paper bag, 266
serration: coin, 225; key, 459
server, dessert, 245
service, tea, 245
service area: highway, 114; jai alai cancha, 314; railroad yard, 96; volleyball court, 319
service article, magazine, 170
service box, handball, 313; squash, 313
service cabinet, elevator, 78
service cap, military uniform, 496
service coupon, magazine, 171
service court: badminton, 319; barn, 104; handball, 313
service deli, supermarket, 103
service door, gas pump, 112
service line: handball, 313; jai alai, 314; squash, 313; tennis, 312
service mast, space shuttle, 152
service revolver, police gun belt, 499
service ribbon, military uniform, 496
service road, highway, 114
service sideline, tennis court, 312
service sign, road, 505
service station island, 112
service structure, launch pad, 152
service time, military, 496
service vehicle, airport, 95

service zone, handball, 313
serving, bow, 466
serving cap, maid's uniform, 489
serving player's line, jai alai, 314
serving silverware drawer, sideboard, 243
serving tray, 245; baby's high chair, 286
servopneumatic altimeter, pilot's instrument panel, 481
set: scale weights, 446; stage, 350; tea, 245; television, 185
setback, skyscraper, 77
set-in cap, magazine, 170
set-in sleeve: blouse, 197; jacket, 196
set of tail, dog, 36
setscrew: barbell, 344; faucet, 273
settee: patio, 288; sailboat, 135
setting: clock radio, 233; light meter, 176; ring, 219
setting dots, sewing machine, 278
setting indicator, ski binding, 326
setting lotion, hair, 214
setup: bowling lane, 317; chess, 345
7/8 mile chute, harness racetrack, 337
7/8 pole, harness racetrack, 337
747 cockpit, 150-151
seven furlong chute, harness racetrack, 337
seven pin, bowling, 317
70mm camera: lunar rover, 155; spacesuit, 155
sewer valve, camper, 130
sewing hole: hook and eye, 208; snap fastener, 208
sewing machine, 278
sewing pattern, 388
sew-through button, 209
sextant, 137
sforzando, organ, 360
shackle: block and tackle, 461; padlock, 459; pocket knife, 426
shade: and composition, 368; lamp, 238, 239; stagecoach, 131; track lighting 239; window covering, 240
shading: relief map, 21; and texture, composition, 369
shading key, globe, 1
shadow: and composition, 368; makeup, 216, 217; sundial, 389
shadow pin, compass, 136
shaft: arrow, 466; billiard cue, 320; bird feather, 39; boot, 206; bridge, 97; can opener, 251; cave, 11; column, 73; croquet mallet, 318; dart, 322; destroyer, 476; drum major's baton, 495; electric meter, 399; elevator, 78; golf club, 310; Hansom cab, 131; halberd, 464; harness racing, 337; ice ax, 334; ice hockey stick, 295; internal combustion engine, 406; javelin, 303; lacrosse stick, 298; lamp, 239; lance, 464; longbow, 466; metronome, 367; music stand, 367; oar, 133; obelisk, 71; pin, 208; printing press, 376, 377; ski pole, 326; squash racket, 313; stagecoach, 131; tennis racket, 312; umbrella, 230; underwater tunnel, 98; White House, 75
shaftment, arrow, 466

shake, wooden roofing shingle, 68
shakedown, cowboy, 490
shake-hands grip, Ping-Pong racket, 321
shaker: kitchen tool, 260; salt, 261
shako, drum major, 495
shallow gouge, woodcarving, 372
Shanghai, darts, 322
shank: anchor, 132; bolt, 411; boot, 206; brasses, 358; button, 209; cat, 37; chicken, 35; chisel, 420; shank, drill, 419; fishhook, 341; gimlet, 418; gouge, 374; hoe, 427; human, 25; lamb, 33; latch needle, 386; nail, 410; needle, 384; pipe, 229; ring, 219; screw, 410; screwdriver, 413; shoe, 204, 205; trombone, 358; type, 166
shape, pipe, 229
sharp: music, 352; organ, 360
sharpening oil, woodcarving, 372
sharpening steel, 256
sharpening stone: gouge, 374; woodcarving, 372
shaver, 210
shaving brush, 210
shawl, Jewish prayer vestment, 486
shawl collar, sweater, 199
shears, 384; gardening, 427
sheath: cat, 37; grass, 58; knife, 463; nerve, 29; safety pin, 208; skin diving, 331; snake fang, 42; wire, 423
sheathing, house, 60
sheave: block and tackle, 461; elevator shaft, 78
shed, oil drilling platform, 101
sheep, 33
sheer line, powerboat, 139
sheet: ambulance, 123; bedding, 271; kite, 323; postage stamps, 159
sheet-fed press, printing, 166
sheet music notation, 352-353
sheet-transfer cylinder, offset-lithography, 166
shelf: cupboard, 243; fireplace, 232; igloo, 85; refrigerator, 249; stove oven, 248; telescope, 443
shelfback, book, 167
shelf break, continental margin, 15
shelf mount, telescope, 443
shelf sign, aisle display, 102
shell: attaché case, 285; baseball catcher's mask, 290; bivalve, 47; block and tackle, 461; brace chuck, 418; coconut, 262; cupboard, 243; drill, 419; drum, 364; egg, 262; fire extinguisher, 284; football helmet, 292; iron, 279; lamp, 238; lobster, 47; necktie, 192; nuclear reactor, 392; parka, 201; pea, 54; plug fuse, 399; quiche, 263; sleeping bag, 343; tambourine, 364; tart, 264; toaster, 253; turtle, 43; univalve, 47; vacuum tube, 396
shellfish, 47
shell fuse, aerial shell, 383
shell plate, mandolin, 362
shel rosh, Jewish ritual item, 486
shelter, destroyer, 477
shel yad, tefillin, 486
shield: car seat, 286; chain saw muffler, 431; coat of arms,

503; drag racing driver's fire suit, 339; drum major's coat, 495; hollow wall fastener, 411; lantern, 342; medieval, 464; merry-go-round, 93; mower, 429; nuclear, 392; police, 498; racing car, 338; tank, 475; toll basket, 114; tunnel, 98
Shield of David, 88, 508
shift, doppler, 2
shifter, bicycle, 128
shifting head, theodolite, 436
shift key, typewriter, 161
shift lever, bulldozer, 435
shimagi, torii, 70-71
shin, human, 24
shin boot, harness racing pacer, 337
shin pad, soccer, 297
shiner, brick wall, 69
shingle, roofing, 68
shinguard: baseball, 290; football, 292; ice hockey, 295
shin pad, ice hockey, 295
Shinto temple gateway, 70-71
ship: aircraft carrier, 478; cargo, 140-141; passenger, 142-143; submarine, 479; surface fighting, 476-477
shipboard lines, canal lock, 99
shipping lane, 476
shirring: blouse, 197; woman's pants, 196
shirt, 189; baseball, 290; cowboy, 490; Indian, 490; man's formal attire, 488; military, 496, 497; police, 499; polo, 299; soccer, 297
shirt dress, cook's uniform, 489
shirt-waist dress, cook's uniform, 489
shoaling wave, shoreline, 14
shoat, 34
shock absorber: automobile, 109; motorcycle, 129; single engine airplane, 147; snowmobile, 130
shoe: accessories, 207; blackjack, 347; boxing, 309; bridge, 97; bulldozer track, 435; clown, 493; drag racing driver, 339; drum major, 495; elevator shaft, 78; fencing, 315; football, 292; horse, 38; jai alai, 314; king's regalia, 484; ladder, 425; man's, 204; mechanical sweeper, 127; military, 496; mountain climbing, 334; organ, 360; police, 498; running, 302; sailor, 497; sander, 421; saw, 417; screen, 175; snowshoe, 327; soccer, 297; stagecoach, 131; woman's, 205
shoe brace, guitar, 362
shoe horn, 207
shoelace, 204
shoe shop, prison, 76
shoestring strap, dress, 198
shoe tree, 207
shoot: asparagus, 54; grass, 58
shooter: dice, 346; craps table, 347
shooting star, 2
shootout, soccer, 297
shop: frontier fort, 82; passenger ship, 142; prison, 76; railroad yard, 96
shopping cart, supermarket, 102
shore, 14
shoreline, 14; iceberg, 12; nautical chart, 22
short bar, easel, 370
short bar clamp, 409

short bent gouge, woodcarving, 372
short circuit, fuse box, 399
short lid prop, grand piano, 361
short line, handball, 313
short loin, beef, 32
short ribs, beef, 32
shorts: 191; basketball, 296; men's underwear, 194; soccer, 297
short service line, badminton court, 319
short stick, grand piano, 361
shortstop area, baseball, 291
short-term parking lot, airport, 95
shot, field events equipment, 303
shotgun, 468-469; stagecoach, 131
shotgun chaps, cowboy, 490
shot put, 301, 303
shot timer, basketball backstop, 296
shoulder: bell, iv; bottle, 267; broom, 282; cat, 37; chisel, 420; dog, 36; highway, 114; horse, 38; human, 24; key, 459; lamb, 33; mountain, 8; pencil, 158; pork, 34; razor blade, 210; shovel, 427; suit hanger, 281; tennis racket, 312; type, 166; waterskiing vest, 329; wave, 14; woman's jacket, 196; wristwatch, 220
shoulder bag, 222
shoulder blade: human, 24; stegosaurus, 43
shoulderboard, military uniform, 496
shoulder butt, pork, 34
shoulder harness, drag racing driver, 339
shoulder hook, frame, 379
shoulder pad: football, 292; ice hockey, 295
shoulder pad strap, backpack, 343
shoulder press, universal gym, 344
shoulder protector, ice hockey goalie, 294
shoulder rest, bazooka, 472
shoulder seam, jacket, 188
shoulder sling, mountain climbing, 334
shoulder strap: accordion, 366; brassiere, 195; child's car seat, 286; combat soldier, 497; golf bag, 311; handbag, 222; trench coat, 200
shoulder vise, workbench, 408
shoulder yoke blouse, 197
shovel, 427; fire iron, 232; ski, 326
show, flat racing, 336
shower: bath, 274; thunderstorm, 17; weather map, 19
shrapnel, grenade, 473
shredding disc, food processor, 254
shrimp, 47
shrine, pyramid, 70
shrinkwrap, packaging, 268
shroud: internal combustion engine, 406; parachute line, 333; sailboat, 134
shuffleboard, 318
shutoff handle, pilot's instrument panel, 481
shutoff valve: radiator, 400; standpipe, 59; toilet, 275; water heater, 401
shutter: house, 62, 63; laboratory burner, 447; windmill, 390; window, 241

564

shutter release: camera, **172**; Polaroid, **173**; video-still camera, **173**
shutter scale, light meter, **176**
shutter speed key, camera, **172**
shuttle: badminton, **319**; sewing machine, **278**; space, **152**; tatting, **386**
shuttlecock, badminton, **319**
shuttle race, hand loom, **387**
siamese: hose, **428**; standpipe, **59**
sickle, chicken, **35**
sickle-bar lawn mower, **429**
side: accordion, **366**; basket, **266**; elliptical galaxy, **2**; lumber, **68**; organ, **360**; piano, **361**; skillet, **257**; snap fastener, **208**; violin, **355**
sidearm, **470**; juice extractor, **255**
sidebar: courtroom, **89**; magazine, **170**; pulley block, **461**
side belt, handbag, **222**
side bit: fireboat, **144**; tugboat, **144**
sideboard, **243**; ice hockey rink, **295**; polo grounds, **299**
side body molding, automobile, **107**
sidebones, brassiere, **195**
side broom balance assembly, mechanical sweeper, **127**
sideburns, **211**
side cleft, horse's foot, **38**
side curtains, four-poster bed, **270**
side cushion, sofa, **236**
side cutter, pliers, **414**
side deck, powerboat, **139**
side drop, bedding, **270**
side drum, **364**
side fender, tugboat, **144**
side flight, staircase, **66**
side handle, drill, **418**
side handrail, subway car, **119**
side horse, gymnastics, **307**
side jamb, window, **65**
side leg, playpen, **286**
sidelight: door, **64**; Hansom cab, **131**; house, **62**; stagecoach, **131**
sideline: basketball, **296**; fencing strip, **315**; football, **293**; lacrosse field, **298**; Ping-Pong, **321**; polo grounds, **299**; soccer field, **297**; volleyball, **319**
side link, chain saw chain, **431**
sidelit composition, **368**
side-loading collection truck, **127**
side loading door, stove, **404**
side loop, handbag, **222**
side marker: automobile, **106**; bus, **118**; tow truck, **126**
side panel: bureau, **272**; bus, **118**; curtain, **240**; lounger, **235**; package, **268**; sideboard, **243**; tractor, **434**
side pieces, furniture, **243**
side plate: pulley block, **461**; racing car, **338**; revolver, **470**
side pocket, backpack, **343**
side pod, racing car, **338**
side rail: bed, **270**; child's wagon, **287**; ladder, **47**
skin diving fin, **331**; sled, **328**; slide, **287**; surgical table, **450**; truck van, **121**
side seam: boot, **206**; trousers, **191**
side shell, block and tackle, **461**
sideshow, circus, **90**
side sign: bus, **118**; subway car, **119**

side slats, sled, **328**
side span, bridge, **97**
sidestand, motorcycle, **129**
side stretcher, rocking chair, **234**
side vent, volcano, **10**
sideview mirror: automobile, **106**; mechanical sweeper, **127**
sidewalk, moving, **79**
sidewall: can, **267**; circus tent, **91**; horse's hoof, **38**; man's hair, **211**; slalom water ski, **329**; squash, **313**; swimming pool, **316**; tire, **105**; truck van, **121**
side welt, boot, **206**
side whiskers, **211**
side window: bus, **118**; camper, **130**
siding: house, **62**, **63**; railroad yard, **96**
sidur, Jewish prayer book, **486**
sieve, **260**
sifter, **260**
sight: armor, **465**; automatic weapons, **470**, **471**; bazooka, **472**; crossbow, **466**; pool table, **320**; rifle, **469**; tank, **474**
sight bracket, mortar, **472**
sight cut, bayonet, **463**
sight glass, furnace, **400**
sightseeing bus, **118**
sign: bus, **118**; music, **352**, **353**; public, **506-506**; road, **504-505**; subway car, **119**
signal: automobile, **106**; bus, **118**; railroad crossing, **115**; traffic light, **113**
signal ahead, road sign, **505**
signal baton, drum major, **495**
signal bridge, destroyer, **477**
signal deck, passenger ship, **143**
signal halyard, destroyer, **477**
signal intensity meter, metal detector, **445**
signal light: automobile, **106**; bus, **118**; coffee maker, **252**; mechanical sweeper, **127**; motorcycle, **129**; taxi, **119**
signal meter, phonograph, **179**
signal processor, synthesizer, **363**
signal shelter, destroyer, **477**
signal strength indicator, cellular telephone, **181**
signal tower, passenger ship, **143**
signature: baseball bat, **291**; cartoon, **380**; letter, **159**; music, **352**; prescription, **451**
sign: taxi roof light, **119**; toll booth, **114**; zodiac, **509**
sign language, **512**
sign-off, magazine article, **170**
silencer, **470**
silent alarm, vault, **457**
silent anti-reverse housing, fishing reel, **340**
silicon photodiode, Polaroid, **173**
silk: corn, **58**; flat racing, **336**
silk screen, **375**
silk threads, spider, **40**
sill: dam, **100**; door, **64**; house, **60**, **61**, **62**; volcano, **10**
sill cock, standpipe, **59**
silo, **104**; ballistic missile launch deck, **479**
silver amalgam, dental, **455**
silver-bullion embroidered cuff, king's regalia, **484**
silver certificate, paper money, **224**
silverware, **244**

silverware drawer, sideboard, **243**
simple eye, grasshopper, **41**
simple microscope, **442**
simple miter, bishop, **487**
sin bin, ice hockey rink, **295**
since, symbol, **511**
single-breasted jacket, **188**
single corner, checkerboard, **345**
single cuff, shirt, **189**
single engine airplane, **147**
single lens reflex camera, **172**
single-membered foot, ultimate beast, **49**
single pleat, woman's pants, **196**
single quotation mark, **513**
single ring, dart board, **322**
single-score ring, dart board, **322**
single service court, badminton, **319**
singles sideline: badminton, **319**; tennis, **312**
single system movie sound camera, **174**
sinister side, coat of arms, **503**
sinister supporter, coat of arms, **503**
sink, **62**, **247**, **273**; sailboat, **135**; sidepiece, **243**
sinker, fishing, **341**
sinus, leaf, **52**
siphon: clam, **47**; octopus, **46**
sire, horse, **38**, **336**
siren: fire engine, **124**, **125**; police car, **122**
sirloin, beef, **32**
sissy bar, motorcycle, **129**
sitar, **362**
situation display indicator, pilot's instrument panel, **481**
six pin, bowling, **317**
six-shooter, cowboy, **490**
16mm camera, lunar rover, **155**
sixteenth note, music, **352**
sixteenth-of-a-mile pole, harness racetrack, **337**
sixty-fourth note, music, **353**
60-yard line, polo grounds, **299**
size: electrician's wire, **423**; nail, **410**; painting brush, **371**; tire, **105**; type, **166**
sizer, football helmet, **292**
size selector, phonograph turntable, **178**
skate: ice, **325**; ice hockey, **295**
skateboard, **324**
skeg: outboard engine, **137**; sailboat, **134**; surfboard, **330**; waterskiing, **329**; windsurfer, **330**
skein: ballista cord, **467**; knitting yarn, **386**
skeleton: coral polyp, **46**; human, **26**; skyscraper, **77**; umbrella, **230**
skeleton key, **459**
skeleton tower, buoy, **132**
sketch box, painting, **371**
skewback: arch, **72**; handsaw, **416**
skew chisel, woodcarving, **372**
skewer, **259**
ski, **326**, **327**, **329**; snowmobile, **130**
skid, glider, **147**
skiff, **133**
skiing: cross-country, **327**; downhill, **326**; water, **329**
skillet, **257**
skimmer, **259**
skimming brush, **259**
skin: fruit, **55**; geodesic dome, **85**; igloo, **85**; skyscraper, **77**;

tepee, **84**; vegetables, **54**, **262**; yurt, **70**
skin diving, **331**
skink, **42**
skip rope, body building, **344**
skirt: badminton shuttlecock, **319**; bedding, **270**; bureau, **272**; drag racing driver's helmet, **339**; dress, **198**; escalator, **79**; fishing jig, **341**; fishing reel, **340**; gas pump, **112**; girdle, **195**; hot air balloon, **332**; hovercraft, **145**; missile, **482**; octopus, **46**; palm, **52**; racing car, **338**; Revolutionary War general's coat, **492**; saddle, **335**; skin diving mask, **334**; window, **65**; window shade, **240**; woman's, **197**
skull: armor, **465**; human, **26**
skull cap: flat racing, **336**; Jewish prayer vestment, **486**
skull temple, eyeglasses, **221**
sky, **2**
skydiver, **333**
sky drop, stage, **350**
skyline, newspaper, **168**
skyscraper, **77**
slab: house, **60**; lumber, **68**
slacks, **191**
slalom skiing, **326**, **329**
slant: gouge, **374**; grammatical symbol, **513**; type, **165**
slant-front desk, **276**
slash, grammatical symbol, **513**
slash pocket, trousers, **191**
slat: fence, **67**; lobster pot, **433**; rocking chair, **234**; screen, **175**; sled, **328**; train stock car, **117**; venetian blind, **241**; window, **65**; window shade, **241**
sled, **328**
sleeper, railroad track, **115**
sleeping bag, backpacking, **343**
sleeping box, truck cab, **120**
sleeping car, passenger train, **116**
sleeping shelf, igloo, **85**
sleep key, television, **185**
sleet, **17**
sleeve: baluster, **73**; barbell, **344**; blouse, **197**; bridal gown, **488**; cardigan, **199**; fencing, **315**; jacket, **188**, **196**; jackhammer, **436**; lamp, **238**, **239**; overhead power line, **396**; parka, **201**; queen's regalia, **484**; scriber, **375**; shirt, **189**; sponge mop, **282**; telescope, **443**; trenchcoat, **200**; windsurfer mast, **330**
sleeve protector, banjo, **362**
slice: bread, **263**; cake, **264**; pizza, **265**; quiche, **263**
slicer, vegetable, **261**
slicing disc, food processor, **254**
slick, racing, **338**, **339**
slicker, cowboy, **490**
slide: backyard equipment, **287**; cigar cutter, **228**; cornet, **359**; cowboy hat, **202**; desk, **276**; film, **172**; French horn, **331**; hand loom, **387**; laboratory, **447**; pistol, **470**; projector, **175**; rule, **424**, **441**; string tie, **192**; suspenders, **190**; traverse rod, **240**; trombone, **358**, **359**; trumpet, **359**; tuba, **358**; vise, **409**; zipper, **209**
slide bed, **287**
slide bolt, chain lock, **458**

slide bracket, hand shower, 274
slide fastener, 209
slide handle, shotgun, 468
slide holder, microscope, 442
slide hook, garbage disposal, 247
slide-out shelf, refrigerator, 249
slide plate, sewing machine, 278
slide projector, 175
slider, parachute, 333
slide rail, snowmobile, 130
slide rule, 441
slide support, 286
slide switch, minivacuum, 283
sliding block, steam engine, 405
sliding cover, desk, 276
sliding door: barn, 104; helicopter, 146; powerboat, 139
sliding eyepiece, ear scope, 448
sliding jaw, monkey wrench, 415
sliding pond, backyard, 287
sliding tandem wheels, truck, 121
slim fin, skin diving, 331
slim skirt, 197
sling: bazooka, 472; elevator shaft, 78; golf bag, 311; ice hammer, 334; mountain climbing, 334; rifle, 468
sling shoe, woman's, 205
slingshot dragster, 339
sling swivel, rifle, 468
slipcase, book, 167
slip-joint pliers, 414
slip nut, sink drain, 273
slipper, ballet, 494
slippery when wet, road sign, 505
slip printer, cash register, 440
slip ring, automatic rifle, 471
slip seat, rocking chair, 234
slip stitched seam, necktie, 192-193
slit: cheese plane, 256; man's underpants, 194; tepee, 84
slit pocket, skirt, 197
slogan, coat of arms, 503
slogan sign, aisle display, 102
sloop, sail, 136
slope: continental, 15; mountain, 8; permanent fort, 83; suit hanger, 281
slope indicator, runway, 94
sloping dormer, house, 62
slot: blackjack, 347; checkbook clutch, 223; clothespin, 280; dental brace, 453; electrical receptacle, 398; electrical switch, 398; hasp, 460; hovercraft, 145; parking meter, 113; pliers, 414; razor, 210; roulette wheel, 346; sandal, 206; screw head, 410; sketch box, 371; slot machine, 346; table saw, 417; telephone, 180; toaster, 253; toggle bolt, 411; toll basket, 114; wallet, 223
slot machine, 346
slotted lifter, kitchen tool, 259
slow down, music notation, 352
slow forward, remote control unit, 184
slow-motion control knobs, telescope, 443
slow-moving vehicle symbol, hitch and harrow, 434
SLR, 172
slug: book page, iv; cartridge, 470; magazine, 171; and parking meter, 113
sluice gate: canal lock, 99; dam, 100
slur, music notation, 352
small intestine, human, 27
small of back, human, 25
small of stock, shotgun, 468
small saphenous vein, human, 28
smock mill, 390
smoke alarm, 284
smoke bomb discharger, tank, 475
smoke chamber, fireplace, 232
smoke detector, 284
smoked sausage, 265
smoke ejector, fire engine, 124
smoke flap, tepee, 84
smoke grenade, 473
smokehouse, 104
smoke path, stove, 404
smoke shelf, fireplace, 232
smokestack, locomotive, 116
smoke-wagon, cowboy, 490
smooth bore, shotgun, 468
smoothbore firing tube, bazooka, 472
smooth-soled climbing shoe, 334
SMV symbol, hitch and harrow, 434
snack food, 265
snail, 47
snake, 42-43; plumbing tool, 422
snap, fishhook, 341
snap bar, suit hanger, 281
snap fastener, 208; fireman's coat, 500; parka, 201; spacesuit, 155; waterskiing vest, 329
snap lock, starting block, 304
snare drum, 364
snaste, candlewick, 237
sneaker, basketball, 296
snifter, 245
snood, 203; turkey, 35
snooker, billiards, 320
snooze alarm, clock radio, 233
snorkel, skin diving, 331
snorkel tube, submarine, 479
snot, candlewick, 237
snout: fish, 45; alligator, 42; crocodile, 42; glacier, 12; pig, 34; stingray, 45
snow, 19
snow block, igloo, 85
snow couloir, 8
snow cuff, ski boot, 327
snowfield, 9, 12
snow gully, 8
snowmobile, 130
snow plow, garbage truck, 127; hockey skate, 325
snow spoiler, snowmobile, 130
snow ring, ski pole, 326
snowshoe, 327
snuff, candlewick, 237
snuffbox, anatomical, 31
snuffer, candle, 237
soap dish: bathtub, 274; sink, 273
soap dispenser, 247
soaring, glider, 147
soccer, 297
sock, 207; baseball, 290; basketball, 296; drag racing driver, 339; fencing, 315; football, 292; ice hockey, 295; skiing, 327; soccer, 297; windsurfer, 330
socket: bayonet, 463; camera, 174; candlestick, 237; eye, 30; guitar, 363; lamp, 238; movie projector, 175; nozzle, 428; operating table, 450; rowboat, 133; shovel, 427;
snap fastener, 208; teeth, 456
socket wrench, 415
sod, hogan, 84
soda-acid fire extinguisher, 284
soda straw, cave, 11
sofa, 236
soffit, house, 61
soft, music notation, 352, 353
softback book, 167
softbound book, 167
softcover book, 167
soft dorsal fin, fish, 45
soft ground, printmaking, 377
soft lens, contact lens, 221
softnose, canal lock, 99
soft ray, fish, 45
soft suction connection hose, pumper, 125
soft tissue, and denture, 453
software, computer, 438
solar flare, 3
solar heating system, 391
solar panel: satellite, 186; weather station, 18
solar plexus, 25
solar power system, 391
solar prominence, 3
solar radiation sensor, weather station, 18
solar time, 5
solar system, 2-3
solder, plumbing, 422
soldering iron, 378
soldier: brick wall, 69; uniform, 496, 497
sole: ballet slippers, 494; boot, 206; golf club, 310; horse's foot, 38; human foot, 31; ice climbing boot, 334; ice skates, 325; man's shoe, 204; plane, 420; running shoe, 302; sailboat, 135; sandal, 206; sock, 207; woman's shoe, 205
soleplate: house, 61; iron, 279; rollerskate, 324
soleus, human, 26
solid body, guitar, 363
solid-rocket booster, space shuttle, 152
solid spoke wheel, motorcycle, 129
solitary confinement, prison, 76
solleret, armor, 465
solrad, cartoon, 381
solution: contact lens, 221; magazine puzzle, 171
sommelier, corkscrew, 251
sonar, 444
sonar autofocus transducer, Polaroid, 173
sonar dome, destroyer, 477
sonar rangefinder, Polaroid, 173
sostenuto pedal, piano, 361
soul, human, 25
sound, movie film, 174
sound box: dulcimer, 362; lyre, 355
sound hole: guitar, 260; violin, 355
sounding, nautical chart, 22
sounding board, guitar, 362
sounding datum reference, nautical chart, 22
soundome, sonar, 444
sound-test button, movie camera, 174
soundtrack, movie film, 174
soup spoon, 244
source: composition lighting, 369; coupon, 103
source code, magazine mailing label, 169
source lake, river, 13
sousaphone, 358
South Equatorial Current, ocean, 6
south fork, river, 13
south latitude, globe, 5
South Pole pin, globe, 1
south wing, Capitol, 74
sow, 34
space: music clef, 353; proofreader's mark, 514
space bar, typewriter, 161
space mark, basketball court, 296
spacer: typewriter, 161; wheelchair, 452
space shuttle, 152-153
spacesuit, 155
spade, 427; playing cards, 348
spade bit, drill, 418
spading fork, 427
spaghetti spoon, 259
spaghetti strap, dress, 198
spaghetti tongs, 259
spall, brick, 68
span: arch, 72; bowling ball, 317; bridge, 97
spandrel: arch, 72; mosque, 71
spandrel ornament, grandfather clock, 233
spangle, 219
spanner screw, mortise lock, 458
span wire, traffic light, 113
spar: kite, 323; sailboat, 134
spareribs, 34
spare tire, automobile, 106
spare wheel, truck, 120
spark-arrester: chain saw, 431; fireplace, 232
sparkgap trigger, gas laser, 395
spark plug: automobile engine, 111; internal combustion engine, 406
sparring, 309
spats, drum major, 495
spatula, 259
spawning, fish, 45
speaker: CB radio, 183; guitar amplifier, 363; House of Representatives, 74; metal detector, 445; phonograph, 179; projector, 175; sonar, 444; tape recorder, 177; telephone, 180; television, 185; theatre, 351
speaker grill, portable radio/cassette player, 182
speakerphone, answering machine, 181
speaker selector: phonograph, 179; police car, 122
spear: asparagus, 54; window shade roller, 241
spear blade: partisan, 464; pocket knife, 426
spearhead, partisan, 464
spear point, fence, 67
special-effect pedal, guitar, 363
special effects, synthesizer, 363
special-feature photo treatment, magazine, 170
special function button, telephone, 180
special instructions card holder, elevator car, 78
specialist, space shuttle, 153
specification: electric motor, 399; internal combustion engine, 406
specific edition, book, 167
specific product code, Universal Product Code, 440
specimen holder, microscope, 442
spectacles, 221
spectator seating, courtroom, 89

spectrometer, **445**; satellite, **186**
speculum, **448**
speech balloon, comic strip, **380**
speech selector, tape recorder, **177**
speed, jet fighter, **480**
speed bit, drill, **419**
speed controls: blender, **254**; car, **110**; motorcycle, **129**; phonograph turntable, **178**; police car, **122**; 747 cockpit, **150**; tape recorder, **177**
speedway racing, **338**
spell out, proofreader's mark, **514**
spelunking, **11**
sphericasia, cartooning, **380**
sphygmomanometer, **449**
spice, **263**
spider, **40**; lampshade, **238**
spigot, **247**, **273**
spike, **410**; baseball batter, **290**; castle portcullis, **81**; fence, **67**; football field, **293**; halberd, **464**; ice climbing, **334**; mace, **464**; pineapple, **55**; railroad track, **115**; stegosaurus, **43**; track shoe, **302**; volleyball, **319**
spiked foot, camera tripod, **176**
spiked heel, woman's shoe, **205**
spikelet, grass, **58**
spillway, dam, **100**
spinal cord, human, **29**
spinal nerve, human, **29**
spindle: faucet, **273**; movie projector, **175**; phonograph turntable, **178**; rocking chair, **234**; roulette wheel, **346**; screwdriver, **413**; sewing machine, **278**; spinning wheel, **387**; stethoscope, **449**; typewriter, **161**; weather vane, **19**
spindle hole, diskette, **162**
spindle locking plate, workbench vise, **408**
spindrift, wave, **14**
spine: book, **167**; cactus, **56**; dust jacket, **167**; hair comb, **314**; kite, **323**; starfish, **46**; stegosaurus, **43**; stingray, **45**
spinnaker, sail, **136**
spinner: dominos, **345**; seeder, **430**; single engine airplane, **147**
spinneret, spider, **40**
spinning reel, **340**
spinning rod, **340-341**
spinning wheel, **387**
spiny dorsal fin, fish, **45**
spiny ray, fish, **45**
spiracle: grasshopper, **41**; tadpole, **44**
spiral: spider web, **40**; staircase, **66**
spiral bone, girdle, **195**
spiral brush, vacuum cleaner, **283**
spiral galaxy, **2**
spiral ratchet screwdriver, **413**
spiral tip, drain cleaner, **422**
spire: church, **86**; kokoshniki, **70**; mountain, **9**; univalve shell, **47**
spirit level, **424**
spit, of land, **7**, **15**, **22**
spit curl, **211**
spit key: trombone, **359**; trumpet, **359**
spitter, toll basket, **114**
spitz, glacier, **12**
splashboard: Hansom cab, **131**; sink, **247**
splash guard: truck, **120**, **121**, **126**; washing machine, **280**

splash pan, potter's wheel, **373**
splash rim, sink, **273**
splat, rocking chair, **234**
splayed leg, butterfly table, **242**
spleen, human, **25**, **27**
splint, **123**, **451**
split ballot, voting, **437**
split end, paint brush bristle, **425**
split line, pill, **451**
split-rail fencing, barnyard, **104**
split-rim wheel, tow truck, **126**
split rudder, space shuttle, **152**
split screen, picture-in-picture viewing, **185**
splitter, table saw, **417**
splitting tool, stonecutting, **372**
spoiler: glider, **147**; jumbo jet, **148**; racing car, **338**; snowmobile, **130**
spoke: bicycle, **128**; Ferris wheel, **93**; geodesic dome, **85**; harness racing sulky, **337**; spider web, **40**; stagecoach, **131**
sponge: cannon, **467**; mop, **282**
sponge face, Ping-Pong racket, **321**
sponge mop, **282**
sponge-tip applicator, **217**
sponson, helicopter, **146**
spool, **384**; film roll, **172**; fishing reel, **340**; typewriter, **161**
spool pin, sewing machine, **278**
spoon: golf club, **311**; hand grenade, **473**; kitchen, **258**, **259**; pipe tool, **259**; table setting, **244**
spore, fern, **57**
sports car, **106**
sports coupe, **108**
sports deck, passenger ship, **143**
sports wagon, **108**
spot: billiard table, **320**; blackjack, **347**; bowling lane, **317**; dice, **347**; ice hockey rink, **295**; label, **269**; playing card, **348**; sun, **3**
spot label, **268**
spotlight: circus, **91**; pumper, **125**; stage, **350**; truck bed, **126**
spot-meter reading index, light meter, **176**
spotter, gymnastics, **306**
spot weld, tweezers, **215**
spout: bathtub, **274**; beaker, **447**; coffee maker, **252**; faucet, **273**; gas pump automatic nozzle, **112**; Jacuzzi, **274**; juice extractor, **255**; package, **268**; pot, **373**; sink, **247**, **273**; tea kettle, **245**
spray: bathtub, **274**; dishwasher, **250**; iron, **279**; lawn sprinkler, **428**; paint, **425**; pistol nozzle, **428**; shower, **274**; sink, **247**
spray adjuster, hand shower, **274**
spread: book, **167**; canapé, **263**; magazine, **170-171**; sandwich, **263**; shirt collar, **189**
spreader: gardening tool, **430**; ladder, **425**; powerboat, **139**; sailboat, **134**; saw, **417**
spreading spinner, seeder, **430**
spring: automobile, **109**; ballpoint pen, **158**; bear trap, **433**; bed, **271**; chest pull, **344**; clothespin, **280**; etching press, **377**; gardening shears, **427**; gas pump nozzle, **112**; hair clip,

214; internal combustion engine, **406**; lamp, **239**; mousetrap, **433**; pencil sharpener, **277**; pistol magazine, **470**; racing car, **338**; sewing machine, **278**; shoe tree, **207**; sponge mop, **282**; stapler, **277**; trampoline, **308**; truck, **120**; umbrella, **230**
spring-bar, wristwatch, **220**
spring beard needle, **386**
springboard: diving, **316**; gymnastics, **307**; trampoline, **308**
spring catch, swivel, **218**
spring clamp, **409**
spring clip: juice extractor, **255**; woodcarving, **372**
spring earclip, **218**
springer, arch, **72**
spring guide, pistol, **470**
spring hanger, lamp, **239**
spring headband, headphones, **182'**
spring hinge, **460**
springhouse, barnyard, **104**
spring slot, clothespin, **280**
spring wing, toggle bolt, **411**
sprinkle: cake, **264**; ice cream cone, **265**
sprinkler, **428**
sprocket, motorcycle, **129**
sprocket drive housing, bulldozer, **435**
sprocket hole: film, **172**; movie film, **174**
sprocket-tip cutting bar, chain saw, **417**
spud, laboratory burner, **447**
spur: auger bit, **419**; chicken, **35**; flat racing, **336**; polo, **299**; revolver hammer, **470**; riding equipment, **335**
spurl, cartoon, **381**
spyglass, **443**
squall cloud, **17**
square: cannon carriage, **467**; chessboard, **345**; combination, **424**; Manchu court dress, **491**; shuffleboard court, **318**
square nut, **411**
square up, proofreader's mark, **514**
square root: calculator key, **441**; symbol, **511**
square shank, screwdriver, **413**
squash, vegetable, **54**
squash court, **313**
squean, cartoon, **381**
squeegee, silk screen, **375**
squeeze bottle, **268**
squeezer, kitchen tool, **261**
squelch control, CB radio, **183**
squid, **46**
S/RF meter, CB radio, **183**
stabilizer: destroyer, **477**; fire engine, **124**; glider, **147**; helicopter, **146**; jet fighter, **480**; jumbo jet, **149**; missile, **482**; parachute, **333**; passenger ship, **143**; single engine airplane, **147**
stabilizer block, football helmet, **292**
stabilizer trim, 747 cockpit, **150**
stable, frontier fort, **82**
stack: destroyer, **476**; fireboat, **144**; furnace, **400**; passenger ship, **142**; racing car, **338**
stacker, high-speed printer, **439**
stadia circle, theodolite, **436**
stadium, baseball, **291**
staff: cardinal, **487**; destroyer, **476**, **477**; flag, **502**; halberd,

464; lance, **464**; music, **352-353**; royal scepter, **485**; weather vane, **19**
stage, **350-351**; microscope, **442**; missile, **482**
stagecoach, **131**
staggeration, cartoon, **380**
staggered starting line for distance events, track and field, **300**
stained glass, **378**
staircase design, house, **66**
stairs: **66**; house blueprint, **62**; jumbo jet, **148**; White House, **75**
stake: basket frame, **266**; croquet, **318**; tent, **91**, **342**
stake pockets, truck platform, **121**
stalactite, **11**
stalagmite, **11**
stalk: asparagus, **54**; celery, **262**; corn, **58**; flower, **53**; mushroom, **57**; seaweed, **57**
stalk end, tomato, **54**
stall: railroad yard, **96**; shower, **274**
stallion, **38**
stamen, flower, **53**
stamp: coin, **225**; envelope, **159**; house blueprint, **62**
stamp board, track and field, **300**
stamp plate number, envelope, **159**
stanchion: barn, **104**; basketball backstop, **296**; ice skates, **325**; sailboat, **134**; tow truck, **126**
stand: cellular telephone, **181**; chafing dish, **245**; child's car seat, **286**; courtroom, **89**; curling iron, **214**; cymbal, **364**; etching press, **377**; frame, **379**; hammock, **288**; kiln, **373**; laboratory, **447**; lithographic press, **376**; movie camera microphone, **174**; music, **367**; pencil sharpener, **277**; slot machine, **346**
standard: armor, **465**; football goalpost, **293**; hose nozzle, **428**; pole vault, **305**; sled, **328**; spinning wheel, **387**; theodolite, **436**
standard desk phone, **180**
standard ratchet screwdriver, **413**
stand brace, table saw, **417**
standby altimeter, 747 cockpit, **150**
standby altitude indicator, pilot's instrument panel, **481**
standby compass: pilot's instrument panel, **481**; 747 cockpit, **151**
stand by/talk switch, cordless phone, **180**
standee window, bus, **118**
standing collar: butler's uniform, **489**; drum major's coat, **495**; man's formal attire, **488**
standing rigging, sailboat, **134**
standing sail, **136**
stand leg, table saw, **417**
standpipe, fire hydrant, **125**
stang, fire engine, **124-125**
staple, **410**; hasp, **460**; silk screen frame, **375**
stapler, **277**
star: Milky Way, **2-3**; sea, **46**
starboard: boat, **132**; powerboat, **138**
star button, telephone, **180**
star case, rocket, **383**

567

star diagonal, telescope, **443**
star facet, cut gemstone, **218**
starfish, **46**
star fort, **83**
star note, paper money, **224**
Star of David, **88, 508**
star of order, queen's regalia, **484**
stars, aerial shell, **383**
start button, copier, **164**
starter: automobile, **108, 111**; barbecue, **288**; bulldozer, **435**; chain saw, **431**; clothes dryer, **281**; elevator, **78**; internal combustion engine, **406**; mower, **429**; outboard engine, **137**; phonograph, **178**; 747 cockpit, **151**; stopwatch, **304**
starting block: racing, **304**; swimming pool, **316**
starting gate, flat racing, **336**
starting light, drag racing, **339**
starting line: drag racing, **339**; running track, **300**
state abbreviation, magazine mailing label, **169**
state dining room, White House, **75**
state political division, thematic map, **21**
state prescription number, prescription, **451**
stateroom: passenger ship, **142**; sailboat, **135**
state route: road map, **20**; road sign, **504**
statesman's name, paper money, **225**
static discharge wick, jumbo jet, **148**
static line, parachuting, **333**
station: dam, **100**; nautical chart, **22**; subway, **119**; universal gym, **344**
stationary front, weather map, **19**
stationary jaw, wrench, **415**
stationary leaf, table, **242**
stationary rings, gymnastics, **307**
stationery, **159**
stationery rack, desk, **276**
station guide, picture-in-picture viewing, **185**
station model, weather map, **19**
station wagon, **106, 108**
Statue of Freedom, Capitol, **74**
stave, barrel, **267**
stay: bicycle, **128**; checkbook clutch, **223**; girdle, **195**; running shoe, **302**; shirt collar, **189**; sousaphone, **358**; wallet, **223**
stay rope, bridge, **97**
staysail, sailboat, **134**
stealth bomber, **480**
steam-and-dry iron, **279**
steam engine, **405**
steamer, pot, **257**
steamer cap, fire hydrant, **125**
steam generator, nuclear reactor, **392**
steam heat, furnace, **400**
steam line, nuclear reactor, **392**
steam locomotive, **116**
steam main, furnace, **400**
steel: jackhammer, **436**; sharpening, **256**
steel blade, food processor, **254**
steel burr, dental, **455**
steel cage, circus, **90**
steel guitar, **363**
steel helmet, combat soldier, **497**

steel inner shell, nuclear reactor, **392**
steel pin, and carpet, **246**
steel shield, tunnel, **98**
steeplechase: harness racetrack, **337**; hurdle, **304**; track and field, **300**
steeple-crowned hat, wizard, **492**
steer, **32**
steerable front strut, hydrofoil, **145**
steerable high-gain antenna, satellite, **186**
steering: automobile, **108, 110**; bulldozer, **435**; bumper car, **92**; fireboat, **144**; fire engine, **125**; outboard engine, **137**; 747 cockpit, **150**; sled, **328**; snowmobile, **130**
stegosaurus, **43**
stela, architecture, **71**
stem: apple, **55**; bicycle, **128**; cactus, **56**; candelabrum, **237**; carrot, **54**; celery, **262**; faucet, **273**; fern, **57**; fishing reel, **340**; flower, **53**; grass, **58**; hose nozzle, **428**; laboratory burner, **447**; latch needle, **386**; leaf, **52**; lettuce, **54**; mushroom, **57**; music, **353**; onion, **54**; pepper, **262**; percolator brewing basket, **252**; pipe, **229**; potato, **54**; powerboat, **138**; razor blade injector, **210**; rowboat, **133**; royal orb, **485**; steamer basket, **257**; glassware, **244**; spring beard needle, **386**; thermometer, **449**; tuning fork, **367**; type, **165-166**; watch, **220**
stem press, incandescent bulb, **238**
stemware, **244**
stencil, silk screen, **375**
stenographer's table, courtroom, **89**
step: cannon carriage, **467**; church, **87**; escalator, **79**; fire engine, **124**; gallows, **462**; Hansom cab, **131**; house, **63**; ladder, **425**; locomotive, **116-117**; medical examination table, **450**; sailboat, **135**; shoreline, **14**; shovel, **427**; staircase, **66**; tractor, **434**; truck, **120, 126**; windsurfer mast, **330**
stepladder, **425**
step well, bus, **118**
stereo camera, lunar rover, **155**
stereo display, portable radio/cassette player, **182**
stereo indicator light, phonograph receiver, **179**
stereo key, television, **185**
stereo/mono button, Walkman, **182**
stereo sound LED display, VCR, **184**
stereo speaker, television, **185**
sterilizing flame, dental, **455**
stern: boat, **132**; destroyer, **476**; dog, **36**; sailboat, **134**; tugboat, **144**; windsurfer, **330**
sterndrive engine, **137**
sternocleidomastoid, human, **26**
sternum, human, **26**
stet, proofreader's mark, **514**
stethoscope, **449**
stetson, cowboy hat, **490**
steward, circus, **90**
steward, corkscrew, **251**
stew pot, **257**
stick: ambulance, **123**; beauty product, **217**; billiard bridge,

320; car shift, **110**; craps table, **347**; folding rule, **424**; golf course, **311**; ice hockey, **295**; internal combustion engine, **406**; lacrosse, **298**; piano, **361**; pilot's instrument panel, **481**; polo, **299**; rocket, **383**; space shuttle, **153**; subway motorman's cab, **119**; violin bow, **355**; walking, **452**
stick glove, ice hockey goalie, **294**
stickman, craps table, **347**
stick pin, **192**
stick umbrella, **230**
stiff backing, frame, **379**
stiffening truss, bridge, **97**
stifle: cow, **32**; dog, **36**; horse, **38**
stigma, flower pistil, **53**
stile: door, **64**; rocking chair, **234**; shutters, **241**; sideboard, **243**; window, **65**
stiletto heel, **205**
stilling basin, dam, **100**
stimulator tip, toothbrush, **215**
sting, bee, **41**
stingray, **45**
stipe: fern, **57**; mushroom, **57**
stipule, leaf, **52**
stirrup: crossbow, **466**; medical examination table, **450**; saddle, **335-337**
stirrup sock, baseball batter, **290**
stitch and stitching, **384**; baseball, **290**; boot, **206**; broom, **282**; checkbook clutch, **223**; decorative, **385**; handbag, **222**; knitting, **386**; man's belt, **190**; sandal, **206**; sewing machine, **251**; sleeping bag, **343**; sock, **207**; suspenders, **190**
stitching line, sewing pattern, **388**
stock: anchor, **132**; bagpipe, **365**; bell, **iv**; crossbow, **466**; rifle, **468, 471**; shotgun, **468**; slide rule, **441**; windmill, **390**
stockade, frontier fort, **82**
stockcar, train, **117**
stock grip cap, shotgun, **468**
stocking: Beefeater, **483**; soccer, **297**
stock pot, **257**
stock saddle, **335**
stogies, **228**
stole, bishop, **487**
stolon, grass, **58**
stomach: human, **27, 31**; jellyfish, **46**
stomach teeth, **456**
stone: backgammon, **345**; dominos, **345**; lithographic press, **376**; peach, **55**; pendant, **219**; ring, **219**; wall, **69**; woodcarving, **372**
stonecutting, **372**
stool: boxing, **309**; window, **65**
stool bed, cannon carriage, **467**
stoop, **66**; door, **64**; house, **63**
stop: dam, **100**; dog, **36**; drill press, **419**; elevator car, **78**; etching press, **377**; gardening shears, **427**; mower, **429**; organ, **360**; remote control unit, **184**; road sign, **504**; subway, **119**; tape recorder, **177**; typewriter, **161**; window, **65**; zipper, **209**
stop-act, clown, **493**
stop action, picture-in-picture viewing, **185**
stopboard, shot put, **301**

stop button: compact disc player, **178**; Walkman, **182**
stoplight, truck, **121, 126**
stopper: backpack, **343**; bathtub, **274**; hypodermic syringe, **451**; sink, **273**
stopping medium, silk screen, **375**
stop plate, internal combustion engine, **406**
stop sign, road, **505**
stop signal, traffic light, **113**
stopwatch, **220, 304**
stop wire, umbrella runner, **230**
storage: ambulance, **123**; buoy, **132**; camper, **130**; car, **110**; fire engine, **124, 125**; garbage disposal, **247**; gasoline pump, **112**; laboratory scale, **447**; nuclear reactor, **392**; oil drilling platform, **101**; pool table, **320**; refrigerator, **249**; stagecoach, **131**; tanker, **140**
storage area, supermarket, **102-103**
storage drawer, oven, **248**
storage solution, contact lens, **221**
store ad space, supermarket, **102**
storm, **19**
storm door: house, **63**; subway car, **119**
storm flap, backpack, **343**
storm igloo, **85**
storm patch, trench coat, **200**
storm surge, **14**
story: minaret, **70**; newspaper, **168**; skyscraper, **77**
stove: camping, **342**; kitchen, **248**; sailboat, **135**; woodburning, **404**
stovepipe leg, woman's pants, **196**
stowage: jumbo jet, **148**; lunar rover, **155**; tank, **474**
stowed derrick bracket, tanker, **141**
straight arm, bobby pin, **214**
straightaway, roller coaster, **92**
straighten type horizontally, proofreader's mark, **514**
straight gouge, **374**
straight jaw, pliers, **414**
straight leg: trousers, **191**; woman's pants, **196**
straight-line course, drag racing, **339**
straight-line sander, **421**
straight of goods, sewing pattern, **388**
straight pin, **208**
straight razor, **210**
straight run, staircase, **66**
straight side, grand piano, **361**
straight ticket, voting, **437**
straight tray, slide projector, **175**
straight-up ribbed top, sock, **207**
strainer: dishwasher, **250**; juice extractor, **255**; kitchen tool, **260**
strain insulator, overhead power line, **396**
strain reliever: curling iron cord, **214**; hand drill cord, **419**; toaster oven cord, **253**
strait, **7**
strand: barbed wire, **432**; basket, **266**; electrician's wire, **423**; hair, **213, 214**; land feature, **7**; mop, **282**; rope, **132**; thread, **384**
strap: accordion, **366**; athletic supporter, **194**; backpack,

343; baseball catcher, 290; bicycle, 128; block and tackle, 461; boot, 206; brassiere, 195; chain saw chain, 431; child's car seat, 286; cinch fastener, 208; cowboy hat, 202; drag racing driver, 339; dress, 198; electrical wall switch, 398; electric chair, 462; fencing half-jacket, 315; football helmet, 292; glove, 200, 313; golf bag, 311; hasp, 460; ice climbing boot, 334; ice hockey player, 295; man's undershirt, 194; motorcycle, 129; operating table, 450; overnight bag, 285; photographic, 176; police uniform, 499; sandal, 206; handbag, 222; saddle, 335; sandal, 206; skin diving gear, 331; ski pole, 326; stationary rings, 307; subway car, 119; tefillin, 486; trench coat, 200; umbrella, 230; waterskiing vest, 329; woman's shoe, 205; wristwatch, 220

strap hinge, 460
strapping, chaise longue, 288
strap lug, camera, 172
stratocumulus cloud, 16, 17
stratosphere, 4
stratus cloud, 16
straw, cave, 11
strawberry, 55
stream: mountain, 8; ocean, 6; river, 13; topographic map, 22
streamer: drum major's waist sash, 495; flagpole, 502
street, city plan, 20
street address, magazine mailing label, 169
street cleaner, 127
street zip, mailing label, 169
stretcher: ambulance, 123; brick wall, 69; drop-leaf table, 242; fire engine, 124; painting canvas, 370; rocking chair, 234; umbrella, 230; workbench, 408
stretch limo, 109
stretch pants, skiing, 326
strike: bell, iv; lock, 458
strike pocket, bowling, 317
striker, croquet, 318
striker plate, door lock, 458
striker wheel, cigarette lighter, 228
striking weapons, medieval, 464
string: balloon, 493; cowboy hat, 490; double bass, 355; frankfurter, 265; guitar, 362, 363; jai alai cesta, 314; kite, 323; mandolin, 362; orchestra section, 354; polo, 299; saddle, 335; sitar, 362; squash racket, 313; tennis racket, 312; tie, 192; tub fiddle, 366; violin, 355
string bass, 354
string brace, kite, 323
stringed instruments, 355, 362
string hole: tennis racket, 312; tub fiddle, 366
string tie, 192
strip: bath, 274; cartridge fuse, 399; fence, 67; fencing, 315; Indian shirt, 490; kite, 323; matchbook, 228; postage stamps, 159; roofing shingle, 68; staples, 277; tackless, carpet, 246; wheelbarrow, 430; window shutters, 241

stripe: enlisted man's uniform, 496; powerboat, 138; runway, 94; toll booth, 114
striped morning trousers, butler's uniform, 489
stripper, wire, 423
strip title, comic strip, 380
strobe, photographic, 176
strobe flasher, locomotive, 117
stroller, child's, 286
strongbox, 457
strongbox storage, stagecoach, 131
strop, razor, 210
structural unit, piano, 361
structure: domed, 85; launch pad, 152; pyramids, 70
strut: bulldozer, 435; destroyer, 476; geodesic dome, 85; helicopter, 146; house, 61; hydrofoil, 145; racing car, 338; sled, 328
stub: candle, 237; pliers, 414; ticket, 189
stubble, beard, 211
stud: house, 61; man's formal attire, 488; organ, 360; running shoe tread, 302
stud hole, shirt, 189
stud side, snap fastener, 208
stuffing box, steam engine, 405
stuffsack, backpacking, 343
stump: rocking chair, 234; tree, 50
stupa, pagoda, 71
style: art, 368; flower pistil, 53; pea, 54
styled man's hat, 202
stylet, mosquito, 41
stylus, phonograph turntable, 178
styptic pencil, 210
subcategory, book page, iv
subclavian artery, human, 28
subclavian vein, human, 28
sub-control panel, VCR, 184
subdued unit patch, combat soldier, 497
subflooring, house, 60
subhead: book page, iv; magazine, 169-170; newspaper, 168
subject, work of art, 368
subleaflet, fern, 57
submarine, 479
submarine tender, 477
submerged foil hydrofoil, 145
submerged rock, nautical chart, 22
submersible watch, skin diving, 331
subnuclear particle, 3394
subordinate illustration, book page, iv
subscriber, magazine, 169
subsidiary coin, 225
subsidiary road, 114
substitute box area, basketball court, 296
substitute letter, proofreader's mark, 514
subtract, symbol, 510
subtraction, with abacus, 441
subtractive process, stone sculpture, 372
subway, 119; city plan, 20
succulent, 56
sucker, octopus, 46
suction cup, plumber's plunger, 422
suction machine, ambulance, 123
suction unit, paramedic equipment, 123
sudden death, darts, 322
sudden-death overtime, soccer, 297
suffix letter, paper money, 225

sugar bowl, 245
sugar cone, ice cream, 265
sugar shaker, 260
suicide king, playing cards, 348
suit: basketball, 296; chauffeur, 489; drag racing driver, 339; playing cards, 348; sails, 136
suitcase, 285
suit hanger, 281
suite, passenger ship, 143
sulky, harness racing, 337
summer berm, shoreline, 14
summer squash, 54
summer uniform, police, 499
summit, mountain, 8
summons pouch, police, 498
sump, nuclear reactor, 392
sun, 3
sundae, 264
sun deck, passenger ship, 142
sundial, 389
sunglasses, baseball gear, 290
sunglasses pocket, spacesuit, 155
sun roof, automobile, 106
sunshade: satellite, 186; sextant, 137; telescope, 443
sun spot, 3
sun visor, car, 110
super collider, 394
supercombo, 102
superconducting magnet, accelerator, 394
supercooled water, thundercloud, 17
supergiant star, 2
superior mesenteric artery, human, 28
superior slope, permanent fort, 83
superior vena cava, human, 28
supermarket, 102-103
supernova, 3
supersport, passenger car, 109
superstore, 102
superstructure, tanker, 141
super tanker, 140-141
supertweeter, phonograph speaker, 179
Super-Vee racing car, 338
supply duct, heat exchanger, 403
supply line, water heater, 401
supply pipe: solar collector panel, 391; space shuttle, 152; water heater, 401
supply reel: movie camera, 174; projector, 175; tape recorder, 177
support: backyard equipment, 287; camp stove, 342; citrus juicer, 255; desk, 276; Ferris wheel, 93; helicopter, 146; hot air balloon, 332; mailbox, 231; playpen, 286; pole vault, 305; pool table, 320; power line, 396; power saw, 417; pulley block, 461; rocking chair arm, 234; stroller, 286; traverse rod, 240; vacuum tube, 396; wheelbarrow, 430
support bar, drag racing dragster, 339
support beam: bus, 118; subway car, 119
supporter: athletic, 194; coat of arms, 503
support hose, 207
supporting members, fence, 67
supporting plate, land mine, 473
supportive devices, 452
support lacing, lacrosse glove, 298
support leg, truck, 121

support post, Ping-Pong net, 321
support system, racing car, 338
support tube, lamp, 239
support unit, basketball backstop, 296
support wire, incandescent bulb, 238
suppressor, automatic weapon flash, 471
sural nerve, human, 29
surbase, column pedestal, 73
surcingle, flat racing, 336
surf, 14
surface: brick, 68; desk, 276; diving platform, 316; lithographic press, 376; parachute, 333; and perspective, 368; pool table, 320; printing, 166; solar power system, 391; starfish, 46; table saw, 417; type, 166
surface fighting ship, 476-477
surface heating unit, oven, 248
surface-piercing hydrofoil, 145
surface search radar: aircraft carrier, 478; destroyer, 477
surface-to-air missiles, 476
surface-to-surface missiles, 476
surface wave, 14
surfboard, 331
surfing, 330
surgical table, 450
surname: basketball player, 296; magazine mailing label, 169
surplice, minister, 487
surveyor, and transit, 436
suspended ceiling, elevator car, 78
suspender, harness racing gear, 337
suspender cable, bridge, 97
suspenders, 190; ice hockey player, 294
suspension: phonograph turntable, 178; racing car, 338
suspension bridge, 97
suspension cable, stationary rings, 307
suspension line, parachute, 333
suspension pivot, laboratory scale, 447
suspension rope, hot air balloon, 332
suspension system: automobile, 108; football helmet, 292
suspension wheel, snowmobile, 130
sutler, frontier fort, 82
su-tshu, Manchu court dress, 491
suture, univalve shell, 47
swab, cannon, 467
swagger bag, 222
swalloop, cartoon, 380
swallowtail: flag, 502; surfboard, 330
swallowtail pennant, 502
swami belt, mountain climbing, 334
swamp: coastline, 15; river, 13
swan neck, house, 63
swash, wave, 14
swatch, fabric, 388
swastika, symbol, 508
sweatband, beret, 202
sweater, 199; skiing, 326, 327
sweat sock, 207
sweat soldering, plumbing, 422
sweep: brace, 418; windmill, 390
sweeper: carpet, 282; lawn, 429
sweep indicator, pilot's instrument panel, 481

sweet goods, 264
sweet spot, tennis racket, 312
sweet tooth, 456
swell, 14; saddle, 335
swelling, lance, 464
swell keyboard, organ, 360
swell shoe, organ, 360
swept-back wing, combat
    aircraft, 480
swim fin, skin diving, 331
swimming, 316
swimming foot, bird, 39
swine, 34
swing, backyard, 287
swing-away bar, suit hanger,
    281
swing chain, 287
swing gouge, woodcarving,
    372
swing hanger, 287
swinging gate, drop-leaf table,
    242
swing mirror, dressing table,
    272
swing seat, 287
Swiss army knife, 426
switch: accordion, 366;
    calculator, 441; camera, 172;
    car directional signal, 110;
    CB radio, 183; clothes dryer,
    281; cow, 32; curling iron,
    214; dental unit, 454;
    dishwasher, 250; drill press,
    419; electric, 398; electric
    hairbrush, 212; electric
    razor, 210; elevator, 78; fax
    machine, 164; finishing
    sander, 421; food processor,
    254; guitar amplifier, 363;
    hair dryer, 212; jackhammer,
    436; kiln, 373; lamp, 238,
    239; laser printer, 163;
    microphone, 183;
    minivacuum, 283; movie
    camera, 174; organ, 360;
    outboard engine, 137;
    phonograph receiver, 179;
    pilot's instrument panel,
    481; portable radio/cassette
    player, 182; radar, 444;
    railroad yard, 96; saw, 417,
    431; 747 cockpit, 150, 151;
    tape measure, 424; tape
    recorder, 177; telephone,
    180; toaster oven, 253;
    Walkman, 182
swivel: camera tripod, 176;
    C-clamp, 409; field events
    hammer, 303; fishhook, 341;
    hasp, 460; jewelry findings,
    218; jump rope, 344; mortar,
    472; peeler, 256; pulley
    block, 461; rifle, 468, 469;
    stationary rings, 307;
    stroller, 286; suit hanger,
    281; vise, 409
swivel holster, police gun belt,
    499
swivel mount, hand shower,
    274
sword, 463, 492
sword point position,
    windmill, 390
sword-swallower, circus, 90
symbol: grammatical, 513;
    label, 268, 269; of life, 508;
    mah-jongg tile, 345; map,
    20; religious, 508; science,
    business, and commerce,
    510-511
symbolia, cartoon, 381
symbolic date, coin, 225
symbolic decoration, minister,
    487
symbolic language, 512
sympathetic string, sitar, 362
symphony orchestra, 354
synagogue, 88, 486

synchronized dubbing,
    portable radio/cassette
    player, 182
synodic period, moon, 4
synoptic chart, weather, 19
synthesizer, 363
synthetic coil, zipper, 209
synthetic porcelain, dental, 455
syringe: dental, 454, 455;
    hypodermic, 451; kitchen,
    259; paramedic, 123
syrup, sundae, 264
system control panel, Polaroid,
    173
system diagram, portable
    radio/cassette player, 182

T

T: braille, 512; sign language,
    512; windsurfer, 330
tab: electrical receptacle, 398;
    eyeglasses, 221; handbag,
    222; package, 268; parka,
    201; powerboat, 138; racing
    car, 338; razor, 210; roofing
    shingle, 68; wallet, 223;
    zipper, 209
tabernacle, church, 87
table, 242; basketball court,
    296; courtroom, 89; cut
    gemstone, 218; dental, 455;
    drill press, 419; medical,
    450; Ping-Pong, 321; pocket
    billiards, 320; sailboat, 135;
    saw, 417; violin, 355
table arm, dental, 455
table lamp, 238
table lock, camera tripod, 176
table-locking clamp, drill
    press, 419
table position selector, surgical
    table, 450
table saw, 417
table setting, 244-245
tablet: computer workstation,
    438; medicinal, 451; organ,
    360; tombstone, 516
table tennis, 321
tabletop, dressing table, 272
tabling, mainsail, 136
tabloid newspaper, 168
tabulator control, typewriter,
    161
TACAN antenna, destroyer,
    476
Tacan navigation system,
    aircraft carrier, 478
tace, armor, 465
tach, car, 110
tachometer: car, 110;
    motorcycle, 129; pilot's
    instrument panel, 481;
    powerboat, 138
tack, 410; carpet, 246;
    mainsail, 136; necktie, 193;
    racehorse, 336; tambourine,
    364; umbrella, 230
tack cloth, painting, 425
tackle, fishing, 341
tackless strip, carpet, 246
taco, jai alai cesta, 314
tactical information display,
    pilot's instrument panel, 481
tadpole, 44
taenia, column entablature, 73
taffrail, sailboat, 134
tag: attaché case, 285; combat
    soldier's uniform, 461
tail: allosaurus, 43; cat, 37;
    coffin, 516; coin, 225; comet,
    3; cow, 32; dog, 36;
    fireworks, 383; fish, 45;
    horse, 38; house, 61; kite,
    323; lobster, 47; pelt, 201;
    pig, 34; single engine
    airplane, 147; skateboard,
    324; ski, 326, 329; snowshoe,
    327; stegosaurus, 43;

stingray, 45; surfboard, 330;
    ultimate beast, 48; weather
    station vane, 18; windsurfer,
    330
tail coat: circus ringmaster, 90;
    drum major, 495; man's
    formal attire, 488
tail crest, tadpole, 44
tail fan, lobster, 47
tail feather, 35, 39
tail fin: automobile, 107; cruise
    missile, 482; fish, 45; jet
    fighter, 480; jumbo jet, 149
tailgate piston, garbage truck,
    127
tailhead, cow, 32
taillight: automobile, 107;
    locomotive, 117; motorcycle,
    129; truck, 121, 126
tail nozzle, jet fighter, 480
tailored pillow, sofa, 236
tailor shop, prison, 76
tailor's loop, shirt, 189
tailpiece: banjo, 362; sink
    drain, 273; violin, 355
tailpipe, tow truck, 126
tail plane, jumbo jet, 149
tail pylon, helicopter, 146
tail rocker, slalom water ski,
    329
tail rotor, helicopter, 146
tail section: flute, 356;
    snowmobile, 130; torpedo,
    479
tail service mast, space shuttle,
    152
tail vise, workbench, 408
tail water, dam, 100
tail wheel, helicopter, 146
taintor gate, dam, 100
takeoff area, high jump, 305
takeoff board, track and field,
    300
takeoff engine, lunar lander,
    154
takeoff fan, high jump, 300
take out space, proofreader's
    mark, 514
take-up motion handle, hand
    loom, 387
take-up reel: movie camera,
    174; movie projector, 175;
    tape recorder, 177
take-up spool, typewriter, 161
talk switch, CB radio
    microphone, 183
tall-case clock, 233
tallith, Jewish prayer vestment,
    486
tallow, candle, 237
tally clerk, House of
    Representatives, 74
tally man, cattle ranch, 432
tallywhacker, sailor's uniform,
    497
talon: allosaurus, 43; bird, 39
talus slope, mountain, 8
tambourine, 354, 364
tamer, circus, 90
Tamid, 88, 486
tamper, pipe tool, 229
tandem wheels, truck, 121
tang: drill bit, 419; file, 420;
    knife, 244, 256, 463; rake,
    427; rasp, 420; skillet, 257
tangential section, lumber,
    68
tank, 474-475; ambulance, 123;
    automobile, 107, 108, 109;
    barbecue grill, 288; camper,
    130; camp stove, 342; chain
    saw, 431; drag racing
    dragster, 339; fire engine,
    124; garbage truck, 127;
    gasoline storage, 112;
    internal combustion engine,
    406; iron, 279; lantern, 342;
    lunar lander, 154; mower,

429; nuclear reactor, 392; oil
    drilling platform, 101;
    railroad yard, 96; skin
    diving, 331; solar heating
    system, 391; space shuttle,
    152; submarine ballast, 479;
    toilet, 275; truck, 120, 121;
    water heater, 401
tank car, train, 116
tanker, ocean-going, 140-141
tank forward bay, space
    shuttle, 152
tap, 273
tape: Band-Aid, 451; baseball
    bat, 291; boxing, 309; cash
    register, 440; cassette, 177;
    coat of arms, 503; envelope,
    159; garment seam, 196;
    measuring, 424; mountain
    climbing, 334; package, 269;
    Ping-Pong net, 321;
    skateboard, 324; tennis net,
    312; typewriter, 161; Velcro,
    209; venetian blind, 241;
    volleyball net, 319; zipper,
    209
tape control, portable
    radio/cassette player, 182
tape control button, Walkman,
    182
tape measure, 424
tape mode selector, portable
    radio/cassette player, 182
tape-monitor switch,
    phonograph receiver, 179
taper, 237
tape recorder, 177
tapered leg, woman's pants,
    196
tapered winder, staircase, 66
tape reel, magnetic tape
    subsystem, 439
taphole, keg, 267
tapper: buoy, 132; glass cutter,
    378
taproot, 51; carrot, 54
tare poise, laboratory scale,
    446
target: medieval shield, 464;
    radar, 444; railroad crossing
    signal, 115
target arrow, bowling lane,
    317
target designate switch, pilot's
    instrument panel, 481
target lock, sonar, 444
tassel: drum major's boot top,
    495; king's regalia, 484;
    Manchu court dress, 491;
    venetian blind, 241; window
    shade, 240; woman's hat,
    203
tasset, armor, 465
taste buds, tongue, 30
tasting spoon, 259
tatting shuttle, 386
tattooed lady, circus, 90
tau cross, symbol, 508
Taurus, zodiac, 509
taxi roof light, 119
taxi stand, public sign, 506
taxiway, airport, 95
t-bar, truck bed, 126
tea ball, 260
teacup, 245
tea infuser, 260
team insignia, soccer uniform,
    297
team logo, baseball, 290
team number, jai alai, 314
team race, swimming pool,
    316
team shirt, polo, 299
teamsters' mess, frontier fort,
    82
teamsters' quarters, frontier
    fort, 82
teapot, 245

tear-away jersey, football
uniform, 292
tear drop, surfboard, 330
tear duct, eye, 30
tear gland, eye, 30
tear tape, package, 269
teased hair, woman's, 213
teaser: magazine, 171; stage,
350
tea set, 245
tea spoon, 245
tea strainer, 260
teat: cow, 32; pig, 34
technical magazine, 169
technician's set, ambulance,
123
tee: golf, 310; pagoda, 71
teepee, 84
teeterboard, circus, 90
teeter-totter, backyard, 287
teeth, see tooth
tefillin, Jewish ritual items, 486
teflon pad, baren, 374
telegraph aerial, tanker, 141
telegraph key, 157
telemetry radio, ambulance,
123
telephone, 180; public sign,
506; road sign, 504
telephone handset: answering
machine, 181; fax machine,
164
telephone line, fax machine,
164
telephone line hook-up, fax
machine, 164
telephone line jack, fax
machine, 164
telephone monitor, tape
recorder, 177
telephone pushbutton,
answering machine, 181
telescope, 443; satellite, 186;
sextant, 137; tank, 475;
theodolite, 436
telescopic helicopter hangar,
destroyer, 476
telescopic sight, rifle, 469
television, 184-185; antenna,
house, 63; mast, skyscraper,
77
television monitor, video-still
camera, 173
telex number, business card,
160
telltale: mainsail, 136; squash
court, 313
telson, lobster, 47
tempera, painting medium,
370
temperature: 747 cockpit, 150;
thermometer, 18; weather
map, 19
temperature control: air
conditioner, 403; dryer, 281;
iron, 279; microwave oven,
248; toaster oven, 253;
washing machine, 280
temperature gauge, car engine,
110
temperature prediction,
weather map, 19
temperature scale, volt-ohm
meter, 423
temperature sensor: microwave
oven, 248; weather station,
18
temple: eyeglasses, 221;
human, 24; Jewish, 88, 486;
Muslim, 70-71
temple gateway, Shinto, 70
temple memorial band, Jewish
prayer shawl, 486
temporal lobe, brain, 29
temporary traffic-control
device, toll booth, 114
tempura rack, wok, 257
tenant floor, skyscraper, 77

tender, 133; locomotive, 116
tenderloin, pork, 34
tender truck, locomotive, 116
tendon, human foot, 31
tendon guard: hockey skate,
325; skate, 295
tendril, hair, 213
ten-gallon hat, 202, 490
tennis, 312
10-off square, shuffleboard
court, 318
tenon, bagpipe, 365
tenor drone, bagpipe, 365
tenor drum, 364
tenor joint, bassoon, 37
tenpins, bowling, 317
tension adjustment pin,
gardening shears, 427
tension arm, bobby pin, 214
tension bar: razor, 210; steel
chain fence gate, 67
tension clamp, lamp, 239
tension control knob, snare
drum, 364
tension cord, Ping-Pong net,
321
tension guide, sewing
machine, 278
tension hoop, banjo, 362
tension ring, dome, 85
tension rod: bass drum, 364;
man's buckle, 190
tension screw: banjo, 362;
kettledrum, 364; paramedic
equipment, 123
tension sheave, elevator shaft,
78
tension wheel, bicycle, 128
tent, 342; circus, 90; oxygen,
452; yurt, 70
tentacle: coral polyp, 46;
jellyfish, 46; octopus, 46;
starfish, 46
10-yard chain, football, 293
10-yard line, football field, 293
10.5-inch magnetic tape,
computer tape, 439
10.5-inch magnetic tape drive,
computer system, 439
tepal, flower, 53
tepee, 84
terminal: airport, 95; electrical
wall switch, 398; fax
machine, 164; fence gate, 67;
railroad yard, 96
terminal block, stove, 248
terminal bud, tree, 50
terminal moraine, 8, 12
terminology, nautical, 132
terminus, glacier, 12
terrace: house, 63; shoreline,
14
terrace server, 245
terreplein, permanent fort, 83
territory, baseball field, 291
tertiary root, 51
test area, aircraft carrier, 478
test button: police car, 122;
smoke alarm, 284
test lead jack, volt-ohm meter,
423
test panel, pilot's instrument,
481
test tube, 447
tether line, hot air balloon, 332
text: book, 167; magazine, 170
textblock, book page, iv
texture, and composition, 369
thalamus, brain, 29
T-handle, pommel horse, 307
theatre, 351; passenger ship,
41
the end, gesture, 507
thematic map, 21
thenar eminence, human
hand, 31
theodolite, 436
therefore, symbol, 511

thermal dot, curling iron, 214
thermal energy, steam engine,
405
thermal-storage tank, solar
heating system, 391
thermistor, weather station, 18
thermometer, 449; dual scale,
18; kitchen, 258; laboratory,
447
thermosphere, earth, 4
thermostat: refrigerator, 249;
solar heating system, 391;
stove, 404; water heater, 401
thick stroke, type, 165
thick-walled inert laser
pressure vessel, 395
thigh: bird, 39; cat, 37;
chicken, 35; cow, 32; dog,
36; frog, 44; horse, 38;
human, 24; poultry, 35
thigh pad, football uniform,
292
thigh machine, universal gym,
344
thimble, 384; harness racing,
337; stove, 404
thin stroke, type, 165
third base, baseball field, 291
third eye, tuatara, 42
third molar, 456
third quarter moon, 4
third rail, subway, 119
third stage, missile, 482
third toe, human foot, 31
third valve, trumpet, 359
third valve slide: French horn,
358; trumpet, 359
3480 magnetic tape cartridge,
computer tape, 439
3480 magnetic tape drive,
computer system, 439
thirty-second-inch mark, tape
measure, 424
thirty-second note, music, 353
30-yard line, polo grounds,
299
thong: cowboy holster, 490;
police nightstick, 498;
sandal, 206
thoracic nerve, human, 29
thorax, grasshopper, 41
thorn, ultimate beast, 48
thoroughbrace, stagecoach,
131
thoroughbred, flat racing, 336
thought balloon, cartoon, 380
thread: bolt, 411; plug fuse,
399; screw, 410; sewing, 384;
spider, 40; weaving, 387
threaded fitting, nozzle, 428
threaded handle, paint roller,
425
threaded neck, bottle, 268
threaded pipe, 422
thread guide, sewing machine,
278
3-band display, portable
radio/cassette player, 182
3-band equalizer, Walkman,
182
three dimensions, stone
sculpture, 372
3/8 pole, harness racetrack,
337
301, darts, 322
three pin, bowling, 317
three-point line, basketball
court, 296
three-point perspective, 368
3/4 pole, harness racetrack,
337
3.25-inch disk format, diskette,
162
three-ring circus, 90
three-second lane, basketball
court, 296
3/16 pole, harness racetrack,
337

three suit, domino, 345
three-way light bulb, 238
three-way syringe, dental, 455
three-yard line, football, 293
threshold: airport runway, 94;
door, 64; house, 62
throat: anchor, 132; auger bit,
419; bird, 39; clamp, 409;
cornet, 359; fireplace, 232;
human, 24, 25, 30; lacrosse
stick, 298; latch needle, 386;
salamander, 44; saw, 416;
shoe, 204, 205; squash
racket, 313; tennis racket,
312
throat-cutting, gesture, 507
throat doctor, examination
equipment, 448
throat fan, lizard, 43
throating, church, 86
throat latch strap, trenchcoat,
200
throat opening, vise, 408
throatpiece, tennis racket, 312
throat plate, sewing machine,
278
throat protector, baseball
catcher, 290
throat pump, paramedic
equipment, 123
throttle: car, 110; horse, 38;
internal combustion engine,
406; motorcycle, 129;
outboard engine, 137; pilot's
instrument panel, 481;
powerboat, 138
throttle latch, chain saw, 431
throw: bedding, 270; track and
field, 301
throwing circle, shot put, 301
throwing sector, javelin, 300
thrown pot, 373
throw rug, 246
thrust cone, jumbo jet, 149
thruster: lunar lander, 154;
passenger ship, 143; space
shuttle, 152
thrusting and cutting weapon,
463
thrust lever, 747 cockpit, 151
thrust ring, missile, 482
thrust tube, ballpoint pen, 158
thruway, 114
thumb: baseball glove, 291;
dog, 36; frog, 44; human
hand, 31
thumbhole: bowling ball, 317;
painter's palette, 371
thumbpiece, revolver safety
catch, 218
thumb press, curling iron, 214
thumb rest: hypodermic
syringe, 451; iron, 279
thumbscrew: blood pressure
gauge, 449; clarinet
mouthpiece, 357; drain
cleaner, 422; earring, 218;
laboratory clamp, 446
thumb-string peg, banjo, 362
thunder, 17
thundercloud, 17
thunderhead, 16, 17
thunderstorm, 17, 19
thurl, cow, 32
thwart, rowboat, 133
thyratron, gas laser, 395
tiara, 219, 484, 485
tibia: frog, 44; grasshopper, 41;
human, 26; spider, 40
tibialis anterior, 26
tibialis posterior, 26
tibial nerve, human, 29
ticket, 349; police, 498; voting,
437
ticket pocket flap, jacket, 188
ticket spitter, toll basket, 114
tidal inlet, 15
tidal marsh, 15

tidal wave, 14
tide, 15
tie: man, 192-193, 488; military, 496; music notation, 353; package, 269; police, 499; railroad track, 115; saddle, 335; skirt, 197; wall, 69
tieback, curtain, 240
tie bar, 192
tie beam: house, 61; incline track, 92
tie brace, bridge, 97
tie clasp, 192
tie closure: blouse, 197; umbrella, 230
tie-down, inflatable, 133
tie holder, suitcase, 285
tie plate: railroad track, 115; stapler, 277
tie rod end, automobile, 108
tie strap, chain saw chain, 431
tie wing, dental brace, 453
tiger, circus, 90
tightener, dental, 455
tightrope act, circus, 90
tights, ballet dancer, 494
tight spiral, staircase, 66
tilde, grammatical symbol, 513
tile: domino, 345; mah-jongg, 345
till, cash register, 440
tiller: boat, 134; grass, 58; 747 cockpit, 150
tilt control, sonar, 444
tilt cord, venetian blind, 241
tilting arbor handwheel, saw, 417
tilting base, saw, 417
tilting knob, movie projector, 175
tilt lock, saw, 417
tilt rod, window shutters, 241
timber, 68; castle portcullis, 81
timbered joint, Japanese building, 70
timberline, 8
time: drag racing, 339; map, 5; parking meter, 113
time belt, 5
time cord, dental x-ray unit, 454
time dial, globe, 1
time dot, music, 353
timekeeper: House of Representatives, 74; ice hockey, 295
time lock, vault, 457
timer: basketball, 296; clothes dryer, 281; dishwasher, 250; kitchen, 258; parking meter, 113; skin diving, 331; stove, 248; traffic light, 113
timer digital display, microwave oven, 248
timer key, television, 185
timer set control, microwave oven, 248
times, symbol, 510
time signature, music, 352
Times Square, prison, 76
time zone, map, 5
time zone display control, wristwatch, 220
timing case cover, automobile engine, 111
timpani, 354, 364
tin, squash court, 313
tin can, surface fighting ship, 476
tine: fork, 244; hitch and harrow, 434; rake, 427
tip: arrow, 466; asparagus, 54; ballpoint pen, 158; bicycle, 128; billiard cue, 320; bobby pin, 214; bow, 466; cheese plane, 256; crutch, 452; curling iron, 214; dental

unit, 454; drain cleaner, 422; drum major's baton, 495; fencing foil, 315; fishing rod, 341; grass, 58; hypodermic syringe, 451; iceberg, 12; icing nozzle, 259; javelin, 302; knife, 256, 463; leaf, 52; man's belt, 190; nose, 30; outboard engine, 137; peeler, 256; pelt, 201; pliers, 414; saw, 431; screwdriver, 413; sharpening steel, 256; ski, 326, 329; soldering iron, 378; sword, 463; tent pole, 342; toothbrush, 215; tweezers, 215; umbrella, 230; univalve shell, 47; violin bow, 355; woman's shoe, 205
tip contact, incandescent bulb, 238
tip guard, hockey skate, 325
tipi, 84
tip-in, magazine, 171
tip-on label, 268
tippet, minister, 487
tipping, necktie, 193
tipping lever, wheelchair, 452
tip top, fishing rod, 341
tire, 105; automobile, 106, 107; bicycle, 128; bus, 118; drag racing dragster, 339; harness racing sulky, 337; motorcycle, 129; seeder, 430; stagecoach, 131; tractor, 434; truck, 120; wheelbarrow, 430
tissue: and denture, 453; fruit, 255; meat, 262; photographic supplies, 176; succulent, 56
Titan, 3
titanium salute, fireworks, 382
title: book, 167; business card, 160; comic strip, 380; magazine, 169, 170, 171; map, 21; music, 352; nautical chart, 22; phonograph record, 178
title block, house blueprint, 62
T-neck, ski clothes, 327
TNT, hand grenade, 473
toad, 44
toadstool, 57
toaster, 253
toaster oven, 253
tobacco, 228
tobacco pouch, 229
toboggan, 328
toe: bird, 39; boot, 206; cat, 37; chicken, 35; dog, 36; frog, 44; hockey skate, 325; golf club, 310; horseshoe, 38; horse's hoof, 38; human, 24, 31; ice skate, 325; man's shoe, 204; panty hose, 195; piano, 361; plane, 420; roller skate, 324; running shoe, 302; saw, 416; shotgun, 468; ski, 326, 327, 329; snowshoe, 327; sock, 207
toeboard, shot put, 301
toe cap, skate, 295
toe clip: bicycle, 128; horse's hoof, 38
toe disc, toad, 44
toe guard: elevator shaft, 78; mower, 429
toe-height adjustment screw, ski binding, 326
toenail: cat, 37; human, 31; turkey, 35; ultimate beast, 49
toe-piece release, ski binding, 326
toe plate: baseball pitcher, 290; refrigerator, 249
toe rail, sailboat, 134
toeshoe, ballet dancer, 494
toe strap, bicycle, 128

toe stud, organ, 360
toga, 491
toggle bolt, 411
toggle lever, pliers, 414
toggle link, sponge mop, 282
togglelock, backpack, 343
toilet, 275
toilet mirror, dressing table, 272
token, collector, 225
toll basket, 114
toll booth, highway, 114
tom, turkey, 35
tomato, 54
tomato sauce, pizza, 265
tomb, 516
tombolo, 7
tombstone, 516
tomcat, 37
tom-tom, 364
tone: tuning fork, 367; woodwind, 356, 358, 359
tone arm, phonograph turntable, 178
tone control: guitar, 363; tape recorder, 177
tone generator, synthesizer, 363
tone unit, piano, 361
tone-up wheel, body building, 344
tong(s): kitchen, 259; lunar rover, 155; oil drilling platform, 101; revolver safety catch, 218
tongue: bolt ring, 218; child's wagon, 287; cow, 32; curling iron, 214; film, 172; flag, 502; human, 30; Jew's harp, 366; L-shaped square, 424; man's belt, 190; man's shoe, 204; running shoe, 302; skate, 295, 324, 325; sled, 328; snake, 42
tongue-and-groove pliers, 414
tongue blade, 123, 449
tongue depressor, 449
tonsil, 30
tool: ice climbing, 334; pipe, 229; pocket knife, 426; police car, 122; sculpting, 372
tool stowage: bulldozer, 435; jackhammer, 436; lunar rover, 155; motorcycle, 129; tow truck, 126; workbench, 408
tooth, 456; allosaurus, 43; bear trap, 433; corrugated fastener, 410; denture, 453; fern, 57; file, 420; hair comb, 212; ice hammer, 334; knee kicker, 246; lobster, 47; pliers, 414; rake, 427; rasp, 420; saw, 416, 417; scissors, 384; scrimshaw, 375; snake, 42; suspenders, 190; tank drive wheel, 475; zipper, 209
toothbrush, 215
toothed chisel, 372
toothpick, pocket knife, 426
top: automobile, 107; balance beam, 306; battery, 397; button, 209; can, 267; circus, 90; desk, 276; fishing rod, 341; flag, 502; golf bag, 311; handbag, 222; horizontal bar, 306; hurdle, 304; juice extractor, 255; laboratory burner, 447; lettuce, 262; medical examination table, 450; microscope limb, 442; mountain, 8; parachute, 333; parallel bars, 306; piano, 361; rocking chair, 234; sideboard, 243; skyscraper, 77; sock, 207; stove, 404;

thimble, 384; violin, 355; workbench, 408; zipper, 209
top block, window shutters, 241
top cover, dot matrix printer, 163
tope, pagoda, 71
top exit, elevator, 78
top fabric, quilting, 385
top hat: circus ringmaster, 90; miser, 492
top housing, electric razor, 210
top link, hitch and harrow, 434
top lip, lacrosse stick, 298
toplit composition, 368
top-loading washing machine, 280
top margin, book page, 167
topographic map, 22
top pad, child's car seat, 286
top pillow, stagecoach, 131
topping: canapé, 263; dessert, 264
top plate: house, 61; typewriter, 161; violin, 355
top pocket flap, backpack, 343
top rail: backyard equipment, 287; bureau, 272; door, 64; fence gate, 67; playpen, 286; staircase, 66; window, 65
top ring, fishing rod, 341
top roller, etching press, 377
topsail, sailboat, 134
top sheet, bedding, 271
top spring, umbrella, 230
top stitching: checkbook clutch, 223; handbag, 222; man's belt, 190
top thread guide, sewing machine, 278
top tube, bicycle, 128
toque, 203
Torah, 88, 486
torch, propane, 422
torii, 70-71, 508
tormentor: fire engine, 124; stage, 350
tornado, 17
torpedo, 479
torsade, wrought iron fence, 67
torse, coat of arms, 503
torso: cow, 32; human, 24; space suit, 155
tortoise, 43
torus, column, 73
tossut, igloo, 85
total air temperature, 747 cockpit, 150
totalizer, gas pump, 112
totalizer board, flat racing, 336
total reflector, laser, 395
tote board, horseracing, 336, 337
touchdown area, airport runway, 95
touch line: polo grounds, 299; soccer field, 297
touch-tone button: pay phone, 180; telephone, 180
toupee, 211
touring, ski, 327
tourist section, jumbo jet, 149
tournament darts, 322
towboat, 144
tow-cable pulley, tow truck, 126
towel bar: barbecue grill, 288; oven, 248
towel clip, dental, 455
towel rack, bathtub, 274
tower: aircraft carrier, 478; bridge, 97; castle, 80, 81; church, 86, 87; destroyer, 476; Ferris wheel, 93; fireboat, 144; frontier fort,

572

82; globe, 1; mountain, 9; nautical chart, 22; passenger ship, 143; polygonal, 71; powerboat, 139; power network, 396; prison, 76; railroad yard, 96; slide, 287; windmill, 390
tower bin, silo, 104
tower control, airport, 95
tower ladder, 124
towing gear: glider, 147; fire engine, 124, 125; tank, 475; tow truck, 126; tugboat, 144
towing light: destroyer, 477; tugboat, 144
towing ring, kite, 323
towline, waterskiing, 329
town: magazine mailing label, 169; map, 20; nautical chart, 22
towpath, canal lock, 99
tow ring, fire engine, 124, 125
tow truck, 126
tracery, church, 86
track: baseball field, 291; bulldozer, 435; canal lock, 99; circus, 90-91; dishwasher, 250; Grand Prix, 338; horseracing, 336, 337; incline, 92; lighting, 239; movie film, 174; passenger ship, 142; railroad, 96, 115; roller coaster, 92; snowmobile, 130; subway, 119; tank, 474; traverse rod, 240
track and field, 300-301
track cueing, compact disc player, 178
tracking adjuster, belt sander, 421
tracking-force dial, phonograph turntable, 178
track lighting, 239
track shoe, 302; bulldozer, 435
traction splint, 123
tractor, 434; bulldozer, 435; truck, 120
tractor dial, dot matrix printer, 163
tractor wheel, roller coaster, 92
trade magazine, 169
trademark: bank card, 226; baseball bat, 286; book, 167; credit card, 227; label, 268
trade winds, 6
trading post, 82
traffic control, 113; airport, 94, 95; toll booth, 114
traffic light, 113
traffic police officer, 498
traffic signals, 113
traffic ticket, 498
tragus, outer ear, 30
trail: public sign, 506; road sign, 504
trail bike, 129
trailer, 130
trailer connecter, truck, 120
trailing edge, jumbo jet, 148
trailing truck, locomotive, 116
trail rope, hot air balloon, 332
trail shoe, snowshoe, 327
train: bridal gown, 488; railroad, 96, 116-117; roller coaster, 92; subway, 119
trainer: circus, 90; flat racing entry, 336; running shoe, 302
training shoe, 302
tramp, merchant ship, 140
trampolets, 308
trampoline, 308
tranquilizer, 123
transaction button, automatic teller machine, 226
transaction receipt slot,

automatic teller machine, 226
transceiver: CB radio, 183; radar antenna, 444
transducer, sonar, 444
transept, church, 87
transfer call, answering machine, 181
transfer scale, light meter, 176
transfer to local elevator, skyscraper, 77
transformer, nuclear reactor, 393
transistor chip, 396
transit, 436
transit system, 119
transmission: automobile, 109; bulldozer, 435; tank, 474
transmit light, CB radio, 183
transmitter, telephone, 180
transom: door, 64; elevator car, 78; powerboat, 139; rowboat, 133
transom clamp, outboard engine, 137
transparency: film slide, 172; projector, 175
transparent balustrade, escalator, 79
transparent roof, bus, 118
transponder, 747 cockpit, 151
transportation, public sign, 506
transportation office, Capitol building, 74
transpose, proofreader's mark, 514
transverse arch, human foot, 31
transverse piece, kite, 323
trap, 433; clothes dryer, 281; gallows, 462; sink drain, 273
trapdoor: Hansom cab, 131; stage, 350
trapeze artist, circus, 90
trapezius, human, 26
trap plug, sink drain, 273
trapunto, quilting, 385
trash basket, 247
trash compactor, 247
trauma box, paramedic equipment, 123
traveler: sailboat, 134; stage, 350
traveler's check, 227
traverse arm, overhead power line, 396
traverse rod, 240
traversing gear, mortar, 472
tray: baby's high chair, 286; copier, 164; cosmetic case, 285; dental unit, 454; easel, 370; house painting, 425; slide projector, 175; tea set, 245; toaster, 253
tread: planetary wheel, 434; running shoe, 302; staircase, 66; stirrup, 335; tire, 105
treadboard, escalator, 79
treadle: hand loom, 387; spinning wheel, 387
treasure box, stagecoach, 131
Treasury seal, paper money, 225
treatment, magazine photo, 170
treatment aids, medical, 451
treble clef, music, 352
treble dial, phonograph receiver, 179
treble hook, fishing plug, 341
treble part, accordion, 366
treble pick-up, guitar, 363
tree, 50; saddle, 335; shoe, 207
tree of life, Torah, 486
trefoil: church, 86; drum major's coat, 495; medal, 501
tremolo arm, guitar, 363

trench: continental margin, 15; underwater funnel, 98
trench coat, 200
tress, 25, 213
trestle, guillotine, 462
triangle: orchestra, 354; shuffleboard court, 318
tributary, river, 13
triceps, human, 26
triceps exerciser, body building, 344
trick, spring beard needle, 386
trick ski, waterskiing, 329
tricorne, pirate, 492
tricycle, 128
trifecta, flat racing, 336
trifocal lenses, eyeglasses, 221
triforium, church, 86
trigger: bear trap, 433; chain saw, 431; crossbow, 466; drill, 419; gas pump automatic nozzle, 112; movie camera, 174; paint spray gun, 425; sander, 421; slalom water ski, 329; weapon, 468, 470, 471, 472
trigger control, gas laser, 395
trig-loop post, laboratory scale, 447
trim: automobile, 107; baseball uniform, 290; cake, 264; door, 64; drum major's uniform, 495; fencing mask, 315; Manchu court dress, 491; pendant, 219; pool table, 320; queen's regalia, 484; running shoe, 302; 747 cockpit, 150; stove, 248; tennis racket, 312; window shade, 240; woman's hat, 203; woman's shoe, 205
trim-adjustment rack, outboard engine, 137
trimline phone, 180
trimmer: body building, 344; lawn, 429; razor, 210
trimming, woman's hat, 203
trimming end, clay modeling tool, 372
trim tab: powerboat, 138; racing car, 338
trip, fishing reel, 340
trip handle, toilet, 275
trip indicator, nuclear reactor control room, 393
triple jump, track and field, 300
triple ring, dart board, 322
triple-score ring, dart board, 322
triplet, music notation, 352
tripod: machine gun, 471; music stand, 367; photographic, 176; screen, 175; telescope, 443; transit, 436
trip odometer, car, 110
trochanter: grasshopper, 41; spider, 40
trolley, girdle, 195
trolley pole, bumper car, 92
trolling gear, fishing, 344
trombone, 354, 358-359
trophy, 289; king's regalia, 484; medal, 501
tropical storm, 19
troposphere, earth, 4
trotter, harness racing, 35
trough: barn, 104; humidifier, 402; longshore, 14; wave, 14
trousers, 191; bull denim, 490; butler, 489; cowboy, 490; jai alai player, 314; king's regalia, 484; man's formal attire, 488; military uniform, 496, 497; paramedic equipment, 123; police uniform, 498

trowel, 427
truck, 120-121; airport, 95; cannon carriage, 467; fire engine, 124; flagpole, 502; garbage, 127; locomotive, 116, 117; platform, 121; roller skate, 324; semitrailer, 121; skateboard, 324; tractor, 120
truck bed, tow truck, 126
true air speed indicator, 747 cockpit, 150
true bias, fabric, 388
true edge: knife, 463; sword, 463
true north, 22
true vertical, transit, 436
true-zero hook, tape measure, 424
trumpet, 354, 359
trunk: automobile, 107; cactus, 56; fish, 45; grandfather clock, 233; human, 24; octopus, 46; palm, 52; police car, 122; powerboat, 138; and root, 51; sailboat, 134; tree, 50; ultimate beast, 49
trunks, boxing, 309
trunnion: bulldozer, 435; cannon barrel, 467
truss: bridge, 97; roof, 61
trysail, 136
try square, 424
T-shirt, man's, 194
tsunami, 14
tuatara, 42
tub: bath, 274; dishwasher, 250; tub fiddle, 366; washing machine, 280
tuba, 354, 358
tube: ambulance, 123; automobile engine, 111; bazooka, 472; beauty product, 217; bicycle, 128; blood pressure gauge, 449; bolt ring, 218; dental unit, 454; dispenser, 267; eyedropper, 451; fire extinguisher, 284; food processor, 254; hurdle, 304; icing nozzle, 259; jet fighter, 480; laboratory burner, 447; laboratory clamp, 446; lamp, 238, 239; lawn sprinkler, 428; light bulb, 238; microscope, 442; mortar, 472; pen, 158; pitch pipe, 367; radiator, 400; screen, 175; shoe tree, 207; shotgun, 469; sketch box, 371; sleeping bag, 343; solar collector panel, 391; stethoscope, 449; submarine, 479; subway, 119; tank gun, 475; telescope, 443; television, 185; test, 447; thermometer, 449; toilet, 275; vacuum, 396; wave, 14
tuber, potato, 54
tubercles, stingray, 45
tube sock, 207
tub fiddle, 366
tubing: backyard glider, 287; dental, 455; plumbing, 422; stethoscope, 449
tub ring and filter, washing machine, 280
tuck: blouse, 197; cigar, 228
tucker, queen's regalia, 484
tuck flap, package, 269
tuft: lounger, 235; man's hair, 211; sofa, 236; toothbrush, 215
tug, 144; airport, 95
tugboat, 144
tumbling, trampoline, 308
tumbrel, execution vehicle, 462
tummy, human, 25

tuna tower, powerboat, 139
tuner: audio, 179; television, 185
tunic: Beefeater, 483; king's regalia, 484
tuning fork, 367
tuning gear: cornet, 359; dulcimer, 362; French horn, 358; guitar, 362; phonograph receiver, 179; radar, 444; sitar, 362; trombone, 358-359; trumpet, 359
tunnel, 98; igloo, 85; prison, 76; railroad, 115; subway, 119; super collider, 394; wave, 14
tunnel bottom, waterski, 329
tunnel visor, traffic light, 113
turban, woman's, 203
turbine: combustion jet engine, 407; nuclear reactor, 392
turbine engine, helicopter, 146
turbine locomotive, 116
turbofan engine, cruise missile, 482
turbofan jet engine, 149, 407
turboprop jet engine, 407
turf: baseball field, 291; polo grounds, 299; racetrack, 336, 337
turkey, 35
turn: lamp, 239; racetrack, 337
turnback, suit hanger, 281
turnback cuff: blouse, 197; jacket, 196
turnbuckle, boxing ring, 309
turned step, shovel, 427
turner, kitchen utensil, 259
turn indicator, 747 cockpit, 480
turning, drop-leaf table, 242
turning gear, can opener, 251
turning signal, automobile, 106
turning stake, croquet, 318
turning wall, swimming pool, 316
turn-lock, handbag, 222
turnouts, fireman, 500
turnover, 264
turnover collar, king's regalia, 484
turn signal light: bus, 118; truck, 120, 121
turntable: fire engine, 124; phonograph, 178; railroad yard, 96
turret: castle, 80; stethoscope, 449; tank, 475
turtle, 43
turtleneck: clothes, 327; sweater, 199
tusche stencil, silk screen, 375
tush, ultimate beast, 49
tusk, ultimate beast, 49
tutu, ballerina, 494
tuxedo, man's formal attire, 488
TV camera: aircraft carrier, 478; lunar rover, 155; satellite, 186
TV monitor, prison, 76
TV optical unit, jet fighter, 480
TV power status, space shuttle, 153
TV/VCR mode, remote control unit, 184
tweeter, audio speaker, 179
tweezers, 215; pocket knife, 426
twelve foot marker, bowling lane, 317
21, layout, 347
25-point ring, dart board, 322
20mm cannon, jet fighter, 48
24-second clock, basketball, 296
twig, tree, 50

twilight zone, cave, 11
twin bed, 270
twine, frankfurter, 265
twine tie, aerial shell, 383
twinned stories, newspaper, 168
twins, zodiac, 509
twist: drill bit, 418, 419; paper clip, 277
twisted handle, paper bag, 266
twister, 17; body building, 344
twist-off cap, bottle, 269
twist tie, package, 269
two-button closing, woman's jacket, 196
two-color eye pencil, 217
two-cycle internal combustion engine, 406
two-deck head, magazine, 171
2-door coupe, 108
2-piece casing, capsule, 451
two-point perspective, 368
two-pronged fork, 259
two-suiter, 285
two-stick kite, 323
two-way traffic, road sign, 505
two-way zipper, 209
two-yard line, football, 293
typanum: church, 86; frog, 44; grasshopper, 41; toad, 44
type, 165; magazine, 170, 171; printing, 166; typewriter, 161; wine label, 267
type display window, laser printer, 163
type of subscription code, magazine mailing label, 169
typewriter, 161
typhoon, 17
typist's initials, letter, 159
typography, 165
tzit, Torah, 486

U

U: braille, 512; sign language, 512
U-boat, 479
udder, cow, 32
U-gouge, 374
UHF radio, pilot's instrument panel, 481; 747 cockpit, 150
ullage, bottle, 267
ulna, human, 26
ulnar nerve, human, 29
ultimate beast, 48-49
ultraviolet spectrometer, satellite, 186
umbilical: space shuttle, 152; spacesuit, 155
umbilical system bag, lunar rover, 155
umbilicus, human, 24
umbo, shield, 464
umbo, clam, 47
umbrella, 230; golf, 311; pipe, 229; silo, 104
umlaut, grammatical symbol, 513
umpire, polo, 299
umpire's area, baseball field, 291
una corda pedal, piano, 361
unattended reception capability, fax machine, 164
undercarriage, stagecoach, 131
undercarriage protector, tow truck bed, 126
undercarriage wheels, helicopter, 146
undercoat, bird, 39
undercut, razor blade, 210
underline, grammatical symbol, 513
underpants, 194
underpass, 114
underpinnings, queen's regalia, 484

underscore, grammatical symbol, 513
under-seat bag stowage, lunar rover, 155
underserve line, jai alai cancha, 314
undershirt, 194, 290
underwater tunnel, 98
underwear, man's, 194
underwiring, brassiere, 195
uneven parallel bars, 306
unexposed film, movie camera, 174
unicycle, 128
uniform: baseball, 290; basketball, 296; boxer, 309; drag racing driver, 339; fencing, 315; football, 292; ice hockey, 294, 295; jai alai, 314; jockey, 336, 337; military, 496-497; police, 498-499; Revolutionary War general, 492; skiing, 326, 327; skin diving, 331
unimproved road, topographic map, 22
union: flag, 502; water heater, 401
unistrut, Ferris wheel, 93
unit: ambulance, 195; masonry, 68
unit citation, military uniform, 496
unit column, abacus, 441
unit crest, military cap, 496
US insignia, military uniform, 496
United States notes, paper money, 17
U.S. interstate route number, road map, 20
U.S. route, road sign, 504
unit number, fireman's helmet, 500
unit patch, military uniform, 496, 497
unit point, abacus, 441
unit value, thematic map, 21
univalve shell, 47
universal cross connection, traffic light, 113
universal drive joint, hitch and harrow, 434
universal gym, 344
universal joint: automobile, 109; windsurfer, 330
Universal Product Code, 440; symbol, label, 269
Universal Transverse Mercator grid marking, topographic map, 22
universal veil, remnants, mushroom, 57
universe, 2-3
UPC code, coupon, 103
UPC label, 440
updraft, tornado, 17
uphaul, windsurfer, 330
upholstery: sofa, 236; wheelchair, 452
upper: ice skate, 325; man's shoe, 204; running shoe, 302; sandal, 206
upper arm: dog, 36; frog, 44; human, 24; traffic light, 113
upper back-stick, easel, 370
upper ball joint, automobile, 108
upper blade guard, saw, 417
upper bolt, pulley block, 461
upper bout, viola, 355
upper bow, bear trap, 433
upper case, type, 165
upper chord, bridge, 97
upper control arm, automobile, 108
upper control line, parachute, 333

upper deck, passenger ship, 143
upper eyelid, frog, 44
upper face, zipper, 209
upper frame, piano, 361
upper gate, canal lock, 99
upper-girdle facet, cut gemstone, 218
upper grid, nuclear reactor, 392
upper grip ring, sword hilt, 463
upper handle, mower, 429
upper hatch, lunar lander, 154
upper header, solar collector panel, 391
upper housing, sander, 421
upper jaw, fish, 45
upper joint, clarinet, 357
upper limb, bow, 466
upper lounge, jumbo jet, 148
upper magnet, dipole magnet, 394
upper mandible, bird, 39
upper panel, piano, 361
upper plate, theodolite, 436
upper shell, turtle, 43
upper spray arm, dishwasher, 250
upper tail crest, tadpole, 44
upper teeth, 456
upper thigh, dog, 36
upper pool, canal lock, 99
upper rack, dishwasher, 250
upper rail, balustrade, 73
upper receiver, rifle, 471
upper rudder, jumbo jet, 149
upper sash, window, 65
upper side-rail, truck van, 121
upper windshield, bus, 118
upright: basketball backstop, 296; croquet wicket, 318; easel, 370; etching press, 377; football, 293; guillotine, 462; hand loom, 387; horizontal bar, 306; hurdle, 304; lithographic press, 376; parallel bars, 306; pole vault, 305; pommel horse, 307; roller coaster, 92; tow truck, 126
upright handlebar, bicycle, 128
upright piano, 361
upright pole, tent, 342
upright standard, theodolite, 436
upright vacuum cleaner, 283
uprush, wave, 14
upstop wheel, roller coaster, 92
upstream, river, 13
upstream gate, canal lock, 99
Uranus, planet, 3
urine transfer connector, spacesuit, 155
urn, bed finial, 270
uropod, lobster, 47
usage register, electric meter, 399
use, label, 268
used-blade box, razor blade injector, 210
utility belt, police, 498-499
utility pocket: cowboy, 490; spacesuit, 155
uvula, 30

V

V: braille, 512; sign language, 512
VAC scale, volt-ohm meter, 423
vacuum cleaner, 283
vacuum gauge, gas laser, 395
vacuum hose, automobile engine, 111
vacuum jar, laboratory, 447

vacuum mount, pencil sharpener, 277
vacuum relief valve, tanker, 140, 141
vacuum tube, 396
valance: curtain, 240; stage, 350; theater, 351
valley, 7; house roof, 63; non-glaciated, 12; river, 13
valley glacier, 12
value: coin, 225; thematic map, 21
value range, isarithmic map, 21
valve: automobile engine, 111; bicycle, 128; blood pressure gauge, 449; camper, 130; camp stove, 342; clam, 47; cornet, 359; drag racing dragster, 339; dental unit, 454; faucet, 273; football, 292; French horn, 358; furnace, 400; hot air balloon, 332; inflatable, 133; laboratory burner, 447; lantern, 342; motorcycle, 129; nuclear reactor, 392; playing cards, 348; plumber's torch, 422; radiator, 400; scallop, 47; skin diving, 331; solar heating system, 391; standpipe, 59; steam engine, 405; subway motorman's cab, 119; tanker, 140, 141; toilet, 275; trumpet, 359; water heater, 401
vambrace, armor, 465
vamp: boot, 206; man's shoe, 204; running shoe, 302; sandal, 206; woman's shoe, 205
van, truck, 121
Vandyke beard, 211
vane: barn, 104; bird feather, 39; missile, 482; weather, 18, 19; windmill, 390
vanishing point, perspective, 368
vanity, dresser, 272
vanogan, 108
varashield, truck cab, 120
variable range marker, radar and sonar, 444
variable spacer, typewriter, 161
variable-speed control, saw, 417
variable sweep wing, jet fighter, 480
variable wing, combat aircraft, 480
vase, church, 87
VASI, airport runway, 94
vastus medialis, human, 26
vault: bank, 457; burial chamber, 516; dome, 85; parking meter, 113; pay telephone, 180; pole, 300, 305
vaulter: gymnastics, 307; pole vault, 305
vaulting board, 307
vaulting horse, 307
V-berth, sailboat, 135
V-bottom hull, powerboat, 138
VCR, 184
VDC scale, volt-ohm meter, 423
vegetable, 54, 55, 262; juice extractor, 255; refrigerator compartment, 249
vegetable organ, grass, 58
vegetable slicer, 261
vehicle: airport, 95; armor-plated, 474-475
V-8 automobile engine, 111
veil: bride's, 488; nun's, 487; remnants of universal,

mushroom, 57; woman's hat, 203
vein: human, 27, 28; leaf, 52
Velcro closure, 209; football helmet, 292; parka cuff, 201
velocity indicator: pilot's instrument panel, 481; space shuttle, 153
velocity stack, racing car, 338
velvet cap, royal crown, 485
venetian blind, 241
vent: automobile, 107; Band-Aid, 451; battery, 397; bus, 118; cannon barrel, 467; furnace, 400; hair dryer, 212; hot air balloon, 332; house gable, 63; jacket, 188; paint spray gun, 425; radiator, 400; shoe tree, 207; skin diving fin, 331; stove, 248; truck van, 121; volcano, 10; water heater, 401
vent field astragal and filets, cannon barrel, 467
ventilated rib, shotgun, 469
ventilation building, underwater tunnel, 98
ventilation hatch, bus, 118
ventilation-heating controls, car, 110
ventilation pack, hovercraft, 145
ventilation umbilical, spacesuit, 155
ventilator: barn, 104; lantern, 342; locomotive, 117; subway car, 119; tank, 475
venting arm, launch pad, 152
vent pipe: house, 62; pressure cooker, 257
vent port, drag racing driver's fire suit, 339
ventral fin: fish, 45; jet fighter, 480
ventral scale, snake, 42
vent screw, outboard engine, 137
venturi windshield, powerboat, 139
venule, human, 28
Venus, planet, 3
veranda, house, 63
verge, barn, 104
vergeboard, house, 63
Vermeil Room, White House, 75
vernier, theodolite, 436
verso, book page, 167
vertebral column, human, 26
vertebral shield, turtle, 43
vertex, pyramid, 71
vertical, transit, 436
vertical adjustment, speculum, 448
vertical aerial, volleyball net, 319
vertical angulation dial readout, dental x-ray unit, 454
vertical brace: bridge, 97; oil drilling platform, 101
vertical centering, radar, 444
vertical circle, theodolite, 436
vertical exhaust, truck tractor, 120
vertical fin: blimp, 156; glider, 147; single engine airplane, 147
vertical gauge, carpenter's level, 424
vertical reduction, theodolite, 436
vertical speed indicator, 747 cockpit, 150
vertical stabilizer, jumbo jet, 149
vertical tail fin, jet fighter, 480
vertical updraft, tornado, 17

vertical velocity indicator, pilot's instrument panel, 481
very high frequency antenna, destroyer, 476
very soft, music notation, 353
vessel, 132
vest, 188; cowboy, 490; man's formal attire, 488; police, 499; ski clothes, 327, 329; sweater, 199
vestibule, vault, 457
vestment, Jewish ritual, 486
vestry, church, 87
V-gouge, 374
VHF aerial, jumbo jet, 148
VHF antenna: destroyer, 476, 477; helicopter, 146; lunar lander, 154
VHF radio, 747 cockpit, 151
vial: carpenter's level, 424; theodolite, 436
vibration damper pulley, automobile engine, 111
vibrissa: cat, 37; ultimate beast, 48
vice president, Senate, 74
victory, gesture, 507
video camera, 184
video cassette, 184
video key, television, 185
video recorder, 184
video screen, personal computer, 162
video-still camera, 173
video-still camera adaptor, 173
viewfinder: camera, 172; Polaroid, 173; telescope, 443
viewing hood, radar, 444
vignette: book, 167; label, 268
vintage, wine label, 267
viola, 354, 355
violation flag, parking meter, 113
violin, 354, 355
violoncello, 355
virgule, grammatical symbol, 513
virgin, zodiac, 509
Virgo, zodiac, 509
viscid spiral, spider web, 40
vise, 409; workbench, 408
visor: armor, 465; drum major's busby, 495; fireman's helmet, 500; man's cap, 202; spacesuit, 155; traffic light, 113
visual-approach slope indicator light, airport runway, 94
visual code, coupon, 103
visual display, personal computer, 162
vite, cartoon, 380
vitellus, egg, 262
vitreous body, eye, 30
vitreous humor, eye, 30
V-neck, sweater, 199
vocational rehabilitation, prison, 76
voice, organ, 360
void, type, 165
volcanic rock, brazier, 288
volcano, 7, 10
volleyball court, 319
voltmeter: powerboat, 138; symbol, 510
volt-ohm meter, 423
volt-ohm milliameter, 423
volume: stringed instruments, 355; wine label, 267
volume control: CB radio, 183; guitar, 363; hearing aid, 452; metal detector, 445; movie projector, 175; police radio, 122; portable radio/cassette player, 182; sonar, 444; tape recorder, 177; Walkman, 182

volume dial, audio receiver, 179
volume graduation, beaker, 447
volume key, television, 185
volume number, newspaper, 168
volume slider, synthesizer, 363
volume unit meter, tape recorder, 177
voluntary muscle, human, 26
volva, mushroom, 57
voting booth, 437
voting machines, mechanized, 437
votive candle, 237
voussoir, arch, 72
VRM range-intensity control, radar, 444
V-sign, gesture, 507
V-tail, surfboard, 330
V-waist, queen's regalia, 484

W

W: braille, 512; sign language, 512
wafer, Communion, 87
wafer ice cream cone, 265
waffle ice cream cone, 265
waftarom, cartoon, 381
wagon, child's toy, 287
wagon masters' quarters, frontier fort, 82
wagon pole, stagecoach, 131
wah-wah pedal, guitar, 363
waist: ant, 41; bell, iv; guitar, 362; hourglass, 185; human, 24; queen's regalia, 484; skirt, 197; viola, 355; woman's pants, 196
waistband: athletic supporter, 194; man's formal attire, 488; man's underpants, 194; panty hose, 195; skirt, 197; trousers, 291; woman's pants, 196
waistcoat: man's formal attire, 488; Revolutionary War general, 492
waistline: bridal gown, 488; dress, 198
waist trimmer, body building, 344
walk, house, 63
walk-around, clown, 493
walk board, roller coaster, 92
walkie-talkie radio, 183
walking leg, lobster, 47
walking race, 300
walking stick, 452
Walkman, 182
wall: barn, 104; baseball field, 291; brick, 69; canal lock, 99; and carpet, 246; cave, 11; circus tent, 91; dam, 100; dustpan, 282; elevator car, 78; fort, 83; handball court, 313; horse's hoof, 38; house, 60, 62; jai alai cancha, 314; mah-jongg, 345; lacrosse stick, 298; mountain, 9; oil drilling platform, 101; pea, 54; pepper, 262; prison, 76; safe, 457; squash court, 313; stage, 350; swimming pool, 316; tomato, 54; truck, 121; wave, 14
wallaby pouch, ultimate beast, 48
wallet, 223
wall fastener, 411
wall flange: aneroid barometer, 18; sink drain, 273
wall socket, electrical, 398
wall switch, electrical, 398
wall tent, 342
wall-to-wall carpet, 246

wand: venetian blind, 241;
  wizard, 492
waning moon, 4
war bonnet, Indian, 490
ward, castle, 80, 81
warding, key, 459
wardrobe, 272
warehouse store, 102
warhead: missile, 482; torpedo,
  479
warm front, weather map, 19
warming element, percolator,
  252
warming grid, barbecue grill,
  288
warming unit, coffee maker,
  252
warm liquid pipe, heat
  exchanger, 403
warm-up jersey, baseball
  batter, 290
warm-up suit, basketball, 296
warning, dental x-ray unit, 454
warning light: car, 110; fire
  engine, 124, 125; pilot's
  instrument panel, 481;
  railroad crossing signal, 115;
  747 cockpit, 150, 151; space
  shuttle, 153; tractor, 434
warning lines, fencing strip,
  315
warning sign, road, 505
warning track, baseball field,
  291
warp, hand loom, 387
war paint, Indian, 490
warship, 476
warts, toad, 44
washbasin, sailboat, 135
washcloth rack, bathtub, 274
washer, 411; aerial shell, 383;
  faucet, 273; hose coupling,
  428; lamp, 238; levigator,
  376; parking meter, 113
washing machine, 280
washline, 280
washout plug, locomotive
  boiler, 116
washtub, 280
waste disposal, dental, 455
watch, 220; skin diving, 331
watchband, 220
watch cap, sailor's, 497
watch pocket: skirt, 197;
  trousers, 191; vest, 188
watchtower, train caboose, 117
water: dam, 100;
  thundercloud, 17
water bearer, zodiac, 509
water buffalo horn, ultimate
  beast, 49
water closet, sailboat, 135
watercolor, painting medium,
  370
water control, dental unit, 454
watercourse, river, 13
water droplet, cave, 11
waterfalls, 13
water fill: camper, 130; iron,
  279
watergate: castle, 81; frontier
  fort, 82
water glass, 244
water hazard: golf course,
  310-311; steeplechase race,
  304
water heater, 401; camper, 130
water hook, harness racing,
  337
water jet, Jacuzzi, 274
water kettle, tea set, 245
water key: trombone, 359;
  trumpet, 359
water level sight glass,
  furnace, 400
waterline: boat, 132; destroyer,
  477
water pipe, 229

water pressure gauge, pumper,
  125
water regulator, dental, 455
water reservoir, coffee maker,
  252
water return pipe, furnace, 400
waterskiing, 329
water spray: mechanical
  sweeper, 127; tooth cleaner,
  215
water tank: iron, 279; railroad
  yard, 96; water heater, 401
water temperature gauge,
  powerboat, 138
watertight bulkhead,
  passenger ship, 142
watertight door, destroyer, 476
water tower, nautical chart, 22
wattage selector, CB radio, 183
wattle: chicken, 35; turkey, 35
wattmeter, symbol, 510
watts, phonograph, 179
wave, 14; radio, 3
wave-cut platform, iceberg, 12
waveguide, radar antenna, 444
wave height, 14
wavelength, 14; laser beam,
  395
wax: candle, 237; ski, 327
waxing moon, 4
way, permanent fort, 83
W.C., sailboat, 135
weaponry, 463-482; combat
  soldier, 497; defensive
  guided, 476
weather boarding, barn, 104
weather deck, passenger ship,
  143
weather ear, newspaper, 168
weather forecast, 18
weather map, 19
weather radarscope, 747
  cockpit, 150
weather stripping, window, 65
weather vane, 19; barn, 104
weaving, 387
web: bird foot, 35, 39; circus
  aerialist, 90; horseshoe, 38;
  human hand, 31; knife, 256;
  spider, 40; toad, 44;
  weaving, 387
web area, wrench, 415
webbing: baseball glove, 291;
  suspenders, 190
web-fed press, printing, 166
web sling, bazooka, 472
wedding bouquet, bride, 488
wedge: cannon carriage, 467;
  crossbow, 466; dental, 455;
  hammer, 412; quiche, 263;
  running shoe, 302;
  sawhorse, 408; snowmobile,
  130
weep hole: brick wall, 69;
  fence, 67
weft, weaving, 387
weight: barbell, 344; baseball
  bat, 290; bowling ball, 317;
  discus, 303; flat racing, 336;
  grandfather clock, 233;
  guillotine, 462; hurdle, 304;
  laboratory scale, 446, 447;
  lobster, 433; metronome,
  367; skin diving, 331;
  tractor, 434; type, 165;
  universal gym, 344
weight floor, stage, 350
weights and measures
  certification, gas pump, 112
weight to be carried, flat
  racing entry, 336
weiner, 265
weld: link chain, 461;
  tweezers, 215
welded channel, backyard
  glider, 287
well: automobile, 106, 109; bus
  steps, 118; cigarette lighter,

228; ink, 158; magazine, 169;
  powerboat, 139; saucer, 245;
  Senate, 74; toaster, 253;
  workbench, 408
well-contents measuring tool,
  oil drilling platform, 101
welt: boot, 206; shoe, 204
welting: baseball glove, 291;
  lounger, 235; handbag, 222;
  mattress, 271
welt pocket flap, jacket, 188
West Australia Current, ocean,
  6
West Coast mirror, truck, 120
westerlies, wind, 6
western pocket, trousers, 191
western saddle, 335
western yoke shirt, cowboy,
  490
west front, church, 87
west longitude, 5
west portico, Capital, 74
west wind drift, ocean, 6
wet boot, slalom water ski, 329
wet compass, 747 cockpit, 151
wet suit, skin diving, 331
whaleboat, destroyer, 476
whalebone carving,
  scrimshaw, 375
whale's tooth, scrimshaw, 375
wharf, castle, 80, 81
wheat, 58
wheel: automobile, 106, 107;
  balance beam, 306; ballista,
  467; bicycle, 128; blimp, 156;
  body building, 344; bumper
  car, 92; cannon carriage,
  467; can opener, 251; child's
  wagon, 287; cigarette lighter,
  228; drag racing dragster,
  339; Ferris, 93; glass cutter,
  378; hand loom, 387;
  helicopter, 146; humidifier,
  402; locomotive, 116;
  motorcycle, 129; mower,
  429; pastry cutter, 261;
  potter's, 373; powerboat,
  138; roller coaster, 92; roller
  skate, 324; roulette, 346;
  sailboat, 134; seeder, 430;
  single engine airplane, 147;
  skateboard, 324; slide
  projector, 175; slot machine,
  346; snowmobile, 130;
  spinning, 387; stagecoach,
  131; stroller, 286; tank, 474,
  475; tire, 105; tractor, 434;
  truck, 120, 121, 126; vacuum
  cleaner, 283; wheelbarrow,
  430; wheelchair, 452
wheelbarrow, 430
wheelchair, 452
wheelhouse: hydrofoil, 145;
  tanker, 141
wheel of fortune, 346
wheels-flaps position
  indicator, pilot's instrument
  panel, 481
wheel speed fairing, single
  engine airplane, 147
wheel window, church, 86
whey, and cheese, 263
whip: flat racing, 336; harness
  racing, 337; stagecoach, 131;
  windmill, 390
whip roll, hand loom, 387
whirlpool bath, 274
whirlpool jet, bath, 274
whirlybird, 146
whisk, kitchen tool, 258
whiskers: cat, 37; man, 211;
  ultimate beast, 48
whistle: destroyer, 477;
  locomotive, 116; police gun
  belt, 499; subway
  motorman's cab, 119
white, egg, 262
whitecap, wave, 14

white dwarf star, 3
whiteface, clown, 493
White House, 75
white inner table,
  backgammon board, 345
white line, horse's foot, 38
white outer table,
  backgammon board, 345
white paint, sketch box, 371
white room, launch pad, 152
white square, chessboard, 345
white tie, man's, 488
whitewall tire, automobile, 107
white wine glass, 244
white wire, electrical
  receptacle, 398
whole note, music, 352
whole note rest, music, 352
whole-timbered building, 70
whorl: human fingertip, 31;
  univalve shell, 47
wick: candle, 237; jumbo jet,
  148; Molotov cocktail, 473
wicket, croquet, 318
wickiup, 84
wide swing gouge,
  woodcarving, 372
wide tire, tractor, 434
width, and perspective, 368
widow, bowling pin, 317
widow's peak, hair, 211
widow's walk, house, 62
width, type, 165
wig, 211, 492
wiggle nail, 410
wigwag, symbolic language,
  512
wigwam, 84
wild card, 348
wimple, nun, 487
win, flat racing, 336
winch: oil drilling platform,
  101; sailboat, 134; tanker,
  140; tow truck, 126
wind: fishing rod, 340;
  thunderstorm, 17
windage adjustment knob,
  rifle scope, 469
wind baffle, camp stove, 342
windbag, bagpipe, 365
windbreaker, automobile, 107
wind chest, organ, 360
wind direction sensor, weather
  station, 18
wind-door, garbage truck, 127
wind drift, ocean, 6
wind indicator, destroyer, 477
winding, fishing rod, 340
winding road, road sign, 505
wind instruments: brass,
  358-359; wood, 356-357
windlass: ballista, 467;
  sailboat, 134; tanker, 140
windmill, 390
window, 65; airport control
  tower, 95; automobile, 106,
  107; bridge, 97; bus, 118;
  camper, 130; checkbook
  clutch, 223; church, 86;
  house, 62, 63; igloo, 85; light
  meter, 176; lunar lander,
  154; mainsail, 136; mat, 379;
  microwave oven, 248;
  package, 269; parking meter,
  113; plug fuse, 399;
  powerboat, 139; slot
  machine, 346; stove oven
  door, 248; subway car, 119;
  tank, 475; tractor, 434;
  wallet, 223; washing
  machine door, 280;
  windsurfer, 330
window control, car, 110
window coverings, 240, 241
window flap, tent, 342
window shade, 240, 241
wind patterns, 6
windscreen: passenger ship,

142; 747 cockpit, 150; single engine airplane, 147
windshaft, windmill, 390
windshield: automobile, 106, 107; bus, 118; jet fighter, 480; powerboat, 139; 747 cockpit, 150; single engine airplane, 147; snowmobile, 130; space shuttle, 153; truck, 120
windshield defroster, 110
windshield frame, pilot's instrument panel, 481
windshield wiper: bus, 118; car, 106, 110; locomotive, 117; subway motorman's cab, 119
Windsor knot, necktie, 192
wind speed sensor, weather station, 18
windsurfer, 330
wind system, 390
wind turbine, 390
wind vane, 18, 19
wind wall, oil drilling platform, 101
windward side, boat, 132
wine, consecrated, 87
wine bin, sideboard, 243
wine cellar, passenger ship, 143
wine department, supermarket, 102
wine district, wine label, 267
wine drawer, sideboard, 243
wine glass, 244
wine label, bottle, 267
wine selector, wine label, 267
wine steward's corkscrew, 251
wing: baseball catcher's shinguard, 290; bassoon, 357; bird, 39; bow tie, 192; Capitol, 74; cruise missile, 482; dental braces, 453; destroyer bridge, 477; easel, 370; grasshopper, 41; house, 63; hydrofoil, 145; ice hockey, 295; jet fighter, 480; lamp, 238; poultry, 35; racing car, 338, 339; safety razor, 210; scallop, 47; single engine airplane, 147; space shuttle, 152; stroller, 286; tanker, 141; theatre, 351; toggle bolt, 411; turkey, 35; wallet, 223
wing area, lacrosse field, 298
wing-back cuff link, 218
wing fixed glove, jet fighter, 480
wing nut, 411; hacksaw, 416; hurdle, 304; Ping-Pong net, 321
wing strut, racing car, 338
wing sweep indicator, pilot's instrument panel, 481
wing tip: man's shoe, 204; single engine airplane, 147
wing type, combat aircraft, 480
winter berm, shoreline, 14
winter cap, Manchu court dress, 491
winter squash, 54
winter uniform, police, 498
wipe, cowboy, 490
wiper: bus windshield, 118; car windshield, 106, 110; locomotive windshield, 117
wire: automobile engine, 111;

barbed, 432; circuit breaker box, 399; dental, 453; earring, 218; electrical receptacle, 398; electrician's, 423; field events hammer, 303; fire engine, 124; frame, 379; horizontal bar, 306; incandescent bulb, 238; plug fuse, 399; railroad crossing signal, 115; size, 423; stationary rings, 307; toaster, 253; traffic light, 113; trumpet, 359; typewriter 161; vacuum tube, 396
wire cutter: electrician's wire stripper, 423; pliers, 414
wire end, clay modeling tool, 372
wire hood, champagne cork, 267
wire knob, seeder, 430
wireless aerial, tanker, 141
wireline-logging unit, oil drilling platform, 101
wire stripper: electrician's, 423; pocket knife, 426
wire support, camp stove, 342
wiring tube, lamp, 239
wisdom teeth, 456
wishbone, poultry, 35
wishbone boom, windsurfer, 330
wisp, woman's hair, 213
withdrawals, automatic teller machine, 226
withers: cow, 32; dog, 36; sheep, 33
witness cone, potting, 373
witness stand, courtroom, 89
wizard, costume, 492
wok, 257
woman's hair, 213
woman's hat, 203
woman's jacket, 196
woman's pants, 196
woman's shoe, 205
woman's skate, 325
women's tee, golf course, 310
wood, jai alai cancha, 314
wood block, 374, 461
woodburning stove, 404
wood carrier, fireplace, 232
woodcarving tool, 372
wood clamp, 409
woodcut printing, 374
wooded marsh, topographic map, 22
wooden beam, tow truck bed, 126
wooden mallet, woodcarving, 372
wooden pipe, levigator, 376
wooden roofing shingle, 68
wooden siding, house, 62
wooden spoon, 259
wood fence, 67
wood form, etching press, 377
wood saw, pocket knife, 426
wood shaft, umbrella, 230
wood splice, house, 61
woodwind, 354, 356-357
woodworking vise, 409
woodyard, frontier fort, 82
woof, weaving, 387
woofer, audio speaker, 179
wool collar, trench coat, 200
word, book page, iv
word processor, 162

workbench, 408
work bowl, food processor, 254
work experience, résumé, 160
working drawing, house, 62
workingman, circus, 90
workingman's suspenders, 190
working surface, balance beam, 306
workshelf, potter's wheel, 373
work spotlight, tow truck bed, 126
workstation, computer, 438
work surface, desk, 276
worktop, kitchen sink, 247
worm: cannon, 467; corkscrew, 251
worm gear, venetian blind, 241
woven backing, carpet, 246
woven basket, guillotine, 462
woven side, basket, 266
woven wire fabric, steel chain fence, 67
wrap: boxing, 309; packaging, 269
wrap belt, cardigan, 199
wrapper: cigar, 228; paperback book, 167; Torah, 88
wrapping, dabber, 377
wreath: medal, 501; tombstone, 516
wreck, nautical chart, 22
wrecker, 126
wrench, 415
wringer, 280
wrist: cat, 37; human, 24, 29; steam engine crank, 405
wristband, soccer, 297
wristpad, lacrosse glove, 298
wrist sling, ice hammer, 334
wrist strap, ski pole, 326
wristwatch, 220
wrist weight, body building, 344
write-in, voting, 437
write-protect hole & slider, diskette, 162
write-protect notch, diskette, 162
writer's initials, letter, 159
writing area, desk, 276
writing arm, rocking chair, 234
writing slide, desk, 276
writing tip, pen, 158
wrought iron fence, 67

X

X: braille, 512; sign language, 512
x-height, type, 165
x-indication, voting booth, 437
x-ray cassette, operating room table, 450
x-ray dental unit, 454
xylem, tree, 50
xylography, 374

Y

Y: braille, 512; sign language, 512
yacht, 133
yackety-yak, gesture, 507
yad, Torah, 486
y adjusting lever, plane, 420
yankee, sailboat, 134
yard: barn, 104; frontier fort, 82; house, 62; prison, 76
yardarm, destroyer, 477

yard goods, fabric, 388
yard line, football field, 293
yardmaster, railroad yard, 96
yarmulke, Jewish prayer vestment, 486
yarn: knitting, 386; rope, 132; weaving, 387
yarn loop, 246
year of birth: flat racing entry, 336; tombstone, 516
year of death, tombstone, 516
yellow traffic light, 113
yen, symbol, 511
Yeoman warder, 483
yield, road sign, 504
Yin-Yang, symbol, 508
yod, tefillin, 486
yoke: blouse, 197; dental x-ray unit, 454; dress, 198; 747 cockpit, 150; shirt, 189; tennis racket, 312; tuning fork, 367; window, 65
yoke cable, bicycle caliper brake, 128
yoke shirt, cowboy, 490
yolk, egg, 262
you're out, gesture, 507
yurt, 70

Z

Z: braille, 512; sign language, 512
zebra coat, ultimate beast, 49
zecher lechurban, Jewish prayer vestment, 486
Zeppelin, 156
zero adjust knob, volt-ohm meter, 423
zero mark, wristwatch, 220
zester, kitchen tool, 261
ziggurat, pyramid, 70
zigzag rule, 424
zinc carbon cell, 397
zip code: envelope, 159; magazine mailing label, 169
zip-out robe lining, overcoat, 200
zipper, 209; backpack, 343; mainsail, 136; package, 268; parka, 201; skirt, 197; sleeping bag, 343; trousers, 191; woman's pants, 196
zippered door, tent, 342
zipper foot, sewing machine, 278
zipper line, sewing pattern, 388
zip plus four, mailing label, 169
zizith, Jewish prayer shawl, 486
zonal pattern, wind, 6
zone: envelope, 159; football field, 293; glacier, 12; handball court, 313; ice hockey rink, 295; shuffleboard court, 318; time, 5
zone marking, ice hockey rink, 295
zoom collar, zoom lens, 172
zoom control, video camera, 184
zooming ring, movie projector, 175
zoom lens, 172; movie camera, 174; video camera, 184
zoom ring: movie camera, 174; video camera, 184

Credits

pages **2-3**, illustration by Neal Adams; **5**, time zone map courtesy of Hammond Incorporated, Maplewood, NJ; **8-9**, illustration by Dee Molenaar; **18**, photo courtesy of Science Associates Inc.; **20-21**, Japan map courtesy of Hammond Inc., thematic map of "Number of Irish Foreign Born 1930" courtesy of Carnegie Institution of Washington; **28, 29, 30**, anatomy cross sections courtesy of Hammond Inc.; **60-61**, illustrations courtesy of American Plywood Assoc.; **62**, illustration by Charles Addams, blueprint by Carl Hribar; **74-75**, photos by David Burnett, courtesy of Contact Press Images, Inc.; **76**, photo courtesy of State of N.Y. Dept. of Correctional Services; **77**, top photo courtesy of The Port Authority of New York & New Jersey, lower photo courtesy of Empire State Building; **78**, elevator shaft illustration courtesy of Westinghouse Elevator, elevator car illustration courtesy of Williamsburg Steel Products, Co.; **80**, photo courtesy of British Information Service; **86-87**, illustrations courtesy of Cathedral Church of St. John the Divine, N.Y.C.; **88**, courtesy of Temple Emanuel, N.Y.C.; **90-91**, courtesy of Ringling Brothers and Barnum & Bailey; **92-93**, roller coaster courtesy of Magic Mountain Amusement Park, Ferris wheel and merry-go-round courtesy of Rye Playland; **94-95**, airport photo courtesy of American Airlines; **96**, photo courtesy of Association of American Railroads; **97**, photos courtesy of Triborough Bridge and Tunnel Authority; **101**, photo by Carroll S. Grevemberg, Grevy Photography, New Orleans, LA; **102-103**, supermarket plan courtesy of *Progressive Grocer*, coupon courtesy of Folger's Coffee; **106-107**, AnyCar photos courtesy of Manufacturers Hanover Trust, N.Y.C.; **108-109**, photo courtesy of Buick Division, General Motors Corp.; **110**, photo courtesy of Alfa Romeo; **111**, photo courtesy of Bradford La Riviera Inc.; **114**, courtesy of Triborough Bridge & Tunnel Authority; **116-117**, steam locomotive photo courtesy of Association of American Railroads, turbine engine photo courtesy of National Railroad Passenger Corporation, panels courtesy of The Train Shop, Ltd.; **118**, coach courtesy of American Eagle, commuter bus interior courtesy of NY Metropolitan Transit Authority; **119**, courtesy of NY Metropolitan Transit Authority Museum; **120-121**, photos courtesy of Mack Trucks Corp.; **124-125**, photos courtesy of New York City Fire Department; **126**, tow truck courtesy of LST Towing, N.Y.C.; **127**, courtesy of NYC Department of Sanitation; **129**, photo courtesy of Kawasaki Motorcycles; **130**, camper photo courtesy of Winnebago Industries, Inc., snowmobile photo courtesy of Yamaha Motor Corp.; **131**, stagecoach courtesy of Wells Fargo Bank History Dept., hansom cab courtesy of The New-York Historical Society; **133**, photo courtesy of Dyer Jones, Warren, RI; **134-135**, illustrations courtesy of CSY Yacht Corp., Tampa, FL; **136**, compass photo courtesy of Aqua Meter Instrument Corp., Roseland, NJ; **137**, outboard photo courtesy of Mariner Outboards, Fond du Lac, WI, sextant photo courtesy of Weems & Plath, Annapolis, MD; **138-139**, illustration courtesy of Bertram Yachts, Miami, FL; **142-143**, illustration courtesy of Cunard Line Ltd., N.Y.C.; **144**, tugboat courtesy of Moran, fireboat courtesy of NYC Fire Department; **145**, hovercraft photo courtesy of British Hovercraft Corp. Ltd.; **146**, photo courtesy of Sikorsky; **147**, airplane photo courtesy of Piper Aircraft Corp.; **148-149**, illustration courtesy of Boeing; **150-151**, photo courtesy of Boeing; **152-153**, photo and illustration courtesy of NASA; **154-155**, illustrations courtesy of NASA; **156**, photo courtesy of Goodyear; **159**, calligraphy by Melissa, text by Sean Kelly; **161**, manual typewriter photo courtesy of Royal Business Machines, Inc.; **162**, top photo courtesy of Apple Computer Inc., bottom right photo courtesy of Sharp Electronics Corp.; **163**, top photo courtesy of Fujitsu America, San Jose, CA, bottom illustration after NEC Information Systems, Inc.; **164**, fax machine and copier photos courtesy of Sharp Electronics Corp.; **166**, illustrations courtesy of International Paper Company; **168**, courtesy of *The New York Times*, N.Y.C.; **169**, *Time* cover reprinted by permission from *Time* The Weekly Newsmagazine, copyright Time Inc., 1980, contents page reprinted courtesy of *Sports Illustrated* from the March 3, 1980 issue, copyright (c) 1980, Time, Inc.; **170-171**, prepared by *New York* Magazine, N.Y.C.; **172**, zoom lens photo courtesy of Tokina Optical Ltd.; **173**, video still camera photo courtesy of Sony; **174**, photo courtesy of Minolta Camera Co., Ltd.; **175**, movie projector photo courtesy of Minolta, slide projector photo courtesy of Kodak, screen courtesy of Da-Lite Screen Co.; **176**, light meter courtesy of Gossen-Luna Pro, electronic flash courtesy of Vivitar Corp., tripod courtesy of E. Leitz Inc.; **177**, reel-to-reel recorder photo courtesy of Pioneer Electronics, cassette tape photo courtesy of Sony; **178**, turntable photo courtesy of Pioneer Electronics Corp.; **179**, audio photos courtesy of Pioneer Electronics Corp.; **181**, cellular telephone photo courtesy of Panasonic, answering machine photo courtesy of Sony; **182**, bottom photo courtesy of Sharp Electronics Corp.; **183**, photo courtesy of Radio Shack; **184**, VCR photo courtesy of Panasonic, video camera courtesy of Sharp Electronics; **185**, television photo courtesy of Sony; **186**, illustration courtesy of NASA; **195**, panty hose photo courtesy of Hanes Corp.; **196-197**, illustrations by Calvin Klein; **201**, fur photo courtesy of Rosette, NY; **205**, courtesy of Andy Warhol; **207**, sock photo courtesy of Alexander Lee Wallan Inc.; **209**, photo courtesy of Velcro USA; **210**, electric razor photo courtesy of Sunbeam Corp.; **212**, hair dryer photo courtesy of Conair; **214**, curling iron photo courtesy of Conair; **216-217**, products courtesy of Avon Products, Inc., make-up by Tom Gearhard; **218-219**, ring and pendant illustrations courtesy of Jane Evans; **220**, wristwatch courtesy of Chronosport Inc., Rowayton, CT; **227**, traveler's check courtesy of Barclay's Bank, N.Y.C.; **237**, candle snuffer courtesy of Fortunoff Department Store, N.Y.C.; **244**, place setting courtesy of Rosenthal China Co.; **245**, dessert setting courtesy of Rosenthal China, panels courtesy of Gorham Division of Textron Inc.; **247**, sink courtesy of Elkay Manufacturing Co., disposal unit courtesy of Hobart Co.; **248**, stove and microwave oven photos courtesy of General Electric Co.; **251**, electric opener courtesy of Oster Corp., can piercer courtesy of Ekco Industries; **255**, vegetable juicer courtesy of Hamilton Beach, automatic juicer courtesy of Oster Corp., manual juicer courtesy of Acme Juicer Mfg. Corp.; **257**, pressure cooker courtesy of National Presto Industries, electric wok courtesy of Farberware; **258-261**, courtesy of H&P Mayer Corp.; **267**, pump dispenser courtesy of Calmar Division/Diamond Int'l.; **268-269**, illustration by The Schecter Group; **278**, courtesy of Viking Sewing Machine Co.; **279**, courtesy of Proctor-Silex; **281**, dryer courtesy of General Electric; **283**, vacuum cleaner courtesy of Hoover Co., minivacuum courtesy of Black & Decker; **284**, fire extinguisher courtesy of Amerex Corp., smoke alarm courtesy of General Electric; **286**, stroller

courtesy of Perego/Pines, Milan, Italy, playpen and car seat courtesy of Century Products, Los Angeles, CA; **287**, wagon illustration courtesy of Flexible Flyer; **288**, barbecue courtesy of King Seeley Co.; **290**, models: Rod Carew, California Angels (batter), Ossie Virgil Jr., Philadelphia Phillies (catcher); **291**, glove courtesy of Rawlings Sporting Goods; **292**, model: James Ramey, New York Jets, helmet courtesy of Bike Athletic Co.; **294-295**, models: Ken Morrow (defenseman) and Billy Smith (goalie), New York Islanders; **296**, model: Mike Glenn, New York Knickerbockers; **298**, photos courtesy of STX Company; **299**, photo courtesy of *Polo* Magazine; **302**, running shoe courtesy of Adidas; **306-307**, photos courtesy of Nissen/Walter Kidde & Co.; **309**, model: Wendal Newton; **310-311**, equipment photos courtesy of Northwestern Golf Co.; **314**, courtesy of Bridgeport, Conn., Jai Alai, model: Donald Mazza; **315**, piste courtesy of George Santelli Fencing School, N.Y.C.; **320**, photo courtesy of Brunswick Corp.; **322**, courtesy of Darts Unlimited, N.Y.C.; **324**, photo courtesy of Chicago Roller Skates Inc.; **326**, equipment courtesy of Scandinavian Ski Shop; **327**, cross-country equipment courtesy of Scandinavian Ski Shop, snowshoe courtesy of The Snowcraft Corp.; **329**, ski courtesy of Connelly Skis, Inc.; **331**, equipment courtesy of Atlantic Divers World, NY; **332**, photo courtesy of The Balloon Works, Statesville, NC; **333**, parachute courtesy of Para-Flite Inc., US Parachuting Assoc., hang glider courtesy of United States Hang Gliding Assoc.; **334**, photos courtesy of George Willig, Topanga, CA; **335**, Western saddle courtesy of H. Kauffman and Sons, Inc., English saddle by Crosby, courtesy of Millers, N.Y.C.; **336**, program entry courtesy of Pimlico Race Track; **337**, Meadowlands Racetrack, East Rutherford, NJ, model: Courtney Foos; **338**, illustration by Jack Lane, courtesy of L'Art et L'Automobile Gallery, 354 E. 66th Street, N.Y.C., Jacques Vaucher; **339**, photos courtesy of National Hot Rod Association; **340-341**, fishing reel photo courtesy of Penn Reels, rod photo courtesy of Shakespeare Fishing Rods; **342**, photos courtesy of Coleman Co.; **343**, backpack photo courtesy of Johnson/Camp Trails; **344**, universal gym photo courtesy of Nissen; **346-347**, courtesy of Mr. Lucky Equipment, Rosedale, NY; **349**, ticket courtesy of Globe Ticket Co.; **351**, photo of the Bardavon Theatre courtesy of Robert Paul Molay; **352-353**, *Theme From What's What Book* written by John Hill, John Hill Music Inc.; **354**, illustration and photo courtesy of Chicago Symphony Orchestra; **360**, photo courtesy of Rodgers Organ, N.Y.C.; **365**, bagpipes courtesy of Larry Cole; **366**, accordion courtesy of Stuyvesant Music; **369**, painting courtesy of the Metropolitan Museum of Art, N.Y.C.; **370-371**, painting equipment courtesy of Grumbacher; **372**, Sculpture House, N.Y.C.; **374**, equipment courtesy of Rembrant Graphic Arts, NJ; **376-377**, courtesy of Rembrant Graphic Arts, NJ and Charles Brand Machinery Inc., NY; **378**, equipment courtesy of Glassmaster Guild; **380-381**, cartoon by Mike Witte, comic strip by Mort Walker, copyright 1978 King Features Syndicate, Inc.; **382**, photo courtesy of Fireworks By Grucci Inc., Brookhaven, NY; **383**, top and bottom right photos courtesy of Fireworks By Grucci Inc., Brookhaven, NY, center and bottom left photos courtesy of Zambelli Fireworks Mfg. Co., Inc., New Castle, PA; **385**, quilt courtesy of Fairfield Processing; **386**, shuttle courtesy of C.J. Bates & Son, Inc.; **387**, loom courtesy of LaClerc Weaving Looms; **390**, wind turbine photo courtesy of Grumman Corp.; **394**, super collider illustrations and photo courtesy of Universities Research Assoc., Washington, DC; **395**, gas laser diagram after *Lumonics*, hologram photo courtesy of AT&T Archives; **396**, transistor photo courtesy of Bell Laboratories; **402**, courtesy of Hampton Sales; **406**, courtesy of Teledyne Wisconsin Motor; **409**, photos courtesy of Adjustable Clamp Co.; **417**, table saw photo courtesy of ToolKraft, circular saw photo courtesy of Ski, saber saw photo courtesy of Rockwell International; **421**, sander photo courtesy of Rockwell International, belt sander courtesy of Black & Decker; **423**, voltmeter courtesy of Amprobe Instruments; **424**, folding rule courtesy of Stanley Tools, carpenter's level courtesy of ToolKraft; **425**, spray painter courtesy of Spray Tech Corp.; **426**, photo courtesy of Hoffritz; **427**, courtesy of Douglas Products; **428**, photos courtesy of L.R. Nelson Corp.; **429**, photo courtesy of Sears, Roebuck & Company; **430**, wheelbarrow courtesy of Jackson Mfg. Co., seeder courtesy of Cyclone Seeder Co., Inc.; **431**, chainsaw photo courtesy of Ski Corp.; **434**, tractor photo courtesy of J.I. Case; **436**, theodolite courtesy of Dietzgen Corp., jackhammer courtesy of Bosch Power Tools; **437**, photos courtesy of R.F. Shoup Corp., Radnor, PA; **438**, computer workstation photo courtesy of Intergraph Corp., Huntsville, AL; **439**, computer system and computer tapes photos courtesy of IBM Corp., White Plains, NY, circuit board photo courtesy of Intergraph Corp.; **440**, courtesy of NCR Corporation; **442**, photo courtesy of Carl Zeiss Inc.; **443**, telescope photo courtesy of Unitron Instruments Inc., binoculars photo courtesy of Minolta Camera Co., Ltd.; **444**, photos courtesy of Furuno U.S.A., Inc.; **445**, metal detector photo courtesy of White Electronics Inc., geiger counter photo courtesy of EDA Instruments; **446-447**, burner courtesy of Fisher Scientific Co., scale courtesy of Ohaus Scale Corp.; **448**, photos courtesy of Welch Allyn, Skaneateles Falls, NY; **449**, photos courtesy of Sybron Corp.; **450**, courtesy of Affiliated Hospital Products; **451**, prescription form courtesy of Scriptech; **452**, wheelchair photo courtesy of Invacare Corp., hearing aid photo courtesy of Dahlberg Electronics, pacemaker photo courtesy of Medtronic, Inc.; **453**, denture photo courtesy of Sterndent Corp., braces bracket photo courtesy of 'A' Company, Inc.; **454**, courtesy of Ritter Dental Corp.; **455**, courtesy of Dr. Herbert Spasser; **457**, photos courtesy of Mosler Safe Co.; **458**, Safe Hardware Corporation, Emhart Industries Inc.; **459**, lock photo courtesy of Medico Security Locks Inc.; **460**, hasp photo courtesy of Lawrence Brothers, Inc.; **461**, chains courtesy of Diamond Chain Co., block and pulley courtesy of The Crosby Group; **476-477**, illustration of DE 1092 courtesy of officers and men of *USS Thomas C. Hart*, drawings of ship types after *Jane's Fighting Ships*; **478-479**, photos courtesy of US Navy Department; **480-481**, fighter aircraft photos courtesy of Grumman; **482**, cruise missile photo courtesy of Boeing Aerospace; **483**, illustration courtesy of James Burrough Ltd., N.Y.C.; **484**, costumes courtesy of Eaves-Brooks Costume Co.; **486**, photo courtesy of Irving Fisher; **487**, minister photo courtesy of The Very Reverend Francis B. Sayre; **488**, photo courtesy of After Six Formal Wear; **489**, photos courtesy of Masterpiece Theatre, LWT, N.Y.C.; **490**, costume courtesy of Eaves-Brooks Costume Co., Indian courtesy of the Museum of the American Indian, N.Y.C.; **491**, Manchu Court Dress courtesy of Reginald Bragonier, Arab dress courtesy of Bill Ashe, model: Jan Leighton; **492**, model: Jan Leighton, pirate photograph by BODI, miser photograph by Michael Weiss; **493**, illustration by Ted Geisel; **494**, photo courtesy of Lois Greenfield/Capezio Ballet Makers; **496-497**, photos by Phil Koenig, soldiers courtesy of US Army, sailor courtesy of US Navy; **500**, photo courtesy of New York City Fire Department; **503**, courtesy of Government of Canada; **506**, symbols courtesy of *Handbook of Pictorial Symbols*, Rudolph Modley, Dover Publications, Inc., N.Y.C.; **514**, courtesy of Mary Grace and Maria Maggi; **516**, casket courtesy of Simmons Casket Co./Gulf and Western Casket Co.

Acknowledgements

The editors wish to express their special appreciation to the late Hugh Johnson for his friendship and support. Without him, WHAT'S WHAT would not exist.

Harold Adler, Adler Monument and Granite Works; Roslyn Alexander, librarian, Charles Evans Hughes High School; Jack Arnoff; Dave Lipsky, Juana Torres and Frank Coppinger, Army Corps of Engineers; Martin Bacheller, Hammond Inc.; Gwen Baker, Hammond Inc.; Roberta Baker, *Life* Magazine; Barney's Clothing Store; Sandy Bartram; Susan Bates Inc.; David Baxley, Triborough Bridge & Tunnel Authority; Mitch Becker, Globe Ticket Corp.; Paul Berkovitz, Algoma Net Company; Randy Black, Bike Athletic Corp.; Mitchell and George Tepper, Bond Street Suspender Inc.; Bonny Products; Carol Boswell and Gina Frantz, Boswell-Frantz Public Relations; Jerry Boxer, Abraham Boxer and Sons; Lee Bracy, Westinghouse Elevator Inc.; Benjamin Bragonier; Dana Bragonier; queen model Penelope Bragonier; Bill and Betty Brennan; Andreas Brown, Gotham Book Store; Donna Grucci Butler, Grucci Inc.; Cadillac Meat Company; Camrod Motorcycles; Carez Health Care Corp.; cross-country skiing model Catherine Carlen; Zack Carr, Calvin Klein Ltd.; Celeste Champagn, LWT Int'l.; Robert E. Lewis and William S. DeArment, Channellock Corp.; Betty Charak, Personality Hanger Inc.; Jerry Charles, Hollco Tools Coats and Clark, Inc.; accordion supplied by Larry Cole; Phil Colicchio, Oreo Cookies; Dita Comacho; Nancy Conforti, H & P Mayer Inc.; H. C. Cook, Inc., Division of Gem Products; Ron Coplon, Rubin Gloves Inc.; Richard Curtis, Richard Curtis Associates; Elmer Danch and Elaine Harr, Da-Lite Movie Screen Company; Frank Davis; John and Jessica Dorfman; Rose Dreger; Alfred Dunhill Inc.; Alex Dupuy, Columbia Computer Lab; Blaise Dupuy, The Box Studio; Ken Durst, Rawlings Inc.; John Edelmann; EKCO Housewares Corp.; Lt. Juan Torres and Ray Florida, NYC Emergency Medical Service; Lee Entwhistle, Eaves-Brooks Costumes Inc.; Herbert Eskelson, Para-Flite Inc.; Eye Center Inc.; Penny Farber, Foxmore Inc.; staff of Fashion Institute of Technology library; Arthur Ferguson, Metropolitan Transit Authority; Steve Fineberg, Feinberg Associates; Ira Finke, Ira Finke Photography; Nini Finkelstein, Ringling Brothers and Barnum & Bailey Circus; Irving and Sylvia Fisher; Anthony Forgione, Consolidated Wafer and Cone Corp.; Joann Forster, International School of Harness Racing at Roosevelt Raceway; William Free Advertising Agency; Bill Freeman, The Gill Track and Field Equipment Company; Steve Friedman; Lois Fry, Shakespeare Fishing Equipment; Fuller Brush Corp.; Louise Gaither, Executive Services Advertising; Gary Galante, Museum of the American Indian; cosmetic model make-up by Tom Gearhard; Irv Goldfinger, Forsyth Monument Works; Matthew Goldman; Bob Goldstein, M & F Hanger; Brian Goodman; Mary Grace; Kathy Graham, Bridgeport, Conn., Jai Alai; Thomas Grasso, Kay Jeep Eagle; J. F. Grgula, Structo Division, King-Seeley Thermos Co.; John Growth, School of Visual Arts; Mike Gue, Ethics Automobile Racing; Walter Guslawski, Williamsburg Steel Products; Stephen A. Halls, Jr., Digital Equipment Corp.; Dana Hammond, Hammond Inc.; Dean Hammond, President, Hammond Inc.; Kathy Hammond, Hammond Inc.; Stuart Hammond, Hammond Inc.; management and staff of Hampton Sales; Harvey Sound Corp.; Irving Heiberger, Marshall Clark Inc.; Joyce Heiberger, JBH Advertising; Kenneth Heinz, Welch-Allyn Corporation; Paul Heller, International Creative Management; Katharine Hill; Hoffritz Inc.; Ernst Hofmann, Hammond Inc.; Anne S. Hopkins, *Time* Magazine; Edward Irrizarry; Chris Jones, Hammond Inc.; Edward M. Kalail, Diebold Inc.; PO Ken Kaufman, NYPD, coauthor of *The Incredible Scooter Cops*; Scrooge's letter by Sean Kelly, former editor of *The National Lampoon*; Chris Kelly; Jessie O. Kempter, IBM; cowboy model by William Ketchum, Jr., author of *Western Memorabilia*; George Klauber, George Klauber Graphic Arts Studio; Morris and Ruth Kleinman; Drew Kuber, Hammond Inc.; Barbara Lach, Fermilab; Richard and Elyse Langsam; Larry Letizia, Joyson Motors; Leaf Tent and Sail Inc.; Charles Leib; Leland-Penn; Patricia Lewis; Robert Lewis, Chrysler Corporation; Teresa Longhitano; Mel and Cheryl London, authors of *Bread Winners*; Lionel V. Lorona, New York Public Library; Candace Love; Donald A. Macaulay; Joseph W. Maresca, Jr., SRI Institute; Daniel Mazzarella, Science Associates Inc.; Ken McAdams; Kay McDowell, US Postal Data Center; Frank 'Tug' McGraw, Philadelphia Phillies; Dave McNamara, Wilson Sporting Goods, Inc.; The Meadowlands Racetrack management; Jennifer Meyer, Hammond Inc.; John Meyers, Fisher Scientific Company; Ray Miller, VISA; Mr. Lucky School of Gambling; Macmillan Publishing Corp.; Captain Don Mitchell, Eastern Airlines; Jenny Moradfar; Ruth Grevey and Larry Osterman, Mosler Safe Corp.; Edward J. Murphy, Edward J. Murphy Corp.; Neckwear Association of America; Steve Nesbitt, Mark Hess, Tom Jacqua, NASA; New York Jets; New York Knickerbockers; New York Yankees; Don Morris and Suzanne Eagle, *New York* Magazine; PO George Legas and Steve Berenhaus, NYPD; John Nicholson; C. Michael Oldenberg, Centennial Management Corp.; Joan Rubin and Christine Martorana, Omega Fashions Ltd.; John Pace, National Cash Register; Shirley Palmer, *Progressive Grocer*; Rolando Pena; Arthur and Lois Perschetz, LTC Gerald Perschetz, U.S. Army (Ret.); Clarence Peskac, Dietzgen Corp.; Allen Petersen, Petersen Manufacturing Co., Inc.; Robert Pledge, Contact Press Images; Brigit Polk, The Factory; Marian Powers, *Time* Magazine; Andrew W. Prescott, Hammond Inc.; Donald Quest, Southwest Texas Drilling Co.; James Ramey, New York Jets; Jim Ramsey, Rodgers Organ Corp.; Mitch Rapaport, Scriptech; Mark Resnick, Hammond Inc.; Malcolm Ritter, Associated Press; Rock of Ages Corp.; Rosemary Rodgers, John Hill Music, Inc.; Linda Rosenblatt, R.D.H.; Joan Evanish, Judith Johnson and Canon West, Cathedral Church of St. John the Divine; Teddi Sann, Avon Products, Inc.; Gene Sayet, Executive Recording Ltd.; Frank and Harriet Sayre; Rosette Schecter, Furs by Rosette; Leslie Schwartz, Hammond Inc.; Deputy Police Commissioner 'Mickey' Schwartz, NYPD; Ann Scott, *Sports Illustrated*; Elizabeth Scott, Chicago Symphony Orchestra; Ray Scroggins, Wisconsin-Teledyne; Esther R. Selby, Zambelli Fireworks Mfg. Co.; Dr. John H. Seward, MD EENT; Joel Shaffer, Hammond Inc.; J. Ronald Shumate, Association of American Railroads; Craig Siebert; Harold Silver, Caldwell Button Corp.; Robert Simon, Wan, Simon and Black; Robert Smith; NY-NJ Port Authority; Dr. Herbert Spasser, D.D.S.; cosmetics model Tina Stahle; Stappers Equipment Corp.; Stuyvesant Music; Tom Szobe, Paragon Sporting Goods; Bob Taylor, Hedstrom Baby Furniture; Technigraph Studio; Marilyn Tempkins, Vivitar Inc.; calligraphy letterhead on Scrooge's letter by Melissa Topping; Tower Manufacturing; Paul Schulhaus, Russ Levin, Train Shop Ltd.; Bobbie Tupper, Park West Chapel; Helen Turi, General Motors Corp.; Helen Tutt, American Eagle; Tina T. Underwood, Intergraph; Universal Fastenings Inc.; Anna Urband, US Navy Public Relations; officers and men of the *USS Thomas C. Hart* (DE 1092); Jacques Vaucher, L'Art et L'Automobile Gallery; Ossie Virgil, Jr., Philadelphia Phillies; Dan Walden, Consolidated Edison Corp.; John Wanamaker; Sam Weinstein, Color Group; Western Union Corp.; Janet L. Wetmore, AT&T Archives; George Willig; king model Robert Wills; PO 'Scooter' Joe Wins, NYPD, coauthor of *The Incredible Scooter Cops*; John Wisdom; Laurie Wolford; Janet Wygall; Will Yolin, author of *The Complete Book of Kites and Kite Flying*; Richard Ziskin, American Umbrella Co.; Roger Zissu, Cowan, Liebowitz & Latman; Nell Znamierowski, Fashion Institute of Technology; and special thanks to the Hammond staff for their numerous contributions and assistance in producing this book.

Afterword

When we first created WHAT'S WHAT in 1981, it was
a major new undertaking, the first visual glossary
to appear in more than a century. While we were
confident that our research was meticulous, we also
recognized that errors were bound to creep into such
an ambitious project. So we asked readers to share
their special knowledge and observations with us.
Hundreds did. Most of the mail was embarrassing in
its flattery, much of it was touching. Letters from
parents of deaf children or children with learning
disabilities, for example, described the benefits and
pleasures derived by a very special reading audience.
Dozens of other letters proffered thoughtful criticism
that proved extremely valuable in preparing this
revision. We are indebted to all who wrote, and we
invite you to correspond with us in the future, for
whatever reason.

David Fisher
WHAT'S WHAT
357 West 19th St.
New York, N.Y., 10011